THE JERUSALEM TALMUD
THIRD ORDER: NAŠIM
TRACTATE *YEBAMOT*

STUDIA JUDAICA

FORSCHUNGEN ZUR WISSENSCHAFT
DES JUDENTUMS

HERAUSGEGEBEN VON
E. L. EHRLICH UND G. STEMBERGER

BAND XXIX

WALTER DE GRUYTER · BERLIN · NEW YORK

THE JERUSALEM TALMUD
תלמוד ירושלמי

THIRD ORDER: NAŠIM
סדר נשים
TRACTATE *YEBAMOT*
מסכת יבמות

EDITION, TRANSLATION, AND COMMENTARY

BY

HEINRICH W. GUGGENHEIMER

WALTER DE GRUYTER · BERLIN · NEW YORK

ISBN 978-3-11-068116-1
e-ISBN (PDF) 978-3-11-091926-4

This volume is text- and page-identical with the hardback published in 2004.

Library of Congress Control Number: 2020942698

Bibliographic information published by the Deutsche Nationalbibliothek
The Deutsche Nationalbibliothek lists this publication in the
Deutsche Nationalbibliografie;
detailed bibliographic data are available on the Internet at http://dnb.dnb.de.

Printing and binding: CPI books GmbH, Leck

www.degruyter.com

Preface

The present volume is the sixth in this series on the Jerusalem Talmud, the first in a five volume edition, translation, and commentary of the Third Order of this Talmud. The principles of the edition regarding text, vocalization, and Commentary have been spelled out in detail in the Introduction to the first volume. The text in this volume is based on the recently published manuscript text of the Yerushalmi by the Academy of the Hebrew Language, Jerusalem 2001.

The extensive Commentary is not based on emendations; where there is no evidence from manuscripts or early prints to correct evident scribal errors, the correction is given in the Notes. One objective of the Commentary is a study of the relation of the Babli to the Yerushalmi; this is discussed in more detail in the Introduction.

Again I wish to thank my wife, Dr. Eva Guggenheimer, who acted as critic, style editor, proof reader, and expert on the Latin and Greek vocabulary. Her own notes on some possible Latin and Greek etymologies are identified by (E. G.).

Contents

Introduction to Tractate Yebamot 1

Chapter 1, חמש עשרה נשים
Halakhah 1 9
Halakhah 2 38
Halakhah 3 49
Halakhah 4 50
Halahkah 5 51
Halakhah 6 54

Chapter 2, כיצד
Halakhah 1 70
Halakhah 2 76
Halakhah 3 83
Halakhah 4 85
Halakhah 6 96
Halakhah 7 101
Halakhah 8 102
Halakhah 9 105
Halakhah 10 106
Halakhah 11 109
Halakhah 12 110

Chapter 3, ארבעה אחין
Halakhah 1 117
Halakhah 2 133
Halakhah 3 135
Halakhah 4 139
Halakhah 6 142
Halakhah 7 144
Halakhah 8 144
Halakhah 9 147
Halakhah 10 152
Halakhah 11 155
Halakhah 12 156

Chapter 4, החולץ
Halakhah 1 161
Halakhah 2 169
Halakhah 3 179
Halakhah 4 183
Halakhah 5-6 185
Halakhah 7 186
Halakhah 8 189
Halakhah 9 192
Halakhah 10 193
Halakhah 11 194
Halakhah 12 209
Halakhah 13 213
Halakhah 14 214
Halakhah 15 220

Chapter 5, רבן גמליאל
Halakhah 1 222
Halakhah 2 231
Halakhah 3 234

Halakhah 4 235
Halakhah 5 239
Halakhah 7 242

Chapter 6, הבא על יבמתו
Halakhah 1 246
Halakhah 2 253
Halakhah 3 256
Halakhah 4 261
Halakhah 5 267
Halakhah 6 270

Chapter 7, אלמנה לכהן גדול
Halakhah 1 278
Halakhah 2 289
Halakhah 4 296
Halakhah 5 300
Halakhah 6 305
Halakhah 7 308
Halakhah 8 309

Chapter 8, הערל
Halakhah 1 312
Halakhah 2 339
Halakhah 3 352
Halakhah 5 365
Halakhah 6 369

Chapter 9, יש מותרות
Halakhah 1 376
Halakhah 2 380
Halakhah 5 382

Halakhah 6 388
Halakhah 9 392

Chapter 10, האשה שהלך
Halakhah 1 396
Halakhah 3 409
Halakhah 4 414
Halakhah 5 420
Halakhah 7 421
Halakhah 8 424
Halakhah 14 432
Halakhah 17 443

Terumot Chapter 11, נושאין
Halakhah 1 449
Halakhah 2 463
Halakhah 3 471
Halakhah 4 473
Halakhah 5 474
Halakhah 6 477
Halakhah 7 480

Chapter 12, מצות חליצה
Halakhah 1 490
Halakhah 2 502
Halakhah 3 511
Halakhah 4 513
Halakhah 5 514
Halakhah 6 516
Halakhah 7 518

Chapter 13, בית שמאי
Halakhah 1 526
Halakhah 2 537
Halakhah 3 546
Halakhah 4 547
Halakhah 6 548
Halakhah 8 552
Halakhah 9 557
Halakhah 10 559
Halakhah 11 559
Halakhah 12 560
Halakhah 14 562
Halakhah 15 564
Halakhah 16 567

Chapter 14, חרש שנשא
Halakhah 1 571
Halakhah 3 576
Halakhah 4 578
Halakhah 6 579
Halakhah 7 581
Halakhah 8 581
Halakhah 10 582

Chapter 15, האשה שהלכה
Halakhah 1 585
Halakhah 2 590
Halakhah 3 593
Halakhah 4 604
Halakhah 5 609
Halakhah 7 617
Halakhah 8 619

Halakhah 10 621
Halakhah 11 625
Halakhah 12 627

Ma'serot Chapter 16, האשה שהלך
Halakhah 1 629
Halakhah 2 632
Halakhah 3 635
Halakhah 4 641
Halakhah 5 646
Halakhah 6 650
Halakhah 7 656
Halakhah 9 659
Halakhah 11 660

Indices
Index of Biblical Quotations 663
Index of Talmudical Quotations
Babylonian Talmud 665
Tosephta 667
Other Talmudic Sources 668
Index of Greek, Latin, Hebrew, and Arabic, Words 668
General Index 669

Introduction to Tractate Yebamot

The main topic of this Tractate, as the title "Sisters-in-Law" indicates, are the rules of levirate marriage by the widow of a man who died without issue (*Deut.* 25:5-9). Since the levirate marriage is in obvious contradiction to the incest prohibition of the sister-in-law (*Lev.* 18:16), all incest prohibitions become topics for discussion. A child born from an incestual relationship is by consensus of all Jewish groups identified as the *mamzer* who is excluded from endogamous marriage (*Deut.* 23:3); therefore Judaism as a marriage community is to a large degree defined by the incest rules. While the Mishnah and both of its Talmudim have defined these rules for the last 2000 years, it is difficult to ascertain what the operative rules were during the Second Commonwealth. In certain respects, the Mishnah defines itself as the sectarian document of the House of Hillel even in the Pharisee community (Mishnah 1:4). The Talmud texts (cf. Chapter 1, Notes 192-196 and Babli *Qiddušin* 75a/76b) note that the Samaritans follow an interpretation of the levirate laws which eliminates any conflict between *Deut.* 25:5 and *Lev.* 18:16; the Yerushalmi implies that this interpretation was adopted by at least part of the Pharisee school of Shammai. For lack of sources, it is impossible to ascertain the position of Sadducee schools in this matter. The Samaritan interpretation is consistent with the Hebrew text of *Deut.* 25:5 but not with the Greek of the LXX. Possibly many of the complicated cases introduced in the Mishnah are not intellectual exercises but anti-Sadducee polemics directed against the Sadducee prohibition of polygamy and the marriage of an uncle to his niece, spelled out in the Damascus Document, CD iv 20-v 11.

A considerable part of the Tractate does not deal with levirate marriage but with its avoidance, known as *ḥălîṣah* "pulling off", the widow removing the levir's shoe, prescribed by *Deut.* 25:6-9 in case the levir refuses to marry his brother's widow. In a majority of cases mentioned, the levir is forced to refuse to marry his brother's widow. (In current rabbinical practice, the levir is always forced to refuse to marry his brother's widow.) A considerable part is also dedicated to the role of marriage in giving women access to the privileges of priesthood (*Lev.* 22:10-13).

The first Chapter starts with an enumeration of the incest prohibitions which in varying degrees free the childless widow for remarriage outside the family without formality, the expansive interpretation of these rules by the House of Hillel, and the restrictive one of the House of Shammai. The position of the House of Shammai is mentioned afterwards only infrequently.

The second Chapter starts with a definition of the notion of "levir" and continues with a discussion of forbidden marriages which are not incestuous and rabbinic extensions of biblical incest prohibitions. Then follows a discussion of the complications arising if several men contract preliminary marriages (cf. *Peah*, Chapter 6, Note 46) with a group of sisters but one does not know which sister belongs to which man. Finally, there are rabbinic rules on undue influence or conflicts of interest in contracting marriage.

The third Chapter is entirely dedicated to the complications that arise if a group of brothers marry a group of sisters and one brother dies without issue. It has been noted that in isolated communities this might have represented real problems.

The fourth Chapter deals with the complications in the case of a widow presumed to be childless but who actually was pregnant at the time of her husband's death, the pregnancy having been noted later than usual, as well as rules intended to avoid these complications. Then follow the implications of levirate marriage and *ḥălîṣah* for the disposition of the inheritance of the deceased. At the end of the Chapter follows the definition of the *mamzer* who is permanently excluded from the Jewish marriage community.

The fifth Chapter deals with the complications caused by inconsistent actions by the levir with respect to his sister-in-law, including the rabbinic betrothal required before the actual marriage by levirate.

The sixth Chapter notes that levirate marriage becomes valid, in biblical terms, only by consummation of the marriage. This leads to a discussion of those acts which constitute incest or adultery, and the corresponding rules for marriages prohibited to priests. The topic is continued in Chapter Seven which discusses the consequences of permitted or prohibited priestly marriages, mainly with respect to the status of the wife's dowry which could be either common property of the couple or remain separate property of the wife. This leads to a general discussion of what enables or disables a wife to become part of the priestly clan with access the priestly prebends.

The eighth Chapter deals with disabilities, either of a priest who cannot exercise the duties of priesthood or persons who are barred from marriage in the community.

The first part of Chapter Nine is an exercise in the combinations of women or men who are permitted/forbidden to husband/levir or wife/sister-in-law. The second part continues topics of the previous Chapters about the access of non-priestly and non-levitic women married to priests or levites to heave and tithes.

A completely new topic is introduced in Chapter Ten: Permission for a widow to remarry if her husband's death is not certified by two witnesses of good standing. In that case, one requires the woman to satisfy herself beyond a reasonable doubt that she truly is a widow before she remarries because if her husband turns out to be alive her second marriage is adulterous, her children from the second husband are *mamzerim*, she has to be divorced by both husbands and has no monetary claim on either one. On the other hand, the rabbinate is not supposed to interfere with her remarriage based on incomplete information. Also discussed is the case of the husband who marries his wife's sister after the report of his wife's death. Finally, the marital status of a boy between the ages of nine and thirteen years is discussed (a girl can be married if she is older than three years).

Chapter Eleven deals first with the problem whether incest prohibitions are created by rape and seduction, with the status of children who were mixed up at birth, or with children whose paternity is indeterminate since their mother remarried too soon after her husband's death.

Chapter Twelve describes the details of the act of *ḥălîṣah*.

Chapter Thirteen first details the rules of repudiation of a marriage by an underage girl who was married off by her mother or brothers after her father's death. The marriage of an underage girl contracted by her father is biblically valid and can be dissolved only by a formal divorce; the marriage contracted by her mother or brothers is only rabbinically valid.

The second half of the Chapter investigates the consequences of repudiation for levirate and *ḥălîṣah.*

Chapter Fourteen investigates the marital situation of deaf-mutes of both sexes. Their marital status is ambiguous because deaf-mutes are considered as legally incompetent but their marriages are rabbinically approved. However, the levirate of a deaf-mute with the widow of his hearing brother is a biblically valid marriage.

Chapter Fifteen returns to the topic of Chapter Ten. The main thrust is that testimony as to the death of a husband (and distribution of his inheritance) is accepted from everybody, including slaves, but to the exclusion of women who might want to goad the presumed widow into a forbidden second marriage: a co-wife and her children, the mother-in-law and her daughters, a sister-in-law, and a stepdaughter. The existence of co-wives again leads to great complications.

The last Chapter finally details the rules governing identification of corpses and additional rules for the court that permit to declare a missing person as dead.

The Commentary explains the text within the talmudic setting. No attempt has been made to connect the text to extratalmudic sources since, as stated at the beginning, the Tractate is essentially a sectarian document. A considerable part of the Commentary is devoted to the relation of the Babli to the Jerusalem Talmud. This subject needs careful study. Historically, we find that, from the late Severan dynasty of Rome all through the Military Anarchy and the reign of Diocletian, there was a steady stream of Babylonian scholars into Galilee. In fact, the successors of R. Joḥanan as heads of the Academy of Tiberias for three generations were Babylonians. The situation changed with the reign of Constantius, when the Christian Roman Empire turned against the Jews. From then on, there is a stream of Galilean scholars emigrating to Babylonia. The Babylonian Talmud reports many discussions which Rava (Rav Abba bar Rav Josef bar Ḥama) had with two of the most prominent emigrants, Rebbi Dimi (Eudaimon) and Rabin (Rebbi Abun). Z. M. Dor[1] has documented many cases in which Rava did adopt the Galilean point of view; a few more are pointed out in the present commentary. E. M. Ziany has identified influences of the Yerushalmi in the editorial work of the Saboreans and early Geonim[2]. But as the Commentary will make clear, the core Babylonian Talmud treats mostly those topics mentioned in the Yerushalmi with whom it disagrees, either in the law or in its argumentation. One has to conclude that much of the core Babli was formulated in conscious opposition to the teachings of the Yerushalmi; a thorough investigation of the Babli concentrating on its implicit polemic against Yerushalmi sources has still to be undertaken.

Sources for this Tractate are as always the Leiden ms. (referred to in the Commentary as ms. L) and the *editio princeps*; in places the latter source is based on manuscripts different from the Leiden one. In several Chapters, important information is given in the Ashkenazic ms. fragments (referred to as ms. A) edited by Jacob Sussman[3], which by a few corruptions show that they are derived from the same archetype as the Leiden ms. As explained in the Introduction to the first volume in this

---

1 Cf. Chapter 1, Note 19.

2 הרב ד״ר אליהו רחמים זייני, רבנן סבוראי וכללי ההלכה, חיפה תשנב (1992).

3 יעקב זוסמן, שרידי ירושלמי - כ״י אשכנזי; קבץ על יד יב(כב), מקיצי נרדמים תשנד, Jerusalem 1994.

series, evidence contained in medieval (mostly Spanish and Provençal) texts is most valuable for information and interpretation but cannot be considered as evidence to the exact wording of the text.

Of the classical commentaries, the most useful guides are קרבן העדה by R. David Fraenckel and the frequent references to the Yerushalmi in the novellae of Rashba (R. Salomon ibn Adrat) and Meïri (R. Menaḥem ben Šelomo Lebēt Meïr).

חמש עשרה נשים פרק ראשון

(fol. 2a) **משנה א:** חֲמֵשׁ עֶשְׂרֵה נָשִׁים פּוֹטְרוֹת צָרוֹתֵיהֶן וְצָרוֹת צָרוֹתֵיהֶן מִן הַחֲלִיצָה וּמִן הַיִּבּוּם עַד סוֹף הָעוֹלָם. וְאֵלּוּ הֵן בִּתּוֹ וּבַת בִּתּוֹ וּבַת בְּנוֹ בַּת אִשְׁתּוֹ וּבַת בְּנָהּ וּבַת בִּתָּהּ חֲמוֹתוֹ וְאֵם חֲמוֹתוֹ וְאֵם חָמִיו אֲחוֹתוֹ וַאֲחוֹת אִמּוֹ וַאֲחוֹת אִשְׁתּוֹ אֵשֶׁת אָחִיו מֵאִמּוֹ וְאֵשֶׁת אָחִיו שֶׁלֹּא הָיָה בְעוֹלָמוֹ וְכַלָּתוֹ.

Mishnah 1: Fifteen [categories of] women[1] free their co-wives[2] and the co-wives of their co-wives from *ḥalîṣah* and levirate forever[3]. They are the following: one's daughter[4], his daughter's daughter and his son's daughter[5], his wife's daughter and her daughter's daughter and her son's daughter[6], his mother-in-law and his mother-in-law's mother and his father-in-law's mother, his sister[7] and his maternat aunt[8] and his wife's sister[9], his maternal halfbrother's wife[10], the wife of his brother who did not live in his world[11], and his daughter-in-law[12].

1 *Deut.* 25:5 requires that the widow of any man who died without legitimate or illegitimate issue be married by the man's brother. If, however, that brother is forbidden one of the deceased's wives by the incest prohibition of *Lev.* 18 or the rules of *Deut.* 25:5-10, she may not be married by the brother to whom she is forbidden.

2 The House of Hillel hold that if one widow is forbidden, all co-widows are forbidden. This is not accepted by the House of Shammai, Mishnah 6.

3 If one of three brothers had married the second brother's daughter and another woman, died childless, the other wife was married by the third brother who already had another wife, if the third also dies childless both of his widows are forbidden because one of them is forbidden. This scenario can

be extended to *n* polygamous brothers; *n* arbitrary.

4 This statement seems to be needed only for an illegitimate daughter, except the daughter from a gentile or a slave woman who are not legally his relatives (Rashi *ad loc.*). Legitimate children are covered by *Lev.* 18:17. However, the Yerushalmi (Note 135) does not make any distinction between legitimate and illegitimate daughters.

Sadducees (followed by Karaites and Christians) did forbid marriage with a niece since marriage with an aunt is a biblical prohibition and they held that the incest prohibitions of *Lev.* 18 are gender symmetric. Pharisaic opinion is that "one does not introduce punishable offence by argument;" what is written is forbidden, what is not written is not (biblically) forbidden.

5 *Lev.* 18:10.

6 *Lev.* 18:17: "The genitals of a women and her daughter (including mother-in-law and wife) you may not [both] uncover, her son's daughter (wife's granddaughter or wife as paternal grandmother's daughter) or her daughter's daughter (this forbids the wife's maternal grandmother) you may not marry to uncover her genitals; they are relatives, it is tabu."

7 This is needed only for the maternal halfsister (*Lev.* 18:9) married to a paternal halfbrother. It will be established that the levirate applies only to paternal brothers; the first marriage of the halfsister was legitimate.

8 *Lev.* 18:13.

9 *Lev.* 18:18.

10 *Lev.* 18:16. It is assumed that the halfbrother died or divorced his wife who then married a paternal halfbrother of the man in question to whom she was not related. The earlier marriage to the maternal halfbrother forbade her permanently to the levir, the brother-in-law on the husband's side.

Since in *Deut.* 25, "brother" is assumed to mean "paternal brother", it needs some discussion in the Halakhah why in *Lev.* 18 "brother" may mean "maternal or paternal brother" since the usual stance is that in legal texts one word can have only one meaning.

11 *Deut.* 25:5 introduces the rules of the levirate with the statement "If brothers live together". This means that a brother born after the death of another cannot marry the widow of the deceased, i. e., the childless widow does not have to wait until the newborn baby grows up to marry her but, if

there is no other brother, she may immediately marry outside the family.

12 This is obvious (*Lev.* 18:15) except for the case that the son had died and his widow married a brother of her father-in-law unrelated to her. The prohibition of 18:15 is permanent; the earlier marriage to the son forbade her permanently to the father-in-law.

הלכה א: חֲמֵשׁ עֶשְׂרֵה נָשִׁים פּוֹטְרוֹת צָרוֹתֵיהֶן כול׳. כְּתִיב מַצּוֹת תֵּאָכֵל. לְפִי שֶׁהָיְתָה בִּכְלַל הֵיתֵר וְנֶאֶסְרָה וְחָזְרָה וְהוּתְּרָה. יָכוֹל תַּחֲזוֹר לְהֵיתֵירָהּ הָרִאשׁוֹן. תַּלְמוּד לוֹמַר מַצּוֹת תֵּאָכֵל. מִצְוָה. כְּיוֹצֵא בוֹ יְבָמָהּ יָבוֹא עָלֶיהָ. מִצְוָה. לְפִי שֶׁהָיְתָה בִּכְלַל הֵיתֵר וְנֶאֶסְרָה וְחָזְרָה וְהוּתְּרָה. יָכוֹל תַּחֲזוֹר לְהֵיתֵירָהּ הָרִאשׁוֹן. תַּלְמוּד לוֹמַר יְבָמָהּ יָבוֹא עָלֶיהָ. מִצְוָה.

Halakhah 1: "Fifteen [categories of] women free their co-wives", etc. [13]It is written[14] "unleavened it must be eaten". Since it was permitted[15] and then forbidden[16], when it became permitted again[17] should one think it returned to its prior permission? The verse states "unleavened it should be eaten" as commandment. Similarly, "her levir shall come upon her" as a commandment. Since she was permitted and then forbidden, when she became permitted again should one think she returned to her prior permission[18]? The verse states "her levir shall come upon her" as commandment.

13 *Sifra Ṣaw Parashah* 2(9-10); another version of 2(10) in Babli *Yebamot* 39b. The basis of the argument is the 12th exegetical rule of R. Ismael [Introduction to *Sifra* (2)]: If anything was in some set and was removed from it for another purpose, you cannot return it to that set unless the verse returns it explicitly. See *Midraš Gen. rabba* 85(6) for a formulation of 2(10) referring more directly to the rule. (For an introduction to these rules, see H. Guggenheimer, *Logical Problems in Jewish Tradition*, in: Confrontations with Judaism, Ph. Longworth, ed., London 1966, pp. 171-196; *Über ein bemerkenswertes logisches System aus*

der Antike, Methodos 1951, pp. 150-161.) What exactly was permitted, became forbidden, and is now commanded is a matter of interpretation in the next paragraphs.

14 *Lev.* 6:9, speaking of the leftovers of cereal offerings in the Tabernacle. These leftovers must be eaten by priests, in the holy precinct, and unleavened, after the prescribed rites were performed.

15 Before dedication as offering, the flour was profane and permitted to everybody. It is in the set of unrestricted permitted food.

16 After dedication and before the prescribed rites were performed, the flour is forbidden to everybody, including priests. It is no longer in any set of permitted food.

17 After the prescribed rites were performed, it cannot return to the set of unrestricted permitted food.

18 A rhetorical question; this is impossible by rule 12.

רִבִּי יוֹסֵי פָּתַר מַתְנִיתָא. מַצּוֹת תֵּאָכֵל. מִצְוָה. לְפִי שֶׁהָֽיְתָה בִּכְלַל הֵיתֵר עַד שֶׁלֹּא הִקְדִּישָׁהּ. רוֹצֶה לוֹכַל אוֹכֵל. שֶׁלֹּא לוֹכַל אֵינוֹ אוֹכֵל. הִקְדִּישָׁהּ וְנֶאֶסְרָה קָרַב קוֹמְצָהּ וְחָֽזְרָה וְהוּתְּרָה. יָכוֹל תַּחֲזוֹר לְהֵיתֵירָהּ הָרִאשׁוֹן. רוֹצֶה לוֹכַל אוֹכֵל. שֶׁלֹּא לוֹכַל אֵינוֹ אוֹכֵל. תַּלְמוּד לוֹמַר מַצּוֹת תֵּאָכֵל. מִצְוָה. כְּיוֹצֵא בוֹ יְבָמָהּ יָבוֹא עָלֶיהָ. מִצְוָה. לְפִי שֶׁהָֽיְתָה בִּכְלַל הֵיתֵר עַד שֶׁלֹּא נִישֵּׂאת לְאָחִיו. רָצָה לִכְנוֹס כּוֹנֵס. שֶׁלֹּא לִכְנוֹס אֵינוֹ כוֹנֵס. נִישֵּׂאת לְאָחִיו וְנֶאֶסְרָה וּמֵת אָחִיו בְּלֹא בָנִים חָֽזְרָה וְהוּתְּרָה. יָכוֹל תַּחֲזוֹר לְהֵיתֵירָהּ הָרִאשׁוֹן. רָצָה לִכְנוֹס כּוֹנֵס. שֶׁלֹּא לִכְנוֹס אֵינוֹ כוֹנֵס. תַּלְמוּד לוֹמַר יְבָמָהּ יָבוֹא עָלֶיהָ. מִצְוָה.

Rebbi Yose[19] explains the *baraita*: "Unleavened it must be eaten". Since it was permitted before it was dedicated, if one wants to eat it, he eats, not to eat, he does not eat. When he dedicated it became forbidden. When the fistful[20] was brought it became permitted again; should one think it returned to its prior permission? If he wants to eat it, he eats, not to eat, he does not eat[21]? The verse states "unleavened it must be eaten" as commandment. Similarly, "her levir shall come upon her" as a commandment. Since she was permitted before she was married to his brother, if he wanted to bring her into his house[22], he could bring her, not to bring her into his house, he would not bring her. When she was married to his brother she became forbidden. When his brother died childless she became permitted again. Should one think she returned to her prior permission, if he wanted to bring her into his house, he could bring her, not to bring her into his house, he would not bring her? The verse states "her levir shall come upon her" as commandment[23].

19 The Amora. In the Babli, *Yebamot* 40a, the parallel arguments, in inverse order, are attributed to Rava, a preeminent authority. He is known sometimes to represent Yerushalmi positions, cf. צבי דור, תורת ארץ ישראל בבבל, דביר, תל אביב 1971.

20 A fistful of the offering with all the incense, *Lev*. 6:8, brought to the altar to be burned. Once the offering starts to burn, the remainder is permitted to the priests.

21 This is also Rava's argument in the Babli. The Babli corrects the statement since the obligation to eat the remainders of the offering is repeated several times in *Ex*. and *Lev*.

22 As his bride.

23 He *has* to marry her whether he likes her or not.

רִבִּי הוּנָא פָּתַר מַתְנִיתָא. מַצּוֹת תֵּאָכֵל. מִצְוָה. לְפִי שֶׁהָיְתָה בִּכְלַל הֵיתֵירָה עַד שֶׁלֹּא הִקְדִּישָׁהּ. רוֹצֶה לוֹכַל חָמֵץ אוֹכֵל. מַצָּה אוֹכֵל. תַּלְמוּד לוֹמַר מַצּוֹת יֵאָכֵל. מִצְוָה. (fol. 2b) כְּיוֹצֵא בוֹ יְבָמָהּ יָבוֹא עָלֶיהָ. מִצְוָה. לְפִי שֶׁהָיְתָה בִּכְלַל הֵיתֵר עַד שֶׁלֹּא נִישֵּׂאת לְאָחִיו. רָצָה לִכְנוֹס לְשֵׁם תּוֹאַר כּוֹנֵס. לְשֵׁם מָמוֹן כּוֹנֵס. נִישֵּׂאת לְאָחִיו וְנֶאֶסְרָה. מֵת אָחִיו בְּלֹא בָנִים חָזְרָה וְהוּתְּרָה. יָכוֹל תַּחֲזוֹר לְהֵיתֵירָהּ הָרִאשׁוֹן. רָצָה לִכְנוֹס לְשֵׁם תּוֹאַר כּוֹנֵס. לְשֵׁם מָמוֹן כּוֹנֵס. תַּלְמוּד לוֹמַר יְבָמָהּ יָבוֹא עָלֶיהָ. מִצְוָה.

Rebbi Huna[24] explains the *baraita*: "Unleavened it must be eaten". Since it was permitted before it was dedicated, if one wants to eat it leavened, he eats it, unleavened, he eats it. [25] The verse states "unleavened it should be eaten" as commandment. Similarly, "her brother-in-law shall come upon her" as commandment. Since she was permitted before she was married to his brother, if he wanted to bring her into his house because of her shapeliness, he could bring her, because of her money, he could bring her. When she was married to his brother she became forbidden. When his brother died childless she became permitted again. Should one think she returned to her prior permission, if he wanted to bring her into his house because of her shapeliness, he could bring her, because of her money, he could bring her? The verse states "her levir shall come upon her" as commandment[26].

24 In the Babli (*l. c.* 39b) this is the opinion of Rav Isaac ben Eudaimon, a minor figure. Here also, the author R. Huna of this paragraph does not have the authority of R. Yose of the preceding paragraph.

25 The argument of the preceding paragraph has to be inserted here. Since the corrector of the ms. did not insert anything here, it probably was not in the ms. before the copyist; the lacuna can be replaced by three dots.

26 She remains forbidden if the levir has any intention other than to fulfill the commandment. This means that in practice the brother has to refrain from marrying the sister-in-law to avoid enjoying her sexually.

אַתְיָא דְרִבִּי חוּנָא כְּאַבָּא שָׁאוּל. דְּתַנָּא אַבָּא שָׁאוּל אוֹמֵר. הַכּוֹנֵס אֶת יְבִימְתּוֹ לְשׁוּם נוֹי אוֹ לְשׁוּם דְּבָרִים אֲחֵרִים הֲרֵי זֶה בְּעִילַת זְנוּת וְקָרוֹב לִהְיוֹת הַוְּולָד מַמְזֵר.

It turns out that Rebbi Ḥuna follows Abba Shaul, as we have stated[27]: "Abba Shaul says, one who brings his sister-in-law into his house because of beauty or another reason[28] commits intercourse of prostitution and the child is close to be a bastard[29]."

27 A different formulation, stressing the opposition of the anonymous majority, in Babli 39b.

28 Other than fulfilling the biblical commandment.

29 Who is forbidden to marry a Jewish partner, *Deut*. 23:3.

מַה אַבָּא שָׁאוּל כְּרִבִּי עֲקִיבָה. דְּרִבִּי עֲקִיבָה אָמַר. יֵשׁ מַמְזֵר בִּיבָמָה. מַה דְאָמַר רִבִּי עֲקִיבָה בִּיבָמָה שֶׁזִּינָת. מַה דְאָמַר אַבָּא שָׁאוּל בִּיבִמְתּוֹ. אַתְיָא כְּרִבִּי יוֹסֵי בֶּן חֲלַפְתָּא. דְּרִבִּי יוֹסֵי בֶּן חֲלַפְתָּא יִיבֵּם אֶת אֵשֶׁת אָחִיו. חָמֵשׁ חֲרִישׁוֹת חָרַשׁ וְחָמֵשׁ נְטִיעוֹת נָטַע וְדֶרֶךְ סַדִּין בָּעַל. אֵילוּ הֵן. רִבִּי יִשְׁמָעֵאל בֵּירִבִּי יוֹסֵי רִבִּי לֶעְזָר בֵּירִבִּי יוֹסֵי רִבִּי מְנַחֵם בֵּירִבִּי יוֹסֵי וְרִבִּי חֲלַפְתָּא בֵּירִבִּי יוֹסֵי רִבִּי אֶבְדִּימוֹס בֵּירִבִּי יוֹסֵי.

Does Abba Shaul hold with Rebbi Aqiba? Since Rebbi Aqiba said, there exists a bastard from a sister-in-law! What Rebbi Aqiba said refers to a sister-in-law who whored[30]. What Abba Shaul said refers to his sister-in-law[31]. It comes like Rebbi Yose ben Ḥalaphta[32] since Rebbi Yose ben Ḥalaphta contracted a levirate marriage with his brother's wife. He ploughed five times and planted five saplings and had intercourse using a bedsheet[33]. These are they: Rebbi Ismael ben Rebbi Yose, Rebbi Eleazar ben Rebbi Yose[34], Rebbi Menaḥem ben Rebbi Yose, and Rebbi Ḥalaphta ben Rebbi Yose, Rebbi Eudaimon ben Rebbi Yose.

30 R. Aqiba holds that any child born of any forbidden union is a bastard; the majority opinion is that bastards are created only by incestuous relations that either are capital crimes or sanctioned by extirpation (cf. Halakhot 4:15, 11:1). Since it is written (*Deut*. 25:5) "the wife of the deceased may not belong to any outside unrelated man" he holds that any marriage of a widow not released from levirate duty to another man is invalid and her relationship is one of whoring.

A parallel, but more differentiated, statement is in the Babli 92a.

31 In a completely legal situation.

32 The Tanna, who is a much more important authority than the older Abba Shaul. The formulation as a story implies that R. Yose followed Abba Shaul as a matter of personal piety but did not impose his discipline on others.

33 He avoided direct contact with his levirate wife following Abba Shaul. In a regular marriage, such behavior permits the wife to force a divorce (Babli *Ketubot* 48a). The story contradicts Mishnah 4:4 which states that once married, the sister-in-law becomes a wife *in all respects*, including the husband's duty to satisfy her sexual needs. Tosaphot (Babli *Šabbat* 118b) discuss the Yerushalmi versions but they read that R. Yose contracted levirate marriages *with the widows of his brothers* implying that he married five widows, had with each of them only the one biblically required intercourse (*Deut.* 25:5) and then divorced them. This custom was followed by some Jewish Berber groups in the Atlas mountains to modern times. (R. Moses Margalit restricts the avoidance of direct contact to the first intercourse in fulfillment of the biblical command. R. David Fraenckel concludes that R. Yose rejects Mishnah 4:4 except that he agrees that the wife acquired in levirate can be divorced by the rules applying to any other wife.)

The parallel in Babli *Šabbat* 118b, formulated as personal statement of R. Yose does not mention either the sheet or levirate marriage, and appears in a completely different context.

34 Only the first two are renowned; R. Ismael ben R. Yose was the teacher of R. Yehudah the Prince.

כְּתִיב עֶרְוַת אֵשֶׁת אָחִיךָ לֹא תְגַלֵּה. מַשְׁמַע הוּא בֵּין אֵשֶׁת אָחִיו מֵאָבִיו בֵּין אֵשֶׁת אָחִיו מֵאִמּוֹ. בֵּין אֵשֶׁת אָחִיו שֶׁהָיָה בְעוֹלָמוֹ בֵּין אֵשֶׁת אָחִיו שֶׁלֹּא הָיָה בְעוֹלָמוֹ. בֵּין לְחַיִּים בֵּין לְאַחַר מִיתָה. בֵּין שֶׁיֵּשׁ לוֹ בָנִים בֵּין שֶׁאֵין לוֹ בָנִים. הוּתְּרָה מִכְּלָלָהּ עַל יְדֵי יִיבּוּם. יָכוֹל לְכָל־דָּבָר. נֶאֱמַר כָּאן כִּי יֵשְׁבוּ אַחִים יַחְדָּיו. וְנֶאֱמַר לְהַלָּן שְׁנֵים־עָשָׂר עֲבָדֶיךָ אַחִים אֲנַחְנוּ. מַה אַחִים שֶׁנֶּאֱמַר לְהַלָּן בְּאַחִים מִן הָאָב הַכָּתוּב מְדַבֵּר. אַף אַחִים שֶׁנֶּאֱמַר כָּאן בְּאַחִים מִן הָאָב.

It is written[35]: "The genitals of your brother's wife you may not uncover." One understands both his paternal and his maternal brothers' wives, both the wife of a brother who lived concurrently with him or one who did not live concurrently with him, whether he had children or did not have children[36] She became permitted, excluded from this set, by levirate. Should I think unconditionally? It is said here[37]: "When brothers live together"; and it is said there[38]: "We, your servants, are twelve brothers." Since the "brothers" mentioned there are paternal brothers, so the "brothers" mentioned here must be paternal brothers.

35 *Lev.* 18:16.

36 The verse is discussed in the Babli, 55a, independently from the verse quoted next. Therefore, the Babli engages in a series of arguments to indicate that "brother" in this verse has a wider meaning than "brothers" in *Deut.* 25:5; among them a reference to *Lev.* 18:9, where "sister" is expressly defined as at least a halfsister from any side. [A tannaitic source, *Sifra Qedošim Pereq* 11(3), restricts the meaning of "brother" in this verse to that in *Deut.* 25:5. Cf. R. Abraham ben David's commentary ad loc.] The Yerushalmi has no need for an additional argument since this paragraph is still a continuation of the first one in this Halakhah, an application of the 12th exegetical rule (Note 13), only that the argument is inverted. Since we know that if something was permitted, forbidden, and permitted again, the set of second permissions must be a proper subset of that of first permissions, it is necessary that the restrictions applied to the meaning of "brother" in the second set cannot apply to the prohibition. [The Babli avoids using rules 7-13 of R. Ismael and never has systematic comparisons between arguments following R. Ismael and those following R. Aqiba.]

37 *Deut.* 25:5.

38 *Gen.* 42:13. להלן is a Babylonism; in true Galilean style it would be תמן. The parallel argument is in Babli 17b; because the constructive framework of the Yerushalmi is missing in the Babli, the latter has a lengthy discussion why the definition of "brother" for levirate is narrower than that for incest prohibitions.

יַחְדָיו. פְּרָט לְאֵשֶׁת אָחִיו שֶׁלֹּא הָיָה בְעוֹלָמוֹ. וּמֵת אֶחָד מֵהֶן. הֵן בַּחַיִּים. אֲפִילוּ גֵירְשָׁהּ וּמֵת זוּ פְטוּרָה. וּבֵן אֵין לוֹ. הָא אִם יֵשׁ לוֹ בֵן פְּטוּרָה.

[39]"Together", this excludes the wife of his brother who did not live in his world. "And one of them died", of those who lived. Even if he divorced her and then died? This one is exempted[40]. "Without child". Therefore, if he has a child she is exempted.

39 *Deut.* 25:5. The parallel in the Babli, 17b, follows *Sifry Deut.* #288 in inferring from "together" not only to exclude the wife of a predeceased brother but also the wife of the maternal halfbrother who in a patriarchal world would not live in their clan.

40 Exempted from the rules of the levirate.

כְּתִיב כִּי אֶת־כָּל־אֲשֶׁר יַעֲשֶׂה מִכֹּל הַתּוֹעֵבוֹת הָאֵל וְנִכְרְתָה. וַהֲלֹא אֵשֶׁת אָחִיו בִּכְלָל כָּל־הָעֲרָיוֹת הָיְתָה וְהוּתְּרָה מִכְּלָלָהּ עַל יְדֵי יִיבּוּם. יָכוֹל אַף שְׁאָר כָּל־הָעֲרָיוֹת הוּתְּרוּ מִכְּלָלָן עַל יְדֵי יִיבּוּם. רִבִּי זְעוּרָה בְשֵׁם רִבִּי יוֹסֵי בֶּן חֲנִינָה. עָלֶיהָ עָלֶיהָ. יְבָמָהּ יָבֹא עָלֶיהָ. מַה עָלֶיהָ שֶׁנֶּאֱמַר לְהַלָּן בְּאַחִים מִן הָאָב הַכָּתוּב מְדַבֵּר. אַף עָלֶיהָ שֶׁנֶּאֱמַר כָּאן בְּאַחִים מִן הָאָב הַכָּתוּב מְדַבֵּר.

It is written[41]: "For anyone who is acting out any of these abominations will be extirpated"[42]. Was not the brother's wife in the set of all incest prohibitions and was removed from this set by the levirate? Could one say that all other incest prohibitions were removed from this set by levirate? Rebbi Ze'ira in the name of Rebbi Yose ben Ḥanina: "upon her[43]", "upon her[44]": "her levir shall come upon her.[44]" Since with respect to "upon her" which was said there, the verse speaks about paternal brothers, so with respect to "upon her" which was said here[43], the verse speaks about paternal brothers[45].

41 *Lev.* 18:29. The verse is not quoted exactly. The argument is in *Sifra Qedošim Pereq* 10(10). A similar version in Babli 3b.

42 The argument is made explicit (in the name of the 5th generation Galilean Amora R. Jonah) in Babli 8a: The verse considers all incest prohibitions as equivalent.

43 *Lev.* 18:18: "Do not take a woman in addition to her sister to be 'bundle' together, to uncover her genitals in addition [to the sister's] in her lifetime." Cf. also Note 51.

44 *Deut.* 25:5.

45 This implies (a) that a sister which also is a sister-in-law cannot be subject to the levirate and (b) no woman subject to an incest prohibition of *Lev.* 18 can be subject to the levirate, as spelled out in the Mishnah.

רִבִּי בִּנְיָמִין בַּר גִּידַל וְרִבִּי אָחָא הֲווּ יָתְבִין. אָמַר רִבִּי אָחָא הָדָא דְּרִבִּי יוֹסֵי בֶּן חֲנִינָה. אָמַר לֵיהּ רִבִּי בִּנְיָמִין בַּר גִּידַל. אוֹ מַה עָלֶיהָ שֶׁנֶּאֱמַר לְהַלָּן בְּשֶׁאֵינָהּ יְבָמָה הַכָּתוּב מְדַבֵּר. אַף עָלֶיהָ שֶׁנֶּאֱמַר כָּאן בְּשֶׁאֵינָהּ יְבָמָה הַכָּתוּב מְדַבֵּר. אָמַר לֵיהּ רִבִּי אָחָא. הַתּוֹרָה אָמְרָה בִּיבָמָה וְאַתְּ אוֹמֵר בְּשֶׁאֵינָהּ יְבָמָה. אָמַר לֵיהּ רִבִּי בִּנְיָמִין בַּר גִּידַל. הַתּוֹרָה אָמְרָה בְּשֶׁאֵינָהּ יְבָמָה וְאַתְּ אוֹמֵר בִּיבָמָה. וְאִיקְפִּיד רִבִּי אָחָא לְקוֹבְלֵיהּ. אָמַר רִבִּי יוֹסֵי. לֹא דְּרִבִּי אָחָא פְּלִיג אֶלָּא דְהוּא מְפַקֵּד עַל לִישְׁנָא דְּשַׁמַע מִן רַבֵּיהּ. מַה כְדוֹן. יְבָמָהּ יָבֹא עָלֶיהָ. מַה עָלֶיהָ שֶׁנֶּאֱמַר לְהַלָּן בְּ(שֶׁאֵינָהּ)[46] יְבָמָה. אַף עָלֶיהָ שֶׁנֶּאֱמַר כָּאן אֲפִילוּ יְבִמְתּוֹ.

Rebbi Benjamin ben Gidal and Rebbi Aḥa were sitting together. Rebbi Aḥa mentioned the statement of Rebbi Yose ben Ḥanina. Rebbi Benjamin bar Gidal said to him: Or maybe: Since with respect to "in addition" which was said there[43], the verse speaks about one who is not a sister-in-law, so with respect to "in addition" which was said here[44], does the verse speak about one who is not a sister-in-law[47]? Rebbi Aḥa said to him: The Torah mentions[44] the brother's wife and you say, the verse speaks about one who is not a sister-in-law! Rebbi Benjamin bar Gidal said to him: The Torah mentions[43] one who is not a sister-in-law and you say a sister-in-law[48]! Rebbi Aḥa was offended by him. Rebbi Yose said, not that Rebbi Aḥa disagreed but he insisted on the formulation he had heard from his teacher. What about it? Since "in addition" mentioned there[44] is about a brother's widow, so "in addition" here[43] is even about a brother's widow[49].

46 The argument of all commentators is accepted that this word is a slip of the pen and should be disregarded.

47 Since an argument based on the invariable meaning of words in legal texts must work both ways and *Lev.* 18:18 obviously includes the prohibition of a sister-in-law who is not a brother's wife, R. Yose ben Ḥanina's argument seems illogical.

48 The implication from *Deut.* to *Lev.* would restrict the prohibition of the sister-in-law to a brother's widow!

49 The correct implication, parallel to the argument of R. Yose ben Ḥanina, is that *Lev.* 18:18 applies even to the widow of the childless brother as claimed in the Mishnah.

אָמְרָה תוֹרָה וְאִשָּׁה עַל אֲחוֹתָהּ לֹא תִקָּח. אֵין לִי אֶלָּא הִיא. צָרָתָהּ מְנַיִין. תַּלְמוּד לוֹמַר לִצְרוֹר. לֹא לְצָרָתָהּ וְלֹא לְצָרַת צָרָתָהּ. אֵין לִי אֶלָּא אֲחוֹת אִשְׁתּוֹ. שְׁאָר כָּל־הָעֲרָיוֹת מְנַיִין. רִבִּי זְעוּרָה בְּשֵׁם רִבִּי יוֹסֵה בַּר חֲנִינָה. קַל וָחוֹמֶר. מַה אֲחוֹת אִשְׁתּוֹ מְיוּחֶדֶת עֶרְוָה שֶׁיֵּשׁ לָהּ הֵיתֵר לְאַחַר אִיסוּרָהּ הֲרֵי הִיא אֲסוּרָה לְהִתְיַיבֵּם. שְׁאָר כָּל־הָעֲרָיוֹת שֶׁאֵין לָהֶן הֵיתֵר לְאַחַר אִיסוּרָן לֹא כָּל־שֶׁכֵּן. מַה זוֹ עֶרְוָה פּוֹטֶרֶת צָרָתָהּ אַף שְׁאָר כָּל־הָעֲרָיוֹת פּוֹטְרוֹת צָרוֹתֵיהֶן. עַד כְּדוֹן כְּרִבִּי עֲקִיבָה.

The Torah said[50]: "Do not take a woman in addition to her sister". Not only her, her co-wife from where? The verse says "to 'bundle' together", not her co-wife nor her co-wife's co-wife[51]. Not only his wife's sister, all other incest prohibition from where? Rebbi Ze'ira in the name of Rebbi Yose ben Ḥanina: A conclusion *de minore ad majus*[52]. Since his wife's sister, who is under an incest prohibition which may be lifted after being imposed[53], nevertheless is prohibited from the levirate, all other women under incest prohibitions which cannot be lifted after being imposed not much more so! Since in the first case the incest prohibition exempts the prohibited co-wife, all other incest prohibitions also exempt their co-wives[54]. This follows Rebbi Aqiba.

50 *Lev.* 18:18.

51 The problem is the verb form לִצְרוֹר which has been translated as "to 'bundle' together" (from צרר II, Arabic صرّ) but which might also be taken as "to be a co-wife" (from צרה II, Arabic ضرّ). The Yerushalmi opts for the first version. In the Babli, 13a, the argument is that the verb appears in two forms, צרר here and צור in *Deut.* 14:25. The duplication of consonants is taken to imply "many bundlings together", to exclude the co-wives' co-wives. That argument is more in the line of R. Aqiba's teaching than the bare argument here.

52 The first of R. Ismael's rules (cf. Note 13) which is universally accepted, also by R. Aqiba.

53 After the wife's death.

54 Since there is no argument pointing to the opposite conclusion.

כְּרִבִּי יִשְׁמָעֵאל. תַּנֵּי רִבִּי יִשְׁמָעֵאל. קַל וָחוֹמֶר. מָה אֲחוֹת אִשְׁתּוֹ מְיוּחֶדֶת עֶרְוָה שֶׁחַייָבִין עַל זְדוֹנָהּ כָּרֵת וְעַל שִׁגְגָתָהּ חַטָּאת הֲרֵי הִיא אֲסוּרָה לְהִתְייַבֵּם. אַף כָּל־עֶרְוָה שֶׁחַייָבִין עַל זְדוֹנָהּ כָּרֵת וְעַל שִׁגְגָתָהּ חַטָּאת תְּהֵא אֲסוּרָה לְהִתְייַבֵּם. מַה (fol. 2c) נְפַק מִן בֵּינֵיהוֹן. אַלְמָנָה לְכֹהֵן גָּדוֹל. מָאן דָּמַר עֶרְוָה שֶׁיֵּשׁ לָהּ הֵיתֵר לְאַחַר אִיסּוּרָהּ. זוֹ הוֹאִיל וְאֵין לָהּ הֵיתֵר לְאַחַר אִיסּוּרָהּ הֲרֵי הִיא אֲסוּרָה לְהִתְייַבֵּם. מָאן דָּמַר עֶרְוָה שֶׁחַייָבִין עָלֶיהָ זְדוֹנָהּ כָּרֵת וְעַל שִׁגְגָתָהּ חַטָּאת הֲרֵי זֶה אֲסוּרָה לְהִתְייַבֵּם. זֶה הוֹאִיל וְאֵין חַייָבִין עַל זְדוֹנָהּ כָּרֵת וְעַל שִׁגְגָתָהּ חַטָּאת תְּהֵא מוּתֶּרֶת לְהִתְייַבֵּם.

Following Rebbi Ismael? [55]Rebbi Ismael stated an argument *de minore ad majus.* Since his wife's sister is particular being under incest prohibition for whose violation one is punished if intentional by extirpation, if in error by an obligation to bring a purification offering, and is barred from the levirate, all other women under incest prohibitions for whose violation one is sanctioned if intentional by extirpation, if in error by the obligation to bring a purification offering, should be barred from the levirate.

What is the difference between them? A widow for the High Priest. For him who says, a woman under an incest prohibition which may be lifted after being imposed, this one, not being permitted after being prohibited[56], should be barred from the levirate. For him who says, a woman under an incest prohibition for which one is punished if intentional by extirpation, if in error by the obligation to bring a purification offering, is barred from the levirate, in this case since one is not sanctioned if intentional by extirpation, if in error by the obligation of a purification offering, should be permitted for the levirate[57].

55 *Sifra Qedošim Pereq* 11(10); a version combining the argument with the argument excluding the co-wives in Babli 3b. Both sources are anonymous.

56 A widow is forbidden for the High Priest as a new wife, *Lev.* 21:14. No sanction in mentioned in this case, in contrast to violations of incest prohibitions whose punishment is detailed in Chapter 20. On the other hand, following the principle that "one ascends in holiness but does not descend", a High Priest may become inactive but he cannot return to the status of common priest permitted to marry a widow.

57 This conclusion has to be shown to be faulty.

רִבִּי אַיְיבוּ בַּר נַגָּרִי קְרִיסְפִּי בְּשֵׁם רִבִּי שִׁמְעוֹן בֶּן לָקִישׁ. לֹא תִהְיֶה אֵשֶׁת הַמֵּת הַחוּצָה לְאִישׁ זָר. זוֹ אִשָּׁה שֶׁהִיא זָרָה לוֹ. אָמְרָה הַתּוֹרָה. לֹא תִהְיֶה לוֹ לְאִשָּׁה אֲפִילוּ מִצְוָה. מֵעַתָּה לֹא תְהֵא צְרִיכָה חֲלִיצָה. אָמַר רִבִּי יִרְמְיָה. יְבִימְתּוֹ יְבִימְתּוֹ. הַתּוֹרָה רִיבְתָה בַּחֲלִיצָה. אִי יְבִימְתּוֹ יְבִימְתּוֹ הַתּוֹרָה רִיבְתָה בַּיִּיבּוּם. תַּנֵּי רִבִּי יִשְׁמָעֵאל. מָאֵן יַבְמִי. זוֹ שֶׁמֵּיאֵן יַבְמִי. לֹא שֶׁמֵּיאֵינוֹ שָׁמַיִם. מֵעַתָּה לֹא

תְּהֵא צְרִיכָה חֲלִיצָה. הֲוֵי צוֹרְכָה לְהֵין דְּאָמַר רִבִּי יִרְמְיָה. יְבִימְתּוֹ יְבִימְתּוֹ. הַתּוֹרָה רִיבְתָה בַּחֲלִיצָה.

Rebbi Ayvu bar Naggari, Crispus, in the name of Rebbi Simeon ben Laqish. "The dead man's wife should not be outside, to a strange man[58]." That is a wife who is a stranger to him. The Torah said, she should not be his wife even in case of a commandment. That being, she should not need *ḥalîṣah*! Rebbi Jeremiah[59] said: "his sister-in-law, his sister-in-law", the Torah increased the cases of *ḥalîṣah*[60]! If from "his sister-in-law, his sister-in-law", did the Torah not increase the cases of levirate[61]? Rebbi Ismael stated[62]: "My levir refuses". That is, my levir refused, not that Heaven refused for him. In that case, she should not need *ḥalîṣah*! That means, the statement of Rebbi Jeremiah is needed, "his sister-in-law, his sister-in-law", the Torah increased the cases of *ḥalîṣah*!

58 *Deut.* 25:5. "To be" referring to a woman means "to be married", *Deut.* 24:2. זר "strange" means "outside the clan", cf. *Num.* 17:5. This is interpreted here to mean "outside her marriage group", e. g., the High Priest for the widow.

59 In the differently formulated Babli parallel, 20a, the author is Rav. It seems therefore that one should read "Rav Jeremiah" (first generation Babylonian) rather than "Rebbi Jeremiah" (fifth generation Galilean).

60 *Deut.* 25:7 reads: "If the man does not want to take his sister-in-law, then his sister-in-law shall go to the elders at the gate and she shall say: My levir refuses to sustain his brother's name in Israel, my levir does not agree." The second "sister-in-law" seems unnecessary; if it were written "then she shall go" it would have the same meaning. Since we hold that no word in the Torah is unnecessary, R. Jeremiah concludes that there is a sister-in-law who goes even though the levir did not refuse but Heaven refused for him. This is the subject of the next paragraph.

61 Since *Deut.* 25:7 also repeats "levir", should there not be a levir who marries his sister-in-law even though

the union otherwise would be forbidden?

62 *Sifry Deut.* #289. There, the second "levir" is used to express what R. Jeremiah concluded from the first part of the verse: "My *levir* does not agree," to exclude the case that the Omnipresent does not agree.

רִבִּי בּוּן בַּר חִייָה בְּעָא קוֹמֵי רִבִּי זְעוּרָא. אַלְמָנָה לְכֹהֵן גָּדוֹל מַהוּ שֶׁתְּהֵא צְרִיכָה חֲלִיצָה. אָמַר לֵיהּ. אֶיפְשַׁר לוֹמַר קִידּוּשִׁין תּוֹפְסִין בָּהּ וְאַתְּ אוֹמֵר. אֵינָהּ צְרִיכָה חֲלִיצָה. אָמַר לֵיהּ. הֲרֵי אַיילוֹנִית קִידּוּשִׁין תּוֹפְסִין בָּהּ וְאַתְּ אוֹמֵר. אֵינָהּ צְרִיכָה חֲלִיצָה. אָמַר לֵיהּ. הֲרֵי אַיילוֹנִית מִטַּעַם אַחֵר הוּצֵאתָה. אֲשֶׁר תֵּלֵד. יָֽצְתָה זוֹ שֶׁאֵינָהּ יוֹלֶדֶת.

Rebbi Bun bar Ḥiyya asked before Rebbi Ze'ira: Does a widow need *ḥalîṣah*? He said to him, is it possible to say that her *qiddushin*[63] are legally recognized[64] and you say she may not need *ḥalîṣah*? He answered him: But *qiddushin* of a she-ram[65] are legally recognized and one says that she does not need *ḥalîṣah*! He said to him, the she-ram was removed because of another reason: "she will bear[66]", this excludes the one who cannot have children.

63 A Jewish marriage is performed in two stages. The first, *qiddushin*, requires the groom to hand over to the bride an object of value (today, a gold ring) or a written promise of marriage and to declare before two witnesses that the woman is betrothed to him. From that moment on they are married as far as penal law is concerned. In antiquity, the prospective bride (who probably was in her early teens) did not prepare any trousseau. Hence, after *qiddushin* she was given adequate time to prepare and then was married to live with her husband in a second public ceremony, *nissuïn*, the execution of the *ketubah* document, in which the groom mortgages all his possessions and earnings for the upkeep of his wife and the care of his children, followed by the public recitation of seven benedictions (in the presence of 10 adult males). From that moment on, the couple is required to live in intimacy.

Today, the two ceremonies are separated only by the reading of the *ketubah* and, sometimes, by a rabbi's sermon. The period between *qiddushin* and *nissuïn* is one in which the groom is legally married, but as he is forbidden marital relations with his wife, as yet has no financial responsibility. After *nissuïn*, since the wife has a claim on his property enforceable in court, he receives administration of her estate. The "preliminary marriage" contracted by *qiddushin*, in Greek speaking communities called πρωτογαμία (cf. *Demay* 6, Note 19), can be dissolved only by a valid bill of divorce.

64 Incestual *qiddushin* (where the relationship is punished by extirpation by the Heavenly court or as a capital crime by the earthly court) are null and void. Forbidden marriages for which no particular penalties are indicated, such as marriages of priests with unsuitable women or marriages of bastards, are sinful but valid. Since the marriage of a High Priest with a widow would be valid, it is clear that a levirate union would be sinful but valid and, therefore, the widow needs *ḥalîṣah*.

65 A woman lacking secondary feminine sex characteristics held to be infertile.

66 *Sifry Deut.* #289, quoted in Babli 12a. *Deut.* 25:6: "It shall be that the firstborn *she will bear* should replace the name of his dead brother".

עַד שֶׁאַתְּ לָמֵד כָּל־הָעֲרָיוֹת מֵאֲחוֹת אִשְׁתּוֹ לְאִיסּוּר. לְמַד כָּל־הָעֲרָיוֹת מֵאֵשֶׁת אָחִיו לְהֵיתֵר. אָמַר רִבִּי מָנָא. לְמֵידִין שְׁנֵי אִיסּוּרִין מִשְּׁנֵי אִיסּוּרִין. וְאֵין לְמֵידִין שְׁנֵי אִיסּוּרִין מֵאִיסּוּר אֶחָד. רִבִּי לְעָזָר בְּשֵׁם רִבִּי אָבוּן. כָּל־דָּבָר שֶׁהוּא בָּא מַחְמַת הַגּוֹרֵם בָּטֵל הַגּוֹרֵם בָּטֵל הָאִיסּוּר. וְדָבָר שֶׁאֵינוֹ בָא מַחְמַת הַגּוֹרֵם אַף עַל פִּי שֶׁבָּטֵל הַגּוֹרֵם הָאִיסּוּר בִּמְקוֹמוֹ. וּמַה אִית לָךְ. אָמַר רִבִּי יוֹסֵי בֵּירִבִּי בּוּן. כְּגוֹן אֵילוּ חֲמֵשׁ עֶשְׂרֵה נָשִׁים. שֶׁלֹּא תֹאמַר בִּתּוֹ עַד שֶׁלֹּא נִישֵּׂאת לְאָחִיו אֲסוּרָה לוֹ. נִישֵּׂאת לְאָחִיו מוּתֶּרֶת לוֹ.

Instead of inferring from his wife's sister that all women under incest prohibitions remain prohibited[67], deduce from his brother's wife that all women under incest prohibitions become permitted[68]! Rebbi Mana[69] said, one infers two prohibitions from two prohibitions[70] but one does not infer two prohibitions from one prohibition[71]. Rebbi Eleazar in the name of Rebbi Abun: For anything induced by a cause, if the cause is removed the prohibition is removed. But for anything not induced by a cause, if the cause is removed the prohibition remains. What is that? Rebbi Yose ben Rebbi Bun said, e. g., those fifteen categories of women. That you should not say that his daughter is forbidden to him before she is married to his brother; once she is married to his brother she is permitted to him.

67 For levirate; see above, Notes 50-55.

68 That the prohibitions are eliminated by the duty of levirate. The argument is repeated in the Babli, 8a, by Amoraim of the last Babylonian generation who add an additional argument.

69 Since the authors quoted in the following are of early generations, this must be R. Mana I.

70 One pre-existing prohibition to which was added the additional prohibition of adultery when she married the brother.

71 In the case of an unrelated woman, the prohibition of adultery and that of marrying the brother's wife are one and the same.

לֵוִי בַּר סוּסַיי בְּעָא קוֹמֵי רִבִּי. נִיתְנֵי שֵׁשׁ עֶשְׂרֵה נָשִׁים. אִמּוֹ אֲנוּסַת אָבִיו נְשׂוּאָה לְאָחִיו מֵאָבִיו. אָמַר לֵיהּ. נִיכַּר אוֹתוֹ הָאִישׁ שֶׁאֵין לוֹ מוֹחַ בְּקָדְקֳדוֹ. וְלָמָּה. אָמַר לֵיהּ. בְּגִין דְּרִבִּי יוּדָה. דְּרִבִּי יוּדָה אוֹסֵר בַּאֲנוּסַת אָבִיו וּמְפוּתַּת אָבִיו. וְלֹא מוֹדֵי רִבִּי יְהוּדָה שֶׁאִים קִידְּשָׁהּ שֶׁתָּפְסוּ בָהּ קִידּוּשִׁין. אֶלָּא בְגִין דְּתַנִּינָן שֵׁשׁ עֲרָיוֹת חֲמוּרוֹת מֵאֵילּוּ. מִפְּנֵי שֶׁהֵן נְשׂוּאוֹת לַאֲחֵרִים צָרוֹתֵיהֶן מוּתָּרוֹת. וְתַנֵּי רִבִּי חִייָה כֵן. אִם יְכוֹלוֹת לְהִינָּשֵׂא לְאָחִיו שֶׁלֹּא בַעֲבֵירָה צָרוֹתֵיהֶן פְּטוּרוֹת מִן הַחֲלִיצָה וּמִן הַיִּיבּוּם. וּמִכּוּלָּם אֵין לָךְ אֶלָּא אִמּוֹ אֲנוּסַת אָבִיו נְשׂוּאָה לְאָחִיו מֵאָבִיו. לָמָּה לֹא תַנִּיתָהּ. בְּגִין דְּתַנִּיתָהּ רִבִּי חִייָה לֹא נִיתְנִינָהּ. כָּל־שֶׁכֵּן נִיתְנִינָהּ. אֶלָּא בְגִין דְּתַנִּינָן. אֲחוֹתָהּ שֶׁהִיא יְבִמְתָּהּ אוֹ

חוֹלֶצֶת אוֹ מִתְיַיבֶּמֶת. וְאַתְּ מַשְׁכַּח בְּכוּלְּהוֹן אֲחוֹתוֹ שֶׁהִיא יְבִימְתּוֹ מִתְיַיבֶּמֶת. חוּץ מֵאִמּוֹ אֲנוּסַת אָבִיו נְשׂוּאָה לְאָחִיו מֵאָבִיו.

[72]Levi bar Sisi asked before Rebbi: Should we not state "sixteen women"? One's mother who was raped by his father married to his paternal halfbrother[73]. He said to him, it is evident that this person has no brain in his head. And why? He said to him, because of Rebbi Jehudah, because Rebbi Jehudah forbids the one who was raped or seduced by his father. Does Rebbi Jehudah not agree that if [the halfbrother] gave her *qiddushin*, the preliminary marriage is legally recognized? But because we have stated[74]: "Six incest prohibitions more severe than these; because they are married to others their co-wives are free." And Rebbi Ḥiyya stated thereupon: [75]"If they may marry his brother without sin their co-wives are freed from *ḥalîṣah* and levirate." And among all of them there is only his mother who was raped by his father married to his paternal halfbrother. Why did we not state this? Because Rebbi Ḥiyya stated it, should we not state it? Certainly we should state it! But because we have stated[76]: "Her sister who also is her sister-in-law either takes *ḥalîṣah* or accepts the levirate." We find in all cases[77] that her sister who also is her sister-in-law accepts the levirate except for his mother who was raped by his father married to his paternal halfbrother.

72 Babli 9a. There, many other interpretations are given and the discussion extends up to fol. 10b.

73 According to the majority interpretation, *Deut.* 23:1 does not forbid the unmarried mother of a son to his paternal halfbrothers. R. Jehudah disagrees but even he must hold that the prohibition of the unwed mother to the halfbrothers of her son is not severely penalized and therefore, a marriage would be legally valid. The incest prohibitions of *Lev.* 18 all speak of the "father's wife".

74 Mishnah 1:5.

75 Tosephta *Yebamot* 1:7. In that case, the marriage is valid and the co-wives are freed as co-wives of a forbidden one. But if the "marriage" of the brother was in sin, it was in deadly sin and the marriage was not legally recognized. In that case, the brother was not married to the forbidden woman and the so-called co-wife was in fact the only wife and subject to the laws of the levirate.

76 Babli 9b, in the name of R. Ḥiyya.

77 The complicated scenario for all 15 cases of the Mishnah is given in detail by Rashi in his Commentary to *Yebamot* 9b. In the 16th case, if the raped woman married a son of the man who raped her, her sister cannot marry her son since the maternal aunt is forbidden in *Lev.* 18:13. Therefore, her sister cannot be her sister-in-law in a case involving prohibited levirate.

יִצְחָק בַּר אִיסְטַייָה אָמַר. רִבִּי שִׁמְעוֹן בֶּן לָקִישׁ בָּעֵי. נִיתְנֵי. שֵׁשׁ עֶשְׂרֵה נָשִׁים. חֲלִיצָה פּוֹטֶרֶת צָרָתָהּ. אָמַר רִבִּי יַעֲקֹב דְּרוֹמַייָא קוֹמֵי רִבִּי יוֹסֵי. וְלָמָּה לֹא תַנֵּינָתָהּ. בְּגִין רִבִּי עֲקִיבָה. דְּאָמַר רִבִּי עֲקִיבָה. יֵשׁ מַמְזֵר בַּחֲלוּצָה. נִיתְנִינָהּ עַל דְּרַבָּנָן. לֹא אָתִינָן מִיתְנֵי אֶלָּא מִילִין דְּכָל־עַמָּא מוֹדֵיי בְהוֹן. אַתְיָיא דְּיִצְחָק בַּר אִיסְטַייָה כְּרִבִּי אִמִּי. רִבִּי יָסָא אָמַר. אִיתְפַּלְּגוֹן רִבִּי יוֹחָנָן וְרִבִּי שִׁמְעוֹן בֶּן לָקִישׁ. רִבִּי יוֹחָנָן אָמַר הוּא אֵינוֹ חַייָב עַל הַחֲלוּצָה וְהָאַחִין חַייָבִין עַל הַחֲלוּצָה. בֵּין הוּא וּבֵין אַחִים חַייָבִין עַל הַצָּרָה. רִבִּי שִׁמְעוֹן בֶּן לָקִישׁ אָמַר. בֵּין הוּא בֵּין אַחִין אֵינָן חַייָבִין לֹא עַל הַחֲלוּצָה וְלֹא עַל הַצָּרָה. רִבִּי אִימִּי מַחֲלִיף שְׁמוּעָתָא. אָמַר רִבִּי זְעִירָא קוֹמֵי רִבִּי יָסָא. וְהָא רִבִּי אִימִּי מַחֲלִיף שְׁמוּעָתָא. אֶלָּא דֵעוֹן דֵּעוֹן אִית לֵיהּ לְרִבִּי יוֹחָנָן. וַאֲפִילוּ תֹאמַר. דֵעוֹן דֵּעוֹן אִית לֵיהּ לְרִבִּי יוֹחָנָן. דֵעוֹן דֵּעוֹן אִית לְרִבִּי שִׁמְעוֹן בֶּן לָקִישׁ. מִילְתֵיהּ דְּיִצְחָק בַּר אִיסְטַייָה מְסַייְעָא לְרִבִּי אִמִּי וּמִילֵּיהוֹן דְּרַבָּנָן מְסַייְעִין לְרִבִּי יָסָא. דְּאָמַר רִבִּי יִרְמְיָה רִבִּי בָּא תְּרֵיהוֹן בְּשֵׁם רִבִּי חִייָא בַּר בָּא. הַכֹּל מוֹדִין בְּצָרָה שֶׁהוּא חַייָב. מַה פְּלִיגִין. בַּחֲלוּצָה. רִבִּי יוֹחָנָן אָמַר. הוּא אֵינוֹ חַייָב עַל הַחֲלוּצָה וְהָאַחִין חַייָבִין עַל הַחֲלוּצָה.

Isaac, the son of the isatis grower[78], said that Rebbi Simeon ben Laqish asked, should we state sixteen women? *Ḥalîṣah* frees her co-wife[79]! Rebbi Jacob the Southerner said before Rebbi Yose, why was this not stated? Because of Rebbi Aqiba, since Rebbi Aqiba said there is a bastard from a woman who got *ḥalîṣah*[80]. One should have stated it for the rabbis[81]! We came to state only things everybody agreed to. It turns out that Isaac, the son of the isatis grower, holds with Rebbi Immi. Rebbi Yasa said, Rebbi Joḥanan and Rebbi Simeon ben Laqish disagreed[82]. Rebbi Joḥanan said, he is not guilty[83] for the woman who got *ḥalîṣah*, but the brothers are guilty for the woman who got *ḥalîṣah*. Both he and the brothers are guilty for the co-wife[84]. Rebbi Simeon ben Laqish said, neither he nor the brothers are guilty for the woman who got *ḥalîṣah* or for the co-wife[85]. Rebbi Immi switches the attributions[86]. Rebbi Ze'ira said before Rebbi Yasa, does not Rebbi Immi switch the attributions? But Rebbi Joḥanan had several opinions[87]. Did Rebbi Simeon ben Laqish have several opinions[88]? The statement of Isaac, the son of the isatis grower, supports Rebbi Immi and the statements of the rabbis support Rebbi Yasa, as both Rebbi Jeremiah, Rebbi Abba, said in the name of Rebbi Ḥiyya bar Abba: Everybody agrees about the co-wife that one is guilty. Where do they disagree? About the woman who got *ḥalîṣah*. Rebbi Joḥanan said, he is not guilty for the woman who got *ḥalîṣah*, but the brothers are guilty for the woman who got *ḥalîṣah*.

78 His name appears only here.

79 This cryptic argument is explicit in Babli 10b in the form of a discussion between R. Joḥanan and R. Simeon ben Laqish. It is generally agreed that when a levir freed his brother's widow from the levirate by the ceremony of *ḥalîṣah*, she is forbidden to him and all other brothers. The majority opinion is that she is forbidden not as his

brother's wife since that prohibition was eliminated when levirate became possible but because it is written in *Deut.* 25:5 אֲשֶׁר לֹא־יִבְנֶה אֶת־בֵּית אָחִיו which is interpreted not as "who *would* not build his brother's house but as "who *will* not build"; if he refused once he will not build in the future. If the brother who performed *ḥalîṣah* nevertheless afterwards marries his sister-in-law, that marriage is recognized since no special penalties are attached to this prohibition. If he then dies childless, according to R. Simeon ben Laqish she is forbidden to any remaining brothers as wife of the first brother since for them that prohibition was never lifted. Since she is severely forbidden, the co-wife is free without ceremony.

80 R. Aqiba, who denies any difference between severely or simply forbidden marriages, declares all children born from all kinds of forbidden marriages as bastards forbidden to marry untainted Jewish partners.

81 Who disagree with R. Aqiba.

82 The Babli quotes only the tradition here attributed to R. Immi.

83 "Guilty" of the severe sin of incest with the brother's wife.

84 Since she was not selected for the ceremony, her status vis-à-vis the brother performing *ḥalîṣah* is not different from that vis-à-vis the other brothers.

85 Since any of the brothers could have performed the ceremony, the severe prohibition was lifted for all of them and was never re-instituted.

86 Since the position of R. Simeon as quoted by R. Yasa contradicts the position of R. Simeon quoted by R. Isaac the isatis grower's.

87 He taught different positions to different students (R. Immi and R. Yasa).

88 Should he have changed his position just to oppose R. Joḥanan?

מִילֵּיהוֹן דְּרַבָּנִין אָֽמְרִין. חֲלוּצָה פְטוֹר. שִׁמְעוֹן בַּר בָּא בְּעָא קוֹמֵי רִבִּי יוֹחָנָן. מַה בֵּין חוֹלֵץ וּמַה בֵּין מְגָרֵשׁ. אָמַר לֵיהּ. אַתְּ סָבוּר חֲלִיצָה קִנְיָין. אֵינָהּ אֶלָּא פְטוֹר. אֵין הָאַחִין חַייָבִין עָלֶיהָ מִשֵּׁם אִשְׁתּוֹ שֶׁלְּחוֹלֵץ אֲבָל חַייָבִין עָלֶיהָ מִשֵּׁם אִשְׁתּוֹ שֶׁל מֵת.

[89]The words of the rabbis mean that *ḥalîṣah* is freeing. Simeon bar Abba asked before Rebbi Joḥanan: What is the difference between having *ḥalîṣah* and divorcing[90]? He said to him: You think that *ḥalîṣah* is acquisiton, but it is only freeing. The brothers are not guilty[91] for her under the category of "wife of the one acting in *ḥalîṣah*" but they are guilty under the category of "wife of the deceased".

89 This paragraph belongs to Halakhah 3:1 where the main discussion is whether *ḥalîṣah* gives the widow the additional status of divorcee, a position endorsed by Rebbi. Samuel holds that *ḥalîṣah* is simply the removal of an impediment for the widow to remarry and does not create new marriage restrictions.

90 Since in relation to a Cohen the woman freed by *ḥalîṣah* is at least rabbinically treated as a divorcee.

91 If they would engage in sexual relations with her.

רִבִּי יוּדָן בְּעָא. כְּמַה דְאָמַר. בֵּין הוּא בֵּין אַחִין אֵין חַייָבִין עַל הַחֲלוּצָה אֲבָל חַייָבִין עַל הַצָּרָה. נִיחָא הוּא אֵינוֹ חַייָב עַל הַחֲלוּצָה. שֶׁכְּבָר נִרְאָה לִפְטוֹר בָּהּ. וְחַייָב עַל הַצָּרָה. שֶׁלֹּא נִרְאָה לִפְטוֹר בָּהּ. אַחִין מַה בֵּין חֲלוּצָה אֶצְלוֹ מַה בֵּין צָרָה אֶצְלוֹ. חָזַר וְאָמַר. אֵין אַתְּ יוֹדֵעַ מִשֵּׁם מַה אַתְּ מְחַייְבוֹ. אִי מִשּׁוּם אִשְׁתּוֹ שֶׁכְּחוֹלֵץ אִי מִשּׁוּם אִשְׁתּוֹ שֶׁל מֵת. אָמַר רִבִּי יוֹסֵי מַה אַתְּ סָבוּר חֲלִיצָה קִנְייָן. אֵינָהּ אֶלָּא פְטוֹר. אֵין הָאַחִין חַייָבִין עָלֶיהָ מִשֵּׁם אִשְׁתּוֹ שֶׁלַּחוֹלֵץ אֲבָל חַייָבִין עָלֶיהָ מִשֵּׁם אִשְׁתּוֹ שֶׁכַּמֵּת.

Rebbi Yudan asked: Following him who says, neither he nor the brothers are guilty for the woman who got *ḥalîṣah* but are guilty for the co-wife. It is fine that he is not guilty about the woman who got *ḥalîṣah* since he was cleared to have her freely[92]. He is guilty about the co-wife since he was never cleared to have her freely. What is the difference for one of the brothers between the woman who got *ḥalîṣah* and the co-wife?

He turned around and said, you do not know under which head to declare him guilty, whether as wife of the one performing *ḥalîṣah* or wife of the deceased. Rebbi Yose said, do you think *ḥalîṣah* is acquisiton? But it is only freeing. The brothers are not guilty for her under the category of "wife of the one acting in *ḥalîṣah*" but they are guilty under the category of "wife of the deceased".

92 Since he could have married her in levirate. The Babli, 9a, rejects this kind of argument since any one of the brothers could have acted as levir of any of the widows which, therefore, were potentially available to all brothers and none of them could be accused of incest with any of the women.

רִבִּי יוּדָן בָּעֵי. כְּמָאן דְּאָמַר. הַכֹּל מוֹדִין בְּצָרָה שֶׁהוּא חַייָב. קִידֵּשׁ אֶחָד מִן הַשּׁוּק אֶת אַחַת מֵהֶן וּבָא הַיָּבָם וְחָלַץ לָהּ וּבָא עָלֶיהָ. וּפָקְעוּ מִמֶּנּוּ קִידּוּשִׁין. חָלַץ לַחֲבֵירָתָהּ וּבָא עָלֶיהָ. לְמַפְרֵיעָה חָלוּ עָלֶיהָ קִידּוּשִׁין. אָמַר רִבִּי שַׁמַּי. לֹא כֵן אָמַר רִבִּי יַנַּאי. נִימְנוּ שְׁלֹשִׁים וְכַמָּה זְקֵינִים. מְנַיִין שֶׁאֵין קִידּוּשִׁין תּוֹפְסִין בִּיבָמָה. תַּלְמוּד לוֹמַר לֹא תִהְיֶה אֵשֶׁת הַמֵּת הַחוּצָה לְאִישׁ זָר. שֶׁלֹּא יְהֵא לָהּ הֲוָייָה אֵצֶל אַחֵר. אָמַר לֵיהּ רִבִּי יוֹחָנָן. וְלֹא מַתְנִיתָה הִיא. אוֹ לְאַחַר שֶׁיַּחֲלוֹץ לֵיךְ יַבְמֵיךְ. אֵינָהּ מְקוּדֶּשֶׁת. וְהָיָה רִבִּי יוֹחָנָן מְקַלֶּס לָהּ. הַזָּלִים זָהָב מִכִּיס. בְּנִי אַל יָלוּזוּ מֵעֵינֶיךָ. חֲכַם בְּנִי וְשַׂמַּח לִבִּי. תֵּן לְחָכָם וְיֶחְכַּם עוֹד. יִשְׁמַע חָכָם וְיוֹסֵף לֶקַח. אָמַר רִבִּי שִׁמְעוֹן בֶּן לָקִישׁ בָּתַר כָּל־אִילֵּין קִילּוּסַיָּא יְכוֹל אֲנָא פָּתַר לָהּ כְּרִבִּי עֲקִיבָה. דְּרִבִּי עֲקִיבָה אוֹמֵר. יֵשׁ מַמְזֵר בִּיבָמָה. אֶלָּא תַּמָּן יְבָמָה אַחַת וְהָכָא שְׁתֵּי יְבָמוֹת. שַׁנְייָא הִיא אִיסּוּר יְבָמָה אַחַת שַׁנְייָא הִיא אִיסּוּר שְׁתֵּי יְבָמוֹת.

Rebbi Yudan asked: Following him who says that everybody agrees about the co-wife that he is guilty, if somebody from the market gave *qiddushin* to one of them and then the levir came and performed *ḥalîṣah* with her or had intercourse with her, did the *qiddushin* become invalid? If he performed *ḥalîṣah* with her companion but then had intercourse with her, were *qiddushin* validated retroactively? Rebbi Shammai said, did not Rebbi Yannai say the following: More than 30 elders voted, from where that *qiddushin* have no legal effect on a sister-in-law? The verse says, [93]"the wife of the deceased may not belong to any outside unrelated man", that she cannot have any existence with another man[94]. Rebbi Joḥanan said to him, is that not a Mishnah? [95]"Or after your levir will have performed *ḥalîṣah* with you, she is not preliminarily married." And Rebbi Yannai[96] praised him "those who pour out gold from the wallet[97]," "my son, they should not be removed from your eyes,[98]" "get wise, my son, and make me happy[99]", "give to the wise that he shall become wiser[100]," "let the wise listen that he increase in knowledge.[101]" Rebbi Simeon ben Laqish said, after all these praises I can explain it following Rebbi Aqiba since Rebbi Aqiba said that there exists a bastard from a sister-in-law[30]! But there[102] is one sister-in-law, here are two sisters-in-law. The prohibition of a single sister-in-law is different from that of two sisters-in-law[103]!

93 *Deut.* 25:5.

94 This is the unquestioned doctrine of the Yerushalmi. In the Babli, 92b, it is the position only of Rav; Samuel doubts whether the verse invalidates *qiddushin* or simply makes them sinful like other non-incestuous forbidden unions. The editors of the Babli explicitly follow Samuel and reject the opinion of the Yerushalmi. That a transgression which is not a capital crime either before the human or the heavenly court is invalid is a very exceptional statement.

95 *Qiddušin* 3:5. The Mishnah enumerates situations in which consummation of the marriage is impossible at the moment but may become possible later on. If consummation of the marriage is

impossible then *qiddushin* are impossible since they make the bride a wife for all aspects of criminal law. She becomes a wife for matters of civil law only by entering the husband's house in *nissuïn*, the marriage ceremony. (R. Meïr disagrees and acknowledges inoperative *qiddushin* which become activated once the impediment to marriage is removed. The second question of R. Yudan must refer to R. Meïr's position.)

96 The text here reads "R. Johanan". This has been changed in the translation following the parallel text in *Soṭah* 2:1 and a similar text in *Kilaim* 8:1 (p. 258).

97 *Is.* 46:6.

98 *Prov.* 3:21.

99 *Prov.* 27:11.

100 *Prov.* 9:9.

101 *Prov.* 1:5

102 Mishnah *Qiddušin*.

103 The biblical argument of R. Yannai does not imply anything about the status of a co-wife; cf. Note 92 for the opposition of the Babli.

רִבִּי יוּדָן בְּעָא. כְּמָאן דְּאָמַר. הוּא אֵינוֹ חַייָב עַל הַחֲלִיצָה אֲבָל חַייָב הוּא עַל הַצָּרָה. חֲלִיצָה פְּטוֹר. בִּיאָה פְּטוֹר. כְּמַה דְתֵימַר. חָלַץ לָהּ נֶאֶסְרָה לָאַחִין. וְדִכְווָתָהּ בָּא עָלֶיהָ נֶאֶסְרָה לָאַחִין. תַּנֵּי רִבִּי חִייָה. מֵת הָרִאשׁוֹן יְיַבֵּם הַשֵּׁינִי. מֵת הַשֵּׁינִי יְיַבֵּם הַשְּׁלִישִׁי. אָמַר רִבִּי יוֹסֵי מַה אַתְּ סָבַר. הִיא חֲלִיצָה הִיא (fol. 2d) בִּיאָה. כֵּיוָן שֶׁחָלַץ לָהּ נֶעֶקְרָה הִימֶּינָּה זִיקַּת הַמֵּת לְמַפְרֵיעָה. לְמַפְרֵיעָה חָל עָלֶיהָ אִיסּוּרוֹ שֶׁלְּמֵת אֵצֶל הָאַחִין. אֲבָל אִם בָּא עָלֶיהָ אִשְׁתּוֹ הִיא. וְתַנֵּי רִבִּי חִייָה. מֵת הָרִאשׁוֹן יְיַבֵּם הַשֵּׁינִי. מֵת הַשֵּׁינִי יְיַבֵּם הַשְּׁלִישִׁי.

Rebbi Yudan asked: Following him who said, a man is not guilty for the woman who got *ḥalîṣah* but he is guilty for the co-wife, *ḥalîṣah* is freeing; is intercourse freeing[104]? As you say, if he performed *ḥalîṣah* with her, she became forbidden to the brothers. Similarly, if he had intercourse with her, she became forbidden to the brothers. Rebbi Ḥiyya stated: If the first husband died, the second brother shall take her in levirate. If the second dies, the third shall take her in levirate[105]! Rebbi Yose said, what do you think? That *ḥalîṣah* is the same as intercourse? Once he performed *ḥalîṣah*, the claim of the dead is removed from her retroactively. Retroactively fell on her the prohibition[106] of the dead man regarding the brothers. But if he had intercourse with her, she is his wife[107]. On that did Rebbi Ḥiyya state: If the first husband died, the second brother shall take her in levirate. If the second dies, the third shall take her in levirate[108].

104 Intercourse is the only way a sister-in-law can be married, *Deut.* 25:5. The act not only is one of binding the woman to him but also of freeing him from the incest prohibition of the brother's wife.

105 How can the third man marry her if she is forbidden to him by the levirate of the second?

106 The incest prohibition.

107 "In every respect", Mishnah 4:4. Her relationship with the first husband is legally dissolved.

108 But if two husbands die (except in war or during an epidemic) she is considered a danger to a husband's life and must have *ḥalîṣah*.

אֲרוֹתוֹ מֵאִמּוֹ. נְשׂוּאָה לְאָחִיו מֵאָבִיו. אֲחוֹת אִמּוֹ. גְּבַר וּבְרֵיהּ נָסְבִין תַּרְתֵּין אַחֲוָן. אֲחוֹת אִשְׁתּוֹ. תְּרֵין אַחִין נְסִיבִין לְתַרְתֵּיי אַחֲוָון.

"His maternal halfsister," married to his paternal halfbrother. "His mother's sister," a man and his son married two sisters. "His wife's sister," two brothers being married to two sisters[109].

109 From here to the end of the Halakhah one constructs cases in which the prohibitions of levirate can actually apply.

וְאֵשֶׁת אָחִיו מֵאִמּוֹ. נֶאֱמַר כָּאן אַחֲוָה וְנֶאֱמַר לְהַלָּן שְׁנֵים־עָשָׂר עֲבָדֶיךָ אַחִים אֲנַחְנוּ. מַה אַחִים שֶׁנֶּאֱמַר לְהַלָּן בְּאַחִים מִן הָאַב הַכָּתוּב מְדַבֵּר. אַף אַחִים שֶׁנֶּאֱמַר כָּאן בְּאַחִים מִן הָאַב הַכָּתוּב מְדַבֵּר. אָמַר רִבִּי יוֹנָתָן. נֶאֱמַר כָּאן

יְשִׁיבָה וְנֶאֱמַר לְהַלָּן יְשִׁיבָה. וִירִשְׁתָּהּ וְיָשַׁבְתָּ בָּהּ. מַה יְשִׁיבָה שֶׁנֶּאֱמַר לְהַלָּן יְשִׁיבָה שֶׁיֵּשׁ עִמָּהּ יְרוּשָּׁה. אַף יְשִׁיבָה שֶׁנֶּאֱמַר כָּאן יְשִׁיבָה שֶׁיֵּשׁ עִמָּהּ יְרוּשָּׁה. רִבִּי אָבוּן בַּר בִּיסְנָא בְשֵׁם רִבִּי יוֹנָתָן דְּבֵית גּוּבְרִין. יֵשְׁבוּ. אֶת שֶׁיְּשִׁיבָתָן בְּבַיִת אֶחָד. יָצְאוּ אַחִים מִן הָאֵם שֶׁזֶּה הוֹלֵךְ לְבֵית אָבִיו וְזֶה הוֹלֵךְ לְבֵית אָבִיו.

"His maternal halfbrother's wife.[110]" It mentions here brotherhood and it is said there: "We, your servants, are twelve brothers." Since the "brothers" mentioned there are paternal brothers, so the "brothers" mentioned here must be paternal brothers[111]. Rebbi Jonathan said, it is said here dwelling and it says there dwelling. "You will inherit and dwell there[112]." Since with "dwelling" mentioned there, inheritance is connected. so with "dwelling" mentioned here, inheritance is connected. Rebbi Abun bar Bisna in the name of Rebbi Jonathan from Bet Gubrin: "they dwell[113]". Those whose dwelling is in one house. This excludes maternal halfbrothers where one goes to his own father's house and the other one goes to his own father's house.

110 One explains why the scenario described in Note 10 is intended, that there is no levirate among maternal halfbrothers.

111 See above, Note 37.

112 *Deut.* 17:13.

113 *Deut.* 25:5. The argument is based on the expression "dwell *together*". Cf. *Sifry Deut.* #288, first paragraph. The argument is hinted at in the Babli, 17b, as a side remark.

יַחְדָּיו. פְּרָט לְאֵשֶׁת אָחִיו שֶׁלֹּא הָיָה בְעוֹלָמוֹ. רִבִּי בּוּן בַּר חִיָּיה אָמַר. רִבִּי בָּא בַּר מָמָל בָּעֵי. אַיילוֹנִית וְאֵשֶׁת אָחִיו שֶׁלֹּא הָיָה בְעוֹלָמוֹ הָיוּ בְפָרָשָׁה. מֶה חָמִית מֵימַר. אַיילוֹנִית צָרָתָהּ מוּתֶּרֶת וְאֵשֶׁת אָחִיו שֶׁלֹּא הָיָה בְעוֹלָמוֹ צָרָתָהּ אֲסוּרָה. אָמַר לֵיהּ. אַיילוֹנִית מִטַּעַם אַחֵר הוּצֵאתָהּ. אֲשֶׁר תֵּלֵד. יָצְתָה זוֹ שֶׁאֵינָהּ יוֹלֶדֶת. לֹא דַייֵךְ שֶׁאֵינָהּ מִתְייַבֶּמֶת אֶלָּא שֶׁאַתְּ מְבַקֵּשׁ לֶאֱסוֹר צָרָתָהּ. אֲבָל אֵשֶׁת אָחִיו

שֶׁלֹּא הָיָה בְּעוֹלָמוֹ עֶרְוָה הִיא וְעֶרְוָה פּוֹטֶרֶת צָרָתָהּ. אַסִּי אָמַר. צָרַת אַיילוֹנִית אֲסוּרָה. מַתְנִיתָא פְלִיגָא עַל אַסִּי. וְכוּלָּן אִם מֵתוּ אוֹ מֵיאֵינוּ אוֹ נִתְגָּרְשׁוּ אוֹ שֶׁנִּמְצְאוּ אַיילוֹנִיּוֹת צָרוֹתֵיהֶן מוּתָּרוֹת. רִבִּי בּוּן בַּר חִיָּיה בְּשֵׁם רִבִּי בָּא בַּר מָמָל. מַה דָמַר אַסִּי כְּרִבִּי מֵאִיר. דְּרִבִּי מֵאִיר אָמַר. כֹּל שֶׁאֵין אַתְּ מְייַבְּמֵנִי אֵין אַתְּ מְייַבֵּם צָרָתִי.

"Together", this excludes the wife of his brother who did not live in his world[11,39]. Rebbi Abun bar Ḥiyya said, Rebbi Abba bar Mamal asked: The she-ram[65] and the wife of his brother who did not live in his world were in the paragraph. Why do you see fit to say that the co-wife of the she-ram is permitted but the co-wife of the wife of his brother who did not live in his world is forbidden? He said to him, the she-ram was removed because of another reason: "she will bear", this excludes the one who cannot have children[66]. Is it not enough that she cannot be eligible for the levirate but you also want to forbid her co-wife? But the wife of his brother who did not live in his world is under an incest prohibition and any incest prohibition frees the co-wife. Assi[114] said, the co-wife of a she-ram is forbidden. The Mishnah[115] disagrees with Assi: "All of these, if they died, or refused, or were divorced, or turned out to be she-rams, their co-wives are permitted." Rebbi Abun bar Ḥiyya in the name of Rebbi Abba bar Mamal: Assi follows Rebbi Meïr since Rebbi Meïr said, in any case where you cannot take me in levirate you cannot take my co-wife[116].

114 He is Rav Assi; his statement is in Babli 12b. Since he is Babylonian and slightly older than Rav for whom the title of "Rav" was invented, it seems correct to leave him without title.

115 Mishnah 1:2.

116 The Babli holds that the Mishnah speaks about a girl whose first husband never realized that she was congenitally sterile. Therefore, we assume that had he known this, he would not have married her; the

marriage act was in error and she is not his widow. But if he knowingly married a sterile woman she is his wife and her co-wife is forbidden (accepting R. Meir's reasoning without quoting him.)

וְכַלָּתוֹ. אָמַר רִבִּי יוֹסֵי. זֹאת אוֹמֶרֶת שֶׁמּוּתָּר לָאָדָם לִישָּׂא אֶת אֵשֶׁת בֶּן אָחִיו.

"And his daughter-in-law." Rebbi Yose said, this implies that a man is permitted to marry his brother's son's wife[117].

117 A daughter-in-law becomes a sister-in-law only if the son dies or divorces her and she marries a brother. The statement is attributed to R. Ḥaggai in Halakhah 11:4.

(fol. 2a) **משנה ב:** הֲרֵי אֵילּוּ פּוֹטְרוֹת צָרוֹתֵיהֶן וְצָרוֹת צָרוֹתֵיהֶן מִן הַחֲלִיצָה וּמִן הַיִּיבּוּם עַד סוֹף הָעוֹלָם. וְכוּלָּם אִם מֵתוּ אוֹ מֵיאֲנוּ אוֹ נִתְגָּרְשׁוּ אוֹ שֶׁנִּמְצְאוּ אַיילוֹנִיּוֹת צָרוֹתֵיהֶן מוּתָּרוֹת. וְאֵי אַתְּ יָכוֹל לוֹמַר בַּחֲמוֹתוֹ וּבְאֵם חֲמוֹתוֹ שֶׁנִּמְצְאוּ אַיילוֹנִיּוֹת אוֹ שֶׁמֵּיאֵינוּ.

Mishnah 2: All these free their co-wives and the co-wives of their co-wives from *ḥalîṣah* and levirate forever[3]. And all of these, if they died, or repudiated[118], or were divorced, or found to be she-rams, their co-wives are permitted[119]. But you cannot say about his mother-in-law or his mother-in-law's mother that they were found to be she-rams or that they had repudiated[120].

118 Only a father can give his minor daughter in marriage. If the father died, mother or brother can marry her off, but this marriage is rabbinic only and the girl can walk out of the marriage as long as she is a minor by a simple declaration that she refuses to be married to this man.

119 An impediment to levirate must exist at the moment of death of the childless brother. If the relationship with the brother was dissolved before his death, it no longer has any influence.

120 If they had a daughter they must have had marital relations when adult.

(fol. 2d) **הלכה ב:** הֲרֵי אֵילּוּ פּוֹטְרוֹת צָרוֹתֵיהֶן וְצָרוֹת צָרוֹתֵיהֶן מִן הַחֲלִיצָה וּמִן הַיִּיבּוּם כול׳. רִבִּי יוֹחָנָן אָמַר. מְמָאֶנֶת הִיא בְּיָבָם לַעֲקוֹר זִיקַת הַמֵּת לְהַתִּיר צָרָה לְאָבִיהָ וְכַלָּה לְחָמִיהָ. רַב וְרִבִּי שִׁמְעוֹן בֶּן לָקִישׁ תְּרֵיהוֹן אָמְרִין. אֵינָהּ מְמָאֶנֶת בְּיָבָם לַעֲקוֹר זִיקַת הַמֵּת לְהַתִּיר צָרָה לְאָבִיהָ וְכַלָּה לְחָמִיהָ. רַב וְרִבִּי שִׁמְעוֹן בֶּן לָקִישׁ כְּבֵית שַׁמַּי. דְּבֵית שַׁמַּי אוֹמְרִים בְּבַעַל. מָה אֲנָן קַיָּימִין. אִם בְּאוֹמֶרֶת. אִי אֶיפְשִׁי לֹא בְנִישּׂוּאֵיךְ וְלֹא בְנִישּׂוּאֵי אָחִיךָ. כָּל־עַמָּא מוֹדֵיי שֶׁהִיא[121] עוֹקֶרֶת. אֶלָּא כֵן אֲנָן קַיָּימִין בְּאוֹמֶרֶת. אֵיפְשִׁי בְנִישּׂוּאִין. רִבִּי יוֹחָנָן אָמַר. אִי אֶיפְשִׁי לֹא בְנִישּׂוּאֵיךְ וְלֹא בְנִישּׂוּאֵי אָחִיךָ. רַב וְרִבִּי שִׁמְעוֹן בֶּן לָקִישׁ תְּרֵיהוֹן אָמְרִין. בְּאוֹמֶרֶת. אִי אֶיפְשִׁי בְנִישּׂוּאֵיךְ אֲבָל בְּנִישּׂוּאֵי אָחִיךָ רוֹצָה אֲנִי. מַתְנִיתָא פְלִיגָא עַל רִבִּי יוֹחָנָן. וְכוּלָּן אִם מֵתוּ אוֹ מֵיאֵינוּ אוֹ נִתְגָּרְשׁוּ אוֹ שֶׁנִּמְצְאוּ אַיילוֹנִיּוֹת צָרוֹתֵיהֶן מוּתָּרוֹת. נִתְגָּרְשׁוּ וְלֹא הִימֵּינוּ. וְדִכְוָותָהּ מֵיאֵינוּ הִימֵּינוּ. תַּנֵּי רִבִּי חִיָּיא כֵן. אִם מֵיאֵינוּ אוֹ נִתְגָּרְשׁוּ בְחַיֵּי הַבַּעַל צָרוֹתֵיהֶן מוּתָּרוֹת. לְאַחַר מִיתַת הַבַּעַל צָרוֹתֵיהֶן חוֹלְצוֹת וְלֹא מִתְיַיבְּמוֹת.

Halakhah 2: "All these free their co-wives and the co-wives of their co-wives from *ḥalîṣah* and levirate, etc." [121]Rebbi Johanan said, she may repudiate the levir to invalidate the claim of the dead brother, to permit the co-wife to her father, and the daughter-in-law to her father-in-law[122]. Rav and Rebbi Simeon ben Laqish both say, she may not repudiate the levir to invalidate the claim of the dead brother, to permit the co-wife to her father, and the daughter-in-law to her father-in-law. Do Rav and Rebbi Simeon ben Laqish follow the house of Shammai, since the House of Shammai say "the husband"[123]? Where do we hold? If she says, I can stand neither the marriage with your brother nor with you, everybody agrees that she invalidates[124]. But we hold in case she says "I cannot stand marriage[125]". Rebbi Joḥanan said, I can stand neither the marriage with your brother nor with you. Rav and Rebbi Simeon ben Laqish both say, she says I cannot stand marriage with you but marriage with your brother I want. The Mishnah disagrees with Rebbi Joḥanan: "And all of these, if they died, or repudiated, or were divorced, or found to be she-rams, their co-wives are permitted." Was she not divorced from him? Similarly, she repudiated him[126]. Rebbi Ḥiyya stated: If they repudiated or were divorced in the husband's lifetime, their co-wives are permitted[127]. After the husband's death their co-wives perform *ḥalîṣah* but not levirate.

121 The main place of this Halakhah is Halakhah 13:1.

122 If the girl walks out of the marriage, the marriage did never exist. The co-wife after *ḥalîṣah* is permitted to the girl's father in case the father had lost his guardianship over the daughter (see below). She herself is permitted to her non-husband's father.

The Babli, 12a, agrees that repudiation of the levir invalidates the marriage to the dead brother but nevertheless in this case forbids the girl to the father-in-law (a Babylonian *baraita*).

123 Mishnah 13:1; the House of Shammai limit repudiation strictly to the husband even if the widow is a minor. It would be very unusual if practice were to follow the House of Shammai against the declared opinion of the House of Hillel.

124 Reading of Halakhah 13:1. The ms. here reads "does not invalidate". The practice is that of the House of Hillel.

125 Without spelling out which marriage.

126 The first husband in his lifetime.

127 To the brothers in levirate. The marriage of a minor except through the father is only rabbinic and cannot eliminate the biblical requirement of levirate or *ḥalîṣah*. But levirate cannot be tolerated since that would show that the rabbinically valid marriage is a sham.

אָמַר רִבִּי יוּדָן אָבוֹי דְּרִבִּי מַתָּנְיָה. תִּיפְתָּר שֶׁמֵּתוּ וְלֹא מֵיאֲנוּ. דְּמַתְנִיתָא. כָּל־הַיְּכוֹלָה לְמָאֵן וְלֹא מֵיאֵינָה צָרָתָהּ חוֹלֶצֶת וְלֹא מִתְיַבֶּמֶת. כֵּן מַתְנִיתָא. כָּל־הַיְּכוֹלָה לְמָאֵן וְלֹא מֵיאֲנָה וּמֵתָה צָרָתָהּ חוֹלֶצֶת וְלֹא מִתְיַבֶּמֶת. אָמַר רִבִּי אַבָּא מָרִי. אֲפִילוּ תֵימַר בְּקַיֶּימֶת. תִּיפְתָּר שֶׁאֵין שָׁם יָבָם אַחֵר אֶלָּא אָבִיהָ.

Rebbi Yudan, the father of Rebbi Mattaniah said: Explain it when they died without having repudiated since there is a Mishnah[128]: "If a woman could repudiate but did not do so, her co-wife performs *ḥalîṣah* but cannot be married in levirate[127]." So is the Mishnah: "If a woman could repudiate but did not dies, her co-wife performs *ḥalîṣah* but cannot be married in levirate." Rebbi Abba Mari said, you may even say if she still lives; explain it if her father is the only levir[129].

128 Mishnah 1:4.

129 Since at the moment of the husband's death the rabbinic marriage of the daughter was still presumed to be valid and the daughter cannot repudiate her father, there is no way to circumvent the prohibition of levirate.

רִבִּי יוֹנָה אָמַר. בִּלְבַד מִן הָאֵירוּסִין. רִבִּי יוֹסֵה אָמַר. אַף מִן הַנִּישּׂוּאִין. בְּמַחֲזִירָה תִנְיָנָא חָזַר בּוֹ רִבִּי יוֹסֵי. אָמַר לֵיהּ רִבִּי פִּינְחָס. לֹא כֵן אִלְּפָן רִבִּי. מִן הַנִּישּׂוּאִין. אָמַר לֵיהּ. וְהִיא קְבוּעָה גַּבָּךְ כְּמַסְמְרָא.

Rebbi Jonah said, only after *qiddushin*[130]. Rebbi Yose said, even after final marriage. In the second repetition[131], Rebbi Yose changed his mind. Rebbi Phineas said to him, did the Rabbi not teach us "after final marriage"? He answered him is that fixed in you like a nail[132]?

130 This refers to the she-ram married to the dead brother. R. Jonah holds that after consummation of the marriage the husband would recognize that his wife had no secondary sex characteristics and that she was congenitally sterile. If he did not claim that the marriage was in error (since

usually people marry with a view to have children), the marriage was valid and it is not clear why an incest prohibition for the she-ram should be irrelevant for the co-wife.

131 The second time R. Yose taught *Yebamot*.

132 He refused to be bound by his prior opinion.

אָמַר רִבִּי זְעוּרָה קוֹמֵי רִבִּי מָנָא. יֵאוּת אָמַר רִבִּי יוֹסֵי עַד לֹא יַחֲזוֹר בָּהּ. אִילּוּ בִתּוֹ מִן הַנִּישּׂוּאִין בְּלֹא אַיילוֹנִית צָרָתָהּ אֲסוּרָה. מִפְּנֵי שֶׁנִּיתּוֹסַף לָהּ אַיילוֹנִית צָרָתָהּ מוּתֶּרֶת. אָמַר לֵיהּ. אַיילוֹנִית כְּמִי שֶׁאֵינָהּ בָּעוֹלָם. אִילּוּ שְׁתֵּי יְבָמוֹת אַחַת אַיילוֹנִית וְאַחַת שֶׁאֵינָהּ אַיילוֹנִית וּבָא הַיָּבָם וְחָלַץ לָהּ וּבָא עָלֶיהָ. שֶׁמָּא פָּטַר בַּחֲבֶרְתָּהּ כְּלוּם. הֲוֵי אַיילוֹנִית כְּמִי שֶׁאֵינָהּ בָּעוֹלָם.

Rebbi Ze'ira said before Rebbi Mana, did not Rebbi Yose say correctly before he changed his mind? Once a man's daughter is married without being a she-ram, her co-wife is forbidden. If in addition she is a she-ram, does her co-wife become permitted[133]? He said to him, the she-ram is as if non-existent. If there are two sisters-in-law, one a she-ram and one not a she-ram, if the levir comes and performs *ḥalîṣah* or has intercourse with the first[134], did he free her companion of anything? That shows that the she-ram is as if non-existent.

133 The daughter married to a brother is forbidden to her father. A she-ram is forbidden to all brothers (cf. Notes 65, 66). Since when do two prohibitions add up to a permission?

134 Who is forbidden for levirate.

בִּתּוֹ. וּבִתּוֹ מְמָאֶנֶת. וְלֹא כְנִישּׂוּאֵי תוֹרָה הִיא. אֶת בִּתִּי נָתַתִּי לָאִישׁ הַזֶּה. רִבִּי הוּנָא בְשֵׁם רִבִּי שִׁמְעוֹן בֶּן לָקִישׁ. תִּיפְתָּר בִּקְטַנָּה שֶׁהִשִּׂיאָהּ אָבִיהָ וְנִתְגָּרְשָׁה. שֶׁהִיא כִיתוֹמָה בְחַיֵּי אָבִיהָ.

"His daughter". How can his daughter repudiate, is she not married by Torah standards, "my daughter I gave to this man[135]"? Rebbi Huna in the name of Rebbi Simeon ben Laqish: Explain it by a minor, who was married off by her father[136] and divorced, who is like an orphan while her father is alive.

135 *Deut.* 22:16. From the text it is clear that the marriage is valid in all respects. The verse implies that the father has the right to marry off his daughter, but only the Babli (*Soṭah* 23b) infers from it that the mother does not have this right, even though the Yerushalmi accepts that ruling in practice.

136 She is emancipated from her father by the marriage but not able to validly contract while under age. This is quoted cryptically in Babli *Qiddušin* 44b.

רִבִּי אָחָא רִבִּי חֲנִינָה בְּשֵׁם רִבִּי שִׁמְעוֹן בֶּן לָקִישׁ. זֹאת אוֹמֶרֶת שֶׁאֵין קְטַנָּה יוֹלֶדֶת. דְּלֹא כֵן תַּמְתִּין עַד שֶׁתַּגְדִּיל[137] וּתְמָאֵן בְּבַעֲלָהּ וְתַתִּיר צָרָתָהּ לַחֲתָנָהּ. כַּלָּתוֹ שֶׁל רִבִּי יִשְׁמָעֵאל מֵיאֲנָה וּבְנָהּ עַל כְּתֵיפָהּ. רִבִּי חִזְקִיָּה בְּשֵׁם רִבִּי אַבָּהוּ. רִבִּי יוּדָה וְרִבִּי שִׁמְעוֹן וְרִבִּי יִשְׁמָעֵאל אָמְרוּ דָּבָר אֶחָד. תַּנֵּי. עַד אֵימָתַי הַבַּת מְמָאֶנֶת. עַד שֶׁתָּבִיא שְׁתֵּי שְׂעָרוֹת. דִּבְרֵי רִבִּי מֵאִיר. רִבִּי יוּדָה אוֹמֵר. עַד שֶׁיִּרְבֶּה הַשָּׁחוֹר. רִבִּי שִׁמְעוֹן אוֹמֵר. עַד שֶׁתִּתְפַּשֵּׁט הַכַּף. רִבִּי זְעוּרָא רִבִּי חִיָּיא בְּשֵׁם רִבִּי שִׁמְעוֹן בֶּן לָקִישׁ. עַד שֶׁתִּתְפַּשֵּׁט הַכַּף וִיהֵא הַשָּׁחוֹר רָבָה עַל הַלָּבָן.

Rebbi Aḥa, Rebbi Ḥanina, in the name of Rebbi Simeon ben Laqish: This means[138] that a minor cannot give birth; because otherwise she could wait until she grew up, repudiate her husband, and permit her co-wife to her son-in-law. The daughter-in-law[139] of Rebbi Ismael repudiated while her son was on her shoulder. Rebbi Ḥizqiah in the name of Rebbi Abbahu: Rebbi Jehudah, Rebbi Simeon, and Rebbi Ismael[140] said the same. It was stated[141]: Until when may the daughter repudiate? Until she grows two pubic hairs[142], the words of Rebbi Meïr. Rebbi Judah says until the black covers most. Rebbi Simeon says until the hill of Venus expands. Rebbi Ze'ira, Rebbi Ḥiyya[143] in the name of Rebbi Simeon ben Laqish: Until the mons Veneris enlarges and the black be more than the white[144].

137 Reading of the parallel in 13:1. Text here: שיתגדל.

138 The statement that the mother-in-law could not have repudiated her husband since she had a daughter from him.

139 In Babli *Niddah* 52a, the daughter.

140 In the Babli, *loc. cit.*, R. Ismael is quoted to hold that no biblically invalid marriage bars the woman from walking out. It is also stated that the action of the daughter was in accordance with her deceased father's opinion. Since according to the Yerushalmi that opinion is nowhere recorded formally, the Babli's explanation is one of the possibilities mentioned in the paragraph after the next as R. Ismael's.

141 A slightly different version is in Babli *loc. cit.* and Tosephta *Niddah* 6:11.

142 Alternatively, the breasts as indicators of puberty are described in Mishnaiot *Niddah* 5:7-8, 6:1.

143 R. Ḥiyya bar Abba.

144 Corrected version of R. Simeon's opinion.

רִבִּי אַבָּהוּ רִבִּי לָעְזָר בְּשֵׁם רִבִּי הוֹשַׁעְיָה. הֲלָכָה כְּרִבִּי יוּדָן. רִבִּי יְהוֹשֻׁעַ בֶּן לֵוִי אָמַר. הֲלָכָה כְּרִבִּי יוּדָה. אָתָא עוֹבְדָא קוֹמֵי רִבִּי יַסָּא. אָמַר. אֵיזִלוֹן לְגַבֵּי רִבִּי אַבָּהוּ דְּאִית לֵיהּ אוּלְפָן. הֲלָכָה כְּרִבִּי יוּדָה. אֲנָן לֵית לָן אוּלְפָן. הֲלָכָה כְּרִבִּי יוּדָה. רִבִּי חֲנִינָה אָמַר. הֲלָכָה כְּרִבִּי יוּדָה. רִבִּי יוֹחָנָן אָמַר לְצִיפּוֹרַיָּיא. אַתּוּן אָמְרִין בְּשֵׁם רִבִּי חֲנִינָה. הֲלָכָה כְּרִבִּי יוּדָה. וְלֵית הִיא כֵן. מַאי כְדוֹן. חֲבֵרַיָּיא בְּשֵׁם רִבִּי חֲנִינָה. מוֹדֵיי רִבִּי יְהוּדָה שֶׁאִם נִבְעֲלָה מִשֶּׁהֵבִיאָה שְׁתֵּי שְׂעָרוֹת שֶׁאֵין יְכוֹלָה לְמָאֵין. רִבִּי זְעוּרָה בְּשֵׁם רִבִּי חֲנִינָה. מוֹדֵיי רִבִּי יְהוּדָה שֶׁאִם נִתְקַדְּשָׁה מִשֶּׁהֵבִיאָה שְׁתֵּי שְׂעָרוֹת שֶׁאֵינָהּ יְכוֹלָה לְמָאֵין. עַל דַּעְתֵּיהּ דְּרִבִּי זְעוּרָה דְּאָמַר. נִתְקַדְּשָׁה מִשֶּׁהֵבִיאָה שְׁתֵּי שְׂעָרוֹת. הָא אִם נִתְקַדְּשָׁה עַד שֶׁלֹּא הֵבִיאָה שְׁתֵּי

שְׂעָרוֹת וְנִבְעֲלָה מִשֶּׁהֵבִיאָה שְׁתֵּי שְׂעָרוֹת יְכוֹלָה הִיא לְמֵאֵין. נִיחָא. עַל דַּעְתִּין דַּחֲבֵרַיָּא דְּאִינּוּן אָמְרִין. נִבְעֲלָה מִשֶּׁהֵבִיאָה שְׁתֵּי שְׂעָרוֹת. הָא אִם נִבְעֲלָה עַד שֶׁלֹּא הֵבִיאָה שְׁתֵּי שְׂעָרוֹת יְכוֹלָה הִיא לְמֵאֵין.

Rebbi Abbahu, Rebbi Eleazar, in the name of Rebbi Hoshaia: Practice follows Rebbi Jehudah[145]. Rebbi Joshua ben Levi said, practice follows Rebbi Jehudah. A case came before Rebbi Yasa; he said, go to Rebbi Abbahu since he has learned that practice follows Rebbi Jehudah; we did not learn that practice follows Rebbi Jehudah. Rebbi Ḥanina said, practice follows Rebbi Jehudah. Rebbi Joḥanan said to the Sepphoreans, you say in the name of Rebbi Ḥanina that practice follows Rebbi Jehudah, but it is not so. How is it? The colleagues[146] in the name of Rebbi Ḥanina: Rebbi Jehudah agrees that if she had intercourse after she grew two hairs, she cannot repudiate[147]. Rebbi Ze'ira in the name of Rebbi Ḥanina: Rebbi Jehudah agrees that if she received *qiddushin* after she grew two hairs, she cannot repudiate[148]. According to Rebbi Ze'ira who said "she received *qiddushin* after she grew two hairs", it follows that if she received *qiddushin* before she grew two hairs and had intercourse after she grew two hairs, she can repudiate[149]. That fits[150]. According to the colleagues who say "she had intercourse after she grew two hairs", it follows that if she had intercourse before she grew two hairs, she can repudiate[151].

145 In the Babli, *Niddah* 52a, the statement is Rebbi Abbahu in the name of Rebbi Eleazar and includes that of the colleagues below.

146 Rav Ḥanania and his brother Rav Oshaia.

147 He agrees that the criterion of R. Meïr is valid to give her the right to contract marriage but if she is not forced to make a decision her right to repudiation remains in force; cf. Rashi in *Niddah* 52a.

148 This opinion, the more important one in the Yerushalmi, is ignored in the Babli.

149 The Babli, *Niddah* 46a, disagrees.

150 As explained in the next paragraph, one holds with R. Simeon that the rabbinic marriage of the minor becomes biblically valid only by a conscious act, for example intercourse to confirm the marriage. Since people usually think that a rabbinic marriage is all they need, simple intercourse does not satisfy the requirement. Therefore, R. Ismael's daughter-in-law could repudiate even as an adult.

151 By the same reason as given in the previous paragraph. But for them, if she was married as a minor and the marriage was not consummated until she produced two pubic hairs, she cannot repudiate.

וְזֶה אֵימָתַי. עִיבְּרָה וְיָלְדָה עַד שֶׁלֹּא הֵבִיאָה שְׁתֵּי שְׂעָרוֹת. וְחָיָה הִיא. לֹא כֵן
אָמַר רִבִּי רְדִיפָא רִבִּי יוֹנָה בְּשֵׁם רִבִּי אִילָא. אִיתָא. עִיבְּרָה וְיָלְדָה עַד שֶׁלֹּא
הֵבִיאָה שְׁתֵּי שְׂעָרוֹת הִיא (fol. 3a) וּבְנָהּ מֵתִים. מִשֶּׁהֵבִיאָה שְׁתֵּי שְׂעָרוֹת הִיא
וּבְנָהּ חַיִּים. עִיבְּרָה עַד
שֶׁלֹּא הֵבִיאָה שְׁתֵּי שְׂעָרוֹת וְיָלְדָה מִשֶּׁהֵבִיאָה שְׁתֵּי שְׂעָרוֹת הִיא חָיָה וּבְנָהּ מֵת.
מַאי כְדוֹן. רִבִּי יִשְׁמָעֵאל כְּרִבִּי יוּדָה. עַד שֶׁיִּרְבֶּה שָׁחוֹר כְּרִבִּי שִׁמְעוֹן. עַל תְּנַאי
קִידּוּשׁ הָרִאשׁוֹן וּבָעַל. עַל דַּעְתֵּיהּ דְּרִבִּי מֵאִיר וְרִבִּי יוּדָה. דְּאָמְרֵי. בְּסִימָנִין
הַדָּבָר תָּלוּי. נִיחָא. עַל דַּעְתֵּיהּ דְּרִבִּי שִׁמְעוֹן דּוּ אָמַר. לִכְשֶׁיּוֹסִיף בָּהּ קִנְיָן אֶחָד.
מֵעַתָּה אֲפִילוּ גְדוֹלָה. אָמַר רִבִּי יִצְחָק. וְכֵינִי. אֶלָּא כְדֵי שֶׁלֹּא יִתְפָּרְצוּ בְּנוֹת
יִשְׂרָאֵל בְּזִימָּה.

When was it[152]? She became pregnant and gave birth before she grew two hairs. Could she have lived? Did not Rebbi Redifa, Rebbi Jonah, say in the name of Rebbi Hila[153]: If a woman became pregnant and gave birth before she grew two hairs, she and her son will die. After she grew two hairs, she and her son will live. If she became pregnant before she grew two hairs and gave birth after she grew two hairs, she will live but her son will die. How is the situation? Rebbi Ismael follows Rebbi

Jehudah, until the black covers most[154] [and] Rebbi Simeon, that intercourse occurred with the idea of the prior *qiddushin*[150]. Following the opinions of Rebbi Meïr and Rebbi Jehudah who say that her status depends on the signs of development, it fits[155]. Following the opinion of Rebbi Simeon who says, if he adds another act of acquisition, then even if she is an adult! Rebbi Isaac said, that is so[156]. Only that the daughters of Israel should not be unbridled in breaking tabus[157].

152 The daughter-in-law of R. Ismael who had a child and wanted to repudiate her husband following her father's rules.

153 The Babli, *Yebamot* 12b, rejects a similar (Galilean) statement; the Babylonian Rav Saphra declares that pregnancy is a sign of puberty.

154 In all these criteria, he will replace "two hairs" with "most of the mons Veneris is black".

155 As explained above, the daughter-in-law could have had a baby and still be a minor according to R. Jehudah [not according to R. Meïr; he is mentioned here only to reject the implied opinion of R. Saphra (Note 152).]

156 The daughter-in-law of R. Ismael could have been an adult if no conscious validation of the marriage took place after her reaching adulthood (Note 150).

157 The rejection of this interpretation in practice is rabbinic; the Babli (cf. Note 140) takes this as a reason to reject R. Ismael's position.

אַתְיָיא עוֹבְדָא קוֹמֵי רִבִּי יוֹסֵי. אָמַר יִבְדְּקוֹ דַדֶּיהָ. מַה. כְּרִבִּי יוּדָה. דְּרִבִּי יוּדָה אָמַר. עַד שֶׁיַּרְבֶּה שָׁחוֹר. וְהוּא דְאָמַר כְּרִבִּי יְהוֹשֻׁעַ בֶּן לֵוִי. אֵין בֵּין יְמוֹת הַנַּעֲרוּת לִימוֹת הַבַּגְרוּת אֶלָּא ו׳ חֳדָשִׁים בִּלְבַד. וְאָמַר רִבִּי אַבָּהוּ בְשֵׁם רִבִּי יוֹחָנָן. אֵין עוֹשִׂין מַעֲשֶׂה. הָדָא דְתֵימַר בְּתוֹךְ הַזְּמָן. אֲבָל לְאַחַר הַזְּמַן עוֹשִׂין מַעֲשֶׂה. בְּרַם הָכָא סָפֵיק רָבָה שָׁחוֹר סָפֵיק לֹא רָבָה שָׁחוֹר כּוֹפוֹ אֲנִי לִיתֵּן גֵּט. רָבָה הַשָּׁחוֹר אֵינוֹ נוֹגֵעַ בַּגֵּט.

There came a case before Rebbi Yose[158]. He said: One should examine her breasts[159]. How? Following Rebbi Jehudah! Since Rebbi Jehudah said, until the black covers most. Is not that what Rebbi Joshua ben Levi said, between maidenhood and adulthood thare are only six months[160], and Rebbi Abbahu said in the name of Rebbi Joḥanan, one does not act on this[161]? This means during that period[162]. But after that period one acts[163]. But in this case where there was a doubt whether the black covered most or the black did not cover most, I force him to give a bill of divorce[164]. When the black covers most one does not touch a bill of divorce.

158 Of a girl repudiating when it was doubtful whether or not she was an adult.

159 Mishnah *Niddah* 5:7-8 explains the progress of puberty from minority to adulthood through the state called נערות "maidenhood" when she is an adult and legally responsible for her actions but still under the authority of her father. This paragraph identifies the beginning of maidenhood with the growing of two pubic hairs and adulthood with the covering of the mons Veneris by hair. This means that R. Meïr permits repudiation only during minority and R. Jehudah during minority and maidenhood.

160 In the Babli, *Niddah* 65a, this is a statement of the contemporary Babylonian Samuel.

161 How can Rebbi Yose follow R. Jehudah when according to R. Meïr any marriage contracted by the repudiating girl would be adultery and R. Joḥanan forbids to follow R. Jehudah (even if in the abstract R. Jehudah might be correct).

162 When she is no longer a minor but not an adult, the court does not act either to permit repudiation or to deny it, as explained later.

163 Six months after the first signs of puberty one forbids repudiation without checking for signs of adulthood. The Babli, *Niddah* 46a, which disregards R. Jehudah's opinion and forbids repudiation by maidens, holds that after the age of 12 full years no examination is necessary to establish the fact of maidenhood.

164 Since one cannot deny repudiation according to R. Jehudah and cannot permit it following R. Meïr, the court forces the husband to confirm the repudiation by a formal divorce. Then the girl can remarry without problems. But once she is an adult, she cannot force a divorce in court (except for infertility or serious misbehavior of the husband.)

(fol. 2a) **משנה ג:** בְּאֵי זֶה צַד פּוֹטְרוֹת צָר͏ֹתֵיהֶן. הָיְתָה בִתּוֹ אוֹ אַחַת מִכָּל־הָעֲרָיוֹת הָאֵילוּ נְשׂוּאָה לְאָחִיו וְלוֹ אִשָּׁה אֲחֶרֶת וָמֵת כְּשֵׁם שֶׁבִּתּוֹ פְּטוּרָה כָּךְ צָרָתָהּ פְּטוּרָה. הָלְכָה צָרַת בִּתּוֹ וְנִשֵּׂאת לְאָחִיו הַשֵּׁנִי וְלוֹ אִשָּׁה אֶחֶרֶת וָמֵת כְּשֵׁם שֶׁצָּרַת בִּתּוֹ פְּטוּרָה כָּךְ צָרַת צָרָתָהּ פְּטוּרָה אֲפִילוּ הֵן מֵאָה.

Mishnah 3: How do they free their co-wives? If a man's daughter or one of the incest-prohibited women[165] was married to his brother who has another wife and dies, just as his daughter is free so her co-wife is free[166]. If his daughter's co-wife went and was married to a second brother[167] who then died, just as his daughter's co-wife is freed, so the co-wife's co-wife is freed; even if this is repeated a hundred times.

165 Forbidden to him but not to his brother.

166 If the man is the only brother of the deceased.

167 Since the daughter is not forbidden to his brother, her co-wife is also permitted. The brother could have married his niece in levirate.

(fol. 3a) **הלכה ג:** כֵּיצַד פּוֹטְרוֹת צָרוֹתֵיהֶן. הָיְתָה בִתּוֹ אוֹ אַחַת מִכָּל־הָעֲרָיוֹת הָאֵילוּ כול'. הִיא מַתְנִיתָא כָּל־הַיְכוֹלוֹת לְמָאֵן וְלֹא מֵיאֵינָה צָרָתָהּ חוֹלֶצֶת וְלֹא מִתְיַבֶּמֶת.

Halakhah 3: "How do they free their co-wives? If a man's daughter or one of the incest-prohibited women,", etc. That is the *baraita*[168]: "If a woman could repudiate but did not do so, her co-wife performs *ḥalîṣah* but cannot be married in levirate[127]."

168 This is not the text of the next Mishnah since here the daughter is still alive. A similar text is in Tosephta 1:2. It refers to the second case in the Mishnah, if there are at least three brothers. If there is only one brother and the daughter is still a minor one might teach her to repudiate the former marriage (cf. Mishnah 13:7) and her co-wife will be permitted to her father.

(fol. 2a) **משנה ד:** בְּאֵי זֶה צַד אִם מֵתוּ הֵן צָרוֹתֵיהֶן מוּתָּרוֹת. הָיְתָה בִתּוֹ אוֹ אַחַת מִכָּל־הָעֲרָיוֹת הָאֵילּוּ נְשׂוּאָה לְאָחִיו וְלוֹ אִשָּׁה אֲחֶרֶת מֵתָה בִתּוֹ אוֹ נִתְגָּרְשָׁה וְאַחַר כָּךְ מֵת אָחִיו צָרָתָהּ מוּתֶּרֶת. וְכָל־הַיְכוֹלָה לְמָאֵן וְלֹא מֵיאֵינָה וּמֵתָה צָרָתָהּ חוֹלֶצֶת וְלֹא מִתְיַבֶּמֶת.

Mishnah 4: How are their co-wives permitted[169] if they die? If his daughter or one of the incest-prohibited women was married to his brother who has another wife, if his daughter died and then his brother died her co-wife is permitted. And if a woman could repudiate but did not do so, when she died her co-wife performs *ḥalîṣah* but cannot be married in levirate[127].

169 To the levir in levirate.

(fol. 3a) **הלכה ד:** כֵּיצַד אִם מֵתוּ הֵן צְרוֹתֵיהֶן מוּתָּרוֹת כול'. כֵּינִי מַתְנִיתָא כָּל־הַיְכוֹלוֹת לְמָאֵן וְלֹא מֵיאֵנָה וּמֵתָה צָרָתָהּ חוֹלֶצֶת וְלֹא מִתְיַבֶּמֶת.

Halakhah 4: "How are their co-wives permitted if they die," etc. That is the Mishnah: "If a woman could repudiate but did not do so, when she died her co-wife performs *ḥalîṣah* but cannot be married in levirate[170]."

170 This is the Mishnah text "when she died", in contrast to the *baraita* text of the preceding Halakhah which presumes the daughter to be a widow.

(fol. 2a) **משנה ה:** שֵׁשׁ עֲרָיוֹת חֲמוּרוֹת מֵאֵילּוּ מִפְּנֵי שֶׁנִּשּׂוּאוֹת לָאֲחֵרִים צָרוֹתֵיהֶן מוּתָּרוֹת. אִמּוֹ וְאֵשֶׁת אָבִיו וַאֲחוֹת אָבִיו אֲחוֹתוֹ מֵאָבִיו. וְאֵשֶׁת אֲחִי אָבִיו וְאֵשֶׁת אָחִיו מֵאָבִיו.

Mishnah 5: Six incest prohibitions are more stringent than these[171] since they [concern women who] must be married to others[172], their co-wives are permitted[173]: A man's mother, his father's wife, his father's sister, his paternal sister, his paternal aunt, and his paternal brother's wife[174].

171 Than the 15 mentioned in Mishnah 1.

172 They are equally forbidden to all paternal brothers and never can be parties to levirate.

173 If they were widowed or divorced and married an unrelated husband, their co-wives from this marriage are unrelated to the brothers since co-wives can become forbidden only in cases of levirate.

174 Who had children or was divorced.

(fol. 3a) **הלכה ה:** שֵׁשׁ עֲרָיוֹת חֲמוּרוֹת מֵאֵילּוּ מִפְּנֵי שֶׁנִּשּׂוּאוֹת לָאֲחֵרִים כול'. מַה אֵינָהּ חֲמוּרָה. הָכָא כָּרֵת וְהָכָא כָּרֵת. הָכָא מַמְזֵר וְהָכָא מַמְזֵר. מַהוּ חֲמוּרוֹת. שֶׁאֵינָן יְכוֹלוֹת לְהִינָּשֵׂא לָאַחִים שֶׁלֹּא בַעֲבֵירָה. וְתַנֵּי רִבִּי חִיָּיא כֵן.

וְכוּלָּן אִם יְכוֹלוֹת לְהִינָּשֵׂא לָאַחִין שֶׁלֹּא בַעֲבֵירָה צָרוֹתֵיהֶן פְּטוּרוֹת מִן הַחֲלִיצָה וּמִן הַיִּבּוּם.

"Six incest prohibitions are more stringent than these since they [concern women who] must be married to others", etc. In what are they more stringent? Here there is extirpation, there is extirpation[175]. Here there is bastardy, there there is bastardy[176]. What is more stringent? That they cannot be married to the brothers without transgression. And Rebbi Ḥiyya stated thus: For all women who may be married to the brothers without transgression, their co-wives are free from *ḥalîṣah* and levirate[177].

175 Incest with some of the women is a capital crime. Even these are subject to divine extirpation if there are no two witnesses to the act.

176 The child of any of the forbidden unions is a bastard excluded from marriage with natural-born Jews.

177 A slightly different version in Tosephta 1:7.

תַּנֵּי רִבִּי חִייָה. אֵין צָרָה אֶלָּא מֵאָח בִּלְבַד. אָמַר רִבִּי יוֹסֵי. מַתְנִיתָא אָמְרָה כֵן. מִפְּנֵי שֶׁהֵן נְשׂוּאוֹת לָאֲחֵרִים צָרוֹתֵיהֶן מוּתָּרוֹת. רִבִּי יִרְמְיָה בָּעֵי. וּתְהֵא צָרָה מִן הַשּׁוּק. אָמַר רִבִּי יוֹסֵה. לֹא שְׁמִיעַ רִבִּי יִרְמְיָה הָדָא דְתַנֵּי רִבִּי חִייָה. לֹא שְׁמִיעַ לְמַתְנִיתִין מִפְּנֵי שֶׁהֵן נְשׂוּאוֹת לַאֲחֵרִים צָרוֹתֵיהֶן מוּתָּרוֹת. חָזַר וָמַר. אִין דִּשְׁמִיעַ. אֶלָּא כְּאִינַשׁ דִּשְׁמִיעַ מִילָּה וּמַקְשֵׁי עֲלָהּ.

Rebbi Ḥiyya stated[177]: "A co-wife is only from a brother". Rebbi Yose said, our Mishnah says the same: "Since they must be married to others[178], their co-wives are permitted." Rebbi Jeremiah asked: Why can there not be a co-wife from the market place[179]? Rebbi Yose said, did Rebbi Jeremiah not hear what Rebbi Ḥiyya said, did he not hear our Mishnah, "since they must be married to others, their co-wives are permitted"[180]? He turned around and said, certainly did he hear. But he is a person who hears something and questions it[181].

178 Others than the brothers.

179 If an incest-prohibited woman is married to a total stranger, why should her co-wife, if divorced or widowed, not be forbidden also to the family of the other wife?

180 It is impossible to become an ordained rabbi without knowing the Mishnah.

181 The Yerushalmi leaves this without an answer. Two different answers are given in *Sifra Qedošim Pereq* 11(12), Babli *Yebamot* 8a/b.

רִבִּי יִרְמְיָה בָּעֵי. הַבָּא עַל הַצָּרָה מַהוּ שֶׁיְּהֵא חַיָּב עָלֶיהָ מִשּׁוּם אֵשֶׁת אַח. אָמַר רִבִּי יוֹסֵי. אִילּוּ אֶיפְשַׁר לְצָרָה בְּלֹא אֵשֶׁת אַח יְאוּת. אֶיפְשַׁר לְאֵשֶׁת אַח בְּלֹא צָרָה. אֵיפְשַׁר לְצָרָה בְּלֹא אֵשֶׁת אַח.

Rebbi Jeremiah asked: If one has intercourse with a co-wife[182], is he guilty because of his brother's wife[183]? Rebbi Yose said, if a co-wife were possible without a brother's wife, that would be a valid question[184]. It is possible to be a brother's wife without a co-wife. It is impossible to be a co-wife without a brother's wife[185].

182 Widow of his brother whom he cannot marry because of the incest prohibition regarding the other wife.

183 In general, the brother's wife is forbidden under penalty of divine extirpation. But if levirate is possible, the widows of the dead brother become potentially permitted. If one of them is married by a brother, the others are forbidden since *Deut.* 25:5-9 speaks only of one sister-in-law and one house to build. The question is, does the brother who sleeps with the excluded co-wife infringe on the prescription (regarding a single levirate) of *Deut.* 25 or the incest prohibition of *Lev.* 18? The problem does not appear in the Babli since it derives all prohibitions directly from *Lev.* 18.

184 In the sense of R. Jeremiah's first question.

185 As R. Ḥiyya stated. Therefore, the prohibition of the co-wife is no separate prohibition, but only that one of the dead brother's wives gets a special dispensation from the incest prohibition of *Lev.* 18:16.

וְאֵשֶׁת אָח לֹא יְבִימְתּוֹ הִיא. אָמַר רִבִּי יוֹסֵה בֵּירִבִּי בּוּן. תִּיפְתָּר שֶׁהָיָה לָהּ בָּנִים מֵאַחִים.

Is the brother's wife not his sister-in-law? Rebbi Yose bar Abun said, explain it if she had children from a brother[174].

(fol. 2a) **משנה ו:** בֵּית שַׁמַּאי מַתִּירִין הַצָּרוֹת לָאַחִים. וּבֵית הִלֵּל אוֹסְרִין. חָלְצוּ בֵּית שַׁמַּאי פּוֹסְלִין מִן הַכְּהוּנָּה וּבֵית הִלֵּל מַכְשִׁירִין. נִתְייַבְּמוּ בֵּית שַׁמַּאי מַכְשִׁירִין וּבֵית הִלֵּל פּוֹסְלִין. אַף עַל פִּי שֶׁאֵלּוּ אוֹסְרִין וְאֵלּוּ מַתִּירִין אֵלּוּ פּוֹסְלִין וְאֵלּוּ מַכְשִׁירִן לֹא נִמְנְעוּ בֵּית שַׁמַּאי מִלִּישָּׂא נָשִׁים מִבֵּית הִלֵּל וְלֹא בֵּית הִלֵּל מִבֵּית שַׁמַּאי. כָּל־הַטְּהָרוֹת וְהַטּוּמְאוֹת שֶׁהָיוּ אֵילּוּ מְטַהֲרִין וְאֵילּוּ מְטַמְּאִין לֹא נִמְנְעוּ עוֹשִׂין טְהָרוֹת אֵילּוּ עַל גַּבֵּי אֵילּוּ.

Mishnah 6: The House of Shammai permit the co-wives to the brothers[186], but the House of Hillel forbid. If they took *ḥalîṣah*, the House of Shammai disqualify them for the priesthood[187] but the House of Hillel declare them qualified[188]. If they entered levirate, the House of Shammai declare them qualified[189] but the House of Hillel as disqualified. Even though these forbid and those permit, these declare disqualified and those qualified, the House of Shammai did not refrain from marrying women from the House of Hillel nor the House of Hillel from the House of Shammai. Regarding all purities and impurities which these were declaring as pure and those as impure[190], these did not refrain to process pure foods with the help of those[191].

186 They dispute the validity of Mishnaiot 1-4. The schools of Hillel and Shammai existed for about 100 years in the first Century C. E The Babli (17a) dates the public permission of the co-wives to the brothers to the short time of ascendancy of the House of Shammai shortly before the outbreak of the revolt against the Romans.

187 A divorcee is forbidden to a Cohen (*Lev.* 21:7) and *ḥalîṣah* is the equivalent of a divorce (Mishnah 2:4).

188 Since the marriage is impossible, so is the corresponding divorce. *Lev.* 21:7 prohibits the marriage of a Cohen with "a woman divorced from her husband", but not a woman divorced from a non-husband.

189 The children are legitimate. For the House of Hillel the children are bastards and excluded from endogamous marriage.

190 The differences in the interpretation of laws of purity are noted in the sixth order of the Mishnah.

191 They lent one another pure vessels.

(fol. 3a) **הלכה ו:** בֵּית שַׁמַּאי מַתִּירִין אֶת הַצָּרוֹת לָאַחִין, כול׳. רִבִּי סִימוֹן בְּשֵׁם רִבִּי יוֹסֵי בְּשֵׁם נְהוֹרַיי. טַעֲמוֹן דְּבֵית שַׁמַּי לֹא תִהְיֶה אֵשֶׁת הַמֵּת הַחוּצָה לְאִישׁ זָר. הַחִיצוֹנָה לֹא תִהְיֶה לְאִישׁ זָר. אַתְיָיה דְבֵית שַׁמַּי כְּאִילֵּין כּוּתַיָּא שֶׁהֵן מְיַבְּמִין אֶת הָאֲרוּסוֹת וּמוֹצִיאִין אֶת הַנְּשׂוּאוֹת. דְּאִינּוּן דָּרְשִׁין. חוּצָה הַחִיצוֹנָה. מַה מְקַיְּמִין בֵּית שַׁמַּי וּבֵן אֵין לוֹ. אָמַר רִבִּי יַעֲקֹב דְּרוֹמַיָּא קוֹמֵי רִבִּי יוֹסֵי. וּבֵן אֵין לוֹ מִן הַנְּשׂוּאָה. הַחִיצוֹנָה לֹא תִהְיֶה לְאִישׁ זָר. אָמַר לֵיהּ. לֹא יְחַסְּדוּנָךְ כּוּתָאֵי דְאַתְּ מְקַיֵּים דְּרָשֵׁיהוֹן. תַּנֵּי רִבִּי שִׁמְעוֹן בֶּן אֶלְעָזָר. נוּמֵיתִי לְסוֹפְרֵי כּוּתִים. מִי גָרַם לָכֶם לִטְעוֹת. דְּלֵית אַתּוּן דָּרְשִׁין כְּרִבִּי נְחֶמְיָה. דְּתַנֵּי בְשֵׁם רִבִּי נְחֶמְיָה. כָּל־דָּבָר שֶׁהוּא צָרִיךְ לַמֶּ״ד מִתְּחִילָּתוֹ וְלֹא נִיתָּן לוֹ. נִיתֵּן לוֹ הֵ״א בְסוֹפוֹ. כְּגוֹן לַחוּץ חוּצָה. לִשְׂעִיר שְׂעִירָה. לְסוּכּוֹת סוּכּוֹתָה. מְתִיבִין לְרִבִּי נְחֶמְיָה. וְהָא כְתִיב יָשׁוּבוּ רְשָׁעִים לִשְׁאוֹלָה. אָמַר רָבָא בַּר זַבְדָּא. לְדַיִיטֵי הַתַּחְתּוֹנָה שֶׁלִּשְׁאוֹל.

Halakhah 6: "The House of Shammai permit the co-wives to the brothers," etc. Rebbi Simon in the name of Rebbi Yose in the name of

Nehorai: The reason of the House of Shammai, "the outside wife of the deceased shall not belong to a strange man[192]," the "outer one" should not be another man's. It turns out that the House of Shammai hold like those Samaritans who perform levirate with the betrothed but remove the married, for they explain "outside" as "the outer one[193]." How do the House of Shammai[194] confirm "when he has no child[195]"? Rebbi Jacob the Southerner said before Rebbi Yose, "when he has no child" from the married one, "the outer one shall not belong outside to a strange man.[196]" He said to him, will not the Samaritans love you that you confirm their interpretations! Rebbi Simeon ben Eleazar stated: I told the learned Samaritans, what did cause you to err? That you did not explain following Rebbi Neḥemiah, since it was stated in the name of Rebbi Neḥemiah: Anything which needs a ל as a prefix but did not get it, we give it a ה at the end, e. g., to the outside חוּצָה, to Se‘ir[197] שֵׂעִירָה, to Succoth[198] סוּכּוֹתָה . They objected to Rebbi Neḥemiah, is it not written: "The wicked shall return to the pit לִשְׁאוֹלָה[199]." Rabba bar Zabda said, to the lowest living space[200] in Sheol.

192 *Deut.* 25:5. The verse reads לֹא־תִהְיֶה אֵשֶׁת הַמֵּת הַחוּצָה לְאִישׁ זָר. In the masoretic text, הַחוּצָה is adverbial לֹא־תִהְיֶה אֵשֶׁת הַמֵּת הַחוּצָה לְאִישׁ זָר and therefore is stressed on the penultimate syllable. The House of Shammai read an unlikely adjective לֹא־תִהְיֶה אֵשֶׁת הַמֵּת הַחוּצָה לְאִישׁ זָר. Following masoretic grammar, הַחוּצָה then should be stressed on the last syllable. As E. Y. Kutscher has shown in his study of the Isaiah scroll, one may assume that in the last century of the Jewish state the stress was penultimate irrespective of meaning. Therefore, in Mishnaic times there may not have been an audible difference between the two versions.

The House of Shammai would translate: "The deceased man's wife who is outside [the family of the levir] shall not be to a strange man," implying that only the widow who already belongs to the levir's family is free from the obligations of the levirate. The argument is quoted in the Babli, 13b.

193 Having received *qiddushin* but not yet finally married, she is not yet part of the family. This interpretation avoids any appearance of conflict between *Lev.* 18:16, declaring relations with the brother's wife incestuous, and *Deut.* 25:5, requiring marriage to the brother's wife.

In rabbinic Hebrew, א־וסה "the betrothed one", is a seldom used synonym of מקודשת "who had received *qiddushin*".

194 The commentators want to replace "House of Shammai" by "Samaritans", but it was stated before that the House of Shammai accepts the reading of the Samaritans while giving it another interpretation.

195 *Deut.* 25:5. You do not expect a man to have a child before marriage.

196 In this interpretation, the "outside" wife is the woman betrothed, legally a wife, but not married to live in her husband's family. For them, a woman widowed after marriage is never subject to levirate, only one becoming a widow from betrothal to a childless man. This eliminates any conflict between *Deut.* 25:5 and *Lev.* 18:16. The practice of the Samaritans is confirmed in the Babli, *Qiddušin* 75b-76a.

197 *Gen.* 33:16.

198 *Gen.* 33:17.

199 *Ps.* 9:18; one of the two signs of direction is superfluous.

200 Greek δίαιτα.

אָמַר רִבִּי יוֹחָנָן בֶּן נוּרִי. רְאֵה הֵיאַךְ הֲלָכָה זוֹ רוֹוַחַת בְּיִשְׂרָאֵל. אִם לְקַייֵם דִּבְרֵי בֵית שַׁמַּי הַוּוֹלָד מַמְזֵר מִדִּבְרֵי בֵית הִלֵּל. אִם לְקַייֵם דִּבְרֵי בֵית הִלֵּל הַוּוֹלָד מַמְזֵר מִדִּבְרֵי בֵית שַׁמַּי. בּוֹאוּ וּנְתַקֵּן שֶׁיְּהוּ הַצָּרוֹת חוֹלְצוֹת וְלֹא מִתְייַבְּמוֹת. תַּנֵּי. לֹא הִסְפִּיקוּ לְהַתְקִין עַד שֶׁנִּכְרְפָה הַשָּׁעָה. אָמַר רַבָּן שִׁמְעוֹן בֶּן גַּמְלִיאֵל. וְאִם כֵּן מַה נַּעֲשֶׂה לְצָרוֹת הָרִאשׁוֹנוֹת שֶׁנִּשְּׂאוּ.

[201]Rebbi Johanan ben Nuri said, look how this practice is widespread in Israel! If one upholds the words of the House of Shammai, the child is a bastard following the words of the House of Hillel[202]. If one upholds the words of the House of Hillel, the child is a bastard[203] following the words

of the House of Shammai. Come and let us institute that the co-wife perform *ḥalîṣah* but not be admitted to levirate[204]. It was stated: They did not manage to institute this before the time became unsuitable[205]. Rabban Simeon ben Gamliel said, if it were so, what would one have done with the earlier co-wives who married[206]?

201 Tosephta 1:9-10, Babli 14b, 27a, 13b.

202 For them the co-wife is forbidden because of the incest prohibition.

203 In Tosephta and Babli: "damaged"; of questionable origin and unfit for the priesthood but not a bastard. The co-wife who married outside the husband's family did breach a simple prohibition, *Deut*. 25:5, which only R. Aqiba declares to result in bastards. The *baraita* of the Yerushalmi must come from R. Aqiba's school and cannot represent practice.

204 *Ḥalîṣah* would let the co-wife marry outside the family for the House of Shammai and be ineffective for the House of Hillel.

205 The revolt of Bar Kokhba and its aftermath intervened.

206 After the restitution of the patriarchate, R. Simeon ben Gamliel refused to follow R. Joḥanan ben Nuri since he would characterize women who had married following the House of Shammai as lawbreakers. The Babli, 27a, asserts that later generations followed R. Joḥanan ben Nuri. This is not the position of the Yerushalmi.

אָמַר רִבִּי לָעְזָר. אַף עַל פִּי שֶׁנֶּחְלְקוּ בֵּית שַׁמַּי וּבֵית הִלֵּל בְּצָרוֹת מוֹדִין הָיוּ שֶׁאֵין הַוְולָד מַמְזֵר. שֶׁאֵין מַמְזֵר אֶלָּא מֵאִשָּׁה שֶׁהִיא אֲסוּרָה עָלָיו אִיסּוּר עֶרְוָה וְחַיָּבִין עָלֶיהָ כָּרֵת. אָמַר רִבִּי טַרְפוֹן. תָּאֵב אֲנִי שֶׁיְּהֵא לִי צָרַת הַבַּת שֶׁאַשִּׂיאֶהָ לִכְהוּנָּה. שָׁאֲלוּ אֶת רִבִּי יְהוֹשֻׁעַ. בְּנֵי צָרַת הַבַּת מַה הֵן. אָמַר לָהֶן. הֲרֵי אַתֶּם מַכְנִיסִין אֶת רֹאשִׁי בֵּין שְׁנֵי הֶהָרִים הַגְּבוֹהִים בֵּין דִּבְרֵי בֵית שַׁמַּי וּבֵין דִּבְרֵי בֵית הִלֵּל בִּשְׁבִיל שֶׁיָּרִיצוּ אֶת מוֹחִי. אֲבָל מֵעִיד אֲנִי עַל מִשְׁפַּחַת בֵּית עֲנוּבַיי מִבֵּית צְבוֹעִים וְעַל מִשְׁפַּחַת בֵּית נְקִיפַי מִבֵּית קוֹשֵׁשׁ שֶׁהָיוּ בְּנֵי צָרוֹת. וְהָיוּ בְּנֵי בְנֵיהֶם כֹּהֲנִים גְּדוֹלִים עוֹמְדִין וּמַקְרִיבִין עַל גַּבֵּי הַמִּזְבֵּחַ.

[207]Rebbi Eleazar said, even though the House of Hillel and the House of Shammai disagreed about co-wives, they agree that the child is not a bastard[208], since a bastard is only from a woman which is forbidden to [a man] by an incest prohibition and one is subject to extirpation for [sinning with] her[209]. Rebbi Tarphon said, I would love to have a daughter's co-wife to marry her into priesthood[210]. They asked Rebbi Joshua, what are children of a daughter's co-wife? He said to them, you bring my head between two large mountains, between the words of the House of Shammai and those of the House of Hillel, that they should smash my brain. But I testify about the family 'Anubai from Bet Ṣeba'im and the family Neqipai from Bet Meqošeš[211] that they were sons of co-wives and their grandchildren were High Priests officiating on top of the altar[212].

207 Tosephta 1:10 (which proves that R. Eleazar ben Shamua, the Tanna, is the author); Babli 14a.

208 The House of Shammai agree with the House of Hillel, against R. Aqiba and R. Joḥanan ben Nuri, that the child of a co-wife married according to the House of Hillel is not a bastard since even for the House of Shammai only a simple prohibition is involved. In the shortened version of the Babli it is easy to read into the text a one-sided version, implying that the children according to the House of Shammai are indeed bastards. It is difficult to read this into the Yerushalmi and the Tosephta text

209 This extends even to incestuous relationships that are capital crimes since in absence of two witnesses to the forbidden act, when there can be no prosecution, the guilty pair still faces divine retribution in the form of extirpation.

210 In the Babli, "that I would marry her", being a Cohen, to invalidate the position of the House of Shammai.

211 In the Tosephta (1:10): בית עלובי (עליבאי) מבית צבאים (צביים), בית קיפאי (קיפא) מביה מקושש. In the Babli (15b): משפחת בית צבועים מבן עכמאי ומשפחת בית קופאי מבן מקושש. The town of צבעים is mentioned in *Neh.* 11:34 as settled by the returnees from the tribe of

Benjamin; cf. B. Z. Luria, ערי הכהנים בימי בית שני, HUCA 44 (1973) א-יח.

212 Even though he did not want to express any opinion of the co-wives themselves, he was adamant that the children were untainted.

רִבִּי יַעֲקֹב בַּר אִידִי בְשֵׁם רִבִּי יְהוֹשֻׁעַ בֶּן לֵוִי. מַעֲשֶׂה שֶׁנִּכְנְסוּ זְקֵינִים אֵצֶל רִבִּי דוֹסָא בֶּן הָרְכֵּינַס לִשְׁאוֹל לוֹ עַל צָרַת הַבַּת. אָֽמְרוּ לוֹ. אַתְּ הוּא שֶׁאַתְּ מַתִּיר בְּצָרוֹת. אַמַר לוֹן. מַה שְׁמַעְתּוֹן. דוֹסָא בֶּן הָרְכֵּינַס. אָֽמְרוּ לוֹ בֶּן הָרְכֵּינַס. אָמַר לוֹן יוֹנָתָן אָחִי הֲוָה בְּכוֹר שָׂטָן הֲוָה וּמִתַּלְמִידֵי בֵית שַׁמַּי. הִיזָּהֲרוּ מִמֶּנּוּ. שְׁלֹשׁ מֵאוֹת תְּשׁוּבוֹת יֶשׁ לוֹ עַל צָרַת הַבַּת. אָֽזְלוֹן לְגַבֵּיהּ. שָׁלַח וְכָתַב לֵיהּ. הִיזָּהֵר שֶׁחַכְמֵי יִשְׂרָאֵל נִכְנָסִין אֶצְלָךְ. עָלוֹן וְיָתִיב לָהֶן קוֹמוֹי. הֲוָה מַסְבִּיר לְהוֹן וְלָא סָֽבְרִין. מִיסְבַּר לְהוֹן וְלָא סָֽבְרִין. שָׁרִייָן מִתְנַמְנְמִין. אָמַר לָהֶן. מַה אַתּוּן מִתְנַמְנְמִין. שָׁרֵי מִישְׁדֵּי עֲלֵיהוֹן צְרִירִין. וְאִית דָּֽמְרִין. בְּחַד תְּרַע עָלוֹן וּבִתְלָתָא נָֽפְקִין. שָׁלַח אָמַר לֵיהּ. מַה שָׁלַחְתָּ לִי בְּנֵי נַשׁ בָּעוֹ מֵילַף. וְאָמַרְתָּ לִי. אִינּוּן חַכְמֵי יִשְׂרָאֵל. אָתוֹ לְגַבֵּיהּ אָֽמְרוּן לֵיהּ. אַתְּ מַה אַתְּ אָמַר. אָמַר לָהֶן. עַל הַמְּדוֹכָה הַזֹּאת יָשַׁב חַגַּי הַנָּבִיא וְהֵעִיד שְׁלֹשָׁה דְבָרִים. עַל צָרַת הַבַּת שֶׁתִּינָּשֵׂא לִכְהוּנָּה. וְעַל עַמּוֹן וּמוֹאָב שֶׁהֵן מְעַשְּׂרִין מַעֲשַׂר עָנִי בַּשְּׁבִיעִית. וְעַל גֵּירֵי תַּדְמוֹר שֶׁהֵן כְּשֵׁירִין לָבוֹא בַקָּהָל. תָּלוֹן עֵינַיי דְנֵיחְמֵי לְחַכְמֵי יִשְׂרָאֵל. רָאָה אֶת רִבִּי יְהוֹשֻׁעַ. וְקָרָא עָלָיו אֶת מִי יוֹרֶה דֵיעָה. זָכוּר אֲנִי שֶׁהָֽיְתָה אִמּוֹ מוֹלֶכֶת עֲרִיסָתוֹ לְבֵית הַכְּנֶסֶת בִּשְׁבִיל שֶׁיִּתְדַּבְּקוּ אָזְנָיו בְּדִבְרֵי תוֹרָה. אֶת רִבִּי עֲקִיבָה. וְקָרָא עָלָיו כְּפִירִים רָשׁוּ וְרָעֵבוּ. מַכִּירוֹ אֲנִי שֶׁאָדָם גִּיבּוֹר בַּתּוֹרָה הוּא. רָאָה אֶת רִבִּי לָֽעְזָר בֶּן עֲזַרְיָה. וְקָרָא עָלָיו נַעַר הָיִיתִי וְגַם זָקַנְתִּי. מַכִּירוֹ אֲנִי שֶׁהוּא דוֹר עֲשִׂירִי לְעֶזְרָא. וְעֵינוֹי דָֽמְיִין (fol. 3b) לְדִידֵיהּ. אָמַר רִבִּי חֲנִינָה דְצִיפּוֹרִין. אַף רִבִּי טַרְפוֹן הָיָה עִמָּהֶן וְקָרָא עָלָיו הָדָא דְרִבִּי לָֽעְזָר בֶּן עֲזַרְיָה.

[213]Rebbi Jacob bar Idi in the name of Rebbi Joshua ben Levi: It happened that the Sages visited Rebbi Dosa ben Hyrkanos[214] to ask him about the daughter's co-wife. They said to him, are you the one who permits co-wives? He said to them, what did you hear? Dosa ben

Hyrkanos? They said to him, ben Hyrkanos. He said to them, my brother Jonathan is exceedingly sharpminded[215] and of the students of the House of Shammai. Be careful with him, he has three hundred arguments about the daughter's co-wife. They went to him. He sent and wrote to him[216], be careful because the Sages of Israel will visit you. They came and he placed them before him. He lectured[217] but they did not understand, repeatedly. They started to get drowsy. He said to them, why are you getting drowsy? He started pelting them with pebbles. But some people said, they entered in one door and left in three[218]. He sent to say to him[219], why did you send to me, the people want to learn and you said to me, these are the Sages of Israel? They came to him[220] and said to him, what do you say in the matter? He said, on this stone[221] sat the prophet Ḥaggai and testified to three things: On the daughter's co-wife that she can be married into priesthood[222], on Ammon and Moab that they tithe for the poor in a Sabbatical year[223], and on proselytes of Palmyra that they are acceptable to marry into the congregation[224]. He said, lift my eyelids so I can see the Sages of Israel. He saw Rebbi Joshua and said to him: "To whom will one teach knowledge[225]?" I remember that his mother brought his crib to the Synagogue that his ears should cling to the words of the Torah. [He saw] Rebbi Aqiba, and said to him: "Lion cubs will be poor and hungry[226]." I know of him that he is a man strong in Torah. He saw Rebbi Eleazar ben Azariah and said to him: "I was a youth but became an elder[227]." I know of him that he is the tenth generation from Ezra and their eyes are similar. Rebbi Ḥanina from Sepphoris said, Rebbi Tarphon also was with them and he addressed him as he did Rebbi Eleazar ben Azariah.

213 A different version of the entire paragraph in Babli, 16a.

214 A contemporary of Rabban Joḥanan ben Zakkai, already old at the time of the destruction of the Temple. He was almost blind in his old age.

215 Interpretation of Rashi.

216 R. Dosa to Jonathan.

217 About his 300 reasons to permit the co-wives to the brothers.

218 Defeated.

219 Jonathan to Dosa.

220 R. Dosa.

221 A stone used to crush spices.

222 Following the House of Hillel.

223 Mishnah *Yadayim* 3:3.

224 They are reputedly the children of Gentiles from Jewish women. The statement objects to the opinion (Halakhah 7:6) that the child of a Gentile and a Jewish woman, who certainly has to be counted as Jewish, is a bastard. It is known from the Babli that the soldiers of Odenathus of Palmyra in his campaigns in Babylonia abducted Jewish women for their own use.

225 *Is.* 28:9. "To whom will one teach knowledge, to whom impart understanding, to those weaned from milk, removed from the breasts." This determines the start of school for outstanding scholars at age 2. As usual, the part of the verse not quoted is the one intended.

226 *Ps.* 34:11: "Lion cubs will be poor and hungry, but those who seek the Lord will not lack any good thing." R. Aqiba at the outset was an ignorant seeker of the Lord.

227 *Ps.* 37:25. A pun is intended; זָקַנְתִּי "I grew old" is turned into "I was appointed as an elder" at age 16, cf. *Berakhot* 4:1, Note 118.

רַב נַחְמָן בַּר יַעֲקֹב אָמַר. מְקַבְּלִין גֵּרִים מִן הַקַּרְדּוּיִין וּמִן הַתַּדְמוֹרִיים. רִבִּי אַבָּהוּ בְשֵׁם רִבִּי יוֹחָנָן. מַתְנִיתָא אָמְרָה כֵן שֶׁגֵּירֵי תַדְמוֹר כְּשֵׁירִין. תַּמָּן תַּנִּינָן כָּל־הַכְּתָמִים הַבָּאִין מֵרֶקֶם טְהוֹרִין. הָא גֵירֵי תַדְמוֹר כְּשֵׁירִין.

[229]Rav Naḥman bar Jacob said, one accepts proselytes from Kurds[230] and Palmyrenians. Rebbi Abbahu in the name of Rebbi Joḥanan: A Mishnah said that the proselytes from Palmyra are acceptable[231]. There, we have stated[232]: "All stains coming from Petra are pure." Therefore[233], the proselytes from Palmyra are acceptable.

229 A similar text in Babli *Yebamot* 16a/b, *Niddah* 56b.

230 From Corduene. Again, the problem exists only for those who hold that the child of a Gentile from a Jewish mother is a bastard.

231 As marriage partners for Jews.

232 Mishnah *Niddah* 7:6, 56b. If a stain is found on a garment, it might be from menstrual blood and therefore would be impure. As a precaution, any stain on a garment from Jewish sources is considered impure. Gentiles are unable to be impure in biblical law; their impurity is only rabbinical. Considering stains of Gentile origin to be impure would be superimposing one rabbinical decree over another, which is inadmissible.

233 This looks like a *non sequitur*. One has to admit the version, tentatively offered in the Babli, "from Petra and Palmyra". This would either clear the inhabitants of Palmyra from any suspicion of Jewishness (Rashi's opinion) or make it clear that the descendents of Jewish mothers were raised as Jews but that a Jewish woman would not give away an unwashed cloth (opinion of Tosaphot, R. Elieser from Tuchheim). Therefore, even following Tosaphot, a proselyte will never be a bastard.

רִבִּי יַעֲקֹב אָמַר שְׁמוּעָתָא. רִבִּי חֲנִינָה וְרִבִּי יְהוֹשֻׁעַ בֶּן לֵוִי חַד מַכְשִׁיר וְחַד מְקַבֵּל. מָאן דְּמַכְשִׁיר מְקַבֵּל. וּמָאן דִּמְקַבֵּל לֹא מַכְשִׁיר. רִבִּי יוֹסֵי בֵּירִבִּי בּוּן בְּשֵׁם רִבִּי נַחְמָן בַּר יַעֲקֹב. אבל לְיוּחֲסִין עַד נָהָר זרוק. רִבִּי יוֹסֵי בֵּירִבִּי בּוּן אָמַר. רַב וּשְׁמוּאֵל חַד אָמַר עַד נָהָר זְרוֹק. וְחוֹרֵינָה אָמַר עַד נָהָר וָואנִיי. רִבִּי יְהוּדָה אָמַר. בֵּין הַנְּהָרוֹת כְּגוֹלָה לְיוּחֲסִין. רִבִּי חֲנִינָה בְּרוֹקָא בְּשֵׁם רִבִּי יְהוּדָה. בְּנֵי מֵישָׁא לֹא חָשׁוּ לְהוּ אֶלָּא מִשֵּׁם סְפֵק חֲלָלוֹת. וְכֹהֲנִים שֶׁשָּׁם לֹא הִקְפִּידוּ עַל הַגְּרוּשׁוֹת. תַּמָּן קַרְיִין לְמֵישָׁא מֵתָה. לְמָדַי חוֹלָה. עֵילָם וגוובאי גוֹסְסוֹת. חֶבֶל יָמָא תְכִילְתָא דְבָבֶל. שניות עווניא וגווכייא וצוצרייה תְכִילְתָא דְחֶבֶל יָמָא.

Text of the parallel *Qiddušin* 4:1:

רִבִּי יַעֲקֹב **בַּר אָחָא** אָמַר שְׁמוּעָתָא. רִבִּי חֲנִינָה וְרִבִּי יְהוֹשֻׁעַ בֶּן לֵוִי חַד מַכְשִׁיר וְחַד מְקַבֵּל. מָאן דְּמַכְשִׁיר מְקַבֵּל. וּמָאן דִּמְקַבֵּל לֹא מַכְשִׁיר. רִבִּי **יוֹסֵה** בֵּירִבִּי בּוּן בְּשֵׁם רִבִּי נַחְמָן. **בָּבֶל** לְיוּחֲסִין עַד נָהָר **יזק**. רִבִּי יוֹסֵי בֵּירִבִּי בּוּן אָמַר. רַב וּשְׁמוּאֵל חַד אָמַר עַד נָהָר **יזק**. וְחוֹרוֹנָה

אָמַר. עַד נְהַר יואני. אָמַר רַב יְהוּדָה. בֵּין הַנְּהָרוֹת כְּגוֹלָה לְיוּחֲסִין. רִבִּי חֲנִינָה בֶּן בְּרוֹקָא בְּשֵׁם רַב יְהוּדָה. בְּנֵי מֵישָׁא לֹא חָשׁוּ לָהֶם אֶלָּא מִשּׁוּם סָפֵק חֲלָלוֹת. וְכֹהֲנִים שֶׁשָּׁם לֹא הִקְפִּידוּ עַל הַגְּרוּשׁוֹת. תַּמָּן אָמְרִין מֵישָׁא מֵתָה מָדַי חוֹלָה. עֵילָם וגבביי גּוֹסְסוֹת. חֲבִיל יָמָא תְּכִילְתָא דְבָבֶל. שנייא וגבביא וצרדייא תְּכִילְתָא דְחֲבִיל יָמָא.

[234]Rebbi Jacob bar Aḥa presented traditions: Rebbi Ḥanina and Rebbi Joshua ben Levi, one declares permissible and the other admits. He who declares permissible admits. But he who admits does not declare admissible[235]. Rebbi Yose ben Rebbi Abun in the name of Rebbi Naḥman bar Jacob: Babylonia, as far as family pedigree is concerned, extends up to the *zrvq*[236] canal. Rebbi Yose ben Rebbi Abun said, Rav and Samuel, one said up to the *zrvq* canal, the other said up to the *Wani* canal. Rav Jehudah said, between the rivers is like Nahardea[237] as far as family pedigree is concerned. Rebbi Ḥanina ben Beroqa in the name of Rav Jehudah: The people of Mesene[238] are questionable only because of doubts of desecrated women[239]. The Cohanim amongst them did not care about divorcees. There[240], they called Mesene dead, Media sick, Elam and *gbby* dying. The maritime district[241] is the purple-blue of Babylonia. *Šny', gbby', and ṣrry*[242] are purple-blue of the maritime district.

234 A parallel to the paragraph in Babli *Qiddušin* 71b. The origin of the paragraph is in *Qiddušin*, the readings of the parallel from there seem to be slightly better. Since the canals of Antiquity all decayed after the Arab conquest, the names cannot be reconstructed.

235 Anybody can become a proselyte. But only a person not descendent from Jews is sure not to be really Jewish and, according to the earlier opinion, a bastard. This problem is most urgent in Media, place of exile of the Ten Tribes, but also in Palmyra, part of Solomon's empire.

236 In the Babli: עזק.

237 The place of exile of King Jojachin and the nobles of Jerusalem, usually called "exile". The rivers are

Euphrates and Tigris.

238 The province of the confluence of Tigris and Euphrates.

239 Women desecrated by a forbidden union with Coharim: Divorcees, harlots, and daughters of such marriages.

240 In Babylonia. There seems to be a pun involved if מחה and מישא both are pronounced *mēsā*. Neubauer (*La Géographie du Talmud*, Paris 1868, p. 325) thinks that the pun about Media connects the name of Media with the root דוה "to be unwell".

241 It might be "the Western district", but the West of Babylonia is desert. Neubauer conjectures that it might be the lake region of upper Mesopotamia. Since the meaning and location is unknown, the places cannot be determined. Purple-blue is the most costly of colors.

242 In the Babli, *Qiddušin* 72b, שוניא גוביא, ציצורא

אַף עַל פִּי שֶׁנֶּחְלְקוּ בֵּית שַׁמַּי וּבֵית הִלֵּל בְּצָרוֹת וּבָאֲחָיוֹת וּבְגֵט יָשָׁן וּבִסְפֵק אֵשֶׁת אִישׁ וּבִמְקַדֵּשׁ בְּשָׁוֶה פְרוּטָה. וְהַמְגָרֵשׁ אֶת אִשְׁתּוֹ וְלָנָה עִמּוֹ בְּפוּנְדָּקִי. וְהָאִשָּׁה מִתְקַדֶּשֶׁת בְּדֵינָר וּבְשָׁוֶה דֵינָר. לֹא נִמְנְעוּ בֵית שַׁמַּי מִלִּישָּׂא נָשִׁים מִבֵּית הִלֵּל וְלֹא בֵית הִלֵּל מִבֵּית שַׁמַּי אֶלָּא נוֹהֲגִין בֶּאֱמֶת וּבְשָׁלוֹם. שֶׁנֶּאֱמַר וְהָאֱמֶת וְהַשָּׁלוֹם אֶהָבוּ. מַמְזֵירוּת בֵּינְתַיִים וְאַתְּ אָמַר הָכֵין. הֵיךְ עֲבִידָא. קִידֵּשׁ הָרִאשׁוֹן בְּשָׁוֶה פְרוּטָה וְהַשֵּׁינִי בְדֵינָר. עַל דַּעְתֵּיהּ דְּבֵית שַׁמַּי מְקוּדֶּשֶׁת לַשֵּׁינִי וְהַוּוֹלָד מַמְזֵר מִן הָרִאשׁוֹן. עַל דַּעְתֵּיהּ דְּבֵית הִלֵּל מְקוּדֶּשֶׁת לָרִאשׁוֹן וְהַוּוֹלָד מַמְזֵר מִן הַשֵּׁינִי. רִבִּי יַעֲקֹב בַּר אָחָא בְשֵׁם יוֹחָנָן. מוֹדִין בֵּית שַׁמַּי לְבֵית הִלֵּל לְחוּמְרִין. מֵעַתָּה בֵּית שַׁמַּי יִשְׂאוּ נָשִׁים מִבֵּית הִלֵּל דְּאִינּוּן מוֹדֵיי לְהוֹן. וּבֵית הִלֵּל לֹא יִשְׂאוּ נָשִׁים מִבֵּית שַׁמַּי דְּלֵית אִינּוּן מוֹדֵיי לְהוֹן. רִבִּי הִילָא בְשֵׁם רִבִּי יוֹחָנָן. אֵילוּ וְאֵילוּ כַהֲלָכָה הָיוּ עוֹשִׂין. אִם כַּהֲלָכָה הָיוּ עוֹשִׂין בְּדָא תַנִּינָן. שָׁלְחוּ לָהֶן בֵּית שַׁמַּי וּפְחָתוּהָ. שֶׁבֵּית שַׁמַּי אוֹמְרִים. עַד שֶׁיִּפָּחוֹת אֶת רוּבָּהּ. אָמַר רִבִּי יוֹסֵי בֵּירִבִּי בוּן. עַד שֶׁלֹּא בָא מַעֲשֶׂה אֵצֶל בֵּית הִלֵּל הָיוּ בֵית שַׁמַּי נוֹגְעִין בּוֹ. מִשֶּׁבָּא מַעֲשֶׂה אֵצֶל בֵּית הִלֵּל לֹא הָיוּ בֵית שַׁמַּי נוֹגְעִין בּוֹ. אָמַר רִבִּי אַבָּמָרִי. יְאוּת. מַה תַנִּינָן. טִימְּאוּ טָהֳרוֹת לְמַפְרֵעַ. לֹא מִכָּן וּלְהַבָּא. רִבִּי יוֹסֵי בֵּירִבִּי בוּן אָמַר. רַב וּשְׁמוּאֵל. חַד אָמַר. אֵילוּ וְאֵילוּ כַהֲלָכָה הָיוּ עוֹשִׂין. וְחַד אָמַר. אֵילוּ

כְּהִילְכָתָן וְאֵילּוּ כְהִילְכָתָן. מַמְזֶרֶת בֵּינְתַיִים וְאַתְּ אָמַר הָכֵין. הַמָּקוֹם מְשַׁמֵּר וְלֹא אוּרַע מַעֲשֶׂה מֵעוֹלָם.

[243]"Even though the House of Shammai and the House of Hillel disagreed about co-wives[244], and sisters[245], and an old bill of divorce[246], and a woman doubtfully married[247], and one who gives *qiddushin* in the value of a *peruṭa*,[248] i. e., he who divorces his wife and spends the night with her in a hostelry, and that a woman receives *qiddushin* for at least a *denar* or the value of a *denar*, the House of Shammai did not refrain from marrying women from the House of Hillel or the House of Hillel from the House of Shammai but they behave truthfully and in peace, as it is said[249]: 'Love truth and peace.'" Bastardy is between them and you say so? How is that? If a first man gives her *qiddushin* for a *peruṭa* and a second for a *denar*, in the opinion of the House of Shammai she is betrothed to the second and the child of the first is a bastard. In the opinion of the House of Hillel she is betrothed to the first and the child of the second is a bastard[250]. Rebbi Jacob bar Aḥa in the name of Rebbi Joḥanan: The House of Shammai concede to the House of Hillel as a restriction[251]. In that case, the House of Shammai should marry women from the House of Hillel since they concede to them. But the House of Hillel should not marry women from the House of Shammai since they do not concede to them. Rebbi Hila in the name of Rebbi Joḥanan: They all followed the same practice[252]. If they followed the same practice, in this case we stated[253]: "The House of Shammai sent and diminished it, since the House of Shammai says unless most of it is missing?" Rebbi Yose ben Rebbi Abun said, the House of Shammai acted before the question came before the House of Hillel. After a question came before the House of

Hillel, the House of Shammai were not touching it. Rebbi Abba Mari said, that is correct. Did we not state[254]: "They declared impure all purities from before", but not in the future. Rebbi Yose ben Rebbi Abun said, Rav and Samuel, one said both acted according to valid practice[252]; the other said, each party followed its own practice. Bastardy is between them and you say so? The Omnipresent watched and no case ever happened[255].

243 Tosephta 1:10, Babli 14b.

244 Discussed in the Mishnah here.

245 Mishnah 3:1, about two sisters married to two brothers who both die childless at the same time.

246 The House of Hillel hold that if a man divorces his wife and then spends time with her under circumstances that permit sexual relations, the bill of divorce is invalidated and the woman needs a new one to marry again. The House of Shammai disagree and hold that if they sleep with one another they do it in intended promiscuity. What the Tosephta calls "an old bill of divorce", Mishnah *Giṭṭin* 8:8 calls "he who divorces his wife and spends the night with her in a hostelry."

247 There are several cases of disagreement about the status of a woman in the Mishnah, and Rashi, R. Ḥananel, and S. Lieberman all have their own preferences. Probably this refers to all instances.

248 Mishnah *Qiddušin* 1:1. In *qiddushin*, the man has to give the woman something of value to make the act legally binding. The value according to the House of Hillel must be at least a *peruṭah*, the smallest copper coin in Hasmonean times, long out of circulation in Mishnaic times. The House of Shammai require a *denar*, the larger Roman silver coin in the early Empire.

249 *Zach.* 8:19.

250 In the Babli, the discussion is about the more realistic case of the daughter's co-wife, where the child is a bastard for the House of Hillel in a levirate following the House of Shammai but only damaged (unfit for a Cohen) for the House of Shammai if married outside following the House of Hillel.

251 They would never permit a new marriage if an existing one is valid for the House of Hillel. There remains the difference that, if it happened, the *qiddushin* of the second are invalid, the woman remains permitted to the first, but for the House of Shammai the court would have to force the second to write a bill of divorce.

252 Following the House of Hillel.

253 Mishnah *Miqwa'ot* 4:5. If there is a trough in a rock too small to be a *miqweh* (40 *seah*), one may drill holes in the rock to lead the water to a *miqweh*. The House of Hillel require that the hole be slightly more than 2 fingers in diameter; the House of Shammai require that most of the bottom be removed. In a case in Jerusalem known as "trough of Jehu", the House of Shammai actually did enlarge the hole even though practice should follow the House of Hillel.

254 It is unknown where this is stated.

255 The Babli, 14a, disagrees and holds that they informed one another in case the child of a family should not be married by a person of the other House. Since the ascendancy of the House of Shammai was so shortlived, the position of the Yerushalmi seems justified. One has to wonder what the rules were for marriages between Sadducees and Pharisees in late Temple times.

כְּהָדָא דְתַנֵּי. כָּל־הָרוֹצֶה לְהַחֲמִיר עַל עַצְמוֹ לִנְהוֹג כְּחוּמְרֵי בֵית שַׁמַּי וּכְחוּמְרֵי בֵית הִלֵּל עַל זֶה נֶאֱמַר וְהַכְּסִיל בָּחוֹשֶׁךְ הוֹלֵךְ. כְּקוּלֵּי אֵילּוּ וָאֵילּוּ נִקְרָא רָשָׁע. אֶלָּא אוֹ כְדִבְרֵי בֵית שַׁמַּי כְּקוּלֵּיהֶם וּכְחוּמְרֵיהֶן אוֹ כְדִבְרֵי בֵית הִלֵּל כְּקוּלֵּיהֶם וּכְחוּמְרֵיהֶן. הָדָא דְתֵימַר עַד שֶׁלֹּא יָצָאת בַּת קוֹל. אֲבָל מִשֶּׁיָּצָאת בַּת קוֹל לְעוֹלָם הֲלָכָה כְבֵית הִלֵּל. וְכָל־הָעוֹבֵר עַל דִּבְרֵי בֵית הִלֵּל חַייָב מִיתָה. תַּנֵי יָצָאת בַּת קוֹל וְאָמְרָה. אֵילּוּ וְאֵילּוּ דִבְרֵי אֱלֹהִים חַיִּים הֵם אֲבָל הֲלָכָה כְבֵית הִלֵּל לְעוֹלָם. בְּאֵיכָן יָצָאת בַּת קוֹל. רַב בֵּיבַי בְשֵׁם רִבִּי יוֹחָנָן אָמַר. בְּיַבְנֶה יָצָאת בַּת קוֹל.

In this matter[256], it was stated[257]: "About anybody who wants to take upon himself the stringencies both of the House of Shammai and the House of Hillel it was said[258]: 'The silly one walks in darkness'. The leniencies of both of them, he is called wicked. Only either following the words of the House of Shammai in their leniencies and stringencies, or following the words of the House of Hillel in their leniencies and stringencies." That is, before there came the disembodied voice[259]. But after the disembodied voice was heard, "practice follows the House of Hillel forever[257]." And any who transgresses the words of the House of Hillel is deserving of death[260]. It was stated: There came the disembodied voice and said: Both of them are the words of the Living God, but practice follows the House of Hillel forever. Where was the disembodied voice heard? Rav Bebai in the name of Rebbi Johanan: The disembodied voice was heard at Yabneh[261].

256 As R. Moses Margalit points out, this kind of reference fits the style of the Yerushalmi. Those who want to delete כהדא ד are lead astray by the style of the Babli.

257 Tosephta *Sukkah* 2:3, *Yebamot* 1:13, *Idiut* 2:3. Babli *Eruvin* 6b, *Roš Haššanah* 14b, *Ḥulin* 43b.

258 *Eccl.* 2:14.

259 The collective agreement of the people, over the heads of the rabbinic establishment.

260 Cf. Mishnah *Berakhot* 1:7.

261 Between the two wars against the Romans.

כיצד פרק שני

(fol. 3b) **משנה א:** כֵּיצַד אֵשֶׁת אָחִיו שֶׁלֹּא הָיָה בְעוֹלָמוֹ. שְׁנֵי אַחִים וּמֵת אֶחָד מֵהֶם וְנוֹלַד לָהֶן אָח וְאַחַר כָּךְ יִבֵּם הַשֵּׁנִי אֶת אֵשֶׁת אָחִיו וָמֵת. הָרִאשׁוֹנָה יוֹצֵאת מִשּׁוּם אֵשֶׁת אָחִיו שֶׁלֹּא הָיָה בְעוֹלָמוֹ וְהַשְּׁנִייָה מִשּׁוּם צָרָתָהּ. עָשָׂה בָהּ מַאֲמָר וָמֵת שְׁנִייָה חוֹלֶצֶת וְלֹא מִתְייַבֶּמֶת.

Mishnah 1: In which way[1] "the wife of his brother who did not live in his world"? There were two brothers, one of them died, then a brother was born to them[2], and after that the second brother took his brother's wife in levirate[3], and died. The first woman[4] leaves as widow of his brother who did not live in his world and the second one[5] because she is her co-wife. If he had "bespoken" her[6], the second performs *ḥalîṣah* but not levirate.

1 In which way does the wife of his brother who did not live in his world free her co-wife?, cf. Mishnah 1:1.

2 To whom the widow now is forbidden. She remains forbidden.

3 Having already another wife. He then died childless.

4 The widow taken in levirate.

5 The original wife of the second brother.

6 In biblical law, only cohabitation makes the sister-in-law the wife of the levir (*Deut.* 25:5). Since it was felt that having sex without prior ceremony was unbecoming, there is a requirement (rabbinic for the Babli, possibly biblical for the Yerushalmi) to go through the formalities of *qiddushin*; cf. Chapter 1, Note 63. *Qiddushin* make a free woman a wife for the purposes of criminal law. But for the sister-in-law, the act is invalid by biblical standards (cf. Chapter 1,

Note 94); the wife of the second brother does not become co-wife of the sister-in-law through the latter's *qiddushin* by the standards of criminal law. Therefore, the act is not called *qiddushin* but מאמר "bespeaking": she is reserved for the brother claiming her; all other brothers are excluded from levirate with her. "Bespeaking" is not preliminary marriage since it is voided not by a bill of divorce but by *ḥalîṣah* (but it needs a rabbinic bill of divorce).

The other woman is not freed as co-wife but, rabbinically, one does not admit levirate since she is almost a co-wife.

הלכה א: (fol. 3c) כֵּיצַד אֵשֶׁת אָחִיו שֶׁלֹּא הָיָה בְעוֹלָמוֹ כול׳. יַחְדָּיו. פְּרָט לְאֵשֶׁת אָחִיו שֶׁלֹּא הָיָה בְעוֹלָמוֹ. דְּלֹא כֵן מַה אֲנָן אָמְרִין. מֵת בְּלֹא בָנִים תְּהֵא אִשְׁתּוֹ אֲסוּרָה לְהִינָּשֵׂא. שֶׁמָּא יוֹלִיד אָבִיו בֵּן וּתְהֵא אִשְׁתּוֹ זְקוּקָה לְיִיבּוּם. מֵעַתָּה אֲפִילוּ מֵתָה אִמּוֹ תְּהֵא אִשְׁתּוֹ אֲסוּרָה לְהִינָּשֵׂא. שֶׁמָּא יֵלֵךְ אָבִיו וְיִשָּׂא לוֹ אִשָּׁה אַחֶרֶת וְיוֹלִיד בֵּן וּתְהֵא אִשְׁתּוֹ זְקוּקָה לְיִיבּוּם. וְיֹאמַר קִרְיָיה וּבֵן וְאַב אֵין לוֹ. אֶלָּא כֵן אֲנָן קַייָמִין כְּשֶׁמֵּת וְהִנִּיחַ אֶת אִשְׁתּוֹ מְעוּבֶּרֶת. שֶׁלֹּא תֹאמַר. אִילּוּ מֵת וְהִנִּיחַ אֶת אִשְׁתּוֹ מְעוּבֶּרֶת שֶׁמָּא אֵינָהּ צְרִיכָה לְהַמְתִּין וְלֵידַע אִם בֶּן קַייָמָא הוּא וְאִם אֵינוֹ בֶּן קַייָמָא. אַף הָכָא תְּהֵא צְרִיכָה לְהַמְתִּין וְלֵידַע אִם בֶּן קַייָמָא הוּא וְאִם אֵינוֹ בֶּן קַייָמָא. לְפוּם כֵּן צָרַךְ מֵימַר יַחְדָּיו. פְּרָט לְאֵשֶׁת אָחִיו שֶׁלֹּא הָיָה בְעוֹלָמוֹ.

Halakhah 1: Why "the wife of his brother who did not live in his world"[7]? "Together', this excludes the wife of his brother who did not live in his world[8]. Because if it were not so, what would we say? If he died childless, his widow would be forbidden to remarry, for maybe his father would have another son and his widow would then be a candidate[9] for the levirate! Even if [the deceased's] mother had died, his widow would be forbidden to remarry, [because] maybe the father would go and marry a new wife who could have a son and the widow would then be a candidate for the levirate! Then the verse would have to read[10]: "He has neither father nor son"! One would compare this to the case that he left his widow pregnant; does she not have to wait to know whether the child is viable or not[11]? Here also, should she not have to wait to know whether the child is viable or not? Therefore it was necessary to say "together"; this excludes the wife of his brother who did not live in his world.

7 Mentioned in Mishnah 1:1. In contrast to all other cases enumerated there, this is not based on a direct incest prohibition.

8 Cf. Chapter 1, Note 39.

9 The one under obligation of levirate or *ḥalîṣah* is always called זקוקה, the fact of obligation זיקה. It does not seem reasonable to connect this meaning to biblical זקק "to refine, purify"; maybe the root is related to Arabic زقّ، زقق "to feed (a bird his young)", that she is fodder for the levirate, or even Akkadic *zāqiqum* "ghost; necromancer". {Jewish Berber tribes held that a brother who rejects levirate will be punished by the ghost of his dead brother.}

10 To free her for remarriage.

11 A posthumous child who does not survive for 30 days does not free its mother from levirate or *ḥalîṣah*.

יְבָמָהּ יָבֹא עָלֶיהָ. זֶה הַבִּיאָה. וּלְקָחָהּ לוֹ לְאִשָּׁה. זֶה הַמַּאֲמָר. יָכוֹל יְהֵא כְשֵׁם שֶׁהַבִּיאָה גוֹמֶרֶת בָּהּ כָּךְ יְהֵא הַמַּאֲמָר גוֹמֵר בָּהּ. תַּלְמוּד לוֹמַר וְיִבְּמָהּ. עוֹרָה אֶת כָּל־הַפָּרָשָׁה כּוּלָּהּ לְיִיבּוּם. הַבִּיאָה גוֹמֶרֶת בָּהּ וְאֵין הַמַּאֲמָר גוֹמֵר בָּהּ. אִם כֵּן מַה הוֹעִיל בָּהּ מַאֲמָר. לְאוֹסְרָהּ לָאַחִין.

"Her levir shall come upon her[12]", that is cohabitation. "And take her as wife for himself", that is "bespeaking"[13]. I might think that just as cohabitation is final so "bespeaking" is final[14]; the verse says "and act as levir towards her." This directs the entire paragraph towards levirate. Cohabitation is final, "bespeaking" is not final. Then what is "bespeaking" good for? To forbid her to the brothers[15].

12 *Deut.* 25:5.

13 A better translation, if one identifies biblical and rabbinic Hebrew, would be: "Acquires her as a wife for himself", by giving her some valuables as for legally valid *qiddushin.*

14 Cohabitation makes the widow his wife; her marriage to him can be terminated only by death or by a bill of divorce. "Bespeaking" does not remove the obligation of *ḥalîṣah* if the levir changes his mind, in contrast to *qiddushin* which can be undone only by a bill of divorce.

Tosephta 3:1: "*Qiddushin* are final, 'bespeaking' is not final".

The Babli, 54a, formulates: "Cohabitation is final, money or a document are not final." Cohabitation is final even if in error or unintentional (Mishnah 6:1); money or a document are not final even if given as *qiddushin* and not as "bespeaking".

15 After "bespeaking", she remains forbidden to the other brothers even if the "bespeaker" changes his mind.

רִבִּי שִׁמְעוֹן אוֹמֵר. הַמַּאֲמָר אוֹ קוֹנֶה אוֹ לֹא קוֹנֶה. מַה טַעֲמָא דְרִבִּי שִׁמְעוֹן. יְבָמָהּ יָבֹא עָלֶיהָ. זוֹ הַבִּיאָה. וּלְקָחָהּ לוֹ לְאִשָּׁה. זֶה הַמַּאֲמָר. וּכְשֵׁם שֶׁהַבִּיאָה גוֹמֶרֶת בָּהּ כָּךְ הַמַּאֲמָר גּוֹמֵר בָּהּ. אוֹ יְבָמָהּ יָבֹא עָלֶיהָ וַהֲרֵי הִיא לְקוּחָה לוֹ וְהַמַּאֲמָר לֹא הוֹעִיל בָּהּ. כְּלוּם.

Rebbi Simeon says, "bespeaking" either acquires[16] or does not acquire[17]. What is the argument of Rebbi Simeon? "Her levir shall come upon her", that is cohabitation. "And take her as wife for himself", that is "bespeaking". Just as cohabitation is final so "bespeaking" is final. Or "her levir shall come upon her", then she has been acquired by him and "bespeaking" was of no use to her[18].

16 As a biblically required act. This is the opinion of the House of Shammai, cf. Halakhah 3:5, Babli 18a.

17 As a rabbinic institution. In the Babli, 18b-19b, the question whether R. Simeon's problem is rabbinic or biblical is only marginally hinted at.

18 Since in the interpretation given above, "bespeaking" is mentioned in the verse after intercourse. This is incomprehensible since everybody agrees that cohabitation makes the

widow the full wife of the levir without any "bespeaking". If "bespeaking" is not needed, it cannot be a biblical requirement and "take her as wife for himself" does not refer to "bespeaking" but that "she is his wife in every respect" (Mishnah 4:4).

רִבִּי לְעָזָר בֶּן עֲרָךְ אוֹמֵר. הַמַּאֲמָר קוֹנֶה קִנְיָין גָּמוּר בִּיבָמָה. מַה טַעֲמָה דְּרִבִּי לְעָזָר בֶּן עֲרָךְ. וּלְקָחָהּ לוֹ לְאִשָּׁה. הֲרֵי הִיא כְקִידּוּשֵׁי אִשָּׁה. מַה קִידּוּשֵׁי אִשָּׁה קוֹנִין קִנְיָין גָּמוּר. אַף הַמַּאֲמָר קוֹנֶה קִנְיָין גָּמוּר בִּיבָמָה. אֵי זוֹ הִיא מַאֲמָר בִּיבָמָה. הֲרֵי אַתְּ מְקוּדֶּשֶׁת לִי בְּכֶסֶף וּבְשָׁוֶה כֶסֶף.

Rebbi Eleazar ben Arakh says, "bespeaking" acquires a sister-in-law completely. What is the argument of Rebbi Eleazar ben Arakh? "And take her as wife for himself", the same expression is used as for *qiddushin* of a woman[19]. Just as *qiddushin* acquire completely, so "bespeaking" acquires a sister-in-law completely. What is the formula for "bespeaking" a sister-in-law? "You are betrothed to me by money or money's worth.[20]"

19 *Deut*. 22:13, "If a man takes a wife".

20 The same formula as for *qiddushin*; Babli 52a, Tosephta 1:1 (the latter also has the formula for "bespeaking" by document).

בֵּין רַבָּנִין בֵּין רִבִּי שִׁמְעוֹן מוֹדֵיי בָהּ. כְּרַבָּנִין. צַד שֶׁקָּנָה בָהּ מַאֲמָר כְּנֶגְדּוֹ אָסוּר בְּצָרָה. וְצַד שֶׁלֹּא קָנָה בָהּ מַאֲמָר כְּנֶגְדּוֹ הֵיתֵר בְּצָרָה. לְפִיכָךְ חוֹלֶצֶת וְלֹא מִתְיַבֶּמֶת. כְּרִבִּי שִׁמְעוֹן. קָנָה מַאֲמָר שְׁתֵּיהֶן מוּתָּרוֹת. לֹא קָנָה מַאֲמָר הָרִאשׁוֹנָה אֲסוּרָה וְהַשְּׁנִייָה מוּתֶּרֶת. מִסָּפֵק חוֹלֶצֶת וְלֹא מִתְיַבֶּמֶת. מַה נְפִיק מִן בֵּינֵיהוֹן. בָּא עַל הַשְּׁנִייָה. עַל דַּעְתִּין דְּרַבָּנִין בִּיאוֹת עֶרְוָה. מִפְּנֵי שֶׁעָשָׂה בָהּ מַאֲמָר. הָא אִם לֹא עָשָׂה בָהּ מַאֲמָר מִתְיַבֶּמֶת וְאֵין לוֹ זִיקָה בָהּ. אָמַר רִבִּי חַגַּיי. קִיַּמְתָּהּ בְּהַהוּא דָמַר רִבִּי יַעֲקֹב בַּר אָחָא בְשֵׁם רִבִּי לְעָזָר. שׁוֹמֶרֶת יָבָם שֶׁמֵּתָה מוּתָּר בְּאִמָּהּ. זִיקָה הָיְתָה לוֹ בָהּ. כֵּיוָן שֶׁמֵּתָה בָטְלָה זִיקָתָהּ. וְהָכָא כֵּיוָן שֶׁמֵּת בָּטְלָה זִיקָתוֹ.

Both the rabbis and Rebbi Simeon agree to the following[21]. According to the rabbis, the aspect which "bespeaking" acquires is forbidden in the co-wife, the aspect which "bespeaking" does not acquire is permitted in the co-wife; therefore, the latter has to have *ḥalîṣah* but not levirate[22]. According to Rebbi Simeon, if "bespeaking" acquires, both are permitted[23]. If "bespeaking" does not acquire, the first one is forbidden but the second one permitted. Out of doubt, she has to have *ḥalîṣah* but not levirate. What is the difference between them[24]? If he slept with the second one[25]. In the opinion of the rabbis, an incestuous intercourse because he[26] had "bespoken". Therefore, if he had not "bespoken" she may have levirate and there is no candidacy at all[27]. Rebbi Ḥaggai said, I explained that following what Rebbi Jacob bar Aḥa said in the name of Rebbi Eleazar: If a woman waiting for her levir died, her mother is permitted to him[28]. He had in her an interest of candidacy. When she died, the candidacy was eliminated. And here, when he died, the candidacy was eliminated[29].

21 Two different reasonings lead to the same practical result.

22 Since "bespeaking" is neither final nor useless, the wife of the brother becomes possibly a co-wife of his sister-in-law; if he dies she is excluded from levirate since that is possible only for a woman certainly permitted to the (newly born) levir. She cannot leave the family without *ḥalîṣah* since she was not a full co-wife of the forbidden woman.

23 If "bespeaking" preceded the birth of the next brother, the widow of the first brother already was the wife of the second and after his death will be permitted to the third. If the birth of the next brother preceded bespeaking, both are forbidden: the first as widow of a brother who did not live in his world, the second as her co-widow. Whether one wants to emend the text here, from "permitted" to "forbidden", depends on which case one chooses.

24 Is there any case where there is

a practical difference between the rabbis and Rebbi Simeon?

25 If the third brother sleeps with the woman to whom he should give *ḥalîṣah*, this is to some degree incestuous intercourse, he cannot acquire her in levirate, and a child from this union is a bastard.

26 The second brother.

27 The simple fact that the widow may not marry outside the family without *ḥalîṣah* does not establish a relationship with any one of the brothers. In the Babli, 17b, this is the minority opinion ascribed to Rav Huna in the name of Rav.

28 Quoted many times affirmatively in the Yerushalmi (*Yebamot* 4:8, 4:16; *Soṭah* 2:5), rejected in the Babli, 17b.

The position of R. Simeon is not explained but is clear: The relationship is possibly incestuous, the child is only possibly a bastard and cannot be forbidden by the court to marry inside the congregation.

29 Rejected in the Babli, 18a: "Candidacy cannot disappear without action."

(fol. 3b) **משנה ב:** שְׁנֵי אַחִים וּמֵת אֶחָד מֵהֶן וְיִיבֵּם הַשֵּׁנִי אֶת אֵשֶׁת אָחִיו וְאַחַר כָּךְ נוֹלַד לָהֶן אָח וָמֵת. הָרִאשׁוֹנָה יוֹצֵאת מִשּׁוּם אֵשֶׁת אָחִיו שֶׁלֹּא הָיָה בְעוֹלָמוֹ וְהַשְּׁנִייָה מִשּׁוּם צָרָתָהּ. עָשָׂה בָהּ מַאֲמָר וָמֵת שְׁנִייָה חוֹלֶצֶת וְלֹא מִתְיַבֶּמֶת. רַבִּי שִׁמְעוֹן אוֹמֵר מְיַיבֵּם לְאֵיזוֹ שֶׁיִּרְצֶה אוֹ חוֹלֵץ לְאֵיזוֹ שֶׁיִּרְצֶה.

Mishnah 2: There were two brothers, one of them died and the second[30] took his brother's widow in levirate; afterwards a brother was born to them, and he died. The first woman[31] leaves as wife of his brother who did not live in his world and the second one as her co-wife. If [the second brother] had bespoken [the widow of the first] when he died, the second performs *ḥalîṣah* but cannot have levirate[32]. Rebbi Simeon says, he may take in levirate any one he wants or performs *ḥalîṣah* with any one he wants[33].

30 Who already has a wife. If he has no wife, the rules for the widow of the first brother do not change.

31 The widow. The author of this Mishnah holds that the widow does not lose her status as widow of the first by her marriage to the second brother. She leaves the family of her dead husbands and is free to marry any outsider without further ceremony.

32 As explained in the preceding paragraph.

33 As shown in the next paragraph, this must refer to the first case and R. Simeon must hold that the marriage to the second brother erases her status as widow of the first.

(fol. 3c) **הלכה ב:** שְׁנֵי אַחִים וּמֵת אֶחָד מֵהֶן כול׳. רִבִּי שִׁמְעוֹן אוֹמֵר. הַמַּאֲמָר אוֹ קוֹנֶה אוֹ לֹא קוֹנֶה וְאַתְּ אָמַר אָכֵין. וּמְייַבְּמִין לְבַעֲלַת מַאֲמָר. וְחָשׁ לוֹמַר שֶׁמָּא לֹא קָנָה מַאֲמָר וְנִמְצָא מִתְחַייֵב עָלֶיהָ מִשֵּׁם אֵשֶׁת אָחִיו שֶׁלֹּא הָיָה בְעוֹלָמוֹ. וְחוֹלְצִין לְבַעֲלַת מַאֲמָר. וְחָשׁ לוֹמַר שֶׁמָּא קָנָה מַאֲמָר וְנִמְצֵאת הַשְּׁנִייָה זְקוּקָה לוֹ. הֲוֵיי מַה דְּאָמַר רִבִּי שִׁמְעוֹן עַל רֵישֵׁיהּ.

Halakhah 2: "If there were two brothers, one of them died", etc. Rebbi Simeon says, "bespeaking" either acquires or does not acquire, and you say so[34]? May one permit levirate with the "bespoken" woman? One should suspect that "bespeaking" does not acquire; then he[35] would be guilty because of "wife of his brother who did not live in his world." Can the "bespoken" one perform *ḥaliṣah?* Should one not suspect that "bespeaking" does acquire; then the second {widow} is a candidate for [the third brother][36]. It must be that Rebbi Simeon refers to the first case.

34 Could R. Simeon refer to the woman "bespoken" when the second brother died?

35 The youngest brother born after the death of the first.

36 According to R. Simeon, see Note 33. Another argument with the same result is in the Babli, 18b.

אָמַר רִבִּי יוֹחָנָן. מוֹדֶה רִבִּי שִׁמְעוֹן בָּרִאשׁוֹנָה. אַשְׁכָּח תַּנֵּי. עוֹד הִיא בְּמַחֲלוֹקֶת. מַה בֵּין רִאשׁוֹנָה וּמַה בֵּין שְׁנִייָה. רִאשׁוֹנָה בָּא וּמְצָאָהּ בְּאִיסּוּר. וְהַשְּׁנִייָה בָּא וּמְצָאָהּ בְּהֵיתֵר. רִבִּי יוֹחָנָן בָּעֵי. אֵשֶׁת אָבִיו שֶׁמְּצָאָהּ לִפְנֵי אֶחָד מִן הַשּׁוּק מַה אָמַר בָּהּ רִבִּי שִׁמְעוֹן. מִפְּנֵי שֶׁמְּצָאָהּ בְּהֵיתֵר מוּתֶּרֶת. לֹא אָמַר רִבִּי שִׁמְעוֹן אֶלָּא עַל יְדֵי אַחִין מִן הָאַב. רִבִּי יַעֲקֹב בַּר אָחָא אָמַר רִבִּי שִׁמְעוֹן בֶּן לָקִישׁ בָּעֵי. אֵשֶׁת אָחִיו מֵאִמּוֹ שֶׁמְּצָאָהּ לִפְנֵי אֶחָד מִן הַשּׁוּק מַה אָמַר בָּהּ רִבִּי שִׁמְעוֹן. מִפְּנֵי שֶׁמְּצָאָהּ בְּהֵיתֵר מוּתֶּרֶת. לֹא אָמַר רִבִּי שִׁמְעוֹן אֶלָּא עַל יְדֵי אַחִים מֵאָב. רִבִּי יוּדָן בָּעֵי. צָרַת אֲחוֹת אִמּוֹ שֶׁמְּצָאָהּ לִפְנֵי אֶחָד מִן הַשּׁוּק. מִפְּנֵי שֶׁמְּצָאַת בְּהֵיתֵר מוּתֶּרֶת. רִבִּי אָבִין בָּעִין *(sic!)*. גְּרוּשָׁה שֶׁנַּעֲשֵׂית אַלְמָנָה. אַתְּ אָמַר מַה דְאָמַר רִבִּי שִׁמְעוֹן עַל רֹאשָׁהּ.

Rebbi Joḥanan said, Rebbi Simeon agrees in the first case[37]. It was found stated, that also is in disagreement. What is the difference between the first and second cases? In the first case he came and found her forbidden[38], in the second he came and found her permitted[39]. Rebbi Joḥanan asked, if he found his father's wife[40] married to an outsider, what does Rebbi Simeon say about her? Because he came and found her permitted, is she permitted? Rebbi Simeon said that only relative to paternal brothers[41]. Rebbi Jacob bar Aḥa said, Rebbi Simeon ben Laqish asked: His maternal halfbrother's wife which he found married to an outsider, what does Rebbi Simeon say about her? Because he came and found her permitted, is she permitted? Rebbi Simeon said that only relative to paternal brothers. Rebbi Yudan asked, a co-wife of his maternal aunt which he found married to an outsider? Because he came and found her permitted, is she permitted? Rebbi Abin asked, if a divorcee became a widow[42]? You have to say that Rebbi Simeon referred to the first case.

37 The case of Mishnah 1, when the third brother was born after the death of the first and before the second brother married the widow in levirate.

38 "He" is the newly born brother, "she" is the widow of the first brother. The argument shows that R. Simeon could not possibly disagree with Mishnah 1.

39 As wife of a living brother. The text is from Tosephta 3:1; the same argument is found in Babli, 19b.

40 A man with two wives dies, leaving one of them pregnant while the other is already married to an outsider when the pregnant widow gives birth to a boy. Is the remarried one still "his father's wife" (*Lev.* 18:8)?

41 The answer is readily understood but not the question. *Deut.* 25:5 cancels the prohibition of *Lev.* 18:16 but no other prohibition from *Lev.* 18; the same conclusion in Babli, 20a.

In the Babli, 20a, the impossible question is about a maternal halfsister married to a paternal halfbrother when the new baby was born.

42 This is a different case altogether. A Cohen is forbidden to marry a divorcee (*Lev.* 21:7). If a Cohen was born when a certain woman who had been divorced had remarried and now was a widow, is she a widow or a divorcee for him? No answer is given since she is both a divorcee and a widow.

מַה אָמַר רִבִּי שִׁמְעוֹן בְּבַעֲלַת מַאֲמָר. נִישְׁמְעִינָהּ מִן הָדָא. רִבִּי שִׁמְעוֹן אוֹמֵר. בִּיאָתָהּ וַחֲלִיצָה שֶׁלְּאַחַת מֵהֶן פּוֹטֶרֶת צָרָתָהּ. וְאִם חָלַץ לְבַעֲלַת מַאֲמָר אַף הַשְּׁנִיָּיה צְרִיכָה חֲלִיצָה. אַתְּ אָמַר. בִּיאָתָהּ אוֹ חֲלִיצָתָהּ שֶׁלְּאַחַת מֵהֶן פּוֹטֶרֶת צָרָתָהּ. מַה נַפְשָׁךְ. קָנָה מַאֲמָר שְׁתֵּיהֶן נָשָׁיו. נִפְטְרָה בַּחֲלִיצַת חֲבֵירָתָהּ. לֹא קָנָה מַאֲמָר אֵין הָרִאשׁוֹנָה צְרִיכָה חֲלִיצָה. וְאִם חָלַץ לְבַעֲלַת מַאֲמָר אַף הַשְּׁנִיָּיה צְרִיכָה חֲלִיצָה. שֶׁמָּא לֹא קָנָה מַאֲמָר וְלֹא נֶגְעָה בָהּ חֲלִיצָה וְיִיבּוּם שֶׁמָּא קָנָה מַאֲמָר וְנִפְטְרָה בַּחֲלִיצַת חֲבֵירָתָהּ. מַה נְפִיק מִי בֵּינֵיהוֹן. חָלַץ לָרִאשׁוֹנָה וּבָא עַל הַשְּׁנִיָּיה. עַל דַּעְתִּין דְּרַבָּנִין בִּיאַת עֶרְוָה. עַל דַּעְתֵּיהּ דְּרִבִּי שִׁמְעוֹן אֵינָהּ בִּיאַת עֶרְוָה. בָּא עַל הָרִאשׁוֹנָה וּבָא עַל הַשְּׁנִיָּיה. עַל דַּעְתִּין דְּרַבָּנָן הָרִאשׁוֹנָה בִּיאַת עֶרְוָה וְהַשְּׁנִיָּיה צְרִיכָה גֵט וַחֲלִיצָה. עַל דַּעְתֵּיהּ דְּרִבִּי שִׁמְעוֹן שְׁתֵּיהֶן

צְרִיכוֹת גֵּט. הָרִאשׁוֹנָה צְרִיכָה גֵט שֶׁמָּא קָנָה מַאֲמָר. וְהַשְּׁנִייָה צְרִיכָה גֵט שֶׁמָּא קָנָה יִיבּוּם שֶׁמָּא קָנָה מַאֲמָר נִפְטֶרֶת מֵחֲלִיצַת חֲבֵירָתָהּ.

What does Rebbi Simeon say about the "bespoken" woman[43]? Let us hear from the following: "Rebbi Simeon says, the cohabitation or the *ḥalîṣah* of one of them[44] frees her co-wife but if he performed *ḥalîṣah* with the "bespoken" woman, her colleague also needs *ḥalîṣah*[45]. You say, the cohabitation or the *ḥalîṣah* of one of them frees her co-wife. However one argues, if "bespeaking" acquires, both are his wives and any one of them becomes free by her colleague's *ḥalîṣah*. If "bespeaking" does not acquire, the first one does not need *ḥalîṣah*, but if he performed *ḥalîṣah* with the "bespoken" one, the second one also needs *ḥalîṣah*. Maybe "bespeaking" does not acquire, then *ḥalîṣah* or levirate do not apply to her. Maybe "bespeaking" does acquire; then she is freed by her colleague's *ḥalîṣah*. What is the difference between them[46]? If he performed *ḥalîṣah* with the first and cohabited with the second[47]. In the opinion of the rabbis it was an incestuous cohabitation[48]. In the opinion of Rebbi Simeon it was not an incestuous cohabitation[49]. If he cohabited both with the first and the second widow, in the opinion of the rabbis with the first it was incest[44] and the second needs a bill of divorce and *ḥalîṣah*[50]. In the opinion of Rebbi Simeon, both need a bill of divorce. The first one needs a bill of divorce; perhaps the "bespeaking" did acquire. The second one needs a bill of divorce; perhaps levirate did acquire; if "bespeaking" did acquire, she was freed by her colleague's *ḥalîṣah*[51].

43 The second case in the Mishnah, when the additional brother was born after the second brother bespoke his brother's widow and before his death.

44 A slightly confusing wording. "One of them" means "a certain one of

them", viz., the brother's original wife.

45 Since it is doubtful whether the "bespoken" one was his wife it is doubtful whether her *ḥalîṣah* means anything.

46 Are there additional practical differences between the theories of the rabbis as given in the Mishnah and R. Simeon?

47 Again, "the first" is the widow of the first brother, "the second" the wife of the second brother. "He" is the third brother born after the death of the first.

48 "If he performed *ḥalîṣah* with the first" means "even if" since for the rabbis *ḥalîṣah* of the first is legally impossible and therefore irrelevant. The relation with the second was certainly partially incestuous.

49 Since the second one is permitted, Note 44.

50 With the sister-in-law in a case not covered by *Deut*. 25:5.

51 Since for the rabbis "bespeaking" is partial acquisition of the widow as a wife, the second, the original wife of the second brother, was partially co-wife of the widow of the first brother. That aspect of her which was not that of co-wife is acquired by the third brother in levirate and needs a divorce; then she also needs *ḥalîṣah* for that aspect which was not acquired. In no case can she be permitted to stay with the third brother.

52 That means that the first one needs both divorce and *ḥalîṣah*.

רִבִּי זְעוּרָה בְשֵׁם רַב שֵׁשֶׁת. תַּנֵּי תַמָּן. דִּבְרֵי רִבִּי שִׁמְעוֹן שְׁתֵּיהֶן אֲסוּרוֹת. וְקַשְׁיָא. קָנָה מַאֲמָר שְׁתֵּיהֶן (fol. 3d) מוּתָּרוֹת. לֹא קָנָה מַאֲמָר אֶלָּא זִיקָה. וְקַשְׁיָא. קָנָה זִיקָה שְׁתֵּיהֶן מוּתָּרוֹת. לֹא קָנָה זִיקָה הָרִאשׁוֹנָה אֲסוּרָה וְהַשְּׁנִייָה מוּתֶּרֶת. שֶׁמָּא זִיקַת רִבִּי שִׁמְעוֹן כְּמַאֲמָר דְּרַבָּנָן. כְּמָה דְרַבָּנָן אָמְרֵי. הַמַּאֲמָר קָנָה וּמְשַׁייֵר. כֵּן אָמַר. זִיקָה קוֹנָה וּמְשַׁייֶרֶת. וְקַשְׁיָא. צַד שֶׁקּוֹנָה זִיקָה כְּנֶגְדּוֹ אָסוּר בַּצָּרָה. צַד שֶׁלֹּא קָנָה זִיקָה כְּנֶגְדּוֹ הֵיתֵר בַּצָּרָה. אָמַר שַׁמַּי. וְכִי מַה נַפְשָׁךְ בָּעֲרָיוֹת. מַהִיא בְהוֹן. כְּהִיא דְאָמַר רִבִּי אָחָא בְשֵׁם רִבִּי בּוּן בַּר חִיָּיה. כָּל־יְבָמָה שֶׁאֵין כּוּלָּהּ לְפָנִים צַד הַקָּנוּי שֶׁבָּהּ נִידּוֹן לְשֵׁם עֶרְוָה. וְעֶרְוָה פּוֹטֶרֶת צָרָתָהּ.

Rebbi Ze'ira in the name of Rav Sheshet: There[53], one stated: The words of Rebbi Simeon are that both are forbidden. This is difficult. If "bespeaking" acquires, are not both permitted? This is a question of acquiring not by "bespeaking" but by candidacy. This is difficult. If candidacy acquires, both are permitted. If candidacy does not acquire, the first one is forbidden but the second permitted. Maybe candidacy for Rebbi Simeon is like "bespeaking" for the rabbis. Just as the rabbis say, "bespeaking" acquires but leaves a remainder, so Rebbi Simeon says, candidacy acquires but leaves a remainder. This is difficult. That aspect which is acquired by candidacy implies a prohibition of an equal part of the co-wife, that part which is not acquired by candidacy implies permission of an equal aspect of the co-wife! Shammai[54] said, is this kind of argument applicable to incest prohibitions? What does he mean? As Rebbi Aḥa said in the name of Rebbi Abun bar Ḥiyya, the aspect acquired in any sister-in-law which is not totally inside [the family] is considered to be under the incest prohibition and an incest prohibition frees her co-wife[55].

53 In Babylonia. No similar statement is found in the Babli. In the discussion there, whether candidacy has any legal consequences other than preventing the widow to marry outside the clan, the name of R. Simeon is not mentioned.

54 Rebbi Shammai, the late Amora.

55 This statement is stronger than that ascribed to the Sages about "bespeaking". The lifting of the incest prohibition of *Lev.* 18:16 applies only to a brother who can marry the widow without doubt. If any condition of the levirate is not fully met, there can be no levirate and the co-wife is freed without *ḥalîṣah*.

משנה ג: כְּלָל אָמְרוּ בִיְבָמָה כָּל־שֶׁהִיא אֲסוּרָה אִיסּוּר עֶרְוָה לֹא חוֹלֶצֶת (fol. 3b) וְלֹא מִתְייַבֶּמֶת. אִיסּוּרָהּ אִיסּוּר מִצְוָה וְאִיסּוּר קְדוּשָּׁה חוֹלֶצֶת וְלֹא מִתְייַבֶּמֶת. אֲחוֹתָהּ שֶׁהִיא יְבִמְתָּהּ אוֹ חוֹלֶצֶת אוֹ מִתְייַבֶּמֶת.

Mishnah 3: They formulated a principle about a sister-in-law: Any woman forbidden by an incest prohibition has neither *ḥalîṣah* nor levirate[56]. If she is forbidden by a commandment prohibition[57] or one of sanctity[58], she has *ḥalîṣah* but not levirate. Her sister who is also her sister-in-law has either *ḥalîṣah* or levirate[59].

56 Since the rules of *Deut*. 25:5 do not apply to her.

57 Simple biblical prohibition as well as rabbinic prohibitions, explained in the next Mishnah.

58 A woman prohibited to a Cohen by the laws of *Lev*. 21:1-14. In these two cases, while marriage is sinful, the act of marriage is not void.

59 If two sisters married to two brothers become widows and there is a third brother to whom one of the sisters is forbidden by one of the incest prohibitions, her sister may be married in levirate since the rules of *Deut*. 25:5 do not apply to the forbidden one; an example is given in the Halakhah.

הלכה ג: (fol. 3d) כְּלָל אָמְרוּ בִּיְבָמָה כָּל־שֶׁהִיא אֲסוּרָה כול'. אָמַר רִבִּי זְעִירָא. עַד דַּאֲנָן תַּמָּן אַפְּקִינָן אַרְבַּע עֶשְׂרֵה מִן דְּעַד אֲחוֹתָהּ שֶׁהִיא יְבִמְתָּהּ מִתְייַבֶּמֶת חוּץ מִבִּתּוֹ. דְּסַלְקִינָן לְהָכָא שְׁמָעִינָן הָכָא דְתַנֵּי רִבִּי חִייָה. דְּתַנֵּי רִבִּי חִייָה. בִּתּוֹ מֵאֲנוּסָתוֹ נְשׂוּאָה לְאָחִיו מֵאָבִיו וְלוֹ אָחוֹת מֵאֵם מֵאִישׁ אַחֵר נְשׂוּאָה לְאָחִיו הַשֵּׁינִי וּמֵת בְּלֹא בָנִים. הֲרֵי זֶה אָסוּר בְּבִתּוֹ וּמוּתָּר בַּאֲחוֹתָהּ. הָדָא הִיא אֲחוֹתָהּ שֶׁהִיא יְבִמְתָּהּ מִתְייַבֶּמֶת.

Halakhah 3: "They formulated a principle about a sister-in-law: Any woman forbidden," etc. Rebbi Ze'ira said: When I was still there[60], we extracted fourteen cases from "her sister which is also her sister-in-law has levirate", except his daughter[51]. When we came up here, we heard what

Rebbi Ḥiyya stated, since Rebbi Ḥiyya stated: His daughter from a woman he raped was married to a paternal halfbrother; she[62] also has a maternal sister from a different father married to a second brother who died childless. His daughter is forbidden to him but her sister, who is her sister-in-law, is permitted to him[63]. That is, "her sister which is also her sister-in-law has levirate".

60 In Babylonia.

61 From the 15 cases of Mishnah 1:1, excluded from the laws of levirate.

62 לו read as לה, as in Tosephta, Chap. 2. The use of the masculine for the feminine is not uncommen in the Yerushalmi; the substitution is most likely *not* a scribal error.

63 Since he never was married to her mother and the prohibition of a woman and her daughter is formulated in terms of "taking", i. e., marriage. In the Tosephta, Chapter 2, "she either has *ḥalîṣah* or is taken in levirate".

פְּשִׁיטָא הָדָא מִילְתָא. אִיסּוּר מִצְוָה וְאִיסּוּר קְדוּשָּׁה חָלַץ נִפְטְרָה צָרָתָהּ. וּבָא עָלֶיהָ. רִבִּי יוֹסֵה אָמַר. אִיתְפַּלְגוּן רִבִּי לָעְזָר וְרִבִּי יוֹחָנָן אָמַר. לֹא נִפְטְרָה צָרָתָהּ. רִבִּי שַׁמַּי מַחְלִף שְׁמוּעָה. מִסְתַּבְּרָה עַל דְּרִבִּי שַׁמַּי דִּבְכָל־אָתָר רִבִּי לָעְזָר סָמַךְ לְרִבִּי חִיָּה רַבָּה. דְּתַנֵּי רִבִּי חִיָּה. אִיסּוּר מִצְוָה וְאִיסּוּר קְדוּשָּׁה חָלַץ לָהּ וּבָא עָלֶיהָ נִפְטְרָה צָרָתָהּ.

It is obvious that if somebody had *ḥalîṣah* with a woman forbidden by a commandment or because of sanctity, the co-widow was freed[64]. When he had intercourse with her? Rebbi Yose said, Rebbi Eleazar and Rebbi Joḥanan disagree; they say the co-widow was not freed[65]. Rebbi Shammai switches the [names] of this tradition. The position of Rebbi Shammai is reasonable since everywhere Rebbi Eleazar seeks support from the great Rebbi Ḥiyya and Rebbi Ḥiyya stated for women forbidden by a commandment or because of sanctity, if he had *ḥalîṣah* or intercourse with her, the co-widow was freed[66].

64 Since marriage would be valid, *ḥalîṣah* must be valid.

65 In this interpretation, Rebbis Eleazar and Joḥanan agree with one another but disagree with everybody else (interpretation of פני משה). Another way would be to postulate a lacuna: "R. Eleazar and R. Joḥanan disagree, *R. Joḥanan said, the co-widow was freed, R. Eleazar said,* the co-widow was not freed" (קרבן העדה). The Babli is no help; the Venice text (20b) asserts that R. Joḥanan and R. Eleazar disagree in the matter but it is unsure who said what (parallel the Yerushalmi, supporting קרבן העדה), but Tosaphot (fol. 5a, s. v. ואכתי) reads "Rebbi Aḥa and Rebbi Eleazar", supporting פני משה.

The people denying that the co-widow was freed must hold that this is a rabbinic ordinance since "commandments" and "sanctity" are treated together. The Babli, 20b/21a, treats only the prohibition of a widow to the High Priest which is simultaneously a prohibition and the transgression of a positive commandment (to marry a virgin) and therefore in a different category.

66 Statement not found in Tosephta.

(fol. 3b) **משנה ד:** אִיסּוּר מִצְוָה שְׁנִיּוֹת מִדִּבְרֵי סוֹפְרִים. אִסּוּר קְדוּשָּׁה אַלְמָנָה לְכֹהֵן גָּדוֹל גְּרוּשָׁה וַחֲלוּצָה לְכֹהֵן הֶדְיוֹט מַמְזֶרֶת וּנְתִינָה לְיִשְׂרָאֵל. וּבַת יִשְׂרָאֵל לְנָתִין וּלְמַמְזֵר.

Mishnah 4: Commandment prohibition: Secondary prohibitions[67] instituted by the Sopherim. Holiness prohibiton: A widow for the High Priest[68], a divorcee[69] or one who had *ḥalîṣah*[70] for a simple priest, a bastard[71] or a Gibeoness[72] to an Israel, a Jewish woman to a Gibeonite or a bastard[73].

67 For any biblical incest prohibition of *Lev*. 18, one more generation is forbidden by common law, a tradition ascribed to the "Sopherim",

the colleagues and successors of Ezra in reconstituting Judaism in Israel after the Babylonian exile.

68 *Lev.* 21:14.

69 *Lev.* 21:7.

70 The identification of *ḥalîṣah* with divorce is rabbinic for the majority, possibly biblical for R. Simeon; cf. Note 17.

71 *Deut.* 23:3.

72 A popular tradition ascribes the exclusion of Gibeonites from the Jewish marriage community to their cruel behavior towards the family of Saul when it was decided that "the Gibeonites are not part of Israel" (*2S.* 21:2). They are called "given" for Joshua "gave" them as hewers of wood and drawers of water (*Jos.* 9:27).

73 Both of them could be illegitimate paternal halfbrothers of the deceased obligated by the laws of *Deut.* 25.

(fol. 3d) **הלכה ד:** אִיסּוּר מִצְוָה עֲרָיוֹת מִדִּיבְרֵי סוֹפְרִים מִצְוָה מִן הַתּוֹרָה לִשְׁמוֹעַ אֶת דִּבְרֵי סוֹפְרִים. וְאִיסּוּר קְדוּשָּׁה. אַלְמָנָה לְכֹהֵן גָּדוֹל גְּרוּשָׁה וַחֲלוּצָה לְכֹהֵן הֶדְיוֹט. אֵלֶּא הַמִּצְוֹת. כָּל־שֵׁם מִצְוָה אַחַת. וְקִדַּשְׁתּוֹ כִּי אֶת לֶחֶם אֱלֹהֶיךָ הוּא מַקְרִיב. וְאִית דִּמְחַלְּפִין. אַלְמָנָה לְכֹהֵן גָּדוֹל גְּרוּשָׁה וַחֲלוּצָה לְכֹהֵן הֶדְיוֹט. אֵלֶּא הַמִּצְוֹת וְכָל־שֵׁם מִצְוָה אַחַת. וְאִיסּוּר קְדוּשָּׁה. עֲרָיוֹת מִדִּיבְרֵי סוֹפְרִים.

Halakhah 4: Commandment prohibition: Incest prohibitions instituted by the Sopherim; it is a biblical commandment to listen to the words of the Sopherim. And Holiness prohibition: A widow for the High Priest, a divorcee or one who had *ḥalîṣah* for a simple priest. "These are the commandments,[74]" all commandments are one. "[75]You should sanctify him, for he brings the bread of your God." But some[76] do switch: A widow for the High Priest, a divorcee or one who had *ḥalîṣah* for a simple priest, "you should sanctify him, for he brings the bread of your God." "These are the commandments," all commandments are one[77]. And holiness prohibitions, incest prohibitions instituted by the Sopherim[78].

74 *Lev.* 27:35. The last verse of *Lev.* includes all commandments contained in the book. This sentence is redundant here; it belongs to the argument of those who switch the attributions.

75 *Lev.* 21:8; this explains the expression "holiness prohibitions".

76 In the Babli, 20a, the first interpretation is that of the rabbis, the second that of Rebbi Jehudah.

77 The special rules for priests are called "commandment prohibitions".

78 *Lev.* 19:2, "you shall be holy", is taken as general injunction to the religious leadership to institute "fences around the law" to which the secondary prohibitions belong.

אָמַר רִבִּי יוּדָה בֶּן פָּזִי. וְלָמָּה סָמַךְ הַכָּתוּב פָּרָשַׁת עֲרָיוֹת לְפָרָשַׁת קִידּוּשִׁין. לְלַמֶּדְךָ שֶׁכָּל־מִי שֶׁהוּא פוֹרֵשׁ מִן הָעֲרָיוֹת נִקְרָא קָדוֹשׁ. שֶׁכֵּן שׁוּנַמִּית אוֹמֶרֶת לְאִישָׁהּ הִנֵּה נָא יָדַעְתִּי כִּי אִישׁ אֱלֹהִים קָדוֹשׁ הוּא. אָמַר רִבִּי יוֹנָה קָדוֹשׁ הוּא. וְאֵין תַּלְמִידוֹ קָדוֹשׁ. רִבִּי אָבִין אָמַר. שֶׁלֹּא הִבִּיט בָּהּ. וְרַבָּנָן אָמְרִין. שֶׁלֹּא רָאָה טִיפַּת קֶרִי מִיָּמָיו. אַמְּתֵיהּ דְּרִבִּי שְׁמוּאֵל בַּר רַב יִצְחָק אָמְרָה. מִן יוֹמוֹי לָא חָמַת מִילָּה בִּישָׁא עַל מָנוֹי דְמָרִי. כְּתִיב וַיִּגַּשׁ גֵּיחֲזִי לְהָדְפָהּ. מַהוּ לְהָדְפָהּ. אָמַר רִבִּי יוֹסֵה בֶּן חֲנִינָה. שֶׁנָּתַן יָדוֹ בְּהוֹד שֶׁבְּיוֹפְיָהּ. בֵּין דַּדֶּיהָ.

Rebbi Jehudah ben Pazi said, why did Scripture put the incest chapter next to the holiness chapter[79]? To teach you that every one who shies away from incest[80] is called "holy". In this sense, the woman of Shunem said to her husband: "[81]Lo, I know that he is a holy man of God". Rebbi Jonah said, "he is holy", but not his student. Rebbi Abin said, that he never looked at her. But the rabbis say that he he never had an involuntary emission. {The slave girl of Rebbi Samuel ben Rav Isaac said, I never saw a bad thing on my master's garments.}[82] It is written "Geḥazi drew near to push her away[83]". What is לְהָדְפָהּ[84]? Rebbi Yose ben Ḥanina said, he put his hand on her beauty spot[85], between her breasts.

79 *Lev.* 19.

80 "Incest" always includes adultery.

81 *2K.* 4:9. The parallel is in Babli *Berakhot* 10b, mostly in the name of R. Yose ben Ḥanina.

82 The statement is added to explain how the Sunamite could know that Elisa was holy..

83 *2K.* 4:27.

84 A poetic contraction of לַהֲדוֹף אוֹתָהּ, somewhat out of place in a prose text.

85 In the Babli, בְּהוֹד יוֹפְיָהּ, better suited as expansion of הודפה.

מְנַיִין לִשְׁנִיּוֹת. רִבִּי חוּנָא אָמַר. הָאֵל. קָשׁוֹת. מִיכָּן שֶׁיֵּשׁ לְמַטָּה מֵהֶן. וְאֵילוּ הֵן הַשְּׁנִיּוֹת. אֵם אָבִיו. אֵם אִמּוֹ. אֵשֶׁת אֲבִי אָבִיו. וְאֵשֶׁת אֲבִי אִמּוֹ. אֵשֶׁת בֶּן בְּנוֹ. וְאֵשֶׁת בֶּן בִּתּוֹ. אֵשֶׁת אֲחִי אִמּוֹ. וְאֵשֶׁת אֲחִי אָבִיו מֵאִמּוֹ.

How can one prove secondary prohibitions? Rebbi Ḥuna said: "These[86]", the strong ones. This implies that there are weaker ones[87]. The following are the secondary prohibitions[88]: His paternal grandmother and his maternal grandmother, his paternal grandfather's wife and his maternal grandfathers wife, his grandson's wife whether from son or daughter, the wife of his mother's brother and the wife of his father's maternal brother.

86 *Lev.* 18:27, כִּי אֶת־כָּל־הַתּוֹעֵבוֹת הָאֵל "all these abominations", *these* should have been written הָאֵלֶּה, the short form is taken as a hint of the root אל "power" (the meaning of the word commonly but wrongly translated as "God").

87 In the Babli, 21a, the argument is in the name of Rava.

88 Babli 21a, Tosephta 3:1 (parallels the Babli in content and the Yerushalmi in language), *Derekh Ereṣ Rabba* 1, extended to contain most of the next paragraph.

תַּנֵּי. רִבִּי חָנִין אוֹמֵר. כּוּלְהוֹן אֵין לָהֶן הֶפְסֵק חוּץ מֵאֵשֶׁת אָבִיו מֵאִמּוֹ. בַּר קַפָּרָא אָמַר. כּוּלְהוֹן יֵשׁ לָהֶן הֶפְסֵק. דְּבַר קַפָּרָא מוֹסִיף אֵם אֲבִי אִמּוֹ וְאֵם אֲבִי אָבִיו. רַב אָמַר. כַּלַּת בְּנוֹ יֵשׁ לָהּ הֶפְסֵק. מַה פְּלִיג. כַּלַּת בְּנוֹ מִמָּקוֹם אַחֵר

בָּאת. רַב אָמַר. זֶרַע הַיּוֹצֵא מִמֶּנּוּ אָסוּר. אָמַר רִבִּי יוֹסֵי בֵּירִבִּי בּוּן. טַעֲמָא דְרַב. אַבְרָהָם אָסוּר בְּכָל־נְשֵׁי יִשְׂרָאֵל. שָׂרָה אֲסוּרָה בְכָל־אַנְשֵׁי יִשְׂרָאֵל.

It was stated: Rebbi Ḥanin said, all of them have no limit[89] except for the wife of his maternal grandfather[90]. Bar Qappara said, all of them have a limit, since Bar Qappara added the mother of his maternal grandfather and the mother of his paternal grandfather[91]. Rav said, his son's daughter-in-law is the limit[92]. Why does he disagree? His son's daughter-in-law comes under a different category[93]. Rav said, his [grandson's] issue from her is forbidden[94]. Rebbi Yose ben Rebbi Abun said, the reason of Rav is that all Jewish women are forbidden for Abraham and all Jewish men are forbidden for Sarah.

89 This sentence has no formal equivalent in the Babli but is understood there since the exceptions to the rule are discussed at length, 21a-22a.

"No limit" means no limit to the number of generations to which it applies. Not only the grandmother is forbidden but also the great-grandmother and all her female ancestors. Daughter and granddaughter are biblically forbidden, the great-granddaughter and all her descendants are rabbinically forbidden.

90 The text reads "the mother of his maternal father." This makes no sense. The translation follows the Babli (21a), where Ze'iri tentatively interprets a statement of Rav that the wife of his maternal grandfather is the last in her line but her female ancestors are permitted.

91 It is not claimed that Bar Qappara made a formal statement to this effect but, since he found it necessary to include an extra generation in some cases, it is clear that he assumes that only the cases enumerated are forbidden. The statement is also in *Derekh Ereṣ Rabba* 1.

92 In the Babli, 21a, Rav declares a limit in the number of generations to exist only in 3 or four cases: the wives of any maternal uncle (whether maternal or paternal (half)brother of his mother), his daughterin-law (per

mitting her daughter who is not his granddaughter), and possibly the case quoted by R. Ḥanin.

93 She is no blood relative.

94 The great-granddaughter and all her descendants are rabbinically prohibited since the granddaughter is biblically prohibited (*Lev*. 18:17).

רַב אָמַר. כָּל־שֶׁאִילּוּ נְקֵיבָה מִן הַתּוֹרָה אֲסוּרָה כְּיוֹצֵא בוֹ זָכָר אִשְׁתּוֹ אֲסוּרָה. אֲחוֹת אָבִיו נְקֵיבָה אֲסוּרָה. אֲחִי אָבִיו זָכָר אִשְׁתּוֹ אֲסוּרָה.. אֲחוֹת אִמּוֹ נְקֵיבָה אֲסוּרָה. אֲחִי אִמּוֹ זָכָר אִשְׁתּוֹ אֲסוּרָה. בַּת בְּנוֹ נְקֵיבָה אֲסוּרָה. בֶּן בְּנוֹ זָכָר אִשְׁתּוֹ אֲסוּרָה. בַּת בִּתּוֹ נְקֵיבָה אֲסוּרָה. בֶּן בִּתּוֹ זָכָר אִשְׁתּוֹ אֲסוּרָה. אָמַר רִבִּי יַעֲקֹב דְּרוֹמַייָא קוֹמֵי רִבִּי יוֹסֵי. אִית לָךְ אַף תַּרְתֵּי. אִמּוֹ תוֹרָה. אֵם אִמּוֹ שְׁנִיָּיה לָהּ. אָסְרוּ אֵם אָבִיו מִפְּנֵי אֵם אִמּוֹ. אֵשֶׁת בְּנוֹ תוֹרָה. אֵשֶׁת בֶּן בְּנוֹ שְׁנִיָּיה לָהּ. אָסְרוּ אֵשֶׁת בֶּן בִּתּוֹ מִפְּנֵי אֵשֶׁת בֶּן בְּנוֹ. אָמַר רַב מַתַּנְיָיא. אִית לָךְ אַף תַּרְתֵּי. אֵשֶׁת אָבִיו תּוֹרָה. אֵשֶׁת אֲבִי אָבִיו שְׁנִיָּה לָהּ. אָסְרוּ אֵשֶׁת אֲבִי אִמּוֹ מִפְּנֵי אֵשֶׁת אֲבִי אָבִיו. אֵשֶׁת אֲחִי אָבִיו מֵאָבִיו תּוֹרָה. אֵשֶׁת אֲחִי אָבִיו מֵאִמּוֹ שְׁנִיָּיה לָהּ. אָסְרוּ אֵשֶׁת אֲחִי אִמּוֹ מֵאִמּוֹ מִפְּנֵי אֵשֶׁת אֲחִי אָבִיו מֵאִמּוֹ.

Rav said[95]: In all cases where the female is forbidden by the Torah, the wife of the corresponding male is forbidden. The father's sister is forbidden as female; the wife of the father's brother, the corresponding male, is forbidden[96]. The mother's sister is forbidden as female[97]; the wife of the mother's brother, the corresponding male, is forbidden His son's daughter is forbidden as female[98]; the wife of his son's son, the corresponding male, is forbidden His daughter's daughter is forbidden as female[98]; the wife of his daughter's son, the corresponding male, is forbidden Rebbi Jacob the Southerner said before Rebbi Yose, there are another two. His mother is biblical[99]. His mother's mother is secondary to her. They forbade his father's mother because of his mother's mother[100]. His son's wife is biblical[101]. His son's son's wife is secondary to her. They forbade his daughter's son's wife because of his son's son's wife. Rebbi Mattaniah said, there are another two. His father's wife is biblical[102]. His paternal grandfather's wife is secondary to her. They forbade his maternal grandfather's wife because of his paternal grandfather's wife. His father's paternal brother's wife is biblical[103]. His father's maternal brother's wife is secondary to her. They forbade his mother's maternal halfbrother's wife because of his father's maternal brother's wife.

95 In the Babli, 21b, this is reported as a Galilean statement which is rejected because it is not valid in all cases.

96 Both cases are biblical, *Lev.* 18: 12,14. It seems that Rav claims biblical status for his statement

97 *Lev.* 18:13. The second case is a secondary prohibition.

98 *Lev.* 18:17.

99 *Lev.* 18:7.

100 She is in the list of secondary prohibitions. As the Babli notes, 21b, in general one does not admit fences around fences of the law (cf. Note 72), so without Rav's rule, she should be permitted. The Babli has a special explanation for the prohibitions, because grandmother and grandfather are called grand *mother* and grand *father* by the grandchildren, which gives them status of father and mother. The Yerushalmi disagrees and holds that there is never a fence for a fence of the law. In the next paragraph one proves the biblical prohibition of some so-called secondaries.

101 *Lev.* 18:15.

102 *Lev.* 18:8.

103 *Lev.* 18:14. It was stated in Halakhah 1:1 that "brother" means "paternal brother".

רִבִּי חוּנָה שָׁמַע כּוּלְהוֹן מִן הָדָא קִרְיָיא עֶרְוַת אִשָּׁה וּבִתָּהּ לֹא תְגַלֶּה אֶת בַּת בְּנָהּ וְאֶת בַּת בִּתָּהּ. זִימָּה זִימָּה לִגְזֵירָה שָׁוָה. מַה לְמַטָּן שְׁלֹשָׁה דוֹרוֹת. אַף לְמַעֲלָן שְׁלֹשָׁה דוֹרוֹת. מַה לְמַטָּן בְּלֹא תַעֲשֶׂה. אַף לְמַעֲלָן בְּלֹא תַעֲשֶׂה. מַה לְמַעֲלָן דֶּרֶךְ נִישּׂוּאִין. אַף לְמַטָּן דֶּרֶךְ נִישּׂוּאִין. מַה לְמַעֲלָן בִּשְׂרֵיפָה אַף לְמַטָּן בִּשְׂרֵיפָה.

מַה לְמַטָּן עָשָׂה בַת זָכָר כְּבַת נְקֵיבָה. אַף לְמַעְלָן עָשָׂה אֵם זָכָר כְּאֵם נְקֵיבָה. מָה אִית לָךְ לְמֵימַר. אֵם חָמִיו וְאֵם חֲמוֹתוֹ. לֹא תְהֵיֶה אֵם אָבִיו כְּאֵם חָמִיו. לֹא תְהֵיֶה אֵם אִמּוֹ כְּאֵם חֲמוֹתוֹ. אָסְרוּ אֵשֶׁת אֲבִי אָבִיו מִפְּנֵי אֵם אָבִיו. אָסְרוּ אֵשֶׁת אֲבִי אִמּוֹ מִפְּנֵי אֵם אִמּוֹ. לֹא תְהֵיֶה אֵשֶׁת בֶּן בְּנוֹ כְּבַת בֶּן אִשְׁתּוֹ. לֹא תְהֵיֶה אֵשֶׁת בֶּן בִּתּוֹ כְּבַת בַּת אִשְׁתּוֹ.

Rebbi Ḥuna understood all of them from this verse[104]: "The genitals of a woman and her daughter you should not uncover; her son's daughter or her daughter's daughter." Taboo - taboo, for an equal cut[105]. Since there are three generations downwards, so there are three generations upwards[106]. Since there is a prohibition downwards, so there is a prohibition upwards. Since upwards one requires marriage, so downwards one requires marriage[107]. Since upwards they are burned, so downwards they are burned. Since downwards, He[108] gave the male's daughter the same status as the female's daughter[104], so upwards He gave the male's mother the same status as the female's mother. What is this about? His father-in-law's mother and his mother-in-law's mother. Should not his father's mother be like his father-in-law's mother[109]? Should not his mother's mother be like his mother-in-law's mother[110]? They forbade his father's father's wife because of his father's mother. They forbade his mother's father's wife because of his mother's mother. Should not his son's son's wife be like his wife's son's daughter? Should not his daughter's son's wife be like his wife's daughter's daughter?

104 *Lev.* 18:17. "The genitals of a woman and her daughter you should not uncover; her son's daughter or her daughter's daughter you should not *take* to uncover her genitals, they are relatives, this is *taboo*." *Take* means "to marry".

105 In v. 20:14 one reads: "If a man *take* a woman and her mother, it is taboo, in fire they should burn him and

them, so that there be no taboo amongst you." In contrast to v. 18:17 which speaks "downwards" of future generations, that verse speaks "upwards" of preceding generations. They are connected by the word *taboo* (Accadic *zamū* "to exclude from something, to refuse something to somebody") which must "cut" the same way in both cases. The argument is refuted in Babli *Sanhedrin* 75a/b since it contradicts verses dealing with earlier generations which seem to insist that the kinds of sin and their punishments are not comparable.

106 Wife, her mother, and grandmothers as well as himself, his mother and grandmothers.

107 To make it a capital crime.

108 The Lawgiver.

109 His mother-in-law's mother is under a biblical prohibition since his wife is her granddaughter. Since the verse puts the daughter's daughter on the same level as the son's daughter, the paternal grandmother also must be forbidden.

110 So there is only one fence, not two. The same argument holds for all the rhetorical questions; all the prohibitions are reduced to single fences.

הֲתִיב רִבִּי חַגַּיי קוֹמֵי רִבִּי יוֹסֵי. וְהָא מַתְנִיתָא פְּלִיגָא עַל רַב. מוּתָּר הוּא אָדָם בְּאֵשֶׁת חוֹרְגוֹ וְאָסוּר בְּבִתּוֹ. אֶלָּא חוֹרְגָתוֹ שֶׁמָּא אֵינוֹ אָסוּר בָּהּ. הֲרֵי חוֹרְגוֹ זָכָר וְאִשְׁתּוֹ מוּתֶּרֶת.

Rebbi Ḥaggai objected before Rebbi Yose: Does not a *baraita* contradict Rav? "A person's stepson's wife is permitted to him but the latter's daughter is forbidden.[111]" Is his stepdaughter not forbidden to him[112]? The stepson is the corresponding male but his wife is permitted[113]!

111 Tosephta 3; Babli 21a; *Sifra Aḥare Mot Pereq* 13 (15).

112 Babli 21a. A biblical prohibition; she is his wife's daughter.

113 Babli 21b.

רִבִּי זְרִיקָן בְּשֵׁם רִבִּי חֲנִינָה. אֵשֶׁת חָמִיו אֲסוּרָה מִפְּנֵי מַרְאִית הָעַיִן. אִי תֵימַר תּוֹרָה. הֲרֵי דָוִד שֶׁנָּשָׂא רִיצְפָּה בַּת אַיָּה. שֶׁנֶּאֱמַר וָאֶתְּנָה לְךָ אֶת בֵּית אֲדוֹנֶיךָ וְאֶת נְשֵׁי אֲדוֹנֶיךָ בְּחֵיקֶיךָ. רִבִּי יִרְמְיָה בְּשֵׁם רִבִּי לָעְזָר. שְׁנֵי חוֹרְגִים שֶׁגָּדְלוּ בְבַיִת אֶחָד אֲסוּרִין לְהִינָּשֵׂא מִפְּנֵי מַרְאִית הָעַיִן. אָתָא עוֹבְדָא קוֹמֵי רִבִּי חֲנִינָה בְּרֵיהּ דְּרִבִּי אַבָּהוּ. אָמַר. יִסְבּוּן בְּאָתַר דְּלָא חָכְמִין לְהוֹן.

Rebbi Zeriqan in the name of Rebbi Ḥanina: His father-in-law's wife[114] is forbidden because of the bad impression. If[115] you want to say it is biblical, did not David marry Riṣpah bat Ayyah[116]? As it was said[117]: "I gave you your master's house and your master's wives in your bosom." Rebbi Jeremiah in the name of Rebbi Eleazar: Two stepchildren who grow up in the same house[118] are forbidden to marry because of the bad impression. A case came before Rebbi Ḥanina ben Rebbi Abbahu. He said, they should marry in a place where they are not known[119].

114 Who is not his wife's mother. The Babli disagrees, 21a. Tosaphot report that Rabbenu Tam did follow the Yerushalmi in a case at Provins (Champagne), but his contemporaries objected.

115 The word was missing in the text; it was inserted by the corrector. It probably should have been אִין since אִי meaning "if" is Babylonian.

116 His father-in-law Saul's concubine.

117 *2S.* 12:8.

118 And are not related.

119 In line with the general attitude of the Yerushalmi, cf. *Kilaim* 9, Notes 34ff.

תַּמָּן תַּנִּינָן. רִבִּי יוֹסֵי אוֹמֵר. אִם עָבַר הַזָּקֵן וּנְשָׂאָהּ. מַה עָבַר. עָבַר עַל דִּבְרֵי סוֹפְרִים. רִבִּי יוֹסֵי בְּשֵׁם רִבִּי אַבָּהוּ שָׁאַל לְרִבִּי יוֹחָנָן. הָדָא אָמְרָה. שְׁנִיּוֹת אֵין לָהֶן הֶפְסֵק. אָמַר לֵיהּ. וְכִי שְׁנִייָה לִשְׁנִיּוֹת שָׁנִינוּ לֹא שְׁנִיָּה לְדִבְרֵי תוֹרָה. וְכוּלְּהוֹן מִשּׁוּם כַּלַּת בְּנוֹ. רִבִּי חִזְקִיָּה בְּשֵׁם רִבִּי יוֹנָה. רִבִּי אַבָּהוּ לֹא אָמַר כֵּן אֶלָּא רִבִּי לָעְזָר שָׁאַל לְרִבִּי יוֹחָנָן. שְׁמוֹנֶה שְׁנִיּוֹת שָׁנִינוּ וְזֶה הֲרֵי תֵשַׁע וְכוּלְּהוֹן מִשּׁוּם כַּלַּת בְּנוֹ.

There, we have stated[120]: "Rebbi Yose says, if the grandfather transgressed and married her.' What did he transgress? He transgressed the words of the Sopherim[121]. Rebbi Yose in the name of Rebbi Abbahu, he asked Rebbi Johanan: Does this mean that secondary prohibitions have no limit? He said to him, did we learn "secondaries to secondaries"? No. Secondaries to the words of the Torah, and all of them because of his son's daughter-in-law[122]. Rebbi Ḥizqiah in the name of Rebbi Jonah, Rebbi Abbahu did not say so, but Rebbi Eleazar asked Rebbi Joḥanan, did we not learn of eight secondaries, and here they are nine! But all of them because of his son's daughter-in-law[123].

120 *Keritut* Mishnah 3:5. The Mishnah speaks of the grandfather's grandson's daughter's daughter who was married to his brother. If that brother dies without issue, the widow is forbidden to her great-grandfather by a secondary prohibition. If the old man marries her in levirate instead of having *ḥalîṣah* as required, since the prohibition is rabbinic she is married and, if the son sleeps with her, Rebbi Yose the Tanna declares him guilty both for his granddaughter and his father's wife, committing two sins in one act.

121 Three generations are biblically forbidden. She would be secondarily forbidden to the father. Since the Mishnah does not mention the father but "the old man", generally interpreted as "grandfather", this is one generation more than that spelled out in the Tosephta. Does this support R. Ḥanin that these prohibitions are unlimited in the number of generations?

122 Rebbi Yose the Tanna does not refer to the first part of the Mishnah speaking of a granddaughter but has a new case where the woman was the son's daughter-in-law before marrying the father's brother who is permitted to her.

123 Since this case is the root of all secondary prohibitions it was not spelled out before; Babli *Yebamot* 21b.

משנה ה: מִי שֶׁיֵּשׁ לוֹ אָח מִכָּל־מָקוֹם זוֹקֵק אֶת אֵשֶׁת אָחִיו לַיִּיבּוּם(fol. 3b) וְאָחִיו לוֹ לְכָל־דָּבָר חוּץ מִמִּי שֶׁיֵּשׁ לוֹ מִן הַשִּׁפְחָה וּמִן הַנָּכְרִית.

Mishnah 5: Any [male] who has a brother anywhere[124] makes his brother's wife a candidate[9] for levirate and he is his brother in every respect[125], except if he were from a slave woman[126] or a non-Jew.

משנה ו: מִי שֶׁיֵּשׁ לוֹ בֵּן מִכָּל־מָקוֹם פּוֹטֵר אֶת אֵשֶׁת אָבִיו מִן הַיִּיבּוּם וְחַיָּב עַל מַכָּתוֹ וְעַל קִלְלָתוֹ וּבְנוֹ לוֹ לְכָל־דָּבָר חוּץ מִמִּי שֶׁיֵּשׁ לוֹ מִן הַשִּׁפְחָה וּמִן הַנָּכְרִית.

Mishnah 6: Any person who has a child[124] anywhere frees [the child's] father's wife from levirate; [the child] would be guilty for wounding or cursing [the father][127]; he is his child in every respect[125] except if he were from a slave woman[126] or a non-Jew.

124 Even illegitimate or bastard.

125 Including inheritance.

126 If she is not his own property. In the latter case, one might assume that he freed the mother of his child. She is a semi-Jew who upon manumission and immersion in a *miqweh* becomes a full Jew. Therefore, she is not in the same category as a non-Jewish woman.

127 *Ex*. 21:15,17.

(fol. 3d) **הלכה ו:** מִי שֶׁיֵּשׁ לוֹ בֵּן מִכָּל־מָקוֹם כול׳. רִבִּי אָבִין בָּעֵי וּבְנוֹ לְכָל־דָּבָר. אֲפִילוּ לְפִירְיָיה וְרִבְיָיה. וְלֹא שַׁנְיָיה בֵּן גּוֹי שֶׁבָּא עַל בַּת יִשְׂרָאֵל וְיָלְדָה. בֵּן יִשְׂרָאֵל שֶׁבָּא עַל גּוֹיָה וְיָלְדָה. משום בת[128] יִשְׂרָאֵל וְיָלְדָה. בְּכוֹר לְנַחֲלָה וְאֵינוֹ בְּכוֹר לַכֹּהֵן.

Halakhah 6: "Any person who has a child anywhere", etc. Rebbi Avin asked: "His child in every respect", even for being fruitful and multiplying[129]? Is there no difference[130] between a Gentile who came to a Jewish woman and she gave birth and a Jew who came to a Gentile woman and she gave birth[131]? "When she became Jewish and gave birth it is a first-born for inheritance but not a first-born for the Cohen.[132]"

128 This text is corrupt. The translation takes the sentence to be a quote from Mishnah *Bekhorot* 8:1 and reads מִשֶּׁבָּאת.

129 Cf. Mishnah 6:6. Since no answer is given, it seems obvious that a bastard counts as a child. This is the interpretation of R. Mose Isserls.

130 The Spanish tradition, from Nachmanides to R. Nissim, reads לפריה ולרביה ולשניות "for being fruitful and multiplying and secondary prohibitions".

131 In both cases, of the three partners in the creation of a child, father, mother, and God (*Peah*, Chapter 1, Note 116), the child has only two since legally it has no father.

132 Mishnah *Bekhorot* 8:1. If the Gentile first has a child as a Gentile, then converts and marries the father of her child, the next child, if male, will be the father's firstborn (since he is no relative of the other child) but does not have to be redeemed (*Ex.* 34:20) since he is not the first child of the mother.

גּוֹי שֶׁבָּא עַל גּוֹיָה וְיָֽלְדָה. רִבִּי יוֹחָנָן אָמַר. גּוֹיִם יֵשׁ לָהֶם יְחָסִים. רִבִּי שִׁמְעוֹן בֶּן לָקִישׁ אָמַר. גּוֹיִם אֵין לָהֶן יְחָסִין. וְהָא כְתִיב בָּעֵת הַהִיא שָׁלַח מְרוֹדַךְ־בַּלְאֲדָן בֶּן בַּלְאֲדָן מֶלֶךְ בָּבֶל סְפָרִים וּמִנְחָה אֶל חִזְקִיָּהוּ. עַל יְדֵי שֶׁכִּיבֵּד זְקֵינוֹ זָכָה לְהִתְיָחֵס. וְהָא כְתִיב וַיִּשְׁלַח הַמֶּלֶךְ אָסָא אֶל בֶּן הֲדַד בֶּן טַבְרִימוֹן בֶּן חֶזְיוֹן מֶלֶךְ אֲרָם הַיּוֹשֵׁב בְּדַמֶּשֶׂק לֵאמֹר. קוֹצֵץ בֶּן קוֹצֵץ. כְּמָה דְאַתְּ אָמַר כִּי הָמָן בֶּן הַמְּדָתָא. וְכִי בֶּן הַמְּדָתָא הָיָה. אֶלָּא צוֹרֵר בֶּן צוֹרֵר. אוּף הָכָא קוֹצֵץ בֶּן קוֹצֵץ. אָמַר רִבִּי תַנְחוּמָא. כָּךְ מֵשִׁיב רִבִּי שִׁמְעוֹן בֶּן לָקִישׁ אֶת רִבִּי יוֹחָנָן. וְהָא כְתִיב וּלְצִיבָא שִׁשָּׁה עָשָׂר בָּנִים וְעֶשְׂרִים עֲבָדִים. וַעֲבָדִים יֵשׁ לָהֶן יִיחוּס. בָּא לִמְנוֹת שׁוֹמְטִין שֶׁלִּמְפִיבוֹשֶׁת.

A Gentile came to a Gentile woman and she gave birth. Rebbi Joḥanan said, Gentiles have family relationships[133]. Rebbi Simeon ben Laqish said, Gentiles have no family relationships. But is it not written[134]: "At that time, Merodakh-Baladan, son of Baladan, king of Babylon, sent letters and a gift to Ḥizqiah." Since he honored his elder[135], he was honored with a family relationship. But is it not written[136]: "At that time, king Asa sent to Ben-Hadad, son of Tabrimon, son of Ḥezayon, king of Damascus, as follows." Destroyer son of a destroyer. As you say[137]: "For Haman ben Hamedata was". Was he the son of Hamedata? That means, oppressor son of an oppressor. So here also, destroyer son of a destroyer. Rebbi Tanḥuma said, so did Rebbi Simeon ben Laqish answer Rebbi Joḥanan, but is there not written[138]: "Ṣiba had sixteen sons and twenty slaves." Do slaves have family relationships[139]? It is to enumerate those who served Mephiboshet together.

133 The verse *Gen.* 2:24: "Therefore, a man abandons his father and his mother and clings to his wife so they will be one flesh" is interpreted to mean that, by the laws of Creation, incest between parents and children, adultery (with a wife not his own) and possibly homosexuality are forbidden. The question is whether a court can enforce the incest prohibition between father and daughter. If there is no recognized legal relationship, that cannot be enforced. R. Joḥanan holds that any court on earth, even a Jewish one, can punish incest between Gentile father and daughter. R. Simeon ben Laqish disagrees.

In the Babli, 62a, the parallel discussion is on a completely different topic, whether the firstborn of a proselyte who converted together with his father is entitled to the customary double portion of the inheritance. R. Joḥanan answers in the affermative, R. Simeon ben Laqish in the negative.

134 *Is.* 39:1.

135 Babli *Sanhedrin* 96a reports that Baladan was incapacitated and Merodakh added his father's name to his own so that all acts of his regency should also be in his father's name.

136 *1K.*. 15:18. The text is contaminated with *2Chr.* 16:2..

137 *Esth.* 9:24. In *Targum Šeni* 3:1, the family tree of Haman is given up to his ancestor Esaw. It is not clear there

whether "Hamedata the Agagite" is intended as a name or a title. In the latter case, Haman's father's name was Seraḥ.

138 *2S.* 9:10. In v. 2, Ṣiba is called "*'ebed* of the House of Saul". Since in v. 9 he is called "esquire of Saul", it seems that *'ebed* represents the usage of the time the book was finally edited, the later kingdom of Judah, when *'ebed* was the recognized title of officials directly responsible to the king.

139 Not being able to legally marry, they are empowered to be promiscuous without guilt.

שִׁפְחָה. הָאִשָּׁה וִילָדֶיהָ תִּהְיֶה לַאדוֹנֶיהָ. נָכְרִית. רִבִּי יוֹחָנָן אָמַר בְּשֵׁם רִבִּי שִׁמְעוֹן בַּר יוֹחַי. כְּתִיב לֹא תִתְחַתֵּן בָּם וּכְתִיב כִּי יָסִיר אֶת בִּנְךָ מֵאַחֲרַי. בִּנְךָ מִיִּשְׂרָאֵלִית קָרוּי בִּנְךָ. וְאֵין בִּנְךָ מִגּוֹיָה קָרוּי בִּנְךָ אֶלָּא בְּנָהּ.

A slave woman: "The woman and her children shall belong to her owner.[140]" A Gentile woman Rebbi Joḥanan said in the name of Rebbi Sineon ben Iohai, it is written[141]: "You shall not conclude marriage with them". And it is written: "For he will divert your son from after Me." Your son from a Jewish woman is called your son; but your son from a Gentile woman is not called your son but her son.

140 *Ex.* 18:4, speaking of the Jewish indentured servant who has to serve for six years. If the children he had during that time with a slave woman were his, they would have to be freed with him at the end of his servitude.

141 *Deut.* 7:3-4. Since only the masculine is used, "he will divert", but not the feminine, it is concluded that the verse speaks only about the Gentile husband. Therefore, the child of the Jewish husband and the Gentile wife is not the husband's child.

The parallel to this paragraph is in the Babli 23a.

יַעֲקֹב אִישׁ כְּפַר נַבּוֹרַיָּה אֲזַל לְצוֹר. אַתּוֹן שָׁאֲלִין לֵיהּ. מַהוּ מִיגְזָר בְּרֵיהּ דַּאֲרָמִייְתָא בְּשׁוּבְתָּא וְסָבַר מִישְׁרֵי לוֹן מִן הָדָא וַיִּתְיַלְדוּ עַל מִשְׁפְּחוֹתָם לְבֵית

אֲבוֹתָם. שָׁמַע רִבִּי חַגַּיי אָמַר. יֵיתֵי. אַיְיתוּנֵיהּ דִּילְקֵי. אָמַר לֵיהּ. מֵאֵיכָן אַתָּה מַלְקֵינִי. אָמַר לֵיהּ. מִן הָדָא דִכְתִיב וְעַתָּה נִכְרוֹת בְּרִית לֵאלֹהֵינוּ. אָמַר לֵיהּ. מִן הַקַּבָּלָה אַתְּ מַלְקֵינִי. אָמַר לֵיהּ. וְכַתּוֹרָה יֵעָשֶׂה. אָמַר לֵיהּ. מִן הֵדָא אוֹרַיְיָה. אָמַר לֵיהּ. מִן הַהִיא דְּאָמַר רִבִּי יוֹחָנָן בְּשֵׁם רִבִּי שִׁמְעוֹן בַּר יוֹחַי. כְּתִיב לֹא תִתְחַתֵּן בָּם וּכְתִיב כִּי יָסִיר אֶת בִּנְךָ מֵאַחֲרַיי. בִּנְךָ מִיִּשְׂרְאֵלִית קָרוּי בִּנְךָ. וְאֵין בִּנְךָ מִגּוֹיָה קָרוּי בִּנְךָ אֶלָּא בְּנָהּ. אָמַר לֵיהּ. חֲבוֹט חַבְטָךְ דְּהוּא טָבָא בְּקֶלְטָא.

[142]Jacob from Kefar Naboraia went to Tyre. They came to ask him, may one circumcise the son of a Gentile woman[143] on the Sabbath? He wanted to permit it from the verse[144]: "They determined their genealogies for their families according to their fathers' houses." Rebbi Ḥaggai heard it and said, he shall come. They brought him in order to be whipped. He said to him, for what reason do you whip me? He said, from what is written[145]: "Now we shall make a covenant for our God". He said, you want to whip me based on tradition[146]? He said, "and it should be done according to the Torah." He said to him, from which teaching? He said, from that which Rebbi Joḥanan said in the name of Rebbi Simeon ben Iohai, it is written: "You shall not conclude marriage with them". And it is written: "For he will divert your son from after Me." Your son from a Jewish woman is called your son; but your son from a Gentile woman is not called your son but her son. He said to him, whip your whipping, because it is good to impress[147].

142 Parallels in *Qiddušin* 3:14; *Gen. rabba* 7(3); *Eccl. rabba* 7:26; *Bemidbar rabba, Tanḥuma,* both *Pesiqtot,* to *Ḥuqqat* (*Parah*).

143 The son of a Jewish father born on the Sabbath, converted at birth.

144 *Num.* 1:18, which determines the clan by patrilinear descent. The principle is expressed in Mishnah *Qiddušin* 3:12: "If there is a possibility of marriage without sin, the child follows its father", even if the parents

are not married.

145 *Ezra* 10:3: "Now we shall make a covenant for our God to expel all these [foreign] women and what was born to them, as counseled by the Lord, by those who fear the commandments of our God; it should be done according to the Torah". As usual, the main point is the part not quoted.

146 "Tradition" is the name for the books of Prophets and Hagiographs which are not books of law. The most one can infer from a text of tradition is how Torah laws were handled in later times.

147 To impress upon him the lesson he should not forget.

(fol. 3b) **משנה ז:** מִי שֶׁקִּידֵּשׁ אַחַת מִשְּׁתֵּי אֲחָיוֹת וְאֵינוֹ יוֹדֵעַ אֵיזֶה מֵהֶן קִידֵּשׁ נוֹתֵן גֵּט לָזוֹ וְגֵט לָזוֹ. מֵת וְלוֹ אָח אֶחָד חוֹלֵץ לִשְׁתֵּיהֶן. הָיוּ לוֹ שְׁנַיִם אֶחָד חוֹלֵץ וְאֶחָד מְיַיבֵּם. קָדְמוּ וְכָנְסוּ אֵין מוֹצִיאִין מִיָּדָם.

Mishnah 7: If somebody gave *qiddushin* to one of two sisters but he does not know to which one of them, he gives a bill of divorce to each[148]. If he died and has one brother, that one has to perform *ḥalîṣah* with both sisters[149]. If he had two [brothers], one performs *ḥalîṣah* and one may marry in levirate[150] If both married without asking, one[151] does not remove [the women] from them.

148 Both are forbidden to him since each one is possib.y hi
his sister-in-law's sister.

150 If the one who performed *ḥalîṣah* had received *qiddushin* from the deceased, the other one is free to marry his brother. If she did not get *qiddushin*, then the levirate is valid.

151 The court does not intervene since one has correctly married in levirate and the other is free to marry his brother since she had no *qiddushin*.

(fol. 4a) **הלכה ז:** מִי שֶׁקִּידֵּשׁ אַחַת מִשְּׁתֵּי אֲחָיוֹת וְאֵינוֹ יוֹדֵעַ אֵיזֶה מֵהֶן קִידֵּשׁ נוֹתֵן גֵּט לָזוֹ וְגֵט לָזוֹ. מֵת וְלוֹ אָח אֶחָד חוֹלֵץ לִשְׁתֵּיהֶן. בְּכָל־אָתָר אַתְּ אוֹמֵר. אֵין חֲלִיצָה אַחַר חֲלִיצָה. וְהָכָא אַתְּ אָמַר הָכֵין. כָּאן בְּוַדַּאי כָּאן בְּסָפֵק. הָיוּ לוֹ שְׁנַיִם אֶחָד חוֹלֵץ וְאֶחָד מְיַיבֵּם. בְּכָל־אָתָר אַתְּ אָמַר. בְּכָל־מָקוֹם שֶׁאוֹמְרִים לוֹ. יַיבֵּם. אֵין אוֹמְרִים לוֹ. חֲלוֹץ. וְהָכָא אַתְּ אָמַר אָכֵין. כָּאן בְּוַדַּאי כָּאן בְּסָפֵק. קָדְמוּ וְכָנְסוּ אֵין מוֹצִיאִין מִיָּדָן.

Halakhah 7: "If somebody gave *qiddushin* to one of two sisters but he does not know to which one of them, he gives a bill of divorce to each. If he died and has one brother, that one has to perform *ḥalîṣah* with both sisters." Everywhere else you say[152] "there cannot be *ḥalîṣah* after *ḥalîṣah*" but here you say so? There if it is certain, here one is in doubt[153]. "If he had two [brothers], one performs *ḥalîṣah* and one may marry in levirate." Everywhere else you say, in any case one asks him to perform the levirate one does not say perform *ḥalîṣah;* but here you say so? There if it is certain, here one is in doubt. "If both married without asking, one does not remove [the women] from them."

152 Mishnah 5:1.

153 It is impossible to do otherwise.

(fol. 3b) **משנה ח:** שְׁנַיִם שֶׁקִּידְּשׁוּ שְׁתֵּי אֲחָיוֹת זֶה אֵינוֹ יוֹדֵעַ אֵיזוֹ קִידֵּשׁ וְזֶה אֵינוֹ יוֹדֵעַ אֵיזוֹ קִידֵּשׁ. זֶה נוֹתֵן שְׁנֵי גִיטִּין וְזֶה נוֹתֵן שְׁנֵי גִיטִּין. מֵתוּ לָזֶה אָח וְלָזֶה אָח זֶה חוֹלֵץ לִשְׁתֵּיהֶן וְזֶה חוֹלֵץ לִשְׁתֵּיהֶן. לָזֶה אֶחָד וְלָזֶה שְׁנַיִם. הַיָּחִיד חוֹלֵץ לִשְׁתֵּיהֶן וְהַשְּׁנַיִים אֶחָד חוֹלֵץ וְאֶחָד מְיַיבֵּם. קָדְמוּ וְכָנְסוּ אֵין מוֹצִיאִין מִיָּדָן.

Mishnah 8: If two[154] [men] gave *qiddushin* to two sisters and neither of them knows to which one he gave his, each one of them gives two bills of divorce[155]. If they died and each one had a brother, each [brother] performs *ḥalîṣah* with both [sisters][156]. If one had one [brother] but the other had two, the single one performs *ḥalîṣah* with both [sisters], but of the two brothers one performs *ḥalîṣah* and the other may marry in levirate[157]. If both married without asking, one does not remove [the women] from them[151].

154 Unrelated.

155 Both sisters are forbidden to both men since each relation would possibly be adultery. Of the two bills each of the women gets, one is valid and the other, given by a man not her husband, is as if it had not been written; only they do not know which is which.

156 They are forbidden to both of them for each one is possibly a candidate for levirate with the other man's brother.

157 The second sister which did not perform *ḥalîṣah* with his brother since she either is his sister-in-law or an unrelated person.

(fol. 4a) **הלכה ח**: שְׁנַיִם שֶׁקִּידְּשׁוּ שְׁתֵּי אֲחָיוֹת כול׳. תַּנֵּי. אֶחָד יִשְׂרָאֵל וְאֶחָד כֹּהֲנִים כְּסֶדֶר הַזֶּה. הָדָא דְאַתְּ אָמַר בְּשֶׁחָלַץ וְאַחַר כָּךְ יִיבֵּם. אֲבָל אִם יִיבֵּם בַּתְּחִילָּה אָסוּר. שֶׁמָּא יָמוּת אָחִיו וְנִמְצָא כְּבָא עַל אֲחוֹת יְבִימְתּוֹ. אָמַר רַב חִסְדָּא. הָדָא אָמְרָה הַבָּא עַל אֲחוֹת יְבִימְתּוֹ[158] לֹא פְסָלָהּ מִן הַכְּהוּנָּה. אָמַר רִבִּי יוֹסֵי בַּר בָּא. תַּנֵּי רִבִּי חִייָה. הַבָּא עַל אֲחוֹת חֲלוּצָתוֹ לֹא פְסָלָהּ מִן הַכְּהוּנָּה.

Halakhah 8: "If two [men] gave *qiddushin* to two sisters," etc. It was stated: These rules apply both for Israel and for Cohanim[159]. That is, if *ḥalîṣah* was performed first and the levirate afterwards. But to perform levirate first is forbidden; maybe his brother will die and it will turn out that he cohabited with the sister of his sister-in-law[160]. Rav Ḥisda said, that means that having relations with the sister of his sister-in-law[161] does not make her unfit for [marriage into] priesthood. Rebbi Yose bar Abba said, Rebbi Ḥiyya stated: He who cohabited with the sister of a woman for whom he had performed *ḥalîṣah* did not make her unfit for [marriage into] priesthood.

158 Reading of ms. A (see the Introduction) confirming a conjecture by R. M. Margalit. In the ms: חלוצתו, as in the next sentence.

159 Babli 24a, with an explanation: Since for priests, *ḥalîṣah* is treated like divorce, one should assume that both sisters are forbidden to priests. But since this treatment is only a rabbinic enhancement of the priest's status, it is not applied to cases of doubt.

160 Who still is bound to him as a candidate for levirate. Babli 23b.

161 Who is not known certainly to be his sister-in-law. The conclusion is reached since all parts of this Mishnah are approved if one of the men is a Cohen.

מֵתוּ לָזֶה אָח וְלָזֶה אָח זֶה חוֹלֵץ לִשְׁתֵּיהֶן וְזֶה חוֹלֵץ שְׁתֵּיהֶן. בְּכָל־אָתָר אַתְּ אוֹמֵר. אֵין חֲלִיצָה אַחַר חֲלִיצָה. וְהָכָא אַתְּ אָמַר הָכֵין. כָּאן בְּוַדַּאי כָּאן בְּסָפֵק. לָזֶה אֶחָד וְלָזֶה שְׁנַיִם. הַיָּחִיד חוֹלֵץ לִשְׁתֵּיהֶן וְהַשְּׁנַיִים אֶחָד חוֹלֵץ וְאֶחָד מְיַיבֵּם. בְּכָל־אָתָר אַתְּ אוֹמֵר. בְּכָל־מָקוֹם שֶׁ(אֵין) אוֹמְרִים לוֹ. יַיבֵּם. אֵין אוֹמְרִים לוֹ. חֲלוֹץ. וְהָכָא אַתְּ אָמַר אָכֵין. כָּאן בְּוַדַּאי כָּאן בְּסָפֵק. קָדְמוּ וְכָנְסוּ אֵין מוֹצִיאִין מִיָּדָן.

"If they died and each one had a brother, each [brother] performs *ḥalîṣah* with both [sisters]. Everywhere else you say "there cannot be *ḥalîṣah* after *ḥalîṣah*" but here you say so? There if it is certain, here one is in doubt. "If one had one [brother] but the other had two, the single one performs *ḥalîṣah* with both [sisters], but of the two brothers one performs *ḥalîṣah* and the other may marry in levirate. Everywhere else you say, in any case one asks him to perform the levirate one does not say perform *ḥalîṣah;* but here you say so? There if it is certain, here one is in doubt.

"If both married without asking, one does not remove [the women] from them."

(fol. 3b) **משנה ט:** לָזֶה שְׁנַיִם וְלָזֶה שְׁנַיִם אָחִיו שֶׁלָּזֶה חוֹלֵץ לָאַחַת וְאָחִיו שֶׁלָּזֶה חוֹלֵץ לָאַחַת. אָחִיו שֶׁל זֶה מְיַיבֵּם חֲלוּצָתוֹ שֶׁלָּזֶה. אָחִיו שֶׁל זֶה מְיַיבֵּם חֲלוּצָתוֹ שֶׁלָּזֶה. קָדְמוּ הַשְּׁנַיִם וְחָלְצוּ לֹא יְיַבְּמוּ הַשְּׁנַיִם אֶלָּא אֶחָד חוֹלֵץ וְאֶחָד מְייַבֵּם. קָדְמוּ וְכָנְסוּ אֵין מוֹצִיאִין מִיָּדָם.

Mishnah 9: If each [of the deceased] had two brothers, one brother of each [of the deceased] performs *ḥalîṣah* with one [of the sisters] and the other brother takes the other [sister] in levirate[162]. If two [brothers] both performed *ḥalîṣah*[163], the other two should not [both] marry in levirate[164] but one of them performs *ḥalîṣah* and the other one may take in levirate. If both married without asking, one does not remove [the women] from them.

162 If the *ḥalîṣah* of his brother was correct, then the other brother marries an unrelated widow. If it was incorrect then he enters a valid levirate marriage.

163 Each of them for another woman.

164 Since one of them might marry the sister of a candidate of levirate with him. But if they married without asking, one of them certainly executed a valid levirate and the other married an unrelated woman.

(fol. 4a) **הלכה ט:** לָזֶה שְׁנַיִם וְלָזֶה שְׁנַיִם. הָדָא דְאַתְּ אָמַר בְּיִשְׂרָאֵל אֲבָל בְּכֹהֲנִים אָסוּר.

Halakhah 9: "If each [of the deceased] had two brothers". That is, for Israel, but for Cohanim they are forbidden[165].

165 If the first pair of brothers both performed *ḥalîṣah* and the second are Cohanim then one of the second pair certainly will marry a woman freed by *ḥalîṣah*, who is considered a rabbinic divorcee. The Babli, 24a, seems to extend the permission given to Cohanim (Note 159) even to this case since for each single person there is only a 50/50 chance that he married a woman with a legally valid *ḥalîṣah*.

(fol. 3c) **משנה י**: מִצְוָה בַגָּדוֹל לְייַבֵּם וְאִם קָדַם הַקָּטָן זָכָה. הַנִּטְעָן עַל הַשִּׁפְחָה וְנִשְׁתַּחְרְרָה אוֹ עַל הַנָּכְרִית וְנִתְגַּייְרָה הֲרֵי זֶה לֹא יִכְנוֹס וְאִם כָּנַס אֵין מוֹצִיאִין מִיָּדוֹ. הַנִּטְעָן עַל אֵשֶׁת אִישׁ וְהוֹצִיאוּהָ מִתַּחַת יָדוֹ אַף עַל פִּי שֶׁכָּנַס יוֹצִיא.

Mishnah 10: The obligation of levirate is on the oldest [brother] but if a younger one got the start on him, he acquired. If somebody is accused in matters of a slave woman[166] and she was manumitted, or of a Gentile and she converted, he should not marry her but if he married her one does not remove her from him. If somebody is accused in matters of a married woman and she was forcibly divorced from [her husband], even if he married her he must divorce her[167].

166 That he has an affair with the slave.

167 An adulteress is permanently forbidden both to the husband and the adulterer (Mishnah *Soṭah* 5:1).

(fol. 4a) **הלכה י**: מִצְוָה בַגָּדוֹל לְיַיבֵּם וְאִם קָדַם הַקָּטָן זָכָה כול׳. מִצְוָה בַגָּדוֹל לְיַיבֵּם. שֶׁנֶּאֱמַר וְהָיָה הַבְּכוֹר אֲשֶׁר תֵּלֵד. מַה אֲנָן קַיימִין. אִם בְּנוֹלָד. יֹאמַר קִרְייָה יָקוּם עַל שֵׁם אָבִיו הַמֵּת. אֶלָּא עַד שֶׁיְּהֵא הַנּוֹלָד בְּכוֹר. מֵעַתָּה אֲפִילוּ הָיוּ לוֹ בָנִים וּמֵתוּ וְאַחַר כָּךְ מֵת הוּא לֹא תִהְיֶה אִשְׁתּוֹ זְקוּקָה לְיִיבּוּם. וְיֹאמַר קִרְייָה וּבָנִים לֹא הָיוּ לוֹ. אֶלָּא אִם אֵינוֹ עִנְיָין לַנּוֹלָד תְּנֵיהוּ עִנְיָין לַמְיַיבֵּם. מִצְוָה בַגָּדוֹל לְיַיבֵּם.

"The obligation of levirate is on the oldest [brother] but if a younger one got the start on him, he acquired, etc." "The obligation of levirate is on the oldest," since it is said[168], "the firstborn she will bear shall . . .". How do we hold? If about the newborn, the verse should read "he should rise in the name of his dead father.[169]" But it must be that the newborn is a firstborn. In that case, even if he had children and they died before he died, his widow should not be a candidate for levirate! Then the verse should have said, 'he never had children[164]". But if it cannot refer to the newborn; let it refer to the levir, "the obligation of levirate is on the oldest."

168 *Deut.* 25:6: "The firstborn she will bear shall rise in the name of his dead brother." This seems to imply that the child should be called X son of Y, where Y is not the biological father but the dead first husband.

The Babli, 24a, discusses the same verse in a different manner, based on *Sifry Deut.* #289.

169 The first hand in the ms. had יקום על שם אחיו המת which is exactly the biblical text and therefore cannot have been meant. The corrector changed this into יקום על שם אביו המת as given in the text. Ms. A reads יקום על שם אחיו אביו המת "shall rise on the name of his dead brother-father" and this seems to be the superior reading; cf. Note 168.

170 The clause (v. 5) וּבֵן אֵין לוֹ "he [is] without issue" implies that at the moment of death no descendants are living.

הַנִּטְעָן עַל הַשִּׁפְחָה וְנִשְׁתַּחְרְרָה אוֹ עַל הַנָּכְרִית וְנִתְגַּייְרָה הֲרֵי זֶה לֹא יִכְנוֹס. קִידֵּשׁ כְּמִי שֶׁכָּנַס. אָמַר [מִדִּין][171] שֶׁלֹּא לִכְנוֹס וְכָנַס מוֹצִיאוֹ מִיָּדוֹ. גֵּירַשׁ מַהוּ שֶׁיַּחֲזִיר. אִם אוֹמֵר אַתְּ כֵּן לֹא נִמְצֵאת מוֹצִיא לִיזָּה עַל בָּנֶיהָ. הַנִּטְעָן עַל אֵשֶׁת אִישׁ. רַב אָמַר בְּנִטְעָן בְּעֵדִים. רִבִּי יוֹסֵי בָּעֵי. אִם בְּנִטְעָן בְּעֵדִים בְּהָא תַנֵּי וְהוֹצִיאָהּ[172] מִתַּחַת יָדוֹ. אַף עַל פִּי שֶׁכָּנַס יוֹצִיא. וּמִתַּחַת יְדֵי אַחֵר יְקַיֵּים. אִם בְּנִטְעָן בְּעֵדִים אֲפִילוּ מִתַּחַת יְדֵי אַחֵר יוֹצִיא. אֶלָּא כֵן אֲנָן קַייָמִין בְּנִטְעָן שֶׁלֹּא בְעֵדִים וְהוֹצִיאָהּ[172] מִתַּחַת יְדֵי אַחֵר יְקַיֵּים.

"If somebody is accused in matters of a slave woman and she was manumitted, or of a Gentile and she converted, he should not marry her but if he married her one does not remove her from him." If he agreed lawfully not to marry her and [nevertheless] married her, she is forcibly removed from him[173]. If he divorced her, may he take her back? If you would say that, would you not defame her children[174]? "If somebody is accused in matters of a married woman," Rav said, that is, he was accused by witnesses[175]. Rebbi Yose asked, if he was accused by witnesses, is that what was stated: If *he*[176] divorced her, even if he[177] married her, he must divorce her? If somebody else divorced her[178], he can keep her! If he was accused by witnesses, even if somebody else divorced her, he must divorce her[167]! But that is what we deal with: If he was accused not by witnesses, if somebody else divorced her, he may keep her[179].

171 Reading of ms. A, missing ms. L and *editio princeps*, but necessary for the understanding of the text.

172 Reading of ms. A; in the Leiden ms. as in the Mishnah והוציאוה; since the statement is qualified as a *baraita*, some deviation from the text of the Mishnah must be expected. This *baraita* is quoted by Rabba bar Rav Nahman in Babli 25a and seems to be underlying Tosephta 4:5.

173 But without a confession of guilt by the husband, the rabbinic authority cannot interfere.

174 If she was divorced and one would prohibit remarriage (as long as she had no other husband in between), at the same time one would declare her children from that man as bastards. This is unacceptable.

175 Only for adultery proven in court is the marriage with the presumed adulterer forbidden. A parallel statement in Babli, 24b.

176 The husband. He may divorce her for suspected adultery and refuse to pay her anything. If she goes to court for the money, he can defend himself by circumstantial evidence permitted in civil law.

177 The adulterer.

178 After her divorce, she married a party other than the presumed adulterer.

179 Tosephta 4:5.

(fol. 3c) **משנה יא:** הַמֵּבִיא גֵט מִמְּדִינַת הַיָּם וְאָמַר בְּפָנַי נִכְתַּב וּבְפָנַי נֶחְתַּם לֹא יִשָּׂא אֶת אִשְׁתּוֹ. מֵת הֲרַגְתִּיו אוֹ הֲרַגְנוּהוּ לֹא יִשָּׂא אֶת אִשְׁתּוֹ. רַבִּי יְהוּדָה אוֹמֵר הֲרַגְתִּיו לֹא תִינָּשֵׂא אִשְׁתּוֹ הֲרַגְנוּהוּ תִינָּשֵׂא אִשְׁתּוֹ.

Mishnah 11: If somebody brings a bill of divorce from overseas and says "it was written and signed in my presence", he shall not marry the wife[180]. "He died[181]", "I killed him", or "we killed him", he shall not marry the wife. Rebbi Jehudah said, "I killed him", the wife cannot be married[182], "we killed him", the wife can be married[183].

180 A bill of divorce brought from another country is valid only if the person who delivers the document can testify to the circumstances in which it was executed (Mishnah *Giṭṭin* 1:1). If the witness would marry the divorcee, his testimony would be suspect because of his interest in the validity of the divorce.

181 If the husband died far from home and somebody testifies to his death to free the widow for another marriage, he cannot marry her because of conflict of interests. The same holds

for the other cases.

182 The killer cannot testify since he declares himself to be wicked and persons officially declared wicked cannot be witnesses (*Ex.* 23:1). Therefore, there is no evidence of the death and the wife cannot claim to be a widow.

183 The witness only says that he was with a group containing a killer, not that he himself is a killer. His testimony is valid; cf. Mishnah 15:4.

(fol. 4a) **הלכה יא**: הַמֵּבִיא גֵט מִמְּדִינַת הַיָּם וְאָמַר. בְּפָנַיי נִכְתַּב וּבְפָנַיי נֶחְתַּם כול'. מַהוּ נֶאֱמָן. שְׁמוּאֵל אָמַר. נֶאֱמָן לִיתֵּן גֵּט. אַסִּי אָמַר נֶאֱמָן לִכְנוֹס. רַב הוּנָא אָמַר בְּשֵׁם רַב. נֶאֱמָן לִכְנוֹס. רִבִּי יוֹחָנָן אָמַר נֶאֱמָן לִכְנוֹס וְאֵין לְמֵידִין הֵימֶינּוּ דָּבָר אַחֵר. מַהוּ אֵין לְמֵידִין הֵימֶינּוּ דָּבָר אַחֵר. אַחַת מִשְּׁדוֹתַיי מָכַרְתִּי וְאֵינִי יוֹדֵעַ לְמִי מְכַרְתִּיהָ. וּבָא אֶחָד וְאָמַר. אֲנִי הוּא שֶׁלְּקַחְתִּיהָ. לֹא כָל־הֵימֶינּוּ. אַף בְּקִידּוּשִׁין כֵּן. אַחַת מִבְּנוֹתַיי קִידַּשְׁתִּי וְאֵינִי יוֹדֵעַ לְמִי קִידַּשְׁתִּיהָ. וּבָא אֶחָד וְאָמַר. אֲנִי קִידַּשְׁתִּיהָ. לֹא כָל־הֵימֶינּוּ. מַתְנִיתִין פְּלִיגָא עַל רַב. הַמֵּבִיא גֵט מִמְּדִינַת הַיָּם וְאָמַר. בְּפָנַיי נִכְתַּב וּבְפָנַיי נֶחְתַּם. לֹא יִשָּׂא אֶת אִשְׁתּוֹ. תַּמָּן חוּחְזְקָה אֵשֶׁת אִישׁ בִּפְנֵי הַכֹּל. בְּרַם הָכָא לֹא חוּחְזְקָה אֵשֶׁת אִישׁ אֶלָּא בִּפְנֵי שְׁנַיִם. לִכְשֶׁיָּבוֹאוּ שְׁנַיִם וְיֹאמְרוּ. זֶה הוּא שֶׁקִּידֵּשׁ. מַתְנִיתָא פְּלִיגָא עַל רִבִּי יוֹחָנָן. זֶה אוֹמֵר. אֲנִי קִידַּשְׁתִּיהָ. וְזֶה אוֹמֵר. אֲנִי קִידַּשְׁתִּיהָ. שְׁנֵיהֶן נוֹתְנִין גֵּט. וְאִם רָצוּ אֶחָד נוֹתֵן גֵּט וְאֶחָד כּוֹנֵס. פָּתַר לָהּ בְּאוֹמֵר. לְאֶחָד מִשְּׁנֵי אֵילּוּ קִידַּשְׁתִּיהָ וְאֵינִי יוֹדֵעַ אֵי זֶה הוּא. רִבִּי זְעִירָא רִבִּי יָסָא בְּשֵׁם רִבִּי יוֹחָנָן. קָדַם אֶחָד מֵהֶן וְכָנַס (אֵין)[184] מוֹצִיאִין מִיָּדוֹ. הָדָא דְאַתְּ אָמַר. בְּשֶׁזֶּה אוֹמֵר. אֲנִי קִידַּשְׁתִּיהָ. וְזֶה אוֹמֵר. אֲנִי קִידַּשְׁתִּיהָ. וְקָדַם אֶחָד מֵהֶן וְכָנַס. אֲבָל אִם אָמַר אֲנִי קִידַּשְׁתִּיהָ. וּכְנָסָהּ. וּבָא אַחֵר וְאָמַר. אֲנִי קִידַּשְׁתִּיהָ. לֹא כָל־הֵימֶינּוּ. וְתַנֵּי כֵן. אִם מִשֶּׁכְּנָסָהּ בָּא אַחֵר וְאָמַר. אֲנִי קִידַּשְׁתִּיהָ. לֹא כָל־הֵימֶינּוּ.

[185]"If somebody brings a bill of divorce from overseas and says", etc. About what is he trustworthy? Samuel says, he is trusted to give a bill of divorce[186]. Assi said, he is trusted to marry[187]. Rav Huna said in the

name of Rav: He is trusted to marry. Rebbi Joḥanan said, he is trusted to marry but one does not infer from this ruling anything for another case. What means, one does not infer from this ruling anything for another case? I sold one of my fields but I do not remember to whom I sold it. If someone comes and says, I bought it, he is not trusted in any way. In *qiddushin*, the same holds. "[188]I betrothed one of my daughters but I do not remember to whom I betrothed her. If someone comes and says, I gave her *qiddushin*," he is not trusted in any way[189]. The Mishnah disagrees with Rav: "If somebody brings a bill of divorce from overseas and says, it was written and signed in my presence, he shall not marry the wife[190]." There, she is considered by everybody to be a married woman. Here, she is considered to be a married woman only by two persons[191]. One waits until these two come and say, this is the man who gave her *qiddushin*. The Mishnah disagrees with Rebbi Joḥanan[192]: "[188]This one says, I gave her *qiddushin*, and that one says, I gave her *qiddushin*. Both of them give a bill of divorce, but if they agree, one gives a bill of divorce and the other one marries.[193]" He explains this, if [the father] says, I did betroth her to one of these two but I do not remember which one it was. Rebbi Ze'ira, Rebbi Yasa, in the name of Rebbi Joḥanan: If one of them jumped the gun and married her, one does remove her from him. That is, if this one says, I gave her *qiddushin*, and that one says, I gave her *qiddushin*[194] and one of them jumped the gun and married her. But if he said, I gave her *qiddushin* and married her, and another one comes[195] and says, I gave her *qiddushin*, he is not trusted in any way. It was stated thus: If after the marriage another man comes and says, I gave her *qiddushin*, he is not trusted in any way.

184 Missing in the parallel in *Qiddušin*; the context requires that the word be deleted even though ms. A also has it.

185 This paragraph is a copy of the parallel in *Qiddušin* 3:7 on the Mishnah quoted later, "I betrothed one of my daughters but I do not remember to whom I betrothed her. If someone comes and says, I gave her *qiddushin*, he is trustworthy."

186 But without further evidence he is not allowed to marry the girl since he is testifying in his own behalf. In the Babli, *Qiddušin* 63b, this is the opinion of Rav; Samuel is not mentioned there.

187 Without evidence to the contrary, we do not accuse him of attempted adultery.

188 Mishnah *Qiddušin* 3:7.

189 To marry her; this is the point made by Samuel. The text in *Qiddušin* reads לא הכל ממנו "is not everything from him?"; the father's evidence is nothing and everything depends on the word of the suitor. This seems to be the correct version even though the two mss. agree in *Yebamot*.

190 The person on whose word the woman becomes free to marry may not marry her; why should a person whose word frees the girl from being unable to marry anybody in the world be allowed to marry her?

191 The two witnesses without whom any *qiddushin* are invalid. If they come and testify, there will be no doubt; the testimony of the suitor is verifiable. In the case of the divorce, everybody knows that the woman is married and the testimony is unverifiable.

192 In *Qiddušin*: Samuel. This is the correct version even though the two mss. agree in *Yebamot*. If one of the two suitors is permitted to marry the girl, the rest of the world is excluded and both are trustworthy even for marriage.

193 End of Mishnah *Qiddušin* 3:7, about the father who btrothed his daughter to an unknown suitor.

194 They both came at the same time, or at least the existence of both of them was known when one of them married the girl.

195 He comes later; his identity was not known at the time of marriage.

מַה נַפְשָׁךְ. קְטָלֵיהּ. הֶחָשׁוּד עַל הַדָּבָר לֹא דָנוֹ וְלֹא מְעִידוֹ. לֹא קְטָלֵיהּ. בַּחַיִּים הוּא.

[196]As you take it, if he killed him, a suspect in a case can neither judge nor testify in it. If he did not kill him, the person is alive.

196 In both mss. the reference to the Mishnah is missing, that R. Jehudah bars the one who says, I killed the husband, from marrying the widow. It is explained here that such testimony is always invalid.

הֲרַגְנוּהוּ. מֵעַתָּה קְטָלֵיהּ. תִּינָּשֵׂא לַאֲחֵרִים וְלֹא לוֹ. אָמְרוּ לִפְנֵי רִבִּי יוּדָה. מַעֲשֶׂה בְּלִיסְטֵיס אֶחָד שֶׁנִּתְפַּס בְּקֵיסָרִין שֶׁבְּקַפָּדוֹקִיָּא. (fol. 4b) אִם כְּשֶׁהוּא יוֹצֵא לִיהָרֵג אָמַר לָהֶן. צְאוּ וְאִמְרוּ לְאִשְׁתּוֹ שֶׁלְּשִׁמְעוֹן בֶּן כָּהֲנָא שֶׁהֲרַגְתִּיו בִּכְנִיסָתוֹ לְלוֹד. וּבָא מַעֲשֶׂה לִפְנֵי חֲכָמִים וְקִייְמוּ אֶת דְּבָרָיו. אָמַר לָהֶן רִבִּי יוּדָה. מִשָּׁם רְאָייָה. וַהֲלֹא לֹא אָמַר אֶלָּא הֲרַגְנוּהוּ.

"We killed him," she should be married to others but not to him[197]. [198]"They said before Rebbi Jehudah, it happened that a robber was caught in Kappadokian Caesarea[199]. When he went out to be executed, he said to them, go and tell the wife of Simeon ben Cahana that I killed him when he was coming into Lydda. The case came before the Sages and they confirmed his words. Rebbi Jehudah said to them: Is that a proof? He only said, we killed him."

197 Even though R. Jehudah says only that the woman can remarry; he will agree that she cannot marry the person upon whose testimony she becomes a widow.

198 Tosephta 4:5; a somewhat different version in Babli, 25b. The Babli insists that the robber explicitly dissociated himself from the killers. This is not the position of the Yerushalmi; a possibility that he was not the killer is enough, given all the leniencies admitted in testimonies concerning women whose husbands had disappeared.

199 Today Kaisarie.

(fol. 3c) **משנה יב:** הֶחָכָם שֶׁאָסַר אֶת הָאִשָּׁה בְּנֶדֶר עַל בַּעֲלָהּ הֲרֵי זֶה לֹא יִשָּׂאֶנָּה. מֵיאֵינָה אוֹ שֶׁחָלְצָה בְּפָנָיו יִשָּׂאֶנָּה. מִפְּנֵי שֶׁהוּא בֵית דִּין. וְכוּלָּן שֶׁהָיוּ לָהֶן נָשִׁים וָמֵתוּ מוּתָּרוֹת לְהִינָּשֵׂא לָהֶן וְכוּלָּן שֶׁנִּישְּׂאוּ לַאֲחֵרִים וְנִתְגָּרְשׁוּ אוֹ שֶׁנִּתְאַלְמְנוּ מוּתָּרוֹת לְהִינָּשֵׂא לָהֶם. וְכוּלָּן מוּתָּרוֹת לִיבְנֵיהֶם וְלַאֲחֵיהֶם.

Mishnah 12: A rabbi who forbade a woman to her husband because of a vow[200] cannot marry her. If she repudiated or performed *ḥalîṣah* before him he may marry her since he acts as a court[201]. And all who had wives who [subsequently] died may marry them[202]. And to all who were married to others and were divorced or widowed, they can be married. All are permitted to their sons or brothers[203].

200 A woman made a vow that she will have no usufruct from her husband. This is a vow the husband cannot dissolve since it is not a "vow of deprivation" (*Num.* 30:2-17). She can go to a competent rabbi who may find a way to relieve her from her vow if she sincerely repents. If he did not find a way to repeal the vow, the husband will divorce her (obviously, he need not pay her anything.) Since the refusal of the rabbi to annul the vow forces the divorce, he cannot profit from his act or people will suspect him of bending the law for his own profit.

201 In this case, he does not act alone since a repudiation needs 3 and *ḥalîṣah* 5 judges. In the other cases of the Mishnah, the availability of the woman for marriage depends on unforseeable circumstances.

202 The rabbi who forces the divorce or the witnesses who testified that she was a widow. If they were married at the time of the action, they may marry the woman after the death of their wives since death is an unpredictable event. In this case, it is presumed that the marriage contract of the rabbi or any member of the court forbade the husband to take an additional wife without the first wife's consent. Then the members of the court are truly disinterested parties. *Ketubot* of this kind are known from the Cairo *Genizah*.

203 Nobody sins for the profit of others; see the Halakhah.

הלכה יב: הֶחָכָם שֶׁאָסַר אֶת הָאִשָּׁה בְּנֶדֶר עַל בַּעֲלָהּ כול'. הֶחָכָם(fol. 4b) שֶׁאָסַר אֶת הָאִשָּׁה בְּנֶדֶר עַל בַּעֲלָהּ הֲרֵי זֶה לֹא יִשָּׂאֶנָּה. אוֹמֵר אֲנִי. לְכָךְ מִתְכַּוֵּן מִתְּחִילָּה. מֵיאֲנָה אוֹ שֶׁחָלְצָה בְּפָנָיו יִשָּׂאֶינָּה מִפְּנֵי שֶׁהוּא בֵּית דִּין. שֶׁאֵין שְׁנַיִם מְצוּיִין לַחֲטוֹא מִפְּנֵי אֶחָד. תַּמָּן תַּנִּינָן. הַמַּפְקִיד פֵּירוֹת אֵצֶל חֲבֵירוֹ אֲפִילוּ הֵן אוֹבְדִין לֹא יִגַּע בָּהֶן. רַבָּן שִׁמְעוֹן בֶּן גַּמְלִיאֵל אוֹמֵר. יִמְכּוֹר בִּפְנֵי בֵית דִּין מִפְּנֵי הָשֵׁב אֲבֵידָה לַבְּעָלִים. אָמַר רִבִּי[204] אַבָּא בַּר יַעֲקֹב בְּשֵׁם רִבִּי יוֹחָנָן. הֲלָכָה כְּרַבָּן שִׁמְעוֹן בֶּן גַּמְלִיאֵל. מַה יְהֵא בְדָמִים. רַב יְהוּדָה אָמַר. מַחֲלוֹקֶת רִבִּי עֲקִיבָה וְרִבִּי טַרְפוֹן. תְּנַיי בֵּית דִּין. לֹא יִקְחוּ. רִבִּי עֲקִיבָה אָמַר. רִבִּי חִיָּה בַּר שַׁבְּתַי מַקְשֶׁה. הָכָא אַתְּ אָמַר מֵיאֲנָה אוֹ שֶׁחָלְצָה בְּפָנָיו יִשָּׂאֶינָּה מִפְּנֵי שֶׁהוּא בֵּית דִּין. וְהָכָא אַתְּ אָמַר הָכֵין. אָמַר רִבִּי יוֹסֵי. תַּמָּן הַמִּקָּח דַּרְכּוֹ לְהִשְׁתַּלֵּשׁ. בְּרַם הָכָא אֵין שְׁנַיִם מְצוּיִין לַחֲטוֹא מִפְּנֵי אֶחָד.

Halakhah 12: 'A rabbi who forbade a woman tc her husband because of a vow", etc. "A rabbi who forbade a woman to her husband because of a vow cannot marry her." I would say, that was his intention from the start. "If she repudiated or performed *ḥalîṣah* before him he may marry her since he acts as a court", because two will not usually sin for the benefit of a third. There[205], we have stated: "If somebody deposits fruit with another person, that one should not touch it even if it spoils. Rabban Simeon ben Gamliel said, he shall sell it under the supervision of a court because one is obliged to return a find to its owners." Rebbi Abba bar Jacob said in the name of Rebbi Johanan, practice follows Rabban Simeon ben Gamliel[206]. What does one do with the money? Rav Jehudah said, the disagreement of Rebbi Aqiba and Rebbi Ṭarphon[207]. It is a condition that the members of the court cannot buy. Rebbi Aqiba[208] said, Rebbi Ḥiyya ben Rebbi Sabbatai[208] asked: Here, you say, "if she repudiated or performed *ḥalîṣah* before him he may marry her since he acts as a court," and here, you say so[209]? Rebbi Yose said, there, the buy could be in thirds[210], but here, two will not usually sin for the benefit of a third.

204 Correct reading of ms. A. Ms. L: רב.

205 *Baba Meṣi'a*, Mishnah 3:7.

206 Babli *Baba Meṣi'a* 39b (R. Abba ben R. Jacob in the name of R. Johanan). In the Babli, the circumstances of this ruling are very much in dispute.

207 Mishnah *Baba Meṣi'a* 2:7. If somebody finds perishables (with characteristics that might allow the indentification of the lawful owner), he sells them under the supervision of a court. R. Tarphon holds that he uses the money in his own business; therefore he is totally responsible for it. R. Aqiba says, he may not touch the money; therefore, he is not responsible if it is stolen.

208 An otherwise unknown Amora.

209 Why are the members of the court forbidden to buy the produce to be sold under their supervision?

210 Every judge could profit from the transaction.

וְכוּלָּן שֶׁהָיוּ לָהֶן נָשִׁים וָמֵתוּ מוּתָּרוֹת לְהִינָּשֵׂא לָהֶן. לֹא אָמַר אֶלָּא מֵתוּ. הָא אִם נִתְגָּרְשׁוּ לֹא. וְכוּלָּן שֶׁנִּישְּׂאוּ לַאֲחֵרִים וְנִתְגָּרְשׁוּ אוֹ שֶׁנִּתְאַלְמְנוּ מוּתָּרוֹת לְהִינָּשֵׂא לָהֶם. שֶׁאֵין אָדָם מָצוּי לַחֲטוֹא לְאַחַר זְמָן. וְכוּלָּן מוּתָּרוֹת לִיבְנֵיהֶן וְלַאֲחֵיהֶן. שֶׁאֵין אָדָם מָצוּי לַחֲטוֹא לֹא מִפְּנֵי בְנוֹ וְלֹא מִפְּנֵי אָחִיו.

""And all who had wives who [subsequently] died may marry them." It only says "who died"; therefore, not if they were divorced. "And to all who were married to others and were divorced or widowed, they can be married", since usually nobody sins for an uncertain future. "All are permitted to their sons or brothers," since usually nobody sins for the benefit of either his son ot his brother.

ארבעה אחין פרק שלישי

(fol. 4b) **משנה א:** אַרְבָּעָה אַחִין שְׁנַיִים מֵהֶן נְשׂוּאִין שְׁתֵּי אֲחָיוֹת. מֵתוּ אֶת הַנְּשׂוּאִין אֶת הָאֲחָיוֹת הֲרֵי אֵלּוּ חוֹלְצוֹת וְלֹא מִתְייַבְּמוֹת. וְאִם קָדְמוּ וְכָנְסוּ יוֹצִיאוּ. רִבִּי לְעֶזֶר אוֹמֵר בֵּית שַׁמַּאי אוֹמְרִים יְקַייְמוּ וּבֵית הִלֵּל אוֹמְרִים יוֹצִיאוּ.

Mishnah 1: There are four brothers, two of whom are married to two sisters. If those married to the sisters died[1], [the sisters] have *ḥalîṣah* but not levirate. If [the remaining brothers] jumped the gun and married, they must divorce them. Rebbi Eliezer said, the House of Shammai say, they shall keep them[2], but the House of Hillel say, they have to divorce.

1 One possible explanation is that they died childless at the same time; then each of the sisters is a candidate for levirate for either one of the surviving brothers, i. e., each is a sister of a sister-in-law and potentially forbidden.

2 According to him the House of Shammai must hold that candidacy has no other legal consequences (cf. Note 19). Therefore, if they married the sisters against the rules, no biblical precept has been violated. In contrast, cf. Halakhah 5.

(fol. 4c) **הלכה א:** אַרְבָּעָה אַחִין שְׁנַיִים מֵהֶן נְשׂוּאִין שְׁתֵּי אֲחָיוֹת כול׳. אִילּוּ אַרְבָּעָה אַחִין שְׁנַיִים מֵהֶן נְשׂוּאִין שְׁתֵּי נָכְרִיּוֹת שֶׁמָּא אֵינָן מִתְייַבְּמוֹת. שַׁנְיָיא הִיא הָכָא שֶׁיֵּשׁ בּוֹ אִיסּוּר אֲחָיוֹת. מֵעַתָּה לֹא יְהוּ צְרִיכוֹת הֵימֶינּוּ חֲלִיצָה. אָמַר רִבִּי מַתַּנְיָה. עַל יְדֵי זִיקָה. וְאֵין בּוֹ אִיסּוּר אֲחָיוֹת בְּרוּרוֹת.

Halakhah 1: 'Four brothers, two of whom are married to two sisters," etc. If there were four brothers, two of whom are married to unrelated women, would they not be subject to levirate? There is a difference, since here there is the prohibition of sisters. In that case, they should not need *ḥalîṣah* from them! Rebbi Mattaniah said, it is because of candidacy and the prohibition of sisters is not clear[3].

3 It is not clear whether the fact that the sisters become candidates for levirate at the same time makes them forbidden; cf. Chapter 2, Notes 27-29.

תַּמָּן תַּנִּינָן. שׁוֹמֶרֶת יָבָם שֶׁקִּידֵּשׁ אָחִיו אֶת אֲחוֹתָהּ. מִשּׁוּם רִבִּי יוּדָה בֶּן בָּתֵירָה אָמְרוּ. אוֹמֵר לוֹ. הַמְתֵּן עַד שֶׁיַּעֲשֶׂה מַעֲשֶׂה. חָלְצוּ אַחִים אוֹ כָּנְסוּ (. . .)[4] מֵת הַיָּבָם מוֹצִיא אֶת אִשְׁתּוֹ בְּגֵט וְאֶת אֵשֶׁת אָחִיו בַּחֲלִיצָה. לֹא אָמַר אֶלָּא מֵתָה יְבִמְתּוֹ מוּתָּר בְּאִשְׁתּוֹ. אֲבָל מֵתָה אִשְׁתּוֹ אָסוּר בִּיבִמְתּוֹ. [אָמַר רִבִּי יוֹחָנָן. זוֹ דִבְרֵי רִבִּי לִעֶזֶר. אֲבָל דִּבְרֵי חֲכָמִים מֵתָה אִשְׁתּוֹ מוּתָּר בִּיבִמְתּוֹ. מֵתָה יְבִמְתּוֹ מוּתָּר בְּאִשְׁתּוֹ.][5] אָמַר רִבִּי יוֹחָנָן. דִּבְרֵי חֲכָמִים כָּל־דָּבָר שֶׁהוּא בָא מֵחֲמַת הַגּוֹרֵם בָּטַל הַגּוֹרֵם בָּטַל הָאִיסּוּר. וּדְרִבִּי לִעֶזֶר. אֲפִילוּ בָּטַל הַגּוֹרֵם הָאִיסּוּר בִּמְקוֹמוֹ.

[6]There, we have stated: "If a brother gave *qiddushin* to the sister of a woman waiting for the levir[7], they said in the name of Rebbi Jehudah ben Bathyra: One says to him, wait until your brother has acted. If [one of the] brothers performed *ḥalîṣah* or married her, he may marry his wife[8]. If the sister-in-law died, he may marry his wife. If the levir died, he has to send away his wife by a bill of divorce and his brother's widow by *ḥalîṣah*.[9]" It says only: If the sister-in-law died, his wife is permitted to him. But if his wife died, his sister-in-law is forbidden to him. Rebbi Joḥanan said, these are the words of Rebbi Eliezer[10]. But the Sages say, if his sister-in-law died, his wife is permitted to him, if his wife died, his sister-in-law is permitted to him. Rebbi Joḥanan said[11], the Sages hold that for anything

induced by a cause, if the cause is removed the prohibition is removed. But for Rebbi Eliezer, if the cause is removed the prohibition remains.

4 In both mss., the middle of the Mishnah is indicated only by a few words. Ms. L: וכנס היבם מן. Ms. A: יכנוס ח' ייב' הייבום. The full text, translated in small print, reads: מֵתָה. יִכְנוֹס אֶת אִשְׁתּוֹ. הַיְּבָמָה יִכְנוֹס.

5 Missing in the L text here, taken from the parallel in Halakhah 4:10. Most of the text is in ms. A.

6 Mishnah 4:10.

7 After the death of the brother, when the sister-in-law's sister was prohibited to him since the widow is a candidate for levirate with any one of the brothers.

8 Since the candidacy obstacle to marriage was removed. The same holds if the widow dies.

9 Only if he is the only remaining brother. Then he is forbidden to marry his betrothed and has to divorce her. The widow becomes the sister of a woman divorced by him and cannot be married.

10 The source of the argument is Mishnah 13:6. In the tradition of the Babli, the author is R. Eleazar (ben Arakh, the Tanna). The Babli disagrees (41a) and holds that both opinions are compatible with the position of the Sages who in this case might agree with R. Eleazar that a woman whom a brother could not marry for one moment is permanently forbidden to him.

11 In Chapter 1 (Note 71), this is a statement of R. Eleazar (the Amora) in the name of R. Abun. In the Babli, 27b, R. Johanan disagrees and holds that any sister-in-law who cannot be married in levirate at the moment of death of her husband can never be a party to levirate.

רִבִּי יוֹסֵי בֵּירִבִּי חֲנִינָה בְּעָא קוֹמֵי רִבִּי יוֹחָנָן. הָכָא אַתְּ אָמַר. מֵתָה יְבִמְתּוֹ מוּתָּר בְּאִשְׁתּוֹ. מֵתָה אִשְׁתּוֹ מוּתָּר בִּיבִמְתּוֹ. וְהָכָא אַתְּ אָמַר אָכֵין. אָמַר לֵיהּ. אֵינִי יוֹדֵעַ טַעַם אֲחָיוֹת מָה הֵן. רִבִּי בָּא רִבִּי חִייָה בְּשֵׁם רִבִּי יוֹחָנָן. אֵינִי יוֹדֵעַ טַעַם אֲחָיוֹת יְבָמוֹת מַה הֵן. רִבִּי הִילָא רִבִּי יָסָא בְּשֵׁם רִבִּי יוֹחָנָן. לֹא דוֹמֶה אִיסּוּר אֲחָיוֹת יְבָמוֹת לְאִיסּוּר אֲחָיוֹת שֶׁאֵינָן יְבָמוֹת. אָמַר רִבִּי יִרְמְיָה. תִּיפְתָּר

שֶׁנָּפַל הַבַּיִת עַל שְׁנֵיהֶן כְּאַחַת. רִבִּי יוֹסֵה בָּעֵי. אִם בְּשֶׁנָּפַל הַבַּיִת עַל שְׁנֵיהֶן כְּאַחַת בְּדָא אָמַר רִבִּי יוֹחָנָן. אֵינִי יוֹדֵעַ טַעַם אֲחָיוֹת יְבָמוֹת מָהֵן[12]. אֶלָּא בְּשֶׁמֵּתוּ בְּזֶה אַחַר זֶה. הֲוון בָּעֵיי מֵימַר. מַה צְרִיכָה לְרִבִּי יוֹחָנָן מֵתָה הַשְּׁנִייָה לָמָּה אֵינוֹ מוּתָּר בָּרִאשׁוֹנָה. אֲבָל אִם מֵתָה הָרִאשׁוֹנָה יְהֵא אָסוּר בַּשְּׁנִייָה. אָמַר רִבִּי יוּדָן.[12] הִיא דָא הִיא דָא. צְרִיכָה לֵיהּ. וְלֵית זִיקָה כְּלוּם. אִילּוּ שְׁלֹשָׁה אַחִין. שְׁנַיִם מֵאָב וְלֹא מֵאֵם. שְׁנַיִם מֵאֵם וְלֹא מֵאָב. מֵת בְּנוֹ שֶׁלָּאָב תְּחִילָּה. לֹא הִסְפִּיק הַשֵּׁינִי לְהַחֲלִיץ וּלְייַבֵּם עַד שֶׁמֵּת וְנֶפְלָה לִפְנֵי אָחִיו מֵאִמּוֹ. שֶׁמָּא אֵינוֹ מוּתָּר בָּהּ. אִין מַאֲמָר זִיקָה כְּלוּם. יְהֵא אָסוּר בָּהּ מִשּׁוּם אֵשֶׁת אָחִיו מֵאִמּוֹ.

Rebbi Yose ben Ḥanina asked before Rebbi Joḥanan: Here[13], you say, if his sister-in-law died, his wife is permitted to him, if his wife died, his sister-in-law is permitted to him, and here[14] you say so? He said to him, I do not know the reason for [the rule regarding] sisters[15]. Rebbi Abba, Rebbi Ḥiyya, in the name of Rebbi Joḥanan: I do not know the reason for [the rule regarding] sisters who are sisters-in-law[16]. Rebbi Hila, Rebbi Yasa, in the name of Rebbi Joḥanan: The prohibition of sisters who are sisters-in-law cannot be compared to the prohibition of sisters who are not sisters-in-law. Rebbi Jeremiah said, explain it that the house fell on both [brothers] at the same time[17]. Rebbi Yose asked, did Rebbi Joḥanan say, I do not know the reason for [the rule regarding] sisters who are sisters-in-law if the house fell on both [brothers] at the same time? Only if they died one after the other. They wanted to say, what was the problem of Rebbi Joḥanan? If the second one died, why should the first one not be permitted to him? But if the first one died, the second should be forbidden to him. Rebbi Yudan said, both cases are the same problem for him. And candidacy counts for nothing since if there are three brothers, two of them paternal but not maternal halfbrothers, and two maternal but not paternal halfbrothers. If the paternal halfbrother died first[18] and the second brother had no time to perform *ḥalîṣah* or levirate before he died, and she became eligible for his maternal halfbrother, may he not take her[19]? This shows that candidacy is nothing, [otherwise] she should be forbidden as the maternal halfbrother's wife.

12 Reading of ms. A. In ms. L: 'ר' יודה, unknown as Amora.

13 Mishnah 4:10.

14 Mishnah 3:1. If one of the brothers performs *ḥalîṣah* with the woman who became a widow later, the sister who first became a widow should be permitted to the other brother by the rule spelled out by R. Joḥanan; see below.

15 In the Babli, 27b, R. Joḥanan is quoted as saying that he does not know the author of Mishnah 3:1. This means he is unable to analyze the hidden premisses on which the ruling is based.

16 He spelled out that his criticism refers to Mishnah 3 1, not 4:10.

17 Cf. Note 1. In that case, we do not know which of the two brothers died first; there are no discernible first and second widows to apply the rule of Mishnah 4:10. A similar argument in the Babli, 28a.

18 Brother 2 is paternal half-brother of brother 1 and maternal half-brother of brother 3. There is no relationship between 1 and 3. If 1 dies childless, his widow becomes a candidate for levirate with 2.

19 If candidacy had given her some status comparable a wife of 2, she would be forbidden to 3. Since this case is never mentioned, one has to conclude that for 3 she is the widow of an unrelated man. In the Babli, *Nedarim* 74a, this position is ascribed to R. Aqiba, but not accepted by the other Sages.

מַהוּ שֶׁיְּהֵא לָהּ צָרָה. רִבִּי הִילָא בְשֵׁם רִבִּי אֲבִינָא. קַל וָחוֹמֶר. מַה אִם אָחוֹת חֲלוּצָתוֹ שֶׁהִיא[20] מִדִּבְרֵיהֶם נָתְנוּ לָהּ חֲכָמִים צָרָה. כָּאן שֶׁיֵּשׁ כַּאן אִיסּוּר אֲחָיוֹת לֹא כָּל־שֶׁכֵּן. בִּתּוֹ פְּשִׁיטָא לָךְ שֶׁיְּהֵא לָהּ צָרָה. רִבִּי בּוּן בַּר חִיָּיה בְשֵׁם רִבִּי אֲבִינָא. תַּנֵּי תַמָּן. חָלְצוּ הַצָּרוֹת נִפְטְרוּ הָאֲחָיוֹת. (לא)[21] חָלְצוּ הָאֲחָיוֹת לֹא

נִפְטְרוּ הַצָּרוֹת. וּכְמַה דְאַתְּ אָמַר. חָלְצוּ הַצָּרוֹת נִפְטְרוּ הָאֲחָיוֹת. וְדִכְוָותָהּ אֲפִילוּ חָלְצוּ אֲחָיוֹת יִפָּטְרוּ צָרוֹת. אֶלָּא כְּרִבִּי יוֹחָנָן בֶּן נוּרִי. דְּרִבִּי יוֹחָנָן בֶּן נוּרִי אוֹמֵר. בּוֹאוּ וּנְתַקֵּן שֶׁיְּהוּ צָרוֹת חוֹלְצוֹת וְלֹא מִתְייַבְּמוֹת. וְהִתְקִינוּ. לֹא כֵן תַּנֵּי. לֹא הִסְפִּיקוּ לְהַתְקִין עַד שֶׁנִּטְרְפָה הַשָּׁעָה. אֶלָּא כְבֵית שַׁמַּי. דְּבֵית שַׁמַּי מַתִּירִין אֶת הַצָּרוֹת לָאַחִין. אָמַר רִבִּי פִינְחָס קוֹמֵי רִבִּי יוֹסֵי. אִין כְּבֵית שַׁמַּי (אלא)[21] אֲפִילוּ חָלְצוּ הַצָּרוֹת לֹא נִפְטְרוּ אֲחָיוֹת. וְתַנִּינָן. רִבִּי לְעָזָר אוֹמֵר. מִשּׁוּם בֵּית שַׁמַּי אוֹמְרִים. יְקַיֵּימוּ. וּבֵית הִלֵּל אוֹמְרִים. יוֹצִיאוּ. הֲווּ[22] תְּרֵין תַּנָּאִין אִינּוּן עַל דְּבֵית שַׁמַּי. חַד אָמַר. חָלְצוּ צָרוֹת נִפְטְרוּ אֲחָיוֹת. וְחָרָנָה אָמַר. חָלְצוּ צָרוֹת לֹא נִפְטְרוּ אֲחָיוֹת.

What if there is a co-wife[23]? Rebbi Hila in the name of Rebbi Avina: It is an inference *de minore ad majus.* If the Sages gave a co-wife to the sister of a woman with whom one performed *ḥalîṣah*, which is rabbinic[24], here, where there is the prohibition of sisters[25], not so much more? It is obvious that the rule of co-wives applies to his daughter[26]. Rebbi Abun in the name of Rebbi Avina: One has stated there[27], "if the co-wives performed *ḥalîṣah*, the sisters were freed; if the sisters performed *ḥalîṣah*, the co-wives were not freed." But as you say, if the co-wives performed *ḥalîṣah*, the sisters were freed, so it should be that even if the sisters performed *ḥalîṣah*, the co-wives should be freed[28]. But it must follow Rebbi Joḥanan ben Nuri, since Rebbi Joḥanan ben Nuri said, come and let us institute that the co-wife perform *ḥalîṣah* without being admitted to levirate[29]. Did they institute that? Was it not stated: They did not manage to institute this before the time became unsuitable. But it must follow the House of Shammai[30] since the House of Shammai permit the co-wives to the brothers. Rebbi Phineas said to Rebbi Yose: If it follows the House of Shammai, even if the co-wives performed *ḥalîṣah*, the sisters should not be freed[31]! But we have stated: Rebbi Eliezer said, the House of Shammai say, they shall keep them, but the House of Hillel say, they have to divorce. There are two Tannaïm interpreting the House of Shammai, one said if the co-wives performed *ḥalîṣah*, the sisters were freed, the other one said if the co-wives performed *ḥalîṣah*, the sisters were not freed.

20 Reading of ms. A. Ms. L: בשיהא.

21 Missing in ms. A; devoid of sense in the context.

22 Reading of ms. A and the first hand of ms. L. Miscorrected text in L: הוי.

23 Since none of the sisters can be married (Mishnah 3:1), could any co-wife of one of them be married?

24 The imputation of the status of divorcee to any woman having performed *ḥalîṣah* is purely rabbinic. Therefore, the prohibition of the sister of a woman with whom he had performed *ḥalîṣah* and her co-wives is not biblical.

25 *Lev.* 18:18.

26 Since this is a case of Mishnah 1:1, the sentence is superfluous. It is missing in ms. A.

27 A *baraita* referring to the case of Mishnah 3:1, partially quoted in Babli, 27a.

28 Since the House of Hillel hold that a woman forbidden for levirate gives the same status to her co-wives, it seems illogical to give the co-wives a status different from that of the sisters.

29 Chapter 1, Notes 200-204.

30 Same conclusion in Babli, 27a.

31 If *ḥalîṣah* of the sisters is worthless for the co-wives then *ḥalîṣah* of the co-wives should be worthless for the sisters since the House of Shammai validate a marriage of the sisters

תַּנֵּי. אַבָּא שָׁאוּל אוֹמֵר. קוֹל הֲוֵוי בֵית הִלֵּל בַּדָּבָר הַזֶּה. מַה. לִגְנַאי. לִשְׁבָח. מְלִיזִים. מַה אִיסּוּר יֵשׁ כָּאן. אַשְׁכַּח תַּנֵּי בְשֵׁם רִבִּי שִׁמְעוֹן. אִם קָדְמוּ וְכָנְסוּ יְקַיְּימוּ. וְהֵן שֶׁבָּעֲלוּ שְׁנֵיהֶן כְּאַחַת. עַל דַּעְתֵּיהּ דְּאַבָּא שָׁאוּל מוּתָּר לִבְעוֹל כַּתְּחִילָּה. עַל דַּעְתֵּיהּ דְּרִבִּי שִׁמְעוֹן וְהוּא שֶׁעָבַר וּבָעַל. כָּנַס הָרִאשׁוֹן וּבָעַל אוֹמֵר

לַשֵּׁינִי שֶׁיִּבְעוֹל. לֹא בָעַל הָרִאשׁוֹן אָסוּר לִבְעוֹל בְּעִילָה שְׁנִיָּה. שֶׁמָּא יָמוּת אֶחָד מֵהֶן וְנִמְצָא כְבָא עַל אַחוֹת יְבִמְתּוֹ. תַּנֵּי מֵת[32] הַשֵּׁינִי הָרִאשׁוֹן מוֹצִיא אֶת אִשְׁתּוֹ בְּגֵט וְאֶת אֵשֶׁת אָחִיו בַּחֲלִיצָה אֲפִילוּ מֵת הַשֵּׁינִי. לֹא רִבִּי שִׁמְעוֹן הִיא. דְּרִבִּי שִׁמְעוֹן פּוֹטֵר אֶת הַשְּׁנִיָּה מִן הַחֲלִיצָה וּמִן הַיִּיבּוּם. אָמַר רִבִּי זְעוּרָה. קִייַּמְתִּיהָ. כָּל־יְבָמָה שֶׁנִּרְאֵית לָצֵאת בַּחֲלִיצָה אֵינָה מוּתֶּרֶת בְּלֹא חֲלִיצָה.

It was stated[33]: "Abba Shaul says, the House of Hillel made this easy[34]." Is that a criticism? It is a praise, since people were saying, what is the prohibition here[35]? It was found stated in the name of Rebbi Simeon[33]: "If they jumped the gun and married, they should keep them." But that is only if they had intercourse at the same time[36]. In the opinion of Abba Shaul it is permitted to have intercourse without asking. In the opinion of Rebbi Simeon only if he transgressed and had intercourse. If the first [brother] married and had intercourse, he tells the second also to have intercourse. If that one did not have intercourse, the first [brother] is forbidden to have intercourse a second time[37]; maybe one of them will die and it turns out that he had intercourse with the sister of *his*[38] sister-in-law. It was stated: If the second [brother] died, the first one had to divorce his wife with a bill of divorce and his brother's wife by *ḥalîṣah*[39]. Even if the second one died? Does this not follow Rebbi Simeon? But Rebbi Simeon frees the second [sister] from *ḥalîṣah* and levirate[40]! Rebbi Ze'ira said, I confirmed this: Any sister-in-law who was to be freed by *ḥalîṣah* will never be permitted without *ḥalîṣah*[41].

32 Reading of ms. A. Ms. L: מה.

33 Tosephta 5:1, quoted in Babli 28a.

34 In his opinion, the House of Hillel permit the sisters to the brothers without problems, not only if they married without asking; they are more lenient than the House of Shammai.

35 If candidacy without "bespeaking" has no influence, there is no reason

why the two brothers should not marry the two sisters in levirate since no biblical precept could be violated.

36 Since levirate is valid only through intercourse (Mishnah 6:1), and R. Simeon has doubts whether "be-speaking" makes the woman a wife (Halakhah 2:1), he will require to do away with "bespeaking" and marriage ceremony. If each brother has intercourse with the corresponding sister at the same time, they both become wives of the respective brothers and neither of them is an impediment to the other's marriage.

37 Which does not fulfill the biblical requirement to marry the widow of the childless brother.

38 The one who from the start was a candidate to be taken by him in levirate. Then both of them are forbidden to him.

39 The wife of the first brother becomes forbidden as the sister of a woman who is a candidate for levirate with him. This Tanna holds that since the levirate of the first sister was illegal, it does not exclude the second sister from becoming a candidate. The expression "his brother's wife" means "his brother's potential wife". If the second brother had taken the second sister in levirate, the problems would have disappeared and when he died childless, his widow would be free of levirate or *ḥalîṣah* without problems.

40 Mishnah 3:4. The second sister should be able to marry outside the family without any formality.

41 Since both sisters did require *ḥalîṣah* when they became widows, the intervening incomplete action by one of the brothers cannot remove that requirement.

הָיְתָה[42] לָרִאשׁוֹנָה צָרָה חָלַץ לָהּ. נִפְטְרָה צָרָתָהּ וּבָא עָלֶיהָ. בִּיאַת אִיסּוּר הִיא וְלֹא נִפְטְרָה צָרָתָהּ. חָלַץ לָהּ וּבָא עָלֶיהָ. מַה נַפְשָׁךְ. אִם בַּחֲלִיצָה הִיא תַּתִּיר. אִם בְּבִיאָה הִיא תַתִּיר. אָמַר רִבִּי יוּדָן. קִייַמְתִּי כְהָדָא. הַכּוֹנֵס אֶת יְבִמְתּוֹ וְנִמְצֵאת מְעוּבֶּרֶת. כְּמַה דְתֵימַר תַּמָּן. צָרָתָהּ לֹא תִינָּשֵׂא עַד שֶׁתֵּדַע בְּמַה הִיא נִיתֶּרֶת אִם בְּעוּבָּר אִם בְּבִיאָה. אַף הָכָא צָרָתָהּ לֹא תִינָּשֵׂא עַד שֶׁתֵּדַע בְּמַה הִיא נִיתֶּרֶת אִם בַּחֲלִיצָה אִם בְּבִיאָה.

If the first [sister] had a co-wife, one [of the brothers] performs *ḥalîṣah*, the co-wife is freed. If then he had intercourse with her[43], this is forbidden intercourse and the co-wife is not freed[44]. If he performed *ḥalîṣah* and then had intercourse with her, as you look at it, either *ḥalîṣah* should free or intercourse should free[45]! Rebbi Yudan said, I confirmed it following "If somebody married his sister-in-law and she turns out to be pregnant[46]", as you say there, the co-wife should not marry until she knows by which means she is permitted, whether through the fetus or through intercourse[47]; so here also the co-wife should not marry until she knows by which means she is permitted, whether through *ḥalîṣah* or through intercourse[48].

42 Reading of ms. A; ms L: הא.

43 The sister who had *ḥalîṣah*.

44 Even for R. Simeon.

45 If *ḥalîṣah* was valid, then the intercourse is sinful but otherwise without consequence; if *ḥalîṣah* was not valid, then the intercourse makes the sister a wife and the co-wife is automatically freed.

46 Cf. Mishnah 4:2.

47 The same statement appears in Halakhah 4:1. The only parallel is in Tosephta 6:3: If somebody "bespeaks" his sister-in-law and she turns out to have been pregnant (from the deceased husband), her co-wife should not marry until it will be known that the fetus has developed into a viable child since no child frees unless it came into the air. That version must be Babylonian since it does not support R. Yudan.

48 That would require the decision of a court of law.

הָיָה לַשְּׁנִיָּיה צָרָה. כּוֹנֵס אֶת הַצָּרָה וּמְקַיֵּים אֶת אִשְׁתּוֹ וְאָסוּר בַּשְּׁנִיָּיה. הָדָא הִיא מוּתָּר אָדָם בַּאֲחוֹת צָרַת חֲלוּצָתוֹ. וִיהֵא אָסוּר בַּצָּרָה מִשּׁוּם צָרַת אֲחוֹת חֲלוּצָתוֹ. אָמַר רִבִּי יוּדָן. אִילּוּ בִיקֵּשׁ לִבְעוֹל אֶת הַצָּרָה עַד שֶׁלֹּא כָנַס שֶׁמָּא אֵינוֹ מוּתָּר בָּהּ. כַּתְּחִילָּה הוּא מוּתָּר בָּהּ וּבְסוֹף הוּא אָסוּר. אִם אוֹמֵר אַתְּ כֵּן נִמְצֵאתָה עוֹשֶׂה צָרָה לְאַחַר מִיתָה. וְאֵין צָרָה לְאַחַר מִיתָה.

If the first [sister] had a co-wife, he can marry the co-wife, keep his wife, but the second [sister] is forbidden to him[49]. That is "the sister of the co-wife of one for whom he performed *ḥalîah* is permitted to a person.[50]" Should the co-wife not be forbidden to him as co-wife of the sister[51] of one for whom he performed *ḥalîṣah*? Rebbi Yudan said, if he wanted to have intercourse with the co-wife before he married[52], would he not have been permitted? At the start, he is permitted; at the end, he is prohibited? If you say so, you are making a co-wife after death[53] and there can be no co-wife after death.

49 This still refers to the case of the Mishnah where the first brother performed levirate with the first sister but the second brother did nothing with respect to the second sister.

50 In Mishnah 4:7: "The relative of the co-wife of one for whom he performed *ḥalîṣah*".

51 In ms. A: "relative", cf. Note 50.

52 Take her in levirate. This would be the easiest solution since then the second sister is eliminated as co-wife of one married in levirate and the first sister is permitted to the remaining brother.

53 By treating candidacy as equivalent of marriage, the co-wife of the second sister would become co-wife of the first, an impossible proposition.

הָיוּ חֲמִשָּׁה אַחִין שְׁלֹשָׁה מֵהֶן נְשׂוּאִין לְשָׁלֹשׁ אֲחָיוֹת וָמֵתוּ. רַב אָמַר זֶה חוֹלֵץ לְאַחַת וְזֶה חוֹלֵץ לְאַחַת וְהַשְּׁלִישִׁית חוֹלֶצֶת מֵאֵיזֶה מֵהֶן שֶׁיִּרְצֶה. שְׁמוּאֵל אָמַר. זֶה חוֹלֵץ לְאַחַת וְזֶה חוֹלֵץ לְאַחַת וְהַשְּׁלִישִׁית חוֹלֶצֶת מִשְּׁנֵיהֶן. רַב אוֹמֵר חֲלִיצָה קִינְיָין שְׁמוּאֵל אָמַר. חֲלִיצָה פְטוֹר. רִבִּי זְעִירָא אָמַר. חֲלִיצָה קִינְיָין. רִבִּי הִילָא אָמַר. חֲלִיצָה פְּטוֹר. מִילֵּיהוֹן דְּרַבָּנִין אָמְרִין. חֲלִיצָה פְטוֹר. שִׁמְעוֹן בַּר בָּא בְּעָא קוֹמֵי רִבִּי יוֹחָנָן. מַה בֵּין חוֹלֵץ וּמַה בֵּין מְגָרֵשׁ. אָמַר לֵיהּ. אַתְּ סָבוּר חֲלִיצָה (fol. 4d) [54]קִנְיָין. אֵינָהּ אֶלָּא פְטוֹר. אֵין הָאַחִין חַיָּבִין עָלֶיהָ מִשּׁוּם אִשְׁתּוֹ שֶׁלַּחוֹלֵץ אֲבָל חַיָּבִין עָלֶיהָ מִשּׁוּם אִשְׁתּוֹ שֶׁלַּמֵּת. לֵוִי אָמַר. זִיקָה קִנְיָין. וְכָל־אַחַת וְאַחַת צְרִיכָה חֲלִיצָה מִשְּׁנֵיהֶן.

If there were five brothers of whom three married three sisters and died[55]: Rav said, each one [of the remaining brothers] performs *ḥalîṣah* for one of them, and the third [sister] performs *ḥalîṣah* with whom she wants[56]. Samuel says, each one [of the remaining brothers] performs *ḥalîṣah* for one of them, and the third performs *ḥalîṣah* with both of them[57]. Rav said that *ḥalîṣah* is acquisition. Samuel said that *ḥalîṣah* is freeing. Rebbi Ze'ira said that *ḥalîṣah* is acquisition. Rebbi Hila said that *ḥalîṣah* is freeing.

[58]The words of the rabbis mean that *ḥalîṣah* is freeing. Simeon bar Abba asked before Rebbi Joḥanan: What is the difference between having *ḥalîṣah* and divorcing? He said to him: You think that *ḥalîṣah* is acquisiton, but it is only freeing. The brothers are not guilty for her under the category of "wife of the one acting in *ḥalîṣah*" but they are guilty under the category of "wife of the deceased".

Levi said, candidacy is acquisition and each {sister] has to perform *ḥalîṣah* with both [brothers][59].

54 Reading of ms. A. Ms L: חליצה אינו קניין

55 All childless. The text here and the parallel one in the Babli, 26b, are totally incompatible (as noted by Rashba, חידושי יבמות, מוסד הרב קוק, ירושלים תשמט, ע' קסז) since the Babli attributes to Rav the statement given here to Samuel and then bases everything on candidacy which has been proven to be irrelevant (Note 19).

56 As explained here, Rav holds that *ḥalîṣah* is acquisition, i. e., it is as if the brother had married the sister-in-law and immediately divorced her. The third sister should be freed automatically were it not for the argument that no obligation of *ḥalîṣah* can vanish into thin air.

57 Samuel holds that *ḥalîṣah* is freeing; the third sister has to obtain *ḥalîṣah* from both brothers since she is equally forbidden to both of them. The Babli (26b, 51b, 53a) states that an

impossible *ḥalîṣah*, like that of the third sister, necessitates *ḥalîṣah* from all brothers. This is not found in the Yerushalmi.

58 This paragraph was explained in Chapter 1, Notes 89-91.

59 Levi holds that each sister became a forbidden quasi-wife of each of the surviving brothers at the death of each husband and therefore needs freeing from each of them. This statement is not discussed since its premiss had been rejected.

מַתְנִיתָא פְּלִיגָא עַל שְׁמוּאֵל. הַחוֹלֵץ לִיבִמְתּוֹ הוּא אָסוּר בִּקְרוֹבוֹתֶיהָ וְהִיא אֲסוּרָה בִקְרוֹבָיו. שַׁנְיָיא הִיא הָכָא שֶׁכְּבָר נִרְאָה לִפְטוֹר בָּהּ. מַתְנִיתָא פְלִיגָא עַל רַב. הַחוֹלֵץ לִיבִמְתּוֹ וְנָשָׂא אָחִיו אֶת אֲחוֹתָהּ[60] וָמֵת חוֹלֶצֶת וְלֹא מִתְייַבֶּמֶת. הָדָא מְסַייְעָא לְמָאן דְּאָמַר. חֲלִיצָה פְטוֹר. בְּרַם הָכָא כְּמָאן דְּאָמַר. חֲלִיצָה קִינְייָן. וְיֵשׁ אָדָם מִתְכַּוֵּין לִקְנוֹת שְׁתֵּי אֲחָיוֹת כְּאַחַת. פָּתַר לָהּ. לְאַחַר מִיתָה. אֵין לְאַחַר מִיתָה יִיבּוּם. פָּתַר לָהּ כְּרִבִּי לָעְזָר. אַף עַל פִּי שֶׁבָּטֵל הַגּוֹרֵם הָאִיסּוּר בִּמְקוֹמוֹ. מַתְנִיתָא פְלִיגָא עַל רַב. שְׁלֹשָׁה אַחִין שְׁנַיִם מֵהֶן נְשׂוּאִין שְׁתֵּי אֲחָיוֹת וְאֶחָד מוּפְנֶה. מֵת אֶחָד מִבַּעֲלֵי אֲחָיוֹת וְעָשָׂה בָהּ הַמּוּפְנֶה מַאֲמָר וְאַחַר כֵּן מֵת אָחִיו הַשֵּׁינִי. בֵּית שַׁמַּי אוֹמְרִים. אִשְׁתּוֹ עִמּוֹ וְהַלֵּזוּ תֵצֵא מִשּׁוּם אֲחוֹת אִשָּׁה. בֵּית הִלֵּל אוֹמְרִים מוֹצִיא אֶת אִשְׁתּוֹ בְגֵט וּבַחֲלִיצָה[61] וְאֶת אֵשֶׁת אָחִיו בַּחֲלִיצָה. הָדָא מְסַייְעָא לְמָאן דְּאָמַר. חֲלִיצָה קִנְייָן.[62] [בְּרַם כְּמָאן דְּאָמַר חֲלִיצָה קִנְייָן.] וְיֵשׁ אָדָם מִתְכַּוֵּין לִקְנוֹת שְׁתֵּי אֲחָיוֹת כְּאַחַת. פָּתַר לָהּ לְאַחַר מִיתָה. וְאֵין לְאַחַר מִיתָה יִיבּוּם. פָּתַר לָהּ כְּרִבִּי לָעְזָר. דְּרִבִּי לָעְזָר אָמַר. אַף עַל פִּי שֶׁבָּטֵל הַגּוֹרֵם הָאִיסּוּר בִּמְקוֹמוֹ. מַתְנִיתָא פְלִיגָא עַל רַב. שׁוֹמֶרֶת יָבָם שֶׁקִּידֵּשׁ אָחִיו אֶת אֲחוֹתָהּ. מִשּׁוּם רִבִּי יוּדָה בֶּן בְּתֵירָה אָמְרוּ. אוֹמֵר לוֹ. הַמְתֵּן עַד שֶׁיַּעֲשֶׂה מַעֲשֶׂה. חָלְצוּ אַחִין אוֹ כָנְסוּ יַכְנִסוּ אֶת אִשְׁתּוֹ. מֵתָה הַיְבָמָה יַכְנִיס. מֵת הַיָּבָם מוֹצִיא אֶת אִשְׁתּוֹ בְגֵט וְאֶת אֵשֶׁת אָחִיו בַּחֲלִיצָה. הָדָא מְסַייְעָא לְמָאן דְּאָמַר. חֲלִיצָה פְטוֹר. בְּרַם כְּמָאן דְּאָמַר חֲלִיצָה קִנְייָן. יֵשׁ אָדָם מִתְכַּוֵּין לִקְנוֹת שְׁתֵּי אֲחָיוֹת כְּאַחַת. פָּתַר לָהּ כְּרִבִּי לָעְזָר. דְּרִבִּי לָעְזָר אָמַר. אַף עַל פִּי שֶׁבָּטֵל הַגּוֹרֵם הָאִיסּוּר בִּמְקוֹמוֹ. מַתְנִיתָא פְלִיגָא עַל רַב. כֹּהֵן גָּדוֹל שֶׁמֵּת אָחִיו. חוֹלֵץ וְלֹא

מְייַבֵּם. הָדָא מְסַייְעָא לְמָאן דְּאָמַר. חֲלִיצָה פְטוֹר. בְּרַם כְּמָאן דְּאָמַר חֲלִיצָה קִנְיָין. אוֹמְרִים לוֹ. עֲבוֹר עַל דִּבְרֵי תוֹרָה. הָתִיב רִבִּי חָמָא חֲבֵרִין דְּרַבָּנָן. וְהָא מַתְנִיתָא פְלִיגָא עַל רַב. שְׁלֹשָׁה אַחִין. שְׁנַיִם מֵהֶן נְשׂוּאִין שְׁתֵּי אֲחָיוֹת אוֹ אִשָּׁה וּבִתָּהּ אוֹ אִשָּׁה וּבַת בִּתָּהּ אוֹ אִשָּׁה וּבַת בְּנָהּ. הֲרֵי אֵילוּ חוֹלְצוֹת וְלֹא מִתְייַבְּמוֹת. שַׁנְייָא הִיא אִיסּוּר אִשָּׁה וּבִתָּהּ בֵּין בַּחַיִּים בֵּין לְאַחַר מִיתָה. אִילֵּין תְּרֵין אַחֲרִייָתָא פְלִיגֵי עַל רַב וְלֵית לְהוֹן קִייוּם.

[63]A Mishnah disagrees with Samuel: [64]"If somebody performs *ḥalîṣah* with his sister-in-law, her relatives are forbidden to him and his relatives are forbidden to her.[65]" There is a difference here, since he already is available to free himself from her[66].

A Mishnah disagrees with Rav: [67]"If somebody performs *ḥalîṣah* with his sister-in-law, then his brother marries her sister and dies, she performs *ḥalîṣah* but cannot have levirate." This supports him who says that *ḥalîṣah* is freeing. But according to him who says, *ḥalîṣah* is acquisiton, is there anybody who wants to acquire two sisters together[68]? Explain it, after her[69] death. Is there no levirate after death? Explain it following Rebbi Eleazar, since Rebbi Eleazar said, if the cause is removed the prohibition remains[70].

A Mishnah disagrees with Rav: [71]"Three brothers, two of them are married to two sisters and the third is free. One of the sisters' husbands died, the free [brother] "bespoke" her, then the second brother died. The House of Shammai say, his wife is with him[72] and the other one should leave as the wife's sister. The House of Hillel say, he divorces his wife with a bill of divorce (and *ḥalîṣah*), and his wife's sister with *ḥalîṣah*[73]. This supports him who says that *ḥalîṣah* is (acquisiton) [freeing][62]. But according to him who says, *ḥalîṣah* is acquisiton, is there anybody who wants to acquire two sisters together? Explain it, after her death. Is there no levirate after death? Explain it following Rebbi Eleazar, since Rebbi Eleazar said, if the cause is removed the prohibition remains.

A Mishnah disagrees with Rav: [74]"If a brother gives *qiddushin* to the sister of a woman waiting for the levir, they said in the name of Rebbi Jehudah ben Bathyra: One says to him, wait until your brother has acted. If one of the brothers performed *ḥalîṣah* or married her, he may marry his wife. If the sister-in-law died, he may marry his wife. If the levir died, he has to remove his wife by a bill of divorce and his brother's widow by *ḥalîṣah*.". This supports him who says that *ḥalîṣah* is freeing. But according to him who says, *ḥalîṣah* is acquisiton, is there anybody who wants to acquire two sisters together? Explain it following Rebbi Eleazar, since Rebbi Eleazar said, if the cause is removed the prohibition remains.

A Mishnah disagrees with Rav: [75]"If a brother of the High Priest dies, he performs *ḥalîṣah* but not levirate." This supports him who says that *ḥalîṣah* is freeing. But according to him who says, *ḥalîṣah* is acquisiton, does one say to him, transgress the words of the Torah?

Rebbi Ḥama, the colleague of the rabbis, objected: Does not a Mishnah disagree with Rav? [76]"Three brothers, two of them married to two sisters or a woman and her daughter or a woman and her daughter's or her son's daughter. These perform *ḥalîṣah* but not levirate." There is a difference since the prohibition of a woman and her daughter applies both when she is alive as also after her death. These last two disagree with Rav and one cannot explain them away

60 Reading of ms. A. Ms. L: אחותו.

61 The word is missing in the Mishnah and is deleted in ms. L by the corrector; therefore it is missing in the

editio princeps. It is found in ms. A. From Halakhah 3:4 it is clear that the word was omitted from the Mishnah by a scribal error (cf. א. שכטר, המשנה בבבלי ובירושלמי, מוסד הרב קוק, י-ם תשיט) and was wrongly eliminated from the text.

62 It is clear that one must read פטור instead of קיניין. The next sentence is missing in ms. L; it is clear that the scribe of ms. L already had the error before him since ms. A also reproduces it. The sentence in brackets is only in ms. A, it is missing in ms. L since its scribe left out a sentence from קיניין to קיניין. It is unlikely that the insertion in A is a deliberate correction.

63 This paragraph is missing in ms. A and in the text reproduced by Rashba (Note 55).

64 Mishnah 4:7.

65 All relatives of his wife forbidden to a husband are forbidden to the levir who performs *ḥalîṣah*. Therefore, it seems that *ḥalîṣah* turns the widow into an ex-wife.

66 This sentence is unintelligible and none of the commentators has an acceptable explanation. The only sensible way is to translate שכבר נראה not in the singular, "since he already is available", but "since they (both brothers) are available" and neither has an advantage over the other as participant in *ḥalîṣah*. The question raised by the text is not answered since the prohibition is clearly rabbinic and independent of the nature of *ḥalîṣah*.

67 Mishnah 4:8. The widow is biblically permitted to her levir but rabbinically forbidden; therefore, she needs *ḥalîṣah*. If *ḥalîṣah* were acquisition, she would be freed without ceremony.

68 Since everybody knows that one cannot be married to two sisters simultaneously.

69 If the first sister died, the second one is permited. Then one does not understand why she cannot have levirate.

70 If the first widow was alive when the second husband died, the second widow cannot have levirate. If then the first widow died, the situation is not changed for R. Eleazar.

71 Mishnah 3:5.

72 The House of Shammai hold that "bespeaking" acquires like a betrothal; parallel the opinion of R. Eleazar ben Arakh (Halakhah 5, cf. Halakhah 1). Therefore, the first widow is his wife; the second is forbidden to him biblically and leaves the family without formality.

73 The House of Hillel hold that "bespeaking" is purely rabbinical and

that the only legal consequence of "bespeaking" is to forbid the sister-in-law to the other brothers. Therefore, now the "bespoken" and the new widow have conflicting claims on him; he has to give *ḥalîṣah* to both of them and in addition a rabbinic bill of divorce for the rabbinic betrothal to the first widow.

74 Mishnah 4:9, explained in Notes 7-9.

75 Mishnah 6:4. The High Priest may marry only a virgin. The verse (*Lev.* 21:14) reads: "A widow, a divorcee, a harlot, and a desecrated one he shall not acquire . . .". Since marriage is formulated in terms of acquisition, if *ḥalîṣah* were acquisition, the widow of the High Priest's brother either should be free without *ḥalîṣah* or never could be freed.

76 Mishnah 3:4. The second widow has to have *ḥalîṣah* if the first widow did. If the first was married in levirate, the second goes free without ceremony.

(fol. 4b) **משנה ב:** הָיְתָה אַחַת מֵהֶן אֲסוּרָה עַל הָאֶחָד אִיסּוּר עֶרְוָה אָסוּר בָּהּ וּמוּתָּר בַּאֲחוֹתָהּ וְהַשֵּׁנִי אָסוּר בִּשְׁתֵּיהֶן. אִיסּוּר מִצְוָה אוֹ אִיסּוּר קְדוּשָּׁה חוֹלְצוֹת וְלֹא מִתְייַבְּמוֹת. הָיְתָה אַחַת מֵהֶן אֲסוּרָה עַל זֶה אִיסּוּר עֶרְוָה וְהַשְּׁנִייָה אֲסוּרָה עַל זֶה אִיסּוּר עֶרְוָה. הָאֲסוּרָה לָזֶה מוּתֶּרֶת לָזֶה וְהָאֲסוּרָה לָזֶה מוּתֶּרֶת לָזֶה. וְזוֹ הִיא שֶׁאָמְרוּ אֲחוֹתָהּ שֶׁהִיא יְבִמְתָּהּ אוֹ חוֹלֶצֶת אוֹ מִתְייַבֶּמֶת.

Mishnah 2: If one of them was forbidden to one of them by an incest prohibition, that one is forbidden for him but her sister is permitted to him[77]. Both are forbidden to the second [brother]. In case of a commandment prohibition or a holiness prohibition, they have *ḥalîṣah* but not levirate[78]. If one of [the sisters] was forbidden to that one [brother] by an incest prohition and the other [sister] was forbidden to the [other brother] by an incest prohition, the one who is forbidden for one might be permitted to the other and vice-versa. That is what they said, "Her sister who is her sister-in-law can have *ḥalîṣah* or be married in levirate."

77 Since one of the sisters is not available to him, the other is not the sister of a candidate for levirate. If they both become candidates at the same time (or at least before the other brother had married one in levirate), they both are sisters of a candidate and therefore forbidden to the second brother.

78 Mishnah 3:4. Since a marriage would not be void, *ḥalîṣah* is necessary.

(fol. 4d) **הלכה ב:** הָיְתָה אַחַת מֵהֶן אֲסוּרָה כול׳. אָנַס אִשָּׁה וְיָֽלְדָה בַּת וְהָלְכָה וְנִישֵּׂאת לְאָחִיו וְלָהּ אָחוֹת מֵאֵם מֵאִישׁ אַחֵר נְשׂוּאָה לְאָחִיו הַשֵּׁינִי וּמֵת בְּלֹא בָנִים. הֲרֵי זֶה אָסוּר בְּבִתּוֹ וּמוּתָּר בַּאֲחוֹתָהּ. הָדָא הִיא אֲחוֹתָהּ שֶׁהִיא יְבִמְתָּהּ מִתְייַבֶּמֶת.

Halakhah 2: "If one of them was forbidden," etc. If a man raped a woman and she had a daughter who married one of his brothers while [the daughter's] half-sister from another man is married to a second brother: When they died without children, his daughter is forbidden to him but her sister is permitted to him[79]. This exemplifies: "Her sister who is her sister-in-law can be married in levirate[80]."

הלכה ג: הָיְתָה אַחַת מֵהֶן אֲסוּרָה כול׳. אָנַס אִשָּׁה וְיָֽלְדָה בַּת וּבָא אָחִיו וַאֲנָסָהּ וְיָֽלְדָה בַת וְנָֽשְׂאוּ שְׁתֵּיהֶן לִשְׁנֵי אַחִים מֵאָב אֲבָל לֹא מֵאֵם. זֶה אָסוּר בְּבִתּוֹ וּמוּתָּר בַּאֲחוֹתָהּ וְזֶה אָסוּר בְּבִתּוֹ וּמוּתָּר בַּאֲחוֹתָהּ. הָדָא הִיא הָאָסוּר לָזֶה מוּתָּר לָזֶה וְהָאָסוּר לָזֶה מוּתָּר לָזֶה.

Halakhah 3: "If one of them was forbidden," etc. If one of them raped a woman and she had a daughter, [the woman] in turn was raped by his brother and also had a daughter and both [daughters] married [these] brothers who were paternal but not maternal halfbrothers: Each one of them is forbidden his own daughter but permitted her sister. That exemplifies: The one forbidden for one is permitted to the other and vice-versa[80].

79 Since she is not his wife's daughter.

80 That case never can happen if he is married to the mother of the girl (Babli 28b). All these rules are valid only for cases which probably never occur.

(fol. 4b) **משנה ג:** שְׁלֹשָׁה אַחִין. שְׁנַיִם מֵהֶן נְשׂוּאִין שְׁתֵּי אֲחָיוֹת אוֹ אִשָּׁה וּבִתָּהּ אוֹ אִשָּׁה וּבַת בִּתָּהּ אוֹ אִשָּׁה וּבַת בְּנָהּ. הֲרֵי אֵילוּ חוֹלְצוֹת וְלֹא מִתְיַיבְּמוֹת. וְרַבִּי שִׁמְעוֹן פּוֹטֵר. הָיְתָה אַחַת מֵהֶן אֲסוּרָה עַל הָאֶחָד אִיסּוּר עֶרְוָה אָסוּר בָּהּ וּמוּתָּר בַּאֲחוֹתָהּ. אִיסּוּר מִצְוָה אוֹ אִיסּוּר קְדוּשָּׁה חוֹלְצוֹת וְלֹא מִתְיַיבְּמוֹת. וְרַבִּי שִׁמְעוֹן פּוֹטֵר.

Mishnah 3: [76]Three brothers, two of them married to two sisters or a woman and her daughter or a woman and her daughter's or her son's daughter: These perform *ḥalîṣah* but not levirate, but Rebbi Simeon frees them[81]. If one of them was forbidden to one of them by an incest prohibition, that one is forbidden for him but her sister is permitted to him[77]. In case of a commandment prohibition or a holiness prohibition, they have *ḥalîṣah* but not levirate[78]. But Rebbi Simeon frees them[82].

81 If both women become widows before one of them is married in levirate or performs *ḥalîṣah*.

According to the Babli, 28b-29a, R. Simeon reads *Lev.* 18:18: "Do not take a wife together with her sister to tie into one bundle" that the common candidacy of a woman and her sister destroys both candidacies so that even the one who was widowed first would be freed by her sister. This is not the position of the Yerushalmi which holds that the candidacy of the first widow excludes the second from candidacy, as explained in the Halakhah.

82 This sentence is not in the Mishnah of the Babli; the Babli holds that in this case, R. Simeon agrees with the majority.

(fol. 4d) **הלכה ד:** שְׁלֹשָׁה אַחִין. שְׁנַיִם מֵהֶן נְשׂוּאִין שְׁתֵּי אֲחָיוֹת כול'. עוּלָּה בַּר יִשְׁמָעֵאל אָמַר. כָּךְ פֵּירְשָׁהּ רִבִּי הוֹשַׁעְיָה אֲבִי הַמִּשְׁנָה. רִבִּי שִׁמְעוֹן פּוֹטֵר אֶת הַשְּׁנִייָה מִן הַחֲלִיצָה וּמִן הַיִּיבּוּם. אָמַר רִבִּי יוֹחָנָן. חֲבוּרָה הָיְתָה מַקְשָׁה שֶׁלֹּא עָלַת עַל דַּעַת שֶׁיִּקְנֶה אָדָם שְׁתֵּי אֲחָיוֹת כְּאַחַת. אָמַר רִבִּי חֲנִינָא קוֹמֵי רִבִּי מָנָא וּפְלִיגָא. וְלָמָּה רִבִּי שִׁמְעוֹן פּוֹטֵר אֶת הַשְּׁנִייָה מִן הַחֲלִיצָה וּמִן הַיִּיבּוּם. אָמַר לֵיהּ. שֶׁלֹּא עָלַת עַל דַּעַת שֶׁיִּקְנֶה אָדָם שְׁתֵּי אֲחָיוֹת כְּאַחַת. תַּמָּן אָמְרִין. דִּבְרֵי רִבִּי שִׁמְעוֹן אֵין זִיקָה נוֹפֶלֶת בִּמְקוֹם זִיקָה. רִבִּי בָּא בְשֵׁם רִבִּי לָעְזָר. וְהוּא שֶׁעָבַר וּבָעַל. הֵיךְ עֲבִידָא. קִידֵּשׁ אֶחָד מִן הַשּׁוּק אֶת הַשְּׁנִייָה. עַל דַּעְתִּין דְּרַבָּנִן קִידּוּשִׁין גְּמוּרִין. עַל דַּעַת דְּרִבִּי לָעְזָר קִידּוּשִׁין תְּלוּיִין. לִכְשֶׁיִּבְעוֹל אֶת הָרִאשׁוֹנָה קִידּוּשִׁין תּוֹפְסִין אֶת הַשְּׁנִייָה. בָּא עַל הַשְּׁנִייָה. עַל דַּעְתִּין דְּרַבָּנִן בִּיאַת עֶרְוָה. עַל דַּעְתֵּיהּ דְּרִבִּי לָעְזָר אֵינָהּ בִּיאַת עֶרְוָה. מֵתָה הָרִאשׁוֹנָה. עַל דַּעְתִּין דְּרַבָּנִין מוּתָּר בַּשְּׁנִייָה.

Halakhah 4: "Three brothers, two of them married to two sisters," etc. Ulla bar Ismael said, so explained Rebbi Hoshaia, the father of the Mishnah[83]: Rebbi Simeon frees the second one from *ḥalîṣah* and levirate[81]. Rebbi Joḥanan said, the group asked, would anybody think that a man could acquire two sisters together[84]? Rebbi Ḥanina said before Rebbi Mana and disagreed: Why does Rebbi Simeon free the second one from *ḥalîṣah* and levirate? He said to him, because nobody thinks that a man could acquire two sisters together. There they said, the words of

Rebbi Simeon imply that no candidacy can come after another candidacy[85]. Rebbi Abba in the name of Rebbi Eleazar: Only if he sinned and had intercourse[86]. What is the difference? If somebody from the market gave *qiddushin* to the second sister. Following the rabbis, perfect *qiddushin*[87]. Following Rebbi Eleazar, suspended *qiddushin*. When he[88] has intercourse with the first, the *qiddushin* become valid for the second. If he had intercourse with the second, following the rabbis it is an incestuous act. Following Rebbi Eleazar, it is not an incestuous act[89]. If the first one died, following the rabbis the second is permitted to him[90].

83 In the Babli, he and the elder R. Ḥiyya are given as the source of reliable *baraitot*.

84 They held that any *ḥalîṣah* mentioned in the Mishnah is only rabbinic (a view also held in the Babli, 28b/29a). Since nobody assumes that anyone might contract incestuous marriages, that rabbinic institution seems superfluous.

85 This statement, attributed to Babylonian sources, is not found in the Babli. Here it is referred to as "the opinion of the rabbis" in the interpretation of R. Simeon.

86 R. Eleazar holds that R. Simeon considers candidacy only as tentative (cf. Chapter 2, Note 47). Therefore, the second widow is freed only if the first becomes unquestionably the wife of the third brother; this she can become only by having intercourse which under the circumstances is sinful.

87 Since the second widow leaves the family without ceremony.

88 The third brother.

89 At least not an act which certainly would be incestuous.

90 To the third brother, but only in the case of two sisters.

הָיָה לָרִאשׁוֹנָה צָרָה. כּוֹנֵס צָרָה וּמְקַיֵּים אֶת אִשְׁתּוֹ וְאָסוּר בַּשְּׁנִייָה. הָדָא הִיא מוּתָּר הוּא אָדָם בָּאֲחוֹת צָרַת חֲלוּצָתוֹ. וִיהֵא אָסוּר בַּצָּרָה מִשּׁוּם צָרַת קְרוֹבַת חֲלוּצָתוֹ. אָמַר רִבִּי יוּדָן. אִילּוּ בִיקֵּשׁ לִבְעוֹל אֶת הַצָּרָה עַד שֶׁלֹּא כָנַס שֶׁמָּא

אֵינוֹ מוּתָּר בָּהּ. כַּתְּחִילָּה הוּא מוּתָּר בָּהּ וּבַסּוֹף הוּא אָסוּר. אִם אוֹמֵר אַתְּ כֵּן נִמְצֵאת עוֹשֶׂה צָרָה לְאַחַר מִיתָה. וְאֵין צָרָה לְאַחַר מִיתָה.

If the first [sister] had a co-wife, he can marry the co-wife, keep his wife, but the second [sister] is forbidden to him[49]. That is "the sister of the co-wife of one with whom he performed *ḥalîṣah* is permitted to a person.[50]" Should the co-wife not be forbidden to him as co-wife of a relative of one with whom he performed *ḥalîṣah*? Rebbi Yudan said, if he wanted to have intercourse with the co-wife before he married[52], would he not have been permitted? At the start, he is permitted; at the end, he is prohibited? If you say so, you are creating a co-wife after death[53] and there can be no co-wife after death.

מִחְלְפָה שִׁיטָּתֵיהּ דְּרִבִּי שִׁמְעוֹן. תַּמָּן הוּא אָמַר. מְיַיבֵּם לְאֵי זוֹ שֶׁיִּרְצֶה וְחוֹלֵץ לַשְּׁנִייָה. וְהָכָא הוּא אָמַר אָכֵין. אָמַר רִבִּי זְעִירָא. עַד אֲנָן תַּמָּן שְׁמָעִית טַעֲמָא. תַּמָּן זִיקַת שְׁנֵי יְבָמִין אֵינָהּ זִיקָה וְזִיקָה נוֹפֶלֶת לִמְקוֹם זִיקָה. בְּרַם הָכָא זִיקַת יָבָם אֶחָד וְאֵין זִיקָה נוֹפֶלֶת לִמְקוֹם מַאֲמָר. אָמַר רִבִּי מַתַּנְיָה. מַה אִיכְפְּלִין אֲחָיוֹת גַּבֵּי נָכְרִיּוֹת. אִין אַתְּ בְּעֵי מִקְשַׁייָא קְשִׁיתָהּ עַל הַהִיא דְּרִבִּי זְעוּרָא בְּשֵׁם רַב שֵׁשֶׁת. תַּנֵּיי תַּמָּן דִּבְרֵי רִבִּי שִׁמְעוֹן שְׁתֵּיהֶן אֲסוּרוֹת. מִחְלְפָה שִׁיטָּתֵיהּ דְּרִבִּי שִׁמְעוֹן. תַּמָּן הוּא אָמַר. שְׁתֵּיהֶן אֲסוּרוֹת. וְהָכָא אַתְּ אָמַר. שְׁתֵּיהֶן מוּתָּרוֹת.

The argument of Rebbi Simeon seems to be inverted. There[91], he says, "he marries in levirate the one he wants and performs *ḥalîṣah* with the other," and here, he says so? Rebbi Ze'ira said, when I was still there[92], I learned the reason: There, the candidacy for two brothers-in-law does not interfere and one candidacy can be added to another, but here it is candidacy for one levir and no candidacy can come after a "bespeaking"[93]. Rebbi Mattania said, are not sisters different from unrelated women? If you want a difficulty, find it in what Rebbi Ze'ira said in the name of Rav

Sheshet: They stated there that Rebbi Simeon forbade both of them[94]. The argument of Rebbi Simeon seems to be inverted. There he says, both are forbidden, and here[91] you says, both are permitted[95].

91 Mishnah 3:10 where R. Simeon completely disregards "bespeaking" while here he even considers candidacy as obstacle.

92 In Babylonia. In the Babli, 31b, this argument is labelled rabbinic, not biblical.

93 A comparison with the earlier quote (Note 85) shows that candidacy and "bespeaking" are put on one and the same level.

94 Halakhah 2:2, Note 47. In that case, Rebbi Simeon accepts "bespeaking" as marriage.

95 No answer is given since the earlier explanation of R. Ze'ira is also valid here.

(fol. 4b) **משנה ד:** שְׁלֹשָׁה אַחִין שְׁנַיִם מֵהֶן נְשׂוּאִים שְׁתֵּי אֲחָיוֹת וְאֶחָד מוּפְנֶה מֵת אֶחָד מִבַּעֲלֵי אֲחָיוֹת וְעָשָׂה בָהּ מוּפְנֶה מַאֲמָר וְאַחַר כֵּן מֵת אָחִיו הַשֵּׁינִי בֵּית שַׁמַּי אוֹמְרִים אִשְׁתּוֹ עִמּוֹ. וְהַלָּז תֵּצֵא מִשּׁוּם אֲחוֹת אִשָּׁה. בֵּית הִלֵּל אוֹמְרִים מוֹצִיא אֶת אִשְׁתּוֹ בְגֵט וְאֶת אֵשֶׁת אָחִיו בַּחֲלִיצָה. זוֹ הִיא שֶׁאָמְרוּ אוֹי לוֹ עַל אִשְׁתּוֹ וְאוֹי לוֹ עַל אֵשֶׁת אָחִיו.

Mishnah 4: Three brothers, two of whom are married to two sisters and the third is a bachelor. One of the sisters' husbands died; the bachelor "bespoke" her; then the second brother died. The House of Shammai say, his wife is with him[72] and the other one should leave as the wife's sister. The House of Hillel say, he divorces his wife with a bill of divorce[61], and his wife's sister with *ḥalîṣah*[73]. That is what people say, he is unlucky with his wife and with his brother's wife[96].

96 A popular saying about somebody who loses everything without having done anything wrong.

(fol. 4d) **הלכה ד:** שְׁלֹשָׁה אַחִין. שְׁנַיִם מֵהֶן נְשׂוּאִין שְׁתֵּי אֲחָיוֹת כול'. בֵּית שַׁמַּי אוֹמְרִים כְּרִבִּי לָעְזָר בֶּן עֲרָךְ. דְּרִבִּי לָעְזָר בֶּן עֲרָךְ אָמַר. הַמַּאֲמָר קוֹנֶה קִנְיָן גָּמוּר בִּיבָמָה. אִין כְּרִבִּי לָעְזָר בֶּן עֲרָךְ. גֵּירַשׁ לְבַעֲלַת מַאֲמָר לֹא תְהֵא צְרִיכָה חֲלִיצָה. וְאָמַר רִבִּי הִילָא בְשֵׁם רִבִּי לָעְזָר. מוֹדֵיי בֵית שַׁמַּי שֶׁאִם גֵּירַשׁ לְבַעֲלַת מַאֲמָר שֶׁהִיא צְרִיכָה מִמֶּנּוּ חֲלִיצָה. אֶלָּא כְּרִבִּי שִׁמְעוֹן. דְּרִבִּי שִׁמְעוֹן אָמַר. הַמַּאֲמָר אוֹ קוֹנֶה אוֹ לֹא קוֹנֶה. אִין כְּרִבִּי שִׁמְעוֹן. מַה נַפְשָׁךְ. קָנָה מַאֲמָר וְאֵין אַחֲרָיו כְּלוּם. לֹא קָנָה מַאֲמָר לָמָּה לִי אִשְׁתּוֹ עִמּוֹ וְהַלָּז תֵּצֵא מִשּׁוּם אֲחוֹת אִשָּׁה. שֶׁמָּא מַאֲמָר דְּבֵית שַׁמַּי כְּזִיקַת רִבִּי שִׁמְעוֹן. עַל דַּעְתִּין דְּרַבָּנִין דְּתַמָּן. כְּמָה דְרַבָּנִין דְּתַמָּן אָמְרִין. הַמַּאֲמָר קוֹנֶה וּמְשַׁיֵּיר. כֵּן רִבִּי שִׁמְעוֹן אוֹמֵר. קוֹנָה וּמְשַׁיֵּירֶת. רִבִּי שִׁמְעוֹן אוֹמֵר. אֵין זִיקָה נוֹפֶלֶת לִמְקוֹם זִיקָה. כֵּן בֵּית שַׁמַּי אוֹמְרִים הָכָא. אֵין זִיקָה נוֹפֶלֶת לִמְקוֹם מַאֲמָר.

"Three brothers, two of whom are married to two sisters," etc. Do the House of Shammai follow Rebbi Eleazar ben Arakh[97], since Rebbi Eleazar ben Arakh says, "bespeaking" acquires a sister-in-law completely? If they would follow Rebbi Eleazar ben Arakh, in case he had divorced the "bespoken" widow, she would not need *ḥalîṣah*! But Rebbi Hila said in the name of Rebbi Eleazar[98], the House of Shammai agree that if he divorced the "bespoken", she needs *ḥalîṣah*! It must be they follow Rebbi Simeon, since Rebbi Simeon says, "bespeaking" either acquires or does not acquire. If they would follow Rebbi Simeon, in any case, if "bespeaking" acquires, nothing follows it[99]. If "bespeaking" does not acquire, why "his wife is with him and the other one should leave as the wife's sister"[100]? Maybe "bespeaking" for the House of Shammai is like candidacy for Rebbi Simeon in the interpretation of the rabbis there. As the rabbis there[101] say, "bespeaking" acquires and leaves a remainder, so Rebbi Simeon says, [candidacy] acquires and leaves a remainder. Rebbi Simeon says, no candidacy can come after a candidacy, so the House of Shammai say here, no candidacy can come after a "bespeaking".

97 The positions of Rebbis Eleazar ben Arakh and Simeon are explained in Halakhah 2:1, Notes 10-13; their agreement is asserted in the Babli, 29b.

98 The Amora, who lived about 150 years after the disappearance of the House of Shammai. His opinion is in the Babli, 29a.

99 She is his wife as if there were *qiddushin*; there is no question that the sister is free without ceremony.

100 They would have to agree to the position of the House of Hillel.

101 In Chapter 2, Note 47 ff.

רִבִּי יוּדָן בָּעֵי. קִידֵּשׁ אִשָּׁה מֵעַכְשָׁיו (fol. 5a) לְאַחַר שְׁלֹשִׁים יוֹם וְנָפְלָה לוֹ אֲחוֹתָהּ בְּתוֹךְ שְׁלֹשִׁים יוֹם אֲפִילוּ כֵן אִשְׁתּוֹ עִמּוֹ וְהַלָּז תֵּצֵא מִשּׁוּם אֲחוֹת אִשָּׁה. אָמַר. לֹא אָמְרוּ בֵית שַׁמַּי אֶלָּא עַל יְדֵי זִיקָה וְעַל יְדֵי מַאֲמָר. וְהַהִיא דְאָמַר רִבִּי אַבָּהוּ בְּשֵׁם רִבִּי יוֹחָנָן. אֲפִילוּ קִידּוּשִׁין מֵאָה תּוֹפְשִׂין בָּהּ וְלֹא כְבֵית שַׁמַּי.

Rebbi Yudan asked: If somebody gave *qiddushin* to a woman "from now and after thirty days"[102] and her sister became a candidate for levirate with him during these thirty days, is even in this "his wife with him and the other one should leave as the wife's sister"[103]? He said, the House of Shammai said that only after candidacy and "bespeaking". But that what Rebbi Abbahu said in the name of Rebbi Johanan, even a hundred *qiddushin* are valid for her[104], does not follow the House of Shammai[105].

102 Mishnah *Qiddušin* 3:1 If somebody gives something of value to a woman and says, "be betrothed to me after thirty days", if another man comes in the meantime and gives her *qiddushin*, she is the wife of the second

man and after 30 days, when she should become the wife of the first, she already is married and betrothal with a married man is void. But if the first had said, "from now after thirty days", he reserved his rights to her from the moment of the transaction but she becomes his wife in civil and criminal law only after 30 days. If anybody else gives her *qiddushin* in that period, she is tentatively betrothed to both of them and both have to divorce her.

103 Following the House of Shammai.

104 Babli *Qiddušin* 60a, Yerushalmi *Qiddušin* fol. 63c, 3:1. It is a little difficult to accomodate 100 *qiddushin*. The general idea is that the first man says, from now in 30 days, the next day another says, from now in 29 days, etc.

105 Since the House of Shammai hold that "bespeaking", which is a very weak imitation of *qiddushin*, suffices to make the woman a wife in relation to female competitors, they should hold that *qiddushin* "from now to 30 days" also are enough to eliminate male competitors.

(fol. 4b) **משנה ה:** שְׁלֹשָׁה אַחִין שְׁנַיִם מֵהֶן נְשׂוּאִים שְׁתֵּי אֲחָיוֹת וְאֶחָד נָשׂוּי נָכְרִית. מֵת אֶחָד מִבַּעֲלֵי אֲחָיוֹת וְכָנַס הַנָּשׂוּי נָכְרִית אֶת אִשְׁתּוֹ וָמֵת. שְׁנִיָּה יוֹצִיא מִשּׁוּם אֲחוֹת אִשְׁתּוֹ וְרִאשׁוֹנָה מִשּׁוּם צָרָתָהּ. עָשָׂה בָהּ מַאֲמָר וָמֵת נָכְרִית חוֹלֶצֶת וְלֹא מִתְייַבֶּמֶת.

Mishnah 5: Of three brothers, two are married to two sisters and one to an unrelated woman. One of the sisters' husbands died, the husband of the unrelated married his widow, and died. [The dead brother's] second [wife] leaves as his wife's sister, the first one as her co-wife. If he had "bespoken" her, the unrelated woman performs *ḥalîṣah* but cannot have levirate.

הלכה ו: שְׁלֹשָׁה אַחִין שְׁנַיִם מֵהֶן נְשׂוּאִין לִשְׁתֵּי אֲחָיוֹת כול'. בֵּין רַבָּנִין(fol. 5a) בֵּין רִבִּי שִׁמְעוֹן מוֹדִין בָּהּ. כְּרַבָּנִין צַד שֶׁקָּנָה מַאֲמָר כְּנֶגְדָּהּ אָסוּר בַּצָּרָה. וְצַד שֶׁלֹּא קָנָה מַאֲמָר כְּנֶגְדּוֹ אָסוּר בַּצָּרָה. לְפִיכָךְ חוֹלֶצֶת וְלֹא מִתְיַיבֶּמֶת. כְּרִבִּי שִׁמְעוֹן קָנָה מַאֲמָר שְׁתֵּיהֶן מוּתָּרוֹת. לֹא קָנָה מַאֲמָר הָרִאשׁוֹנָה אֲסוּרָה וְהַשְּׁנִיָּה מוּתֶּרֶת מִסָּפֵק חוֹלֶצֶת וְלֹא מִתְיַיבֶּמֶת.

Halakhah 6: "Of three brothers, two are married to two sisters," etc. Both the rabbis and Rebbi Simeon will agree in this case. For the rabbis, the part of the co-wife parallel to that which "bespeaking" acquired [in the widow] is forbidden. Also, the part of the co-wife parallel to that which "bespeaking" did not acquire [in the widow] is [still] forbidden[106]. Therefore, she performs *ḥalîṣah* but cannot have levirate. Following Rebbi Simeon, if "bespeaking" acquires, both are permitted[107]. If "bespeaking" does not acquire, the first is forbidden but the second permitted. Because of the doubt, she[108] performs *ḥalîṣah* but cannot have levirate.

106 Since no woman can be the wife of two men; since she cannot have partial levirate, she cannot have levirate at all.

In this Mishnah and the next, the only question is why the unrelated woman has to perform *ḥalîṣah*. These Mishnaiot require the third brother to be married.

107 To marry outside the family without formalities.

108 The first, unrelated, wife is forbidden for outsiders without *ḥalîṣah*. {The Mishnah in the Babli switches the places of "first" and "second" in the Mishnah; students of the Babli consider this paragraph corrupt.}

משנה ו: שְׁלֹשָׁה אַחִין שְׁנַיִם מֵהֶן נְשׂוּאִין שְׁתֵּי אֲחָיוֹת וְאֶחָד נָשׂוּי(fol. 4b) נָכְרִית. מֵת הַנָּשׂוּי נָכְרִית וְכָנַס אֶחָד מִבַּעֲלֵי אֲחָיוֹת אֶת אִשְׁתּוֹ וָמֵת. רִאשׁוֹנָה יוֹצְאָה מִשּׁוּם אֲחוֹת אִשְׁתּוֹ וּשְׁנִיָּה מִשּׁוּם צָרָתָהּ. עָשָׂה בָהּ מַאֲמָר וָמֵת נָכְרִית חוֹלֶצֶת וְלֹא מִתְיַיבֶּמֶת.

Mishnah 6: Of three brothers, two are married to two sisters and one to an unrelated woman. The husband of the unrelated died, one of the sisters' husbands married his widow, and died. His first [wife] leaves as his wife's sister, the second one as her co-wife. If he had "bespoken" her, the unrelated woman performs *ḥalîṣah* but cannot have levirate.

(fol. 5a) **הלכה ז:** שְׁלֹשָׁה אַחִין שְׁנַיִם מֵהֶן נְשׂוּאִין לִשְׁתֵּי אֲחָיוֹת כול׳. בֵּין רַבָּנִין בֵּין[109] רִבִּי שִׁמְעוֹן מוֹדֵיי בָהּ.

Halakhah 7: "Of three brothers, two are married to two sisters," etc. Both the rabbis and Rebbi Simeon will agree in this case.

109 In the ms.: ‘ביר, a copyist's error (not caught by the editors).

(fol. 4b) **משנה ז:** שְׁלֹשָׁה אַחִין שְׁנַיִם מֵהֶן נְשׂוּאִין שְׁתֵּי אֲחָיוֹת וְאֶחָד נָשׂוּי נָכְרִית. מֵת אֶחָד מִבַּעֲלֵי אֲחָיוֹת וְכָנַס נָשׂוּי נָכְרִית אֶת אִשְׁתּוֹ וּמֵתָה אִשְׁתּוֹ שֶׁלַּשֵּׁינִי וְאַחַר כָּךְ מֵת נָשׂוּי נָכְרִית הֲרֵי זֶה אֲסוּרָה עָלָיו עוֹלָמִית הוֹאִיל וְנֶאֶסְרָה עָלָיו שָׁעָה אַחַת.

Mishnah 7: Three brothers, two of them are married to two sisters and one to an unrelated woman. One of the sisters' husbands died, the husband of the unrelated married his widow, the wife of the second brother died and then the husband of the unrelated died. She[110] is permanently forbidden to him[111] since she was forbidden one moment.

110 The widow of the first brother is forbidden to the second even though in general the deceased wife's sister is permitted to her husband (*Lev*. 18:18). The reason is that when her first husband died, she was forbidden to the second brother as sister of his wife and, as will be explained later, any brother who cannot "build his brother's house" at the first opportunity can never build after that.

111 The only surviving brother.

(fol. 5a) **הלכה ח:** שְׁלֹשָׁה אַחִין כול'. אָמַר רִבִּי אֲבִינָא. הָדָא דְאָמַר רִבִּי יוֹסֵי בְּשֵׁם רִבִּי יוֹחָנָן. לֹא דוֹמֶה אִיסּוּר אֲחָיוֹת יְבָמוֹת לְאִיסּוּר אֲחָיוֹת שֶׁאֵינָן יְבָמוֹת.

Halakhah 8: "Of three brothers," etc. Rebbi Avina said, that is what Rebbi Yose said in the name of Rebbi Johanan: The prohibition of sisters who are sisters-in-law does not compare with the prohibition of sisters who not are sisters-in-law[112].

112 These are always permitted to the widower of the sister.

(fol. 4b) **משנה ח:** שְׁלֹשָׁה אַחִין שְׁנַיִם מֵהֶן נְשׂוּאִין שְׁתֵּי אֲחָיוֹת וְאֶחָד נָשׂוּי נָכְרִית. גֵּירַשׁ אֶחָד מִבַּעֲלֵי אֲחָיוֹת אֶת אִשְׁתּוֹ וּמֵת הַנָּשׂוּי נָכְרִית וּכְנָסָהּ הַמְגָרֵשׁ וּמֵת. זוֹ הִיא שֶׁאָמְרוּ וְכוּלָּן שֶׁמֵּתוּ אוֹ שֶׁמֵּיאֵינוּ אוֹ נִתְגָּרְשׁוּ אוֹ שֶׁנִּמְצְאוּ אַיְילוֹנִיּוֹת צָרוֹתֵיהֶן מוּתָּרוֹת.

Mishnah 8: Of three brothers, two are married to two sisters and one to an unrelated woman. If one of the sisters' husbands divorced his wife, when the one married to an unrelated woman died and the divorcer married her[113] and then died, that is what they said: Of all of these, if they died, or repudiated, or were divorced, or turned out to be she-rams, the co-wives are permitted[114].

113 The unrelated woman, now his brother's widow.

114 If at the moment of the husband's death there is no impediment to levirate, anything that happened before is unimportant. Cf. Chapter 1, Note 115.

In the Babli and most Mishnah mss., the text is short "if they died or were divorced" as in the quote in the Halakhah.

(fol. 5a) **הלכה ח:** שְׁלֹשָׁה אַחִין כול׳. רִבִּי חַגַּיי בְּשֵׁם רִבִּי זְעִירָא. לֹא סוֹף דָּבָר בְּשֶׁגֵּירַשׁ וְאַחַר כָּךְ כָּנַס. אֶלָּא אֲפִילוּ כָּנַס וְאַחַר כָּךְ גֵּירַשׁ. הָדָא הוּא דְתַנִּינָן שֶׁאִם מֵתוּ אוֹ נִתְגָּרְשׁוּ צָרוֹתֵיהֶן מוּתָּרוֹת.

Halakhah 8: "Of three brothers," etc. Rebbi Ḥaggai said in the name of Rebbi Ze'ira, not only if he divorced and after that married, but even if he married and after that divorced[115]. That is what we had stated: "Of all of these, if they died or were divorced, their co-wives are permitted.[116]"

115 The Babli, 30a/b, considers this only as a possibilty, to be disregarded. That Talmud requires that the two women never were potential co-wives, i. e., if the first brother divorced his wife only after the third brother had died and the unrelated woman was a potential co-wife of the first's wife, she is permanently forbidden to the second brother.

116 A shortened version, possibly due to Babylonian influence, cf. Note 114.

אָמַר רִבִּי יוּדָן. אַף רִבִּי לְעָזָר מוֹדֶה. אָמַר רִבִּי יוֹסֵה. וְיֵאוּת. אִילּוּ מִי שֶׁהָיוּ לוֹ בָנִים וּמֵתוּ וְאַחַר כָּךְ מֵת הוּא שֶׁמָּא אֵין אִשְׁתּוֹ זְקוּקָה לְיִיבּוּם. תַּמָּן וְהוּא שֶׁהָיוּ לוֹ בָנִים בִּשְׁעַת מִיתָה. וְהָכָא וְהוּא שֶׁתְּהֵא צָרָה לְאַחַר מִיתָה.

Rebbi Yudan said, even Rebbi Eliezer[117] agrees. Rebbi Yose said, that is correct. Because, if somebody had children but they died before he died, is his widow not a candidate for levirate? There, if he had children at the moment of death. Here, if they were co-wives after his death[118].

117 Who holds in Halakhah 1 (Note 10) that a prohibition remains even if its cause has disappeared.

118 Only the status at the moment of the husband's death counts in matters of levirate. Everybody reads in *Deut.* 25:5: "one of them died while he left no child." Only the status at the moment of death counts; the prior history is irrelevant.

(fol. 4b) **משנה ט:** וְכוּלָּן שֶׁהָיוּ בָהֶן קִידּוּשִׁין אוֹ גֵירוּשִׁין בְּסָפֵק הֲרֵי אֵילּוּ חוֹלְצוֹת וְלֹא מִתְייַבְּמוֹת. כֵּיצַד סְפֵק קִידּוּשִׁין זָרַק לָהּ קִידּוּשֶׁיהָ סָפֵק קָרוֹב לוֹ סָפֵק קָרוֹב לָהּ זֶהוּ סְפֵק קִידּוּשִׁין. כֵּיצַד סְפֵק גֵירוּשִׁין כָּתַב בִּכְתָב יָדוֹ וְאֵין עָלָיו עֵדִים יֵשׁ עָלָיו עֵדִים וְאֵין בּוֹ זְמַן יֵשׁ בּוֹ זְמַן וְאֵין בּוֹ אֶלָּא עֵד אֶחָד זֶהוּ סְפֵק גֵירוּשִׁין.

Mishnah 9: In all cases[119] in which there were questionable *qiddushin* or divorces, the [co-wives] must perform *halîsah* but cannot have levirate. What are questionable *qiddushin*? If he threw the betrothal gift to her and there is a doubt whether it fell closer to him or to her, that are questionable *qiddushin*[120]. What is a questionable divorce? If [the divorce document] was written in his handwriting but without witnesses, or there are witnesses but no date, or there is a date but only one witness, these are questionable divorces[121].

119 If the relationship with any one of the 15 categories of prohibited women enumerated in Mishnah 1:1 was predicated on a marriage whose validity or dissolution was questionable, the co-wife cannot automatically be freed since the relationship might be nonexistent but she cannot have levirate since the relationship might be valid.

120 *Qiddushin* have two parts: Delivery of a gift to the prospective bride and a declaration by the groom that the gift is intended to make the

woman his bride. If a person stands in the public domain, it is assumed that any object within a circle of radius of 4 cubits with her in the center is acquired by that person upon expression of her will to receive that object. If now both stand in the public domain exactly 8 cubits apart and he throws the gift to her in the presence of two witnesses and it lands in the middle, it is impossible to determine up to the last micron whether most of it landed within her domain. {If both stand on his property, the gift must be properly delivered; if on her property, her property will acquire for her if she wants it. If they are more than 8 cubits apart and the gift is not completely inside her circle of acquisition, there are no *qiddushin*.}

In the Tosephta, 5:7, *qiddushin* are questionable because it was not established that the gift had the monetary value of at least a *peruta*.

121 These are all cases of illegal divorces which can be validated only in urgent cases (if the woman remarried on the basis of the document and is now pregnant.)

(fol. 5a) **הלכה ט:** וְכוּלָּן שֶׁהָיוּ בָהֶן קִידּוּשִׁין אוֹ גֵירוּשִׁין בְּסָפֵק הֲרֵי אֵילּוּ חוֹלְצוֹת וְלֹא מִתְייַבְּמוֹת כול'. לֵית כָּאן סְפֵק גֵירוּשִׁין מַמָּשׁ. כֵּיצַד סְפֵק קִידּוּשִׁין. זָרַק לָהּ קִידּוּשֶׁיהָ סָפֵק קָרוֹב לוֹ סָפֵק קָרוֹב לָהּ זֶהוּ סְפֵק קִידּוּשִׁין. וְהָכָא זָרַק לָהּ גִּיטָּהּ סָפֵק קָרוֹב לוֹ סָפֵק קָרוֹב לָהּ זֶהוּ סְפֵק גֵירוּשִׁין.

Halakhah 9: [122]"In all cases in which there were questionable *qiddushin* or divorces, the [co-wives] must perform *ḥalîṣah* but cannot have levirate," etc. There really is no questionable divorce here[123]. What are questionable *qiddushin*? If he threw the betrothal gift to her and there is a doubt whether it fell closer to him or to her, that are questionable *qiddushin*. And here, if he threw the divorce document to her[124] and there is a doubt whether it fell closer to him or to her, that is a questionable divorce.

122 The entire Halakhah is copied in *Giṭṭin* 9:2.

123 As noted, the divorce documents are formally defective but can be validated in hardship cases. Therefore, if the forbidden woman has remarried based on such a document and now has children from another man, there is no reason why Mishnah 8 should not be invoked by the former co-wife. Therefore, for matters of levirate such a divorce is valid under all circumstances. The corresponding text in *Giṭṭin* 9:2 (fol. 50b) reads: "There really is no questionable divorce but a real divorce." See the next paragraph.

124 A divorce document can be valid by biblical standards only when delivered to the woman (or her duly appointed representative), *Deut.* 24:1. This is a condition which cannot be waived.

רִבִּי יוֹחָנָן בְּשֵׁם רִבִּי חֲלַפְתָּא דְמִן הוה. וְכוּלָּן אִם נִשֵּׂאת בּוֹ לֹא תֵצֵא. שֶׁלֹּא לְהוֹצִיא לִיזָּה עַל בָּנֶיהָ. בִּתּוֹ שֶׁנִּשֵּׂאת לַשּׁוּק בְּגֵט זֶה לֹא תֵצֵא כְּדֵי לַזּוּק צָרָתָהּ לְאָבִיהָ. צָרָתָהּ שֶׁנִּשֵּׂאת לַשּׁוּק בְּגֵט זֶה תֵצֵא. בִּתּוֹ שֶׁנִּשֵּׂאת לְאָחִיו בְּגֵט זֶה תֵצֵא. צָרָתָהּ שֶׁנִּשֵּׂאת לְאָחִיו בְּגֵט זֶה אֲפִילוּ לְאָבִיהָ לֹא תֵצֵא.

Rebbi Joḥanan in the name of Rebbi Ḥalaphta from Haifa[125]: Any who were married on the basis of such a document should not leave[126] in order not to give a bad reputation to her children. His daughter who was married outside on the basis of such a document should not leave in order to damage her co-wife to her father[127]. Her co-wife who was married outside on the basis of such a document has to leave[128]. His daughter who married his brother on the basis of such a document has to leave[129]. Her co-wife who was married to his brother on the basis of such a document, or even to her father, should not leave[127].

125 The place name is corrupt in most sources. In the Babli, *Giṭṭin* 86 b, the statement appears in very abbreviated form.

126 Her marriage based on the flawed document should not be terminated to avoid tainting her children from the second husband as bastards.

127 If his daughter was married to his brother and divorced by one of these questionable documents, if later her ex-husband dies childless, her co-wife is permitted to her father in levirate. If the rabbinical establishment would force the termination of a second marriage, the co-wife would have to perform *ḥalîṣah* as possible co-wife of his daughter.

128 If his daughter was married to his brother and divorced by one of these questionable documents, if later her ex-husband dies childless, her former co-wife is permitted to her father and any outside marriage she contracts without *ḥalîṣah* is null and void.

129 If his daughter was married to his brother and divorced by one of these questionable documents, if later her ex-husband dies childless, any marriage of this daughter to one of the other paternal uncles is incestuous.

תַּנֵּי שְׁלֹשָׁה שְׁטָרוֹת הַלָּלוּ גוֹבֶה מִבְּנֵי חוֹרִין וְאֵינוֹ גוֹבֶה מִן הַמְשׁוּעֲבָדִים. אָמַר רִבִּי בָּא. הָדָא דְתֵימַר בְּשֶׁלֹּא הוּחְזַק בִּשְׁטָר בְּיַד הַמַּלְוֶה. אֲבָל הוּחְזַק הַשְּׁטָר בְּיַד הַמַּלְוֶה גוֹבֶה. רִבִּי יוֹסֵה בָּעֵי. אִם שֶׁלֹּא הוּחְזַק הַשְּׁטָר בְּיַד הַמַּלְוֶה אֲפִילוּ מִבְּנֵי חוֹרִין לֹא יִגְבֶּה. אֶלָּא כֵן אֲנָן קַיָּמִין בְּשֶׁהוּחְזַק הַשְּׁטָר בְּיַד הַמַּלְוֶה. וְלָמָּה אֵינוֹ גוֹבֶה. אָמַר רִבִּי בִּיסְנָא. מִפְּנֵי קֶינוֹנִיָּא. רִבִּי אָבוּן אָמַר. מִפְּנֵי שֶׁהוּא פָסוּל. עַד כְּדוֹן בְּשֶׁלָּוָה הַזָּקֵן וְשִׁיעְבֵּד הַזָּקֵן. לָוָה הַזָּקֵן וְשִׁיעְבֵּד הַבֵּן. אִית לָךְ מֵימָר מִפְּנֵי קֶינוֹנִיָּא. לֹא מִפְּנֵי שֶׁהוּא פָסוּל. וְהָכָא מִפְּנֵי שֶׁהוּא פָסוּל. אָמַר רִבִּי אָבוּן. וְהָא תַנֵּי אַף בְּגִיטֵּי נָשִׁים כֵּן. אִית לָךְ מֵימָר מִפְּנֵי קֶינוֹנִיָּא. לֹא מִפְּנֵי שֶׁהוּא פָסוּל. וְהָכָה מִפְּנֵי שֶׁהוּא פָסוּל.

It was stated: [A claim based on] any of these three types of documents[130] can be collected only from unincumbered property[131], not from mortgaged property. Rebbi Abba said, that means, if the document in the hand of the lender has not been confirmed. But if the document in the hand of the lender has been confirmed, he may collect[132]. Rebbi Yose asked: If the document in the hand of the lender has not been confirmed, he should not be able to collect even from unincumbered property! But one must deal with a document confirmed in the hand of the lender. And why can he not collect? Rebbi Bisna said, because of action in partnership[133]. Rebbi Abun said, because it is invalid. So far, if the old man took the loan and [later] the old man mortgaged[134]. But if the old man took the loan and [later] the son mortgaged, can you say because of a conspiracy? No, because it is invalid. And here, because it is invalid. Rebbi Abun said, and was it not stated[135]: The same holds for bills of divorce. Can you say there, because of action in partnership? No, because it is invalid. And here[136], because it is invalid.

130 A bill of debt executed in the manner of any of the three types of bills of divorce declared questionable in the Mishnah. In talmudic practice, mortgages were usually not executed for specified pieces of real estate but were liens on all real estate of the debtor (in his possession at the date of the document) to be satisfied in the order of execution (except for the money due to a wife at the dissolution of a marriage by divorce or death of the husband, which always takes precedence). Therefore, the date of a bill of debt determines its rank as a mortgage.

The problem is touched on very lightly in Babli, *Baba Batra* 176a.

131 Real estate acquired after any other bill of debt was executed.

132 No mortgage can be foreclosed unless the document and its signatures have been found to be genuine by a competent court.

133 Greek κοινωνία, used by LXX as translation (*Lev.* 5:21) of Hebrew תְשׂוּמֶת יָד, derived from the verb κοινωνέω, one of whose meanings is "to act in partnership". In talmudic literature, the word always has a pejorative meaning, "a criminal conspiracy". The lender and the borrower might conspire to defraud an earlier mortgage holder by predating the document. A sale of real estate cannot invalidate mortgage liens executed before the time of the sale. The lender and the borrower might also conspire to defraud any buyer of unincumbered real estate by pretending that the later loan predates the earlier sale. Since they would not find witnesses in good

standing to sign a predated document (and to testify before a court), they take their chance with an undated bill in the borrower's hand.

134 There might be a conspiracy if the borrower and the writer of the bill of debt are one and the same person. But if the borrower was the parent and the writer an heir, the *baraita* should have validated the document in this exceptional case just as the defective divorce document is validated in an exceptional case.

135 Quoted in slightly different form in Babli, *Baba Batra* 176a. This is all part of R. Abun's argument.

136 In the case of a bill of debt.

(fol. 4b) **משנה י:** שְׁלֹשָׁה אַחִים נְשׂוּאִין לְשָׁלֹשׁ נָשִׁים נָכְרִיּוֹת וּמֵת אֶחָד מֵהֶן וְעָשָׂה בָהּ שֵׁינִי מַאֲמָר וָמֵת הֲרֵי אֵילּוּ חוֹלְצוֹת וְלֹא מִתְייַבְּמוֹת שֶׁנֶּאֱמַר יְבָמָהּ יָבוֹא עָלֶיהָ. שֶׁעָלֶיהָ זִיקַת יָבָם אֶחָד וְלֹא שֶׁעָלֶיהָ זִיקַת שְׁנֵי יְבָמִין. רִבִּי שִׁמְעוֹן אוֹמֵר מְייַבֵּם לְאֵי זוֹ שֶׁיִּרְצֶה וְחוֹלֵץ לַשְּׁנִייָה.

Mishnah 10: Three brothers are married to three unrelated women. If one of them died, his second brother "bespeaks" her and then dies, these[137] perform *ḥalîṣah* but not levirate, as it is said: "Her levir shall come to her[138]," if on her is the candidacy from one brother but not from two. Rebbi Simeon says, he takes in levirate the one he prefers and performs *ḥalîṣah* with the other[139].

137 The two widows who now are candidates for levirate with the third brother. If the second brother had not "bespoken" the first widow, he would have been free to marry both of the widows. Now that the first widow is quasi-married to the second brother, she cannot be married by the third brother; therefore the quasi-co-wife also is barred. But since the first widow is only partially forbidden, both require *ḥalîṣah*.

138 *Deut*. 25:5. The Mishnah in the Babli and most Mishnah mss. also quote

the beginning of the verse: "If brothers live together and *one* of them dies, . . ."

139 Rebbi Simeon holds that bespeaking either acquires completely or not at all (Halakhah 2:1). If it acquires completely, both widows are widows of the second brother, and the influence of the first is eliminated; the third may marry one in levirate and then the other would be freed without ceremony. If "bespeaking" does not acquire, the two women are widows of different brothers and both are permitted to the third in levirate. Because of the doubt, the third can marry only one of the widows and has to perform *ḥalîṣah* with the other.

(fol. 5a) **הלכה י:** שְׁלֹשָׁה אַחִין נְשׂוּאִין לְשָׁלֹשׁ נָשִׁים כול'. אִילּוּ שׁוֹמֶרֶת יָבָם שֶׁנָּפְלָה לִפְנֵי כַמָּה יְבָמִים שֶׁמָּא אֵינָהּ מִתְייַבֶּמֶת. תַּנֵּי רִבִּי חִייָא. אֵשֶׁת אֶחָד מִתְייַבֶּמֶת. לֹא אֵשֶׁת שְׁנֵי מֵתִים. נִיחָא חוֹלֵץ לְבַעֲלַת מַאֲמָר. עַל שֵׁם אֵשֶׁת מֵת אֶחָד מִתְייַבֶּמֶת וְלֹא אֵשֶׁת שְׁנֵי מֵתִים. שְׁנִייָה לָמָּר אֵינָהּ מִתְייַבֶּמֶת. אָמַר רִבִּי לְעָזָר. דְּרִבִּי מֵאִיר הִיא. דְּאָמַר רִבִּי מֵאִיר. כָּל־שֶׁאֵין אַתְּ מְייַבְּמֵנוֹ אֵין אַתְּ מְייַבֵּם צָרָתוֹ. אָמַר רִבִּי יוֹחָנָן. אִם אֲמָרָהּ רִבִּי לְעָזָר מִנִּי שְׁמָעָהּ וַאֲמָרָהּ. אָמַר רִבִּי יוֹסֵי. מַתְנִיתָא אָמְרָה כֵן. בֶּן תֵּשַׁע שָׁנִים וְיוֹם אֶחָד שֶׁבָּא עַל יְבִמְתּוֹ מִשֶּׁהִגְדִּיל וְנָשָׂא אִשָּׁה אַחֶרֶת. אִם לֹא יָדַע אֶת הָרִאשׁוֹנָה מִשֶּׁהִגְדִּיל הַשְּׁנִייָה אוֹ חוֹלֶצֶת אוֹ מִתְייַבֶּמֶת. הָרִאשׁוֹנָה חוֹלֶצֶת וְלֹא מִתְייַבֶּמֶת. הָכָא אַתְּ אוֹמֵר. חוֹלֶצֶת. וְהָכָא אַתְּ אוֹמֵר. מִתְייַבֶּמֶת. הָא דְאַתְּ אָמַר חוֹלֶצֶת רִבִּי מֵאִיר וְרִבִּי שִׁמְעוֹן. וְהֵן דְּאַתְּ אָמַר מִתְייַבֶּמֶת רִבִּי שִׁמְעוֹן וְרַבָּנָן. רִבִּי אָבוּן רִבִּי בִּיסְנָא בְשֵׁם רִבִּי אָחָא. וְהוּא שֶׁייִבֵּם וְאַחַר כָּךְ חָלַץ. אֲבָל אִם חָלַץ בַּתְּחִילָּה אָסוּר. שֶׁמָּא קָנָה מַאֲמָר וְנִפְטְרָה בַּחֲלִיצַת חֲבֵירָתָהּ.

Halakhah 10: "Three brothers married to three women," etc. Can a woman waiting for a levir who became available to several brothers-in-law not be married in levirate[140]? Rebbi Ḥiyya stated: The wife of one [dead husband] is married in levirate, not the wife of two dead[137]. One understands that he has to perform *ḥalîṣah* with the "bespoken" because the wife of one [dead husband] is married in levirate, not the wife of two dead. Why can the other one not be married in levirate? Rebbi Eleazar said, this follows Rebbi Meïr, since Rebbi Meïr said, of any one you cannot marry in levirate, you cannot marry the co-wife in levirate[141]. Rebbi Joḥanan said, if Rebbi Eleazar formulated this, he formulated what he had heard from me[142]. Rebbi Yose said, a Mishnah said so: "[143]A boy at least nine years and one day old who had intercourse with his sister-in-law[144] and when he grew up he married another wife; if he never had intercourse with the first again after he became an adult[145], the second [wife] may perform *ḥalîṣah* or be married in levirate[146]. The first one must perform *ḥalîṣah* and cannot be married in levirate." Here you say, she performs *ḥalîṣah*; there you say, she is married in levirate[147]! Where you say she performs *ḥalîṣah*, Rebbi Meïr and Rebbi Simeon; where you say, she is married in levirate, Rebbi Simeon and the rabbis[148]. Rebbi Abun bar Bisna in the name of Rebbi Aḥa, but only if first he[149] married in levirate and then performed *ḥalîṣah*. But if he performed *ḥalîṣah* first, it is forbidden; perhaps "bespeaking" acquired and she was freed by her co-wife's *ḥalîṣah*.

140 Since the verse also speak of the levir in the singular, one might infer that the laws of levirate apply only to a single levir. But this is certainly not the case.

141 Also quoted in Chapter 1, cf. Note 116.

142 Cf. Berakhot 2, Note 53.

143 Mishnah 10:9.

The sex act of a minor less than 9 years old has no legal consequences. If the boy is at 9 years and one day old, his sex act counts (if a married woman sleeps with him, she is criminally liable for adultery but he is not responsible since he is a minor.) A minor cannot acquire in general; therefore, his sex act corresponds to "bespeaking" for adults and the disagreement between the rabbis and Rebbi Simeon about the legal consequences of "bespeaking" extends to those of the sex act by a minor close to puberty.

144 Widow of an older brother who had died childless.

145 For the rabbis, she is partially his wife; for R. Simeon, she either is his wife or she is not his wife.

146 With a third brother, if the second brother also dies childless.

147 In Mishnah 3:10, neither woman can be married. In Mishnah 10:9, one of them can be married even though the legal situation is the same!

148 In both Mishnaiot, R. Simeon holds that the third brother may marry one of the widows without restriction. In Mishnah 3:10, the anonymous Tanna is Rebbi Meïr; in Mishnah 10:9 he is another Tanna who admits the possibility that only one of the widows may be a candidate for levirate. In Tosephta 5:7, R. Yose (ben Ḥalaphta) holds that in the situation of Mishnah 3:10, the second widow may be married, parallel to the opinion of the Tanna of 10:9.

149 The third brother. In the Tosephta, this is a tannaitic statement attributed to R. Eleazar ben Rebbi Simeon, following his father's doctrine. The *ḥalîṣah* of one of the widows frees the other; the marriage of the second has no influence on the status of the first.

(fol. 4b) **משנה יא:** שְׁנֵי אַחִין נְשׂוּאִין לִשְׁתֵּי אֲחָיוֹת וּמֵת אֶחָד מֵהֶן וְאַחַר כָּךְ מֵתָה אִשְׁתּוֹ שֶׁלַּשֵּׁנִי הֲרֵי זוֹ אֲסוּרָה עָלָיו עוֹלָמִית הוֹאִיל וְנֶאֶסְרָה עָלָיו שָׁעָה אַחַת.

Mishnah 11: Two brothers are married to two sisters. If one of them died and then the wife of the other died, she[150] is eternally forbidden to him since she was forbidden one moment.

150 The wife of the first brother who had died childless. Since at the time of death of the first the wife of the second was alive, there could not

have been any levirate. If levirate is forbidden at the time of death of the husband, it is permanently forbidden (since in *Deut*. 25:5 both the death of one and the marriage of the other are mentioned.)

(fol. 5a) **הלכה יא:** שְׁנֵי אַחִין נְשׂוּאִין לִשְׁתֵּי אֲחָיוֹת כול׳. אָמַר רִבִּי אֲבִינָא. הָדָא הִיא דְאָמַר רִבִּי הִילָא רִבִּי יוֹסֵי בְּשֵׁם רִבִּי יוֹחָנָן. לֹא דוֹמֶה אִיסּוּר אֲחָיוֹת יְבָמוֹת לְאִיסּוּר אֲחָיוֹת שֶׁאֵינָן יְבָמוֹת.

Halakhah 11: "Two brothers married to two sisters," etc. Rebbi Avina said, that is what Rebbi Hila, Rebbi Yose, said in the name of Rebbi Joḥanan: The prohibition of sisters who are sisters-in-law does not compare with the prohibition of sisters who not are sisters-in-law[112].

(fol. 4b) **משנה יב:** שְׁנַיִם שֶׁקִּידְּשׁוּ שְׁתֵּי נָשִׁים וּבִשְׁעַת כְּנִיסָתָן לַחוּפָּה הֶחֱלִיפוּ אֶת שֶׁלָּזֶה בָּזֶה וְאֶת שֶׁלָּזֶה לָזֶה. הֲרֵי אֵילּוּ חַייָבִין מִשּׁוּם אֵשֶׁת אִישׁ הָיוּ אַחִין חַייָבִין אַף מִשּׁוּם אֵשֶׁת אָח. וְאִם הָיוּ אֲחָיוֹת חַייָבִין אַף מִשּׁוּם אִשָּׁה עַל אֲחוֹתָהּ. וְאִם הָיוּ נִידּוֹת חַייָבִין אַף מִשּׁוּם נִידּוֹת. וְכוּלָּן (fol. 4c) מַפְרִישִׁין אוֹתָן שְׁלֹשָׁה חֳדָשִׁים שֶׁמָּא מְעוּבָּרוֹת הֵן וְאִם הָיוּ קְטַנּוֹת שֶׁאֵינָן רְאוּיִין לֵילֵד מַחֲזִירִין אוֹתָן מִיָּד. וְאִם הָיוּ כוֹהֲנוֹת נִפְסְלוּ מִן הַתְּרוּמָה.

Mishnah 12: If two men gave *qiddushin* to two women and when they entered the bridal chamber[151] they switched each of them to the other[152], they are guilty of [adultery with] a married woman. If they were brothers, they also are guilty because of [the prohibition of] the brother's wife. If they were sisters, they are guilty also because of [the prohibition of] "a woman in addition to her sister". If they were menstruating, they are guilty also because of [the prohibition of] menstruating women[153].

And all of these one separates for three months to see whether they are pregnant. If they were minors not able yet to have children one returns them at once. If they were from priestly families they are disabled for heave[154].

151 The act of marriage itself which was preceded by a public ceremony and which validates the marriage in terms of civil law. The meaning of "bridal canopy" given today to the word חוּפָּה is comparatively recent, not older than about 1000 years. In terms of criminal law, the couple are married from the time of qiddushin; therefore, the marriage with the wrong wife constitutes adultery.

152 Inadvertently, maybe because they never had seen their brides beforehand.

153 It is possible to commit 4 deadly sins in one act; this would require 8 purification offerings per pair.

154 *Lev.* 22:13 states that the daughter of a Cohen married to a non-Cohen who becomes a widow may return to her family to eat from holy food only is she is "as in her maidenhood", that she could be married by a Cohen. But a woman who had illicit sex, even as a rape victim, is forbidden to a Cohen.

(fol. 5a) **הלכה יא:** אִם בָּא עַל הַשְּׁנִייָה חַייָב שְׁתַּיִים. מִשּׁוּם אֵשֶׁת אָח וּמִשּׁוּם אִשָּׁה עַל אֲחוֹתָהּ.

Halakhah 11: If he had intercourse with the second he is two times guilty, for the brother's wife and for "a woman in addition to her sister"[155].

155 The formulation is elliptic. It is asserted (1) that entering the bridal chamber is not sinful, only the intercourse is; (2) that prohibited acts can be added together. The Babli has great difficulties with multiple guilt for one act; that problem is not mentioned in the Yerushalmi except for procedural problems in criminal law.

תַּנֵּי רִבִּי חִייָא. פְּעָמִים אַרְבַּע פְּעָמִים שְׁמוֹנֶה פְּעָמִים שְׁתֵּים עֶשְׂרֵה פְּעָמִים שֵׁשׁ עֶשְׂרֵה. הֲרֵי אֵילּוּ חַייָבִין מִשֵּׁם אֵשֶׁת אִישׁ הָהֵן תַּרְתֵּיי הָהֵן תַּרְתֵּיי. הָיוּ אַחִין מִשֵּׁם אֵשֶׁת אָח הָהֵן אַרְבַּע וְהָהֵן אַרְבַּע. אִם הָיוּ אֲחָיוֹת מִשֵּׁם אִשָּׁה עַל אֲחוֹתָהּ הָהֵן שִׁיתָא וְהָהֵן שִׁיתָא. אִם הָיוּ נִידּוֹת מִשֵּׁם נִידָּה הָהֵן תְּמָנֵי וְהָהֵן תְּמָנֵי. הֵן קְטַנִּים וְהֵן גְּדוֹלוֹת פְּטוּרִין. וְכוּלָּן הֵן גְּדוֹלִין וְהֵן קְטַנּוֹת חַייָבִין שְׁתַּיִים שְׁתַּיִים מִשּׁוּם נִידָּה. וְאִם הִשִּׂיאָן אֲבִיהֶן מִשּׁוּם שְׁמוֹנֶה. הָיוּ אֶחָד גָּדוֹל וְאֶחָד קָטוֹן. הַנִּבְעֶלֶת מִן הַקָּטָן חַייֶבֶת מִשּׁוּם אִשְׁתּוֹ שֶׁלַּגָּדוֹל. הַנִּבְעֶלֶת מִן הַגָּדוֹל פְּטוּרָה מִשּׁוּם אִשְׁתּוֹ שֶׁלַּקָּטָן.

Rebbi Ḥiyya stated[156]: Sometimes four times, sometimes eight times, sometimes twelve times, sometimes sixteen times[157]. They are guilty under the heading of adultery with a married woman, each couple for two. If they were brothers, under the heading of "brother's wife", each couple for four. If they were sisters, under the heading of "a wife together with her sister", each couple six. If they were menstruating, under the heading of "menstruating", each couple eight. If the men are minors and the women adults, they are free[158]. If the men are adults and the women minors, they are obligated two by two because of menstruation[159]. If their father married them off, for all eight. If one of the men was an adult and the other a minor, the one who had intercourse with the minor is guilty as wife of the adult but the one who had intercourse with the adult is free as wife of the minor.

156 Tosephta 5:8-9, in a slightly different wording. A very short quote of the Tosephta in Babli, 33b.

157 Since four persons are involved, each transgression implies punishment for four people. The total number of crimes (or purification sacrifices) must be a multiple of four.

158 The minors cannot legally marry; it is impossible to commit adultery with their wives.

159 Since a minor girl cannot legally

marry except if given in marriage by her father, in the absence of a father the only inadvertent crime possible is that of intercourse with a menstruating woman. But if the father married the girls off, they are legally married and all four sins are possible.

רִבִּי בָּא בְשֵׁם רִבִּי יִרְמְיָה. אֲנוּסָה אֵינָהּ צְרִיכָה לְהַמְתִּין שְׁלֹשָׁה חֳדָשִׁים. וְהָא תְנָן. מַפְרִישִׁין אוֹתָן שְׁלֹשָׁה חֳדָשִׁים שֶׁמָּא מְעוּבָּרוֹת הֵן. אִם הָיוּ קְטַנּוֹת שֶׁאֵינָן רְאוּיִין לְוָלָד מַחֲזִירִין אוֹתָן מִיָּד. שַׁנְיָיא הִיא מִפְּנֵי תִּיקּוּן הַוָּלָד.

Rebbi Abba in the name of Rebbi Jeremiah: A rape victim does not have to wait three months[160]. But did we not state: "One separates them for three month to see whether they are pregnant. If they were minors not yet able to have children one returns them at once." That is different, it is for the benefit of the child[161].

160 That statement is tannaitic in the Babli, 35a, and ascribed to the Tanna R. Yose. R. Jehudah is reported to require separation of a raped wife from her husband for three months. R. Yose, in the interpretation of Abbai, is confident that the rape victim will know how to rid herself of the unwanted semen. That argument seems so obvious to the Yerushalmi that it is not necessary to mention it.

161 If the woman is pregnant from the unintended adultery, the child is a bastard and permitted to marry another bastard. If she were allowed immediately to return to her husband, any child would be a possible bastard and forbidden to marry either a regular person or a bastard.

אִם הָיוּ כּוֹהֲנוֹת נִפְסְלוּ מִן הַתְּרוּמָה. אָמַר רִבִּי יוֹסֵי. זֹאת אוֹמֶרֶת שֶׁהָאוֹנְסִין פּוֹסְלִין בִּכְהוּנָּה כְּאֵשֶׁת אִישׁ.

"If they were from priestly families they are disabled for heave." Rebbi Yose said, this implies that rape disables in priestly families like adultery[162].

162 Mishnah 6:5 quotes the opinion of the anonymous majority that the "harlot" forbidden to a Cohen in *Lev.* 21:7 is either a libertine or a woman "subject to illegitimate sexual relations" without any consideration of intent. While a non-priestly husband keeps his raped wife, the Cohen is forced to divorce her, even against his will.

החולץ פרק רביעי

(fol. 5b) **משנה א:** הַחוֹלֵץ לִיבִמְתּוֹ וְנִמְצֵאת מְעוּבֶּרֶת וְיָלְדָה בִּזְמַן שֶׁהַוְּלָד שֶׁלְּקַייָמָא הוּא מוּתָּר בִּקְרוֹבוֹתֶיהָ וְהִיא מוּתֶּרֶת בִּקְרוֹבָיו. וְלֹא פְסָלָהּ מִן הַכְּהוּנָּה. אֵין הַוְּלָד שֶׁלְּקַייָמָא הוּא אָסוּר בִּקְרוֹבוֹתֶיהָ וְהִיא אֲסוּרָה בִּקְרוֹבָיו. וּפְסָלָהּ מִן הַכְּהוּנָּה.

Mishnah 1: If somebody performed *ḥalîṣah* with his sister-in-law but she turns out to have been pregnant and gives birth, if it is a live birth her relatives are permitted to him and his relatives are permitted to her; he has not disabled her [from marrying into] priesthood[1]. If it is a still birth, her relatives are forbidden to him and his relatives are forbidden to her; he has disabled her [from marrying into] priesthood[2].

1 Even though usually וולד של קיימא denotes a child surviving more than 30 days; in case of levirate, Mishnah *Niddah* 5:3 states that a one day old baby causes levirate (if the husband died childless one day after a brother was born to him) and frees from levirate (if the pregnant widow gave birth to a live baby). Then her late husband potentially had a child when he died, there can be no levirate or *ḥalîṣah* and, legally, the ceremony never happened.

2 The ceremony is valid; she is (rabbinically) under all rules of a divorcee from the brother.

הלכה א: הַחוֹלֵץ לִיבִמְתּוֹ וְנִמְצֵאת מְעוּבֶּרֶת כול'. בְּשֶׁעָבַר הָא כַתְּחִילָּה לֹא. דֵּי מַתְנִיתָא הַיְּבָמָה לֹא תַחֲלוֹץ וְלֹא תִתְיַבֵּם עַד שֶׁיְּהֵא לָהּ שְׁלֹשָׁה חֳדָשִׁים. וְתַחֲלוֹץ מִיָּד. מַה נַפְשָׁךְ. אִם בֶּן קַייָמָא הוּא לֹא נָגְעָה בָהּ חֲלִיצָה. אִם אֵינוֹ בֶּן קַייָמָא הוּא הֲרֵי חֲלִיצָתָהּ בְּיָדָהּ. רִבִּי זְעִירָה רִבִּי חִייָה בְּשֵׁם רִבִּי בּוּן בְּשֵׁם רִבִּי יוֹחָנָן. שֶׁלֹּא תְהֵא צְרִיכָה כְרוּז לִכְהוּנָּה. רִבִּי בָּא רִבִּי יַעֲקֹב בַּר אִידִי בְּשֵׁם רִבִּי

הוֹשַׁעְיָה. שֶׁלֹּא תְהֵא צְרִיכָה כְרוּז לִכְהוּנָּה. תַּנֵּי רִבִּי הוֹשַׁעְיָה. מֵאֵן יְבָמִי. אֶת שֶׁאוֹמְרִים לוֹ. יַיבֵּם. אוֹמְרִים לוֹ. חֲלוֹץ. וְאֶת שֶׁאֵין אוֹמְרִים לוֹ. יַיבֵּם. אֵין אוֹמְרִים לוֹ. חֲלוֹץ. מַה נְפַק מִן בֵּינֵיהוֹן. הָיְתָה כְשֵׁירָה וְנִתְחַלְּלָה. כְּגוֹן אַלְמָנָה לְכֹהֵן גָּדוֹל וּגְרוּשָׁה וַחֲלוּצָה לְכֹהֵן הֶדְיוֹט. מָאן דְּאָמַר. שֶׁלֹּא תְהֵא צְרִיכָה כְרוּז לִכְהוּנָּה. וְזוּ (fol. 5c) הוֹאִיל וְאֵינָהּ צְרִיכָה כְּרוּז לִכְהוּנָּה חוֹלֶצֶת. מָאן דְּאָמַר. אֶת שֶׁאוֹמְרִים לוֹ יַיבֵּם. אוֹמְרִים לוֹ. חֲלוֹץ.

Halakhah 1: "If somebody performed *ḥalîṣah* with his sister-in-law but she turns out to have been pregnant," etc. If he transgressed, but not from the start[3]. That follows the Mishnah[4]: "The widow should not perform *ḥalîṣah* or have levirate until after three months." Why can she not have *ḥalîṣah* immediately? As you take it, if she has a live birth, *ḥalîṣah* did not affect her[1]. If she has a still birth, she holds *ḥalîṣah* in her hand. Rebbi Ze'ira, Rebbi Ḥiyya, Rebbi Abun in the name of Rebbi Joḥanan, that she should not need a proclamation for the priesthood[5]. Rebbi Abba, Rebbi Jacob bar Idi, in the name of Rebbi Hoshaiah, that she should not need a proclamation for the priesthood. Rebbi Hoshaiah stated: "My levir refuses[6]." To the one to whom one says: perform levirate, to him one says: perform *ḥalîṣah*; but to the one to whom one cannot say: perform levirate, to him one cannot say: perform *ḥalîṣah*! What is the difference between them? If she had been acceptable and was desecrated[7], e. g., a widow for the High Priest or a divorcee or one who had performed *ḥalîṣah* for a common priest. According to him who says that she should not need a proclamation for the priesthood; that one, who does not need a proclamation for the priesthood, should have *ḥalîṣah*. According to him who says that to the one to whom one says: perform levirate, to him does one say: perform *ḥalîṣah*?[8]

3 The Mishnah is formulated "if it happened", not that it should be the rule.

4 Mishnah 4:11. To ascertain that the widow is not pregnant. Before that time, *ḥalîṣah* is not needed since she could not remarry even if she had children, for the same reason.

5 Since *ḥalîṣah* prevents a woman from marrying a priest, an invalid *ḥalîṣah* demands public proclamations by the town crier (a herald, Greek κῆρυξ), to make sure people would not think that her children from a Cohen are desecrated. The same argument in Babli 41b. Cf. also Chapter 16, Note 11.

6 *Deut.* 25:7. As long as the levir is not required to marry her, she cannot claim that he refused. The same argument in Babli 41b.

7 By a marriage contracted in violation of the holiness prohibitions, *Lev.* 21:7,14.

8 The answer, that still even a desecrated woman cannot remarry for 90 days after her husband's death, is missing. This is either a scribal omission or it is assumed that everybody will be able to supply the rest of the argument.

חָלַץ בְּתוֹךְ שְׁלֹשָׁה חֳדָשִׁים מַהוּ שֶׁתְּהֵא צְרִיכָה לְאַחַר שְׁלֹשָׁה חֳדָשִׁים. נִישְׁמְעִינָהּ מִן הָדָא. קְטַנָּה שֶׁחָלְצָה תַּחֲלוֹץ מִשֶּׁתַּגְדִּיל. וְאִם חָלְצָה חֲלִיצָתָהּ כְּשֵׁירָה. רִבִּי מָנָא אָמַר לָהּ סְתָם. רִבִּי יִצְחָק בְּרֵיהּ דְּרִבִּי חִייָה מָטֵי בָהּ בְּשֵׁם רִבִּי יוֹחָנָן. דְּרִבִּי מֵאִיר הִיא. דְּרִבִּי מֵאִיר אָמַר. אֵין חוֹלְצִין וְאֵין מְייַבְּמִין אֶת הַקְּטַנָּה שֶׁמָּא תִימָּצֵא אַיילוֹנִית. כְּמַה דְּאַתְּ אָמַר תַּמָּן אַף עַל פִּי שֶׁחָלְצָה חוֹלֶצֶת. וְהָכָא נַמִּי אַף עַל פִּי שֶׁחָלְצָה חוֹלֶצֶת.

If there was *ḥalîṣah* during these three months, does she need another one after three months? Let us hear from the following[9]: "A minor who performed *ḥalîṣah* should perform *ḥalîṣah* after she grows up; if she performed [only one] *ḥalîṣah*, the *ḥalîṣah* she performed is valid[10]." Rebbi Mana said it anonymously, Rebbi Isaac the son of Rebbi Ḥiyya brought it in the name of Rebbi Joḥanan[11]; this is Rebbi Meïr's, since Rebbi Meïr says one does neither perform *ḥalîṣah* nor levirate with a minor: maybe she would turn out to be a she-ram[12]. As you say there, even though she already performed *ḥalîṣah*, she again performs *ḥalîṣah*; so here also though she did perform *ḥalîṣah*, she performs *ḥalîṣah*[13].

9 Mishnah 12:5.

10 In a plurality of mss. of the Babylonian Mishnah, "not valid". A minor cannot perform acts that are legally valid, but the essence of *ḥalîṣah* is the declaration of the levir, by necessity an adult, that he refuses to marry the widow.

11 In the parallel in Chapter 12, R. Jonah instead of R. Joḥanan.

12 R. Meïr is known in many cases to require attention to possibilities that are seldom realities. For a she-ram, levirate is forbidden and *ḥalîṣah* unnecessary. The same argument in Babli *Bekhorot* 19b; a detailed discussion in Tosaphot *ad. loc., s. v.* **איש**.

13 If *ḥalîṣah* was performed early, against the rules, it has to be performed again after the three months have passed but, in case this was not done, the first *ḥalîṣah* is valid.

רִבִּי יוּדָן בָּעֵי. חָלַץ לָהּ מְעוּבֶּרֶת וְהִפִּילָה. נִישְׁמְעִינָהּ מִן הָדָא. הֲרֵי שֶׁמֵּת וְהִנִּיחַ אֶת אִשְׁתּוֹ מְעוּבֶּרֶת יָכוֹל תְּהֵא זְקוּקָה לְיָבָם. תַּלְמוּד לוֹמַר וְלֹא יִמָּחֶה שְׁמוֹ מִיִּשְׂרָאֵל. אֶת שֶׁשְּׁמוֹ מָחוּי. תַּלמוּד לוֹמַר. לְהָקִים לְאָחִיו שֵׁם בְּיִשְׂרָאֵל. עַד שֶׁתֵּדַע אִם בֶּן קַייָמָה הוּא אִם אֵינוֹ בֶּן קַייָמָה. יָכוֹל אַף אֵשֶׁת סָרִיס תְּהֵא צְרִיכָה לְיִיבּוּם. תַּלְמוּד לוֹמַר וְלֹא יִמָּחֶה שְׁמוֹ מִיִּשְׂרָאֵל. אֶת שֶׁאֵין שְׁמוֹ מָחוּי. יָצָא זֶה שֶׁ(אין)[14] שְׁמוֹ מָחוּי.

Rebbi Yudan asked: If he performed *ḥalîṣah* with a pregnant woman and she had a miscarriage[15]? Let us hear from the following: If somebody died and left a pregnant widow, should I think that she must have recourse to her levir[16]? The verse says, "that his name should not be extinguished from Israel," only one whose name is extinguished[17]. The verse says, "to establish a name in Israel for his brother," until you know whether there is a live child or not[18]. I could think that the wife of an eunuch should need levirate, the verse says "that his name should not be extinguished from Israel," only one whose name is not extinguished; this excludes this one whose name was already extinguished[19].

14 Scribal error, copying a frequent expression; it is not reasonable to follow the commentators in simply deleting the word. The sentence is a copy of the corresponding one in *Sifry Deut.* #289: יָצָא זֶה שֶׁכְּבָר שְׁמוֹ מָחוּי. This makes eminent sense and is the basis of the translation.

15 Is the procedure valid if intended as a precaution in case the woman had a miscarriage?

16 At the moment of death, the husband was childless.

17 But not one who had the potential of offspring at the time of his death.

18 The early *ḥalîṣah* is of no legal value.

19 Before his death.

יָכוֹל אוֹמֵר. צָרָתָהּ מוּתֶּרֶת לְהִינָּשֵׂא. הַכּוֹנֵס אֶת יְבִימְתּוֹ וְנִמְצֵאת מְעוּבֶּרֶת כְּמָה דְאַתְּ אָמַר. צָרָתָהּ לֹא תִינָּשֵׂא עַד שֶׁתֵּדַע בְּמָה הִיא מוּתֶּרֶת אִם בְּעִיבּוּר אִם בְּבִיאָה. אַף בַּחֲלוּצָה כֵן. חֲלִיצָה פְטוֹר וּבִיאָה פְטוֹר. כְּמָה דְתֵימַר בְּבִיאָה כָּךְ אִיתְאֲמַר בַּחֲלִיצָה.

Could I say, her[20] co-wife may remarry? "[21]He who marries his sister-in-law and she turns out to be pregnant," as you say, "her co-wife cannot marry until you know by which means she is permitted, whether by pregnancy or by intercourse[22]" The same is valid for the one who performed *ḥalîṣah*. *Ḥalîṣah* frees and intercourse frees[23]. As you said it for intercourse so it was said for *ḥalîṣah*.

20 The pregnant woman who performed *ḥalîṣah*.

21 Similar *baraitot* are in Babli, 36a, Tosephta 6:3.

22 Whether the deceased finally had a posthumous child and the rules of levirate do not apply or whether she is freed by the levirate of her co-wife, which is justified after the fact if the widow has a miscarriage or a still birth.

23 The co-wife.

שְׁמוּאֵל אָמַר. זָכִין בָּעוּבָּרִין. רִבִּי לְעָזָר אָמַר. אֵין זָכִין בָּעוּבָּרִין. אָמַר רִבִּי יוֹסֵי. אַף עַל גַּב דִּשְׁמוּאֵל אָמַר זָכִין לָעוּבָּרִין. מוֹדֵי הוּא שֶׁיָּצָא רֹאשׁוֹ וְרוּבּוֹ

בְּחַיִּים. דֵּי מַתְנִיתָא הַחוֹלֵץ לִיבִמְתּוֹ וְנִמְצֵאת מְעוּבֶּרֶת. כְּמָה דְאַתְּ אָמַר כָּאן. הוּא לְמַפְרֵעַ לֹא נָֽגְעָה בָהּ חֲלִיצָה. וְהָכָא בֵּ(י)ן[24] הוּא לְמַפְרֵעַ וְהוּא שֶׁיִּזְכֶּה. תַּמָּן תַּנִּינָן. הָאוֹמֵר. אִם יָֽלְדָה אִשְׁתִּי זָכָר יִטּוֹל מָנֶה. יָֽלְדָה זָכָר נוֹטֵל מָנֶה. אִם נְקֵיבָה מָאתַיִם. יָֽלְדָה נְקֵיבָה נוֹטֶלֶת מָאתַיִם. רִבִּי לָֽעְזָר אָמַר. לֹא אָֽמְרוּ אֶלָּא בְנוֹ. הָא אַחֵר לֹא. רִבִּי יוֹסָה אָמַר. אֲפִילוּ אַחֵר. עַל דַּעְתֵּיהּ דְּרִבִּי לָֽעְזָר וּבִלְבַד שְׁכִיב מְרַע. הָא בָרִיא לֹא. בִּלְבַד בְּמִטַּלְטְלִין. הָא קַרְקָעוֹת לֹא. מַתְנִיתָא פְלִיגָא עַל רִבִּי לָֽעְזָר. גֵּר שֶׁמֵּת וּבִיזְבְּזוּ יִשְׂרָאֵל אֶת נְכָסָיו. וְנוֹדַע שֶׁיֵּשׁ לוֹ בֵן בִּמְדִינַת הַיָּם אוֹ שֶׁהָֽיְתָה עִיבְּרָה. הַכֹּל חַייָבִין לְהַחֲזִיר. מַה עָבַד לָהּ רִבִּי לָֽעְזָר. שַׁנְייָא הִיא הָכָא שֶׁהוּא בְנוֹ. וְסֵיפָה פְלִיגָא עַל שְׁמוּאֵל מִן הָדָא דְרִבִּי יוֹסָה. הֶחֱזִירוּ הַכֹּל. אַחַר כָּךְ מֵת הַבֵּן אוֹ שֶׁהִפִּילָה. כָּל־הַקּוֹדֵם בָּאַחֲרוֹנָה זָכָה. בָּרִאשׁוֹנָה לֹא זָכָה. אֲפִילוּ בָרִאשׁוֹנָה לֹא יִזְכֶּה. לֹא כֵן אָמַר רִבִּי יוֹסֵה. אַף עַל גַּב דִּשְׁמוּאֵל אָמַר. זָכִין לָעוּבָּרִין. מוֹדֵי וְהוּא שֶׁיָּצָא רֹאשׁוֹ וְרוּבּוֹ בַחַיִּים. הֲרֵי אֵינוֹ בֶּן קַייָמָה. אָמַר רִבִּי יִצְחָק בַּר אֶלְעָזָר. מִשּׁוּם יֵיאוּשׁ. רַבָּנִין דְּקֵיסָרִין רִבִּי חִייָה בַּר וָא בְשֵׁם רִבִּי אַבָּא בַּר נָתָן. חָזַר בָּהּ רִבִּי נָתָן. מִן מַתְנִיתָא. אִם זָכָר מָנֶה. אִם נְקֵיבָה מָאתַיִם. וּנְקֵיבָה גַּבָּהּ לֹא בְעִנְייָן כְּאַחֵר הוּא. תַּנֵּי בַּר קַפָּרָא. בֶּן יוֹמוֹ זָכִין לוֹ.

Samuel said, one can transfer benefits to fetuses; Rebbi Eleazar said, one cannot transfer benefits to fetuses[24]. Rebbi Yose[25] said, even though Samuel said, one can transfer benefits to fetuses, he agrees that most of [the fetus's] head and body must come out alive[26]. That is the Mishnah, "if somebody performed *ḥalîṣah* with his sister-in-law but she turns out to have been pregnant," as you say here, retroactively *ḥalîṣah* did not touch her, so retroactively the child is a son and receives the benefit[27]. There, we have stated: "If somebody says, if my wife gives birth to a male, he shall take a mina[28], if she gave birth to a male, [the male baby] will take a mina. If a female, 200 [drachmae], if she gave birth to a female, that one will take 200." Rebbi Eleazar said, this is only for his son, but not for any other. Rebbi Yasa[29] said, even any other. In the opinion of Rebbi Eleazar, only from a sick person, but not a healthy one; only movables but not real estate[30]. A *baraita* disagrees with Rebbi Eleazar. "[31]If a proselyte died and Jews plundered his estate, then it became known that he had a son overseas or that [his wife] was pregnant, everybody is required to return [what he took]." What does Rebbi Eleazar do with this[32]? There is a difference because it is his child. The second part [of the Mishnah] disagrees with Samuel in the interpretation of Rebbi Yose: "If they returned everything and then the son died[33] or she had a miscarriage[34], anybody who takes first *after that* acquires it." The first group did not acquire. Even at the beginning they should not have acquired! Did not Rebbi Yose say, even though Samuel said, one can transfer benefits to fetuses, he agrees that most of [the fetus's] head and body must come out alive. He was not living[35]! Rebbi Isaac bar Eleazar[36] said, because of abandoning[37]. The rabbis of Caesarea, R. Ḥiyya bar Abba, Rebbi Abba bar Natan[38]: Rebbi Natan changed his mind because of that Mishnah: "If a male, a mina, if a female, 200." Is a female in this situation not like an outsider[39]? Bar Qappara stated: "On transfers benefit to a one day old.[40]"

24 The question whether an unborn child can inherit and receive gifts is discussed in Babli *Baba Batra* 141b/142a, Yerushalmi *Baba Batra* 9:1 in a similar way. The opinion of R. Eleazar is attributed to (the slightly older) Rav Huna in the Babli.

25 R. Yose, the fifth generation Amora, colleague of R. Jonah. In ms. A, the name appears as ר' יונסה, a confluence of both names.

26 In Babli *Baba Batra* 142a, that a gift to a minor is acquired only at the time of birth is the opinion of Rav Naḥman, Samuel's foremost student in matters of civil law.

27 After birth, the gift is valid from the time it was given but it is not acquired (and cannot be invested by the baby's trustees) before birth.

28 100 drachmae. In the parallel, *Baba batra* 141b, only the male baby is mentioned. In Yerushalmi *Baba batra* 9:2, edited by a different group, and

Tosephta *Baba batra* 9:5, a different text, the male gets double the amount of the female.

29 It seems here that instead of 'ר' יוסה' (in both mss.) one should read 'ר' יסה'; he is R. Yasa (Assi), contemporary of R. Eleazar.

30 The rules of emergency wills, which are much more lenient than those of standard wills, are detailed in tractates *Giṭṭin* and *Baba batra.* Real estate can be acquired only if all rules are followed; since the fetus cannot perform the act of acquisition, no real estate can be transferred to him on the death bed.

31 A similar *baraita* in Babli *Baba batra* 142a. If a proselyte has no children after he became Jewish, his estate has no heirs; so anybody who wants to may take it. It is assumed here that if the deceased had a wife, he died without a will and she was not present since either way she immediately could lay claim to the entire property. Therefore, it is stated that only later it became known that the widow was pregnant.

32 The unborn baby inherits his father's estate. This is a biblical decree (*Num.* 27:8).

33 And again there are no legal heirs.

34 If a fetus cannot acquire, then the first group of people who had returned what they had taken, simply should be given back what they had returned. If a fetus can acquire, then the first group took the possession illegally and they should not be considered as owners.

35 In the interpretation of R. Yose, the return was in error and the people who took first should take their property back.

36 In *Baba batra* 9:1 this is an anonymous statement of the editors. In ms A: R. Eleazar. Cf. *Berakhot* 7:117.

37 The owners had given up hope to recover their property. Then they had given up ownership. Loss of ownership by giving up hope of recovery is the topic of *Baba meṣi'a* 2.

38 A Babylonian in Galilee, older than R. Ḥiyya bar Abba, student of Rav Huna. The next name, R. Nathan, seems to be corrupt; possibly one should read "R. Eleazar". Unfortunately, two lines are missing here in ms. A.

39 Since in the presence of sons she does not inherit (but can claim support from the estate and a dowry).

40 He denies that an unborn child can inherit or receive gifts; cf. Mishnah *Niddah* 5:3.

משנה ב: הַכּוֹנֵס אֶת יְבִמְתּוֹ וְנִמְצֵאת מְעוּבֶּרֶת וְיָלְדָה בִּזְמַן שֶׁהַוּוֹלָד שֶׁל(fol. 5b) קַיְימָא יוֹצִיא וְחַייָבִין בְּקָרְבָּן. וְאִם אֵין הַוּוֹלָד שֶׁל קַייָמָא יְקַייֵם. סָפֵק בֶּן תֵּשַׁע לָרִאשׁוֹן סָפֵק בֶּן שִׁבְעָה לָאַחֲרוֹן יוֹצִיא וְהַוּוֹלָד כָּשֵׁר וְחַייָבִין בְּאָשָׁם תָּלוּי.

Mishnah 2: If somebody marries his sister-in-law but she turned out to have been pregnant and gave birth. If the child is alive, [the levir] has to divorce her and they must bring a sacrifice[41]. If the child is not alive, he may keep her. If it is doubtful whether [the child is] a nine-month child of the first [brother] or a seven-month of the second, he has to divorce her, the child is legitimate, and they are obligated to bring a reparation offering for an uncertain case[42].

41 His marriage to her is incestuous; she is forbidden to him as sister-in-law with children. The sacrifice is a purification sacrifice, חַטָּאת (*Lev.* 4). One has to assume that the marriage was entered into without any suspicion of pregnancy.

42 His marriage to her is possibly incestuous; he must divorce her. A child is either a bastard or not a bastard; legally no children exist that *possibly* are bastards. The reparation offering is the אָשָׁם required if it is uncertain whether a sin was committed or not (*Lev.* 5:17-19).

(fol. 5c) **הלכה ב:** אָמַר רִבִּי יוֹסֵי. כָּל־שֶׁאֶיפְשַׁר כָּךְ לַעֲמוֹד עַל וַדָּאוֹ אֵין חַייָבִין עַל סְפֵיקוֹ אָשָׁם תָּלוּי. הֵיךְ עֲבִידָא. הָיוּ לְפָנָיו שְׁנֵי זֵיתִים אֶחָד שֶׁלְּחֵלֶב וְאֶחָד שֶׁלְּשׁוּמָּן וְאָכַל אֶחָד מֵהֶן וַחֲבֵירוֹ מוּנָּח בְּתוֹכָהּ.[43] וְאָמַר. מֵאַחַר שֶׁאִילּוּ אֶמְצָא אֶת הַמַּפְתֵּחַ יָכוֹל אֲנִי לַעֲמוֹד עַל וַדָּאוֹ מַהוּ שֶׁיְּהוּ חַייָבִין עַל סְפֵיקוֹ אָשָׁם תָּלוּי. נִישְׁמְעִינָהּ מִן הָדָא. הַכּוֹנֵס אֶת יְבִמְתּוֹ וְנִמְצֵאת מְעוּבֶּרֶת עַד שֶׁלֹּא יִוָּדַע לוֹ אִם בֶּן קַיְימָא הוּא אִם אֵינוֹ בֶּן קַייָמָא מֵבִיא. הָדָא אָמְרָה שֶׁאֵינוֹ מֵבִיא.

Halakhah 2: Rebbi Yose[44] said, in any case where the true fact can be ascertained, one does not have to bring a reparation offering because of doubt. How is that? If there were before him two olive-sized pieces, one of suet[45] and one of fat[46], he ate one of them and the other is locked up.

He says, since I could determine the true fact if I would find the key, does one have to bring a reparation offering in this case of doubt[47]? Let us hear from the following: "If somebody marries his sister-in-law but she turned out to have been pregnant", as long as it is not known whether the child lives or does not live, does he have to bring a reparation offering because of the doubt[48]? This means that he does not bring.

43 Either this word is misspelled (some suggestions are בחינה, בתה), or a word is missing.

44 He cannot be either the late Amora or the Tanna; it seems that he is the Babylonian who in the Babli is called Rav Assi. The Babli (*Keritut* 17b) by implication attributes to Rav Assi the opinion that a reparation offering is due if the true situation cannot be ascertained.

45 From the back part of a domestic animal. Since suet of a sacrifice has to be burned on the altar, it is forbidden as food from all animals that can be sacrifices (*Lev.* 7:27). Eating an olive-sized piece of suet inadvertently requires a purification offering.

46 Fat permitted as food.

47 Theoretically, the true situation could be ascertained, whether a purification offering is due or no sin has been committed, but practically it cannot. Does one follow theory or practice?

48 No, the Mishnah requires them to wait until the eventual necessity for a purification offering is decided.

רַב אָמַר. כָּל־שֶׁאֵיפְשַׁר לוֹ לַעֲמוֹד עַל וַדָּייו אֵין חַייָבִין עַל סְפֵיקוֹ אָשָׁם תָּלוּי. הֵיךְ עֲבִידָא. הָיוּ לְפָנָיו שְׁנֵי זֵיתִים אֶחָד שֶׁלְּחֵלֶב וְאֶחָד שֶׁלְּשׁוּמָּן וְאָכַל אֶחָד מֵהֶן. וּבָא עוֹרֵב וְאָכַל אֶת הַשֵּׁינִי. מֵאַחַר שֶׁאֵינוֹ יָכוֹל לַעֲמוֹד עַל וַדָּייו אֵין חַייָבִין עַל סְפֵיקוֹ אָשָׁם תָּלוּי. אֲבָל אִם אָכַל עוֹרֵב תְּחִילָּה וְאַחַר כָּךְ אָכַל הוּא. מֵאַחַר שֶׁהוּא יָכוֹל לַעֲמוֹד עַל וַדָּייו וְחַייָבִין עַל סְפֵיקוֹ אָשָׁם תָּלוּי. לֹא כֵן אָמַר רַב. וְהוּא שֶׁיּוֹכִיחַ לְפָנָיו חֵלֶב בָּרוּר. אַף עַל גַּב דְּרַב אָמַר. וְהוּא שֶׁיּוֹכִיחַ לְפָנָיו חֵלֶב בָּרוּר. מוֹדֶה הוּא הָכָא. שֶׁיָּכוֹל לַעֲמוֹד עַל וַדָּאוֹ. מַתְנִיתָא פְלִיגָא עַל רַב. כְּרִבִּי לְעָזָר אוֹמֵר. חַייָבִין עַל חֶלְבּוֹ אָשָׁם תָּלוּי. מַה עֲבַד רַב. פָּתַר לָהּ. חֲלוּקִין

עַל דִּבְרֵי רִבִּי לָעְזָר. מַתְנִיתָא פְלִיגָא עַל רַב. חֲתִיכָה שֶׁלְּחוּלִין וַחֲתִיכָה שֶׁלְּקוֹדֶשׁ. אָכַל אֶת אַחַת מֵהֶן וְאֵין יָדוּעַ אֶת אֵי זֶה מֵהֶן אָכַל מֵבִיא אָשָׁם תָּלוּי. אָכַל אֶת הַשְּׁנִייָה מֵבִיא אָשָׁם וַדַּאי. אָכַל אֶת הָרִאשׁוֹנָה וּבָא אַחֵר וְאָכַל אֶת הַשְּׁנִייָה זֶה מֵבִיא אָשָׁם תָּלוּי וְזֶה מֵבִיא אָשָׁם תָּלוּי. נִיחָא רִאשׁוֹן מֵבִיא אָשָׁם תָּלוּי. שֵׁינִי לָמָּה. אָמַר רִבִּי יוֹסֵה. תִּיפְתָּר שֶׁהָיְתָה חֲתִיכָה גְדוֹלָה וְאָכַל חֶצְיָיהּ וְהִנִּיחַ חֶצְיָיהּ. מַתְנִיתָא פְלִיגָא עַל רַב. סָפֵק בֶּן תֵּשַׁע לָרִאשׁוֹן סָפֵק בֶּן שִׁבְעָה לָאַחֲרוֹן יוֹצִיא וְהַוְולָד כָּשֵׁר וְחַייָבִין אָשָׁם תָּלוּי. הֲרֵי אִיפְשַׁר לָךְ לַעֲמוֹד עַל וַדָּייוֹ וְחַייָבִין עַל סְפֵיקוֹ אָשָׁם תָּלוּי. אָמַר רִבִּי יוֹסֵה. קִייֶמָהּ רִבִּי זְעִירָא קוֹמֵי רִבִּי חִייָא בַּר וָוא. רִבִּי חִזְקִיָּה רִבִּי חִייָא בַּר בָּא. קִייְמָהּ רִבִּי זְעוּרָה קָמִינָן. מֵאַחַר שֶׁהוּא יָכוֹל לְהֶעָרוֹת וְלִפְרוֹשׁ וְלֵידַע אִם מִמֶּנּוּ הוּא אִם מֵאַחֵר הוּא. כְּמִי שֶׁהוּא[49] יָכוֹל לַעֲמוֹד עַל וַדָּייוֹ.

Rav said, in any case where the true fact can never be established, one does not have to bring a reparation offering for the doubt[50]. How is that? If there were before him two olive-sized pieces, one of suet[45] and one of fat[46], he ate one of them, and then a raven ate the other. Since he cannot ascertain the true fact, one does not have to bring a reparation offering for this doubt. But if the raven ate first and then he ate, since he could have ascertained the true fact[51], one has to bring a reparation offering for the doubt. But did not Rav say, only if he made sure that it certainly was suet[52]? Even though Rav said, only if he made sure that it certainly was suet, he agrees here that he could have ascertained the true fact. A *baraita* disagrees with Rav: "As Rebbi Eleazar says, one must bring a reparation offering for the doubt of suet[53]." What does Rav do with that? They[54] disagree with the words of Rebbi Eleazar. A *baraita* disagrees with Rav[55]: "If there were both a piece of profane [meat] and a piece of sacrificial [meat], he ate one of them and it is not known which one, he brings a reparation offering for the doubt. If he [then] ate the second piece, he brings a reparation offering for a certain transgression[56]. If he ate the first piece and another person came and ate the second, each one brings a reparation offering for the doubt." One understands that the first brings a reparation offering for the doubt. Why the second? Rebbi Yose said, explain it that the piece was large, he ate half of it and left the other half[57]. A Mishnah disagrees with Rav[58]: "If it is doubtful whether [the child is] a nine-month child of the first [brother] or a seven-month of the second, he has to divorce her, the child is legitimate, and they are obligated for a reparation offering for the doubt." Here it is impossible to ascertain the true fact and they are obligated for a reparation offering for the doubt! Rebbi Yose said, Rebbi Ze'ira explained it before Rebbi Ḥiyya bar Abba; Rebbi Ḥizqiah, Rebbi Ḥiyya bar Abba: Rebbi Ze'ira explained it before us. Since he could just have touched her[59] and then separated, he could have known whether it is his or the other's, it is as if he could have ascertained the true fact!

49 Reading of ms. A. Ms. L and *editio princeps*: במשהו "in the least amount".

50 The same statement in *Bikkurim* 2:8, Babli *Keritut* 17b. (The commentators who did not recognize that Yerushalmi אֵיפשר = Babli אי אפשר had to rewrite the text; cf. *Peah*, Chapter 7, Note 170.)

51 By having the piece analyzed by a competent butcher.

52 The Babli, *Keritut* 17b, quotes a similar statement in the name of Ḥiyya bar Rav, that the offering for a doubt is due only if there were two pieces, one permitted, one forbidden, whose history can be traced and their true status ascertained. But if there is only one piece whose status is indeterminate (the case of Rebbi Yose, Rav Assi), the offering for a doubt does not apply.

53 *Bikkurim* 2:8, quoted in Babli *Keritut* 17b. The animal is the *koy*, for which it is impossible to ascertain whether it is domestic (whose suet is forbidden) or wild (whose suet is permitted).

54 The majority of Sages disagree with the Tanna R. Eleazar ben Shamua.

55 Similar texts are in Mishnah *Keritut* 5:4; Tosephta *Keritut* 3:1. Neither of these texts is identical with

the *baraita* quoted here.

56 It is assumed that the person who ate is not a Cohen and commits a sin by eating sacrificial meat. The reparation offering is for unauthorized use of sacred property, *Lev.* 5:14-16. Both texts quoted in Note 55 require two sacrifices, one a reparation sacrifice for the use of sacred meat, the other a purification sacrifice (*Lev.* 4:27-35) for the sin.

57 It is impossible to explain that both people ate from one large piece since that is the case in which Rav denies that a reparation offering is due. If must be that one piece was eaten completely but of the other enough is left that it could be analyzed. (This is the explanation rejected by קרבן העדה).

58 This quote is the reason the entire discussion is placed here.

59 In rabbinic Hebrew, the expression הערה in *Lev.* 20:17 is taken to mean "touched (the female genital by the male genital)", not the etymologically more likely "bared". Mishnah 6:1 will explain that the biblically required act of validation of the marriage with the sister-in-law is the touching of the two genitals. They could have performed this act without ejaculation to be married (and make the brother financially responsible for the sister-in-law) and then waited the prescribed 90 days to ascertain the paternity of an eventual child.

מַה אֲנָן קַיָּמִין. אִם כְּשֶׁבָּא עָלֶיהָ לְאַחַר מִיתַת בַּעֲלָהּ מִיַּד הוּכָּר עוּבְרָהּ לְאַחַר שְׁנֵי חֳדָשִׁים. נִיתְנֵי. בֶּן תִּשְׁעָה לָזֶה וְלָזֶה בֶּן שִׁבְעָה לָזֶה וְלָזֶה. אֶלָּא כֵן אֲנָן קַיָּמִין בְּשֶׁבָּא עָלֶיהָ לְאַחַר שְׁנֵי חֳדָשִׁים וְהוּכָּר עוּבְרָהּ לְאַחַר שְׁלֹשָׁה חֳדָשִׁים. נִיתְנֵי. הַיְּבָמָה לֹא תַחֲלוֹץ וְלֹא תִתְיַבֵּם עַד שֶׁיְּהוּ לָהּ חֲמִשָּׁה חֳדָשִׁים. אֶלָּא כֵן אֲנָן קַיָּמִין. כְּשֶׁבָּא עָלֶיהָ לְאַחַר אַרְבָּעִים יוֹם וְהוּכָּר עוּבְרָהּ לְאַחַר חֲמִשִּׁים יוֹם. הֲרֵי יֵשׁ כָּאן שְׁלֵימִין לָרִאשׁוֹן וּמְקוּטָעִין לַשֵּׁינִי. שְׁמַע מִינָּהּ שֶׁהָאִשָּׁה יוֹלֶדֶת לֶחֳדָשִׁים שְׁלֵימִים. אַתְּ שְׁמַע מִינָּהּ שֶׁהֵן שְׁתֵּי יְצִירוֹת. אַתְּ שְׁמַע מִינָּהּ שֶׁהָאִשָּׁה יוֹלֶדֶת לֶחֳדָשִׁים מְקוּטָעִין. אַתְּ שְׁמַע מִינָּהּ שֶׁהָאִשָּׁה מְעוּבֶּרֶת וְחוֹזֶרֶת וּמִתְעַבֶּרֶת. אַתְּ שְׁמַע מִינָּהּ שֶׁהָאִשָּׁה אֵינָהּ מְעֻבֶּרֶת מִשְּׁנֵי בְנֵי אָדָם כְּאַחַת. וּפְלִיגָא עַל דְּרַבָּנָן דַּאֲגַדְתָּא. דְּרַבָּנָן דַּאֲגַדְתָּא אוֹמְרִים. וַיֵּצֵא אִישׁ הַבֵּינַיִים. מִמַּעַרְכוֹת פְּלִשְׁתִּים. מִמֵּאָה עָרְלוֹת פְּלִשְׁתִּים. שֶׁהֶעֱרוּ בָהּ מֵאָה עָרְלוֹת פְּלִשְׁתִּים. אָמַר רִבִּי מַתַּנְיָיָה. וְלָא פְלִיגִין. עַד שֶׁלֹּא נִסְרַח (fol. 5d) הַזֶּרַע הָאִשָּׁה מְעוּבֶּרֶת מִשְּׁנֵי בְנֵי אָדָם כְּאַחַת. מִשֶּׁנִּסְרַח הַזֶּרַע אֵין הָאִשָּׁה מְעוּבֶּרֶת מִשְּׁנֵי בְנֵי אָדָם כְּאַחַת.

How do we hold[60]? If he came to her immediately after her husband's death, and the fetus was recognized after two months, one should have stated: A nine-month child of either one of them or a seven-month of either one of them! But it may be that he came to her after two months and the fetus was recognized after three months[61], one should have stated: The sister-in-law should not perform *ḥalîṣah* or be married in levirate until after five months! But it must be that he came to her after 40 days and the fetus was recognized after 50 days. That would be complete months for [a child of] the first [brother] and incomplete ones for the second[62]. This implies that a woman may give birth after full months. This implies that there are two creations[63]. This implies that a woman may give birth after incomplete months. This implies that a woman may become pregnant repeatedly[64]. This implies that a woman cannot become pregnant simultaneously from two men[65]. And it disagrees with the sermonizing rabbis, since the sermonizing rabbis say "the middleman" "from the orders of the Philistines", from 100 prepuces of Philistines, that 100 prepuces of Philistines touched her[66]. Rebbi Mattaniah said, there is no disagreement. As long as the semen is not spoiled, a woman can become pregnant from several men simultaneously. After the semen is spoiled, a woman cannot become pregnant from several men simultaneously.

60 Here starts the discussion of the last sentence of the Mishnah, how xan a child be a nine-months child or a seven-months child with equal probabilities.

61 Since a widow should not be married in levirate earlier than 3 months after the husband's death (Mishnah 4:11) in order to avoid situations like the one discussed in the Mishnah, it follows that there are pregnancies that are recognized only after three months.

62 If the child was born exactly

nine months after the death of the husband, then this would be 7 months and 10 days after the levir had intercourse with her.

63 Certain regular pregnancies are terminated naturally during the seventh month; certain others only after 9 full months.

64 The Babli, *Niddah* 27a, disagrees and holds that Jehudah and Ḥizqiah, children of Rebbi Ḥiyya, who were born 3 months apart, were twins; the one a seven-months child and the other a nine-months child.

65 Since the Mishnah excludes the possibility that, even if there were twins, they could come from both brothers as fathers. In that case, according to Rav there would be no reparation offering for a doubt.

66 Midrash *Ruth* 2(21), Midrash *Samuel* ed. Buber 20(4), Babli *Sotah* 42b in the name of R. Johanan. These sermons identify (1) the Moabite Orpah, the daughter-in-law of Noemi who did not follow her to Bethlehem, with the Philistine Haraphah (*2S.* 21:22), and (2) Goliat mentioned in *2S.* 21 with the warrior in *1S.* 17:23. The latter is introduced in the written text as אִישׁ הַבֵּנַיִם מִמַּעַרְוֹת פְּלִשְׁתִּים interpreted in a slightly pornographic way as "a man [created] in between the touchings (cf. Note 59) of the Philistines", explaining that Orpah, once she had decided not to become Jewish, went to the enemies of the Jews, the Philistines of Gath, and slept with 100 of their warriors (מִמֵּאָה הֶעָרוֹת = מִמַּעַרְוֹת) in one night to create a super-warrior; in the words of R. Johanan, 100 fathers and one mother. One can construct such a sermon only if all gutturals had become silent and *pataḥ, qāmeṣ* assimilated to one another.

מְנַיִין שְׁתֵּי יְצִירוֹת. רִבִּי זְעִירָא בְשֵׁם רִבִּי הוּנָא. וַיִּיצֶר. יְצִירָה לְשִׁבְעָה וִיצִירָה לְתִשְׁעָה. נוֹצָר לְשִׁבְעָה וְנוֹלָד לִשְׁמוֹנָה חַיי. כָּל־שֶׁכֵּן לְתִשְׁעָה. נוֹצָר לְתִשְׁעָה וְנוֹלָד לִשְׁמוֹנָה אֵינוֹ חַיָּיה. נוֹצָר לְתִשְׁעָה וְנוֹלָד לְשִׁבְעָה.[67] אִיתָא חֲמִי. אִם לִשְׁמוֹנָה אֵינוֹ חַיָּיה לֹא כָּל־שֶׁכֵּן לְשִׁבְעָה. בָּעוֹן קוֹמֵי רִבִּי אַבָּהוּ. מְנַיִין לְבֶן שִׁבְעָה שֶׁהוּא חַיָּיה. אָמַר לוֹן מִדִּידְכוֹן אֲנָא יְהִיב לְכוֹן. זוטא אבטא זוטא אבטא.

From where the two creations? Rebbi Ze'ira in the name of Rebbi Huna: "He created[68]", a creation for seven and a creation for eight. If he was created for seven but born at eight, he lives; so much more if [born] by nine. If he was created for nine and born at eight, he does not live. If he was created for nine and born at seven? Come and see, if he does not live at eight, so much less at seven! They[69] asked before Rebbi Abbahu. From where that a seven-month baby lives? he said to them, from yours I am giving to you: ζῇ τὰ ἑπτὰ, ζῇ τὰ ἑπτὰ[70].

67 Reading of *editio princeps*. In ms. L: לשמונה.

68 *Gen*. 2:7. In the creation of Man, it is written וייצר, in that of the animals, 2:19, only ויצר. The two letters י symbolize the two creations. A more detailed exposition of this sermon is in *Gen. rabba* 14(2).

69 Some Greek speakers.

70 "It lives at seven, it lives at seven". In all other sources, *Gen. rabba* 14(2), 20(13), *Tanḥuma Bemidbar* 18, *Tanḥuma Buber Bemidbar* 21, *Bemidbar rabba* 4(3), the reading seems to be זיטא אפטא איטא אוכטא for the interpretation of which S. Lieberman (יוונית ויוונות בארץ ישראל, Jerusalem 1962, p. 209) prefers the reading of A. Crusius: ζῇ τὰ ἑπτὰ <μᾶλλον> ἤ τὰ ὀκτώ "the life-expectancy of that of seven [is better than] that of eight," a medical maxim. The formulation is a pun on the Hellenistic numeral values of letters, *zeta* ζ' = 7, *eta* η' = 8.

בָּא הַסָּפֵק לִיטּוֹל אֶת חֶלְקוֹ שֶׁלְּאָבִיו. אָמְרִין לֵיהּ. הַנֵּי אָבִיךְ. בָּא הַיָּבָם לִיטּוֹל חֶלְקוֹ שֶׁלְּאָחִיו. אוֹמְרִים לֵיהּ. הַנֵּי בְּרֵיהּ. הָא כֵיצַד. עוֹשִׂין שִׁיפִּיּוּת בֵּינֵיהֶן וּמְחַלְּקִין נִיכְסֵי הַמֵּת. נִמְצֵאת אוֹמֵר. שִׁיפִּיּוּת לְאָחִיו הֶפְסֵד לָאַחִין. תַּחֲרוּת בָּאַחִין שֶׁבֶּר בָּאַחִין. מֵת הַזָּקֵן הֲרֵי יֵשׁ בָּאִים בָּנִים בְּוַדַּאי וּבֶ(י)ן בֵּן בְּסָפֵק. מֵת הַסָּפֵק הֲרֵי יֵשׁ אֲחִי אָב בְּוַדַּאי וְאֵם בְּסָפֵק. מֵת אֶחָד מִן הָאַחִין הֲרֵי יֵשׁ בֶּן בְּוַדַּאי וּבֵ(י)ן אָח בְּסָפֵק. מֵתָה אִמּוֹ שֶׁלְּסָפֵק הֲרֵי יֵשׁ כָּאן בֵּן בְּוַדַּאי וּבַעַל בְּסָפֵק. מֵת הַסָּפֵק וְאַחַר כָּךְ מֵתָה אִמּוֹ הֲרֵי יֵשׁ בֶּן אֲחִי אֵם בְּוַדַּאי וּבַעַל בְּסָפֵק. מֵת הַיָּבָם וּבָא הַסָּפֵק לִיטּוֹל חֶלְקוֹ שֶׁלְּאָבִיו. אִי הֲוָה קַדְמַיְיָא מִיסְכֵּן אָמְרִין לֵיהּ. הַנֵּי אָבוּךְ. אִין הֲוֵי עָתִיר אָמְרִין לֵיהּ. כּוּלָּן אַחִין בְּנֵי אַחִין. בּוֹאוּ וְנִירַשׁ חֶלְקוֹ שֶׁלְּאָבִיבוּ וְחֶלְקוֹ שֶׁלַּאֲחִי אָבִינוּ.

If the uncertain [son] comes to take his part in his father's[71] [inheritance]. one says to him, the other one is your father. If the levir comes to take his part in his brother's [inheritance], one says to him, that one is his son. How is that? They compromise between themselves and split the property of the deceased[72]. One finds, compromise with his brother is loss to the brothers; competition between the brothers is catastrophy for the brothers[73]. If the old man dies, one finds that certain sons and an uncertain grandson come[74]. If the uncertain [son] dies there exists a certain son of his father's brother and an uncertain mother[75]. If one of the brothers dies, there is a certain son and an uncertain son of a brother[76]. If the mother of the uncertain [son] dies, there is a certain son and an uncertain husband[77]. If first the uncertain [son] dies and after that his mother, a son of the mother's brother is certain but the husband uncertain[77]. If the levir dies and the uncertain [son] comes to take his part in his father's inheritance, if the first one was poor, they tell him, that one is your father. If he was rich, the tell him, we all are brothers, sons of his brother. Come and let us inherit our father's part and the part of our father's brother[78].

71 The putative father, his mother's first husband.

72 The Babli, 37b, notes that the inheritance of the deceased brother is "money which is in doubt and money in doubt one splits in the middle". The Yerushalmi has no explicit rule on how the compromise is reached.

73 The compromise splits the inheritance between the uncertain son and his uncertain father; this excludes the other brothers from the inheritance of their childless brother. The rules of inheritance in the cases of *ḥalîṣah* and levirate are spelled out in Mishnaiot 3-4. If there is no compromise, nobody gets anything.

74 Inheritance of the grandfather goes to his children and grandchildren *per stirpes*. If the grandson cannot prove who his father was, he cannot inherit in the presence of sons or

grandsons of known fathers.

75 The mother is certain but she does not inherit. The sons of the levir inherit either as brothers or as cousins of the deceased. The other sons of the mother could inherit his part from his mother's estate only if there were no relatives from the family of the possible fathers.

76 The uncertain son cannot claim a part in the inheritance of a childless uncle since he cannot prove whether he should get the full part of the first husband or a share with the other brothers of the levir.

77 The levir cannot inherit since he cannot prove that the woman was his legal wife.

78 In the Babli, 37b, there is a serious disagreement whether the inheritance of the first husband remains separate after the levir and the uncertain son did compromise (Note 72). In practice, the Babli holds that the uncertain son cannot inherit more than what he got under the compromise since he cannot prove that he was the levir's son.

תַּנֵּי הָרִאשׁוֹן רָאוּי לִהְיוֹת כֹּהֵן גָּדוֹל וְהַשֵּׁינִי מַמְזֵר בְּסָפֵק. רִבִּי לִיעֶזֶר בֶּן יַעֲקֹב אוֹמֵר. אֵין מַמְזֵר בְּסָפֵק. מוֹדֶה רִבִּי לִיעֶזֶר בֶּן יַעֲקֹב בִּסְפֵק כּוּתִים וּבִסְפֵק חֲלָלִים. כְּהַהִיא דְתַנִּינָן תַּמָּן. עֲשָׂרָה יוּחֲסִין עָלוּ מִבָּבֶל. עַל דַּעְתֵּיהּ דְּרִבִּי לִיעֶזֶר בֶּן יַעֲקֹב שְׁמוֹנֶה. עַל דַּעְתִּין דְּרַבָּן גַּמְלִיאֵל וְרִבִּי לִיעֶזֶר תִּשְׁעָה. עַל דַּעְתִּין דְּרַבָּנִן עֲשָׂרָה.

It was stated[79]: "The first son could be High Priest, any second son possibly is a bastard[80]. Rebbi Eliezer ben Jacob said, there is no such thing as a possible bastard.[81]" Rebbi Eliezer ben Jacob agrees in cases of doubt of Samaritans and desecrated persons[82]. This refers to what we have stated there: "Ten classes returned from Babylonia.[83]" In the opinion of Rebbi Eliezer ben Jacob, eight. In the opinion of Rabban Gamliel and Rebbi Eliezer, nine. In the opinion of the rabbis, ten.

79 Tosephta 6:2, quoted in Babli 37a.

80 If the first child is the son of the first husband, he certainly is in order. If he is the son of the levir, the first husband died childless and the levirate was legitimate. But any second child is the issue of a union which

possibly is incestuous and punishable by divine extirpation.

81 He is considered a bastard, permitted to marry a bastard partner, since he cannot marry a legitimate Israel partner; cf. *Qiddushin* 4:3.

82 As noted before, Samaritans have different interpretations of incest and marriage laws; a child of a marriage with a Samaritan is not automatically excluded but subject to inquiry. The text speaks of Samaritans since in talmudic times they were the only remnants of Sadducee traditions. (Today, of the other tribes of Sadducee traditions, Ethiopians have accepted rabbinic rules and Karaites are legitimate marriage partners if they accept rabbinic rules.)

"Desecrated" children are children of the marriage of a Cohen with a divorcee or a prostitute; such a marriage is not incestuous and stringent exclusionary rules do not apply.

83 Mishnah *Qiddushin* 4:1: 'Ten classes returned from Babylonia, Cohanim, Levites, Israel, desecrated, proselytes, freed slaves, bastards, Gibeonites, people of unknown paternity, and foundlings. Cohanim, Levites, Israel may marry one another. Levites, Israel, desecrated, proselytes, and freed slaves, may marry one another. Proselytes, freed slaves, bastards, Gibeonites, people of unknown paternity, and foundlings, may marry one another."

For R. Eliezer ben Jacob, bastards, people of unknown paternity, and foundlings, all form one group.

In Mishnah *Ketubot* 1:8, Rabban Gamliel and R. Eliezer hold that the unmarried mother of a child of unknown paternity is believed if she asserts that the father was one of the first six categories (or a Gentile). For them, the special category of "child of unknown paternity" does not exist since the child inherits the status of his mother.

(fol. 5c) **משנה ג:** שׁוֹמֶרֶת יָבָם שֶׁנָּפְלוּ לָהּ נְכָסִים מוֹדִין בֵּית שַׁמַּי וּבֵית הִלֵּל שֶׁמּוֹכֶרֶת וְנוֹתֶנֶת וְקַיָּם. מֵתָה מַה יֵּעָשֶׂה בִּכְתוּבָּתָהּ וּבִנְכָסִים הַנִּכְנָסִין וְהַיּוֹצְאִין עִמָּהּ. בֵּית שַׁמַּי אוֹמְרִים יַחֲלוֹקוּ יוֹרְשֵׁי הַבַּעַל עִם יוֹרְשֵׁי הָאָב. וּבֵית הִלֵּל אוֹמְרִים הַנְּכָסִים בְּחֶזְקָתָן. כְּתוּבָּה בְחֶזְקַת יוֹרְשֵׁי הַבַּעַל. וּנְכָסִים הַנִּכְנָסִין וְהַיּוֹצְאִין עִמָּהּ בְּחֶזְקַת יוֹרְשֵׁי הָאָב.

Mishnah 3: If property came to a woman waiting for her levir[84], the House of Shammai agree with the House of Hillel that she may sell or give away and it is valid[85]. If she dies, what does one do with her *ketubah* and property that enters and leaves with her[86]? The House of Shammai say, the husband's heirs should split with her father's heirs. But the House of Hillel say that all property remains where it is; the *ketubah* in the hands of the husband's heirs[87] and property that enters and leaves with her in the hands of her father's heirs[88].

84 She waits to be married in levirate or to be freed by *ḥalîṣah*. In the meantime, the *ketubah*, the money due her at the dissolution of her marriage (her dowry and the capital due her from her husband) is not payable since concerning money matters levirate is considered as continuation of the first marriage. The capital due from the husband is at least 200 *zuz* for a virgin, defined in Mishnah *Peah* 8:8 as sufficient to disqualify her from public assistence.

85 During the marriage, the husband has the administration and usufruct of her property. This power is not automatically transferred to the levir; it comes only with the actual levirate. Since the marriage with the first husband is now terminated, the administration of the properties is solely in her hands.

86 Property she inherited or otherwise received during her marriage. In contrast to the dowry, for which the husband assumes responsibility in the *ketubah* contract and whose value only has to be returned at the dissolution of the marriage, these remain her property and, during marriage, may be sold or mortgaged only by the common action of the wife as owner and the husband as administrator. These properties are called נִכְסֵי מְלוֹג (Accadic *mulūgu* "wife's property"), cf. Mishnah 8:1.

87 Her dowry remains in the husband's family. (This is a matter of civil law, not a religious precept. In the Middle Ages, many communities promulgated rules that returned all or part of the dowry of a childless marriage of short duration to the wife's family.)

88 They never were the husband's property.

הלכה ג: שׁוֹמֶרֶת יָבָם שֶׁנָּפְלוּ לָהּ נְכָסִים וכו׳. הָכָא אַתְּ אָמַר. מוֹכֶרֶת(fol. 5d) וְנוֹתֶנֶת וְקַיָּם. מֵתָה מַה יֵעָשֶׂה בִּכְתוּבָּתָהּ. וְהָכָא אַתְּ אָמַר. יַחֲלֹקוּ יוֹרְשֵׁי הַבַּעַל עִם יוֹרְשֵׁי הָאָב. אָמַר רִבִּי יוֹסֵי בֶּן חֲנִינָה. הֵן דְּאַתְּ אָמַר מוֹכֶרֶת וְנוֹתֶנֶת וְקַיָּם. כְּשֶׁנָּפְלוּ לָהּ עַד שֶׁלֹּא הָיְתָה שׁוֹמֶרֶת יָבָם. וְהָא דְאַתְּ אָמַר יַחֲלֹקוּ יוֹרְשֵׁי הַבַּעַל עִם יוֹרְשֵׁי הָאָב. בְּשֶׁנָּפְלוּ לָהּ מִשֶּׁנַּעֲשֵׂית שׁוֹמֶרֶת יָבָם. נָפְלוּ לָהּ עַד שֶׁלֹּא נַעֲשֵׂית שׁוֹמֶרֶת יָבָם וְעָשׂוּ פֵּירוֹת מִשֶּׁנַּעֲשֵׂית שׁוֹמֶרֶת יָבָם כְּמִי שֶׁנָּפְלוּ לָהּ מִשֶּׁנַּעֲשֵׂית שׁוֹמֶרֶת יָבָם. אָמַר רִבִּי זְעִירָא. הָהֵן יָבָם דְּהָכָא צְרִיכָא דְבֵית שַׁמַּי כְּבַעַל הוּא אוֹ אֵינוֹ כְבַעַל. אִין כְּבַעַל הוּא יוֹרֵשׁ אֶת הַכֹּל. אִם אֵינוֹ כְבַעַל לֹא יוֹרֵשׁ כְּלוּם. מִסָּפֵק יַחֲלוֹקוּ יוֹרְשֵׁי הַבַּעַל עִם יוֹרְשֵׁי הָאָב. בֵּית הִלֵּל פְּשִׁיטָא לֵיהּ כְּבַעַל. וְיוֹרֵשׁ אֶת הַכֹּל. שֶׁכֵּן אֲפִילוּ אָחִיו אֵין לוֹ אֶלָּא אֲכִילַת פֵּירוֹת בִּלְבַד.

Halakhah 3: "If property came to a woman waiting for her levir," etc. Here, you say "she may sell or give away and it is valid. If she dies, what does one do with her *ketubah*?" And you also say "the husband's heirs should split with her father's heirs!"[89] Rebbi Yose ben Ḥanina said[90], when do you say "she may sell or give away and it is valid"? If they came to her before she became a woman waiting for her levir. When do you say "the husband's heirs should split with her father's heirs"? If they came to her after she became a woman waiting for her levir. If they came to her before she became a woman waiting for her levir and produced revenue after she became a woman waiting for her levir, [that revenue is as if] they came to her after she became a woman waiting for her levir. Rebbi Ze'ira[91] said, the levir in this situation is a problem for the House of Shammai. If he is a husband, he inherits everything. If he is not a husband, he inherits nothing. Because of the doubt, "the husband's heirs should split with her father's heirs." For the House of Hillel it is obvious that he is a husband and inherits everything. For even his brother had only the usufruct[92].

89 If she can dispose of the property without the consent of the husband's family, the property belongs to her family. Why, according to the House of Shammai, should the late husband's family get anything of the widow's separate property?

90 In the Babli, 38b, this is quoted as the opinion of Abbai (middle 4th Cent.), with a belated acknowledgment (39a) of the priority of R. Yose ben Ḥanina (middle 3rd Cent.). As Levy Ginzburg has pointed out, in the Babylonian Talmud the Babylonian authors are always mentioned before the Galileans; chronological order is followed within each group separately.

The wife of a childless man who has a brother becomes "a woman waiting for her levir" at the moment she is widowed.

91 This opinion is not mentioned in the Babli. There, the opinion opposed to that of Abbai is that of Rava, who holds that the widow can only dispose of her property before "bespeaking". For him, "bespeaking" for the House of Shammai makes the widow a wife in civil but not in criminal matters, while *qiddushin* makes the unencumbered woman a wife in criminal but not in civil matters.

92 This sentence is the answer to an unasked question: If the husband inherits from his wife, why does the widow's separate property return to her family? The answer is that this property, in contrast to the dowry, never was the husband's. He only was the administrator and had the usufruct during her lifetime. The levir's hand cannot be stronger than the husband's. (The husband received the usufruct since he was under the obligation to provide for his wife a lifestyle appropriate to her social standing. This is one of the major topics of Tractate *Ketubot*.)

תַּנֵּי רִבִּי הוֹשַׁעְיָה. יִירְשׁוּ הַיּוֹרְשִׁין אֶת כְּתוּבָתָהּ חַייָבִין בִּקְבוּרָתָהּ. אָמַר רִבִּי יוֹסֵה. אִילוּלֵי דְתַנִּיתָהּ רִבִּי הוֹשַׁעְיָה הֲוָות צְרִיכָה לוֹן. מֵאַחַר שֶׁאֵין לָהּ כְּתוּבָּה אֵין לָהּ קְבוּרָה. וְקַשְׁיָא. אִילּוּ אִשָּׁה שֶׁאֵין לָהּ כְּתוּבָּה שֶׁמָּא אֵין לָהּ קְבוּרָה. אִשָּׁה אַף עַל פִּי שֶׁאֵין לָהּ כְּתוּבָּה יֵשׁ לָהּ קְבוּרָה. בְּרַם הָכָא אִם יֵשׁ לָהּ כְּתוּבָּה יֵשׁ לָהּ קְבוּרָה. אִם אֵין לָהּ כְּתוּבָּה אֵין לָהּ קְבוּרָה.

Rebbi Hoshaia stated: The heirs of her *ketubah* are obliged to bury her[93]. Rebbi Yose said, if Rebbi Hoshaia had not stated this, we would have had a problem. If she had no *ketubah*, do they not have to bury her? This is difficult. If a woman has no *ketubah*, does she not have to be buried[94]? A wife, even if she has a *ketubah*, must be buried. This one, if she has a *ketubah*, is entitled to burial costs. But here, if she does not have a *ketubah*, she is not entitled to burial costs[95].

93 This is also quoted in Babli *Ketubot* 81a. The discussion there is irrelevant for the Yerushalmi.

The heirs of the *ketubah* are the heirs of the husband since her death terminates the obligation of *ketubah*. Since the husband is freed from the obligation of paying the *ketubah*, he has to pay all costs connected with her funeral.

94 For example, if she sold her right to *ketubah* in case of dissolution of the marriage to her husband for current cash, nevertheless the husband is required to bear the expenses of her funeral. She must have had a *ketubah* to be married.

95 In this case, the expenses have to be covered from her estate, and if she leaves no estate, from her family.

(fol. 5b) **משנה ד:** כְּנָסָהּ הֲרֵי הִיא כְאִשְׁתּוֹ לְכָל־דָּבָר וּבִלְבַד שֶׁתְּהֵא כְתוּבָּתָהּ עַל נִכְסֵי בַּעֲלָהּ הָרִאשׁוֹן.

Mishnah 4: If he married her, she is his wife in every respect except that her *ketubah* is a lien on the property of her first husband[96].

96 If the levir married his sister-in-law he does not write her a new *ketubah*. Therefore, he did not mortgage his own property to her.

(fol. 5d) **הלכה ד:** כְּנָסָהּ הֲרֵי הִיא כְאִשְׁתּוֹ לְכָל־דָּבָר כול׳. כֵּיצַד הוּא עוֹשֶׂה. כּוֹנֵס וּמְגָרֵשׁ וּמַחֲזִיר וְהִיא שׁוֹבֶרֶת לוֹ עַל כְּתוּבָּתָהּ. אָמַר רִבִּי יוֹסֵה. לִצְדָדִין הִיא מַתְנִיתָא. אוֹ שׁוֹבֶרֶת לוֹ עַל כְּתוּבָּתָהּ. רִבִּי זְעִירָא בְשֵׁם רַב הַמְנוּנָא. כְּנָסָהּ וְגֵירְשָׁהּ וְהֶחֱזִירָהּ. אִם חִידֵּשׁ לָהּ כְּתוּבָּה כְּתוּבָּתָהּ עַל נְכָסָיו. וְאִם לָאו כְּתוּבָּתָהּ

עַל נִכְסֵי בַּעֲלָהּ הָרִאשׁוֹן. רִבִּי יוֹסֵי אָמַר בְּשֵׁם רַב חִסְדָּא. מַתְנִיתָא אָמְרָה כֵן שֶׁהַמְגָרֵשׁ אֶת הָאִשָּׁה וְהֶחֱזִירָהּ. עַל מְנָת כְּתוּבָּה הָרִאשׁוֹנָה הֶחֱזִירָהּ. סוֹף עַד שֶׁיַּכְנִיס וִיגָרֵשׁ וְיַחֲזִיר. דְּרוּבָּה אָתָא מֵימָר לָךְ. אֲפִילוּ כְּנָסָהּ וְגֵירְשָׁהּ וְהֶחֱזִירָהּ. אִם חִידֵּשׁ לָהּ כְּתוּבָּה עַל נְכָסָיו. וְאִם לָאו כְּתוּבָּה עַל נִכְסֵי בַּעֲלָהּ הָרִאשׁוֹן.

Halakhah 4: "If he married her, she is his wife in every respect", etc. What does he do? "He marries her, he may divorce her and take her back, and she writes him a receipt for her *ketubah*."[97] Rebbi Yose said, the *baraita* has two possibilities. "Or she writes him a receipt for her *ketubah*."[98] Rebbi Ze'ira in the name of Rav Hamnuna: If he married her, divorced her, and took her back, if he wrote her a new *ketubah*, the lien is on his property; otherwise, it is on the property of her first husband. Rebbi Yose said in the name of Rav Ḥisda, a Mishnah said so: "For he who takes back his wife, takes her back under the terms of her first *ketubah*[99]." At the end, if he married her, divorced her, and took her back? He tells you something new. Even if he married her, divorced her, and took her back, if he wrote her a new *ketubah*[100], the lien is on his property; otherwise, it is on the property of her first husband.

97 Babli 39a, *Ketubot* 82b. The Babli points out that it is not obvious from the biblical text that the levir has the right to take his divorced sister-in-law back since she might be forbidden to him as sister-in-law.

98 If he takes her back before she received the payment of her *ketubah*, she obviously does not write a receipt. R. Yose wants to point out that the *baraita* quoted here is *not* the Tosephta *Ketubot* 9:1: "If somebody died and left his widow waiting for the levir, even if his estate is a hundred minas and her *ketubah* only one mina, the heirs cannot sell anything since her *ketubah* is a lien on the entire estate. What can he do? He marries her, divorces her, and she writes a receipt for her *ketubah*."

99 Mishnah *Ketubot* 9:9.

100 If she refuses to come back under the old terms, her lien extends to the entire property of the levir.

רִבִּי זְעוּרָא בְּשֵׁם רִבִּי הַמְנוּנָא אָמַר. אֲרוּסָה שֶׁמֵּתָה אֵין לָהּ כְּתוּבָּה. שֶׁלֹּא הוּתְּרָה לְהִינָּשֵׂא לַשּׁוּק. שֶׁלֹּא תֹאמַר. יֵעָשֶׂה כְּמִי שֶׁגֵּירֵשׁ וִיהֵא לֵיהּ כְּתוּבָּה. לְפוּם כָּךְ צָרִיךְ מֵימַר אֵין לָהּ כְּתוּבָּה.

Rebbi Ze'ira in the name of Rav Hamnuna said[101]: A betrothed woman who died does not have a *ketubah* since she was not permitted to marry outside[102]. That you should not say [the case] should be considered as if he divorced her and she should have a *ketubah*; therefore it was necessary to say that she does not have a *ketubah*.

101 This paragraph belongs to the material of *Ketubot*; it has no bearing on the rules of levirate since it was noted in Halakha 1:4 that women between *qiddushin* and marriage are not subject to levirate. The material is inserted here because this is the only other case where Rebbi Ze'ira quotes Rav Hamnuna (of the students of Rav).

102 This is a matter of great controversy in the Babli, which frequently (*Yebamot* 29b, 43; *Ketubot* 53, 89; *Baba mesi'a* 18a; *Sanhedrin* 28a) quotes a *baraita* to the effect that if she dies, the husband does not inherit but if he dies, she collects her *ketubah*. Since a *ketubah* is not necessary for *qiddushin* but only for *nissuin*, the actual marriage, there is a problem only if the *ketubah* was already written at the time of *qiddushin*, which also implies that the dowry was determined or even delivered at that time. Then it is clear that at the groom's death the betrothed woman can recover the dowry recorded in the *ketubah*. For the amount due from the husband, even though they disagree in the case of *ketubah* written at the betrothal, both Talmudim [*Ketubot*, Yerushalmi 5:1 (fol. 29c), Babli 56a] agree that any sum agreed to above the statutory minimum can be collected only after the consummation of the marriage.

(fol. 5b) **משנה ה** (fol. 5d) **הלכה ה:** מִצְוָה בַּגָּדוֹל לְיַיבֵּם לֹא רָצָה מְהַלְּכִין עַל כָּל־הָאַחִין. לֹא רָצוּ חוֹזְרִין אֵצֶל הַגָּדוֹל וְאוֹמְרִים לוֹ עָלֶיךָ מִצְוָה אוֹ חֲלוֹץ אוֹ יַיבֵּם.

Mishnah 5: The obligation of levirate is on the oldest [brother][103]. If he refuses, one[104] goes to all the other brothers. If they refuse, one returns to the oldest and tells him, the obligation is yours, either give *ḥalîṣah* or marry in levirate.

(fol. 5b) **משנה ו**: תָּלָה בַקָּטָן עַד שֶׁיַּגְדִּיל וּבַגָּדוֹל עַד שֶׁיָּבוֹא מִמְּדִינַת הַיָּם וּבַחֵרֵשׁ וּבַשּׁוֹטֶה אֵין שׁוֹמְעִין לוֹ אֶלָּא אוֹמְרִים לוֹ עָלֶיךָ מִצְוָה אוֹ חֲלוֹץ אוֹ יַיבֵּם.

Mishnah 6: If he[105] made it dependent on a minor until he grows up, or on the oldest when he returns from overseas, or on a deaf-mute or on an insane [brother], one does not listen to him but tells him, the obligation is yours, either give *ḥalîṣah* or marry in levirate.

103 Already stated in Mishnah 2:8.

104 The local rabbinic court whose obligation it is to enforce the rules; cf. Maimonides, *Hilkhot Yibum* 2:7.

105 The brother available at the place of the widow.

(fol. 5b) **משנה ז**: הַחוֹלֵץ לִיבִמְתּוֹ הֲרֵי הוּא כְאֶחָד מִכָּל־הָאַחִין לַנַּחֲלָה. וְאִם יֵשׁ שָׁם אָב הַנְּכָסִים שֶׁלָּאָב. הַכּוֹנֵס אֶת יְבִמְתּוֹ זָכָה בְנִיכְסֵי אָחִיו. רַבִּי יְהוּדָה אוֹמֵר בֵּין כָּךְ וּבֵין כָּךְ אִם יֵשׁ שָׁם אָב הַנְּכָסִים שֶׁלָּאָב.

Mishnah 7: He who performs *ḥalîṣah* with his sister-in-law is like any of the other brothers for the inheritance and, if there is a father, the property goes to the father[106]. He who marries his sister-in-law acquires his brother's property. Rebbi Jehudah says, in any case if there is a father, the property goes to the father[107].

106 The father is not mentioned in the biblical rules of inheritance (*Num.* 27:6-11) but since the paternal uncles are mentioned it is clear that one assumes that the father died before his son. Since the rules imply that the

descendants of the son rank before all other relatives, it is logical to assume that the father ranks before all his descendants and other relatives; *Baba batra* 8:2.

107 Subject to the lien of the widow's *ketubah*. The problem does not appear in the case of *ḥalîṣah* since the widow has to be paid in full before the inheritance is distributed. In the Tosephta, 6:3, R. Jehudah also denies that the levir gets all the inheritance if there is no father.

(fol. 5d) **הלכה ז:** הַחוֹלֵץ לִיבִמְתּוֹ הֲרֵי הוּא כְאֶחָד מִכָּל־הָאַחִין לַנַּחֲלָה כול'. שֶׁלֹּא תֹאמַר. חֲלִיצָה פְטוֹר וּבִיאָה פְטוֹר. כְּמָה דְתֵימַר הַכּוֹנֵס אֶת יְבִמְתּוֹ זָכָה בְנִיכְסֵי אָחִיו. וְדִכְוָותָהּ הַחוֹלֵץ לִיבִמְתּוֹ זָכָה בְנִיכְסֵי אָחִיו. לְפוּם כָּךְ צָרִיךְ מֵימַר הֲרֵי הוּא כְאֶחָד מִכָּל־הָאַחִין לַנַּחֲלָה.

Halakhah 7: "He who performs *ḥalîṣah* with his sister-in-law is like any of the other brothers for the inheritance," etc. That one should not say, *ḥalîṣah* is freeing, intercourse is freeing[108]; just as you say, "he who marries his sister-in-law acquires his brother's property," so he who performs *ḥalîṣah* with his sister-in-law acquires his brother's property. Therefore, it is necessary to say "he is like any of the other brothers for the inheritance".

108 Chapter 1, Note 104. The argument is quoted in Babli, 40a, and refuted. The accepted argument is that one might think that the levir who refuses to honor his duty of levirate should be punished by being excluded from inheriting his part, but this is not so.

רַב יְהוּדָה אָמַר בְּשֵׁם שְׁמוּאֵל. הָעוֹשֶׂה מַאֲמָר בִּיבִמְתּוֹ לֹא זָכָה בְנִיכְסֵי אָחִיו. וְאַף בֵּית שַׁמַּי מוֹדֵיי בָהּ. וְאַף רִבִּי שִׁמְעוֹן מוֹדֵיי בָהּ. וְלֹא כְרִבִּי לָעְזָר בֶּן עֲרָךְ. דְּרִבִּי לָעְזָר בֶּן עֲרָךְ אוֹמֵר. הַמַּאֲמָר קוֹנֶה קִנְייָן גָּמוּר בִּיבָמָה. הָיוּ שְׁתֵּי יְבָמוֹת. עָשָׂה מַאֲמָר בְּזוֹ וּבָעַל לְזוֹ. מַה נַּפְשָׁךְ. אִם בְּמַאֲמָר יִזְכֶּה אִם בְּבִיאָה יִזְכֶּה. אָמַר רִבִּי יוֹסֵה. מֵאַחַר שֶׁאֵינוֹ יָכוֹל לְקַיֵּים אֶת אַחַת מֵהֶן לֹא זָכָה בְנִיסְכֵי אָחִיו.

Rav Jehudah said in the name of Samuel: He who "bespeaks" his sister-in-law does not acquire his brother's property[109]. Even the House of Shammai agree to that[110]; even Rebbi Simeon agrees to that, but not Rebbi Eleazar ben Arakh. As Rebbi Eleazar ben Arakh said, "bespeaking" acquires the sister-in-law totally. If there were two sisters-in-law, he "bespoke" one and came to the other. As you take it, either by "bespeaking" he acquires or by intercourse he acquires. Rebbi Yose said, since he cannot keep either one[111], he did not acquire his brother's property.

109 Since *qiddushin* do not give the husband any property rights, the weaker "bespeaking" cannot do it either.

110 They hold that "bespeaking" is a biblical requirement for levirate. Still they cannot hold that "bespeaking" is stronger than *qiddushin*. The same argument is good for R. Simeon who only allows for the possibility that "bespeaking" might be like *qiddushin* (Chapter 2, Note 16).

111 The second one is forbidden to him rabbinically for the House of Hillel, biblically for the House of Shammai. The first one is forbidden to him biblically for the House of Hillel.

רִבִּי יִצְחָק בַּר טֶבֶלַיי בְּשֵׁם רִבִּי לָעְזָר. טַעֲמָא דְרִבִּי יְהוּדָה וְהָיָה הַבְּכוֹר אֲשֶׁר תֵּלֵד. מַקִּישׁוֹ לַבְּכוֹר. מַה הַבְּכוֹר אֵינוֹ יוֹרֵשׁ בְּחַיֵּי אָבִיו אַף זֶה אֵינוֹ יוֹרֵשׁ בְּחַיֵּי אָבִיו. אִי מַה בְּכוֹר יוֹרֵשׁ אַחַר מִיתַת אָבִיו אַף זֶה יוֹרֵשׁ אַחַר מִיתַת אָבִיו. אָמַר רִבִּי זְעוּרָא. מִינָהּ. מַה הַבְּכוֹר לֹא יוֹרֵשׁ בְּשָׁעָה שֶׁהוּא רָאוּי לֵירֵשׁ אַף זֶה אֵינוֹ יוֹרֵשׁ בְּשָׁעָה שֶׁהוּא רָאוּי לֵירֵשׁ. עוֹד אֵינוֹ יוֹרֵשׁ. רִבִּי אַבָּא בַּר כַּהֲנָא רִבִּי חִייָה בַּר אַשִׁי בְּשֵׁם רַב. הֲלָכָה כְּרִבִּי יְהוּדָה. רִבִּי יְהוֹשֻׁעַ בֶּן לֵוִי אָמַר. הֲלָכָה כְּרִבִּי יוּדָה. רִבִּי אַבָּהוּ רִבִּי לָעְזָר בְּשֵׁם רִבִּי הוֹשַׁעְיָה. הֲלָכָה כְּרִבִּי יוּדָה. אָמַר רִבִּי יוֹחָנָן. זִימְנִין סַגִּין יָתְבִית קוֹמֵי רִבִּי הוֹשַׁעְיָה וְלֹא שָׁמְעִית מִינֵּיהּ הָדָא מִילְתָה. אָמַר לֵיהּ. וְלֵית בַּר נַשׁ דּוּ שָׁמַע מִילָּה וְלֵית חַבְרֵיהּ שְׁמִיעַ לֵיהּ.

Rebbi Isaac ben Tevele in the name of Rebbi Eleazar: The reason of Rebbi Jehudah: "[112]The first-born whom she will bear shall be"; He compared it to a first-born. Since the first-born does not inherit during his father's lifetime, so this one does not inherit during his father's lifetime. But since the first-born inherits after his father's death, does this one inherit after his father's death[113]? Rebbi Ze'ira said, since the first-born does not inherit when it was time to inherit, so this one does not inherit when it was time to inherit[114]. Afterwards he cannot inherit. Rebbi Abba bar Cahana, Rebbi Ḥiyya bar Ashi in the name of Rav: Practice follows Rebbi Jehudah. Rebbi Joshua ben Levi said, practice follows Rebbi Judah. Rebbi Abbahu, Rebbi Eleazar in the name of Rebbi Hoshaia, practice follows Rebbi Judah. Rebbi Joḥanan said, many times I sat before Rebbi Hoshaia and never heard that from him. He said to him, does nobody exist who heard something his partner did not hear[115]?

112 *Deut.* 25:6. The verse connects the birth of a first-born with the inheritance of the dead brother.

113 Since the first-born inherits an extra portion from the estate, does the levir inherit the separate inheritance of his wife's first husband separately?

114 The separate inheritance of the first-born is restricted (*Deut.* 21:17) to "all that is found of his property." This is interpreted as excluding claims that are not yet collected; cf., e. g., Babli *Baba batra* 55a. Since the inheritance of the dead brother is under his wife's lien for her *ketubah*, it is not considered as "found of his property".

115 The Babli, 40a, strongly disagrees since practice follows the anonymous majority. This is the position of R. Joḥanan's teacher R. Yannai.

(fol. 5b) **משנה ח:** הַחוֹלֵץ לִיבִמְתּוֹ הוּא אָסִיר בִּקְרוֹבוֹתֶיהָ וְהִיא אֲסוּרָה בִקְרוֹבָיו. הוּא אָסוּר בְּאִמָּהּ וּבְאֵם אִמָּהּ וּבְאֵם אָבִיהָ בְּבִתָּהּ בְּבַת בִּתָּהּ וּבְבַת

בְּנָהּ וּבְאֲחוֹתָהּ בִּזְמַן שֶׁהִיא קַייֶמֶת. הָאַחִין מוּתָּרִין. הִיא אֲסוּרָה בְאָבִיו בַּאֲבִי אָבִיו בִּבְנוֹ וּבְבֶן בְּנוֹ בְּאָחִיו וּבְבֶן אָחִיו. מוּתָּר אָדָם בִּקְרוֹבַת צָרַת חֲלוּצָתוֹ וְאָסוּר בְּצָרַת קְרוֹבַת חֲלוּצָתוֹ.

He who performs *ḥalîṣah* with his sister-in-law is forbidden her relatives and his relatives are forbidden to her[116]. Forbidden to him are her mother and her mother's mother, her father's mother, her daughter, her daughter's daughter and her son's daughter, and her sister as long as she is alive. The brothers are permitted. Forbidden to her are his father, his father's father, his son and his son's son, his brother and his brother's son. The relative of a co-wife of a person who had *ḥalîṣah* with him is permitted to him, but the co-wife of a relative of a person who had *ḥalîṣah* with him is forbidden[117].

116 All relatives forbidden after a divorce (biblical or rabbinic) are rabbinically forbidden after *ḥalîṣah*; cf. also Mishnah 4:13.

117 Mishnah 1:1.

(fol. 5d) **הלכה ח:** הַחוֹלֵץ לִיבִמְתּוֹ כול'. מִפְּנֵי שֶׁחָלַץ לָהּ. הָא לֹא חָלַץ לָהּ וּמֵתָה מוּתָּר בְּאִמָּהּ. אָמַר רִבִּי אֲבִינָא. הָדָא הִיא דָמַר רִבִּי יַעֲקֹב בַּר אָחָא בְשֵׁם רִבִּי לְעָזָר. שׁוֹמֶרֶת יָבָם שֶׁמֵּתָה מוּתָּר בְּאִמָּהּ. זִיקָה הָיְתָה לוֹ בָהּ. כֵּיוָן שֶׁמֵּתָה בָטְלָה (fol. 6a) לוֹ זִיקָתָהּ. וְהָכָא כֵּיוָן שֶׁמֵּת בָּטְלָה זִיקָתוֹ. רִבִּי אָבוּן שָׁמַע לָהּ מִן דְּבַתְרָהּ. וּבַאֲחוֹתָהּ בִּזְמַן שֶׁהִיא קַייֶמֶת וְהָאַחִין מוּתָּרִין. וַאֲחוֹתָהּ אֵצֶל הָאַחִין לֹא כְמֵתָה הִיא.

"He who performs *ḥalîṣah* with his sister-in-law," etc. Because he performed *ḥalîṣah* with her. Therefore, if he did not perform *ḥalîṣah* with her but she died, her mother is permitted to him. [118]That is what Rebbi Jacob bar Aḥa said in the name of Rebbi Eleazar: If a woman waiting for her levir died, her mother is permitted to him. He had in her an interest of candidacy. When she died, the candidacy was eliminated.

And here, when he died, the candidacy was eliminated. Rebbi Abun understood it from what follows: "And her sister as long as she is alive, but the brothers are permitted." Is her sister's position relative to the brothers not as if[119] she herself had died?

118 Chapter 2, Notes 28-29.

119 Relative to the brother chosen to perform *ḥalîṣah*.

אֲסוּרָה בְּאַבִיו וּבַאֲבִי אָבִיו בִּבְנוֹ וּבְבֶן בְּנוֹ בְּאָחִיו וּבְבֶן אָחִיו. הָדָא אָמְרָה שֶׁנִּיתְּנוּ שְׁנִיּוֹת לַחוֹלֵץ. וְהַיְידָא אָמְרָה דָא. בִּבְנוֹ וּבְבֶן בְּנוֹ בְּאָחִיו וּבְבֶן אָחִיו. הָדָא אָמְרָה שֶׁנִּיתְּנוּ שְׁנִיּוֹת לַחוֹלֵץ.

"Forbidden to her are his father, his father's father, his son and his son's son, his brother and his brother's son." Does this imply that secondary prohibitions are imposed on the one performing *ḥalîṣah*? That says it, "his son and his son's son, his brother and his brother's son." That implies that secondary prohibitions are imposed on the one performing *ḥalîṣah*[120].

120 It seems that the first quote is too long and should only refer to his father's father. The Babli, 40b, also raises the question why the paternal grandfather is forbidden and answers that the prohibition has nothing to do with *ḥalîṣah* since that grandfather was forbidden to her from the moment she married her husband. But the son's and the brother's sons are secondary prohibitions. This is also the conclusion of the Babli which, however, restricts secondary prohibitions arising from *ḥalîṣah* strictly to those enumerated in the Mishnah.

כֵּינִי מַתְנִיתָא. מוּתָּר הוּא אָדָם בִּקְרוֹבַת צָרַת חֲלוּצָתוֹ וְאָסוּר בְּצָרַת קְרוֹבַת חֲלוּצָתוֹ. הָדָא מְסַייְעָא לְהַהִיא דְאָמַר רִבִּי הִיָּא בְשֵׁם רִבִּי אֲבִינָא. קַל וָחוֹמֶר. מַה אֲחוֹת חֲלוּצָתוֹ שֶׁהוּא מִדִּבְרֵיהֶן נָתְנוּ לָהּ חֲכָמִים צָרָה. כָּאן שֶׁיֵּשׁ כָּאן אִיסּוּר אָחִיו לֹא כָּל־שֶׁכֵּן.

So is the Mishnah: "The relative of a co-wife of a person who had *ḥalîṣah* with him is permitted to him, but the co-wife of a relative of a person who had *ḥalîṣah* with him is forbidden[121]". [122]Rebbi Hila in the name of Rebbi Avina: It is an inference *de minore ad majus*. If the Sages gave a co-wife to the sister of a woman for whom he performed *ḥalîṣah*, which is rabbinic, here, where there is the prohibition of sisters, not so much more?

121 This is the text of the Mishnah. It seems that the intent of this note is not to correct the text but to reject the formulation "the sister of a co-wife . . .", quoted in Chapter 3 (Note 50).

122 The text is from Chapter 3; explained there in Notes 24, 25.

(fol. 5b) **משנה ט**: הַחוֹלֵץ לִיבִמְתּוֹ וְנָשָׂא אָחִיו אֶת אֲחוֹתָהּ וָמֵת חוֹלֶצֶת וְלֹא מִתְיַיבֶּמֶת. וְכֵן הַמְגָרֵשׁ אֶת אִשְׁתּוֹ וְנָשָׂא אָחִיו אֶת אֲחוֹתָהּ וָמֵת הֲרֵי זוֹ פְטוּרָה.

Mishnah 9: If somebody performs *ḥalîṣah* with his sister-in-law while his brother had married her sister and then died, she must perform *ḥalîṣah* but not levirate[123]. Similarly, if somebody divorces his wife while his brother had married her sister and then died, she is free[124].

123 She is prohibited to the levir by Mishnah 8. But these prohibitions are rabbinical. Since by biblical standards she could have been married in levirate, she needs *ḥalîṣah*.

124 The widow of the brother is forbidden to the levir by biblical standards, there can be no levirate and, therefore, no *ḥalîṣah*.

(fol. 6a) **הלכה ט**: וְכֵן הַמְגָרֵשׁ אֶת אִשְׁתּוֹ כול׳. שִׁמְעוֹן בַּר בָּא בְּעָא קוֹמֵי רִבִּי יוֹחָנָן. מַה בֵין חוֹלֵץ וּמַה בֵין מְגָרֵשׁ. אָמַר לֵיהּ. מָה אַתְּ סָבוּר חֲלִיצָה קִנְיָן.

אֵינָהּ אֶלָּא פְטוֹר. אֵין הָאַחִין חַייָבִין עָלֶיהָ מִשּׁוּם אִשְׁתּוֹ שֶׁלַּחוֹלֵץ. אֲבָל חַייָבִין עָלֶיהָ מִשּׁוּם אִשְׁתּוֹ שֶׁלַּמֵּת.

"Similarly, if somebody divorces his wife," etc. [125]Simeon bar Abba asked before Rebbi Joḥanan: What is the difference between having *ḥalîṣah* and divorcing[90]? He said to him: You think that *ḥalîṣah* is acquisiton, but it is only freeing. The brothers are not guilty[91] for her under the category of "wife of the one acting in *ḥalîṣah*" but they are guilty under the category of "wife of the deceased".

125 Chapter 1, Notes 90, 91.

(fol. 5b) **משנה י:** שׁוֹמֶרֶת יָבָם שֶׁקִּידֵּשׁ אָחִיו אֶת אֲחוֹתָהּ. מִשּׁוּם רִבִּי יְהוּדָה בֶּן בְּתֵירָה אָמְרוּ. אוֹמֵר לוֹ הַמְתֵּן עַד שֶׁיַּעֲשֶׂה אָחִיךָ הַגָּדוֹל מַעֲשֶׂה. חָלְצוּ לָהּ אַחִין אוֹ כָנְסוּ יִכְנוֹס אֶת אִשְׁתּוֹ. מֵתָה הַיְּבָמָה יִכְנוֹס. מֵת הַיָּבָם מוֹצִיא אֶת אִשְׁתּוֹ בְּגֵט וְאֵשֶׁת אָחִיו בַּחֲלִיצָה.

Mishnah 10: If a brother gave *qiddushin* to the sister of a woman waiting for the levir, they said in the name of Rebbi Jehudah ben Bathyra: One says to him wait until your older brother has acted. If [one of the] brothers performed *ḥalîṣah* or married her, he may marry his wife. If the sister-in-law died, he may marry. If the levir died, he has to remove himself from his wife by a bill of divorce and his brother's widow by *ḥalîṣah*.

(fol. 6a) **הלכה י:** שׁוֹמֶרֶת יָבָם כול'. לֹא אָמְרוּ אֶלָּא מֵתָה יְבִמְתּוֹ מוּתָּר בְּאִשְׁתּוֹ. אֲבָל מֵתָה אִשְׁתּוֹ אָסוּר בִּיבִמְתּוֹ. אָמַר רִבִּי יוֹחָנָן. זוֹ דִבְרֵי רִבִּי לְעָזָר. אֲבָל דִּבְרֵי חֲכָמִים מֵתָה יְבִמְתּוֹ מוּתָּר בְּאִשְׁתּוֹ. מֵתָה אִשְׁתּוֹ מוּתָּר בִּיבִמְתּוֹ. אָמַר

רִבִּי יוֹחָנָן. דִּבְרֵי חֲכָמִים. כָּל־דָּבָר שֶׁהוּא בָא מֵחֲמַת הַגּוֹרֵם בָּטַל הַגּוֹרֵם בָּטַל הָאִיסּוּר. וְדִבְרֵי רִבִּי לִעֶזֶר. אֲפִילוּ בָּטַל הַגּוֹרֵם הָאִיסּוּר בִּמְקוֹמוֹ.

It says only: If the sister-in-law died, his wife is permitted to him. But if his wife died, his sister-in-law is forbidden to him. Rebbi Joḥanan said, these are the words of Rebbi Eliezer. But the Sages say, if his sister-in-law died, his wife is permitted to him, if his wife died, his sister-in-law is permitted to him. Rebbi Joḥanan said, the Sages hold that for anything induced by a cause, if the cause is removed the prohibition is removed. But for Rebbi Eliezer, if the cause is removed the prohibition remains[126].

126 Text and explanation in Chapter 3, Notes 6-11.

(fol. 5b) **משנה יא**: הַיְבָמָה לֹא תַחֲלוֹץ וְלֹא תְיַיבֵּם עַד שֶׁיְּהֵא לָהּ שְׁלֹשָׁה חֳדָשִׁים. וְכֵן כָּל־שְׁאָר הַנָּשִׁים לֹא יִנָּשְׂאוּ וְלֹא יִתְאָרְסוּ עַד שֶׁיְּהוּ לָהֶן שְׁלֹשָׁה חֳדָשִׁים. אַחַת בְּתוּלוֹת וְאַחַת בְּעוּלוֹת אַחַת אַלְמָנוֹת וְאַחַת גְּרוּשׁוֹת אַחַת נְשׂוּאוֹת וְאַחַת אֲרוּסוֹת. רִבִּי יְהוּדָה אוֹמֵר הַנְּשׂוּאוֹת יִתְאָרְסוּ וְהָאֲרוּסוֹת יִנָּשְׂאוּ. חוּץ מִן הָאֲרוּסוֹת שֶׁבִּיהוּדָה מִפְּנֵי שֶׁלִּבּוֹ גַס בָּהּ. רִבִּי יוֹסֵי אוֹמֵר כָּל־הַנָּשִׁים יִתְאָרְסוּ חוּץ מִן הָאַלְמָנָה מִפְּנֵי הָאִיבּוּל.

Mishnah 11: No sister-in-law should be a party to *ḥalîṣah* or levirate until after three months. Similarly, no woman[127] should be married or receive *qiddushin* until after three months, whether virgin or not virgin, widow or divorcee, married or betrothed. Rebbi Jehudah says, those that had been married may receive *qiddushin*[128] and those that had received *qiddushin* can be married except those that had received *qiddushin* in Judea because he is familiar with her[129]. Rebbi Yose said, any woman may receive *qiddushin* except a widow because of her mourning.

127 Who had been married. Included are preliminarily married women either as a matter of discipline or because of women betrothed in Judea (Note 129).

128 Since they cannot actually be married until 90 days after the death of the first husband, there is no danger that she will bear a child of undetermined paternity.

129 It is explained in Mishnah *Ketubot* 1:5 that in Judea one permitted the betrothed couple to be together unchaperoned. Therefore, one may assume that they slept together.

(fol. 6a) **הלכה יא:** הַיְבָמָה לֹא תַחֲלוֹץ כול׳. עַד כַּמָּה הַכָּרַת הָעוּבָּר. סוּמְכוֹס אוֹמֵר מִשּׁוּם רִבִּי מֵאִיר. עַד שְׁלֹשָׁה חֳדָשִׁים. אַף עַל פִּי שֶׁאֵין רְאָיָיה לַדָּבָר זֵיכֶר לַדָּבָר שֶׁנֶּאֱמַר וַיְהִי כְּמִשְׁלֹשׁ חֳדָשִׁים. אָמַר רִבִּי יוּדָן. אֲפִילוּ מְעוּבֶּרֶת רוּחַ. הָרִינוּ חַלְנוּ כְּמוֹ יָלַדְנוּ רוּחַ. תַּהֲרוּ חֲשַׁשׁ תֵּלְדוּ קַשׁ. רִבִּי זְעִירָא רִבִּי בָּא בַּר זוּטְרָא אָמַר רִבִּי חֲנִינָה בְשֵׁם רִבִּי חִייָה רַבָּה. אֲפִילוּ רוּבּוֹ שֶׁלָּרִאשׁוֹן וְרוּבּוֹ שֶׁלָּאַחֲרוֹן וְהָאֶמְצָעִי שָׁלֵם. רִבִּי אַסִּי אָמַר. תִּשְׁעִים יוֹם שְׁלֵימִין. שְׁמוּאֵל אָמַר הֵן עִיבּוּרֵיהֶן. אָתָא עוּבְדָא קוֹמֵי רַבָּנָן דְּתַמָּן דְּלָא יָדְעִין אִם שְׁלֹשָׁה עָשָׂר מִן הָרִאשׁוֹן וְשִׁבְעָא עָשָׂר מִן הָאַחֲרוֹן. אוֹ שִׁבְעָא עָשָׂר מִן הָרִאשׁוֹן וּשְׁלֹשָׁה עָשָׂר מִן הָאַחֲרוֹן.[130] וַחֲמִשָּׁה שְׁלֵימִין בָּאֶמְצַע. וּבִקְשׁוּ לִיגַּע בַּוָּולָד מִשּׁוּם סָפֵק מַמְזֵרוּת. אָמַר לוֹן רַב נַחְמָן בַּר יַעֲקֹב. בְּהָהֵין עוּבְדָא אָתָא קוֹמֵי רַבָּה בַּר בָּא וְאַכְשְׁרוֹ. אַבָּא בַּר וָוא פְּלִיג עַל שְׁמוּאֵל בְּרֵיהּ. אָמַר רַבָּא. שַׁנְיָיא הִיא הַכָּרַת הָעוּבָּר שַׁנְיָיא הִיא לֵידָתוֹ. הַכָּרַת הָעוּבָּר לַחֳדָשִׁים שְׁלֵימִין וְלֵידָתוֹ לַחֳדָשִׁים מְקוּטָעִין. תַּמָּן תַּנִּינָן. וְכַמָּה הִיא כִּישּׁוּיָהּ. רִבִּי מֵאִיר אוֹמֵר. אֲפִילוּ אַרְבָּעִים חֲמִשִּׁים יוֹם. רִבִּי יוּדָה אוֹמֵר. דַּיָּיהּ חָדְשָׁהּ. רִבִּי יוֹסֵי וְרִבִּי שִׁמְעוֹן אוֹמְרִים. אֵין קִישּׁוּי יוֹתֵר מִשְׁתֵּי שַׁבָּתוֹת. רִבִּי יוֹסֵה בְשֵׁם רִבִּי וָוא. זֹאת אוֹמֶרֶת שֶׁהָאִשָּׁה יוֹלֶדֶת לַחֳדָשִׁים מְקוּטָעִין. דְּלֹכֵן נִיתְנֵי שְׁלֹשִׁים יוֹם. רִבִּי יוֹסֵה בֵּירִבִּי בּוּן בְּשֵׁם רִבִּי וָוא זֹאת אוֹמֶרֶת שֶׁהָאִשָּׁה יוֹלֶדֶת לַחֳדָשִׁים שְׁלֵימִין. דְּתַנִּינָן דַּיָּיהּ חָדְשָׁהּ.

Halakhah 11 "No sister-in-law should be a party to *ḥalîṣah*," etc. [131]How long is it until a pregnancy is recognized? [132]Symmachos said in the name of Rebbi Meïr: After three months. Even though it is no proof, there is a hint: "It was after about three months.[133]" Rebbi Yudan said, even for a phantom pregnancy, "we were pregnant, we were sick, as if we gave birth to wind,[134]" "get pregnant with dry grass, give birth to straw[135]." Rebbi Ze'ira, Rebbi Abba bar Zuṭra said, Rebbi Ḥanina in the name of the Great Rebbi Ḥiyya: Even most of the first, most of the last, and the middle one complete[136]. Rav Assi said, a full 90 days. Samuel said, they in their fulness[137]. A case came before the rabbis there; we do not know if thirteen of the first and seventeen of the last or seventeen of the first and thirteen of the last, and five complete ones in the middle; they wanted to touch the child because of a doubt of bastardy[138]. Rav Naḥman bar Jacob told them, such a case came before Abba bar Abba[139] and he declared it acceptable. Does Abba bar Abba disagree with his son Samuel? Rebbi Abba said, there is a difference between recognizing a pregnancy and giving birth. A pregnancy is recognized after full months, a birth can happen after fractional months. There, we have stated[140]: "How long can labor be[141]? Rebbi Meïr said, even 40 to 50 days. Rebbi Jehudah said, her month is sufficient. Rebbi Yose and Rebbi Simeon say, no labor is longer than two weeks." Rebbi Yose in the name of Rebbi Abba: This implies that a woman gives birth after fractional months. Since otherwise one should have stated "thirty days". Rebbi Yose ben Rebbi Abun in the name of Rebbi Abba: This implies that a woman gives birth after full months[142]. Since we have stated: "Her month is sufficient."

130 Reading of ms. A. In ms. L, this sentence is identical with the preceding.

131 The text of Symmachos is also in Babli *Niddah* 8b, but the meaning is different there.

In the Babli, the discussion is not about recognizing a pregnancy for the question of remarriage; that question is settled by the proviso that a woman must wait 90 days after her husband's death (as explained in the Mishnah here) and, if she turns out to be pregnant, she cannot remarry as long as the child is not weaned (*Ketubot* 5:6, *Sotah* 4:4; Babli *Ketubot* 60a,b). The statement there is to the effect that if a woman has missed her period three times and is visibly pregnant, then, starting three months after her last period, any bleeding does not follow the general rules of menstrual flow but the special rules of pregnant women. There is no discussion of the rule and it is not claimed that the rule represents any medical validity.

But in the Yerushalmi it appears from the sequel that one sees in the rule a statement of biological fact. The Halakhah, up to Note 155, is copied in *Niddah* 1:4.

132 Tosephta *Niddah* 1:7, including the statement attributed here to Rebbi Yudan.

133 *Gen.* 38:24.

134 *Is.* 26:18; as the Babli points out, this statement is addressed to males and therefore not a good support. In the interpretation of the Babli (Note 131), a fake delivery ("delivery of wind") after recognition of the pregnancy does not change the status of the woman in matters of impurity.

135 *Is.* 33:11.

136 If the pregnancy is recognizable, the rules of pregnancy are applicable after 61 days.

137 Samuel says the same of Rav Assi, three full (i. e., 30days long) months.

138 A woman gave birth to a live baby exactly 180 days after her marriage. The rabbis wondered whether such a short pregnancy was possible for a live baby or whether the short time was proof that the woman had committed adultery in the time between *qiddushin* and her actual marriage, which would make the child a bastard.

139 The most famous of Jewish medical men of his age. Presumably Samuel, also a doctor by profession, learned most of his medical knowledge from his father.

140 Mishnah *Niddah* 4:5.

141 As a matter of principle, blood lost during labor is neither menstrual nor of the impure type known as *zivah* (*Lev.* 15:25). The disagreement is on how long the exemption from impurity can be claimed.

142 See above, Note 63, and in the next paragraph.

רִבִּי יוּדָן בָּעֵי. סוֹף דָּבָר עַד שֶׁתֵּלֵד. לֹא אֲפִילוּ הִפִּילָה.

Rebbi Yudan asked: Does this hold until she gives birth? No, even if she had a miscarriage[143].

143 If the woman has a miscarriage, is her blood retroactively classified as *zivah* blood which requires a purification offering? The Babli declares that miscarriages and stillborn babies make their mother impure retroactively (*Niddah* 38b).

אָמַר רִבִּי מָנָא. שְׁמָעִית בְּשֵׁם שְׁמוּאֵל. הִיא הַכָּרַת הָעוּבָּר הִיא לֵידָתוֹ. וְלֵית אֲנָא יְדַע מִן מַה שְׁמָעִת. אָמַר רִבִּי בָּא בַּר כֹּהֵן קוֹמֵי רִבִּי יוֹסֵי. רִבִּי יִרְמְיָה אֲמְרָהּ. אָמַר לֵיהּ רִבִּי חִזְקִיָּה. לֹא אֲמְרָהּ רִבִּי יִרְמְיָה. וְאִיקְפִּיד רִבִּי יוֹסֵי לְקִיבְלֵיהּ. אָמַר לֵיהּ. שֶׁכֵּן אֲפִילוּ יְהוֹשֻׁעַ שֶׁהָיָה קָשׁוּר לְמֹשֶׁה לֹא אָמַר כֵּן. וְאַתְּ אוֹמְרָהּ כֵּן. חֲזַר וְאָמַר. אִין דַּאֲמְרָהּ אֶלָּא כְאִינָשׁ דְּשָׁמַע מִילָּה וּמַקְשֵׁי עָלֶיהָ. וְאַבָּא בַּר וָוא פַּלִּיג עַל שְׁמוּאֵל בְּרֵיהּ. רִבִּי בֶּרֶכְיָה בְּשֵׁם שְׁמוּאֵל. לְעוֹלָם אֵין הָאִשָּׁה יוֹלֶדֶת אוֹ לְמָאתַיִם וְשִׁבְעִים וְאֶחָד אוֹ לְמָאתַיִם וְשִׁבְעִים וּשְׁנַיִם אוֹ לְמָאתַיִם וְשִׁבְעִים וּשְׁלֹשָׁה אוֹ לְמָאתַיִם וְשִׁבְעִים וְאַרְבָּעָה. אָמַר לֵיהּ רִבִּי מָנָא. מְנָן שָׁמַע רִבִּי הָדָא מִילְּתָא. אָמַר לֵיהּ. מִן רִבִּי בָּא. מִחְלְפָא שִׁיטָּתֵיהּ דְּרִבִּי בָּא. תַּמָּן הוּא אָמַר. שַׁנְיָיא הִיא הַכָּרַת הָעוּבָּר שַׁנְיָיא הִיא לֵידָתוֹ. וְהָכָא אָמַר הָכֵין. רִבִּי אַבָּא בַּר זוּטְרָא בְּשֵׁם שְׁמוּאֵל. {כָּל־שֶׁהוּא בְהֵ״י רַבָּה. כָּל־שֶׁהוּא בְאַלֶ״ף רָבָא.} כָּל־שֶׁהוּא בְהַרְבֶּה הֲרֵי הוּא בְאַרְבֶּה.

Rebbi Mana said, I heard in the name of Samuel that there is no difference between recognizing a pregnancy and giving birth, but I do not remember from whom I heard this. Rebbi Abba bar Cohen said before Rebbi Yose, Rebbi Jeremiah said this. Rebbi Ḥizqyah said to him, Rebbi Jeremiah did not say this; Rebbi Yose was offended by him. He said to him: Even Joshua who was bound to Moses would not have said so, but you said so[144]! He checked himself and said, it is true that he said that but as a person who quotes something and questions it; does Abba bar Abba disagree with his son Samuel? Rebbi Berekhiah in the name of Samuel: A woman gives birth only either after 271, 272, 273, or 274, days[145]. Rebbi Mana said to him, from whom did the rabbi hear this? He said to him, from Rebbi Abba. The position of Rebbi Abba seems inverted. There, he says, there is a difference between recognizing a pregnancy and giving birth[146], and here, he says so? Rebbi Abba bar Zuṭra in the name of Samuel: {If with ה Rabba, with א Rava.}[147] Everything which is "many" is 208[148].

144 To claim that he knew absolutely everything his teacher ever said.

145 After her last period. In the Babli, *Niddah* 38b, Mar Zuṭra is quoted that a 9 months pregnancy is 271 days, the numerical value of הריון "pregnancy" in the Alexandrian system.

146 That the length of a pregnancy is not counted in full months, and here he even counts them in full months of 30 days each.

147 The text in braces is the text from *Yebamot*; it is a gloss from a student of the Babli to distinguish between quotes of Rabba רבה (Rav Abba bar Naḥmani) and Rava רבא (Rav Abba bar Rav Joseph bar Ḥama), assuming the copyists made no mistakes.

148 This is the text from *Niddah* and it makes sense, that if in the Pentateuch there is a promise of הרבה ארבה (cf. *Gen.* 16:10, 22:17) it implies a seven month birth after ה+ב+ר+א = 1+200+2+5 days. In Babli *Niddah* 38b, Mar Zuṭra reads *1S.* 1:20 that Hanna gave birth to Samuel after 2 seasons (of $91^1/_4$ days each) and two days, or 184.5 days, barely more than 6 full months.

רַב חִייָה בַּר אַשִׁי הֲוָה יְתִיב קוֹמֵי דְרַב. חֲמִיתֵיהּ מַבְעֵת. אָמַר לֵיהּ. מַהוּ כֵן. אָמַר לֵיהּ. חֲמָרְתִּי מְעַבְּרָה וְהִיא בְעָיָא מֵילַד וַאֲנָא בָעֵי מִרְבַּעְתָּהּ עַד דְּלָא תְצַנֵּן. אָמַר לֵיהּ. אֵימָתַי עָלָה עָלֶיהָ הַזָּכָר. אָמַר לֵיהּ. בְּיוֹם פְּלָן. וְחָשַׁב אָמַר לֵיהּ. בְּעָיָא הִיא עַד כְּדוֹן. וְתַנֵּי כֵן. חֲמָרְתָא פוֹחֶתֶת אֵינָהּ פוֹחֶתֶת מִימוֹת הַלְּבָנָה וְהַמּוֹסֶפֶת אֵינָהּ מוֹסֶפֶת עַל יְמוֹת הַחַמָּה. מִילְתֵיהּ דְּרִבִּי יְהוֹשֻׁעַ בֶּן לֵוִי פְלִיגָא. דְּאָמַר רִבִּי יְהוֹשֻׁעַ בֶּן לֵוִי. בָּקוֹרֶת שֶׁלַּמַּלְכוּת עִיבְּרָה וְהִרְבִּיעִי שֶׁלְּבֵית רִבִּי מִמֶּנָּה[149] שְׁוָרִים. וְיֵשׁ מֵהֶן שֶׁיָּלְדוּ עַכְשָׁיו וְיֵשׁ מֵהֶן שֶׁיָּלְדוּ לְאַחַר זְמָן. כָּאן

בִּבְהֵמָה טְהוֹרָה כָּאן בִּבְהֵמָה טְמֵיאָה. וְהָא כְתִיב הֲיָדַעְתָּ עֵת לֶדֶת יַעֲלֵי סָלַע וגו׳. תִּסְפּוֹר יְרָחִים תְּמַלֶּאנָה וְיָדַעְתָּ עֵת לִדְתָּנָה. הֲיָדַעְתָּ עֵת לֶדֶת. חַיָּה טְהוֹרָה כִבְהֵמָה טְמֵאָה.

Rab Ḥiyya bar Ashi was sitting before Rav who saw him disturbed. He said to him, what is the matter? He said to him, my female donkey is pregnant and will give birth; then I have to get her to copulate before she is out of heat. He said to him, when did the male mount her? He said, on day X. He calculated and said, she still has some time until then. It was stated so: A quick female donkey does not need less than the days of the moon[150] and one who is late is not later than the days of the sun[151]. The words of Rebbi Joshua ben Levi disagree, since Rebbi Joshua ben Levi said, the cattle herd of the government[152] was there for copulating and those of the house of Rebbi took bulls from them to copulate. Some of them gave birth soon and some of them later[153]. Here it is about a pure animal, there about an impure animal. But is it not written, "do you know the time the mountain goats will give birth, etc." "Count months, make them complete, you will know the time of their giving birth[154]." "Do you know the time of giving birth?" A pure wild animal is like a domestic impure animal[155].

149 Reading of ms. A. Ms. L: ממנא.

150 354 days in a lunar year.

151 365 days in a solar year. The Babli, *Bekhorot* 8a, simply states that impure domestic animals have a gestation period of 12 months.

152 In *Niddah* 1:4: "of Antoninus"; cf. *Kilaim*, Chapter 9, Note 79.

153 It seems, later than the 11 days' difference allowed by Rav.

154 *Job* 39:1-2.

155 This supports the prior assertion of Rav and excludes only domestic pure animals from predicting the exact time of gestation. The Babli, *Baba batra* 16a/b, uses *Job* 39:1 to prove that the time of birth of wild animals is unpredictable. Elsewhere, *Bekhorot* 8a, the gestation period of great predators (lions, wolves, bears, panthers) as well as apes and marmosets is given as three years.

רִבִּי מֵאִיר חָשַׁשׁ לְגִיטִּין. רִבִּי יוּדָה חָשַׁשׁ לִוְולָד. רִבִּי יוֹסֵי חָשַׁשׁ לַגִּיטִּין וְלִוְולָד. אִין תֵּימַר דְּלֵית רִבִּי מֵאִיר. חוֹשֵׁשׁ לַגִּיטִּין. דְּתְנָן. אֲרוּסוֹת יִנָּשְׂאוּ מִיָּד. רִבִּי זְעוּרָא בְּשֵׁם רִבִּי גְּדוּלָה. מְמָאֶנֶת אֵינָהּ צְרִיכָה לְהַמְתִּין שְׁלֹשָׁה חֳדָשִׁים. [הַיּוֹצְאָה בְּגֵט צְרִיכָה לְהַמְתִּין שְׁלֹשָׁה חֳדָשִׁים.][156] הָדָא מְסַיְּיעָא לְרִבִּי מֵאִיר. דְּרִבִּי מֵאִיר חָשַׁשׁ לְגִיטִּין. רִבִּי בָּא בְּשֵׁם רִבִּי אַבָּא בַּר יִרְמְיָה. אֲנוּסָה אֵינָהּ צְרִיכָה לְהַמְתִּין שְׁלֹשָׁה חֳדָשִׁים. מְסַיְּיעָא לְרִבִּי יוֹסֵי. דְּרִבִּי יוֹסֵי חָשַׁשׁ לַגִּיטִּין וְלִוְולָד. תַּנֵּי הַגִּיּוֹרֶת וְהַשְּׁבוּיָה וְהַשִּׁפְחָה שֶׁנִּפְדּוּ וְשֶׁנִּתְגַּיְּירוּ וְשֶׁנִּשְׁתַּחְרְרוּ צְרִיכוֹת לְהַמְתִּין שְׁלֹשָׁה חֳדָשִׁים. דִּבְרֵי רִבִּי יוּדָה. רִבִּי יוֹסֵי אוֹמֵר. אֵינָן צְרִיכוֹת לְהַמְתִּין. וּבְדָמִים. רִבִּי יוּדָה אוֹמֵר. מְטַמֵּא מֵעֵת לָעֵת. רִבִּי יוֹסֵי אוֹמֵר. דַּיָּיהּ שַׁעְתָּהּ. אָמַר רִבִּי. נִרְאִין דִּבְרֵי רִבִּי יוּדָה בְדָמִים וְדִבְרֵי רִבִּי יוֹסֵי בִוְולָד. אָמַר רִבִּי חֲנִינָה בְּרֵיהּ דְּרִבִּי אַבָּהוּ. אַבָּא הֲוָה לֵיהּ עוֹבְדָא וְשָׁלַח שָׁאַל לְרִבִּי חִיָּיה וּלְרִבִּי יוֹסָה[157] וּלְרִבִּי אִמִּי וְהוֹרוֹן לֵיהּ כְּרִבִּי יוֹסֵי בִּוְלָד. דְּלֹא כֵן מַה אֲנָן אָמְרִין. רִבִּי יוּדָה וְרִבִּי יוֹסֵי אֵין הֲלָכָה כְּרִבִּי יוֹסֵי. אֶלָּא בְגִין דְּאָמַר רִבִּי. נִרְאִין. לֹא כֵן אָמַר רִבִּי בָּא בְּשֵׁם רִבִּי זְעוּרָה. כָּל־מָקוֹם שֶׁשָּׁנָה רִבִּי. נִרְאִין. עֲדַיִין הַמַּחֲלוֹקֶת בִּמְקוֹמָהּ חוּץ מֵעִיגּוּל שֶׁלִּדְבֵילָה. דְּדִין מוֹדֵי לְדִין וְדֵין מוֹדֵי לְדִין. אָמַר רִבִּי יוֹסֵי. כַּשִׁיטָּתָהּ כּוֹמֵי רִבִּי חֲנִינָה בְּרֵיהּ דְּרִבִּי אַבָּהוּ. אֲפִילוּ דָבָר בָּרִיא שֶׁנִּבְעֲלוּ. (fol. 6b) אָמַר לוֹ. וּסְתָם גּוֹיוֹת לֹא כִבְעוּלוֹת הֵן. שִׁמְעוֹן בַּר בָּא אָמַר. אָתָא עוֹבְדָא קוֹמֵי רִבִּי יוֹחָנָן וְהוֹרֵי כְּרִבִּי יוֹסֵי. וַהֲוָה רִבִּי לָעְזָר מִצְטָעֵר. אָמַר. שָׁבְקִין סְתָמָא וְעָבְדִין כִּיחִידָייָא. אַשְׁכַּח תַּנֵּי לָהּ רִבִּי חִיָּיה בְּשֵׁם רִבִּי מֵאִיר. כְּרִבִּי שִׁמְעוֹן שָׁמַע לָהּ דְּתַנֵּי לָהּ רִבִּי חִיָּיה בְּשֵׁם רִבִּי מֵאִיר אָמַר. יְאוּת סַבָּא יְדַע פִּירְקֵי גִיטָּא.

Rebbi Meïr[158] is suspicious about bills of divorce[159]. Rebbi Jehudah is suspicious about a child[160]. Rebbi Yose is suspicious about bills of divorce and a child[161]. Could you say that Rebbi Meïr is not suspicious about bills of divorce, as we have stated[162]: "Those that had received *qiddushin* can be married.[163]" Rebbi Ze'ira in the name of Rebbi Gedula[164]: The one who repudiates does not have to wait three months; the one who leaves by a bill of divorce needs to wait three months[165]. This supports Rebbi

Me'ir since Rebbi Meïr is suspicious about bills of divorce. Rebbi Abba in the name of Rebbi Abba bar Jeremiah: A woman who has been raped does not have to wait three months[166]. This supports Rebbi Yose, since Rebbi Yose is suspicious about bills of divorce and a child. It was stated[167]: The proselyte, the captive, and the slave woman who were redeemed, or converted, or freed, have to wait three months, the words of Rebbi Judah. Rebbi Yose says, they do not have to wait. Their blood[168], Rebbi Jehudah says, makes impure 24 hours retroactively; Rebbi Yose says, from its moment onwards. Rebbi said, the words of Rebbi Judah are reasonable for the blood, and the words of Rebbi Yose for the child. Rebbi Ḥanina ben Rebbi Abbahu said, my father had a case and he asked Rebbi Ḥiyya, Rebbi Yasa, and Rebbi Immi, and they instructed him following Rebbi Yose for the child. For if it were not so, what could we say? Between Rebbi Jehudah and Rebbi Yose, practice does not follow Rebbi Yose[169]? But because Rebbi said, "they are reasonable"[170]. Did not Rebbi Abba say in the name of Rebbi Ze'ira, every time Rebbi taught "they are reasonable", the disagreement is unresolved except in the case of the fig cake where each party to the controversy accepts the opposition's argument[171]. Rebbi Yose said, I stated a difficulty before Rebbi Ḥanina ben Rebbi Abbahu: Even if it is certain that they had sex? He said to him, is a normal Gentile not like one who had sex? Simeon bar Abba said, there came a case before Rebbi Joḥanan and he instructed following Rebbi Yose. Rebbi Eleazar was sorry about this; he said, one disregards the anonymous [Mishnah] and follows an isolated opinion! He found that Rebbi Ḥiyya[172] stated it in the name of Rebbi Meïr. He understood that following Rebbi Simeon[173], he found that Rebbi Ḥiyya stated it in the name of Rebbi Meïr. He said, the old man[174] certainly understands the chapters about bills of divorce.

156 From ms. A, missing in ms. L; necessary for the context

157 From ms. A; ms. L: יוסי, since clearly the reference is to R. Yasa (Assi); that reading has to be rejected.

158 He is the author of the anonymous opinion in the Mishnah, as asserted by R. Simeon ben Laqish in the paragraph after the next. N. Rabbinovicz in *Diqduqe Soferim Erubin* 47a (Note כ) indicates that the Soncino edition, in the quote of the Mishnah here, has "the words of Rebbi Meïr", a reading rejected by Rashi *ad loc.* It seems that the Soncino text is the correct quote of a parallel Mishnah.

159 He is afraid that a man who had divorced his childless wife would notice too late that she was pregnant and say that, if he had known this, he never would have divorced her. This could invalidate the bill of divorce and make the divorcee and the second husband adulterers and the child a bastard. {Therefore, in modern divorce proceedings, one lets the husband state three times before witnesses that any later action to invalidate the bill will be null and void.}

160 He requires waiting only in cases where there could be a question of the paternity of a child. Since bills of divorce should be handled only by a competent authority, he is confident that the case behind R. Meïr's restrictions is not justified.

161 The "and" is taken in the strict sense: Only if there is a simultaneous question about a bill of divorce *and* paternity.

162 תנן is an error of the corrector under the influence of the Babli instead of תנינן.

163 Since this is stated as R. Jehudah's opinion, it follows that R. Meïr objects. To dissolve a preliminary marriage, a bill of divorce is needed even though there normally should not be any chance of pregnancy.

164 Usually, he is called Rav Gidul; a Babylonian of the second generation, student of Rav, who immigrated into Galilee.

165 Both statements are about underage girls, too young to have children. If the girl had been married off by her father, she cannot repudiate her husband but needs a bill of divorce. R. Meïr requires a waiting period for all divorcees even if there is no question of a possible pregnancy. In the Babli, 34b, this is a statement of Samuel.

166 In the Babli, 35a, this is a tannaitic statement attributed to R. Yose, whose opinion is interpreted to assume that she will know how to rid herself of the unwanted semen. R.

Jehudah is quoted as requiring her to wait three months; his opinion is interpreted as questioning the efficacy of means to rid herself of the unwanted semen.

167 In the parallels, only the first part, dealing with waiting before marriage, is quoted. A shortened version is in Tosephta 6:6. The text quoted here is in the Babli, 35a, with the same lack of coordination between nouns and verbs.

168 Their menstrual blood which is an original source of impurity. Gentiles cannot impart impurity by biblical standards; the impurity of menstruation certainly is not applicable to Gentiles. Therefore, a Gentile who converts to Judaism (or becomes fully Jewish in the case of the manumitted slave) really should not be a retroactive source of impurity. In the Tosephta, *Niddah* 1:3, the attributions are switched, and this seems to be the background both for the remark of Rebbi (not in the Tosephta) and the later discussion since in a switched version, Rebbi seems to prefer the stringency of R. Judah in the matter of remarriage. But it is difficult to change the text against the testimony of both mss. (which, however, represent the same *Vorlage*.)

The Babli has no possible interest in this discussion since it holds (*Avodah zarah* 36b) that all Gentile women are rabbinically permanently menstruating {and biblically married, since in talmudic theory, *Sanhedrin* 58b, a Gentile is married to the first partner he or she is copulating with, without possibility of divorce (a position which seems to be adopted by the Apostle Paul).}

169 In the practical rules of preference, Rebbi Yose ranks over all other students and colleagues of Rebbi Aqiba (Yerushalmi *Terumot* 3:1, Notes 20-26; Babli *Erubin* 46b).

170 This question makes sense only if Rebbi's preference is formulated so it endorses R. Jehudah for the rules of remarriage.

171 This seems to refer to the disagreement between rabbis Eliezer and Joshua over pressed figs among which some heave was lost; *Terumot* Halakhah 4:10, Tosephta 5:11. In neither source is there a reference to the position taken by Rebbi.

172 The Great R. Ḥiyya, not R. Ḥiyya bar Abba mentioned earlier in this paragraph.

173 R. Simeon ben Laqish, cf. Note 158. The question mark put in the text by the editor of the ms. is unnecessary.

174 R. Joḥanan.

רִבִּי מָנָא בְּעָא קוֹמֵי רִבִּי יוּדָן. תַּמָּן אָמַר רִבִּי חִזְקִיָּה רִבִּי אַבָּהוּ בְּשֵׁם רִבִּי לָעְזָר. כָּל־מָקוֹם שֶׁשָּׁנָה רִבִּי מַחֲלוֹקֶת וְחָזַר וְשָׁנָה סְתָם הֲלָכָה כִסְתָם מִשְׁנָה. וְהָכָא אַתְּ אָמַר הָכֵין. אָמַר לֵיהּ. לֹא רִבִּי דִּילְמָא חוֹרָן אָמַר. מִן מַה הֵן דְּשָׁנָה רִבִּי מַתְנִיתִין מַחֲלוֹקֶת וְחָזַר וְשָׁנָה סְתָם הֲלָכָה כִסְתָם. אַתְּאֵי דְּלָא אַשְׁכַּח רִבִּי מַחֲלוֹקֶת אֶלָּא אֲחֵרִים שָׁנוּ מַחֲלוֹקֶת וְרִבִּי שָׁנָה סְתָם לֹא כָּל־שֶׁכֵּן תְּהֵא הֲלָכָה כִסְתָם. אָתָא רִבִּי חִזְקִיָּה וְרִבִּי יַעֲקֹב בַּר אָחָא וְרִבִּי שִׁמְעוֹן בַּר אַבָּא בְּשֵׁם רִבִּי לָעְזָר וַאֲפִילוּ שָׁנוּ אֲחֵרִים מַחֲלוֹקֶת וְרִבִּי שָׁנָה סְתָם הֲלָכָה כִסְתָם. וְלָמָּה הוּא מוֹרֵי לֵיהּ כִּיחִידַיָּא. רִבִּי שְׁמוּאֵל בַּר אִינַיָּא בְּשֵׁם רִבִּי אָחָא. הָדָא דְתֵימַר בְּשֶׁאֵין מַחֲלוֹקֶת אֵצֶל סְתָם. אֲבָל אִם יֵשׁ מַחֲלוֹקֶת אֵצֶל סְתָם לֹא בְדָא הֲלָכָה כִסְתָם. רִבִּי יוֹסֵי בֵּירִבִּי בּוּן בְּשֵׁם רִבִּי אָחָא. הָדָא דְתֵימַר בְּיָחִיד אֵצֶל יָחִיד. אֲבָל בְּיָחִיד אֵצֶל חֲכָמִים לֹא בְדָא הֲלָכָה כִסְתָם.

Rebbi Mana asked before Rebbi Yudan: There Rebbi Ḥizqiah, Rebbi Abbahu, said in the name of Rebbi Eleazar: Every place where Rebbi taught a disagreement and afterwards taught it anonymously, practice follows the anonymous Mishnah[175]. And here, you say so? He said to him, if not Rebbi, maybe somebody else said it? Since when Rebbi taught a disagreement and afterwards taught it anonymously, practice follows the anonymous [text]. It must be that Rebbi did not find a disagreement in the Mishnah; but if others taught it in disagreement and Rebbi taught it anonymously, certainly practice follows the anonymous [text]. There come Rebbi Ḥizqiah, Rebbi Jacob bar Abba and Rebbi Simeon bar Abba, in the name of Rebbi Eleazar: Even if others taught a disagreement but Rebbi taught it anonymously, practice follows the anonymous [text]. Why does he agree here with a dissenting opinion? Rebbi Samuel ben Inaya in the name of Rebbi Aḥa. That means, if no diagreement is stated together with the anonymous [text], but if a disagreement is stated together with the anonymous [text], practice does not follow the anonymous [opinion]. Rebbi Yose ben Rebbi Abun in the name of Rebbi Aḥa. That is, if individual disagrees with individual. But if an individual disagrees next to[176] the [anonymous] Sages, practice does not follow the anonymous [text].

175 The Babli, *Yebamot* 42b, *Baba qama* 102a, *Avodah zarah* 7a, *Niddah* 11b, quotes the corresponding statement (in the name of R. Johanan) in a very succinct way: Disagreement followed by anonymous statement implies practice follows the anonymous statement; anonymous statement followed by disagreement implies practice does not follow the anonymous statement. Therefore, the Babli has no problem to follow R. Yose in this Halakhah. The same conclusion is reached here in the last sentence of the paragraph.

176 Meaning "after".

אָמַר רִבִּי יוֹחָנָן. כָּל־מָקוֹם שֶׁשָּׁנָה סְתָם מִשְׁנָיוֹת דְּרַבָּנָן עַד שֶׁיְּפָרֵשׁ לוֹ רַבּוֹ. רִבִּי שִׁמְעוֹן בֶּן לָקִישׁ אוֹמֵר. כָּל־סְתָם מִשְׁנָיוֹת דְּרִבִּי מֵאִיר עַד שֶׁיְּפָרֵשׁ לוֹ רַבּוֹ. אָמַר רִבִּי זְעִירָא קוֹמֵי רִבִּי רִבִּי יוֹסָה.[157] לֹא דְרִבִּי שִׁמְעוֹן בֶּן לָקִישׁ פְּלִיג אֶלָּא דוּ חֲמֵי רוֹב סְתָם מִשְׁנָיוֹת דְּרִבִּי מֵאִיר. רִבִּי זְעִירָא בְּעָא קוֹמֵי רִבִּי מָנָא. הֵידֵינוּ רַבָּה. רַבָּה דְמַתְנִיתָא רַבָּה דְאוּלְפָּנָא. לֵית מִילְתָא דְרִבִּי לָעְזָר אָמְרָה רַבָּה דְמַתְנִיתָא. כְּרִבִּי שִׁמְעוֹן דְּתַנֵּי לָהּ רִבִּי חִייָה בְשֵׁם רִבִּי מֵאִיר אָמַר. יְאוּת סַבָּא יְדַע פִּירְקֵי גַרְמֵה. נֹאמַר אוּלְפָּן קְבִיל מִן רַבָּה דְמַתְנִיתָא. כַּד שָׁמַע דְּתַנֵּי לָהּ רִבִּי חִייָה בְּשֵׁם רִבִּי מֵאִיר.

Rebbi Johanan said, everywhere one taught anonymous Mishnaiot, it follows the rabbis unless one's teacher explains it [differently]. Rebbi Simeon ben Laqish says, all anonymous Mishnaiot follow Rebbi Meïr unless one's teacher explains it [differently][177]. Rebbi Ze'ira said before Rebbi Yasa, not that Rebbi Simeon ben Laqish disagrees, only he saw that most anonymous Mishnaiot follow Rebbi Meïr. Rebbi Ze'ira asked before Rebbi Mana: What kind of teacher? The teacher of the *baraita* or the teacher of study[178]? Does not the story of Rebbi Eleazar imply, the teacher of the *baraita*? "Following Rebbi Simeon[173], he found that Rebbi

Ḥiyya stated it in the name of Rebbi Meïr. He said, the old man[174] certainly understands his chapters." We have to say that he received instruction from the teacher of the *baraita*[179] when he understood that Rebbi Ḥiyya stated it in the name of Rebbi Meïr.

177 In the Babli, both statements are attributed to R. Joḥanan: Practice follows the anonymous Mishnah as consensus of the majority (*Hulin* 43a), the formulation usually is due to R. Meïr (*Sanhedrin* 86a). The attributions of texts in other tannaitic works stated in the latter source have no parallels in Yerushalmi sources.

178 A tannaitic source or the Amora, his personal teacher?

179 When R. Eleazar questioned the decision of his teacher R. Joḥanan, he certainly did not get his information from the latter. So the "teacher' must be the author of a *baraita* to be discovered by independent research.

הַחוֹלֶצֶת מוֹנָה מִשְּׁעַת מִיתָה. הַיּוֹצְאָה בְגֵט מוֹנָה מִשְּׁעַת נְתִינַת גִּיטָּהּ. רִבִּי חֲנִינָה אָמַר. מִשְּׁעַת נְתִינַת גִּיטָּהּ. רִבִּי יוֹחָנָן אָמַר. מִשְּׁעַת כְּתִיבָה. רַב וּשְׁמוּאֵל. רַב כְּרִבִּי חֲנִינָה. וּשְׁמוּאֵל אָמַר כְּרִבִּי יוֹחָנָן. מָתִיב שְׁמוּאֵל לְרַב. עַל דַּעְתָּךְ דְּאַתְּ אָמַר מִשְּׁעַת נְתִינָה. מִשּׁוּם מָה אַתְּ חוֹשֵׁשׁ. מִשּׁוּם שֶׁנִּתְיַיֲחְדָה בֵּנְתַיִים. וְנִיחוּשׁ לָהּ לְגֵט יָשָׁן. מַתִיב רִבִּי חֲנִינָה לְרִבִּי יוֹחָנָן. עַל דַּעְתָּךְ דְּאַתְּ אָמַר מִשְּׁעַת כְּתִיבָה. הָיוּ שְׁנֵי גִיטִּין. אֶחָד נִכְתָּב עַכְשָׁיו וְאֶחָד נִכְתָּב לְאַחַר זְמָן וְנִיתְּנוּ שְׁנֵיהֶן בְּיוֹם אֶחָד. לַזּוֹ אַתְּ אוֹסֵר וְלַזּוֹ אַתְּ מַתִּיר. מִן דַּהֲוָה מוֹתְבָה רַב לִשְׁמוּאֵל הָתִיב רִבִּי חֲנִינָה לְרִבִּי יוֹחָנָן. מִן[180] דַּהֲוָה מוֹתְבָה רִבִּי יוֹחָנָן לְרִבִּי חֲנִינָה הָתִיב שְׁמוּאֵל לְרַב. וַהֲלָכָה מוֹנֶה לְגֵט מִשְּׁעַת כְּתִיבָה אִם לֹא נִתְיַיחֵד עִמָּהּ.

The woman who performs *ḥalîṣah* counts from the moment of death[181]. The one who leaves by a bill of divorce counts from the moment of delivery of her bill. Rebbi Ḥanina said, from the moment of delivery of her bill. Rebbi Joḥanan said, from the moment of writing. Rav and Samuel, Rav like Rebbi Ḥanina, Samuel like Rebbi Joḥanan[182].

Samuel objected to Rav: According to you, since you say from the moment of delivery, about what are you suspicious? Because in the meantime she was alone with him! Then one should worry about an old bill of divorce[183]! Rebbi Ḥanina objected to Rebbi Joḥanan: According to you, since you say from the moment of writing, if there were two bills of divorce, one written now and one later, and both delivered on the same day. This one you prohibit and that one you permit![184] What Rav objected to Samuel, Rebbi Ḥanina objected to Rebbi Joḥanan. What Rebbi Joḥanan objected to Rebbi Ḥanina, Samuel objected to Rav. Practice: She counts from the time of writing if he never was alone with her[185].

180 Reading of ms. A. Ms. L: מאן.

181 Since she cannot be freed before three months, she may remarry immediately after *ḥalîṣah*. The Babli, 42a, follows the Tosephta, 6:7, that a sister-in-law who performed *ḥalîṣah* within the first three months must wait another three months.

182 Babli 42a.

183 An bill of divorce is old at the moment of delivery if husband and wife were alone together at a place where they could have intercourse. For the House of Hillel, the bill is invalid and the woman is not divorced (Mishnah *Giṭṭin* 8:4). According to Samuel, Rav should not permit the delivery of a bill of divorce if husband and wife are at the same place and the bill was not delivered on the day it was written and signed.

184 The same argument in Babli *Giṭṭin* 18a.

185 The Babli agrees, 42a; *Giṭṭin* 18a.

חוּץ מִן הָאַלְמָנָה מִפְּנֵי הָאִיבּוּל. וְכַמָּה הוּא הָאִיבּוּל. שְׁלֹשִׁים יוֹם. הָדָא דְתֵימַר בַּנָּשִׁים. אֲבָל בָּאֲנָשִׁים שְׁלֹשָׁה רְגָלִים. בְּשֶׁיֵּשׁ לוֹ בָנִים. אֲבָל אִם אֵין לוֹ בָנִים מִיָּד. בְּשֶׁיֵּשׁ לוֹ מִי שֶׁיְּשַׁמְּשֶׁנּוּ. אֲבָל אִם אֵין לוֹ מִי שֶׁיְּשַׁמְּשֶׁנּוּ מִיָּד. בְּשֶׁאֵין לוֹ בָנִים קְטַנִּים. אֲבָל אִם הָיוּ בָנָיו קְטַנִּים מִיַּד. כְּהָדָא. מַעֲשֶׂה שֶׁמֵּתָה אִשְׁתּוֹ

שֶׁלְּרִבִּי טַרְפוֹן. עַד כְּשֶׁרוּא בְּבֵית הַקְּבָרוֹת אָמַר לַאֲחוֹתָהּ. הִכָּנְסִי וְגַדְּלִי אֶת בְּנֵי אֲחוֹתֵיךְ. אַף עַל פִּי כֵן כְּנָסָהּ וְלֹא הִכִּירָהּ עַד שֶׁעָבְרוּ עָלֶיהָ שְׁלֹשִׁים יוֹם.

"Except the widow because of her mourning." How much does mourning last? Thirty days[186]. That is, for women. But for men[187], three holidays. If he has children; but if he does not have children immediately. If he has somebody to serve him; but if he has nobody to serve him, immediately. If he does not have small children; but if he has small children, immediately, as in the following: It happened that Rebbi Ṭarphon's wife died. While he still was in the cemetery, he said to her sister: Come into my house and raise your sister's children. Even though he married her, he did not know her until 30 days had passed.

186 The same in Babli, 43b.

187 All this, including the story (attributed to Joseph the Cohen), in Babli *Mo'ed Qaṭan* 23a. (Except when he has nobody to serve him; current practice follows the Yerushalmi.)

(fol. 5b) **משנה יב**: אַרְבָּעָה אַחִין נְשׂוּאִין לְאַרְבַּע נָשִׁים וָמֵתוּ אִם רָצָה הַגָּדוֹל שֶׁבָּהֶם לְיַיבֵּם אֶת כּוּלָּן הָרְשׁוּת בְּיָדוֹ. מִי שֶׁהָיָה נָשׂוּי לִשְׁתֵּי נָשִׁים וָמֵת בִּיאָתָהּ אוֹ חֲלִיצָתָהּ שֶׁל אַחַת מֵהֶן פּוֹטֶרֶת צָרָתָהּ. הָיְתָה אַחַת כְּשֵׁירָה וְאַחַת פְּסוּלָה אִם הָיָה חוֹלֵץ חוֹלֵץ לַפְּסוּלָה וְאִם הָיָה מְיַיבֵּם מְיַיבֵּם לַכְּשֵׁירָה.

Mishnah 12: If four brothers[188] were married to four women and died, if their oldest [brother] wants to marry all of them in levirate, he is permitted to do so. If somebody was married to two women and he died, intercourse or *ḥalîṣah* with one of them frees the co-wife. If one was acceptable and the other blemished[189], if he performs *ḥalîṣah*, he performs it with the blemished; if he takes in levirate, he takes the acceptable one.

188 The text in the Halakhah, "four of the brothers", is a better formulation since one speaks of a large group of brothers.

189 One was eligible to marry a Cohen; the other (e. g., a divorcee) was blemished in this respect. Since a woman freed by *ḥalîṣah* is considered a divorcee for a Cohen, the chances of remarriage of the acceptable one should not be diminished. For levirate, he may take either one.

(fol. 6b) **הלכה יב:** אַרְבָּעָה מֵאַחִין כול׳. דְּלֹמָה. תְּלַת עָשָׂר אַחִין הֲוִיָּן וּמֵתִין תְּרֵין עָשָׂר דְּלָא בְּבִין. אַתְיוּן בְּעַיּוּן מִתְייַבְּמָה קוֹמֵי רִבִּי. אֲמַר לֵיהּ רִבִּי. אֵיזִיל יַיבֵּם. אֲמַר לֵיהּ. לֵית בְּחֵיילִי. וְהֵם אוֹמְרוֹת. כָּל־חָדָא וְחָדָא אֲנָא מְזַייְנְנָא יַרְחִי. אֲמַר. וּמָאן זַיֵּין הַהוּא יַרְחָא דְעִיבּוּרָא. אֲמַר רִבִּי. אֲנָא זַייְנְנָא יַרְחָא דְעִיבּוּרָא. וְצַלִּי עֲלֵיהוֹן וְאֶזְלוּן לְהוֹן. בְּתַר תְּלַת שְׁנִין אָתוּן טְעִינִין תַּלְתִּין וְשִׁיתָא מֵיינוּקִין. אָתוּן וְקַמְנוּ לָהֶן קוֹמֵי דָּרְתָה דְרִבִּי. סָלְקִין וְאָמְרִין לֵיהּ. לְרַע קַרְיָיא דְמֵיינוּקִין בְּעַיָּין מִישְׁאוֹל בִּשְׁלָמָךְ. אוֹדִיק רִבִּי מַן כַּוְּותָא וְחַמְתּוֹן. אֲמַר לוֹן. מַה עִיסְקֵיכוֹן. אָמְרִין לֵיהּ. אֲנָן בְּעַיָּין תֵּיתִין לָן הַהוּא יַרְחָא דְעִיבּוּרָא. וִיהִיב לְהוֹן הַהוּא יַרְחָא דְעִיבּוּרָא.

Halakhah 12: "Four of the brothers," etc. Explanation: There were thirteen brothers, of whom twelve died childless. They [the widows] came and wanted to be married in levirate before Rebbi. He said to him, go and take in levirate. He said to him, it overtaxes my means. But each one of them said, I will support during my month. He said, and who will support during that intercalary month? Rebbi said, I shall support during that intercalary month. He prayed for them and they went from him. After three years they came, carrying 36 toddlers. They came and stood in front of Rebbi's dwelling. [People] went in and told [Rebbi], outside are rural toddlers who want to greet you. Rebbi looked down from the window and saw them. He asked them, for what are you here? They said to him, we beg that you give us [support for] that intercalary month; he gave them [support for] that intercalary month.

כְּתִיב וַיֵּשֶׁב אֲרוֹן יי עִם עוֹבֵד אֱדוֹם בְּבֵיתוֹ שְׁלֹשָׁה חֳדָשִׁים וַיְבָרֶךְ יי וגו׳. בְּמָה בֵּירְכוֹ. בְּבָנִים. הָדָא הוּא דִכְתִיב כָּל־אֵלֶּא מִבְּנֵי עוֹבֵד אֱדוֹם הֵמָּה וּבְנֵיהֶם וַאֲחֵיהֶם אִישׁ חַיִל בַּכֹּחַ לַעֲבוֹדָה שִׁשִּׁים וגו׳. דַּהֲוָות כָּל־חָדָא מִנְּהֶן יָלְדָה תְּרֵיי בְּכָל־יַרְחָא. הָא כֵיצַד. טְמֵאָה שִׁבְעָה וּטְהוֹרָה שִׁבְעָה וְילֵדַת. טְמֵאָה שִׁבְעָה וּטְהוֹרָה שִׁבְעָה וִילֵדַת. שִׁית עֲשַׂר לְכָל־יֶרַח. לִתְלָתָא יַרְחִין הָא אַרְבָּעִין וּתְמַנְיָיא. וְהוּא אֲשְׁתִּין. הָא חַמְשִׁין וְאַרְבַּע. וְתַמְנוּתְהוֹן. הָא אֶשְׁתִּין וּתְרֵיי. הָדָא הִיא דִכְתִיב שִׁשִּׁים וּשְׁנַיִם לְעוֹבֵד אֱדוֹם.

It is written: "[190]The ark of the Eternal dwelt in the house of Obed Edom for three months, and the Eternal blessed," etc. By what did he bless him? With sons. That is what is written: "[191]All these were from the sons of Obed Edom, they, their sons and relatives, strong men for the service, sixty" etc., because each one of them gave birth to two every month. How was that? She was impure for seven days[192], pure for seven days, and gave birth, was impure for seven days, pure for seven days, and gave birth. Sixteen every month[193], in three months 48. And he, six[194]. This makes 54 together. And those eight, sum total 62. That is what was written: "[191]62 for Obed Edom".

190 An inexact quote of *1Car.* 13:14, *2S.* 6:10.

191 *1Chr.* 26:8.

192 Since all children were males, *Lev.* 12:2.

193 16 grandchildren since Obed Edom had 8 sons (*1Chr.* 26:4-5)

194 His own wife bore him six more sons. Together with the original 8, that makes 62 in all. In the Babli, *Berakhot* 63b/64a, the wife and all her daughters-in-law each had one birth of sextuplets.

אָמַר רִבִּי בָּא בַּר זַבְדָּא. כְּתִיב וְנִקְרָא שְׁמוֹ בְּיִשְׂרָאֵל בֵּית חֲלוּץ הַנָּעַל. בַּיִת שֶׁהוּא נִיתָּר בַּחֲלִיצָה אַחַת. אַף בְּבִיאָה כֵן. חֲלִיצָה פוֹטֵר וּבִיאָה פוֹטֵר. כְּמָה דְאַתְּ אָמַר בַּחֲלִיצָה כֵּן אַתְּ אָמַר בְּבִיאָה.

Rebbi Abba bar Zavda said, it is written: "His house should be called in Israel the house of the shoe-stripped." A house which was permitted by one stripping. The same is true for intercourse. Stripping frees and intercourse frees. What you say about stripping you say about intercourse[195].

195 This refers to the sentence in the Mishnah that action by one of the widows frees the others without more ceremony. The argument is based on the singular describing the shoe which was stripped from the levir. A similar but more involved argument in Babli 44b, based on the same verse.

וּמַהוּ לְהַעֲרִים. וְכִי רִבִּי טַרְפוֹן אֲבִיהֶן שֶׁלְּכָל־יִשְׂרָאֵל לֹא הֶעֱרִים. קִידֵּשׁ שְׁלֹשׁ מֵאוֹת נָשִׁים בִּימֵי רַעֲבוֹן עַל מְנַת לְהַאֲכִילָן תְּרוּמָה. תַּמָּן אֵין כָּל־אַחַת וְאַחַת רְאוּיָה לוֹכַל בִּתְרוּמָה. בְּרַם הָכָא כָּל־אֶחָד וְאֶחָד רָאוּי לְיַיבֵּם. רִבִּי יוּדָן בֵּירִבִּי יִשְׁמָעֵאל עָבְדִין לֵיהּ כֵּן.

May one apply a trick[196]? Did Rebbi Ṭarphon, the father of all of Israel, not apply a trick? He gave *qiddushin* to 300 women in times of famine to let them eat heave[197]! There, every one of them was able to eat heave. But here, is each one able to perform levirate? Rebbi Yudan the son of Rebbi Ismael: One deals with him is such a way[197].

196 It is not clear what kind of trick is intended. From the context, it seems that the reference is to the last clause in the Mishnah, that in case of *ḥalîṣah* the one who cannot marry a Cohen should perform *ḥalîṣah*. If the older brother insists on having *ḥalîṣah* with the other widow, may one intervene to direct another brother to consent to the more desirable *ḥalîṣah*?

197 This must have been during the time of the Temple since later generations forbade any non-priestly woman marrying a Cohen to eat sacred

food before the actual marriage (Mishnah *Ketubot* 5:3) and R. Ṭarphon formally acquired all 300 women but married none of them.

198 The court may misinform a recalcitrant brother-in-law in order to obtain a satisfactory *ḥalîṣah*.

(fol. 5b) **משנה יג**: הַמַּחֲזִיר אֶת גְּרוּשָׁתוֹ וְהַנּוֹשֵׂא אֶת חֲלוּצָתוֹ וְהַנּוֹשֵׂא אֶת קְרוֹבַת חֲלוּצָתוֹ יוֹצִיא וְהַוְולָד מַמְזֵר דִבְרֵי רַבִּי עֲקִיבָא. וַחֲכָמִים אוֹמְרִים אֵין הַוְולָד מַמְזֵר. וּמוֹדִים בְּנוֹשֵׂא אֶת קְרוֹבַת גְּרוּשָׁתוֹ שֶׁהַוְולָד מַמְזֵר.

Mishnah 13: He who takes back his divorcee[199], or marries the woman with whom he performed *ḥalîṣah*[200], or marries a relative of the woman with whom he performed *ḥalîṣah*[201], has to divorce her[202] and any child is a bastard, the words of Rebbi Aqiba[203]. But the Sages say, it is not a bastard. But they agree that the child of one who marries a relative of his divorcee[204] is a bastard.

199 After she had married another man, *Deut*. 24:4. This is a simple prohibition.

200 Since she was a candidate for levirate, the incest prohibition of a sister-in-law does not apply. She is only forbidden because of the implication of *Deut*. 25:9 that he is a man "who will not build his brother's house." This excludes any belated levirate with a woman with whom he performed *ḥalîṣah* as a simple prohibition.

201 She is only forbidden by rabbinic decree according to most authorities.

202 This is accepted universally.

203 R. Aqiba holds that any child of a prohibited union is a bastard, irrespective of the severity of the prohibition, and that the prohibition of the relatives of a woman with whom he performed *ḥalîṣah* is biblical.

204 All relatives of a wife that are forbidden are also forbidden of an ex-wife.

הלכה יג: הַמַּחֲזִיר אֶת גְּרוּשָׁתוֹ כול׳. רִבִּי חִייָה בְּשֵׁם רִבִּי יוֹחָנָן.(fol. 6b) הַמַּחֲזִיר אֶת גְּרוּשָׁתוֹ מִשֶּׁנִּשֵּׂאת פְּסָלָהּ מִן הַכְּהוּנָּה. בְּלֹא כָךְ אֵינָהּ פְּסוּלָה מִן הַכְּהוּנָּה. אֶלָּא פְּסוּלָה מִלּוֹכַל בִּתְרוּמָה. רִבִּי זְעִירָא רִבִּי חִייָה בְּשֵׁם רִבִּי יוֹחָנָן. הַמַּחֲזִיר אֶת גְּרוּשָׁתוֹ מִשֶּׁנִּשֵּׂאת בִּתָּהּ כְּשֵׁירָה לִכְהוּנָּה. וּמַאי טַעֲמָא. כִּי תוֹעֵבָה הִיא. תוֹעֵבָה הִיא וְאֵין הַוְּלָד תּוֹעֵבָה.

Halakhah 13: "He who takes back his divorcee," etc. Rebbi Ḥiyya in the name of Rebbi Joḥanan: He who takes back his divorcee after she had remarried makes her blemished for the priesthood. Without that, is she not blemished for the priesthood[205]? But, she is blemished in that she cannot eat heave[206]. Rebbi Ze'ira, Rebbi Ḥiyya in the name of Rebbi Joḥanan: The daughet of a man who takes back his divorcee after she had remarried is acceptable for the priesthood. What is the reason? "She is an abomination[207]". She is an abomination, the child is not an abomination.

205 Any divorcee is barred from marrying a Cohen.

206 A childless daughter of a Cohen married to an Israel can return to her parent's house and partake of their sacred food if she is not in any way desecrated.

207 *Deut*. 24:4. The parallel to this paragraph is in Babli 11b, where the first statement of R. Ḥiyya is quoted as tannaitic and a disagreement is noted whether *qiddushin* or marriage with another man triggers the prohibition.

(fol. 5b) **משנה יד**: וְאֵי זֶהוּ מַמְזֵר כָּל־שְׁאֵר בָּשָׂר שֶׁהוּא בְלֹא יָבוֹא דִּבְרֵי רִבִּי עֲקִיבָא. שִׁמְעוֹן הַתִּימְנִי אוֹמֵר כָּל־שֶׁחַייָבִים עָלָיו כָּרֵת בִּידֵי שָׁמַיִם וַהֲלָכָה כִדְבָרָיו. רִבִּי יְהוֹשֻׁעַ אוֹמֵר כָּל־שֶׁחַייָבִים עָלָיו מִיתַת בֵּית דִּין.

משנה טו: אָמַר רִבִּי שִׁמְעוֹן בֶּן עַזַּאי מָצָאתִי מְגִילַּת יוֹחֲסִין בִּירוּשָׁלֵם וְכָתוּב בָּהּ אִישׁ פְּלוֹנִי מַמְזֵר מֵאֵשֶׁת אִישׁ לְקַיֵּים דִּבְרֵי רִבִּי יְהוֹשֻׁעַ.

Mishnah 14: And what is a bastard? Any [child of a] blood-relation to whom he is forbidden to come, the words of Rebbi Aqiba. Simeon from Timna[208] says, any [child of a relation] for which one is subject to extirpation by heaven's action[209], and practice follows him. Rebbi Joshua said, any [child of a relation] which is a capital crime.

Mishnah 15: Rebbi Simeon ben Azai said, I found a genealogical list in Jerusalem and it was written in it: The man X is a bastard from a[210] married woman, to support the words of Rebbi Joshua.

208 One of the youngest members of the Academy at Jabne.

209 As detailed in *Lev*. 20, also including capital crimes.

210 From the adultery of a married woman.

(fol. 6b) **הלכה טו:** אֵי זֶהוּ מַמְזֵר כול׳. אָמַר רִבִּי שִׁמְעוֹן בֶּן עַזַּאי כול׳. רִבִּי יוֹסֵי בֶּן חֲנִינָה אוֹמֵר. וְכוּלְּהֶם מֵאֵשֶׁת אָב לָמְדוּ. לֹא יִקַּח אִישׁ אֶת אֵשֶׁת אָבִיו וְלֹא יְגַלֶּה כְּנַף אָבִיו. רִבִּי עֲקִיבָה דוֹרֵשׁ. מַה אֵשֶׁת אָבִיו מְיוּחֶדֶת שֶׁהִיא בְּלֹא יָבוֹא הַוּוֹלָד מַמְזֵר. אַף כָּל־שֶׁהוּא בְּלֹא יָבוֹא הַוָּלָד מַמְזֵר. הָתִיבוּן. הֲרֵי אַלְמָנָה לְכֹהֵן גָּדוֹל. שַׁנְייָא הִיא שֶׁפֵּירַשׁ בָּהּ חָלָל. שִׁמְעוֹן הַתִּימְנִי דָרַשׁ. מַה אֵשֶׁת אָבִיו מְיוּחֶדֶת שֶׁחַייָבִין עָלֶיהָ כָּרֵת בִּידֵי שָׁמַיִם הַוּוֹלָד מַמְזֵר. אַף כָּל־שֶׁחַייָבִין עָלֶיהָ כָּרֵת בִּידֵי שָׁמַיִם הַוּוֹלָד מַמְזֵר. הָתִיבוּן. הֲרֵי נִידָּה. שַׁנְייָא הִיא שֶׁאֵין כָּתוּב בָּהּ שְׁאֵר בָּשָׂר. רִבִּי יְהוֹשֻׁעַ דָּרַשׁ. מַה (fol. 6c) אֵשֶׁת אָבִיו מְיוּחֶדֶת שֶׁחַייָבִים עָלֶיהָ מִיתַת בֵּית דִּין וְהַוּוֹלָד מַמְזֵר. אַף כָּל־שֶׁחַייָבִין עָלֶיהָ מִיתַת בֵּית דִּין הַוּוֹלָד מַמְזֵר.

Halakhah 15: "What is a bastard," etc; 'Rebbi Simeon ben Azai said," etc. Rebbi Yose ben Ḥanina said, all of them learned from the father's wife. "A man shall not take his father's wife and not uncover his father's garment's wing.[211]" Rebbi Aqiba explains: Just as his father's wife is special in that she is a forbidden relation from which the child is a bastard, so in any case there is a forbidden relation, the child is a bastard. They objected, is there not a widow for the High Priest[212]? There is a difference, since desecration is spelled out. Simeon from Timna explained: Just as his father's wife is special in that one is subject to extirpation for her[213], the child is a bastard, so in any case that one is subject to extirpation for her, the child is a bastard. They objected, is there not the menstruating woman[214]? There is a difference, since "blood-relation" is not written in reference to her. Rebbi Joshua explained: Just as his father's wife is special in that one is subject to the death penalty for her, the child is a bastard, so in any case that one is subject to the death penalty for her, the child is a bastard.

211 *Deut.* 23:1. This is only half the basis of the arguments. The other is verse 3: No bastard shall come into the community of the Eternal. Since v. 2 speaks of men who cannot have children, v. 3 is taken to refer to v. 1, that the child of a man and his stepmother is a bastard. This is spelled out in detail in the Babli, 49a.

212 *Lev.* 21:14. Everybody agrees that the child is not a bastard from any of the priestly prohibitions since it is spelled out in v. 15 that the children would be desecrated, barred from the priesthood. This case is not discussed in the Babli.

213 In case there are no eye witnesses for the forbidden sex act, when there can be no criminal prosecution.

214 *Lev.* 20:18. In the Babli, this refers to an amoraic statement.

אַף עַל גַּב דְּרִבִּי יְהוֹשֻׁעַ אָמַר הַבָּא עַל אֲחוֹתוֹ[215] הַוְּלָד כָּשֵׁר. מוֹדֶה שֶׁאִם הָיְתָה הַוְּלָד נְקֵיבָה שֶׁהִיא פְּסוּלָה מִן הַכְּהוּנָּה. אַף עַל גַּב דְּרִבִּי שִׁמְעוֹן בֶּן יְהוּדָה מִשּׁוּם רִבִּי שִׁמְעוֹן. גּוֹי וְעֶבֶד שֶׁבָּאוּ עַל בַּת יִשְׂרָאֵל הַוְּלָד כָּשֵׁר. מוֹדֵי שֶׁאִם הָיְתָה נְקֵיבָה שֶׁהִיא פְּסוּלָה מִן הַכְּהוּנָּה. חַד בַּר נַשׁ אָתָא לְגַבַּת רַב אָמַר. בְּנִין דִּילֵידַת אִמָּא דְהַהוּא גַּבְרָא אֲרַמַּאי. אָמַר לֵיהּ. כָּשֵׁר. אָמַר לֵיהּ רַב חָמָא בַּר

גּוּרְיָא. הֵן דְּעֵייְמָךְ רַגְלֵיךְ עַד דְּלָא יֵתֵיי שְׁמוּאֵל וִיפְסָלִינָךְ. אַף עַל גַּב דְּרַב אָמַר. גּוֹי וְעֶבֶד שֶׁבָּאוּ עַל בַּת יִשְׂרָאֵל הַוּוֹלָד כָּשֵׁר. מוֹדֵי שֶׁאִם הָיְתָה נְקֵיבָה שֶׁהִיא פְסוּלָה מִן הַכְּהוּנָּה.

Even though Rebbi Joshua said, the child of him who sleeps with his sister[216] is acceptable, he agrees that if the child was female that she is blemished for the priesthood[217]. Even though Rebbi Simeon ben Jehudah [says] in the name of Rebbi Simeon: If a Gentile or a slave came to a daughter of Israel, the child is acceptable, they agree that if she was female, she is blemished for the priesthood. A man came to Rav and said, since the children of this man's mother are from an Aramean? He said, acceptable. Rav Hama bar Guria said to him, let your feet carry you away before Samuel comes[218] and declares you blemished. Even though Rav said, if a Gentile or a slave came to a daughter of Israel, the child is acceptable, he agrees that if she was female, she is blemished for the priesthood.

215 Reading of the parallel to this paragraph in Halakhah *Qiddushin* 3:14. The reading here, הכא על אחות חלוצתו, is impossible since for everybody except R. Aqiba the sister of the performer of *ḥalîṣah* is forbidden only rabbinically and her child is acceptable to marry into the priesthood.

216 A paradigm for all relations punishable by divine extirpation but not capital crimes.

217 By rabbinic standards.

218 In the Babli, 45a, Samuel agrees with Rav that the child is acceptable. The opinion expressed here, that the child is permitted only to marry outside the priesthood is attributed in the Babli to R. Joshua ben Levi. The Yerushalmi decides here against its own masters, R. Johanan and R. Eleazar, who hold in Halakhah 7:6 that the child is a bastard.

וּמָה רָאוּ לוֹמַר. הֲלָכָה כְּרִבִּי שִׁמְעוֹן הַתִּימְנִי. אָמַר רִבִּי יוֹסֵי בֵּירִבִּי חֲנִינָא. מָקוֹם שֶׁנִּכְלְלוּ כָּל־הָעֲרָיוֹת לְהִיכָּרֵת. יָצָאת אֵשֶׁת אָב לְלַמְּדָךְ עַל הַמַּמְזֵר.

מְחְלְפָּה שִׁיטָּתֵיהּ דְּרִבִּי יוֹסֵי בֵּירִבִּי חֲנִינָה. תַּמָּן הוּא יְלִיף לֵיהּ מִכְּלָלָא וְהָכָא הוּא יְלִיף לֵיהּ מִפְּרָטָא. דְּתַנֵּי מִצְוֹת יי. הָיִיתִי אוֹמֵר. אַף אוֹכְלֵי שְׁקָצִים וּרְמָשִׂים בִּכְלָל. הֲרֵי אַתְּ דָּן לוֹמַר. נֶאֱמַר כָּאן מֵעֵינֵי וְנֶאֱמַר לְהַלָּן מֵעֵינֵי. מַה עֵינֵי שֶׁנֶּאֱמַר לְהַלָּן דָּבָר שֶׁחַייָבִין עַל שִׁגְגָתוֹ חַטָּאת וְעַל זְדוֹנוֹ כָּרֵת. אַף מֵעֵינֵי שֶׁנֶּאֱמַר כָּאן חַייָבִין עַל זְדוֹנוֹ כָּרֵת וְעַל שִׁגְגָתוֹ חַטָּאת. אִי מַה עֵינֵי שֶׁנֶּאֱמַר לְהַלָּן שֶׁיֵּשׁ בּוֹ מִיתַת בֵּית דִּין אַף מֵעֵינֵי שֶׁנֶּאֱמַר כָּאן דָּבָר שֶׁיֵּשׁ בּוֹ מִיתַת בֵּית דִּין. אָמַר רִבִּי יוֹסֵי בֵּירִבִּי חֲנִינָה. מָקוֹם שֶׁיָּצָאת עֲבוֹדָה זָרָה לְלַמֵּד עַל מְחוּייָבִין כְּרִיתוּת לֹא יָצָא עִמָּם כָּרֵת אֶלָּא כָּרֵת בִּלְבַד. אֲבָל מִיתָה מִמָּקוֹם אַחֵר בָּאת. מְחְלְפָה שִׁיטָּתֵיהּ דְּרִבִּי יוֹסֵי בֵּירִבִּי חֲנִינָה. תַּמָּן הוּא יְלִיף לֵיהּ מִכְּלָלָא וְהָכָא הוּא יְלִיף לֵיהּ מִפְּרָטָא. תַּמָּן נִכְלְלוּ כָּל־הָעֲרָיוֹת לְקָרְבָּן. יָצָאת עֲבוֹדָה זָרָה לְלַמֵּד עַל מְחוּייָבֵי קָרְבָּנוֹת. אִית לָךְ מֵימַר. הָכָא נִכְלְלוּ כָּל־הָעֲרָיוֹת לְמַמְזֵר. יָצָאת אֵשֶׁת אָב לְלַמֵּד עַל הַמַּמְזֵר.

Why did they say, practice follows Rebbi Simeon from Timna? [219]Rebbi Yose ben Ḥanina said, from a place where all incest prohibitions were taken as one set [of sins] causing extirpation, the father's wife came out to tell you about the bastard[220]. The method of Rebbi Yose ben Ḥanina seems inverted. There, he infers from the set and here[221] he infers from one of its members. As we have stated: "The commandments of the Eternal,[222]" I could think that this includes also those who eat abominations and crawling things[223]. You argue, saying that here it says "from the eyes[224]" and there it says "from the eyes". Just as "from the eyes" mentioned there means something for which one is obligated for a purification sacrifice in case of inadvertent sin and extirpation in case of intentional sin, also "from the eyes" mentioned here means something for which one is obligated for a purification sacrifice in case of inadvertent sin and extirpation in case of intentional sin. But since "from the eyes" mentioned there is a case[225] involving the death penalty, does "from the eyes" mentioned here involve the death penalty? Rebbi Yose ben Ḥanina said, from the place from which idolatry was singled out to teach about all who are subject to extirpation, there was no mention of anything but extirpation[226]. But the death penalty is written elsewhere. The method of Rebbi Yose ben Ḥanina seems inverted. There, he infers from the set and here he infers from one of its members! There, all incest prohibitions were taken together as to the duty of sacrifice. Idolatry was singled out to teach who is obligated for a sacrifice[227]. What can you say? Here, all incest prohibitions were taken together concerning of bastards. The father's wife was singled out to teach about the bastard.

219 A very shortened version is in *Horaiot* 2:4; much more truncated in Babli *Horaiot* 8a.

220 All incest prohibitions (including adultery) promulgated under one heading, as one set, in *Lev.* Chapter 18 are punishable by divine extirpation as made clear in Chapter 20. The verses about the connection between the father's wife and the bastard are in *Deut.* 23. The father's wife represents a single element of the set of incest prohibitions. *Deut.* 23 has no penalties spelled out. It is presumed that the penalty common to all sins mentioned in *Lev.* 18 is also understood in *Deut.* 23. Cf. Chapter 11, Note 63.

221 The topic of *Horaiot* 2:4, for which transgressions a purification sacrifice is due, *viz.*, those under penalty of divine extirpation. [Simple transgressions are expiated either by the punishment imposed by the court or by sincere repentance and the Day of Atonement (Mishnah *Yoma* 8:7)].

222 *Lev.* 4:2, the introduction to the laws of the purifying sacrifice: "If a person sins inadvertently *against any of the Eternal's commandments* about what should not be done, but he did one of these.

223 Forbidden in *Lev.* 11; these are simple prohibitions, at most punishable by whipping.

224 "Here" is the purification offering of the congregation due (*Lev.* 4:13) "if the entire congregation of Israel errs and something is hidden *from the eyes* of the community and they do one of the actions which by the commandments of the Eternal should not be done, and they do damage." This is part of a series of 5 different statements on purification offerings.

"There" is the isolated statement about the particular purification offering due for the sin of apostasy (i. e., idolatry, *Num.* 15:22-28). *Num.* 15:24 reads: "If *from the eyes* of the congregation it was done in error." By the hermeneutic rule of גזירה שוה "equal cut", parallel expressions imply parallel meanings.

225 Idolatry.

226 The only penalty mentioned is extirpation in *Num.* 15:30 for the blasphemer and idolator, offenses which at other places are classified as capital crimes.

227 Since for idolatry the sacrifices are different from those for all other sins, it is necessary to treat this separately.

(fol. 5b) **משנה טז**: אִשְׁתּוֹ שֶׁמֵּתָה מוּתָּר בַּאֲחוֹתָהּ. גֵּירְשָׁהּ וָמֵתָה מוּתָּר בַּאֲחוֹתָהּ. נִשֵּׂאת לְאַחֵר וָמֵתָה מוּתָּר בַּאֲחוֹתָהּ. יְבִמְתּוֹ שֶׁמֵּתָה מוּתָּר בַּאֲחוֹתָהּ. חָלַץ לָהּ וָמֵתָה מוּתָּר בַּאֲחוֹתָהּ.

Mishnah 16: If his wife died, her sister is permitted to him. If he divorced her and she died, her sister is permitted to him[228]. If she had married another man and died, her sister is permitted to him. If his sister-in-law died, her sister is permitted to him. If he performed *ḥalîṣah* with her and she died, her sister is permitted to him.

228 *Lev.* 18:18. If she was his wife for one minute, her sister is forbidden to him during her lifetime, by biblical standards. The same holds for the sister-in-law from a childless brother by rabbinic standards.

(fol. 6c) **הלכה טז:** אִשְׁתּוֹ שֶׁמֵּתָה מוּתָּר בַּאֲחוֹתָהּ כול׳. הָא בְאִמָּהּ אָסוּר. לֹא כֵן אָמַר רִבִּי יַעֲקֹב בַּר אָחָא בְשֵׁם רִבִּי לָעְזָר. שׁוֹמֶרֶת יָבָם שֶׁמֵּתָה מוּתָּר בְּאִמָּהּ. אֶלָּא בְגִין דְּתַנִּינָן. חָלַץ לָהּ וָמֵתָה מוּתָּר בַּאֲחוֹתָהּ. הָא בְאִמָּהּ אָסוּר. לְפוּם כֵּן תַּנָּא אֲחוֹתָהּ.

Halakhah 16: "If his wife died, her sister is permitted to him," etc. That means, her mother is forbidden to him[229]. Did not Rebbi Jacob bar Aḥa say in the name of Rebbi Eleazar: If a woman waiting for her levir died, her mother is permitted to him[230]. But since we stated: "If he performed *ḥalîṣah* with her and she died, her sister is permitted to him," therefore he stated "her sister[231]."

229 The prohibition of the sister is the only incest prohibition lifted after the death of the wife.

230 Since there was only candidacy and that becomes void with the death of the sister-in-law; Halakhot 2:1, 4:8, *Soṭa* 2:5.

231 Since rabbinically, all close relatives of the sister-in-law except the sister remain forbidden.

רבן גמליאל פרק חמישי

(fol. 6c) **משנה א:** רַבָּן גַּמְלִיאֵל אוֹמֵר אֵין גֵּט אַחַר גֵּט וְלֹא מַאֲמָר אַחַר מַאֲמָר וְלֹא בְעִילָה אַחַר בְּעִילָה וְלֹא חֲלִיצָה אַחַר חֲלִיצָה. וַחֲכָמִים אוֹמְרִים יֵשׁ גֵּט אַחַר גֵּט וּמַאֲמָר אַחַר מַאֲמָר אֲבָל לֹא אַחַר בְּעִילָה וְלֹא אַחַר חֲלִיצָה כְּלוּם.

Mishnah 1: Rabban Gamliel says, there is no bill of divorce after a bill of divorce, no "bespeaking" after "bespeaking", no copulation after copulation, and no *ḥalîṣah* after *ḥalîṣah*[1]. But the Sages say, there is a bill of divorce after a bill of divorce and "bespeaking" after "bespeaking", but nothing after copulation or after *ḥalîṣah*[2].

1 If the childless brother left two widows and either brother gave a bill of divorce to both of them, or two brothers each gave a bill of divorce to one of them, the second bill of divorce has no legal value; the giver of the bill may marry any of the relatives of the sister-in-law who received the invalid document.

While a bill of divorce has no standing in levirate proceedings, it is an old rabbinic tradition that the delivery of a bill of divorce by one of the brothers prohibits all the widows from marrying any of the brothers as if it were a bill of *ḥalîṣah*. For the freeing of the widows, *ḥalîṣah* is still needed.

Similarly, if one of the brothers "bespoke" one of the widows, any later "bespeaking" of any other widow is null and void.

The parallel statement for *ḥalîṣah* is obvious since by biblical standards the act prohibits all widows for all brothers for all times.

2 The Sages hold that no act which is only rabbinically valid has the power to eliminate biblical requirements; only levirate or *ḥalîṣah* can be final.

הלכה א: רַבָּן גַּמְלִיאֵל אוֹמֵר אֵין גֵּט אַחַר גֵּט כול׳. [3]יְבָמָהּ יָבוֹא עָלֶיהָ. זֶה הַבִּיאָה. וּלְקָחָהּ לוֹ לְאִשָּׁה. זֶה הַמַּאֲמָר. יָכוֹל כְּשֵׁם שֶׁהַבִּיאָה גוֹמֶרֶת בָּהּ כָּךְ יְהֵא הַמַּאֲמָר. תַּלְמוּד לוֹמַר יְבָמָהּ יָבֹא עָלֶיהָ. עוֹרָה אֶת כָּל־הַפָּרָשָׁה כוּלָּהּ לְיִיבּוּם. הַבִּיאָה גוֹמֶרֶת בָּהּ וְאֵין הַמַּאֲמָר גוֹמֵר בָּהּ. אִם כֵּן מַה הוֹעִיל בָּהּ מַאֲמָר. לְאוֹסְרָהּ לָאַחִין.

רִבִּי שִׁמְעוֹן אוֹמֵר. הַמַּאֲמָר אוֹ קוֹנֶה אוֹ לֹא קוֹנֶה. מַה טַעֲמָא דְרִבִּי שִׁמְעוֹן. יְבָמָהּ יָבֹא עָלֶיהָ. זֶה הַבִּיאָה. וּלְקָחָהּ לוֹ. זֶה הַמַּאֲמָר. וּכְשֵׁם שֶׁהַבִּיאָה גוֹמֶרֶת בָּהּ כָּךְ הַמַּאֲמָר גוֹמֵר בָּהּ. אוֹ יְבָמָהּ יָבֹא עָלֶיהָ וַהֲרֵי הִיא לְקוּחָה לוֹ. וְהַמַּאֲמָר לֹא הוֹעִיל בָּהּ כְּלוּם.

רִבִּי לָעְזָר בֶּן עֲרָךְ אוֹמֵר. הַמַּאֲמָר קוֹנֶה קִנְיָין גָּמוּר בִּיבָמָה. מַה טַעֲמָה דְרִבִּי לָעְזָר בֶּן עֲרָךְ. וּלְקָחָהּ לוֹ לְאִשָּׁה. הֲרֵי הִיא כְקִידּוּשֵׁי אִשָּׁה. מַה קִידּוּשֵׁי אִשָּׁה קוֹנִין קִנְיָין גָּמוּר אַף הַמַּאֲמָר קוֹנֶה קִנְיָן גָּמוּר. אֵי זֶה מַאֲמָר בִּיבָמָה. הֲרֵי אַתְּ מְקוּדֶּשֶׁת לִי בְּכֶסֶף וּבְשָׁוֶה כֶסֶף.

"Her levir shall come upon her", that is cohabitation. "And take her as a wife for himself", that is "bespeaking". I might think that just as cohabitation is final so "bespeaking" is final; the verse says "her levir shall come upon her." This directs the entire paragraph towards levirate. Cohabitation is final, "bespeaking" is not final. Then what is "bespeaking" good for? To forbid her to the brothers.

Rebbi Simeon says, "bespeaking" either acquires or does not acquire. What is the argument of Rebbi Simeon? "Her levir shall come upon her", that is cohabitation. "And take her for himself", that is "bespeaking". Just as cohabitation is final so "bespeaking" is final. Or "her levir shall come upon her", then she has been acquired by him and "bespeaking" was of no use to her.

Rebbi Eleazar ben Arakh says, "bespeaking" acquires a sister-in-law completely. What is the argument of Rebbi Eleazar ben Arakh? "And take her as wife for himself", the same expression is used as for *qiddushin* of a woman[19]. Just as *qiddushin* acquire completely, so "bespeaking" acquires a sister-in-law completely. What is the formula for "bespeaking" a sister-in-law? "You are betrothed to me by money or money's worth."

3 The text (with minor changes) is from Halakhah 2:1 and explained there, Notes 12-20.

כְּמָה דְרַבָּנִן אָמְרִין. הַמַּאֲמָר קוֹנֶה וּמְשַׁייֵר. כֵּן אִינּוּן (fol. 6d) אָמְרִין. הַגֵּט פּוֹטֵר וּמְשַׁייֵר. וְיִפְטוֹר הַגֵּט פְּטוֹר גָּמוּר בִּיבָמָה מִקַּל וְחוֹמֶר. מַה אִם הָאִשָּׁה שֶׁאֵין חֲלִיצָה פּוֹטֶרֶת בָּהּ הַגֵּט פּוֹטֵר בָּהּ. יְבָמָה שֶׁחֲלִיצָה פּוֹטֶרֶת בָּהּ אֵינוֹ דִין שֶׁיְּהֵא הַגֵּט פּוֹטֵר בָּהּ. תַּלְמוּד לוֹמַר וְחָלְצָה. בַּחֲלִיצָה הִיא נִתֶּרֶת וְאֵינָהּ נִתֶּרֶת בְּגֵט. וְלֹא תִפְטוֹר בָּהּ כְּלוּם. כְּתִיב וְלֹא תִהְיֶה לְאִישׁ זָר. מַה אֲנָן קַייָמִין. אִם בְּשֶׁבָּא עָלֶיהָ אִשְׁתּוֹ הִיא. אִם בְּשֶׁחָלַץ לָהּ תֵּלֵךְ וְתִינָּשֵׂא לְאִישׁ זָר. אֶלָּא כֵן אֲנָן קַייָמִין בְּשֶׁנָּתַן לָהּ גֵּט. וְתַנֵּי חִזְקִיָּה כֵן. מְנַיִין לַנּוֹתֵן גֵּט לִיבִמְתּוֹ שֶׁהִיא אֲסוּרָה עָלָיו וְעַל אֶחָיו. אֶצְלוֹ אֲנִי קוֹרֵא אֲשֶׁר שִׁלְּחָהּ. אֵצֶל הָאַחִין אֲנִי קוֹרֵא אֲשֶׁר שִׁלְּחָהּ. וְתַתִּיר חֲלִיצָה בְּאִשָּׁה מִקַּל וָחוֹמֶר. מַה אִם הַיְּבָמָה שֶׁאֵין הַגֵּט פּוֹטֵר בָּהּ חֲלִיצָה פּוֹטֵר בָּהּ. אִשָּׁה שֶׁהַגֵּט פּוֹטֵר בָּהּ אֵינוֹ דִין שֶׁתְּהֵא חֲלִיצָה פּוֹטֶרֶת בָּהּ. תַּלְמוּד לוֹמַר וְכָתַב לָהּ סֵפֶר כְּרִיתוּת וגו'. בְּגֵט הִיא נִתֶּרֶת וְאֵינָהּ נִתֶּרֶת בַּחֲלִיצָה. וְתִפְטוֹר בָּהּ וּתְשַׁייֵר. תַּמָּן כְּתִיב וְלוֹ תִהְיֶה לְאִשָּׁה. לֹא תִהְיֶה לְאִישׁ זָר. הָכָא מַה אִית לָךְ.

Since the rabbis say, "bespeaking" acquires but not completely, so they say, a bill of divorce frees but not completely. [4]Should not a bill of divorce completely free a sister-in-law by an argument *de minore ad majus*? Since *ḥalîṣah* does not free a wife[5] but a bill of divorce does, is it not logical that a sister-in-law, who is freed by *ḥalîṣah*, should be freed by a bill of divorce? The verse says, "she shall pull off.[6]" By pulling off she is freed; she is not freed by a bill of divorce. So it should free anything! It is written[7]: "She shall not belong . . . to a strange man." Where do we hold? If he came upon her, she is his wife. If he performed *ḥalîṣah* with her, she should go and marry an outsider. So we must hold that he gave her a bill of divorce. Also Ḥizqiah stated thus: From where that the sister-in-law is forbidden to himself and his brothers if he gave her a bill of divorce? For him, I read "whom he had sent away[8]". For the brothers, I read "whom he had sent away". Then should not *ḥalîṣah* free a wife by an argument *de minore ad majus*? Since a bill of divorce does not free a sister-in-law but *ḥalîṣah* does, is it not logical that a wife, who is freed by a bill of divorce, should be freed by *ḥalîṣah*? The verse says, "[9]he shall write her a bill of divorce." By a bill of divorce she is freed; she is not freed by *ḥalîṣah*. So [*ḥalîṣah*] should free partially There, it is written, "she shall not belong . . . to a strange man." Here, what do you have[10]?

4 The arguments of this paragraph (except the last one) are repeated in a few short lines in Babli *Qiddushin* 14a.

5 To marry another man.

6 Pulling off the levir's shoe; *Deut*. 25:9. The Babli points to another part of the same verse, "*so* it should be done", so and not otherwise.

7 *Deut*. 25:5.

8 *Deut*. 24:4, speaking about the divorced wife.

9 *Deut*. 24:1.

10 There is no verse indicating any action of *ḥalîṣah* on the status of a married woman.

כְּמָה דְרִבִּי שִׁמְעוֹן אוֹמֵר. הַמַּאֲמָר אוֹ קוֹנֶה אוֹ לֹא קוֹנֶה. כֵּן הוּא אוֹמֵר. הַגֵּט פּוֹטֵר אוֹ לֹא פּוֹטֵר. נִישְׁמְעִינָהּ מִן הָדָא. רִבִּי שִׁמְעוֹן אוֹמֵר. הַבְּעִילָה בִּזְמַן שֶׁהִיא בַּתְּחִילָּה אֵין אַחֲרֶיהָ כְּלוּם. הָא בְסוֹף יֵשׁ אַחֲרֶיהָ כְּלוּם. בִּבְעִילָה שֶׁהִיא לְאַחַר הַגֵּט. אֲבָל בִּבְעִילָה שֶׁהִיא לְאַחַר מַאֲמָר מַה נַפְשֵׁךְ. קָנָה מַאֲמָר אֵין אַחֲרָיו כְּלוּם. לֹא קָנָה מַאֲמָר תִּקְנֶה הַבִּיאָה וְלֹא יְהֵא אַחֲרֶיהָ כְּלוּם. אֶלָּא כֵן אֲנָן קַיָּימִין בִּבְעִילָה שֶׁהִיא לְאַחַר הַגֵּט. הָדָא אָמְרָה שֶׁהַגֵּט פּוֹטֵר וּמְשַׁיֵּיר.

Since Rebbi Simeon says, "bespeaking" either acquires or does not acquire, does he say similarly that a bill of divorce frees or does not free? Let us hear from the following: Rebbi Simeon says, there is nothing after copulation if it is primary[11]. Therefore, if it is secondary, there is something afterwards. That must deal with copulation after a bill of divorce. For if it were copulation after "bespeaking", what could you say? If "bespeaking" acquired, there is nothing after that. If "bespeaking" did not acquire, intercourse will acquire and there is nothing after that. So we must speak about copulation after a bill of divorce[12]. This implies that a bill of divorce frees partially[13].

11 Cf. Mishnah and Halakhah 7.

12 If he gave a bill of divorce to one of the widows and afterwards had intercourse with the second, the second is his wife and the first, who is forbidden to him, needs *ḥalîṣah* in addition to her bill of divorce.

13 He is certain that *ḥalîṣah* is required after the bill of divorce; it is not a matter of doubt.

רַבָּן גַּמְלִיאֵל כְּרַבִּי[14] שִׁמְעוֹן אוֹמֵר. הַמַּאֲמָר אוֹ קוֹנֶה אוֹ לֹא קוֹנֶה. וְהָכָא מִדְּרַבִּי שִׁמְעוֹן הַגֵּט פּוֹטֵר אוֹ לֹא פוֹטֵר. נִישְׁמְעִינָהּ מִן הָדָא. מוֹדֶה רַבָּן גַּמְלִיאֵל לַחֲכָמִים שֶׁיֵּשׁ גֵּט אַחַר מַאֲמָר וּמַאֲמָר אַחַר גֵּט. גֵּט אַחַר בִּיאַת מַאֲמָר וּמַאֲמָר אַחַר בִּיאַת הַגֵּט. גֵּט אַחַר בִּיאַת מַאֲמָר הֵיךְ עֲבִידָא. הָיוּ שָׁלֹשׁ יְבָמוֹת. עָשָׂה מַאֲמָר בְּזוֹ וּבָעַל לְזוֹ וְנָתַן גֵּט לַשְּׁלִישִׁית. הָדָא אָמְרָה שֶׁהַמַּאֲמָר קוֹנֶה וּמְשַׁיֵּיר. אִי תֹאמַר. הַמַּאֲמָר אוֹ קוֹנֶה אוֹ לֹא קוֹנֶה. מַה נַפְשָׁךְ. קָנָה מַאֲמָר אֵין אַחַר זוֹ כְּלוּם. לֹא קָנָה מַאֲמָר תִּקְנֶה הַבִּיאָה וְלֹא יְהֵא אַחֲרֶיהָ כְּלוּם. הָדָא אָמְרָה שֶׁהַמַּאֲמָר קוֹנֶה וּמְשַׁיֵּיר. מַאֲמָר אַחַר בִּיאַת גֵּט הֵיךְ עֲבִידָא. הָיוּ שָׁלֹשׁ יְבָמוֹת. נָתַן גֵּט לְזוֹ וּבָעַל לְזוֹ וְעָשָׂה מַאֲמָר בַּשְּׁלִישִׁית. הָדָא אָמְרָה שֶׁהַגֵּט פּוֹטֵר וּמְשַׁיֵּיר. וְאִם תֹּאמַר. הַגֵּט פּוֹטֵר אוֹ לֹא פוֹטֵר. מַה נַפְשָׁךְ. פָּטַר הַגֵּט אֵין אַחֲרָיו כְּלוּם. לֹא פָטַר הַגֵּט תִּקְנֶה הַבִּיאָה וְלֹא יְהֵא אַחֲרֶיהָ כְּלוּם. הָדָא אָמְרָה שֶׁהַגֵּט פּוֹטֵר וּמְשַׁיֵּיר. הֵיךְ רַבָּן גַּמְלִיאֵל כְּרַבִּי שִׁמְעוֹן. וְאֵין מַאֲמָר אַחַר מַאֲמָר בִּיבָמָה כְּרַבִּי שִׁמְעוֹן הִיא. אֶלָּא דְלֵית טַעֲמָא דְהֵן כְּטַעֲמָא דְהֵן. טַעֲמָא דְהֵן דְּרַבָּן גַּמְלִיאֵל כָּל־מַה שֶׁמַּאֲמָר הַשֵּׁינִי עָתִיד לִקְנוֹת כְּבָר קָנָה הָרִאשׁוֹן. כָּל־מַה שֶׁהַגֵּט הַשֵּׁינִי עָתִיד לִפְטוֹר כְּבָר פָּטַר הָרִאשׁוֹן. טַעֲמָא דְרַבִּי שִׁמְעוֹן קָנָה

הָרִאשׁוֹן קָנָה הַשֵּׁינִי. לֹא קָנָה הָרִאשׁוֹן אַף הַשֵּׁינִי לֹא קָנָה. פָּטַר הָרִאשׁוֹן פָּטַר הַשֵּׁינִי. לֹא פָּטַר הָרִאשׁוֹן אַף הַשֵּׁינִי לֹא פָּטַר.

Does Rabban Gamliel follow Rebbi Simeon to say that "bespeaking" either acquires or does not acquire? And here, against Rebbi Simeon that a bill of divorce frees or does not free? Let us hear from the following[15]: "Rabban Gamliel agrees with the Sages that there may be a bill of divorce after 'bespeaking'[16] and 'bespeaking' after a bill of divorce[17], a bill of divorce after intercourse and 'bespeaking', and 'bespeaking' after intercourse and a bill of divorce." How can there be a bill of divorce after intercourse and "bespeaking"? There were three sisters-in-law. He "bespoke" one, had intercourse with another, and gave a bill of divorce to the third[18]. This implies that "bespeaking" acquires partially. If you would say that "bespeaking" either acquires or does not acquire then, as you take it, if "bespeaking" acquired, there can be nothing after that. If "bespeaking" did not acquire, intercourse should acquire and there should be nothing after that[19]. This implies that "bespeaking" acquires partially[20]. How can there be "bespeaking" after intercourse and a bill of divorce? If there were three sisters-in-law. He gave a bill of divorce to one, had intercourse with another, and "bespoke" the third. This implies that a bill of divorce frees partially. If you would say that a bill of divorce either frees or does not free then, as you take it, if a bill of divorce frees, there can be nothing after that. If a bill of divorce does not free, intercourse should acquire and there should be nothing after that[19]. This implies that a bill of divorce frees partially[20]. Does Rabban Gamliel follow Rebbi Simeon? There is no "bespeaking" after "bespeaking" a sister-in-law following Rebbi Simeon. But the argument of one is different from the argument of the other. The argument of Rabban Gamliel: any part which a "bespeaking" of the the second could acquire in the future, the first already had acquired[21]. Any part which a bill of divorce from the second [brother] could free in the future, the bill of divorce of the first already had freed. The reasoning of Rebbi Simeon: If the first [brother] acquired, so did the second[22]. If the first [brother] did not acquire, neither did the second. If the first [bill of divorce] did not free, neither did the second[23].

14 Reading of Rashba. In *editio princeps*, רבן גמליאל בר' שמעון but the edition of the ms. indicates that the letter ב is not a safe reading. The reading of Rashba is required since the full name of Rabban Gamliel would have to be either רבן גמליאל ברבן שמעון or רבן גמליאל בן שמעון following the style of his son רבן שמעון בן גמליאל.

15 Tosephta 7:3, Babli 51a.

16 If there were two widows, and he "bespoke" the first and gave a bill of divorce to the second, the first and the relatives of both of them are now forbidden to him.

17 If he gave a bill of divorce to the first and "bespoke" the second, the second also needs a bill of divorce.

18 The bill of divorce is not meaningless; the relatives of the third widow are forbidden to him.

19 In both cases, the divorce document is meaningless and there is no relationship between the levir and the third widow. Cf. Tosephta 7:5 and Note 99.

20 This makes the intercourse with the second widow partially incestuous.

21 Since the form of the legal action of "bespeaking" is not dependent on the person who acts.

22 The second brother cannot acquire anything since he was preempted by the first.

23 If one levir gave bills of divorce to two sisters-in-law, neither of them goes free without *ḥalîṣah* for herself.

עַל דַּעְתֵּיהּ דְּרַבָּן גַּמְלִיאֵל מַהוּ שֶׁיְּהֵא הַגֵּט לְאַחַר גִּיטּוֹ שֶׁלְּמַאֲמָר וּמַאֲמָר אַחַר גִּיטּוֹ שֶׁלְּמַאֲמָר. הַגֵּט לְאַחַר גִּיטּוֹ שֶׁלְּמַאֲמָר הֵיךְ עֲבִידָא. הָיוּ שְׁתֵּי יְבָמוֹת. עָשָׂה מַאֲמָר לְזוֹ וְנָתַן לָהּ גֵּט וְנָתַן גֵּט לַשְּׁנִיָּיה. אִם תֹּאמַר. הַגֵּט פּוֹטֵר. כָּל־מַה שֶׁקָּנָה מַאֲמָר כְּמִי שֶׁיֵּשׁ שָׁם גֵּט וְאֵין גֵּט לְאַחַר גִּיטּוֹ שֶׁלְּמַאֲמָר. אִם תֹּאמַר. אֵין הַגֵּט פּוֹטֵר. כָּל־מַה שֶׁקָּנָה מַאֲמָר כְּמִי שֶׁאֵין כָּאן גֵּט וְיֵשׁ גֵּט לְאַחַר גִּיטּוֹ שֶׁלְּמַאֲמָר. מַאֲמָר אַחַר גִּיטּוֹ שֶׁלְּמַאֲמָר הֵיךְ עֲבִידָא. הָיוּ שְׁתֵּי יְבָמוֹת. עָשָׂה מַאֲמָר לְזוֹ וְנָתַן

לָהּ גֵּט עָשָׂה מַאֲמָר לַשְּׁנִייָה. אִם תֹּאמַר. הַגֵּט פּוֹטֵר יוֹתֵר מִמַּה שֶׁקָּנָה מַאֲמָר. כְּמִי שֶׁאֵין כָּאן מַאֲמָר וְיֵשׁ מַאֲמָר אַחַר גִּטּוֹ שֶׁלְּמַאֲמָר. וְאִם תֹּאמַר. אֵין הַגֵּט פּוֹטֵר יוֹתֵר מִמַּה שֶׁקָּנָה מַאֲמָר. כְּמִי שֶׁיֵּשׁ כָּאן מַאֲמָר וְאֵין מַאֲמָר לְאַחַר גִּיטּוֹ שֶׁלְּמַאֲמָר.

Is there a possibility of a bill of divorce after a bill of divorce for "bespeaking" or of "bespeaking" after a bill of divorce for "bespeaking" for Rabban Gamliel? What is a bill of divorce after a bill of divorce for "bespeaking"? If there were two sisters-in-law, he "bespoke" one of them and gave her a bill of divorce; then he gave a bill of divorce to the second. If you say that a bill of divorce frees, anything "bespeaking" had acquired is subject to the bill of divorce; there is no bill of divorce after a bill of divorce for "bespeaking"[24]. If you say that a bill of divorce does not free, for anything "bespeaking" had acquired there is no bill of divorce; there is a bill of divorce after a bill of divorce for "bespeaking"[25]. What is "bespeaking" after a bill of divorce for "bespeaking"? If there were two sisters-in-law, he "bespoke" one of them and gave her a bill of divorce; then he "bespoke" the second. If you say that a bill of divorce frees more than anything "bespeaking" had acquired, it is as if there were no "bespeaking" and there may be "bespeaking" after a bill of divorce for "bespeaking"[26]. But if you say that a bill of divorce does not free more than he had acquired by "bespeaking", there is "bespeaking" but no "bespeaking" after a bill of divorce for "bespeaking".

24 The second divorce is invalid and the levir may marry any relative of the second widow.

25 Both widows and their relatives are forbidden to the levir.

26 This is a theory not found elsewhere, that a divorce after (rabbinic) "bespeaking" should annul the consequences of "bespeaking" both for him, that all co-wives of the bespoken are no longer forbidden, and seemingly also for the other brothers,

that the widows become permitted again for the "bespeaking" by another brother.

Since practice does not follow Rabban Gamliel, no answer is given. For the Sages, the answer is given in the next Halakhah.

עַל דַּעְתֵּיהּ דְּרַבָּן גַּמְלִיאֵל מַהוּ שֶׁתְּהֵא בִּיאָה פְסוּלָה אַחַר בִּיאָה פְסוּלָה. בִּיאַת בֶּן תֵּשַׁע אַחַר בִּיאַת בֶּן תֵּשַׁע. בִּיאָה פְסוּלָה לְאַחַר בִּיאַת בֶּן תֵּשַׁע. בִּיאַת בֶּן תֵּשַׁע לְאַחַר בִּיאָה פְסוּלָה. מַהוּ שֶׁיּוֹדוּ חֲכָמִים לְרַבָּן גַּמְלִיאֵל וְאֵין מַאֲמָר אַחַר מַאֲמָר בִּיבָמָה אַחַת. הֵיךְ עֲבִידָא. עָשָׂה מַאֲמָר בִּיבִמְתּוֹ וְנָתַן לָהּ גֵּט וְעָשָׂה מַאֲמָר. אִם תֹּאמַר. יֵשׁ מַאֲמָר אַחַר מַאֲמָר. לֹא נִפְטְרָה בְּאוֹתוֹ הַגֵּט. אִם תֹּאמַר. אֵין מַאֲמָר אַחַר מַאֲמָר. נִפְטְרָה בְּאוֹתוֹ הַגֵּט.

In the opinion of Rabban Gamliel, can there be invalid intercourse after invalid intercourse[27], or the intercourse of a nine-years-old after the intercourse of [another] nine-years-old[28], or invalid intercourse[29] after the intercourse of a nine-years-old, or intercourse of a nine-years-old after invalid intercourse? Do the Sages agree with Rabban Gamliel that there cannot be "bespeaking" after "bespeaking" for one sister-in-law? How is that? If he "bespoke" his sister-in-law, gave her a bill of divorce[30], and "bespoke" her again. If you say, there can be "bespeaking" after "bespeaking", she did not become free by that bill of divorce[31]. If you say, there cannot be "bespeaking" after "bespeaking", she was freed by that bill of divorce[32].

27 For example, the intercourse with the second of three widows discussed above. The question is whether a second intercourse would be unquestionably incestuous.

28 Cf. Chapter 3, Note 143. Both children between 9 and 13 years old are supposed to be levirs of the widow.

29 By an adult.

30 For the Sages, this makes the widow forever forbidden to all brothers.

31 She needs a divorce and *ḥalîṣah*.

32 She still needs *ḥalîṣah* since she was not married in levirate.

רִבִּי יוּדָן בָּעֵי. קִידֵּשׁ אִשָּׁה מֵעַכְשָׁיו לְאַחַר שְׁלֹשִׁים יוֹם וְנָפְלָה לוֹ אֲחוֹתָהּ בְּתוֹךְ שְׁלֹשִׁים יוֹם אֲפִילוּ כֵן אֵין מַאֲמָר אַחַר מַאֲמָר. אֲמַר. לֹא אָמַר רַבָּן גַּמְלִיאֵל אֶלָּא עַל יְדֵי גֵט וְעַל יְדֵי מַאֲמָר. וְהַהוּא דָמַר רִבִּי אַבָּהוּ בְשֵׁם רִבִּי יוֹחָנָן. אֲפִילוּ קִידּוּשִׁין מֵאָה תוֹפְשִׂין בָּהּ. דְּלֹא כְרַבָּן גַּמְלִיאֵל.

[33]Rebbi Yudan asked: If somebody gave *qiddushin* to a woman "from now and after thirty days" and her sister became a candidate for levirate with him during these thirty days, is there even in this case no "bespeaking" after "bespeaking[34]? He said, Rabban Gamliel said only "after a bill of divorce and 'bespeaking'"[35]. But what Rebbi Abbahu said in the name of Rebbi Johanan, even a hundred *qiddushin* are valid for her, does not follow Rabban Gamliel.

33 A similar paragraph in Chapter 3, Notes 102-105.

34 Since biblical *qiddushin* are certainly stronger that rabbinic "bespeaking", is his wife immune to the influence of her sister who became a candidate for levirate?

35 Rabban Gamliel did not mention *qiddushin* as excluding further action. Therefore, the claim of her sister forbids the woman to her prospective husband.

For the statement of R. Abbahu, cf. Chapter 3, Notes 102-105.

(fol. 6c) **משנה ב:** כֵּיצַד עָשָׂה מַאֲמָר בִּיבִמְתּוֹ וְנָתַן לָהּ גֵּט צְרִיכָה הֵימֶינּוּ חֲלִיצָה עָשָׂה מַאֲמָר וְחָלַץ צְרִיכָה הֵימֶינּוּ גֵט. עָשָׂה בָהּ מַאֲמָר וּבָעַל הֲרֵי זוֹ כְמִצְוָתָהּ.

Mishnah 2: How[36]? If he "bespoke" his sister-in-law and gave her a bill of divorce, she needs *ḥalîṣah* from him[37]. If he "bespoke" and participated in *ḥalîṣah,* she needs a bill of divorce from him[38]. If he "bespoke" her and copulated, that is as it is commanded.

36 How are the rules of *ḥalîṣah* handled? This Mishnah is not a continuation of the previous one.

37 Since he started to divorce her, she is forbidden to him. He must perform *ḥalîṣah* with her and may not take her in levirate.

38 Since "bespeaking" is the formal equivalent of *qiddushin*, it can be dissolved only by (rabbinic) divorce.

(fol. 6d) **הלכה ב:** כֵּיצַד. עָשָׂה מַאֲמָר כול׳. הָדָא אָמְרָה שֶׁהַגֵּט פּוֹטֵר יוֹתֵר מִמָּה שֶׁקָּנָה מַאֲמָר. אִם תֹּאמַר. אֵין הַגֵּט פּוֹטֵר יוֹתֵר מִמַּה שֶׁקָּנָה מַאֲמָר. יָבָם אָמַר. לֹא יִפְטוֹר גִּיטִּי אֶלָּא מַה שֶׁקָּנָה מַאֲמָרִי. וַאֲפִילוּ מַה שֶׁקָּנָה מַאֲמָרִי לֹא פָּטַר גִּיטִּי. כְּרִיתוּת. אֵין זֶה כְרִיתוּת.

Halakhah 2: "How? If he "bespoke" his sister-in-law," etc. That means[39] that a bill of divorce frees more than anything "bespeaking" had acquired. If you would say that a bill of divorce does not free more than "bespeaking" had acquired, the levir could say: My bill of divorce shall not free more than my "bespeaking" had acquired[40]. But then the bill of divorce did not even free what my "bespeaking" had acquired! "Cutting off[41]." That is no cutting off!

39 The Mishnah which demands *ḥalîṣah* after "bespeaking" and divorce. Since it excludes levirate, it shows that the bill of divorce invalidated both "bespeaking" and candidacy.

40 By excluding candidacy, he wants to reserve the right to levirate. This would prevent the widow from marrying outside the family. The entire proceeding is invalidated since a divorce is only valid if the divorcee has the unconditional right of remarriage.

41 *Deut*. 24:1; the divorcing husband has to write "a document of cutting off" all his ties with her. The Babli, 52b, notes that the rules of a purely rabbinic bill of divorce cannot well be grounded in biblical verses. The argument has to be classified as an intimation, rather than a proof.

חֲלִיצָה פְסוּלָה פּוֹטֶרֶת. וּלְהֵידָא מִילָּה. שֶׁאִם יָבוֹא אַחֵר וְקִידֵּשׁ הַצָּרָה תָּפְשׂוּ בָהּ קִידּוּשִׁין. בָּא אַחֵר וְקִידְּשָׁהּ. מִכֵּיוָן שֶׁנֶּעֶקְרָה הֵימֶינָּה זִיקַת הַמֵּת תָּפְשׂוּ בָהּ קִידּוּשִׁין אוֹ מֵאַחַר שֶׁהִיא צְרִיכָה גֵט לְמַאֲמָרוֹ לֹא תָפְשֵׂי בָהּ קִידּוּשִׁין.

Ḥalîṣah against the rules frees[42]. In which respect? That if an outsider comes and gives *qiddushin* to her co-wife, they will lay hold of her[43]. If an outsider came and gave her[44] *qiddushin*, since the candidacy from the deceased was removed from her[45], the *qiddushin* will lay hold of her, or maybe, since she still needs a bill of divorce for her "bespeaking", the *qiddushin* will not lay hold of her?

42 The *ḥalîṣah* of a woman who was "bespoken" and did not yet receive her divorce document.

43 She certainly is freed by her co-wife's *ḥalîṣah*. *Qiddushin* "lay hold of" a woman if the marriage is valid and the woman is forbidden to any other man by the laws of adultery. In this case, it is not only valid but also legal.

44 The widow who was "bespoken" and performed *ḥalîṣah*.

45 By biblical law, she is forbidden to all levirs.

אָמַר רִבִּי בָּא בַּר מָמָל. הָדָא אָמְרָה שֶׁמִּצְוָה לְקַדֵּשׁ וְאַחַר כָּךְ לִבְעוֹל. מָה אִם שֶׁאֵין כָּתוּב בָּהּ קִידּוּשִׁין אַתְּ אוֹמֵר. הֲרֵי זוֹ כְמִצְוָתָהּ. הָאִשָּׁה שֶׁכָּתוּב בָּהּ קִידּוּשִׁין לֹא כָּל־שֶׁכֵּן.

Rebbi Abba bar Mamal said, this means that there is an obligation first to give *qiddushin* and only after that to cohabit. Since here, where *qiddushin* are not written, you say "that is as it is commanded", for a wife, where it is written, not so much more[46]!

46 This refers to the last statement of the Mishnah, that an orderly levirate is preceded by "bespeaking". It is asserted that an orderly regular marriage is also preceded by *qiddushin* since *Deut*. 22:13 prescribes that a man has to acquire a wife before cohabiting with her: "If a man acquires a wife and

comes to her . . ." Even though in theory a marriage could be effected in criminal law and consummated in civil law by one act of cohabitation, this is frowned upon since the act is only valid if performed in the presence of two witnesses; the Babli agrees emphatically (52a).

(fol. 6c) **משנה ג:** נָתַן גֵּט וְעָשָׂה מַאֲמָר צְרִיכָה גֵט וַחֲלִיצָה. נָתַן גֵּט וּבָעַל צְרִיכָה גֵט וַחֲלִיצָה. נָתַן גֵּט וְחָלַץ אֵין אַחַר חֲלִיצָה כְּלוּם.

Mishnah 3: If he delivered a bill of divorce and then "bespoke", she needs a bill of divorce and *ḥalîṣah.* If he delivered a bill of divorce and then cohabited, she needs a bill of divorce and *ḥalîṣah.* If he delivered a bill of divorce and then performed *ḥalîṣah*, after *ḥalîṣah* nothing more is needed.

(fol. 6d) **הלכה ג:** נָתַן גֵּט וְעָשָׂה מַאֲמָר כול'. גֵּט לְמַאֲמָרוֹ וַחֲלִיצָה לְזִיקָתוֹ.

"If he delivered a bill of divorce and then "bespoke", etc. A bill of divorce for his "bespeaking" and *ḥalîṣah* for her candidacy[47].

47 The bill of divorce is only enough to forbid the widow to himself and all brothers but it does not fulfill the requirements of *Deut.* 25:5-9. Since "bespeaking" is rabbinic, the bill of divorce will be rabbinic (Babli 50b).

הָדָא אָמְרָה. בִּיאָה פְסוּלָה אֵינָהּ פּוֹטֶרֶת. אִיתָא חֲמִי. חֲלִיצָה פְסוּלָה פּוֹטֶרֶת וּבִיאָה פְסוּלָה אֵינָהּ פּוֹטֶרֶת. חֲלִיצָה עַל יְדֵי שֶׁעִיקָּרָהּ פְּסוּלָה פּוֹטֶרֶת. בִּיאָה עַל יְדֵי שֶׁאֵין עִיקָּרָהּ פְּסוּלָה אֵינָהּ פּוֹטֶרֶת. וְלֹא תִפְטוֹר בָּהּ לַקּוּל וְתִפְטוֹר בָּהּ לַחוֹמֶר. וְלֵיי דֶה מִילָּה. שֶׁאִם בָּא אֶחָד וְקִידֵּשׁ אֶת הַצָּרָה תָּפְשׂוּ בָהּ קִידּוּשִׁין. אָמַר רִבִּי יוּדָן. קִייַמְתִּיהָ. כָּל־יְבָמָה שֶׁאֵין כּוּלָּהּ לַחוּץ לְעוֹלָם הִיא בִפְנִים עַד שֶׁתֵּצֵא לַחוּץ.

That means[48] that invalid intercourse does not free. Come and see, invalid *ḥalîṣah*[49] frees but invalid intercourse does not free! Since the purpose of *ḥalîṣah* is invalidation, it frees. Intercourse, whose purpose is not invalidation, does not free. It should not free for leniency but might free for restriction. In which respect? If somebody came and gave *qiddushin* to the co-wife, these should lay hold on her. Rebbi Yudan said, I explained it. Any sister-in-law who is not totally outside remains inside until she leaves for the outside[50].

48 This refers to the statement that intercourse after divorce is invalid; it is incestuous. The sister-in-law may not become his wife. Therefore, a co-wife is not freed to marry outside the family.

49 An invalid *ḥalîṣah* is one where levirate is impossible, as in the last case of the Mishnah. As the Mishnah notes, a *ḥalîṣah* is always final.

50 Since a widow under the obligation of levirate in unable to contract another marriage before the candidacy for levirate is lifted for her, no widow can remarry outside the family as long as not all required ceremonies have been performed.

(fol. 6c) **משנה ד:** חָלַץ וְעָשָׂה בָהּ מַאֲמָר נָתַן גֵּט וּבָעַל אוֹ בָּעַל וְעָשָׂה מַאֲמָר נָתַן גֵּט וְחָלַץ אֵין אַחַר חֲלִיצָה כְּלוּם. אַחַת יְבָמָה אַחַת וְאַחַת שְׁתֵּי יְבָמוֹת.

Mishnah 4: If he performed *ḥalîṣah*, "bespoke" her, gave a bill of divorce, and cohabited[51], or cohabited, "bespoke", gave a bill of divorce, and performed *ḥalîṣah*, nothing is valid after *ḥalîṣah*[52]. There is no difference between one sister-in-law or two sisters-in-law[53].

51 After *ḥalîṣah*, no transaction is legal between the levir and the widow. "Bespeaking" and the bill of divorce become nonexistent, and the inter

course incestuous.

52 In this case, "bespeaking" and *ḥalîṣah* are nonexistent. He married and then divorced the sister-in-law.

53 This really is an introduction to the following Mishnaiot.

(fol. 7a) **הלכה ד:** חָלַץ וְעָשָׂה מַאֲמָר כול׳. אַף עַל פִּי שֶׁאָֽמְרוּ. אֵין חֲלִיצָה אַחַר חֲלִיצָה. אֲבָל בִּיאָה שֶׁלְּאַחַר חֲלִיצָה פּוֹסְלָתָהּ מִן הַכְּהוּנָּה. בְּלֹא כָּךְ אֵינָהּ פְּסוּלָה מִן הַכְּהוּנָּה. אֶלָּא פְּסוּלָה מִלּוֹכַל בִּתְרוּמָה. הַבָּא עַל חֲלוּצָתוֹ חֲלוּצָתוֹ פְּסָלָהּ מִלֹּאכַל בִּתְרוּמָה. אֶלָּא שֶׁבָּאוּ אֶחָיו עָלֶיהָ. נִיחָה כְּמָאן דָּמַר. הוּא אֵינוֹ חַיָּב עַל חֲלוּצָה וְהָאַחִין חַיָּבִין עַל חֲלוּצָה. בְּרַם כְּמָאן דָּמַר. בֵּין הוּא בֵּין הָאַחִין אֵינָן חַיָּבִין עַל חֲלוּצָה. אֶלָּא כְּשֶׁבָּא עַל הַצָּרָה. נִיחָה כְּמָאן דָּמַר. הַכֹּל מוֹדִין בַּצָּרָה שֶׁהוּא חַיָּב. בְּרַם כְּמָאן דָּמַר. הוּא אֵינוֹ חַיָּב לֹא עַל חֲלוּצָה וְלֹא עַל הַצָּרָה. אֶלָּא שֶׁבָּאוּ אַחִין עָלֶיהָ. נִיחָה כְּמָאן דָּמַר בֵּין הוּא בֵּין אַחִין אֵינָן חַיָּבִין עַל הַחֲלוּצָה אֲבָל חַיָּבִין עַל הַצָּרָה. בְּרַם כְּמָאן דָּמַר. בֵּין הוּא בֵּין אַחִין אֵינָן חַיָּבִין לֹא עַל הַחֲלוּצָה וְלֹא עַל הַצָּרָה. אֶלָּא כְּרִבִּי עֲקִיבָה. דְּרִבִּי עֲקִיבָה אוֹמֵר. יֵשׁ מַמְזֵר בַּחֲלוּצָה. אָמַר רִבִּי יוֹסֵי. תִּיפְתָּר שֶׁהָיָה יְבָמָהּ כֹּהֵן וּבָא עָלֶיהָ וְחִילְּלָהּ.

Halakhah 4: "If he performed *ḥalîṣah*, 'bespoke'," etc. Even though they said there is no *ḥalîṣah* after *ḥalîṣah*, intercourse after *ḥalîṣah* disables her from priesthood[54]. Is she not disabled from priesthood anyhow[55]? But she is disabled from eating heave[56]. If he had intercourse with the woman with whom he had performed *ḥalîṣah*, did he disable her from eating heave[57]? It must be that his brothers copulated with her. That agrees with the position that he is not guilty about the woman with whom he had performed *ḥalîṣah*, but his brothers are guilty about the woman with whom he had performed *ḥalîṣah*. But following the position that neither he nor his brothers are guilty about the woman with whom he had performed *ḥalîṣah*? It must be that he had intercourse with the co-wife. That agrees with the position that everybody agrees that he is guilty about the co-wife. But following the position that neither he nor his brothers are guilty about the co-wife? It must be that his brothers had intercourse with the co-wife. That agrees with the position that neither he nor his brothers are guilty about the woman with whom he had performed *ḥalîṣah* but are guilty about the co-wife. But following the position that neither he nor his brothers are guilty about either the woman with whom he had performed *ḥalîṣah* or the co-wife? It must follow Rebbi Aqiba, since Rebbi Aqiba says that a bastard may come from a woman who had performed *ḥalîṣah*[58]. Rebbi Yose said, explain it that the levir was a Cohen, had intercourse with her and desecrated her[59].

54 A second *ḥalîṣah* is invalid; it is as if it had never happened. But illicit sex always has consequences, whether in connection with levirate or not. The statement is in Tosephta 7:5.

55 Since *ḥalîṣah* rabbinically is considered an equivalent of divorce, the widow of a childless man is always forbidden to marry a Cohen unless she is married in levirate.

56 If she is the childless daughter of a Cohen; cf. Chapter 4, Note 206.

57 The argument is predicated on the arguments in Chapter 1, Notes 80-88, where it is held that probably for R. Johanan sexual contact of a levir with the widowed sister-in-law is never punishable. If it is not punishable, it cannot exclude the childless widow from returning to her priestly family.

58 Chapter 1, Note 80.

59 Once she is considered a divorcee in relation to a Cohen, *any* sexual relation with a Cohen desecrates her; cf. Chapter 1, Note 239.

נָתַן גֵּט וְחָלַץ אֵין אַחַר חֲלִיצָה כְּלוּם. וְלֹא כְבָר תַּנִּיתָן. אֵין לְאַחַר חֲלִיצָה כְּלוּם. בְּגִין נִיתְנִינֵיהּ דְּבַתְרָא אֶחָד יְבָמָה וְאֶחָד שְׁתֵּי יְבָמוֹת. אִילּוּ הַמְקַדֵּשׁ חֲלוּצָתוֹ שֶׁמָּא תָּפְשׂוּ בָהּ קִידּוּשִׁין. תִּיפְתָּר אִי כְרִבִּי שֶׁלֹּא לְדַעַת. אוֹ דִבְרֵי הַכֹּל בְּמִתְכַּוֵּין לִקְנוֹתָהּ לְשׁוּם מַאֲמָר יְבִמְתּוֹ וְאֵינָהּ יְבִימְתּוֹ. אָמַר רִבִּי בָּא. וְתַנֵּי כֵן. הַמַּאֲמָר קוֹנֶה בֵּין לְדַעַת בֵּין שֶׁלֹּא לְדַעַת. דִּבְרֵי רִבִּי. וַחֲכָמִים אוֹמְרִים. אֵין קוֹנִין אֶלָּא לְדַעַת. מוֹדֶה רִבִּי בְקִידּוּשִׁין שֶׁאֵינָן קוֹנִין אֶלָּא לדַעַת. וּמַאי טַעֲמָא דְרִבִּי.

בִּיאָה קוֹנָה וּמַאֲמָר קוֹנֶה. מַה בִּיאָה קוֹנָה בֵּין לְדַעַת בֵּין שֶׁלֹּא לְדַעַת אַף הַמַּאֲמָר קוֹנֶה בֵּין לְדַעַת בֵּין שֶׁלֹּא לְדַעַת. וּכְמַה דְרִבִּי אוֹמֵר. הַמַּאֲמָר קוֹנֶה בֵּין לְדַעַת בֵּין שֶׁלֹּא לְדַעַת. כָּךְ הוּא אוֹמֵר. הַגֵּט פּוֹטֵר בֵּין לְדַעַת בֵּין שֶׁלֹּא לְדַעַת. וְלָמָּה רִבִּי אוֹמֵר. הַמַּאֲמָר קוֹנֶה בֵּין לְדַעַת בֵּין שֶׁלֹּא לְדַעַת. שֶׁכֵּן בִּיאָה בְגָדוֹל קוֹנָה בֵּין לְדַעַת בֵּין שֶׁלֹּא לְדַעַת. וְיִפְטוֹר הַגֵּט שֶׁלֹּא לְדַעַת וַחֲלִיצָה אֵינָהּ פּוֹטֶרֶת אֶלָּא לְדַעַת.

"If he gave a bill of divorce, and *ḥalîṣah*, nothing is valid after *ḥalîṣah*," etc. Did we not state already[60] "there is nothing after *ḥalîṣah*"? Because we stated after that, "whether there is one sister-in-law or two sisters-in-law[61]". If somebody gave *qiddushin* to the one with whom he performed *ḥalîṣah*, would they not lay hold on her[62]? Explain it either following Rebbi if he did not intend it or according to everybody if he intended to acquire as "bespeaking" of a sister-in-law but she was not his sister-in-law[63]. Rebbi Abba said, this was stated[64]: "'Bespeaking' acquires whether intentional or not intentional, the words of Rebbi. But the Sages say, it acquires only with intention[65]. Rebbi agrees that *qiddushin* acquire only with intention." What is Rebbi's reason? Intercourse acquires, "bespeaking" acquires. Just as intercourse acquires whether intentional or not intentional[66], so "bespeaking" acquires whether intentional or not intentional. And just as Rebbi says, "bespeaking" acquires whether intentional or not intentional, so he says the bill of divorce[67] frees whether intentional or not intentional. And why does Rebbi say that "bespeaking" acquires whether intentional or not intentional? Since intercourse of an adult[68] acquires whether intentional or not intentional. Even if the bill of divorce would free even if not intentional, *ḥalîṣah* can free only if it is intentional[69].

60 Mishnah 1.

61 From Mishnah 1 it is not clear that after *ḥalîṣah* of one widow all actions with regard to the other are also as if nonexistent.

62 Since it was established in Chapter 1 that the widow is at most forbidden by a simple prohibition, not threatened by divine extirpation, it is clear that *qiddushin* by one of the brothers will be illegal but valid.

63 While "bespeaking" has the external form of *qiddushin*, their rules are quite different. After *ḥalîṣah*, any "bespeaking" is impossible; an action of "bespeaking" is null and void but the same action with the intent of *qiddushin* in valid. The same position is taken in the Babli, 52b.

64 A different but parallel formulation in Babli, 19b.

65 For them, "bespeaking" follows the rules of *qiddushin* as closely as possible.

66 Mishnah 6:1.

67 The divorce document for "bespeaking", which cannot exist without the groom's initiative, can be delivered without getting the widow's attention. Nothing is implied for divorce of an original marriage.

68 But not of a minor. Since a minor can act in practice but not in law, "bespeaking", *qiddushin*, and divorce are not applicable to minors.

69 *Ḥalîṣah* is enacted by both parties; it cannot happen without conscious participation of both parties.

(fol. 6c) **משנה ה:** בְּאֵי זֶה צַד עָשָׂה מַאֲמָר בְּזוֹ וּמַאֲמָר בְּזוֹ שְׁנֵי גִיטִּין וַחֲלִיצָה. מַאֲמָר בְּזוֹ וּבָעַל לְזוֹ שְׁנֵי גִיטִּין וַחֲלִיצָה. מַאֲמָר בְּזוֹ וְגֵט לְזוֹ צְרִיכָה גֵט וַחֲלִיצָה. מַאֲמָר בְּזוֹ וְחָלַץ לְזוֹ הָרִאשׁוֹנָה צְרִיכָה גֵט.

Mishnah 5: How? If he "bespoke" both of them they need two bills of divorce and a *ḥalîṣah*[70]. If he "bespoke" one and copulated with the other, they need two bills of divorce and a *ḥalîṣah*[71]. If he "bespoke" one and gave a bill of divorce to the other, [the first one] needs a bill of divorce and *ḥalîṣah*[72]. If he "bespoke" one and performed *ḥalîṣah* with the other, the first one needs a bill of divorce[73].

מִשְׁנָה ו: גֵּט לְזוֹ וְגֵט לְזוֹ צְרִיכוֹת הַיְּמֵינוּ חֲלִיצָה. גֵּט לְזוֹ וּבָעַל לְזוֹ צְרִיכָה גֵּט וַחֲלִיצָה. גֵּט לְזוֹ וּמַאֲמָר לְזוֹ צְרִיכָה גֵּט וַחֲלִיצָה. גֵּט לְזוֹ וְחָלַץ לְזוֹ אֵין אַחַר חֲלִיצָה כְּלוּם.

Mishnah 6: If there are bills of divorce for both of them, they need a *ḥalîṣah*[74]. If there is a bill of divorce to one and he copulated with the other, [the latter] needs a bill of divorce and *ḥalîṣah*[75]. If he gave a bill of divorce to one and "bespoke" the other, [the second one] needs a bill of divorce and *ḥalîṣah*[71]. If he gave a bill of divorce to one and performed *ḥalîṣah* with the other, nothing follows after *ḥalîṣah*.

70 By "bespeaking" one of them, he forbade the co-wife for himself (and the other brothers). By "bespeaking" both, he forbade both for himself and has to perform *ḥalîṣah* with one of them.

71 The intercourse was illegal, he may not keep his wife and has to divorce her. The first one needs a rabbinic divorce for her rabbinic "bespeaking".

72 Giving a bill of divorce to a sister-in-law forbids her and her co-wives to himself. Therefore, he is forbidden to marry the one he "bespoke" and has to free her by both a divorce and *ḥalîṣah*.

73 She became forbidden to him by the other's *ḥalîṣah*.

74 As if no divorce had happened. However, both are forbidden to him and to any Cohen.

75 See Note 72. The case is repeated to show that the order in which the acts follow one another is irrelevant.

(fol. 7a) **הלכה ה:** כֵּיצַד עָשָׂה מַאֲמָר כול'. עַל דַּעְתֵּיהּ דְּרִבִּי מַהוּ לְמַאֲמָרוֹ שֶׁיְּהֵא מַאֲמָר לְבֶן תֵּשַׁע. בִּיאַת גָּדוֹל גּוֹמְרָתוֹ מַאֲמָרוֹ קוֹנֶה וּמְשַׁיֵּיר. בִּיאַת קָטָן גּוֹמֶרֶת מַאֲמָרוֹ קוֹנֶה וּמְשַׁיֵּיר. מַה בֵּין בִּיאָתוֹ לְמַאֲמָרוֹ. וְאִית דְּבָעֵי מֵימַר. מַה בֵּין מַאֲמָרוֹ שֶׁלַּגָּדוֹל לְמַאֲמָרוֹ שֶׁלַּקָּטָן. שְׁמוּאֵל אָמַר. דִּבְרֵי רִבִּי מֵאִיר. עָשׂוּ בִיאַת בֶּן תֵּשַׁע שָׁנִים וְיוֹם אֶחָד כְּמַאֲמָר בְּגָדוֹל. וּכְמָה דְאַתְּ אָמַר. עָשׂוּ בִיאַת בֶּן תֵּשַׁע שָׁנִים וְיוֹם אֶחָד כְּמַאֲמָר בְּגָדוֹל. וְדִכְוָותָהּ נַעֲשִׂית חֲלִיצַת בֶּן תֵּשַׁע שָׁנִים וְיוֹם אֶחָד כְּמַאֲמָר בְּגָדוֹל. וְרַבָּנָן אָמְרֵי. אֵין חֲלִיצַת בֶּן תֵּשַׁע שָׁנִים וְיוֹם אֶחָד

כְּלוּם. וְלָמָּה עָשׂוּ בִיאַת בֶּן תֵּשַׁע שָׁנִים וְיוֹם אֶחָד כְּמַאֲמָר בְּגָדוֹל. שֶׁכֵּן בִּיאָה בְגָדוֹל קוֹנָה בֵּין לְדַעַת בֵּין שֶׁלֹּא לְדַעַת. נַעֲשֵׂית חֲלִיצַת בֶּן תֵּשַׁע שָׁנִים וְיוֹם אֶחָד כְּגֵט בְּגָדוֹל. וַחֲלִיצָה בְגָדוֹל אֵינָהּ פּוֹטֶרֶת אֶלָּא לְדַעַת.

Halakhah 5: "How? If he 'bespoke'," etc. [76]In the opinion of Rebbi, what about his "bespeaking", may a nine-year-old "bespeak"? The intercourse of an adult is final; his "bespeaking" partially acquires. The intercourse of a minor is final[77]; does his "bespeaking" partially acquire? What is the difference between his intercourse and his "bespeaking"[78]? But some want to formulate: What is the difference between "bespeaking" of an adult and "bespeaking" of a minor? Samuel said, the words of Rebbi Meïr: They made the intercourse of a child of nine years and one day like "bespeaking" of an adult[79]. And as you said, they made the intercourse of a child of nine years and one day like "bespeaking" of an adult, they made the *ḥalîṣah* of a child of nine years and one day like "bespeaking" of an adult. But the rabbis said, the *ḥalîṣah* of a child of nine years and one day is nothing[80]. And why did they make the intercourse of a child of nine years and one day like "bespeaking" of an adult? Because the intercourse of an adult acquires whether intentional or not intentional[81]. The *ḥalîṣah* of a child of nine years and one day was made like a bill of divorce by an adult[82]. But *ḥalîṣah* by an adult can free only if it is intentional[83].

76 This is a direct continuation of the previous paragraph.

77 It is not really final since a minor cannot acquire. However, since the sister-in-law becomes a wife of the levir by the fact of cohabitation irrespective of any thought process, the only way she might be freed from the underage levir is by divorce, which requires an adult partner. So, while she becomes the wife of the levir to the effect that adultery on her part will be a capital crime only through intercourse after he will have reached

the age of 13 years and one day, in all other aspects she is his wife from the day of her first copulation.

78 The answer is too simple to need spelling out: Intercourse is an act of reality which is in the power of the minor; "bespeaking" is a legal act outside the power of a minor.

79 In the Babli, 96a, this is generally accepted. "Bespeaking" which does not lead to marriage has to be dissolved by divorce, which is outside the power of a minor.

80 The last two sentences have no parallel in the Babli.

81 The mind of neither party has to be engaged in this activity; therefore, it is applicable to a minor.

82 This is R. Meïr's opinion in the Babli, 96a. The divorce of a "bespoken" woman is insufficient to free her for outside marriage; so is the *ḥalîṣah* of the minor. She remains forbidden for everyone, levir or unrelated, until she is freed after the minor grows up.

83 Probably addition by the scribe from the preceding paragraph.

(fol. 6c) **משנה ז:** חָלַץ וְחָלַץ חָלַץ וְעָשָׂה מַאֲמָר נָתַן גֵּט וּבָעַל אוֹ בָּעַל וּבָעַל אוֹ בָּעַל וְעָשָׂה מַאֲמָר. נָתַן גֵּט וְחָלַץ אֵין אַחַר חֲלִיצָה כְּלוּם. בֵּין יָבָם אֶחָד לִשְׁתֵּי יְבָמוֹת בֵּין שְׁנֵי יְבָמִים לִיבָמָה אַחַת.

If he performed *ḥaliṣah* with both of them[84], performed *ḥaliṣah* and "bespoke"[85], gave a divorce document and copulated[71], or copulated with both of them[86], or copulated and "bespoke"[87], gave a divorce document and performed *ḥaliṣah*[88], nothing comes after *ḥalîṣah,* whether there are two sisters-in-law and one levir or two levirs with one sister-in-law[89].

משנה ח: חָלַץ וְעָשָׂה מַאֲמָר נָתַן גֵּט וּבָעַל אוֹ בָּעַל וְעָשָׂה מַאֲמָר נָתַן גֵּט וְחָלַץ אֵין אַחַר חֲלִיצָה כְּלוּם. בֵּין בַּתְּחִילָּה בֵּין בָּאֶמְצַע בֵּין בַּסּוֹף. וְהַבְּעִילָה בִּזְמַן שֶׁהִיא בַּתְּחִילָּה אֵין אַחֲרֶיהָ כְּלוּם. רִבִּי נְחֶמְיָה אוֹמֵר אֶחָד בְּעִילָה וְאֶחָד חֲלִיצָה בֵּין בַּתְּחִילָּה בֵּין בָּאֶמְצַע בֵּין בַּסּוֹף אֵין אַחֲרֵיהֶן כְּלוּם.

Mishnah 8: If he performed *ḥaliṣah* and "bespoke", gave a divorce document and copulated, or copulated and "bespoke", gave a divorce document and performed *ḥaliṣah*, nothing comes after *ḥalîṣah*, whether at the beginning, in the middle, or at the end[90]. But in the case of copulation, nothing comes after it when it is at the start[91,92]. Rebbi Neḥemiah says, nothing comes after copulation or *ḥalîṣah*, whether at the beginning, in the middle, or at the end[93].

84 This Mishnah deals with the case of one levir and two sisters-in-law. It is understood that in any group, the first action refers to the first widow, the second to the second, but not both to one woman sequentially.

85 The second *ḥaliṣah* is void; the second widow is not forbidden for a Cohen nor are her close relatives forbidden to the levir.

86 He is married to the first; the relationship with the second was incestuous and no marital relationship was established with her.

87 The act of "bespeaking" is legally nonexistent.

88 Case already treated in Mishnah 5:3.

89 The second case is treated at the beginning of the next Mishnah in a repetetive manner.

90 Since *ḥalîṣah* removes the widow from the family for good, no action of any levir after *ḥaliṣah* can establish a marriage relationship or dissolve one. "In the middle" is only possible if there are more than two widows or levirs.

91 Since the widow is married to the levir.

92 The anonymous majority holds that the intercourse required by the verse is one with an otherwise unencumbered widow. But if the widow has any claim or prohibition concerning another levir on her, they deny that any intercourse can have the status of fulfillment of the requirement of *Deut*. 25:5.

93 For him, the first intercourse always has biblical status except if it comes after *ḥaliṣah* when it is incestuous. *Ḥaliṣah* after intercourse is meaningless; the marriage can be dissolved only by a regular divorce.

הלכה ז: חָלַץ וְחָלַץ חָלַץ וְעָשָׂה מַאֲמָר כול׳. חָלַץ וְעָשָׂה מַאֲמָר כול׳.(fol. 7a) תַּמָּן אָמְרִין. דִּבְרֵי רִבִּי נְחֶמְיָה בִּיאָה פְסוּלָה פוֹטֶרֶת. עַל דַּעְתִּין דְּרַבָּנִן דְּתַמָּן בִּיאָה בֵּין שֶׁהִיא לְאַחַר הַמַּאֲמָר בֵּין שֶׁהִיא לְאַחַר הַגֵּט פוֹטֶרֶת. וְעַל דַּעְתִּין דְּרַבָּנִן דְּהָכָא בִּיאָה שֶׁהִיא לְאַחַר הַמַּאֲמָר פוֹטֶרֶת. שֶׁהִיא לְאַחַר הַגֵּט אֵינָהּ פוֹטֶרֶת. וְלֹא שְׁמָעָן[94] דְּאָמַר רִבִּי הִילָא בְשֵׁם רִבִּי יוֹחָנָן. רִבִּי נְחֶמְיָה וְרִבִּי שִׁמְעוֹן וְרִבִּי יִשְׁמָעֵאל אָמְרוּ דָבָר אֶחָד. דְּתַנֵּי.[95] שָׁלֹשׁ יְבָמוֹת לְיָבָם אֶחָד. עָשָׂה מַאֲמָר בְּזוֹ וּבָעַל לְזוֹ וְנָתַן גֵּט לַשְּׁלִישִׁית. רִבִּי נְחֶמְיָה אוֹמֵר. הָרִאשׁוֹנָה צְרִיכָה גֵט וַחֲלִיצָה וְאֵין אַחַר בְּעִילָה כְּלוּם. קַל וָחוֹמֶר. מָה אִם חֲלִיצָה שֶׁהִיא פוֹסְלָתָהּ מִן הַכְּהוּנָּה אֶחָד בְּעוּלָה וְאֶחָד חֲלוּצָה אֵין אַחֲרֶיהָ כְּלוּם. בִּיאָה שֶׁאֵינָהּ פוֹסְלָתָהּ מִן הַכְּהוּנָּה אֶחָד בְּעוּלָה וְאֶחָד חֲלוּצָה אֵינוֹ דִין שֶׁלֹּא יְהֵא אַחֲרֶיהָ כְּלוּם. וְרַבָּנִן. אָסוּר בִּקְרוֹבוֹת שְׁלָשְׁתָּן וּצְרִיכוֹת שְׁלֹשָׁה גִיטִּין וַחֲלִיצָה לְאַחַת מֵהֶן.

Halakhah 7: "If he performed *ḥaliṣah* with both of them, performed *ḥaliṣah* and 'bespoke'," etc. "If he performed *ḥaliṣah* and 'bespoke'," etc. There[96], they say: The words of Rebbi Neḥemiah that an improper copulation frees. In the opinion of the rabbis there copulation frees, whether after "bespeaking" or after a bill of divorce. In the opinion of the rabbis here, intercourse after "bespeaking" frees; after a bill of divorce it does not free[97]. They did not hear that Rebbi Hila said in the name of Rebbi Joḥanan: Rebbi Neḥemiah, Rebbi Simeon, and Rebbi Ismael all said the same[98]. As it was stated[99]: "If there were three sisters-in-law for one levir, he 'bespoke' one, copulated with the second, and gave a bill of divorce to the third. Rebbi Neḥemiah says, the first one needs a bill of divorce and *ḥalîṣah,* but after copulation there is nothing. An argument *de minore ad majus.* If nothing comes after *ḥalîṣah*, which excludes her from the priesthood, whether she copulated or performed *ḥalîṣah*, then it is only logical that nothing should come after intercourse which does not exclude her from the priesthood, whether she copulated or performed *ḥalîṣah*. But for the rabbis he is forbidden the relatives of all three of them and they need three bills of divorce and *ḥalîṣah* for one of them[100]."

94 Reading of ms. A. Ms. L שמע.

95 Reading of ms. A. Ms. L: דתניא, a lapse into Babylonian spelling.

96 In Babylonia. The statement is in the Babli, 111a. This is the simple understanding one has of the Mishnah since copulation is improper if it does not occur at the beginning.

97 No reason is given for the distinction. The Babli gives reasons why there should be a difference, *viz.*, as a "fence around the law". There is no indication that the Yerushalmi considers any statement about the consequences of "bespeaking" or divorce as being about "fences around the law".

98 The name tradition is uncertain. Ms. A reads: ר' נחמיה ור' שנ'ע ור' שמוא'. The Babli (51a) has: רבן גמליאל ובית שמי ובן עזאי ורבי נחמיה. Rabban Gamliel's opinion is stated in Mishnah 1. R. Simeon holds that maybe "bespeaking" acquires completely; this would imply that in the case of the Tosephta, the intercourse of the second does not free the first widow. Similarly, for the House of Shammai, "bespeaking" acquires by biblical standards. The relevant statement of R. Ismael is not recorded.

99 Tosephta 7:5.

100 Since the intercourse is invalid; the second widow is his wife but he must divorce her.

הבא על יבמתו פרק ששי

(fol. 7a) **משנה א:** הַבָּא עַל יְבִמְתּוֹ בֵּין בְּשׁוֹגֵג בֵּין בְּמֵזִיד בֵּין בְּאוֹנֶס בֵּין בְּרָצוֹן אֲפִילוּ הוּא שׁוֹגֵג וְהִיא מְזִידָה הוּא מֵזִיד וְהִיא שׁוֹגֶגֶת הוּא אָנוּס וְהִיא לֹא אֲנוּסָה הִיא אֲנוּסָה וְהוּא לֹא אָנוּס. אֶחָד הַמְּעָרֶה וְאֶחָד הַגּוֹמֵר קָנָה וְלֹא חָלַק בֵּין בִּיאָה לְבִיאָה.

Mishnah 1: If somebody comes to his sister-in-law[1], whether in error[2], or criminally[3], or under duress[4], or willingly[5], even if he is in error and she acts criminally, or he does it criminally but she is in error, or he is under duress but she is not, or she is under duress but he is not, whether he touched or completed[6], he acquired her and there is no difference between intercourse and intercourse.

1 Widow of his childless brother.

2 He did not realize that she was his sister-in-law.

3 Either he intended extramarital intercourse or he did not know that she was permitted to him.

4 Someone forced him to have intercourse.

5 He intended to fulfill the biblical commandment. That case is not needed but it is mishnaic style always to mention באונס וברצון together.

6 The exact meaning of this term is discussed in the Halakhah. Cf. also Chapter 4, Note 59.

(fol. 7b) **הלכה א:** הַבָּא עַל יְבִמְתּוֹ כול׳. אֲנָן תַּנִּינָן. אֲפִילוּ הוּא שׁוֹגֵג וְהִיא מְזִידָה. הוּא מֵזִיד וְהִיא שׁוֹגֶגֶת. תַּנֵּי רִבִּי חִיָּא. אֲפִילוּ שְׁנֵיהֶן שׁוֹגְגִין אֲפִילוּ שְׁנֵיהֶן מְזִידִין. הֲוֹון בָּעֵיי מֵימַר בְּפִיקֵּחַ שֶׁיֵּשׁ בּוֹ דַעַת שֶׁהוּא קוֹנֶה בֵּין לְדַעַת בֵּין שֶׁלֹּא לְדַעַת. וְחֵרֵשׁ שֶׁאֵין בּוֹ דַעַת לֹא יִקְנֶה אֶלָּא לְדַעַת. אַשְׁכַּח תַּנֵּי רִבִּי חִיָּה. אֶחָד הַחֵרֵשׁ וְאֶחָד הַשּׁוֹטֶה שֶׁבָּעֲלוּ קָנוּ וּפָטְרוּ אֶת הַצָּרוֹת.

Halakhah 1: "If somebody comes to his sister-in-law," etc. We have stated: "Even if he is in error and she acts criminally, or he does it criminally but she is in error." Rebbi Ḥiyya stated[7]: Even if both act in error, even if both act criminally. They wanted to say, a hearing person who is competent acquires both if he has the intention and if he does not have the intention but the deaf-mute, who is not competent, should acquire only if he has the intention. It was found that Rebbi Ḥiyya stated: Both the deaf-mute and the insane who copulated acquired [the widow] and freed the co-wives[8].

7 Quoted also in the Babli, 53b.

8 Since *Deut*. 25:5 requires only that "the levir should come upon her" for valid levirate. Marriage needs the intentional participation of both partners. Therefore the mentally incompetent cannot marry by biblical standards. But levirate of a mentally incompetent person is marriage by biblical standards.

יְבָמָהּ יָבוֹא עָלֶיהָ לְדַעְתּוֹ. וּלְקָחָהּ לוֹ לְאִשָּׁה שֶׁלֹּא לְדַעְתּוֹ. וְיִבְּמָהּ אֲפִילוּ עַל כּוֹרְחוֹ. יְבָמָהּ יָבוֹא עָלֶיהָ לְדַעְתָּהּ. וּלְקָחָהּ לוֹ לְאִשָּׁה שֶׁלֹּא לְדַעְתָּהּ. וְיִבְּמָהּ אֲפִילוּ עַל כּוֹרְחָהּ. יְבָמָהּ יָבוֹא עָלֶיהָ כְּדַרְכָּהּ. וּלְקָחָהּ לוֹ לְאִשָּׁה שֶׁלֹּא כְּדַרְכָּהּ. וְיִבְּמָהּ אֲפִילוּ מִן הַצַּד. יְבָמָהּ יָבוֹא עָלֶיהָ בִּיאָה גְמוּרָה. וּלְקָחָהּ לוֹ לְאִשָּׁה בִּיאָה שֶׁאֵינָהּ גְּמוּרָה. וְיִבְּמָהּ אֲפִילוּ בְּהֶעֱרָייָה.

[9]"Her levir shall come upon her", when he is aware of it. "And take her as a wife for himself", when he is not aware of it. "And take her in levirate", even against his will. "Her levir shall come upon her", when she is aware of it. "And take her as a wife for himself", when she is not aware of it. "And take her in levirate", even against her will. "Her levir shall come upon her", in the usual way. "And take her as a wife for himself", not in the usual way. "And take her in levirate", even from the side[10]. "Her levir shall come upon her", in a completed intercourse. "And take

her as a wife for himself", in incomplete intercourse. "And take her in levirate", even if only touching.

9 The multiple explanation of the multiple expressions in *Deut.* 25:5 is also in the Babli, 54a, in a different formulation.

10 The expression "her levir shall come *upon* her" is not to be taken to mean that the act is only valid if the levir actually lies on top of the woman.

אֵי זוֹ הִיא הָעֲרָייָה. רַב יְהוּדָה בְשֵׁם רִבִּי שְׁמוּאֵל. עַד כְּדֵי שֶׁתְּהֵא אֶצְבַּע נִרְאֵית בֵּין הַשְּׂפָיוֹת. רִבִּי יוֹחָנָן אָמַר עַד שֶׁתִּיכָּנֵס הָעֲטָרָה. רִבִּי בָּא בַּר חִייָה בְשֵׁם רִבִּי יוֹחָנָן. נִכְנְסָה הָעֲטָרָה זוֹ הִיא גְמַר בִּיאָה. מַה אֲנָן קַייָמִין. אִם בִּשְׁאָר כָּל־הָעֲרָיוֹת. עָשָׂה בָהֶן אֶת הַמְּעָרֶה כְגוֹמֵר. אִם בְּשִׁפְחָה חֲרוּפָה. עַד שֶׁיִּפְלוֹט. וְאָמַר רִבִּי יִרְמְיָה רִבִּי בָּא בַּר מָמָל בְּשֵׁם רַב. שִׁכְבַת זֶרַע עַד שֶׁיִּפְלוֹט. אֶלָּא כֵן אֲנָן קַייָמִין בְּאַלְמָנָה לְכֹהֵן גָּדוֹל. הֶעֱרָה בָהּ חַייָב מִשּׁוּם חֲלָלָה. נִכְנְסָה עֲטָרָה חַייָב מִשּׁוּם בִּיאָה. גָּמַר אֶת הַבִּיאָה חַייָב מִשּׁוּם וְלֹא יְחַלֵּל זַרְעוֹ בְּעַמָּיו.

What is touching[11]? Rav Jehudah in the name of Samuel: That the finger should be seen between the lips. Rebbi Joḥanan said, until the gland enters. Rebbi Abba bar Ḥiyya in the name of Rebbi Joḥanan: When the gland has entered that is completion of intercourse. What are we dealing with[12]? If about incest prohibitions, He made the one who touches equal to him who finishes[13]. If for a bound slave girl[14], until he ejaculates, since Rebbi Jeremiah, Rebbi Abba bar Mamal, said in the name of Rav: "Flow of semen", until he ejaculates. But we must deal with a widow for the High Priest. When he touched her, he became guilty for desecrating her. When the gland entered, he became guilty for having intercourse. When he ejaculated, he became guilty because "he shall not desecrate his semen in his people.[15]"

11 In the Babli, 55b, the statement of Samuel is formulated more graphically, that touching the female genital by the male must necessarily make a small indentation which is the act of acquisition. The opinion of R. Johanan is quoted in rather confusing three ways.

12 The two statements of R. Johanan must refer to two different categories of laws.

13 In the list of punishments for sexual offenses, "touching" is mentioned as the offense in *Lev*. 20:18-19.

14 *Lev*. 19:20-22. The quasi adultery of a man with a slave girl which was somehow betrothed before she was manumitted is punishable only if there was ejaculation. (Tosaphot, Babli 55b, *s. v.* אינו, interprets the Babli as making the intercourse punishable in the moment an ejaculation leading to a pregnancy was possible even if none actually occured. It is impossible to read this into the text of the Yerushalmi.)

15 *Lev*. 21:15. Since the three sins are committed at three different times, he can be indicted and punished for three different crimes without any question of competition of laws. In the Babli, *Qiddushin* 78a, it is noted that the language of *Lev*. 21:14 implies that he can be punished for the second offense only if he actually had married the widow.

תַּמָּן תַּנִּינָן. כָּל־הַנָּשִׁים מְטַמּוֹת בְּבֵית הַחִיצוֹן. אֵי זֶה בֵּית הַחִיצוֹן. רִבִּי יוֹחָנָן אָמַר. עַד מָקוֹם שֶׁהַתִּינוֹקוֹת יוֹשְׁבוֹת לַמַּיִם וְנִרְאוֹת. אָמַר לֵיהּ רִבִּי שִׁמְעוֹן בֶּן לָקִישׁ. וַהֲלֹא כָּל־הַטֻּמְאוֹת שֶׁהִיא מְטַמָּא אֵינָהּ מְטַמְּאָה אֶלָּא עַד בֵּית הַשִּׁינַּיִים. תַּנֵּי רִבִּי זַכַּיי. עַד בֵּית הַשִּׁינַּיִים וּמִבֵּין הַשִּׁינַּיִים וּלְפְנִים. רִבִּי יוֹסֵי בְּרִבִּי בּוּן בְּשֵׁם שְׁמוּאֵל. כָּל־בֵּית הַבּוֹשֶׁת קָרוּי בֵּית הַחִיצוֹן.

There[16], we have stated: "All women become impure in the outer cavity[17]." What is the outer cavity? Rebbi Johanan said, up to the place which is seen when girls sit down to urinate. Rebbi Simeon ben Laqish said to him, but in all impurities particular to her, she becomes impure only up to the place of teeth[18]. Rebbi Zakkai stated: Up to the place of teeth, and from between the teeth to the inside. Rebbi Yose ben Rebbi

Abun in the name of Samuel: The entire genitals are called "outer cavity"[19].

16 Mishnah *Niddah* 5:1. In the Babli, *Niddah* 41b, the names between R. Joḥanan and R. Simeon ben Laqish are switched.

17 The impurity of menstrual blood is not dependent on the blood being visible outside her body; it is enough to be close to the vagina.

18 Impurities cannot be transmitted inside body cavities. For food, this means that impure food thrown into one's mouth will not result in any impurity of the eater if it touches the walls of the mouth behind the tetth (except carcass meat). By analogy, anything happening in the womb of a woman inside of a place which can be considered corresponding to the teeth in the mouth cannot have any influence on her status of purity. The Yerushalmi to *Niddah* 5 is lost; in the Babli, Rav Jehudah defined the "teeth" as the place reached by the male organ during intercourse. That place is defined as being open to the outer world since *Lev.* 15:18 decrees that semen causes impurity in the body of the woman.

19 This statement has no parallel in the Babli.

קָנָה וְלֹא חָלַק[20] בֵּין בִּיאָה לְבִיאָה. מַה קָנָה. שְׁמוּאֵל אָמַר. לֹא קָנָה אֶלָּא בִּדְבָרִים הָאֲמוּרִים בַּפָּרָשָׁה. לֵירֵשׁ בְּנִיכְסֵי הַמֵּת וּלְאָרְסָהּ לְאָחִיו וּלְהַתִּיר צָרָתָהּ לַשּׁוּק. רִבִּי יוֹחָנָן אָמַר. קָנָה כָל־הַדְּבָרִים. אָמַר רִבִּי יִצְחָק בַּר אֶלְעָזָר. מַה פְלִיגִין. בְּשֶׁהֶעֱרָה בָהּ. אֲבָל אִם גָּמַר אֶת הַבִּיאָה כָּל־עַמָּא מוֹדֵיי שֶׁקָּנָה בְּכָל־הַדְּבָרִים. אָמַר רִבִּי מַתַּנְיָיא. מַה פְלִיגִין. בְּבָא עָלֶיהָ עוֹדָהּ בְּבֵית אָבִיהָ. אֲבָל אִם בָּא עָלֶיהָ עוֹדָהּ בְּבֵית בַּעֲלָהּ כָּל־עַמָּא מוֹדֵיי שֶׁקָּנָה בְּכָל־הַדְּבָרִים. אָמַר רִבִּי יוֹסֵי. מַתְנִיתָא אָמְרָה. כְּנָסָהּ הֲרֵי הִיא כְאִשְׁתּוֹ לְכָל־דָּבָר.

"He acquired her and there is no difference between intercourse and intercourse." What did he acquire[21]? Samuel said, he acquired only the things spelled out in the paragraph: To inherit the deceased's property, (to be betrothed by a brother)[22], and to permit her co-wife to the outside[23]. Rebbi Joḥanan[24] said, he acquired everything. Rebbi Isaac ben Eleazar said, when do they disagree? If he touched her. But if he completed the intercourse, everybody agrees that he acquired everything. Rebbi Mattaniah said, when do they disagree? If he had intercourse with her still in her father's house. But if he had intercourse with her still in her husband's house[25], everybody agrees that he acquired everything. Rebbi Yose said, the Mishnah[26] said: If he married her, she is his wife in every respect.

20 Reading of the Mishnah and ms. A. Ms. L: חלץ.

21 In any of the kinds of intercourse, incomplete or involuntary, which would not be valid as betrothal of an unincumbered woman.

22 This clause is questionable. It makes sense that any of the questionable kinds of intercourse is valid only as a betrothal (cf. Chapter 1, Note 63), not as marriage (cf. Chapter 1, Note 95). However, the clause is missing in ms. A (confirmed by *Tosaphot Sens*), and is quoted as לאוסרה לאחיו "to forbid her to his brothers" in *Arukh*, *s. v.* דבר א'. One may assume that a compilor of a dictionary is more careful in his quotes than any other medieval author.

23 But if she died before the actual marriage, he would not inherit from her.

24 In the Babli, 56a, this is the position of Rav. He and R. Joḥanan hold that intercourse, even of a questionable kind, with the sister-in-law effects marriage, not betrothal.

25 Either the deceased first husband's (which becomes the levir's property by this intercourse) or the levir's. It is agreed that in this situation, there is marriage not betrothal.

26 Mishnah 4:4.

מַהוּ שֶׁתֹּאכַל בִּתְרוּמָה. רִבִּי בָּא בְשֵׁם שְׁמוּאֵל. נִרְאִין הַדְּבָרִים. אִם הָיְתָה אוֹכֶלֶת בִּתְרוּמָה בְחַיֵּי בַעֲלָהּ אוֹכֶלֶת. וְאִם לָאו אֵינָהּ אוֹכֶלֶת. רִבִּי יוֹחָנָן אָמַר. אֲפִילוּ לֹא אָכְלָה אוֹכֶלֶת. רִבִּי יוֹסֵי אוֹמֵר. אֲפִילוּ נִרְאֵית לֶאֱכוֹל. מַתְנִיתָא מְסַייְעָא לְדֵין מַתְנִיתָא מְסַייְעָא לְדֵין. מַתְנִיתָא מְסַייְעָא לִשְׁמוּאֵל. בַּת יִשְׂרָאֵל פִּיקַּחַת שֶׁנִּישֵּׂאת לְכֹהֵן חֵרֵשׁ אֵינָהּ אוֹכֶלֶת בִּתְרוּמָה. מֵת וְנָפְלָה לִפְנֵי הַיָּבָם.

אִם הָיָה פִּיקֵחַ אוֹכֶלֶת. חֵרֵשׁ אֵינָהּ אוֹכֶלֶת.[27] מַתְנִיתָא מְסַייְעָא לְרִבִּי יוֹחָנָן. בַּת יִשְׂרָאֵל פִּיקַּחַת שֶׁנִּתְאָֽרְסָה לְכֹהֵן פִּיקֵּחַ. לֹא הִסְפִּיק לְכוֹנְסָהּ לְחוּפָּה שֶׁלְּנִישּׂוּאִין עַד שֶׁיֶּחֱרַשׁ הוּא אוֹ עַד שֶׁנִּתְחָֽרְשָׁה הִיא אֵינָהּ אוֹכֶלֶת בִּתְרוּמָה. מֵת וְנָֽפְלָה לִפְנֵי הַיָּבָם אֲפִילוּ חֵרֵשׁ אוֹכֶלֶת. בְּזֶה יִיפָּה כוֹחַ הַיָּבָם מִכּוֹחַ הַבַּעַל. שֶׁהַיָּבָם חֵרֵשׁ מַאֲכִיל וְהַבַּעַל חֵרֵשׁ אֵינוֹ מַאֲכִיל.

May she eat heave[28]? Rebbi Abba in the name of Samuel: It is reasonable that she should eat if she was eating during her husband's lifetime; otherwise she may not eat. Rebbi Johanan said, she eats even if she did not eat before. Rebbi Yose said, even if she was only able to eat[29]. There is a *baraita* in support of either one. There is a *baraita* supporting Samuel[30]: A hearing[31] daughter of an Israel who married a deaf-mute Cohen does not eat heave. If he died and she came before the levir, if he is hearing[32], she eats, deaf-mute does not eat. There is a *baraita* supporting Rebbi Johanan[33]: A hearing daughter of an Israel who became engaged to a hearing Cohen, who did not manage to bring her to the bridal chamber before he became deaf-mute or before she became deaf-mute[34], does not eat heave. If he died and she came before a levir she eats even if he is deaf-mute[35]. In this He increased the power of the levir over that of the husband since the deaf-mute levir enables her to eat, but the deaf-mute husband does not enable her to eat.

27 Reading of ms. A. In ms. L and the *editio princeps*, the last clause is formulated in the feminine for both parties: אם היתה פיקחת אוכלת. חרשת אינה אוכלת!

28 After an unintentional intercourse. This is a direct continuation of the previous discussion since if the levir acquires every power the husband had, then his wife eats heave and other sanctified food by biblical decree (*Lev.* 22:11). In the Babli, 56a, the position of R. Johanan is again represented by Rav.

29 Since the main act of acquisition is *qiddushin*, the Israel bride should be able to eat the Cohen's food after betrothal. In praxi she is not allowed

to use that food until she enters the Cohen's household where everything is organized to vouchsafe the holiness of the sanctified food.

R. Yose clarifies the position of R. Johanan; he is not a third party in the disagreement.

30 Partial quote of Tosephta 10:1.

31 She is of sane mind and therefore legally responsible for her actions in contrast to the deaf-mute. The *qiddushin* of a deaf-mute person are invalid since he has no standing in law. His marriage by cohabitation is valid but it is not an acquisition in the legal sense. Therefore, his wife cannot eat sanctified food under the terms of *Lev.* 22:11.

32 The part of the Tosephta not quoted here specifies that she may eat heave only after intercourse that was *intended* to fulfill the conditions of *Deut.* 25:5. This supports the position of Samuel that the consequences of unintended intercourse are very limited.

33 Tosephta 10:1, Babli 56a.

34 And who therefore was not acquired in the meaning of civil law.

35 No intercourse of the deaf-mute can have the legal status of being intentional. If *Deut.* 25:5 nevertheless decrees that the widow become the wife of the deaf-mute, it cannot make a distinction between intentional and unintentional intercourse. The Babli agrees that Samuel cannot explain this Tosephta (but its terminology implies that this is no reason for him to change his mind.)

(fol. 7a) **משנה ב:** וְכֵן הַבָּא עַל אַחַת מִכָּל־הָעֲרָיוֹת הָאֲמוּרוֹת בַּתּוֹרָה אוֹ פְסוּלוֹת אַלְמָנָה לְכֹהֵן גָּדוֹל גְּרוּשָׁה וַחֲלוּצָה לְכֹהֵן הֶדְיוֹט מַמְזֶרֶת וּנְתִינָה לְיִשְׂרָאֵל וּבַת יִשְׂרָאֵל לְמַמְזֵר וּלְנָתִין פָּסַל וְלֹא חָלַק בֵּין בִּיאָה לְבִיאָה.

Mishnah 2: Similarly, anybody who comes upon any of the incest-prohibited women specified in the Torah, or of the disqualified ones, [i. e.,] a widow for the High Priest or a divorcee or one who had participated in *ḥalîṣah* for a private[36] Cohen, a bastard[37] or Gibeonite[38] female for an

Israel, or an Israel woman for a male bastard or Gibeonite, disqualified her[39] and there is no difference between intercourse and intercourse[40].

36 Greek ἰδιώτης.

37 Cf. Chapter 1, Note 29.

38 Cf. Chapter 2, Note 72.

39 She is disqualified from marrying a Cohen, or, if she is the daughter of a Cohen, from eating sanctified food.

40 Any intercourse in the list of Mishnah 1 which would acquire the sister-in-law in levirate will disqualify any woman from marrying into the priesthood. {There are slight legal differences between the cases enumerated in *Lev.* 21:7. Any infraction of the "holiness prohibitions" (Mishnah 2:4) desecrates the woman; the others formally make her a prostitute.}

(fol. 7b) **הלכה ב:** וְכֵן הַבָּא עַל אַחַת מִכָּל־הָעֲרָיוֹת כול'. אַלְמָנָה לֹא יִקָּח. יָכוֹל אֲפִילוּ אוֹנֶס.[41] תַּלְמוּד לוֹמַר לֹא יְחַלֵּל זַרְעוֹ בְּעַמָּיו. יָכוֹל אֲפִילוּ הֶעֱרָה. תַּלְמוּד לוֹמַר לֹא יָחִיל[42] וְלֹא יְחַלֵּל. אֲפִילוּ בְאוֹנְסִין. לֹא יָחִיל[42] וְלֹא יְחַלֵּל. אֲפִילוּ בְהֶעֱרָיָיה. עַד כְּדוֹן כְּרִבִּי עֲקִיבָה. כְּרִבִּי יִשְׁמָעֵאל. תַּנֵּי רִבִּי יִשְׁמָעֵאל. נֶאֱמַר כָּאן לְקִיחָה וְנֶאֱמַר לְהַלָּן לְקִיחָה בִּשְׁאָר כָּל־הָעֲרָיוֹת. מַה לְקִיחָה שֶׁנֶּאֶמְרָה בִשְׁאָר כָּל־הָעֲרָיוֹת עָשָׂה בָהֶן אֶת הַמְּעָרֶה כְגוֹמֵר. אַף לְקִיחָה שֶׁנֶּאֶמְרָה כָּאן נַעֲשֶׂה בָהּ אֶת הַמְּעָרֶה כְגוֹמֵר. רִבִּי חַגַּיי בָּעֵי. אִי מַה לְקִיחָה שֶׁנֶּאֶמְרָה בִשְׁאָר כָּל־הָעֲרָיוֹת עָשָׂה בָהֶן אֶת הַמְּעָרֶה כְגוֹמֵר וְהַוְּולָד מַמְזֵר. אַף לְקִיחָה שֶׁנֶּאֶמְרָה כָּאן נַעֲשֶׂה בָהּ אֶת הַמְּעָרֶה כְגוֹמֵר וְהַוְּולָד יְהֵא מַמְזֵר. אָמַר רִבִּי יוֹסֵה. לֵיידָה מִילָּה אִתְמַר חָלָל. לֹא דְמַמְזֵר רוֹב מִן הֶחָלָל. אָתָא רִבִּי בּוּן בַּר בִּיסְנָה בְשֵׁם רִבִּי בָּא בַּר מָמָל. נֶאֱמַר כָּאן לְקִיחָה וְנֶאֱמַר לְהַלָּן לְקִיחָה בְּשׁוֹמֶרֶת יָבָם. מַה לְקִיחָה שֶׁנֶּאֶמְרָה בְּשׁוֹמֶרֶת יָבָם עָשָׂה בָהֶן אֶת הַמְּעָרֶה כְגוֹמֵר וְהַוְּולָד כָּשֵׁר. אַף לְקִיחָה שֶׁנֶּאֶמְרָה כָּאן נַעֲשֶׂה בָהּ אֶת הַמְּעָרֶה כְגוֹמֵר וְהַוְּולָד כָּשֵׁר. דְּאָמַר רִבִּי בָּא בַּר מָמָל. הֶעֱרָה בָהּ חַייָב מִשּׁוּם חֲלָלָה. נִכְנְסָה הָעֲטָרָה חַייָב מִשּׁוּם בִּיאָה. גָּמַר אֶת הַבִּיאָה חַייָב מִשּׁוּם מְחַלֵּל.

Halakhah 2: "Similarly, anybody who comes upon any of the incest-prohibited women," etc. "He should not take a widow[43]." Even if under duress? The verse says, "he shall not desecrate his seed in his people." Even if he touched? The verse does not say לא יחול but לא יחלל, even under duress; לא יחול but לא יחלל, even by touching. So far following Rebbi Aqiba[44]. Following Rebbi Ismael[45]? Rebbi Ismael stated: It says here[46] "taking" and it says there "taking" referring to incest prohibitions[47]. Since regarding "taking" referred to by incest prohibitions He treated the one who touched as equal to the one who completed[5], so also regarding "taking" referred to here we should treat the one who touched as equal to the one who completed. Rebbi Ḥaggai asked, if regarding "taking" referred to by incest prohibitions He treated the one who touched as equal to the one who completed and the child is a bastard, so also regarding "taking" referred to here we should treat the one who touched as equal to the one who completed and treat the child as a bastard[48]. Rebbi Yosa said, for which purpose was "desecrated" written? Is not bastard worse than desecrated[49]? Rebbi Abun bar Bisna came in the name of Rebbi Abba bar Mamal. It says here "taking" and it says there "taking" referring to the woman waiting for the levir. Since regarding "taking" referring to the one waiting for the levir He treated the one who touched as equal to the one who completed and the child is acceptable, so also regarding "taking" referred to here we should treat the one who touched as equal to the one who completed and treat the child as acceptable[50], since Rebbi Abba bar Mamal said: When he touched, he became guilty because of the desecrated one. When the gland entered, he became guilty for having intercourse. When he ejaculated, he became guilty because of desecrating[15].

41 Reading of ms. A. Ms. L and *editio princeps*: אנס "he raped"

42 Reading of ms. A. Ms. L and *editio princeps*: חול.

43 A fragment of *Lev*. 21:14.

44 Rebbi Aqiba considers every *pillel* or *polel* verb an extension of an original *ayin waw* or *ayin yod* form. {The reading of ms. A is preferable since a חיל form of חלל is used in *Lev*. 21:4.} On the one hand, "to take" means "to marry". On the other hand , the use of the *pillel* in v. 15 means an extension of the framework. This is taken as authorization of the judicial establishment to extend the range of the acts prohibited.

45 The basis of the argument is the 3rd exegetical rule of R. Ismael [Introduction to *Sifra* (2)]: The technical meaning of a word does not change from topic to topic.

46 The marriage restrictions imposed on the High Priest, *Lev*. 21:14, are formulated as prohibitions to "take" certain women.

47 *Lev*. 18:17-18.

48 This would be the correct application of R. Ismael's rule, leading to a result contradicting practice. A similar argument in the Babli, 54a, is explicitly based on comparison with the menstruating woman whose children are not bastards, circumventing R. Ḥaggai's objection.

49 Since the child of a disapproved union of the High Priest is defined as "desecrated" it cannot be a bastard since everything forbidden to a desecrated person is forbidden to a bastard but not vice-versa. Therefore, the rule of R. Ismael cannot be applied in this form.

50 At least for non-priestly unions.

(fol. 7a) **משנה ג:** אַלְמָנָה לְכֹהֵן גָּדוֹל גְּרוּשָׁה וַחֲלוּצָה לְכֹהֵן הֶדְיוֹט מִן הָאֵירוּסִין לֹא יֹאכְלוּ בַּתְּרוּמָה. רִבִּי אֶלְעָזָר וְרִבִּי שִׁמְעוֹן מַכְשִׁירִין. נִתְאַלְמְנוּ אוֹ נִתְגָּרְשׁוּ מִן הַנִּישׂוּאִין פְּסוּלוֹת מִן הָאֵרוּסִין כְּשֵׁירוֹת.

Mishnah 3: A widow[51] betrothed to the High Priest, a divorcee or one who had participated in *ḥalîṣah* to a private Cohen are not permitted to eat heave; Rebbi Eleazar and Rebbi Simeon declare them able. When they were widowed or divorced, after marriage they are disabled, after betrothal they are enabled[52].

51 The women here are daughters of priests who may eat heave in their fathers' houses. The majority hold that once they are acquired by a man whose sex act will irrevocably disqualify them from the priesthood, they have lost all their privileges. The dissenting rabbis hold that they retain their status until they are actually desecrated.

52 Even the majority will follow here the reasoning of the dissenters.

(fol. 7b) **הלכה ג:** אַלְמָנָה לְכֹהֵן גָּדוֹל כול׳. מַה טַעֲמוֹן דְּרַבָּנִין. נֶאֱמַר כָּאן הֲוָייָה וְנֶאֱמַר לְהַלָּן הֲוָייָה כִּי יִהְיֶה נַעֲרָה מְאוֹרָסָה לְאִישׁ. מַה הֲוָייָה שֶׁנֶּאֱמְרָה לְהַלָּן אֵירוּסִין אַף כָּאן אֵירוּסִין. מַה טַעֲמוֹן דְּרִבִּי לָעְזָר וְרִבִּי שִׁמְעוֹן. נֶאֱמַר כָּאן הֲוָייָה וְנֶאֱמַר לְהַלָּן וּבַת כֹּהֵן כִּי תִהְיֶה לְאִישׁ זָר. מַה הֲוָייָה שֶׁנֶּאֱמְרָה לְהַלָּן נִישּׂוּאִין אַף כָּאן נִישּׂוּאִין. אָמַר רִבִּי יוֹסָה. מְנָא לְרִבִּי לָעְזָר וְרִבִּי שִׁמְעוֹן בַּת כֹּהֵן שֶׁנִּתְאָרְסָה לְיִשְׂרָאֵל שֶׁאֵינָהּ אוֹכֶלֶת בִּתְרוּמָה. לֹא מִן הָדֵין קְרִייָא וּבַת כֹּהֵן כִּי תִהְיֶה לְאִישׁ זָר. הָכָא אִינּוּן עָבְדִין לֵיהּ אֵירוּסִין (fol. 7c) וְהָכָא אִינּוּן עָבְדִין לֵיהּ נִישּׂוּאִין. מַה טַעֲמוֹן דְּרַבָּנָן. לְאִישׁ לְאִישׁ הַמַּאֲכִיל. וַהֲלֹא דִין הוּא. מַה אִם בְּיִשְׂרָאֵל שֶׁאֵין בִּיאָתוֹ פּוֹסְלָתָהּ מִן הַכְּהוּנָּה בִּיאָתוֹ פּוֹסְלָתָהּ מִן הַתְּרוּמָה. כֹּהֵן גָּדוֹל שֶׁבִּיאָתוֹ פּוֹסְלָתָהּ מִן הַכְּהוּנָּה אֵינוֹ דִין שֶׁתְּהֵא בִּיאָתוֹ פּוֹסְלָתָהּ מִן הַתְּרוּמָה. לֹא. אִם אָמַרְתָּ בְּיִשְׂרָאֵל שֶׁאֵינוֹ מַאֲכִיל אֶת אֲחֵירוֹת. תֹּאמַר בְּכֹהֵן גָּדוֹל שֶׁמַּאֲכִיל אֶת אֲחֵירוֹת. הוֹאִיל וְהוּא מַאֲכִיל אֶת אֲחֵירוֹת לֹא תְהֵא בִּיאָתוֹ פּוֹסְלָתָהּ מִן הַתְּרוּמָה. נִשְׁבַּר קַל וָחוֹמֶר וְחָזַרְתָּ לָךְ לְמִקְרָא. לְפוּם כֵּן צָרִיךְ כּוֹמַר לְאִישׁ. לְאִישׁ הַמַּאֲכִיל. [מַאי טַעֲמָא דְּרִבִּי לָעְזָר וְרִבִּי שִׁמְעוֹן מִשּׁוּם רָאוּי הוּא לֶאֱכוֹל אוֹ מִשּׁוּם רָאוּי לְהַאֲכִיל. נִשְׁמְעִנָהּ מִן הָדָה אִם לֹא יָדְעָהּ מִשֶּׁנַּעֲשֶׂה פְּצוּעַ דַּכָּא וּכְרוּת שָׁפְכָה הֲרֵי אִילּוּ יַאֲכִילוּ. אָמַר רִבִּי לָעְזָר דְּרִבִּי לָעְזָר וְרִבִּי שִׁמְעוֹן הִיא. אִית לָךְ מֵימַר הָכָא מִשּׁוּם שֶׁהוּא רָאוּי לְהַאֲכִיל וְהָכָא מִשּׁוּם שֶׁאֵינוֹ רָאוּי לְהַאֲכִיל. אָמַר רִבִּי יוֹסֵיה בֵּירִבִּי בּוּן. לֹא סוֹף דָּבָר מִן הָאֵרוּסִין וְלֹא סוֹף דָּבָר מִן הַנִּישּׂוּאִין. נִבְעֲלוּ בֵּין מִן הָאֵרוּסִין בֵּין מִן הַנִּישּׂוּאִין פּוֹסְלוֹת. לֹא נִבְעֲלוּ בֵּין מִן הָאֵרוּסִין בֵּין מִן הַנִּישּׂוּאִין כְּשֵׁירוֹת.][53]

Halakhah 3: "A widow to the High Priest," etc. What is the reason of the rabbis? "Being" is mentioned here[54] and "being" is mentioned there, "if a girl *will be* betrothed to a man[55]." Just as "being" there means betrothal, so "being" here means betrothal[56]. What is the reason of Rebbi Eleazar and Rebbi Simeon? "Being" is mentioned here[54] and "being" is mentioned there, "if the daughter of a Cohen *will be* an outside man's[57]". Just as "being" there means marriage, so "being" here means marriage. Rebbi Yosa said, from where do Rebbi Eleazar and Rebbi Simeon know that the daughter of a Cohen betrothed to an Israel may not eat heave[58]? Not from that verse, "if the daughter of a Cohen *will be* an outside man's"? Here they make it betrothal, there they make it marriage![59] What is the reason of the rabbis? "A man's", the man who enables to eat[60]. Is it not an argument *de minore ad majus*[61]? Since an Israel, whose intercourse does not disable her[62] from the priesthood, by intercourse will disable her from eating heave[63], the High Priest, whose intercourse does disable her from the priesthood[64], it should be logical that his intercourse will disable her from eating heave. No. If you argue about an Israel who cannot enable others to eat, what can you say about the High Priest who can enable others to eat? Since he can enable others to eat, his intercourse should not disable her from eating heave. The argument *de minore ad majus* is broken, and one has to return to the verse. Therefore, it must say "a man's"; *viz.*, the man who enables her to eat. [53]What is the reason of Rebbi Eleazar and Rebbi Simeon[65], because he may eat or because he may enable to eat? Let us hear from the following[66]: "If he did not know her after his testicles became injured or his penis cut off, these they enable to eat." Rebbi Eleazar said, this follows Rebbi Eleazar and Rebbi Simeon[67]. You have to say, here it is because he[68] enables to eat, there[69] because he cannot enable to eat. Rebbi Yose ben Rebbi Abun said, not really from betrothal or marriage. If they had copulated whether betrothed or married, they are disabled; if they had not copulated whether betrothed or married, they are enabled[70].

53 Text from ms. A.

Ms. L and *editio princeps*: מַה טַעֲמָא לֹא אָמְרוּ רִבִּי לָעְזָר וְרִבִּי שִׁמְעוֹן נִישּׂוּאִין פּוֹסְלִין אוֹתָהּ מִלּוֹכַל בִּתְרוּמָה. מַה עֲבַד לָהּ רִבִּי לָעְזָר וְרִבִּי שִׁמְעוֹן. מִשּׁוּם שֶׁהוּא רָאוּי לוֹכַל אוֹ מִשּׁוּם שֶׁאֵינוֹ רָאוּי לוֹכַל. נִשְׁמְעִינָהּ מִן הָדָא אִם לֹא יְדָעָהּ מִשּׁוּם מַה נַעֲשֶׂה פְּצוּעַ דַּכָּא וּכְרוּת שָׁפְכָה הֲרֵי יֹאכֵלוּ. אָמַר רִבִּי לָעְזָר. דְּרִבִּי לָעְזָר וְרִבִּי שִׁמְעוֹן הִיא. אִית לָךְ מֵימַר. הָדָא מִשּׁוּם שֶׁהוּא רָאוּי לֶאֱכוֹל וְהָכָא מִשּׁוּם שֶׁהוּא רָאוּי לְהַאֲכִיל. אָמַר רִבִּי יוֹסֵי בֵּירִבִּי בּוּן. לֹא סוֹף דָּבָר מִן הַנִּישּׂוּאִין. נִבְעֲלוּ בֵּין מִן הָאֵרוּסִין בֵּין מִן הַנִּישּׂוּאִין פְּסוּלוֹת. לֹא נִבְעֲלוּ בֵּין מִן הָאֵרוּסִין בֵּין מִן הַנִּישּׂוּאִין כְּשֵׁירוֹת.

What is the reason that Rebbi Eleazar and Rebbi Simeon did not say that marriage disables them from eating heave? What do Rebbi Eleazar and Rebbi Simeon in this case? Because he may eat or because he is not fit to eat? Let us hear from the following: "If he did not know her why his testicles became injured or his penis cut off, these they enable to eat." Rebbi Eleazar said, this follows Rebbi Eleazar and Rebbi Simeon. You have to say, here it is because he enables to eat, there because he enables to eat. Rebbi Yose ben Rebbi Abun said, not only from marriage. If they had copulated whether betrothed or married, they are disabled; if they had not copulated whether betrothed or married, they are enabled.

The text is seen to be corrupt.

54 *Lev*. 21:7: "[The Cohen] *shall be* holy for you."

55 *Deut*. 22:23, a shortened quote.

56 The status of sanctity of a woman entering a Cohen's house is determined by her betrothal. The argument follows R. Ismael's rule. Note 45.

57 *Lev*. 22:12.

58 In Mishnah 7:4 it is stated without opposition that betrothal of a Cohen's daughter to an Israel disables her from eating have (but does not enable a daughter of an Israel engaged to a Cohen to eat heave).

59 The question remains unanswered, the arguments presented up to here are inconsistent.

60 *Sifra Emor Parashah* 5(7): "'If the daughter of a Cohen will be an outside man's', this includes not only a bastard, from where even to a Levi or an Israel? The verse says, 'an outside man's'. From where a widow to the High Priest, a divorcee or one who had participated in *ḥalîṣah* to a private Cohen? The verse says 'a man's', a man's who enables to eat."

The rather cryptic argument here and in *Sifra* makes reference to the rule (Mishnah 7:3) that only a man can enable a (non-priestly) woman to eat heave, not a fetus. An Israel woman married to a Cohen eats heave as long as her husband is alive or after his death if she has children, but not if she is the pregnant widow of an otherwise childless man. She will only regain her status as member of the priestly clan after she has given birth. This explains the emphasis of the verse which is formulated לאיש זר and not simply לזר.

For the rabbis, the entire verse refers to betrothal.

61 *Sifra Emor Parashah* 5(8). The Babli, 56b, tries an equally invalid argument.

62 A (widowed) daughter of a Cohen married to an Israel may return to her priestly status if she becomes a childless widow.

63 Once she is married to an Israel by intercourse, she is barred from eating heave.

64 He desecrates any widow by his intercourse.

65 Interpreting the same verse as do the majority rabbis.

66 Mishnah 8:1. Since men with injured testicles or torn-off penis cannot marry (*Deut.* 23:2), if they are Cohanim their intercourse desecrates. They themselves are also barred from eating sanctified food. If they were healthy when they married, their wives retain their priestly status even if the priest who brought them into the priesthood loses his.

67 The Amora R. Eleazar holds that the rabbis, who exclude the betrothed in a forbidden union from eating heave even though betrothal is an acquisition, must also exclude the wife of a man whose intercourse will disable her. The statement is quoted in the Babli, 75a, and contrasted (as in the Yerushalmi, Halakhah 8:1) with the opinion of R. Joḥanan that the rabbis can agree because she started to eat with permission; that permission cannot disappear without anything happening involving her person. According to R. Joḥanan, nothing is proven here.

68 The Cohen before his accident.

69 The High Priest who never could enable a widow.

70 In the Babli, 57b, this is the opinion of Samuel, interpreting the position of the rabbis (against the authoritative opinion of Rav).

(fol. 7a) **משנה ד:** כֹּהֵן גָּדוֹל לֹא יִשָּׂא אֶת הָאַלְמָנָה בֵּין אַלְמָנָה מִן הָאֵירוּסִין בֵּין אַלְמָנָה מִן הַנִּישּׂוּאִין. וְלֹא יִשָּׂא אֶת הַבּוֹגֶרֶת רִבִּי אֶלְעָזָר וְרִבִּי שִׁמְעוֹן מַכְשִׁירִין בְּבוֹגֶרֶת. לֹא יִשָּׂא אֶת מוּכַּת עֵץ. אֵרַס אֶת הָאַלְמָנָה וְנִתְמַנָּה לִהְיוֹת כֹּהֵן גָּדוֹל יִכְנוֹס. וּמַעֲשֶׂה בִּיהוֹשֻׁעַ בֶּן גַּמְלָא שֶׁקִּידֵּשׁ אֶת מָרְתָא בַּת בָּיְיתוֹס וּמִנָּהוּ הַמֶּלֶךְ לִהְיוֹת כֹּהֵן גָּדוֹל וּכְנָסָהּ. שׁוֹמֶרֶת יָבָם לְכֹהֵן הֶדְיוֹט וְנִתְמַנָּה לִהְיוֹת כֹּהֵן גָּדוֹל אַף עַל פִּי שֶׁעָשָׂה בָהּ מַאֲמָר לֹא יִכְנוֹס. כֹּהֵן גָּדוֹל שֶׁמֵּת אָחִיו חוֹלֵץ וְלֹא מְייַבֵּם.

Mishnah 4: The High Priest shall not marry a widow, whether a widow from betrothal or a widow from marriage[71]. He shall not marry an adult; Rebbi Eleazar and Rebbi Simeon enable the adult[72]. He shall not marry one injured[73] by a piece of wood. If he gave *qiddushin* and afterwards was elected High Priest, he shall marry her[74]; it happened that Joshua ben Gamla had given *qiddushin* to Martha bat Boetos[75] when the king appointed him as High Priest and he married her. If a woman was waiting for her Cohen levir when he was elected High Priest, even though he "bespoke" her, he may not marry her[76]. If the brother of a High Priest died, he performs *ḥalîṣah* but not levirate.

71 The prohibition of the widow is in *Deut.* 21:14. Since *qiddushin* are the marriage in criminal law, they can be dissolved only by a bill of divorce which makes the recipient a divorcee. Consequently, if the groom dies between betrothal and marriage, she becomes a widow.

72 *Lev.* 21:13 is interpreted to mean "he shall take a woman with an intact hymen." It is held that an adult, older than 12.5 years, has a softened hymen so that the act of deflowering might not be recognizable.

73 Her hymen injured.

74 Since *qiddushin* are the acquisition understood by the root לקח in the verses, she has already been acquired when he was appointed and verses 13-14 do not apply to him.

75 The richest woman of her time, from a priestly family. According to the Babli, 61a, she bought her husband's the appointment from king

Agrippa I for 3 *qab*, about 6.5 liter, of gold denars. In *Midraš Ekha Rabbati* 1(50), her name is Miriam bat Boethos. Elsewhere in the Babli (*Giṭṭin* 56a, *Ketubot* 104a), her name is that of a legendary superrich woman.

A different story appears in Jesephus *Antiquities* xv, 320 ff., where king Herod dismisses the incumbent High Priest from office and replaces him with Simon ben Boethos, because he wants to marry Simon's daughter (the granddaughter of a Boethos).

In addition to the similarities of names and subject, the sources also agree about the prevailing corruption. The note that the High Priest was appointed, not elected by his fellow priests, is an intended slur.

76 "Bespeaking" is only rabbinical. Since he has the possibility to fulfill all biblical requirements by *ḥalîṣah*, he may not marry the widow.

(fol. 7c) **הלכה ד:** כֹּהֵן גָּדוֹל לֹא יִשָּׂא אֶת הָאַלְמָנָה כול׳. אַלְמָנָה לֹא יִקָּח. בֵּין מִן הָאֵירוּסִין בֵּין מִן הַנִּישּׂוּאִין. גְּרוּשָׁה לֹא יִקָּח. בֵּין מִן הָאֵירוּסִין בֵּין מִן הַנִּישּׂוּאִין.

"The High Priest shall not marry a widow," etc. "A widow he shall not take", whether from betrothal or from marriage. "A divorcee he shall not take," whether from betrothal or from marriage[77].

77 The prescription of *Lev*. 21:14 is absolute, referring to any woman who is called widow or divorcee. An extended argument parallel to this one is in the Babli, 59a.

לֹא יִשָּׂא אֶת הַבּוֹגֶרֶת רִבִּי אֶלְעָזָר וְרִבִּי שִׁמְעוֹן מַכְשִׁירִין בְּבוֹגֶרֶת. שָׁוִין שֶׁלֹּא יִקַּח אֶת מוּכַּת עֵץ. מַה בֵּין בּוֹגֶרֶת מַה בֵּין מוּכַּת עֵץ. בּוֹגֶרֶת כָּלוּ בְתוּלֶיהָ בְּמֵיעֶיהָ. מוּכַּת עֵץ יָצְאוּ בְתוּלֶיהָ לַחוּץ. וְאִית דִּמְחַלְּפִין. לֹא יִשָּׂא אֶת מוּכַּת עֵץ. רִבִּי אֶלְעָזָר וְרִבִּי שִׁמְעוֹן מַכְשִׁירִין בְּמוּכַּת עֵץ. וְשָׁוִין שֶׁלֹּא יִשָּׂא אֶת הַבּוֹגֶרֶת. מַה בֵּין בּוֹגֶרֶת מַה בֵּין מוּכַּת עֵץ. בּוֹגֶרֶת עָבְרוּ יְמֵי נְעוּרִים. מוּכַּת עֵץ לֹא עָבְרוּ יְמֵי נְעוּרִים.

"He shall not marry an adult; Rebbi Eleazar and Rebbi Simeon enable the adult." They agree that he shall not marry one injured by a piece of wood. What is the difference between the adult and the one injured by a piece of wood? The hymen of an adult dissolved in her body. The hymen of one injured by a piece of wood came outside[78]. Some switch: He shall not marry one injured by a piece of wood; Rebbi Eleazar and Rebbi Simeon enable one injured by a piece of wood." They agree that he shall not marry an adult. What is the difference between the adult and the one injured by a piece of wood? An adult is no longer young. The one injured by a piece of wood is still young.

78 In the Babli, 59b, the disagreement between the majority and rabbis Eleazar and Simeon is described as one of the interpretation of *Lev.* 21:13; parallel to the discussion here in the next paragraph. The switched version is not found elsewhere.

אָחוֹת מוּכַּת עֵץ. רִבִּי מֵאִיר וְרִבִּי שִׁמְעוֹן אוֹמְרִים. לֹא יִטַּמָּא לָהּ. וַחֲכָמִים אוֹמְרִים. יִטַּמָּא לָהּ. יְאוּת רִבִּי מֵאִיר וְרִבִּי שִׁמְעוֹן עַל דַּעְתִּין דְּאִילֵּין תַּנַּייָא. מְחַלְּפָתָה שִׁיטָּתִין דְּרַבָּנָן. תַּמָּן אִינּוּן אָמְרִין. נַעֲרָה וְלֹא בוֹגֶרֶת. בְּתוּלָה וְלֹא מוּכַּת עֵץ. וְהָכָא אִינּוּן אָמְרִין הָכֵין. אָמַר רִבִּי הִילָא. כָּל־הַמִּדְרָשׁ בְּעִנְייָנוֹ. תַּמָּן וְלַאֲחוֹתוֹ הַבְּתוּלָה פְּרָט לָאֲנוּסָה וְלִמְפוּתָּה. אוֹ יָכוֹל שֶׁאֲנִי[79] מוֹצִיא אֶת מוּכַּת עֵץ. תַּלְמוּד לוֹמַר אֲשֶׁר לֹא הָיְתָה לְאִישׁ. אֶת שֶׁהָיְתָה בִידֵי אִישׁ. לֹא שֶׁהָיְתָה בְדָבָר[80] אַחֵר. הַקְּרוֹבָה לְרַבּוֹת אֶת הָאֲרוּסָה. אֵלָיו לְרַבּוֹת אֶת הַבּוֹגֶרֶת. מְחַלְּפָה שִׁיטָּתִין דְּרַבָּנִין. תַּמָּן אִינּוּן אָמְרִין. [81] קָרוֹב וְלֹא אֲרוּסָה. אֵלָיו וְלֹא גְרוּשָׁה. וְהָכָא אִינּוּן אָמְרִין הָכֵין. אָמַר רִבִּי הִילָא. כָּל־הַמִּדְרָשׁ בְּעִנְייָנוֹ. אֲחוֹתוֹ לְעוֹלָם הִיא בִפְנִים עַד שֶׁתֵּצֵא לַחוּץ. אֲרוּסָתוֹ לְעוֹלָם הִיא בַחוּץ עַד שֶׁתִּיכָּנֵס לִפְנִים.

A sister injured by a piece of wood, Rebbi Meïr and Rebbi Simeon say, he shall not defile himself for her, but the Sages say, he must defile himself for her[82]. Rebbi Meïr and Rebbi Simeon follow well what they have stated, but the argument of Sages seems inverted. There[83], they say "a girl", not an adult, "a virgin", not one injured by a piece of wood; and here, they say so? Rebbi Hila said, every interpretation follows its context. There[84], "and for his virgin sister", that excludes the raped and the seduced one. Or maybe I should exclude the one injured by a piece of wood? The verse says, "who had not been a man's." Who became [deflowered] through the action of a man, not one who became it through something else. "The close one", to include the betrothed one[85]. "To him", to include the adult. The argument of Sages seems inverted. There[86], they say "the close one", to exclude the betrothed one[87], "to him", to exclude the divorcee[88]. And here, they say so[89]? Rebbi Hila said, every interpretation follows its context. "His sister" is always inside [the family] until she leaves; his betrothed is always outside until she enters.

79 Reading of ms. A. Ms. L: שאינו.

80 Reading of ms. A. Ms. L: על ידי אחר.

81 Text of the first hand of ms. L and ms. A. The corrector of ms. L inserted נַעֲרָה וְלֹא בוֹגֶרֶת. בְּתוּלָה וְלֹא מוּכַּת עֵץ, a dittography which makes no sense here.

82 This refers to the rules *Lev.* 21:1-4, that a Cohen may not defile himself by the impurity of the dead except for his close relative. His sister is included in the list as long as she belongs to his clan, i. e., as long as she is not married. The language of v. 3 is involved: "And for his virgin sister who is close to him, who never had been a man's, for her he must defile himself", inviting a close analysis of the meaning of the conditions attached.

In the Babli, 60a, this is only R. Simeon's opinion.

83 It is not clear what the reference is. It could be *Deut.* 22:23, "If there was a virgin girl . . ." The statement of the rabbis referred to is not otherwise recorded.

84 *Lev.* 21:3. The argument is quoted in the Babli, 60a.

85 In the Babli, 60a/b, the divorced sister is included.

86 In the interpretation of *Lev.* 21:3

in *Sifra Emor* 0(4); the Cohen may not defile himself by the impurity of the dead, "except for his flesh close to him, for his mother and his father, his son and his daughter, and his brother."

87 "His flesh close to him" is his wife after the marriage, not his betrothed.

88 The Cohen is not permitted to defile himself for a wife forbidden to him.

89 His betrothed sister is included, his own betrothed is excluded. (Instead of ארוסתו, ms. A has the synonym בלתו.)

אֲנוּסָתוֹ וּמְפוּתָּתוֹ לֹא יִכְנוֹס[90] וְאִם כָּנַס אֵין מוֹצִיאִין מִיָּדוֹ. אֲנוּסַת חֲבֵירוֹ וּמְפוּתַּת חֲבֵירוֹ לֹא יִכְנוֹס וְאִם כָּנַס מוֹצִיאִין מִיָּדוֹ. לֹא יִשָּׂא אֶת הַקְּטַנָּה אֲבָל נוֹשֵׂא אֶת הַמְּמָאֶנֶת. וּמְמָאֶנֶת לֹא כִקְטַנָּה הִיא. מַמְתִּינִין לָהּ עַד שֶׁתַּגְדִּיל.

His own rape victim or seduced woman he should not marry but if he married her one does not remove her from him. Somebody else's rape victim or seduced woman he should not marry but if he married her one does remove her from him[91]. He should not marry a minor[92] but he may marry the one who repudiated[93]. Is the one who repudiated not a minor? One waits until she grows up.

90 Reading of ms. A. Ms. L יכניס.

91 In the Babli, 59b, there is a related *baraita*: "His own rape victim or seduced woman he should not marry but if he married her he is married. Somebody else's rape victim or seduced woman he should not marry but if he married her, R. Eliezer ben Jacob said, their child is desecrated, but the Sages say, their child is enabled."

92 Babli 61b. This restricts the unmarried High Priest to girls older than 12 years when they are no longer minors, but not older than 12 years 6 months, when they become adults.

93 If she repudiated the prospective husband after betrothal and still is a virgin.

אֵירַס אֶת הָאַלְמָנָה וְנִתְמַנָּה לִהְיוֹת כֹּהֵן גָּדוֹל יִכְנוֹס. וְדִכְוָותָהּ אֵירַס אֶת הַקְּטַנָּה וְנִתְמַנָּה לִהְיוֹת כֹּהֵן גָּדוֹל יִכְנוֹס.[90] קוֹרֵא אֲנִי עָלֶיהָ אִשָּׁה. לֹא קְטַנָּה.

"If he gave *qiddushin* and afterwards was elected High Priest, he shall marry her." Similarly, If he gave *qiddushin* to a minor and afterwards was elected High Priest, shall he marry her? I am reading for her "a woman[94]", not a minor.

94 *Lev.* 21:13: "And he shall take a *woman* with an intact hymen."

הַעֲרָמָה עָשָׂה. שְׁאִיל בדיומה וְאַייתִב לְאִמֵּיהּ בְּגַוָּהּ[95]. שְׁמַעַת וְקִבְּלַת עָלֶיהָ. וְתַנִּינָן. יָצָא שְׁמָהּ בָּעִיר מְקוּדֶּשֶׁת הֲרֵי זוֹ מְקוּדֶּשֶׁת.

He tricked her[96]. He borrowed a בדיומה and seated his mother next to her. She heard and accepted. And we have stated: "If she has a reputation in town to be betrothed, then she is betrothed."

95 Reading of ms. A. Ms. L: שאל פיריו מהו ייתב לאמה בגויה.

96 Joshua ben Gamla went into debt in order to marry a rich wife.. It is unclear what he borrowed.

The Mishnah quoted, *Giṭṭin* 9:9, is explained in its Halakhah to mean that a big engagement feast is a kind of proof that a betrothal did in fact take place. If despite the rich gift no betrothal has taken place, a bill of divorce is nevertheless necessary to free the woman for marriage to another man.

If Martha bat Boethos had rejected the gift, as a "divorcee" this daughter of a High Priest would have been barred from marrying another priest.

The word in the recently discovered ms. A, בדיומה, is a *hapax* and probably corrupt. The text of A was chosen because at least the remainder of the sentence represents correct and coherent grammar.

The unintelligible word in ms. L פיריו מהו has been read as פירייומה which in different contexts has been explained as Greek φέρετρον (from the root φέρω "to bear, carry") meaning a litter, or as περιωμίς meaning a garment covering the shoulders. Perhaps here it should be read as Greek φερνάριον, τό, diminutive of φερνή "gift to the wife, bridal gifts" (also from φέρω); also cf. the word παράφερνα "bride's goods", from which Latin "paraphernalia" derives (E. G.).

אַף בֵּית שַׁמַּי מוֹדֶה בָהּ. וְאַף רִבִּי שִׁמְעוֹן מוֹדֶה בָהּ. וְלֹא כְרִבִּי לְעָזָר בֶּן עֲרָךְ. דְּרִבִּי לְעָזָר בֶּן עֲרָךְ אוֹמֵר. הַמַּאֲמָר קוֹנֶה קִנְייָן גָּמוּר בִּיבָמָה.

Also the House of Shammai agree, also Rebbi Simeon agrees but not Rebbi Eleazar ben Arakh, since Rebbi Eleazar ben Arakh says, "bespeaking" acquires a sister-in-law completely[96].

96 This refers to the statement that the High Priest is not permitted to marry a sister-in-law he had "bespoken" while being allowed to marry a widow to whom he had given *qiddushin*. For the position of R. Eleazar ben Arakh, cf. Halakhah 2:1, Notes 13-14.

כֹּהֵן גָּדוֹל שֶׁמֵּת אָחִיו חוֹלֵץ וְלֹא מְייַבֵּם. הָדָא מְסַייְעָא לְמָאן דְּאָמַר. חֲלִיצָה פְּטוֹר. בְּרַם כְּמָאן דְּאָמַר חֲלִיצָה קִנְייָן. אוֹמְרִים לוֹ. עֲבוֹר עַל דִּבְרֵי תוֹרָה.

"If a brother of the High Priest dies, he performs *ḥalîṣah* but not levirate." This supports him who says that *ḥalîṣah* is freeing. But according to him who says *ḥalîṣah* is acquisiton, does one say to him, transgress the words of the Torah?[97]

97 This is from Halakhah 3:1, at Note 75.

(fol. 7a) **משנה ה:** כֹּהֵן הֶדְיוֹט לֹא יִשָּׂא אֶת אַיילוֹנִית אֶלָּא אִם כֵּן יֵשׁ לוֹ אִשָּׁה וּבָנִים. רִבִּי יְהוּדָה אוֹמֵר אַף מִי שֶׁיֵּשׁ לוֹ אִשָּׁה וּבָנִים לֹא יִשָּׂא אֶת אַיילוֹנִית שֶׁהִיא זוֹנָה הָאֲמוּרָה בַתּוֹרָה. וַחֲכָמִים אוֹמְרִים אֵין זוֹנָה אֶלָּא גִיּוֹרֶת וּמְשׁוּחְרֶרֶת וְשֶׁנִּבְעֲלָה בְּעִילַת זְנוּת.

Mishnah 5: A private priest should not marry a she-ram[98] unless he has a wife and children. Rebbi Jehudah says, even one who has a wife and children should not marry a she-ram since she is the harlot mentioned in the Torah[99]. But the Sages say, a harlot is only a convert, a freedwoman, and one who copulated in harlotry[100].

98 Who visibly is sterile.

99 *Lev.* 21:7,14. For R. Jehudah, every sex act which is not one of possible procreation is harlotry.

100 "Copulating in harlotry" is any sex act between people who either could not marry (close relatives, Gentiles, Slaves, or in adultery) or whose marriage would be sinful. The convert and the libertine will be excluded from marrying into the priesthood by their sexual contacts before becoming full Jews.

(fol. 7c) **הלכה ה:** כֹּהֵן הֶדְיוֹט לֹא יִשָּׂא אֶת אַיילוֹנִית כול׳. הָא יִשְׂרָאֵל שֶׁאֵין לוֹ אִשָּׁה וּבָנִים מוּתָּר בָּהּ. עוֹד הוּא אָסוּר בָּהּ. אֶלָּא בְגִין דְּתַנִּינָן תַּמָּן אֵין זוֹנָה הָאֲמוּרָה בַּתּוֹרָה אֶלָּא גִיּוֹרֶת וּמְשׁוּחְרֶרֶת וְשֶׁנִּבְעֲלָה בְּעִילַת זְנוּת. וְכוּלְּהוֹן לַכֹּהֵן. לְפוּם כֵּן לֹא תַנִּינָהּ.

Halakhah 5: "A private priest should not marry a she-ram," etc. Does that mean that an Israel without wife and children may marry her? Still he is forbidden. But since we stated afterwards that "a harlot mentioned in the Torah is only a convert, a freedwoman, and one who copulated in harlotry," all of which refer only to priests, for this reason it was not stated[101].

101 The same argument in Babli 61a.

אָמַר רִבִּי יְהוּדָה בֶּן פָּזִי. כְּתִיב בֵּין שׁוּרוֹתָם יַצְהִירוּ וְלֹא יִפְנֶה דֶּרֶךְ כְּרָמִים. שֶׁלֹּא הָיְתָה בְּעִילָתָן לְשׁוּם בָּנִים. אָמַר רִבִּי סִימוֹן. כְּתִיב וְאָכְלוּ וְלֹא יִשְׂבָּעוּ הִזְנוּ וְלֹא יִפְרוֹצוּ. שֶׁלֹּא הָיְתָה בְּעִילָתָן לְשֵׁם בָּנִים. כְּתִיב וַיִּקַּח לוֹ לֶמֶךְ שְׁתֵּי נָשִׁים. עָדָה. שֶׁהָיְתָה מִתְעַדֵּן בְּגוּפָהּ. צִילָּה. שֶׁהָיְתָה יוֹשֶׁבֶת בְּצִילָּן שֶׁל בָּנִים.[102]

Rebbi Jehudah ben Pazi said, it is written: "Between their rows they make oil,[103]" "they to not turn to the way of vineyards[104]", that their copulation was not for children. Rebbi Simon said, it is written: "They ate and were not satiated, they whored and did not spread,[105]" that their copulation was not for children. It is written: "Lemekh took for himself two wives[106]", "Adah" who was beautifying her body. "Ṣillah", who was sitting in the shadow of children.

102 Reading of ms. A. Ms. L: שֶׁהָיָה יוֹשֵׁב בְּצִילָּהּ שֶׁל בָּנִים. It may be that this "masculine" sentence is the original text.

103 *Job* 24:11. In this pornographic sermon, the rows are the female's legs, the oil is semen.

104 *Job* 24:18. The evildoers are not interested in harvesting.

105 *Hos*. 4:10. In the words of the Babli, 61b, "any intercourse not intended to spread (the human race)" is sinful.

106 *Gen*. 4:19. The intimation is that Adah "the jewel" was not supposed to have children to preserve her beauty. Ṣillah "the shadow" was shadowed by her children. In *Gen. rabba* 23(3), the roles of Adah and Ṣillah are reversed.

מְתִיבִין לְרִבִּי יוּדָה. הַגַּע עַצְמָךְ שֶׁהָיְתָה עֲקָרָה וְאֵין סוֹפָהּ לֵילֵד. הַגַּע עַצְמָךְ שֶׁהָיְתָה זְקֵינָה. תַּנֵּי. רִבִּי לָעְזָר אוֹמֵר. אַף הַפָּנוּי הַבָּא עַל הַפְּנוּיָה שֶׁלֹּא לְשֵׁם אִישׁוּת הֲרֵי זֶה בְעִילַת זְנוּת. אָמַר רִבִּי בָּא בַּר מָמָל. הָדָא אָמְרָה. כֹּהֵן גָּדוֹל שֶׁקִּידֵּשׁ אִשָּׁה בִבְעִילָה אֵינוֹ כְבָא עַל הַבְּעוּלָה.

They objected to Rebbi Jehudah: Think of it, if she was sterile and could not give birth. Think of it, if she was old[107]. Rebbi Eleazar said, intercourse of an unmarried man with an unmarried woman not with the intent of marriage is intercourse of harlotry[108]. Rebbi Abba bar Mamal said, that implies that the High Priest who performed *qiddushin* by copulation is not having intercourse with a deflowered one[109].

107 A very feminine-looking person can be sterile, as were Sarah, Rebecca, and Rachel. It is not sinful to marry a beautiful woman. An elderly widower is encouraged to marry an elderly woman, not a young girl whom he

cannot satisfy.

108 Babli 61b. A later Babylonian authority is emphatic that this is not practice.

109 It is possible to save the money for *qiddushin* by having intercourse with intent of marriage (Mishnah *Qiddushin* 1:1). If "intercourse" means completed intercourse then by "touching" the High Priest would have desecrated the woman and the later ejaculation would be sinful. Since R. Eleazar explicitly authorizes intercourse of unmarried persons for the purpose of marriage, it follows that the act of marriage is the beginning of intercourse and is available to the High Priest.

(fol. 7a) **משנה ו:** לֹא יִבָּטֵל אָדָם מִפְּרִייָה וְרִבְייָה אֶלָּא אִם כֵּן יֵשׁ לוֹ בָנִים. בֵּית שַׁמַּאי אוֹמְרִים שְׁנֵי זְכָרִים וּבֵית הִלֵּל אוֹמְרִים זָכָר (fol. 7b) וּנְקֵיבָה שֶׁנֶּאֱמַר זָכָר וּנְקֵיבָה בְּרָאָם. נָשָׂא אִשָּׁה וְשָׁהֲתָה אִמּוֹ עֶשֶׂר שָׁנִים וְלֹא יָלְדָה אֵינוֹ רַשַּׁאי לִבָּטֵל. גֵּירְשָׁהּ מוּתֶּרֶת לִינָּשֵׂא לְאַחֵר וְרַשַּׁאי הַשֵּׁנִי לִשְׁהוֹת עִמָּהּ עֶשֶׂר שָׁנִים וְאִם הִפִּילָה מוֹנָה מִשָּׁעָה שֶׁהִפִּילָה. הָאִישׁ מְצוּוֶּה עַל פְּרִייָה וְרִבְייָה אֲבָל לֹא הָאִשָּׁה. רִבִּי יוֹחָנָן בֶּן בְּרוֹקָה אוֹמֵר עַל שְׁנֵיהֶם הוּא אוֹמֵר וַיְבָרֶךְ אוֹתָם אֱלֹהִים וַיֹּאמֶר לָהֶם אֱלֹהִים פְּרוּ וּרְבוּ וגו'.

Mishnah 6: A man should not rest from being fruitful and multiply unless he has children. The House of Shammai say two males, but the House of Hillel say a male and a female, as it is said "male and female He created them[110]." If he married a wife and she stayed with him for ten years and had no child he is not permitted to rest. If he divorced her[111], she is permitted to marry another and the second [husband] is permitted to stay with her for ten years, and if she had a miscarriage she counts from the moment of the miscarriage. The man is commanded to be fruitful and multiply but not the woman. Rebbi Joḥanan ben Beroqa said, for both of them it says "God blessed them and God said to them, be fruitful and multiply,[112]" etc.

110 *Gen.* 1:27.

111 He also might take a second wife.

112 *Gen.* 1:28.

(fol. 7c) **הלכה ו:** לֹא יִבָּטֵל אָדָם מִפְּרִיָּה וְרִבְיָּה כול׳. בֵּית שַׁמַּי אוֹמְרִים. שְׁנֵי זְכָרִים. שֶׁנֶּאֱמַר בְּמֹשֶׁה גֵּרְשׁוֹם וֶאֱלִיעֶזֶר. בֵּית הִלֵּל אוֹמְרִים. זָכָר וּנְקֵיבָה מִבְּרִייָתוֹ שֶׁלְּעוֹלָם. שֶׁנֶּאֱמַר זָכָר וּנְקֵיבָה בְּרָאָם. אָמַר רִבִּי בּוּן. לָכֵן צְרִיכָה אֲפִילוּ זָכָר וּנְקֵיבָה. דל׳ כֵן הִיא מַתְנִיתָא מִקּוּלֵּי בֵית שַׁמַּי וּמֵחוּמְרֵי בֵית הִלֵּל. בְּנֵי בָנִים כְּבָנִים. בְּנֵי בָנוֹת אֵינָם כְּבָנִים. בֶּן בֵּן וּבַת בַּת עוֹלִין. בַּת בֵּן וּבֶן בַּת אֵינָן עוֹלִין. אַיילוֹנִית וְהַסָּרִיס וְשֶׁאֵינָן רְאוּיִין לְווָלָד אֵינָן עוֹלִין.

Halakhah 6: "A man should not rest from being fruitful and multiply," etc. The House of Shammai say two males, since "Gershom and Eliezer"[113] are mentioned for Moses. The House of Hillel say a male and a female the way the world was created, as it is said "male and female He created them[110]." Rebbi Abun said, one has to understand "even a male and a female". If it were not so, it should have been a Mishnah[114] about the leniencies of the House of Shammai and the stringencies of the House of Hillel. Sons of sons are counted as sons[115], sons of daughters are not counted as sons[116]. The son's son and the daughter's daughter count; the son's daughter and the daughter's son do not count. A she-ram, a castrate, and those who cannot have children are not counted.

113 *1Chr.* 23:15. The argument is in Babli 61b, Tosephta 8:4, Tanhuma Buber *Bereshit* 26. Nobody has to be more strict than Moses.

114 In Tractate *Idiut*. It must be that the House of Hillel accept either two males or male and female.

115 Tosephta 8:4, Babli 62b.

116 In the Babli, 62b, this is the opinion of Abbai: it is rejected by the authoritative Rava (Rav Abba bar Rav Yosef bar Ḥama).

רִבִּי אִמִּי בְשֵׁם רִבִּי שִׁמְעוֹן בֶּן לָקִישׁ. טַעֲמָא דְהֵן תַּנָּיָיא מִקֵּץ עֶשֶׂר שָׁנִים לְשֶׁבֶת אַבְרָם בְּאֶרֶץ כְּנָעַן. צֵא שָׁנִים שֶׁעָשָׂה בְחוּצָה לָאָרֶץ. וְתַנֵּי כֵן. חָלְתָה הִיא אוֹ שֶׁחָלָה הוּא אוֹ שֶׁהָלַךְ לוֹ לִמְדִינַת הַיָּם אֵינָן עוֹלִין. נִישְּׂאֵת לָרִאשׁוֹן וְלֹא יָלְדָה יֵשׁ לָהּ כְּתוּבָּה. לַשֵּׁינִי יֵשׁ לָהּ כְּתוּבָּה. לַשְּׁלִישִׁי יֵשׁ לָהּ כְּתוּבָּה. לָרְבִיעִי וְלַחֲמִישִׁי אֵין לָהּ כְּתוּבָּה. רִבִּי חֲנִינָה בַּר עָגוּל בְּשֵׁם רִבִּי חִזְקִיָּה. לַשְּׁלִישִׁי עַצְמוֹ אֵין לָהּ כְּתוּבָּה. נִישֵּׂאת לָרְבִיעִי וְלַחֲמִישִׁי וְלֹא יָלְדָה מַה דְיַחְזְרוּן קַדְמָאֵי עָלֶיהָ. יְכָלָה הִיא מֵימַר. כְּדוֹן אִיתְעַקָּרַת הַהִיא אִיתְּתָא. נִישֵּׂאת לַחֲמִישִׁי וְיָלְדָה מַהוּ תַחֲזִיר עַל רְבִיעָיָיה. אוֹמֵר לָהּ. שְׁתִיקוּתֵיךְ יָפָה מִדִּיבּוּרֵיךְ.

Rebbi Immi in the name of Rebbi Simeon ben Laqish. The reason of that Tanna: "At the end of ten years since Abram lived in the Land of Canaan[117]." Deduct the years outside the Land[118]. We also have stated: [The time during which] she was sick or he was sick, or he went overseas, does not count[119]. If she was married to the first [husband] and did not give birth, she receives *ketubah*[120]; from the second she receives *ketubah*, from the third she receives *ketubah*, from the fourth and fifth she has no *ketubah*. Rebbi Ḥanina bar 'Agil in the name of Rebbi Ḥizqiah: From the third himself she has no *ketubah*[121]. [122]If she was married to a fourth or fifth and did not give birth, may the earlier ones have regress on her[123]? She can say, only now did this woman become sterile[124]. If she was married to the fifth and gave birth, has she regress on the fourth? He says to her, your silence is better than your talk[125].

117 *Gen.* 16:3; Sarah gave her husband a second wife to have children.

118 Tosephta 8:5, Babli 64a as tannaitic statement. In both sources, the verse is designated as hint, not as proof since Isaac waited 20 years for his children. The rule does not apply outside the Land in any case.

119 Tosephta 8:6, Babli 64a.

120 Cf. Chapter 4, Note 84.

121 In the Babli, 65a: As a third husband, she should marry only a man with children. If she married a childless man, she has no *ketubah*.

122 In the Babli, 65a, this statement is characterized as tannaitic.

123 Since it is now proven that she is sterile and most people would not marry a woman knowing that she was sterile. May they ask the *ketubah* money back?

124 The claimants would have to prove that she was sterile before.

125 The fourth husband could say, had I known you were not sterile, I never would have given you a bill of divorce. This threatens retroactively to invalidate the divorce and to make her child a bastard (Babli 65a).

נִבְעֶלֶת וְרוֹאָה דָם נִבְעֶלֶת וְרוֹאָה דָם. אִית תַּנָּיֵי תַנֵּי שְׁנִייָה תִיבָּעֵל שְׁלִישִׁית לֹא תִיבָּעֵל. וְאִית תַּנּוּיֵי תַנֵּי שְׁלִישִׁית תִּיבָּעֵל רְבִיעִית לֹא תִיבָּעֵל. הֲוֹון בְּעַייָן מֵימַר. מַה דָמַר. שְׁנִייָה תִבָּעֵל וּשְׁלִישִׁית (fol. 7d) לֹא תִיבָּעֵל. כְּמָאן דָּמַר. שְׁלִישִׁית אֵין לָהּ כְּתוּבָּה. בְּרַם כְּמָאן דָּמַר. שְׁלִישִׁית תִּיבָּעֵל רְבִיעִית לֹא תִיבָּעֵל. כְּמָאן דָּמַר. שְׁלִישִׁית יֵשׁ לָהּ כְּתוּבָּה. הָיְתָה יוֹלֶדֶת זְכָרִים וְהָיוּ נִימוֹלִים וּמֵתִים. אִית תַּנָּיֵי תַנֵּי. שֵׁנִי יָמוֹל שְׁלִישִׁי לֹא יָמוֹל. אִית תַּנָּיֵי תַנֵּי. שְׁלִישִׁי יָמוֹל רְבִיעִי לֹא יָמוֹל. הֲוֹון בְּעַייָן מֵימַר. מָאן דָמַר. שֵׁינִי יָמוֹל שְׁלִישִׁי לֹא יָמוֹל. כְּמָאן דָּמַר. הַשְּׁלִישִׁית אֵין לָהּ כְּתוּבָּה. מָאן דָּמַר. הַשְּׁלִישִׁי יָמוֹל הָרְבִיעִי לֹא יָמוֹל. כְּמָאן דָּמַר. הַשְּׁלִישִׁית יֵשׁ לָהּ כְּתוּבָּה. אֲפִילוּ כְּמָאן דָּמַר. הַשְּׁלִישִׁית יֵשׁ לָהּ כְּתוּבָּה. מוֹדֵי הוּא הָכָא שֶׁלֹּא יָמוֹל מִפְּנֵי סַכָּנָה. תַּנֵּי. אָמַר רִבִּי נָתָן. מַעֲשֶׂה שֶׁהָלַכְתִּי לְקֵיסָרִין שֶׁלְּקַפּוֹטְקִייָא. וְהָיְתָה שָׁם אִשָּׁה וְהָיְתָה יוֹלֶדֶת זְכָרִים וְהָיוּ נִימוֹלִים וּמֵתִים. וּמָלַת אֶת הָרִאשׁוֹן וָמֵת שֵׁינִי וָמֵת שְׁלִישִׁי וָמֵת. רְבִיעִי הֱבִיאָתוֹ לְפָנַיי. נִסְתַּכַּלְתִּי בוֹ וְלֹא רָאִיתִי בוֹ דַם בְּרִית. אֲמַרְתִּי לָהֶם. הֲנִיחוּהוּ לְאַחַר זְמָן. וְהֵנִיחוּהוּ וּמָלוּהוּ וְנִמְצָא בֶן קַייָמָא. וְהָיוּ קוֹרִין אוֹתוֹ נָתָן בִּשְׁמִי.

If she had intercourse and saw blood repeatedly. Some Tannaïm state, a second time she may have intercourse, a third time she may not. But some Tannaïm state, a third time she may have intercourse, a fourth time she may not[126]. They wanted to say[127] that he who says, a second time she may have intercourse, a third time she may not, holds with him who says that a third time she has no *ketubah*. But he who says, a third time she may have intercourse, a fourth time she may not, holds with him who says that the third time she has *ketubah.* If one gave birth to male childen and they died when being circumcised. Some Tannaïm state, a second time one should circumcise, a third time one should not circumcise. Some Tannaïm state, a third time one should circumcise, a fourth time one should not circumcise[128]. They wanted to say that he who says, a second time one should circumcise, a third time one should not circumcise, holds with him who says that a third time she has no *ketubah.* He who says, a third time one should circumcise, a fourth time one should not circumcise, holds with him who says that the third time she has *ketubah.* Even he, who says that the third time she has *ketubah* agrees here that one should not circumcise because of the danger[129]. It was stated[130]: Rebbi Nathan said, it happened that I went to Kappadokian Caesarea, and there was a woman who gave birth to male children and they died when being circumcised. She circumcised the first [child] and he died, the second and he died, the third and he died. She brought the fourth one before me, I looked at him and saw that he did not have enough blood for circumcision. I told them, wait for later. They waited, circumsised him, he turned out to be living, and they called him Nathan after me.

126 The Babli, *Niddah* 65b/66a, and Tosephta *Niddah* 8:1-2 know only of the more lenient opinion. This does not deal with a virgin but a woman who reacts to intercourse with interior bleeding that might be menstrual. After three consecutive episodes she may not have any more intercourse with this husband.

127 A conjecture, not a statement.

128 In the Babli, 64b and other places, and Tosephta *Shabbat* 15:8 the person who holds that in matters of physical danger two cases are proof is Rebbi, and the one who requires three is his father, Rabban Simeon ben Gamliel.

129 The Babli, 64b, agrees that it is most careless not to follow Rebbi in matters of dangers to life. A warning

example is Abbai, who died after he married a very beautiful twofold widow.

130 Tosephta *Shabbat* 15:8, Babli *Shabbat* 134a. In both of these sources, the *third* child was brought before R. Nathan (the Babylonian), the baby was called Nathan the Babylonian, and it happened in Kappadokian Mazaca (pre-Roman name of Caesarea).

הָיוּ לָהּ בָּנִים וּמֵתוּ מוֹנָה מִשְּׁעַת מִיתָה. יְכוֹלָה הִיא מֵימַר. רוּחָא חֲנְקַת בָּנֶיהָ דְּהַהִיא אִיתְּתָא וַעֲקָרְתָהּ.

If she had children but they died, she counts from the time of death[131]. She can say, a spirit strangled the children of this woman and made me sterile[132].

131 This refers to the statement in the Mishnah that after a miscarriage there starts a new period of 10 years.

132 Since she was not sterile at the moment of marriage, her *ketubah* is due her in any case.

רִבִּי לָעְזָר בְּשֵׁם רִבִּי יוֹסֵי בֶּן זִימְרָה. טַעֲמָא דְהֵן תַּנָּייָא. פְּרוּ וּרְבוּ וּמִלְאוּ אֶת הָאָרֶץ וְכִבְשׁוּהָ. וּכְבָשָׁהּ כְּתִיב. מִי דַרְכּוֹ לִכְבּוֹשׁ. הָאִישׁ. לֹא הָאִשָּׁה. רִבִּי יִרְמְיָה רִבִּי אַבָּהוּ רִבִּי יִצְחָק בַּר מַרְיוֹן בְּשֵׁם רִבִּי חֲנִינָה. הֲלָכָה כְּרִבִּי יוֹחָנָן בֶּן בְּרוֹקָה. רִבִּי יַעֲקֹב בַּר אָחָא וְרִבִּי יַעֲקֹב בַּר אִידִי רִבִּי יִצְחָק בַּר חֲקוּלָה בְּשֵׁם רִבִּי יוּדָן נְשִׂיָיא. אִם תּוֹבַעַת לְהִינָּשֵׂא הַדִּין עִמָּהּ. רִבִּי לָעְזָר בְּשֵׁם רִבִּי חֲנִינָה. הֲלָכָה כְּרִבִּי יוֹחָנָן בֶּן בְּרוֹקָה. אָמַר לֵיהּ רִבִּי בָּא בַּר זַבְדָּא. עִמָּךְ הָיִיתִי. לֹא אִיתְאֲמָרַהּ אֶלָּא אִם הָיְתָה תוֹבַעַת לְהִינָּשֵׂא הַדִּין עִמָּהּ. הָדָא הוּא דְתַנִּינָן קַמָּן. שַׁבָּת שֶׁחָלָה תִשְׁעָה בְאַב לִהְיוֹת בְּתוֹכָהּ אֲסוּרִיי מִלְּסַפֵּר וּמִלְּכַבֵּס. וּבַחֲמִישִׁי מוּתָּרִין מִפְּנֵי כְבוֹד הַשַּׁבָּת. רִבִּי בָּא בַּר זַבְדָּא בְּשֵׁם רִבִּי חֲנִינָה. בִּיקֵּשׁ רִבִּי לַעֲקוֹר תִּשְׁעָה בְאַב וְלֹא הִנִּיחוּ לוֹ. אָמַר לוֹ רִבִּי לָעְזָר. עִמָּךְ הָיִיתִי. לֹא אִיתְאֲמָרַת אֶלָּא בִּיקֵּשׁ רִבִּי לַעֲקוֹר תִּשְׁעָה בְאַב שֶׁחָל לִהְיוֹת בְּשַׁבָּת וְלֹא הִנִּיחוּ לוֹ. אָמַר. הוֹאִיל וְנִדְחֶה יִדָּחֶה. אָמְרוּ לוֹ יִדָּחֶה לְמָחָר. וְקָרָא עֲלֵיהֶם טוֹבִים הַשְּׁנַיִם מִן הָאֶחָד.

Rebbi Eleazar in the name of Rebbi Yose ben Zimra: The reason of that Tanna[133]: "Be fruitful and multiply, fill the earth and conquer it." It is written "he shall conquer it.[134]" Who usually conquers? The man, not the woman. Rebbi Jeremiah, Rebbi Abbahu, Rebbi Isaac bar Marion, in the name of Rebbi Ḥanina: Practice follows Rebbi Joḥanan ben Beroqa. Rebbi Jacob bar Aḥa and Rebbi Jacob bar Idi, Rebbi Isaac bar Ḥaqula in the name of Rebbi Jehudah Neśia: If she requests to be married, she has the law on her side[135]. Rebbi Eleazar in the name of Rebbi Ḥanina: Practice follows Rebbi Joḥanan ben Beroqa. Rebbi Abba bar Zavda said to him, I was with you and it was only said that if she requests to be married, she has the law on her side. In a similar case[136], referring to what we have stated there[137]: "In the week in which the Ninth of Av[138] falls, it is forbidden to get a haircut and to wash. But on Thursday one is permitted, in preparation for the Sabbath." Rebbi Abba bar Zavda in the name of Rebbi Ḥanina: Rebbi wanted to do away with the Ninth of Av but they did not let him. Rebbi Eleazar said to him, I was with you and it was only said that Rebbi wanted to do away with the Ninth of Av which happened to be on the Sabbath but they did not let him. He said, since it is pushed away, let it be pushed away. They said to him, it should be pushed to the next day. He recited on these[139]: "Two are better than one."

133 The last clause in the Mishnah, that only men are obligated to have children. The entire paragraph has its parallel in the Babli, 65b.

134 *Gen.* 1:28. The last word is written וכבשה which can be read as defective plural or regular singular.

135 If a woman was childlessly married to a man for 10 years and requests a divorce in order to be able to have a child with a more potent man, the court is required to force the husband to divorce her with a full *ketubah*. The Babli is explicit in this matter, that she must claim to need children who will care for her in her old age. Such a statement is needed only if practice does *not* follow R.

Joḥanan ben Beroqa.

136 Involving R. Eleazar and R. Abba bar Zavda and an erroneous statement. In the Babli, *Megillah* 5a/b, the wrong statement is again given by R. Eleazar and the correction by R. Abba bar Zavda. From the insistence that the two cases are parallel, it seems that this should be the reading here also. But the text given here is confirmed by the parallel in *Megillah* 1:1.

137 Mishnah *Ta'aniot* 4:9.

138 The day of mourning for the destruction of the Temple.

139 *Eccl.* 4:9. From the text in *Megillah*, it seems that "he" is a third person, possibly R. Ḥaninah,

אלמנה לכהן פרק שביעי

(fol. 7d) **משנה א:** אַלְמָנָה לְכֹהֵן גָּדוֹל גְּרוּשָׁה וַחֲלוּצָה לְכֹהֵן הֶדְיוֹט הִכְנִיסָה לוֹ עַבְדֵי מְלוֹג וְעַבְדֵי צֹאן בַּרְזֶל. עַבְדֵי מְלוֹג לֹא יֹאכְלוּ בַתְּרוּמָה עַבְדֵי צֹאן בַּרְזֶל יֹאכְלוּ בַתְּרוּמָה. וְאֵילוּ הֵן עַבְדֵי מְלוֹג אִם מֵתוּ מֵתוּ לָהּ וְאִם הוֹתִירוּ הוֹתִירוּ לָהּ. אַף עַל פִּי שֶׁהוּא חַיָּב בִּמְזוֹנוֹתָן הֲרֵי אֵילוּ לֹא יֹאכְלוּ בַתְּרוּמָה. וְאֵילוּ הֵן עַבְדֵי צֹאן בַּרְזֶל אִם מֵתוּ מֵתוּ לוֹ וְאִם הוֹתִירוּ הוֹתִירוּ לוֹ. הוֹאִיל וְהוּא חַיָּב בְּאַחֲרָיוּתָן אֵילוּ יֹאכְלוּ בַתְּרוּמָה.

Mishnah 1: If a widow [married] to a High Priest, or a divorcee or one freed by *ḥalîṣah* [married] to a simple priest, brought him slaves as paraphernalia or as mortmain[1]: The slaves of separate property may not eat heave[2], the slaves of mortmain may eat heave. These are slaves of paraphernalia: If they died, they died as her property, if they increased, they increased as her property. Even though he is responsible for their upkeep, they may not eat heave. These are slaves of mortmain: If they died, they died as his property, if they increased, they increased as his property. Since he guarantees them, they may eat heave.

1 Mortmain ("inalienable property", 'iron flock', in German law *eisern Vieh*) whose value was determined in the marriage contract (*ketubah*) as *dos aestimata*, upon marriage became the husband's property. At the termination of the marriage their value was due back to the wife.

Paraphernalia [from the Greek παράφερνα, Middle Latin *paraphernalia (bona)*, as a legal term relevant here "bride's goods beyond her dowry," equivalent to Late Latin *parapherna* "bride's property." (For the etymology of מְלוֹג, Ashkenazic מְלוּג, cf.

Note 45, also Chapter 4, Note 86). These goods are *res non aestimata*, property not entered in the marriage contract, of which the husband has administration for the duration of the marriage. He must maintain the value of this property and is compensated by receiving its usufruct but has no property rights.

Since in any irregular union (such as described in the Mishnah) the wife of a Cohen is barred from all sanctified food, her property is barred with her. But the property of a Cohen is entitled to share in his sanctified food (*Lev.* 22:11).

The expression צאן ברזל "iron flock" for "inalienable, private property" may also be compared to Latin *peculium* "private property" which is derived from *pecus, -oris* "cattle" but used as a legal term for property in general.

2 And all other sanctified food that may be eaten outside the Temple precinct.

אַלְמָנָה לְכֹהֵן גָּדוֹל כול׳. מְנַיִין לְכֹהֵן שֶׁנָּשָׂא אִשָּׁה וְקָנָה לוֹ עֲבָדִים שֶׁיֹּאכְלוּ בַּתְּרוּמָה. תַּלְמוּד לוֹמַר וְכֹהֵן כִּי יִקְנֶה נֶפֶשׁ קִנְייַן כַּסְפּוֹ וגו׳. מְנַיִין לְאִשְׁתּוֹ שֶׁקָּנְתָה עֲבָדִים (fol. 8a) וַעֲבָדֶיהָ עֲבָדִים שֶׁיֹּאכְלוּ בַּתְּרוּמָה. תַּלְמוּד לוֹמַר וְכֹהֵן כִּי יִקְנֶה נֶפֶשׁ קִנְייַן כַּסְפּוֹ. אַף קִנְייָנוֹ שֶׁקָּנָה קִנְייָן אוֹכֵל. רִבִּי יַעֲקֹב בַּר אָחָא רִבִּי הִילָא בְשֵׁם רִבִּי לָעְזָר. הֵם יֹאכְלוּ וְהֵם יַאֲכִילוּ. בְּעֶבֶד שֶׁקָּנָה עֲבָדִים עַל מְנָת שֶׁיִּהְיֶה לְרַבּוֹ רְשׁוּת בָּהֶן הִיא מַתְנִיתָא. אֲבָל בְּעֶבֶד שֶׁקָּנָה עֲבָדִים עַל מְנָת [שֶׁלֹּא יְהֵא][3] לְרַבּוֹ רְשׁוּת בָּהֶן קִנְייָנוֹ הוּא. רִבִּי יַעֲקֹב בַּר אָחָא רִבִּי הִילָא בְשֵׁם רִבִּי לָעְזָר. עֶבֶד שֶׁקָּנָה עֲבָדִים עַל מְנָת שֶׁלֹּא יְהֵא לְרַבּוֹ רְשׁוּת בָּהֶן וּמֵת. כָּל־הַקּוֹדֵם בָּהֶן זָכָה. וְהָכָא לֹא קִנְייָן קִנְייָנוֹ הוּא.

"A widow [married] to a High Ptiest," etc. From where that a priest who married a wife or bought slaves enables them to eat heave? The verse says "and if a priest buys a person as his money's acquisition[4]," etc. From where that if his wife bought slaves, and her slaves [bought] slaves, that they may eat heave? The verse says "and if a priest buys a person as his money's acquisition," etc. Also his acquisition which bought an acquisition enables him to eat[5]. Rebbi Jacob bar Aḥa, Rebbi Hila in the name of Rebbi Eleazar. "They shall eat[4]", they shall enable to eat. The *baraita* speaks about a slave who acquired slaves within the power of his master. But if a slave acquired slaves on condition that his master have no power over them, they are his property[6]. Rebbi Jacob bar Aḥa, Rebbi Hila in the name of Rebbi Eleazar. If a slave acquired slaves on condition that his master have no power over them and he died, the first person who comes can grab them[7]. In that case, [that slave] is not his property's property[8].

3 Reading of the Spanish authors, Nachmanides and Rashba (to Babli, 66a). Ms. L: שיהיה, making this and the preceding sentences identical.

4 *Lev.* 22:11: "And if a priest buys a person as his money's acquisition, he shall eat of it; and the one born in his house, *they* shall eat of his food." The wife is acquired by the *qiddushin* money.

5 Note the incongruous plural in *Lev.* 22:11. Up to here the text is a *baraita*; Babli 66a, *Sifra Emor Parasha* 5(1).

6 Anything a slave buys is his owner's property. Usually, what he otherwise acquires is also his owner's property. But if he received something as a gift (e. g., money to buy his freedom) with the express stipulation that his master shall have no claim to it, then it is the slave's direct property. If the slave received other slaves as such a gift, these are not the master's acquisition and are barred from eating sanctified food.

7 They are ownerless. Since a slave can become free only by an act of manumission, these slaves are not freed by the death of their master and can be taken by anybody.

8 The slave's slave is not the slave's master's property.

רִבִּי הִילָא בְשֵׁם רִבִּי לָעְזָר. הֵם יֹאכְלוּ וְהֵם יַאֲכִילוּ. הָרָאוּי לוֹכַל מַאֲכִיל וְשֶׁאֵינוֹ רָאוּי לוֹכַל אֵינוֹ מַאֲכִיל. רִבִּי יוֹחָנָן אָמַר. מִשּׁוּם קְנָס. מַה נְפַק מִן בֵּינֵיהוֹן. עֶבֶד עָרֵל שֶׁקָּנָה לוֹ עֲבָדִים. אִין תֵּימַר קְנָס. אֵין כָּאן קְנָס. אִין תֵּימַר הָרָאוּי לֶאֱכוֹל מַאֲכִיל. וְזֶה הוֹאִיל וְאֵינוֹ רָאוּי לֶאֱכוֹל אֵינוֹ מַאֲכִיל.

Rebbi Hila in the name of Rebbi Eleazar: "They shall eat", they shall enable to eat[9]. The one who may eat enables to eat, the one who may not eat cannot enable to eat[10]. Rebbi Joḥanan says, because of a fine[11]. What is the difference between them? If an uncircumcised slave[12] buys slaves. If you say, it is a fine, here there is no fine[13]. If you say the one who may eat enables to eat, this one, since he is not able to eat, cannot enable to eat.

9 Cf. Note 4. They read יאכלו as יַאֲכִלוּ. In *Sifra Emor Parashah* 5(6), this is a tannaitic argument of R. Simeon.

10 Since the divorcee becomes desecrated by her marriage to any priest, she never can herself eat heave nor cause her slaves to eat.

11 By *qiddushin*, the divorcee was acquired by the priest. Her property was acquired with her. Therefore, by biblical standards her slaves could eat but it is a traditional fine imposed on irregular marriages that they should not confer the same advantages as a regular one.

12 He cannot eat sanctified food (*Ex*. 12:48); the rules are spelled out in Halakhah 8:1.

13 On condition that the slave remain uncircumcised in a way accepted in Jewish law.

14 In the Babli, the opinion of R. Eleazar is quoted in the name of Ravina I and that of R. Joḥanan by Rava. (Maimonides, who identifies the author of the first opinion as the authoritative Ravina II, decides following R. Eleazar).

רִבִּי יַעֲקֹב בַּר אָחָא אָמַר. בְּעַבְדֵי צֹאן בַּרְזֶל פְּלִיגִין. רִבִּי יוֹחָנָן אָמַר. מִכָּרָן אֵינָן מְכוּרִין. אָמַר לֵיהּ רִבִּי לָעְזָר. אוֹכְלִין בַּתְּרוּמָה מִכּוֹחוֹ וְאַתְּ אָמְרַתְּ אָכֵין. אָמַר לֵיהּ. הֲרֵי עַבְדֵי מְלוֹג הֲרֵי הֵן אוֹכְלִין תְּרוּמָה מִכּוֹחוֹ. וְאַתְּ אָמַר. מִכָּרָן אֵינָן מְכוּרִין. מִשֶּׁלָּךְ נָתְנוּ לָךְ. בְּדִין הוּא שֶׁלֹּא יֹאכַל בַּתְּרוּמָה. וְהֵן אָמְרוּ שֶׁיֹּאכַל. וְהֵן אָמְרוּ. מִכָּרָן אֵינָן מְכוּרִין. רִבִּי יַעֲקֹב בַּר אָחָא בְּשֵׁם רִבִּי יֹאשִׁיָּה. מַתְנִיתָא מְסַיְּיעָא לְדִין וּמַתְנִיתָא מְסַיְּיעָא לְדֵין. מַתְנִיתָא מְסַיְּיעָא לְרִבִּי אֶלְיעֶזֶר. עַבְדֵי מְלוֹג יוֹצְאִין בְּשֵׁן וָעַיִן לָאִשָּׁה אֲבָל לֹא לָאִישׁ. וְעַבְדֵי צֹאן בַּרְזֶל יוֹצְאִין בְּשֵׁן וָעַיִן לָאִישׁ אֲבָל לֹא לָאִשָּׁה. מַה עֲבַד לָהּ רִבִּי יוֹחָנָן. קַל הוּא

בְּשִׁחְרוּר. כְּהָדָא דְתַנֵּי. הָעוֹשֶׂה עַבְדּוֹ אֲפּוֹתֵיקִי. מְכָרוֹ אֵינוֹ מָכוּר. שִׁיחְרְרוֹ מְשׁוּחְרָר. מַתְנִיתָא מְסַייְעָא לְרִבִּי יוֹחָנָן. אֶחָד עַבְדֵי מְלוֹג וְאֶחָד עַבְדֵי צֹאן בַּרְזֶל אֵינָן בְּיוֹם וְיוֹמַיִם וְאֵינָן יוֹצְאִין בְּשֵׁן וָעַיִן בֵּין לָאִישׁ בֵּין לָאִשָּׁה. מַה פְלִיגִין. בְּשֶׁמְּכָרָן לְעוֹלָם אוֹ בְשֶׁמְּכָרָן לְשָׁעָה. אִין תֵּימַר. בְּשֶׁמְּכָרָן לְעוֹלָם וְלֹא מְכָרָן לְשָׁעָה. דִּבְרֵי הַכֹּל מְכוּרִין. אִין תֵּימַר. בְּשֶׁמְּכָרָן לְשָׁעָה אֲבָל לֹא מְכָרָן לְעוֹלָם. דִּבְרֵי הַכֹּל אֵינָן מְכוּרִין. נִישְׁמְעִינָהּ מִן הָדָא. הָעוֹשֶׂה שָׂדֵהוּ אֲפּוֹתֵיקִי לְאִשָּׁה בִּכְתוּבָּתָהּ וּלְבַעַל חוֹבוֹ עַל חוֹבוֹ. מְכָרָהּ הֲרֵי זוֹ מְכוּרָה. הַלּוֹקֵחַ יָחוּשׁ לְעַצְמוֹ. רַבָּן שִׁמְעוֹן בֶּן גַּמְלִיאֵל אוֹמֵר. לָאִשָּׁה בִּכְתוּבָּתָהּ אֵינָהּ מְכוּרָה. שֶׁלֹּא עָלְתָ עַל דַּעַת שֶׁתְּהֵא אִשָּׁה מְחַזֶּרֶת עַל בָּתֵּי דִינִין. אָמְרוּ. אַתְיָא דְרִבִּי לָעְזָר כְּרַבָּנִן. דְּרִבִּי יוֹחָנָן כְּרַבָּן שִׁמְעוֹן בֶּן גַּמְלִיאֵל. הֲוֵי בְּשֶׁמְּכָרָן לְשָׁעָה אֲנָן[15] קַייָמִין. אֲבָל אִם מְכָרָן לְעוֹלָם דִּבְרֵי הַכֹּל אֵינָן מְכוּרִין.

Rebbi Jacob bar Aḥa said, there is disagreement about mortmain slaves. Rebbi Joḥanan said, if he sold them, they are not sold[16]. Rebbi Eleazar said to him, they are eating heave by his power and you say so? He answered, do not paraphernalia slaves also eat by his power, and one says that if he sold them, they are not sold[17]. From your own they[18] gave to you. It would be logical that one[19] should not eat heave. But they said that he eats[20], and they said, if he sold them, they are not sold. Rebbi Jacob bar Aḥa in the name of Rebbi Josiah. A *baraita* supports one and another *baraita* supports the other. A *baraita* supports Rebbi Eleazar: Paraphernalia slaves are freed on account of "tooth and eye"[21] from the wife but not the husband. Mortmain slaves[22] are freed by "tooth and eye" from the husband but not the wife. What does Rebbi Joḥanan do with this? They are quick to manumit[23], as we have stated[24]: If somebody mortgages[25] a slave and later sold him, he is not sold[26]; if he freed him, he is freed[27]. A *baraita* supports Rebbi Joḥanan: Neither mortmain slaves nor paraphernalia slaves are under the rules of "one or two days"[28] and are freed by "tooth or eye" from neither the husband nor the wife. Where do they disagree? When he sold them forever or sold them for some time[29]? If you say that he sold them permanently rather than temporarily, does everybody agree that they are sold? If you say that he sold them temporarily rather than permanently, does everybody agree that they are not sold? Let us hear from the following: [30]If somebody mortgages his field to his wife for her *ketubah* or to a creditor for his claim and then sells it, it is sold and the buyer should beware for himself[31]. Rabban Simeon ben Gamliel says, for the *ketubah* of the wife it is not sold since it is unthinkable that a woman[32] should run around at courts of law. They said, Rebbi Eleazar parallels the rabbis, Rebbi Johanan Rabban Simeon ben Gamliel[33]. That means, we deal with a temporary sale. But if he sold permanently, everybody agrees that they are not sold.

15 Reading of *editio princeps*. Ms. L: אינן

16 Tosaphot in *Giṭṭin* 41a, *s. v.* אשה, are of the opinion that the Babli concurs.

17 If the wife is not from a priestly family, then her slaves can eat only because he made her his wife. He cannot sell them since nobody can sell what is not his; Tosephta 9:1.

18 The developers of rabbinic doctrine.

19 A paraphernalia slave who is not property of a Cohen.

20 As if he were the property of a Cohen.

21 If a slave loses a body part through his owner's fault, he gains his freedom (*Ex.* 21:26). Paraphernalia slaves are property of the wife but not the husband. This part of the *baraita* is quoted in the Babli. *Baba Qama* 89a.

22 This *baraita* holds that they are the husband's property; therefore, he must have the absolute power to sell them, against R. Johanan.

23 The Babli agrees without a dissenting opinion.

24 Quoted as tannaitic text also in *Giṭṭin* 4:4 (fol. 45b), as amoraic in the Babli, *Baba Qama* 11b. 33b; *Baba Meṣi'a* 44b.

25 Greek ὑποθήκη "mortgage".

26 The creditor can foreclose on the slave in the hands of the buyer.

27 The creditor has to sue the borrower for damages; he cannot put his hand on the ex-slave.

28 *Ex.* 21:20. The exemption for the owner who hits his slave which provided that he is not prosecutable if the slave survives for two days is not available to either wife or husband. This *baraita* defines "owner" as a person who has both the right to and disposition of his property.

This text is also in the Babli *Baba Qama* 89b.

29 "Selling temporarily" is not selling the property but leasing the use of the property for a limited period.

30 *Ševi'it* 10:1 (Notes 22-24), in a slightly different version Babli *Giṭṭin* 41a.

31 The buyer has to insure himself against the possibility that the creditor or the wife at the dissolution of her marriage will foreclose the property and he will have to sue the seller for restitution of the sale price.

32 Without a male protector. Then the law has to protect her.

33 Since the wife has a lien on the mortmain slaves, the husband cannot alienate them without her consent, just as he cannot alienate real estate put up as collateral for her *ketubah*.

Rosh (R. Asher ben Iehiel) in his commentary on this Yerushalmi (*Yebamot* 7 #1) holds that the husband is prevented even from leasing the property without his wife's consent. Rif (R. Isaac Fasi), *Giṭṭin* #472 holds that the husband may not sell but may lease for a limited time.

וְלַד בְּהֶמַת מְלוֹג לְבַעַל. וְלַד שִׁפְחַת מְלוֹג לָאִשָּׁה. חֲנַנְיָה בֶּן אֲחִי יְהוֹשֻׁעַ אָמַר. וְלַד בְּהֶמַת מְלוֹג כִּוְולַד שִׁפְחַת מְלוֹג. רִבִּי לָעְזָר אָמַר לַחֲבֵרָייָא. הֲוֹון יָדְעִין דּוּ רִבִּי יוֹחָנָן כַּחֲנַנְיָה בֶּן אֲחִי יְהוֹשֻׁעַ. רַב וּשְׁמוּאֵל. רַב כְּרַבָּנִן וּשְׁמוּאֵל כַּחֲנַנְיָה בֶּן אֲחִי יְהוֹשֻׁעַ. מָתִיב שְׁמוּאֵל לְרַב. עַל דַּעְתָּךְ דְּאַתְּ אָמַר מִשֶּׁלָּאִשָּׁה הֵן. מֵאַתָּה לֹא יִטּוֹל הַבְּכוֹר פִּי שְׁנַיִם. הַגַּע עַצְמָךְ שֶׁהִכְנִיסָן קְטַנִּים וְגָֽדְלוּ הֲרֵי הֵן שֶׁלָּאִשָּׁה הֵן. וְאַתְּ מוֹדֶה לִי שֶׁהַבְּכוֹר נוֹטֵל פִּי שְׁנַיִם.

[34]The offspring of a paraphernalia animal belongs to the husband, that of a paraphernalia slave girl belongs to the wife. Ḥanania the nephew of Rebbi Joshua said, the offspring of a paraphernalia animal is like that of a paraphernalia slave girl[35]. Rebbi Eleazar said to the colleagues, you should know that Rebbi Joḥanan follows Ḥanania the nephew of Rebbi

Joshua. Rav and Samuel, Rav follows the rabbis, but Samuel follows Ḥanania the nephew of Rebbi Joshua[36]. Samuel objected to Rav: According to you who says, they belong to the wife, should the first-born not take a double portion[37]? Think of it, if she brought them when they were small and they grew up, are they not the wife's, and you agree with me that the first-born takes a double portion[38]!

34 In the Babli, *Ketubot* 79b, this is a *baraita*. Since first generation Amoraim disagree over the rule, it seems that the Yerushalmi also presents this as a *baraita*.

35 In the Babli, the formulation is: "the offspring of a paraphernalia slave girl is like that of a paraphernalia animal." In the Babli, the child of the slave girl belongs to the husband; in the Yerushalmi, everything belongs to the wife.

In the Babli, the straight argument of Ḥanania is that the husband has the usufruct. In the Babli the argument of the rabbis is that if the slave girl dies, the wife is left with nothing but if an animal dies, she is left with the value of the hide. There is no reason to transfer the argument of the Babli to the Yerushalmi. From the next paragraph it seems rather that the rabbis hold that the wife's slaves belong to her father's household and have to be treated as family heirlooms, and any increase in their number is increase of the value of the stock (which is the wife's), not yield (which is the husband's).

36 In the Babli (Note 34) only Samuel's opinion (opposite in meaning to his position here) is noted, without opposition.

37 The first-born takes a double portion of the inheritance (*Deut.* 21:17, reading פי שנים as "double", not "$^2/_3$".) However, the first-born takes a double portion only from what is available at the father's death. For example, property leased to others is available, debts collectable are not available (since the payer may default. Most modern authorities hold that sovereign debt is available.) In the Babli, *Baba Batra* 123b, an anonymous *baraita* is quoted which in a different form is a Tosephta, *Bekhorot* 6:16, that the first-born gets a double interest in the calf of a cow who was pregnant at the father's death. This must mean that the calf is increase of the value of the stock, of which the first-born gets a

double portion, not yield after the father's death, of which he would get only a simple portion. It does not make any sense that Rav denies the young of the animal to the wife when he gives the first-born a double portion.

38 Here everybody agrees that this represents increase in the stock, not yield.

תַּנֵּי הִכְנִיסָתָן יְלָדִים נוֹטְלָתָן נְעָרִים. הִכְנִיסָה לוֹ שְׁנֵי כֵלִים. הָיָה אֶחָד יָפֶה כִכְתוּבָּתָהּ נוֹטְלָתוֹ בִכְתוּבָּתָהּ. הָיָה אֶחָד וּמֶחֱצָה יָפֶה כִכְתוּבָּתָהּ רַב הוּנָא וְרַב נַחְמָן בַּר יַעֲקֹב. חַד אָמַר. הוּא נוֹתֵן דְּמֵי הַשֵּׁינִי וְנוֹטְלוֹ. וְחוֹרָנָה אָמַר. הִיא נוֹתֶנֶת דְּמֵי הַשֵּׁינִי וְנוֹטְלָתוֹ. רִבִּי אַבָּא בַּר כַּהֲנָא אָמַר קוֹמֵי רִבִּי אִמִּי רִבִּי יַעֲקֹב בַּר אָחָא בְשֵׁם רִבִּי יָסָא. אֲפִילוּ הָיָה יָפֶה אֶחָד וּמֶחֱצָה בִכְתוּבָּתָהּ הִיא נוֹתֶנֶת דְּמֵי הַשֵּׁינִי וְנוֹטְלָתוֹ. שֶׁלֹּא עָלַת עַל דַּעַת שֶׁיִּשְׁתַּמְּשׁוּ אֲחֵרִים בְּכֵלֶיהָ. רִבִּי יַעֲקֹב בַּר אָחָא בְשֵׁם רִבִּי זְעוּרָה. מַתְנִיתָא אָמְרָה כֵן. הִכְנִיתָתָן בְּדָמִים נוֹטְלָתָן בְּדָמִים.

It was stated[39]: If she brought them when they were small, she takes them when they are lads. If she brought him two vessels[40]. If one of them was worth the value of her marriage contract, she takes it for her marriage contract[41]. If one and a half was the value of her marriage contract, [disagreement of] Rav Huna and Rav Naḥman bar Jacob. One of them said, he pays for the second vessel and takes it; the other one says, she pays for the second vessel and takes it[42]. Rebbi Abba bar Cahana said before Rebbi Immi, Rebbi Jacob bar Aḥa in the name of Rebbi Yasa[43]: Even if one was worth one and a half times the value of her marriage contract, she pays for the second vessel and takes it, because it is unthinkable that others should use her vessels. Rebbi Jacob bar Aḥa in the name of Rebbi Ze'ira: A *baraita* says so: If she brought them for their monetary value, she takes them for their monetary value[44].

39 Tosephta 9:1. The Tosephta deals with mortmain slaves and states that the wife has the right at the dissolution of the marriage to take the offspring of her slaves, even if their value today is greater than the value at which they were recorded in the marriage contract. She will have to indemnify her ex-husband for the difference in value but, since they are family heirlooms, he has no right to retain them against her will. This right extends to inanimate objects.

40 As mortmain property.

41 *Ketubah* in this connection denotes the entire value of the marriage contract, the statutory *ketubah* sum, the value of mortmain property, and the additional fee he agreed to pay in case of a dissolution of the marriage. For this reason the translation does not simply state "*ketubah*". We are dealing with a state of rampant inflation, as it was recorded during the military anarchy of the Roman empire, where the sum stated in the contract would have lost most of its buying power over time.

42 They are not mentioned in the Babli, 66b/67a There, Rav Jehudah holds that the wife always has the right to take her dowry back and pay the difference but Rebbi Ammi (Immi) holds that it is the husband's choice what to give her, in contrast to the position he is quoted for in the Yerushalmi. In the final decision after a lenghty discussion, the Babli sides with the Yerushalmi.

43 The colleague of R. Immi in their separate place of study in Tiberias.

44 Tosephta 9:1. Therefore in times of inflation it is preferable to specify the property, not the monetary value, in marriage contracts.

רִבִּי חִייָה בַּר אָדָא בְּעָא קוֹמֵי רִבִּי מָנָא. מַהוּ עַבְדֵי מְלוֹג. אָמַר לֵיהּ. כְּמָה דְאַתְּ אָמַר. מְלִיג. מְלִיג.

Rebbi Ḥiyya bar Ada asked Rebbi Mana: What is the etymology of "*mĕlōg* slaves"? He said to him, as you say: strip off, strip off[45]!

45 In *Gen. rabba* 45(2) the etymology appears in the name of R. Simeon ben Laqish and it is explained that Hagar was a paraphernalia personal slave of Sarah whom Abraham had to feed but could not get services from. In the interpretation of *Arukh*, the simile here is the other way:

since the husband has the usufruct of the property he is like somebody who strips the feathers off a chicken but cannot eat the meat.

The root מלג means "strip off (feathers, hair, etc.)" in Syriac. Ostensibly the word is Accadic *mulūgu* "paraphernalia", which appears in the same meaning as an Eastern Semitic loanword *mlg* in Ugaritic (Canaanite); languages long dead by Talmudic times. The relation between Arabic مَלַגַ ملج "to drink from the breast (baby)", to Greek ἀμέλγω, Latin *mulgeo*, "to milk", is not clear. But possibly the notion of "milking" associated with property of one kind contrasted with the notion of "flock" associated with another goes back to ancient images from times when property mainly consisted of livestock.

תַּמָּן תַּנִּינָן הַמְקַבֵּל צֹאן בַּרְזֶל מִן הַגּוֹי. הַוְולָדוֹת פְּטוּרִין. וְוְלָדֵי וְולָדוֹת חַייָבִין. רִבִּי יִרְמְיָה בָּעֵי. תַּמָּן אַתְּ אָמַר. הַוְולָדוֹת לָרִאשׁוֹן. וְהָכָא אַתְּ אָמַר. הַוְולָדוֹת לַשֵּׁינִי. אָמַר רִבִּי יוֹסָה. תַּמָּן עַל יְדֵי שֶׁעִיקָּרוֹ לָרִאשׁוֹן הַוְולָדוֹת לָרִאשׁוֹן. בְּרָם הָכָא עַל יְדֵי שֶׁעִיקָּרוֹ לַשֵּׁינִי הַוְולָדוֹת לַשֵּׁינִי.

[46]There, we have stated: "If somebody receives [a flock] under mortmain conditions from a Gentile, the young are free, the young's young are obligated." [47] Rebbi Jeremiah asked: There you say, the young are for the first, and here you say, the young are for the second[48]! Rebbi Yosa said, there, because the property rights are with the first, the young belong to the first. But here, because the property rights are with the second, the young belong to the second[49].

46 Mishnah *Bekhorot* 2:4. It is not totally clear what mortmain conditions for a shepherd are; cf. the extensive discussion in S. Lieberman, תוספתא כפשוטה בבא קמא-בבא מציעא New York 1988, pp. 217-219.

The Yerushalmi *Baba Meṣi'a* 5:7, quoting Tosephta *Bekhorot* 5:1,14, explains: "What is a mortmain flock? If [the owner] had 100 sheep and said [to the shepherd]: these are stipulated to be worth 100 gold denars, their lambs, their milk, and their shearings are yours, if they die, you are responsible, and for each one you give me a tetradrachma at the end, it is forbidden." It is forbidden to the shepherd to receive a flock under these conditions from a Jew since most owners will structure the contract so they will make money, which turns the final payment (which accompanies the return of the flock to the owner) into a money-making proposition which looks like interest since the shepherd pays for the use of the flock which he received on credit. It is forbidden to pay interest to Jews. The same kind of contract is permitted with Gentiles.

47 The parallel text is in *Baba Meṣi'a* 5:7 (fol. 10b).

48 In the Mishnah in *Bekhorot*, lambs are exempt because they belong to the Gentile even though the entire flock is the shepherd's responsibility whereas the Mishnah here states that mortmain lambs belong to the husband who also carries the same responsibility as the shepherd.

49 The contract of the shepherd specifies that the flock must be returned intact at a specified time; the interest of the Gentile is there all the time. In the case of marriage, if the wife predeceases her husband, he inherits from her; his obligation to return the dowry is conditional.

(fol. 7d) **משנה ב:** בַּת יִשְׂרָאֵל שֶׁנִּישֵּׂאת לְכֹהֵן וְהִכְנִיסָה לוֹ בֵין עַבְדֵי מְלוֹג בֵּין עַבְדֵי צֹאן בַּרְזֶל הֲרֵי אֵילּוּ יֹאכלוּ בַתְּרוּמָה וּבַת כֹּהֵן שֶׁנִּשֵּׂאת לְיִשְׂרָאֵל וְהִכְנִיסָה לוֹ בֵין עַבְדֵי מלוֹג בֵּין עַבְדֵי צֹאן בַּרְזֶל הֲרֵי אֵילּוּ לֹא יֹאכֵלוּ.

Mishnah 2: If a daughter of an Israel married a Cohen and brought him paraphernalia or mortmain slaves, they may eat heave. But if a daughter of a Cohen married an Israel and brought him paraphernalia or mortmain slaves, they may not eat[50].

משנה ג: בַּת יִשְׂרָאֵל שֶׁנִּישֵּׂאת לְכֹהֵן וּמֵת וְהִנִּיחָהּ מְעוּבֶּרֶת לֹא יֹאכְלוּ עֲבָדֶיהָ בַּתְּרוּמָה מִפְּנֵי חֶלְקוֹ שֶׁלָּעוּבָּר. הָעוּבָּר פּוֹסֵל וְאֵינוֹ מַאֲכִיל דִּבְרֵי רִבִּי יוֹסֵי. אָמְרוּ לוֹ מֵאַחַר שֶׁהֵיעַדְתָּ בָנוּ עַל בַּת יִשְׂרָאֵל לְכֹהֵן וְאַף בַּת כֹּהֵן לְכֹהֵן וּמֵת וְהִנִּיחָהּ מְעוּבֶּרֶת לֹא יֹאכְלוּ עֲבָדֶיהָ בַּתְּרוּמָה מִפְּנֵי חֶלְקוֹ שֶׁלָּעוּבָּר.

Mishnah 3: If a daughter of an Israel married a Cohen who then died and left her pregnant, her slaves[51] may not eat heave because of the share of the fetus. A fetus disqualifies[52] but cannot enable to eat, the words of Rebbi Yose. They said to him, after you testified before us about the daughter of an Israel [married] to a Cohen, even if a daughter of a Cohen [was married] to a Cohen who died and left her pregnant, her slaves may not eat heave because of the share of the fetus[53].

50 Heave may be eaten by "every pure person in [the Cohen's] household" (*Num.* 18:11); this includes his wife and her circumcised slaves. But the daughter of a Cohen who marries outside the clan is barred from eating heave (*Lev.* 22:12) and so are her slaves.

51 Mortmain slaves who become the property of her child once he will be born.

52 A widowed, pregnant, otherwise childless daughter of a Cohen married to an Israel is precluded from returning to "her father's house" because of the fetus who, once born, will not be a Cohen.

53 Even if she has other children, the fetus will be co-heir of the mortmain slaves and, since he is not a person, cannot have a "house" in which they eat heave.

(fol. 8a) **הלכה ב:** אָמַר רִבִּי אֶלְעָזָר. כֵּינִי מַתְנִיתָא. עֲבָדֶיהָ יֹאכֵלוּ. עֲבָדָיו לֹא יֹאכֵלוּ. דְּלֹ כֵן הִיא אוֹכֶלֶת וַעֲבָדֶיהָ אֵינָן אוֹכְלִין. רִבִּי יֹאשִׁיָּה בְשֵׁם רִבִּי יוֹחָנָן. אִם מִזּוֹ אֲפִילוּ הִיא לֹא תֹאכֵל. אָמַר רִבִּי חַגַּיי קוֹמֵי רִבִּי יוֹסֵה. לֹא דְרִבִּי יוֹחָנָן פְּלִיג. לֹא אָמַר אֶלָּא מִזּוֹ אֲפִילוּ הִיא לֹא תֹאכֵל. אָתָא עוֹבְדָא קוֹמֵי רִבִּי יְהוֹשֻׁעַ בֶּן לֵוִי. אָמַר. צֵא וּרְאֵה הֵיאַךְ הַצִּיבּוּר נוֹהֵג. רִבִּי אָבוּן בְּשֵׁם רִבִּי יְהוֹשֻׁעַ בֶּן לֵוִי. וְלֹא דְבַר הֲלָכָה זוֹ. אֶלָּא כָּל־הֲלָכָה שֶׁהִיא רוֹפֶפֶת בְּבֵית דִּין וְאֵין אַתְּ יוֹדֵעַ מַה טִיבָהּ צֵא וּרְאֵה מַה הַצִּיבּוּר נוֹהֵג וּנְהוֹג. וַאֲנָן חָמֵיי צִיבּוּרָא דְּלָא מֵיכְלוֹן. אָמַר רִבִּי יוֹסֵה. הָדָא אָמְרָה אֵין הָעֶבֶד פּוֹסֵל אֶת מִי שֶׁהוּא רָאוּי לֶאֱכוֹל וְלֹא מַאֲכִיל אֶת מִי שֶׁאֵינוֹ רָאוּי לֶאֱכוֹל.

Halakhah 2: Rebbi Eleazar said, so is the Mishnah: Her slaves[54] may eat, his slaves[55] may not eat For if it were not so, she would eat[56] but her slaves would not eat! Rebbi Josia in the name of Rebbi Joḥanan: If it is from this, she also should not eat[57]. Rebbi Ḥaggai said before Rebbi Yose: Not that Rebbi Joḥanan disagrees, he only said, for if it were not so, she would eat but her slaves would not eat. There came a case before Rebbi Joshua ben Levi. [58]He said, go out and look how the public behaves. Rebbi Abin said in the name of Rebbi Joshua ben Levi, not only this practice, but in any practical question which is weak in court and you do not know how to decide, go out and see how the public acts, and act accordingly. And we see that they do not eat. Rebbi Yose said, this means that [the fetus] does not disable anybody able to eat and does not enable anybody unable to eat[59].

54 Paraphernalia slaves. The Tosephta, 9:1, disagrees except if she has other children (since otherwise if for any reason the pregnancy did not result in a viable baby she had left the priestly clan at her husband's death). The Babli, 67a, formulates: "Paraphernalia slaves eat if and only if she eats."

55 Mortmain slaves.

56 Since the Mishnah mentions only her slaves but not herself. The childless widow of a Cohen reverts to her status before marriage with regard to heave. On the other hand, the Mishnah does not state that the rule applies only to a widow without other children. If she has children from the Cohen then certainly she remains part of his house and eats heave. There is no reason why the paraphernalia slaves should not eat because of her status.

57 One could find an argument that if the fetus disables her slaves it must disable her also.

58 This text, position, and argument is from *Peah* 7, Note 137.

59 This disproves R. Joḥanan's attempted argument. Since the Mishnah does not mention her but mentions her mortmain slaves, the fetus does not disable her but cannot enable her slaves whose enabler has died and was not yet replaced.

תַּנֵּי רִבִּי יִשְׁמָעֵאל בַּר יוֹסֵף מִשּׁוּם אַבָּיי. הָיָה בַת מַאֲכֶלֶת. רִבִּי אִימִּי בְשֵׁם רִבִּי יוֹחָנָן. שֶׁכֵּן הָיָה רְאוּיָה לְתוֹפְשָׂן מִן הַמְּזוֹנוֹת. וְאִשָּׁה אֵינָהּ רְאוּיָה לְתוֹפְשָׂן מִן הַמְּזוֹנוֹת. רְאוּיָה הִיא לִתְבּוֹעַ כְּתוּבָּתָהּ וּלְאַבֵּד כְּתוּבָּתָהּ. וְקַשְׁיָא כְּתוּבָּה מִדְּבַר תּוֹרָה וּמְזוֹן הַבָּנוֹת מִדִּבְרֵיהֶן וְדִבְרֵיהֶן עוֹקְרִין דְּבַר תּוֹרָה. כְּמָאן דָּמַר. מֵאֵילֵיהֶן קִבְּלוּ עֲלֵיהֶן אֶת הַמַּעְשְׂרוֹת.

Rebbi Ismael ben Rebbi Yose stated in the name of his father: If there was a daughter, she enables to eat[60]. Rebbi Immi in the name of Rebbi Johanan: Because she is able to take her upkeep away from them. Is a wife not also able to take her upkeep away from them[61]? She might request her *ketubah* be paid or lose her *ketubah*[62]. This is difficult! The *ketubah* is a biblical institution[63], the upkeep of the daughters is rabbinical; do their institutions uproot a word of the Torah? It follows him who said that they accepted tithes voluntarily[64].

60 Tosephta 9:1; Babli 67a. In both sources it is emphasized that only a daughter lets mortmain slaves eat during the pregnancy of her mother but not sons. As R. Moses Margalit points out, the thrust of the argument of the Babli (not its details) must be understood also in the Yerushalmi that a daughter enables only in the presence of a son. By biblical rules (*Num.* 27:6-11), a daughter inherits only in the absence of sons, but the standard marriage contract assures the upkeep of unmarried daughters as a lien on the estate (Mishnah *Ketubot* 4:11). This means that the claim of the daughter to be fed as a member of the priestly clan is prior to and independent of any claim of the male heirs; since she is fed, the slaves who secure her claim also may eat. But if there are no male heirs, the daughters are heirs according to biblical standards. If the fetus is male, he becomes the sole heir. If female, she becomes a co-heir and the slaves cannot eat because of her part. If there are male heirs, a female fetus has no influence since the marriage contract stipulates only support for living daughters.

61 The widow has a choice of either claiming her *ketubah* or staying in her house and being supported by the estate (Mishnah *Ketubot* 4:12).

62 By any of the transactions mentioned in Mishnah *Ketubot*.

63 At least for a virgin bride, *Ex.* 22:16. The rabbinic document is reported to be an institution of Simeon ben Šetah, cf. *Ketubot*, Yerushalmi 8:11 (fol. 32c), Babli 82b. The opinion that the origin of the *ketubah* of a virgin (not the details of the text) is rabbinic is found only in the Babli, attributed to R. Jehudah (*Ketubot* 56a, 10a).

64 The laws connected with the distribution of land after the first conquest became moot with the Babylonian exile. They were voluntarily reintroduced in the times of Ezra; cf. *Ševi'it* 7:1, Note 11.

אַשְׁכָּחַת אָמַר. רִבִּי יִשְׁמָעֵאל בֵּירִבִּי יוֹסֵה חָלוּק עַל ר' אבון. דְּאָמַר רִבִּי סִימוֹן בְּשֵׁם חִילְפַיי. רִבִּי וְרִבִּי יִשְׁמָעֵאל בֵּי רִבִּי יוֹסֵי וּבַר הַקַּפָּר נִמְנוּ עַל אֲוִיר אַשְׁקְלוֹן וְטִיהֲרוּהוּ מִפִּי רִבִּי פִּינְחָס בֶּן יָאִיר שֶׁאָמַר. יוֹרְדִין הָיִינוּ לְסִירְקִי שֶׁלְּאַשְׁקְלוֹן וְלוֹקְחִין חִטִּים וְעוֹלִין לְעִירֵנוּ וְטוֹבְלִין וְאוֹכְלִים בִּתְרוּמָתֵינוּ. לְמָחָר בִּיקְשׁוּ לְהִמָּנוֹת עָלֶיהָ לְפוֹטְרוֹ מִן הַמַּעְשְׂרוֹת וּמָשַׁךְ רִבִּי יִשְׁמָעֵאל בֵּי רִבִּי יוֹסֵי אֶת יָדָיו. שֶׁהָיָה מִסְתַּמֵּךְ עַל בֶּן הַקַּפָּר. אָמַר לוֹ. בְּנִי. לָמָּה לֹא אָמַרְתָּ לִי. לֹא מָשַׁכְתָּ אֶת יָדֶיךָ. הָיִיתִי אוֹמֵר לָךְ. אֶתְמוֹל אֲנִי סִימֵּאתִי וַאֲנִי טִיהַרְתִּי. עַכְשָׁיו אֲנִי אוֹמֵר לָךְ. שֶׁמָּה שֶׁנִּתְכַּבְּשָׁה מִדְּבַר תּוֹרָה הֵיאַךְ אֲנִי פוֹטְרָהּ מִדְּבַר תּוֹרָה. אֵימָתַי הִיא טְמֵיאָה מִשּׁוּם אֶרֶץ הָעַמִּים. אַשְׁכַּח תַּנֵּי בְשֵׁם אַבָּיֵי. מֵאֵילֵיהֶן קִבְּלוּ עֲלֵיהֶן אֶת הַמַּעְשְׂרוֹת. וְאָמַר. יְאוּת מַעְשְׂרוֹת מִדִּבְרֵיהֶן וּמָזוֹן הַבָּנוֹת מִדִּבְרֵיהֶן וְדִבְרֵיהֶן עוֹקְרִין אֶת דִּבְרֵיהֶן.

We find that Rebbi Ismael ben Rebbi Yose disagrees with his father[65] [66]since Rebbi Simon said in the name of Hilfai: Rebbi, Rebbi Ismael ben Rebbi Yose and Ben Qappara voted on the airspace of Ascalon and declared it pure from the testimony of Rebbi Phineas ben Yaïr who said, we were descending to the Saracen [market] at Ascalon where we bought wheat, returned to our town, immersed ourselves and ate our heave. The next day they wanted to vote to free it from tithes but Rebbi Ismael ben Rebbi Yose removed his hand.[67] He was leaning on Ben Qappara. He said to him, my son, why did you not say to me: did you not remove your hand? I would have told you that yesterday I was he who declared it impure, I am he who declared it pure. But now I am saying, maybe it was conquered within the meaning of the Torah, how can I free it from the meaning of the Torah? [68]When is it impure because of territory of Gentiles? But we found that he stated in the name of his father that they accepted tithes voluntarily[69]! And he said, it is correct that if tithes are from their words and the food of the daughters is of their words that their words may uproot their words[70].

65 Conjectural reading required by the context.

66 This paragraph is from *Ševi'it*, Halakhah 7:1, explained there in Notes 52-57.

67 He declined to vote positively.

68 The following sentence was copied in error; it belongs to the next item in *Ševi'it*.

69 In the previous paragraph it was shown that R. Yose must hold that all rules of heave are rabbinical since biblical heave would require that every farmer till his ancestral soil given to the family by Joshua. In the present paragraph, R. Ismael holds that the rules are biblical.

70 In rabbinic institutions it is of the essence that the originators can settle the order of precedence.

הָיוּ שָׁם זְכָרִים (fol. 8b) מַאֲכִילִין. נְקֵיבוֹת אֵין מַאֲכִילוֹת. הָיוּ שָׁם זְכָרִים מַאֲכִילִין. שֶׁהוּא סָפֵק אֶחָד. זָפֵק זָכָר זָפֵק נְקֵיבָה. וְסָפֵק מִדְּבַר תּוֹרָה לְהַחֲמִיר. נְקֵיבוֹת אֵין מַאֲכִילוֹת. שֶׁהֵן שְׁנֵי סְפֵיקוֹת. זָפֵק זָכָר זָפֵק נְקֵיבָה. מִשֶּׁנִּתְאָרְסָה סָפֵק עַד שֶׁלֹּא נִתְאָרְסָה. וְסָפֵק דִּבְרֵיהֶן הָקֵל. מַה נַפְשָׁךְ. זָכָר הוּא כּוּלָּהּ דִּידֵיהּ. נְקֵיבָה הִיא נָסְבָה חוּלְקָהּ עִימְּהוֹן.

[70]"If there are males they enable to eat, females do not enable to eat." [71]If there are males, they enable to eat since there is one doubt, whether he is male or female[72]. A doubt in biblical matters forces restriction[73,74]. Females[75] do not enable to eat since there are two doubts[76], whether he is male or female, (after she was betrothed or maybe before she was

betrothed.)[77] A doubt regarding their words forces leniency[73]. However you take it, if he is male, everything is his[78]. Female, she takes her part with them[79].

70 A quote from Tosephta 9:1, in the name of R. Simeon (ben Iohai). He disagrees with the Mishnah and states that a pregnancy does not deprive mortmain slaves of heave if the husband left male heirs.

71 The following text does not make much sense. The discussion in the Babli, 67a/b, is too hypothetical to be of much help here.

72 As Rashi (*Ketubot* 67a) points out, there are two doubts, whether the pregnancy leads to a live birth or not and if there is a live birth whether it will be a male or a female. If there is no live birth, the males are the heirs and the slaves may eat because of them. If the baby is female, again the existing males are the heirs. The Yerushalmi probably holds that the miscarriages and female births just about equal the male births so that there are equal probabilities that the existing males are all heirs and the slaves may or may not eat because of them.

73 A generally accepted principle, Babli *Beṣah* 3a.

74 If heave were a biblical precept, the slaves could not eat if there was a male heir; if heave is rabbinic, they are enabled by him.

75 The deceased had only daughters, no son.

76 There is only one doubt but it has two sides, both of which support the position of R. Simeon.

77 The text in parentheses makes no sense here; it belongs to another category of doubts, discussed at length in Tractate *Ketubot*, cf., e.g., Mishnah *Ketubot* 1:6-7.

78 Then the slaves are disabled since before the birth they have no master who might enable them.

79 This parallels the case of boys. In this case there is a doubt concerning the applicability of biblical law which requires restrictive interpretation.

משנה ד: הָעוּבָּר וְהַיָּבָם וְהָאֵירוּסִין וְהַחֵרֵשׁ וּבֶן תֵּשַׁע שָׁנִים וְיוֹם אֶחָד(fol. 7d) פּוֹסְלִין וְלֹא מַאֲכִילִין. סָפֵק שֶׁהוּא בֶן תֵּשַׁע שָׁנִים וְיוֹם אֶחָד סָפֵק שֶׁאֵינוֹ סָפֵק הֵבִיא שְׁתֵּי שְׂעָרוֹת סָפֵק שֶׁלֹּא הֵבִיא. נָפַל הַבַּיִת עָלָיו וְעַל בַּת אָחִיו וְאֵין יָדוּעַ אֵי זֶה מֵהֶן מֵת רִאשׁוֹן צָרָתָהּ חוֹלֶצֶת וְלֹא מִתְייַבֶּמֶת.

Mishnah 4: The fetus[80], the levir[81], the betrothal[82], the deaf-and-dumb[83], and the male nine years and one day old[84] disable but do not enable to eat. If there was a doubt whether or not he had reached nine years and one dayt[85]; whether or not he had grown two pubic hairs[86]; when the house fell on him and his brother's daughter and it is not known who of them died first, her co-wife performs *ḥalîṣah* but not levirate[87].

80 As explained in the previous Mishnah.

81 The (not priestly) childless widow of a Cohen who waits for the levir is prevented from eating heave, Mishnah *Ketubot* 5:3.

82 The daughter of a Cohen betrothed to a non-Cohen is disabled.

83 Since the deaf-and-dumb cannot legally acquire, his marriage is only of rabbinic validity.

84 Who had intercourse with a woman, cf. Chapter 5, Note 79. If he is a Cohen and marries the woman rabbinically, he cannot enable her to eat heave until he grows two pubic hairs.

85 If he did not reach the age of nine years and one day, his intercourse is inoperative and he did not disable a priest's daughter. If he did reach that age, she is disabled.

86 If he had not grown two pubic hairs his betrothal is not valid by biblical standards. If he is an Israel betrothed to the daughter of a Cohen she is not disabled. If he had grown two pubic hair his betrothal is valid by biblical standards and his betrothed is disabled. If the male is a Cohen and his wife an Israel, she can start eating heave only after he reaches adulthood (in the opinion of the Babli, once he had intercourse with her after growing two pubic hairs.)

87 If he died first, the niece who was his wife frees the co-wife from the obligation of *ḥalîṣah* and levirate. If she died first, the co-wife is permitted to the levirs.

הלכה ד: הָעוּבָּר וְהַיָּבָם וְהָאֵירוּסִין כול'. אָמַר רִבִּי שִׁמְעוֹן. בְּזוֹ מִידַּת (fol. 8b) הַדִּין לוֹקָה. שֶׁאִם מַעֲשֶׂה הוּא לִפְסוֹל יְהֵא מַעֲשֶׂה לְהַאֲכִיל. וְאִם אֵינוֹ מַעֲשֶׂה לִפְסוֹל. לֹא יְהֵא מַעֲשֶׂה לְהַאֲכִיל. יְאוּת אָמַר רִבִּי שִׁמְעוֹן. וּמַה טַעֲמוֹן דְּרַבָּנִין. הֵם יֹאכְלוּ וְהֵם יַאֲכִילוּ. הָרָאוּי לוֹכַל מַאֲכִיל. וְשֶׁאֵינוֹ רָאוּי לוֹכַל אֵינוֹ מַאֲכִיל. הָתִיבוּן. הֲרֵי מַמְזֵר הֲרֵי אֵינוֹ רָאוּי לֶאֱכוֹל וּמַאֲכִיל. שַׁנְיָיא הִיא. דִּכְתִיב יְלִיד בַּיִת. מֵעַתָּה הַיָּלוּד מַאֲכִיל וְשֶׁאֵינוֹ יָלוּד אֵינוֹ מַאֲכִיל. שַׁנְיָיא הִיא. דִּכְתִיב וְשָׁבָה אֶל בֵּית אָבִיהָ. פְּרָט לְשׁוֹמֶרֶת יָבָם. בִּנְעוּרֶיהָ פְּרָט לִמְעוּבֶּרֶת. אָמַר רִבִּי יוֹסֵה. הָדָא אָמְרָה. הַעִיבּוּר עָשׂוּ אוֹתוֹ כְּמַמָּשׁ לִפְסוֹל וְלֹא עָשׂוּ אוֹתוֹ כְּמַמָּשׁ לְהַאֲכִיל. מִילֵּיהוֹן דְּרַבָּנִין פְּלִיגִין. דָּמַר זְעִירָא. תַּנֵּי תַמָּן. אֲרוּסָה וְשׁוֹמֶרֶת יָבָם וּמְעוּבֶּרֶת מְשַׁלְּמוֹת אֶת הַקֶּרֶן וְאֵינָן מְשַׁלְּמוֹת אֶת הַחוֹמֶשׁ. מַה אֲנָן קַיָּמִין. אִם בְּבַת כֹּהֵן שֶׁנִּישֵּׂאת לְיִשְׂרָאֵל אֲפִילוּ יוֹלֶדֶת הֵימֶינּוּ בָנִים אֵינָהּ זָרָה לוֹ. אֶלָּא כֵן אֲנָן קַיָּמִין בְּבַת יִשְׂרָאֵל שֶׁנִּישֵּׂאת לְכֹהֵן. אִם אוֹמֵר אַתְּ. הָעוּבָּר עָשׂוּ אוֹתוֹ כְּמַמָּשׁ לִפְסוֹל וְלֹא עָשׂוּ אוֹתוֹ כְּמַמָּשׁ לְהַאֲכִיל. לָמָּה מְשַׁלְּמוֹת אֶת הַקֶּרֶן וְאֵינָן מְשַׁלְּמוֹת אֶת הַחוֹמֶשׁ וִישַׁלְּמוּ קֶרֶן וְחוֹמֶשׁ.

Halakhah 4: "The fetus, the levir, the betrothal," etc. Rebbi Simeon said, here the logic is deficient, for if it is action to disable it also should be action to enable, and if it is not action to disable it also should not be action to enable[88]. Rebbi Simeon is correct; what is the reason of the rabbis? "They shall eat", they shall enable to eat. The one who may eat enables to eat, the one who may not eat cannot enable to eat[89]. They objected: there is the bastard who may not eat and he enables to eat[90]! There is a difference, since it is written "born in the house[91]". Then the born should enable, the not born should not enable! There is a difference, [92]since it is written "and she returns to her father's house", to exclude the one waiting for the levir, "in her youth", to exclude the pregnant one. Rebbi Yose said, that[93] means that they considered pregnancy to be real to disable but did not consider it real to enable to eat. The words of the rabbis disagree since Ze'ira[94] said, there[95] they state that the betrothed, the one waiting for the levir, and the pregnant, pay the capital but not the fifth[96]. What are we speaking about? If about the daughter of a Cohen married to an Israel, even if she had children from him she is not an outsider for it. But we must deal with the daughter of an Israel married to a Cohen. If you say, they considered the fetus to be real to disable but did not consider it real to enable to eat, why does she pay the capital but not the fifth, should she not pay capital and fifth[97]?

88 The wording is correct in Tosephta 9:3: "For if it is action to disable it also should be action to enable, and if it is not action to enable it also should not be action to disable." S. Lieberman (*Tosephta ki-fshutah Yebamot*, pp. 83-85) shows that the question is restricted to the fetus.

89 See above, Notes 9-10. Since in *Sifra* this is an argument of R. Simeon, S. Lieberman (*l. c.*) concludes that the objection of R. Simeon is a rhetorical device.

90 This is a quote from *Sifra Emor Pereq* 5(4), quoted in Babli 69b; the scenario is elaborated in Mishnah 7. According to Halakhah 6, Gentile or slave disable the woman partner from the priesthood; whether the child is a bastard is a matter of dispute (in Galilee, not in Babylonia). One has to assume that the desecrated mother of the disabled child has died. Since the verses *Lev*. 22:11,12 speak only of "born in the house" and "descendants" without qualifications, the child from an improper union is as good as one from a proper union for the rules of eating heave. The biological fathers do not disable since they cannot be legal fathers; the child is the child of his mother and God alone, cf. *Peah* 1:1, Note 116, Babli *Niddah* 31a.

91 *Lev*. 22:11. The simple meaning of the text is that slaves of a Cohen may eat heave, whether they are born in the house or bought by the master. The expression "born in the house" is extended here to disqualified children of the house.

92 *Sifra Emor Pereq* 6(1) on *Lev*. 22:12, speaking about the issueless daughter of a Cohen returning to her father's house to eat sanctified food. The text is also quoted in Babli 67b.

93 The language is not quite appropriate; it is influenced by the context of the quote at the end of the paragraph. R. Yose notes that the Tanna of *Sifra* interprets the biblical

verse as implying the status of the fetus as described in the sentence; he should have said "the verse considers . . .' The formulation as given is appropriate for the version of Ze'ira/the rabbis who refer to rabbinic rules "they" are the men of the Great Assembly who voluntarily reintroduced the rules of heave and tithes.

94 Cf. *Berakhot* 2:1, Note 54.

95 In Babylonia. No parallel to this statement is found.

96 If a person who is not enabled to eat heave transgresses and eats it, in general he is liable to pay for the amount he took plus a 25% fine to the priesthood; cf. *Terumot*, Chapters 6,7. Mishnah *Terumot* 7:2 states that the daughter of a Cohen never loses her priestly status, even if she is disabled from eating heave, to the effect that she never pays the fine.

97 Since even the marriage of the daughter of an Israel to a Cohen does not free her from the fine incurred before her marriage, Mishnah *Terumot* 6:2. This proves that the rule cannot be biblical; the reference to the verse is not a proof.

חֵרֵשׁ פּוֹסֵל. לֹא כֵן תַּנֵּי רִבִּי חִייָה. אִשְׁתּוֹ שֶׁלְּחֵרֵשׁ וְשֶׁלְּשׁוֹטֶה טוֹבֶלֶת מְחֵיק בַּעֲלָהּ וְאוֹכֶלֶת. רִבִּי אַבָּא מָרִי וְרִבִּי מַתַּנְיָה. חַד אָמַר. בְּחֵרֵשׁ פּוֹסֵל. וְחוֹרָנָה אָמַר בְּחֵרֵשׁ יָבָם.

"The deaf-and-dumb disables." Did not Rebbi Ḥiyya state: "The wife of the deaf-and-dumb or the insane immerses herself from her husband's bosom and eats[98]"? Rebbi Abba Mari and Rebbi Mattaniah, one said, a disqualified deaf-and-dumb[99], the other said, a deaf-and-dumb levir[100].

98 In Tosephta 9:4: "The sane daughter of a Cohen married to an insane Israel . . ." Since marriages of the deaf-and-dumb or the insane are not valid, the woman does not lose her priestly status. She has to immerse herself after intercourse with her husband (*Lev.* 15:18) but is not disabled from eating heave. This contradicts the Mishnah.

99 A person whose intercourse would disable the woman even if he were hearing.

100 He disqualifies as levir, whose standing is not different from a hearing man; cf. Chapter 6, Note 35.

סָפֵק שֶׁהוּא בֶן תֵּשַׁע שָׁנִים וְיוֹם אֶחָד סָפֵק שֶׁאֵינוֹ. כְּמִי שֶׁהוּא בֶן תֵּשַׁע שָׁנִים וְיוֹם אֶחָד לִפְסוֹל. סָפֵק הֵבִיא שְׁתֵּי שְׂעָרוֹת סָפֵק שֶׁלֹּא הֵבִיא. כְּמִי שֶׁהֵבִיא שְׁתֵּי שְׂעָרוֹת לְהַאֲכִיל.

"Whether he had reached nine years and one day or not", he is as if he were nine years and one day old to disable[85]; "whether he had grown two pubic hairs or not", he is as if he had grown two pubic hairs to make her eat[86,101].

נָפַל הַבַּיִת עָלָיו וְעַל בַּת אָחִיו וְאֵין יָדוּעַ אֵי זֶה מֵהֶן מֵת רִאשׁוֹן. צָרָתָהּ חוֹלֶצֶת וְלֹא מִתְיַיבֶּמֶת. וְהָכָא אֲתִינָן מִתְנֵי סְפֵיקוֹת. אֶלָּא בְגִין דְּתַנִּינָן צָרוֹת תַּנִּינָן סְפֵק צָרוֹת.

"When the house fell on him and his brother's daughter and it is not known who of them died first, her co-wife performs *ḥalîṣah* but not levirate." Why do we come here to state doubts? Since we had stated [the rules for] co-wives, we now state for doubts concerning co-wives.

101 The Yerushalmi states here that a young man whose vows are valid can marry by biblical standards, an open question in the Babli. Cf. Mishnah *Terumot* 1:3, Note 105; Babli *Niddah* 46b.

(fol. 7d) **משנה ה:** הָאוֹנֵס וְהַמְפַתֶּה וְהַשּׁוֹטֶה לֹא פוֹסְלִים וְלֹא מַאֲכִילִים. וְאִם אֵינָם רְאוּיִין לָבוֹא בְיִשְׂרָאֵל הֲרֵי אֵילּוּ פוֹסְלִין. בְּאֵי זֶה צַד יִשְׂרָאֵל שֶׁבָּא עַל בַּת כֹּהֵן תֹּאכַל בַּתְּרוּמָה עִיבְּרָה לֹא תֹאכַל. נִתְחַתֵּךְ הָעוּבָּר בְּמֵעֶיהָ תֹּאכַל. הָיָה כֹהֵן שֶׁבָּא עַל בַּת יִשְׂרָאֵל לֹא תֹאכַל בַּתְּרוּמָה. עִיבְּרָה לֹא תֹאכַל. יָלְדָה תֹאכַל. נִמְצָא כוֹחוֹ שֶׁלַּבֵּן גָּדוֹל מִשֶּׁלָּאָב.

Mishnah 5: The rapist, the seducer, and the insane[102] do neither disable nor enable to eat, but if they are unable to marry in Israel they disable. How is that? If an Israel came upon the daughter of a Cohen, she may eat heave, if she became pregnant she may not eat. If the fetus was cut into pieces in her body[103] she may eat. If a Cohen came upon the daughter of an Israel, she may not eat heave, if she became pregnant she may not eat, if she gave birth she may eat[104]. It turns out that the son's power is greater than the father's.

102 Even if he is married to her since the insane cannot enter into any contract, not even a marriage.

103 In that case, she did not give birth. If she has a child from a non-Cohen, the child prevents her from eating heave.

104 The relationship of the child to his father does not depend on the marital status of the mother; cf. Mishnah 2:5.

(fol. 8b) **הלכה ה:** הָאוֹנֵס וְהַמְפַתֶּה כול׳. הָדָא אָמְרָה שֶׁאֵין אוֹנְסִין פּוֹסְלִין בִּכְהוּנָּה בִּפְנוּיָה.

Halakhah 5: "The rapist, the seducer," etc. This means that rape does not disable an unmarried priestly woman[104].

104 But the Cohen is forced to divorce his wife if she was raped, cf. *Ketubot* 2:10.

הָדָא מְסַיְיְעָא לְהַהוּא דְתַנֵּי רִבִּי חִיָּה. אִשְׁתּוֹ שֶׁלְּחֵרֵשׁ וְשֶׁלְּשׁוֹטֶה טוֹבֶלֶת מֵחֵיק בַּעְלָהּ וְאוֹכֶלֶת. וּדְלֹא כְרִבִּי לָעְזָר. דְּרִבִּי לָעְזָר אוֹמֵר. אַף הַפָּנוּי שֶׁבָּא עַל הַפְּנוּיה שֶׁלֹּא לְשֵׁם אִישׁוּת הֲרֵי זוֹ בְעִילַת זְנוּת.

This supports what Rebbi Ḥiyya stated[98]: The wife of the deaf-and-dumb or the insane immerses herself from her husband's bosom and eats, against Rebbi Eleazar, since Rebbi Eleazar said, also if an unmarried man had intercourse with an unmarried woman not for the purpose of marriage it is copulation of harlotry[105].

105 Cf. Chapter 6, Note 108. The woman would be disabled from marrying into the priesthood. Quoted in Babli 61b, 59b; *Sanhedrin* 51a, *Temurah* 30a.

רִבִּי בָּא בְשֵׁם רִבִּי אַבָּא בַּר יִרְמְיָה. אֲנוּסָה אֵינָהּ צְרִיכָה לְהַמְתִּין שְׁלֹשָׁה חֳדָשִׁים. אֲמָרָהּ רִבִּי יוֹנָה קוֹמֵי רִבִּי יוֹסֵה. אָמַר לֵיהּ. לֹא תְקַבֵּל עָלָיו. קַל הוּא בַאֲכִילַת תְּרוּמָה. אִילּוּ בַּת כֹּהֵן שֶׁנִּישֵּׂאת לְיִשְׂרָאֵל וְהָלַךְ בַּעֲלָהּ לִמְדִינַת הַיָּם וְשָׁמְעָה עָלָיו שֶׁמֵּת שֶׁמָּא אֵינָהּ אוֹכֶלֶת בַּתְּרוּמָה מִיָּד. וּלְעִנְיַין הָעוּבָּר צְרִיכָה לְהַמְתִּין שְׁלֹשָׁה חֳדָשִׁים.

Rebbi Abba in the name of Rebbi Abba bar Jeremiah: A woman who has been raped does not have to wait three months[106]. Rebbi Jonah said this before Rebbi Yose[107]. He said to him, do not accept that from here, they were lenient for eating heave. If a daughter of a Cohen was married to an Israel, her husband went overseas, and she received notice that he died, does she not immediately eat heave[108]? But because of a fetus she has to wait three months.

106 Cf. Chapter 4, Note 166.

107 He wanted to prove the statement of R. Abba from the Mishnah since a Cohen's daughter who was raped continuous to eat heave until it is ascertained that she is pregnant; the Mishnah does not say that for three months after the rape she could not eat heave.

108 If she has no child, *Lev*. 22:13. But even though the husband left more than three months before his death, the widow must wait three months before remarrying. The argument is rejected in the Babli, 69b.

אִם אֵינָם רְאוּיִין לָבוֹא בְיִשְׂרָאֵל הֲרֵי אֵילּוּ פְסֵלִין. וְאֵילּוּ הֵן. בֶּן תֵּשַׁע שָׁנִים וְיוֹם אֶחָד גֵּר עֲמוֹנִי וּמוֹאָבִי וּמִצְרִי וְעֶבֶד וּמַמְזֵר חָלָל נָתִין כּוּתִי וְגוֹי שֶׁבָּאוּ עַל בַּת יִשְׂרָאֵל עַל בַּת כֹּהֵן עַל בַּת לֵוִי פְּסוּלָה מִן הַכְּהוּנָּה. רִבִּי יוֹסֵי אוֹמֵר. כָּל־שֶׁזַּרְעוֹ פָּסוּל בִּיאָתוֹ פוֹסֶלֶת. כָּל־שֶׁאֵין זַרְעוֹ פָּסוּל אֵין בִּיאָתוֹ פוֹסֶלֶת. רַבָּן שִׁמְעוֹן בֶּן גַּמְלִיאֵל אוֹמֵר. כַּל־שֶׁאַתְּ מוּתָּר בְּבִתּוֹ מוּתָּר בְּאַלְמָנָתוֹ. וְכָל־שֶׁאֵין

אַת מוּתָּר בְּבִתּוֹ אֵין אַתְּ מוּתָּר בְּאַלְמָנָתוֹ. וּמַה בֵּינֵיהוֹן. רִבִּי יוֹחָנָן אוֹמֵר. גֵּר עֲמוֹנִי וּמוֹאָבִי בֵּינֵיהוֹן. מָאן דְּאָמַר. כָּל־שֶׁזַּרְעוֹ פָּסוּל בִּיאָתוֹ פוֹסֶלֶת. זֶה הוֹאִיל וְזַרְעוֹ פָּסוּל בִּיאָתוֹ פוֹסֶלֶת. מָאן דְּאָמַר. כַּל־שֶׁאַתְּ מוּתָּר בְּבִתּוֹ (אֵין)[109] אַתְּ מוּתָּר בְּאַלְמָנָתוֹ. וְזֶה הוֹאִיל וְ(אֵין)[109] אַתְּ מוּתָּר בְּבִתּוֹ (אֵין) אַתְּ מוּתָּר בְּאַלְמָנָתוֹ. דִּבְרֵי חֲכָמִים. רִבִּי יִרְמְיָה בְּשֵׁם [רַבָּנִן][110] רִבִּי בָּא תְּרֵיהוֹן אָמְרִין. בַּ[ת][110] גֵּר עֲמוֹנִי וּמוֹאָבִי וּבַת דּוֹר שֵׁינִי מִצְרִי אַף עַל פִּי שֶׁאַתְּ מוּתָּר בְּבִתּוֹ אַתְּ אָסוּר בְּאַלְמָנָתוֹ. רִבִּי זַכַּיי רִבִּי אֲלֶכְסַנְדְּרִיה מִשְׁלַח שְׁאוֹל. בַּת גֵּר עֲמוֹנִי וּבַת דּוֹר שֵׁינִי שֶׁל מִצְרִי. אָמַר לֵיהּ רִבִּי יוֹסֵה. לֹא שְׁמִיעַ לְהַהוּא דָּמַר רִבִּי יִרְמְיָה בְּשֵׁם רַבָּנִין וְרִבִּי בָּא תְּרֵיהוֹן אָמְרִין. בַּת גֵּר עֲמוֹנִי וּבַת דּוֹר שֵׁינִי מִצְרִי אַף עַל פִּי שֶׁאַתְּ מוּתָּר בְּבִתּוֹ אַתְּ אָסוּר בְּאַלְמָנָתוֹ. וְכָל־שֶׁזַּרְעוֹ פָּסוּל בִּיאָתוֹ פְּסוּלָה. לֹא כֵן צְרִיכָה בְּשֶׁהָיְתָה אִמָּהּ מִיִּשְׂרָאֵל. שֶׁלֹּא תֹאמַר. כְּשֵׁם שֶׁנִּתְחַלְּלָה אִמָּהּ כָּךְ נִתְחַלְּלָה בִּתָּהּ. וְעוֹד מִן הָדָא דְאָמַר רִבִּי יַעֲקֹב בַּר אָחָא. פְּלִיגִין רִבִּי יוֹחָנָן וְרִבִּי שִׁמְעוֹן בֶּן לָקִישׁ. בַּת גֵּר עֲמוֹנִי וּבַת דּוֹר הַשֵּׁינִי מִצְרִי. רִבִּי יוֹחָנָן אָמַר. כְּשֵׁירוֹת. רֵישׁ־לָקִישׁ אָמַר פְּסוּלוֹת. רִבִּי יוֹסֵי בֵּירִבִּי בּוּן אָמַר. בִּזְקֵינוֹת פְּלִיגִין. רִבִּי יוֹחָנָן אָמַר. כְּשֵׁירוֹת. רֵישׁ־לָקִישׁ אָמַר פְּסוּלוֹת.

"If they are unable to marry in Israel they disable." These are[111]: "A child of nine years and one day[112], an Ammonite, Moabite, or Egyptian[113] proselyte, or a bastard, desecrated, Gibeonite[114], Samaritan[115], and Gentile who had intercourse with the daughter of an Israel, a Cohen, or a Levite, disqualified her for the priesthood. Rebbi Yose said, everybody's intercourse disqualifies whose descendant would be disqualified; his intercourse does not disqualify those whose descendant would not be disqualified. Rabban Simeon ben Gamliel says, in all cases, if his daughter is permitted to you, so is his widow[116]; if his daughter is not permitted to you, neither is his widow." In what do they differ? Rebbi Johanan says, an Ammonite or Moabite proselyte[117] is between them. For him who says, everybody's intercourse disqualifies whose descendant would be disqualified, here since his descendant[118] would be disqualified, his intercourse disqualifies. For him who says, if you may marry his daughter you may marry his widow, here since you may marry his daughter you may marry his widow. The words of the Sages? Rebbi Jeremiah in the name of [the rabbis], Rebbi Abba, both say: Regarding the daughter of an Ammonite or Moabite proselyte or the daughter of a second-generation Egyptian[119], even though his daughter is permitted to you, his widow is forbidden to you. Rebbi Zakkai: Rebbi Alexander sent to ask [about] the daughter of an Ammonite proselyte and the daughter of a second-generation Egyptian. Rebbi Yose said to him, did you not hear that Rebbi Jeremiah in the name of the rabbis, Rebbi Abba, both say: Regarding the daughter of an Ammonite proselyte or the daughter of a second-generation Egyptian, even though his daughter is permitted to you, his widow is forbidden to you. And everybody's intercourse disqualifies whose descendant would be disqualified. Do we not need it when her mother was from Israel? That you should not say that since her mother was desecrated so her daughter was desecrated. In addition, Rebbi Joḥanan and Rebbi Simeon ben Laqish disagreed, the daughter of an Ammonite proselyte or the daughter of a second-generation Egyptian[120], Rebbi Joḥanan said, they are acceptable, Rebbi Simeon ben Laqish said, they are disqualified. Rebbi Yose ben Abun said, they disagree about the old women[121]: Rebbi Joḥanan said, they are acceptable[122], Rebbi Simeon ben Laqish said, they are disqualified.

109 A scribal error.

110 Missing in the text, supplied from the second quote in this paragraph.

111 Babli 68a, Tosephta *Yebamot* 8:1, *Niddah* 6:1.

112 Mishnah 4.

113 Mishnah *Yadaim* 4:4 notes that modern Ammonites, Moabites, and Egyptians are no longer the peoples living in these places at the time of the Exodus; therefore, the prohibitions of

Deut. 23:4-9 are no longer operative. All arguments based on these rules are theoretical exercises of retrospection.

114 Cf. Chapter 2, Note 72.

115 Their problems are discussed in the next Halakhah.

116 For a Cohen, not necessarily for anybody else.

117 A female Moabite or Ammonite was never prohibited from marrying a Jew (Mishnah 8:3; *Sifry Deut.* 249.). The same argument in Babli 69a.

118 If he is a male (Mishnah 8:3).

119 Any third generation Egyptian, male or female, is permitted; *Deut.* 23:9; Mishnah 8:3.

120 From a Jewish mother.

121 The mother, the wife of an Ammonite or second generation Egyptian.

122 He follows Rabban Simeon ben Gamliel. Rebbi Alexander's question is not answered since it is moot anyhow.

(fol. 7d) **משנה ו:** הָעֶבֶד פּוֹסֵל מִשּׁוּם בִּיאָה וְאֵינוֹ פּוֹסֵל מִשּׁוּם זֶרַע. בְּאֵי זֶה צַד בַּת יִשְׂרָאֵל לַכֹּהֵן בַּת כֹּהֵן לְיִשְׂרָאֵל וְיָלְדָה מִמֶּנּוּ בֵן וְהָלַךְ הַבֵּן וְנִכְבַּשׁ עַל הַשִּׁפְחָה וְיָלְדָה מִמֶּנּוּ בֵן הֲרֵי זֶה עֶבֶד. הָיְתָה אֵם אָבִיו בַּת יִשְׂרָאֵל לַכֹּהֵן לֹא תֹאכַל בַּתְּרוּמָה בַּת כֹּהֵן לְיִשְׂרָאֵל תֹּאכַל בַּתְּרוּמָה.

Mishnah 6: A slave disables because of intercourse[123] but not because of descendants. How is this? A daughter of an Israel [married] to a Cohen [or] the daughter of a Cohen [married] to an Israel had a son from him. The son went and was pressed on a slave girl who had a son from him; the latter is a slave[124]. If his father's mother was a daughter of an Israel [married] to a Cohen, she cannot eat heave[125], the daughter of a Cohen [married] to an Israel may eat heave[126].

123 Since a free woman cannot marry a slave, her intercourse with him is a form of prostitution.

124 He has no legal relationship with his father.

125 If her husband and all her descendants except that slave had died, she has no descendants in the

priesthood and is barred from heave.

126 If her husband and all her descendants except that slave had died, she has no descendants outside the priesthood and may eat heave.

(fol. 8b) **הלכה ו:** הָעֶבֶד פּוֹסֵל מִשּׁוּם בִּיאָה כול'. הָעֶבֶד מְנַיִין שֶׁבִּיאָתוֹ פּוֹסֶלֶת. רִבִּי יוֹחָנָן אָמַר בְּשֵׁם רִבִּי יִשְׁמָעֵאל. וּבַת כֹּהֵן כִּי תִהְיֶה אַלְמָנָה וּגְרוּשָׁה וְזֶרַע אֵין לָהּ. שֶׁיֵּשׁ עָלָיו אַלְמָנוּת וְגֵירוּשִׁין חוֹזֶרֶת. אֶת שֶׁאֵין לָהּ עָלָיו אַלְמָנוּת וְגֵירוּשִׁין אֵינָהּ חוֹזֶרֶת. הָתִיב רִבִּי יִרְמְיָה. הֲרֵי אַלְמָנָה שֶׁזִּינְתָה הֲרֵי אֵין לָהּ אַלְמָנוּת וְגֵירוּשִׁין וְחוֹזֶרֶת. רִבִּי יוֹסֵי לֹא אָמַר כֵּן אֶלָּא מְחַלְפָה שִׁיטָּתֵיהּ דְּרִבִּי יוֹחָנָן. בְּגִיטִּין הוּא אָמַר. כּוּתִין מִשּׁוּם מַה הֵן פְּסוּלִין. רִבִּי יוֹחָנָן בְּשֵׁם רִבִּי יִשְׁמָעֵאל. מִשּׁוּם גּוֹי וְעֶבֶד הַבָּא עַל בַּת יִשְׂרָאֵל הַוָּולָד מַמְזֵר. בְּקִידּוּשִׁין הוּא אָמַר. רִבִּי יוֹחָנָן וְרִבִּי שִׁמְעוֹן בֶּן לָקִישׁ תְּרֵיהוֹן אָמְרִין. הַוָּולָד מַמְזֵר. הָכָא אָמַר לֵיהּ מִשּׁוּם גַּרְמֵיהּ וְהָכָא אָמַר לָהּ מִשּׁוּם רִבִּי יִשְׁמָעֵאל. שֶׁכֵּן לְדִבְרֵי חֲכָמִים הַוָּולָד מַמְזֵר. רִבִּי חִזְקִיָּה לֹא אָמַר כֵּן אֶלָּא מְחַלְפָה שִׁיטָּתֵיהּ דְּרִבִּי יוֹחָנָן. בְּגִיטִּין הוּא אָמַר. כּוּתִין מִשּׁוּם מַה הֵן פְּסוּלִין. רִבִּי יוֹחָנָן בְּשֵׁם רִבִּי יִשְׁמָעֵאל. מִשּׁוּם גּוֹי וְעֶבֶד הַבָּא עַל בַּת יִשְׂרָאֵל הַוָּולָד מַמְזֵר. בְּקִידּוּשִׁין הוּא רִבִּי יוֹחָנָן וְרִבִּי שִׁמְעוֹן בֶּן לָקִישׁ תְּרֵיהוֹן אָמְרִין. הַוָּולָד מַמְזֵר. וְהָכָא הוּא אָמַר. אֶת שֶׁיֵּשׁ עָלָיו אַלְמָנוּת וְגֵירוּשִׁין חוֹזֶרֶת וְאֶת שֶׁאֵין לָהּ עָלָיו אַלְמָנוּת וְגֵירוּשִׁין אֵינָהּ חוֹזֶרֶת. אָמַר רִבִּי מַתַּנְיָיה. סָלְקִית לִסְחוֹרָה וּשְׁמָעִית רִבִּי יוֹחָנָן וְרִבִּי יִשְׁמָעֵאל בְּנֵי יֵישׁוּעַ. וּבַת כֹּהֵן כִּי תִהְיֶה אַלְמָנָה וּגְרוּשָׁה וְזֶרַע אֵין לָהּ. אֶת שֶׁיֵּשׁ לָהּ עָלָיו אַלְמָנוּת וְגֵירוּשִׁין חוֹזֶרֶת. וְאֶת (fol. 8c) שֶׁאֵין לָהּ עָלָיו אַלְמָנוּת וְגֵירוּשִׁין אֵינָהּ חוֹזֶרֶת. וְאָמְרִת יָאוּת. אֵין מַמְזֵר כְּרִבִּי יְהוֹשֻׁעַ. שֶׁאֵין מַמְזֵר אֶלָּא מֵאִשָּׁה שֶׁהִיא אֲסוּרָה עָלָיו אִיסּוּר עֶרְוָה וְחַיָּיבִין עָלֶיהָ כָּרֵת.

"A slave disables because of intercourse," etc. From where that the intercourse with a slave disables? Rebbi Johanan said in the name of Rebbi Ismael: "If a Cohen's daughter becomes a widow or a divorcee without issue,[127]" from [a man] with whom she has widowhood or divorce she returns, from [a man] with whom she has no relation of widowhood or divorce she does not return. Rebbi Jeremiah objected: But if a widow whored she has no widowhood or divorce and she returns[128]! Rebbi Yose did not say so, but [he held] that the argument of Rebbi Johanan is reversed. In *Giṭṭin* he says, why are Samaritans disqualified? Rebbi Johanan in the name of Rebbi Ismael: Because if a Gentile or a slave has intercourse with a Jewish woman, the child is a bastard[129]. In *Qiddushin* one says, Rebbi Johanan and Rebbi Simeon ben Laqish both say, the child is a bastard. Here he says it in his own name but there he says it in the name of Rebbi Ismael! For also according to the words of the Sages the child is a bastard. Rebbi Ḥizqiah did not say so, but: the argument of Rebbi Johanan is reversed. In *Giṭṭin* he says, why are Samaritans disqualified? Rebbi Johanan in the name of Rebbi Ismael: Because if a Gentile or slave has intercourse with a Jewish woman, the child is a bastard. In *Qiddushin* one says, Rebbi Johanan and Rebbi Simeon ben Laqish both say, the child is a bastard. Here he says, from [a man] with whom she has widowhood or divorce she returns, from [a man] with whom she has no relation of widowhood or divorce she does not return[130]. Rebbi Mattaniah said, I went to Seḥora and heard: Rebbi Johanan and Rebbi Ismael the sons of Jesua: "If a Cohen's daughter becomes a widow or a divorcee without issue,[127]" from [a man] with whom she has widowhood or divorce she returns, from [a man] with whom she has no relation of widowhood or divorce she does not return. And I said, that is correct, there is no bastard, following Rebbi Joshua[131], for a bastard is only from a woman which is for him under an incest prohibition and for whom one is punished by divine extirpation.

127 *Lev.* 22:13. "If a Cohen's daughter becomes a widow or a divorcee without issue, when she returns to her father's house as in her

youth, she shall eat from her father's food."

128 If she is not married she cannot become a widow or be divorced. The objection is too stupid to deserve an answer since it is only required that she could have a marriage relationship, not that she actually must have had one.

129 In our text, *Giṭṭin* 1:5, the statement is by R. Johanan in the name of R. Eleazar (the Tanna), in *Qiddushin* 3:14 it is an anonymous *baraita*. In the Babli, 45a, the statement is by R. Joḥanan and R. Eleazar (the Amora); a parallel statement in the name of Rebbi.

There is no doubt in the Yerushalmi that the original Samaritans were Jews. They consider the children of a Jewish mother from a Gentile as Jewish, as is accepted as practice, under Babylonian influence, in the next Halakhah and as already was decided in Halakhah 4:15.

130 This implies that the child of a Gentile or a slave is not a bastard since the only person to be affected is the mother who cannot return to her priestly status if she was the daughter of a Cohen.

131 It really is following R. Simeon from Timna (Mishnah 4:14), but the more liberal R. Joshua will certainly agree that there is no hint of bastardy attached to the child. If the child is a girl, she will be disqualified from the priesthood, cf. Halakhah 4:15.

(fol. 7d) **משנה ז:** מַמְזֵר פּוֹסֵל וּמַאֲכִיל. בְּאֵי זֶה צַד בַּת יִשְׂרָאֵל לַכֹּהֵן בַּת כֹּהֵן לְיִשְׂרָאֵל וְיָלְדָה מִמֶּנּוּ בַת וְהָלְכָה הַבַּת וְנִשֵּׂאת לְעֶבֶד אוֹ לְנָכְרִי וְיָלְדָה מִמֶּנּוּ בֵּן הֲרֵי זֶה מַמְזֵר. הָיְתָה אֵם אִמּוֹ בַּת יִשְׂרָאֵל לַכֹּהֵן תֹּאכַל בַּתְּרוּמָה בַּת כֹּהֵן לְיִשְׂרָאֵל לֹא תֹאכַל בַּתְּרוּמָה.

Mishnah 7: A bastard disables and enables to eat. How is this? A daughter of an Israel [married] to a Cohen [or] the daughter of a Cohen [married] to an Israel had a daughter from him. If the daughter went and married a slave or a Gentile and had a son from him, that is a bastard[132]. If his mother's mother was a daughter of an Israel [married] to a Cohen, she can eat heave[133], the daughter of a Cohen [married] to an Israel cannot eat heave[134].

132 In practice, he is an unblemished Jew.

133 If the grandmother's husband and her daughter had died, the grandson is descended from a Cohen and keeps his grandmother in the priestly clan.

134 If the grandmother's husband and her daughter had died, the grandson is descended from an Israel and keeps his grandmother out of the priestly clan.

(fol. 8c) **הלכה ז:** מַמְזֵר פּוֹסֵל כול׳. לֵית הָדָא פְלִיגָא עַל רַב. דְּרַב אָמַר. גּוֹי וְעֶבֶד הַבָּא עַל בַּת יִשְׂרָאֵל הַוְּלָד כָּשֵׁר. פָּתַר לָהּ בְּגוֹי פָּסוּל וּבְעֶבֶד פָּסוּל.

Halakhah 7: "A bastard disables," etc. Does that not disagree with Rav, since Rav said that if a Gentile or a slave has intercourse with a Jewish woman, the child is acceptable. Explain it that the Gentile disables and the slave disables[135].

135 While the Mishnah speaks of a bastard, the interpretation following the current practice is that both the daughter and the grandchild become disabled for the priesthood; cf. Halakhah 4:15. The Babli, 70a, simply states that the Mishnah either follows R. Aqiba or that Rebbi holds that the grandchild is a bastard by rabbinic standards since there is a general biblical prohibition of sexual relations with a person whom one could not marry, *Deut*. 23:18.

(fol. 7d) **משנה ח:** כֹּהֵן גָּדוֹל פְּעָמִים שֶׁהוּא פוֹסֵל. כֵּיצַד בַּת כֹּהֵן נִשֵּׂאת לְיִשְׂרָאֵל וְיָלְדָה מִמֶּנּוּ בַּת הָלְכָה הַבַּת וְנִשֵּׂאת לְכֹהֵן וְיָלְדָה מִמֶּנּוּ בֵּן הֲרֵי זֶה רָאוּי לִהְיוֹת כֹּהֵן גָּדוֹל וְעוֹמֵד וּמְשַׁמֵּשׁ עַל גַּבֵּי הַמִּזְבֵּחַ מַאֲכִיל אֶת אִמּוֹ וּפוֹסֵל אֶת אֵם אִמּוֹ. זֹאת אוֹמֶרֶת לֹא כִבְנִי כֹּהֵן גָּדוֹל שֶׁהוּא פוֹסְלֵנִי מִן הַתְּרוּמָה.

Mishnah 7: Sometimes the High Priest disables. How is this? A Cohen's daughter was married to an Israel and had a daughter from him. The daughter went and was married to a Cohen and had a son from him. The latter possibly is a High Priest serving on top of the altar. He enables his mother to eat and disables his mother's mother[136]. The latter says, not like my son the High Priest who disables me from heave[137].

136 If he is the only surviving descendent, he keeps his grandmother out and his mother in the clan of priests.

137 This seems to have been a proverb describing a paradoxical situation.

(fol. 8c) **הלכה ח**: כֹּהֵן גָּדוֹל כול'. תַּנֵּי בַּר קַפָּרָא. בֶּן יוֹמוֹ פוֹסֵל וּמַאֲכִיל.

Halakhah 8: "The High Priest," etc. Bar Kappara stated: A one-day-old disables and enables to eat[138].

138 For the situation described in the Mishnah, it is not necessary that the grandson be an adult admitted to the Temple service.

לֹא כְבֶן בִּתּוֹ כֹהֵן גָּדוֹל שֶׁהוּא פוֹסְלָתוֹ מִן הַתְּרוּמָה. הָא כֵיצַד. בַּת כֹּהֵן שֶׁנִּשֵּׂאת לְיִשְׂרָאֵל וְיָלְדָה מִמֶּנּוּ בַת וּבַת יִשְׂרָאֵל שֶׁנִּשֵּׂאת לְכֹהֵן וְיָלְדָה מִמֶּנּוּ בֵן. וְנִשְּׂאוּ שְׁנֵיהֶן זֶה לָזֶה וְהוֹלִידוּ בֵן. הֲרֵי זֶה רָאוּי לִהְיוֹת כֹּהֵן גָּדוֹל עוֹמֵד וּמְשַׁמֵּשׁ עַל גַּבֵּי הַמִּזְבֵּחַ. מַאֲכִיל אֶת אִמּוֹ וּפוֹסֵל אֶת אֵם אִמּוֹ. זֹאת אוֹמֶרֶת לֹא כְבֶן בִּתּוֹ כֹהֵן גָּדוֹל שֶׁהוּא פוֹסְלֵינִי מִן הַתְּרוּמָה.

"Not like my son the High Priest who disables me from heave.[139]" So is the Mishnah: A Cohen's daughter was married to an Israel and had a daughter from him; an Israel's daughter was married to a Cohen and had a son from him. The two married and had a son. The latter possibly is a High Priest serving on top of the altar. He enables his mother to eat and disables his mother's mother[140]. The latter says, not like my son the High Priest who disables me from heave.

139 The text has some slight copying errors.

140 To get the maximum effect from the rearrangement of the Mishnah, it should read "He enables his paternal grandmother (who was born Israel) and disables his maternal grandmother (who was born priestly)." It simply means that only the husband's affiliation counts.

הערל פרק שמיני

(fol. 8c) **משנה א:** הֶעָרֵל וְכָל־הַטְּמֵאִים לֹא יֹאכְלוּ בִתְּרוּמָה נְשֵׁיהֶם וְעַבְדֵיהֶם יֹאכְלוּ. פְּצוּעַ דַּכָּא וּכְרוּת שָׁפְכָה הֵן וְעַבְדֵיהֶן יֹאכְלוּ וּנְשֵׁיהֶן לֹא יֹאכְלוּ. וְאִם לֹא יְדָעָהּ מִשֶּׁנַּעֲשָׂה פְּצוּעַ דַּכָּא וּכְרוּת שָׁפְכָה הֲרֵי אֵילּוּ יֹאכְלוּ.

Mishnah 1: The uncircumcised and any impure persons may not eat heave; their wives and slaves may eat. Someone injured in his testicles or with cut-off penis and his slaves may eat, his wives may not eat; but if he did not know her carnally after he was injured in his testicles or his penis was cut off, they may eat[1].

1 No uncircumcised person may eat any sanctified food (*Ex.* 12:48) nor any impure (*Lev.* 22:3). If these persons belong to the priestly clan they are not excluded by their disability (assuming the the Cohen is legally uncircumcised, e. g., as a hemophiliac). But the rules of entitlement to heave follow only the rules of membership in the priestly clan. The person injured in his testicles is prevented from marrying inside the congregation; therefore, his intercourse disables his otherwise entitled sex partner from heave.

The numerical inconsistency in the last sentence is in the Mishnah.

הלכה א: הֶעָרֵל וְכָל־הַטְּמֵאִים כול'. אִישׁ אִישׁ לְרַבּוֹת אֶת הֶעָרֵל. אוֹ אִישׁ אִישׁ לְרַבּוֹת אֶת הָאוֹנֵן. אָמַר רִבִּי יוֹסֵה בֶּן חֲנִינָה. כְּתִיב כָּל־זָר לֹא יֹאכַל קוֹדֶשׁ. מִשּׁוּם זָרוּת אֲסַרְתִּי לָךְ וְלֹא אָסַרְתִּי לָךְ מִשּׁוּם עָרְלָה. רִבִּי טִיוֹפָא סִמּוּקָא בָּעֵי קוֹמֵי רִבִּי יוֹסֵי. אוֹ נֹאמַר. זָרוּת אָסַרְתִּי וְלֹא אָסַרְתִּי מִשּׁוּם עָרְלָה וּמִשּׁוּם אֲנִינָה. אָמַר לֵיהּ. מֵאַחַר שֶׁכָּתוּב אֶחָד מַרְבֶּה וְאֶחָד מְמָעֵט. מַרְבֶּה אֲנִי אֶת הֶעָרֵל שֶׁהוּא מְחוּסָּר מַעֲשֶׂה בְגוּפוֹ. וּמוֹצִיא אֶת הָאוֹנֵן שֶׁאֵינוֹ מְחוּסָּר מַעֲשֶׂה בְגוּפוֹ. עַד כְּדוֹן כְּרִבִּי עֲקִיבָה. כְּרִבִּי יִשְׁמָעֵאל. תַּנֵּי רִבִּי יִשְׁמָעֵאל. נֶאֱמַר תּוֹשָׁב

וְשָׂכִיר בְּפֶסַח וְנֶאֱמַר תּוֹשָׁב וְשָׂכִיר בִּתְרוּמָה. מַה תּוֹשָׁב וְשָׂכִיר הָאָמוּר בְּפֶסַח פָּסַל בּוֹ אֶת הֶעָרֵל. אַף תּוֹשָׁב וְשָׂכִיר הָאָמוּר בִּתְרוּמָה פָּסַל בּוֹ אֶת הֶעָרֵל. רִבִּי חַגַּיי בְּעָא. אִי מַה תּוֹשָׁב וְשָׂכִיר הָאָמוּר בְּפֶסַח פָּסַל בּוֹ אֶת הָאוֹנֵן. אַף תּוֹשָׁב וְשָׂכִיר הָאָמוּר בִּתְרוּמָה נִפְסוֹל בּוֹ אֶת הָאוֹנֵן. אָמַר רִבִּי הִילָא. לֹא לָמְדוּ תַּחַת תַּחַת אֶלָּא דְבָרִים הָאֲמוּרִין בַּפָּרָשָׁה. טוּמְטוּם וְאַנְדְרוֹגִינוֹס מִמָּקוֹם אַחֵר בָּאוּ. אוֹנֵן מִמַּעֲשֵׂר שֵׁינִי בָא.

Halakhah 1: "The uncircumcised and any impure persons," etc. "Every man[2]", to include the uncircumcised[3]. Or "every man" to include the mourner[4]? Rebbi Yose ben Ḥanina said, it is written, "no outsider shall eat sanctified [food][5]". I forbade to you because of outside status, I did not forbid because of prepuce[6]. The reddish Rebbi Tiufa[7] asked before Rebbi Yose: may we not say, I did not forbid because of prepuce and because of mourning? He said to him, since one verse includes and the other excludes[8], I am including the uncircumcised who is missing some procedure performed on his body and excluding the mourner who is not missing some procedure performed on his body. So far following Rebbi Aqiba. Following Rebbi Ismael? Rebbi Ismael stated[9]: It said "sojourner and hireling" with regard to Passover[10] and "sojourner and hireling" with regard to heave[11]. Since "sojourner and hireling" with regard to Passover implies disabling the uncircumcised, so "sojourner and hireling" with regard to heave must imply disabling the uncircumcised[12]. Rebbi Ḥaggai questioned: If "sojourner and hireling" with regard to Passover is in a group of laws disabling the mourner, also "sojourner and hireling" with regard to heave should imply disabling the mourner[13]. Rebbi Hila answered: They inferred from "under, under" only items mentioned in the paragraph[14]. The sexless and the hermaphrodite came under another category[15]. The mourner comes from second tithe[4].

2 *Lev*. 22:4. The verse excludes impure persons from sanctified food. The inclusive "*every* man" implies that every man of the descendents of Aaron is included among the prospective eaters of heave since every man is exluded when impure. Verse 7 notes that after immersion in water he may eat the sanctified food after sundown; this refers to heave which does not require a prior purification sacrifice.

3 Quoted in the Babli (70a, 71a, 74a) and *Sifra Emor Pereq* 4(18) in the name of R. Aqiba. He takes the emphatic expression "*every* man" to mean that in addition to the persons excluded in the text there must be some category of excluded persons not mentioned in the text.

4 The mourner during the period between the death of a relative and his burial, who is excluded from all religious duties except the care for the burial. As R. Hila points out at the end, the exclusion of the mourner is mentioned only in the declaration of tithes (*Deut*. 26:14), which implies that even the Israel farmer may not eat his sanctified food (the Second Tithe) while in mourning. From there, it is inferred that the Cohen certainly is disabled during his mourning.

5 *Lev*. 22:10: "No outsider (a non-priestly Jew; cf. *Num*. 18:4) shall eat sanctified [food], a Cohen's sojourner (foreign worker) and hireling shall not eat sanctified [food]." The verse clearly disqualifies persons because of their intrinsic status, not because of a temporary disability. *Sifra Emor Pereq* 4(16) also classifies the bastard as an outsider.

6 In the Babli 71a, "I did not forbid because of mourning" which is immediately corrected to "say: not lack of circumcision." One may not correct the Yerushalmi text according to the first version of the Babli (done by most commentators and the editors of the Zhitomir/Wilna text), since not only the principle of *lectio difficilior* but also the next sentence in the text, and the parallel discussion in the Babli preclude such an approach. It is clear from the start that both the uncircumcised and the mourner are forbidden heave, and the entire discussion is one of hermeneutics. No temporary disabilities have any place in the interpretation of vv. 10-13. The question is only whether the rather arbitrary approach of R. Aqiba has any justification.

7 A Galilean Amora of the fourth generation; his name appears also as Ṭaifa. His sobriquet may mean that he was a redhead.

8 It is the general method of R.

Aqiba to analyze verses for expressions of inclusion and exclusion. The expression in 22:4: אִישׁ אִישׁ "man, man" (translated as "every man") implies that some man is included in the set of persons excluded from heave who is not mentioned in the verse. On the other hand, if the verse had simply read אִישׁ אִישׁ מִזֶּרַע אַהֲרֹן צָרוּעַ אוֹ זָב the same meaning as in the actual verse אִישׁ אִישׁ מִזֶּרַע אַהֲרֹן וְהוּא צָרוּעַ אוֹ זָב could have been expressed in correct grammar with one less word. This is taken as an exclusion, "*only if he be* a leper or sick with gonorrhea", which decreases the size of the excluded set. The verse deals only with temporary disabilities. The verse 22:10 dealing with permanent disabilities has no exclusion. It is therefore acceptable to include a permanently disabled person in the excluded set and to exclude from that set an additional temporarily disabled person.

9 *Sifra Emor Pereq* 4(18). In the Babli (70a) and the *Mekhilta deR. Ismael, Bo* (ed. Horovitz-Rabin, p. 54), the argument is presented in the name of R. Eliezer, adding to the arguments of B. Z. Wacholder [*The date of the Mekhilta de-R. Ishmael*, HUCA 39(1968) 117-144] about the dependence of that Mekhilta on the Babli.

10 *Ex.* 12:45.

11 *Lev.* 22:10.

12 An application of the principle of גזרה שוה, R. Ismael's rule 2: One word found in two different laws which in neither of them are needed for the understanding of the law, are written to permit the transfer of rules from one to the other.

13 However, Mishnah *Pesaḥim* 8:8, explained in *Pesaḥim* [Yerushalmi 8:8 (fol. 36b), Babli 92a] states that the mourner is excluded by biblical decree only from services during daytime. This means that the mourner (as long as he is not impure) is admitted to the Passover meal. R. Haggai attempts to discredit R. Ismael's approach.

14 While the argument of R. Hila is almost understandable, this sentence is not. Neither in the laws of Passover nor in those of heave is the word חתך used. The Babli, in a somewhat similar discussion (71a, 74a) discusses the seemingly superfluous inclusion of three expressions "ממנו" in the laws of the Passover sacrifice offered in Egypt (*Ex.* 12:9,10). The argument there is not applicable here. All R. Hila seems to say is that one does not derive laws not touched upon in *Ex.* 22:43-50 from there.

15 The sexless is excluded from sacrifices since he probably is a male

with an ingrown penis and therefore uncircumcised. The hermaphrodite is circumcised and accepted. His inclusion here has to be rated an editorial or scribal error since "sexless and hermaphrodite" is a frequently occurring combination. (A priest hermaphrodite is excluded from the sacrifices reserved for men and admitted to those open to women; Tosephta 10:2.)

רִבִּי אָבוּן בָּעֵי. וּתְהֵא תְרוּמָה אֲסוּרָה לְאוֹנֵן מִקַּל וָחוֹמֶר. וּמַה אִם הַמַּעֲשֵׂר שֶׁהוּא מוּתָּר לְזָרִים הֲרֵי הוּא אָסוּר לְאוֹנֵן. תְּרוּמָה שֶׁהִיא אֲסוּרָה לְזָרִים אֵינוֹ דִין שֶׁתְּהֵא אֲסוּרָה לְאוֹנֵן. לֹא. אִם אָמַרְתָּ בְמַעֲשֵׂר שֶׁהוּא טָעוּן מְחִיצָה. תֹּאמַר בִּתְרוּמָה שֶׁאֵינָהּ טְעוּנָה מְחִיצָה. הָא לְפִי שֶׁיֵּשׁ בָּזֶה מַה שֶׁאֵין בָּזֶה וּבָזֶה מַה שֶׁאֵין בָּזֶה לֹא צָרְכוּ לְלַמֵּד זֶה מִזֶּה.

Rebbi Abun asked: Should not heave be forbidden to the mourner by an inference *de minore ad majus*? Since tithe[16], which is permitted to outsiders, is forbidden to the mourner[4], should not heave, which is forbidden to outsiders, be forbidden to the mourner? No. If you said it about tithe which needs an enclosure[17], what can you say about heave which does not need an enclosure? Therefore, since each of them has an aspect missing in the other, they cannot teach an inference from one to the other.

16 Second tithe, which has to be eaten by the farmer's family who are not priestly (cf. Tractate *Ma'aser Šeni*).

17 Inside the walls of Jerusalem or, earlier, of Siloh.

קֳדָשִׁים מַהוּ שֶׁיְּהוּ אֲסוּרִים בְּעָרֵל. לְלַמֵּד מִן הַפֶּסַח אֵין אַתְּ יָכוֹל שֶׁאֵין בּוֹ שְׁבִירַת הָעֶצֶם. וְלֹא מִן הַתְּרוּמָה שֶׁהוּא לֶמֶד מִן הַלֶּמֶד. הֲוֵי סוֹפָךְ (fol. 8d) לוֹמַר מִמֶּנּוּ וּמִמֶּנּוּ. מַה מִמֶּנּוּ שֶׁנֶּאֱמַר בְּפֶסַח פּוֹסֵל בּוֹ אֶת הֶעָרֵל. אַף מִמֶּנּוּ שֶׁנֶּאֱמַר בְּקֳדָשִׁים פּוֹסֵל בּוֹ אֶת הֶעָרֵל. קֳדָשִׁים מַהוּ שֶׁיְּהוּ אֲסוּרִין לְאוֹנֵן. מִמֶּנּוּ מִמֶּנּוּ. מַה מִמֶּנּוּ שֶׁנֶּאֱמַר בְּמַעֲשֵׂר פּוֹסֵל בּוֹ אֶת הָאוֹנֵן. אַף מִמֶּנּוּ שֶׁנֶּאֱמַר בְּפֶסַח פּוֹסֵל בּוֹ אֶת הָאוֹנֵן.

Are sacrifices forbidden for the uncircumcised? One cannot deduce the answer from Passover since they are not subject to [the prohibition of] breaking a bone[18], neither from heave since that would be inference after inference[19]. At the end, you have to say "from it, from it[20]." Since "from it"[21] which was said in the laws of Passover implies that the uncircumcised is disqualified, so "from it"[22] which was said in the laws of sacrifices must imply that the uncircumcised is disqualified. Are sacrifices forbidden for the mourner?[23] "From it, from it." Since "from it" which was said in the laws of tithe[24] states that the mourner is disqualified, so "from it" which was said in the laws of Passover[25] must imply that the mourner is disqualified.

18 No bone may be broken of the Passover sacrifice; *Ex.* 12:46. The bone marrow of other sacrificial animals is not forbidden. Therefore, no argument *de minore ad majus* is possible from Passover to other sacrifices.

19 In general, the rules of R. Ismael may be combined with one another; an exeption are the rules of sacrifices and sanctified matter. This is discussed in detail in the Babli, *Zebaḥim* Chapter 5, which has no parallel in the Yerushalmi. Even though the authorities quoted there are all Babylonian, the reference here shows that the basis of the arguments is a Yerushalmi tradition. It is stated in Babli, *Zebaḥim* 50a, that rules 2 and 3 in the scheme of R. Ismael cannot be used one after the other. Since the exclusion of the uncircumcised from heave was an application of rule 2 (Note 12), the result cannot be used as premiss for an argument of type 3. An attempt to formulate the rules in an extension of symbolic logic is in H. Guggenheimer, *Über ein bemerkenswertes logisches System aus der Antike*, Methodos 1951, 150-164.

20 An application of rule 2 (Note 12).

21 *Ex.* 12:9 (once), 10 (twice). The Babli must reject this argument since it deduces laws of Passover from all three instances of the word.

22 *Lev.* 7:14. The verse is quoted in Mishnah *Menaḥot* 8:2.

23 There is no inference to be drawn from *Lev.* 10:6 since, after the death of Nadab and Abihu, Aaron and

his sons were commanded not to mourn.

24 The Second Tithe, *Deut.* 26:14.

25 This word indicates an oversight by editor or copyist since (1) from the laws of Passover nothing can be inferred for other sacrifices and (2) the mourner (whose relative died outside of Jerusalem so that he could not defile himself) is admitted to the Passover sacrifice. It most probably should read "sacrifices" (Note 22).

וּמוּפְנֶה הוּא. וַהֲלֹא דְרוּשָׁה הִיא. כְּהָדָא דְתַנֵּי. תּוֹשָׁב זֶה קָנוּי קִנְיַן עוֹלָם. שָׂכִיר זֶה קָנוּי קִנְיַן שָׁנִים. יֹאמַר תּוֹשָׁב. מַה תַלְמוּד לוֹמַר שָׂכִיר. הַקָּנוּי קִנְיַן עוֹלָם אֵינוֹ אוֹכֵל. וְהַקָּנוּי קִנְיַן שָׁנִים אוֹכֵל. אִילּוּ כָךְ הָיִיתִי אוֹמֵר. תּוֹשָׁב זֶה קָנוּי קִנְיַן שָׁנִים. וּכְשֶׁהוּא אוֹמֵר שָׂכִיר בָּא הַשָּׂכִיר לְלַמֵּד עַל הַתּוֹשָׁב שֶׁהוּא קִנְיַן עוֹלָם. אָמַר רִבִּי מַתְיָה. מִכֵּיוָן דִּכְתִיב וְכָל־עָרֵל לֹא יֹאכַל בּוֹ כְּמִי שֶׁהוּא מוּפְנֶה מִצַּד אֶחָד.

Is it free[26]? Has it not been used for a derivation? As it was stated[27]: "Sojourner", that is the one who is permanently acquired, "hireling" the one temporarily acquired[28]. It should only say "sojourner"; why does the verse mention "hireling"? Should the one who is permanently acquired be forbidden to eat and the one temporarily acquired be permitted? But I would have said that "sojourner" means the one temporarily acquired; the mention of the "hireling" teaches that "sojourner" means the one permanently acquired. Rebbi Mathias[29] said, since it is written "no uncircumcised person may eat from it,[30]" it is as if free from one side[31].

26 This refers back to the argument (Notes 9-12) that the uncircumcised is barred from eating heave. It is claimed that the conditions for application of rule 2, גזרה שוה, are not fulfilled.

27 Babli 70a, *Qiddushin* 4a, *Zebaḥim* 62a; *Sifra Emor Pereq* 4(17).

28 *Lev.* 22:10: "A Cohen's sojourner or hireling shall not eat from sanctified food." Who are sojourner and hireling? They cannot be Gentiles; these were excluded in the first part of v. 10. They cannot be slaves; these are included (when circumcised) in v. 11. They must be Hebrew "slaves", i. e.,

indentured servants. The verse states that the money paid in acquiring a Hebrew slave is paid not to acquire his person but his working and earning power. Therefore, they are not able to partake of sanctified food. The Hebrew slave who is permanently acquired is the one who refuses to leave when his six years of indenture are passed; *Ex*.. 21:5-6, *Deut*. 15:15-17.

According to tradition, the institution of Hebrew slaves disappeared with the first commonwealth and could never be re-introduced. The argument here is purely one of biblical interpretation, not of actual law.

29 He is mentioned only here.

30 *Ex*. 12:48.

31 While the verse in *Lev*. is used for clarification about the Hebrew slave, *Ex*. 12:46 cannot speak about him since no circumcised Jew is excluded from the Passover sacrifices. Therefore, the verse is not used for other deductions and the application of rule 2 might be justified.

The Yerushalmi does not clarify the difference between a straight גזרה שוה in which neither part is used for other implications (cf. Note 12), and a conditional one in which only one of the conditions is fulfilled, which may be rejected on logical grounds. This is made explicit in the Babli, 70b.

עַל דַּעְתֵּיהּ דְּרִבִּי עֲקִיבָה לְאֵי זֶה דָבָר נֶאֱמַר תּוֹשָׁב וְשָׂכִיר בַּתְּרוּמָה. כְּהַהִיא דְאָמַר רִבִּי אִילָא בְשֵׁם רִבִּי יָסָא. הַלּוֹקֵחַ עֲבָדִים עֲרֵילִים מִן הַגּוֹי עַל מְנָת לְמוֹהֲלָן. רִבִּי יָסָא בְשֵׁם רִבִּי יוֹחָנָן שִׁמְעוֹן בַּר בָּא בְשֵׁם רִבִּי יוֹחָנָן. הַלּוֹקֵחַ עֲבָדִים עֲרֵילִים מִן הַגּוֹי עַל מְנָת לְמוֹהֲלָן אֲפִילוּ מָלָן לֹא יֹאכְלוּ בַתְּרוּמָה. רִבִּי יוֹסִי בְשֵׁם רִבִּי יוֹחָנָן שִׁמְעוֹן בַּר בָּא בְשֵׁם רִבִּי יוֹחָנָן. הַלּוֹקֵחַ עֲבָדִים מִן הַגּוֹי עַל מְנָת לְמוֹהֲלָן וְחָזְרוּ בָהֶן מְגַלְגֵּל עִמָּהֶן שְׁנֵים עָשָׂר חוֹדֶשׁ. אִם קִיבְּלוּ עֲלֵיהֶן הֲרֵי יָפֶה וְאִם לָאו מוּתָּר לְמוֹכְרָן לְגוֹי. רִבִּי יִצְחָק בַּר נַחְמָן בְּשֵׁם רִבִּי יְהוֹשֻׁעַ בֶּן לֵוִי. מַעֲשֶׂה בְאֶחָד שֶׁלָּקַח עִיר אֶחָד שֶׁלַּעֲבָדִים עֲרֵלִים מִן הַגּוֹי עַל מְנָת לְמוֹהֲלָן וְחָזְרוּ בָהֶן. אָתָא שָׁאַל לְרַבָּנִין. אָמְרוּ לֵיהּ. גַּלְגֵּל עִמָּהֶן שְׁנֵים עָשָׂר חוֹדֶשׁ. אִם קִיבְּלוּ עֲלֵיהֶן הֲרֵי יָפֶה וְאִם לָאו הַכֹּל כְּמִנְהַג הַמְּדִינָה.

In the opinion of Rebbi Aqiba, for which reason were "sojourner or hireling" written for heave[32]? Like what Rebbi Hila said in the name of Rebbi Yasa, if somebody bought uncircumcised slaves from a Gentile with the understanding that he would circumcise them[33]. Rebbi Yose in the name of Rebbi Joḥanan, Rebbi Simeon bar Abba in the name of Rebbi Joḥanan: If somebody bought uncircumcised slaves from a Gentile with the understanding that he would circumcise them, they [still] cannot eat heave even if circumcised[34]. Rebbi Yose in the name of Rebbi Joḥanan, Rebbi Simeon bar Abba in the name of Rebbi Joḥanan: If somebody bought slaves from a Gentile with the understanding that he would circumcise them but they changed their minds, he keeps them for twelve months. If they accept, it is fine; otherwise, he may sell them to a Gentile[35]. Rebbi Isaac bar Naḥman in the name of Rebbi Joshua ben Levi: It happened that somebody bought a village full of uncircumcised slaves from a Gentile with the understanding that he would circumcise them but they changed their minds. He came and asked the rabbis. They said to him, keep them for twelve months. If they accept, it is fine; otherwise one follows the local customs.

32 He derives the exclusion of the uncircumcised from another verse, cf. Note 8. For him there is no necessity to explain "sojourner and hireling" as (no longer applicable) Jewish slaves; he takes "sojourner and hireling" both with respect to heave as with respect to Passover as Gentiles who have not completed the process of conversion.

33 That sentence seems to be incomplete. The following rules imply that nobody can be forced to be circumcised against his will. (This is the majority opinion in the Babli, 48a). A Jewish buyer will prefer to buy slaves only with their prior agreement to be circumcised.

34 If the buyer is a Cohen, the slave can become part of his household only if he became Jewish by circumcision followed by immersion in a *miqweh*. If the last step is missing, the conversion is void. A lawful conversion is necessary since upon manumission the slave becomes a full Jew.

35 But a converted slave cannot be sold to a Gentile under any circumstances. This rule and the following story also are in the Babli,

48b. The Babli also quotes R. Aqiba to the effect that one does not buy or keep a slave who did not give his prior agreement to be circumcised.

וְאָמַר רִבִּי יִצְחָק בַּר נַחְמָן. רִבִּי יְהוֹשֻׁעַ בֶּן לֵוִי הָיָה בְּלָדוֹקֵיָא. וַהֲוָה תַּמָּן רִבִּי יְהוּדָה נְשִׂיאָה. בְּעָא מִיקְרוֹץ. אָמַר לֵיהּ. הַמְתֵּן וְאָנוּ מַטְבִּילִין אֶת הַגִּיּוֹרֶת הַזּוֹ לְמָחָר. רִבִּי זְעִירָא שָׁאַל לְרִבִּי יִצְחָק בַּר נַחְמָן. לָמָּה. מִפְּנֵי כְבוֹד הַזָּקֵן אוֹ מִשּׁוּם שֶׁאֵין מַטְבִּילִין אֶת הַגִּיּוֹרֶת בַּלַּיְלָה. אָמַר לֵיהּ. מִשּׁוּם שֶׁאֵין מַטְבִּילִין אֶת הַגִּיּוֹרֶת בַּלַּיְלָה. אָתָא עוֹבְדָא קוֹמֵי דְרִבִּי יוֹסֵי. מַהוּ לְהַטְבִּיל אֶת הַגֵּרִים בַּלַּיְלָה. וְלֹא הוֹדוּ.

Rebbi Isaac bar Naḥman also said: Rebbi Joshua ben Levi was in Laodicea and met there Rebbi Jehudah the Patriarch[36]. He[37] wanted to leave early, when he[38] said to him wait for us tomorrow to immerse this woman convert. Rebbi Zera[39] asked Rebbi Isaac bar Naḥman: Was that to honor the old man[37] or because one does not immerse a woman convert at night? He said to him, because one does not immerse a woman convert at night. A case came before Rebbi Yose whether one may immerse converts at night. They could not agree[40].

36 The grandson of Rebbi.

37 R. Joshua ben Levi.

38 R. Jehudah Neśia.

39 He might be R. Ze'ira, name written in Babylonian style.

40 In the Babli, 46b, the Galilean authorities are quoted without dissent that conversion needs a court of three judges and must be executed during daytime since "judgment" is written in this respect (*Num.* 15:16).

עֶבֶד תּוֹשָׁב לְעוֹלָם. גֵּר תּוֹשָׁב הֲרֵי הוּא כְגוֹי לְכָל־דָּבָר. רִבִּי שְׁמוּאֵל בַּר חִיָּיה בַּר יְהוּדָה בְּשֵׁם רִבִּי חֲנִינָה. גֵּר (וְ)תוֹשָׁב מְגַלְגְּלִין עִמָּהֶן שְׁנֵים עָשָׂר חוֹדֶשׁ. אִם חָזַר בּוֹ הֲרֵי יָפֶה וְאִם לָאו הֲרֵי הוּא כְגוֹי לְכָל־דָּבָר. רִבִּי שְׁמוּאֵל בַּר חִיָּיה בַּר יְהוּדָה רִבִּי חֲנִינָה בְּשֵׁם רִבִּי. גֵּר תּוֹשָׁב צָרִיךְ לְקַבֵּל עָלָיו עַל מְנָת שֶׁיְּהֵא אוֹכֵל נְבֵילוֹת. אָמַר רִבִּי הִילָא יֵאָמְרוּ הַדְּבָרִים כִּכְתָבָן. מַה יֵאָמְרוּ הַדְּבָרִים כִּכְתָבָן. אָמַר רִבִּי

יוֹסֵה בַּר חֲנִינָה. לֹא תֹאכְלוּ כָל־נְבֵילָה לַגֵּר אֲשֶׁר בִּשְׁעָרֶיךָ תִּתְּנֶנָּה וַאֲכָלָהּ. אִית תַּנָּיֵי תַנֵּי. גֵּר תּוֹשָׁב אֵין מְקַבְּלִין אוֹתָן עַד שֶׁיְּקַבֵּל אֶת כָּל־הַמִּצְוֹת שֶׁכְּתוּבוֹת בַּתּוֹרָה. אִית תַּנָּיֵי תַנֵּי. גֵּר תּוֹשָׁב אֵין מְקַבְּלִין אוֹתוֹ עַד שֶׁיִּכְפּוֹר בָּעֲבוֹדָה זָרָה שֶׁלּוֹ. רִבִּי אַבָּא בְשֵׁם רִבִּי חִייָה בַּר אַשִּׁי. גֵּר תּוֹשָׁב אֵין מְקַבְּלִין אוֹתוֹ עַד שֶׁיִּכְפּוֹר בָּעֲבוֹדָה זָרָה כְּגוֹי. אָמַר רִבִּי זְעִירָא. מִדִּבְרֵי כּוּלְּהוֹן עַד שֶׁיִּכְפּוֹר בָּעֲבוֹדָה זָרָה כְּגוֹי. דִּל כֵּן מַה אֲנָן אָמְרִין. הוֹאִיל וְהוּא מְצוּוֶּה עַל עֲבוֹדָה זָרָה לֹא יְבַטֵּל. וְגוֹיִים אֵינָן מְצוּוִּים עַל עֲבוֹדָה זָרָה וּמְבַטְּלִין. אָמַר רִבִּי יוֹסֵה. שֶׁלֹּא תֹאמַר. וְהוּא שָׁוֶה לְיִשְׂרָאֵל בִּשְׁלֹשָׁה דְבָרִים. בְּלֹא תַעֲשׂוֹק וְלֹא תוֹנֶה וְגוֹלֶה כְיִשְׂרָאֵל. הוּא לֹא יְבַטֵּל. לְפוּם כֵּן צָרִיךְ מֵימַר. מְבַטֵּל עֲבוֹדָה זָרָה כְּגוֹי. מָאן תַּנָּא בְּלֹא יַעֲשׂוֹק. רִבִּי יוֹסֵה בֵּירִבִּי יְהוּדָה. דְּתַנֵּי. גֵּר תּוֹשָׁב הֲרֵי בְלֹא תַעֲשֶׂה. דִּבְרֵי רִבִּי יוֹסֵה בֵּירִבִּי יְהוּדָה.

A slave may be a permanent sojourner[41]. A sojourner is like a Gentile in every respect[42]. Rebbi Samuel bar Ḥiyya bar Jehudah in the name of Rebbi Ḥanina: One keeps the sojourner for twelve months. If he changes his mind, that is fine; otherwise he is like a Gentile in all respects[43]. Rebbi Samuel bar Ḥiyya bar Jehudah, Rebbi Ḥanina in the name of Rebbi: The sojourner has to accept on condition that he may eat cadaver meat[44]. Rebbi Hila said, one would then say, the words are [interpreted] as they are written. What does it mean, the words are [interpreted] as they are written? Rebbi Yose ben Ḥanina said, "You shall not eat any cadaver; to the sojourner in your midst you shall give it that he eat it[45]." Some Tannaim state: One does not receive a sojourner unless he accepts all commandments written in the Torah[44]. Some Tannaim state: One does not receive a sojourner unless he renounces his idolatry[46]. Rebbi Abba in the name of Rebbi Ḥiyya bar Ashi: One does not receive a sojourner unless he renounces his idolatry as a Gentile[47]. Rebbi Ze'ira said, from their consensus: unless he renounces his idolatry as a Gentile. For if it were not so, what would we say? Since he is forbidden idolatry he cannot render profane. But are Gentiles not also forbidden[48] idolatry and they do render profane? Rebbi Yose said, that you should not say, since he is equal to an Israel in three respects, do not oppress[49], do not cheat[50], and he is exiled like an Israel[51], that he has no power to render profane. Therefore, it was necessary to spell out that he renders idols profane like a Gentile. Who is the Tanna who includes "do not oppress"? He is Rebbi Yose ben Rebbi Jehudah, as it was stated[52]: The sojourner is protected by the prohibition, the words of Rebbi Yose ben Rebbi Jehudah.

41 A slave may refuse to be circumcised and stay in the Jewish household as a "sojourner", a Gentile who has accepted the seven Noahide commandments (prohibition of idolatry, murder, adultery and incest with direct descendents; eating flesh torn from living beings, blasphemy; prohibition of robbery, duty to live under the rule of a civil law). As such he is under the protection of the often repeated commandment to treat the sojourner well and he can be tolerated in a Jewish household since his touch does not make wine prohibited (Babli *Avodah zarah* 64b).

In the Babli, 48b, this is the position taken by R. Ismael; R. Aqiba (48b) and R. Eliezer (71a) prohibit keeping uncircumcised slaves.

42 This is not meant to be a generally valid statement; the idolator is not protected by the Covenant of the sojourner. What is meant is a rather technical detail. It is stated repeatedly in the Torah, e. g. *Deut.* 13:18, that statues and other idolatrous objects are prohibited for any use by a Jew. Therefore, valuables of an idolatrous character may only be used by Jews (for example, melted down for their precious metal content) if they come into the hand of a Jew already profaned, i. e., if a non-Jew has treated them contemptuously, preferably damaging them. The Yerushalmi holds that the sojourner still has the power of a Gentile to render profane objects of idolatry even though he is a monotheist, and make them available for a Jew to use. The Babli, *Avodah zarah* 64b/65a, explains away all the reasons quoted in this paragraph and decides that only an idolator can effectively render idols profane.

43 This statement, that the status of sojourner is only temporary and should lead to full conversion is not found

anywhere else.

44 In the Babli, *Avodah zarah* 64b, the opinion of "others" is that the sojourner has to accept all commandments in the Torah except those of kosher food.

45 *Deut.* 14:21: "You shall not eat any cadaver; to the sojourner in your midst you shall give it that he eat it, or sell it to a stranger." This seems to imply that cadaver meat must be donated to the sojourner or sold to the Gentile. Whether it may be sold to the sojourner or donated to the Gentile is a matter of controversy in the Babli (*Pesaḥim* 21b, *Avodah zarah* 20a) and *Sifry Deut* # 104. R. Hila wants to decide following the majority that a sale to the sojourner is permitted.

46 In the Babli *Avodah zarah* 64b, this is the opinion of R. Meïr. The operative majority opinion there, that he has to accept all seven Noahide commandments, is not mentioned in the Yerushalmi.

47 This is the same statement as the preceding one, only it emphasizes that the sojourner has not lost his power to render idols profane which was his as an idolator.

48 The Noahide precepts are supposed to be valid for all mankind.

49 *Deut.* 24:14: "Do not oppress the poor hireling, or the deprived, from your brothers or the stranger in your land, in your gates." The stranger who has the right of permanent residence in your gates is the approved sojourner.

51 The exile of the homicide to one of the cities of refuge, *Num.* 35:15: "For the children of Israel and the sojourner in their midst should these six cities be a refuge."

50 *Deut.* 23:17: "With you he shall dwell in your midst, at the place which he will chose, where he feels well within one of your gates; do not cheat him."

51 The exile of the homicide to the city of refuge. In *Num.* 35:15 these cities are declared to be for "the children of Israel and the sojourner in their midst."

52 More explicit in Babli *Baba meṣi'a* 111b, Tosephta *Baba meṣi'a* 10:4. In the latter source, it is explained that the prohibition of oppression includes the obligation to pay the day-laborer immediately.

רִבִּי יוּדָה אוֹמֵר. גֵּר תּוֹשָׁב בְּשַׁבָּת כְּיִשְׂרָאֵל בְּיוֹם טוֹב. מַה יִשְׂרָאֵל בְּיוֹם טוֹב אוֹפֶה וּמְבַשֵּׁל וְאָסוּר בְּכָל־מְלָאכָה אַף גֵּר תּוֹשָׁב בְּשַׁבָּת כֵּן. רִבִּי יוֹסֵי אוֹמֵר. גֵּר תּוֹשָׁב בְּשַׁבָּת כְּיִשְׂרָאֵל בְּחוּלוֹ שֶׁלְּמוֹעֵד. מַה יִשְׂרָאֵל בְּחוּלוֹ שֶׁל מוֹעֵד מְגַבֵּב עַל פְּנֵי הַשָּׂדֶה וְאָסוּר בְּכָל־מְלֶאכֶת הַשָּׂדֶה אַף גֵּר תּוֹשָׁב בְּשַׁבָּת כֵּן. רִבִּי שִׁמְעוֹן אוֹמֵר. גֵּר תּוֹשָׁב בְּשַׁבָּת כְּיִשְׂרָאֵל בִּשְׁאָר יְמוֹת הַשָּׁנָה. מַה יִשְׂרָאֵל בִּשְׁאָר יְמוֹת הַשָּׁנָה חוֹרֵשׁ וְזוֹרֵעַ וְקוֹצֵר אַף גֵּר תּוֹשָׁב בְּשַׁבָּת כֵּן. רַב אָדָא רַב הַמְנוּנָא רַב אָדָא בַּר אַחֲוָה בְּשֵׁם רַב. הֲלָכָה כְּרִבִּי שִׁמְעוֹן.

Rebbi Jehudah says, the sojourner on a Sabbath is like a Jew on a holiday. Just as a Jew bakes and cooks but is forbidden to work, so is the sojourner on the Sabbath[53]. Rebbi Yose says, the sojourner on a Sabbath is like a Jew on the intermediate days of a holiday[54]. Just as a Jew on the intermediate days of a holiday collects from the field but is forbidden agricultural work, so is the sojourner on the Sabbath. Rebbi Simeon says, the sojourner on a Sabbath is like a Jew on the remaining days of the year[55]. Just as a Jew on the remaining days of the year ploughs, sows, and harvests, so does the sojourner on the Sabbath. Rav Ada, Rav Hamnuna, Rav Ada bar Aḥawa in the name of Rav: Practice follows Rebbi Simeon[56].

53 In the Babli, *Keritut* 9a, this is the opinion of R. Aqiba.

54 In the Babli, this is the opinion of the anonymous majority.

55 In the Babli, he explicitly includes the sojourner-slave working for himself; work for the Jewish owner is forbidden.

56 In the Babli, quoted by *Šiṭṭa Mequbeṣet* from manuscript: Rav Idi bar Naḥman in the name of Rav Ada bar Ahava (cf. *Berakhot*, Chapter 1, Note 161.)

כְּתִיב וְכָל־עֶבֶד אִישׁ מִקְנַת כֶּסֶף וגו'. עֶבֶד אִישׁ אַתְּ מוֹהֲלוֹ בְּעַל כּוֹרְחוֹ. בֶּן אִישׁ אֵין אַתְּ מוֹהֲלוֹ בְּעַל כּוֹרְחוֹ. רִבִּי יוֹחָנָן בָּעֵי. הָא בֶּן קָטָן אַתְּ מוֹהֲלוֹ עַל כּוֹרְחוֹ. אֲפִילוּ כִּבְנוֹ שֶׁלְּאוֹרְכְנֵיס. רִבִּי חִזְקִיָּה בְּשֵׁם רַבָּא. הָא כֵיְנִי. מָצָא בְתוֹכָהּ תִּינוֹק

מוּשְׁלָךְ. הִטְבִּילוֹ לְשׁוּם עֶבֶד אַתְּ מוֹהֲלוֹ לְשׁוּם עֶבֶד. לְשׁוּם בֶּן חוֹרִין אַתְּ מוֹהֲלוֹ לְשׁוּם בֶּן חוֹרִין. רִבִּי יוֹחָנָן בָּעֵי. לְשׁוּם עֶבֶד הֲרֵי הוּא כְעֶבֶד. אֲפִילוּ כְבְנוֹ שֶׁלְּאוֹרְכְנֵיס. רִבִּי אַבָּהוּ וְרִבִּי אֶלְעָזָר בְּשֵׁם רִבִּי הוֹשַׁעְיָה לֹא אָמַר כֵּן אֶלָּא וְכָל־עֶבֶד אִישׁ מִקְנַת כָּסֶף. עַבְדָּךְ אִישׁ אַתְּ מוֹהֲלוֹ בְּעַל כּוֹרְחוֹ. בִּנְךָ אִישׁ אֵין אַתְּ מוֹהֲלוֹ בְּעַל כּוֹרְחוֹ. כְּהָהִיא דָמַר רִבִּי הִילָא בְשֵׁם רִבִּי יָסָא. הַלּוֹקֵחַ עֲבָדִים עֲרֵילִים מִן הַגּוֹיִם עַל מְנָת לְמְהוֹל. מַה נַפְשֵׁךְ. כְּעֶבֶד אִישׁ הוּא אַתְּ מוֹהֲלָן עַל כּוֹרְחָן עַל מְנָת שֶׁלֹּא לְמוֹהֲלָן. כְּבֵן אִישׁ הוּא אֵין אַתְּ מוֹהֲלוֹ עַל כּוֹרְחוֹ.

It is written: "Any slave who is a man bought by money[57]." You circumcise by force a slave who is a man[58], you do not circumcise by force a son who is a man[59]. Rebbi Joḥanan asked, does this imply that you may circumcise a minor by force? Even like one of undescended testicles[60]? Rebbi Ḥizqiah in the name of Rebbi Abba: It is so. "If he found there a foundling. If he immersed him as a slave, he circumcises him as a slave; [if he immersed him] as a free person, he circumcises him as a free person.[61]" Rebbi Joḥanan asked, as a slave, he circumcises him as a slave; even like one of undescended testicles? Rebbi Abbahu and Rebbi Eleazar in the name of Rebbi Hoshaia did not say so, but "any slave who is a man bought by money." If your slave is a man, you circumcise him by force. If your son is a man, you do not circumcise him by force. This refers to what Rebbi Hila said in the name of Rebbi Yasa: If somebody buys uncircumcised slaves from Gentiles on condition that he will circumcise them, in any case if they are slaves who are men, you circumcise them by force. On condition[62] that he will not circumcise them, he is like a son who is a man, you do not circumcise him by force.

57 *Ex.* 12:44: "Any slave who is a man bought for money, when you have circumcised him, then he may eat from [the Passover sacrifice]." In the Babli (*Yebamot* 48a) the anonymous opinion here is the minority opinion of R. Simeon ben Eleazar. The *Mekhilta dR. Simeon ben Iohai* follows the

Yerushalmi; the *Mekhilta dR. Ismael* follows the Babli (*Yebamot* 71a) in referring the sentence "then he may eat from [the Passover sacrifice]" to the owner who in that interpretation is barred from the sacrifice as long as not all his slaves are circumcised. (Cf. Note 41, the position of R. Aqiba).

58 The verse notes only the activity of the owner.

59 A proselyte may only circumcise his minor sons with him.

60 The word אורכנים has a number of explanations in the dictionaries which do not fit since they denote persons of high social standing. It is difficult to see how a foundling can be a son of a "ruler" (Mussaphia) or a "chief leader" (Kohut), etc. According to the context, one may translate בן not as "son" but "endowed with a certain quality" and take אורכנים as a composite of Greek ὀρχίς "testicles", such as ὀρχιπέδη "restraint of testicles, impotence" (E. G.).

61 Mishnah *Makhshirin* 2:7 explains that in a city where Jews and Gentiles dwell together, a foundling has the status of the majority (according to R. Jehudah the majority of those who abandon their children; in Tosephta *Makhshirin* 1:8 he declares the foundling to be a Gentile or a slave if only one Gentile or female slave of childbearing age lives there.)

62 A condition negotiated with the slave trader.

הַמָּשׁוּךְ וְהַנּוֹלָד מָהוּל וְהַמָּל עַד שֶׁלֹּא נִתְגַּיֵּיר לֹא יֹאכְלוּ בַתְּרוּמָה. רִבִּי זְרִיקָן רִבִּי יַנַּאי בֵּירִבִּי יִשְׁמָעֵאל בְּשֵׁם רִבִּי יוֹחָנָן. מִשּׁוּם קְנָס. רִבִּי יִרְמְיָה רִבִּי שְׁמוּאֵל בַּר רַב יִצְחָק בְּשֵׁם רַב. גְּזֵירָה גָּזְרוּ. מַה נְפַק מִן בֵּינֵיהוֹן. מָשַׁךְ לוֹ אַחֵר עָרְלָה אוֹ שֶׁנִּמְשְׁכָה מֵאֵילֶיהָ. אִין תֵּימַר קְנָס. אֵין כָּאן קְנָס. אִין תֵּימַר גְּזֵירָה גָּזְרוּ. אֲפִילוּ כֵן גְּזֵירָה גָּזְרוּ.

The one drawn [circumcised][63], the one born circumcised[64], and the circumcised before he converted[64] may not eat heave[65]. Rebbi Zeriqan, Rebbi Yannay ben Rebbi Ismael, in the name of Rebbi Joḥanan: As a fine. Rebbi Jeremiah, Rebbi Samuel ben Rav Isaac in the name of Rav: They instituted a fence[66]. What is the difference between them? If another person drew it[67], or that it regrew by itself. If you want to say, it is a fine, there is no place for a fine. If you say they instituted a fence, nevertheless they instituted a fence.

63 A circumcised person who extended the skin of his penis that it should look like a prepuce and he should not be recognized as a Jew.

64 His circumcision had no connection with Judaism. He cannot be circumcised for fear that his penis would be injured. If one drop of blood can be drawn from him, then he is considered fully circumcised; see below.

65 In the first two cases, if the man is a Cohen.

66 In the Babli, 72a, Rav Huna states that the drawn [circumcised] is forbidden heave only by rabbinic standards; everybody in the Yarushalmi will agree.

67 Against the will of the person on whom the procedure is executed.

הִמּוֹל יִמּוֹל. גְּזֵירָה לִשְׁתֵּי מִילוֹת. אֶחָד לְמִילָה וְאֶחָד לִפְרִיעָה. אַחַת לִפְרִיעָה וְאַחַת לְצִיצִין. עַד כְּדוֹן כְּרִבִּי עֲקִיבָה דוּ אָמַר. לְשׁוֹנוֹת רִבּוּיִין הֵן. כְּרִבִּי יִשְׁמָעֵאל דוּ אָמַר. לְשׁוֹנוֹת כְּפוּלִין הֵן. הַתּוֹרָה דִיבְּרָה כְדַרְכָּהּ. הָלוֹךְ הָלַכְתָּ. כִּי נִכְסֹף נִכְסַפְתָּ. גֻּנֹּב גּוּנַּבְתִּי. מְנָלָן. אָמַר רִבִּי יוּדָה בַּר פָּזִי. אָז אָמְרָה חֲתַן דָּמִים לַמּוּלוֹת. מִיכָּן לִשְׁתֵּי מִילוֹת. אַחַת לְמִילָה וְאַחַת לִפְרִיעָה. אַחַת לְמִילָה וְאַחַת לְצִיצִין. רַב אָמַר. הִמּוֹל יִמּוֹל. מִיכָּן לְנוֹלָד כְּשֶׁהוּא מָהוּל שֶׁצָּרִיךְ לְהַטִּיף מִמֶּנּוּ דַם בְּרִית. הִמּוֹל יִמּוֹל. מִיכָּן לְיִשְׂרָאֵל עָרֵל שֶׁלֹּא יִמּוֹל עַד שֶׁיִּמּוֹל. וְאֵין צָרִיךְ לוֹמַר גּוֹי עָרֵל. אָמַר רִבִּי לֵוִי. כְּתִיב וְאַתָּה אֶת בְּרִיתִי תִשְׁמוֹר. אַתָּה וְכָל־כְּיוֹצֵא בָךְ.

"Circumcising he shall circumcise[68]." A decision for two circumcisions, one for the circumcision, the other for the uncovering[69]. One for the uncovering, the other for the fibers[70]. So far following Rebbi Aqiba who said, these are expressions of additions[71]. From where for Rebbi Ismael who said, these are double expressions in the style of the Torah, "going you went, desiring you desired, by stealing I was stolen[72]"? Rebbi Judah bar Pazi said, "then she said, a blood bridegroom for circumcisions[73]," from here that there are two circumcisions, one for the circumcision, the other for the uncovering; one for the uncovering, the other for the fibers. Rav said, "circumcising he shall circumcise," from here that one has to draw a drop of covenant blood from one born circumcised. "Circumcising he shall circumcise," from here that an uncircumcised Jew cannot circumcise until he circumcises himself; not to speak of an uncircumcised Gentile[74]. Rebbi Levi said, it is written: "But you have to keep my covenant." You and yours[75].

67 *Gen.* 17:13.

68 The follow-up to the act of circumcision in which the skin is cut and plied back to uncover the corona.

70 Eventual fibers of the prepuce which have to be cleaned from the wound. The same argument in the Babli, 72a.

71 This interpretation of double expressions is also attributed to R. Aqiba in the Babli, *Shevuot* 27b.

72 *Gen.* 31:30, a speech of Laban; 40:15, Josef's address to the cup-bearer. Both verses are without legal implications; this proves that the repetitions are a literary device to express emphasis. The same argument in Babli, *Avodah zarah* 27a.

73 *Ex.* 4:26, the inference is from the plural form מולות. {Modern interpreters take the words of the Ismaelite Ṣippora to be Arabic, "poor circumcised one, may it be for opulence".}

74 In *Gen. rabba* 46(8), this is the argument of R. Joḥanan.

75 In *Gen. rabba* 46(8), this is the argument of Rav Huna. In the Babli, *Avodah zarah* 27a, it is attributed to Rebbi.

תַּנֵי. יִשְׂרָאֵל מָל אֶת הַכּוּתִי (fol. 9a) וְהַכּוּתִי אֵינוֹ מָל אֶת יִשְׂרָאֵל מִפְּנֵי שֶׁהוּא מָהוּל לְשׁ֖ם הַר גְּרִיזִים. דִּבְרֵי רִבִּי יוּדָה. אָמַר לוֹ רִבִּי יוֹסֵה. וְכִי אֵיכָן מָצִינוּ בַּתּוֹרָה שֶׁהַמִּילָה צְרִיכָה כַוָּנָה. אֶלָּא יְהֵא מָל וְהוֹלֵךְ לְשֵׁם הַר גְּרִיזִים עַד שֶׁתֵּצֵא נַפְשׁוֹ. הַמּוֹשֵׁךְ לֹא יָמוֹל שֶׁלֹּא יָבוֹא לִידֵי סַכָּנָה. דִּבְרֵי רִבִּי יוּדָה. אָמַר לוֹ רִבִּי יוֹסֵי. הַרְבֵּה מְשׁוּכִין הָיוּ בִימֵי בֶּן כּוֹזְבָה וְכוּלָּן מָלוּ וְחָיוּ וְהוֹלִידוּ בָנִים וּבָנוֹת. הַמּוֹשֵׁךְ וְהַנּוֹלָד מָהוּל וְהַמָּל עַד שֶׁלֹּא נִתְגַּייֵר צָרִיךְ לְהַטִּיף מִמֶּנּוּ דַם בְּרִית. תַּנֵּי

רִבִּי שִׁמְעוֹן בֶּן אֶלְעָזָר. לֹא נֶחְלְקוּ בֵית שַׁמַּי וּבֵית הִלֵּל עַל שֶׁנּוֹלָד מָהוּל שֶׁצָּרִיךְ לְהַטִּיף מִמֶּנּוּ דַם בְּרִית מִפְּנֵי שֶׁהִיא עָרְלָה כְבוּשָׁה. עַל מַה נֶחְלְקוּ. עַל גֵּר שֶׁנִּתְגַּייֵר מָהוּל. שֶׁבֵּית שַׁמַּי אוֹמְרִים. צָרִיךְ לְהַטִּיף מִמֶּנּוּ דַם בְּרִית. וּבֵית הִלֵּל אוֹמְרִים. אֵין צָרִיךְ לְהַטִּיף מִמֶּנּוּ דַם בְּרִית. רִבִּי יִצְחָק בַּר נַחְמָן בְּשֵׁם רִבִּי הוֹשַׁעְיָה. הֲלָכָה כְדִבְרֵי הַתַּלְמִיד. אָתָא עוֹבְדָא קוֹמֵי רַב וְאָמַר. מָן הָא דְתַנֵּי. מִפְּנֵי שֶׁהִיא עָרְלָה כְבוּשָׁה. הָדָא אָמְרָה. עָרֵל בָּרוּר הוּא וְדוֹחִין עָלָיו אֶת הַשַּׁבָּת. רִבִּי אַבָּהוּ אָמַר. אֵין דּוֹחִין עָלָיו אֶת הַשַּׁבָּת וְצָרִיךְ לְהַטִּיף מִמֶּנּוּ דַם בְּרִית. רַב אָדָא בַּר אַחֲוָה אִתְיְלִיד לֵיהּ חַד בַּר נַשׁ כֵּן. מִיסְמֵס בֵּהּ מִית. אָמַר רִבִּי אָבִין נַעֲשֶׂה כְּרוּת שָׁפְכָה וְנִתְעַנֶּה עָלָיו שֶׁיָּמוּת. רַבָּנִין דְקֵיסָרִין אָמְרִין נַעֲשֶׂה פְּצוּעַ דַּכָּא וְנִתְעַנֶּה עָלָיו שֶׁיָּמוּת.

It was stated[76]: "A Jew may circumcise a Samaritan but a Samaritan may not circumcise a Jew since he is circumcised in the name of Mount Gerizim, the words of Rebbi Jehudah. Rebbi Yose said to him, where do we find in the Torah that circumcision needs intent? Let him continue to circumcise in the name of Mount Gerizim until he dies!" "The drawn should not circumcise [again] lest he get into danger, the words of Rebbi Jehudah. Rebbi Yose said to him, many drawn[77] ones were in the days of Ben Koziba, they all circumcised, lived, and begat sons and daughters. One has to draw a drop of covenant blood from the drawn [circumcised][63], the one born circumcised[64], and the circumcised before he converted.[64] Rebbi Simeon ben Eleazar stated: The House of Shammai and the House of Hillel did not disagree that one has to draw a drop of covenant blood from the one born circumcised since that is a compressed prepuce; what did they disagree about? About the convert who converted when already circumcised, for the House of Shammai said one has to draw a drop of covenant blood from him, but the House of Hillel say, one does not have to draw a drop of covenant blood from him."[78] Rebbi Issac bar Naḥman said in the name of Rebbi Hoshaia: Practice follows the words of the student[79]. There came a case before Rav, who said: Who is he who said that it is a compressed prepuce[80]? That means[81], he certainly is uncircumcised and one pushes the Sabbath away for him[82]. Rebbi Abbahu said, one does not push the Sabbath away for him but one has to draw a drop of covenant blood from him[83]. A male child was born to Rav Ada bar Ahawa in that condition[84]. He squeezed it, he died. Rebbi Abin said, his penis was damaged and he fasted for him that he should die. The rabbis of Caesarea said, his testicles became injured and he fasted for him that he should die.

76 Babli *Avodah zarah* 27a, Tosephta *Avodah zarah* 3:13.

77 They might have been forcibly circumcised in the general conscription ordered by Bar Kokhba.

78 *Sifra Tazria' Pereq* 1(7); also Tosephta *Shabbat* 15:9; Babli *Shabbat* 135a; *Gen. rabba* 46(9).

79 R. Simeon ben Eleazar, a student of R. Jehudah who is quoted in a *baraita* in the Babli as stating that the Houses of Shammai and Hillel disagree about the child born without prepuce.

80 Also in the Babli, *Shabbat* 135a, he is quoted as deciding practice following R. Jehudah.

81 The statement of R. Simeon ben Eleazar, who asserts flatly that the baby apparently without prepuce has a compressed prepuce, not that possibly he has one.

82 As explained in the next paragraph, a child born on the Sabbath is circumcised on the following Sabbath (if he is healthy enough to be circumcised on the eighth day.)

83 This is the uncontested anonymous decision of the Babli.

84 Babli *Shabbat* 135a. There, R. Ada bar Ahava accused himself of being punished for not following the ruling of his teacher Rav.

עָרְלָתוֹ וַדַּאי דּוֹחָה אֶת הַשַּׁבָּת. וְאֵין הַסָּפֵק דּוֹחֶה אֶת הַשַּׁבָּת. עָרְלָתוֹ וַדַּאי דּוֹחָה אֶת הַשַּׁבָּת. אֵין אַנְדְּרוֹגִינוֹס דּוֹחֶה אֶת הַשַּׁבָּת. שֶׁהָיָה רִבִּי יוּדָה אוֹמֵר. אַנְדְּרוֹגִינוֹס דּוֹחִין עָלָיו אֶת הַשַּׁבָּת וְחַיָּיבִין עָלָיו כָּרֵת. עָרְלָתוֹ וַדַּאי דּוֹחָה אֶת הַשַּׁבָּת וְאֵין בֵּין הַשְּׁמָשׁוֹת דּוֹחֶה אֶת הַשַּׁבָּת. עָרְלָתוֹ

וַדַּאי דוֹחָה אֶת הַשַּׁבָּת. אֵין שֶׁנּוֹלַד מָהוּל דוֹחֶה אֶת הַשַּׁבָּת. שֶׁבֵּית שַׁמַּי אוֹמְרִים. צָרִיךְ לְהַטִּיף מִמֶּנּוּ דַּם בְּרִית.

A certain prepuce pushes away the Sabbath, but a doubtful one does not push away the Sabbath. "His prepuce[85]", his certain prepuce pushes away the Sabbath, but the hermaphrodite does not push away the Sabbath even though Rebbi Jehudah said one pushes away the Sabbath for the hermaphrodite and is punished for him by divine extirpation[86]. "His prepuce", his certain prepuce pushes away the Sabbath, but the one born at dusk does not push away the Sabbath[87]. "His prepuce", his certain prepuce pushes away the Sabbath, but the one born circumcised does not push away the Sabbath even though the House of Shammai say one has to draw a drop of covenant blood from him[88].

85 *Lev.* 12:3: "On the eighth day, one circumcises the prepuce of his flesh." "The flesh" is the penis as boneless member; cf. *Ez.* 23:20. Since the commandment is unconditional, a baby boy born on the Sabbath has to be circumcised on the following Sabbath even though without the commandment it would be a desecration of the Sabbath and a capital crime.

From here to the end of the Halakhah, most of the text is also found in *Shabbat*, Chapter 18.

The text is from *Sifra Tazria' Pereq* 1(5), also quoted in Babli *Shabbat* 134b. The details are only applications of the general principle stated at the start.

86 He considers the hermaphrodite as a certain male. Therefore, cohabitation of a male with the female aspect of an hermaphrodite nevertheless is homosexual behavior; cf. Notes 243 ff.

87 When it is not clear whether the child was born on the Sabbath which starts at nightfall, which time is not well defined; cf. *Berakhot* Chapter 1, Notes 20 ff.

88 This disproves the earlier statement that the child apparently born without prepuce has a compressed one.

תַּמָּן תַּנִּינָן. הַכֹּל חַייָבִין בִּרְאִייָה חוּץ מֵחֵרֵשׁ שׁוֹטֶה וְקָטָן וטוּמְטוּם וְאַנְדְּרוֹגִינֹס. מַה אָמַר בָּהּ רִבִּי יוּדָה. נִישְׁמְעִינָהּ מִן הָדָא. רִבִּי יוֹחָנָן בֶּן דַּהֲבַאי אָמַר מִשּׁוּם רִבִּי יוּדָה. אַף הַסּוּמָא. לֵית בַּר נַשׁ אָמַר אַף אֶלָּא דוּ מוֹדֶה עַל קַדְמִייָתָא. מִחְלְפָא שִׁיטָּתֵיהּ דְּרִבִּי יוּדָה. תַּמָּן אָמַר פְּרָט. וְהָכָא אָמַר לְרַבּוֹת. רִבִּי יוּדָה וְרַבָּנִין מִקְרָא אֶחָד הֵן דּוֹרְשִׁין. רַבָּנִן דּוֹרְשִׁין. עָרֵל. מַה תַּלְמוּד לוֹמַר זָכָר. עַד שֶׁיְּהֵא כּוּלּוֹ זָכָר. רִבִּי יוּדָה דָּרַשׁ. זָכָר. מַה תַּלְמוּד לוֹמַר עָרֵל. וַאֲפִילוּ מִקְצָתוֹ עָרֵל. בְּרַם הָכָא כָּל־זְכוּרְךָ. פְּרָט לְאַנְדְּרוֹגִינֹס.

There[89], we have stated: "Everybody is required to be seen except the deaf-and-dumb, the insane, the minor, the sexless, and the hermaphrodite[90]." What says Rebbi Jehudah in this respect? Let us hear from the following. Rebbi Johanan ben Dahavai said in the name of Rebbi Jehudah, "also the blind one."[91] Nobody says "also" unless he agrees with the preceding statement. The argument of Rebbi Jehudah seems to be inverted. There he says to exclude, but here he says to include[92]. Rebbi Jehudah and the rabbis explain the same verse[93]. The rabbis explain "uncircumcised", why does the verse add "male"? Only if he is totally male[94]. Rebbi Jehudah explains "male", why does the verse add "uncircumcised"? Even if he is partially male[95]. But here, "all your maleness", that excludes the hermaphrodite.

89 Mishnah *Ḥagigah* 1:1. This refers to the duty of pilgrimage. *Ex.* 23:17: "Three times a year all your male population *should be seen* before the Lord, the Eternal."

90 The first three are not subject to commandments, the last two may not be males.

91 Tosephta *Ḥagigah* 1:1, Babli *Ḥagigah* 2a, 4b; *Sanhedrin* 4b; *Arakhin* 2b.

92 For the pilgrimage he agrees that the person whose masculinity is questionable is excluded but for circumcision he includes him as male.

93 *Gen.* 17:14: "An uncircumcised male who refuses to circumcise the prepuce of his flesh . . ."

94 They disregard the existence of societies practicing female

circumcision. *Shabbat* 136b/137a.

95 The same argument in the Babli,

תַּמָּן תַּנִּינָן. קָטָן הַחוֹלֶה אֵין מוֹלִין אוֹתוֹ עַד שֶׁיַּבְרִיא. שְׁמוּאֵל אָמַר. אֲפִילוּ אֲחָזָתוֹ הַחַמָּה שָׁעָה אַחַת מַמְתִּינִין לוֹ עַד שְׁלֹשִׁים יוֹם. וְאוֹתָן שְׁלֹשִׁים יוֹם מַהוּ לְהַאֲכִילוֹ מֵחֲלָבָהּ שֶׁלַּתְּרוּמָה. מַהוּ לְסוֹכוֹ שֶׁמֶן שֶׁלַּתְּרוּמָה. נִישְׁמְעִינָהּ מִן הָדָא. הֶעָרֵל וְכָל־הַטְּמֵאִים לֹא יֹאכְלוּ בִתְרוּמָה נְשֵׁיהֶם וְעַבְדֵיהֶם יֹאכְלוּ. רִבִּי אָחָא בְשֵׁם רִבִּי תַנְחוּם בֵּירִבִּי חִייָה. אֵין עָרְלָה אֶלָּא מִשְּׁמִינִי וְהָלְאָה. וְתַנֵּי כֵן. כָּל־שְׁלֹשִׁים יוֹם אָסוּר לְהַאֲכִילֹה חֲלָבָהּ שֶׁלַּתְּרוּמָה וְאָסוּר לְסוֹכוֹ בְּשֶׁמֶן שֶׁלַּתְּרוּמָה. לֵילֵי שְׁמִינִי מַה אַתְּ עֲבַד לָהּ. מִן מַה דְתַנֵּי. לֵילֵי שְׁמִינִי הַנִּכְנַס לַדִּיר לְהִתְעַשֵּׂר. הָדָא אָמְרָה. לֵילֵי שְׁמִינִי כִשְׁמִינִי הוּא. וְתַנֵּי כֵן. כָּל שִׁבְעַת הַיָּמִים מוּתָּר לְהַאֲכִילוֹ חֲלָבָהּ שֶׁלַּתְּרוּמָה וְאָסוּר לְסוֹכוֹ בְּשֶׁמֶן שֶׁלַּתְּרוּמָה.

There[96], we have stated: "One does not circumcise a sick baby until he gets well." Samuel said, even if he runs a fever for one hour one waits with him up to one month[97]. May one feed him with milk-substitute[98] from heave? May one rub him with heave oil? Let us hear from the following: "The uncircumcised and any impure persons may not eat heave; their wives and slaves may eat." Rebbi Aḥa in the name of Rebbi Tanḥum: The prepuce is counted only from the eighth day onward[99]. It was stated so: For the entire thirty days it is forbidden to feed him with milk-substitute from heave and forbidden to rub him with heave oil. How do you treat the night of the eighth day? Since it was stated: In the night of the eighth day it enters the corral to be tithed[100], that means that the night of the eighth is treated like the eighth day. It was stated so: All seven days long one is permitted to feed him with milk-substitute from heave and permitted to rub him with heave oil.

96 Mishnah *Shabbat* 19:5.

97 In the Babli, 71a and *Shabbat* 137a, he gives a minimum of 7 times 24 hours.

98 Some baby food made from heave grain.

99 The Babli, 71a, asserts the opposite, that uncircumcised babies of Cohanim may not be fed heave products.

100 A newborn animal is acceptable as sacrifice only after eight days. If a calf can be counted for tithing already in the night of the eighth day, that proves that one does not have to wait until it is daytime; Babli *Zebaḥim* 12a. Therefore, the baby may not be fed heave products between nightfall of the eighth day and the time of circumcision on the next morning.

תַּמָּן תְּנִינָן. אֵילּוּ הֵן הַצִּיצִין הַמְעַכְּבִין אֶת הַמִּילָה. רִבִּי אֲבִינָא בְשֵׁם רִבִּי יִרְמְיָה. בְּחוֹפֶה רוֹב גּוֹבְהָהּ שֶׁלָּעֲטָרָה. רִבִּי יוֹסֵי בֶּן יוֹסֵי אָמַר. בְּחוֹפֶה רוֹב גַּגָּהּ שֶׁלָּעֲטָרָה. רִבִּי טֵבִי בְשֵׁם שְׁמוּאֵל. בּוֹדְקִין אוֹתוֹ בְּשָׁעָה שֶׁהוּא מַקְשֶׁה. מָל וְלֹא פָרַע אֶת הַמִּילָה כִּילּוּ לֹא מָל. תַּנֵּי וְעָנוּשׁ כָּרֵת. רִבִּי אָחָא בְשֵׁם רִבִּי אַבָּהוּ. הָדָא דְתֵימַר בְּשֶׁאֵין בַּיּוֹם כְּדֵי לְמָרֵק. אֲבָל אִם יֵשׁ בַּיּוֹם כְּדֵי לְמָרֵק מְמָרֵק וְאֵינוֹ חוֹשֵׁשׁ.

There[101], we have stated: "These are the fibers which invalidate the circumcision." Rebbi Avina in the name of Rebbi Jeremiah: If it covers most of the height of the corona[102]. Rebbi Yose ben Yose[103] said, if it covers most of the top of the corona. Rebbi Tebi in the name of Samuel: One checks at the time of an erection[104]. "If he circumcised and did not fold back, it is as if he did not circumcise.[101]" It was stated: He is subject to divine extirpation[105]. Rebbi Aha in the name of Rebbi Abbahu: That is to say if there is no time left in the day to correct it. But if there is time left in the day to correct, he corrects without hesitation.

101 Mishnah *Shabbat* 19:6: These are the fibers which invalidate the circumcision: flesh that covers most of the corona. If he was fat, one has to fix it because of the bad appearance. If he circumcised and did not fold back, it is as if he did not circumcise.

102 Making clear that "most" in the Mishnah refers to the vertical, not the horizontal. In the Babli, *Shabbat* 137b, this is a statement of Rebbi Avina in the name of (the Babylonian) Rav

Jeremiah bar Abba. This is the correct version since R. Avina lived two generations before Rebbi Jeremiah (cf. *Berakhot* Chapter 6, Note 148).

103 Since he was a Galilean Amora of the last generation, his statement makes sense only if the preceding statement was Babylonian, i. e., that the Yerushalmi version also read "Rav Jeremiah bar Abba."

104 This refers to the fat baby mentioned in the Mishnah; if only the uncovered part of his corona is visible, nothing has to be done. In the Babli, *Shabbat* 137b, this is a statement of Samuel, modifying a tannaitic statement of Rabban Simeon ben Gamliel (Tosephta *Shabbat* 15:9).

105 The person who performs an invalid circumcision on the Sabbath.

תַּנֵּי. כָּל־שָׁעָה שֶׁהוּא עוֹסֵק בְּמִילָה חוֹזֵר. בֵּין עַל צִיצִין הַמְעַכְּבִין אֶת הַמִּילָה בֵּין עַל צִיצִין שֶׁאֵין מְעַכְּבִין אֶת הַמִּילָה. פֵּירַשׁ אֵינוֹ חוֹזֵר אֶלָּא עַל צִיצִין הַמְעַכְּבִין אֶת הַמִּילָה. אָמַר רִבִּי יוֹחָנָן. דִּבְרֵי רִבִּי יוֹסֵי אֲפִילוּ פֵּירַשׁ חוֹזֵר אֲפִילוּ עַל צִיצִין שֶׁאֵין מְעַכְּבִין אֶת הַמִּילָה. הֵיידָן רִבִּי יוֹסֵי הַהִיא דְתַנִּינָן תַּמָּן. רִבִּי יוֹסֵי אוֹמֵר. יוֹם טוֹב רִאשׁוֹן שֶׁלֶּחָג שֶׁחָל לִהְיוֹת בַּשַּׁבָּת. שָׁכַח וְהוֹצִיא אֶת הַלּוּלָב בִּרְשׁוּת הָרַבִּים פָּטוּר. מִפְּנֵי שֶׁהוֹצִיאוֹ בִרְשׁוּת. אַף בְּסַכִּין שֶׁלַּמִּילָה כֵן. אַף בְּמַצָּה כֵן. מִן מַה דְאָמַר רִבִּי יוֹחָנָן דִּבְרֵי רִבִּי יוֹסֵי אֲפִילוּ פֵּירַשׁ חוֹזֵר אֲפִילוּ עַל צִיצִין שֶׁאֵין מְעַכְּבִין אֶת הַמִּילָה. הָדָא אָמְרָה. אַף בְּסַכִּין שֶׁלַּמִּילָה כֵן אַף בְּמַצָּה כֵן.

It was stated[106]: As long as he is occupied with the circumcision, he may return both to fibers which invalidate the circumcision as also to fibers that do not invalidate the circumcision. Once he has stopped, he may return only to fibers which invalidate the circumcision. Rebbi Joḥanan said, the words of Rebbi Yose imply that even after he has stopped he may return even to fibers that do not invalidate the circumcision. Which [statement of] Rebbi Yose? That which we had stated there[107]: "Rebbi Yose said, if the first day of Tabernacles falls on a Sabbath and somebody forgot [that it was the Sabbath] and took the palm branch into the public domain he is free [from punishment] since he took it out with permission." Is it the same for the knife of circumcision, for a *maṣṣah*? Since Rebbi Joḥanan said, the words of Rebbi Yose imply that even after he has stopped he may return even to fibers that do not invalidate the circumcision, that means the same holds for the knife of circumcision, for a *maṣṣah*.

106 A *baraita* also quoted in Babli *Shabbat* 133b and determined there to disagree with R. Yose (the Tanna).

107 Mishnah *Sukkah* 3:14. R. Yose holds that since the Torah requires one to take a palm branch on the first day of Tabernacles (*Lev.* 23:40), even taking it out on the Sabbath cannot be punishable. The same then holds for the knife for a circumcision which must be performed on the Sabbath and the unleavened bread which *must* be eaten during the first night of Passover even if that happens to be on a Sabbath. (The remainder of Passover, leavened matter is forbidden but consumption of unleavened bread is not commanded.)

אִם לֹא יְדָעָהּ מִשֶּׁנַּעֲשָׂה פְצוּעַ דַּכָּא וּכְרוּת שָׁפְכָה הֲרֵי אֵילּוּ יֹאכְלוּ. אָמַר רִבִּי לָעְזָר. דְּרִבִּי לָעְזָר וְרִבִּי שִׁמְעוֹן הִיא. אָמַר רִבִּי יוֹחָנָן. דִּבְרֵי הַכֹּל הִיא. שַׁנְיָיא הִיא הָכָא שֶׁלֹּא הוֹסִיף בָּהּ קִינְיָין אֶחָד לִפְסוֹל. אַתְיָין אִילֵּין פְּלוּגְוָותָא כְּאִינּוּן פְּלוּגְוָותָא. דְּאִיתְפַּלְּגוֹן. שׁוֹמֶרֶת יָבָם כּוֹהֶנֶת שֶׁנָּפְלָה לִפְנֵי שְׁנֵי כֹּהֲנִים יְבָמִים. עָשָׂה בָהּ אֶחָד מֵהֶן מַאֲמָר. לֹא הִסְפִּיק לְכוֹנְסָהּ לַחוּפָּה שֶׁלַּנִּישּׂוּאִין עַד שֶׁנַּעֲשֶׂה פְצוּעַ דַּכָּא וּכְרוּת שָׁפְכָה. אָמַר רִבִּי שִׁמְעוֹן בֶּן לָקִישׁ. מִכֵּיוָן שֶׁהִיא זְקוּקָה לְבִיאָה פְסוּלָה פּוֹסֶלֶת. רִבִּי יוֹחָנָן אָמַר. לִכְשֶׁיִּבְעוֹל. הָיָה אֶחָד מֵהֶן כָּשֵׁר וְאֶחָד פָּסוּל אַף רִבִּי יוֹחָנָן מוֹדֶה. רִבִּי חִיָּיה בַּר אָדָא בְּעָא קוֹמֵי רִבִּי מָנָא. עָשָׂה בָהּ הַכָּשֵׁר מַאֲמָר. אָמַר לֵיהּ. מַחֲלוֹקֶת רִבִּי יוֹחָנָן וְרִבִּי שִׁמְעוֹן בֶּן לָקִישׁ.

"If he did not know her carnally after he was injured in his testicles or his penis was cut off, they may eat." Rebbi Eleazar said, this is Rebbi Eleazar's and Rebbi Simeon's[108]. Rebbi Joḥanan said, it is everybody's opinion; there is a difference since he did not add an acquisition to disable[109]. It turns out that this disagreement parallels the other disagreement, since they disagreed: A priestly woman waiting for her levir who became eligible to two priestly levirs. If one of them "bespoke" her but did not have occasion to bring her to the marriage chamber before he became injured in his testicles or his penis was damaged[110], Rebbi Simeon ben Laqish said, since she is a candidate for disabling intercourse, she is disabled. Rebbi Joḥanan said, when he will copulate[111]. If one of them was qualified but the other disqualified, even Rebbi Joḥanan agrees[112]. Rebbi Ḥiyya bar Ada asked before Rebbi Mana, if the qualified one "bespoke" her? He said to him, the disagreement of Rebbi Joḥanan and Rebbi Simeon ben Laqish[113].

108 They say in Mishnah 6:3 that a priestly woman who is disqualified for marriage to a priest but nevertheless betrothed to a priest may continue to eat heave up to the time of the actual marriage. A similar discussion is in the Babli, 75a.

109 The case is not comparable to that of a widow betrothed to a High Priest. In the latter case, the act of betrothal is an illegitimate act of acquisition which disqualifies the woman. But in the case here there was no transaction between the man and the woman which could change the latter's status.

110 Her situation is bad. If she goes ahead with the now forbidden marriage, she is disqualified from priestly prebends. If she does not go ahead, she needs a (rabbinic) divorce and becomes disqualified.

111 If she stays engaged permanently, neither married nor divorced, she can continue to eat heave indefinitely.

112 Her first husband's death confers on her the equal candidacy of both levirs. This is a disabling change of status.

113 But everybody will agree that marriage to the qualified levir will remove her temporary disability.

(fol. 8c) **משנה ב:** אֵי זֶהוּ פְּצוּעַ דַּכָּא. כָּל־שֶׁנִּפְצְעוּ הַבֵּצִים שֶׁלּוֹ וַאֲפִילוּ אַחַת מֵהֶן. וּכְרוּת שָׁפְכָה כַּל־שֶׁיִּכָּרֵת הַגִּיד וְנִשְׁתַּייֵר בָּעֲטָרָה אֲפִילוּ כְּחוּט כָּשֵׁר. פְּצוּעַ דַּכָּא וּכְרוּת שָׁפְכָה מוּתָּרִין בַּגִּיּוֹרֶת וּבַמְשׁוּחְרֶרֶת וְאֵינָן אֲסוּרִין אֶלָּא מִלָּבוֹא בַקָּהָל שֶׁנֶּאֱמַר לֹא יָבוֹא פְּצוּעַ דַּכָּא וּכְרוּת שָׁפְכָה בִּקְהַל יי.

Mishnah 2: Who is injured in his lower parts[114]? Everyone whose testicles are injured, even one of them. The one whose urethra[115] is cut off, anyone whose penis is cut, but he is qualified if there is a thread's[116] [breath] left of the corona. The ones injured in their testicles or with cut-off urethra are permitted [to marry] a convert or a manumitted woman; they are only forbidden to marry into the congregation[117], as it was said[118]: "No one with a damaged testicle or with cut-off penis may marry into the Eternal's congregation."

114 The Halakhah will investigate why דכא means the testicles. The Babli, 75b, and most moderns hold that the word means "crushed", the object crushed being understood without being mentioned. In the opinion of the Yerushalmi, the root of the word is דך "downtrodden", the lowest organ of the body.

115 Really "discharge pipe"; this meaning is used in the Halakhah.

116 In the Babli: A hair's breadth.

117 The definition of "congregation" is discussed in the Halakhah.

118 *Deut*. 23:2.

(fol. 9a) **הלכה ב:** אֵי זֶהוּ פְּצוּעַ דַּכָּא כול'. פְּצוּעַ. הָיִיתִי אוֹמֵר. עֵינוֹ. תַּלְמוּד לוֹמַר שָׁפְכָה. פָּצוּעַ שֶׁבְּצַד שָׁפְכָה. אִם פָּצוּעַ שֶׁבְּצַד שָׁפְכָה עֵינוֹ שֶׁבְּצַד חוֹטְמוֹ. תַּלְמוּד לוֹמַר דַּכָּא. שֶׁבָּא בֵין עֲקֵיבָיו. אָמַר רִבִּי חַגַּיי קוֹמֵי רִבִּי יוֹסֵי. אֵין לָךְ נָמוּךְ בָּאָדָם בְּשָׁעָה שֶׁהוּא יוֹשֵׁב אֶלָּא בֵיצָיו בִּלְבַד. אָמַר רִבִּי יוֹסֵי בֵּירִבִּי בוּן. וְיֵאוּת. תֵּדַע לָךְ שֶׁהוּא כֵן. שֶׁבְּכוּלָּן כְּתִיב דּוֹרוֹת חוּץ מִזֶּה שֶׁאֵינוֹ מוֹלִיד. וְלֹא סוֹף דָּבָר נִפְצְעָה אֶלָּא אֲפִילוּ נִימוֹקָה אֲפִילוּ יָבְשָׁה אֲפִילוּ חֲסֵרָה. תַּנֵּי. רִבִּי יִשְׁמָעֵאל בְּנוֹ שֶׁל רִבִּי יוֹחָנָן בֶּן בְּרוֹקָה אוֹמֵר. שָׁמַעְתִּי בְכֶרֶם בְּיַבְנֶה. כָּל־שֶׁאֵין לוֹ אֶלָּא בֵיצָה אַחַת אֵינוֹ מוֹלִיד וְהוּא סָרִיס חַמָּה. אָמַר רִבִּי יוֹסֵי. שָׁמַעְתִּי

הֲלָכָה כְרִבִּי יוֹחָנָן בֶּן בְּרוֹקָה. וְלֵית אֲנָא יְדַע מִן מַה שְׁמָעִית. אָמַר רִבִּי אִימִּי. לֹא הֲוָה רִבִּי יוֹסֵי שְׁמַע לָהּ מִן בַּר נַשׁ זָעִיר. שְׁמוּאֵל אָמַר. אִם יָבוֹא לְפָנַיי בַּעַל בֵּיצָה אַחַת אֲנִי מַכְשִׁירוֹ. רִבִּי חוּנָה אָמַר. דּוּ סָבַר כְּרִבִּי יִשְׁמָעֵאל בְּנוֹ שֶׁל רִבִּי יוֹחָנָן. אָמַר רִבִּי יוּדָן בַּר חָנִין. (fol. 9b) וּבִלְבַד שֶׁל יָמִין. אָתָא עוֹבְדָא קוֹמֵי רִבִּי אִימִּי. אָמַר לָהּ. אִין בְּרַתִּי דְּאַתְּ שַׁרְיָיה לֵיהּ. אֶלָּא הֲוֵי יְדָעָה דְלָא מוֹלִיד. וַהֲוָה רִבִּי זְעִירָא מְקַלֵּס לָהּ דּוּ מֵשִׂים מִילְּתָא עַל בְּרָרָא.

Halakhah 2: "Who is injured in his lower parts," etc. "Injured," I would have said in his eye. The verse says "discharge pipe[119]", he is injured in the neighborhood of the discharge pipe. If he is injured in the neighborhood of the discharge pipe it might be his eye in the neighborhood of his nose[120]! The verse says, "the lowly". What comes between his heels. Rebbi Ḥaggai said before Rebbi Mana, a man's lowest part when he sits down are his testicles. Rebbi Yose ben Rebbi Abun said, that is correct. You should know that this is so since in all other cases "generations" are written except in this case since he is infertile[121]. And not only if [a testicle] is injured but also if it is gangrenous, or dried up, or missing[122]. It was stated: Rebbi Ismael ben Rebbi Joḥanan ben Beroqa says: I heard in the vineyard at Jabne that nobody [born] with only one testicle can be fertile and he is a "sun eunuch"[123]. Rebbi Yose said, I heard that practice follows Rebbi Joḥanan ben Beroqa but I do not remember from whom I heard it. Rebbi Immi said, certainly Rebbi Yose did not hear it from a minor personality. Samuel said, if a person with only one testicle will come before me, I shall declare him qualified. Rebbi Ḥuna said, because he thinks like Rebbi Ismael ben Rebbi Joḥanan. Rebbi Yudan ben Ḥanin said, but only the one of the right hand side[124]. There came a case before Rebbi Immi. He said, yes, my daughter, you are permitted to him. But you should know that he is infertile. Rebbi Ze'ira praised him for making the case clear.

119 The original meaning of שפכה, translated in the Mishnah as "urethra".

120 Which also is a conduit for body discharges.

121 In all other marriage prohibitions in that group, *Deut.* 23:3-9, the prohibition includes descendants. Only in v. 2 there is no mention of descendants. This is the only argument accepted in the Babli, 75b.

122 A slightly different text, including punctured and excluding dried-up testicles, is in Tosephta 10:3 and Babli 75a.

123 A person infertile by natural causes is not forbidden to marry into the congregation. Rashba, in his commentary to the Babli 75a, has the version: "Rebbi Ismael ben Rebbi Joḥanan ben Beroqa says: I heard in the vineyard at Jabne that a person [born] with only one testicle *and* infertile is a 'sun eunuch'". The language in the Babli, 75a, seems to indicate that even a person who had one testicle removed with the second intact is not prohibited from marrying into the congregation.

124 Tosaphot *Yebamot* 75a/b, *s. v.* שאין read וּבִלְבַד שְׁלֵימִין "only if intact". This is by far the better reading but it is not accepted in the halakhic tradition.

אִית תַּנָּיֵי תַנֵּי. בִּידֵי אָדָם פָּסוּל בִּידֵי שָׁמַיִם כָּשֵׁר. אִית תַּנָּיֵי תַנֵּי. בֵּין בִּידֵי אָדָם וּבֵין בִּידֵי שָׁמַיִם פָּסוּל. מָאן דְּאָמַר. בִּידֵי אָדָם פָּסוּל בִּידֵי שָׁמַיִם כָּשֵׁר. יְלִיף לָהּ מִמַּמְזֵר. לֹא יָבֹא מַמְזֵר. לֹא יָבוֹא פְצוּעַ דַּכָּא. מַה מַמְזֵר בִּידֵי אָדָם אַף פְּצוּעַ דַּכָּא בִּידֵי אָדָם. מָאן דְּאָמַר. בֵּין בִּידֵי אָדָם וּבֵין בִּידֵי שָׁמַיִם פָּסוּל. מְנָן לֵיהּ. אָמַר רִבִּי מָנָא. מֵהָכָא. לֹא יָבוֹא פְצוּעַ דַּכָּא לְעוֹלָם. אָמַר רִבִּי יוֹסֵי בֵּירִבִּי בּוּן. עוֹד הוּא יְלִיף לָהּ מִמַּמְזֵר. לֹא יָבֹא מַמְזֵר. לֹא יָבוֹא פְצוּעַ דַּכָּא. מַה מַמְזֵר בִּידֵי שָׁמַיִם. אַף פְּצוּעַ דַּכָּא בִּידֵי שָׁמַיִם. וּמַמְזֵר בִּידֵי שָׁמַיִם. יְצִירָתוֹ בִּידֵי שָׁמַיִם. הֲוֹון בָּעֵיי מֵימַר. מָאן דְּאָמַר. בִּידֵי אָדָם פָּסוּל בִּידֵי שָׁמַיִם כָּשֵׁר. רִבִּי יִשְׁמָעֵאל בְּנוֹ שֶׁלְּרִבִּי יוֹחָנָן בֶּן בְּרוֹקָה. מָאן דְּאָמַר. בֵּין בִּידֵי אָדָם וּבֵין בִּידֵי שָׁמַיִם פָּסוּל כְּרַבָּנִן. אָמַר רִבִּי אָחָא בַּר פַּפֵּי קוֹמֵי רִבִּי זְעִירָא. כּוּלָּהּ דְּרַבָּנִן. הֲרֵי שֶׁעָלַת חַטָּטִין מְחַכֵּךְ בָּהּ אוֹ מַסִּיָּית. וַהֲרֵי הוּא בִּידֵי אָדָם כְּמִי שֶׁהִיא בִּידֵי שָׁמַיִם.

Some Tannaïm state: Through human action he is disqualified, through Heaven's action he is qualified[125]. Some Tannaïm state: He is disqualified both through human or Heaven's action[126]. He who said, through human action he is disqualified, through Heaven's action he is qualified, infers it from a bastard. "A bastard may not marry," "no one with a damaged testicle may marry." Just as a bastard is created by human action[127], so the one injured in a testicle is created by human action. He who said, he is disqualified both through human or Heaven's action, from where does he infer it? Rebbi Mana said, from here: "No one with a damaged testicle may marry," ever. Rebbi Yose ben Rebbi Abun said, he still infers it from a bastard. "A bastard may not marry," "no one with a damaged testicle may marry." Just as a bastard is created by Heaven's action, so the one injured in a testicle is created by Heaven's action. Is the bastard created by Heaven's action? His formation is by Heaven's action. They wanted to say that he who said, through human action he is disqualified, through Heaven's action he is qualified, follows Rebbi Ismael the son of Rebbi Johanan ben Beroqa; he who said, he is disqualified both through human or Heaven's action, [follows] the rabbis. Rebbi Aḥai bar Pappaios[128] said before Rebbi Ze'ira, all follows the rabbis. For instance, if scab developed and he rubbed or squeezed it off, that is human action induced by Heaven's action.

125 This is the only opinion reported in the Babli, 75b.

126 In the Tosephta, 10:3, this is the opinion of R. Joḥanan ben Beroqa.

127 There is no bastard without human incest or adultery. The same argument in the Babli, 75b.

128 Elsewhere, he is called R. Aḥa bar Pappus.

וּכְרוּת שָׁפְכָה כַּל־שֶׁנִּכְרַת הַגִּיד וְנִשְׁתַּיֵּיר בָּעֲטָרָה אֲפִילוּ כְּחוּט כָּשֵׁר. רִבִּי יוֹסֵי בְּשֵׁם רִבִּי חֲנִינָה. בָּעֲטָרָה הָעֶלְיוֹנָה. רִבִּי חִיָּיה בְּשֵׁם רִבִּי חֲנִינָה. בָּעֲטָרָה הַתַּחְתּוֹנָה. רִבִּי יְהוֹשֻׁעַ בֶּן לֵוִי אָמַר. בָּעֲטָרָה הַתַּחְתּוֹנָה. תַּמָּן אָמְרֵי. הֶעָשׂוּי כְּמַרְזֵב כָּשֵׁר. רִבִּי הִילָא בְשֵׁם רִבִּי יוֹחָנָן. כְּקוֹלְמוֹס הֲרֵי זֶה כָּשֵׁר. כְּקוֹלְמוֹס הָפוּךְ הֲרֵי זֶה פָּסוּל. נִיקַּב בּוֹ נֶקֶב. מִבִּפְנִים פָּסוּל מִבַּחוּץ כָּשֵׁר. רִבִּי בָּא בְשֵׁם רַב יְהוּדָה. מִן הָעֲטָרָה וְלִפְנִים. מִבַּחוּץ. מִן הָעֲטָרָה וְלַחוּץ. נִיקַּב הֲרֵי זֶה פָּסוּל. נִיסְתַּם הֲרֵי זֶה כָּשֵׁר. נִיקַּב הֲרֵי זֶה פָּסוּל מִפְּנֵי שֶׁהוּא שׁוֹפֵךְ. נִיסְתַּם הֲרֵי זֶה כָּשֵׁר מִפְּנֵי שֶׁהוּא מוֹלִיד. וְזֶהוּ פְּסוּל הַחוֹזֵר לְהֶכְשֵׁרוֹ. תַּנֵּי אֵין בֵּין פְּצוּעַ דַּכָּא לְבֵין כְּרוּת שָׁפְכָה אֶלָּא הִלְכוֹת רוֹפְאִין. שֶׁפְּצוּעַ דַּכָּא חוֹזֵר. שֶׁבִּכְרוּת שָׁפְכָה אֵינוֹ חוֹזֵר. כֵּיצַד הוּא עוֹשֶׂה. רִבִּי יַעֲקֹב בַּר אָחָא בְשֵׁם רִבִּי יוּדָה. מֵבִיא נֵימוֹלִין וּמַשְׁכִין וְקוֹצֵץ.

"The one whose urethra is cut off, anyone whose penis is cut, but he is qualified if there is a thread's [breath] left of the corona," etc. Rebbi Yose in the name of Rebbi Ḥanina: Of the upper side of the corona. Rebbi Ḥiyya in the name of Rebbi Ḥanina: Of the lower side of the corona. Rebbi Joshua ben Levi said, of the lower side of the corona[129]. There[130], they said, if it has the shape of a drainpipe, he is qualified. Rebbi Hila in the name of Rebbi Joḥanan, if it has the shape of a writing reed, he is qualified, of an inverted writing reed, he is disqualified[131]. If it is punctured, from the inside he is disqualified, from the outside he is qualified. Rebbi Abba in the name of Rav Jehudah, "inside" [means] from the corona towards the body; "outside" [means] from the corona away from the body. If it is punctured, he is disqualified; if it became blocked, he is qualified. If [the urethra] is punctured, he is disqualified, because it pours out; if it became blocked, he is qualified because he can be fertile[132]. That is a disqualification which can revert to a qualification. The only difference between one injured in his lower parts and one whose testicles are injured are medical rules since an injured testicle may heal, an injured urethra does not heal. What can he do? Rebbi Jacob bar Aḥa in the name of Rav Jehudah: He brings ants, lets them bite, and cuts them off[133].

129 In the Babli, 75b, it is only required that a hair's breadth of the corona be left along the greater part of the circumference of the penis.

130 In Babylonia. In the Babli, 75b, there are different opinions in the matter. Maimonides interprets the Babli as being parallel to the Yerushalmi; R. Jacob ben Asher (*Ṭur*) holds that the Babli opposes the Yerushalmi. A drainpipe is cut at a right angle to the pipe.

131 A writing reed (and a quill) is cut to be short at the top and long at the bottom; that is acceptable. But if the penis is cut short at the bottom and long at the top, it might not be possible to deliver the semen into the vagina and the man is disqualified for marriage.

132 Babli 76a.

133 Babli 76a. One clips off the bodies of the ants while they still hold the flesh together in their fangs.

רִבִּי חִלְקִיָּה רִבִּי סִימוֹן בְּשֵׁם רִבִּי יְהוֹשֻׁעַ בֶּן לֵוִי. לֹא שָׁנוּ אֶלָּא פְּצוּעַ דַּכָּא יִשְׂרָאֵל אֲבָל פְּצוּעַ דַּכָּא כֹהֵן לֹא בְדָא. תַּמָּן תַּנִּינָן. כָּל־הָאֲסוּרִין לָבוֹא בַקָּהָל פְּטוּרִין לָבוֹא זֶה בָזֶה. רִבִּי יוּדָה אוֹסֵר. רִבִּי יִרְמְיָה אָמַר. כְּלָלָא פְּצוּעַ דַּכָּא יִשְׂרָאֵל מוּתָּר לוֹ לִישָּׂא מַמְזֶרֶת. אָמַר רִבִּי יוֹסֵי. בִּלְבַד פְּסוּל מִשְׁפָּחָה. הָא פְּסוּל גּוּף לֹא בְדָא. חֵיילֵיהּ דְּרִבִּי יוֹסֵי מִן הָדָא דְּאָמַר רִבִּי חִלְקִיָּה רִבִּי סִימוֹן בְּשֵׁם רִבִּי יְהוֹשֻׁעַ בֶּן לֵוִי. לֹא שָׁנוּ אֶלָּא פְּצוּעַ דַּכָּא יִשְׂרָאֵל אֲבָל פְּצוּעַ דַּכָּא כֹהֵן כְּמַה דְאַתְּ אָמַר תַּמָּן. אִם כֹּהֵן בָּרוּר הוּא פְּסוּל לוֹ לִישָּׂא גִיּוֹרֶת. אַף הָכָא יִשְׂרָאֵל בָּרוּר אָסוּר לִישָּׂא מַמְזֶרֶת.

Rebbi Ḥilqiah, Rebbi Simon in the name of Rebbi Joshua ben Levi: One did state this[134] only for an Israel with an injured testicle, but not a Cohen with an injured testicle. There, we have stated[135]: "All those forbidden to marry into the congregation may marry one another; Rebbi Jehudah forbids." [136]Rebbi Jeremiah said, as a matter of principle, an

Israel with an injured testicle may marry a female bastard[137]. Rebbi Yose said, it[135] applies only to family blemishes, not to bodily defects. The strength of Rebbi Yose comes from the statement of Rebbi Ḥilqiah, Rebbi Simon in the name of Rebbi Joshua ben Levi: One did state this only for an Israel with an injured testicle, but not a Cohen, since, as you say there, if he is certainly a Cohen it is disabling if he married a convert[138]; here also, he is certainly an Israel and forbidden to marry a female bastard.

134 The statement in the Mishnah that people injured in their testicles may marry people forbidden to marry into the congregation. The injured Cohen remains a Cohen and may not marry at all; Babli 76a.

135 Mishnah *Qiddushin* 4:3.

136 This and the following paragraphs form Halakhah *Qiddushin* 4:3.

137 Since both are excluded from marrying into the congregation.

138 According to R. Joshua ben Levi, if he marries a convert (who is assumed to have had illicit sex before she converted) he becomes disabled for heave. For the Babli, 76a, a Cohen injured in his testicles is disabled for heave and may marry a convert, siding with R. Jeremiah.

עַל דַּעְתֵּיהּ דְּרִבִּי יוּדָה מַמְזֵר לֹא יִשָּׂא מַמְזֶרֶת. נִישְׁמְעִינָהּ מִן הָדָא דָּמַר רִבִּי אִימִּי תַּנֵּי רִבִּי יַעֲקֹב גֶּבַלָּיָא קוֹמֵי רִבִּי יוֹחָנָן רִבִּי יִצְחָק בַּר טֶבְלַיי בְּשֵׁם רִבִּי שִׁמְעוֹן בֶּן לָקִישׁ. דִּבְרֵי רִבִּי יְהוּדָה מַמְזֵר לֹא יִשָּׂא מַמְזֶרֶת כְּדֵי שֶׁיִּתְכַּלּוּ מַמְזֵירִין מִן הָעוֹלָם. וְדִכְוָותָהּ עֲמוֹנִי לֹא יִשָּׂא עֲמוֹנִית. אָמַר רִבִּי יוֹסֵי בֵּירִבִּי בּוּן. עַל דְּרַבָּנִין נִצְרְכָה. דְּאִין יִסְבּוֹר רִבִּי יוּדָה גֵּירִין פְּסוּלִין קְהַל יי אִינּוּן. לִישָּׂא עֲמוֹנִית אֵינוֹ יָכוֹל שֶׁהוּא קְהַל יי אֶצְלָהּ. לִישָּׂא מִצְרִית אֵינוֹ יָכוֹל שֶׁהוּא קְהַל יי אֶצְלָהּ. אָמַר רִבִּי מַתַּנְיָה. מְשַׁחְרְרִין לוֹ שִׁפְחָה. וְדִכְוָותָהּ מִצְרִי לֹא יִשָּׂא מִצְרִית. נִישְׁמְעִינָהּ מִן הָדָא. תַּנֵּי רִבִּי אַבָּהוּ קוֹמֵי רִבִּי יוֹחָנָן. אָמַר רִבִּי יוּדָה. בִּנְיָמִין גֵּר מִצְרִי הָיָה מִתַּלְמִידָיו שֶׁלְּרִבִּי עֲקִיבָה. אָמַר. אֲנִי גֵּר מִצְרִי נָשׂוּי לְגִיּוֹרֶת מִצְרִית. בְּנִי בֶן גֵּר מִצְרִי וַאֲנִי מַשִּׂיאוֹ לְגִיּוֹרֶת מִצְרִית. נִמְצָא בֶן בְּנִי כָּשֵׁר לָבוֹא בְקָהָל. אָמַר לוֹ רִבִּי עֲקִיבָה. לֹא בְנִי. אֶלָּא אַף אַתָּה הַשִּׂיאוֹ לְבַת גִּיּוֹרֶת מִצְרִית כְּדֵי שֶׁיְּהוּ שְׁלֹשָׁה דוֹרוֹת מִיכָּן וּשְׁלֹשָׁה דוֹרוֹת מִיכָּן.

In the opinion of Rebbi Jehudah, may a male bastard not marry a female bastard[139]? Let us hear from the following, as Rebbi Immi said, Rebbi Jacob from Gebal stated before Rebbi Joḥanan, Rebbi Isaac bar Tevele in the name of Rebbi Simeon ben Laqish: Rebbi Jehudah stated that a male bastard should not marry a female bastard so that bastards should disappear from the world[140]. Similarly, is an Ammonite man forbidden to marry an Ammonite woman? Was that needed for the rabbis? For if Rebbi Jehudah would think that disqualified converts form one of the Eternal's congregations, then [the Ammonite] could not marry an Ammonite woman since for her he would be of the Eternal's congregation[141]. He could not marry an Egyptian woman since for her he would be of the Eternal's congregation[142]. Rebbi Mattania said, one frees a slave girl for him. Similarly, could an Egyptian man not marry an Egyptian woman? Let us hear from the following, as Rebbi Abbahu stated before Rebbi Joḥanan: "Rebbi Jehudah said, Benjamin, an Egyptian convert, was a student of Rebbi Aqiba. He said, I am an Egyptian convert married to an Egyptian convert. My son is an Egyptian convert; I shall marry him to an Egyptian convert so that my grandson will be qualified to marry into the congregation[143]. Rebbi Aqiba said to him, my son, it is not so. But you marry him to the daughter of an Egyptian woman convert so that there should be three generations on every side.[144]"

139 In Mishnah *Qiddushin* 4:3 (Note 135), R. Jehudah makes a sweeping statement that no two people disqualified from marrying into the congregation may marry one another. The rabbis also will agree that a Moabite or Ammonite cannot marry a Moabite or Ammonite woman, cf. Mishnah 3. R. Jehudah may hold that converts form a congregation of their own and therefore bastards are prohibited from marrying them but are permitted to marry bastards, or he may hold, as is asserted later in the

Halakhah, that bastards should not marry any Jew and are prohibited from marrying other bastards.

140 In Mishnah *Qiddushin* 3:13, R. Tarphon counsels the male bastard to live with a slave girl whose children will be slaves not legally connected with him. If he converts (and therefore frees) his biological children at birth they will be converts, free from the taint of bastardy. The female bastard may marry a convert; since this marriage is legal and untainted, the child will be a convert, not a bastard (Mishnah *Qiddushin* 3:12).

141 The text given is the corrector's. The uncorrected text is inconsistent: שהוא קהל יי אצלו which probably should be שהיא קהל יי אצלו "for she belongs to the Eternal's congregation [forbidden] to him," cf. Mishnah 3.

142 For R. Jehudah only.

143 In the Babli, 78a, Rabba bar bar Ḥana justifies Benjamin against R. Aqiba since Mishnah *Qiddushin* 3:12 states that in all marriages that are perfectly lawful the status of the child is determined by that of the father alone.

144 The text (without R. Aqiba's remark) is in the Babli, *Yebamot* 76b, 78a; *Soṭah* 9a. A full text is in Tosephta *Qiddushin* 5:4. There, the text is up-to-date, following Mishnah *Yadaim* 4:5: "Rebbi Aqiba told him: Benjamin, you erred in the practice. Since Sanherib came and mixed all peoples {by mass deportations}, neither Ammonites and Moabites {permanently barred} nor Egyptians and Edomites {barred for two generations} are in their places . . . but everybody may marry one of any family on earth." But in Tosephta *Yadaim* 4:18 it is stated that from all peoples only the restrictions on Egyptians are valid since Ezechiel (29:13) certified that the Egyptians returned to their land. In any case, it is clear that R. Aqiba asserts that an Egyptian woman may marry an Egyptian man.

רַב יְהוּדָה בְשֵׁם רַב. הֲלָכָה כְרִבִּי לְעֶזֶר דִּבְרֵי חֲכָמִים. רִבִּי יִרְמְיָה בְשֵׁם רִבִּי שְׁמוּאֵל בַּר רַב יִצְחָק. כְּתִיב לֹא יָבֹא מַמְזֵר בִּקְהַל יי. בְּקָהָל בָּרוּר אֵינוֹ בָא. בָּא הוּא בִקְהַל סָפֵק.

Rav Jehudah in the name of Rav: Practice follows Rebbi Eliezer[145]. The words of the Sages[146]? Rebbi Jeremiah in the name of Rebbi Samuel bar Rav Isaac, it is written: "No bastard shall marry into the Eternal's congregation". He cannot marry into a congregation which is certain. He may marry if the membership in the congregation is questionable[147].

145 In Mishnah *Qiddushin* 4:3 he states that people who certainly are barred from marrying into the congregation may marry one another but that those of unclear status, foundlings and Samaritans, cannot marry. This and the next paragraphs are from *Qiddushin* 4:3.

146 Who permit people who are certainly excluded to marry those who are excluded only because of doubt.

147 The same argument is in Babli *Qiddushin* 73a.

תַּמָּן תַּנִּינָן סָפֵק בֶּן תֵּשַׁע לָרִאשׁוֹן סָפֵק בֶּן שִׁבְעָה לָאַחֲרוֹן. יוֹצִיא וְהַוְּלָד כָּשֵׁר וְחַיָּבִין בְּאָשָׁם תָּלוּי. תַּנֵּי. הָרִאשׁוֹן כָּשֵׁר לִהְיוֹת כֹּהֵן גָּדוֹל וְהַשֵּׁינִי מַמְזֵר בְּסָפֵק. רִבִּי אֱלְעָזָר בֶּן יַעֲקֹב אוֹמֵר. אֵין מַמְזֵר בְּסָפֵק. מוֹדֶה רִבִּי לִיעֶזֶר בֶּן יַעֲקֹב בִּסְפֵק כּוּתִים וּבִסְפֵק חֲלָלִים. כְּהַהִיא דְתַנִּינָן תַּמָּן. עֲשָׂרָה יוּחֲסִין עָלוּ מִבָּבֶל. עַל דַּעְתֵּיהּ דְּרִבִּי לִיעֶזֶר בֶּן יַעֲקֹב שְׁמוֹנֶה. עַל דַּעְתִּין דְּרַבָּן גַּמְלִיאֵל וְרִבִּי לִיעֶזֶר תִּשְׁעָה. עַל דַּעְתִּין דְּרַבָּנִן עֲשָׂרָה.

[148]There, we have stated: "If it is doubtful whether [the child is] a nine-month's child of the first [brother] or a seven-month's of the second, he has to divorce her, the child is legitimate, and they are obligated for a reparation offering for a possible sin." [149]It was stated: "The first son could be High Priest, any second son possibly is a bastard. Rebbi Eliezer ben Jacob said, there is no such thing as a possible bastard." Rebbi Eliezer ben Jacob agrees in cases of doubt of Samaritans and desecrated persons. This refers to what we have stated there: "Ten classes returned from Babylonia." In the opinion of Rebbi Eliezer ben Jacob, eight. In the opinion of Rabban Gamliel and Rebbi Eliezer, nine. In the opinion of the rabbis, ten.

148 Mishnah 4:2.

149 Halakhah 4:2, Notes 79-83.

אָמַר רִבִּי חִינְנָא. מַתנִיתָא דְלָא כְרִבִּי יוּדָה. דְּרִבִּי יוּדָה אָמַר. אַרְבָּעָה קְהִילוֹת אִינּוּן קָהָל. קְהַל כֹּהֲנִים. קְהַל לְוִיִּם. קְהַל יִשְׂרָאֵל. קְהַל גֵּרִים. מֵתִיבִין דְּרִבִּי יוּדָה. וְהָכְתִיב לֹא יָבֹא פְצוּעַ דַּכָּא פְּסוּל גּוּף אִינּוּן. וְהָכְתִיב בָּנִים אֲשֶׁר יִוָּלְדוּ לָהֶם דּוֹר שְׁלִישִׁי יָבֹא לָהֶם. בַּעֲשֵׂה אִינּוּן. וְרַבָּנִין אָמְרִין. שְׁלֹשָׁה קְהִילוֹת אִינּוּן. קְהַל כֹּהֲנִים. קְהַל לְוִיִּם. קְהַל יִשְׂרָאֵל. לֹא יָבֹא. לֹא יָבֹא. לֹא יָבֹא.

Rebbi Ḥinena said, the Mishnah[150] does not follow Rebbi Jehudah[151], since Rebbi Jehudah said that four congregations are called "congregation", the congregation of Cohanim, the congregation of Levites, the congregation of Israelites, the cogregation of converts. They objected to Rebbi Jehudah[152], but is it not written, "one injured in his testicles should not come"? That refers to bodily blemishes[153]. But is it not written, "children that will be born to them, the third generation shall come from them"? That is a positive commandment[154]. But the rabbis said, there are three congregations, the congregation of Cohanim, the congregation of Levites, the congregation of Israelites; "they shall not come, they shall not come, they shall not come[155]."

150 *Qiddushin* 4:1. The paragraph is from there, Halakhah 4:1.

151 The Mishnah states that converts may marry anybody, including bastards.

152 In verses *Deut*. 23:2-9, the expression "the Eternal's congregation" appears 6 times. Should there not be 6 congregations?

153 *Deut*. 23:2. This is a personal exclusion, not a generic one. This verse is not counted. Cf. Note 135.

154 *Deut*. 23:9. The prohibition of Egyptians and Edomites is only by inference. Since it is a positive commandment to let Egyptian converts of the third generation marry into the congregation, it follows that the first two may not. But as a positive commandment, an infraction of the rule is not prosecutable. R. Jehudah counts only mentionings of "the Eternal's congregation" connected to explicit prohibitions of groups.

155 The rabbis agree that four times one finds the expression לא יבא בקהל י״י, but only three are left for symbolical inferences since at least one is needed for the fact of the prohibition.

דִּלְמָה. רִבִּי הוֹשַׁעְיָה רוֹבָה וְרִבִּי יוּדָן נְשִׂיָּא הֲווֹן יְתִיבִין. רָהַט רִבִּי יוֹחָנָן וְלָחַשׁ לֵיהּ בְּאוּדְנָא דְּרִבִּי הוֹשַׁעְיָה רוֹבָה. פְּצוּעַ דַּכָּא כֹּהֵן מַהוּ שֶׁיִּשָּׂא בַּת גֵּרִים. אָמַר לֵיהּ. מַה אָמַר לָךְ. אָמַר לֵיהּ. מִילָּה דְנַגָּר בַּר נַגָּרִין לֹא מְפָרֵיק לֵיהּ. לֹא אָמַר לִי גִּיּוֹרֶת שֶׁהִיא כְּזוֹנָה אֶצְלוֹ. וְלֹא בַת יִשְׂרָאֵל שֶׁהִיא כְחַלָּלָה. לֹא אָמַר לִי אֶלָּא בַת גֵּרִים. וּבַת גֵּרִים לֹא כְיִשְׂרָאֵל הִיא. פָּתַר לָהּ כְּרִבִּי יוּדָה. דְּרִבִּי יוּדָה אוֹמֵר. בַּת גֵּר זָכָר כְּבַת חָלָל זָכָר.

Example. The elder Rebbi Hoshaia and Rebbi Judah Neśia were sitting together. Rebbi Joḥanan ran und whispered into Rebbi Hoshaia the elder's ear: May a Cohen who is injured in his testicles marry the daughter of converts? He[156] asked him, what did he tell you? He answered, a question which a carpenter, son of carpenters[157], cannot resolve. He did not ask me about a convert, since she is like a whore for him[158]. He did not ask about an Israelite daughter, for she will be desecrated[159]. He asked only about the daughter of converts! Is the daughter of converts not an Israel[160]? You have to explain it following Rebbi Jehudah, since Rebbi Jehudah says, the daughter of a male convert has the status of a desecrated male[161].

156 R. Jehudah Neśia.

157 A Sage, son of Sages.

158 Mishnah 6:5.

159 Since he remains a Cohen, he desecrates any woman forbidden to him.

160 Mishnah *Qiddushin* 4:6. If she was conceived after conversion, she is an Israel for everybody except R. Jehudah who excludes descendants of converts from the priesthood on basis of *Ez.* 44:22. Cf. *Bikkurim*, Chapter 1, Notes 96, 104.

161 Since R. Jehudah is not followed in practice, R. Joḥanan's question is answered in the negative even by a minor capacity such as R. Jehudah Neśia.

כֹּהֵן שֶׁבָּא עַל גְּרוּשָׁה וְהוֹלִיד בַּת וּבַת בַּת מַהוּ. רִבִּי חֲנַנְיָה וְרִבִּי מָנָא. חַד אָמַר. כְּשֵׁירָה. וְחַד אָמַר. פְּסוּלָה. מָתִיב מָאן דְּאָמַר כְּשֵׁירָה לְמָאן דְּאָמַר פְּסוּלָה. בַּת חָלָל זָכָר אֵינָהּ חֲלָלָה מִכְּהוּנָּה. אֵינָהּ מִיִּשְׂרָאֵל. מָה אַתְּ פּוֹסְלָהּ.

If a Cohen had intercourse with a divorcee and had a daughter, and the daughter a daughter, what is her status? Rebbi Ḥanania and Rebbi Mana, one said she is qualified, the other said she is disqualified. The one who said she is qualified objected to the one who said she is disqualified: The daughter of a desecrated male is desecrated for the priesthood. Is this one[162] not from an Israel? Why do you declare her disqualified?

162 The Cohen's granddaughter from an Israel son-in-law is explicitly qualified for the priesthood by Mishnah *Qiddushin* 4:6. An extended discussion of this case is in Halakhah *Qiddushin* 4:6.

רִבִּי יַעֲקֹב בַּר אִידִי בְּשֵׁם רִבִּי יְהוֹשֻׁעַ בֶּן לֵוִי. מַעֲשֶׂה בְּמִשְׁפָּחָה אַחַת בְּרוֹדוֹס שֶׁהָיוּ קוֹרִין עָלֶיהָ עִרְעֵר וְשָׁלַח רִבִּי אֶת רִבִּי רוֹמָנוּס לְבוֹדְקָהּ. וּבָדַק וּמָצָא שֶׁנִּתְגַּיְּירָה זְקֵינָתָהּ פָּחוֹת מִבַּת שָׁלֹשׁ שָׁנִים וְיוֹם אֶחָד. וְהִכְשִׁירָהּ לִכְהוּנָּה. רַב הוֹשַׁעְיָא אָמַר כְּרִבִּי שִׁמְעוֹן הִכְשִׁירָהּ. אָמַר רִבִּי זְעִירָא. דִּבְרֵי הַכֹּל הִיא הָכָא. דְּאָמַר רִבִּי זְעִירָה בְּשֵׁם רַב אָדָא (fol. 9c) בַּר אֲחָוָה רִבִּי יוּדָן מַטֵּי בָהּ בְּשֵׁם רַב. רִבִּי אַבָּהוּ בְּשֵׁם רִבִּי יוֹחָנָן. וּוְלַד בּוֹגֶרֶת כָּשֵׁר. שֶׁהִיא בְלֹא תַעֲשֶׂה שֶׁהוּא בָא מִכֹּחַ עֲשֵׂה. וְהוּא אִשָּׁה בִבְתוּלֶיהָ יִקָּח וְלֹא בוֹגֶרֶת. כָּל־לֹא תַעֲשֶׂה שֶׁהוּא בָא מִכֹּחַ עֲשֵׂה עֲשֵׂה הוּא. וְדִכְוָותָהּ כִּי אִם בְּתוּלָה מֵעַמָּיו יִקַּח אִשָּׁה וְלֹא גִיּוֹרֶת.[163] כָּל־לֹא תַעֲשֶׂה שֶׁבָּא מִכֹּחַ עֲשֵׂה עֲשֵׂה הוּא. הָתִיב רִבִּי הוֹשַׁעְיָה. הֲרֵי שֵׁינִי לְמִצְרִי הֲרֵי הוּא בְלֹא תַעֲשֶׂה שֶׁבָּא מִכֹּחַ עֲשֵׂה עֲשֵׂה הוּא. חָזַר רִבִּי הוֹשַׁעְיָה וְאָמַר. לֹא דוֹמֶה עֲשֵׂה בְּיִשְׂרָאֵל לַעֲשֵׂה שֶׁבַּכֹּהֲנִים. עֲשֵׂה שֶׁבְּיִשְׂרָאֵל אָסוּר בַּכֹּל. וַעֲשֵׂה שֶׁבַּכֹּהֲנִים אָסוּר בַּכֹּהֲנִים וּמוּתָּר בִּלְוִיִּם וּבְיִשְׂרָאֵל.

[164]Rebbi Jacob bar Idi in the name of Rebbi Joshua ben Levi: It happened that a family in Rhodes was in bad reputation. Rebbi sent Rebbi Romanus to investigate them. He investigated and found that a

grandmother had been converted at less than three years and a day of age, and he declared them fit for the priesthood. Rav Hoshaia said, he declared them fit following Rebbi Simeon. Rebbi Zeïra said, here it is everybody's opinion since Rebbi Zeïra said in the name of Rav Ada bar Ahava, Rebbi Judan brings it in the name of Rebbi Abbahu in the name of Rebbi Joḥanan: The child of an adult is fit since it is a prohibition deduced from a positive commandment. (*Lev.* 21:13) "But he shall take a wife in her virginity," which is a prohibition deduced from a positive commandment. Similarly, (*Lev.* 21:14) "only a virgin from among his people he shall take as wife," not a proselyte. Any prohibition deduced from a positive commandment is a positive commandment. Rebbi Hoshaia objected: But the second generation of an Egyptian is under a prohibition deduced from a positive commandment! Rebbi Hoshaia turned around and said, a positive commandment for an Israel cannot be compared to a positive commandment for Cohanim. A positive commandment for an Israel implies a prohibition for everybody. A positive commandment for Cohanim implies a prohibition for Cohanim but a permission for Levites and Israel.

163 Reading of the parallels. Text here: בוגרת by dittography from the preceding sentence.

164 Parallel text in *Bikkurim* 1:6, explained there in Notes 101-106, and *Qiddushin* 4:7.

(fol. 8c) **משנה ג:** עַמּוֹנִי וּמוֹאָבִי אֲסוּרִין וְאִיסוּרָן אִיסּוּר עוֹלָם אֲבָל נְקֵיבוֹתֵיהֶן מוּתָּרוֹת מִיָּד. מִצְרִי וַאֲדוֹמִי אֵינָם אֲסוּרִים אֶלָּא עַד שְׁלֹשָׁה דוֹרוֹת אֶחָד זְכָרִים וְאֶחָד נְקֵיבוֹת. אָמַר רִבִּי שִׁמְעוֹן קַל וְחוֹמֶר הַדְּבָרִים וּמָה אִם בִּמְקוֹם שֶׁאָסַר

אֶת הַזְּכָרִים אִיסּוּר עוֹלָם הִתִּיר אֶת הַנְּקֵיבוֹת מִיָּד. מָקוֹם שֶׁלֹּא אָסַר אֶת הַזְּכָרִים אֶלָּא עַד שְׁלֹשָׁה דוֹרוֹת אֵינוֹ דִין שֶׁנַּתִּיר אֶת הַנְּקֵיבוֹת מִיָּד. אָמְרוּ לוֹ אִם הֲלָכָה נְקַבֵּל וְאִם לַדִּין יֵשׁ תְּשׁוּבָה. אָמַר לָהֶם לֹא כִי הֲלָכָה אֲנִי אוֹמֵר. מַמְזֵירִין וּנְתִינִין אֲסוּרִים וְאִיסּוּרָן אִיסּוּר עוֹלָם אֶחָד זְכָרִים וְאֶחָד נְקֵיבוֹת.

Mishnah 3: Ammonites and Moabites are eternally forbidden but their females are immediately permitted. Egyptians and Edomites are forbidden only for three generations, both males and females. Rebbi Simeon said, is it not an argument *de minore ad majus*? If He permitted the females immediately in a case where the males are eternally forbidden, should we not permit the females in a case where He forbade the males only for three generations? They said to him: If it is practice[165], we shall accept this; if it is a logical argument, there is a counter-argument. He said to them, in fact, I am declaring practice. Bastards and Gibeonites are eternally forbidden, both males and females.

165 What in the Babli usually is called "practice going back to Moses on Mount Sinai", meaning accepted practice whose origin lies so far back that its originator can no longer be ascertained. The Mishnah speaks only of Jews.

(fol. 9c) **הלכה ג:** עַמּוֹנִי וּמוֹאָבִי אֲסוּרִין כול׳. עַמּוֹנִי וְלֹא עַמּוֹנִית. מוֹאָבִי וְלֹא מוֹאָבִית. וְדִכְוָותָהּ אֲדוֹמִי וְלֹא אֲדוֹמִית. מִצְרִי וְלֹא מִצְרִית. כְּתִיב עַל דְּבַר אֲשֶׁר לֹא קִדְּמוּ אֶתְכֶם בַּלֶּחֶם וּבַמַּיִם. הָיָה לָהֶם לַנָּשִׁים לְקַדֵּם. כְּתִיב אֲשֶׁר שָׂכַר עָלֶיךָ וַאֲשֶׁר יָעַץ. מִי דַרְכּוֹ לִשְׂכּוֹר. הָאִישׁ וְלֹא הָאִשָּׁה. מִי דַרְכּוֹ לִיָעֵץ. הָאִישׁ וְלֹא הָאִשָּׁה.

Halakhah 3: "Ammonites and Moabites are forbidden," etc. "Ammonite[166]," but not female Ammonite. "Moabite[166]," but not female Moabite. Similarly, "Edomite[167]" but not female Edomite, "Egyptian[167]" but not female Egyptian? It is written: "Because they did not receive you with bread and water[168]," should the women have received? "Who hired against you[169]," "who took counsel," who usually hires? Males but not females. Who usually sits in counsel? Males but not females.

166 *Deut.* 23:4.

167 *Deut.* 23:8.

168 *Deut.* 23:5, the reason for the exclusion of Ammonites and Moabites, even if converted.

169 *Micah* 6:5, speaking of Bileam being hired to curse the Israelites. The argument is slightly extended in *Sifry Deut.* #249, 250.

כְּתִיב וְשַׁחֲרַיִם הוֹלִיד בִּשְׂדֵה מוֹאָב מִן שִׁלְחוֹ אוֹתָם חוּשִׁים וְאֶת בַּעֲרָה נָשָׁיו. שַׁחֲרַיִם זֶה בּוֹעַז שֶׁהָיָה מְשׁוּחְרָר מִן הָעֲוֹנוֹת. הוֹלִיד בִּשְׂדֵה מוֹאָב שֶׁנָּשָׂא אֶת רוּת הַמּוֹאֲבִיָּה. מִן שִׁלְחוֹ אוֹתָם שֶׁהָיָה מִשִּׁבְטוֹ שֶׁלִּיהוּדָה. דִּכְתִיב בֵּיהּ וְאֶת יְהוּדָה שָׁלַח לְפָנָיו וגו'. חוּשִׁים וְאֶת בַּעֲרָה נָשָׁיו. וְכִי יֵשׁ לָךְ אָדָם שֶׁהוּא מוֹלִיד אֶת נָשָׁיו. אֶלָּא שֶׁחָשׁ כְּנָמֵר וּבֵיאֵר אֶת הֲלָכָה. וַיּוֹלֶד מִן חוֹדֶשׁ אִשְׁתּוֹ. לֹא צוֹרְכָה דְלֹא וַיּוֹלֶד מִן בַּעֲרָה נָשָׁיו. אֶלָּא עַל יָדֶיהָ נִתְחַדְּשָׁה הֲלָכָה. עַמּוֹנִי וְלֹא עַמּוֹנִית. מוֹאָבִי וְלֹא מוֹאָבִית.

It is written: "Shaḥaraim fathered children in the fields of Moab, after he had sent them, Ḥushim and Ba'arah his wives[170]." "Shaḥaraim," that is Boaz who was freed from sins. "He fathered children in the fields of Moab" because he married Ruth the Moabite. "After he had sent them,[171]" he was from the tribe of Judah, of whom it is written, "he sent Jehudah before him[172]". "Ḥushim and Ba'arah his wives," can anybody father his wives? But it means that he was quick as a panther and explained the practice. "He fathered from New Moon his wife[173]," should it not have been: he fathered from Baarah, one of his wives[174]? But through her, practice was newly defined: "Ammonite," and but female Ammonite. "Moabite," but not female Moabite.

170 *1Chr.* 8:8, speaking of the tribe of Benjamin. The verse probably means that he fathered children from a new Moabitic wife after he had divorced his two Benjaminite wives. The same text also in *Ruth rabba* 4:1.

171 The masoretic text reads מִן שִׁלְחוֹ אוֹתָם "after he had divorced them".

172 *Gen.* 46:28.

173 *1Chr.* 8:9. It might also mean: He fathered from his new wife.

174 The children of Ḥushim are mentioned in *1Chr.* 8:11; no children of Ba'arah are mentioned.

כָּתוּב אֶחָד אוֹמֵר. וּשְׁמוֹ יִתְרָא הַיִּשְׂרְאֵלִי. וְכָתוּב אֶחָד אוֹמֵר. יֶתֶר הַיִּשְׁמְעֵאלִי. רִבִּי שְׁמוּאֵל בַּר נַחְמָן אוֹמֵר. יִשְׁמְעֵאלִי הָיָה. וְאַתְּ אוֹמֵר יִשְׂרְאֵלִי. אֶלָּא שֶׁנִּכְנַס לְבֵית דִּינוֹ שֶׁלִּישַׁעְיָה וּמְצָאוֹ יוֹשֵׁב וְדוֹרֵשׁ פְּנוּ אֵלַי וְהִוָּשְׁעוּ כָּל־אַפְסֵי אָרֶץ. וְנִתְגַּייֵר. וְנָתַן לוֹ אֶת בִּתּוֹ. וְרַבָּנִין אָמְרִין. יִשְׂרְאֵלִי הָיָה. וְאַתְּ אוֹמֵר יִשְׁמְעֵאלִי. אֶלָּא שֶׁחָגַר מָתְנָיו כְּיִשְׁמְעֵאלִי וְנָעַץ אֶת הַחֶרֶב בְּבֵית דִּין. אוֹ נַהֲרוֹג אוֹ נֶהָרֵג אוֹ נְקַייֵם דִּבְרֵי רִבִּי. כָּל־מִי שֶׁהוּא עוֹבֵר עַל הֲלָכָה זוֹ בְּחֶרֶב זוֹ אֲנִי הוֹרְגוֹ. עַמּוֹנִי וְלֹא עַמּוֹנִית. מוֹאָבִי וְלֹא מוֹאָבִית. אָמַר רִבִּי שְׁמוּאֵל בַּר נַחְמָן. אֲנִי אֵין לִי אֶלָּא מִשְׁנָה. וַתָּשָׁב נָעֳמִי וְרוּת הַמּוֹאֲבִיָּה כַלָּתָהּ עִמָּהּ הַשָּׁבָה מִשְּׂדֵה מוֹאָב. זוֹ הִיא שֶׁשָּׁבָה מִשְּׂדֵה מוֹאָב תְּחִילָּה. אַחוֹרֵי אָמַר לָהּ. וַתַּעַזְבִי אָבִיךְ וְאִמֵּךְ. אָמַר לָהּ. אִילּוּ בָאת אֶצְלֵנוּ מֵאֶתְמוֹל שִׁלְשׁוֹם לֹא הָיִינוּ מְקַבְּלִים אוֹתָךְ.

One verse[175] says, "his name was Yitra the Israelite;" another verse says, "Yeter the Ismaelite[176]." Rebbi Samuel bar Naḥman said, he was an Ismaelite. And you say, he was an Israelite? But he entered the court of Isaiah[177] and found him sitting and explaining: "turn to me and be saved, all ends of the earth[178]," and converted. Then he gave him his daughter[179]. But the rabbis say, he was an Israelite, and you say, an Ismaelite? But he girded his loins like an Ismaelite and stuck his sword in the earth in court, to kill or be killed, to support the word of my teacher: I shall kill with this sword anybody who transgresses this practice: "Ammonite," and not female Ammonite; "Moabite," and not female Moabite. Rebbi Samuel bar Naḥman said, I have only what I did learn[180]:

"Naomi returned with Ruth the Moabite, her daughter-in-law, who returned from the fields of Moab[181]." She is the one who first returned from the fields of Moab. Afterwards, he[182] told her: "You abandoned your father and your mother." He said to her: If you had come to us yesterday or the day before, we would not have accepted you.

175 *2S.* 17:25.

176 *1Chr.* 2:17. Both names refer to the same person, father of Amasa, nephew of David.

177 It seems that the author of this piece identifies Isay with his descendant Isaiah 500 years later.

178 *Is.* 45:22.

179 It is very doubtful whether David's sisters ever agreed to live under the authority of a husband.

180 It is possible that instead of משנה one should read משׂדה, "I have only 'from the field'", referring to the preceding paragraph that שדה מואב is a catchword for Ruth the Moabite.

181 *Ruth* 1:22.

182 *Ruth* 2:11, a speech of Boaz. The implication is that Boaz was instrumental in declaring Moabite women eligible for marriage before he became involved with Ruth since otherwise he would have had to recuse himself from decision making. In the parallel in the Babli, 77a, the decision is directly attributed to the prophet Samuel.

תַּנָּה רִבִּי זַכַּיי קוֹמֵי רִבִּי יוֹחָנָן. בַּת גֵּר עַמּוֹנִי כְּשֵׁירָה. בַּת גִּיּוֹרֶת עֲמּוֹנִית פְּסוּלָה. אָמַר לֵיהּ רִבִּי יוֹחָנָן. בַּבְלַיְיָא. עָבַרְתָּ בְּיָדְךָ שְׁלֹשָׁה נְהָרִין וְאִתְאַבַּדְתָּ. אֶלָּא הִיא בַּת גֵּר עַמּוֹנִי הִיא בַּת גִּיּוֹרֶת עֲמּוֹנִית כְּשֵׁירָה. רִבִּי יוֹסָה בְשֵׁם רִבִּי יוֹחָנָן. לֹא כֵן צְרִיכָה בְּשֶׁהָיְתָה אִמָּהּ מִיִּשְׂרָאֵל. שֶׁלֹּא תֹאמַר. כְּשֵׁם שֶׁנִּתְחַלְּלָה אִמָּהּ כָּךְ נִתְחַלְּלָה בִתָּהּ. רִבִּי אַבָּהוּ בְשֵׁם רִבִּי יוֹחָנָן. כְּשֵׁירָה אֲפִילוּ לְכֹהֵן גָּדוֹל. מַה טַעֲמָא. בְּעַמָּיו. עַם שֶׁהֵן עֲשׂוּיִין שְׁנֵי עַמְמִין. זְכָרִים אֲסוּרִין וּנְקֵיבוֹת מוּתָּרוֹת. רִבִּי חַגַּיי בְשֵׁם רִבִּי פְדָת. רִבִּי שִׁמְעוֹן בֶּן לָקִישׁ לֹא אָמַר כֵּן אֶלָּא בַּת גֵּר עַמּוֹנִי פְּסוּלָה שֶׁהִיא בָאָה מִטִּיפָּה פְסוּלָה. אָמַר רִבִּי יוֹחָנָן. וְתַנֵּי כֵן. עַמְמִין זֶה בָּזֶה עַד שֶׁלֹּא נִתְגַּיְירוּ זְכָרִים אֲסוּרִין אִיסּוּר עוֹלָם וּנְקֵיבוֹתֵיהֶן מוּתָּרוֹת מִיָּד. נִתְגַּיְירוּ זְכָרִים אֲסוּרִין אִיסּוּר עוֹלָם וּנְקֵיבוֹתֵיהֶן מוּתָּרוֹת לְאַחַר שְׁלֹשָׁה דוֹרוֹת.

רבי חִזְקִיָּה בְּשֵׁם אָחָא. מַתְנִיתָא אָמְרָה כֵן. מְנַיִין אַתָּה אוֹמֵר. אֶחָד מִכָּל־מִשְׁפְּחוֹת הָאֲרָצוֹת שֶׁבָּא עַל אַחַת מִן הַכְּנַעֲנִים וְיָלְדָה מִמֶּנּוּ בֵּן מוּתָּר לִקְנוֹתוֹ עֶבֶד. תַּלְמוּד לוֹמַר אֲשֶׁר הוֹלִידוּ בְּאַרְצְכֶם. וְלֹא מִן הַגָּרִים אֲשֶׁר בָּאָרֶץ.

Rebbi Zakkai stated before Rebbi Joḥanan: The daughter of an Ammonite convert is enabled, the daughter of an Ammonite woman convert is disabled. Rebbi Joḥanan told him: Babylonian, you crossed three rivers on your way and got lost! But both the daughter of an Ammonite convert and the daughter of an Ammonite woman convert are enabled[183]. Rebbi Yosa in the name of Rebbi Joḥanan: The statement is needed only if her mother was from Israel. That you should not say, since her mother was desecrated, so the daughter is desecrated. Rebbi Abbahu in the name of Rebbi Joḥanan, she is enabled even for the High Priest. What is the reason? "In his peoples[184]". A people divided into two peoples, the males are forbidden but their females permitted. Rebbi Ḥaggai in the name of Rebbi Pedat: Rebbi Simeon ben Laqish did not say so, but the daughter of an Ammonite convert is disabled since she comes from a disabled drop[185]. Rebbi Joḥanan said, we have stated thus: Of Gentiles married unconverted, the males are permanently forbidden but their females are immediately permitted. If they converted, the males are permanently forbidden but their females are permitted after three generations[186]. Rebbi Ḥizqiah in the name of [Rebbi] Aḥa: A *baraita* states this: From where can you say that if one of any of the families of the earth cohabited with a Canaanite woman and she gave birth to a son, that you may buy him as a slave? The verse says, "whom they will father in your land,[187]" not from those who dwell in your land.

183 It seems that R. Zakkai only had heard the statement that the daughter of a male Ammonite convert was enabled to be married into the

priesthood and concluded that the insistence on a male would imply the quite unreasonable implication that the daughter of a female Ammonite would be disabled. R. Johanan points out that the statement on the daughter of a male Ammonite convert is needed for itself if the mother is an Israelite woman. Since the marriage of the parents is forbidden, the mother becomes desecrated for the priesthood. It is noteworthy that the disability does not extend to the daughter.

In the Babli, 77b, one version of the statement of R. Zakkai is explicit: The daughter of an Ammonite and an Israelite woman is disabled. This is rejected by R. Johanan.

184 *Lev.* 21:14, speaking of the High Priest, "only a virgin from among his people he may take as a wife." In the Babli, 77b, R. Zakkai is the source of this argument but he wrongly requires the (converted) parents to be from the same people.

185 Babli 77a, a different reason ascribed to him.

186 If an Ammonite and an Egyptian woman married as Gentiles, the children are Ammonites since in permitted marriages the child's status is that of the father. But if they married when converted, the child inherits the disabilities of both parents. Therefore, the daughter, who does not inherit any disability from her father, has the status of a second generation Egyptian from her mother (in the opinion of the rabbis who reject R. Simeon's argument.)

The Babli, 78a, formulates this explicitly: Among Gentiles, the status of the father is determining. If they converted, the more disabled is determining.

187 *Lev.* 25:45. In v. 44 it is stated that slaves may be bought (only) from the surrounding peoples, since Canaanites are not to be tolerated in the Land. It is then stated that a child fathered in the Land can be tolerated if his father was not a Canaanite; the argument is parallel to that of the *baraita* quoted earlier. The same statement is in the Babli, 78a.

שְׁמוּאֵל בַּר אַבָּא בָּעֵי. עֲבָדִים מַהוּ שֶׁיַּעֲלֶה לָהֶם דּוֹרוֹת. הֵיךְ עֲבִידָה. גֵּר עֶבֶד עַמּוֹנִי שֶׁנָּשָׂא לְגִיוֹרֶת שִׁפְחָה מִצְרִית לְאַחַר שְׁלֹשָׁה דוֹרוֹת נִתְגַּייְרוּ. אִין תֵּימַר. עֲבָדִים עָלוּ לָהֶם דּוֹרוֹת זְכָרִים אֲסוּרִין אִיסּוּר עוֹלָם וּנְקֵיבוֹת מוּתָּרוֹת לְאַחַר שְׁלֹשָׁה דוֹרוֹת.

Samuel bar Abba asked: Are generations counted for slaves? How is that? A converted[188] Ammonite slave who married a converted Egyptian slave. After three generations they converted[189]. If you say that generations are counted for slaves, the males are permanently forbidden but the females are permitted after three generations[190].

188 A slave circumcised as property of a Jew who will become a full Jew upon manumission.

189 As it stands, this makes no sense. One may either emend the text to read "were manumitted" instead of "converted" or one may read the fact of manumission into the expression "converted into full Jews".

190 I. e., the females are permitted immediately upon manumission of the third generation.

אָמְרוּ לוֹ אִם הֲלָכָה נְקַבֵּל. אִם לַדִּין יֵשׁ תְּשׁוּבָה. מַה הָיָה לָהֶם לְהָשִׁיב. רִבִּי אַבָּהוּ בְּשֵׁם רִבִּי יוֹסֵי בֵּירִבִּי חֲנִינָה. הֲרֵי בֶן בְּנוֹ וּבֶן בִּתּוֹ הֲרֵי הֵן אֲסוּרִין עַד שְׁלֹשָׁה דוֹרוֹת אֶחָד זְכָרִים וְאֶחָד נְקֵיבוֹת. רִבִּי אַבָּהוּ אָמַר. רִבִּי שִׁמְעוֹן בֶּן לָקִישׁ בָּעֵי. מְשִׁיבִין דָּבָר שֶׁהוּא מַמְזֵר עַל דָּבָר שֶׁאֵינוֹ מַמְזֵר. רִבִּי חַגַּיי אָמַר. רִבִּי אַבָּהוּ בָּעֵי. מְשִׁיבִין דָּבָר שֶׁהוּא כָּרֵת עַל דָּבָר שֶׁאֵינוֹ כָּרֵת. אָמַר לָהֶן לֹא כִי הֲלָכָה אֲנִי אוֹמֵר וּמִקְרָא מְסַייְעֵינִי. בָּנִים. לֹא בָנוֹת.

"They said to him: If it is practice, we shall accept this; if it is a logical argument, there is a counter-argument." What could they have argued? Rebbi Abbahu in the name of Rebbi Yose ben Rebbi Ḥanina: Are not his grandchildren forbidden for three generations, both male and female[191]? Rebbi Abbahu said that Rebbi Simeon ben Laqish questioned, does one argue a matter concerning bastardy in a matter not concerning bastardy? Rebbi Ḥaggai said that Rebbi Abbahu questioned, does one argue a matter concerning extirpation in a matter not concerning extirpation? He said to them, in fact, I am declaring practice and a verse supports me. "Sons," not daughters[192].

191 In *Lev.* 18:17, incest with direct descendents is forbidden for three generations, equally for males and females. The Babli, 77b, has the same argument. There, the two questions of R. Abbahu are answered in the negative; incest prohibitions which concern capital crimes cannot be used as counter arguments in an argument *de minore ad majus* involving simple prohibitions (regarding Ammonites and Moabites) or prohibitions derived from a positive commandment (regarding Edomites and Egyptians) but they may be used in applications of rules 3 and 4 of R. Ismael (under conditions not recognized by the Yerushalmi.)

192 *Deut.* 23:9: "Sons that will be born to them in the third generation shall come (masc.) for them into the Eternal's congregation." The entire sentence is in the masculine.

רִבִּי יַעֲקֹב בַּר אָחָא בְשֵׁם רִבִּי יֹאשִׁיָּא. דּוֹר אַחַד עָשָׂר שֶׁבְּמַמְזֵר כְּרִבִּי שִׁמְעוֹן כָּשֵׁר. וְלֹא דָרַשׁ עֲשִׂירִי. תַּנֵּי. רִבִּי אֶלְעָזָר בֵּירִבִּי שִׁמְעוֹן אוֹמֵר. דּוֹר אַחַד עָשָׂר שֶׁבְּמַמְזֵר זְכָרִים אֲסוּרִין נְקֵיבוֹת מוּתָּרוֹת. אַף הָכָא זְכָרִים אֲסוּרִין נְקֵיבוֹת מוּתָּרוֹת. רִבִּי שְׁמוּאֵל בְּרֵיהּ דְּרִבִּי יוֹסֵי בֵּירִבִּי בּוּן אָמַר. אַתְיָא דְּרִבִּי לְעְזָר בֵּירִבִּי שִׁמְעוֹן כְּרִבִּי מֵאִיר. כְּמַה דְרִבִּי מֵאִיר אָמַר. גְּזֵירָה שָׁוָה בְּמָקוֹם שֶׁכָּתוּב. כֵּן רִבִּי [ ] בֵּירִבִּי שִׁמְעוֹן אוֹמֵר. גְּזֵירָה שָׁוָה בְּמָקוֹם שֶׁכָּתוּב. מַה לְהַלָּן זְכָרִים אֲסוּרִין נְקֵיבוֹת מוּתָּרוֹת. אַף הָכָא זְכָרִים אֲסוּרִין וּנְקֵיבוֹת מוּתָּרוֹת. מֵעַתָּה אֲפִילוּ מִיָּד. בִּלְבַד מֵעֲשִׂירִי וּלְמַעֲלָן.

Rebbi Jacob bar Aḥa in the name of Rebbi Josia: The eleventh generation of bastards is qualified[193] following Rebbi Simeon; he does not use the principle of *gezerah šawah*[194]. It was stated: Rebbi Eleazar ben Rebbi Simeon says, in the eleventh generation of bastards, the males are forbidden and the females permitted. Here also the males are forbidden and the females permitted[195]. Rebbi Samuel ben Rebbi Yose ben Rebbi Abun said, it turns out that Rebbi Eleazar ben Rebbi Simeon follows the argument of Rebbi Meïr. As Rebbi Meïr said, a *gezerah šawah* is as if written in a verse, so Rebbi [Eleazar] ben Rebbi Simeon says, a *gezerah šawah* is as if written in a verse. Here also, the males are forbidden and the females permitted. In that case, even immediately? Only from the tenth and further.

193 As marriage partners for all Jews.

194 The principle that identical expressions must have identical legal implications (R. Ismael's rule #2). *Deut.* 23:3 forbids the bastard *even up to the tenth generation.* Verse 4 forbids Ammonites and Moabites *even up to the tenth generation, forever.* The rule of *gezerah šawah* is invoked in *Sifry Deut.* #248, 249 to imply that the prohibition of the bastard also is *forever.*

195 R. Eleazar ben R. Simeon disagrees with his father and accepts the *gezerah šawah*, with the automatic consequence that it can be applied only to males since in the case of Ammonites it applies only to males. Female bastards are forbidden only to the tenth generation as stated explicitly in the verse.

שָׁאֲלוּ אֶת רִבִּי אֱלִיעֶזֶר. דּוֹר אַחַד עָשָׂר שֶׁבְּמַמְזֵר מַהוּ. אָמַר לָהֶן. הָבִיאוּ לִי דּוֹר שְׁלִישִׁי וַאֲנִי מְטַהֲרוֹ. וּמַה טַעֲמָא דְּרִבִּי אֱלִיעֶזֶר. דְּלָא הֲוָה אַתְיָיא דְרִבִּי לִיעֶזֶר כְּרִבִּי חֲנִינָה. דְּאָמַר רִבִּי חֲנִינָה. אַחַת לְשִׁשִּׁים וּלְשִׁבְעִים שָׁנָה הַקָּדוֹשׁ בָּרוּךְ הוּא מֵבִיא דֶבֶר בָּעוֹלָם וּמְכַלֶּה מַמְזֵרֵיהֶן וְנוֹטֵל אֶת הַכְּשֵׁירִין עִמָּהֶן שֶׁלֹּא לְפַרְסֵם אֶת חַטָּאֵיהֶן. וְאַייְתִינָהּ כַּיי דָמַר רִבִּי לֵוִי בְשֵׁם רִבִּי שִׁמְעוֹן בֶּן לָקִישׁ. בִּמְקוֹם אֲשֶׁר תִּשָּׁחֵט הָעוֹלָה תִּשָּׁחֵט הַחַטָּאת לִפְנֵי יי. שֶׁלֹּא לְפַרְסֵם אֶת הַחַטָּאִים. וּמַה טַעַם. וְגַם הוּא חָכָם וַיָּבֵא רָע. לֹא מִסְתַּבְּרָה דְלֹא אֶלָּא זֶהוּ וַיָּבֵא טוֹב. אֶלָּא לְלַמְּדָךְ שֶׁאֲפִילוּ רָעָה שֶׁמֵּבִיא הַקָּדוֹשׁ בָּרוּךְ הוּא בָּעוֹלָם בְּחָכְמָה הוּא מְבִיאָהּ. וְאֶת דְּבָרָו לֹא הֵסִיר. כָּל־כָּךְ לָמָּה. וְקָם עַל בֵּית מְרֵיעִים וְעַל עֶזְרַת פּוֹעֲלֵי אָוֶן. וְאַתְיָיא כְּהַהִיא דָמַר רִבִּי לֵוִי בְשֵׁם רִבִּי שִׁמְעוֹן בֶּן לָקִישׁ. בִּמְקוֹם אֲשֶׁר תִּשָּׁחֵט הָעוֹלָה תִּשָּׁחֵט הַחַטָּאת לִפְנֵי יי. שֶׁלֹּא לְפַרְסֵם אֶת הַחַטָּאִים. רַב הוּנָא אָמַר. אֵין מַמְזֵר חַי יוֹתֵר מִשְּׁלֹשִׁים יוֹם. רִבִּי זְעִירָא כַּד סְלַק לְהָכָא שְׁמַע קָלִין קָרְייָן. מַמְזֵירָא וּמַמְזֵירְתָא. אָמַר לוֹן. מַהוּ כֵן. הָא אֲזִילָא הַהִיא דְּרַב הוּנָא. דְּרַב הוּנָא אָמַר. אֵין מַמְזֵר חַי יוֹתֵר מִשְּׁלֹשִׁים (fol. 9d) יוֹם. אָמַר לֵיהּ רִבִּי יַעֲקֹב בַּר אָחָא. עִמָּךְ הָיִיתִי כַּד אָמַר רִבִּי בָּא רַב הוּנָא

בְּשֵׁם רַב. אֵין מַמְזֵר חַי יוֹתֵר מִשְּׁלֹשִׁים יוֹם. אֵימָתַי. בִּזְמַן שֶׁאֵינוֹ מְפוּרְסָם. הָא אִם הָיָה מְפוּרְסָם חַי הוּא.

They asked Rebbi Eliezer, what is the status of the eleventh generation of a bastard? He said to them, bring to me a third generation and I shall declare him pure[196]. What is Rebbi Eliezer's reason since he does not seem to follow Rebbi Ḥanina? As Rebbi Ḥanina said, once every sixty to seventy years the Holy One, praise to Him, brings a plague into the world to finish off the bastards and he takes the qualified ones with them in order not to publicize the sinners[197]. This parallels what Rebbi Levi said in the name of Rebbi Simeon ben Laqish: "In the place where the ascent offering has its throat cut before the Eternal, the purification sacrifice has its throat cut,[198]" in order not to publicize the sinners. What is the reason? "[199]Also He is wise and brings evil;" should it not rather be "brings good"? But to teach you that even the evil that the Holy One, praise to Him, brings to the world, He brings in wisdom. "His word He did not remove," why all this? "He overcomes the house of evildoers and accomplices of workers of iniquity." That parallels what Rebbi Levi said in the name of Rebbi Simeon ben Laqish: "In the place where the ascent offering has its throat cut before the Eternal, the purification sacrifice has its throat cut," in order not to publicize the sinners. Rav Huna said, no bastard lives more than thirty days[200]. When Rebbi Ze'ira immigrated here, he heard voices call "he-bastard, she-bastard". He said, what is this? There goes that of Rav Huna, since Rav Huna said, no bastard lives more than thirty days. Rebbi Jacob bar Aḥa said to him, I was with you when Rebbi Abba, Rav Huna said in the name of Rav: No bastard lives more than thirty days, when? If it is unknown. Therefore, if it is known, he lives[201].

196 The same statement is in the Babli, 78b.

197 This describes the situation in the later Roman Empire where the plague had become endemic during the reign of the emperor Hadrian.

198 *Lev.* 6:18; the purification sacrifice atones for inadvertent sins. In the Babli, *Soṭah* 32b, the statement is by R. Joḥanan in the name of R. Simeon bar Iohai.

199 *Is.* 31:2.

200 A convenient legal fiction which allows every male to marry every female without investigating his or her background. The same statement in the Babli, 78b.

201 In the parallel, *Qiddushin* 3:13, the argument is by Rebbi Uqba bar Aḥa. In the Babli, 78b, the entire argument is R. Ze'ira's, based on a statement of his teacher Rav Jehudah.

רִבִּי יָסָא בְשֵׁם רִבִּי יוֹחָנָן. אַף לְעָתִיד לָבוֹא אֵין הַקָּדוֹשׁ בָּרוּךְ הוּא נִזְקַק אֶלָּא לְשִׁבְטוֹ שֶׁלְּלֵוִי. מֵאי טַעֲמָא. וְיָשַׁב מְצָרֵף וּמְטַהֵר כֶּסֶף וְטִהַר אֶת בְּנֵי לֵוִי וְזִקַּק אוֹתָם כול׳. אָמַר רִבִּי זְעוּרָא. כְּאָדָם שֶׁהוּא שׁוֹתֶה בְּכוֹס נָקִי. אָמַר רַב הוֹשַׁעְיָה. בְּגִין דַּאֲנָן לְוִיִּים נַפְסִיד. אָמַר רִבִּי חֲנִינָה בְּרֵיהּ דְּרִבִּי אַבָּהוּ. אַף לְעָתִיד לָבוֹא הַקָּדוֹשׁ בָּרוּךְ הוּא עוֹשֶׂה עִמָּהֶן צְדָקָה. וּמַה טַעֲמָא. וְהָיוּ לַיי מַגִּישֵׁי מִנְחָה בִּצְדָקָה.

Rebbi Yasa in the name of Rebbi Joḥanan: In the future, the Holy One, praise to Him, will only deal with the tribe of Levi[202]. What is the reason? "[203]The refiner will sit, the purifier of silver, and will refine them," etc. Rebbi Ze'ira said, like a man who only drinks from a clean cup. Rav Hoshaia said, because we are Levites, should we lose? Rebbi Ḥanina the son of Rebbi Abbahu said, also in the future, the Holy One, praise to Him, will deal with them charitably. What is the reason? "[203]They will be for the Eternal presenters of an offering in charity."

202 He denies that all bastards automatically disappear (cf. *Qiddushin* 3:13) and holds that in the days of the Messiah only from the tribe of Levy will they be eliminated by divine action.

In the Babli, *Qiddushin* 70b, the same verse is used to declare that the tribe of Levi is cleansed of bastards first of all the tribes.

203 *Mal.* 3:3.

אָמַר רִבִּי יוֹחָנָן. כָּל־מִשְׁפָּחָה שֶׁנִּשְׁתַּקֵּעַ בָּהּ פְּסוּל אֵין מְדַקְדְּקִין אַחֲרֶיהָ. אָמַר רִבִּי שִׁמְעוֹן בֶּן לָקִישׁ. מַתְנִיתָא אָמְרָה כֵן. מִשְׁפַּחַת בֵּית צְרִיפָה הָיְתָה בְּעֵבֶר הַיַּרְדֵּן וְרִיחֲקָהּ בֶּן צִיּוֹן בִּזְרוֹעַ. וְעוֹד אַחֶרֶת הָיְתָה שָׁם וְקֵרְבָהּ בֶּן צִיּוֹן בִּזְרוֹעַ. אַף עַל פִּי כֵן לֹא בִיקְשׁוּ חֲכָמִים לְפַרְסְמָן. אֲבָל חֲכָמִים מוֹסְרִין אוֹתָן לִבְנֵיהֶן וּלְתַלְמִידֵיהֶן פַּעֲמַיִים בַּשָּׁבוּעַ. אָמַר רִבִּי יוֹחָנָן. הָעֲבוֹדָה שֶׁאֵינִי מַכִּירָן וְנִשְׁתַּקְּעוּ בָהֶן גְּדוֹלֵי הַדּוֹר. אָמַר רִבִּי יְהוֹשֻׁעַ בֶּן לֵוִי. חֲמֵשֶׁת אֲלָפִים עֲבָדִים הָיוּ לוֹ לְפַשְׁחוּר בֶּן אִמֵּר הַכֹּהֵן וְכוּלָּן נִשְׁתַּקְּעוּ בִכְהוּנָּה גְדוֹלָה. הֵן הֵן עַזֵּי פָנִים שֶׁבַּכְּהוּנָּה. אָמַר רִבִּי לָעְזָר. עִיקַּר טִירוֹנִיָּא שֶׁבָּהֶן וְעַמְּךָ כִּמְרִיבֵי כֹהֵן. אָמַר רִבִּי אַבָּהוּ שְׁלֹשׁ עֶשְׂרֵה עֲיָרוֹת נִשְׁתַּקְּעוּ בַּכּוּתִיִּים בִּימֵי הַשְּׁמָד. אָמְרִין הָדָא עִירוֹ דְמוֹשְׁהָן מִינְּהוֹן.

Rebbi Joḥanan said, one does not investigate a family in which a family disqualification[204] has disappeared. Rebbi Simeon ben Laqish said, a Mishnah says so: "There was a family in Bet Ṣerifa in Transjordan who was forcibly distanced by Ben Ṣion. Another [family] was there who was forcibly integrated by Ben Ṣion.[205]" Nevertheless, the Sages did not want to make their names public[206]. But the Sages transmit them to their sons and students two times in a Week[207]. Rebbi Joḥanan said, by the Temple service, I know them[208] and the leading personalities of the generation have disappeared in them. Rebbi Joshua ben Levi said, Pashḥur ben Immer the priest had 5000 slaves[209], and their traces have disappeared in the high priesthood. These are the insolent in the priesthood. Rebbi Eleazar said, their main training[210]: "Your people is like quarrelsome priests." Rebbi Abbahu said, Samaritans[211] disappeared in thirteen villages in the times of persecution. They said, the village of Moshhan[212] is one of them.

204 Either a disqualification of bastardy or a disqualification for the priesthood.

205 Mishnah *Idiut* 8:7. It is not known who this Ben Ṣion was. The text states that one family was deemed unworthy of marrying into priesthood against the will of the rabbis and one was declared worthy also against the will of the rabbis. Cf. Babli *Qiddushin* 70a.

206 This proves R. Joḥanan's point that one may not investigate accepted families for disqualifications.

207 A sabbatical period of 7 years.

208 Reading אני for the ms. איני, following the *editio princeps*. Another formulation of the same statement in the Babli, *Qiddushin* 70a.

209 4000 in the Babli, *Qiddushin* 70a. Cf. *Jer.* 20:1.

210 In modern Hebrew טִירוֹנוּת, from Latin *tiro* "recruit", cf. *Ma'aser Šeni* p.

214. The verse, *Hos.* 4:4, proves that priest were quarrelsome long before Jeremiah's time and strong-armed behavior is ingrained in Cohanim even without any admixture of slaves. The same argument by R. Eleazar in the Bablim *Qiddushin* 69b.

211 Who might be bastards in the rabbinic view; cf. Chapter 4, Note 82.

212 The village and the time of persecution are not identified.

(fol. 8c) **משנה ד:** אָמַר רִבִּי יְהוֹשֻׁעַ שָׁמַעְתִּי שֶׁהַסָּרִיס חוֹלֵץ וְחוֹלְצִין אֶת אִשְׁתּוֹ וְהַסָּרִיס לֹא חוֹלֵץ וְלֹא חוֹלְצִין אֶת אִשְׁתּוֹ וְאֵין לִי לְפָרֵשׁ. אָמַר רִבִּי עֲקִיבָה אֲנִי אֲפָרֵשׁ סְרִיס אָדָם חוֹלֵץ וְחוֹלְצִין אֶת אִשְׁתּוֹ מִפְּנֵי שֶׁהָיְתָה לוֹ שְׁעַת הַכּוֹשֶׁר. סְרִיס חַמָּה לֹא חוֹלֵץ וְלֹא חוֹלְצִין אֶת אִשְׁתּוֹ מִפְּנֵי שֶׁלֹּא הָיְתָה לוֹ שְׁעַת הַכּוֹשֶׁר. רִבִּי אֱלִיעֶזֶר אוֹמֵר לֹא כִי אֶלָּא סְרִיס חַמָּה חוֹלֵץ וְחוֹלְצִין אֶת אִשְׁתּוֹ מִפְּנֵי שֶׁיֵּשׁ לוֹ רְפוּאָה. סְרִיס אָדָם לֹא חוֹלֵץ וְלֹא חוֹלְצִין אֶת אִשְׁתּוֹ מִפְּנֵי שֶׁאֵין לוֹ רְפוּאָה. הֵעִיד רִבִּי יְהוֹשֻׁעַ בֶּן בְּתֵירָה עַל בֶּן מְגֵיסָה שֶׁהָיָה בִירוּשָׁלַםִ סְרִיס אָדָם וְיִיבְּמוּ אֶת אִשְׁתּוֹ לְקַיֵּים דִּבְרֵי רִבִּי עֲקִיבָה.

Mishnah 4: Rebbi Joshua said, I heard[213] that the castrate performs *ḥalîṣah* and one performs *ḥalîṣah* for his wife, and that the castrate does not perform *ḥalîṣah* and one does not perform *ḥalîṣah* for his wife, and I cannot explain. Rebbi Aqiba said, I shall explain it. A castrate by human action performs *ḥalîṣah*[214] and one performs *ḥalîṣah* for his wife since he had been qualified; a congenital castrate[215] does not perform *ḥalîṣah* and one does not perform *ḥalîṣah* for his wife since he never had been qualified. Rebbi Eliezer said, it is not so, but a congenital castrate performs *ḥalîṣah* and one performs *ḥalîṣah* for his wife since he might be healed, a castrate by human action does not perform *ḥalîṣah* and one does not perform *ḥalîṣah* for his wife since he cannot be healed. Rebbi Joshua ben Bathyra testified about Ben Megisa in Jerusalem that he was a castrate by human action and they instructed that levirate be performed for his wife, to endorse the words of Rebbi Aqiba.

משנה ה: הַסָּרִיס לֹא חוֹלֵץ וְלֹא מְיַיבֵּם וְכֵן אַיילוֹנִית לֹא חוֹלֶצֶת וְלֹא מִתְייַבֶּמֶת. הַסָּרִיס שֶׁחָלַץ לִיבִמְתּוֹ לֹא פְסָלָהּ בְּעָלָהּ פְּסָלָהּ מִפְּנֵי שֶׁהִיא בְּעִילַת זְנוּת. וְכֵן אַיילוֹנִית שֶׁחָלְצוּ לָהּ אַחִין לֹא פְסָלוּהָ. בְּעָלוּהָ פְּסָלוּהָ מִפְּנֵי שֶׁבְּעִילָתָהּ בְּעִילַת זְנוּת.

Mishnah 5: The castrate does not perform either *ḥalîṣah* or levirate; similarly, the she-ram does not perform either *ḥalîṣah* or levirate[216]. The castrate who performed *ḥalîṣah* for his sister-in-law did not disable her[217]; if he copulated with her he disabled her because it is incestuous[218]. Similarly, if the brothers performed *ḥalîṣah* for a she-ram, they did not disable her; if they copulated with her they disabled her because it is incestuous.

213 An ancient tradition.

214 He certainly cannot perform levirate since he is not qualified to marry in the congregation. But his widow might be married in levirate.

215 Literal translation: "A sun castrate".

216 This Mishnah overrules the previous one even though usually the statement that a certain action had been executed determines practice.

217 All he did was an empty

gesture.

218 Since levirate is permitted only if the couple can have children (*Deut.* 25:6). Therefore, if one of the partners is certified sterile, the sister-in-law is under the incest prohibition of *Lev.* 18:16.

(fol. 9d) **הלכה ה:** אָמַר רִבִּי יְהוֹשֻׁעַ שָׁמַעְתִּי כול׳. הַסָּרִיס לֹא חוֹלֵץ כול׳. וְכֵן אַיילוֹנִית שֶׁחָלְצוּ כול׳. אֵי זֶהוּ סְרִיס חַמָּה. רִבִּי חִייָה בְשֵׁם רִבִּי יוֹחָנָן. כָּל־שֶׁלֹּא רָאָתוֹ הַחַמָּה בְכוֹשֶׁר אֲפִילוּ שָׁעָה אַחַת. הוֹשִׁיט יָדוֹ וְסֵירְסוֹ מִבִּפְנִים. דִּבְרֵי הַכֹּל אָסוּר לָבוֹא בַקָּהָל וְאֵינוֹ לֹא חוֹלֵץ וְלֹא מְייַבֵּם. נוֹתְנִין עָלָיו חוּמְרֵי סְרִיס אָדָם וּסְרִיס חַמָּה בְּמַחֲלוֹקֶת.

Halakhah 5: "Rebbi Joshua said, I heard," etc. "That the castrate does not perform *ḥalîṣah*," etc. "Similarly, if the brothers performed *ḥalîṣah* for a she-ram," etc. What is a sun-castrate? Rebbi Ḥiyya in the name of Rebbi Joḥanan, anybody whom the sun did not see qualified even for one hour[219]. If somebody stretched out his hand and castrated [the not yet born baby] in the womb, everybody agrees that [when born] he is prohibited from marrying into the congregation and he cannot perform either *ḥalîṣah* or levirate. One imposes upon him the restrictions of both castrate by human action and sun-castrate[220] in this disagreement.

219 The same argument in the Babli, 79b/80a.

220 Since he is both.

מִחְלְפָה שִׁיטָּתֵיהּ דְּרִבִּי אֱלִיעֶזֶר. תַּמָּן הוּא אוֹמֵר. לֹא כִּי אֶלָּא סְרִיס חַמָּה חוֹלֵץ וְחוֹלְצִין לְאִשְׁתּוֹ. וְאַתְּ אָמַר הָכֵין. אָמַר רִבִּי אִינְיָא. לֹא אָמַר רִבִּי אֱלִיעֶזֶר אֶלָּא לְעוֹנְשִׁין.

The argument of Rebbi Eliezer is inverted. There, he says "it is not so, but a congenital castrate performs *ḥalîṣah* and one performs *ḥalîṣah* for his wife," and you say so? Rebbi Iniah said, Rebbi Eliezer referred only to criminal responsibility[221].

221 This paragraph is copied from the lost fifth chapter of Tractate *Niddah*. In the Mishnah there, the House of Hillel say that 20 year olds of both sexes who have not developed pubic hair should prove their age and then are declared as congenital castrate or she-ram and unable to perform either *ḥalîṣah* or levirate. The House of Shammai puts the age limit at 18 and R. Eliezer at 18 for the female and 20 for the male. From his silence about levirate one concludes that he agrees that the congenital castrate cannot perform either *ḥalîṣah* or levirate, in contradiction to his statement here in Mishnah 4.

The answer, given in the Babli 80a by the Amora R. Eleazar, is that R. Eliezer only refers to the declaration of adulthood for the sun-castrate and the she-ram; for all other persons adulthood starts with the development of pubic hair.

רִבִּי חִיָּיה בְּשֵׁם רִבִּי יוֹחָנָן. זוֹ דִבְרֵי רִבִּי לִיעֶזֶר וְרִבִּי יְהוֹשֻׁעַ וְרִבִּי עֲקִיבָה. אֲבָל דִּבְרֵי חֲכָמִים אֶחָד סְרִיס אָדָם וְאֶחָד סְרִיס חַמָּה אֵינוֹ לֹא חוֹלֵץ וְלֹא חוֹלְצִין לְאִשְׁתּוֹ. לֹא מְייַבֵּם וְלֹא מְייַבְּמִין אֶת אִשְׁתּוֹ. דּוּ מַתְנִיתָא. הַסָּרִיס שֶׁחָלַץ לִיבִמְתּוֹ לֹא פְסָלָהּ. בְּעָלָהּ פְּסָלָהּ מִפְּנֵי שֶׁהִיא בְּעִילַת זְנוּת. אַנְדְּרוֹגִינֹס שֶׁחָלַץ לִיבִמְתּוֹ לֹא פְסָלָהּ. בְּעָלָהּ פְּסָלָהּ מִפְּנֵי שֶׁהִיא בְּעִילַת זְנוּת. וְכֵן אַיְילוֹנִית שֶׁחָלְצוּ לָהּ אַחִין לֹא פְסָלוּהָ. בְּעָלוּהָ פְּסָלוּהָ מִפְּנֵי שֶׁבְּעִילָתָהּ בְּעִילַת זְנוּת.

Rebbi Ḥiyya in the name of Rebbi Joḥanan: These are the words of Rebbi Eliezer, Rebbi Aqiba, and Rebbi Joshua. But the words of the Sages are that neither the castrate by human action nor the congenital castrate is able to perform *ḥalîṣah* nor does one perform *ḥalîṣah* for his wife[222]. He cannot perform levirate, nor does one marry his wife in levirate. That is the Mishnah: "The castrate who performed *ḥalîṣah* for his sister-in-law did not disable her; if he copulated with her, he disabled her because it is incestuous." The hermaphrodite who performed *ḥalîṣah* for his sister-in-law did not disable her; if he copulated with her, he disabled her because it is incestuous[223]. "Similarly, if the brothers performed *ḥalîṣah* for a she-ram, they did not disable her; if they copulated with her, they disabled her because it is incestuous."

222 The Babli, 80b, disagrees and holds that Mishnah 5 explains Mishnah 4 and refers only to the congenital castrate who parallels the she-ram, following R. Aqiba.

223 The Tosephta 2:6 and 11:2, equates all rules of the hermaphrodite with those of the congenital castrate. It seems that this tradition (ascribed to Rebbis Yose and Simeon in the next Mishnah) considers the hermaphrodite as a congenitally infertile male.

(fol. 8c) **משנה ו:** סְרִיס חַמָּה כֹּהֵן שֶׁנָּשָׂא בַת יִשְׂרָאֵל מַאֲכִילָהּ בַּתְּרוּמָה. רִבִּי יוֹסֵי וְרִבִּי שִׁמְעוֹן אוֹמְרִים אַנְדְּרוֹגִינוֹס כֹּהֵן שֶׁנָּשָׂא בַת יִשְׂרָאֵל מַאֲכִילָהּ בַּתְּרוּמָה. רִבִּי יְהוּדָה אוֹמֵר טוּמְטוּם שֶׁנִּקְרַע וְנִמְצָא זָכָר לֹא יַחֲלוֹץ מִפְּנֵי שֶׁהוּא כְסָרִיס. אַנְדְּרוֹגִינוֹס נוֹשֵׂא אֲבָל לֹא נִישָּׂא. רִבִּי לָעְזָר אוֹמֵר אַנְדְּרוֹגִינוֹס חַייָבִין עָלָיי סְקִילָה כְּזָכָר.

Mishnah 6: A congenital castrate priest who married an Israel daughter enables her to eat heave[224]. Rebbi Yose and Rebbi Simeon say, an hermaphrodite[225] priest who married an Israel daughter enables her to eat heave. Rebbi Jehudah says, a seemingly sexless[226] who was cut open and found to be a male does not perform *ḥalîṣah* since he is like a castrate. The hermaphrodite marries but is not married[227]. Rebbi Eleazar says [a male] is guilty to be stoned for [homosexual intercourse] with an hermaphrodite as with a male.

224 He has a penis but no visible testicles. He is not injured in his testicles and, therefore, able to marry in the congregation.

225 Since he has a penis and testicles, he is a male and may marry. That he also has female breasts and a vagina is irrelevant.

226 He was born without apparent penis or vagina. If it turns out that he has a penis, covered by skin, that can be laid bare, he still is congenitally infertile.

227 A male marries, a female is married.

(fol. 9d) **הלכה ו:** סְרִיס חַמָּה כֹּהֵן כול'. תַּנֵּי. מַאֲכִילָהּ בְּחָזֶה וְשׁוֹק. רִבִּי יוֹחָנָן אוֹמֵר. אוֹכֶלֶת בִּתְרוּמָה וְאֵינָהּ אוֹכֶלֶת בְּחָזֶה וְשׁוֹק. רִבִּי שִׁמְעוֹן בֶּן לָקִישׁ אָמַר. כַּמָּה קוּלֵּי חוֹמְרִין בַּדָּבָר. רִבִּי יוֹסֵי בֵּירִבִּי חֲנִינָה בְּעָא קוֹמֵי רִבִּי שִׁמְעוֹן בֶּן לָקִישׁ. מַהוּ כַּמָּה קוּלֵּי חוֹמְרִין בַּדָּבָר. אָמַר לֵיהּ. פְּתַח פִּיךָ וְקַבֵּל. אָמַר רִבִּי מָנָא. מְגָחֵךְ הֲוָה עִימֵּיהּ. אָמַר רִבִּי אָבוּן. מִילָּה אָמַר לֵיהּ. מַה אִם תְּרוּמָה שֶׁאֵינָהּ רְאוּיָה לְיִשְׂרָאֵל בְּכָל־מָקוֹם הֲרֵי הִיא אוֹכֶלֶת. חָזֶה וְשׁוֹק שֶׁהֵן רְאוּיִן לְיִשְׂרָאֵל בְּכָל־מָקוֹם אֵינוֹ דִין שֶׁתֹּאכַל. רְאוּיִן הָיוּ לְיִשְׂרָאֵל וּכְשֶׁנִּתְחַייְבוּ נִיטְּלוּ מֵהֶן וְנִיתְּנוּ לַכֹּהֲנִים. יָכוֹל כְּשֵׁם שֶׁנִּתְחַייְבוּ וְנִיטְּלוּ מֵהֶן וְנִיתְּנוּ לַכֹּהֲנִים כָּךְ אִם יִזְכּוּ יַחֲזִירוּ לָהֶן. תַּלְמוּד לוֹמַר וָאֶתֵּן אוֹתָם לְאַהֲרֹן וּלְבָנָיו לְחָק עוֹלָם. מַה מַתָּנָה אֵינָהּ חוֹזֶרֶת אַף אֵילּוּ אֵינָן חוֹזְרִין.

Halakhah 6: "A congenital castrate priest," etc. It was stated: He enables her to eat breast and thigh[228]. Rebbi Joḥanan said, he enables her for heave but not for breast and thigh[229]. Rebbi Simeon ben Laqish said, there are several arguments *de minore ad majus* in this matter. Rebbi Yose ben Rebbi Ḥanina asked, what means "there are several arguments *de minore ad majus* in this matter"? He said to him, open your mouth and receive. Rebbi Mana said, he made fun of him. Rebbi Abun said, he gave him an example. [230]"Since she eats heave that never was within the reach of an Israel, is it not logical that she should eat breast and thigh that were within the reach of Israel[231]? Breast and thigh were within the reach of Israel but when they became guilty these were taken from them and given to the priests. I could think, since these were taken from them when they incurred guilt, so they would be given back to them when they acquire merit. The verse[232] says, 'I gave them to Aaron and his sons for an eternal law;' since a gift is not returned, so these are not returned."

228 The part of breast and right front thigh from a well-being offering which has to be given to the Cohen and is eaten by him and his family; *Lev.*

7:34. In the interpretation of the Babli, 81a, "breast and thigh" stands for all gifts to the Cohen which are biblical; "heave" is today's heave which is only a rabbinical obligation. The following discussion in the Yerushalmi shows that this cannot be the Yerushalmi's interpretation.

229 In the Babli, 81a, this position is ascribed to R. Simeon ben Laqish, the opposite statement to R. Joḥanan. Since practice in general follows R. Joḥanan, the two Talmudim take opposite positions in practice. According to the Babli, the entire discussion is about the hermaphrodite Cohen, not the one born without testicles. It seems from the second paragraph following that the Yerushalmi also has to be read in this sense.

230 *Sifra Ṣaw Fereq* 17(5). R. Simeon ben Laqish intimates that there may be more (amoraic) arguments in the vein of the tannaitic statement to be quoted.

231 It is not clear what the argument is. R. Abraham ben David in his commentary to *Sifra* gives two possible explanations. (1) Before the sin of the Golden Calf, first-borns exercised the priestly functions. (2) In the obligatory sacrifices of Passover and animal tithes, the Cohen gets nothing. (In profane slaughter he should get some other parts, *Deut.* 18:3. During the stay in the desert, profane slaughter was forbidden, *Lev.* 17:3-4). Since this shows that there is nothing intrinsic in the nature of a sacrifice which requires a part to be given to the Cohen, the Cohen's parts are in some sense robbed from the Israel and given to the Cohen.

232 *Lev.* 7:34.

רִבִּי יַעֲקֹב בַּר אָחָא אָמַר שְׁמַעְתְּתָא עַל בַּת יִשְׂרָאֵל שֶׁנִּישֵּׂאת לְכֹהֵן. רִבִּי יוֹחָנָן אָמַר. אוֹכֶלֶת בִּתְרוּמָה וְאֵינָהּ אוֹכֶלֶת בְּחָזֶה וָשׁוֹק. רִבִּי שִׁמְעוֹן בֶּן לָקִישׁ אָמַר. כַּמָּה קוּלֵּי חוּמְרִין בַּדָּבָר. רִבִּי יוֹסֵי בֵּירִבִּי חֲנִינָה בְּעָא קוֹמֵי רִבִּי שִׁמְעוֹן בֶּן לָקִישׁ. מַהוּ כַּמָּה קוּלֵּי חוּמְרִין בַּדָּבָר. אָמַר לֵיהּ. פְּתַח פִּיךְ וְקַבֵּל. אָמַר רִבִּי מָנָא. מְגָחֵיךְ הֲוָה עִימֵּיהּ. אָמַר רִבִּי אָבִין. מִילָּה הֲוָה אָמַר לֵיהּ. מַה אִם תְּרוּמָה שֶׁאֵינָהּ רְאוּיָה לְיִשְׂרָאֵל בְּכָל־מָקוֹם הֲרֵי הִיא אוֹכֶלֶת. חָזֶה וָשׁוֹק שֶׁהֵן רְאוּיִן לְיִשְׂרָאֵל בְּכָל־מָקוֹם אֵינוֹ דִין שֶׁתֹּאכַל. רְאוּיִין הָיוּ לְיִשְׂרָאֵל. וּכְשֶׁנִּתְחַיְּיבוּ נִיטְּלוּ מֵהֶן וְנִיתְּנוּ לַכֹּהֲנִים. יָכוֹל כְּשֵׁם שֶׁנִּתְחַיְּיבוּ וְנִיטְּלוּ מֵהֶן וְנִיתְּנוּ לַכֹּהֲנִים כָּךְ אִם יִזְכּוּ יַחְזְרוּ לָהֶן. תַּלְמוּד לוֹמַר וָאֶתֵּן אוֹתָם לְאַהֲרֹן הַכֹּהֵן וּלְבָנָיו לְחָק עוֹלָם. מַה מַּתָּנָה אֵינָהּ חוֹזֶרֶת אַף אֵילּוּ אֵינָן חוֹזְרִין.

Rebbi Jacob bar Aḥa said the argument is about the daughter of an Israel married to a Cohen[233]: Rebbi Joḥanan said, he enables her for heave but not for breast and thigh. Rebbi Simeon ben Laqish said, there are several arguments *de minore ad majus* in this matter. Rebbi Yose ben Rebbi Ḥanina asked, what means "there are several arguments *de minore ad majus* in this matter"? He said to him, open your mouth and receive. Rebbi Mana said, he made fun of him. Rebbi Abun said, he gave him an example. "Since she eats heave that never was within the reach of an Israel, is it not logical that she should eat breast and thigh that were within the reach of Israel? Breast and thigh were within the reach of Israel but when they became guilty these were taken from them and given to the priests. I could think, since these were taken from them when they incurred guilt, so they would be given back to them when they acquire merit. The verse says, 'I gave them to Aaron the priest[234] and his sons for an eternal law;' since a gift is not returned, so these are not returned."

233 The problem is not that of a handicapped Cohen but arises anytime a perfectly normal Cohen marries outside his clan. There is no mention of such a problem anywhere else in the Talmudim.

234 This is the correct quote.

וְאֵין חֲלוּקִין עַל דִּבְרֵי רִבִּי יוּדָה. מִן דְּאָמַר רִבִּי יוֹסֵי בְשֵׁם רִבִּי הִילָא. מְייַבְּמִין אֶת אִשְׁתּוֹ. הָדָא אָמְרָה אֵין חֲלוּקִין עַל דִּבְרֵי רִבִּי יוּדָה. קִידֵּשׁ אֵינָן חוֹשְׁשִׁין לְקִידּוּשָׁיו. נִתְקַדֵּשׁ חוֹשְׁשִׁין לְקִידּוּשָׁיו. נִבְעַל נִפְסַל מִן הַתְּרוּמָה כַּנָּשִׁים. וְקַשְׁיָא. רִבִּי נִיחָא בַּר רִבִּי סָבָא רִבִּי יוֹנָה בְשֵׁם רַב הַמְנוּנָא. אֲפִילוּ מִין בְּמִינוֹ כָּל־שֶׁהוּא. וְקַשְׁיָא. אִם זָכָר הוּא. אֵין זָכָר פּוֹסֵל זָכָר. אִם נְקֵיבָה הִיא. אֵין נְקֵיבָה פּוֹסֶלֶת נְקֵיבָה. צַד זַכְרוּתוֹ שֶׁלָּזֶה פּוֹסֶלֶת צַד נְקֵיבָתוֹ שֶׁלָּזֶה. מַאֲכִיל אֶת נָשָׁיו וְאֵינוֹ מַאֲכִיל אֶת עֲבָדָיו. מַאֲכִיל אֶת נָשָׁיו מִכֹּחַ זַכְרוּתוֹ. וְאֵינוֹ מַאֲכִיל אֶת עֲבָדָיו מִכֹּחַ זֶה וָזֶה. נִתְחַלֵּל צַד נְקֵיבָה שֶׁבּוֹ.

Is there nobody who disagrees with Rebbi Jehudah? Since Rebbi Yose said in the name of Rebbi Hila, one marries his[235] wife in levirate, that means that nobody disagrees with Rebbi Jehudah. If he betrothed, his betrothal is not problematic. If he was betrothed, his betrothal is problematic[236]. If he was copulated with, he becomes disabled from heave like a woman[237]. That is difficult. Rebbi Niḥa bar Rebbi Sava[238], Rebbi Jonah in the name of Rav Hamnuna: Even with his own kind in any case[239]. That is difficult: if he is a male, no male disables a male[240]. If she is a female, no female disables a female[241]. The male aspect of one disables the female aspect of the other[237]. He enables his wives to eat but does not enable his slaves. He enables his wives to eat by his male aspect. But he does not enable his slaves because of his double aspect; his female aspect was desecrated[242].

235 The hermaphrodite's.

236 Since she is forbidden to her male partner, she needs a divorce.

237 Like any woman having intercourse with a man she could not marry.

238 A student of Rebbis Jonah and Yose of the fourth generation.

239 Intercourse of two hermaphrodites disables both of them, whether homosexual or heterosexual.

240 It is inferred from *Lev*. 21:7,14 that the intercourse of a Cohen with a woman forbidden to him in marriage desecrates the woman and her children but not the man [*Sifra Emor Pereq* (7)].

241 In the tradition of the Yerushalmi (*Giṭṭin* 8:10, fol. 49c) a lesbian relationship disables from heave for the House of Shammai but not for the House of Hillel. In the opinion of the Babli, *Yebamot* 76a, lesbianism is undesirable but not sanctionable. [Rabbinic practice follows an obscure *baraita* (*Sifra Emor Parasha* 9(8)), the House of Shammai in the Yerushalmi, and Paul in Romans 1:26.]

242 His female aspect is desecrated and his slaves barred from heave only if he ever had a sexual relationship with either a male or another hermaphrodite.

רִבִּי יַעֲקֹב בַּר זַבְדִּי בְּשֵׁם רִבִּי אַבָּהוּ בְּשֵׁם רִבִּי יוֹחָנָן. וּבִלְבַד מִמְּקוֹם זַכְרוּת. רִבִּי סִימוֹן בְּשֵׁם רִבִּי יְהוֹשֻׁעַ בֶּן לֵוִי. אֲפִילוּ מִמְּקוֹם נְקֵיבָה. רִבִּי יַעֲקֹב בַּר זַבְדִּי בְּשֵׁם רִבִּי אַבָּהוּ. חָזַר בָּהּ רִבִּי יְהוֹשֻׁעַ בֶּן לֵוִי מִן הָדֵין קִרְייָא וְאֶת זָכָר לֹא תִשְׁכַּב מִשְׁכְּבֵי אִשָּׁה. אֶת שֶׁיֵּשׁ לוֹ שְׁנֵי מִשְׁכָּבוֹת כְּאִשָּׁה. וְאֵי זֶה זֶה. זֶה אַנְדְּרוֹגִינוֹס. אָמַר רִבִּי. בִּיקַּשְׁתִּי וְלֹא מָצָאתִי דִבְרֵי בֶּן שַׁמּוּעַ בְּאַנְדְּרוֹגִינוֹס. וְחֶבְרָה עָלַי חֲבוּרָה. וְלָמָּה. מִשּׁוּם שֶׁלֹּא לְגְלוֹעַ בּוֹ אוֹ מִשּׁוּם שֶׁאֵינוֹ כְדַיי. מַה נְפַק מִן בֵּינֵיהוֹן. הָיָה דַרְכּוֹ לְגַלֵּעַ. אִין תֵּימַר שֶׁלֹּא לְגַלֵּעַ בּוֹ. הֲרֵי גִילּוּעוֹ בְיָדוֹ. הֲוֵי לֵית טַעֲמָא דְלֹא מִשּׁוּם שֶׁאֵינוֹ כְדַיי. מַה הָיָה לוֹ לְגַלֵּעַ בּוֹ. יוֹרֵשׁ. מֵעִיד. מִנְחָתוֹ קְרֵיבָה בְּכָלִל. מְזַמְּנִין עָלָיו כְּזָכָר.

Rebbi Jacob bar Zavdi in the name of Rebbi Abbahu in the name of Rebbi Johanan, only from the place of masculinity[243]. Rebbi Simon in the name of Rebbi Joshua ben Levi: even from the female place[244]. Rebbi Jacob bar Zavdi in the name of Rebbi Abbahu: Rebbi Joshua ben Levi retracted this, from the following verse[245]: "And with a male you should not lie in the way of a woman's beddings", one who may lie in two ways, including the female. Who is that? That is the hermaphrodite. Rebbi said, I looked for but did not find words of Ben Shamua about the hermaphrodite, for the entire group ganged up on me[246]. Why? Not to make it public or because he was not worth it? What difference does it make? He usually made public. If you say, it was not to make it public[247], the publicity is already in his hand. The reason must be that he was not worth it. What could he made public? He inherits[248], he testifies[249], his grain offering is burnt completely[250], one says grace with him as with a male.

243 Here starts the discussion of the last sentence in this Mishnah, the assertion of R. Eleazar ben Shamua (in the Babli, R. Eliezer) that for the definition of homosexuality an hermaphrodite is a full male. The position of R. Johanan here is an explicit statement of R. Eleazar (ben

Shamua) in Tosephta 10:2.

244 For him, heterosexual intercourse of a male with an hermaphrodite is still homosexuality. In the Babli, 83b, that is the opinion of Rav.

245 *Lev.* 18:22. As the Babli explains, on the face of it, the verse seems to support the first opinion of R. Joshua ben Levi, but a second look shows that the prohibition is to lie with a male, i. e., the male aspect of the hermaphrodite.

246 Babli 84a; there, "the students of R. Eleazar ben Shamua ganged up on him like chickens in a chicken coop."

247 The uncommon form לגלע instead of the common לגלות seems so be an Arabism, from جلع "to uncover indecently". It seems that the teachings of R. Eleazar ben Shamua's students were esoteric.

248 If there are 2 children, a hermaphrodite and a daughter, at the death of the father the daughter has a claim on the estate for a dowry but the only heir is the hermaphrodite.

The Babli, 83b, which attributes the Mishnah to R. Eliezer, proves from parallel statements that the hermaphrodite is considered a full male only in respect to homosexuality. In all other respects, it is considered a case of doubt whether he is male or female.

249 He can testify formally in cases where a male witness is required (such as the validity of certain legal acts.)

250 The grain offering of a Cohen is burned completely (*Lev.* 6:16); the grain offering of the daughter of a Cohen is treated like the offering of an Israel and most of it is eaten by the Cohanim in the Temple precinct.

יש מותרות פרק תשיעי

משנה א: יֵשׁ מוּתָּרוֹת לְבַעֲלֵיהֶן וַאֲסוּרוֹת לְיִבְמֵיהֶן מוּתָּרוֹת לְיִבְמֵיהֶן (fol. 9d) וַאֲסוּרוֹת לְבַעֲלֵיהֶן מוּתָּרוֹת לָאֵילּוּ וְלָאֵלּוּ וַאֲסוּרוֹת לָאֵילּוּ וְלָאֵלּוּ.

Mishnah 1: There exist women[1] permitted to their husbands but forbidden to their levirs, permitted to their levirs but forbidden to their husbands, permitted to both of them, or forbidden to both.

משנה ב: אֵילּוּ מוּתָּרוֹת לְבַעֲלֵיהֶן וַאֲסוּרוֹת לְיִבְמֵיהֶן כֹּהֵן הֶדְיוֹט שֶׁקִּידֵּשׁ אֶת הָאַלְמָנָה וְיֵשׁ לוֹ אָח כֹּהֵן גָּדוֹל כָּשֵׁר שֶׁנָּשָׂא כְשֵׁירָה וְיֵשׁ לוֹ אָח חָלָל. יִשְׂרָאֵל שֶׁנָּשָׂא יִשְׂרְאֵלִית וְיֵשׁ (fol. 10a) לוֹ אָח מַמְזֵר. מַמְזֵר שֶׁנָּשָׂא מַמְזֶרֶת וְיֵשׁ לוֹ אָח יִשְׂרָאֵל מוּתָּרוֹת לְבַעֲלֵיהֶן וַאֲסוּרוֹת לְיִבְמֵיהֶן.

Mishnah 2: The following are permitted to their husbands but forbidden to their levirs: If a simple priest was betrothed[2] to a widow and has a brother who is High Priest, or a qualified man married a qualified woman and has a disqualified brother[3], or an Israel married an Israelite woman and has a bastard brother, or a bastard married a bastard woman and has an Israel brother, [the women] are permitted to their husbands and forbidden for their levirs.

1 Women who are forbidden but not by an incest prohibition whose marriages are nevertheless valid, cf. Halakhah 2:3.

2 In the Babli: is married to.

3 In the Babli: If a *desecrated* [priest], married to a woman qualified for the priesthood, has a *qualified* brother.

הלכה א: יֵשׁ מוּתָּרוֹת לְבַעֲלֵיהֶן כול׳. רִבִּי נִיחָא בַּר סָבָא בְּעָא קוֹמֵי רִבִּי יוֹנָה. לָמָּה לִי נָשָׂא וַאֲפִילוּ קִידֵּשׁ. לָמָּה לִי אַלְמָנָה וַאֲפִילוּ בְתוּלָה. וְאִילֵּין אִינּוּן. זוֹ וְצָרָה. אִית לִי חוֹרָנִין. צָרַת סוֹטָה מוּתֶּרֶת לְבַעַל וַאֲסוּרָה לְיָבָם. אָחִיו שֶׁבָּא עַל אֲחוֹת חֲלוּצָתוֹ מוּתֶּרֶת לְבַעַל וַאֲסוּרָה לְיָבָם. כָּשֵׁר שֶׁנָּשָׂא כְשֵׁירָה וְיֵשׁ לוֹ אָח חָלָל מוּתֶּרֶת לְבַעַל וַאֲסוּרָה לְיָבָם. הָדָא מְסַייְעָא לְרִבִּי יוֹנָה. דְּרִבִּי יוֹנָה אָמַר. לֵית כְּלָלֵיהּ דְּרִבִּי כְּלָלִין.

Halakhah 1: "There exist women permitted to their husbands," etc. Rebbi Niḥa bar Sava asked before Rebbi Jonah: Why "married"? Even "betrothed"! Why a widow? even a virgin[4]! Are these all? She and her co-wife[5]. I also have others: The co-wife of one suspected of adultery is permitted to her husband and forbidden to her levir[6]. If his brother had slept with the sister of one who had performed *ḥalîṣah* with him, she is permitted to her husband and forbidden to her levir[7]. If a qualified [priest], married to a woman qualified for the priesthood, has a desecrated brother, she is permitted to her husband and forbidden to her levir[8]. This supports Rebbi Jonah, since Rebbi Jonah said, the groupings of Rebbi are not exhaustive[9].

4 The questions show that the Mishnah before the Amoraim was the Babylonian version and that the Mishnah in the Yerushalmi ms. and *editio princeps* is a version modified according to the discussion here.

The questions refer to the Cohen who has a brother who is High Priest. A widow is forbidden to the High Priest even if she is not a sister-in-law. The same questions are asked in the Babli, 84a.

5 He holds that with a woman also the co-wife is forbidden; cf. Mishnah 2:3 and the commentary of Meïri, *Bet Habeḥira, Yebamot*, ed. K. Albeck, p. 89, Note עה.

6 A woman formally charged by her husband as a possible adulteress is forbidden to her husband until she undergoes the ordeal described in *Num.* 5:11-31 (*Sifry Num.* 8). If the husband dies before he can bring his suspected wife to the Temple, she cannot be

married in levirate and neither can her co-wife but the suspicion of adultery of one wife has no bearing on the status of the co-wife in the marriage.

7 Brother A had married the sister of a woman who had performed *ḥalîṣah* with brother B. If A dies childless, his widow is forbidden to B. However, this prohibition is purely rabbinical and its place should be in the discussion of Mishnah 5.

8 While a qualified woman is not forbidden to marry a desecrated or otherwise disqualified man (see the next paragraph) and could have married the disqualified brother in a first marriage, she cannot be married in levirate since her child would be barred from the priesthood and could not come "in place of the deceased" who was a priest. The widow therefore is forbidden to the disqualified brother by the incest prohibition of the sister-in-law.

The mention of this sentence here is not a scribal error as assumed by the commentaries.

9 Accepted by the Babli, 84b.

כָּשֵׁר שֶׁנָּשָׂא כְשֵׁירָה וְיֵשׁ לוֹ אָח חָלָל מוּתֶּרֶת לְבַעַל וַאֲסוּרָה לְיָבָם. לֹא כֵן אָמַר רִבִּי יוֹסֵי בֵּירִבִּי בּוּן בְּשֵׁם רַב. גֵּר וְעֶבֶד מְשׁוּחְרָר וְחָלָל מוּתָּרִין בִּכְהוּנָּה. כֵּינִי מַתְנִיתָא. כָּשֵׁר שֶׁנָּשָׂה כְשֵׁירָה וְיֵשׁ לוֹ אָח חָלָל. רִבִּי יוֹסֵי בֵּירִבִּי בּוּן בְּשֵׁם רַב. גֵּר וְעֶבֶד מְשׁוּחְרָר וְחָלָל מוּתָּרִין בִּכְהוּנָּה. מַאי טַעֲמָא. כְּשֵׁירִין הוּזְהָרוּ עַל הַפְּסוּלוֹת וּפְסוּלִים עַל הַכְּשֵׁירוֹת אֲבָל לֹא פְסוּלוֹת עַל הַכְּשֵׁירִין וְלֹא כְשֵׁירוֹת עַל הַפְּסוּלִין. וְהָא תַנֵּי לֹא יִקָּחוּ לֹא יִקָּחוּ. מְלַמֵּד שֶׁהָאִשָּׁה מוּזְהֶרֶת עַל יְדֵי הָאִישׁ. סָבְרִין מֵימַר כִּכְשֵׁירוֹת עַל הַפְּסוּלוֹת. וְאֵינָן כִּפְסוּלוֹת עַל הַכְּשֵׁירוֹת.

"If a qualified [priest], married to a woman qualified for the priesthood, has a desecrated brother, she is permitted to her husband and forbidden to her levir." Did not Rebbi Yose ben Rebbi Abun say in the name of Rav that a proselyte, a freedman, and a disqualified priest are permitted priestly [wives]? So is the Mishnah: If a qualified [priest], married to a woman qualified for the priesthood, has a desecrated brother. Rebbi Yose ben Rebbi Abun said in the name of Rav: A proselyte, a freedman, and a disqualified priest are permitted priestly [wives]. What is the reason?

Qualified men are warned against disqualified women and disqualified men against qualified women but not disqualified women against qualified men nor qualified women against disqualified men. Did we not state: "they should not take, should not take", which teaches that the woman is warned through the man? They wanted to say, qualified women against disqualified women but it is only disqualified women against qualified women[10].

10 This paragraph is in very bad shape. It seems that it should be corrected as follows:

כָּשֵׁר שֶׁנָּשָׂה כשֵׁירָה וְיֵשׁ לוֹ אָח חָלָל מוּתֶּרֶת לְבַעַל וַאֲסוּרָה לְיָבָם. לֹא כֵן אָמַר רִבִּי יוֹסֵי בֵּירִבִּי בּוּן. גֵּר וְעֶבֶד מְשׁוּחרָר וְחָלָל מוּתָּרִין בִּכְהוּנָּה. כֵּיני מַתְנִיתָא. **חָלָל** שֶׁנָּשָׂא כְשֵׁירָה וְיֵשׁ לוֹ אָח **כָּשֵׁר**. רִבִּי יוֹסֵי בֵּירִבִּי בּוּן בְּשֵׁם רַב. גֵּר וְעֶבֶד מְשׁוּחְרָר וְחָלָל מוּתָּרִין בִּכְהוּנָּה. מַאי טַעֲמָא. כְּשֵׁירִין הוּזְהָרוּ עַל הַפְּסוּלוֹת אֲבָל לֹא פְסוּלוֹת עַל הַכְּשֵׁירִין וְלֹא כְשֵׁירוֹת עַל הַפְּסוּלִין. וְהָא תַנֵּי לֹא יִקָּחוּ לֹא יִקָּחוּ. מְלַמֵּד שֶׁהָאִשָּׁה מוּזְהֶרֶת עַל יְדֵי הָאִישׁ. סָבְרִין מֵימַר בִּכְשֵׁירוֹת עַל הַפְּסוּלִים. וְאֵינָן כִּפְסוּלוֹת עַל הַכְּשֵׁירִים.

"If a qualified [priest], married to a woman qualified for the priesthood, has a desecrated brother, she is permitted to her husband and forbidden to her levir." Did not Rebbi Yose ben Rebbi Abun say that a proselyte, a freedman, and a disqualified priest are permitted priestly [wives][11]? So is the Mishnah: If a *desecrated* [priest], married to a woman qualified for the priesthood, has a *qualified* brother[12]. Rebbi Yose ben Rebbi Abun said in the name of Rav: A proselyte, a freedman, and a disqualified priest are permitted priestly [wives]. What is the reason? Qualified men are warned against disqualified women but not disqualified women against qualified men nor qualified women against disqualified men. Did we not state[13]: "they should not take, should not take", which teaches that the woman is warned through the man? They wanted to say, qualified women against disqualified *men* but it is only disqualified women against qualified *men*[14].

11 Priestly women are not enjoined to stay in their priestly status. The Babli concurs, 84b, also in the name of Rav.

12 Since the wife is disabled for the priesthood by her marriage to the desecrated man, she is forbidden to the brother.

13 Babli 84b, *Sifra Emor Pereq* 1(12). The verse *Lev.* 21:7, "A promiscuous and a desecrated woman *they should not take* and a woman divorced from her husband *they should not take*. . ." The two prohibitions are interpreted as one for the man, not to take a disabled wife, and one for the woman, not to seduce a man into a forbidden marriage.

14 The clause "nor qualified women against disqualified men" is shown to be false.

משנה ג: אֵילּוּ מוּתָּרוֹת לְיִבְמֵיהֶן וַאֲסוּרוֹת לְבַעֲלֵיהֶן כֹּהֵן גָּדוֹל שֶׁקִּידֵּשׁ אֶת הָאַלְמָנָה וְיֵשׁ לוֹ אָח כֹּהֵן הֶדְיוֹט. כָּשֵׁר שֶׁנָּשָׂא חֲלָלָה וְיֵשׁ לוֹ אָח חָלָל. יִשְׂרָאֵל שֶׁנָּשָׂא מַמְזֶרֶת וְיֵשׁ לוֹ אַח מַמְזֵר. מַמְזֵר שֶׁנָּשָׂא בַת יִשְׂרָאֵל וְיֵשׁ לוֹ אָח יִשְׂרָאֵל מוּתָּרוֹת לְיִבְמֵיהֶן וַאֲסוּרוֹת לְבַעֲלֵיהֶן.

Mishnah 3: These are permitted to their levirs and forbidden to their husbands: If a High Priest was betrothed to a widow and has a brother who is a simple priest, or qualified [priest] married a disqualified woman and has a disqualified brother, or an Israel married a bastard woman and has a bastard brother, or a bastard who married an Israel woman and has an Israel brother; [the women] are permitted to their levirs and forbidden to their husbands.

משנה ד: אֲסוּרוֹת לָאֵילּוּ וְלָאֵילוּ. כֹּהֵן גָּדוֹל שֶׁנָּשָׂא אֶת הָאַלְמָנָה וְיֵשׁ לוֹ אָח כֹּהֵן גָּדוֹל אוֹ כֹהֵן הַדְיוֹט. כָּשֵׁר שֶׁנָּשָׂא חֲלָלָה וְיֵשׁ לוֹ אָח כָּשֵׁר. יִשְׂרָאֵל שֶׁנָּשָׂא מַמְזֶרֶת וְיֵשׁ לוֹ אַח יִשְׂרָאֵל. מַמְזֵר שֶׁנָּשָׂא בַת יִשְׂרָאֵל וְיֵשׁ לוֹ אָח מַמְזֵר אֲסוּרוֹת לָאֵילּוּ וְלָאֵילוּ. וּשְׁאָר כָּל־הַנָּשִׁים מוּתָּרוֹת לְבַעֲלֵיהֶן וּלְיִבְמֵיהֶן.

Mishnah 4: Forbidden to both of them: If a High Priest married a widow and has a brother who is a High Priest or a simple priest, or a qualified [priest] married a disqualified woman and has a qualified brother, or an Israel married a bastard woman and has an Israel brother, or a bastard married an Israel woman and has a bastard brother; these [women] are forbidden to both of them and all other women are permitted to their husbands and their levirs.

הלכה ב: אֵילּוּ מוּתָּרוֹת לְבַעֲלֵיהֶן כול׳. לֹא אָמַר אֶלָּא קִידֵּשׁ. הָא אִם בָּעַל נִפְסְלָה בִבְעִילָה. הָדָא דְתַנִּינָן. אֲסוּרוֹת אֵילּוּ וְלָאֵילּוּ.

Halakhah 2: "The following are permitted to their husbands,[15]" etc. He only said "betrothed[16]", but if he copulated with her, the copulation disqualifies her. That is what we stated: "Forbidden to both of them."

15 A quote from Mishnah 2, irrelevant for the sequel.

16 In Mishnah 3, the mention of betrothal is essential; in Mishnah 4 the mention of marriage. In Mishnah 2, either betrothal or marriage may be mentioned for the High Priest's brother.

וְאִילֵּין אִינּוּן. הָא אִית לִי חוֹרָנִיין. הַמַּחֲזִיר אֶת גְּרוּשָׁתוֹ מִשֶּׁנִּישֵּׂאת אֲסוּרָה לַבַּעַל וּמוּתֶּרֶת לְיָבָם. הוּא שֶׁבָּא עַל אֲחוֹת חֲלוּצָתוֹ אֲסוּרָה לְבַעַל וּמוּתֶּרֶת לְיָבָם. פְּצוּעַ דַּכָּא שֶׁנָּשָׂא כְשֵׁירָה וְיֵשׁ לוֹ אָח כָּשֵׁר אֲסוּרָה לְבַעַל וּמוּתֶּרֶת לְיָבָם. הָדָא מְסַייְעָא לְרִבִּי יוֹנָה. דְּרִבִּי יוֹנָה אָמַר. לֵית כְּלָלֵיהּ דְּרִבִּי כְּלָלִין.

Are these all? There are others: If somebody takes back a woman he divorced after she had been married [to another man], she is forbidden to the husband[17] but permitted to the levir. If he slept with the sister of a woman with whom he had performed *ḥaliṣah*, she is forbidden to the husband[18] but permitted to the levir. If a man with injured testicles married a qualified woman, she is forbidden to the husband but permitted to the levir. This supports Rebbi Jonah, since Rebbi Jonah said, the groupings of Rebbi are not exhaustive[9].

17 *Deut.* 24:4.

18 A purely rabbinical prohibition as sister of a quasi-wife; cf. Halakhah 4:7.

וְאִילֵּין אִינּוּן. הָא אִית לָךְ חוֹרָנִין. סוֹטָה אֲסוּרָה לָזֶה וְלָזֶה. חֲלוּצָה אֲסוּרָה לָזֶה וְלָזֶה. פְּצוּעַ דַּכָּא שֶׁנָּשָׂא כְשֵׁירָה וְיֵשׁ לוֹ אָח פְּצוּעַ דַּכָּא אֲסוּרָה לָזֶה וְלָזֶה. הָדָא מְסַייְעָא לְרִבִּי יוֹנָה. דְּרִבִּי יוֹנָה אָמַר. לֵית כְּלָלֵיהּ דְּרִבִּי כְלָלִין.

Are these all[19]? There are others: A woman suspected of adultery[6] is forbidden to both of them. The widow after *ḥalîṣah*[20] is forbidden to both of them. If a man with injured testicles married a qualified woman and has a brother with injured testicles, she is forbidden to both of them. This supports Rebbi Jonah, since Rebbi Jonah said, the groupings of Rebbi are not exhaustive[9].

19 This refers to Mishnah 4.

20 If a woman was freed by *ḥalîṣah* she is forbidden to all levirs. If nevertheless one of the levirs marries her, she remains forbidden to all of them.

משנה ה: שְׁנִיּוֹת מִדִּבְרֵי סוֹפְרִים שְׁנִייָה לַבַּעַל וְלֹא שְׁנִייָה לַיָּבָם אֲסוּרָה לַבַּעַל וּמוּתֶּרֶת לַיָּבָם שְׁנִייָה לַיָּבָם וְלֹא שְׁנִייָה לַבַּעַל אֲסוּרָה לַיָּבָם וּמוּתֶּרֶת לַבַּעַל. שְׁנִייָה לָזֶה וְלָזֶה אֲסוּרָה לָזֶה וְלָזֶה. אֵין לָהּ לֹא כְתוּבָּה וְלֹא פֵירוֹת וְלֹא מְזוֹנוֹת וְלֹא בְלָאוֹת וְהַוְּלָד כָּשֵׁר וְכוֹפִין אוֹתוֹ לְהוֹצִיא. אַלְמָנָה לְכֹהֵן גָּדוֹל גְּרוּשָׁה וַחֲלוּצָה לְכֹהֵן הֶדְיוֹט מַמְזֶרֶת וּנְתִינָה לְיִשְׂרָאֵל. בַּת יִשְׂרָאֵל לְנָתִין וּלְמַמְזֵר וְיֵשׁ לָהֶן כְּתוּבָּה.

Mishnah 5: Secondary prohibitions instituted by the Sopherim[21]. If she is secondarily prohibited to the husband but not to the levir, she is forbidden to the husband but permitted to the levir[22]. Secondarily prohibited to the levir but not to the husband, she is forbidden to the levir but permitted to the husband. Secondarily prohibited to both of them, she is forbidden to both of them. She may claim neither *ketubah*[23] nor usufruct[24] nor upkeep nor wear[25] but the child is qualified[26] and one forces him to divorce her[27]. A widow married to the High Priest, a divorcee of one that performed *ḥalîṣah* married to a simple priest, a female bastard or a Gibeoness married to an Israel, and Israel woman married to a Gibeonite or a bastard have a claim of *ketubah*[28].

21 Cf. Mishnah 2:4.

22 Since the first marriage was legitimate by biblical standards the levirate also will be legitimate by biblical standards.

23 Cf. Chapter 4, Note 84.

24 She cannot reclaim the usufruct the husband had from her dowry during the marriage.

25 If part of the dowry was in the form of vessels or clothing, she cannot claim the diminution in value caused by wear during the marriage.

26 Since the marriage is completely legitimate by biblical standards, the child is qualified even for the office of High Priest.

27 The rabbinic court if it has the power to do so. All these rules are made to dissuade women to consent to such a marriage which otherwise they would have no incentive to refuse since the children are qualified.

28 Since in this case the children are disqualified the woman has every incentive not to agree to such a marriage.

הלכה ה: שְׁנִיּוֹת מִדִּבְרֵי סוֹפְרִים כול׳. הַשְּׁנִיּוֹת מִדִּבְרֵי סוֹפְרִים שְׁנִיָּה לַבַּעַל וְלֹא שְׁנִיָּה לַיָּבָם אֲסוּרָה לַבַּעַל וּמוּתֶּרֶת לַיָּבָם. מַהוּ שֶׁיְּהֵא לָהּ כְּתוּבָּה אֶצֶל הַיָּבָם. מֵאַחַר שֶׁהִיא מוּתֶּרֶת לוֹ יֵשׁ לָהּ כְּתוּבָּה. אוֹ מֵאַחַר שֶׁכְּתוּבָּתָהּ עַל נִיכְסֵי בַּעֲלָהּ הָרִאשׁוֹן וְהִיא אֲסוּרָה לוֹ אֵין לָהּ כְּתוּבָּה.

Halakhah 5: "Secondary prohibitions instituted by the Sopherim," etc. "If she is secondarily, rabbinically, prohibited to the husband but not to the levir, she is forbidden to the husband but permitted to the levir.' Does she have *ketubah* from the levir? Since she is permitted to him, she has *ketubah*, or because the *ketubah* is a lien on the estate of her first husband and she was forbidden to him, does she have no *ketubah*[29]?

29 The question is not answered; in the absence of a rule, no claim of the woman married in levirate can be enforced in court. The Babli, 85a, decides that she has no *ketubah*; in this case, the court will actively prohibit a claim of *ketubah*.

שְׁנִייָה לַיָּבָם וְלֹא שְׁנִיָּה לַבַּעַל אֲסוּרָה לַיָּבָם וּמוּתֶּרֶת לַבַּעַל. מַהוּ שֶׁיְּהֵא לָהּ כְּתוּבָּה אֶצֶל הַיָּבָם. מֵאַחַר שֶׁהִיא אֲסוּרָה לוֹ אֵין לָהּ כְּתוּבָּה. אוֹ מֵאַחַר שֶׁכְּתוּבָּתָהּ עַל נִיכְסֵי בַּעֲלָהּ הָרִאשׁוֹן וְהִיא מוּתֶּרֶת לוֹ יֵשׁ לָהּ כְּתוּבָּה.

"If she is secondarily prohibited to the levir but not to the husband, she is forbidden to the levir but permitted to the husband." Does she have *ketubah* from the levir? Since she is forbidden to him, she does not have *ketubah*, or because the *ketubah* is a lien on the estate of her first husband and she was permitted to him, does she have *ketubah*[30]?

30 The question is not treated in the Babli. Her claim of *ketubah* is not enforceable in court.

וְלֹא פֵּירוֹת. אָמַר רִבִּי יִרְמְיָה. שֶׁאֵין לוֹ עָלֶיהָ אֶלָּא אֲכִילַת פֵּירוֹת בִּלְבַד. תַּנֵּי רִבִּי יוֹסֵי צַייְדָנִייָה קוֹמֵי רִבִּי יִרְמְיָה וּפַלִּיג עַל רִבִּי יִרְמְיָה. וְזַכַּאי בִּמְצִיאָתָהּ וּבְמַעֲשֵׂה יָדֶיהָ וּבְהֵפֵר נְדָרֶיהָ. מַהוּ וְלֹא פֵּירוֹת. שֶׁאֵינָהּ יְכוֹלָה לְהוֹצִיא מִמֶּנּוּ אֲכִילַת פֵּירוֹת שֶׁאָכַל.

[31]"No usufruct." Rebbi Jeremiah said, that he has from her only the usufruct[32]. Rebbi Yose the Sidonian[33] stated before Rebbi Jeremiah, in disgreement with Rebbi Jeremiah[34]: "He has the right to what she finds and earns, and to dissolve her vows." What means "no usufruct"? That she cannot reclaim from him the usufruct he had [from her property].

31 From here to the end of the Halakhah, this is Halakhah *Ketubot* 11:7.

32 This is the only right he has as a husband; he has no right to what she finds or earns, nor may he dissolve any of her vows.

33 An Amora of the fourth

generation; he appears in the Babli as Rav Yosef Ṣidonî.

34 The Tosephta, 2:4, states the opposite: "He has no right to what she finds and earns, and no right to dissolve her vows."

אָמַר רִבִּי יוֹסֵה. כָּל־שָׁעָה הֲוָה רִבִּי הִילָא אָמַר לִי. תְּנֵי מַתְנִיתָךְ. יוֹרְשָׁהּ וּמִיטַּמֵּא לָהּ. וְתַנֵּי כֵן. מְטַמֵּא הוּא אָדָם בְּאִשְׁתּוֹ הַכְּשֵׁירָה. וְאֵינוֹ מִיטַּמֵּא בְּאִשְׁתּוֹ פְּסוּלָה.

Rebbi Yose said: All the time Rebbi Hila told me, state in your *baraita* that he inherits from her and defiles himself for her[35]. We have also stated so: A man defiles himself for his qualified wife but does not become defiled for his disqualified wife[36].

35 Tosephta 2:4.

36 A Cohen is required to become impure for the burial of his close relatives (*Lev.* 21:1-3). The secondarily prohibited is a qualified wife by biblical standards; he must bury her. A divorcee for a Cohen is disqualified; he may not become impure for her.

רִבִּי אָבוּן בְּעָא קוֹמֵי רִבִּי מָנָא. עַבְדֵי שְׁנִיּוֹת מַהוּ שֶׁיֹּאכְלוּ בַתְּרוּמָה. אָמַר לֵיהּ. שְׁתוֹק וְיָפֶה לָךְ. הִיא (fol. 10b) אוֹכֶלֶת וַעֲבָדֶיהָ אֵינָן אוֹכְלִין.

Rebbi Abun asked before Rebbi Mana: May the slaves of a secondarily forbidden [wife][37] eat heave? He said to him, be quiet, it is better for you. She eats[38] but her slaves do not eat[39].

37 The mortmain slaves of the wife of a Cohen.

38 Her marriage is legitimate by biblical standards.

39 Since the husband has no obligation to feed her and her slaves, the acquisition is not complete and the slaves cannot eat from what the Cohen does not have to give them (Maimonides, *Hilkhot Terumah* 6:20, commentary of Radbaz.)

תַּמָּן תַּנִּינָן. גֵּט מְעוּשֶּׂה בְיִשְׂרָאֵל כָּשֵׁר וּבַגּוֹיִם פָּסוּל. שְׁמוּאֵל אָמַר. פָּסוּל וּפוֹסֵל לִכְהוּנָּה. וָמַר שְׁמוּאֵל. אַכְרְזוֹן בְּקִרְוֵיכוֹן. שְׁמוּאֵל אָמַר. אֵין מְעַשִּׂין אֶלָּא פוֹסְלִין. שְׁמוּאֵל אָמַר. אֵין מְעַשִּׂין אֶלָּא כְגוֹן אַלְמָנָה לְכֹהֵן גָּדוֹל. גְּרוּשָׁה וַחֲלוּצָה לְכֹהֵן הֶדְיוֹט. וְהָא תַנִּינָן שְׁנִיּוֹת. לָא בְגִין אָמַר שְׁמוּאֵל. וְהָא תַנִּינָן. הַמַּדִּיר אֶת אִשְׁתּוֹ מִלֵּיהָנוֹת לוֹ. עַד שְׁלֹשִׁים יוֹם יַעֲמִיד פַּרְנָס. יוֹתֵר מִכֵּן יוֹצִיא וְיִתֵּן כְּתוּבָּה. שָׁמַעְנוּ שֶׁהוּא מוֹצִיא. שָׁמַעְנוּ כוֹפִין.

There, we have stated[40]: "A forced bill of divorce is valid in Israel[41]; it is invalid from Gentiles.[42]" Samuel said, it is invalid and disqualifies for the priesthood[43]. And Samuel said, publicize in your towns: It is invalid and disqualifies for the priesthood. Samuel said, one does not force, only disqualify[44]. Samuel said, one does not force except for example a widow married to a High Priest, a divorcee or one freed by *ḥalîṣah* for a simple priest. But did we not state: "Secondarily forbidden"? Did he not say "for example"[45]? But did we not state: "A person who by a vow forbids his wife to have any usufruct from him, up to 30 days he shall appoint a caretaker; after 30 days he shall divorce her and pay *ketubah*"! We heard that he shall divorce; did we hear that one forces him[46]?

40 Mishnah *Giṭṭin* 9:8.

41 If a rabbinic court forces the husband to divorce his wife, the divorce is valid.

42 If the wife appeals to the Gentile court or ruler to force a divorce from her husband, the divorce document is invalid (except, as stated in the Mishnah, if the Gentile court or ruler forces the husband to obey the directives of the rabbinic court.)

43 The woman who uses the instruments of the Gentile government to force a divorce is not divorced but disqualified for the priesthood.

44 In the absence of parallel sources, it is difficult to ascertain the exact text and its meaning.

45 He approves of judicial intervention in the case of any sinful marriage, whether by biblical or rabbinic standards.

46 In this case, only moral pressure is acceptable; one may not jail the recalcitrant husband until he agrees to a divorce.

מַה בֵין אֵילּוּ לָאֵילּוּ. אֶלָּא עַל יְדֵי שֶׁהֵן דִּבְרֵי תוֹרָה וְאֵין דִּבְרֵי תוֹרָה צְרִיכִין חִיזּוּק לְפִיכָךְ יֵשׁ לָהֶן כְּתוּבָּה. וְאֵילּוּ עַל יְדֵי שֶׁהֵן דִּבְרֵי סוֹפְרִין וְדִבְרֵי סוֹפְרִין צְרִיכִין חִיזּוּק לְפִיכָךְ אֵין לָהֶן כְּתוּבָּה. אִית דְּבָעֵי מֵימַר. אֵילּוּ עַל יְדֵי שֶׁקְּנָסָן בְּיָדָן וּבְיַד הַוּוֹלָד וְלֹא קָנְסוּ בָהֶן דָּבָר אַחֵר לְפִיכָךְ יֵשׁ לָהֶן כְּתוּבָּה. וְאֵילּוּ עַל יְדֵי שֶׁאֵין קְנָסָן בְּיָדָן וּבְיַד הַוּוֹלָד וְקָנְסוּ בָהֶן דָּבָר אַחֵר לְפִיכָךְ אֵין לָהֶן כְּתוּבָּה. מַה נְפַק מִן בֵּינֵיהוֹן. הַמַּחֲזִיר אֶת גְּרוּשָׁתוֹ מִשֶּׁנִּישֵּׂאת. מָאן דְּאָמַר. אֵילּוּ עַל יְדֵי שֶׁהֵן דִּבְרֵי תוֹרָה. וְזוֹ הוֹאִיל וְהוּא דְּבַר תּוֹרָה לְפִיכָךְ יֵשׁ לָהּ כְּתוּבָּה. וְאִית דְּבָעֵי מֵימַר. אֵילּוּ עַל יְדֵי שֶׁקְּנָסָן בְּיָדָן וּבְיַד הַוּוֹלָד. וְזֶה הוֹאִיל וְאֵין קְנָסָהּ בְּיָדוֹ וּבְיַד הַוּוֹלָד לְפִיכָךְ אֵין לָהּ כְּתוּבָּה.

What is the difference between these and those[47]? Since these are words of the Torah and the words of the Torah do not need support, therefore they have *ketubah*. Those, because they are words of the Sopherim and the words of the Sopherim need support, therefore they do not have *ketubah*. Some want to say since these are punished together with the child, they did not fine them, therefore they have *ketubah*. Those, since they are not punished together with the child, they fined them, therefore they do not have *ketubah*[48] What is the difference between them? He who remarried his divorced wife after she had remarried[49]. For him who says since these are words of the Torah, and this case is a word of the Torah, therefore she has *ketubah*. For those who want to say since these are punished together with the child, this one, since neither she nor the child is punished, therefore, she has no *ketubah*.

47 Between the disqualified women married to priests who receive *ketubah* at the time of divorce and the secondarily prohibited who do not.

48 A more detailed discussion is in Tosephta 2:4/Babli 85b. Both these sources stress that a disqualified woman has no reason to seek out a Cohen since her child will be desecrated whereas a secondarily forbidden (who might be permitted to him by another sect) might want to be

married by a relative.

49 This case is not discussed in the parallel sources.

רִבִּי יַעֲקֹב בַּר אָחָא אָמַר. רִבִּי זְעִירָא וְרִבִּי הִילָא תְּרֵיהוֹן אָמְרִין. בִּמְזוֹנוֹת פְּלִיגִין. רִבִּי יוֹחָנָן אָמַר. יֵשׁ לָהּ מְזוֹנוֹת. אָמַר לֵיהּ רִבִּי לָעְזָר. אוֹמְרִים לָהּ. הוֹצִיא. וְאַתְּ אָמַר הָכֵין. הֲווֹן בָּעְייָן מֵימַר כֵּן. בִּתְנַיֵי כְתוּבָּה פְלִיגִין. כָּל־עַמָּא מוֹדֵיי שֶׁאֵין לָהּ מְזוֹנוֹת. בְּיוֹרְשֶׁיהָ קָנְסוּ לֹא כָּל־שֶׁכֵּן בָּהּ. וּמָאן דָּמַר. בִּמְזוֹנוֹת פְּלִיגִין. הָא בִּתְנַיֵי כְתוּבָּה לֹא. לָמָּה. בָּהּ קָנְסוּ וְלֹא קָנְסוּ בְּיוֹרְשֶׁיהָ.

Rebbi Jacob bar Aḥa said that Rebbi Ze'ira and Rebbi Hila say that they differ about upkeep[50]. Rebbi Joḥanan said, she may demand upkeep[51]. Rebbi Eleazar said to him, one says to [him][52], divorce her! And you say so? They wanted to say so, they differ about the conditions attached to a *ketubah*[53]. Everybody agrees that she cannot claim support since they even punished her heirs, so much more herself. But for him who says that they differ about upkeep it follows that they do not differ about the conditions attached to a *ketubah*. They fined her but not her heirs.

50 In the case of an irregular marriage of a Cohen.

51 From her husband.

52 Reading לה in the ms. and the *editio princeps* as לו.

53 The general framework of the obligations of a husband towards his wife and her heirs which can be enforced even if not written in the document (Mishnah *Ketubot* Chapter 4).

(fol. 10a) **משנה ו**: בַּת יִשְׂרָאֵל מְאוֹרֶסֶת לְכֹהֵן מְעוּבֶּרֶת מִכֹּהֵן שׁוֹמֶרֶת יָבָם לְכֹהֵן. וְכֵן בַּת כֹּהֵן לְיִשְׂרָאֵל לֹא תֹאכַל בַּתְּרוּמָה. בַּת יִשְׂרָאֵל מְאוֹרֶסֶת לְלֵוִי מְעוּבֶּרֶת מִלֵּוִי שׁוֹמֶרֶת יָבָם לְלֵוִי וְכֵן בַּת לֵוִי לְיִשְׂרָאֵל לֹא תֹאכַל בַּמַּעֲשֵׂר. בַּת לֵוִי

מְאוֹרֶסֶת לְכֹהֵן מְעוּבֶּרֶת מִכֹּהֵן שׁוֹמֶרֶת יָבָם לְכֹהֵן וְכֵן בַּת כֹּהֵן לְלֵוִי לֹא יֹאכְלוּ לֹא בִתְרוּמָה וְלֹא בְמַעֲשֵׂר.

Mishnah 6: An Israel woman betrothed to a Cohen, or pregnant from a Cohen[54], or waiting for her Cohen levir, and also a Cohen woman betrothed to an Israel may not eat heave. An Israel woman betrothed to a Levite, or pregnant from a Levite, or waiting for her Levite levir, and also a Levite woman betrothed to an Israel may not eat tithe. A Levite woman betrothed to a Cohen or pregnant from a Cohen, or waiting for her Cohen levir, and also a Levite woman betrothed to a Cohen may not eat either heave or tithe.

54 A pregnant widow, cf. Mishnah 7:3. All cases will be explained in the Halakhah.

(fol. 10b) **הלכה ו**: בַּת יִשְׂרָאֵל מְאוֹרֶסֶת לְכֹהֵן. כָּל־טָהוֹר בְּבֵיתְךָ יֹאכְלֶנּוּ. וְלֵית הִיא גַו בֵּייתֵיהּ. מִכֹּהֵן. לִילִיד בַּיִת. אֵין בֵּין[55] יְלִיד בַּיִת. לְשׁוֹמֶרֶת יָבָם לְכֹהֵן. כָּל־טָהוֹר בְּבֵיתְךָ יֹאכְלֶנּוּ. וְלֵית הִיא גַו בֵּייתֵיהּ. וְכֵן בַּת כֹּהֵן לְיִשְׂרָאֵל. וּבַת כֹּהֵן כִּי תִהְיֶה לְאִישׁ זָר. מְעוּבֶּרֶת מִיִּשְׂרָאֵל שׁוֹמֶרֶת יָבָם לְיִשְׂרָאֵל. וְשָׁבָה אֶל בֵּית אָבִיהָ פְּרָט לְשׁוֹמֶרֶת יָבָם. כִּנְעוּרֶיהָ. פְּרָט לִמְעוּבֶּרֶת.

"An Israel woman betrothed to a Cohen." "Any pure person in your house may eat it,[56]" but she is not in his house. "From a Cohen", for the one born in his house; this one is not born in his house[57]. "The one waiting for her Cohen levir," "any pure person in your house may eat it," but she is not in his house. 'And also a Cohen woman betrothed to an Israel," "a daughter of a Cohen when she will belong to an outside man[58]." One[59] pregnant from an Israel or waiting for an Israel levir: "When she returns to her father's house[60]," that excludes the one waiting for her levir, "as in her youth[59]," that excludes the pregnant one.

55 This is the text in the ms. and *editio princeps*. Probably one should read כאן as in the next paragraph.

56 *Num*. 18:11, speaking of heave. While she was acquired by her husband (cf. Chapter 1, Note 63), she is not in his house before the actual marriage. She has a claim if the husband drags his feet for the marriage, cf. Mishnah *Ketubot* 5:2-3.

57 This refers to the pregnant widow. The reason given is a misquote from *Lev*. 22:11: "Any born in his house, they should eat from his food." The unborn does not eat.

58 *Lev*. 22:12: "she may not eat from the holy heaves."

59 Speaking of the parallel cases not mentioned in the Mishnah of a Cohen's daughter betrothed to, pregnant from, or waiting for a levir of, an Israel.

60 *Lev*. 22:12: "she may eat from her father's food." The same argument in the Babli, 87a. A longer discussion in *Sifra Emor Pereq* 6(1)

בַּת יִשְׂרָאֵל מְאוֹרֶסֶת לְלֵוִי. אַתֶּם וּבֵיתְכֶם וְלֵית הִיא גַּו בֵּייתֵהּ. מְעוּבֶּרֶת מִלֵּוִי. יְלִיד בַּיִת. וְאֵין כָּאן יְלִיד בַּיִת. אָמַר רִבִּי יוֹסֵי. כְּלוּם כְּתִיב יְלִיד בַּיִת אֶלָּא בְכֹהֵן. כְּמַה דְתֵימַר תַּמָּן הַיִּלּוּד מַאֲכִיל וְשֶׁאֵינוֹ יִלּוּד אֵינוֹ מַאֲכִיל. וְהָכָא נַמֵּי הַיִּלּוּד מַאֲכִיל וְשֶׁאֵינוֹ יִלּוּד אֵינוֹ מַאֲכִיל. שׁוֹמֶרֶת יָבָם לְלֵוִי. אַתֶּם וּבֵיתְכֶם. וְלָאו הוּא גַּו בֵּייתָהּ. וְכֵן בַּת לֵוִי. וּבַת כֹּהֵן כִּי תִהְיֶה לְאִישׁ זָר. וְלֹא בַּת כֹּהֵן כְּתִיב. אָמַר רִבִּי יוֹסֵי. בַּת. אַחַת בַּת כֹּהֵן וְאַחַת בַּת לֵוִי. בַּת כֹּהֵן שֶׁנִּשֵּׂאת לְיִשְׂרָאֵל חוֹזֶרֶת וְאוֹכֶלֶת. בַּת יִשְׂרָאֵל שֶׁנִּשֵּׂאת לְכֹהֵן חוֹזֶרֶת וְאֵינָהּ אוֹכֶלֶת. מְעוּבֶּרֶת מִיִּשְׂרָאֵל שׁוֹמֶרֶת יָבָם לְיִשְׂרָאֵל. וְשָׁבָה אֶל בֵּית אָבִיהָ פְּרָט לְשׁוֹמֶרֶת יָבָם. כִּנְעוּרֶיהָ. פְּרָט לִמְעוּבֶּרֶת.

"An Israel woman betrothed to a Levite," "you and your house[61]" but she is not in his house. "Pregnant from a Levite," "born in the house," this one is not born in his house[57]. Rebbi Yose said, is not "born in the house" written only for a Cohen? As you say there, whoever is born lets eat, whoever is not born does not let eat; here also whoever is born lets eat, whoever is not born does not let eat[62]. "Waiting for her Levite levir," "you and your house," but he is not in her house. "And also a Levite woman": "And a daughter of a Cohen when she will belong to an outside man[58]." Is there not written "daughter of a Cohen"? Rebbi Yose said "daughter", whether she is a Cohen's or a Levi's[63]. The daughter of a Cohen who was married to an Israel may return and eat, the daughter of an Israel who was married to a Cohen may return and not eat. One[64] pregnant from an Israel or waiting for an Israel levir: "When she returns to her father's house," that excludes the one waiting for her levir, "as in her youth," that excludes the pregnant one.

61 *Num.* 18:31.

62 All rules for the Levites are (rabbinically) derived from those of the Cohen; they are not biblical.

63 This argument is a little less cryptic in the Babli, 68b, in the name of R. Abba: Since it is written "*and* a daughter" and not simply "a daughter", following R. Aqiba one has to add another category of daughters who do not eat their part of agricultural produce.

64 Again the case of the Levite is assimilated into that of the Cohen.

בַּת לֵוִי מְאוֹרֶסֶת לְכֹהֵן. כָּל־טָהוֹר בְּבֵיתְךָ יֹאכְלֶנּוּ. וְלֵית הוּא גַו בֵּייתָהּ. מְעוּבֶּרֶת מִכֹּהֵן. יְלִיד בַּיִת. וְאֵין כָּאן יְלִיד בַּיִת. שׁוֹמֶרֶת יָבָם לְכֹהֵן. כָּל־טָהוֹר בְּבֵיתְךָ יֹאכְלֶנּוּ. וְלֵית הוּא גַו בֵּייתָא. וְכֵן בַּת כֹּהֵן לְלֵוִי לֹא יֹאכְלוּ לֹא בַּתְּרוּמָה וְלֹא בַמַּעֲשֵׂר. נִיחָא בַּתְּרוּמָה לֹא תֹאכַל. בְּמַעֲשֵׂר. מַה נַפְשָׁךְ. כֹּהֶנֶת הִיא תֹאכַל. לְוִייָה הִיא תֹאכַל. רִבִּי הִילָא בְשֵׁם רִבִּי יוֹחָנָן. כְּמָאן דְּאָמַר אֵין נוֹתְנִין מַעֲשֵׂר לִכְהוּנָּה. הֲוָה הוּא דְאָמַר נוֹתְנִין מַעֲשֵׂר לִכְהוּנָּה.

"A Levitic woman betrothed to a Cohen." "Any pure person in your house may eat it,[56]" but he is not in her house. "From a Cohen", for the one born in his house; this one is not born in his house[57]. "The one waiting for her Cohen levir," "any pure person in your house may eat it," but she is not in his house. [65]"Similarly, the daughter of a Cohen [betrothed] to a Levite should eat neither heave nor tithe." We understand that she should not eat heave. But tithe any way you take it, if she is a Cohen's daughter she should eat, if she is a Levite's wife she should eat. Rebbi Hila in the name of Rebbi Joḥanan: [It follows] him who says one does not give tithe to Cohanim. That means, he himself says one gives heave to Cohanim[66].

65 This text is copied from *Ma'aser Sheni* 5:9, Notes 176-177.

66 This last sentence is inappropriate here; it refers to the position of R. Joḥanan that the daughter of a Cohen betrothed to a Levite may eat tithe. The discussion in the Babli, 86a/b, remains inconclusive.

(fol. 10a) **משנה ז**: בַּת יִשְׂרָאֵל שֶׁנִּשֵּׂאת לְכֹהֵן תֹּאכַל בַּתְּרוּמָה. מֵת וְלָהּ מִמֶּנּוּ בֵּן תֹּאכַל בַּתְּרוּמָה. נִשֵּׂאת לַלֵּוִי תֹּאכַל בַּמַּעֲשֵׂר. מֵת וְלָהּ מִמֶּנּוּ בֵּן תֹּאכַל בַּמַּעֲשֵׂר. נִשֵּׂאת לְיִשְׂרָאֵל לֹא תֹאכַל לֹא בַּתְּרוּמָה וְלֹא בַּמַּעֲשֵׂר.

Mishnah 7: An Israel woman married to a Cohen shall eat heave. If he died but she had a son from him, she shall eat heave. If [then] she married a Levite, she shall eat tithe. If he died but she had a son from him, she shall eat tithe. If [then] she marries an Israel, she may eat neither heave nor tithe.

משנה ח: מֵת וְלָהּ מִמֶּנּוּ בֵּן לֹא תֹאכַל לֹא בַּתְּרוּמָה וְלֹא בַּמַּעֲשֵׂר. מֵת בְּנָהּ מִיִּשְׂרָאֵל תֹּאכַל בַּמַּעֲשֵׂר. מִלֵּוִי תֹּאכַל בַּתְּרוּמָה. מֵת בְּנָהּ מִכֹּהֵן לֹא תֹאכַל לֹא בַּתְּרוּמָה וְלֹא בַּמַּעֲשֵׂר.

Mishnah 8: If he died but she had a son from him, she may eat neither heave nor tithe. If her son from the Israel died, she may eat tithe[67]. From the Levite, she may eat heave. If her son from the Cohen died, she may eat neither heave nor tithe.

משנה ט: בַּת כֹּהֵן שֶׁנִּשֵּׂאת לְיִשְׂרָאֵל לֹא תֹאכַל בַּתְּרוּמָה. מֵת וְלָהּ מִמֶּנּוּ בֵּן לֹא תֹאכַל בַּתְּרוּמָה. נִשֵּׂאת לַלֵּוִי תֹּאכַל בַּמַּעֲשֵׂר. מֵת וְלָהּ מִמֶּנּוּ בֵּן תֹּאכַל

בַּמַּעֲשֵׂר. נִשֵּׂאת לְכֹהֵן תֹּאכַל בַּתְּרוּמָה. מֵת וְלָהּ מִמֶּנּוּ בֵן תֹּאכַל בַּתְּרוּמָה. מֵת בְּנָהּ מִכֹּהֵן לֹא תֹאכַל בַּתְּרוּמָה. מִלֵּוִי לֹא תֹאכַל בַּמַּעֲשֵׂר. מֵת בְּנָהּ מִיִּשְׂרָאֵל חוֹזֶרֶת לְבֵית אָבִיהָ וְעַל זוֹ נֶאֱמַר וְשָׁבָה אֶל בֵּית אָבִיהָ כִּנְעוּרֶיהָ.

Mishnah 9: A Cohen's daughter married to an Israel may not eat heave. If he died but she had a son from him, she may not eat heave. If [then] she married a Levite, she may eat tithe. If he died but she had a son from him, she may eat tithe. If [then] she married a Cohen, she may eat heave. If he died but she had a son from him, she may eat heave. If her son from the Cohen died, she may eat tithe; from the Levite, she may not eat tithe. If her son from the Israel died, she returns to her father's house and for this case it was said: "She returns to her father's house as in her youth[68]."

67 Not only her child, but all of her child's children. As long as any descendant of the husband is alive, she belongs to the husband's family. This holds for all these cases. This Mishnah presumes that a Cohen, being also a Levite, is free to eat tithe, as are all members of his household.

68 *Lev.* 22:13. "If the daughter of a Cohen becomes a widow or divorcee without issue, she returns to her father's house as in her youth, she shall eat of her father's food, but no outsider may eat of it."

(fol. 10b) **הלכה ט**: בַּת כֹּהֵן שֶׁנִּשֵּׂאת לְיִשְׂרָאֵל כול׳. רִבִּי לֵיוֹנְטֵי בְּעָא קוֹמֵי רִבִּי יוֹנָה. נִיחָא בַּת כֹּהֵן שֶׁנִּשֵּׂאת לְיִשְׂרָאֵל חוֹזֶרֶת וְאוֹכֶלֶת. בַּת יִשְׂרָאֵל שֶׁנִּשֵּׂאת לְכֹהֵן הוֹאִיל וְהִיא רְאוּיָה לוֹכַל לָמָּה אֵינָהּ אוֹכֶלֶת. אָמַר לֵיהּ. כֵּן אָמַר רִבִּי זְעִירָה רַב עָנָן בְּשֵׁם רַב. מַהוּ בַּת כֹּהֵן. מִתְלַמֶּדֶתָהּ שֶׁלַּכֹּהֵן. כְּמַה דְתֵימַר בַּת בָּבֶל הַשְּׁדוּדָה. וְכִי בַּת בָּבֶל הָיְתָה. אֶלָּא שֶׁנַּעֲשֵׂית כְּמַעֲשֵׂה בָבֶל. רִבִּי יוֹסֵי בֵּירִבִּי בּוּן בְּשֵׁם רַב. שְׁתֵּי בָנוֹת אֲמוּרוֹת בַּפָּרָשָׁה. אַחַת חוֹזֶרֶת וְאוֹכֶלֶת וְאַחַת חוֹזֶרֶת וְאֵינָהּ אוֹכֶלֶת. בַּת כֹּהֵן שֶׁנִּשֵּׂאת לְיִשְׂרָאֵל חוֹזֶרֶת וְאוֹכֶלֶת. בַּת יִשְׂרָאֵל שֶׁנִּשֵּׂאת לְכֹהֵן חוֹזֶרֶת וְאֵינָהּ אוֹכֶלֶת. אֱמוֹר מֵעַתָּה. נִשֵּׂאת לְכָשֵׁר חוֹזֶרֶת וְאוֹכֶלֶת. לְפָסוּל חוֹזֶרֶת וְאֵינָהּ אוֹכֶלֶת. רַב אָמַר הֲלָכָה אוֹכֶלֶת בַּתְּרוּמָה וְאֵינָהּ

אוֹכֶלֶת בֶּחָזֶה וָשׁוֹק. רִבִּי יוֹחָנָן אָמַ. אוֹכֶלֶת בֶּחָזֶה וָשׁוֹק. תַּנֵּי רִבִּי חִייָה מְסַייֵעַ לְרַב. מִלֶּחֶם. לֹא כָּל־הַלֶּחֶם. תַּנֵּי רִבִּי שִׁמְעוֹן בַּר יוֹחַי מְסַייֵעַ לְרִבִּי יוֹחָנָן. מִלֶּחֶם אָבִיהָ תֹּאכֵל. לְרַבּוֹת חַלּוֹת תּוֹדָה וּרְקִיקֵי נָזִיר.

Halakhah 9: "A Cohen's daughter married to an Israel," etc. Rebbi Leontes asked before Rebbi Yose: One understands that a Cohen's daughter who was married to an Israel returns to eat. But why does the daughter of an Israel married to a Cohen not eat when she should be enabled to eat[69]? He said to him, so said Rebbi Ze'ira, Rav Anan in the name of Rav: What means "a Cohen's daughter[70]", one who is trained by a Cohen. As you say, "Babylon's ransacked daughter,[71]" was she the daughter of Babylon? But she behaved in Babylon's way. Rebbi Yose ben Rebbi Abun in the name of Rav: Two daughters are mentioned in the paragraph[72]. One returns and eats, the other returns but does not eat. A Cohen's daughter who was married to an Israel returns to eat. A daughter of an Israel married to a Cohen returns but does not eat. Say also, if she was married to a qualified person, she returns and eats, to a disqualified person she returns but does not eat[73]. Rav said, practice is that she returns to eat heave but not to eat breast and foreleg[74]. Rebbi Johanan said, she eats breast and foreleg. Rebbi Ḥiyya stated a support for Rav: "*of* food,[75]" not all the food. Rebbi Simeon ben Iohai stated a support for Rebbi Johanan: "of her father's food she shall eat," to include the loaves of the thanksgiving sacrifice and the cakes of the *nazir*.

69 As long as the Cohen's son is alive she should be able to eat heave since for him she remains in the Cohen's family after her husband's death.

70 *Lev*. 22:13.

71 *Ps*. 137:8, speaking of Edom.

72 *Lev*. 22:12, a daughter who does not eat, *Lev*. 22:13 one who does eat.

73 A Cohen's daughter married to a person disqualified for priesthood remains permanently disabled.

74 Cf. Chapter 8, Note 228.

75 *Lev.* 22:13. "If the daughter of a Cohen becomes a widow or divorcee without issue, she returns to her father's house as in her youth; she shall eat *of* her father's food." As usual, the prefix מ is used as partitive. The same argument (anonymous) in *Sifra Emor Pereq* 6(1), Babli 37a.

האשה שהלך פרק עשירי

(fol. 10b) **משנה א:** הָאִשָּׁה שֶׁהָלַךְ בַּעֲלָהּ לִמְדִינַת הַיָּם וּבָאוּ וְאָמְרוּ לָהּ מֵת בַּעֲלֵיךְ נִשֵּׂאת וְאַחַר כָּךְ בָּא בַּעֲלָהּ תֵּצֵא מִזֶּה וּמִזֶּה וּצְרִיכָה גֵט מִזֶּה וּמִזֶּה וְאֵין לָהּ לֹא כְתוּבָּה. וְלֹא פֵּירוֹת וְלֹא מְזוֹנוֹת וְלֹא בְלָאוֹת עַל זֶה וְעַל זֶה. וְאִם נָטְלָה מִזֶּה וּמִזֶּה תַּחֲזִיר וְהַוְּלָד מַמְזֵר מִזֶּה וּמִזֶּה. וְלֹא זֶה וְזֶה מִטַּמְּאִין לָהּ. וְלֹא זֶה וְזֶה זַכָּאִים לֹא בִמְצִיאָתָהּ וְלֹא בְמַעֲשֵׂה יָדֶיהָ וְלֹא בְהֵפֵר נְדָרֶיהָ. הָיְתָה בַת יִשְׂרָאֵל נִפְסְלָה מִן הַכְּהוּנָּה. וּבַת לֵוִי מִן הַמַּעֲשֵׂר. וּבַת כֹּהֵן מִן הַתְּרוּמָה. וְאֵין יוֹרְשָׁיו שֶׁל זֶה וְלֹא יוֹרְשָׁיו שֶׁל זֶה יוֹרְשִׁין אֶת כְּתוּבָּתָהּ. מֵתוּ אָחִיו שֶׁל זֶה וְאָחִיו שֶׁל זֶה חוֹלְצִין וְלֹא מְיַיבְּמִין.

Mishnah 1: A woman's husband went overseas and some persons[1] came and told her, your husband died. If she remarried[2] and then the husband returned, she has to leave both husbands[3], she needs a bill of divorce from both of them, she has neither *ketubah* nor usufruct nor used clothing from either of them, and if she took anything she must return it. Any child from either of the men is a bastard; neither of them may defile himself for her. Neither man has any claim on what she finds or earns, or on invalidation of her vows[4]. If she was the daughter of an Israel, she is disabled from priesthood, the daughter of a Levite from tithe, the daughter of a Cohen from heave. The heirs of neither man inherit her *ketubah*[5]. If they died[6], the brothers of both of them perform *ḥaliṣah* but not levirate.

1 The language of the Mishnah implies that the wife was told (maybe by hearsay), not that she received testimony that would stand up in court.

This is clear from the following Mishnaiot and the discussion at the end of Halakhah 2.

2 Without having her husband declared dead by a competent court. That a woman may remarry even if her husband's death is not confirmed by two independent witnesses of sterling character (*Deut*. 19:15) is a rabbinic institution.

3 It is clear that she has to leave the second husband since her marriage to him was invalid by biblical standards. As pointed out by both Talmudim, this shows that the rules of the Mishnah are rabbinical.

4 *Num*. 30:14.

5 If the deceased husband had sons from different wives, before the inheritance is distributed the *ketubah* of each wife should be given to her sons; only the remainder is distributed among all sons.

6 Before the divorce documents were executed and there are no children.

(fol. 10c) **הלכה א**: הָאִשָּׁה שֶׁהָלַךְ בַּעֲלָהּ לִמְדִינַת הַיָּם כול'. כְּמָה דְתֵימַר תַּמָּן מַפְרִישִׁין אוֹתָן שְׁלֹשָׁה חֳדָשִׁים שֶׁמָּא מְעוּבָּרוֹת הֵן. וְאִם הָיוּ קְטַנּוֹת וְלֹא הָיוּ רְאוּיוֹת לְוּלָד מַחֲזִירִין אוֹתָן מִיָּד. וְאָמַר אַף הָכָא כֵן. שַׁנְייָא הִיא תַמָּן שֶׁאֲחֵרִים הִטְעוּ בָהֶן. וְהָכָא לֹא אֲחֵרִים הִטְעוּ בָהּ. קְנָס קָנְסוּ בָהּ שֶׁתְּהֵא בוֹדֶקֶת יָפֶה. וְיִקְנְסוּ בָהּ אֵצֶל הַשֵּׁינִי וְלֹא יִקְנְסוּ בָהּ אֵצֶל הָרִאשׁוֹן. אָמַר רִבִּי יוֹחָנָן. מֵרֵיחַ עֶרְוָה נָֽגְעוּ בָהּ. מֵעַתָּה לֹא תְהֵא צְרִיכָה מִמֶּנּוּ גֵט. שַׁנְייָא הִיא שֶׁנִּשֵּׂאת לוֹ דֶרֶךְ הֵיתֵר. שְׁמוּאֵל אָמַר. אוֹמֵר אֲנִי. שֶׁמָּא שִׁילַּח לָהּ גִּיטָּהּ מִמְּדִינַת הַיָּם. הָתִיב רִבִּי חַגַּיי קוֹמֵי רִבִּי זְעִירָה וְהָתַנִּינָן. אָֽמְרוּ לָהּ. מֵת בַּעֲלֵיךְ. וְנִתְקַדְּשָׁה וְאַחַר כָּךְ בָּא בַעֲלָהּ. מוּתֶּרֶת לַחֲזוֹר לוֹ. אִם אוֹמֵר אַתְּ. שֶׁמָּא שִׁילַּח לָהּ גִּיטָּהּ מִמְּדִינַת הַיָּם. תְּהֵא אֲסוּרָה לַחֲזוֹר לוֹ. אֶלָּא כְרִבִּי יוֹסֵי בֶן כִּיפֵּר. דְּרִבִּי יוֹסֵי בֶן כִּיפֵּר אָמַר. מִן הָאֵירוּסִין מוּתֶּרֶת. וְלֹא מוֹדֵי רִבִּי יוֹסֵי בֶן כִּיפֵּר שֶׁאִם נָתַן לָהּ הָאַחֲרוֹן גֵּט לֹא פְסָלָהּ מִן הַכְּהוּנָּה. וְהָתַנִּינָן. עַף עַל פִּי שֶׁנָּתַן לָהּ הָאַחֲרוֹן גֵּט לֹא פְסָלָהּ מִן הַכְּהוּנָּה. רַבָּנִין דְּקֵיסָרִין בְּשֵׁם רִבִּי הִילָא. כְּדֵי לְבָרֵר אִיסּוּרוֹ שֶׁל רִאשׁוֹן.

Halakhah 1: "A woman's husband went overseas," etc. As you say there[7], "these women one separates for three months to see whether they are pregnant. If they were minors not yet able to have a child one returns them at once." Should one not say the same here[8]? There is a difference, since there others deceived them. Did here not also others deceive them? They instituted a fine so that she should investigate carefully[9]. Then they should fine her with respect to the second [husband] but not with respect to the first! Rebbi Joḥanan said, they touched this case because it looks like adultery[10]. Then she should not need a bill of divorce from him[11]! There is a difference since she was married to him in a lawful manner[12]. Samuel said, I say, maybe he sent her a bill of divorce from overseas[13]. Rebbi Ḥaggai objected before Rebbi Ze'ira: Did we not state[14]: "If they said to her, your husband has died, she was betrothed and then her husband came, she is permitted to return to him." If you say, maybe he sent her a bill of divorce from overseas; should she not be forbidden to return to him[15]? But it must follow Rebbi Yose ben Kipper, as Rebbi Yose ben Kipper said, from betrothal it is permitted[16]. Did Rebbi Yose ben Kipper not agree that if the second husband gave her a bill of divorce that she was not disabled from priesthood? As we have stated[14], "even if the second husband gave her a bill of divorce, she was not disabled from priesthood.[17]" The rabbis of Caesarea in the name of Rebbi Hila: In order to make clear the prohibition of the first[18].

7 Mishnah 3:12, speaking of a bride who was switched in the night of the marriage.

8 What is the difference between the bride who was led into the wrong chamber and the wife given wrong information?

9 In biblical standards, there is no difference; she should be able to return to the first husband since the second marriage is nonexistent. By rabbinic decree they made the consequences of error so enormous that the presumed widow should investigate the report of her husband's death very thoroughly.

10 The wife inadvertently committed adultery with the second husband. If it had been intentional she

would be forbidden to both men (Mishnah *Soṭah* 5:1); inadvertent adultery is not a cause of forced divorce unless the husband is a Cohen. They treated the inadvertent adultery in this case under the rules of the intentional. This argument is not found in the Babli.

11 If the second marriage is treated as adulterous, it is invalid and does not require a divorce.

12 Since imperfect witnesses, even slaves, are accepted in court in cases involving a disappeared husband (Mishnah 15:4), the second marriage, based on imperfect witnesses, cannot be declared invalid.

13 The argument is given by Rav Huna, Rav's student, in the Babli (88b). People would think that the woman entered on her second marriage after receiving a bill of divorce from overseas. If she could return from the second husband to the first without formality, people would think that a marriage may be dissolved without formality.

14 Mishnah 10:7. In the Babli, 88b/89a, the argument is anonymous.

15 A divorcee may remarry her ex-husband only if she was not married to another man in the meantime, *Deut*. 24:1-4. The language of the verses makes it clear that this law applies only if the first marriage was consummated. Since, in general, "to take a wife" means to perform a formal betrothal (cf. Chapter 1, Notes 63, 95; *Peah* 6, Note 46), the prohibition is triggered by formal betrothal to the second husband.

16 To remarry one's divorcee who was divorced from a second husband whose marriage was never consummated. This minority opinion is also quoted in the Babli, 88b, as background of Mishnah 10:7.

17 The reason is spelled out in the Mishnah, that the betrothal was invalid and the dissolution of a non-marriage does not turn the woman into a divorcee forbidden to priests.

18 This is a new explanation of the Mishnah. Even though the second marriage is in fact invalid, the court will require a divorce from the second husband to make clear that the woman is forbidden to return to her first husband.

עַד כְּדוֹן בְּיוֹדַעַת שֶׁהִיא אֵשֶׁת אִישׁ. לֹא הָיְתָה יוֹדַעַת שֶׁהִיא אֵשֶׁת אִישׁ. נִישְׁמְעִינָהּ מִן הָדָא. קְטַנָּה שֶׁהִשִּׂיאָהּ אָבִיהָ. נִתְגָּרְשָׁה וְהָלְכָה וְהִשִּׂיאָה אֶת עַצְמָהּ. וְאָמַר רִבִּי אִילָא. תַּנֵּי תַּמָּן. כָּל־הָעֲרָיוֹת אֵינָן צְרִיכוֹת הֵימֶינּוּ גֵט חוּץ

מֵאֵשֶׁת אִישׁ בִּלְבָד. רִבִּי עֲקִיבָה אוֹמֵר. אַף אֲחוֹת אִשְׁתּוֹ וְאֵשֶׁת אָחִיו. שַׁנְייָא הִיא תַּמָּן בֵּין שֶׁהִיא יוֹדַעַת בֵּין שֶׁאֵינָהּ יוֹדַעַת. וְהָכָא לֹא שַׁנְייָא בֵּין שֶׁהִיא יוֹדַעַת בֵּין שֶׁאֵינָהּ יוֹדַעַת.

So far[19] if she knows that she is a married woman. What if she did not know that she was a married woman? Let us hear from the following: An underage girl who was married off by her father. She was divorced[20] and went and married on her own. About this Rebbi Hila said, one states there[21], for incestuous relationships no divorce is needed except for a married woman[22]; Rebbi Aqiba says also from his wife's sister[23] and his brother's wife[24]. Is there a difference? There, whether she knows or does not know, here also whether she knows or does not know[25].

19 The penalties spelled out in the Mishnah apply to a married woman who knowingly enters a relationship that might be adulterous.

20 This clause is a scribal error, induced by the frequent references to a minor who was married off by her father and then divorced. As the text stands, there is no problem at all since by marriage the underage girl is emancipated. If she is divorced as a minor, she becomes "an orphan while her father is living" (Mishnah 13:6) and her subsequent marriage is rabbinically valid.

If the clause is deleted, then we assume that the girl was not informed that her father had betrothed her. While the acts of a minor have no standing in law, the fact that she contracted an invalid marriage necessitates a divorce by the reasoning of R. Hila.

21 In Babylonia. The Babylonian text is quite different (Babli 94b): "For incestuous relationships no divorce is needed except for a married woman {whose husband had disappeared and} *who remarried with the consent of the court*; Rebbi Aqiba says also from his wife's sister and his brother's wife." In all these cases, the marriages would have been valid if the information about the death of husband or wife or absence of a child had been true (explanation of RITBA).

22 Since adultery is included in the chapter (*Lev.* 18) on incest prohibitions, it is technically considered incestuous.

23 Since a man may marry his

deceased wife's sister (*Lev.* 18:18).

24 Who might be married in levirate.

25 This proves only that a formal divorce is needed in all cases. It implies nothing about the material consequences spelled out in the Mishnah. It is to be assumed that the question referred only to the necessity of a divorce which is the subject of the previous discussion.

וְלֹא פֵּירוֹת. וְאָמַר רִבִּי אֲבִינָא. שֶׁאֵינָהּ יְכוֹלָה לְהוֹצִיא מִמֶּנּוּ אֲכִילַת פֵּירוֹת שֶׁאָכַל. הָדָא דְתֵימַר בְּשֶׁאָכַל עַד שֶׁלֹּא בָא הָרִאשׁוֹן. אֲבָל אִם אָכַל מִשֶּׁבָּא הָרִאשׁוֹן מוֹצִיאָה.

"Nor usufruct[26]." Rebbi Avina said, that she cannot recover from him[27] the usufruct he took. That means[28], before the first [husband] returned. But if he took after the return of the first, she can recover[29].

26 The husband upon marriage becomes the administrator of the wife's property; he is indemnified for his care and, e. g., for the obligation to redeem his wife should she be kidnapped, by receiving the usufruct of her properties; cf. Chapter 7, Note 1.

27 The second husband.

28 In the (French) text before Tosafot (85a, *s. v.* אלמנה) "Rebbi Ḥanina said, that means . . ." The ms. text corresponds to the Sephardic text before R. Isaac Fasi (§116 28b in the Wilna edition).

29 Since from the moment of the return of the first husband, the second knew that he had no right to the property.

וְאִם נָטְלָה מִזֶּה וּמִזֶּה תַּחֲזִיר. הָדָא דְתֵימַר בְּשֶׁנָּטְלָה מִשֶּׁבָּא הָרִאשׁוֹן. אֲבָל אִם נָטְלָה עַד שֶׁלֹּא בָא הָרִאשׁוֹן כְּמָא דְלָא מַפְקָה מִינֵּיהּ כֵּן לֹא מַפְקָא מִינָּהּ.

"And if she took anything one takes it away from her." That means, if she took something after the first [husband] returned. But if she took before the first returned, just as she cannot take from him so he cannot take from her[30].

30 In his absence, she naturally administers the estate and takes the usufruct; cf. *Nimmuqe Yosef* on *RIF*, Wilna edition 26b.

וְהַוּוֹלָד מַמְזֵר מִזֶּה וּמִזֶּה. נִיחָא דְוּוֹלָד מַמְזֵר מִן הַשֵּׁינִי. הַוְּלָד מַמְזֵר מִן הָרִאשׁוֹן. רִבִּי בָּא בְשֵׁם רִבִּי זְעִירָה אָמַר. דְּרִבִּי עֲקִיבָה הִיא. דְּרִבִּי עֲקִיבָה אָמַר. הַבָּא עַל סוֹטָתוֹ הַוְּלָד מַמְזֵר. הַמַּחֲזִיר גְּרוּשָׁתוֹ מִשֶּׁנִּשֵּׂאת הַוְּלָד מַמְזֵר. רִבִּי יוֹסֵי בְשֵׁם רִבִּי הִילָא. דִּבְרֵי הַכֹּל הַוְּלָד כָּשֵׁר. כְּגִיטָּהּ כֵּן מַמְזֵירָהּ. מַה נְפַק מִן בֵּינֵיהוֹן. נָתַן לָהּ הַשֵּׁינִי גֵט וְאַחַר כָּךְ בָּא עָלֶיהָ הָרִאשׁוֹן. עַל דַּעְתֵּיהּ דְּרִבִּי בָּא בְשֵׁם רִבִּי זְעִירָה הַוְּלָד מַמְזֵר כְּרִבִּי עֲקִיבָה. עַל דַּעְתֵּיהּ דְּרִבִּי (fol. 10d) יוֹסֵי בְשֵׁם רִבִּי הִילָא דִּבְרֵי הַכֹּל הַוְּלָד כָּשֵׁר.

"Any child from either of the men is a bastard." One understands that the child is a bastard from the second [husband][31]. Is it a bastard from the first[32]? Rebbi Abba in the name of Rebbi Ze'ira, this follows Rebbi Aqiba, since Rebbi Aqiba says if a man copulates with his wife whom he accuses of infidelity[33] the child is a bastard, if a man takes back his divorcee after she had remarried the child is a bastard. Rebbi Yose in the name of Rebbi Hila, according to everybody the child is acceptable[34]; the status of her bill of divorce is the status of her bastardy. What is the difference between them? If the second one gave her a bill of divorce and then the first one copulated with her. In the opinion of Rebbi Abba in the name of Rebbi Ze'ira, the child is a bastard following Rebbi Aqiba; in the opinion of Rebbi Yose in the name of Rebbi Hila, according to everybody the child is acceptable.

31 This child is the result of adultery.

32 The marriage to the first is valid.

33 *Num.* 5:11-31. If the husband formally accuses his wife of infidelity, she is forbidden to him until she is cleared (Mishnah *Soṭah* 1:3). R. Aqiba holds that any child conceived in a union which is not unconditionally permitted is a bastard.

34 Even according to R. Aqiba, the

child of the first husband is not blemished since the wife did not act with criminal intent. The child of the second husband is a bastard by biblical standards; he or she is forbidden to marry an unblemished partner but permitted a bastard. The child of the first husband is a rabbinic bastard; he or she is forbidden to marry an unblemished partner by rabbinic decree and a bastard by biblical standards. This interpretation is explicitly stated in the Babli, 89b.

לֹא זֶה וְזֶה מִיטַּמִּין לָהּ. הָדָא הִיא דְתַנֵּי רִבִּי חִייָה. מִטַּמֵּא הוּא אָדָם לְאִשְׁתּוֹ כְשֵׁירָה. וְאֵינוֹ מִטַּמֵּא לְאִשְׁתּוֹ פְסוּלָה.

"Neither of them may defile himself for her." That is what Rebbi Ḥiyya stated: "A man defiles himself for his acceptable wife but he does not defile himself for his disqualified wife.[35]"

35 If either one of the two husbands is a Cohen, he may not defile himself to bury her. The statement ascribed to R. Ḥiyya is anonymous in the Babli (94b), where the rule is derived from *Lev.* 21:4: "A husband may not defile himself if this desecrates him."

אִית תַּנָּיֵי תַנֵּי. תֵּצֵא בִשְׁלֹשָׁה עָשָׂר דָּבָר. וְאִית תַּנָּיֵי תַנֵּי. תֵּצֵא בְאַרְבָּעָה עָשָׂר דָּבָר. מָאן דָּמַר. תֵּצֵא בִשְׁלֹשָׁה עָשָׂר דָּבָר. עָבֵד בִּמְצִיאָתָהּ וּבְמַעֲשֵׂה יָדֶיהָ חָדָא. וּמָאן דָּמַר. בְּאַרְבָּעָה עָשָׂר דָּבָר. עָבֵד כָּל־חָדָא וְחָדָא מִינְּהוֹן חָדָא.

Some Tannaim state, she leaves under thirteen disabilities, but some Tannaim state, she leaves under fourteen disabilities. He who says that she leaves under thirteen disabilities takes what she finds and what she earns as one case, but he who says under fourteen disabilities takes each one by itself[36].

36 In fact, if one takes all disabilities stated in the Mishnah and the next under 13 or 14 categories, one has to take quite a few statements as one category. The Babli does not try to give a number.

אָמַר רִבִּי יִרְמְיָה. לְוִיָּה שֶׁזִּינָת אוֹכֶלֶת בְּמַעֲשֵׂר. וְתַנֵּי כֵן. לְוִיָּה שֶׁנִּשְׁבֵּית אוֹ שֶׁבָּא עָלֶיהָ אֶחָד מִן הַפְּסוּלִין לָהּ לֹא כָל־הֵימֶנָּה לְפוֹסְלָהּ. לְוִיִּם הַמְזוּהָמִים מֵאִימָּן לֹא חָשׁוּ לָהֶם מִשּׁוּם רֵיחַ פְּסוּל. וְהָתַנִּינָן בַּת לֵוִי מִן הַמַּעֲשֵׂר. אָמַר רִבִּי יוֹסֵי. תִּיפְתָּר שֶׁבָּא עָלֶיהָ יִשְׂרָאֵל וְיָלְדָה מִמֶּנּוּ בֵן.

Rebbi Jeremiah said, the promiscuous levitic woman still eats tithe[37]. One has stated thus: If a levitic woman was kidnapped[38] or if any one barred for her[39] copulated with her, he[40] is not empowered to disable her. One does not suspect even a hint of disability for Levites who were compromised from their mother's side[41]. But did we not state[42]: "the daughter of a Levite from tithe"? Rebbi Yose said, explain it that an Israel came upon her and she bore him a son[43].

37 Tithe in the hands of a Levite is totally profane; its consumption does not require any status of holiness.

38 And presumed raped.

39 Whom she could not legally marry.

40 The male illegally having sex with her. In all these cases, the daughter of a Cohen would be disabled for heave.

41 Whose father was a Levite or Cohen of questionable standing.

42 In Mishnah 1.

43 The status of the mother always follows that of her child; the mother of an Israel is an Israel woman. Cf. Halakhot 7:3-4.

רִבִּי בִּיסְנָא בְּשֵׁם רִבִּי יְהוֹשֻׁעַ בֶּן לֵוִי. כֹּהֶנֶת שֶׁזִּינָת אוֹכֶלֶת בְּמַעֲשֵׂר. וְלֹא מַתְנִיתָא הִיא. בַּת כֹּהֵן מִן הַתְּרוּמָה. הָא בְּמַעֲשֵׂר אוֹכֶלֶת. כְּמָאן דְּאָמַר. אֵין נוֹתְנִין מַעֲשֵׂר לִכְהוּנָּה. אָמַר רִבִּי נָסָא. מִילֵּיהוֹן דְּרַבָּנִין פְּלִיגִין. דְּאָמַר רִבִּי הִילָא שִׁמְעוֹן בֶּן יוֹסִינָא בְשֵׁם רִבִּי הוֹשַׁעְיָה. כֹּהֵן שֶׁבָּא עַל גְּרוּשָׁה וְהוֹלִיד בֵּן וּמֵת הָאָב. בְּתוֹךְ שְׁלֹשִׁים יוֹם הַבֵּן חַיָּיב לִפְדּוֹת אֶת עַצְמוֹ. לְאַחַר שְׁלֹשִׁים יוֹם חֲזָקָה שֶׁפְּדָייוֹ אָבִיו. וְאִם לַאֲחֵרִים הוּא פּוֹדֶה לֹא כָל־שֶׁכֵּן בְּנוֹ.

Rebbi Bisna in the name of Rebbi Joshua ben Levi: A promiscuous priestly woman may eat tithe[44]. Is that not the Mishnah: "the daughter of a Cohen from heave," this implies that she eats tithe. It may follow him who says that tithe is not given to Cohanim[45]. Rebbi Nasa said, the words of the rabbis disagree, since Rebbi Hila, Simeon ben Yosina, in the name of Rebbi Hoshaia said: If a Cohen came upon a divorcee, had a son from her, and died. [If the father died] within thirty days [of the son's birth], the son must redeem himself. After thirty days, the presumption is that his father redeemed him[46]. If he redeems for others, certainly for his son.

44 Since any Cohen is also a Levite (*Deut.* 18:1), he holds that even if a priestly woman loses her priestly status she is still levitic.

45 In that case, no statement about tithe is implied; cf. *Ma'aśer Šeni* 5:9.

46 The children of priests and Levites, as well as priestly or levitic women of good standing, are not redeemed (*Num.* 3:11-13). If the disabled son of a Cohen has to be redeemed, it follows that with the priestly he also lost the levitic status. This disproves R. Bisna's statement.

In the Babli, *Bekhorot* 47b, there is a dissenting opinion that even if the father died before 30 days, the son does not have to give his redemption money to a Cohen since his father, being a Cohen, could not be sued for the money by other Cohanim. This does not change the validity of the argument given here.

וְלֹא כְּבָר תְּנִינָתָהּ. אֵין לָהּ כְּתוּבָּה. אָמַר רִבִּי יוֹסֵי בֶּן יַעֲקֹב. שֶׁלֹּא תֹאמַר. בָּהּ קָנְסוּ וְלֹא קָנְסוּ בְיוֹרְשֶׁיהָ. לְפוּם כָּךְ צָרִיךְ מֵימַר. אֵין לָהּ כְּתוּבָּה.

Had it not already been stated: "she has no *ketubah*"?[47] Rebbi Yose ben Jacob said, that you should not say, they fined her but not her heirs. Therefore it was necessary to say, she has no *ketubah*[48].

47 This refers to the statement in the Mishnah that no children of hers, by any of her husbands, do inherit her claim to *ketubah* if she predeceases the husbands. Since it was stated earlier that she has no claim to any *ketubah* sum, the statement about her children seems superfluous.

48 That means, the first mention of the *ketubah* also refers to the claim of the children (explanation of Rav Papa in Babli 91a).

סוֹטָה כְּשֵׁם שֶׁהִיא אֲסוּרָה לַבַּעַל כָּךְ הִיא אֲסוּרָה לַבּוֹעֵל. כְּשֵׁם שֶׁהִיא אֲסוּרָה לְאָחִיו שֶׁלַּבַּעַל כָּךְ הִיא אֲסוּרָה לְאָחִיו שֶׁלַּבּוֹעֵל. יָכוֹל כְּשֵׁם שֶׁצָּרַת סוֹטָה אֲסוּרָה לְאָחִיו שֶׁלַּבַּעַל כָּךְ תְּהֵא אֲסוּרָה לְאָחִיו שֶׁלַּבּוֹעֵל. נִישְׁמְעִינָהּ מִן הָדָא. הָאִשָּׁה שֶׁהָלַךְ בַּעֲלָהּ לִמְדִינַת הַיָּם. בָּאוּ וְאָמְרוּ לָהּ. מֵת בַּעֲלֵיךְ. וְהָיָה לָהּ יָבָם כָּאן[49] וְיִבְּמָהּ וָמֵת. וְאַחַר כָּךְ בָּא בַּעֲלָהּ. אָסוּר בָּהּ וּמוּתָּר בְּצָרָתָהּ. אָסוּר בָּהּ וּמוּתָּר בְּאֵשֶׁת אָחִיו. וְאֵשֶׁת אָחִיו לֹא כְצָרַת סוֹטָה הִיא. הָדָא אָמְרָה שֶׁצָּרַת סוֹטָה מוּתָּר לְאָחִיו שֶׁלַּבּוֹעֵל. אָמַר רִבִּי יוּדָן.[50] אַתְיָיא כְרַבָּנִן דְּתַמָּן. דְּאָמַר רִבִּי הִילָא וְתַנֵּיי תַמָּן. כָּל־הָעֲרָיוֹת אֵינָן צְרִיכוֹת מִמֶּינּוּ גֵט חוּץ מֵאֵשֶׁת אִישׁ בִּלְבָד. רִבִּי עֲקִיבָה אוֹמֵר. אַף אֲחוֹת אִשְׁתּוֹ וְאֵשֶׁת אָחִיו (לֹא כְצָרַת סוֹטָה הִיא. הָדָא אָמְרָה. צָרַת סוֹטָה מוּתֶּרֶת לְאָחִיו שֶׁל בּוֹעֵל.)[51] בְּרַם כְּרַבָּנִן דְּהָכָא. רִבִּי חִיָּיה[52] אָמַר בְּשֵׁם רִבִּי יוֹחָנָן. הַכֹּל מוֹדִין בְּאֵשֶׁת אָחִיו שֶׁהִיא צְרִיכָה הֵימֶינּוּ גֵט מִשּׁוּם הֲלָכָה אֵשֶׁת אִישׁ קָנָה בָהּ. עֶרְוָה [הִיא].[53] וְעֶרְוָה פּוֹטֶרֶת צָרָתָהּ. אָמַר רִבִּי חֲנַנְיָה. אֲפִילוּ כְרַבָּנִן דְּהָכָא אַתְיָיא הִיא. בָּהּ קָנְסוּ וְלֹא קָנְסוּ בְיוֹרְשֶׁיהָ. אָמַר רִבִּי חֲנַנְיָה בְּרֵיהּ דְּרִבִּי הִילֵל. אִם כְּרַבָּנִן דְּתַמָּן יְהֵא מוּתָּר בָּהּ. רִבִּי זְעִירָה בְּשֵׁם רִבִּי יוֹחָנָן. צָרַת סוֹטָה אֲסוּרָה וְצָרַת גְּרוּשָׁה מוּתֶּרֶת. רִבִּי יַעֲקֹב בַּר אָחָא בְּשֵׁם רִבִּי יוֹחָנָן. כָּל־הַצָּרוֹת מוּתָּרוֹת חוּץ מִצָּרַת סוֹטָה. שְׁמוּאֵל אָמַר. גְּרוּשָׁה עַצְמָהּ מוּתֶּרֶת לְבֵיתָהּ. מַה פְלִיג. בְּגִין דַּהֲווֹן עָסְקִין בְּצָרוֹת לֹא אִדְכָּרִין גְּרוּשׁוֹת. צָרַת סוֹטָה לָמָּה הִיא אֲסוּרָה. רִבִּי יוֹחָנָן אָמַר. מֵרֵיחַ עֶרְוָה נָגְעוּ בָהּ. רַב אָמַר. מִפְּנֵי שֶׁכָּתוּב בָּהּ טוּמְאָה כַעֲרָיוֹת.

Just as the woman accused of infidelity is forbidden to her husband, so she is forbidden to her paramour[54]. Just as she is forbidden to her husband's brother[55], so she is forbidden to her paramour's brother. I might think that just as the co-wife of a woman accused of infidelity is forbidden to her husband's brother[56], so she should be forbidden to her paramour's brother. Let us hear from the following[57]: "A woman's husband went overseas; they came and told her that her husband had died, and she had a levir here; he married her in levirate[58] and died. Then her husband returned. She is forbidden to him but her co-widow is permitted to him; she is forbidden to him but his brother's wife is permitted to him[59]." Is his brother's wife not like the co-wife of a woman accused of infidelity? That means that the co-wife of a woman accused of infidelity is permitted to her paramour's brother. Rebbi Judan said, this follows the rabbis there[60], as Rebbi Hiia said, one states there[21], for incestuous relationships no divorce is needed except for a married woman[22]; Rebbi Aqiba says also from his wife's sister[23] and his brother's wife[24] (not like the co-wife of a woman accused of infidelity? That implies that the co-wife of a woman accused of infidelity is permitted to her paramour's brother.)[51] But following the rabbis here? Rebbi Ḥiyya said in the name of Rebbi Joḥanan, everybody agrees that his brother's wife needs a bill of divorce from him[61] because of the rule of a married wife. He married a person forbidden by the incest rules, and an incest-prohibited woman frees her co-wife. Rebbi Ḥananiah said, it is accepted even according to the rabbis here. They fined her but not her heirs[62]. Rebbi Ḥananiah, the son of Rebbi Hillel, said, according to the rabbis there, she should be permitted to him[63]. Rebbi Ze'ira in the name of Rebbi Joḥanan, the co-wife of a woman accused of infidelity is forbidden, the co-wife of a divorcee[64] is permitted. Rebbi Jacob bar Aḥa in the name of Rebbi Joḥanan: All co-wives[65] are permitted except the co-wife of a woman accused of infidelity. Samuel said, the divorcee herself is permitted in her house[66]. Does he disagree? Since they were discussing co-wives they did not mention divorcees. Why is the co-wife of a woman accused of infidelity forbidden? Rebbi Joḥanan said, they touched this case because it looks like adultery[10]. Rav said, because impurity is written there parallel to incest prohibitions[67].

49 Text from *Soṭah* 1:2. Reading here: בהן.

50 Text from *Soṭah* 1:2. Reading here: יודה.

51 The text in parentheses is dittography and is missing in *Soṭah* 1:2.

52 Text from *Soṭah* 1:2. The reference is to R. Ḥiyya bar Abba. Reading here: אחייה. Probably the Babylonian name Ḥiyya is a contraction of the Biblical Aḥiyya.

53 Word missing here, inserted in *Soṭah* 1:2 by the corrector.

54 Mishnah *Soṭah* 5:1; *Sifry Num.* 19. Unless she is cleared from the accusation, she may not marry her presumed paramour after being divorced or after her husband's death

55 If her husband dies childless and her status was not clarified; Mishnah *Soṭah* 1:2.

56 As explained at the end of this paragraph.

57 Tosephta 14:3.

58 The husband was childless.

59 The two parts of this sentence say the same: the co-widow is the brother's wife.

60 The Tosephta must be Babylonian. Since for the anonymous majority a woman married in incestuous levirate does not need a bill of divorce; she never was a co-wife in the legal sense and her disabilities cannot be transferred to her co-wives.

61 This negates R. Judan's premiss.

62 This sentence is figurative speech. It means that in most cases of fines, the heirs are not responsible, so also in this case her disability is not transferred to her co-wives.

63 Since according to the Babylonian rabbis an erroneous levirate does not necessitate a divorce, the wife committed unintentional adultery which does not cause a forced divorce except for Cohanim.

64 A divorcee remarried by her ex-husband after a second marriage. The remarriage is forbidden but not incestuous. The Babli agrees, 11b.

65 Of a woman in a forbidden but non-incestuous marriage.

66 If the husband died childless, she may be married in levirate.

67 Incestuous relations are declared impure in *Lev.* 18:24. Adultery is declared impure repeatedly in the law of the suspected wife, *Num.* 5:11-31. This argument is the only one given in the Babli, 11a.

משנה ב: רִבִּי יוֹסֵי אוֹמֵר כְּתוּבָּתָהּ עַל נִכְסֵי בַּעֲלָהּ הָרִאשׁוֹן. רִבִּי לָעְזָר (fol. 10b) אוֹמֵר הָרִאשׁוֹן זַכַּאי בִּמְצִיאָתָהּ וּבְמַעֲשֵׂה יָדֶיהָ וּבְהֵפֵר נְדָרֶיהָ. רִבִּי שִׁמְעוֹן אוֹמֵר בִּיאָתָהּ אוֹ חֲלִיצָתָהּ מֵאָחִיו הָרִאשׁוֹן פּוֹטְרוֹת צָרוֹתֶיהָ וְאֵין הַוּוָלָד מִמֶּנּוּ מַמְזֵר. נִשֵּׂאת שֶׁלֹּא בִרְשׁוּת מוּתֶּרֶת לַחֲזוֹר לוֹ.

Mishnah 2: Rebbi Yose says, her *ketubah* is from the property of her first husband[68]. Rebbi Eleazar says, the first [husband] is entitled to what she finds and earns and may annul her vows[69]. Rebbi Simeon says, copulation[70] with her or *ḥaliṣah* with her by a brother of the first [husband] frees her co-wives and a child from him[71] is not a bastard; if she was married without permission[72] she is permitted to return to him.

68 The Tannaïm mentioned in this Mishnah all disagree with Mishnah 1 in some respects. R. Yose must hold that the first husband also must provide for her until she is divorced.

69 He agrees with R. Yose that she is entitled to *ketubah* from the first husband; therefore, the husband is entitled to receive her earnings.

70 If the first husband dies childless in the case she was permitted to return to him, the levir may take her in regular levirate.

71 The first husband. The child from him after his return even if he is not allowed to take her back is never a bastard.

72 She remarried on the basis of the information by two witnesses that her husband had died without asking the court for a declaration that the husband was dead. Then her second marriage was in error and is non-existent; her adultery was unintentional and does not bar her from returning to an Israel husband. But if the second marriage was contracted under the supervision of the court, it cannot be considered non-existent and she cannot return to her first husband parallel to the remarried divorcee. In any case, any sexual relation she may have with the first husband after the dissolution of the second marriage cannot be incestuous (cf. Notes 64,128).

משנה ג: נִישֵּׂאת עַל פִּי בֵית דִּין (fol. 10c) תֵּצֵא וּפְטוּרָה מִן הַקָּרְבָּן. וְשֶׁלֹּא עַל פִּי בֵית דִּין תֵּצֵא וְחַיֶּיבֶת בְּקָרְבָּן. יִיפָּה כֹּחַ שֶׁל בֵּית דִּין שֶׁפְּטוּרָה מִן הַקָּרְבָּן.

הוֹרוּהָ בֵּית דִּין לְהִינָּשֵׂא וְהָלְכָה וְקִלְקְלָה חַיֶּבֶת בַּקָּרְבָּן שֶׁלֹּא הִיתִּירוּהָ אֶלָּא לְהִינָּשֵׂא.

Mishnah 3: If she married by a decision of the court, she must leave but is free from the sacrifice[73]; without a decision of the court, she must leave but must bring the sacrifice[74]. The power of the court frees her from the sacrifice. If the court instructed her to marry but she misbehaved[75], she must bring a sacrifice since they permitted her only to marry.

73 A purification sacrifice is available only to persons acting carelessly (*Lev.* 4:2). Her transgression is neither intentional (for which no sacrifice would atone, *Num.* 15:30-31) nor careless; no guilt is attached to her in the eyes of the earthly or the Heavenly court.

74 Not asking the court to investigate the disappearance of her husband is carelessness.

75 By having unmarried sex; in the opinion of the Babli also by entering a forbidden marriage, e. g., a divorcee marrying a Cohen. The Yerushalmi accepts and the Babli rejects the entire Mishnah.

(fol. 10d) **הלכה ג**: נִישֵּׂאת עַל פִּי בֵית דִּין כול׳. רִבִּי בָּא. רַב הַמְנוּנָא וְרִבִּי זְעִירָא תְּרֵיהוֹן אָמְרִין. זֶהוּ רֹאשׁוֹ שֶׁלַּפֶּרֶק. מַה אָמַר רִבִּי יוֹסֵי בִּשְׁאָר כָּל־הַדְּבָרִים. נִשְׁמְעִינָהּ מִן הָדָא. רִבִּי יוֹסֵי אוֹמֵר. כָּל־שֶׁהוּא פוֹסֵל עַל יְדֵי אֲחֵרִים פּוֹסֵל עַל יְדֵי עַצְמוֹ וְכָל־שֶׁאֵינוֹ פוֹסֵל עַל יְדֵי אֲחֵרִים אֵינוֹ פוֹסֵל עַל יְדֵי עַצְמוֹ. וְאָמַר רִבִּי בָּא. רַב הַמְנוּנָא וְרִבִּי זְעִירָא תְּרֵיהוֹן אָמְרִין. זֶהוּ רֹאשׁוֹ שֶׁלַּפֶּרֶק. הָדָא אָמְרָה. לֹא חָלוּק רִבִּי יוֹסֵי בִּשְׁאָר כָּל־הַדְּבָרִים.

Halakhah 3: "If she married by a decision of the court," etc. [76]Rebbi Abba: Rav Hamnuna and Rebbi Ze'ira both say that this refers to the beginning of the chapter[77]. What does Rebbi Yose say about the other matters? Let us hear from the following: "Rebbi Yose said, anything which disables for others disables for himself; anything which does not disable for others does not disable for himself[78]." And Rebbi Abba said, Rav Hamnuna and Rebbi Ze'ira both say that this refers to the beginning of the chapter. This means that Rebbi Yose does not disagree about the other matters[79].

76 The origin of this paragraph is in Halakhah 8, about other Mishnaiot.

77 Mishnah 3 is a continuation of Mishnah 1, not Mishnah 2.

78 Mishnah 10; Tosephta 11:7. Since the second husband by his intercourse disables the wife for her first husband, he disables her for himself and she must be divorced by both of them as is stated in Mishnah 1. But if a woman went overseas and her husband married her single sister on the erroneous news of his wife's death, since he does not disable the sister for anybody by his invalid marriage he does not disable himself to return to his wife.

79 The only disagreement of R. Yose with the Tanna of Mishnah 1 is that he holds that the wife can collect her *ketubah* from her first husband

מַה אָמַר רִבִּי לָעְזָר בִּכְתוּבָּה. מַה אִם דְּבָרִים שֶׁנָּפְלוּ דֶרֶךְ אִיסּוּר אַתְּ אוֹמֵר זַכַּאי. כְּתוּבָּה שֶׁנָּפְלָה לוֹ דֶרֶךְ הֵיתֵר לֹא כָּל־שֶׁכֵּן.

מִסְתַּבְּרָה דְּרִבִּי לָעְזָר יוֹדֵי לְרִבִּי יוֹסֵי. רִבִּי יוֹסֵי לֹא יוֹדֵי לְרִבִּי לָעְזָר. רִבִּי יוֹסֵי וְרִבִּי לָעְזָר יוֹדוּן לְרִבִּי שִׁמְעוֹן. רִבִּי שִׁמְעוֹן לֹא יוֹדֵי לְרִבִּי יוֹסֵי וּלְרִבִּי לָעְזָר. הָדָא אָמְרָה עַל דְּרִבִּי שִׁמְעוֹן בִּיאָה פְסוּלָה פוֹטֶרֶת.

What does Rebbi Eleazar say about *ketubah*? If you say that he is entitled to things that come to him in prohibition, then *ketubah* that came to him in permission certainly[80]!

It is reasonable to say that Rebbi Eleazar agrees with Rebbi Yose but Rebbi Yose does not agree with Rebbi Eleazar[81]; Rebbi Yose and Rebbi Eleazar agree with Rebbi Simeon but Rebbi Simeon does not agree with Rebbi Yose and Rebbi Eleazar[82]. This means that in the opinion of Rebbi Simeon, invalid intercourse frees[83].

80 If the first husband has the right to his wife's earnings as long as he did not divorce her, then certainly he is obligated to pay the *ketubah* whose obligation he accepted voluntarily when she was permitted to him.

81 In the Babli, 91a, this is the opinion of Rav Huna and is disputed by R. Joḥanan. In Rav Huna's interpretation, for R. Eleazar the first husband can get his wife's earnings only on the basis of the marital contract which is the *ketubah*; R. Yose will hold that the husband gets nothing to induce him to grant a speedy divorce.

82 In the Babli, 91a, this is the opinion of R. Joḥanan and is disputed by Rav Huna. It seems that here only the first statement of R. Simeon is considered (as shown by the next sentence), that if the first husband dies childless before he could divorce his wife, the action of a brother in levirate or *ḥalîṣah* with her is invalid as marriage act but effective to free the co-wives. The reason given in the Babli is that R. Simeon holds that no rabbinic decree exists in this case after the death of the first husband.

The Babli holds that the composition principle in this Mishnah is that direction of agreement is always the same, either the later agree with the former (Rav Huna) or the former agree with the later (R. Joḥanan). This explains the slight deviation in the Mishnah from the chronological principle (R. Simeon is slightly older than R. Eleazar ben Shamua). The Yerushalmi rejects such schematism.

83 Cf. Chapter 5, Notes 96, 98.

לֹא מִסְתַּבְּרָא דְלֹא נִיסֵּית בִּרְשׁוּת מוּתֶּרֶת. שֶׁלֹּא בִרְשׁוּת אֲסוּרָה. אָמַר רִבִּי יוֹחָנָן. דִּבְרֵי רִבִּי שִׁמְעוֹן עָשׂוּ בֵית דִּין הוֹרָייָתָן בְּזָדוֹן אִישׁ וְאִשָּׁה. נִישֵּׂאת שֶׁלֹּא בִרְשׁוּת כִּשְׁגְגַת אִישׁ וְאִשָּׁה. אָמַר רִבִּי יוֹחָנָן. לֵית כָּאן פְּטוּרָה אֶלָּא חַייֶבֶת. הָתִיב רִבִּי חַגַּיי קוֹמֵי רִבִּי יוֹסֵי. וִיהִי כֵן בְּהוֹרָייָה. בְּשֶׁהוֹרוּ מוּתָּר לָבוֹא עַל אֵשֶׁת אִישׁ. וְלֹא עֲקִירַת גּוּף הוּא. בְּשֶׁהוֹרוּ עַד חָמֵשׁ שָׁנִים אֲסוּרָה מִכָּן וְאֵילַךְ מוּתֶּרֶת. וִיהִי כֵן בְּקִילְקוּל. הַקִּילְקוּל דוֹמֶה לַאֲכִילַת חֵלֶב וָדָם. בְּשֶׁהוֹרוּ מוּתָּר לֶאֱכֹל חֵלֶב וָדָם.

[84]Would it not be reasonable that she should be permitted if she remarried with permission, forbidden if she remarried without permission? Rebbi Joḥanan said, the words of Rebbi Simeon [imply] that the court

made their decision like intentional [relations between] man and woman[85], if she remarried without permission[86] like erroneous [relations between] man and woman. Rebbi Johanan said, there is no "free" here but "obligated"[87]. Rebbi Haggai objected before Rebbi Yose: should it not be an act of instruction? When they instructed that it is permitted to sleep with an [otherwise] married woman[88]. Is that not uprooting a principle[89]? When they instructed that she is forbidden for five years, from then on permitted[90]. Then it should be so if she misbehaved! Misbehaving is like eating fat or blood. When they instructed that fat is permitted and [she ate] blood[91].

84 Here starts the discussion of Mishnah 3.

85 Intentional adultery.

86 The only case in which she could remarry without permission of the court is that two witnesses testified to the first husband's death. Since two concurrent witnesses must be believed by biblical standards, her remarriage was an excusable error which can be atoned for by a purification sacrifice.

87 He holds that the woman acted in good faith in both cases and that, therefore, her adultery was unintentional in both cases and can be expiated by a purification sacrifice. This is the position of Ze'iri in the Babli, 92a.

88 Everybody knows that adultery is biblically prohibited and that it is not in the power of the court to permit it.

89 It is agreed that if the supreme court instructs that a biblical commandment is invalidated, no individual has the right to follow that instruction; *Horaiot* 1:3 (fol. 46a), Babli 4a.

90 To declare the husband as dead after five years is within the competence of the court. If the wife remarried after five years, she was behaving correctly.

91 "Any fat or blood" is forbidden to eat (*Lev.* 3:17). However, it is clear from the context that only fat is forbidden which may be burned on the altar (cf., e. g., *Lev.* 4:8). Therefore, a technical ruling is needed to define which fat of cattle, sheep, or goats qualifies as חלב. If the court rules that certain fat that was considered

forbidden is now permitted, a lay person who follows their ruling is excused; the sin is the court's. But if the layman uses the permission of fat to eat of the permitted fat when it still contains blood, he is guilty since the ruling never included permission to eat "unkoshered" fat. Similarly, a permission to remarry does not include permission of promiscuity whose prohibition has biblical roots that have nothing to do with adultery.

The Babli concurs, 92a.

(fol. 10c) **משנה ד**: הָאִשָּׁה שֶׁהָלַךְ בַּעֲלָהּ וּבְנָהּ לִמְדִינַת הַיָּם וּבָאוּ וְאָֽמְרוּ מֵת בַּעֲלֵיךְ וְאַחַר כָּךְ מֵת בְּנֵךְ וְנִישֵּׂאת וְאַחַר כָּךְ אָֽמְרוּ לָהּ חִילּוּף הָיוּ הַדְּבָרִים. תֵּצֵא וְהַוְּולָד הָרִאשׁוֹן וְהָאַחֲרוֹן מַמְזֵר.

Mishnah 4: A woman's husband and son[92] went overseas and people came and told her, your husband died and after that your son died[93], and she remarried. After that, they said to her, the sequence was inverted[94]. Then she must leave and the first[95] and the last[96] children are bastards.

92 The husband's only child.

93 From the last sentence in the Mishnah it follows that there were two separate informations, one about the husband's death and later one about the son's.

94 If the husband had a brother she would need levirate or *ḥalîṣah* to marry outside the family.

95 Everybody agrees that a child conceived while the first husband was still alive is a bastard.

96 Only R. Aqiba holds that a child from a widow remarried without levirate or *ḥalīṣah* is a bastard.

(fol. 10d) **הלכה ד**: הָאִשָּׁה שֶׁהָלַךְ בַּעֲלָהּ וּבְנָהּ לִמְדִינַת הַיָּם כול׳. מָה אַתְּ עֲבַד. כְּעֵידֵי מִיתָה אוֹ כְעֵידֵי גֵירוּשִׁין. אִין תַּעַבְדִּיבָהּ כְּעֵידֵי מִיתָה. פְּלִיגָא עַל רַבָּנָן דְּתַמָּן. אִין תַּעַבְדִּינָהּ כְּעֵידֵי גֵירוּשִׁין פְּלִיגָא בֵּין עַל רַבָּנִין דְּהָכָא בֵּין עַל רַבָּנִין דְּתַמָּן. אָמַר רִבִּי יוֹחָנָן. וְתַנֵּי כֵן. שְׁנַיִם אוֹמְרִים מֵת. וּשְׁנַיִם אוֹמְרִים לֹא מֵת.

לֹא תִינָּשֵׂא. וְאִם נִישֵּׂאת לֹא תֵצֵא. שְׁנַיִם אוֹמְרִים נִתְגָּרְשָׁה. וּשְׁנַיִם אוֹמְרִים לֹא נִתְגָּרְשָׁה. לֹא תִינָּשֵׂא. וְאִם נִישֵּׂאת תֵּצֵא. תַּמָּן אָמְרִין. לֹא שַׁנְייָא. הִיא מִיתָה הִיא גֵירוּשִׁין לֹא תִינָּשֵׂא. וְאִם נִישֵּׂאת לֹא תֵצֵא. עַל דַּעֲתִּין דְּרַבָּנִין דְּתַמָּן נִיחָא. הִיא מִיתָה הִיא גֵירוּשִׁין. עַל דַּעֲתְּהֹם דְּרַבָּנִן דְּהָכָא מַה בֵין מִיתָה מַה בֵין גֵירוּשִׁין. רִבִּי זְעִירָה אָמַר לָהּ סְתָם. רִבִּי חִייָה בְשֵׁם רִבִּי יוֹחָנָן אָמַר. הַדַּעַת מַכְרַעַת בְּעֵידֵי מִיתָה מֵאַחַר שֶׁאִילּוּ יָבוֹא הוּא מַכְחִישׁ. אָמַר רִבִּי חִזְקִיָּה. רַבָּנִן דְּתַמָּן כְּדַעְתִּין. כְּמוֹ דְּרַבָּנִן דְּתַמָּן אוֹמְרִים. בְּשָׁעָה שֶׁיָּצָאת בְּעֵידוּת בְּרוּרָה יָצָאת בּוֹ. כֵּן רַבָּנִין דְּהָכָא אָמְרִין. בְּשָׁעָה שֶׁנִּישֵּׂית בְּעֵידוּת בְּרוּרָה נִישֵּׂית. אָמַר רִבִּי יוֹסֵי. מִסְתַּבְּרָא דְלָא מִחְלְפָא שִׁיטָּתִין דְּרַבָּנִן דְּתַמָּן. לֹא מוֹדֵיי רַבָּנִן דְּתַמָּן שֶׁאִילּוּ מִשָּׁעָה רִאשׁוֹנָה שְׁנַיִם אוֹמְרִים. מֵת אָבִיהָ מִתּוֹכָהּ. וּשְׁנַיִם אוֹמְרִים. לֹא מֵת אָבִיהָ מִתּוֹכָהּ. שֶׁהַשָּׂדֶה בְּחֶזְקַת שֶׁלְּרְאוּבֵן. אִילּוּ אָמְרוּ שְׁנַיִם. נִתְקַדְּשָׁה וְנִתְגָּרְשָׁה וְנִשֵּׂאת. וּשְׁנַיִם אוֹמְרִים לֹא נִתְגָּרְשָׁה. לֹא תֵצֵא. יְאוּת.

Halakhah 4: "If a woman's husband and son went overseas,' etc. How do you consider this situation, comparing[97] to witnesses of death or witnesses of divorce? If you compare it to witnesses of death, it disagrees with the (rabbis there)[98]. If you compare it to witnesses of divorce, it disagrees (both with the rabbis here and those there). [99]Rebbi Joḥanan said, it was stated thus: Two [witnesses] say he died. [later] two witnesses said, he did not die. She shall not remarry, but if she has remarried she should not leave. Two [witnesses] say she was divorced, [later] two witnesses said, she was not divorced. She shall not remarry; if she has remarried she must leave[100]. There, they say, it makes no difference; whether about death or divorce she should not leave[100]. In the opinion of the rabbis there it is understandable, there is no difference between death and divorce. In the opinion of the rabbis here, what is the difference between death and divorce? Rebbi Ze'ira said it without attribution, Rebbi Ḥiyya in the name of Rebbi Joḥanan: It is reasonable to decide in the case of witnesses of death that if he comes he contradicts them[101]. Rebbi Ḥizqiah said, the rabbis there stick to their opinion since the rabbis there say, when the [first] testimony was accepted, it was accepted as certain[102]. So the rabbis here say, at the moment of her remarriage, she remarried based on certain testimony. Rebbi Yose said, it is reasonable that the rabbis there did not change their argument. Do the rabbis there not agree if two [witnesses] say, his father died while in possession, and two say his father died while not in possession, that the field is in Reuben's possession[102]? Therefore, if two say, she was married, divorced, and remarried, and two say[103] she was not divorced, rightly she should not leave.

97 The two pairs of witnesses mentioned in the Mishnah.

98 The argument in the Halakhah shows that the positions of "rabbis there" and "rabbis here and those there" must be switched.

99 From here to the end of the Halakhah, the text is from *Ketubot* 2:2.

100 Babli *Ketubot* 22b; Tosephta 14:1. In the Babli, the position of "the rabbis here" is that of R. Joḥanan only, based on a minor Tanna R. Menaḥem bar Yose.

101 The Babli is a little more explicit. Since a return of the husband is absolute proof that he is alive, the wife will not remarry unless she is absolutely convinced that the witnesses are truthful. But in the case of divorce, if the husband claims that he never divorced her, she can contradict him based on her witnesses.

102 This refers to Mishnah *Ketubot* 2:2: "Rebbi Joshua agrees if somebody says to another person: This field did belong to your father but I bought it from him, one believes him [in the absence of documents] since the mouth which forbade is the mouth which permitted (the person stating that the field was another person's being the same who states that now it belongs to him). But if there are witnesses that it belongs to [the second person's] father and [the first] says I bought it from him, he cannot be believed [without documents].

The situation described in the Yerushalmi is that each party in a court case brings two witnesses; Simeon proves that when his father died the field was still in his possession and Reuben (who is in actual possession) brings two witnesses that the field was not in Simeon's father's possession when he died. In that case, we do not say that the case is undecidable on basis of the evidence before the court and, therefore, the field should be split between the parties (position of Symmachos, in Babli *Baba mesi'a* 2b) but that the burden of proof is on the claimant and, therefore, the field remains in the possession of Reuben.

The situation discussed in the Babli *Ketubot* 22b is different: Reuben is in actual possession of the field the number of years which creates a presumption of ownership, but he has no documentation of his acquisition. Simeon brings two witnesses that his father had died in possession of the field. Since squatting is no proof of ownership, the court puts Simeon in possession. Later, Reuben comes again to court with two witnesses who testify that Simeon's father was not in possession at the time of his death. By the same principle as above, the field remains in the possession of Simeon.

The commentators, following the Babli, require to substitute "Simeon" for "Reuben" at all occurrences here and in *Ketubot*. Such a correction is unwarranted.

102 In the case of remarriage, it is impossible to say that the two pairs of witnesses came to court in the same case, since then the wife would not be permitted to remarry. Therefore, the court permitted her to remarry (or she was not required to go to court) on basis of two uncontested testimonies which have to be accepted as true by biblical standards.

103 Later.

מַתְנִיתָא פְלִיגָא עַל רִבִּי יוֹחָנָן. שְׁנַיִם אוֹמְרִים. נִתְקַדְּשָׁה. וּשְׁנַיִם (fol. 11a) אוֹמְרִים. לֹא נִתְקַדְּשָׁה. לֹא תִינָּשֵׂא. וְאִם נִישֵּׂאת לֹא תֵצֵא. אָמַר רִבִּי הוֹשַׁעְיָה. פָּתַר לָהּ רִבִּי יוֹחָנָן. שְׁנַיִם אוֹמְרִים. נִתְקַדְּשָׁה וְנִתְגָּרְשָׁה. וּשְׁנַיִם אוֹמְרִים. לֹא נִתְגָּרְשָׁה. לֹא תִינָּשֵׂא. וְאִם נִישֵּׂאת לֹא תֵצֵא. מַה בֵּינָהּ לְקַדְמִיתָא. תַּמָּן הוּחְזְקָה אֵשֶׁת אִישׁ בִּפְנֵי הַכֹּל. בְּרַם הָכָא לֹא הוּחְזְקָה אֵשֶׁת אִישׁ אֶלָּא בִּפְנֵי שְׁנַיִם. לִכְשֶׁיָּבוֹאוּ שְׁנַיִם וְיֹאמְרוּ. זֶהִי שֶׁקִּידֵּשׁ.

A *baraita* disagrees with Rebbi Johanan[104]: "If two are saying, she was betrothed[105], and two are saying, she was not betrothed, she should not be married, but if she married she should not leave." Rebbi Hoshaia said, Rebbi Joḥanan may explain it as follows: "If two are saying, she was betrothed and divorced, and two are saying, she was not divorced, she should not be married, but if she married she should not leave." What is the difference between this and the first case[104]? There, she was considered a married woman in everybody's opinion. Here, she is considered a married woman only for two people. If two others would come and identify the man who was betrothed to her[106].

104 His statement that the woman who married on testimony that she was divorced by an absent husband must be divorced by the second husband on contradicting testimony.

105 As a minor by an absent father. The situation should be the same as in the case of witnesses to the divorce.

106 Then the case can be independently investigated and we are no longer dependent on contradictory testimonies.

מַתְנִיתָא פְלִיגָא עַל רִבִּי יוֹחָנָן. שְׁנַיִם אוֹמְרִים. נִשְׁבֵּית וְהִיא טְהוֹרָה. וּשְׁנַיִם אוֹמְרִים. נִשְׁבֵּית וְהִיא טְמֵיאָה. לֹא תִינָּשֵׂא. וְאִם נִישֵּׂאת לֹא תֵצֵא. אָמַר רִבִּי יוֹסֵי. מֵאַחַר שֶׁאֵילּוּ אוֹמְרִים. טְהוֹרָה. וְאֵילּוּ אוֹמְרִים. טְמֵיאָה. כְּמִי שֶׁאֵילּוּ אוֹמְרִים. נִשְׁבֵּית. וְאֵילּוּ אוֹמְרִים. לֹא נִשְׁבֵּית. וְאָנוּ כְּחַיַּן מִפִּיהָ.

A *baraita* disagrees with Rebbi Joḥanan[104]: "If two are saying, she was kidnapped but is pure, and two are saying, she was kidnapped and is impure[107], she should not be married, but if she married she should not leave[108]." Rebbi Yose said, since these say, she is pure, and those say, she is impure, it is as if two said, she was kidnapped, and two said, she was not kidnapped, and we depend on what she says[109].

107 The kidnappers slept with her. She cannot marry a Cohen.

108 A similar text is Tosephta *Ketubot* 2:2.

109 The trustworthiness of a person concerning himself is the topic of Mishnaiot *Ketubot* 1:6-9.

שְׁנַיִם אוֹמְרִים נִתְקַדְּשָׁה. וּשְׁנַיִם אוֹמְרִים לֹא נִתְקַדְּשָׁה. רִבִּי יוֹנָה מְדַמֵּי לָהּ לַחֲלָבִין. אִילּוּ שְׁנַיִם אוֹמְרִים. פְּלוֹנִי אָכַל חֵלֶב. וּשְׁנַיִם אוֹמְרִים. לֹא אָכַל חֵלֶב. שֶׁמָּא אֵינוֹ מֵבִיא אָשָׁם תָּלוּי מִסָּפֵק. וְהָכָא יִתֵּן גֵּט מִסָּפֵק. אָמַר לֵיהּ רִבִּי יוֹסֵי. לֹא תְדַמִּינָהּ לַחֲלָבִין. שֶׁכֵּן אֲפִילוּ אָמַר. לִבִּי נוֹקְרֵינִי. מֵבִיא אָשָׁם תָּלוּי. מַתְנִיתָא פְלִיגָא עַל רִבִּי יוֹסֵי. שְׁנַיִם אוֹמְרִים. נִתְקַדְּשָׁה. וּשְׁנַיִם אוֹמְרִים. לֹא נִתְקַדְּשָׁה. לֹא תִינָּשֵׂא. וְסֵיפָא פְלִיג עַל רִבִּי יוֹנָה. אִם נִשֵּׂאת תֵּצֵא. אָמַר רִבִּי מָנָא. לֹא דְרִבִּי יוֹסֵי אוֹמֵר. תִּינָּשֵׂא. וְלֹא דְרִבִּי יוֹנָה אָמַר אִם נִשֵּׂאת תֵּצֵא. לֹא אָמַר אֶלָּא לֹא תְדַמִּינָהּ לַחֲלָבִים. שֶׁאֲפִילוּ אָמַר. לִבִּי נוֹקְרֵינִי. מֵבִיא אָשָׁם תָּלוּי.

If two are saying, she had been betrothed and two are saying she had not been betrothed. Rebbi Jonah compares that to fat[110]. If two would say, X ate fat, and two would say, X did not eat fat, did he not have to bring a "hung" reparation sacrifice[111] because of the doubt? Here, he[112] should give a bill of divorce because of the doubt. Rebbi Yose said to him, do not compare this to fat, because even if he says my conscience bothers me, he brings a "hung" reparation sacrifice[113]. A *baraita* disagrees with Rebbi Yose: If two are saying she had been betrothed and two are saying she had not been betrothed, she should not be married. The end disagrees with Rebbi Jonah: If she married she must leave. Rebbi Mana said, Rebbi Yose did not say that she may marry, nor did Rebbi Jonah say if she married she must leave, he said only, do not compare this to fat, because even if he says my conscience bothers me, he brings a "hung" reparation sacrifice[114].

110 Cf. Note 91.

111 The sacrifice of expiation for a sin which is only suspected; cf. *Bikkurim* 2, Note 162.

112 The second husband who had married the adult girl under the impression that as a minor she had not been betrothed by her father to a man unknown to her.

113 Even in the absence of witnesses.

114 Their disagreement is one of classification, not of differences in practice.

(fol. 10c) **משנה ה**: אָמְרוּ לָהּ מֵת בְּנֵךְ וְאַחַר כָּךְ מֵת בַּעֲלֵיךְ וְנִתְיַבְּמָה וְאַחַר כָּךְ אָמְרוּ לָהּ חִילּוּף הָיוּ הַדְּבָרִים תֵּצֵא וְהַוָּלָד הָרִאשׁוֹן וְהָאַחֲרוֹן מַמְזֵר.

Mishnah 5: They came and told her, your son died and after that your husband died, and she was married in levirate. After that, they said to her, the sequence was inverted[115]. Then she must leave and the first[95] and the last[96] children are bastards.

115 The husband had a child at the moment of his death and therefore the levir is forbidden to the widow by an incest prohibition (*Lev*. 18:16) punishable by divine extirpation (*Lev*. 21:21), which makes all children of this union bastards, whether conceived before or after the husband's death.

(fol. 11a) **הלכה ה**: אָמְרוּ לָהּ מֵת בְּנֵךְ כול'. לֹא הָיְתָה צְרִיכָה לְהִינָּשֵׂא אֶלָּא לְהִתְייַבֵּם. וְהוּא יְבָמָה שֶׁנִּישֵּׂאת בְּלֹא חֲלִיצָה. רִבִּי יִרְמְיָה אָמַר. זֶה חוֹלֵץ וְזֶה מְקַייֵם. רִבִּי יוּדָה בַּר פָּזִי בְשֵׁם רִבִּי יוֹחָנָן. תֵּצֵא. רִבִּי יוֹסֵי בְּשֵׁם רִבִּי הִילָא. תֵּצֵא. רִבִּי יוֹסֵי שְׁאִיל לְרִבִּי פִּינְחָס. הֵיךְ סָבַר רִבִּי. אָמַר לֵיהּ. כְּרִבִּי יִרְמְיָה. אָמַר לֵיהּ. חֲזוֹר בָּךְ. דְּלֹא כֵן אֲנִי כוֹתֵב עָלֶיךָ. זָקֵן מַמְרֵא. אָמַר רִבִּי זְבִידָא. מַתְנִיתָא מְסַייְעָא לְרִבִּי יוֹחָנָן. תֵּצֵא מִזֶּה וּמִזֶּה וּשְׁלֹשָׁה עָשָׂר דְּבָרִים בָּהּ. כְּדִבְרֵי רִבִּי מֵאִיר שֶׁאָמַר מִשּׁוּם רִבִּי עֲקִיבָה רַבּוֹ. וַחֲכָמִים אוֹמְרִים. אֵין מַמְזֵר בִּיבָמָה. לֹא אָמַר אֶלָּא אֵין מַמְזֵר בִּיבָמָה. הָא לָצֵאת תֵּצֵא. וְהָתַנִּינָן תֵּצֵא. וְאָמַר רִבִּי יוֹחָנָן. תֵּצֵא.

Halakhah 5: "They came and told her, your son died," etc. [116]If she should not have married but entered levirate, this is the case of a sister-in-law who married without *ḥalîṣah*. Rebbi Jeremiah said, this man performs *ḥalīṣah*, the other one keeps her. Rebbi Jehudah ben Pazi in the name of Rebbi Joḥanan: She must leave[117]. Rebbi Yose in the name of Rebbi Hila: She must leave. Rebbi Yose asked Rebbi Phineas, how does the rabbi hold? He said, with Rebbi Jeremiah. He said to him, change your mind, for otherwise I shall publicly call you a rebellious Elder[118]. Rebbi Zevidah said, a *baraita*[119] supports Rebbi Joḥanan: "She must leave both of them and the thirteen items[120] apply to her, following Rebbi Meïr who said it in the name of his teacher Rebbi Aqibah. But the Sages say, there is no bastard from a sister-in-law[121]." They only said, "there is no bastard from a sister-in-law," therefore she must leave. And we have stated, "she must leave". And Rebbi Joḥanan said, she must leave.

116 The same text *Giṭṭin*, Halakhah 8:6. In both places, the problem discussed is not the one stated in the Mishnah. The parallel discussion in the Babli is 92a/b where there is no mention of the position of R. Jeremiah.

117 This is a rabbinic decree since the outside marriage of a woman under obligation of levirate is invalid (Chapter 1, Notes 93, 94); therefore, the widow was not legally married during the levir's lifetime and how can you leave a nonexisting marriage?

118 *Deut*. 17:12.

119 Cf. Tosephta 11:8, *Giṭṭin* 8:6.

120 Enumerated in Mishnah 1.

121 Cf. Halakhah 4:15.

(fol. 10c) **משנה ו**: אָמְרוּ לָהּ מֵת בַּעְלֵיךְ וְנִשֵּׂאת וְאַחַר כָּךְ אָמְרוּ לָהּ קַיָּים הָיָה וּמֵת תֵּצֵא וְהַוְּולָד הָרִאשׁוֹן מַמְזֵר וְהָאַחֲרוֹן אֵינוֹ מַמְזֵר.

Mishnah 6: If they told her, your husband died, and she remarried, and then they told her, he was alive but died, she must leave and the first child[122] is a bastard, but the last is not a bastard.

משנה ז: אָֽמְרוּ לָהּ מֵת בַּעֲלֵיךְ וְנִתְקַדְּשָׁה וְאַחַר כָּךְ בָּא בַעֲלָהּ מוּתֶּרֶת לַחֲזוֹר לוֹ. אַף עַל פִּי שֶׁנָּתַן לָהּ הָאַחֲרוֹן גֵּט לֹא פְסָלָהּ מִן הַכְּהוּנָּה. אֶת זוֹ דָרַשׁ רִבִּי לְעָזָר בֶּן מַתְּיָא. וְאִשָּׁה גְרוּשָׁה מֵאִישָׁהּ. וְלֹא מֵאִישׁ שֶׁאֵינוֹ אִישָׁהּ.

Mishnah 7: If they told her, your husband died; she was betrothed[123] and after that her husband returned, she is permitted to return to him. Even though the second [husband] gave her a bill of divorce he did not disable her from priesthood. This Rebbi Eleazar ben Matthew explained, "a woman divorced from her husband,[124]" and not a woman divorced from a non-husband[125].

122 Any child conceived during the first husband's lifetime.

123 But she never slept with the prospective second husband.

124 *Lev.* 21:7, from the list of women prohibited to a priest.

125 Since betrothal of a married woman has no legal standing.

(fol. 11a) **הלכה ז:** אָֽמְרוּ לָהּ מֵת בַּעֲלֵיךְ כול׳. אָֽמְרוּ לָהּ מֵת בַּעֲלֵיךְ וְנִתְקַדְּשָׁה כול׳. רִבִּי יוֹחָנָן בְּשֵׁם רִבִּי יַנַּאי. אֵין לָהּ אֶלָּא מִשּׁוּם זֵיהוּם כְּהוּנָּה וְאֵין בֵּית דִּין מְזָהֲמִין לָהּ.

Halakhah 7: "If they told her, your husband died," etc. "If they told her, your husband died; she was betrothed," etc. Rebbi Joḥanan in the name of Rebbi Yannai: Her only problem would be aspersion on the priesthood, but the court will not tolerate aspersion[126].

126 The priests, who were very particular about purity of their lineage, might not want to accept the return of a woman for whom one might construe a violation of priestly rules. Even though the courts go along with some of the self-imposed restrictions of Cohanim, such as the prohibition of a toddler convert, this would be one they will reject.

מַה אַתְּ מְקַייֵם לָהּ. בְּעֵד אֶחָד אוֹ בִשְׁנֵי עֵדִים. אִין תְּקַייְמִינָהּ בְּעֵד אֶחָד. נִמְצֵאת אוֹמֵר. עֵד אֶחָד מַתִּירָהּ לְיָבָם. אִין תְּקַייְמִינָהּ בִּשְׁנֵי עֵדִים. הֲוָה פְלִיגָא עַל רַב. דְּאָמַר רַב נַחְמָן בְּשֵׁם רִבִּי יַעֲקֹב בְּשֵׁם רַב. נִישֵּׂאת עַל פִּי שְׁנַיִם אֲפִילוּ דְהוּא אָתֵי אָמְרָה לָהּ. לֵית תני.[129]

How do you explain these[127]? With one witness or with two witnesses? If you explain with one witness, then one witness would permit her to the levir[128]. If you explain with two witnesses, then it disagrees with Rav since Rav Naḥman bar[129] Jacob said in the name of Rav, if she was married by the testimony of two witnesses, even if he returns, she says to him, you are not him.

127 All Mishnaiot of this chapter which deal with a wife remarried on testimony that her husband had died.

128 As explained in Chapter 15, a single witness is accepted to free a widow to remarry. But in that case, Mishnah 5 implies that a single witness can lift the incest prohibition of the sister-in-law by permitting her to the levir. This is against our general rules that biblical prohibitions can be lifted only by two credible independent witnesses. In the Babli, 93b, Rav Ḥisda accepts the argument that a single witness may lift the prohibition of the sister-in-law. It is accepted in the Babli that the restrictions enumerated in Mishnah 1 are intended to make sure the presumed widow checks carefully the truthfulness of a single witness.

129 Reading בר instead of בשם רבי, from the text in Halakhah 15:4. The last word תני is read with Halakhah 15:4 אתנו = אַתְּ (ה)נוּ "you are him".

וּמְנַיִין שֶׁאֵין קִדּוּשִׁין תּוֹפְסִין בְּאֵשֶׁת אִישׁ. רִבִּי אִימִּי בְשֵׁם רִבִּי יַנַּאי. וְיָצְאָה מִבֵּיתוֹ וְהָלְכָה וְהָיְתָה לְאִישׁ אַחֵר. כְּשֶׁתֵּצֵא מִבֵּיתוֹ יְהֵא לָהּ הֲוָיָה אֶצֶל אַחֵר. וּמְנַיִין שֶׁאֵין קִדּוּשִׁין תּוֹפְסִין בְּכָל־הָעֲרָיוֹת. רִבִּי תַנְחוּמָא בְשֵׁם רַב הוּנָא. וְיָצְאָה מִבֵּיתוֹ וְהָלְכָה וְהָיְתָה לְאִישׁ אַחֵר. וּמַה תַלְמוּד לוֹמַר אַחֵר. פְּרָט לְפָרָשַׁת עֲרָיוֹת.

From where that no betrothal is valid for a married woman? Rebbi Immi in the name of Rebbi Yannai: "She left his house, went, and became another man's.[130]" When she leaves his house she may be with another. And from where that no betrothal is valid for incestual relations? Rebbi Tanḥuma in the name of Rav Huna: "She left his house, went, and became another man's." Why does the verse say "another"? To exclude the list of incest relations[131].

130 *Deut.* 24:2.

131 In the Babli, *Qiddušin* 88b, this is quoted in the name of R. Yannai; there the argument is rejected as insufficient. Perhaps for "another" one should translate "an outsider". The Babli always subsumes adultery under incest prohibitions and does not need a separate argument.

(fol. 10c) **משנה ח**: מִי שֶׁהָלְכָה אִשְׁתּוֹ לִמְדִינַת הַיָּם בָּאוּ וְאָמְרוּ לוֹ מֵתָה אִשְׁתְּךָ וְנָשָׂא אֶת אֲחוֹתָהּ וְאַחַר כָּךְ בָּאת אִשְׁתּוֹ מוּתֶּרֶת לַחֲזוֹר לוֹ. הוּא מוּתָּר בִּקְרוֹבוֹת שְׁנִייָה וְהַשְּׁנִייָה מוּתֶּרֶת בִּקְרוֹבָיו. וְאִם מֵתָה הָרִאשׁוֹנָה מוּתָּר בַּשְּׁנִייָה.

Mishnah 8: A man's wife went overseas, they came and told him: your wife died, and he married her sister. If after that his wife returned , she is permitted to return to him. He is permitted [to marry] the relatives of the second, the second is permitted his relatives[132]. If the first [sister] died, the second one is permitted to him[133].

132 Since the marriage to the sister is incestuous (*Lev.* 18:18) it is non-existent and the restrictions detailed in Mishnah 4:8 do not apply.

133 Following the principles of Mishnah 1, she should be prohibited to her brother-in-law.

הלכה ח: מִי שֶׁהָלְכָה אִשְׁתּוֹ לִמְדִינַת הַיָּם כול׳. כְּתִיב וְשָׁכַב אִישׁ(fol. 11a) אוֹתָהּ. שְׁכִיבָתָהּ אוֹסְרָתָהּ וְאֵין שְׁכִיבַת אַחֶרֶת אוֹסְרָתָהּ. וְאָמַר אַף הָכָא תַּחַת אִישֵׁךְ. פְּרָט לְאוֹנְסִין.

Halakhah 8: "If a man's wife went overseas,", etc. It is written: "If a man slept with *her*;[134]" her sleeping prohibits her, the sleeping of another woman does not prohibit her. There, it also says "replacing your husband," that excludes rape cases[135].

134 *Num.* 5:13; written in the paragraph about the wife suspected of unfaithfulness, from where one infers that an adulterous wife is forbidden to her husband. It is implied here that an action of the husband has no influence on her status (but in the paragraph after the next it is pointed out that the husband's action may forbid him to her). *Sifry Num.* 7 (an involved argument in the style of the paragraph after the next), a short parallel in the Babli, 95a.

135 She is forbidden only if her paramour replaces the husband, i. e., if she sleeps with him voluntarily.

אָמַר רִבִּי מַתַּנְיָיה. גָּזְרוּ עַל דָּבָר שֶׁהוּא מָצוּי וְלֹא גָזְרוּ עַל דָּבָר שֶׁאֵינוֹ מָצוּי. דֶּרֶךְ אִישׁ לָצֵאת לִמְדִינַת הַיָּם. וְאֵין דַּרְכָּהּ שֶׁלָּאִשָּׁה לָצֵאת לִמְדִינַת הַיָּם.

Rebbi Mattaniah said, they made a fence about situations that occur frequently but not about rare situations[136]. A man frequently travels overseas; it is infrequent that a woman travels overseas.

136 He explains why the husband is not forbidden to the two sisters following the principles of Mishnah 1. It was shown in the preceding Halakhah that most of Mishnah 1 is purely rabbinical and has the status of "a fence around the law". The problem with this argument is that the rule which is relevant here, that the woman is forbidden to both men, is biblical (*Sifry Num.* 19).

תַּנֵּי. אָמַר רִבִּי יוּדָה. מוֹדִין בֵּית שַׁמַּי וּבֵית הִלֵּל בְּבָא עַל חֲמוֹתוֹ שֶׁפָּסַל אֶת אִשְׁתּוֹ. וְעַל מַה נֶחְלְקוּ. בְּבָא עַל אֲחוֹת אִשְׁתּוֹ. שֶׁבֵּית שַׁמַּי אוֹמְרִים. פָּסַל.

וּבֵית הִלֵּל אוֹמְרִים. לֹא פָּסַל. חֲבֵרַייָא בְשֵׁם רִבִּי יוֹחָנָן. טַעֲמָא דְרִבִּי יוּדָה בָּאֵשׁ יִשְׂרְפוּ אוֹתוֹ וְאֶתְהֶן. מַה נָן קַייָמִין. אִם לְעִנְייָן שְׂרֵיפָה אֵין נִשְׂרֶפֶת אֶלָּא אַחַת. אֶלָּא אִם אֵינוֹ עִנְייָן לִשְׂרֵיפָה תְּנֵיהוּ עִנְייָן לְאִיסּוּר. עַד כְּדוֹן כְּרִבִּי עֲקִיבָה. כְּרִבִּי יִשְׁמָעֵאל. תַּנֵּי רִבִּי יִשְׁמָעֵאל. בָּאֵשׁ יִשְׂרְפוּ אוֹתוֹ וְאֶתְהֶן. הוּא וְאֶת שְׁנִייָה. וְהָיוּ בֵית שַׁמַּי דָנִין. מַה בְמָקוֹם שֶׁבָּא אִיסּוּר הַקַּל עַל אִיסּוּרָה הַקַּלָּה אָסַר אֶת אוֹסְרָיו. כֵּיוָן שֶׁבָּא אִיסּוּר הֶחָמוּר עַל אִיסּוּרָה הַחֲמוּרָה אֵינוֹ דִין שֶׁנֶּאֱסוֹר אֶת אוֹסְרָיו. וְהֵיי דֵין אִיסּוּר קַל. אָמַר רִבִּי יוֹחָנָן. רֹאשָׁה דְפִירְקָא. וְהָהֵן נוּקַל. אֵינוֹ אֶלָּא חוֹמֶר. שַׁנְייָא הִיא שֶׁנִּשֵּׂאת לוֹ דֶרֶךְ הֵיתֵר.

It was stated[137]: Rebbi Jehudah said, the House of Shammai and the House of Hillel agree that one who copulates with his mother-in-law disables his wife. Where did they disagree? If he copulates with his wife's sister; where the House of Shammai say, he disabled her[138], but the House of Hillel say, he did not disable her. The colleagues in the name of Rebbi Joḥanan: The reason of Rebbi Jehudah: "In fire they should burn him and them[139]." Where do we hold? If it is about burning, only one of them is burned[140]. So if it cannot be relevant for burning, let it be relevant for prohibition[141]. So far following Rebbi Aqiba; following Rebbi Ismael? Rebbi Ismael stated: "In fire they should burn him and them," him and the second one[142]. And the House of Shammai was arguing: Since in a case where a slightly prohibited person copulated with a slightly prohibited person the cause of the prohibition became forbidden, if a strongly prohibited person copulated with a strongly prohibited person, it is only logical that the cause of the prohibition is forbidden[143]. Which rule is slight? Rebbi Joḥanan said, the beginning of the chapter[144]. But this is very strong[145]! There is a difference since she was permitted to be married to him[146].

137 A short version of the discussion started here is in the Babli 95a; the very succinct source is in *Sifra Qedošim Pereq* 9(15)-(18).

138 Treating the man's transgression as equal in consequence to the woman's. In their opinion, the husband is forced to divorce his wife and pay her all that is due in a divorce which is his fault.

139 *Lev.* 20:14.

140 As explained in *Sifra*, the prohibition (*Lev.* 18:17) is that of incestuous intercourse the prescription of the punishment (*Lev.* 20:14) deals only with the case that a man marries a woman and her mother. The problem is that if one of them is married to him, he cannot possibly marry the other since any act of incestuous betrothal or final marriage is invalid and legally nonexistent. Therefore, while intercourse with mother and daughter is incestuous and forbidden, it is a capital crime only if the man is married to one of them at the time he sleeps with the other. The innocent wife did not commit any crime and, therefore, cannot be punished. Cf. Chapter 11, Note 46

140 Both the married and the unmarried women are permanently forbidden to him.

141 In *Sifra*, as in the Yerushalmi, this is R. Aqiba's position. In the Babli, 95a, this is an amoraic interpretation of R. Simeon ben Laqish reported by R. Ammi.

142 In *Sifra*, "one of them." He reads the unusual word אתהן (substituting for אותן) as abbreviation of את אחת מהן.

143 This difficult argument is quoted anonymously in *Sifry Num.* 7 as argument that her husband's adulterous relationship with her mother does not prohibit the wife, and explained in detail in *Num. Rabba Našo* 9(35) (most probably a Provençal text): "Since in a case where a slightly prohibited person copulated with a slightly prohibited person, *this refers to adultery since her prohibition is not permanent* (her husband could divorce her), the cause of the prohibition (*the husband*) became forbidden (*he has to divorce his wife*), if a strongly prohibited person copulated with a strongly prohibited person, *this refers to a man sleeping with his mother-in-law whose prohibition is permanent*, it is only logical that the cause of the prohibition (*the wife*) should forbidden", the verse says "with *her*' (cf. Note 134).

A simple and short version is in *Sifre Zuṭa, Midrash Haggadol Num.* 12, ed. Rabbinowitz p. 51.

144 Mishnah 1, the case of careless

adultery.

145 There is no stronger sexual prohibition than that of adultery, the only one mentioned in the Ten Commandments.

146 If the woman remarried on the testimony of one witness, while she took all the risk, the marriage was permitted under our rules. But the sister of the living wife and the mother-in-law are permanently forbidden.

רִבִּי הוֹשַׁעְיָא רַבָּה אָמַר. בְּמַחֲזִיר אֶת גְּרוּשָׁתוֹ מִשֶּׁנִּשֵּׂאת הִיא מַתְנִיתָא. לָמָּה לִי מִשֶּׁנִּשֵּׂאת. אֲפִילוּ מִשְּׁנִּתְאָרְסָה. בְּגִין דְּרִבִּי יוֹסֵי בֶּן כִּיפֵּר. דְּרִבִּי יוֹסֵי בֶּן כִּיפֵּר אָמַר. מִן הָאֵירוּסִין מוּתֶּרֶת. רִבִּי לִיעֶזֶר אוֹמֵר. בִּיבָמָה שֶׁנָּפְלָה לִפְנֵי שְׁנֵי יְבָמִים הִיא מַתְנִיתָא. עָשָׂה בָהּ אֶחָד מַאֲמָר וְאַחַר כָּךְ בָּא עָלֶיהָ הַשֵּׁינִי. לָמָּה לִי עָשָׂה בָהּ מַאֲמָר. אֲפִילוּ לֹא עָשָׂה בָהּ מַאֲמָר. לָמָּה לִי בָּא עָלֶיהָ. אֲפִילוּ לֹא בָּא עָלֶיהָ. בְּגִין בֵּית שַׁמַּי. בְּגִין רִבִּי שִׁמְעוֹן. דְּתַנֵּי. אָמַר רִבִּי שִׁמְעוֹן. לֹא נֶחְלְקוּ בֵּית שַׁמַּי וּבֵית הִלֵּל בְּבָא עַל אֲחוֹת אִשְׁתּוֹ שֶׁלֹּא פָסַל אֶת אִשְׁתּוֹ. וְעַל מַה נֶחְלְקוּ. בְּבָא עַל חֲמוֹתוֹ. שֶׁבֵּית שַׁמַּי אוֹמְרִים. פָּסַל. וּבֵית הִלֵּל אוֹמְרִים. לֹא פָסַל. וְהָיוּ בֵית הִלֵּל דָּנִין. הָאִישׁ מוּתָּר בְּכָל־הַנָּשִׁים וְהָאִשָּׁה מוּתֶּרֶת בְּכָל־הָאֲנָשִׁים. קִידְּשָׁהּ. הוּא אֲסָרָהּ וְהִיא אֲסָרָתָהּ. מְרוּבָּה אִיסּוּר שֶׁאֲסָרָהּ מֵאִיסּוּר שְׁהִיא אוֹסְרָתָהּ. שֶׁהוּא אוֹסְרָהּ לֵילֵךְ לְהִינָּשֵׂא לְאִישׁ זָר. וְהִיא לֹא אֲסָרָתוֹ אֶלָּא עַל קְרוֹבוֹתֶיהָ בִּלְבַד. וַהֲרֵי הַדְּבָרִים קַל וָחוֹמֶר. מַה אִם הִיא שֶׁאֲסוּרָה אִיסּוּר מְרוּבֶּה וְשָׁגְגָה עָלָיו בְּאִיסּוּרָהּ וְלֹא נֶאְסְרָה אֶלָּא לְמוּתָּר לָהּ. הוּא שֶׁאִיסּוּרוֹ אִיסּוּר מְמוּעָט וְשָׁגַג בְּאִיסּוּרוֹ אֵינוֹ דִין שֶׁלֹּא יְהֵא אָסוּר אֶלָּא לְמוּתָּר לוֹ. הָדֵין דִּין בְּשׁוֹגֵג. בְּמֵזִיד מְנַיִין. תַּלְמוּד לוֹמַר אוֹתָהּ. אוֹתָהּ שְׁכִיבָתָהּ אוֹסְרָתָהּ. אֵין שְׁכִיבַת אַחֶרֶת אוֹסְרָתָהּ.

The elder Rebbi Hoshaia[147] said, the *baraita*[148] is about someone who takes back his divorcee after she had been married to another. Why after she had been married, not also after she had been betrothed[149]? Because of Rebbi Yose ben Kipper, since Rebbi Yose ben Kipper said, she is permitted after betrothal[150]. Rebbi Eleazar[151] said, the *baraita* is about a sister-in-law who became eligible before two levirs, when one of them "bespoke" her and then the other copulated with her[152]. Why when one of them "bespoke" her, even if he had not "bespoken" her[153]! Why if he copulated with her, even if he did not copulate with her[154]! Because of the House of Shammai, because of Rebbi Simeon. As it was stated, Rebbi Simeon[155] said, the House of Shammai and the House of Hillel did not disagree that one who copulates with his wife's sister disables his wife. Where did they disagree? If he copulates with his mother-in-law; where the House of Shammai say, he disabled her, but the House of Hillel say, he did not disable her. The House of Hillel were arguing: A man is permitted all women, a woman is permitted all men[156]. When he becomes betrothed to her, he forbids her and she forbids him. The prohibition through which he forbids her is greater than the prohibition through which she forbids him, since he forbids her to go to marry any other man but she forbids him only her relatives. And is that not an argument *de minore ad majus*? If she, whose prohibition is greater, transgressed the prohibition in error, is not forbidden even to the one permitted to her[157], he, whose prohibition is less, if he transgressed the prohibition in error, is it not logical that he should not be forbidden even to the one permitted to him[158]? That works for an error. From where if intentional: [159]The verse says "with *her*;" her sleeping prohibits her, the sleeping of another woman does not prohibit her.

147 In the Babli, 95a, this is attributed to the Babylonian Rav Ḥisda.

148 The "slight prohibition" referred to in the argument of the House of Shammai in the preceding paragraph.

149 The divorcee is forbidden if (*Deut.* 24:2) "she went and was another's". "To be a man's" is everywhere explained as to be formally betrothed to him (cf. Chapter 1, Note 63).

150 Quoted in the Babli, 11b, by R. Yose ben Kipper in the name of R. Eleazar (ben Shamua), in *Sifry Deut.*

270 in the name of R. Eleazar ben Azariah. The reason given is the expression (*Deut.* 24:4) "after she had been defiled" which for the anonymous majority means that a wife divorced for adultery is permanently forbidden to her ex-husband.

151 One has to read לעזר, the word in the text, ליעזר, refers only to the Tanna R. Eliezer (ben Hyrkanos) who cannot be meant here, being a generation older than R. Simeon. His case is not mentioned in the Babli.

152 The intercourse is partially incestuous for R. Simeon and clearly incestuous for the House of Shammai and R. Eleazar ben Arakh as explained at the beginning of Chapters 2 and 5.

153 If the first levir had slept with the widow without bespeaking, she would thereby have become his wife and intercourse with the other levir would be adultery.

154 According to Rabban Gamliel, R. Simeon and the House of Shammai, "bespeaking" acquires absolutely; if the second levir had not slept with the sister-in-law but had "bespoken" her, nothing would have happened, for then it would have been as if somebody became betrothed to an otherwise married woman.

155 In the Babli, 95a, "R. Yose". The difference in names is important; between R. Yose and R. Jehudah, practice always follows R. Yose (cf. Chapter 4, Note 169) whereas between R. Simeon and R. Jehudah, practice usually follows R. Jehudah (*Terumot* Chapter 3, Note 25.) The following argument is closely reproduced in the Babli, 95a.

156 Except close relatives, if they are unmarried.

157 If a married woman sleeps with a man she is tricked into thinking is her husband and she is in error, she is not punishable and not forbidden to her husband (*Soṭah* 4:5, Babli *Yebamot* 56b). The case of Mishnah 1 is classified as negligence, not error.

158 He is permitted to his wife.

159 Cf. above, Note 134.

אִימִּי אָבוֹי דִשְׁמוּאֵל בַּר אִימִּי בְּשֵׁם רַב יְהוּדָה. הֲלָכָה כְרִבִּי שִׁמְעוֹן. אָתָא עוֹבְדָא קוֹמֵי רִבִּי מָנָא וְאַפִּיק לָהּ. דְּהוּא סָבַר כְּרִבִּי יְהוּדָה. אֶלָּא שֶׁהָיְתָה מִתְרַגֶּלֶת לָבוֹא אֶצְלוֹ.

Immi the father of Samuel bar Immi[160] in the name of Rav Jehudah: Practice follows Rebbi Simeon[161]. There came a case before Rebbi Mana and he removed her from him[162]. Does he hold with Rebbi Jehudah? No, she regularly came to him[163].

160 In the Babli the son has the title "Rebbi". A third generation Amora of R. Ze'ira's academy.

161 In the Babli: Rav Jehudah in the name of Samuel. It is difficult to understand why practice has to be declared in the Babli since between R. Yose and R. Jehudah it should be clear that practice follows R. Yose. Probably the statement in the Babli is induced by that in the Yerushalmi.

162 The man was convicted of incest with his mother-in-law and R. Mana forced him to divorce his wife.

163 The mother-in-law regularly visited her daughter; R. Mana felt it was necessary to remove the daughter to keep her mother away from the son-in-law. This is a matter of judgment, not of the strict law. In the Babli, Rav Jehudah had the offender whipped and told him that he would have forced him to divorce if he were not bound by his teacher Samuel's statement.

רִבִּי בָּא. רַב הַמְנוּנָא וְרִבִּי זְעִירָא תְּרֵיהוֹן אָמְרִין. זֶהוּ רֹאשׁוֹ שֶׁל פֶּרֶק. מַה אָמַר רִבִּי יוֹסֵה בִּשְׁאָר כָּל־הַדְּבָרִים. נִישְׁמְעִינָהּ מִן הָדָא. רִבִּי יוֹסֵי אוֹמֵר. כָּל־שֶׁהוּא פוֹסֵל עַל יְדֵי אֲחֵרִים פּוֹסֵל עַל יְדֵי עַצְמוֹ. וְכָל־שֶׁאֵינוֹ פוֹסֵל (fol. 11b) עַל יְדֵי אֲחֵרִים אֵינוֹ פוֹסֵל עַל יְדֵי עַצְמוֹ. וְאָמַר רִבִּי בָּא. וְרַב הַמְנוּנָא וְרִבִּי זְעִירָא תְּרֵיהוֹן אָמְרִין. זֶהוּ רֹאשׁוֹ שֶׁלַּפֶּרֶק.

[164]Rebbi Abba: Rav Hamnuna and Rebbi Ze'ira both say that this refers to the beginning of the chapter. What does Rebbi Yose say about the other matters? Let us hear from the following: "Rebbi Yose said, anything which disables for others disables for himself; anything which does not disable for others does not disable for himself." And Rebbi Abba said, Rav Hamnuna and Rebbi Ze'ira both say that this refers to the beginning of the chapter.

164 This text is from Halakhah 3, Notes 76-78.

(fol. 10c) **משנה ט**: אָמְרוּ לוֹ מֵתָה אִשְׁתְּךָ וְנָשָׂא אֶת אֲחוֹתָהּ וְאַחַר כָּךְ אָמְרוּ לוֹ קַיֶּימֶת הָיְתָה וּמֵתָה הַוְּולָד הָרִאשׁוֹן מַמְזֵר וְהָאַחֲרוֹן אֵינוֹ מַמְזֵר.

Mishnah 9: They said to him, your wife died, and he married her sister; if afterwards they said to him that she was still alive but died later, the first child is a bastard, the last is not a bastard[165].

משנה י: רִבִּי יוֹסֵי אוֹמֵר. כָּל־שֶׁהוּא פוֹסֵל עַל יְדֵי אֲחֵרִים פּוֹסֵל עַל יְדֵי עַצְמוֹ וְכָל־שֶׁאֵינוֹ פוֹסֵל עַל יְדֵי אֲחֵרִים אֵינוֹ פוֹסֵל עַל יְדֵי עַצְמוֹ.

Mishnah 10: Rebbi Yose says, anything which disables for others disables for himself; anything which does not disable for others does not disable for himself[78].

משנה יא: אָמְרוּ לוֹ מֵתָה אִשְׁתְּךָ וְנָשָׂא אֲחוֹתָהּ מֵאָבִיהָ. מֵתָה וְנָשָׂא אֲחוֹתָהּ מֵאִמָּהּ מֵתָה וְנָשָׂא אֲחוֹתָהּ מֵאָבִיהָ. מֵתָה וְנָשָׂא אֲחוֹתָהּ מֵאִמָּהּ וְנִמְצְאוּ כּוּלָּן קַיָּמוֹת מוּתָּר בָּרִאשׁוֹנָה וּבַשְּׁלִישִׁית וּבַחֲמִישִׁית וּפוֹטְרוֹת צָרוֹתֵיהֶן וְאָסוּר בַּשְּׁנִיָּה וּבָרְבִיעִית וְאֵין בִּיאַת אַחַת מֵהֶן פּוֹטֶרֶת צָרָתָהּ.

Mishnah 11: If they said to him "your wife died," and he married her paternal sister[166], "she died[167]" and he married her maternal sister[168], "she died" and he married her paternal sister, "she died" and he married her maternal sister, but it turned out that all were alive, the first, third, and fifth are permitted to him and they would release their co-wives[169]; the second and fourth are prohibited to him[170] and intercourse of any one of these does not release the co-wife.

משנה יב: וְאִם בָּא עַל הַשְּׁנִיָּה לְאַחַר מִיתַת הָרִאשׁוֹנָה מוּתָּר בַּשְּׁנִיָּה וּבָרְבִיעִית וּפוֹטְרוֹת צָרוֹתֵיהֶן וְאָסוּר בַּשְּׁלִישִׁית וּבַחֲמִישִׁית וְאֵין בִּיאַת אַחַת מֵהֶן פּוֹטֶרֶת צָרָתָהּ.

Mishnah 12: If he has intercourse with the second one after the death of the first, the second and fourth are permitted to him and they would release their co-wives; the third and fifth are prohibited to him and intercourse of any one of these does not release the co-wife[171].

משנה יג: בֶּן תֵּשַׁע שָׁנִים וְיוֹם אֶחָד הוּא פוֹסֵל עַל יְדֵי אַחִים וְאַחִים פּוֹסְלִין עַל יָדוֹ. אֶלָּא שֶׁהוּא פוֹסֵל תְּחִילָּה וְאַחִין פּוֹסְלִין תְּחִילָּה וְסוֹף.

Mishnah 13: [A male] nine years and one day old[172] disables for the brothers and the brothers disable for him; only that he disables at the beginning and the brothers disable at beginning and end[173].

משנה יד: כֵּיצַד בֶּן תֵּשַׁע שָׁנִים וְיוֹם אֶחָד שֶׁבָּא עַל יְבִימְתּוֹ פָּסַל עַל יְדֵי אַחִים. בָּאוּ עָלֶיהָ אַחִים עָשׂוּ בָהּ מַאֲמָר נָתְנוּ גֵט אוֹ חָלְצוּ פְּסָלוּ עַל יָדוֹ.

Mishnah 14: How is that? [A male] nine years and one day old who copulated with his sister-in-law disabled her for the brothers. If [any one of] the brothers copulated with her, "bespoke" her, divorced her, or performed *ḥalîṣah* with her, they disabled her for him.

165 Any child conceived by the sister during the first wife's lifetime is a bastard as result of an incestuous union.

166 She is a paternal half-sister.

167 This also is known only by the testimony of a single witness.

168 She is a maternal half-sister of the second wife and unrelated to the first. In this way, the fifth wife is unrelated to the first and third wives.

169 Since they are all legal co-wives, if the husband died childless, the levirate or *ḥalîṣah* of one of them releases all others.

170 The marriage of the second is invalid since it is an incestuous relationship with the sister of the first wife; similarly, the fourth is forbidden because of the third. Since the second and fourth wives are not married to the husband, they do not become widows and their actions with respect to the levirs can have no influence on the status of the legally married ones

171 Since both he and his second wife thought that she was actually married to him, if he sleeps with her after the first wife's death it is with the idea that they are married;

therefore, they are married and the situation becomes identical to that of the preceding Mishnah only with even and odd numbers changing places.

172 Cf. Chapter 3, Note 143, for the status of a male older than 9 years.

173 His action counts only if he acted before any of the adult brothers.

הלכה יד: רִבִּי יוֹסֵי אוֹמֵר. כָּל־שֶׁהוּא פּוֹסֵל כול׳. רִבִּי הִילָא בְשֵׁם רִבִּי שִׁמְעוֹן בֶּן לָקִישׁ. אֲחוֹת אִשְׁתּוֹ נְשׂוּאָה הוֹאִיל וְהוּא פּוֹסֵל עַל יְדֵי אֲחֵרִים פּוֹסֵל עַל יְדֵי עַצְמוֹ. וַאֲחוֹת אִשְׁתּוֹ פְּנוּיָה הוֹאִיל וְאֵינוֹ פּוֹסֵל עַל יְדֵי אֲחֵרִים אֵינוֹ פּוֹסֵל עַל יְדֵי עַצְמוֹ. דָּמַר רִבִּי הִילָא בְשֵׁם רִבִּי שִׁמְעוֹן בֶּן לָקִישׁ. צְרִיכָה הֵימֶינּוּ גֵט.

Halakhah 14: "Rebbi Yose says, anything which disables," etc. Rebbi Hila in the name of Rebbi Simeon ben Laqish: If his wife's sister was married, since he disables her for others, he disables her for himself. But his wife's unmarried sister which he does not disable for others, he does not disable for himself[174]. As Rebbi Hila said in the name of Rebbi Simeon ben Laqish, she needs a bill of divorce from him[175].

174 R. Yose in the Mishnah refers to the preceding Mishnah. If the wife and the sister's husband went overseas and her husband and sister received erroneous notice that the wife and her brother-in-law both had died, the widowed husband and wife's sister married, and then the two who were believed to have died returned, since the husband by his relations with the wife's sister forbade her to her husband, he also forbade his own wife to himself. But if the wife's sister was unmarried, his wife returns to him.

175 They explain the mechanism by which the wife becomes forbidden to him even though R. Yose agrees to the deduction in the preceding Halakhah that intercourse with the wife's sister does not disable the wife. In the first case, the wife's sister must receive a divorce document from him; cf. Note 18. But then the wife becomes the sister of his divorcee and is automatically forbidden to him.

In the Babli, 95b, this is only a conjectural explanation of R. Yose's intention.

אָמְרוּ לוֹ מֵתָה אִשְׁתֶּךָ כול'. וְהֵיךְ עֲבִידָא. גְּבַר אִית לֵיהּ בַּר וְחוֹרְגָּא וְאִינְתּוּ אִית לָהּ בַּר וְחוֹרְגָּה וְאַסְבּוֹן דֵּין לְדֵין וְאוֹלִידוּן בְּרָא. מְשָׁרֵיי מִן חוֹרְגְּתָא דְאִיתְתָא.

"If they said to him "your wife died," etc. How can that be[176]? A man has a daughter and a stepdaughter, a woman has a daughter and a stepdaughter. They married and had a daughter. It starts with the woman's stepdaughter.

[176] How may a man marry five partially related women from one family? Man A has a daughter a1 and a stepdaughter a2 from an earlier marriage. Woman B has a daughter b1 and a stepdaughter b2 from an earlier marriage. They marry and have a daughter c. If an outsider C marries first b2, on her death he may marry her paternal halfsister b1. Then he may marry c, b1's maternal halfsister, afterwards c's paternal halfsister a1 and then a1's maternal halfsister a2.

As known, the Yerushalmi is very weak in the grammar of gender; it uses the masculine as nonspecific universal.

בֶּן תֵּשַׁע שָׁנִים וְיוֹם אֶחָד הוּא פוֹסֵל כול'. הָא בַסוֹף אֵינוֹ פוֹסֵל אֶלָּא אַחַר מַאֲמָרוֹ אֲבָל לְאַחַר בִּיאָתוֹ פוֹסֵל. אֶלָּא שֶׁהוּא פוֹסֵל בְּדָבָר אֶחָד וְהֵן פּוֹסְלִין בְּאַרְבָּעָה דְבָרִים.

"[A male] nine years and one day old disables," etc. At the end he does not disable after his "bespeaking"[177], but after his intercourse he disables. However he can disable only by one act but they may disable by four acts.

[177] The Mishnah which declares that the minor's act counts only if he precedes his adult brothers refers to the legal ceremony of "bespeaking"; but intercourse is a real act which cannot be disregarded under any circumstances and prohibits the widow in all cases.

כֵּיצַד בֶּן תֵּשַׁע שָׁנִים וְיוֹם אֶחָד. וְאִם לִבְנוֹ יִיעָדֶנָּה. לִבְנוֹ הוּא מְיַיַעֲדָהּ. אֵינוֹ מְיַיַעֲדָהּ לָאַחִין. וִיִיעֲדֶינָּהּ לָאַחִין מִקַּל וָחוֹמֶר. מַה אִם הַבֵּן שֶׁאֵינוֹ קָם תַּחְתָּיו לַחֲלִיצָה וּלְיִיבּוּם הֲרֵי הוּא מְיָיעֲדָהּ לוֹ. אָחִיו שֶׁהוּא קָם תַּחְתָּיו לַחֲלִיצָה וּלְיִיבּוּם אֵינוֹ דִין שֶׁמְּיָיעֲדֶנָּה לוֹ. תַּלְמוּד לוֹמַר וְאִם לִבְנוֹ יִיעָדֶנָּה. הוּא מְיָיעֲדָהּ. אֵינוֹ מְיָיעֲדָהּ לְאָחִיו. לֹא. אִם אָמַרְתָּ בְּבֵן שֶׁהוּא קָם תַּחְתָּיו בִּשְׂדֵה אֲחוּזָּה. תֹּאמַר בְּאָחִיו שֶׁאֵינוֹ קָם תַּחְתָּיו בִּשְׂדֵה אֲחוּזָּה. הוֹאִיל וְאֵינוֹ קָם תַּחְתָּיו בִּשְׂדֵה אֲחוּזָּה אֵינוֹ דִין שֶׁיְּיָעֲדֶנָּה לוֹ. תַּלְמוּד לוֹמַר וְאִם לִבְנוֹ יִיעָדֶנָּה. לִבְנוֹ הוּא מְיָיעֲדָהּ וְאֵינוֹ מְיָיעֲדָהּ לְאָחִיו.

[178]"How is that? [A male] nine years and one day old." "If he allots her to his son.[179]" He allots her to his son but may not allot her to the brothers[180]. He should be able to allot her to the brothers by an argument *de minore ad majus*! If he may allot her to his son who may not take his place for *ḥalîṣah* and levirate, should it not be logical that he may allot her to his brother who may take his place for *ḥalîṣah* and levirate[181]? The verse says, "if he allots her to his son." He allots her [to his son] but may not allot her to the brothers. No. If you would accept the son since he will take [the father's] place in a field of inheritance[182], what can you say about his brother who will not take his place in a field of inheritance? Would it be reasonable that he may allot her to him? The verse says, "if he allots her to his son." He allots her to his son but may not allot her to the brothers.

178 This Halakhah is copied from *Qiddushin* 1:2, fol. 59b/c which has a better and more complete text.

179 *Ex.* 21:9, speaking about a minor girl sold by her father as a slave with the understanding that her price would count as betrothal gift in case the owner would desire to marry her or would give her to his son. In that case, the betrothal is called "allotment". If she is not married, she regains her freedom by reaching adulthood at 12 years of age.

180 The argument is reproduced in

Mekhilta deR. Ismael, Masekhta dinziqin 3, *Mekhilta deR. Simeon ben Iohai* Chap. 21 (p. 167); Babli *Qiddushin* 17b.

181 The Babli rejects this argument by noting that levirate presumes the absence of a son.

182 The family estate going back to the distribution of land under Joshua, for which the succession is determined by the rules of *Num.* 27:6-11.

וְאִם לִבְנוֹ יִיעָדֶנָּה. לִבנוֹ הוּא מְייָעֲדָהּ וְאֵינוֹ מְייָעֲדָהּ לְבֶן בְּנוֹ. שְׁמוּאֵל בַּר אַבָּא בְּעָא קוֹמֵי רִבִּי זְעִירָא. בְּפָרָשַׁת נְחָלוֹת אַתְּ עֲבַד בֶּן בֵּן כְּבֵן וְהָכָא לֵית עֲבַד בֶּן בֵּן כְּבֵן. אָמַר רִבִּי זְעִירָא. מָאן דָּמַר לִי הָדָא מִילְּתָה אֲנָא מַשְׁקֵי לֵיהּ קוֹנְדִּיטוֹן. הָתִיב רִבִּי תַּנְחוּם. הֲרֵי פָּרָשַׁת נְחָלוֹת הֲרֵי עָשִׂיתָ אָח כְּבֵן[183] וּשְׁאָר כָּל־הַקְּרוֹבִים כְּבֵן. (וְאֵין)[184] אַתְּ עוֹשֶׂה בֶּן בֵּן כְּבֵן. הָתִיבוֹן רַבָּנִן דְּקַיסָרִין. הֲרֵי פָּרָשַׁת טֻמְאוֹת הֲרֵי עָשִׂיתָה אָח כְּבֵן וּשְׁאָר כָּל־הַקְּרוֹבִים כבֵן. וְאֵין אַתְּ עוֹשֶׂה בֶּן בֵּן כְּבֵן. אָמַר הָא אֲזִיל קוֹנדִּיטוֹן.

"If he allots her to his son;" he allots her to his son but he may not allot her to his grandson. Samuel bar Abba asked before Rebbi Ze'ira: In matters of inheritance you take the grandson like the son but here you do not take the grandson like the son[185]? Rebbi Ze'ira said, if anybody explains this matter, I shall pour him spiced wine[186]. Rebbi Tanḥum[187] answered: In matters of inheritance where the brother can take the place of the son and all others can take the place of the son, the grandson takes the place of the son.[188] The rabbis of Caesarea answered: In matters of impurity you consider the brother like the son and all [near] relatives like the son but not the grandson like the son[189]. He said, there went the spiced wine.

183 Reading of the text in *Qiddushin*. Here: מבן.

184 Missing in *Qiddushin*, out of place here.

185 If the son died before the father, the grandson inherits the son's part.

186 Latin *conditum* (sc., *vinum*),

"spiced wine".

187 In *Qiddushin*: R. Naḥum, a third generation Amora, student of Samuel bar Abba. His name fits into the scheme of things but not the fifth generation R. Tanḥum.

188 Here, a sentence is missing which appears in the text of *Qiddushin*: וְכָאן שֶׁלֹּא עָשִׂיתָ אָח כְּבֵן וּשְׁאָר כָּל־הַקְּרוֹבִים כְּבֵן אֵין אַתְּ עוֹשֶׂה בֶּן בֵּן כְּבֵן "but here, where neither the brother nor the other relatives take the role of the son, the grandson does not take the role of the son."

189 In the list of close relatives who have to defile themselves for the burial of the deceased (*Lev*. 21:2-3), the grandson or grandfather is absent. Among Cohanim, the grandson may not defile himself for his grandfather.

וְאִם לִבְנוֹ יִיעָדֶנָּה. לְדַעַת. אָמַר רִבִּי יוֹחָנָן. לֵית כָּאן לְדַעַת. אָמַר רִבִּי יַעֲקֹב בַּר אָחָא כֵּן. אִית כָּאן כְּרִבִּי יוֹסֵי בֵּירִבִּי יְהוּדָה. אָמַר רִבִּי שְׁמוּאֵל בַּר אֶבְדּוּמָא. אֲפִילוּ תֵימַר אִית כָּאן כְּרִבִּי יוֹסֵי בֵּירִבִּי יְהוּדָה לֹא קָטָן הוּא. אִם לִבְנוֹ יִיעָדֶנָּה. לְדַעַת. רִבִּי יוֹחָנָן אָמַר. מְיָיעֲדֶנָּהּ בֵּין לִבְנוֹ הַגָּדוֹל בֵּין לִבְנוֹ הַקָּטָן בֵּין לְדַעַת בֵּין שֶׁלֹּא מִדַּעַת. רִבִּי שִׁמְעוֹן בֶּן לָקִישׁ אָמַר. אֵינוֹ מְיָיעֲדָהּ אֶלָּא לִבְנוֹ הַגָּדוֹל בִּלְבַד לְדַעַת.

"If he allots her to his son;" with [the girl's] agreement[190]. Rebbi Joḥanan said, there is no agreement here. Rebbi Jacob bar Aḥa said so, the statement follows Rebbi Yose ben Rebbi Jehudah[191]. Rebbi Samuel bar Eudaimon said, even if you say the statement follows Rebbi Yose ben Rebbi Jehudah, is he not a minor[192]? "If he allots her to his son;" with [the latter's] agreement. Rebbi Joḥanan said, he allots her to his minor or adult son, with and without the latter's agreement. Rebbi Simeon ben Laqish said, he allots her only to his adult son with the latter's agreement[193].

190 This is the explicit interpretation of the Babli (*Qiddushin* 19a) which seems to be valid here also and explains the apparent duplication of the argument in this paragraph.

191 He holds in a *baraita* (*Qiddushin* 1:2, fol. 59c; Babli 19a) that the money given to the father does not count as bride money but that the allotment is a legal betrothal since from the moment

of betrothal she is no longer a servant. The money with which she is bought is money with which her services are bought for the duration of her servitude. By allotment, the value of the remainder of the money (computed by the remaining days of her servitude) is given as wedding gift. This implies that on the last day of her servitude she can be allotted to master or son only if at least a *perutah*'s worth of servitude is left (if the day's worth is prorated by hours).

192 Who is not called "a man" and cannot legally acquire. The Babli (19a) refers to the case of a levir aged 9 years and 1 day (Mishnah *Yebamot* 7:4) who by intercourse does acquire preliminarily his sister-in-law by biblical standards, except that his wife cannot be prosecuted for adultery since it is written (*Lev*. 20:10): "A *man* who commits adultery with a *man*'s wife". This implies that there are cases where a woman can be legally married to a male without being a *man*'s wife.

193 In the Yerushalmi, practice should follow R. Johanan. In the Babli, R. Johanan's opinion is not mentioned; what is asserted here in the name of R. Simeon ben Laqish is there attributed to the unquestioned authority of R. Yannai, the teacher of both R. Johanan and R. Simeon ben Laqish.

בֶּן תֵּשַׁע שָׁנִים וְיוֹם אֶרֶד עוֹשֶׂה אַלְמָנָה לְכֹהֵן גָּדוֹל גְּרוּשָׁה וַחֲלוּצָה לְכֹהֵן הֶדְיוֹט. עַל דַּעְתֵּיהּ דְּרִבִּי יוֹחָנָן דְּהוּא פָּתַר לָהּ בְּיִיעוּדִין נִיחָא יִיעוּדִין שֶׁיֵּשׁ לוֹ קִנְייָן בָּהּ עוֹשֶׂה אַלְמָנָה לְכֹהֵן גָּדוֹל גְּרוּשָׁה וַחֲלוּצָה לְכֹהֵן הֶדְיוֹט. עַל דַּעְתֵּיהּ דְּרִבִּי שִׁמְעוֹן בֶּן לָקִישׁ דְּהוּא פָּתַר לָהּ בְּנִישּׂוּאִין תְּהֵא פְטוּרָה מִן הַחֲלִיצָה וּמִן הַיִּיבּוּם. וְהָתַנִּינָן נָשָׂא אִשָּׁה וּמֵת הֲרֵי זוֹ פְטוּרָה. אָמַר רִבִּי אָבִין. אַתְיָא דְּרִבִּי שִׁמְעוֹן בֶּן לָקִישׁ כְּרִבִּי יוֹסֵי בֵּירִבִּי יְהוּדָה. וְתַנֵּי כֵן. בֶּן תֵּשַׁע שָׁנִים וְיוֹם אֶחָד עַד בֶּן שְׁתֵּים עֶשְׂרֵה שָׁנָה וְיוֹם אֶחָד שֶׁהֵבִיא שְׁתֵּי שְׂעָרוֹת הֲרֵי זוֹ שׁוּמָא. רִבִּי יוֹסֵי בֵּירִבִּי יְהוּדָה אוֹמֵר. הֲרֵי אֵילוּ סִימָנִין. רִבִּי יַעֲקֹב בֵּירִבִּי בוּן בְּשֵׁם רִבִּי יוֹסֵי בֶּן חֲנִינָה. וְהֵן שֶׁעָמְדוּ בוֹ בִשְׁעַת סִימָנִין.

"A male nine years and one day old makes[194] a widow for the High Priest or a divorcee or one who performed *ḥalîṣah* for a common priest." In the opinion of R. Joḥanan who will explain this for allotments[195] it is understandable; since he acquires by allotment he makes a widow for the

High Priest or a divorcee or one who performed *ḥalîṣah* for a common priest. In the opinion of Rebbi Simeon ben Laqish[196] who must explain this for a marriage, she should also be free from levirate or *ḥalîṣah*, as we have stated[197]: "If he married a woman, that one is free from levirate or *ḥalîṣah*." Rebbi Abin said, following Rebbi Simeon ben Laqish it[198] comes following Rebbi Yose ben Rebbi Jehudah, as it was stated so: If a male nine years and one day old up to twelve years and one day old grew two pubic hairs, they are warts[199]. Rebbi Yose ben Rebbi Jehudah said, they are indicators[200] [of puberty]. Rebbi Jacob ben Rebbi Abun in the name of Rebbi Yose ben Ḥanina: Only if they were still there at the time of indicators[201].

194 If he marries, the marriage is valid to turn his widow into a woman forbidden to the High Priest and if he divorces her, she becomes forbidden to a common priest.

195 He restricts the validity of the statement to a girl married by allotment since only in that case is his marriage valid by biblical standards.

196 For him, a minor cannot be allotted a wife; therefore, the marriage must be contracted under rabbinic rules and the author of that *baraita* cannot accept the statement in the next Mishnah that the widow of a childless minor is not subject to the laws of levirate.

197 Mishnah 17.

198 The *baraita* which opened this paragraph must follow R. Yose ben R. Jehudah while the Mishnah follows the anonymous majority.

199 Not signs of adulthood defined as onset of puberty. Quoted in Babli *Niddah* 46a.

200 Greek σημεῖον "sign, marker".

201 During his thirteenth year, when the growth of pubic hair is expected. In the Babli, the statement is attributed to a R. Kruspedai ben Sabbatai.

רִבִּי יוֹסֵה בָּעֵי. עָמְדוּ לוֹ בִשְׁעַת סֵימָנִין. לְמַפְרֵיעוֹ הוּא נַעֲשֶׂה אִישׁ אוֹ מִכָּן וּלְהַבָּא. רִבִּי אָבוּן פְּשִׁיטָא לֵיהּ. לְמַפְרֵיעוֹ הוּא נַעֲשֶׂה אִישׁ כָּל־שֶׁכֵּן לָבֹא. דּוּ[202] פָּתַר הָדָא דְּרִבִּי שִׁמְעוֹן בֶּן לָקִישׁ כְּרִבִּי יוֹסֵי בֵּירִבִּי יְהוּדָה. וְלָמָּה לֵית רִבִּי יוֹסֵי

פָּתַר הָדָא דְּרִבִּי שִׁמְעוֹן בֶּן לָקִישׁ כְּרִבִּי יוֹסֵי בֵּירִבִּי יְהוּדָה. אָמַר רִבִּי מָנָא. דְּהִיא צְרִיכָה לֵיהּ. רִבִּי יוֹסֵי בָּעֵי. עָמְדוּ לוֹ בִשְׁעַת סֵימָנִין לְמַפְרֵיעוֹ הוּא נַעֲשֶׂה אִישׁ אוֹ מִכַּן וּלְהַבָּא. נִיחָא אַלְמָנָה. וּגְרוּשָׁה. תִּיפְתָּר שֶׁבָּא עָלֶיהָ מִשֶּׁהִגְדִּיל נָתַן לָהּ גֵּט.[203] חֲלִיצָה. תִּיפְתָּר שֶׁבָּא עָלֶיהָ וָמֵת וְחָלְצוּ לָהּ אַחִין וְעַל יָדָיו הִיא נַעֲשֵׂית חֲלוּצָה. מֵעַתָּה אֲפִילוּ פָּחוֹת מִתֵּשַׁע. אָמַר רִבִּי שְׁמוּאֵל בַּר אֶבְדּוֹמָא. וְכֵינִי. אֶלָּא בְגִין דְּתַנָּא כּוּלְהוֹן תֵּשַׁע תַּנָּא אַף הוּא עִמְּהוֹן.

Rebbi Yose asked: When they[204] remained until the time of indicators, does he retroactively become a man or from that time onward? For Rebbi Abun it is obvious that he becomes a man retroactively, so certainly also for the future, for he explains the position of Rebbi Simeon ben Laqish by Rebbi Yose ben Rebbi Jehudah. Why does Rebbi Yose not explain the position of Rebbi Simeon ben Laqish by Rebbi Yose ben Rebbi Jehudah since he asked, when they remained until the time of indicators, does he retroactively become a man or from that time onward? Rebbi Mana said, because he had difficulty. Rebbi Yose asked: When they remained until the time of indicators, does he retroactively become a man or from that time onward[205]? One understands the case of a widow[206]. But a divorcee[207]? Explain it if he copulated with her after he became an adult and divorced her. *Halîṣah*? Explain it if he copulated with her, died, and the [adult] brothers performed *ḥalîṣah*; she had *ḥalîṣah* because of him. In that case, even if he was younger than nine [years]! Rebbi Samuel ben Eudaimon said, that is correct. But because in all cases one stated "nine", one stated this with them.

202 Reading (דו = דְּהוּא) in *Qiddushin*. Here: די

203 Reading in *Qiddushin*. Here: גיטי

204 The pubic hairs.

205 His difficulty is following R. Yose ben R. Jehudah, not R. Simeon ben Laqish who denies the validity of actions of a minor. His problem is with R. Joḥanan.

206 If his marriage by allotment is sanctioned by biblical decree, if he dies the widow is a widow by biblical standards and unquestionably forbidden to the High Priest.

207 Even if his marriage, effected by his adult father, is valid, a divorce which needs his conscious action is certainly invalid as long as he is a minor.

רִבִּי יְהוּדָה בֶּן פָּזִי בְשֵׁם רִבִּי יְהוֹשֻׁעַ בֶּן לֵוִי. מֵאָחָז לָמַד רִבִּי יוֹסֵי בֵּירִבִּי ווּדָה. דְּתַנֵּי. אָחָז הוֹלִיד בֶּן תֵּשַׁע וְהָרָן[208] בֶּן שֵׁשׁ וְכָלֵב בֶּן עֶשֶׂר. כְּמָאן דָּמַר. הוּא כָּלֵב בֶּן חֶצְרוֹן הוּא כָּלֵב בֶּן יְפוּנֶּה.

Rebbi Jehudah ben Pazi in the name of Rebbi Joshua ben Levi: Rebbi Yose ben Jehudah learned from Aḥaz, as it was stated: Aḥaz produced a child at age nine[209], Haran at age six[210], and Caleb at age ten following him who identifies Caleb ben Ḥeṣron with Caleb ben Yephuneh[211].

208 Reading in *Qiddushin*. Here: הויין "they were".

209 He became king at age 20 and ruled for 16 years (*2K*. 16:2). His son Ḥizqiah became king at age 25 (*2K*. 18:2). That seems to mean that Ḥizqiah was born when his father was 11 years old. However, since the first year of the reign is only counted from the day of accession to the next New Year's Day, it is possible that he was born when his father was 10 and was conceived when he was 9. This computation has no parallel in the sources.

210 The computation is detailed in Babli Sanhedrin 69b and is based on two hypotheses, (1) that Sarah, 10 years younger than Abraham, was Abraham's niece, Haran's daughter, against the explicit testimony of the biblical text that she was his paternal halfsister, and that (2) Haran was the youngest of Teraḥ's sons (*Gen*. 11:27) and at least two years younger than Abraham.

211 This also is detailed in Babli Sanhedrin 69b and is based on the identification of Caleb ben Yephuneh the spy, whose children are enumerated in *1Chr*. 4:15, with Caleb ben Ḥeṣron whose descendants are mentioned in *1Chr*. 2:18-21. Caleb ben Ḥeṣron is described as the great-grandfather of Beṣalel who built the Tabernacle. {The Babli never mentions the problem of the quite impossible identification of the two Calebs.} Since Caleb ben Yephuneh was 40 years of age in the

year after the Exodus (*Jos.* 14:7) and Beṣalel is called "man" in *Ex.* 36:4, he was at least 13 years of age, only 27 years younger than his great-grandfather. That means that Caleb, Uri, and Ḥur all were fathers at age 9. If Caleb was father at age 10, then one of his descendants was father at age 8.

(fol. 10c) **משנה טו:** בֶּן תֵּשַׁע שָׁנִים וְיוֹם אֶחָד שֶׁבָּא עַל יְבִימְתּוֹ וְאַחַר כָּךְ בָּא עָלֶיהָ אָחִיו שֶׁהוּא בֶּן תֵּשַׁע שָׁנִים וְיוֹם אֶחָד פָּסַל עַל יָדוֹ. רִבִּי שִׁמְעוֹן אוֹמֵר לֹא פָסַל.

Mishnah 15: If [a male] nine years and one day old[212] copulated with his sister-in-law and after that his brother, who [also] was nine years and one day old, copulated with her, [the brother] disabled her for [the first levir]. Rebbi Simeon says, he did not disable[213].

משנה טז: בֶּן תֵּשַׁע שָׁנִים וְיוֹם אֶחָד שֶׁבָּא עַל יְבִימְתּוֹ וְאַחַר כָּךְ בָּא עַל צָרָתָהּ פָּסַל עַל יְדֵי עַצְמוֹ. רִבִּי שִׁמְעוֹן אוֹמֵר לֹא פָסַל.

Mishnah 16: If [a male] nine years and one day old copulated with his sister-in-law, and after that he copulated with her co-wife, he disabled her for himself. Rebbi Simeon says, he did not disable.

משנה יז: בֶּן תֵּשַׁע שָׁנִים וְיוֹם אֶחָד שֶׁבָּא עַל יְבִימְתּוֹ וָמֵת חוֹלֶצֶת וְלֹא מִתְיַבֶּמֶת. נָשָׂא אִשָּׁה וָמֵת הֲרֵי זוֹ פְּטוּרָה.

Mishnah 17: If [a male] nine years and one day old copulated with his sister-in-law and died, she performs *ḥalîṣah* but not levirate[214]. If he married a woman and died, she is free[215].

משנה יח: בֶּן תֵּשַׁע שָׁנִים וְיוֹם אֶחָד שֶׁבָּא עַל יְבִימְתּוֹ וּמִשֶּׁהִגְדִּיל נָשָׂא אִשָּׁה אַחֶרֶת וָמֵת אִם לֹא יָדַע אֶת הָרִאשׁוֹנָה מִשֶּׁהִגְדִּיל הַשְּׁנִיָּה אוֹ חוֹלֶצֶת אוֹ מִתְיַבֶּמֶת. וְהָרִאשׁוֹנָה חוֹלֶצֶת וְלֹא מִתְיַיבֶּמֶת. רִבִּי שִׁמְעוֹן אוֹמֵר מְיַיבֵּם לְאֵיזוֹ שֶׁיִּרְצֶה וְחוֹלֵץ לַשְּׁנִיָּה. אֶחָד שֶׁהוּא בֶּן תֵּשַׁע שָׁנִים וְיוֹם אֶחָד וְאֶחָד שֶׁהוּא בֶּן עֶשְׂרִים שָׁנָה וְלֹא הֵבִיא שְׁתֵּי שְׂעָרוֹת.

Miashnah 18: If [a male] nine years and one day old copulated with his sister-in-law and after he became an adult married another woman and died, if he never had intercourse with the first after he became an adult, the second [wife] either performs *ḥalîṣah* or levirate, the first performs *ḥalîṣah* but not levirate[216]. Rebbi Simeon says, he takes in levirate the one he likes and performs *ḥalîṣah* with the other[217]. It makes no difference whether he is nine years and one day or twenty years old, as long as he did not grow two pubic hairs.

212 As explained in Mishnah 18, if he is older than nine full years as long as he did not grow two pubic hairs.

213 As will be repeated in the Halakhah, the majority holds that intercourse of an almost grown up male is like "bespeaking" of an adult and therefore follows the rules of "bespeaking" which disables but does not fully acquire. For R. Simeon, intercourse of a minor either acquires by biblical standards or it does not acquire at all, but we do not know which assertion holds (Halakhah 3:5). If it acquires, then the sister-in-law is the first levir's wife and the action of a minor has no legal consequence; if it does not acquire for the first it did not acquire for the second, both are legally minors and their actions as minors cannot influence the status of the widow when the levirs become grown-ups.

The same argument holds for R. Simeon in the cases following.

214 Since the widow's legal status is one of "bespoken" but not fully married, if the levir dies she becomes the widow of two brothers and may not marry in levirate (cf. Halakhah 3:1).

215 Outside of levirate, the marriage of a minor is invalid; the woman is not a widow.

216 In the Babylonian Mishnah, the order of the actions is inverted. The order of the Yerushalmi is more reasonable. The second is a real wife, who can be married in levirate if the husband dies childless. For the majority, the first one is only "bespoken"; she becomes the widow of two brothers and is disqualified from levirate.

217 For R. Simeon, the first one either was the wife of the deceased or she was not. If she was not, she is the widow of her first husband and can be married in levirate; if she was, she is

the widow of her second husband and can be married in levirate. The second certainly can be married in levirate. But only one of the co-widows can be married. In this case, the other is not free since maybe the first one was not a wife.

(fol. 11b) **הלכה יז**: שְׁמוּאֵל אָמַר. דִּבְרֵי רִבִּי מֵאִיר. עָשׂוּ בִיאַת בֶּן תֵּשַׁע שָׁנִים וְיוֹם אֶחָד כְּמַאֲמָר בְּגָדוֹל. וּכְמַה דְאַתְּ אָמַר. עָשׂוּ בִיאַת בֶּן תֵּשַׁע שָׁנִים וְיוֹם אֶחָד כְּמַאֲמָר בְּגָדוֹל. וְדִכְוָותָהּ נַעֲשָׂה חֲלִיצָה בֶּן תֵּשַׁע שָׁנִים וְיוֹם אֶחָד כְּגֵט בְּגָדוֹל. וְרַבָּנִין אָמְרִין אֵין חֲלִיצַת בֶּן תֵּשַׁע שָׁנִים וְיוֹם אֶחָד כְּלוּם. וְלָמָּה עָשׂוּ בִיאַת בֶּן תֵּשַׁע שָׁנִים וְיוֹם אֶחָד כְּמַאֲמָר בְּגָדוֹל. שֶׁכֵּן בִּיאָה בְגָדוֹל קוֹנָה בֵּין לְדַעַת בֵּין שֶׁלֹּא לְדַעַת. נַעֲשָׂה חֲלִיצָה בֶּן תֵּשַׁע שָׁנִים וְיוֹם אֶחָד כְּגֵט בְּגָדוֹל. וַחֲלִיצָה בְגָדוֹל אֵינָהּ פּוֹטֶרֶת אֶלָּא לְדַעַת.

Halakhah 17: [218]Samuel said, the words of Rebbi Meïr: They made the intercourse of a child of nine years and one day like "bespeaking" of an adult. And as you said, they made the intercourse of a child of nine years and one day like "bespeaking" of an adult, they made the *ḥalîṣah* of a child of nine years and one day like a bill of divorce of an adult. But the rabbis said, the *ḥalîṣah* of a child of nine years and one day is nothing. And why did they make the intercourse of a child of nine years and one day like "bespeaking" of an adult? Because the intercourse of an adult acquires whether intentional or not intentional. The *ḥalîṣah* of a child of nine years and one day was made like a bill of divorce by an adult. But *ḥalîṣah* by an adult can free only if it is intentional.

218 The text is from Halakhah 5:5, Notes 79-83.

אִילּוּ שׁוֹמֶרֶת יָבָם שֶׁנָּפְלָה לִפְנֵי כַמָּה יְבָמִים שֶׁמָּא אֵינָהּ מִתְייַבֶּמֶת. תַּנֵּי רִבִּי חִיָּא. אֵשֶׁת מֵת אֶחָד[219] מִתְייַבֶּמֶת. לֹא אֵשֶׁת שְׁנֵי מֵתִים. שְׁנִיָּה לָמָּה אֵינָהּ מִתְייַבֶּמֶת. אָמַר רִבִּי לָעְזָר. דְּרִבִּי מֵאִיר הִיא. דְּאָמַר רִבִּי מֵאִיר. כָּל־שֶׁאֵינוֹ

מְייַבְּמֵנִי אֵין מְייַבֵּם צָרָתִי. אָמַר רִבִּי יוֹחָנָן. מִינִּי שְׁמָעָהּ רִבִּי אֶלְעָזָר וְאָמְרָהּ. אָמַר רִבִּי יוֹסֵה. מַתְנִיתָא אָמְרָה כֵן. בֶּן תֵּשַׁע שָׁנִים וְיוֹם אֶחָד שֶׁבָּא עַל יְבִמְתּוֹ. מִשֶּׁהִגְדִּיל וְנָשָׂא אִשָּׁה אַחֶרֶת. אִם לֹא יָדַע הָרִאשׁוֹן מִשֶּׁהִגְדִּיל. הַשְּׁנִייָה אוֹ חוֹלֶצֶת אוֹ מִתְייַבֶּמֶת. הָרִאשׁוֹנָה חוֹלֶצֶת וְלֹא מִתְייַבֶּמֶת. הָכָא אִתְּמַר חוֹלֶצֶת. וְהָכָא אִיתְמַר מִתְייַבֶּמֶת. הֵן דְּתֵימַר חוֹלֶצֶת רִבִּי מֵאִיר וְרִבִּי שִׁמְעוֹן. וְהֵן דְּתֵימַר מִתְייַבֶּמֶת רִבִּי שִׁמְעוֹן (fol. 11c) וְרַבָּנִן.

220Can a woman waiting for a levir who became available to several brothers-in-law not be married in levirate? Rebbi Ḥiyya stated: The wife of one dead [husband] is married in levirate, not the wife of two dead. Rebbi Eleazar said, this follows Rebbi Meïr, since Rebbi Meïr said, "any one who cannot marry me in levirate, cannot marry my co-wife in levirate." Rebbi Joḥanan said, Rebbi Eleazar formulated what he had heard from me. Rebbi Yose said, a Mishnah said so: "If [a male] nine years and one day old copulated with his sister-in-law and after he became an adult married another woman and died, if he never had intercourse with the first after he became an adult, the second [wife] either performs *ḥalîṣah* or levirate, the first performs *ḥalîṣah* but not levirate. The first one must perform *ḥalîṣah* and cannot be married in levirate." Here you say, she performs *ḥalîṣah*; there you say, she is married in levirate! Where you say she performs *ḥalîṣah*, Rebbi Meïr and Rebbi Simeon; where you say, she is married in levirate, Rebbi Simeon and the rabbis.

219 Reading of Halakhah 3:10. here: אחר.

220 The text is from Halakhah 3:10, Notes 140-148.

פְּשִׁיטָא הָדָא מִילְּתָא. פָּחוֹת מִבֶּן עֶשְׂרִים שֶׁהֵבִיא שְׁתֵּי שְׂעָרוֹת לְמַפְרֵיעוֹ הוּא נַעֲשֶׂה אִישׁ. וְיוֹתֵר מִבֶּן עֶשְׂרִים שֶׁהֵבִיא שְׁתֵּי שְׂעָרוֹת מִכָּן וְהֵילָךְ הוּא אִישׁ. מַה פְלִיגִין. בְּבֶן עֶשְׂרִים. שְׁמוּאֵל אָמַר. לְמַפְרֵיעוֹ הוּא נַעֲשֶׂה אִישׁ. רַב אָמַר. מִכָּן וְהֵילָךְ הוּא אִישׁ. מַתְנִיתָא פְלִיגָא בֵּין עַל דֵּין בֵּין עַל דֵּין. הַסָּרִיס אֵינוֹ נַעֲשֶׂה

בֶּן סוֹרֵר וּמוֹרֶה שֶׁאֵין בּוֹ הַקָּפַת זָקָן. וְיַתִּיר בּוֹ שֶׁמָּא יָבִיא שְׁתֵּי שְׂעָרוֹת בְּתוֹךְ שְׁלֹשָׁה חֲדָשִׁים. כְּמָאן דָּמַר. אֵין מְקַבְּלִין הַתְרָייָה עַל הַסָּפֵק. מַתְנִיתִין פְּלִיגָא עַל שְׁמוּאֵל. אֶחָד בֶּן תֵּשַׁע שָׁנִים וְיוֹם אֶחָד וְאֶחָד בֶּן שְׁתֵּים עֶשְׂרֵה שָׁנָה וְיוֹם אֶחָד שֶׁלֹּא הֵבִיא שְׁתֵּי שְׂעָרוֹת לְמַפְרֵיעוֹ הוּא נַעֲשֶׂה אִישׁ. כְּמַה דְּתֵימַר. בֶּן תֵּשַׁע שָׁנִים וְיוֹם אֶחָד וְעַד בֶּן שְׁתֵּים עֶשְׂרֵה שָׁנָה וְיוֹם אֶחָד שֶׁהֵבִיא שְׁתֵּי שְׂעָרוֹת לְמַפְרֵיעוֹ הוּא נַעֲשֶׂה אִישׁ. וְדִכְווָתָהּ בֶּן עֶשְׂרִים שָׁנָה שֶׁלֹּא הֵבִיא שְׁתֵּי שְׂעָרוֹת מִכָּן וְהֵילַךְ הוּא נַעֲשֶׂה אִישׁ. מַה עֲבַד לָהּ שְׁמוּאֵל. פָּתַר לָהּ סָמוּךְ לְעֶשְׂרִים שָׁנָה.

The following is obvious: If a person younger than twenty years of age developed two pubic hairs, he becomes a man retroactively. Older than twenty years of age, he becomes a man from that point into the future[221]. Where do they disagree? If he is twenty. Samuel said, he becomes a man retroactively. Rav said, he becomes a man from that point into the future[222]. A *baraita* disagrees with both of them: The castrate cannot become a rebellious son[223] since he has no pubic hair. Should one not warn him, maybe he will develop two pubic hairs within the next three months? Following him who says, one does not accept conditional warnings[224]. Our Mishnah[225] disagrees with Samuel: Does it make no difference whether he is nine years and one day or twelve years and one day old, if by then he did not grow two pubic hairs, he becomes a man retroactively? Could you say: If he did grow two pubic hairs between the ages of nine years and one day until twelve years and one day[226], he becomes a man retroactively? Similarly, if he is older than twenty years of age and did not grow two pubic hairs, he becomes a man from that point into the future. How does Samuel handle this? He explains it: soon after he turns twenty[227].

221 The Babli, 80b and *Niddah* 47b, disagrees and treats the man who at age 20 has no pubic hair and shows the body characteristics of a castrate as

castrated by nature who never will be accepted as a man; otherwise he will be a minor until age 35, half the normal life span. (There is an Amora who disagrees and holds that many cases of impotent men without pubic hair can be treated medically.)

222 In the Babli, 80a, Rav holds that if he or she are late to grow pubic hair but do so before they reach 20, they retroactively become adult and can be prosecuted for any crimes committed earlier; Samuel holds that they remain underage until they grow pubic hair or reach age 18 when they immediately become adults.

223 *Deut.* 21:18-21. Since he is called "son" rather than "child", it is concluded that he must be an adult. The Babli concurs, 80a.

224 The opinion of R. Simeon ben Laqish in the next Chapter; Babli *Makkot* 16a. In the Babli, that opinion is unopposed.

225 That the legal status of one 20 years old is not different from one 9 years old if he did not grow two pubic hairs.

226 Even though the text is formulated in the masculine, it must refer to girls since for a boy standard adulthood is at age 13.

227 But if he grows pubic hair by his 20th birthday, he retroactively becomes an adult from age 13.

נושאין פרק אחד עשר

משנה א: (fol. 11c) נוֹשְׂאִין עַל הָאֲנוּסָה וְעַל הַמְפוּתָּה. הָאוֹנֵס וְהַמְפַתֶּה עַל הַנְּשׂוּאָה חַייָב. נוֹשֵׂא אָדָם אֲנוּסַת אָבִיו וּמְפוּתַּת אָבִיו אֲנוּסַת בְּנוֹ וּמְפוּתַּת בְּנוֹ. רַבִּי יְהוּדָה אוֹסֵר בַּאֲנוּסַת אָבִיו וּבִמְפוּתַּת אָבִיו.

Mishnah 1: One may marry [relatives of] a rape victim or a seduced woman[1]. He who rapes or seduces [a relative of] a married woman is guilty[2]. A person may marry his father's rape victim or seduced woman, his son's rape victim or seduced woman. Rebbi Jehudah prohibits his father's rape victim or seduced woman[3].

1 Incest prohibitions which are not effective at birth can be created only by marriage, not by promiscuity.

2 He is liable not only for rape and seduction but also for incest.

3 The majority considers both parts of *Deut*. 23:1: "Nobody may marry his father's wife, and he should not uncover his father's garment's corner" as one prohibition; R. Jehudah reads the second clause as referring to women with whom his father has extramarital relations.

הלכה א: (fol. 11b) נוֹשְׂאִין עַל הָאֲנוּסָה כול'. כֵּינִי מַתְנִיתִין. נוֹשְׂאִין אַחַר הָאֲנוּסָה וְאַחַר הַמְפוּתָּה אָנַס אִשָּׁה מוּתָּר בְּאִמָּהּ. פִּיתָּה אִשָּׁה מוּתָּר בְּבִתָּהּ.

Halakhah 1: "One may marry [relatives of] a rape victim or a seduced woman," etc. So is the Mishnah: One may marry after a rape victim or seduced woman[4]. If he raped a woman, her mother is permitted; if he seduced a woman, her daughter is permitted[5].

4 The language "...נוֹשְׂאִין עַל" may be interpreted to mean "one marries additionally to . . ." This naturally is not meant here.

5 Quoted as *baraita* in Babli 97a.

הָאוֹנֵס וְהַמְפַתֶּה עַל הַנְּשׂוּאָה חַייָב. אָמַר רִבִּי יוֹחָנָן. דֶּרֶךְ נִישּׂוּאִין שָׁנוּ. נָשָׂה אִשָּׁה וְאַחַר כָּךְ אָנַס אֶת אִמָּהּ חַייָב. נָשָׂה אִשָּׁה וְאַחַר כָּךְ פִּיתֶּה אֶת בִּתָּהּ חַייָב.

"He who rapes or seduces [a relative of] a married woman is guilty." Rebbi Joḥanan said, one stated this for marriage. If he married a woman and then raped her mother, he is guilty. If he married a woman and then seduced her daughter, he is guilty[6].

6 This is obvious, cf. Chapter 10, Notes 139, 140.

תַּמָּן תַּנִּינָן. שְׁחָטָהּ אֶת בַּת בִּתָּהּ וְאַחַר כָּךְ שָׁחַט אֶת בִּתָּהּ. סוֹפֵג אֶת הָאַרְבָּעִים. סוּמָּכוֹס אָמַר מִשּׁוּם רִבִּי מֵאִיר. סוֹפֵג שְׁמוֹנִים. אָמַר רִבִּי. רִבִּי לָעְזָר וְרִבִּי יוֹחָנָן בֶּן נוּרִי שְׁנֵיהֶן אָמְרוּ דָבָר אֶחָד. דְּהָא תַנִּינָן תַּמָּן. רִבִּי יוֹחָנָן בֶּן נוּרִי אוֹמֵר. הַבָּא עַל חֲמוֹתוֹ חַייָב עָלֶיהָ מִשּׁוּם חֲמוֹתוֹ וְאֵם חֲמוֹתוֹ וְאֵם חָמִיו. אָמְרוּ לוֹ. שְׁלָשְׁתָּן שֵׁם אֶחָד הֵן. רִבִּי יוּדָה בַּר פָּזִי בְּשֵׁם רִבִּי יוֹחָנָן. מוֹדֶה סוּמָּכוֹס בָּרִאשׁוֹנָה. אַשְׁכַּח תַּנֵּי. עוֹד הִיא מַחֲלוֹקֶת. מַאי טַעֲמָא דְּרִבִּי יוֹחָנָן בֶּן נוּרִי. מַה אִשָּׁה וּבִתָּהּ וּבַת בִּתָּהּ בִּשְׁנֵי לָאוִין. אַף אִשָּׁה וּבַת בְּנָהּ וּבַת בִּתָּהּ בִּשְׁנֵי לָאוִין. מַה טַעֲמוֹן דְּרַבָּנִין. מַה בַּת בְּנָהּ וּבַת בִּתָּהּ (fol. 11c) בְּלָאו אֶחָד. אַף אִשָּׁה וּבַת בְּנָהּ וּבַת בִּתָּהּ בְּלָאו אֶחָד.

There, we have stated[7]: "If he slaughtered her, her daughter's daughter, and afterwards her daughter, he absorbs forty [lashes].[8] Symmachos said in Rebbi Meïr's name, he absorbs eighty.[9]" Rebbi Eleazar said, [Symmachos][10] and Rebbi Joḥanan ben Nuri said the same thing, since we stated there[11]: "Rebbi Joḥanan ben Nuri said, he who copulates with his mother-in-law may be guilty because of his mother-in-law, his mother-in-law's mother and his father-in-law's mother. They said to him, all three fall under the same law[12]." Rebbi Jehudah bar Pazi in the name of Rebbi Joḥanan: Symmachos agrees to the earlier [part of the Mishnah][13]. If was found stated, it still is in dispute[14]. What is Rebbi Joḥanan ben Nuri's reason? Since a woman and her daughter and a woman and her daughter's daughter fall under two separate prohibitions[15], also a woman and her son's daughter and her daughter's daughter fall under two separate prohibitions. What is the reason of the rabbis? Since a woman and her daughter and a woman and her daughter's daughter fall under one and the same prohibition, also a woman and her son's daughter and her daughter's daughter fall under one and the same prohibition.

7 Mishnah *Ḥulin* 5:3.

8 Really, 39 lashes, the maximum permitted (*Deut.* 25:3). Similarly, Symmachos's 80 are really 78.

9 *Lev.* 22:28: "A cow or a sheep, it and its young you shall not slaughter on the same day." Slaughtering a cow and a second generation calf on the same day is not forbidden. If after that the calf is slaughtered on the same day, with one act he slaughters {the cow and her calf} and {the calf's calf and her mother}. For the rabbis, violating one law by one act can be punished only once. For Symmachos, the order of execution is important; the prohibition of slaughtering the calf after its mother is separate from that of slaughtering the mother after its calf.

10 Missing in the text, required by the context.

11 Mishnah *Keritut* 3:6. R. Eleazar's opinion is quoted in the Babli, *Keritut* 14b.

12 The relevant verse is *Lev.* 18:17: "The genitals of a woman and her daughter you shall not uncover, her son's daughter and her daughter's daughter you shall not take to uncover her nakedness; they are family, it is taboo." The Tosephta (*Keritut* 1:21) explains that R. Joḥanan ben Nuri speaks about a man who married three wives, a woman and her nieces from a sister and a brother; i. e. a daughter and two granddaughters of the same woman. If the man sleeps with his mother-in-law, by one act he sleeps with a woman and her daughter, a woman and her daughter's daughter, and a woman and her son's daughter. If it is three times the same transgression,

he is punished only once; if the one act implies three different paragraphs have been violated, he receives multiple punishment.

13 *Ḥulin* 5:3, where it is stated that everybody agrees that if he slaughtered first the mother and after that two of her calves he is whipped "80" times but if he first slaughtered the two calves and then the mother, he is whipped only "40" times.

14 Tosephta *Ḥulin* 5:7: "If he slaughtered its five calves and then the cow, Symmachos said in the name of Rebbi Meïr he is guilty of five transgressions but he only is guilty for transgression of one prohibition." This shows that Symmachos counts instances of the same prohibition separately; he cannot have the same position as R. Joḥanan ben Nuri. This is the position of Rava in the Babli, *Keritut* 15a; cf. צבי דור, תורת ארץ ישראל בבבל, דביר, תל אביב 1971 , p. 42.

15 For him, the two parts of *Lev.* 18:17 are two separate paragraphs; for the rabbis the verse counts as only one.

כְּתִיב וְאִישׁ אֲשֶׁר יִקַּח אֶת אִשָּׁה וְאֶת אִמָּהּ זִימָּה הִיא. בְּכוּלְּהֹן כְּתִיב שְׁכִיבָה וְכָאן כְּתִיב לְקִיחָה. לְלַמְּדָךְ. לְעוֹלָם אֵינוֹ מִתְחַייֵב עַל הַשְּׁנִייָה עַד שֶׁתְּהֵא הָרִאשׁוֹנָה זְקוּקָה לוֹ. אוֹ אֵינוֹ אֶלָּא דֶרֶךְ נִישּׂוּאִין. כְּבָר אָמַרְנוּ שֶׁאֵין קִידּוּשִׁין בָּעֲרָיוֹת. וְהָכְתִיב לֹא יִקַּח אִישׁ אֶת אֵשֶׁת אָבִיו וְלֹא יְגַלֶּה כְּנַף אָבִיו. בָּא לְהוֹדִיעָךְ שֶׁהָיָה מוּתָּר בָּהּ עַד שֶׁלֹּא נִישֵּׂאת לְאָבִיו. וְהָכְתִיב וְאִישׁ אֲשֶׁר יִקַּח אֶת אֵשֶׁת אָחִיו נִדָּה הִיא. בָּא לְהוֹדִיעָךְ שֶׁהָיָה מוּתָּר בָּהּ עַד שֶׁלֹּא נִישֵּׂאת לְאָחִיו. וְתַנֵּי כֵן. עַל יְדֵי יִיבּוּם. וְהָכְתִיב וְאִשָּׁה עַל אֲחוֹתָהּ לֹא תִקָּח לִצְרוֹר. בָּא לְהוֹדִיעָךְ שֶׁהָיָה מוּתָּר בָּהּ עַד שֶׁלֹּא נָשָׂא אֶת אֲחוֹתָהּ. וְתַנֵּי כֵן. לְאַחַר מִיתַת אֲחוֹתָהּ. וְהָכְתִיב וְאִישׁ אֲשֶׁר יִקַּח אֶת אֲחוֹתוֹ בַּת אָבִיו אוֹ בַת אִמּוֹ וְרָאָה אֶת עֶרְוָתָהּ וְהִיא תִרְאֶה אֶת עֶרְוָתוֹ חֶסֶד הוּא. אָמַר רִבִּי אָבִין. שֶׁלֹּא תֹאמַר. קַיִן נָשָׂא אֶת אֲחוֹתוֹ. הֶבֶל נָשָׂא אֶת אֲחוֹתוֹ. חֶסֶד הוּא. חֶסֶד עָשִׂיתִי עִם הָרִאשׁוֹנִים שֶׁיִּיבָּנֶה הָעוֹלָם מֵהֶן. אָמַרְתִּי עוֹלָם חֶסֶד יִבָּנֶה. וְהָכְתִיב אַלְמָנָה וּגְרוּשָׁה וַחֲלָלָה זוֹנָה אֶת אֵלֶּה לֹא יִקָּח. בָּא לְהוֹדִיעָךְ שֶׁאִם קִידְּשָׁהּ שֶׁתּוֹפְסִין בָּהּ קִידּוּשִׁין.

It is written[16]: "If a man takes a woman and her mother, it is taboo." Everywhere is written "lying with"[17] but here is written "taking", to teach you that he cannot be guilty for the second [woman] unless the first one is prepared[18] for him. Or maybe only by marriage[19]? We already said that there is no incestuous marriage. But is it not written[20]: "Nobody may marry his father's wife, and he should not uncover his father's garment's corner"? This comes to tell you that she was permitted to him before his father married her[21]. But is it not written[22]: "If a man take his brother's wife, it is despicable"? This comes to tell you that she was permitted to him before his brother married her. This is confirmed by levirate[23]. But is it not written[24]: 'You should not take a woman in addition to her sister to make her a co-wife"? This comes to tell you that she was permitted to him before he married her sister. This is confirmed after her sister's death. But is it not written[25]: "A man who would take his sister, his father's daughter or his mother's daughter; he sees her genitals and she sees his genitals, it is *hesed*.' Rebbi Avin said, that you should not say that Kain married his sister, Abel married his sister, "it is charitable", I was charitable with the first generations so the world could be inhabited; "I said, the world was built on *hesed*[26]." But is it not written[27]: "Widow, divorcee, and desecrated, these he shall not take"? This comes to tell you that if he became betrothed to her that the betrothal is valid[28].

16 *Lev.* 20:14

17 In the punishment list of Chap. 20. In the prohibition of Chap. 18, the expression used is mostly "uncovering genitals".

18 Available to him at least by betrothal or obligation of levirate. The criminal sanction cannot be applied if one of the parties was married to him but died.

19 That he had to marry both women. This is impossible since an incestuous marriage has no existence in law.

20 *Deut.* 23:1; neither the term "lying with" nor the term "uncovering genitals" is used. Does this mean that only the marriage with a stepmother is forbidden?

This and the following questions

challenge the assertion that the incest prohibition of a man with mother and daughter is the only one where "taking" is mentioned.

21 The statement that he may not marry her makes sense only if without the father's marriage the son could have married her. This supports the Mishnah.

22 *Lev.* 20:21. This is a relevant question since the verse is also from Chapter 20.

23 She again becomes permitted to the levir.

24 *Lev.* 18:18. The argument following is parallel to that of the verse quoted before this one.

25 *Lev.* 20:17. The argument identifies חסד I "to be well behaved" and חסד II "to act shamefully". A similar argument in Babli *Sanhedrin 58b*.

26 *Ps.* 89:3.

27 *Lev.* 21:7.

28 The marriages forbidden only to priests, "prohibitions of holiness", are not incestuous; they are sinful but valid, cf. Halakhah 2:3.

רִבִּי חוּנָה שָׁמַע כּוֹלְהוֹן מִן הָדָא קִרְיָיא. עֶרְוַת אִשָּׁה וּבִתָּהּ לֹא תְגַלֵּה וגו'. זִימָּה זִימָּה לִגְזֵירָה שָׁוָה. מַה לְמַטָּן שְׁלֹשָׁה דוֹרוֹת אַף לְמַעְלָן שְׁלֹשָׁה דוֹרוֹת. מַה לְמַטָּה בְּלֹא תַעֲשֶׂה אַף לְמַעְלָן בְּלֹא תַעֲשֶׂה. מַה לְמַעְלָה דֶּרֶךְ נִישּׂוּאִין אַף לְמַטָּה דֶּרֶךְ נִישּׂוּאִין. מַה לְמַעְלָן בִּשְׂרֵיפָה אַף לְמַטָּן בִּשְׂרֵיפָה. מַה לְמַטָּן עָשָׂה בַת זָכָר כְּבַת נְקֵיבָה אַף לְמַעְלָן נַעֲשֶׂה אוּם זָכָר אוּם נְקֵיבָה.

[29]Rebbi Ḥuna understood all of them from this verse: "The genitals of a woman and her daughter you should not uncover, etc." Taboo - taboo, for an equal cut. Since there are three generations downwards, so there are three generations upwards. Since there is a prohibition downwards, so there is a prohibition upwards. Since upwards one requires marriage, so downwards one requires marriage. Since upwards they are burned, so downwards they are burned. Since downwards, He gave the male's daughter the same status as the female's daughter, so upwards we give the male's mother the same status as the female's mother.

29 This is from Chapter 2, Notes 104-109.

וּכְדְרַבִּי מֵאִיר. דְּרַבִּי מֵאִיר אוֹמֵר. גְּזֵירָה שָׁוָה בְּמָקוֹם שֶׁבָּת. דּוֹר שְׁלִישִׁי שֶׁלְּמַטָּן מְנַיִין שֶׁהוּא בְלֹא תַעֲשֶׂה. וּכְרַבָּנָן דְּאִינּוּן אָמְרִין. גְּזֵירָה שָׁוָה נֶאֱמַר בָּם. דּוֹר שְׁלִישִׁי שֶׁהִיא לְמַעְלָן מְנַיִין שֶׁהִיא בִשְׂרֵיפָה. בֵּין כְּרַבִּי מֵאִיר בֵּין כְּרַבָּנִין דּוֹר שְׁלִישִׁי שֶׁלְּמַעְלָן שֶׁהִיא בְלֹא תַעֲשֶׂה. מִכֵּיוָן דִּכְתִיב זִמָּה זִמָּה לִגְזֵירָה שָׁוָה כְּמִי שֶׁכּוּלְהֹן כֵּן. דְּכוּלְהֹן כֵּן.

And following Rebbi Meïr? Since Rebbi Meïr said a *gezerah šawah*[30] is at the place it comes from, from where is the third generation (below) forbidden[31]? And following the rabbis, who say, a *gezerah šawah* is said about them[32], from where that the third generation above is punished by burning[33]? Both for Rebbi Meïr and the rabbis, from where that the third generation above is forbidden? Since it is written "taboo, taboo" for a *gezerah šawah*, it is as if all were included; all are included[34].

30 Cf. Chapter 8, Note 195. R. Meïr holds that a *gezerah šawah* is valid only for the rules covered by the respective verses.

31 Instead of "below" one has to read מלמעל "above". In *Lev.* 18:17, the daughter and granddaughter of a woman are forbidden as taboo to a man sleeping with the woman. Therefore, the question can only be whether the grandmother also is forbidden since the pivot of the prohibition is the woman he slept with first and, as a matter of principle, infractions of prohibitions are punishable only if the punishment is stated in the code. The mother is certainly under an incest prohibition whose infraction would be a capital crime; this is stated in *Lev.* 20:14.

32 It refers to all aspects of the laws involved.

33 Since she is not mentioned in the verse.

34 In both Chapters 18 and 20, the prohibition of a woman and either her descendants or ancestors appear in one verse. Therefore, in this case there is no difference in the positions of R. Meïr and the rabbis. The *gezerah šawah* is sufficient to transfer the prohibition of the descendants (18:17) to the ancestors (20:14) and the punishment from the ancestors to the descendants. Cf. Halakhah 2:4. The same argument is in the Babli, *Sanhedrin* 75b.

עַד כְּדוֹן בַּת בִּתּוֹ מִן הַנִּישּׂוּאִין. בַּת בִּתּוֹ מִן הָאוֹנְסִין. עֶרְוַת בַּת בִּנְךָ אוֹ בַת בִּתְּךָ. מַה נָן קַייָמִין. אִם מִן הַנִּישּׂוּאִין כְּבָר הוּא אָמוּר. אֶלָּא אִם אֵינוֹ עִנְייָן לְנִישּׂוּאִין תְּנֵיהוּ עִנְייָן לְאוֹנְסִין. עַד כְּדוֹן לְאַזְהָרָה. לְעוֹנֶשׁ מְנַיִין. אָמַר רִבִּי שְׁמוּאֵל בַּר רַב יִצְחָק. הֵנָּה מֵהֵנָּה. זִמָּה מִזִּמָּה. עַד כְּדוֹן כְּרִבִּי עֲקִיבָה. כְּרִבִּי יִשְׁמָעֵאל. תַּנֵּי רִבִּי יִשְׁמָעֵאל. הֵנָּה מֵאֶתְהֶן. עַד כְּדוֹן בַּת בִּתּוֹ. בִּתּוֹ מְנַיִין. רַב אָמַר. אִם עַל בַּת בִּתּוֹ הוּא מוּזְהָר. לֹא כָּל־שֶׁכֵּן עַל בִּתּוֹ. אִם עַל בַּת בִּתּוֹ הוּא עָנוּשׁ. לֹא כָּל־שֶׁכֵּן עַל בִּתּוֹ.

So far his daughter's daughter from marriage[35]. His daughter's daughter from a rape? "The genitals of your son's daughter or your daughter's daughter[36]." Where do we hold? If from marriage, it already had been said. So it it cannot refer to marriage but must refer to rape. So far for the warning, from where the punishment[37]? Rebbi Samuel bar Rav Isaac said, "they, they; taboo, taboo".[38] That follows Rebbi Aqiba; following Rebbi Ismael? Rebbi Ismael stated: "they", from "them"[39]. So far about his daughter's daughter, from where his daughter[40]? Rav said, if he is forewarned about his daughter's daughter, so much more for his daughter! If for his daughter's daughter he is subject to extirpation, so much more for his daughter[41]!

35 As noted before, both *Lev*. 18:17 and 20:14 contain expressions of marriage.

36 *Lev*. 18:10 prohibits incest with granddaughters. If only legitimate children were intended, the verse would be superfluous. Therefore, it must refer also to all illegitimate children; "rape" is only an example.

37 *Lev*. 18:10 contains no indication of any punishment.

38 *Lev*. 18:10 ends **עֶרְוָתְךָ הֵנָּה** "*they* are your genitals;" *Lev*. 18:17 ends **שַׁאֲרָה הֵנָּה זִמָּה** הִיא "*they* are relatives, it is *taboo*;" *Lev*. 20:14 reads וְלֹא תִהְיֶה **זִמָּה** בְּתוֹכְכֶם "there should be no *taboo* among you." He accepts a *gezerah šawah* between 18:10 and 17 based on the common word הנה and one between 18:17 and 20:14 based on the common word זמה. This concatenation of two transfers is not without problems (cf.

Babli *Zebaḥim* 50a); the Yerushalmi here indicates that it is only acceptable for R. Aqiba, not for R. Ismael. The argument is quoted in the Babli (*Yebamot* 3a and *Sanhedrin* 75b, 76a) in the name of Rav Isaac bar Eudaimon.

39 He makes a direct connection between *Lev.* 18:10 and 20:14, taking the unusual word אתהן (for אותן), the combination of the *nota accusativi* and הן, הנה "they", to indicate the connection. This argument is not quoted in the Babli.

40 *Lev.* 18:10 makes no mention of the daughter as incest prohibition.

41 The Babli, *Sanhedrin* 76a, notes the obvious contradiction to the principle that no punishment can be imposed that is not clearly stated in the text (cf. Note 31) and holds that the argument is so simple that the prohibition must be considered as if it were written in the verse.

בְּעוֹן קוֹמֵי רִבִּי אַבָּהוּ. בַּת בִּתּוֹ מִן הַנִּישׂוּאִין. בַּת בִּתּוֹ מִן הָאוֹנְסִין. אָמַר לוֹן כָּל־שֵׁם בַּת בַּת אַחַת. בְּעוֹן קוֹמֵי רִבִּי אַבָּהוּ. הַבָּא עַל אִשָּׁה וְיָֽלְדָה בַּת וְאַחַר כָּךְ בָּא בְעָלָהּ. חַייָב עָלֶיהָ מִשּׁוּם אִשָּׁה וּבִתָּהּ וּבַת בִּתָּהּ וּבַת בְּנָהּ. אָמַר לוֹן שַׁאֲרָה הֵנָּה זִמָּה הִיא. כּוּלְּהֹן מִשּׁוּם זִימָּה.

They asked before Rebbi Abbahu: His daughter's daughter from a marriage; his daughter's daughter from a rape? He said to them, every "daughter's daughter" falls under the same category[42]. They asked before Rebbi Abbahu: If [a man] came to a woman, she had a daughter, and after that he came and copulated with her[43]. Is he guilty about her because of a woman and her daughter, her daughter's daughter and her son's daughter? He said to them, "they are relatives, it is taboo;" all because of taboo[44].

42 R. Abbahu rejects the argument (Note 36) that the illegitimate offspring needs an extra verse. The simple meaning of the verse includes all daughter's daughters.

43 Something must be missing here. The most simple scenario would be that a man sleeps with his illegitimate daughter when he married two granddaughters of the mother, one from a son and one from another daughter. If the copulation was in

ignorance of the family relationship, how many purification sacrifices does he have to bring?

44 Multiple transgression of the same statute can be punished only once.

רִבִּי חַגַּיי בְּעָא קוֹמֵי רִבִּי יוֹסֵי. לָמָּה לֵית אִינּוּן אָמְרִין. בִּתְּךָ לֹא תְגַלֶּה. בַּת בִּתְּךָ לֹא תְגַלֶּה. אָמַר לֵיהּ. אִילּוּ הֲוָה כְתִיב עֶרְוַת אִשָּׁה וּבַת בִּתָּהּ לֹא תְגַלֵּה הֲוִינָן אָמְרִין. בִּתְּךָ לֹא תְגַלֵּה. בַּת בִּתְּךָ לֹא תְגַלֵּה.

Rebbi Ḥaggai asked before Rebbi Yose: Why do we not say, "your daughter you should not uncover, your daughter's daughter you should not uncover"[45]? He said to him, if it were written "the genitals of a woman and her daughter's daughter you shall not uncover", we would have said, "your daughter you should not uncover, your daughter's daughter you should not uncover"[46].

45 He questions the position of R. Abbahu; why should one not consider *Lev.* 18:17 as containing two separate prohibitions?

46 If the verse had not contained the mention of "taking" (i. e. "marrying") to make the offense a capital crime, one could have considered the caesura in the verse as defining two separate clauses. But now, since the condition of marriage to at least one of them is essential for the definition of criminality of the act, that cannot be the interpretation.

The Babli, 22b, has a totally different take on *Lev.* 18:10: That verse speaks only of *his* granddaughters, but 18:17 deals with the granddaughters of his wife. It is concluded that the granddaughters of a woman with whom he has a child but who is not his wife cannot be under an incest prohibition which is a capital crime. Cf. Chapter 10, Note 195.

רִבִּי אַבָּהוּ רִבִּי לָעְזָר בְּשֵׁם רִבִּי הוֹשַׁעְיָה. שְׁנֵי לָאוִין וְכָרֵת אֶחָד לָאוִין חוֹלְקִין כְּרִיתוּת. מַאי טַעֲמָא עַל בְּשַׂר אָדָם לֹא יִיסָךְ וּבְמַתְכּוּנְתָּהּ לֹא תַעֲשׂוּ כָּמוֹהוּ. וּכְתִיב אִישׁ אֲשֶׁר יִרְקַח כָּמוֹהוּ. הֲרֵי כָאן שְׁנֵי לָאוִין וְכָרֵת אֶחָד. לָאוִין חוֹלְקִין כְּרִיתוּת. וּכְרִבִּי יִשְׁמָעֵאל. דְּרִבִּי יִשְׁמָעֵאל אָמַר. לְמֵידִין מִקַּל וָחוֹמֶר וְאֵין

עוֹנְשִׁין מִקַּל וָחוֹמֶר. מְנָן לֵיהּ. וְאַתְיָיה כְּהַהִיא דְתַנֵּי חִזְקִיָה. וּבַת כֹּהֵן כִּי תֵחֵל לִזְנוֹת. מַה תַלְמוּד לוֹמַר אִישׁ. לְהָבִיא אֶת הַבָּא עַל בַּת בִּתּוֹ מִן הָאוֹנְסִין שֶׁתְּהֵא בִשְׂרֵיפָה. אָמַר רִבִּי יוֹסֵי בֵּירִבִּי בּוּן. אֲפִילוּ לְאַזְהָרָה אַתְּ שְׁמַע מִינָּהּ. אַל תְּחַלֵּל אֶת בִּתְּךָ.

Rebbi Abbahu, Rebbi Eleazar in the name of Rebbi Hoshaiah. If there are two prohibitions and one liability to extirpation, the prohibitions split the extirpation[47]. What is the reason? "On human flesh it may not be rubbed and in its proportions you should not make [a compound] like it.[48]" And it is written: "A man who would compound like it[49]". Here are two prohibitions and one liability to extirpation. The prohibitions divide the extirpation. This follows Rebbi Ismael, since Rebbi Ismael said one infers from an argument *de minore ad majus* but one does not punish from an argument *de minore ad majus*[50]. Where does he have that from? It comes following what Ḥizqiah stated: "If the daughter of a Cohen is desecrated by whoring." Why does the verse say, "a man[51]"? To include him who cohabits with his daughter's daughter from a rape that she should be [under sentence of] burning[52]. Rebbi Yose ben Rebbi Abun said, one may even understand this from the warning: "Do not desecrate your daughter[53]."

47 It is a general principle of hermeneutics in both Talmudim that for every prohibition one verse has to explain what is forbidden and another verse, often at a different place, has to spell out the punishment. If the latter verse refers to several prohibitions at once, the number of sins committed in one act (the number of required cleansing sacrifices if the sin was inadvertent) is counted by the number of prohibitions, not by the number of punishments enumerated separately. In the Babli (*Makkot* 14b, *Keritut* 3a), this is a matter of dispute.

48 *Ex.* 30:32, speaking of the oil used to anoint priests and holy vessels.

49 *Ex.* 30:33: "A man who would compound its likeness or who would apply it on an outside person (who is

not a priest} will be extirpated from his people." There are only two prohibitions since the "human" of v. 32 is defined as "not a priest" in v. 33.

50 A principle spelled out many times in the Babli, cf. *Makkot* 5b, 14a, 17a; *Sanhedrin* 54a.

51 *Lev.* 21:9. "A Cohen man's daughter if she is desecrated by whoring with her father, shall be burned in fire;" cf. Babli *Sanhedrin* 76.

52 It was determined earlier that the prohibition of 20:14 of descendents or progenitors in the direct line applies only if one of the women is married to the man. For priests, this is extended also to extramarital children.

53 *Lev.* 19:29: "Do not desecrate your daughter to cause her to whore." This interpretation is quoted in the Babli, *Sanhedrin* 76a, in the name of R. Abun's father and there is only one of several alternative interpretations.

וּמַה טַעֲמָא דְרִבִּי יוּדָה. לֹא יִקַּח אִישׁ אֶת אֵשֶׁת אָבִיו. זוֹ אֵשֶׁת אָבִיו. וְלֹא יְגַלֶּה כְּנַף אָבִיו. זוֹ אֲנוּסָתוֹ. מַה מְקַיְימִין רַבָּנִן כְּנַף אָבִיו. תַּמָּן אָמְרִין וְלָא יָֽדְעִין מִן מַה שְׁמוּעָה. זוֹ כְּנַף הַסְּמוּכָה לְאָבִיו. בְּלֹא כָךְ אֵינוֹ חַייָב עָלֶיהָ מִשּׁוּם אֵשֶׁת אָב. אָמַר רִבִּי הִילָא. לְהַתְרָייָה. שֶׁאִם הִתְרוּ בָהּ מִשּׁוּם אֵשֶׁת אָב לוֹקֶה. מִשּׁוּם כְּנַף אָבִיו לוֹקֶה. מוֹדֶה רִבִּי יְהוּדָה בְמַכּוֹת. מוֹדֶה רִבִּי יְהוּדָה בְקָרְבָּן. מוֹדֶה רִבִּי יְהוּדָה בִשְׁאָר כָּל־הַסְּפֵיקוֹת שֶׁהוּא פָטוּר. מוֹדֶה רִבִּי יְהוּדָה שֶׁאִים קִידְּשָׁהּ שֶׁתָּפְסוּ בָהּ קִידּוּשִׁין.

What is the reason of Rebbi Jehudah? "[54]A man may not take his father's wife," that refers to his father's wife; "and he should not uncover his father's wing," that is his rape victim. How do the rabbis explain "his father's wing"? There[55], they say and they do not know the origin of the tradition, that refers to a wing which leans on his father[56]. Would he not anyhow be guilty for her because of his father's wife[57]? Rebbi Hila said, because of forewarning[58], that if he was warned because of his father's wife, he will be whipped, and because of his father's wing, he will be whipped[59]. Rebbi Jehudah agrees about whipping. Rebbi Jehudah agrees about sacrifice[60]. Rebbi Jehudah agrees about all other doubtful cases that he is free[61]. Rebbi Jehudah agrees that if he gave her *qiddušin* that these *qiddušin* are legally valid.

54 *Deut*. 23:1. The hermeneutic principles require that two parallel clauses be interpreted as referring to two different situations. If such an interpretation is impossible, then the two clauses count as two separate prohibitions.

55 Babli *Yebamot* 97a, stated in the name of Samuel.

56 The widow of a childless uncle who waits to be married in levirate by his father and in the meantime is forebidden to all other men.

57 For the rabbis who hold that candidacy counts as betrothal; cf. Chapter 2, Note 27.

58 In rabbinic interpretation, no punishment is possible in criminal cases unless criminal intent was established by two witnesses who testify that the perpetrator was duly warned that his intended act was criminal.

59 In the Babli, 97a, an anonymous statement that if we warned for both his father's wife and his father's wing, he transgresses two prohibitions in one act.

60 Since no penalty is stated in the Torah for the man who marries a woman who had unmarried sex with his father, he cannot be punished and, therefore, is unable to bring a sacrifice even if his act is considered sinful.

61 If the woman had sex with any man other than his father, a marriage to whom would make her current marriage incestuous, no punishment can be meted out even according to R. Jehudah since there is no biblical basis for it. Consequently, the marriage is valid.

רִבִּי חַגַּיי בְּעָא קוֹמֵי רִבִּי יוֹסֵי. מַהוּ שֶׁיְּהֵא הַוּוֹלָד מַמְזֵר כְּרִבִּי יוּדָה. אָמַר לֵיהּ. לֹא יָבוֹא פְצוּעַ דַּכָּא וּכְרוּת שָׁפְכָה הִפְסִיק הָעִנְיָין. הִפְסִיק הָעִנְיָין לְעִנְיָין אֵשֶׁת אַב. אָמַר לֵיהּ. אֵשֶׁת אַב בִּכְלַל כָּל־הָעֲרָיוֹת הָיְיתָה וְיָצְאת מִכְּלָלָהּ לְלַמֵּד עַל כָּל־הָעֲרָיוֹת לְמַמְזֵר. וְתֵצֵא אֵשֶׁת אָב וּתְלַמֵּד עַל כָּל־הָעֲרָיוֹת מִמַּמְזֵר. וְתֵצֵא אֲנוּסָה וּתְלַמֵּד עַל כָּל־הָאוֹנְסִין לְאִיסּוּר. אָמַר לֵיהּ. אֵשֶׁת אַב בִּכְלָל כָּל־הָעֲרָיוֹת הָיְיתָה וְיָצְאת מִכְּלָלָהּ לְלַמֵּד עַל כָּל־הָעֲרָיוֹת לְמַמְזֵר. אִית לָךְ לְמֵימַר הָכָא אֲנוּסָה בִּכְלָל כָּל־הָאוֹנְסִין הָיְיתָה וְיָצְאת מִכְּלָלָהּ לְלַמֵּד עַל

כָּל־הָאוֹנְסִין לְאִיסּוּר. וְתֵצֵא אֵשֶׁת אַב וּתְלַמֵּד עַל כָּל־אֲנוּסָתָהּ. אָמַר לֵיהּ. אִם אֵשֶׁת אַב הִיא אֵינָהּ אֲנוּסָה. וְאִם אֲנוּסָה הִיא אֵינָהּ אֵשֶׁת אַב.

Rebbi Ḥaggai asked before Rebbi Yose: Is the child a bastard following Rebbi Jehudah? He said to him, "No one with a damaged testicle or with cut-off penis may marry[62]" interrupts the argument. It interrupted the argument in the matter of the father's wife. He retorted, the father's wife was part of the set of all incest prohibitions; it was selected from this set to teach about bastardy for all incest prohibitions[63]. (Let the father's wife be selected to teach about bastardy for all incests prohibitions.) Similarly, let the rape victim be selected to teach a prohibition concerning all rape victims[64]. He said to him, the father's wife was part of the set of all incest prohibitions; it was selected from this set to teach about bastardy for all incest prohibitions. Can you say that the rape victim was in a set of all rape victims, that it could teach a prohibition concerning all rape victims[65]? Why cannot the father's wife be selected to teach about the rape victims in her case? He said to him, is she is the father's wife, she is not his rape victim; is she is the father's rape victim, she is not his wife.

62 *Deut. 23:2.* The prohibition of the father's wife is verse 1, the rule of bastardy is verse 3; cf. Chaper 4, Note 211.

63 This is an application of Rule 9 of R. Ismael (Introduction to *Sifra*): "Anything in a set which was selected from that set to teach, was not selected to teach only for itself but for the entire set."

The prohibition of the stepmother is contained in the set of all incest prohibitions (*Lev.*, Chapters 18,20). Therefore, if the result of incest with a stepmother is a bastard, the result of any other incestuous relation must be a bastard (cf. Mishnaiot 4:14,15).

64 R. Ḥaggai wants to argue that since according to R. Jehudah, the prohibition of a person who had unmarried sex with his father is written in one verse with the prohibition of the father's wife, all relationships that would be incestuous

in the case of marriage should be prohibited.

65 There does not exist a set of women prohibited as incestuous by extramarital sex; the set to which Rule 9 might be applied contains only the woman who had slept with his father. The parallel reasoning implied by R. Ḥaggai does not work.

(fol. 11c) **משנה ב**: גִּיוֹרֶת שֶׁנִּתְגַּיְּירוּ בָנֶיהָ עִמָּהּ לֹא חוֹלְצִין וְלֹא מְייַבְּמִין אֲפִילוּ הוֹרָתוֹ שֶׁל רִאשׁוֹן שֶׁלֹּא בִקְדוּשָּׁה וְלֵידָתוֹ בִקְדוּשָּׁה וְהַשֵּׁינִי הוֹרָתוֹ וְלֵידָתוֹ בִקְדוּשָּׁה וְכֵן שִׁפְחָה שֶׁנִּשְׁתַּחְרְרוּ בָנֶיהָ עִמָּהּ.

Mishnah 2: The sons of a female convert who converted with her do neither perform *ḥalîṣah* nor levirate[66] even if a first [son] was not conceived in holiness[67] but born in holiness and a second [son] was conceived and born in holiness. The same applies to a slave girl[68] who was freed together with her sons.

66 Even if they biologically are children of the same father, they legally are not since the rules of family relationships are restricted to Jews.

67 Before conversion.

68 Who before manumission already was Jewish as a slave.

(foL 11d) **משנה**: גִּיוֹרֶת שֶׁנִּתְגַּייְרָה כול'. וַהֲלֹא הַגֵּר חַייָב עַל אִמּוֹ וְאֵינוֹ חַייָב עַל אָבִיו כְּדִבְרֵי רִבִּי יוֹסֵי הַגְּלִילִי. רִבִּי עֲקִיבָה אוֹמֵר. אָבִיו וְאִמּוֹ קִלֵּל. אֵת שֶׁהוּא חַייָב עַל אִמּוֹ חַייַב עַל אָבִיו. וְאֵת שֶׁאֵינוֹ חַייָב עַל אִמּוֹ אֵינוֹ חַייָב עַל אָבִיו. מוֹדֶה רִבִּי עֲקִיבָה בִשְׁתוּקִי שֶׁהוּא חַייָב עַל אִמּוֹ אַף עַל פִּי שֶׁאֵינוֹ חַייָב עַל אָבִיו. רִבִּי יַעֲקֹב בַּר אָחָא רִבִּי יָסָא בְשֵׁם רִבִּי יוֹחָנָן. מַה פְלִיגִין. בְּגֵר שֶׁהָיְתָה הוֹרָתוֹ שֶׁלֹּא בִקְדוּשָּׁה וְלֵידָתוֹ בִקְדוּשָּׁה. אֲבָל בְּגֵר שֶׁהָיְתָה הוֹרָתוֹ וְלֵידָתוֹ בִקְדוּשָּׁה אַף רִבִּי יוֹסֵי הַגָּלִילִי מוֹדֶה.

Mishnah: "A female convert who converted," etc. Is not[69] the convert guilty for his mother[70] but not for his father following Rebbi Yose the Galilean? Rebbi Aqiba says, "his father and mother he cursed.[71]" Anybody potentially guilty for his mother is potentially guilty for his father but nobody who cannot be guilty for his mother can be guilty for his father[72]. Rebbi Aqiba agrees that the "silenced[73]" one is potentially guilty for his mother but not for his father. Rebbi Jacob bar Aḥa, Rebbi Yasa in the name of Rebbi Joḥanan: Where do they[74] disagree? About a convert not conceived in holiness but born in holiness. But about a convert conceived and born in holiness even Rebbi Yose the Galilean agrees[75].

69 The interrogative here does not make much sense; the *baraita* text is a copy from *Sifra Qedošim Parašah* 9(9), where the rhetorical question is appropriate.

70 If he injures or curses his mother (*Ex.* 21:15,17). R. Yose the Galilean holds that a Gentile cannot claim relationship with his children, whether the mother is Gentile or Jewish.

71 *Lev.* 20:9: "Any man who would curse his father and (or) his mother shall certainly die; his father and (or) mother he cursed, his blood is on him." R. Aqiba infers from "curse his father", "his mother he cursed", that the rules for father and mother must be identical.

72 In fact, the argument goes the other way, anybody who cannot be guilty for his father cannot be guilty for his mother. Therefore, the child who converted with his mother cannot be prosecuted for injuring or cursing his mother.

73 A person of unknown paternity, who is *silenced* by his mother should he adress any man as his father. If his father were known, he would be a normal Jew.

74 R. Yose the Galilean and R. Aqiba.

75 There is not much to disagree since the child is born as full Jew (even though he is called a proselyte after his father, Mishna *Qiddušin* 3:12)..

רִבִּי יָסָא אֲזַל לְחָמֶץ. אַתּוֹן וּשְׁאָלוֹן לֵיהּ. אִילֵּין דְּבַר עַשְׁתֵּין. גֵּירִין מַהוּ שֶׁיִּיבְּמוּ. אָמַר לוֹן. כֵּן אָמַר רִבִּי יוֹחָנָן. אָסוּר. הֲווֹן בְּעָיֵי מֵימַר. בְּאִשָּׁה שֶׁיֵּשׁ לָהּ בָּנִים. אֲבָל בְּאִשָּׁה שֶׁאֵין לָהּ בָּנִים. מַה נַפְשֵׁךְ. אֵשֶׁת אָחִיו יִיבֵּם. וְאִם אֵינָהּ אֵשֶׁת אָחִיו יְהֵא כְנוֹשֵׂא אִשָּׁה מִן הַשּׁוּק. אָתָא רִבִּי יַעֲקֹב בַּר אָחָא בְּשֵׁם רִבִּי יִצְחָק בַּר נַחְמָן. אֲפִילוּ כֵן אָסוּר. שֶׁלֹּא יְהוּ אוֹמְרִין. מִצְוַת יִיבּוּם רָאִינוּ בְגֵרִים. בַּמֶּה דְבָרִים אֲמוּרִים. בִּזְמָן (fol. 12a) שֶׁהִכִּירָהּ מִשֶּׁנִּתְגַּייֵר. אֲבָל אִם לֹא הִכִּירָהּ מִשֶּׁנִּתְגַּייֵר כָּל־עַמָּא מוֹדֵיי שֶׁהוּא כְנוֹשֵׂא אִשָּׁה מִן הַשּׁוּק.

Rebbi Yasa went to Ḥomṣ[76]. People came and asked him about the family of Ashtin[77] who were converts, might they marry in levirate? He said to them, so says Rebbi Johanan: It is prohibited. They wanted to say, if a woman has children[78]. But if the woman has no children, what can you say? He married his brother's wife in levirate. If she is not his brother's wife[79], should he not be considered as marrying a wife from outside? Rebbi Jacob bar Aḥa came in the name of Rebbi Isaac bar Naḥman: Even so it is forbidden, that people should not say, we saw the commandment of levirate among converts. When has this been said? When he lived with her after he converted[80]. But if he did not live with her after he converted, everybody agrees that it is as if he[81] married a woman from outside.

76 The city in Syria.

77 In *Demai* Chapter 6 they are called Astor.

78 The widow had children but all of them were born while she was a Gentile.

79 If converts born as Gentile brothers are not legally brothers after conversion, the wife of one cannot be forbidden to the other.

80 By the first intercourse after conversion, which certainly was executed as an act between husband and wife, the Gentile marriage became valid in Jewish law.

81 The surviving brother may marry the woman who never was Jewishly married to his brother even if the relationship of brotherhood remained in effect after conversion.

גֵּר שֶׁנִּתְגַּייֵר וְהָיָה נָשׂוּי אִשָּׁה וּבִתָּהּ אוֹ אִשָּׁה וַאֲחוֹתָהּ כּוֹנֵס אַחַת וּמוֹצִיא אַחַת. בַּמֶּה דְבָרִים אֲמוּרִים. שֶׁלֹּא הִכִּיר אַחַת מֵהֶן מִשֶּׁנִּתְגַּייֵר. אֲבָל הִכִּיר אַחַת מֵהֶן מִשֶּׁנִּתְגַּייֵר אוֹתָהּ שֶׁהִכִּיר אִשְׁתּוֹ. וְאִם הִכִּיר אֶת שְׁתֵּיהֶן כֵּיוָן שֶׁהִכִּיר הִכִּיר.

A convert who converted while married to a woman and her daughter, or a woman and her sister, marries one and separates from the other[82]. When has this been said? If he did not live with either of them. But if he lived with one of them after he converted, the one he lived with is his wife. If he lived with both of them, since he lived with them, he lived with them[83].

82 He marries one in Jewish law and separates from the other or divorces her in Gentile law.

83 Since family relationships are dissolved by conversion, the two co-wives are not related in biblical law and, therefore, not prohibited in biblical law. The Babli, 98b, disagrees and holds that if he comes to ask, one tells him to separate from both of them. If he married one of them, he may keep her. It seems from this that the Babli would not tolerate a man to live with two wives who before conversion were mother and daughter or sisters.

גֵּר אֲחוֹתוֹ בֵּין מִן הָאָב בֵּין מִן הָאֵם יוֹצִיא. דִּבְרֵי רִבִּי מֵאִיר. רִבִּי יְהוּדָה אוֹמֵר. אֲחוֹתוֹ מִן הָאֵם יוֹצִיא מֵאָב יְקַייֵם. אֲחוֹת אִמּוֹ יוֹצִיא אֲחוֹת אָבִיו יְקַייֵם. דִּבְרֵי רִבִּי מֵאִיר. רִבִּי יוּדָה אוֹמֵר. אֲחוֹת אִמּוֹ מֵאִמָּהּ יוֹצִיא אֲחוֹת אִמּוֹ מֵאָבִיהָ יְקַייֵם. שְׁאָר כָּל־הָעֲרָיוֹת כָּנַס אֵין מוֹצִיאִין מִיָּדוֹ. לֹא אָמַר אֶלָּא כָּנַס. הָא כַּתְּחִילָּה אָסוּר.

A convert has to separate from his sister, whether paternal or maternal, the words of Rebbi Meïr. Rebbi Jehudah says, he must separate from his maternal halfsister; a paternal halfsister he may keep. He must separate from his mother's sister but may keep his father's sister, the words of Rebbi Meïr. Rebbi Jehudah says, he must separate from his mother's maternal halfsister but may keep his mother's paternal halfsister[84]. If he married any other incest prohibited woman, he may keep her. It was only said, "if he married". Therefore, not from the start[85].

84 If he was married to any one of them at the moment of his conversion. In the Babli, 98b, R. Meïr is quoted as he is here, but instead of R. Jehudah, the anonymous Sages are quoted as permitting all sisters and aunts. In *Gen. Rabba* 18(7), the *baraita* is quoted as it is here, only that instead of R. Jehudah one has the anonymous Sages.

85 If he comes to ask, one does not permit the marriage. In the Babli, all women who are not blood relatives are unconditionally permitted.

גּוֹי אֲחוֹתוֹ בֵּין מֵאָב בֵּין מֵאֵם יוֹצִיא. דִּבְרֵי רִבִּי מֵאִיר. רִבִּי יוּדָה אוֹמֵר. אֲחוֹתוֹ מֵאֵם יוֹצִיא אֲחוֹתוֹ מֵאָב יְקַייֵם. אֲחוֹת אִמּוֹ יוֹצִיא אֲחוֹת אָבִיו יְקַייֵם. דִּבְרֵי רִבִּי מֵאִיר. רִבִּי יוּדָה אוֹמֵר. אֲחוֹת אִמּוֹ מֵאִמָּהּ יוֹצִיא אֲחוֹת אִמּוֹ מֵאָבִיהָ יְקַייֵם. אָמַר רַב חָנִין. פָּשַׁט הוּא לוֹן עַל דִּבְרֵי רִבִּי מֵאִיר. עַל כֵּן יַעֲזוֹב אִישׁ אֶת אָבִיו וְאֶת אִמּוֹ. בְּסָמוּךְ לוֹ מֵאָבִיו בְּסָמוּךְ לוֹ מֵאִמּוֹ. רִבִּי בִּיבִי בְּעָא. מֵעַתָּה אֲחוֹת אָבִיו אֲסוּרָה שֶׁהִיא סְמוּכָה לְאָבִיו. אֲחוֹת אִמּוֹ תְּהֵא אֲסוּרָה מִפְּנֵי שֶׁהִיא סְמוּכָה לְאִמּוֹ. הֲתִיב רִבִּי שִׁמְעוֹן בְּרֵיהּ דְּרִבִּי אַיְיבוּ. וְהָכְתִיב וַיִּקַּח עַמְרָם אֶת יוֹכֶבֶד דּוֹדָתוֹ לוֹ לְאִשָּׁה. מֵעַתָּה אֲפִילוּ כִבְנֵי נֹחַ לֹא הָיוּ יִשְׂרָאֵל נוֹהֲגִין. אָמַר רִבִּי הִילָא. בְּסָמוּךְ לוֹ מֵאָבִיו בְּסָמוּךְ לוֹ מֵאִמּוֹ. מְתִיבִין לְרִבִּי מֵאִיר. וְגַם אָמְנָה אֲחוֹתִי בַת אָבִי הִיא אַךְ לֹא בַת אִמִּי. אָמַר לָהֶן רִבִּי מֵאִיר. מִשָּׁם רְאָיָיה. לֹא וַתְּהִי לִי לְאִשָּׁה.

A Gentile has to separate from his sister, whether paternal or maternal, the words of Rebbi Meïr. Rebbi Jehudah says, he must separate from his maternal halfsister; a paternal halfsister he may keep. He must separate from his mother's sister but may keep his father's sister, the words of Rebbi Meïr. Rebbi Jehudah says, he must separate from his mother's maternal halfsister but may keep his mother's paternal halfsister[86]. Rav Ḥanin said, he[87] explained us the words of Rebbi Meïr simply: "Therefore, a man has to abandon his father and his mother[88]." What is close to him from his father's side, what is close to him from his mother's side. Rebbi Vivian asked: Then his father's sister should be forbidden because she is close to his father! His mother's sister should be forbidden because she is close to his mother[89]! Rebbi Simeon, the son of Rebbi Ayvo objected: "Amram took his aunt Yokhebed as wife[90]." Does that mean that the Israelites did not even behave as descendants of Noah? Rebbi Hila said, what is close to him from his father's side, what is close to him from his mother's side[91]. They objected to Rebbi Meïr: "And truly she is my sister, my father's daughter, but not my mother's.[92]" He said to them: Is a proof from there? Not "she became my wife"[93]?

86 The rules for Gentiles living under Jewish law are identical to those valid for converts; in the Babli they are given in *Sanhedrin* 58a, identical to the rules given for converts in *Yebamot* 98b.

87 This must be Rav, Rav Ḥanin's teacher and father-in-law.

88 *Gen*. 2:24. The common interpretation of the verse as basis of a "natural law" of incest prohibitions is in the sources [Babli *Sanhedrin* 58a, *Gen. rabba* 18(8)]: "Therefore, a man leaves his father (the father's wife who might not be his mother) and his mother and clings to his wife (marriage is effected by intercourse, but after the first intercourse of a woman all sex acts with other people are adulterous since there is no divorce; male homosexual activity is also forbidden) and they will be one flesh (only vaginal intercourse is counted as such)." All other incest prohibitions of *Lev*. are for Jews only. (A minority opinion, that of R. Eliezer in the Babli, identifies the "father" as the father's sisters.)

89 This shows that the opinion of R. Eliezer, quoted in the Babli (see the preceding note) was unknown to the editors of the Yerushalmi.

90 *Ex*. 6:20. According to the rules promulgated by him, Moses was a bastard. This proves (a) that the incest prohibitions of *Lev*. 18 are introduced because of the holiness of the Land or as prohibition of idolatrous practices and (b) the paternal aunt is permitted to a Gentile.

91 Only the father's wives and the mother.

92 *Gen*. 20:12. According to Philo

(*Special Laws III*, 22-25), the practice of marrying halfsisters was recognized in Greece and that of marrying full sisters in Egypt.

93 I am at a loss to understand the argument. The expedient chosen by the talmudic sources that Sarah was not Abraham's sister but his niece, should be excluded out of respect for the biblical text (Cf. Chapter 10, Note 210). This cannot be a general Jewish tradition since Sadducee (Karaite) traditions prohibit the niece to the uncle because the text prohibits the nephew to the aunt.

מַאי כְדוֹן. אָמַר רִבִּי יוֹסֶה. כָּל־עֶרְוָה שֶׁבֵּית דִּין שֶׁלְּיִשְׂרָאֵל מְמִיתִין עָלֶיהָ בְּנֵי נֹחַ מוּזְהָרִין עָלֶיהָ. וְכָל־עֶרְוָה שֶׁאֵין בֵּית דִּין מְמִיתִין עָלֶיהָ אֵין בְּנֵי נֹחַ מוּזְהָרִין עָלֶיהָ. הֲתִיבוּן. הֲרֵי אֲחוֹתוֹ הֲרֵי בֵּית דִּין שֶׁלְּיִשְׂרָאֵל מְמִיתִין עָלֶיהָ וְאֵין בְּנֵי נֹחַ מוּזְהָרִין עָלֶיהָ. רִבִּי הִילָא בְשֵׁם רִבִּי שִׁמְעוֹן בֶּן לָקִישׁ. וּבִגְלַל הַתּוֹעֵבוֹת הָאֵלֶּה יי אֱלֹהֶיךָ מוֹרִישׁ אוֹתָם מִפָּנֶיךָ. מְלַמֵּד שֶׁאֵין הַקָּדוֹשׁ בָּרוּךְ הוּא עוֹנֵשׁ אֶלָּא אִם כֵּן הִזְהִיר.

What about it[94]? Rebbi Yose said, about any incest prohibition which for a Jewish court is a capital crime, a descendant of Noah[95] is forewarned; and about any incest prohibition which for a court is not a capital crime, a descendant of Noah is not forewarned[96]. They objected: Is not a case involving the sister a capital crime for a Jewish court and the descendants of Noah are not forewarned[97]? Rebbi Hila in the name of Rebbi Simeon ben Laqish: "Because of these abominations, the Eternal, your God, uproots them before you.[98]" This teaches that the Holy One, praise to Him, does not punish if He did not warn[99].

94 What is the practice about prohibited Gentile marriages.

95 Any Gentile.

96 This is characterized as R. Meïr's minority opinion in the Babli, *Sanhedrin* 57b.

97 The example is exceedingly bad since incest with one's sister is punished by Heaven with extirpation (*Lev.* 20:17) but is not a capital crime on Earth. Maybe the reference should be to a man married to a woman and

her daughter; cf. Note 82.

98 *Deut.* 18:12, speaking of idolatry.

99 The prohibition of idolatry is universal, valid for all descendants of Noah (Babli *Sanhedrin* 57b). Therefore, Gentiles can be punished for idolatrous practices since they have been warned about them. R. Hila seems to agree that the incest prohibitions which exceed the bare minimum are directed against idolatrous practices.

רִבִּי אִידִי אָמַר קוֹמֵי רִבִּי יוֹסֵי בְּשֵׁם רַב חִסְדָּא. עֶבֶד מוּתָּר בַּאֲחוֹתוֹ. אָמַר לֵיהּ. שָׁמַעְתָּ אֲפִילוּ מֵאֵם. אָמַר לֵיהּ. אִין. אָמַר לֵיהּ. וְהָתַנִּינָן וְכֵן שִׁפְחָה שֶׁנִּשְׁתַּחְרְרוּ בָנֶיהָ עִמָּהּ. לַחֲלִיצָה וּלְיִיבּוּם. רִבִּי פִינְחָס אָמַר קוֹמֵי רִבִּי יוֹסֵי בְּשֵׁם רִבִּי יוֹסֵי. עֶבֶד שֶׁבָּא עַל אִמּוֹ חַיָּיב חַטָּאת. וְאָמַרְתָּ אֲלֵיהֶם לְרַבּוֹת עֲבָדִים. אוֹ נֹאמַר. לַחֲלָבִין אִיתְאֲמָרַת. מַה מָּצִינוּ בְּזִיקַּת אֵם שֶׁעָשָׂה בָהּ צַד שֶׁנִּתְגַּייְרָה בְּצַד שֶׁלֹּא נִתְגַּייְרָה. אַף שִׁפְחָה נַעֲשָׂה בָהּ צַד שֶׁנִּשְׁתַּחְרְרָה בְּצַד שֶׁלֹּא נִשְׁתַּחְרְרָה.

Rebbi Idi said before Rebbi Yose, a slave is permitted his sister[100]. He said to him, did you hear this even if she is from the same mother? He said, yes. He said to him, but did we not state: "The same applies to a slave girl who was freed together with her sons." For *ḥalîṣah* and levirate[101]. Rebbi Phineas said before Rebbi Yose in the name of Rebbi Yasa: A slave who slept with his mother is obligated for a purification sacrifice. "You shall command them[102]," including slaves[103]. Or should we say, this was said about fat[104]? Do we find in his relation to his mother that her converted aspect accompanies the unconverted aspect just as with a slave girl her converted aspect accompanies the unconverted aspect[105]?

100 As the Babli explains (*Sanhedrin* 58b), he is no longer a Gentile but not yet a responsible Jew. He cannot be punished in either law and he cannot legally marry.

101 But not for criminal matters. The convert changed from one set of laws to another; the libertine enters a

set of laws that previously were not applicable to her.

102 *Lev*. 1:2. After the introduction: "Speak to the Children of Israel", the addition "you shall command them" seems superfluous unless it includes people whose inclusion among the Children of Israel is doubtful.

103 Since in theory anything a slaves owns belongs to his master, any obligation of sacrifice would have to be deferred until after the slave's manumission.

104 While a slave is obligated to obey all prohibitions in the Torah, it may be that in matters of sexual relations his status is different (Since slaves cannot marry, as a matter of principle promiscuity is permitted to them; cf. *Terumot* Chapter 8, Note 247.)

105 A betrothed girl is a wife for criminal law; adultery with her is a capital crime (*Deut*. 22:23-24). By contrast, adultery with a half-freed slave girl engaged to be married to a free man (in expectation of her full emancipation; she did belong to two masters one of whom manumitted his share) can be expiated by a reparation offering (*Lev*. 19:20-22; *Sifra Qedošim Pereq* 5). This shows that her semi-free status interferes with the operation of criminal law for free persons. In analogy, we could conjecture that the status of a slave as incompletely converted (since he is not obligated to observe most positive commandments) interferes with the operation of the laws of obligatory sacrifices.

The problem is not resolved, probably because it is not realistic.

(fol. 11c) **משנה ג**: חָמֵשׁ נָשִׁים שֶׁנִּתְעָרְבוּ וַלְדוֹתֵיהֶן הִגְדִּילוּ הַתַּעֲרוֹבוֹת וְנָשְׂאוּ נָשִׁים וָמֵתוּ אַרְבָּעָה חוֹלְצִין לְאַחַת וְאֶחָד מְייַבֵּם אוֹתָהּ. הוּא וּשְׁלֹשָׁה חוֹלְצִים לְאַחֶרֶת וְאֶחָד מְייַבֵּם. נִמְצְאוּ אַרְבַּע חֲלִיצוֹת וְיִיבּוּם לְכָל־אַחַת וְאַחַת.

Mishnah 3: If the children of five women were mixed up, and the mixed-up became adults, married wives, and died, then four perform *ḥalîṣah* and one marries in levirate[106]. This one and three others perform *ḥalîṣah* for another one and another one marries in levirate[107]. It turns out that there are four *ḥalîṣot* and one levirate marriage for every one.

106 It is assumed that each woman had another child whose family membership is clear. If one of the mixed-up children dies childless, then it is not known whose brother he was. Therefore, one brother known to be from each of the families involved performs *ḥalîṣah* with the widow who may be his sister-in-law or four perform *ḥalîṣah* and one marries. The one who marries either performs levirate or he marries an unrelated woman; in both cases the marriage is unquestionably valid.

107 The one who married the first widow might also marry the second one. The number five here is irrelevant; the same rules apply to any number *n* of mixed-up children. The death of a childless man of the mixed-up group causes *n*-1 *ḥalîṣot* and 1 levirate or *n ḥalîṣot*.

(fol. 12a) **משנה**: חָמֵשׁ נָשִׁים שֶׁנִּתְעָרְבוּ וַלְדוֹתֵיהֶן כול׳. בְּכָל־אָתָר אַתְּ אָמַר. אֵין חֲלִיצָה אַחַר חֲלִיצָה. וְהָכָא אַתְּ אָמַר הָכֵין. כָּאן בְּוַדַּאי כָּאן בְּסָפֵק. בְּכָל־אָתָר אַתְּ אָמַר. בְּכָל־מָקוֹם שֶׁאֵין אוֹמְרִים. יַיבֵּם. אֵין אוֹמְרִים. חֲלוֹץ. וְהָכָא אַתְּ אָמַר הָכֵין. כָּאן בְּוַדַּאי כָּאן בְּסָפֵק.

Mishnah: "If the children of five women were mixed up," etc. [107]Everywhere you say, there is no *ḥalîṣah* after *ḥalîṣah*, and here, you say so? There, it is was sure, here it is in doubt. Everywhere you say, if one does not say to him, take in levirate, one does not say, perform *ḥalîṣah*, and here, you say so[108]? There, it is was sure, here it is doubtful.

107 The text is from Halakhah 2:7.

108 The Mishnah is to be interpreted strictly, that the widow is permitted to one of then possible brothers only after all other have performed *ḥalîṣah* with her; otherwise he might marry another man's brother's widow. That means that the four first men must perform *ḥalîṣah* and are forbidden for levirate.

(fol. 11c) **משנה ד**: הָאִשָּׁה שֶׁנִּתְעָרֵב וַלְדָּהּ בְּוָולָד כַּלָּתָהּ. הִגְדִּילוּ הַתַּעֲרוֹבוֹת וְנָשְׂאוּ נָשִׁים וָמֵתוּ. בְּנֵי הַכַּלָּה חוֹלְצִין וְלֹא מְיַיבְּמִין שֶׁהוּא סְפֵק אֵשֶׁת אָחִיו סְפֵק אֵשֶׁת אֲחִי אָבִיו. וּבְנֵי הַזְּקֵינָה אוֹ חוֹלְצִין אוֹ מְיַיבְּמִין שֶׁהוּא אֵשֶׁת אָחִיו וְאֵשֶׁת בֶּן אָחִיו. מֵתוּ הַכְּשֵׁרִים בְּנֵי הַתַּעֲרוֹבוֹת לִבְנֵי הַזְּקֵינָה חוֹלְצִין וְלֹא מְיַיבְּמִין שֶׁהוּא וְאֵשֶׁת אָחִיו סְפֵק אֵשֶׁת אֲחִי אָבִיו. וּבְנֵי הַכַּלָּה אֶחָד חוֹלֵץ וְאֶחָד מְיַיבֵּם.

Mishnah 4: If a woman's child was mixed up with her daughter-in-law's child, the mixed-up children became adults, married wives, and died[109]. The other sons of the daughter-in-law must perform *ḥalîṣah* but not levirate since for them it is doubtful whether [the widow was] a brother's wife or an uncle's wife[110]. But the sons of the old woman may either perform *ḥalîṣah* or levirate since for them she was either a brother's wife or a nephew's wife[111]. If one of the identified ones died, the mixed-up ones must perform *ḥalîṣah* but not levirate for a son of the old woman since there is a doubt whether [the widow was] a brother's wife or an uncle's wife. But for the sons of the daughter-in-law, one performs *ḥalîṣah;* the other may marry in levirate[113].

109 One of the mixed-up sons died childless while being married.

110 If the deceased was the son of the daughter-in-law, his widow could be married in levirate but if he was the son of the mother-in-law, she is forbidden to her husband's nephew. Therefore, one of the other sons of the daughter-in-law must perform *ḥalîṣah* with her.

111 If a son of the daughter-in-law had performed *ḥalîṣah*, then the widow is either the sister-in-law of her husband's brother and can be married in levirate or she is the widow of a nephew who can be married. "Levirate" in this case has to be taken with a grain of salt since unintentional intercourse (cf. Mishnah 5:1) will only possibly make the widow a wife.

113 If the widow already had one *ḥalîṣah*, she is either the sister-in-law or the free widow of a nephew and permitted.

(fol. 12a) **משנה**: הָאִשָּׁה שֶׁנִּתְעָרֵב וַלְדָּהּ כול'. אָמַר רִבִּי יוֹחָנָן. כֵּינִי מַתְנִיתָא. לְנָשֵׁי בְנֵי הַכַּלָּה לְנָשֵׁי בְנֵי הַזְּקֵינָה. אָמַר רִבִּי חַגַּיי. זֹאת אוֹמֶרֶת שֶׁמּוּתָּר אָדָם לִישָּׂא אֶת אֵשֶׁת בֶּן אָחִיו.

Mishnah: "If a woman's child was mixed up," etc. Rebbi Johanan said: So is the Mishnah: The sister-in-law's sons' wives, the old woman's sons' wives[114]. Rebbi Ḥaggai said, this implies that a man may marry a nephew's ex-wife[115].

114 An obvious correction of the language of the Mishnah; one does not speak of the sons of mother-in-law or daughter-in-law but of their childless widows.

115 There is no doubt that such a union is permitted by biblical standards; for some reason it was felt necessary to state that there is no rabbinic restriction in the case.

(fol. 11c) **משנה ה**: כֹּהֶנֶת שֶׁנִּתְעָרֵב וַלְדָּהּ בְּוָלָד שִׁפְחָתָהּ הֲרֵי אֵילּוּ אוֹכְלִין בַּתְּרוּמָה וְחוֹלְקִין חֵלֶק אֶחָד לַגּוֹרֶן וְאֵינָן מִטַּמְּאִין לַמֵּתִים וְאֵינָן נוֹשְׂאִין נָשִׁים בֵּין כְּשֵׁירוֹת בֵּין פְּסוּלוֹת.

Mishnah 5: If the child of a priestly woman was mixed up with the child of her slave girl then both may eat heave; they together take one part from the threshing floor, they may not defile themselves by becoming impure for the dead, and they may not marry women enabled or disabled [for the priesthood][116].

116 Each of them is a possible Cohen. The details are explained in the Halakhah; the removal of the disabilities is the subject of the next Mishnah.

(fol. 12a) **משנה**: כֹּהֶנֶת שֶׁנִּתְעָרֵב וַלְדָּהּ כול׳. הֲרֵי אֵילוּ אוֹכְלִין בִּתְרוּמָה. שֶׁכֵּן עַבְדֵי כֹהֲנִים אוֹכְלִין בִּתְרוּמָה.

Mishnah: "If the child of a priestly woman was mixed up," etc. "Both may eat heave", since slaves of Cohanim eat heave.

וְחוֹלְקִין חֵלֶק אֶחָד עַל הַגּוֹרֶן. הָדָא הִיא דְתַנֵּי רִבִּי חִיָּה. נָשִׁים וַעֲבָדִים אֵינָן חוֹלְקִין עַל הַגּוֹרֶן אֲבָל נוֹתְנִין לָהֶן מַתְּנוֹת כְּהוּנָּה וּלְוִיָּה מִתּוֹךְ הַבַּיִת.

"They together take one part from the threshing floor," that is what Rebbi Ḥiyya stated: One does not distribute to women and slaves on the threshing floor[117] but one gives them the gifts of priesthood and/or those due to Levites from the barn[118].

וְאֵין נוֹשְׂאִין נָשִׁים לֹא כְשֵׁירוֹת וְלֹא פְסוּלוֹת. לֹא כְשֵׁירוֹת מִפְּנֵי הַפָּסוּל. וְלֹא פְסוּלוֹת מִפְּנֵי הַכָּשֵׁר.

"They may not marry women, whether enabled or disabled [for the priesthood]." Not enabled ones because of the disabled one. Not disabled ones because of the enabled one[119].

117 As the Babli (99b) explains, one does not admit women to the public distribution of heave and tithes since a woman may lose her priestly status from one distribution to the next and still receive heave and/or tithes since the farmer may recognize her from former distributions. Slaves are excluded since the entitlement to heave was counted as a proof of priestly status (cf. *Ketubot* 2:7,8).

118 Privately, where no presumption of priestly status is created.

119 The slave cannot marry any woman; the priest is forbidden to marry a woman disabled for the priesthood.

מַהוּ שֶׁיָּבִיאוּ מִנְחָה אַחַת וּתְהֵא קְרֵיבָה בְּכָלִיל. תַּנֵּי. מְבִיאִין מִנְחָה אַחַת וּמַתְנִין עָלֶיהָ וּתְהֵא קְרֵיבָה בְּכָלִיל. מַהוּ שֶׁיָּבִיאוּ שְׁתֵּי מְנָחוֹת אַחַת קְרֵיבָה בְּכָלִיל וְאַחַת נִקְמֶצֶת וְנֶאֱכֶלֶת. תַּנֵּי. מְבִיאִין שְׁתֵּי מְנָחוֹת אַחַת קְרֵיבָה בְּכָלִיל וְאַחַת נִקְמֶצֶת וְנֶאֱכֶלֶת. מַהוּ שֶׁיָּעִידוּ עֵדוּת אַחַת וְתַעֲלֶה לָהֶם עֵדוּת אַחַת. אוֹ

יְבוֹא כְּהַהִיא דָמַר רִבִּי זְעִירָא רַב יִצְחָק בְּשֵׁם רַב אַסִּי. מֵאַחַר שֶׁאִילּוּ יִמְצְאוּ הָעֵדִים זוֹמְמִין אֵין נֶהֱרָגִין וְאֵין הַהוֹרֵג נֶהֱרָג. אַף הָכָא כֵן.

May they bring one cereal offering together that would be totally burned[120]? It was stated: They may bring one cereal offering conditionally that would be totally burned. May they bring two cereal offerings one of which should be burned totally and the other have a handful taken and the rest eaten[121]? It was stated: They may bring two cereal offerings of one which is burned totally and of the other a handful is taken and the rest eaten. May they testify together that it should be counted as testimony of one witness[122]? That would follow the rule of Rebbi Ze'ira, Rav Isaac in the name of Rav Assi: Since if they were to be found perjured they could not be executed, the murderer could not be executed[123]. This applies here also.

120 The cereal offering of a Cohen in the Temple must be burned completely (*Lev.* 6:16). They may bring a cereal offering to the Temple and declare that it should be counted as the offering of the one of them who is a Cohen.

121 They may bring two cereal offerings to the Temple and declare that one should be counted as the offering of the one of them who is a Cohen and the other one as the offering of the slave. A handful of the second offering together with all its incense is burned on the altar and the rest eaten by the Cohanim under the rules of most holy offerings (*Lev.* 6:7-11).

122 Slaves are not admitted as formal witnesses. (They are admitted to ascertain facts, such as the death of a man to permit the widow to remarry.) If their testimonies are identical, may the court accept the testimony of the one who really is a Cohen?

123 A false witness must receive the punishment that would have been meted out to the accused had his testimony been accepted by the court. Since a slave cannot be a witness in a criminal proceeding, he cannot be punished as a perjured witness. Since it is not known who of the two is a slave, neither of them can be punished.

In the formulation of the Babli (*Sanhedrin* 41a): Testimony which is not subject to the penalties of perjuty is no testimony. The remark: "This applies here also" shows that the statement of Rav Assi refers to criminal proceedings in general. The murderer cannot be executed if one of the testimonies to his guilt is not subject to the penalties of perjury.

(fol. 11c) **משנה ו:** הִגְדִּילוּ הַתַּעֲרוֹבוֹת וְשִׁחְרְרוּ זֶה אֶת זֶה נוֹשְׂאִין נָשִׁים רְאוּיוֹת לִכְהוּנָּה וְאֵינָן מִיטַּמְּאִין לַמֵּתִים וְאִם נִטְמְאוּ אֵין סוֹפְגִין אֶת הָאַרְבָּעִים. וְאֵינָן אוֹכְלִין בִּתְרוּמָה וְאִם אָכְלוּ אֵינָן מְשַׁלְּמִין קֶרֶן וְחוֹמֶשׁ. וְאֵינָן חוֹלְקִין עַל הַגּוֹרֶן. וּמוֹכְרִים אֶת הַתְּרוּמָה וְהַדָּמִים שֶׁלָּהֶם. וְאֵינָן רוֹלְקִין בְּקָדְשֵׁי מִקְדָּשׁ. וְאֵין נוֹתְנִין לָהֶם קֳדָשִׁים. וְאֵין מוֹצִיאִין אֶת שֶׁלָּהֶן מִידֵיהֶן. וּפְטוּרִין מִן הַזְּרוֹעַ וּמִן הַלְּחָיַיִם וּמִן הַקֵּיבָה. וּבְכוֹרָן יְהֵא רוֹעֶה עַד שֶׁיִּסְתָּאֵב. וְנוֹתְנִין עֲלֵיהֶן חוּמְרֵי יִשְׂרָאֵל וְחוּמְרֵי כֹהֲנִים.

Mishnah 6: When the mixed-up children became adults and manumitted one another[124] they may marry women appropriate for the priesthood, may not defile themselves for the dead, but if they became defiled they do not suffer forty lashes[125]. They may not eat heave, but if they ate they do not have to pay its value and and additional fifth[126]. They cannot attend distributions on the threshing floor; they have to sell their heave, but the money is theirs[127]. They have no part in the Temple sacrifices, one does not give them sacrifices, but one cannot take theirs from them[128]. They are exempt from the foreleg, the chin, and the first stomach[129]. Their firstborn animal should graze until it develops a blemish[130]. One charges them with the disabilities of an Israel and those of Cohanim[131].

124 Then the slave is manumitted and becomes a full Israel. The manumission of the Cohen is invalid and does not damage him.

125 In order to punish one of them for wilfully desecrating himself, the court would have to prove that the culprit is a Cohen. Since this is impossible, neither of them can ever be punished for any infraction of priestly rules.

126 Since the monetary penalty for unauthorized use of heave has to be given to a Cohen (Mishnaiot *Terumot* 6:1, 7:1), and no Cohen can successfully sue any of them for payment by proving that he is not a Cohen, they do not have to pay.

127 They may not eat heave since the eater may be the former slave. They keep the money since they cannot be sued for it, cf. Note 126.

128 Since a Cohen has the right to sacrifice in the Temple even if he is not on duty there, they have the right to hand over their sacrifices to any certified Cohen and are not obligated to give it to the group of Cohanim currently serving there.

129 The gift to the Cohanim from profane slaughter, *Deut.* 18:3.

130 An unblemished firstborn animal must be given to a Cohen to be sacrificed in the Temple and eaten by the Cohen. Once it is blemished it can be slaughtered locally and eaten by anybody, *Deut.* 15:19-23.

131 This gives the rationale for the entire Mishnah.

(fol. 12a) **משנה**: הִגְדִּילוּ הַתַּעֲרוּבוֹת כול׳. לְשֶׁעָבַר. הָא לְכַתְּחִילָּה לֹא. כֵּינִי מַתְנִיתָא. מוּתָּר לְשַׁחְרֵר כַּתְּחִילָּה. אַף רִבִּי יוֹסֵי הַגָּלִילִי אָמַר. אָסוּר לְשַׁחְרֵר. מוֹדֶה הוּא הָכָא שֶׁהוּא מוּתָּר. מִפְּנֵי תִיקּוּן הַוְולָד. מַהוּ רְאוּיוֹת. לֹא פְסוּלוֹת.

Mishnah: "If the mixed-up children became adults," after it happened[132]. Does that mean, not from the start? So is the Mishnah: It is permitted from the start to manumit[133]. Even Rebbi Yose the Galilean, who said that one is forbidden to manumit[134], will agree here that it is permitted for the benefit of children. What means "appropriate"? Not disabled.

132 One would have expected the Mishnah to read: Once adults, they manumit one another. Does the formulation of the Mishnah imply that the manumission is not recommended?

133 The Babli, 100a, insists that the court forces them to manumit one another.

134 Based on the verse *Lev*. 25:46: "You shall have them work for you forever". In the Babli, this interpretation is quoted in the name of the Amora Rav Jehudah (*Berakhot* 47b), R. Aqiba (*Soṭah* 3b, against R. Ismael who reads "You may have them work for you forever"), Rav Jehudah in the name of Samuel (*Giṭṭin* 38b).

מְנַיִין לְכֹהֵן שֶׁהוּא מַקְרִיב קָרְבְּנוֹתָיו בְּכָל־מִשְׁמָר שֶׁיִּרְצֶה. תַּלְמוּד לוֹמַר וּבָא בְּכָל־אַוַּת נַפְשׁוֹ וְשֵׁרֵת. הָיָה זָקֵן אוֹ חוֹלֶה נוֹתְנוֹ לְכָל־מִשְׁמָר שֶׁיִּרְצֶה וְעוֹרָן וּבְשָׂרָן שֶׁלּוֹ. הָיָה טָמֵא וּבַעַל מוּם נוֹתְנִין לְאַנְשֵׁי הַמִּשְׁמָר וְעוֹרָן וּבְשָׂרָן שֶׁלָּהֶן. אִילֵּין בְּנֵי הַתַּעֲרוּבוֹת מַה אַתְּ עֲבֵד לְהוֹן. כְּזָקֵן וּכְחוֹלֶה אוֹ כְטָמֵא וּבַעַל מוּם. מִסְתַּבְּרָא מֵיעַבְדִינוֹן כְטָמֵא וּכְבַעַל מוּם. וּמַתְנִיתָא עָבְדָא לוֹן כְּזָקֵן וּכְחוֹלֶה. דְּתַנִּינָן. אֵין מוֹצִיאִין אֶת שֶׁלּוֹ מִיָּדוֹ.

From where that a Cohen presents his sacrifices during [the period of duty of] any watch[135] he chooses? The verse says, 'he may come as his heart desires . . . and serve'[136]. If he was old or sick, he may give it to any watch he likes but the hide and meat are his. If he was impure or had a bodily defect, he must give it to the acting watch[137], and the hide and meat are theirs. These mixed-up ones, how do you treat them? Comparing them to the old or sick, or to the impure or to those with a bodily defect. It seems reasonable to compare them to the impure or those having a bodily defect[138]; but the Mishnah compares them to the old or sick, since we have stated: "One cannot take his from him[139]."

135 The land of Israel was divided into 24 districts and the priests from each district came to the Temple for one week (serving as *watch* from the presentation of the shew-bread on one Sabbath to its removal the next Sabbath). The priests were indemnified for their work by

receiving the skins of most holy sacrifices and all gifts to priests during their week of work. A hint of this is found in *Deut.* 18:9.

Even after the destruction of the Temple, the calendar of service of the districts was retained for special occasions, cf. Mishnah *Ta'aniot* 2:7.

136 *Deut.* 18:6-7. Priests acting for themselves are exempt from the obligation to use the watch in charge of the week. The same argument is in Babli *Baba Qama* 109b, where verses are quoted in support of the assertion here that the hide and meat do not belong to the acting watch. In contrast, *Sifry Deut.* 168 restricts the right of the Cohen to participation in the priestly blessing any time he so desires.

137 The old or sick in principle are able to sacrifice by themselves; the impure and disfigured are barred from entering the Temple. The latter cannot sacrifice and in this respect are not different in status from a non-Cohen.

138 They could not possibly be accepted as acting priests in the Temple.

139 This is the language of Mishnah 8.

(fol. 11c) **משנה ז**: מִי שֶׁלֹּא שָׁהֲתָה אַחַר בַּעֲלָהּ שְׁלֹשָׁה חֳדָשִׁים וְנִשֵּׂאת וְיָלְדָה וְאֵין יָדוּעַ אִם בֶּן תִּשְׁעָה לָרִאשׁוֹן. אִם בֶּן שִׁבְעָה לָאַחֲרוֹן. הָיוּ לָהּ בָּנִים מִן הָרִאשׁוֹן בָּנִים מִן הַשֵּׁינִי חוֹלְצִין וְלֹא מְיַיבְּמִין. וְכֵן הוּא לָהֶם חוֹלֵץ וְלֹא מְיַיבֵּם. הָיוּ לוֹ אַחִין מִן הָרִאשׁוֹן וְאַחִין מִן הַשֵּׁינִי. שֶׁלֹּא מֵאוֹתָהּ הָאֵם הוּא חוֹלֵץ וּמְיַיבֵּם. וְהֵן חוֹלְצִין וּמְיַיבְּמִין.

Mishnah 7: [A woman] did not wait three months after [the death of] her husband, married, and gave birth, and it is not known whether it is a nine months' child of the first or a seven months' child of the second. If she had sons from the first and the second, they perform *ḥalîṣah* but not levirate[140]. Similarly, he performs *ḥalîṣah* but not levirate[141]. If he had brothers from the first or from the second not from the same mother, he may perform *ḥalîṣah* or levirate[142] and they may perform *ḥalîṣah* or levirate[143].

140 If the questionable child married and died childless, the widow needs *ḥalîṣah* from both sides. She cannot marry any one of them since her husband might have been the son of the other man and the marriage would then be incestuous.

141 If he had only one brother on one side and that one died childless, he must perform *ḥalîṣah* for the widow but is forbidden levirate.

142 It is obvious that he is not a candidate for either *ḥalîṣah* or levirate if there is another brother who could marry or release a widow without complication. If there was only one brother on one side who died childless, his widow either is a sister-in-law who can be married by the levir or she is an unrelated woman free to marry any man.

143 In the Babli and a number of independent Mishnah mss.: "One performs *ḥalîṣah* and one may marry in levirate." In that version, if the questionable son dies childless, a brother from one side must perform *ḥalîṣah*; then one of the other side either may perform *ḥalîṣah* or marry in levirate since either the widow is his sister-in-law or she is unrelated and free to marry any man. One must assume that the version of the Yerushalmi (and a group of independent Mishnah mss.) is shorthand for the version of the Babli.

משנה ח: הָיָה אֶחָד יִשְׂרָאֵל וְאֶחָד כֹּהֵן נוֹשֵׂא אִשָּׁה רְאוּיָה לַכֹּהֵן וְאֵינוֹ מִטַּמֵּא לַמֵּתִים. וְאִם נִטְמָא אֵינוֹ סוֹפֵג אֶת הָאַרְבָּעִים. וְאֵינוֹ אוֹכֵל בַּתְּרוּמָה וְאִם אָכַל אֵינוֹ מְשַׁלֵּם קֶרֶן וָחוֹמֶשׁ. וְאֵינוֹ חוֹלֵק עַל הַגּוֹרֶן. וּמוֹכֵר אֶת הַתְּרוּמָה וְהַדָּמִים שֶׁלּוֹ. וְאֵינוֹ חוֹלֵק בְּקָדְשֵׁי מִקְדָּשׁ. וְאֵין נוֹתְנִין לוֹ אֶת הַקֳּדָשִׁים. וְאֵין מוֹצִיאִין אֶת שֶׁלּוֹ מִיָּדוֹ. וּפָטוּר מִן הַזְּרוֹעַ וּמִן הַלְּחָיַיִם וּמִן הַקֵּיבָה. וּבְכוֹרוֹ יְהֵא רוֹעֶה עַד שֶׁיִּסְתָּאֵב. וְנוֹתְנִין עָלָיו חוּמְרֵי יִשְׂרָאֵל וְחוּמְרֵי כֹהֲנִים.

Mishnah 8: If one was an Israel and the other a priest[144], he may marry a woman appropriate for the priesthood, may not defile himself for the dead, but if he became defiled he does not suffer forty lashes[125]. He may not eat heave but if he ate, he does not have to pay its value and additional fifth[126]. He cannot attend distributions on the threshing floor. He has to sell his heave but the money is his[127]. He has no part in the

Temple sacrifices, one does not give him sacrifices but one cannot take his from him[128]. He is exempt from the foreleg, the chin, and the first stomach[129]. His firstborn animal should graze until it develops a blemish[130]. One charges him with the disabilities of an Israel and those of Cohanim[131].

144 The two husbands.

משנה ט: הָיוּ שְׁנֵיהֶן כֹּהֲנִים הוּא אוֹנֵן עֲלֵיהֶן וְהֵם אוֹנְנִין עָלָיו. הוּא אֵינוֹ מִיטַּמֵּא לָהֶן וְהֵן אֵינָן מִיטַּמְּאִין לוֹ. הוּא לֹא יוֹרֵשׁ אוֹתָן אֲבָל הֵן יוֹרְשִׁין אוֹתוֹ. וּפָטוּר עַל מַכָּתוֹ וְעַל קִלְלָתוֹ שֶׁל זֶה וְשֶׁל זֶה וְעוֹלֶה בְמִשְׁמָרוֹ שֶׁל זֶה וְשֶׁל זֶה וְאֵינוֹ חוֹלֵק. אִם הָיוּ שְׁנֵיהֶן בְּמִשְׁמָר אֶחָד נוֹטֵל חֵלֶק אֶחָד.

Mishnah 9: If both[144] were Cohanim, he has to mourn intensely for them and they for him[145]. He may not defile himself for them, they may not defile themselves for him. He does not inherit from them[146] but they inherit from him[147]. He is not prosecutable if he injures or curses either one of them[148]. He may serve on the watch of either one but does not participate in distributions[149]. If both were of the same watch, he takes one part.

145 On the day of death of one of his possible fathers, he is forbidden to serve in priestly functions. If he dies, both possible fathers are barred. The disability of a priest on the day of death of a close relative is inferred from the command given to Aaron and his sons on the day Nadab and Abihu died (*Lev.* 10:6) to continue their Temple service. If it were not forbidden in general, no special permission would have been needed.

146 He cannot prove to the other heirs that he is the son of the deceased.

147 If he dies without issue, his father should inherit his property. Since neither of them can prove that he is the father, they split his estate between them.

148 The prosecutor cannot prove that he cursed or injured his father.

149 He is a Cohen for the divine

service but has no property rights since he cannot prove his claim if the fathers belong to different watches.

(fol. 12a) **משנה**: מִי שֶׁלֹּא שָׁהַת אַחַר בַּעֲלָהּ כול׳. הָיוּ שְׁנֵיהֶם כֹּהֲנִים הוּא אוֹנֵן עֲלֵיהֶם כול׳. מַה נָן קַייָמִין. אִם לְאַחַר מִיתָה לֵית יָכִיל. דְּתַנִּינָן. הוּא אוֹנֵן עֲלֵיהֶן וְהֵם אוֹנְנִין עָלָיו. נִיחָא לַשֵּׁינִי אֵינוֹ מִטַּמֵּא שֶׁאֲנִי אוֹמֵר. בְּנוֹ שֶׁלָּרִאשׁוֹן הוּא. לָרִאשׁוֹן לָמָּה אֵינוֹ מִטַּמֵּא. אֶלָּא בְּשֶׁגֵּירַשׁ. מַה נַפְשָׁךְ. בְּנוֹ הוּא יִטַּמֵּא לוֹ. אִם אֵינוֹ בְנוֹ חָלָל הוּא. וּמַה בְכָךְ שֶׁיִּטַּמֵּא. אֶלָּא בְשֶׁאָנַס. לֹא כֵן אָמַר רַבָּא בְשֵׁם אַבָּא בַּר יִרְמְיָה. אֲנוּסָה אֵינָהּ צְרִיכָה לְהַמְתִּין שְׁלֹשָׁה חֳדָשִׁים. וְסַבְרִינָן מֵימַר כְּרַבָּנִן וְהָכָא כְּרִבִּי יוֹסֵי אֲנָן קַייָמִין.

Mishnah: "[A woman] did not wait three months," etc. "If both were Cohanim, he has to mourn intensely for them," etc. Where do we hold[150]? It is impossible after death [of the first] since we have stated: "He has to mourn intensely for them and they[151] for him." One understands that he does not defile himself for the second [husband], I say that he is the son of the first. But why does he not defile himself for the first one? It must be that he divorced. Then, as you take it, if he is his son, he should defile himself for him. If he is not his son, he is desecrated, and what happens if he defiles himself[152]? It must be that he[153] raped. Did not Rebbi Abba say in the name of Abba bar Jeremiah that a rape victim does not have to wait three months[154]? Should we say, following the rabbis, but we follow Rebbi Yose[155]!

150 Under which circumstances did she separate from the first husband?

151 Including the first husband, who then must be alive.

152 If the second husband married a divorcee, his child is not a Cohen and not under the disabilities of Cohanim.

153 The second man is not a husband; then he did not marry a divorcee and his son is a Cohen. The Babli, 100b, expands on the same arguments and concludes that the first might have been a husband who married after an invalid betrothal,

whose wife may walk out on him without a divorce.

154 Chapter 4, Note 166.

155 The Mishnah follows the opinion that a rape victim does have to wait three months before marrying but practice does not follow this opinion.

תַּנֵּי רִבִּי חִייָה. אוֹנְנִין וּמִיטַּמְּאִין עַל הַסָּפֵק. אָמַר רִבִּי יוֹסֵי. מַתְנִיתָא אָמְרָה כֵן. הוּא אוֹנֵן עֲלֵיהֶן וְהֵם אוֹנְנִין עָלָיו. רִבִּי אַשְׁיָין בַּר יָקִים הֲוָה לֵיהּ עוֹבְדָא. שָׁאַל לְרִבִּי יוֹסֵי אֲמַר לֵיהּ. לֵית צְרִיךְ. אֲמַר לֵיהּ. וְהָתַנִּינָן. אָמַר רִבִּי חִייָה. אוֹנְנִין וּמִיטַּמְּאִין עַל הַסָּפֵק. סִימָנִין הָיוּ נִיכָּרִין. לֹא כֵן אָמְרִין חֲבֵרַייָא בְשֵׁם רִבִּי יוֹחָנָן. סִימָנִין בֶּן שְׁמוֹנֶה אֵין עוֹשִׂין מַעֲשֶׂה. סִימָן הָיָה לוֹ שֶׁבָּעַל וּפֵירַשׁ.

Rebbi Ḥiyya stated: One mourns deeply and defiles himself in a case of doubt[156]. Rebbi Yose said, the Mishnah says so: "He has to mourn intensely for them and they for him." Rebbi Ashian bar Yaqim had a case[157]. He asked Rebbi Yose, who told him, you do not have to. He said to him, but did not Rebbi Ḥiyya say, one mourns deeply and defiles himself in a case of doubt? His signs were clear[158]. But did not the colleagues say in the name of Rebbi Joḥanan: One does not act on the signs of an eight months' child[159]? He had a sign that he had intercourse and then separated[160].

156 From the following it seems that this covers two different kinds of doubt: A doubt of paternity and a doubt whether a child is a stillbirth or not. The second problem arises when a child is born after eight months of pregnancy and does not live for 30 days (cf. Chapter 4, Note 70).

157 Of an 8-months' child who did not live.

158 R. Ḥiyya requires full mourning if the child had hair and fingernails (following Rebbi in Tosephta *Sabbath* 15:7). In the Babli, 80b, complete hair and fingernails prove that the child is a living seven-months' baby who just lingered in the womb.

159 The signs does not prove that the child is able to live.

160 The husband went on a trip after having the last intercourse and did not return before the pregnancy

was visible, which gives a lower bound for the duration of pregnancy which came to 8 months and 1 day, i. e., 9 months.

בֶּן שְׁמוֹנֶה הֲרֵי הוּא כְאֶבֶן וְאֵין מְטַלְטְלִין אוֹתוֹ בְּשַׁבָּת. אֲבָל אִמּוֹ שׁוֹחָה עָלָיו וּמֵינִיקָתוֹ. רִבִּי יוֹסֵי בָּעֵי. אִילֵּין תִּינוֹקוֹת סְפֵיקוֹת מַהוּ לְחַלֵּל עֲלֵיהֶן אֶת הַשַּׁבָּת. אָמַר רִבִּי יוֹסֵי בֵּירִבִּי בוּן. וְיָאוּת. מַה נַפְשָׁךְ. בֶּן תִּשְׁעָה הוּא יִמּוֹל. בֶּן שְׁמוֹנֶה נַעֲשָׂה כִמְחַתֵּךְ בָּשָׂר שֶׁלֹּא (fol. 12b) לְצוֹרֶךְ. רַבָּנָן דְּקֵיסָרִין אָמְרֵי. רִבִּי יַעֲקֹב בַּר דּוֹסַאי שָׁאַל. מִי אָמַר שֶׁמּוּתָּר לַחְתּוֹךְ בָּשָׂר שֶׁלֹּא לְצוֹרֶךְ.

An eight months' child is like a stone[161] and one does not move him on the Sabbath, but his mother lies down beside him and nurses him. Rebbi Yose asked: May one push aside the Sabbath for babies that are in doubt[162]? Rebbi Yose ben Rebbi Abun said, it is fine. How you take it, if he is a nine months' child, he must be circumcised. If he is an eight months' child, it is as if he cut flesh without need. The rabbis of Caesarea said, Rebbi Jacob ben Dositheos[163] asked, who permitted to cut flesh without need[164]?

161 Tosephta *Sabbath* 15 5; Babli *Sabbath* 135a, *Yebamot* 80a, *Baba Batra* 20a. He is considered to be dead.

162 May a child which possibly may be an eight-months' child be circumcised on the Sabbath if he was born on the Sabbath? It is clear that the Toseptha *Sabbath* 15:5 was not known to the Yerushalmi since it clearly states: In case of doubt whether it is a seven or an eight months' child, one does not push aside the Sabbath.

163 It seems that he was an Amora of the fourth generation. In other sources, he is called בן דוסאי, בן דוסתאי.

164 They answer the question in the negative; one has to wait until after the Sabbath. It is clear from the next paragraph that one has to wait 30 days to circumcise an eight months' baby. The Babli, *Sabbath* 136a, in the name of R. Ada bar Ahava, follows R. Yose bar Abun here and explains the Tosephta (Note 162) that one may not push aside the Sabbath if one forgot to bring the necessary implements and would have to carry them in the public domain on the Sabbath.

תַּנֵּי. רַבָּן שִׁמְעוֹן בֶּן גַּמְלִיאֵל אָמַר. כָּל־הַמִּתְקַיֵּים בָּאָדָם שְׁלֹשִׁים יוֹם אֵינוֹ נֶפֶל. וּפְדוּיָיו מִבֶּן חוֹדֶשׁ תִּפְדֶּה. וּבְהֵמָה שְׁמוֹנָה יָמִים אֵין זֶה נֶפֶל. וּמִיּוֹם הַשְּׁמִינִי וְהָלְאָה יֵרָצֶה לְקָרְבַּן אִשֶּׁה לַיי. תַּמָּן אָמְרֵי בְשֵׁם שְׁמוּאֵל. הֲלָכָה כְרַבָּן שִׁמְעוֹן בֶּן גַּמְלִיאֵל. אָמַר רִבִּי בָּא. מַה פְלִיגִין. בְּשֶׁלֹּא נוֹלַד לְחֳדָשָׁיו. אֲבָל אִם נוֹלַד לְחֳדָשָׁיו גַּם רַבָּן שִׁמְעוֹן בֶּן גַּמְלִיאֵל מוֹדֶה.

It was stated[165]: Rebbi Simeon ben Gamliel says, any human who lives for thirty days is not a still birth, "all redeemed you shall redeem at the age of one month[166];" and an animal which lives for eight days is not a still birth, "from the eighth day and further it will be welcome as a sacrifice, a gift to the Eternal[167]." There[168], they say that practice follows Rabban Simeon ben Gamliel. Rebbi Abba said, where do they disagree? If he was not born in his months[169]. But if he was born in his months, even Rabban Simeon ben Gamliel will agree.

165 Tosephta *Sabbath* 15:7; Babli *Sabbath* 135a.

166 *Num.* 18:16.

167 *Lev.* 22:27.

168 Babli *Sabbath* 136a. The rabbis hold that any child born alive frees his mother from levirate and *ḥalîṣah*.

169 7 or 9 months. The disagreement is only about an 8 months' child which does not have hair and fingernails. The Babli agrees.

הִכָּה אֶת זֶה וְחָזַר וְהִכָּה אֶת זֶה. קִילֵּל אֶת זֶה וְחָזַר וְקִילֵּל אֶת זֶה פָּטוּר. רִבִּי חֲנַנְיָה בָּעֵי. לֵית הָדָא פְלִיגָא עַל רִבִּי יוֹחָנָן. דְּאִיתְפַּלְּגוֹן בִּשְׁנֵי יָמִים טוֹבִים שֶׁלַּגָּלִיּוֹת. רִבִּי יוֹחָנָן אָמַר. מְקַבְּלִין הַתְרָייָה עַל הַסָּפֵק. רִבִּי שִׁמְעוֹן בֶּן לָקִישׁ אָמַר. אֵין מְקַבְּלִין הַתְרָייָה עַל הַסָּפֵק. אָמַר רִבִּי חֲנִינָא אָמַר רִבִּי. לֵית הִיא פְלִיגָא. תַּמָּן אִיפְשַׁר לָךְ לַעֲמוֹד עָלָיו. בְּרַם הָכָא אִי אֶיפְשַׁר לָךְ לַעֲמוֹד עָלָיו.

"If he injured one and then injured the other, or cursed one and then cursed the other, he cannot be prosecuted."[170] Rebbi Ḥanania asked, does that not disagree with Rebbi Joḥanan? Since they disagree about the second day of holidays in the diaspora. Rebbi Joḥanan said, one accepts forwarning in a case of doubt, Rebbi Simeon ben Laqish said, one does not accept forwarning in a case of doubt[171]. Rebbi Ḥanina said in the name of Rebbi, there is no disagreement. There, it would have been possible to make a determination, here it is impossible to make the determination.

170 Tosephta 12 7; Babli 101a, *Makkot* 16a, *Ḥulin* 82b, 91a.

171 The argument is presented in detail in *Pesaḥim* 5:4 (fol. 32c), *Nazir* 8:1 (fol. 57a); derived from the point of view of R. Jehudah in Babli *Makkot* 16a.

הִכָּה שְׁנֵיהֶן כְּאַחַת קִיקֵּל שְׁנֵיהֶן כְּאַחַת חַיָּיב. רִבִּי יְהוּדָה פּוֹטֵר. רִבִּי יוֹחָנָן בָּעֵי. מִחְלְפָה שִׁיטָּתֵיהּ דְּרִבִּי יוּדָה. דְּתְנָן תַּמָּן. אָכַל מִזֶּה כְּזַיִת וּמִזֶּה כְּזַיִת סוֹפֵג שְׁמוֹנִים. רִבִּי יוּדָה אָמַר. אֵינוֹ סוֹפֵג אֶלָּא אַרְבָּעִים. אָמַר רִבִּי קְרוּסְפִּי. אֵינָהּ מוּחְלֶפֶת. תַּמָּן עִיקַּר לָאוִין סָפֵק הָיָה. בְּרַם הָכָא וַדַּאי הָיָה וְנִסְתַּפֵּק לוֹ. רִבִּי יוּדָה בָּעֵי. מֵעַתָּה נְבֵילָה שֶׁבִּיטְלָהּ בִּשְׁחִיטָה. מֵאַחַר שֶׁוַּדַּאי הָיָה וְנִסְתַּפֵּק לוֹ אָכַל מִמֶּנָּה יְהֵא פָּטוּר. אָמַר רִבִּי יוֹסֵי. מוֹדֶה רִבִּי יוּדָה בִּשְׁאָר כָּל־הַסְּפֵיקוֹת שֶׁהוּא פָּטוּר. בְּרַם הָכָא קִרְיֵי דָרַשׁ. אָבִיו וַדַּאי וְלֹא סָפֵק. אִמּוֹ וַדַּאי וְלֹא סָפֵק.

"If he injured both of them at the same time or cursed them at the same time, he is guilty. Rebbi Jehudah frees him."[172] Rebbi Joḥanan asked: Is not the argument of Rebbi Jehudah inverted? As we have stated there: [173]"If he ate the volume of an olive of one of them and the volume of an olive of the other, he absorbs eighty [lashes]; Rebbi Jehudah says, he absorbs only forty [lashes]." Rebbi Crispus said, it is not inverted. There, it was in doubt what is forbidden. Here, it was certain[174] but it became doubtful for him. Rebbi Judan asked: If it is so, in case carcass meat was mixed up with slaughtered meat, since it was certain but became doubtful for him, should he be free if he ate it[175]? Rebbi Yose said, Rebbi

Jehudah agrees for all other prohibitions that he is (free)[176]. But here, he is interpreting verses: "His father," certain but not uncertain, "his mother", certain but not uncertain[177].

172 In the Babylonian tradition, the position of R. Jehudah is uncertain; cf. Tosephta 12:7, readings of Erfurt ms. and *editio princeps*, and Babli 101a.

173 Mishnah *Ḥulin* 7:3, speaking of the sinew of the hip which is forbidden as food (*Gen.* 32:33). He ate from both sides but did not know which piece was from what side. For the majority it makes no difference since the sinews on both sides are forbidden. For R. Jehudah, the singular used in the verse, "the sinew of the hip" implies that only one is forbidden; in the opinion of the Babli this must be the one on the right hand side. The Yerushalmi must hold that R. Jehudah holds that clearly one of the two sinews is forbidden but it is not decided which one it is. R. Jehudah holds that since he certainly ate a piece of the forbidden sinew, he is guilty. Then the question is why should the eater be prosecutable when the prosecution could not show which piece was the forbidden one?

174 If his mother had waited the prescribed three months, there never would have been any problem.

175 Would R. Jehudah hold that a person who ate all of a portion of meat, of which it was known that it contained both kosher and non-kosher meat, could not be held responsible and would not have to bring a purification sacrifice?

176 One has to read "guilty". The text here is an erroneous copy from Halakhah 1 (Note 61).

177 *Sifra Qedošim Pereq* 9(8), on *Lev.* 20:9.

וְעוֹלֶה בְּמִשְׁמָרוֹ שֶׁלָּזֶה וְשֶׁלָּזֶה. לֹא יַעֲלֶה. רִבִּי אָחָא רִבִּי חִינְנָא בְּשֵׁם רִבִּי יָסָא. מִפְּנֵי פְּגַם מִשְׁפָּחָה.

"He may serve in the watch of either one". He should not serve[178]. Rebbi Aḥa, Rebbi Ḥinena in the name of Rebbi Yasa, because of the damage to the family[179].

178 Why cannot each watch tell him that he does not belong?

179 If it were known that a certain Cohen was not accepted for service in the Temple, nobody would marry any daughter of that family.

תַּנֵּי. וְהֵן שֶׁיְּהוּ שְׁנֵיהֶן בֵּית אַב אֶחָד.

It was stated: Only if they both belong to the same clan[180].

180 This refers to the last statement in the Mishnah, that the son may receive part of the sacrifices if both putative fathers belonged to the same watch. Since each watch was divided into six clans of which one each was serving one day and received all the gifts of that day, he may receive a share only if the fathers belonged to the same clan. Only on the Sabbath they all served together but received no gifts.

The Babli, 101a, agrees to this ruling.

מצות חליצה פרק שנים עשר

(fol. 12b) **משנה א:** מִצְוַת חֲלִיצָה בִשְׁלֹשָׁה דַייָנִים וַאֲפִילוּ שְׁלָשְׁתָּן הֶדְיוֹטוֹת. חָלְצָה בְמַנְעָל חֲלִיצָתָהּ כְּשֵׁרָה בְּאִמְפִּילְיָא חֲלִיצָתָהּ פְּסוּלָה. בְּסַנְדָּל שֶׁיֵּשׁ לוֹ עָקֵב כָּשֵׁר וְשֶׁאֵין לוֹ עָקֵב פָּסוּל. מִן הָאַרְכּוּבָּה וּלְמַטָּה חֲלִיצָתָהּ כְּשֵׁרָה מִן הָאַרְכּוּבָּה וּלְמַעְלָה חֲלִיצָתָהּ פְּסוּלָה.

Mishnah 1: The commandment of *ḥalîṣah* is to be executed before three judges; all three may be lay people[1]. If she performed *ḥalîṣah* with a shoe[2], the *ḥalîṣah* is valid, with a felt slipper[3] it is invalid. With a sandal[4] having a heel it is valid, without a heel it is invalid. Below the knee the *ḥalîṣah* is valid[5], above the knee it is invalid.

1 The procedure has to be executed in front of the town elders (*Deut*. 25:7); this implies that it must be in a judicial setting. Usually, the word "elders" in the Pentateuch is interpreted as "professional judges"; the admissibility of lay judges has to be justified in the Halakhah.

2 Defined as leather shoe or boot enclosing the entire foot, sown together from several pieces of leather, some of it soft, and kept in place by leather shoelaces.

3 Latin *impilia, ium*, (plur.), "felt shoes".

4 Made of a single piece of hard leather covering the sole and some of the sides of the foot, held together with shoe laces fastened tightly over the foot.

Greek σάνδαλον, τό. The word might have been imported with the article from farther East.

5 In the Halakhah the reference is to the way the shoelaces are wound around the leg. The straps may be wound around the lower leg but not around the thigh. The Babli (103a) refers this part of the Mishnah to amputees.

הלכה א: מִצְוַת חֲלִיצָה בִּשְׁלֹשָׁה דַיָּנִים כול׳. כְּתִיב זְקֵינִים וְאַתְּ אָמַר הֶדְיוֹטוֹת. מִצְוָה בִזְקֵינִים. מְנַיִין אֲפִילוּ הֶדְיוֹטוֹת. תַּלְמוּד לוֹמַר חֲלוּץ הַנָּעַל מִכָּל־מָקוֹם.

Halakhah 1: "The commandment of *ḥalîṣah* is to be executed before three judges," etc. It is written "elders", and you say laymen? The commandment is on the elders. From where that even laymen [are acceptable]? The verse says, "stripped of shoe"[6], in any case.

6 *Deut.* 25:10. It seems that the argument refers to the entire verse, "His house shall be known *in Israel* as the house of the stripped of shoe." Any three in Israel may make the fact known. (*Sifry Deut.* 291 may be interpreted as prohibiting a lay person to preside.) The quote from *Deut.* is an introduction to the next paragraph.

The language "the commandment is on the elders" should imply that levirate not before judges is improper but valid; cf. *Midrash Tannaïm* 25:8.

אִית תַּנָּיֵי תַנֵּי. חֲלִיצָה בְגֵרִים כְּשֵׁירָה. וְאִית תַּנָּיֵי תַנֵּי. חֲלִיצָה בְגֵרִים פְּסוּלָה. מָאן דְּאָמַר. חֲלִיצָה בְגֵרִים כְּשֵׁירָה. כְּמָאן דְּאָמַר. בְּיִשְׂרָאֵל לְרַבּוֹת אֶת הַגֵּרִים. מָאן דְּאָמַר. חֲלִיצָה בְגֵרִים פְּסוּלָה. כְּמָאן דְּאָמַר. בְּיִשְׂרָאֵל פְּרָט לַגֵּרִים.

There are Tannaim who state that *ḥalîṣah* in front of converts is valid. And there are Tannaim who state that *ḥalîṣah* in front of converts is invalid[7]. He who says that *ḥalîṣah* in front of converts is valid follows him who says "in Israel[8]" to include converts. He who says that *ḥalîṣah* in front of converts is invalid follows him who says "in Israel" to exclude converts.

7 In *Sifry Deut.* 291 and the Babli, 101b (an Amoraic *baraita*), the reference is to a court composed only of converts. There is no proof that this is also the position of the Yerushalmi.

8 There is no record of such a *baraita* in the parallel texts. In the Babli, those who admit a court composed of converts simply note that *Deut.* 25:10 may be given another

meaning. It is somewhat difficult to accept the validity of a court of converts who themselves are not under the rules of levirate (Mishnah 11:2).

הָכָא אַתְּ אוֹמֵר. פְּרָט לַגֵּרִים. וְהָכָא אַתְּ אוֹמֵר. לְרַבּוֹת אֶת הַגֵּרִים. תַּמָּן הָאֶזְרָח פְּרָט לַגֵּירִים. בְּיִשְׂרָאֵל פְּרָט לַגֵּרִים. מִיעוּט אַחַר מִיעוּט לְרַבּוֹת אֶת הַגֵּרִים. בְּרַם הָכָא בְּיִשְׂרָאֵל לֹא גֵרִים.

Here, you say, to exclude converts. But there[9], you say, to include converts. There, "the citizen" to exclude converts, "in Israel" to exclude converts; an exclusion after an exclusion[10] to include converts. But here, "in Israel", not converts.

9 *Lev.* 23:42. "Every citizen in Israel has to dwell in huts."

10 That an exclusion after an exclusion implies an inclusion is a fundamental principle of R. Akiba's hermeneutics accepted in both Talmudim; cf. *Peah* Chapter 6, Note 154. For this particular example, cf. Babli *Sukkah* 28b; a more complicated argument, taking note of the inclusive "every", in *Sifra Emor Pereq* 17(9).

אִית תַּנָּיֵי תַנֵּי. חֲלִיצָה בִשְׁנַיִם פְּסוּלָה. וְאִית תַּנָּיֵי תַנֵּי. חֲלִיצָה בִשְׁנַיִם כְּשֵׁירָה. מָאן דְּאָמַר. חֲלִיצָה בִשְׁנַיִם פְּסוּלָה. כְּמָאן דָּמַר. חֲלִיצָה בְגֵרִים פְּסוּלָה. מָאן דָּמַר. חֲלִיצָה בִשְׁנַיִם כְּשֵׁירָה. כְּמָאן דָּמַר. חֲלִיצָה בְגֵרִים כְּשֵׁירָה. אֲפִילוּ כְּמָאן דָּמַר. חֲלִיצָה בְגֵרִים כְּשֵׁירָה מוֹדֵיי בִשְׁנַיִם (fol. 12c) שֶׁהִיא פְסוּלָה. שֶׁהֲרֵי דִינֵי מָמוֹנוֹת כְּשֵׁירָה בְגֵירִים וּפְסוּלִין בִּשְׁנַיִם.

There are Tannaim who state that *ḥalîṣah* in the presence of two men is invalid; there are Tannaim who state that *ḥalîṣah* in the presence of two men is valid. Does he who says, *ḥalîṣah* in the presence of two men is invalid, hold that *ḥalîṣah* in front of converts is invalid, and he who says, *ḥalîṣah* in the presence of two men is valid, hold that *ḥalîṣah* in front of converts is valid? Even he who holds that *ḥalîṣah* in front of converts is valid will agree that in the presence of two men it is invalid since judgments in civil matters are valid from converts but invalid from two [judges][11].

11 This is the position of the Yerushalmi, cf. *Sanhedrin* 1:1. The Babli *(Sanhedrin* 3a) follows Samuel in accepting judgments from a court of two; but such a court is called "insolent".

אִית תַּנָּיֵי תַנֵּי. חֲלִיצָה בַּלַּיְלָה כְשֵׁירָה. וְאִית תַּנָּיֵי תַנֵּי. חֲלִיצָה בַּלַּיְלָה פְּסוּלָה. מָאן דְּאָמַר. חֲלִיצָה בַּלַּיְלָה כְּשֵׁירָה. כְּמָאן דָּמַר. חֲלִיצָה בְגֵרִים כְּשֵׁירָה. מָאן דָּמַר. חֲלִיצָה בַּלַּיְלָה פְּסוּלָה. כְּמָאן דָּמַר. חֲלִיצָה בְגֵרִים פְּסוּלָה. אֲפִילוּ כְּמָאן דָּמַר. חֲלִיצָה בְגֵרִים כְּשֵׁירָה. מוֹדֵיי בַּלַּיְלָה שֶׁהִיא פְסוּלָה. שֶׁהֲרֵי דִינֵי מָמוֹנוֹת כְּשֵׁירִין בְּגֵירִים וּפְסוּלִיי בַּלַּיְלָה.

There are Tannaim who state that *ḥalîṣah* in the night is valid[12]; there are Tannaim who state that *ḥalîṣah* in the presence of two men is invalid. Does he who says, *ḥalîṣah* in the night is valid, hold that *ḥalîṣah* in front of converts is valid, and he who says, *ḥalîṣah* in the night is invalid, hold that *ḥalîṣah* in front of converts is invalid? Even he who holds that *ḥalîṣah* in front of converts is valid will agree that in the night it is invalid since judgments in civil matters are valid from converts but invalid in the night[13].

12 Mishnah 12:2. The Tosephta (12:9) reports that R. Ismael presided over an emergency *ḥalîṣah* as sole judge, in the night.

13 Mishnah *Sanhedrin* 4:6 states that civil proceedings have to start during daytime but may be concluded in the night. The Yerushalmi (*Sanhedrin* Halakhah 4:6) holds that this is only a desideratum but that civil suits may be adjudicated any time since it says (*Ex.* 18:26) "they have to judge for the people at all times."

אית תַּנָּיֵי תַנֵּי. וְהֵן שֶׁיְּהוּ הַדַּייָנִים יוֹדְעִין לַקְרוֹת. אית תַּנָּיֵי תַנֵּי. אֲפִילוּ אֵין הַדַּייָנִים יוֹדְעִין לַקְרוֹת. מָאן דְּאָמַר. וְהֵן שֶׁיְּהוּ הַדַּייָנִים יוֹדְעִין לַקְרוֹת. עַד שֶׁלֹּא סָמְכוּהוּ לַמִּקְרָא. וּמָאן דְּאָמַר. אֲפִילוּ אֵין הַדַּייָנִים יוֹדְעִין לַקְרוֹת. מִשֶּׁסָּמְכוּהוּ לַמִּקְרָא. וְעָנְתָה וְאָמְרָה. אֵין עוֹנָה אֶלָּא מִפִּי אֶחָד. אָמַר רִבִּי יוֹסֵי. וּבִלְבַד מִפִּי הַדַּיָּין. וְלָא עָבְדִין כֵּן.

Some Tannaim state, only if the judges know how to instruct what to say[14]. Some Tannaim stated, even if the judges do not know how to instruct what to say. He who said, only if the judges know how to instruct what to say, before they found a hint in Scripture, but he who said, even if the judges do not know how to instruct what to say, after they found a hint in Scripture[15]: "You shall answer and say;" one answers only to a single person. Rebbi Yose said, and only from the mouth of the judge, but one does not follow this.

14 Tosephta 12:9. In the Babli, 101a: Only if they know how to instruct as a judge would do. לקרות is short for להקראת.

15 The hint that only one of the people present has to instruct the participants what to say since their recitation is called "answering". Cf. *Bikkurim*, Chapter 3, Note 83.

חָלְצָה בְמַנְעָל חֲלִיצָתָהּ כְּשֵׁירָה. לְמִי נִצְרְכָה. לְרִבִּי מֵאִיר. וְרִבִּי מֵאִיר אָמַר. אֵין חוֹלְצִין בְּמִנְעָל. תַּנֵּי. אָמַר רִבִּי יוֹסֵי. מַעֲשֶׂה שֶׁהָלַכְתִּי לִנְצִיבִין וְרָאִיתִי שָׁם זָקֵן אֶחָד וְנַמְתִּי לוֹ. בָּקִי לָךְ רִבִּי יְהוּדָה בֶּן בְּתֵירָה מִיָּמֶיךָ. וְנוֹמֶה לִי. שׁוּלְחָנִי הָיִיתִי בְּעִירִי וְעַל שׁוּלְחָנִי הָיָה תָדִיר. וְנַמְתִּי לוֹ. רְאִיתוֹ חוֹלֵץ בְּיָמֶיךָ. בְּמָה הָיָה חוֹלֵץ. בְּמַנְעָל אוֹ בְסַנְדָּל. אָמַר לִי. רִבִּי. וְכִי יֵשׁ סַנְדָּל בִּמְקוֹמֵינוּ. וְאָמַרְתִּי. מָה רָאָה רִבִּי מֵאִיר לוֹמַר. אֵין חוֹלְצִין בְּמַנְעָל.

"If she performed *ḥalîṣah* with a shoe, the *ḥalîṣah* is valid." For whom is this statement needed? For Rebbi Meïr, since Rebbi Meïr said, one does not perform *ḥalîṣah* with a shoe. It was stated[16]: Rebbi Yose said, it happened that I went to Nsebin[17] and saw there an old man to whom I said, did you ever know Rebbi Jehudah ben Bathyra in your lifetime? He told me, I was a banker in my city and he was a constant customer of my bank. I told him, did you ever see him supervising a *ḥalîṣah* in your lifetime and what he did use for *ḥalîṣah*, a shoe or a sandal? He said to me Rabbi, is there a sandal in our place[18]? I wondered, how could Rebbi Meïr say that one does not perform *ḥalîṣah* with a shoe[19]?

16 In the Babli, 102a, and the Tosephta, 12:11, the story is told to exclude shoes from *ḥalîṣah*.

17 In Greek sources, Nisibis; the important border town between the Roman and Persian Empires, seat of the rabbinic family Bene Bathyra for many generations.

18 From antique statuary and pictures, it seems that the sandal was the usual Roman footwear and the shoe the Persian. The high boot was the Roman military footwear.

19 His position would create places where *ḥalîṣah* is not possible.

רִבִּי בָּא רַב יְהוּדָה בְּשֵׁם רַב. אִם יָבוֹא אֵלִיָּהוּ וְיֹאמַר שֶׁחוֹלְצִין בְּמִנְעָל שׁוֹמְעִים לוֹ. שֶׁאֵין חוֹלְצִין בְּסַנְדָּל אֵין שׁוֹמְעִין לוֹ. שֶׁהֲרֵי הָרַבִּים נָהֲגוּ לַחֲלוֹץ בְּסַנְדָּל. וְהַמִּנְהָג מְבַטֵּל אֶת הַהֲלָכָה. רִבִּי זְעִירָה רִבִּי יִרְמְיָה בְּשֵׁם רַב. אִם יָבוֹא אֵלִיָּהוּ וְיֹאמַר שֶׁאֵין חוֹלְצִין בְּמִנְעָל שׁוֹמְעִים לוֹ. שֶׁאֵין חוֹלְצִין בְּסַנְדָּל אֵין שׁוֹמְעִין לוֹ. שֶׁהֲרֵי הָרַבִּים נָהֲגוּ לִהְיוֹת חוֹלְצִין בְּסַנְדָּל. וְהַמִּנְהָג מְבַטֵּל אֶת הַהֲלָכָה.

Rebbi Abba, Rav Jehudah in the name of Rav[20]: If Elijah[21] came and said that one performs *ḥalîṣah* with a shoe, one would listen to him; that one does not perform *ḥalîṣah* with a sandal, one would not listen to him since most people use a sandal for *ḥalîṣah* and usage supersedes practice. Rebbi Ze'ira, Rav[22] Jeremiah, in the name of Rav: If Elijah came and said that one does not perform *ḥalîṣah* with a shoe, one would listen to him; that one does not perform *ḥalîṣah* with a sandal, one would not listen to him since most people use a sandal for *ḥalîṣah* and usage supersedes practice.

20 In the Babli, 102a, the opinion of R. Abba is quoted in the name of Rabba (Rav Abba bar Naḥmani), that of R. Ze'ira in the name of Rav Yosef. The Babli explains that in the opinion of Rabba, one uses a shoe only if one does not have a sandal whereas in the opinion of Rav Yosef one may use a shoe anytime.

21 He was taken in a fiery chariot to be a member of the Heavenly Court and knows all rules how they should be by Heavenly standards.

22 The title "Rebbi" given in the ms. cannot be correct since R. Jeremiah was the foremost student of R. Ze'ira. The reference is to Rav Jeremiah (bar Abba), the colleague of Rav.

רִבִּי זְעִירָא מְחַוֵּי לְרִבִּי בָּא רִבִּי יִצְחָק כֶּפֶף. אָמַר לֵיהּ. וְעָבְדִין כֵּן. אָמַר לֵיהּ. וְעָבְדִין. אָמַר לֵיהּ. הָא רַבָּן כְּפָף.

Rebbi Ze'ira showed the bending[23] to Rebbi Abba, Rebbi Isaac[24]. He said to him: Does one do this? He said to him, one does. He said to him, did not our teacher[25] bend?

23 The meaning of this paragraph is in doubt. It may either mean that the sandal used for *ḥalîṣah* is not a flat piece of leather but must be bent upwards to enclose heel, toes, and part of the sides of the foot [since the sandal must be "slipped *off* the foot" (*Deut.* 25:9) which cannot be done if the sandal is just a flat piece of leather] or whether he bent to show how *ḥalîṣah* is executed.

24 Most commentators emend to "Rebbi Abba bar Isaac" on base of the next paragraph.

25 Probably R. Joḥanan.

רִבִּי זְעִירָא מְחַוֵּי לְרִבִּי בָּא בַּר יִצְחָק. כֵּיצַד הוּא עוֹשֶׂה. קוֹשְׁרוֹ כְּדֵי שֶׁיְּהֵא יָכוֹל לְהַלֵּךְ בּוֹ מֵאֵילָיו. כֵּיצַד הוּא עוֹשֶׂה. אָמַר רִבִּי חֲנַנְיָה בְּרֵיהּ דְּרִבִּי הִילֵּל. עוֹנְבוֹ כְּדֵי שֶׁיָּכוֹל לְהַתִּירוֹ בְּאַחַת מִיָּדָיו. כֵּיצַד הוּא עוֹשֶׂה. מַתָּרָתָן בְּיָמִין וְתוֹפְסָתָן בִּשְׂמֹאל וְשׁוֹמֶטֶת עֶקֶב בְּיָמִין וְגוֹרְרָתָן בְּיָמִין. כְּדֵי שֶׁתְּהֵא חֲלִיצָה וְהַתָּרָה בְּיָמִין.

Rebbi Ze'ira showed Rebbi Abba bar Isaac how it is done. He binds [the shoelaces] that he can walk unaided. How is it done? Rebbi Ḥanania the son of Rebbi Hillel said, he laces it so that she will be able to untie it with one hand. How is it done? She unties with her right hand, grabs [the shoe] with her left hand, slips it off the heel and drags it away with her right hand, so that the slipping off and the unbinding should be done by the right hand[26].

26 The Babli has no parallel to this paragraph. In *Giṭṭin 24b*, it quotes R. Eleazar to the effect that *ḥalîṣah* not done by the right hand (or in the night) forbids the widow to the levir but must be repeated to free the widow for outside marriage.

רַב אָמַר. עִיקַּר חֲלִיצָה הַתָּרַת הָרְצוּעָה. לֹא כֵן אָמַר רִבִּי בָּא בְּשֵׁם רַב יְהוּדָה רִבִּי זְרִיקָן מָטֵי בָהּ בְּשֵׁם רַב. דִּבְרֵי חֲכָמִים. חָלְצָה וְלֹא רָקְקָה. רָקְקָה וְלֹא חָלְצָה. לֹא עָשָׂה כְלוּם עַד שֶׁתַּחֲלוֹץ וְתָרוֹק. אַף עַל גַּב דְּרַב אָמַר. עַד שֶׁתַּחֲלוֹץ וְתָרוֹק. מוֹדֶה רַב. עִיקַּר חֲלִיצָה הַתָּרַת הָרְצוּעוֹת.

Rav said, the essence of *ḥalîṣah*[27] is the untying of the shoelace. Did not Rebbi Abba say in the name of Rav Jehudah, Rebbi Zeriqan turns to it in the name of Rav: The words of the Sages: If she slips off but did not spit, or spat but did not take off, nothing was done unless she slips off and spits[28]. Even though Rav said "unless she slips off and spits" he agrees that the essence of slipping off is untying the shoelaces.

27 As the paragraph shows, this needs a semantic clarification since up to now, the word *ḥalîṣah* designated the entire ceremony by which the widow is freed to marry outside the family. But here, the word designates the action by which the sister-in-law slips the levir's shoe off his foot, which must be followed by her spitting in front of the levir (*Deut.* 25:9). Rav insists that the widow's action is invalid if it does not start with untying the shoelaces.

In the Babli, 102a, Rav insists that

the deciding act is slipping the shoe off the levir's heel.

28 Cf. Mishnah 3.

רַב אָמַר. עִיקַּר חֲזָקָה הַכְנָסַת פֵּירוֹת. לֹא כֵן אָמַר רַב. וְהֵן שֶׁרָאוּ אוֹתוֹ מְנַכֵּשׁ וּמְעַדֵּר. אַף עַל גַּב דְּאָמַר רַב. וְהֵן שֶׁרָאוּ אוֹתוֹ מְנַכֵּשׁ וּמְעַדֵּר. מוֹדֶה רַב. עִיקַּר חֲזָקָה הַכְנָסַת פֵּירוֹת.

Rav said, the main point in acquiring squatters' rights is the bringing in of the yield. Did not Rav say, only if one saw him hoeing and weeding? Even though Rav said, only if one saw him hoeing and weeding, Rav agrees that the main point in acquiring squatters' rights is the bringing in of the yield.

29 In a society in which claims to real estate do not have to be proven exclusively by documents, undisturbed possession for a number of years (in the Talmudim, three full years) counts as proof of ownership when accompanied by a claim of acquisition (by buying, inheriting, or receiving as gift). It is specified here that a claim to agricultural land is valid only if it is supported by testimony that the presumed owner harvested the yield and used it for himself. The importance of this is not diminished by the additional requirement that the claimant also must have been seen tending the field.

The same statement is in *Baba Batra* 3:3. The paragraph is inserted here because of its form which parallels the preceding paragraph.

אָמַר רִבִּי יַנַּאי. חָלַץ הוּא וְהֶחֱזִירָה הִיא. חָלְצָה הִיא וְהִתִּירָהּ הוּא. חֲלִיצָתָהּ פְּסוּלָה. אִם רָצָא לְהַחֲזִיר לֹא יַחֲזִיר. לָמָּה. מִשּׁוּם שֶׁאֵין שְׁתֵּיהֶן בָּהּ אוֹ מִשּׁוּם שֶׁאֵינָן עַל סֵדֶר. מַה נְפַק מִן בֵּינֵיהוֹן. חָזְרָה וְהִתִּירָה. תֹּאמַר מִשּׁוּם שֶׁאֵין שְׁתֵּיהֶן בָּהּ. הֲרֵי שְׁתֵּיהֶן בָּהּ. הֲרֵי לֵית טַעֲמָא דְלֹא מִשּׁוּם שֶׁאֵינָן עַל הַסֵּדֶר.

Rebbi Yannai said, if he took off [his shoe] and she put it on again, or she took it off but he had untied, the *ḥalîṣah* is invalid and if he wants to go back, he may not go back on it[30]. Why? Is it since the two actions are not there together or because they are not in the right order? What is the difference? If she afterwards untied [the shoestrings]. If you say, because the two actions are not there together? They are there together! The reason therefore must be that they are not in the right order.

30 It is not clear what "going back" means. It may mean that if the levir changes his mind after the invalid *ḥalîṣah* and wants to marry the widow that he is barred from doing so; or it may mean that the entire ceremony has to be cancelled and everything started anew. The next paragraphs seem to indicate that the first interpretation is the correct one.

In the Babli, 102 a, the statement of R. Yannai is quoted without the last clause and the extent of the damage by invalid *ḥalîṣah* is not discussed.

אָמַר רִבִּי לָעְזָר. יֵשׁ מֵהֶן שֶׁאָמְרוּ. חֲלִיצָתָהּ פְּסוּלָה וְאִם רָצָא לְהַחֲזִיר יַחֲזִיר. וְיֵשׁ מֵהֶן שֶׁאָמְרוּ. חֲלִיצָתָהּ כְּשֵׁירָה וְאִם רָצָא לְהַחֲזִיר לֹא יַחֲזִיר. בְּאִמְפִּילְיָא וְהַחוֹלְצָה לְקָטָן חֲלִיצָתָהּ פְּסוּלָה. וְאִם רָצָא לְהַחֲזִיר לֹא יַחֲזִיר. חָלְצָה בְּאִמְפִּילְיָא. אִית תַּנָּיֵי תַנֵּי. חֲלִיצָתָהּ כְּשֵׁירָה. אִית תַּנָּיֵי תַנֵּי. חֲלִיצָתָהּ פְּסוּלָה. מָאן דְּאָמַר. חֲלִיצָתָהּ כְּשֵׁירָה. בְּאִמְפִּילְיָא שֶׁלָּעוֹר. מָאן דְּאָמַר. חֲלִיצָתָהּ פְּסוּלָה. בְּאִמְפִּילְיָא שֶׁלַּבֶּגֶד. בְּמַנְעָל בְּאִמְפִּילְיָא. אִית תַּנָּיֵי תַנֵּי. חֲלִיצָתָהּ כְּשֵׁירָה. אִית תַּנָּיֵי תַנֵּי. חֲלִיצָתָהּ פְּסוּלָה. מָאן דְּאָמַר. חֲלִיצָתָהּ כְּשֵׁירָה. כְּשֶׁהָיְתָה בְּאִמְפִּילְיָא שֶׁלַּבֶּגֶד וּמַנְעָל שֶׁלָּעוֹר. מָאן דְּאָמַר. חֲלִיצָתָהּ פְּסוּלָה. כְּשֶׁהָיְתָה אִנְפִּילְיָא שֶׁלָּעוֹר וּמַנְעָל שֶׁלַּבֶּגֶד. אִית תַּנָּיֵי תַנֵּי. יוֹצְאִין בְּאִמְפִּילְיָא בְּיוֹם הַכִּיפּוּרִים. וְאִית תַּנָּיֵי תַנֵּי. אֵין יוֹצְאִין בְּאִמְפִּילְיָא. אָמַר רַב חִסְדָּא. מָאן דְּאָמַר. יוֹצְאִין. בְּאִמְפִּילְיָא שֶׁלַּבֶּגֶד. וּמָאן דְּאָמַר. אֵין יוֹצְאִין. בְּאִמְפִּילְיָא שֶׁלָּעוֹר.

Rebbi Eleazar said, in some cases[31]they said that her *ḥalîṣah* is invalid and if he wants to go back he may go back. And in some cases they said that her *ḥalîṣah* is valid and if he wants to go back he may not go back. [If a woman] performed *ḥalîṣah* with felt slippers or for an underage boy, her *ḥalîṣah* is invalid and if he wants to go back he cannot go back. If she performed *ḥalîṣah* with a slipper, some Tannaim state that the *ḥalîṣah* is valid and some Tannaim state that the *ḥalîṣah* is invalid. He who says that the *ḥalîṣah* is valid, with a leather slipper; he who says that the *ḥalîṣah* is invalid, with a textile slipper[32]. A shoe in a slipper[33], some Tannaim state that the *ḥalîṣah* is valid and some Tannaim state that the *ḥalîṣah* is invalid. For him who holds that the *ḥalîṣah* is valid, the slipper is textile but the shoe leather[34]. For him who holds that the *ḥalîṣah* is invalid, the slipper is leather but the shoe textile. Some Tannaim state that one may wear a slipper of the Day of Atonement[35] and some Tannaim state that one may not wear a slipper. Rav Ḥisda said, For him who holds that one leaves the house [wearing a slipper,] a textile slipper, he who says that one may not leave the house [wearing a slipper,] a leather slipper.

31 The Babli, *Giṭṭin* 24b, states that in the cases discussed here, the valid *ḥalîṣah* implies the prohibition of the widow to the levir and the invalid *ḥalîṣah* is a nonexisting *ḥalîṣah* which does not preclude the possibility of levirate marriage.

32 Babli 102b, a statement of Rava (cf. Chapter 1, Note 21).

33 This case does not appear in the Babli.

34 The leather shoe with which the levir stands on the ground is removed from his heel.

35 Babli 102b, Yerushalmi *Yoma* 8:1 (fol. 44d), *Ta'aniot* 1:6 (fol. 64c). It is held that wearing a textile slipper outside the house does not protect the foot from feeling the stones on the road and therefore does not violate the sanctity of the Day of Atonement as a day of deprivation.

בְּסַנְדָּל שֶׁיֵּשׁ לוֹ עָקֵב כָּשֵׁר. תַּמָּן אָמְרִין. כְּגוֹן אִילֵּין קנסורס. וְרַבָּנָן דְּהָכָא אָמְרֵי. כְּגוֹן אִילֵּין דִּידָן. אָמַר רַב. אִילוּלֵי דְחָמִיי רִבִּי חִייָה רוֹבָא חֲבִיבִי חָלַץ בְּהָדֵין שׁוּרְצִיפָּא דְּשַׁנְצוֹי לָא הֲוָה לִבָּן רָב עֲלֵיהֶן לְמֵיעֲבַד כֵּן. אָחוֹי דְּאִימֵּיהּ דְּרַב כַּהֲנָא חָלַץ בַּלַּיְלָה בְּיָחִיד בְּלֵילֵי שַׁבָּת בְּסַנְדָּל שֶׁלַּשַּׁעַם וּמֵיעוֹמֵד. אָמַר רִבִּי זְרִיקָא. וְלֹא רֶקְקָה. שָׁמַע רַב וְאָמַר. מָאן יַעֲבֵד דָּא אֶלָּא אָחוֹי דְּאִימֵּיהּ דְּרַב כַּהֲנָא.

"With a sandal having a heel it is valid." There, they say, for example those קנסרוס[36]. But the rabbis here say, like ours[37]. Rav said. if I had not seen my uncle, the elder Rebbi Ḥiyya, performing[38] a *ḥalîṣah* with a sandal with plaited straps[39], I would not feel competent to do so. The maternal uncle of Rav Cahana performed[38] *ḥalîṣah* in the night, as single judge, on Friday night, with a cork sandal, and standing; (Rabbi Zeriqa said) and she did not spit. Rav heard that and said, who would ever do that[40] except the maternal uncle of Rav Cahana?

36 A kind of sandal. There is no convincing identification of this word either in Persian or in a Western language. The best so far is I. Löw's Greek κόθορνος, Latin *cothurnus*, "hunting boot laced up in front; high Grecian boot, high shoe worn by actors" for which the first meaning is appropriate here. (Löw credits an author A. Löwinger; I have been unable to find a first reference.) D. Sperber (Sinai 82, 1977/78, p. 168) refers to Latin *cursorius* "belonging to running".

37 The common Roman sandals.

38 I. e., supervising.

39 In the Babli, 102a, סנדל דאית ליה שינצין. The word שורציפא is Semitic, from Syriac רצפא "sandal (to walk on a stone floor)".

40 Every single step being questionable. Since Rav Cahana I was a contemporary of Rav, his uncle belonged to the pre-Amoraic Babylonian scholars. In the Babli, 104a, he is called Rabba bar Ḥiyya from Qaṭosap.

כֵּינִי מַתְנִיתָא. בְּקוֹשֶׁר מִן הָאַרְכּוּבָּה וּלְמַטָּן כְּשֵׁירָה. מִן הָאַרְכּוּבָּה וּלְמַעֲלָן פְּסוּלָה. כְּתִיב וְרָחֲצוּ אַהֲרֹן וּבָנָיו מִמֶּנּוּ אֶת יְדֵיהֶם וְאֶת רַגְלֵיהֶם. וְתַנֵּי עֲלָהּ. בְּיָד עַד הַפֶּרֶק וּבְרֶגֶל עַד הַסּוֹבֶךְ. וְהָכָא אַתְּ אָמַר הָכֵין. שַׁנְיָיא הִיא דִּכְתִיב מֵעַל רַגְלוֹ. מֵעַתָּה אֲפִילוּ מִן הָאַרְכּוּבָּה וּלְמַעֲלָן תְּהֵא כְשֵׁירָה. שַׁנְיָיא הִיא דִּכְתִיב מֵעַל רַגְלוֹ. מֵעַל רַגְלוֹ וְלֹא מִמֵּעַל דִּמְעַל רַגְלוֹ. הָתִיב כַּהֲנָא. וְהָא כְתִיב וּבְשִׁלְיָתָהּ הַיּוֹצֵאת מִבֵּין רַגְלֶיהָ. וְכִי מִבֵּין רַגְלֶיהָ הִיא יוֹצֵאת. אֶלָּא נִרְאֵית כְּמִבֵּין רַגְלֶיהָ. כְּהַהִיא דְתַנִּינָן תַּמָּן. כִּיּוֹר הוּא בֵין הָאוּלָם וְלַמִּזְבֵּחַ וּמָשׁוּךְ כְּלַפֵּי דָרוֹם. וְכִי מִבֵּין הָאוּלָם וְלַמִּזְבֵּחַ הָיָה נָתוּן. אֶלָּא נִרְאֶה כְּבֵין הָאוּלָם וְלַמִּזְבֵּחַ.

So is the Mishnah: "If he ties[41] lower than the knee, it is valid, above the knee it is invalid." It is written: "Aaron and his sons shall wash their hands and feet from it[42]." It was stated about this: The hand up to the wrist, the foot up to the calf; and here you say so[43]? There is a difference, since it is written "from above his foot". In that case, even higher than the knee should be valid! There is a difference, since it is written "from above his foot", and not from higher than above his foot[44]. Cahana objected: Is it not written, "and the afterbirth which comes out from between her feet[45];" does it come out from between her feet? It looks as if it was between her feet; as we have stated there: "The water pit was between the Temple hall and the alter drawn towards the South.[46]" Was it put between the hall and the altar? Only it looked as if between hall and altar.

41 The shoelaces.

42 *Ex.* 30:19.

43 The "foot" of the priests refers only to the calf (in another interpretation to the shinbone) but not to the knee, but for the widow it extends up to the knee!

44 The Babli agrees, 103a.

45 *Deut.* 28:57. Usually, one translates "between her legs"; then one also should translate that the widow has to remove the levir's shoe "from his leg" and shoelaces bound above the knee should be permissible. The same question is quoted in the Babli, 103a.

46 Mishnah *Middot* 3:6. It was between the Southern edge of the hall and the altar.

(fol. 12b) **משנה ב:** חָלְצָה בְסַנְדָּל שֶׁאֵינוֹ שֶׁלּוֹ בְסַנְדָּל שֶׁלְּעֵץ אוֹ בְשֶׁלַּשְּׂמֹאל בְּיָמִין חֲלִיצָתָהּ כְּשֵׁרָה. חָלְצָה בְגָדוֹל שֶׁהוּא יָכוֹל לְהַלֵּךְ בּוֹ אוֹ בְקָטָן שֶׁהוּא חוֹפֶה רוֹב רַגְלוֹ חֲלִיצָתָהּ כְּשֵׁרָה. חָלְצָה בַלַּיְלָה חֲלִיצָתָהּ כְּשֵׁירָה. רִבִּי לִיעֶזֶר פּוֹסֵל. בַּשְּׂמֹאל חֲלִיצָתָהּ פְּסוּלָה וְרִבִּי לִיעֶזֶר מַכְשִׁיר.

Mishnah 2: If she performed *ḥalîṣah* with a sandal that was not his[47], with a wooden sandal[48], or with a left [foot sandal] on the right [foot], the *ḥalîṣah* is valid. If she performed *ḥalîṣah* with [a sandal that was] too large but he could walk in it, or one too small which covers most of his foot[49], the *ḥalîṣah* is valid. If she performed *ḥalîṣah* in the night, the *ḥalîṣah* is valid; Rebbi Eliezer declares it invalid. [If she performed *ḥalîṣah*] with her left hand, the *ḥalîṣah* is invalid but Rebbi Eliezer declares it valid.

47 The levir's.

48 For the Babli, a wooden (or cork) core covered by leather. The Yerushalmi notes that these restrictions are Babylonian.

49 The foot sole.

(fol. 12c) **מתניתין**: חָֽלְצָה בְסַנְדָּל שֶׁאֵינוֹ שֶׁלּוֹ כול'. שׁוֹפָר שֶׁלַּעֲבוֹדָה זָרָה וְשֶׁל עִיר הַנִּדַּחַת. רִבִּי לְעָזָר אוֹמֵר. כָּשֵׁר. תַּנֵּי רִבִּי חִייָה. כָּשֵׁר. תַּנֵּי רִבִּי הוֹשַׁעְיָה. פָּסוּל. הַכֹּל מוֹדִין בְּלוּלָב שֶׁהוּא פָּסוּל. מַה בֵין שׁוֹפָר מַה בֵין לוּלָב. אָמַר רִבִּי יוֹסֵי. בְּלוּלָב כְּתִיב וּלְקַחְתֶּם לָכֶם מִשֶּׁלָּכֶם. לֹא מִשֶּׁלְּאִיסּוּרֵי הֲנָייָה. בְּרַם הָכָא יוֹם תְּרוּעָה יִהְיֶה לָכֶם מִכָּל־מָקוֹם. אָמַר רִבִּי לְעָזָר. תַּמָּן בְּגוּפוֹ הוּא יוֹצֵא. בְּרַם הָכָא בְקוֹלוֹ הוּא יוֹצֵא. וְיֵשׁ קוֹל אָסוּר בַּהֲנָאָה. הַכֹּל מוֹדִין בְּסַנְדָּל שֶׁלָּעִיר הַנִּדַּחַת שֶׁהוּא כָּשֵׁר. דִּכְתִיב חֲלוּץ הַנָּעַל. מִכָּל־מָקוֹם. אָמַר רִבִּי מָנָא. כְּמָא דְאַתְּ אָמַר תַּמָּן יוֹם תְּרוּעָה יִהְיֶה לָכֶם. מִכָּל־מָקוֹם. כֵּן אַתְּ אוֹמֵר הָכָא חֲלוּץ הַנָּעַל. מִכָּל־מָקוֹם.

"If she performed *ḥalîṣah* with a sandal that was not his," etc. [50]Rebbi Eleazar says, a ram's horn[51] belonging to idolatry[52] or to a "seduced city"[53] is valid. Rebbi Ḥiyya stated, it is valid. Rebbi Hoshaia stated, it is invalid[54]. Everybody agrees that such a palmbranch is invalid[55]. What is the difference between a ram's horn and a palmbranch? Rebbi Yose said, for a palmbranch it is written: "You shall take for yourselves[56]," from your own money. But here, "a day of horn blowing it shall be for you[57]," from any source. Rebbi Eleazar said, there he fulfills his obligation with the article itself, but here with its sound. Is any sound forbidden usufruct[58]? Everybody agrees that a sandal from a "seduced city" is valid[59]. For it is written "stripped of shoe," from any source. Rebbi Mana said, as you say there, "a day of horn blowing it shall be for you," from any source, so you say here, "stripped of shoe," from any source.

50 A partial copy of this paragraph is in *Sukkah* 3:1. R. Lazar mentioned here is a Tanna.

51 The ram's horn used on New Year's Day.

52 The usufruct of any implements of idolatrous worship is forbidden. The horn is only permitted since Divine Commandments are not for enjoyment or use. The Babli, *Roš Haššanah* 28a, agrees.

53 A city in the Land of Israel that was seduced to embrace idolatry and defected by a communal vote. This city must be burned to the ground (*Deut.* 13:13-19) with all its belongings, of which any usufruct is forbidden; a case that never happened and never will happen (Tosephta *Sanhedrin* 14:1).

The Babli, *Roš Haššanah* 28a, disagrees in this case since a ram's horn in a "seduced city" must be burned and therefore is considered to be ashes even if not burned. Arguments of this kind are absent in the Yerushalmi.

54 In the Babli, property of an idolatrous temple is undesirable, a dedicated gift to an idolatrous temple is prohibited, as is the shoe from a "seduced city"; 103b/104a.

55 Mishnah *Sukkah* 3:1. The palmbranch stands for the three kinds of branches and the fruit that are taken together on the Festival of Booths (*Lev.* 23:40).

56 *Lev.* 23:40.

57 *Num.* 29:1.

58 R. Eleazar the Amora argues that without reference to Scripture it is obvious that palmbranches from idolatrous property are unusable since the essence of the commandment is the acquisition of the branches.

59 In the Babli, the uncontested rule is promulgated that a shoe from a "seduced city" is invalid: 104a. In the opinion of the Yerushalmi, a shoe may be worn as long as it exists; for the Babli the shoe is legally nonexistent as soon as it has been condemned to be burned, cf. Note 53.

סַנְדָּל שֶׁלָּעֵץ. חֲבֵרַיָּא בְּשֵׁם רַב. וְהֵן שֶׁיְּהוּא חוֹבְטִין שֶׁלְּעֵץ. רִבִּי בָּא בְּשֵׁם רַב. וְהֵן שֶׁיְּהוּ מַעֲמִידִין שֶׁלְּעֵץ. (fol. 12d) תַּמָּן אָמְרִין בְּשֵׁם רַב. וְהֵן שֶׁיְּהוּא תְרְסִיּוֹתָיו שֶׁלְּעֵץ. רִבִּי הִילָא בְּשֵׁם רִבִּי יוֹחָנָן. אֲפִילוּ כוּלּוֹ שֶׁלְּעֵץ כָּשֵׁר. מַתְנִיתִין מְסַייְעָא לְרִבִּי יוֹחָנָן. סַנְדָּל שֶׁל קַשׁ טָמֵא מִדְרָס וְהָאִשָּׁה חוֹלֶצֶת בּוֹ. דִּבְרֵי רִבִּי עֲקִיבָה. אֲבָל חֲכָמִים לֹא הוֹדוּ לְמִדְרָס.

"A wooden sandal." The colleagues in the name of Rav: If only the edges[60] are wooden[61]. Rebbi Abba in the name of Rav: If only the bottom of the sole is wooden. There, they say in the name of Rav: If only the loops[62] are wooden. Rebbi Hila in the name of Rebbi Joḥanan: Even if it is entirely of wood it is valid. A *baraita* supports Rebbi Joḥanan: "[63]A straw sandal becomes impure by being stepped on[64] and a woman may use it for *ḥaliṣah*, the words of Rebbi Aqiba, but the Sages do not agree about impurity by being stepped on[65]."

60 Explanation of the Gaonic commentary to *Tahorot*, Mishnah *Miqwa'ot* 10:3, ed. Epstein: Arabic عرى "border, rim, brim".

61 But the remainder of the sandal must be leather.

62 Explanation of *Arukh*; Arabic שראך "loop, net".

63 Tosephta *Kelim Baba Batra* 4:5. There, the addition "about impurity by stepping on it" is missing. In the Babli, *Sabbat* 66a, "a sandal of whitewashers" (who cannot wear leather sandals which would be destroyed by the whitewash).

64 The impurity of the person with gonorrhea is transferred on anything he puts his weight on even if he does not touch it (*Lev.* 15:5,6,26) and even if same material impervious to impurity separates the person from the object. This is called "impurity by being stepped on." Wooden implements that do not enclose any volume ("flat wooden vessels") cannot accept impurity. R. Aqiba does not agree that flat straw sandals are flat wooden vessels.

65 This version implies that the Sages agree that a flat straw sandal may be used for *ḥaliṣah*. The Tosephta, which omits the last clause, follows the Babylonian tradition that a purely wooden sandal is inadmissible.

סַנְדָּל שֶׁנִּפְסְקוּ אָזְנָיו נִפְסְקוּ חֹבְטָיו נִפְסְקוּ תְּרְסִיּוֹתָיו אוֹ שֶׁפֵּירְשָׁה אַחַת מִכַּפָּיו טָהוֹר. נִפְסְקָה אַחַת מֵאָזְנָיו אַחַת מֵחֹבְטָיו אַחַת מִתְּרְסִיּוֹתָיו אוֹ שֶׁפֵּירְשָׁה רוֹב כַּפָּיו טָמֵא. רִבִּי יוּדָה אָמַר. הַפְּנִימִית טְמֵיאָה וְהַחִיצוֹנָה טְהוֹרָה. רִבִּי יַעֲקֹב בַּר אָחָא רִבִּי טֶבֶלַיי חָנִין בַּר בָּא בְשֵׁם רַב. הֲלָכָה כְּרִיבִּי יוּדָה לְעִנְיַין שַׁבָּת. רִבִּי שְׁמוּאֵל בַּר רַב יִצְחָק הֲוָה לֵיהּ עוֹבְדָא. שְׁלַח שָׁאַל לְרִבִּי יַעֲקֹב בַּר אָחָא לְגַבֵּי רִבִּי חִייָה בַּר בָּא. אָמַר לֵיהּ. כְּשֵׁם שֶׁהֵן חוֹלְקִין בְטוּמְאָה כָּךְ הֵן חוֹלְקִין בְּשַׁבָּת. וְהוֹרֵי לֵיהּ כְּרַבָּנָן. רִבִּי שְׁמוּאֵל בַּר רַב יִצְחָק בָּעֵי וּשְׁמַע מֵימַר. (אֵין) הֲלָכָה כְּרִיבִּי יוּדָה. וְהוּא מוֹרֵי לֵיהּ כְּרַבָּנָן. רִבִּי אָחָא בַר יִצְחָק הֲוָה לֵיהּ עוֹבְדָא. שְׁלַח שָׁאַל לְרִבִּי זְעִירָה. וְשָׁאַל רִבִּי זְעִירָה לְרִבִּי אִימִּי. אָמַר לֵיהּ. אִם כְּדִבְרֵי מִי שֶׁהוּא מְטַמֵּא מוּתָּר לָצֵאת בּוֹ. וְאִם כְּדִבְרֵי מִי שֶׁהוּא מְטָהֵר אָסוּר לָצֵאת בּוֹ. וְלָא אַפֵּק גַּבֵּהּ כְּלוּם.

[66]"[67]A sandal whose holes, edges, or loops are torn or one of whose soles fell off is pure. If one of its holes, edges, or loops is torn or most of it soles fell of it is impure. Rebbi Jehudah says, on the inside it is impure, on the outside it is pure.[68]" Rebbi Jacob bar Aḥa, Rebbi Tevele, Ḥanin bar Abba in the name of Rav: Practice follows Rebbi Jehuda as far as the Sabbath is concerned[69]. A case came before Rebbi Samuel bar Rav Isaac. He sent Rebbi Jacob bar Aḥa to ask Rebbi Ḥiyya bar Abba. He[70] said to him, just as they disagree about impurity so they disagree about the Sabbath, and instructed him following the rabbis. Rebbi Samuel bar Rav Isaac asked himself: One heard saying, practice follows Rebbi Jehuda, and he instructed him following the rabbis? A case came before Rebbi Aḥa bar Isaac. He sent to ask Rebbi Ze'ira and Rebbi Ze'ira asked Rebbi Immi. The latter said to him: Following the words of him who declares impure, it is permitted to go out on it on the Sabbath. Following the words of him who declares pure, it is forbidden to go out on it on the Sabbath. He did not get anything out of him[71].

66 This paragraph and the next are from *Sabbath* 4:2. The paragraph is quoted here because it starts with a quote of the continuation of the *baraita* quoted in the preceding paragraph.

67 Tosephta *Kelim Baba Batra* 4:5; Babli *Sabbath* 112a.

68 Ritual impurity is restricted to Jewish persons, food, vessels and tools, and a leprous house. If a vessel or tool was damaged beyond repair, it becomes ritually pure. In this connection, "impure" means "a possible candidate for impurity" and "pure" "unable to become impure." Rebbi Jehudah holds that people will repair even serious damage to their shoes if it can be done so as not to be noticed in public. The rabbis hold that even in such cases, people will not repair severely damaged shoes.

R. Jehudah holds that a person will repair sandals when the repair is not immediately visible from the outside. Therefore, if a strap or hole for the shoelaces is torn at the instep, towards the other foot, the shoe remains usable. The majority holds that one torn strap or a partially torn sole can always be repaired.

69 The same statement in Babli, *Sabbath* 112b.

70 R. Ḥiyya bar Abba, following his teacher R. Joḥanan (in a first version in Babli, *Sabbath* 112b). The Babli holds that this tradition of R. Joḥanan is not trustworthy. It is possible that the Yerushalmi agrees since R. Joḥanan is not mentioned here, but only his students and later Amoraim.

71 He refused to decide between Rav and the Galilean rabbis. Note that all persons mentioned here are Babylonians; those with the title "Rebbi" are immigrants to Galilee.

תַּנֵּי. אֲבָל מְטַייֵּל הוּא בּוֹ עַד שֶׁהוּא מַגִּיעַ לְפֶתַח חֲצֵירוֹ. רִבִּי אָחָא וְרִבִּי זְעִירָא הֲווֹן מְטַייְלִין בְּאִיסְרָטָן. אַפִּיק סַנְדְּלָא דְּרִבִּי אָחָא. מִן דְּמָטוֹן פִּילֵי אָמַר לֵיהּ רִבִּי זְעִירָא. הַהֵן פֶּתַח חֲצֵירָךְ. רִבִּי אָחָא כָּרַךְ סִבְנָה. רִבִּי אַבָּהוּ כָּרַךְ אַגִּיד מלבניקי. סָבַר רִבִּי אַבָּהוּ. אִגּוּד מלבניקי מִן הַמּוּכָן הוּא. רִבִּי יוֹנָה טָלְקָא לַחֲנוּתָא דַחֲלִיטְרָא. וִיקַר אַף צִיבְחָר הֲוָה. סֵדְדָה יְקַר שֶׁלְּרִבִּי לָעְזָר מְסַלֵּק לָהּ. רִבִּי יִרְמְיָה בְּעָא קוֹמֵי רִבִּי זְעִירָא. מַהוּ לְהַחֲלִיף אֲמַר לֵיהּ שָׁרֵי. אֲפִילוּ כָּךְ אֲמַר לֵיהּ. פּוּק חֲמֵי חַד סָב וּסְמַךְ עֲלוֹי. נְפַק וְאַשְׁכַּח רִבִּי בָּא בַּר מָמָל וּשְׁאַל לֵיהּ וְשָׁרָא. אָמַר רִבִּי יוֹסֵי. מַתְנִיתָא אָמְרָה שֶׁהִיא מִן מַלְבּוּשׁ. אוֹ בְשֶׁלִּשְׂמֹאל

בְּיָמִין חֲלִיצָתָהּ כְּשֵׁירָה. הָדָא דְתֵימַר לְרוֹחַב. אֲבָל לְאוֹרֶךְ צָרִיךְ שֶׁיְּהֵא חוֹפֶה אֶת רוֹב הָרֶגֶל.

It was stated: But he may walk on it until he reaches the entrance of his courtyard[72]. Rebbi Aḥa and Rebbi Ze'ira were walking on the highway. The sandal of Rebbi Aḥa was torn. When they came to the city gate, Rebbi Ze'ira told him, that is the entrance of your courtyard[73]. Rebbi Aḥa wound a fiber around. Rebbi Abbahu wound a bundle of Jew's mallow[74]. Rebbi Abbahu was of the opinion that a bundle of Jew's mallow is ready to be used[75]. Rebbi Jonah threw them away before the fried food store[76]. That is little honor. The honor of Rebbi Eleazar obliged him to take it off[77]. Rebbi Jeremiah asked before Rebbi Ze'ira: May one switch[78]? He said to him, it is permitted. Nevertheless, he told him: go and look for an Elder and rely on him. He went out and found Rebbi Abba bar Mamal, asked him, and he permitted. Rebbi Yose said, the Mishnah said that this is clothing[79]: "Or with a left [foot sandal] on the right [foot], the *ḥalîṣah* is valid."

That means, in width. But in length it must cover most of the foot[80].

72 This paragraph deals only with the rules of the Sabbath. Even if a sandal is torn and no longer is a piece of clothing that may be moved on the Sabbath, one may walk on it until one reaches one's courtyard where it can be left and picked up after the Sabbath.

73 As a rabbi, you must be more strict than people in general.

74 Reading with I. Löw מלכניקי, Arabic ملوخيا *"corchorus olitorius"*, a kitchen vegetable, relative of jute. He derives the name from Greek μολόχη "mallow". In the Babli, *Sabbath* 112a, R. Abbahu told R. Jeremiah to use textile fiber to lightly bind around a torn sandal.

75 As raw textile fiber, its use on the Sabbath would be forbidden. But as kitchen herb it is food and permitted to be used on the Sabbath.

76 The passage is difficult to understand; in the parallel in *Sabbath* the word לחנותא "in the store" is missing.

Since the store is supposed to be closed on the Sabbath, it just indicates that R. Jonah took off his sandals far from his home when a shoelace broke on the Sabbath.

For the translation of חליסר cf. *Shevi'it* Chapter 7, Note 84. It is not necessary to translate טלק "to throw away" (documented from the Targumim), most of the meanings of Arabic طلق will be acceptable, such as "to take off, let go, loosen".

77 Immediately when a shoelace broke.

78 May one switch left and right sandal on the Sabbath if an outside ear was broken to hide the defect from sight?

79 The Mishnah proves that sandal switching is practiced also on weekdays; therefore, it is permitted on the Sabbath since the switched sandals are legitimate pieces of clothing.

80 This has nothing to do with the prior discussion; it shows what is meant in the Mishnah which states that sandals with torn soles are acceptable. The sentence also is copied in *Sabbath*, implying that sandals with partially torn soles may also be worn on the Sabbath.

וּמָה טַעֲמָא דְרִבִּי לִיעֶזֶר. לְעֵינֵי הַזְּקֵנִים. מַה מְקַייְמִין רַבָּנָן לְעֵינֵי הַזְּקֵינִים. פְּרָט לְבֵית דִּין הַסּוּמָא. רִבִּי יוֹחָנָן בָּעֵי. מִחְלְפָה שִׁיטָּתֵיהּ דְּרִבִּי לִיעֶזֶר. תַּמָּן הוּא אָמַר. הַיְמָנִית מְעַכֶּבֶת. וְהָכָא הוּא אָמַר. אֵין הַיְמָנִית מְעַכֶּבֶת. אָמַר רִבִּי יוֹסֵי. תַּמָּן דִּכְתִיב יְמָנִית הַיְמָנִית מְעַכֶּבֶת. בְּרַם הָכָא דְלֵית כְּתִיב יְמָנִית אֵין הַיְמָנִית מְעַכֶּבֶת. תַּנֵּי רִבִּי יוֹסֵי צַיידָנִייָה קוֹמֵי רִבִּי יִרְמְיָה. אָזְנוֹ אָזְנוֹ. מַה אָזְנוֹ שֶׁנֶּאֱמַר לְהַלָּן הַיְמָנִית אַף כָּאן הַיְמָנִית. וְאָמַר רַגְלוֹ רַגְלוֹ. מַאן דְּאִית לֵיהּ אָזְנוֹ אָזְנוֹ. לֵית לֵיהּ רַגְלוֹ רַגְלוֹ. וְהָא תַנֵּי בְשֵׁם רִבִּי לִיעֶזֶר רַגְלוֹ רַגְלוֹ. הֲוֵי תַּרְתֵּי מַתְנִייָן אִינּוּן עַל דִּבְרֵי רִבִּי לִיעֶזֶר. מָאן דְּאִית לֵיהּ אָזְנוֹ אָזְנוֹ. אִית לֵיהּ רַגְלוֹ רַגְלוֹ. מָאן דְּלֵית לֵיהּ אָזְנוֹ אָזְנוֹ. לֵית לֵיהּ רַגְלוֹ. וְהָדָא מַתְנִיתִין דְּלֵית לֵיהּ אָזְנוֹ אָזְנוֹ וְלֹא רַגְלוֹ רַגְלוֹ.

What is the reason of Rebbi Eliezer? "Before the Elders' eyes[81]." How do the rabbis uphold "before the Elders' eyes"? That excludes a court of blind people. Rebbi Joḥanan said, the argument of Rebbi Eliezer seems to be inverted[82]. There[83], he says that the right hand is obligatory, but here, he says that the right hand is not obligatory. Rebbi Yose said, there it is written "the right hand"[84], the right hand is obl;igatory, but here, where "the right hand" is not written, the right hand is notobligatory. Rebbi Yose from Sidon stated before Rebbi Jeremiah: "His ear", "his ear". Since "his ear" mentioned there refers to the right ear, so "his ear" mentioned here means the right ear[85]. It also says "his foot", "his foot". He who infers from "his ear", "his ear" infers from "his foot", "his foot"; he who does not infer from "his ear", "his ear" does not infer from "his foot", "his foot". But it was stated in the name of Rebbi Eliezer: "his foot", "his foot". That means, there are two statements about the words of Rebbi Eliezer[86]. He who argues from "his ear", "his ear" argues from "his foot", "his foot"; he who does not argue from "his ear", "his ear" does not argue from "his foot". And this Mishnah accepts neither "his ear", "his ear" nor "his foot", "his foot"[87].

81 *Deut.* 25:9: "The sister-in-law shall approach him before the elder's eyes". R. Eliezer holds that one sees clearly only during daytime. This argument is not found in any of the parallel sources.

82 The same argument in the Babli, 104a.

83 The purification of a leper requires that blood and oil be put on the right hand thumb and the right big toe of the healed person, *Lev.* 14:14,17. In Mishnah *Nega'im* 14:9, R. Eliezer and R. Simeon disagree about the purification of a person missing his right hand thumb or right big toe; R. Eliezer insists that the right hand must be used in all cases.

84 *Lev.* 14:14,17. In the Babli, 104a, this is the argument of the rabbis. In the Babli, R. Eliezer is defended by the argument that the leper has so many additional ceremonies that it is difficult to transfer any of his ceremonies to other cases.

85 This compares the ceremony of the leper with that of piercing the ear of the Hebrew slave who refuses to regain his freedom, *Ex.* 21:6, *Deut.* 15:17. In the latter verses it is not spelled out which ear has to be pierced. The argument that the ear

must be the right one is quoted anonymously also in Yerushalmi *Qiddušin* Chapter 1, fol. 59d, *Mekhilta dR. Ismael Mišpaṭim* 2, *Mekhilta dR. Simeon bar Iohai Mišpaṭim* p.163, *Sifry Deut.* 122; in the name of R. Eliezer here and in the Babli 104a and *Qiddušin* 15a.

86 In the Mishnah, R. Eliezer accepts the use of the left foot after the fact; in the *baraita* he declares use of the left foot as invalid.

87 That is, for R. Eliezer; but in the opinion of the Babli, the majority base their opinion on the comparison "foot, foot".

(fol. 12b) **משנה ג**: חָלְצָה וְרָקְקָה אֲבָל לֹא קָרָאתָה חֲלִיצָתָהּ כְּשֵׁירָה. קָרָאתָה וְרָקְקָה אֲבָל לֹא חָלְצָה חֲלִיצָתָהּ פְּסוּלָה. חָלְצָה וקָרָאתָה אֲבָל לֹא רָקְקָה רִבִּי אֱלִיעֶזֶר אוֹמֵר חֲלִיצָתָהּ פְּסוּלָה רִבִּי עֲקִיבָה אוֹמֵר חֲלִיצָתָהּ כְּשֵׁרָה.

Mishnah 3: If she stripped off and spat but did not recite, the *ḥalîṣah* is valid[88]. If she recited and spat but did not strip off, the *ḥalîṣah* is invalid. If she stripped off and recited but did not spit, Rebbi Eliezer says, the *ḥalîṣah* is invalid, but Rebbi Aqiba says, the *ḥalîṣah* is valid.

88 All three actions by the widow, first stripping the shoe from the levir's foot, second to spit out in front of him, third to recite: "So should be done to the man who would not build his brother's house" are required in *Deut.* 25:9.

(fol. 12d) **מתניתין**: חָלְצָה וְרָקְקָה כול׳. שְׁמוּאֵל אָמַר. חָלְצָה וְלֹא רָקְקָה תָּרוֹק. וְאַתְיָא כְּרִבִּי לִיעֶזֶר. רִבִּי הִילָא בְשֵׁם רִבִּי לָעְזָר. חָלְצָה אֲבָל לֹא קָרָאתָה וְלֹא רָקְקָה חֲלִיצָתָהּ פְּסוּלָה. עוֹד הִיא דְרִבִּי לִיעֶזֶר. דִּבְרֵי חֲכָמִים רִבִּי בָּא בְשֵׁם רַב יְהוּדָה זְרִיקַן מַטֵי בָהּ בְּשֵׁם רַב. חָלְצָה וְלֹא רָקְקָה רָקְקָה וְלֹא חָלְצָה לֹא עָשָׂה כְּלוּם עַד שֶׁתַּחֲלוֹץ וְתָרוֹק. רִבִּי בָּא בְּעָא קוֹמֵי רִבִּי אִימִּי. הִקְדִּימָה רְקִיקָה לַחֲלִיצָה. אָמַר לֵיהּ. כְּמִי שֶׁהֵן עַל הַסֵּדֶר. קִידֵּשׁ בְּגוּפוֹ שֶׁלְּסוֹפִין. אָמַר לֵיהּ.

בְּתֵנְיָין שֶׁבּוֹ קִידֵּשׁ. מַהוּ לִפְתּוֹחַ חֲלוֹן מִצְרִית לַחֲצַר הַשּׁוּתְפִין לְמַעֲלָה מֵאַרְבַּע אַמּוֹת. אָמַר לֵיהּ. כֵּן אֲנָן אָמְרִין. לִסְתּוֹם אַווירָא בְּעָלְמָא בְּאַפּוֹי. אָמַר רִבִּי נָסָא. כֵּן אָמַר. מָאן דְּבָעֵי מֵיעֲבַד בֵּיתָא כְּמִין שׁוֹבָךְ לֹא שָׁמְעִין לֵיהּ.

Mishnah: "If she stripped off and spat," etc. Samuel said, if she stripped but did not spit, she shall spit[89]. This follows Rebbi Eliezer. Rebbi Hila in the name of Rebbi Eleazar: If she stripped but did not recite nor spit, her *ḥalîṣah* is invalid. Still that is Rebbi Eliezer's. The words of the Sages? Rebbi Abba in the name of Rav Jehudah, Zeriqan turned to it in the name of Rav: If she stripped but did not spit, or spat but did not strip, she did not do anything[90] until she strips and spits. Rebbi Abba asked before Rebbi Immi: If she spat before she stripped? He said, it is as if in the correct order[91]. If he made a betrothal with a cluster of end-of-harvest [figs]? He said to him, with the figs hanging there he made the betrothal[92]. May one open an Egyptian window[93] into a common backyard higher than four cubits[94]? He said to him, so we are saying: He comes simply for the air. Rebbi Nasa said, that is what he said: If somebody wants to build his house in the form of a dovecot[95], does one not listen to him?

89 The missing action can be performed belatedly; the original ceremony was not legally nonexistent.

90 It is legally nonexistent and cannot be fixed belatedly.

91 Anything written in the verse has to be performed but the order in which it is written is not necessarily the order in which the ceremonies have to be performed. In the Babli, 105a, this is a *baraita*.

92 R. Abba continued to address unrelated questions to R. Immi. The question here is not clear, the translation follows the interpretation of *Qorban Ha'edah*. If somebody gave a woman a branch full of figs as betrothal gift (cf. Chapter 1, Note 63), how is the value computed? The betrothal is only valid if the value is at least a *peruṭah*, $^1/_{64}$ of a silver denar. R. Immi specifies that only the figs are

counted for the value, not the wood.

93 Defined in Mishnah *Baba Batra* 3:8 as a hole smaller than a man's head.

94 In general, people can object if a neighbor makes a new window that lets him see their activities that earlier he could not observe. This is called "damage by looking", היזק ראייה ; cf. *Baba Batra* 2:4, Babli *Baba Batra* 2b. But a window higher than 4 cubits (about 2.2 m) is for air, not for looking.

95 Where all openings are very high.

(fol. 12b) **משנה ד**: אָמַר רִבִּי לִיעֶזֶר כָּכָה יֵעָשֶׂה כָּל־דָּבָר שֶׁהוּא מַעֲשֶׂה מְעַכֵּב. אָמַר לוֹ רִבִּי עֲקִיבָה מִשָּׁם רְאָיָה. כָּכָה יֵעָשֶׂה לָאִישׁ כָּל־דָּבָר שֶׁהוּא מַעֲשֶׂה הָאִישׁ.

Mishnah 4: [96]Rebbi Eliezer said, "so it shall be done[97]", anything which is an action is preventing[98]. Rebbi Aqiba said to him, is that a proof? "So it shall be done to the man", any activity of the male [is preventing.]

96 This Mishnah explains the positions of Rebbis Eliezer and Aqiba in Mishnah 3.

97 *Deut*. 25:9: "So should be done to the man who would not build his brother's house". This is the required recitation by the widow. It is taken out of context for emphasis, *so* and not otherwise. This is meant to imply that no *ḥaliṣah* is valid if it is not executed exactly as written.

98 Preventing the validity of the procedure.

(fol. 12d) **מתניתין**: אָמַר רִבִּי לִיעֶזֶר כָּכָה יֵעָשֶׂה לָאִישׁ כול׳. אָמַר רִבִּי יוֹחָנָן. שֶׁאֵינָן יְכוֹלִין לוֹמַר וְאָמַר וְאָמְרָה. וְקִרְיָיה מְעַכֶּבֶת. אָמַר רִבִּי שְׁמוּאֵל בַּר רַב יִצְחָק. הָרָאוּי לִקְרִייָה אֵין קְרִייָה מְעַכֶּבֶת וּשֶׁאֵינוֹ רָאוּי לִקְרִייָה קְרִייָה מְעַכֶּבֶת.

Mishnah: "Rebbi Eliezer said, "so shall be done to the man," etc. Rebbi Joḥanan said, if they cannot fulfill "he shall say, and she shall say"[99]. Does the recitation prevent [validity]? Rebbi Samuel ben Rav Isaac said, for anybody able to recite, the recitation does not prevent [validity] but for anybody unable to recite, the requirement of recitation does prevent[100].

99 This does not refer to the discussion of the Mishnah but to the text quoted as required recitation by the widow. (The levir has to say "I do not like to take her", v. 8). The statement that the verse excludes a person unable to speak from *ḥalîṣah* is attributed to R. Yannai, R. Joḥanan's teacher, in the Babli (104b).

100 In the Babli (104b, *Nedarim* 93a, *Qiddušin* 25a, *Baba Batra* 81b, *Makkot* 18b, *Ḥulin* 83b, *Menaḥot* 18b, 103b, *Niddah* 66b) the rule is attributed to R. Ze'ira: In general, the omission of a required action does not prevent the validity of the ceremony if it would have been possible to perform it as required; cf. *Bikkurim* 1:6, Note 114. This is the source of the next Mishnah.

(fol. 12b) **משנה ה**: הַחֵרֵשׁ שֶׁנֶּחֱלַץ וְהַחֵרֶשֶׁת שֶׁחָלְצָה וְהַחוֹלֶצֶת לַקָּטָן חֲלִיצָתָהּ פְּסוּלָה. קְטַנָּה שֶׁחָלְצָה תַּחֲלוֹץ מִשֶּׁתַּגְדִּיל וְאִם לֹא חָלְצָה חֲלִיצָתָהּ כְּשֵׁירָה.

Mishnah 5: *Ḥalîṣah* is invalid if performed for a deaf-mute man[101], or by a deaf-mute woman, or for an underage male[102]. The underage woman who performed *ḥalîṣah* should repeat *ḥalîṣah* once she becomes of age but if she did not repeat it, the *ḥalîṣah* is valid[103].

101 Since the deaf-mute (who does not understand sign language) cannot perform any legal act, the passive voice is required here.

102 In v. 9 the male is called "man", which means "adult".

103 In the Mishnah in the Babli: "invalid". That version is explained in the Halakhah as representing the opinion of R. Meïr.

(fol. 12d) **מתניתין**: הַחֵרֵשׁ שֶׁנֶּחֱלַץ כול׳. תַּמָּן תַּנִּינָן הַכֹּל חַייָבִין בִּרְאָייָה חוּץ מֵחֵרֵשׁ שׁוֹטֶה וְקָטָן. חֲבֵרַייָא בְשֵׁם רִבִּי לָעְזָר. לְמַעַן יִשְׁמְעוּן וּלְמַעַן יִלְמְדוּן. עַד

כְּדוֹן בִּמְדַבֵּר וְאֵינוֹ שׁוֹמֵעַ. שׁוֹמֵעַ וְאֵינוֹ מְדַבֵּר. רִבִּי הִילָא בְשֵׁם רִבִּי לָעְזָר. לְמַעַן יִלְמְדוּן לְמַעַן יְלַמְּדוּן. אָמַר רִבִּי יוֹנָה. הָדָא אָמְרָה. לֵית כְּלָלִין דְּרִבִּי כְּלָלִין. דְּתַנִּינָן תַּמָּן. חֵרֵשׁ הַמְדַבֵּר וְאֵינוֹ שׁוֹמֵעַ לֹא יִתְרוֹם. וְסָבְרִינָן מֵימַר. מְדַבֵּר וְאֵינוֹ שׁוֹמֵעַ חֵרֵשׁ. שׁוֹמֵעַ וְאֵינוֹ מְדַבֵּר חֵרֵשׁ. וְתַנִּינָן חֵרֵשׁ שֶׁנֶּחֱלַץ וְהַחֵרֶשֶׁת שֶׁחָלְצָה וְהַחוֹלֶצֶת לְקָטָן חֲלִיצָתָהּ פְּסוּלָה. וְאָמַר רִבִּי יוֹחָנָן. שֶׁאֵין יְכוֹלִין לוֹמַר וְאָמַר וְאָמְרָה. וְתַנִּינָן. חֵרֵשׁ שֶׁדִּבְּרוּ בוֹ חֲכָמִים בְּכָל־מָקוֹם שֶׁאֵינוֹ לֹא שׁוֹמֵעַ וְלֹא מְדַבֵּר. הָדָא מְסַיְּיעָא לְרִבִּי יוֹנָה. דְּרִבִּי יוֹנָה אָמַר. לֵית כְּלָלִין דְּרִבִּי כְּלָלִין.

[104]There, we have stated: "Everybody is obligated for appearance except the deaf-mute, the insane, and the minor." The colleagues in the name of Rebbi Eleazar (*Deut.* 31:12): "So they should hear and learn." So far one who speaks but cannot hear; what about one who hears but cannot speak? Rebbi La in the name of Rebbi Eleazar (*Deut.* 31:12): "So they should learn," so they should teach. Rebbi Jonah said, this means that the principles of Rebbi are no principles, since we have stated: "A *ḥereš* who speaks but cannot hear should not give heave," and we thought that one who speaks but does not hear is *ḥereš*, one who hears but does not speak is *ḥereš*. But we have stated: "*Ḥalîṣah* is invalid if performed for a *ḥereš* man, or by a *ḥereš* woman, or for an underage male." And Rebbi Johanan said, because they cannot say (*Deut.* 25:8): "he shall say", (*Deut.* 25:7,9) "she shall say." We also have stated: "A *ḥereš* mentioned anywhere by the Sages is a deaf-mute.' This supports Rebbi Jonah, for Rebbi Jonah said that the principles of Rebbi are no principles.

104 This is from *Terumot* 1:2, Notes 94-102.

רִבִּי יִשְׁמָעֵאל בֵּירִבִּי יוֹסֵי בְּעָא קוֹמֵי רִבִּי. מַה בֵּין קָטָן מַה בֵּין קְטַנָּה. אָמַר לֵיהּ. אִישׁ כָּתוּב בַּפָּרָשָׁה. בְּרַם הָכָא וְנִגְּשָׁה יְבִמְתּוֹ אֵלָיו. מִכָּל־מָקוֹם.

Rebbi Ismael ben Rebbi Yose[105] asked before Rebbi: What is the difference between underage males and females? He said to him, "a man[106]" is written in the paragraph. But about her, "his sister-in-law shall come before him,[105]" in any case.

רִבִּי מָנָא אָמַר לָהּ סְתָם. רִבִּי יִצְחָק בְּרֵיהּ דְּרִבִּי חִיָּיה מַטֵּי בָהּ בְּשֵׁם רִבִּי יוֹנָה. דְּרִבִּי מֵאִיר הִיא דְּאָמַר. אֵין חוֹלְצִין וְלֹא מְייַבְּמִין אֶת הַקְּטַנָּה שֶׁמָּא תִימָּצֵא אַיילוֹנִית.

Rebbi Mana said it without attribution, Rebbi Isaac the son of Rebbi Ḥiyya came to it in the name of Rebbi Jonah: It is[107] Rebbi Meïr's who said that one does not perform *ḥalîṣah* or levirate with an underage girl because she might turn out to be a she-ram[108].

105 In the Babli, 105b, he is reported to say that the Yerushalmi version of the Mishnah is his father's.

106 *Deut*. 25:9. This argument is attributed to "the Rabbis" in the Babli, 105b.

107 The Mishnah which requires that the underage girl repeat the procedure once she grows up.

108 Cf. Chapter 1, Note 65. R. Meïr is reputed to take note of cases which occur only very infrequently. In the Tosephta, 12:12, this is quoted as the opinion of R. Eliezer.

(fol. 12b) **משנה ו:** חָלְצָה בִשְׁנַיִם אוֹ בִשְׁלֹשָׁה וְנִמְצָא אֶחָד מֵהֶן קָרוֹב אוֹ פָסוּל חֲלִיצָה פְסוּלָה. רִבִּי שִׁמְעוֹן וְרִבִּי יוֹחָנָן הַסַּנְדְּלָר מַכְשִׁירִין. מַעֲשֶׂה שֶׁחָלְצָה בֵינָהּ לְבֵינוֹ בְּבֵית הָאֲסוּרִין וּבָא מַעֲשֶׂה לִפְנֵי רִבִּי עֲקִיבָה וְהִכְשִׁיר.

Mishnah 6: If she performed *ḥalîṣah* in front of two [judges][109] or of three when it turned out that one was a relative or unfit[110], the *ḥalîṣah* is invalid; Rebbi Simeon and Rebbi Joḥanan the Alexandrian declare it valid.

If happened that she performed *ḥalîṣah* between herself and him in jail; the case came before Rebbi Aqiba and he declared it valid[111].

109 Which is invalid in the opinion of some authorities, cf. Halakhah 1.

110 According to everybody, a court of law is incompetent if it turns out that one of the judges is a relative of one of the parties or of another judge, or if he had been declared unfit to be a judge.

111 Since this is a report of an actual case, it represents practice (at least in cases of emergency).

(fol. 12d) **מתניתין**: חֲלְצָה בִשְׁנַיִם כול'. בְּבֵית הָאֲסוּרִים הָיָה מַעֲשֶׂה. וּלְבֵית הָאֲסוּרִים בָּא הַמַּעֲשֶׂה. רִבִּי יוֹחָנָן הַסַּנְדְּלָר עֲבַד גַּרְמֵיהּ רוֹכֵל. יוֹמָא עָבַר קוֹמֵי בֵּית חֲבִישָׁה דְּרִבִּי עֲקִיבָה וַהֲוָה מַכְרִיז וְאָמַר. מָאן בָּעֵי מַחֲטִין. מָאן בָּעֵי צִינּוֹרִין. חָלְצָה בֵינָהּ לְבֵינוֹ מַהוּ. אוֹדִיק לֵיהּ רִבִּי עֲקִיבָה מִן כַּוְותָא. אֲמַר לֵיהּ. אִית לָךְ כּוּשִׁין אִית לָךְ כָּשֵׁר.

Mishnah: "If she performed *ḥalîṣah* in front of two," etc. The case happened in a jail and was resolved in a jail[112]. Rebbi Joḥanan the Alexandrian dressed up as a pedlar. One day, he passed in front of the place of confinement of Rebbi Aqiba[113], he cried aloud and said, "who needs needles, who needs hooks, what is if she performed *ḥalîṣah* between herself and him?" Rebbi Aqiba pushed himself tightly to the hole and said: "Do you have spindles? You have valid!"

112 Reported by Amoraim in the Babli, 105b.

113 In the aftermath of the war of Bar Kokhba, when the teaching of Jewish law in Palestine was a capital crime. Therefore, the questions had to be couched in such terms that an Aramaic speaking Gentile would not understand question or answer.

משנה ז: מִצְוַת חֲלִיצָה בָּא הוּא וִיבִמְתּוֹ לְבֵית דִּין וְהֵן נוֹתְנִין לוֹ אֶת(fol. 12b) עֵצָה הֶהָגוּן לוֹ שֶׁנֶּאֱמַר וְקָרְאוּ לוֹ זִקְנֵי עִירוֹ וְדִבְּרוּ אֵלָיו וְהִיא אוֹמֶרֶת מֵאֵן יְבָמִי לְהָקִים לְאָחִיו שֵׁם בְּיִשְׂרָאֵל לֹא אָבָה יַבְּמִי. וְהוּא אוֹמֵר לֹא חָפַצְתִּי לְקַחְתָּהּ. בִּלְשׁוֹן הַקּוֹדֶשׁ הָיוּ אוֹמְרִים. וְנִגְּשָׁה יְבִמְתּוֹ אֵלָיו לְעֵינֵי הַזְּקֵינִים וְחָלְצָה נַעֲלוֹ מֵעַל רַגְלוֹ וְיָרְקָה לְפָנָיו רוֹק שֶׁהוּא נִרְאֶה לַדַּייָנִים. וְעָנְתָה וְאָמְרָה כָּכָה יֵעָשֶׂה לָאִישׁ אֲשֶׁר לֹא יִבְנֶה אֶת בֵּית אָחִיו. עַד כָּאן הָיוּ מַקְרִין. וּכְשֶׁהוּקְרָא רַבִּי הוֹרְקָנוֹס תַּחַת הָאֵלָה בִּכְפַר אָבוּס וְגָמַר אֶת כָּל־הַפָּרָשָׁה הוּחְזְקוּ לִהְיוֹת גּוֹמְרִין כָּל־הַפָּרָשָׁה וְנִקְרָא שְׁמוֹ בְּיִשְׂרָאֵל בֵּית חֲלוּץ הַנָּעַל. מִצְוָה בַדַּייָנִים וְלֹא מִצְוָה בַתַּלְמִידִים. רַבִּי יוּדָה אוֹמֵר מִצְוָה עַל כָּל־הָעוֹמְדִין שָׁם לוֹמַר חֲלוּץ הַנַּעַל חֲלוּץ הַנָּעַל.

Mishnah 7: The commandment of *ḥalîṣah*: He and his sister-in-law come to the court of law and they give him appropriate counsel, as it is said: "The Elders of his city shall call him and speak to him[114]". She says: "My levir refuses to erect a name in Israel for his brother, my levir does not want;[115]" and he says: "I do not desire to take her[114]." They have to speak in the holy language[116]. "His sister-in-law comes to him before the Elders' eyes, strips his shoe from his foot, and spits out before him[117]," spittle that is visible to the judges. She has to declare and say: "So should be done to a man who would not build his brother's house.[117]" Up to this sentence they were reading to them but when it was read for Rebbi Hyrkanos[118] under the oak tree in Kefar Abus he finished the paragraph; they established to finish the entire paragraph, "his house shall be called in Israel the house of the one stripped of shoe[119]." The obligation is on the judges, not on the students[120]. Rebbi Jehudah said, everyone present has the obligation to say,"the one stripped of shoe, the one stripped of shoe[121]".

114 *Deut.* 25:8.

115 *Deut.* 25:7.

116 The entire ceremony must be conducted in Hebrew. Since it is to be assumed that the parties do not know Hebrew, the text has to be read to them by the judges, for them to repeat.

117 *Deut.* 25:9.

118 In the Babli: When R. Hyrkanos was reading it under the oak tree at *Kefar 'Etam.* In other places, the name appears as כפר עיכוס. The place is unidentified.

119 *Deut.* 25:10.

120 The law students who regularly attended court sessions. The judges themselves have to recite "house of the stripped of shoe".

121 In the Babli, the clause is repeated three times.

(fol. 12d) **מתניתין**: מִצְוַת חֲלִיצָה. בָּא הוּא וִיבִמְתּוֹ כול׳. וְהֵן נוֹתְנִין לוֹ עֵצָה אֶת הֶהָגוּן לוֹ. מַהוּ אֶת הֶהָגוּן לוֹ. אִין הֲוָה סָב אוֹמְרִים לָהּ. הָהֵין סָב לְאָן לֵיךְ. אִין הֲוָת סָבְתָא אוֹמְרִים לֵיהּ. הָדָא סָבְתָא לְאָן לֵיךְ. הִיא טַלִיתָא וְהוּא סָב אָמְרִין לֵיהּ. טַלִיתָא הִיא וְהִיא מַכְלְמָה עֲלָךְ. הוּא טַלְיָיא וְהִיא סָבְתָא אוֹמְרִים לָהּ. טַלְיָיא הוּא וְהוּא מַכְלְמָה עֲלָךְ. הוּא רוֹצֶה וְהִיא אֵינָהּ רוֹצָה שׁוֹמְעִין לָהּ. הִיא רוֹצָה וְהוּא אֵינוֹ רוֹצֶה שׁוֹמְעִין לוֹ. כְּלָלוֹ שֶׁלְּדָבָר. כָּל־הַמְעַכֵּב שׁוֹמְעִין לוֹ. הָיוּ שְׁנֵיהֶן רוֹצִין. אָתָא עוֹבְדָא קוֹמֵי רִבִּי יוֹסֵי. אָמַר אַפִּיק לְבַר.

Mishnah: "The commandment of *ḥalîṣah*: He and his sister-in-law come," etc. "They give him appropriate counsel". What means, "they give him appropriate counsel"? If he is old, they tell her, what do you do with an old man like him? If she is old, they tell him, what do you do with that old woman? If she is a girl and he is an old man, they say to him, she is a girl and will bring you shame. If he is a boy and she an old woman, they say to her, he is a boy and will bring you shame. If he wants but she does not, one listens to her. If she wants but he does not, one listens to him. The principle: One listens to the one who wants to prevent. If both of them want, such a case came before Rebbi Yose and he said, throw her out[122].

122 The practice of his court was never to accept levirate. The Babli, 101a, supports levirate for partners that are of similar age. The formulation of the Babli is also that of *Sifry Deut.* 290.

(fol. 13a) רִבִּי יוֹחָנָן בָּעֵי. בִּיבָמָה מִי רוֹדֵף אַחַר מִי. הָתִיב רִבִּי לְעָזָר. וְהָכְתִיב וְעָלְתָה יְבִימְתּוֹ הַשַּׁעְרָה. כַּד שְׁמָעָהּ רִבִּי יוֹחָנָן אָמַר. יָפֶה לִימְּדָנוּ רִבִּי לְעָזָר.

Rebbi Johanan asked, in the case of a sister in law, who runs after whom[123]? Rebbi Eleazar answered: "His sister-in-law shall come to the gate[124]." When Rebbi Johanan heard this, he said, Rebbi Eleazar taught us correctly.

123 If levir and widow live at different places, which court is empowered to deal with the matter?

124 Since the verse requires the widow to take the initiative, the appropriate court is the one at the levir's residence. In the Babli, *Sanhedrin* 31b, this ia a statement of R. Johanan; it is a tannaïtic statement in *Midrash Tannaïm* on *Deut.* 25:8.

וּקְרִייָה מְעַכֶּבֶת. אָמַר רִבִּי שְׁמוּאֵל בַּר רַב יִצְחָק. הָרָאוּי לִקְרִייָה אֵין קְרִייָה מְעַכֶּבֶת וְשֶׁאֵינוֹ רָאוּי לִקְרִייָה קְרִייָה מְעַכֶּבֶת. אָמַר רִבִּי מָנָא. אַף עַל גַּב דְּרִבִּי שְׁמוּאֵל בַּר רַב יִצְחָק אָמַר. אֵין קְרִייָה מְעַכֶּבֶת. מוֹדֶה שֶׁאִם בָּא לְאוֹמְרָן שֶׁהוּא אוֹמֵר עַל הַסֵּדֶר. וּבִלְחוּד דְּלָא תֵימַר. מֵאֵן יְבָמִי לְהָקִים לֹא אָבָה יַבְמִי לֹא חָפַצְתִּי לְקַחְתָּהּ. אֶלָּא מֵאֵן יְבָמִי לְהָקִים לְאָחִיו שֵׁם בְּיִשְׂרָאֵל לֹא אָבָה יַבְמִי לֹא חָפַצְתִּי לְקַחְתָּהּ.

Does the recitation prevent [validity]? Rebbi Samuel ben Rav Isaac said, for anybody able to recite, the recitation does not prevent [validity] but for anybody unable to recite, the recitation does prevent[125]. Rebbi Mana said, even though Rebbi Samuel ben Rav Isaac said, the recitation does not prevent [validity], he agrees that if one recites, he recites in due order; in particular that it should not be said: "My levir refuses to erect, my levir does not want;" "I do not desire to take her", but "my levir refuses to erect a name in Israel for his brother, my levir does not want;" "I do not desire to take her."

125 Cf. Halakhah 4, Note 100.

תַּמָּן אָמְרִין. קָרְבַת קַדָּמָנָא וְשָׁלְפַת סִיָּנֵיהּ מֵעִילוֹי רִגְלֵיהּ דִּימִינָא וְרַקַּת קַדָּמָנָא רוֹק דְּמִתְחֲזֵי עַל אַרְעָא. וְאָמְרָה כָּכָה יֵעָשֶׂה לָאִישׁ אֲשֶׁר לֹא יִבְנֶה אֶת בֵּית אָחִיו. אָמַר רִבִּי אַבָּהוּ. מִכֵּיוָן שֶׁנִּרְאֶה הָרוֹק שֶׁהוּא יוֹצֵא מִתּוֹךְ פִּיהָ אֲפִילוּ הִפְרִיחָתוֹ הָרוּחַ כָּשֵׁר. רָקָה דָם. רִבִּי בָּא בְשֵׁם רַב יְהוּדָה רִבִּי זְרִיקָן מַטֵּי בָהּ. רִבִּי יִרְמְיָה בְשֵׁם אַבָּא בַּר אַבָּא רִבִּי זְעִירָא מַטֵּי בָהּ בְּשֵׁם שְׁמוּאֵל. אִם יֵשׁ בּוֹ צַחְצוּחִית שֶׁלְּרוֹק כָּשֵׁר. הַגִּידֶּמֶת בְּמָה הִיא חוֹלֶצֶת. בְּשִׁינֶּיהָ.

There[126], they say: "She came before us, stripped his shoe from his right foot, spat before us spittle that was visible on the ground, and said: 'So should be done to a man who would not build his brother's house.'" Rebbi Abbahu said, since the spittle was visible when it left her mouth it is valid, even if the wind dissipated it[127]. If she spat blood? Rebbi Abba in the name of Rav Jehudah, Rebbi Zeriqan turned to it, Rebbi Jeremiah in the name of Abba bar Abba[128], Rebbi Ze'ira turned to it in the name of Samuel: If it contains some liquid spittle, it is valid[129]. How does the handless [woman] perform *ḥalîṣah*? With her teeth[130].

126 In Babylonia. In the Babli, 39b, the text of the *ḥalîṣah* document given to the widow is ascribed to Rav Jehudah. In the Tosephta, 12:15, it is quoted as "old text".

127 He disapproves of the formulation that the spittle has to be seen on the ground.

128 He probably is Samuel's father.

129 In the Babli, 105a, no spittle is required since the verse simply says "she shall spit', not "she shall spit spittle".

130 Agreed to in the Babli, 105a, since the verse requires only that the shoe be stripped off but does not prescribe the way it should be done.

בְּנֵי סִימוֹנְיָיא אָתוֹן לְגַבֵּי רִבִּי. אֲמְרִין לֵיהּ. בְּעָא תִתֵּן לָן חַד בַּר נַשׁ דָּרִישׁ דַּיָּין וְחַזָּן סַפָּר מַתְנִיָּין וַעֲבַד לָן כָּל־צָרְכִינָן. וִיהַב לוֹן לֵוִי בַּר סִיסִי. עָשׂוּ לוֹ בִּימָה גְדוֹלָה וְהוֹשִׁיבוּהוּ עָלֶיהָ. אָתוֹן וְשָׁאֲלוֹן לֵיהּ. הַגִּידֶּמֶת בְּמָה הִיא חוֹלֶצֶת. וְלֹא אַגִּיבוֹן. רָקָה דָם. וְלֹא אַגִּיבוֹן. אָמְרִין. דִּילְמָא דְלֵית הוּא מָרֵי אוּלְפָּן. נִישְׁאוֹל לֵיהּ שְׁאֲלוֹן לֵיהּ דַּאֲגָדָה. אָתוֹן וְשָׁאֲלוֹן לֵיהּ. מַהוּ הָדֵין דִּכְתִיב אֲבָל אַגִּיד לְךָ אֶת הָרָשׁוּם בִּכְתַב אֱמֶת. אִם אֱמֶת לָמָּה רָשׁוּם. וְאִם רָשׁוּם לָמָּה אֱמֶת. וְלֹא אַגִּיבוֹן. אָתוֹן לְגַבֵּי דְרִבִּי. אָמְרוּן לֵיהּ. הָדֵין פַּיְיסוּנָא דְפַיְיסַנְתָּךְ. אֲמַר לוֹן. חַיֵּיכוֹן. בַּר נַשׁ דִּכְוָותִי יְהָבִית לְכוֹן. שְׁלַח אַיְיתִיתֵיהּ וּשְׁאַל לֵיהּ. אֲמַר לֵיהּ. רָקָה דָם מַהוּ. אֲמַר לֵיהּ. אִם יֵשׁ בּוֹ צִחְצוּחִית שֶׁלְּרוֹק כָּשֵׁר. הַגִּידֶּמֶת בְּמָה הִיא חוֹלֶצֶת. אֲמַר לֵיהּ. בְּשִׁינֶּיהָ. אֲמַר לֵיהּ. מַהוּ הָדֵין דִּכְתִיב אֲבָל אַגִּיד לְךָ אֶת הָרָשׁוּם בִּכְתַב אֱמֶת. אִם אֱמֶת לָמָּה רָשׁוּם. וְאִם רָשׁוּם לָמָּה אֱמֶת. אֲמַר לֵיהּ. עַד שֶׁלֹּא נִתְחַתֵּם גְּזַר דִּין רָשׁוּם. מִשֶּׁנִּתְחַתֵּם גְּזַר דִּין אֱמֶת. אֲמַר לֵיהּ. וְלָמָּה לֹא אַגִּיבְתִּינוֹן. אֲמַר לֵיהּ. עָשׂוּ לִי בִּימָה גְדוֹלָה וְהוֹשִׁיבוּ אוֹתִי עָלֶיהָ וְטָפַח רוּחִי עָלַי. וְקָרָא עָלָיו אִם נָבַלְתָּ בְהִתְנַשֵּׂא וְאִם זַמּוֹתָ יַד לְפֶה. מִי גָרַם לְךָ לְהִתְנַבֵּל בְּדִבְרֵי תוֹרָה. עַל שֶׁנִּשֵּׂאתָה בָהֶן עַצְמְךָ.

[131]The people of Simonia came to Rebbi and told him, please give us a man who preaches, judges, runs the synagogue, teaches reading, teaches Mishnah, and looks after all our needs. He gave them Levi bar Sisi. They made him a big platform[132] and sat him on it. They came and asked him, how does the handless [woman] perform *ḥalîṣah*? He did not respond. If she spat blood" He did not respond. They said, maybe he is not competent in studies, let us ask him in homiletics. They came and asked him, what is that which is written: "Truly, I shall tell you what is traced in writing, it is true.[133]" If it is true, why is it traced, and if traced, why is it true? He did not respond. They came to Rebbi and told him, that required one we asked you for? He told them, by your lives, I gave you one who is my equal! He sent to bring him and examined him. He asked him, what if she spat blood. He said, if it contains some fluid of spittle it

is valid. How does the handless [woman] perform *ḥaliṣah*? He said, with her teeth. What is that which is written: "Truly, I shall tell you what is traced in writing, it is true." If it is true, why is it traced, and if traced, why is it true? He said, until the decision of the court is sealed, it is traced. After it has been sealed, it is true. He asked him, and why did you not give any answers? He said to him, they made me a big platform and sat me on it; by that my spirit became bloated[134]. He quoted about him: "If you became subject to contempt when you rose, if you planned, hand to mouth[135]"; why did you become contemptible in the words of the Torah? That you used them to aggrandize yourself.

131 A short version of this is in Babli, 105a. There, Levi actually did not know how to respond. The Yerushalmi version is also in *Gen. rabba* 81(2).

132 Greek βῆμα "speaker's platform".

133 *Dan.* 10:21.

134 He forgot all he knew.

135 *Prov.* 30:32.

תַּנֵּי. חֲלִיצָה מוּטְעֵת כְּשֵׁירָה. אֵי זוֹ הִיא חֲלִיצָה מוּטְעֵת. אָמַר רִבִּי שִׁמְעוֹן בֶּן לָקִישׁ. כָּל־שֶׁאוֹמְרִים לוֹ. חֲלוֹץ. וְהִיא נִיתֶּרֶת לָךְ לְאַחַר זְמָן. אָמַר רִבִּי יוֹחָנָן. אֶמֶשׁ הָיִיתִי יוֹשֵׁב וְשׁוֹנֶה. הוּא מִתְכַּוֵּין וְהִיא אֵינָהּ מִתְכַוֶּנֶת. הִיא מִתְכַּוֶּנֶת וְהוּא אֵינָהּ מִתְכַּוֵּין. לְעוֹלָם חֲלִיצָתָהּ פְּסוּלָה עַד שֶׁיְּהוּ שְׁנֵיהֶן מִתְכַּוְּונִין. אֵי זוֹ הִיא חֲלִיצָה מוּטְעֵת. עַל דַּעְתֵּיהּ דְּרִבִּי יוֹחָנָן. כָּל־שֶׁאוֹמְרִים לוֹ. חֲלוֹץ. וְהִיא נוֹתֶנֶת לָךְ מֵאָה מָנֶה. אָמַר רִבִּי מָנָא. אִם אָמַר. עַל מְנָת. נוֹתֶנֶת. אָתָא עוֹבְדָא קוֹמֵי רִבִּי הוּנָא וַעֲבַד כְּרִבִּי שִׁמְעוֹן בֶּן לָקִישׁ. כַּד שָׁמַע דְּרִבִּי יוֹחָנָן פְּלַג חָזַר וְכָפָה וְחָלַץ לָהּ זְמַן הֵינְייָנוּת. אָתָא עוֹבְדָא קוֹמֵי רִבִּי חִיָּיה בַּר וָוא וְאָמַר לֵהּ. בְּנִי. הָאִשָּׁה הַזֹּאת אֵינָהּ רוֹצָה לְהִינָּשֵׂא לוֹ דֶּרֶךְ יִיבּוּם אֶלָּא חֲלוֹץ לָהּ. עֲקוֹר זִיקָתָךְ מִמֶּנָּה. וְהִיא נִישֵּׂאת לָךְ דֶּרֶךְ נִישּׂוּאִין. מִן דְּחָלַץ לָהּ אָמַר לֵיהּ. אִין אֲתֵי מֹשֶׁה וּשְׁמוּאֵל לָא שָׁרֵיי לָךְ. וְקָרָא עָלוֹי חֲכָמִים הֵמָּה לְהָרַע וּלְהֵיטִיב לֹא יָדָעוּ.

It was stated: A mistaken *ḥalîṣah* is valid[136]. What is a mistaken *ḥalîṣah*? Rebbi Simeon ben Laqish said, a case where one told him, perform *ḥalîṣah* and she will be permitted to you after some time. Rebbi Joḥanan said, yesterday I was sitting and learning that "if he has the intention but not she, or she has the intention but not he, *ḥalîṣah* is always invalid unless both of them have the intention![137]" What is a mistaken *ḥalîṣah* for Rebbi Joḥanan? A case where one told him, perform *ḥalîṣah* and she will pay you a hundred talents. Rebbi Mana said, if this was stipulated as a condition, she has to pay[138]. A case came before Rebbi Huna and he followed Rebbi Simeon ben Laqish. When he heard that Rebbi Joḥanan disagreed, he changed his opinion and forced a second *ḥalîṣah*. A case came before Rebbi Ḥiyya bar Abba. He told him, my son, this woman does not want to be married in levirate; therefore perform *ḥalîṣah* and remove your candidacy from her, then she will marry you in a regular marriage. After the *ḥalîṣah*, he said to him: Even if Moses and Samuel came, they could not permit her. He referred to himself as "they are wise to do evil; they do not know how to do good[139]."

136 Tosephta 12:13; quoted in Babli 106a together with the disagreement of R. Simeon ben Laqish and R. Joḥanan.

137 Tosephta 12:13; it is required that both parties act with the intention of freeing the woman for marriage outside the family.

138 If it was a formal stipulation, not a vague promise. The Babli, 106a, disagrees since the levir has the obligation to perform *ḥalîṣah* if levirate is inappropriate in the eyes of the rabbinate and holding up the woman to extort her money is immoral.

139 *Jer.* 4:22.

אִית תַּנָּיֵי תַנֵּי. חֲלִיצָה גְנַאי. אִית תַּנָּיֵי תַנֵּי. חֲלִיצָה שֶׁבַח. אָמַר רַב חִסְדָּא. מָאן דְּאָמַר. חֲלִיצָה גְנַאי. כְּמִשְׁנָה הָרִאשׁוֹנָה. מָאן דְּאָמַר. חֲלִיצָה שֶׁבַח. כְּמִשְׁנָה הָאַחֲרוֹנָה. אָמַר רִבִּי יוֹסֵי. אֲפִילוּ תֵימַר. כָּאן וְכָאן כְּמִשְׁנָה רִאשׁוֹנָה.

כָּאן וְכָאן כְּמִשְׁנָה אַחֲרוֹנָה. מָאן דְּאָמַר. חֲלִיצָה גְנַיי. עַל דָּבָר שֶׁפָּגַם דָּבָר אֶחָד מִן הַתּוֹרָה יָבוֹא וְיִטּוֹל פְּגָמוֹ וְנִקְרָא שְׁמוֹ בְּיִשְׂרָאֵל בֵּית חֲלוּץ הַנָּעַל. וּמָאן דְּאָמַר. חֲלִיצָה שֶׁבַח. נֶאֱמַר כָּאן קְרִייָה וְנֶאֱמַר לְהַלָּן וְיִקָּרֵא בָהֶם שְׁמִי. מַה קְרִייָה שֶׁנֶּאֱמַר לְהַלָּן שֶׁבַח אַף כָּאן שֶׁבַח.

There are Tannaim who state that *ḥalîṣah* is shameful; there are Tannaim who state that *ḥalîṣah* is praiseworthy. Rav Ḥisda said, he who says that *ḥalîṣah* is shameful follows the early Mishnah, that *ḥalîṣah* is praiseworthy follows the late Mishnah[140]. Rebbi Yose said, you might even say, in both cases one follows the early Mishnah, or in both cases one follows the late Mishnah. He who says that *ḥalîṣah* is shameful, since he damaged one thing in the Torah he shall come and take his damage: "his house shall be called in Israel the house of the one stripped of shoe.[117]" He who says that *ḥalîṣah* is praiseworthy, it mentions here "calling" and it is said there: "My name will be called about them[141]". Since "calling" there is a praise, so here it is a praise.

140 Mishnah *Bekhorot* 1:7: "The obligation of levirate has precedence over *ḥalîṣah*. That was in earlier times, when people had the intent to fulfill the commandment, but now, when people do not have the intent to fulfill the commandment (but to enjoy the marriage) they said, the obligation of *ḥalîṣah* has precedence over levirate."

141 *Gen.* 48:16. This verse is a blessing.

בית שמאי פרק שלשה עשר

(fol. 13a) **משנה א:** בֵּית שַׁמַּי אוֹמְרִים אֵין מְמָאֲנִין אֶלָּא אֲרוּסוֹת. בֵּית הִלֵּל אוֹמְרִים אֲרוּסוֹת וּנְשׂוּאוֹת. בֵּית שַׁמַּי אוֹמְרִים בַּבַּעַל וְלֹא בַיָּבָם וּבֵית הִלֵּל אוֹמְרִים בַּבַּעַל וּבַיָּבָם. בֵּית שַׁמַּי אוֹמְרִים בְּפָנָיו וּבֵית הִלֵּל אוֹמְרִים בְּפָנָיו וְשֶׁלֹּא בְּפָנָיו. בֵּית שַׁמַּי אוֹמְרִים בְּבֵית דִּין וּבֵית הִלֵּל אוֹמְרִים בְּבֵית דִּין וְשֶׁלֹּא בְּבֵית דִּין. אָמְרוּ בֵּית הִלֵּל לְבֵית שַׁמַּי מְמָאֶנֶת הִיא קְטַנָּה אֲפִילוּ אַרְבָּעָה וַחֲמִשָּׁה פְּעָמִים. אָמְרוּ לָהֶן בֵּית שַׁמַּי אֵין בְּנוֹת יִשְׂרָאֵל הֶבְקֵר. אֶלָּא מְמָאֶנֶת וּמַמְתֶּנֶת עַד שֶׁתַּגְדִּיל וּתְמָאֵן וְתִנָּשֵׂא.

Mishnah 1: The House of Shammai say, one makes only betrothed girls repudiate[1]. The House of Hillel say, betrothed or married. The House of Shammai say, the husband, but the House of Hillel say, the husband or the levir[2]. The House of Shammai say, in his presence, but the House of Hillel say, in his presence or in his absence. The House of Shammai say, in a court of law, but the House of Hillel say, in a court or outside a court. The House of Hillel said to the House of Shammai: An underage girl may repudiate even four or five times[3]. The House of Shammai said to them: The daughters of Israel are not abandoned property[4]! But she repudiates, waits until she is of age, or repudiates and is married[5].

1 An underage girl can be married off by her father (*Deut*. 22:16). If the father is dead, the girl can be married off by her mother or her brothers under rabbinic rules. Since that marriage is not valid under biblical rules, if the girl dislikes the marriage she can walk out of it by a simple declaration, without formalities (Chapter 1, Note 118). The House of

Shammai restrict this possibility to the betrothed girl. They hold that a consummated marriage can be dissolved only by a bill of divorce, irrespective of how the marriage was contracted.

The active formulation, that one makes a girl repudiate, means that under certain circumstances, explained later in the Mishnah, one tells the girl to repudiate.

2 The House of Shammai and Sadducees restrict levirate to the widowed betrothed girl (Chapter 1, Note 192). They consider candidacy for levirate as binding as marriage.

3 A girl married off by her father becomes an adult by the consummation of marriage. But a girl married off by mother or brothers is not married by biblical standards and, therefore, does not become an adult until she reaches her twelfth year.

4 That she can sleep with any man she chooses and then leave him without formality.

5 Since the House of Shammai do not permit repudiation by married girls, she may remarry as a minor if betrothal and marriage come together.

(fol. 13b) **הלכה א:** בֵּית שַׁמַּי אוֹמְרִים אֵין מְמֵאֲנִין כול׳. תַּמָּן תַּנִּינָן. רִבִּי יוּדָה בַּר אַבָּא הֵעִיד חֲמִשָּׁה דְבָרִים. שֶׁמְּמָאֲנִין אֶת הַקְּטַנּוֹת. וְעַל עֵדוּת חוֹלְקִין. עַל עִיקַּר עֵדוּת חוֹלְקִין. כָּךְ הָיְתָה עִיקַּר עֵדוּתָן. בֵּית שַׁמַּאי אוֹמְרִים. אֵין מְמָאֲנִין אֶלָּא אֲרוּסוֹת. וּבֵית הִלֵּל אוֹמְרִים. אֲרוּסוֹת וּנְשׂוּאוֹת. וְקַשְׁיָא עַל דְּבֵית הִלֵּל. נִישּׂוּאֶיהָ הִתִּירָהּ וְזַכַּאי בִּמְצִיאָתָהּ וּבְמַעֲשֵׂה יָדֶיהָ וּבְהֵפֵר נְדָרֶיהָ כְּאִשְׁתּוֹ לְכָל־דָּבָר. וְאַתְּ אָמַר הָכֵין. מִשֶּׁלָּךְ נָתְנוּ לָךְ. בְּדִין הָיָה שֶׁלֹּא הָיוּ נִישּׂוּאֶיהָ נִישּׂוּאִין. וְהֵן אָמְרוּ שֶׁיְּהוּ נִישּׂוּאֶיהָ נִישּׂוּאִין. וְהֵן אָמְרוּ שֶׁתְּמָאֵן בּוֹ וְתֵצֵא.

Halakhah 1: "The House of Shammai say, one permits repudiation," etc. There[6], we have stated: "Rebbi Jehudah bar Abba testified to five statements: That one makes underage girls repudiate, . . ." Does one disagree with testimony[7]? One disagrees about the essence of the testimony. So was the essence of the testimony: "The House of Shammai say, one makes only betrothed girls repudiate, but the House of Hillel say, betrothed or married". It is difficult following the House of Hillel! Her marriage permitted her[8], he has the right to what she finds and earns[9], to dissolve her vows[10], and she is his wife in every respect. And you say so? They gave you of your own. By right, her marriage should not be a marriage. They[11] said that her marriage is a marriage and they said that she may repudiate him and leave.

6 Mishnah *Idiut* 6:1. In most Mishnah sources, the tradent is R. Jehudah ben Baba.

7 Tractate *Idiut* is a collection of confirmed testimonies an attempt is made to reconstruct a history of early practice. These are recognized as authoritative.

8 The husband's sexual relations with her are meritorious as married sex and not sinful promiscuity.

9 In exchange for the obligations the husband accepted by executing the *ketubah*, he by rabbinic convention acquires the right to the future earnings of his wife.

10 The biblical prerogative of the husband (*Num.* 30:9).

11 The anonymous authors of the institutions of rabbinic Judaism, known as "the men of the great assembly".

מַה טַעֲמוֹן דְּבֵית שַׁמַּי. אִם אוֹמֵר אַתְּ כֵּן נִמְצֵאתָה עוֹשֶׂה כָּל־הַבְּעִילוֹת שֶׁבָּעַל בְּעִילַת זְנוּת. אָמַר רִבִּי אָבִין. אַתְיָא דְבֵית שַׁמַּי כְּרִבִּי לְעָזָר. דְּתַנֵּי. רִבִּי לְעָזָר אָמַר. אַף הַפָּנוּי הַבָּא עַל הַפְּנוּיָה שֶׁלֹּא לְשׁוּם אִישׁוּת הֲרֵי זוֹ בְעִילַת זְנוּת. הָדָא אָמְרָה. עָבְרָה וּמֵיאֲנָה מִן הַנִּישּׂוּאִין עַל דְּבֵית שַׁמַּאי אֵין מֵיאוּנֶיהָ מֵיאוּנִין. נִכְנְסָה לַחוּפָּה וְלֹא נִבְעֲלָה. מַה אַתְּ עֲבַד לָהּ. כַּאֲרוּסָה כִנְשׂוּאָה. אֲרוּסָה שֶׁבִּיהוּדָה שֶׁלִּבּוֹ גַס בָּהּ. מַה אַתְּ עֲבַד לָהּ. כַּאֲרוּסָה כִנְשׂוּאָה.

What is the reason of the House of Shammai? If you say so, you make all intercourse he had with her intercourse of harlotry[13]. Rebbi Abin said, it turns out that the House of Shammai hold with Rebbi Eleazar as Rebbi Eleazar said, intercourse of an unmarried man with an unmarried woman not with the intent of marriage is intercourse of harlotry[14]. That means, for the House of Shammai her repudiation is nothing if she transgressed and repudiated after marriage. If she entered the bridal chamber but had no intercourse yet, what is her status? As betrothed or as married? If she is betrothed in Judea where he is familiar with her[15], what is her status? As betrothed or as married[16]?

13 An outside event would turn legitimate behavior retroactively into sin. The Babli, 107a, in a first explanation formulates that nobody would marry a fatherless underage girl since he does not want to run the risk involved.

14 Chapter 6, Note 108. In the Babli, 107a, the House of Hillel hold that intercourse in a formal marriage can never be sinful.

15 Where betrothed couples were permitted unchaperoned meetings. It is assumed that they slept together; Mishnah *Ketubot* 1:5.

16 The questions are not answered since practice does not follow the House of Shammai. The Babli holds that in all these cases, the House of Shammai would treat her as married.

נִרְאֵית שֶׁלֹּא לְמֵאֵן אֲפִילוּ כֵן חוֹזֶרֶת וּמְמָאֶנֶת נִישְׁמְעִינָהּ מִן הָדָא. קְטַנָּה שֶׁהִשִּׂיאָהּ אָבִיהָ וְנִתְגָּרְשָׁה וְהָלְכָה הִיא וְהִשִּׂיאָה אֶת עַצְמָהּ אֲפִילוּ כֵן חוֹזֶרֶת וּמְמָאֶנֶת.

If she had been in a situation that she could not repudiate, may she go and repudiate? Let us hear from the following: An underage girl who was married off by her father[17] but then was divorced[18], if she went and married by herself she nevertheless can repudiate.

17 This is marriage by biblical standards and can be dissolved only by death or a bill of divorce.

18 She does not return to her father's authority, she is "an orphan during her father's lifetime". Nevertheless, she cannot contract as an adult as long as she is underage. This means any marriage she contracts now, even if arranged by her father, is only rabbinic and subject to repudiation before she reaches the age of 12.

מַה טַעֲמוֹן דְּבֵית שַׁמַּי. בַּעֲלָהּ שֶׁנִּשֵּׂאת לוֹ לִרְצוֹנָהּ מְמָאֶנֶת. יְבָמָהּ שֶׁנָּפְלָה לוֹ עַל כָּרְחָהּ אֵינָהּ מְמָאֶנֶת. מַה טַעֲמוֹן דְּבֵית הִלֵּל. אִם בְּעִקָּר הִיא מְמָאֶנֶת לֹא

כָּל־שֶׁכֵּן בְּיָבָם. רִבִּי יוֹחָנָן אָמַר. מְמָאֶנֶת הִיא בְּיָבָם לַעֲקוֹר זִיקַת הַמֵּת לְהַתִּיר צָרָה לְאָבִיהָ וְכַלָּה לְחָמִיהָ. רַב וְרִבִּי שִׁמְעוֹן בֶּן לָקִישׁ תְּרֵיהוֹן אָמְרִין. אֵינָהּ מְמָאֶנֶת בְּיָבָם לַעֲקוֹר זִיקַת הַמֵּת לְהַתִּיר צָרָה לְאָבִיהָ וְכַלָּה לְחָמִיהָ. רַב וְרִבִּי שִׁמְעוֹן בֶּן לָקִישׁ כְּבֵית שַׁמַּאי. דְּבֵית שַׁמַּאי אוֹמְרִים. בְּבַעַל. מַה אֲנָן קַייָמִין. אִם בְּאוֹמֶרֶת. אֵי אֶיפְשִׁי לֹא בְנִישׂוּאֶיךָ וְלֹא בְנִישׂוּאֵי אָחִיךָ. כָּל־עַמָּא מוֹדֵיי שֶׁהִיא עוֹקֶרֶת. וְאִם בְּאוֹמֶרֶת. אֶפְשִׁי בְנִישׂוּאֶיךָ אֲבָל לֹא בְנִישׂוּאֵי אָחִיךָ. רַב וְרִבִּי שִׁמְעוֹן בֶּן לָקִישׁ תְּרֵיהוֹן אָמְרִין. בְּאוֹמֶרֶת. אֶפְשִׁי בְנִישׂוּאֶיךָ אֲבָל לֹא בְנִישׂוּאֵי אָחִיךָ רוֹצָה אֲנִי. מַתְנִיתָא פְלִיגָא עַל רִבִּי יוֹחָנָן. וְכוּלָּן אִם מֵתוּ אוֹ מֵאֲנוּ אוֹ נִתְגָּרְשׁוּ (fol. 13c) אוֹ שֶׁנִּמְצְאוּ אַיְלוֹנִית צָרוֹתֵיהֶן מוּתָּרוֹת. נִתְגָּרְשׁוּ לֹא הִימֵּינוּ. וְדִכְווָתָהּ מֵאֲנוּ הִימֵּינוּ. תַּנֵּי רִבִּי חִזְקִיָּה כֵן. אִם מֵאֲנוּ בְחַיֵּי הַבַּעַל צָרוֹתֵיהֶן מוּתָּרוֹת. לְאַחַר מִיתַת הַבַּעַל צָרוֹתֵיהֶן חוֹלְצוֹת וְלֹא מִתְייַבְּמוֹת.

What is the reason of the House of Shammai[19]? The husband she may repudiate since she married him with her consent. The levir to whom she was given by an act of God she cannot repudiate. What is the reason of the House of Hillel? If she can repudiate the principal, so much more the levir!

[20]Rebbi Joḥanan said, she may repudiate the levir to invalidate the claim of the dead brother and to permit the co-wife to her father and the daughter-in-law to her father-in-law. Rav and Rebbi Simeon ben Laqish both say, she may not repudiate the levir to invalidate the claim of the dead brother and to permit the co-wife to her father and the daughter-in-law to her father-in-law. Do Rav and Rebbi Simeon ben Laqish follow the house of Shammai, since the House of Shammai say "the husband"? Where do we hold? If she says, I can stand neither the marriage with your brother nor with you, everybody agrees that she invalidates. If she says, I can stand marriage with you but not with your brother? Rav and Rebbi Simeon ben Laqish both say, she says I cannot stand marriage with you but marriage with your brother I want. The Mishnah disagrees with

Rebbi Johanan: "And all of these, if they died, or repudiated, or were divorced, or found to be she-rams, their co-wives are permitted." Was she not divorced from him? Similarly, she repudiated him. Rebbi Ḥiyya stated: If they repudiated or were divorced in the husband's lifetime, their co-wives are permitted. After the husband's death their co-wives perform *ḥalîṣah* but not levirate.

אָמַר רִבִּי יוּדָן אָבוּי דְּרִבִּי מַתַּנְיָיה. תִּיפְתָּר שֶׁמֵּתוּ וְלֹא מֵאֲנוּ. דְּמַתְנִיתָא אָמְרָה כָּל־הַיְכוֹלָה לְמָאֵן וְלֹא מֵאֲנוּ וּמֵתָה צָרָתָהּ חוֹלֶצֶת וְלֹא מִתְייַבֶּמֶת. אָמַר רִבִּי אַבוּדִימִי. אֲפִילוּ תֵימַר בְּקַייֶמֶת. תִּיפְתָּר שֶׁאֵין שָׁם יָבָם אַחֵר אֶלָּא אָבִיהָ.

Rebbi Yudan, the father of Rebbi Mattaniah said: Explain it when they died and did not repudiate since there is a Mishnah: "If a woman could repudiate but did not do so and died, her co-wife performs *ḥalîṣah* but cannot be married in levirate." Rebbi Eudaimon said, you may even say if she still lives; explain it if there is no levir besides her father.

רִבִּי יוֹנָה אוֹמֵר. מִן הָאֵירוּסִין. רִבִּי יוֹסֵה אוֹמֵר. אֲפִילוּ מִן הַנִּישּׂוּאִין. בְּמַחֲזִירָה תִנְיָנָא חָזַר בּוֹ רִבִּי יוֹסֵה. אָמַר לֵיהּ רִבִּי פִּנְחָס. לֹא כֵן אִלְּפָן רִבִּי. אֲפִילוּ מִן הַנִּישּׂוּאִין. אָמַר לֵיהּ. וְהָא קְבִיעָה גַּבָּךְ בְּמַסְמֵירָא.

Rebbi Jonah said, after *qiddušin*. Rebbi Yose said, even after final marriage. In the second repetition, Rebbi Yose changed his mind. Rebbi Phineas said to him, did the rabbi not teach us "after final marriage"? He answered him, is that fixed in you with a nail?

אָמַר רִבִּי זְעִירָה קוֹמֵי רִבִּי מָנָא. יֵאוּת. אָמַר רִבִּי יוֹסֵה עַד לֹא יַחֲזוֹר. מַה אִילּוּ בִתּוֹ מִן הַנִּישּׂוּאִין בְּלֹא אַיילוֹנִית צָרָתָהּ אֲסוּרָה. מִפְּנֵי שֶׁנִּיתּוֹסַף לָאַיילוֹנִית צָרוֹתֶיהֶן מוּתָּרוֹת. אָמַר לֵיהּ. אַיילוֹנִית כְּמִי שֶׁאֵינָהּ בָּעוֹלָם. אִילּוּ שְׁתֵּי יְבָמוֹת אַחַת אַיילוֹנִית וְאַחַת שֶׁאֵינָהּ אַיילוֹנִית וּבָא הַיָּבָם וְחָלַץ לָהּ וּבָא עָלֶיהָ. שֶׁמָּא פָטַר בַּחֲבֵירָתָהּ כְּלוּם. הֲוָה אַיילוֹנִית כְּמִי שֶׁאֵינָהּ בָּעוֹלָם.

Rebbi Ze'ira said before Rebbi Mana, did not Rebbi Yose say correctly before he changed his mind? Once a man's daughter is married without being a she-ram, her co-wife is forbidden. If in addition she is a she-ram, does her co-wife become permitted? He said to him, the she-ram is as if non-existent. If there are two sisters-in-law, one a she-ram and one not a she-ram, if the levir comes and performs *ḥalîṣah* or has intercourse with the first, did he free her companion of anything? That shows that the she-ram is as if non-existent.

בִּתּוֹ מְמָאֶנֶת. וְלֹא נִישׂוּאֵי תוֹרָה הֵן. אֶת בִּתִּי נָתַתִּי לָאִישׁ הַזֶּה. רִבִּי הוּנָא בְּשֵׁם רִבִּי שִׁמְעוֹן בֶּן לָקִישׁ. תִּיפְתָּר בִּקְטַנָּה שֶׁהִשִּׂיאָהּ אָבִיהָ וְנִתְגָּרְשָׁה. שֶׁהִיא כִיתוֹמָה בְּחַיֵּי אָבִיהָ.

"His daughter". How can his daughter repudiate, is she not married by Torah standards, "my daughter I gave to this man"? Rebbi Huna in the name of Rebbi Simeon ben Laqish: Explain it by a minor, who was married off by her father and divorced, who is like an orphan while her father is alive.

רִבִּי אָחָא רִבִּי חִנְּנָה בְּשֵׁם רִבִּי שִׁמְעוֹן בֶּן לָקִישׁ. זֹאת אוֹמֶרֶת שֶׁאֵין קְטַנָּה יוֹלֶדֶת. דְּלֹא כֵן תַּמְתִּין עַד שֶׁתַּגְדִּיל וּתְמָאֵן בְּבַעֲלָהּ וְתַתִּיר צָרָתָהּ לַחֲתְנָהּ. כַּלָּתוֹ שֶׁל רִבִּי יִשְׁמָעֵאל מֵיאֵינָה וּבְנָהּ עַל כְּתֵיפָהּ.

Rebbi Aḥa, Rebbi Ḥinnena, in the name of Rebbi Simeon ben Laqish: This means that a minor cannot give birth; because otherwise she could wait until she grew up, repudiate her husband, and permit her co-wife to her son-in-law. The daughter-in-law of Rebbi Ismael repudiated while her son was on her shoulder.

19 Why do the House of Shammai forbid repudiation of the levir and the House of Hillel permit it?

20 This text is from Chapter 1,

Halakhah 2, Notes 121-139, with small variations, mostly in spelling.

רַב הַמְנוּנָא בְשֵׁם אַסִּי. בִּיבָמָה שֶׁנָּפְלָה לִפְנֵי שְׁנֵי יְבָמִין הִיא מַתְנִיתָא. וְעָשָׂה בָהּ אֶחָד מֵהֶן מַאֲמָר תְּמָאֵן בְּמַאֲמָרוֹ וְתִינָּשֵׂא לַשּׁוּק. וּתְמָאֵן בְּמַאֲמָרוֹ וְתִינָּשֵׂא לְאָחִיו. תִּיפְתָּר בְּאוֹמֶרֶת. אִי אֶיפְשִׁי בָךְ. רִבִּי הִילָא בְשֵׁם רִבִּי שִׁמְעוֹן בֶּן יוֹסִינָא בְשֵׁם רִבִּי הוֹשַׁעְיָא. בִּיבָמָה שֶׁנָּפְלָה לִפְנֵי חֲמִשָּׁה יְבָמִין הִיא מַתְנִיתָא. עָשָׂה בָהּ אֶחָד מֵהֶן מַאֲמָר תְּמָאֵן לְמַאֲמָרוֹ וְתִינָּשֵׂא לְאָחִיו. וּתְמָאֵן בְּמַאֲמָרוֹ וְתִינָּשֵׂא לַשּׁוּק. תִּיפְתָּר בְּשֶׁהִשִּׂיאָהּ אָבִיהָ וְהֵן נִישּׂוּאֵי תוֹרָה.

Rav Hamnuna in the name of Assi: The Mishnah[21] speaks about a sister-in-law who has two levirs. If one of them "bespoke" her, she may repudiate his "bespeaking" and marry on the market place[22]. Why can she not repudiate his "bespeaking" and marry his brother? Explain it, if she says, I cannot stand you[23]. Rebbi Hila in the name of Rebbi Simeon ben Yosina in the name of Rebbi Hoshaia[24]: The Mishnah speaks about a sister-in-law who has five levirs[25]. If one of them "bespoke" her, she may repudiate his "bespeaking" and marry his brother[26]. Why can she not repudiate his "bespeaking" and marry on the market place? Explain it if her father had married her off, this was a marriage by biblical standards[27].

21 The House of Hillel who approve of repudiation of the levir apply this even to the case when there is more than one.

22 In the Babli, 107b, Rav Assi is reported that if she repudiates one of two levirs, she may even be married by the rejected levir himself since the Hose of Hillel will agree that the candidacy (Chapter 2, Note 9) imposed by an act of God cannot be repudiated. What is reported here is in Babli the opinion of Rav, that a repudiation of the levir implies repudiation of the original marriage and elimination of the levirate.

23 Meaning, neither you nor your deceased brother.

24 R. Hila is mentioned in the Babli, 107b, as Ulla who holds that repudiation eliminates candidacy. R. Hoshaia holds there, 107a, that "bespeaking" can be repudiated but not candidacy.

25 There is no difference in law between the case of 2 and that of 5 levirs.

26 The same position taken by R. Hoshaia in the Babli.

27 This contradicts the position ascribed to R. Hoshaia in the Babli; the only candidacy that is not subject to repudiation is one based on the biblical validity of the previous marriage.

אָמְרוּ בֵּית הִלֵּל לְבֵית שַׁמַּי. מַעֲשֶׂה בְּאִשְׁתּוֹ שֶׁלְּפִישׁוֹן הַגַּמָּל שֶׁמֵּיאֲנוּ לָהּ חֲכָמִים שֶׁלֹּא בְּפָנֶיהָ. אָמְרוּ לָהֶן בֵּית שַׁמַּי. מִשָּׁם רְאָיָה. לְפִי שֶׁמָּדַד בִּכְפִישָׁה לְפִיכָךְ מָדְדוּ לוֹ חֲכָמִים בִּכְפִישָׁה. וְקַשְׁיָא. אִילּוּ הָעוֹשֶׂה דָּבָר שֶׁלֹּא כְשׁוּרָה שֶׁמָּא מַתִּירִין עֶרְוָה שֶׁלּוֹ. אָמַר רַב חַסְדָּא. הָדָא אָמְרָה. עָבְרָה וּמֵיאֲנָה מִן הַנִּישּׂוּאִין עַל דְּבֵית שַׁמַּי מֵיאוּנֶיהָ מֵיאוּנִין.

"[28]The House of Hillel said to the House of Shammai: It happened with the wife of the cameldriver Pison that the Sages repudiated for her in her absence[29]. The House of Shammai said to them, is that a proof? Since he measured crookedly, the Sages measured crookedly for him[30]." This is difficult. Because a man behaves incorrectly, does one permit his incest prohibition[31]? Rab Ḥisda said, that means that, if she transgresses and repudiated after marriage, the House of Shammai recognize her act of repudiation[32].

28 Quoted also in the Babli, 107b.

29 In the Babli: "That his wife repudiated him in his absence". In the version of the Yerushalmi, the court acted as the guardian of the orphan.

30 The Babli explained that he was dishonest in administering her property.

31 Since the House of Shammai hold that a married woman cannot repudiate, they seem to lift the prohibition of adultery from Pison's wife. The Babli does not have this problem since it holds that "everybody who marries, marries under rabbinic rules" and that, therefore, a rabbinic court is empowered to annul a marriage as punishment for a severe infraction of the rules (e. g., Babli 90a, 110a, *Giṭṭin* 33a). There is no such claim in the Yerushalmi.

32 This disproves the earlier assertion to the contrary.

רִבִּי בָּא בְּשֵׁם רַב חִיָּיה בַּר אַשִׁי. מַעֲשֶׂה בְתִינּוֹקֶת שֶׁיָּרְדָה לְכַבֵּס בַּנָּהָר. אָֽמְרוּ לָהּ. הָא אָרוּסֵיךְ אִיעֲבַר. אָֽמְרָה. תֵּלֵךְ אִמָּה וְתִינָּשֵׂא לוֹ. וּבָא מַעֲשֶׂה לִפְנֵי חֲכָמִים וְאָֽמְרוּ. אֵין מֵיאוּן גָּדוֹל מִזֶּה. אָמַר רִבִּי חֲנִינָה. מַעֲשֶׂה בְתִינּוֹקֶת שֶׁנִּכְנְסָה לִיטּוֹל פִּשְׁתָּן מִן הַפִּשְׁתָּנִי. אָֽמְרִין לָהּ. הָא אָרוּסֵיךְ אִיעֲבַר. אָֽמְרָה. תֵּלֵךְ אִמָּה וְתִינָּשֵׂא לוֹ. וּבָא מַעֲשֶׂה לִפְנֵי חֲכָמִים וְאָֽמְרוּ. אֵין מֵיאוּן גָּדוֹל מִזֶּה. תַּנֵּי בְשֵׁם רִבִּי יוּדָה. אֲפִילוּ לֹא נִכְנְסָה אֶלָּא לִיטּוֹל חֵפֶץ מִן הַחֶנְוָנִי. וְאָֽמְרָה. אֵי אֶפְשִׁי בִּפְלוֹנִי בַּעֲלִי. אֵין מֵיאוּן גָּדוֹל מִזֶּה.

Rebbi Abba in the name of Rav Ḥiyya bar Ashi: It happened that a girl went to wash at the river when they said to her, your betrothed is passing by. She said, let my mother go and marry him! When the case came before the Sages, they said that there is no repudiation stronger than that. Rebbi Ḥanina said, It happened that a girl went to buy flax from the flax dealer when they said to her, your betrothed is passing by. She said, let my mother go and marry him! When the case came before the Sages, they said that there is no repudiation stronger than that. It was stated in the name of Rebbi Jehudah[33]: "Even if she went to buy something at the store and said, I cannot endure my husband X, there is no repudiation stronger than this.

33 Tosephta 13:1; a similar text in Babli 108a.

וּבֵית דִּין יוֹשְׁבִין בְּמֵיאוּנִין. לֹא כֵן תַּנֵּי. בְּרַח מִן שָׁלֹשׁ וְהִידָּבֵק בְּשָׁלֹשׁ. הִידַּבֵּק בַּחֲלִיצָה וּבְהֵיתֵר נְדָרִים וּבַהֲבָאַת שָׁלוֹם. וּבְרַח מִן הַמֵּיאוּנִין וּמִלְּהִיוֹת עָרֵב וּמִלְּהִיוֹת בַּעַל פִּיקָּדוֹן אָמַר רִבִּי שִׁמְעוֹן בַּר בָּא. לֵית שְׁמָהּ פִּיקָּדוֹן אֶלָּא פּוּק דּוֹן אָמַר רִבִּי בְּרֶכְיָה. בְּנִי אִם עָרַבְתָּ לְרֵעֶךָ. וּבֵית דִּין יוֹשְׁבִין בְּמֵיאוּנִין. תִּיפְתָּר דַּהֲוָיין עֲסוּקִין בְּמִילָּה חוֹרִי וְאָתָא עוֹבְדָא קוֹמֵיהוֹן.

Does a court convene for repudiation[34]? Was it not stated[35]: Flee from three and cling to three. Cling to *ḥalîṣah*, annulling vows, and making peace. But flee from repudiations, from being a guarantor, and from receiving deposits. Rebbi Simeon bar Abba[36] said, its name is not פקדון "deposit" but פק דון "go to court". Rebbi Berekhiah said, "My son, if you became guanrantor for your neighbor." Does a court convene for repudiation? Explain it that they were sitting in another matter and the case came before them[37].

34 This refers to the requirement of the House of Shammai that the court be a party to any repudiation.

35 *Gen. rabba* 93a, in the name of R. Ḥanina. In the Babli, 109a, a statement of Bar Qappara.

36 In *Gen. rabba*, R. Berekhiah in the name of R. Simeon bar Abba.

37 The Babli applies the negative statement only to frivolous repudiations, not to necessary ones.

כֵּינִי מַתְנִיתָא. וּתְמָאֵן בּוֹ וְתִינָּשֵׂא. הָא תִּתְאָרֵס לֹא. הָדָא אָמְרָה. עָבְרָה וּמֵיאֲנָה מִן הַנִּישּׂוּאִין עַל דְּבֵית שַׁמַּי מֵיאוּנֶיהָ מֵיאוּנִין. רִבִּי אָחָא בְּשֵׁם רִבִּי תַנְחוּם בַּר חִייָה. קוֹל יוֹצֵא לַנְּשׂוּאָה וְאֵין קוֹל יוֹצֵא לָאֲרוּסָה. יְכוֹלָה אִשָּׁה לְהַטְמִין עַצְמָהּ וְלוֹמַר. לֹא נִתְאָרַסְתִּי. וְאֵינָהּ יְכוֹלָה לְהַטְמִין עַצְמָהּ וְלוֹמַר. לֹא נִשֵּׂאתִי.

So is the Mishnah: Or she should repudiate him and marry. Therefore, she cannot get herself betrothed. That means, if she transgresses and repudiated after marriage, the House of Shammai recognize her act of repudiation[38]. Rebbi Abba in the name of Rebbi Tanḥum bar Ḥiyya: A rumor spreads for a married woman but not for a betrothed one. A woman might hide herself and say, I was not betrothed, but she will not be able to hide herself and say, I did not marry[39].

38 This opinion must read the statement of the House of Shammai as: If she repudiates, she may remarry in any case.

39 R. Abba reads the statement of the House of Shammai not as a

requirement but as a counsel given to the husband to publicize the marriage in order to make his claim to her widely known. (While betrothal needs only two witnesses, a standard marriage ceremony needs at least ten invitees. They will make the fact of the marriage widely known.)

(fol. 13b) **משנה ב**: אֵי זוֹ הִיא קְטַנָּה שֶׁצְּרִיכָה לְמֵאֵן. כָּל־שֶׁהִשִּׂיאָתָהּ אִמָּהּ וְאַחֶיהָ מִדַּעְתָּהּ. הִשִּׂיאוּהָ שֶׁלֹּא מִדַּעְתָּהּ אֵינָהּ צְרִיכָה לְמָאֵן. רִבִּי חֲנִינָה בֶּן אַנְטִיגְנוֹס אוֹמֵר כָּל־תִּינוֹקֶת שֶׁאֵינָהּ יְכוֹלָה לִשְׁמוֹר קִידּוּשֶׁיהָ אֵינָהּ צְרִיכָה לְמֵאֵן. רִבִּי אֱלִיעֶזֶר אוֹמֵר אֵין מַעֲשֵׂה קְטַנָּה אֶלָּא כִמְפוּתָּה. בַּת יִשְׂרָאֵל לַכֹּהֵן לֹא תֹאכַל בַּתְּרוּמָה בַּת כֹּהֵן לְיִשְׂרָאֵל תֹּאכַל בַּתְּרוּמָה.

Mishnah 2: Which underage girl needs to repudiate? Anyone whom mother or brothers married off with her knowledge[40]. If they married her off without her knowledge[41] she does not have to repudiate. Rebbi Ḥanina ben Antigonos says, any girl who is unable to watch over her marriage gift does not have to repudiate[42]. Rebbi Eliezer says, in all legal respects, the underage girl is like one seduced[43]: The daughter of an Israel married to a Cohen may not eat heave; the daughter of a Cohen married to an Israel may eat heave.

40 She has been informed that she is going to live with that man as his wife.

41 If either she was not informed that she was a wife or she was too young to understand the implications, she may walk out without any formality. The minimum age for a girl to be married is three years and one day (Mishnah *Niddah* 5:4).

42 If she is apt to give her marriage ring away as any other piece of jewelry, she is not married.

43 Since the underage cannot legally enter a contract, her marriage has no legal consequences until she comes of age.

(fol. 13c) **מתניתין:** אֵי זוֹ הִיא קְטַנָּה שֶׁצְּרִיכָה לְמָאֵן כול׳. אֵי זֶהוּ לְדַעְתָּהּ. עָבַד לָהּ גְּנוֹן וּמְלַבְּשִׁין לָהּ קוֹזְמִידִין וּמַדְבְּרִין לָהּ גֶּבֶר.

Mishnah: "Which underage girl needs to repudiate," etc? What means "with her knowledge"? One makes for her a canopy, dresses her in jewelry[44] and leads the man to her.

44 Greek κοσμίδια "jewelry".

מַה חֲלוּקִין עַל רִבִּי חֲנַנְיָה בֶּן אַנְטִיגְנוֹס. מִן מַה דָּמַר רִבִּי יוֹחָנָן. אֵי זוֹ הִיא קְטַנָּה שֶׁהִיא צְרִיכָה לְהִתְגָּרֵשׁ. כָּל־שֶׁנּוֹתְנִין לָהּ גִּיטָּהּ וְדָבָר אַחֵר עִמּוֹ וְהִיא מוֹצִיאָה אוֹתוֹ לְאַחַר זְמָן. הָדָא אָמְרָה. חֲלוּקִין עַל רִבִּי חֲנַנְיָה בֶּן אַנְטִיגְנוֹס.

Do they disagree with Rebbi Ḥananiah ben Antigonos? From what Rebbi Joḥanan said, which is the underage girl that needs a bill of divorce? Anyone who is given her bill of divorce together with something else and she produces it after some time[45]. This implies that they disagree with Rebbi Ḥananiah ben Antigonos.

45 Since a bill of divorce is needed if the girl is able to take care of that bill (which she needs as proof that she is unmarried and can enter a second marriage) irrespective of her maturity when she was married first, it proves that the majority does not require more than that she was made aware that she was being married and reasonably could understand what that meant.

רִבִּי לִיעֶזֶר אוֹמֵר אֵין מַעֲשֵׂה קְטַנָּה כְּלוּם. אֵינוֹ זַכַּאי לֹא בִמְצִיאָתָהּ וְלֹא בְמַעֲשֵׂה יָדֶיהָ וְלֹא בְהֵפֵר נְדָרֶיהָ כִּילּוּ שֶׁאֵינָהּ אִשְׁתּוֹ לְכָל־דָּבָר. אֶלָּא שֶׁהִיא צְרִיכָה מִמֶּנּוּ מֵיאוּנִין. רִבִּי יְהוֹשֻׁעַ אוֹמֵר. זַכַּאי בִּמְצִיאָתָהּ וּבְמַעֲשֵׂה יָדֶיהָ וּבְהֵפֵר נְדָרֶיהָ כִּילּוּ הִיא אִשְׁתּוֹ לְכָל־דָּבָר. אֶלָּא שֶׁהִיא יוֹצְאָה הֵימֶינּוּ בְּגֵט. אָמַר רִבִּי יִשְׁמָעֵאל. חִיזַּרְתִּי עַל כָּל־מִידּוֹת חֲכָמִים וְלֹא מָצָאתִי אָדָם שֶׁמִּידָּתוֹ שָׁוָה בִקְטַנָּה חוּץ מִמִּידַּת רִבִּי אֱלִיעֶזֶר. אֶלָּא שֶׁהוּא אוֹמֵר שֶׁהִיא צְרִיכָה מִמֶּנּוּ מֵיאוּנִין.

[46]Rebbi Eliezer says, the actions of an underage girl have no legal standing. He has no right to what she finds or earns, nor may he dissolve her vows; she is as if not his wife in any respect except that she needs repudiation from him. Rebbi Joshua said, he owns what she finds or earns, he may he dissolve her vows; she is his wife in all respects except that she needs a bill of divorce from him[47]. [48]Rebbi Ismael said, I looked around at all logical systems of Sages and did not find anybody who was consistent in the matter of an underage girl except Rebbi Eliezer, only that he requires repudiation from him.

46 Tosephta 13:3, Babli 108a.

47 In all parallel sources: 'except that she needs repudiation from him." That reading is required by the next sentence, since otherwise R. Joshua would be more logically consistent than R. Eliezer.

48 Tosephta 13:4; in the Babli, this is an Amoraic statement by Samuel.

אָמַר רִבִּי אַבָּהוּ. מַעֲשֶׂה בְּאִמּוֹ שֶׁל רִבִּי לִיעֶזֶר שֶׁהָיְתָה דוֹחֶקֶת בּוֹ לַשֵּׂאת אֶת בַּת אֲחוֹתוֹ. וְהָיָה אוֹמֵר לָהּ. בִּתִּי. לְכִי הִינָּשְׂאִי. בִּתִּי. לְכִי הִינָּשְׂאִי. עַד שֶׁאָמְרָה לוֹ. הֲרֵי אֲנִי שִׁפְחָה לְךָ לִרְחוֹץ רַגְלֵי עַבְדֵי אֲדֹנִי. אַף עַל פִּי כֵן כְּנָסָהּ וְלֹא הִכִּירָהּ עַד שֶׁהֵבִיאָה שְׁתֵּי שְׂעָרוֹת.

Rebbi Abbahu said: It happened that Rebbi Eliezer's mother was pushing him to marry his sister's daughter. He said to [the girl]: go and get married, go and get married, until she said to him: Here I am your slave girl to wash the feet of my master's servants[49]. Even though he married her, he did not sleep with her until she had grown two pubic hairs[50].

49 A slightly garbled version of Abigail's speech, *1S.* 25:41.

50 Since for him, sleeping with an underage girl is tantamount to seducing her, even in a marriage.

עַל דַּעְתֵּיהּ דְּרִבִּי לִיעֶזֶר. מַהוּ שֶׁתְּמָאֵן בּוֹ וְתִיטּוֹל קְנָס מִמֶּנּוּ. עַל דַּעְתֵּיהּ דְּרִבִּי יְהוֹשֻׁעַ. מַהוּ שֶׁתְּמָאֵן בּוֹ וְתִיטּוֹל קְנָס מֵאַחֵר. מַהוּ שֶׁתְּמָאֵן בּוֹ וְתַעֲקוֹר גִּיטָּהּ חֲלָלָה וּמַמְזֶרֶת. רִבִּי יִצְחָק שָׁאַל. מַהוּ שֶׁתְּמָאֵן בּוֹ וְתַחֲזִיר לִמְזוֹנוֹת אָבִיהָ. פְּשִׁיטָה שֶׁאֵינָהּ חוֹזֶרֶת לִמְזוֹנוֹת בַּעֲלָהּ. שֶׁכֵּן הוּא כוֹתֵב לָהּ. וְאַתְּ תְּהַוְיֵין יָתְבָא בְּבֵיתִי וּמִיתְזַנָה מִן נִכְסַיי. וְלֵית הוּא בֵיתָהּ. לֹא צוֹרְכָה דְלֹא. מַהוּ שֶׁתְּמָאֵן בּוֹ וְתַחֲזִיר לִמְזוֹנוֹת אָבִיהָ.

According to Rebbi Eliezer, may she repudiate him and collect a fine from him[51]? According to Rebbi Joshua, may she repudiate him and collect a fine from another man[52]? May she repudiate this one and invalidate her bill of divorce, a desecrated or a bastard[53]? Rebbi Isaac asked, may she repudiate and return to her father's food[54]? It is obvious that she does not return to her husband's food[55] since he writes for her: "You shall live in my house and be fed from my property,[56]" and she is not in his house. Therefore, the only question is, may she repudiate and return to her father's food?

51 Since for R. Eliezer any sex act with a minor girl is a seduction, may she repudiate him and go to court to collect the money due a virgin from her seducer?

52 Assuming she was still a virgin; if she repudiated the man, may she claim never to have been married and therefore be entitled to all the payments the seducer or the rapist of a virgin has to pay?

53 These are different questions taken together. If a Cohen married an underage girl forbidden to him and she repudiated him, does that retroactively free the Cohen from the guilt incurred in the marriage (and its eventual punishment)? Or if she repudiates a second marriage, may she return to the first husband even though for an adult that would be a transgression of a biblical prohibition; cf. Mishnaiot 4-6.

54 The daughter of a Cohen married to an Israel. This is no problem for R. Eliezer since she never stopped eating Cohen's food.

55 After he divorced her. The question whether the repudiating wife has any monetary claim on the husband is also asked in the Babli, *Ketubot* 53b,

and is left unanswared (In the absence of a legal ruling, the claimant cannot prove his case and cannot collect.)

56 Mishnah *Ketubot* 4:12.

תַּמָּן תַּנִּינָן. קָטָן שֶׁלֹּא הֵבִיא שְׁתֵּי שְׂעָרוֹת. רִבִּי יוּדָה אוֹמֵר. תְּרוּמָתוֹ תְרוּמָה. תַּנֵּי בְשֵׁם רִבִּי מֵאִיר. לְעוֹלָם אֵין תְּרוּמָתוֹ תְרוּמָה עַד שֶׁיָּבִיא שְׁתֵּי שְׂעָרוֹת. רִבִּי אָבִין כַּהֲנָא בְּשֵׁם רִבִּי הִילָא. וְלֹא תִשְׂאוּ עָלָיו חֵטְא אֶת שֶׁהוּא בִנְשִׂיאַת עָוֹן תּוֹרֵם. אֶת שְׁאֵינוֹ בִנְשִׂיאַת עָוֹן אֵינוֹ תוֹרֵם. הָתִיבוּן. גוֹיִם הֲרֵי אֵינוֹ בִנְשִׂיאַת עָוֹן וְתוֹרֵם. רִבִּי יוֹסֵי בְּשֵׁם רִבִּי הִילָא. וְנֶחְשַׁב לָכֶם וַהֲרֵמוֹתֶם אֶת שֶׁכָּתוּב בּוֹ מַחֲשָׁבָה תוֹרֵם. וְאֶת שֶׁאֵין כָּתוּב בּוֹ מַחֲשָׁבָה אֵינוֹ תוֹרֵם. הָתִיבוּן. הֲרֵי גוֹיִם הֲרֵי אֵין כָּתוּב בָּהֶן מַחֲשָׁבָה וְתוֹרֵם. תַּנֵּי (fol. 13d) רִבִּי הוֹשַׁעְיָה גוֹיִם אֵין לָהֶן מַחֲשָׁבָה בֵּין לְהַכְשִׁיר בֵּין לִתְרוּמָה.

[57]There, we have stated: Rebbi Jehudah says, the heave given by a minor who has not yet grown two pubic hairs is heave. It was stated in the name of Rebbi Meïr: His heave is never heave unless he grew two pubic hairs. Rebbi Abin, Cahana in the name of the Rebbi Hila (*Num.* 18:32): "You should not carry guilt because of it." He who may carry guilt can give heave, he who cannot carry guilt cannot give heave. They objected: But a Gentile cannot incur guilt, and he may give heave! Rebbi Yose in the name of Rebbi Hila (*Num.* 18:27): "Your heave will be credited to you", (v. 26) "and you shall lift". Anybody for whom "thought" is written may give heave. But anybody for whom "thought" is not written cannot give heave. They objected: But "thought" is not written for Gentiles, and he may give heave! Rebbi Hoshaia stated: Gentiles have no "thought" whether for preparation or for heave.

רִבִּי אָחָא בַּר חִינְנָא בְשֵׁם כַּהֲנָא. כְּדִבְרֵי מִי שֶׁהוּא אוֹמֵר. אֵינוֹ תוֹרֵם וְאֵינוֹ מַקְדִּישׁ. וְלָמָּה לֹא אָמַר. כְּדִבְרֵי מִי שֶׁהוּא אוֹמֵר תּוֹרֵם וּמַקְדִּישׁ. בְּגִין דְּרִבִּי יוּדָה אָמַר. תּוֹרֵם וְאֵינוֹ מַקְדִּשׁ. אָמַר רִבִּי יוֹחָנָן. אֲפִילוּ כְבָאן דְּאָמַר. אֵינוֹ תוֹרֵם מַקְדִּשׁ. מָהוּ מַקְדִּשׁ. עוֹלָה וּשְׁלָמִים. לְהָבִיא חַטָּאת חֵלֶב אֵינוֹ יָכוֹל שֶׁאֵין

לוֹ חַטָּאת חֵלֶב. חַטָּאת דָּם אֵינוֹ יָכוֹל שֶׁאֵין לוֹ חַטָּאת דָּם. מָהוּ שֶׁיָּבִיא קָרְבַּן זִיבָה וְקָרְבַּן צָרַעַת. מֵאַחַר שֶׁהִיא חוֹבָה אֵינוֹ מֵבִיא אוֹ מֵאַחַר שֶׁהוּא מִטַּמֵּא בָּהֶן מֵבִיא. כְּוָתֵי פְּשִׁיטָא לָךְ שֶׁהוּא מֵבִיא. מָהוּ שֶׁיֵּעָשֶׂה בָּהֶן שָׁלִיחַ. מֵאַחַר שֶׁהוּא [מִטַּמֵּא][58] בָּהֶן נַעֲשֶׂה בָּהֶן שָׁלִיחַ אוֹ מֵאַחַר שֶׁאֵינוֹ נַעֲשֶׂה שָׁלִיחַ לְכָל־הַדְּבָרִים אֵינוֹ נַעֲשֶׂה בָּהֶן שָׁלִיחַ. הָתִיב רִבִּי יוּדָן. הֲרֵי יֵשׁ לוֹ טֶבֶל דְּבַר תּוֹרָה. פּוֹטֵר טִבְלוֹ דְּבַר תּוֹרָה. וְהָכָא אַף עַל פִּי שֶׁהוּא מִטַּמֵּא בָּהֶן אֵינוֹ נַעֲשֶׂה שָׁלִיחַ. מָהוּ שֶׁיָּבִיא בִיכּוּרִין כְּרִבִּי יוּדָה. דְּרִבִּי יוּדָה אָמַר הוּקְשׁוּ[59] לְקָדְשֵׁי הַגְּבוּל. אֵינוֹ מֵבִיא. כְּרַבָּנִין. דְּאִינּוּן אָמְרִין הוּקְשׁוּ[59] לְקָדְשֵׁי הַמִּקְדָּשׁ מֵבִיא. מָהוּ שֶׁיָּבִיא חֲגִיגָה מֵאַחַר שֶׁהוּא חוֹבָה אֵינוֹ מֵבִיא אוֹ מֵאַחַר שֶׁהוּא מְשַׁנֶּה לְשֵׁם שְׁלָמִים מֵבִיא. כְּוָתֵי פְּשִׁיטָה לָךְ שֶׁהוּא מֵבִיא. מַהוּ שֶׁיָּבִיא פֶּסַח. מֵאַחַר שֶׁהִיא חוֹבָה אֵינוֹ מֵבִיא אוֹ מֵאַחַר דְּאָמַר רִבִּי שִׁמְעוֹן בֶּן לָקִישׁ בְּשֵׁם רִבִּי הוֹשַׁעְיָה. מֵבִיא הוּא אָדָם פֶּסַח בִּשְׁאַר יְמוֹת הַשָּׁנָה וּמְשַׁנֵּיהוּ לְשֵׁם שְׁלָמִים. מֵבִיא. מָהוּ שֶׁיָּבִיא מַעֲשֵׂר דָּגָן. אִין יִסְבּוֹר כְּרִבִּי מֵאִיר. דְּרִבִּי מֵאִיר אָמַר. מִכֹּל מַעְשְׂרוֹתֵיכֶם. הוּקְשׁוּ מַעְשְׂרוֹת זֶה לָזֶה. כְּשֵׁם שֶׁאֵינוֹ מֵבִיא מַעֲשַׂר דָּגָן כָּךְ אֵינוֹ מֵבִיא מַעֲשַׂר בְּהֵמָה. מָהוּ שֶׁיַּעֲשֶׂה תְּמוּרָה. אִין יִסְבָּר כְּרִבִּי מֵאִיר. דְּאָמַר מִכֹּל מַעְשְׂרוֹתֵיכֶם. הוּקְשׁוּ מַעְשְׂרוֹת זֶה לָזֶה. כְּשֵׁם שֶׁאֵינוֹ מֵבִיא מַעֲשַׂר דָּגָן כָּךְ אֵינוֹ מֵבִיא מַעֲשַׂר בְּהֵמָה. כְּשֵׁם שֶׁאֵינוֹ מֵבִיא מַעֲשַׂר בְּהֵמָה כָּךְ אֵינוֹ עוֹשֶׂה תְּמוּרָה. וְיִסְבּוֹר כְּרִבִּי שִׁמְעוֹן. דְּאָמַר מַעֲשַׂר בְּהֵמָה לִימֵּד עַל כָּל־הַקֳּדָשִׁים לִתְמוּרָה. כְּשֵׁם שֶׁאֵינוֹ מֵבִיא מַעֲשַׂר דָּגָן כָּךְ אֵינוֹ מֵבִיא מַעֲשַׂר בְּהֵמָה. כְּשֵׁם שֶׁאֵינוֹ מֵבִיא מַעֲשַׂר בְּהֵמָה כָּךְ אֵינוֹ עוֹשֶׂה תְּמוּרָה. כְּשֵׁם שֶׁאֵינוֹ עוֹשֶׂה תְּמוּרָה כָּךְ אֵין מֵימַר בּוֹ. כְּשֵׁם שֶׁאֵינוֹ מֵימַר בּוֹ כָּךְ אֵינוֹ מֵימַר בְּכָל־הַקֳּדָשִׁים. מָה הוּא שֶׁיְּהוּא חַיָּבִין עַל קֳדָשָׁיו בַּחוּץ. כַּהֲנָא אָמַר. אֵין חַיָּבִין עַל קֳדָשָׁיו בַּחוּץ. רִבִּי יוֹחָנָן וְרִבִּי שִׁמְעוֹן בֶּן לָקִישׁ תְּרֵיהוֹן אָמְרִין. חַיָּבִין עַל קֳדָשָׁיו בַּחוּץ. וְקַשְׁיָא דְּרִבִּי כַהֲנָא עַל דְּרִבִּי יוּדָה. דְּרִבִּי יוּדָה פּוֹטֵר טִיבְלוֹ דְּבַר תּוֹרָה. וְאַתְּ אָמַר אָכֵן. כְּמָאן דְּאָמַר מֵאֵילֵיהֶן קִבְּלוּ עֲלֵיהֶן אֶת הַמַּעְשְׂרוֹת.

Rebbi Aḥa bar Ḥinena in the name of Cahana: Following the opinion that someone who cannot give heave cannot dedicate to the Temple. Why did he not say: following the opinion that he can give heave, can he dedicate to the Temple? Because of Rebbi Jehudah, for Rebbi Jehudah says he can give heave but cannot dedicate. Rebbi Joḥanan says, even following the opinion that he cannot give heave, he can dedicate. What can he dedicate? Holocaust and well-being offerings. He cannot bring a sin sacrifice for fat because he is not obligated to a sin sacrifice for fat. He cannot bring a sin sacrifice for blood because he is not obligated to a sin sacrifice for blood. May he bring a sacrifice relating to gonorrhea and skin disease? Since it is obligatory can't he bring it, or since he becomes impure by these can he bring it? If it is obvious for you that he brings, can he become an agent for these? Since he may become impure by these, may he become an agent, or since he cannot become an agent for anything else, can't he become an agent for these? Rebbi Yudan objected: His produce is *ṭevel* from the Torah but he can[60] free his *ṭevel* by Torah law! But here, even though he may become impure by them, he cannot become an agent. May he bring First Fruits following Rebbi Jehudah, for Rebbi Jehudah says that First Fruits have the status of territorial consecrated things? He may not bring following the rabbis who say they have the status of things consecrated to the Temple. May he bring a sacrifice of pilgrimage? Since it is obligatory can't he bring it, or since he may change its name to well-being offering, may he bring it? May he bring a Passover sacrifice? Since it is obligatory can't he bring it, or since Rebbi Simeon ben Laqish said in the name of Rebbi Hoshaia, a person may bring a Passover sacrifice any day of the year when he changes its name to well-being offering, may he bring it? May he bring tithes of cereals[61]? If he holds with Rebbi Meïr, since Rebbi Meïr said (*Num.* 18:28): "From all your tithes," that all tithes were bracketed together, then since he cannot bring tithes of grain he cannot bring tithes of animals. May he make substitutions? If Rebbi Meïr is of the opinion that all tithes were bracketed together, then since he cannot bring tithes of grain he cannot bring tithes of animals; since he cannot bring tithes of animals he cannot make substitutions. One may hold with Rebbi Simeon, since Rebbi Simeon says that tithes of animals teach you for all sacrifices about substitutions. That means, since he cannot bring tithes of grain he cannot bring tithes of animals; since he cannot bring tithes of animals he cannot make substitutions; since he cannot make substitutions for these he cannot make substitutions for any sacrifices. Is one guilty sacrificing for him outside the Temple? Cahana said, one cannot be guilty sacrificing for him outside the Temple. Rebbi Joḥanan and Rebbi Simeon ben Laqish both say, one is guilty sacrificing for him outside the Temple. The statement of Cahana disagrees with Rebbi Jehudah, since Rebbi Jehudah frees his *ṭevel* as biblical law. And you say so? We can say he [Cahana] is following him who says they accepted tithes voluntarily.

57 This and the following paragraphs are from *Terumot* Chapter 1, Notes 105-135, with minor differences.

58 Inserted from the text in *Terumot*.

59 Following the text in *Terumot*. Here always הוקדשו "were sanctified".

60 In *Terumot*: "He cannot". He can, following R. Jehudah; he cannot, following the majority.

61 In *Terumot*: "Of animals". The text following shows that the *Terumot* text is correct at this place.

וְקַשְׁיָא דְּרִבִּי יוֹחָנָן עַל דְּרִבִּי יְהוֹשֻׁעַ. נִישּׂוּאֶיהָ תוֹרָה הֵפֵר נְדָרֶיהָ תוֹרָה. וְאַתְּ אָמַר הָכֵין. אָמַר רִבִּי זְעִירָא. לֵית כָּאן הֵפֵר נְדָרִים מִן הָדָא דְּרִבִּי יוֹחָנָן עַל הָדָא דְּרִבִּי יְהוֹשֻׁעַ. רִבִּי נִיסָּא שָׁאַל. וִיהִי כֵן בָּאֲסוּרוֹת. רִבִּי יוֹחָנָן אָמַר. אֵין לוֹקִין עַל הָאֲסוּרוֹת. הֲוֵי הַהִיא דְתַנִּינָן תַּמָּן. קוֹדֶם לַזְּמַן הַזֶּה אַף עַל פִּי שֶׁאָמְרוּ. יוֹדְעִין אָנוּ לְשֵׁם מִי נָדַרְנוּ וּלְשֵׁם מִי הִקְדַּשְׁנוּ. אֵין נִדְרֵיהֶן נְדָרִים וְאֵין הֶקְדֵּישָׁן הֶקְדֵּשׁ. לְאַחַר הַזְּמַן הַזֶּה אַף עַל פִּי שֶׁאָמְרוּ. אֵין אָנוּ יוֹדְעִין לְשֵׁם מִי נָדַרְנוּ וְלֹא לְשֵׁם מִי הִקְדַּשְׁנוּ. נִדְרֵיהֶן נְדָרִים וְהֶקְדֵּישָׁן הֶקְדֵּשׁ. וְהָדָא מַתְנִיתָא

מַהוּ. עַל דַּעְתֵּיהּ דְּכַהֲנָא בְּמַחֲלוֹקֶת. עַל דַּעְתִּין דְּרִבִּי יוֹחָנָן וְרִבִּי שִׁמְעוֹן בֶּן לָקִישׁ דִּבְרֵי הַכֹּל.

Rebbi Yoḥanan had a difficulty with the words of Rebbi Joshua. Is her marriage valid by biblical standards? The dissolution of her vows must be by biblical standards[62]! And you say so! Rebbi Ze'ira said, there is no dissolution of vows here, because of what Rebbi Joḥanan had against the words of Rebbi Joshua. Rebbi Nissa asked: Would it be the same for prohibitions[63]? Rebbi Joḥanan said, one does not whip for prohibitions[64]. Would that be as we stated there: "Before that time, even though they said, we know for Whom we made a vow or to Whom we dedicated, their vows are no vows and their dedications no dedications. After that time, even though they said, we do not know for Whom we made a vow or to Whom we dedicated, their vows are vows and their dedications dedications[65]." What is the status of that Mishnah? For Cahana it is in dispute[66], for Rebbi Joḥanan and Rebbi Simeon ben Laqish it is everybody's opinion[67].

62 This again proves that in the statement of R. Joshua early in the Halakhah, he must agree that the underage girl may walk out of the marriage by simple repudiation. This means that even according to him, the marriage of a minor is only valid by rabbinic standards. But since the annulment of the wife's vows by the husband is a biblical law, it is difficult to see how a rabbinic marriage could confer biblical powers on the husband.

63 If somebody privatly forbade himself certain things or enjoyments. These "vows and oaths of prohibition to deprive oneself" (*Num.* 30:14) are exactly what the husband may hinder his wife to bind herself to.

64 Cf. *Nazir* 1:1, *Nedarim* 1:1. Since the prohibition is purely by words, it is a "prohibition not implying an action", for whose infringement no sacrifice of purification is needed or possible. But then there is no criminal act involved and the court will not get involved. It is well possible that R. Joshua holds that the powers of the husband to eliminate such a minor

prohibition extends to rabbinic marriages. Cf. Babli *Niddah* 46b.

65 Mishnah *Niddah* 5:6. The vows of a girl up to 11 years and a boy up to 12 years are null and void. The vows of a girl over 12 years and a boy over 13 years are valid. In the year in between the validity depends on the ability of the person making the vow to understand what he is doing.

66 Who said earlier that he who cannot give heave cannot dedicate. For him, R. Jehudah will not agree to the lower time limit set by the Mishnah.

67 In the previous paragraphs they had denied the link between ability to tithe and ability to make dedications and vows.

(fol. 13a) **משנה ג**: רִבִּי לִיעֶזֶר בֶּן יַעֲקֹב אוֹמֵר כָּל־עֲכָּבָה שֶׁהִיא מִן הָאִישׁ כְּאִילּוּ הִיא אִשְׁתּוֹ. וְכָל־עֲכָּבָה שֶׁאֵינָהּ מִן הָאִישׁ כְּאִילּוּ אֵינָהּ אִשְׁתּוֹ.

Mishnah 3: Rebbi Eliezer ben Jacob said, every impediment that comes from the man makes her as if she were his wife; every impediment that does not come from the man makes her as if she were not his wife[68].

68 If the marriage of a man with an underage girl is dissolved by the initiative of the man, she is treated as a divorcee forbidden his relatives and forbidden to a Cohen, and he is forbidden her close relatives. But if she walks out on him, there never was any marriage, neither side is forbidden the close relatives of the other, and she is not forbidden to marry a Cohen. This is all explained in the next Mishnah.

(fol. 13d) **מתניתא:** רִבִּי לִיעֶזֶר בֶּן יַעֲקֹב אוֹמֵר כול׳. תַּנֵּי. רִבִּי לִיעֶזֶר בֶּן יַעֲקֹב אוֹמֵר כָּל־עֲכָּבָה שֶׁהִיא מִן הָאִישׁ כְּאִילּוּ הִיא אִשְׁתּוֹ בְּגֵט. וְכָל־עֲכָּבָה שֶׁאֵינָהּ מִן הָאִישׁ כְּאִילּוּ אֵינָהּ אִשְׁתּוֹ בְּמֵיאוּנִים.

Mishnah: "Rebbi Eliezer ben Jacob said," etc. It was stated: "Rebbi Eliezer ben Jacob said, every impediment that comes from the man *by a bill of divorce* makes her as if she were his wife; every impediment that does not come from the man *by repudiation* makes her as if she were not his wife[68]."

(fol. 13a) **משנה ד**: הַמְּמָאֶנֶת בָּאִישׁ הוּא מוּתָּר בִּקְרוֹבוֹתֶיהָ וְהִיא מוּתֶּרֶת בִּקְרוֹבָיו וְלֹא פְסָלָהּ מִן הַכְּהוּנָּה. נָתַן לָהּ גֵּט הוּא אָסוּר בִּקְרוֹבוֹתֶיהָ וְהִיא אֲסוּרָה בִּקְרוֹבָיו וּפְסָלָהּ מִן הַכְּהוּנָּה. נָתַן לָהּ גֵּט וְהֶחֱזִירָהּ מֵאֲנָה בוֹ וְנִשֵּׂאת לְאַחֵר וְנִתְאַלְמְנָה אוֹ נִתְגָּרְשָׁה מוּתֶּרֶת לַחֲזוֹר לוֹ. מֵאֲנָה בוֹ וְהֶחֱזִירָהּ נָתַן לָהּ גֵּט וְנִשֵּׂאת לְאַחֵר וְנִתְאַלְמְנָה אוֹ נִתְגָּרְשָׁה אֲסוּרָה לַחֲזוֹר לוֹ. זֶה הַכְּלָל גֵּט אַחַר מֵיאוּן אֲסוּרָה לַחֲזוֹר לוֹ. מֵיאוּן אַחַר גֵּט מוּתֶּרֶת לַחֲזוֹר לוֹ.

Mishnah 4: If [a girl] repudiates a man, he is permitted [to marry] her relatives and she is permitted [to marry] his relatives; he did not disable her for the priesthood. If he gave her a bill of divorce, he is forbidden [to marry] her relatives and she is forbidden [to marry] his relatives; he did disable her for the priesthood[68]. If he gave her a bill of divorce and later took her back, then she repudiated him[69] and married another man from whom she became widowed or divorced, she is permitted to return to him. If she repudiated him and he took her back, then he gave her a bill of divorce[70] and she married another man from whom she became widowed or divorced, she is prohibited to return to him. That is the principle: By divorce after repudiation she is prohibited to return to him; by repudiation after divorce she is permitted to return to him.

69 This repudiation is applied not only to the second but also to the first marriage; then she is not divorced from him and may marry him anew after divorce or widowhood from another man.

70 This divorce stands, and so stands the prohibition to take back the divorcee who was otherwise married (*Deut*. 24:4).

(fol. 13d) **מתניתא**: הַמְמָאֶנֶת בָּאִישׁ כול'. רִבִּי יוֹחָנָן בְּשֵׁם רִבִּי יַנַּאי. אֵין בָּהּ [אֶלָּא][71] מִשּׁוּם זְהוּם כְּהוּנָּה וְאֵין בֵּית דִּין מְזַהֲמִין אוֹתָהּ.

Mishnah: "If [a girl] repudiates a man, etc." Rebbi Joḥanan in the name of Rebbi Yannai: Her only problem would be aspersion on the priesthood, but the court will not tolerate aspersion[72].

71 Inserted from the parallels in the next Halakhah, Halakha 10:7, and the *editio princeps*.

72 Cf. Chapter 10, Halakhah 7, Note 126. Since the marriage was only rabbinic, the prohibition cannot be biblical.

(fol. 13b) **משנה ה**: הַמְמָאֶנֶת בָּאִישׁ וְנִישֵּׂאת לְאַחֵר וְגֵירְשָׁהּ לְאַחֵר וּמֵיאֲנָה בוֹ. לְאַחֵר וְגֵירְשָׁהּ לְאַחֵר וּמֵיאֲנָה בוֹ. כָּל־שֶׁיָּצָאת מִמֶּנּוּ בְגֵט אֲסוּרָה לַחֲזוֹר לוֹ. בְּמֵיאוּן מוּתֶּרֶת לַחֲזוֹר לוֹ.

Mishnah 5: If [a girl] repudiates a man and marries another who divorces her, another and she repudiates him, another who divorces her, another and she repudiates him, she is forbidden to return to anyone who had divorced her but permitted to return to those she had repudiated.

(fol. 13d) **מתניתא**: הַמְמָאֶנֶת כול'. רִבִּי יוֹחָנָן בְּשֵׁם רִבִּי יַנַּאי. אֵין בָּהּ אֶלָּא מִשּׁוּם זְהוּם כְּהוּנָּה וְאֵין בֵּית דִּין מְזַהֲמִין אוֹתָהּ.

Mishnah: "If [a girl] repudiates," etc. Rebbi Joḥanan in the name of Rebbi Yannai: Her only problem would be aspersion on the priesthood, but the court will not tolerate aspersion[72].

משנה ו: הַמְגָרֵשׁ אֶת הָאִשָּׁה וְהֶחֱזִירָהּ מוּתֶּרֶת לְיָבָם וְרִבִּי לִיעֶזֶר (fol. 13b) אוֹסֵר. וְכֵן הַמְגָרֵשׁ אֶת הַיְּתוֹמָה וְהֶחֱזִירָהּ מוּתֶּרֶת לְיָבָם וְרִבִּי לִיעֶזֶר אוֹסֵר. קְטַנָּה שֶׁהִשִּׂיאָהּ אָבִיהָ וְנִתְגָּרְשָׁה כִּיתוֹמָה בְּחַיֵּי הָאָב הֶחֱזִירָהּ אֲסוּרָה לְיָבָם.

Mishnah 6: If somebody divorced his wife and later took her back, she is permitted to the levir but Rebbi Eliezer forbids her[73]. Similarly, if somebody divorced an orphan girl and took her back, she is permitted to the levir but Rebbi Eliezer forbids her[73]. If an underage girl who was married off by her father was divorced, she is like an orphan during her father's lifetime[74]. If she was taken back, she is prohibited to the levir.

משנה ז: וּמוֹדִין חֲכָמִים לְרִבִּי לְעֶזֶר בִּזְמַן שֶׁגֵּירְשָׁהּ קְטַנָּה וְהֶחֱזִירָהּ קְטַנָּה מִפְּנֵי שֶׁהָיוּ גֵירוּשֶׁיהָ גֵּירוּשִׁין גְּמוּרִין וְלֹא הָיְתָה חֲזָרָתָהּ גְּמוּרָה. אֲבָל אִם גֵּירְשָׁהּ קְטַנָּה וְהֶחֱזִירָהּ גְּדוֹלָה אוֹ שֶׁגִּידְּלָה תַּחְתָּיו מוּתֶּרֶת לְיָבָם.

[75]**Mishnah 7**: The Sages agree with Rebbi Eliezer in case he divorced her as a minor and took her back as a minor, since her divorce is a total divorce but her return was not complete. But if he divorced her as a minor and took her back as an adult or she became an adult while married to him[76], she is permitted to the levir.

73 The second marriage annuls the prior divorce. R. Eliezer holds that she remains forbidden, even if the husband dies childless, since she was forbidden as his brother's divorcee, as explained in the Halakhah. The same explanation is given in the Babli, 109a.

74 She is emancipated from her father's power by her marriage. Since the father has the right to marry off his underage daughter, both betrothal and divorce are valid by biblical standards. But since the remarriage was by an underage girl no longer under tutelage but unable to perform legal acts by reason of her age, everybody agrees that her rabbinic marriage cannot lift the biblical prohibition of the brother's divorcee.

75 This Mishnah is not in the Babli nor in most independent Mishnah mss.

76 Since they live together with the idea of being married, the first intercourse after she reaches the age of 12 years makes her marriage valid by biblical standards.

מתניתא: ומודין חֲכָמִים כול׳. מַאי טַעֲמָא דְּרִבִּי לְעֶזֶר. מִפְּנֵי שֶׁעָמְדָה עָלָיו בְּאִיסּוּר שָׁעָה אַחַת. מוֹדִין חֲכָמִים לְרִבִּי לְעֶזֶר בִּקְטַנָּה שֶׁהִשִּׂיאָהּ אָבִיהָ וְנִתְגָּרְשָׁה שֶׁהִיא כִיתוֹמָה בְּחַיֵּי אָבִיהָ. קִידּוּשֶׁיהָ וְגֵירוּשֶׁיהָ תוֹרָה. חֲזָרָתָהּ אֵינָהּ תוֹרָה. (fol. 13d)

Mishnah: "The Sages agree," etc. What is Rebbi Eliezer's reason? That she was forbidden to him for an hour[73]. [77]The Sages agree with Rebbi Eliezer about the underage girl who was married off by her father and divorced, that she is like an orphan during her father's lifetime. Her betrothal and divorce were by biblical standards; her remarriage was not by biblical standards.

77 Tosephta 13:5.

צָרָתָהּ מַהוּ. רַב אָמַר. צָרָתָהּ אֲסוּרָה. רִבִּי יוֹחָנָן אָמַר. צָרָתָהּ אֲסוּרָה. רִבִּי שִׁמְעוֹן בֶּן לָקִישׁ אָמַר. צָרָתָהּ מוּתֶּרֶת. אָמַר רִבִּי לָעְזָר. חוֹזְרֵת בֵּין עַל רַבָּנָן דְּהָכָא בֵּין עַל רַבָּנָן דְּתַמָּן לָא אַשְׁכָּחִית בַּר נַשׁ דִּכְוָותִי אֶלָּא רִבִּי שִׁמְעוֹן בֶּן לָקִישׁ דּוּ אָמַר. צָרָתָהּ מוּתֶּרֶת. רַב הַמְנוּנָא הֲוָה יְתִיב קוֹמֵי רַב אָדָא בַּר אַחֲוָה. אָמַר. צָרָתָהּ מַהוּ. אָמַר לֵיהּ. מוּתָּר. אָמַר. גֵּירוּשִׁין. אָמַר. אֲסוּרָה. אָמַר. חֲזָרָיו. אָמַר רַבָּא בַּר מָמָל. מִסְתַּבְּרָא כְּמָאן דְּאָמַר. צָרָתָהּ מוּתֶּרֶת. בְּרַם כְּמָאן דְּאָמַר. צָרָתָהּ אֲסוּרָה. מַה נַפְשֵׁךְ. צַד שֶׁקָּנָה בָהּ כְּנֶגְדּוֹ אָסוּר בְּצָרָתָהּ וְצַד שֶׁלֹּא קָנָה בָהּ כְּנֶגְדּוֹ הִתִּיר בְּצָרָתָהּ. אָמַר רִבִּי שַׁמַּי. וְכִי יֵשׁ מַה נַפְשֵׁךְ בַּעֲרָיוֹת. מַהוּ כְדוֹן. כָּל־יְבָמָה שֶׁאֵין כּוּלָּהּ לַחוּץ צַד הַקָּנוּי שֶׁבָּהּ נִידּוֹן מִשּׁוּם עֶרְוָה. וְעֶרְוָה פוֹטֶרֶת צָרָתָהּ.

What is the status of her co-wife[78]? Rav said, her co-wife is forbidden. Rebbi Johanan said, her co-wife is forbidden. Rebbi Simeon ben Laqish said, her co-wife is permitted. Rebbi Eleazar said, I looked around at the rabbis here and at the rabbis there and did not find anybody agreeing with me except Rebbi Simeon ben Laqish who says, her co-wife is permitted.

Rav Hamnuna was sitting before Rav Ada bar Ahava and said, what is the status of her co-wife? He said to him, she is permitted. He asked, divorce? He answered, forbidden[79]. He said, go around[80]. Rebbi Abba bar Mamal said, it is reasonable following him who said that her co-wife is permitted. But following him who said, her co-wife is forbidden, as you take it: The aspect he acquired in her makes the corresponding aspect forbidden in her co-wife, the aspect he did not acquire in her makes the corresponding aspect permitted in her co-wife[81]! Rebbi Shammai said, does one admit that kind of argument in matters of incest prohibitions? What about it? For any sister-in-law who is not totally outside [the family], the acquired aspect of her belongs to an incest prohibition and an incest prohibition forbids the co-wife[82].

78 The co-wife of the girl married off by her father, divorced, and remarried.

79 This is the case of the Mishnah.

80 Look for other opinions in the matter.

81 This text makes no sense. It seems that the correct text is the one quoted by Nahmanides (*The wars of the Eternal* on Alfasi, 37b in the Wilna edition): צַד שֶׁקָּנָה בָהּ כְּנֶגְדּוֹ מוּתָּר בְּצָרָתָהּ וְצַד שֶׁלֹּא קָנָה בָהּ כְּנֶגְדּוֹ הִתִּיר בְּצָרָתָהּ. "The aspect he acquired in her *permits* the corresponding aspect in her co-wife, the aspect he did not acquire in her was permitted in the corresponding aspect in her co-wife." The argument is based on the doctrine that the marriage of an underage girl not arranged by her father results in partial acquisition of the girl by the husband. This doctrine is stated explicitly in the Babli (110b, 111a) but not in the Yerushalmi. If the girl was married, then the prior divorce was annulled and both she and her co-wife are permitted to the levir. Is the girl was not married, then she is not a widow; the co-wife is the only widow and as such subject to the levirate.

82 This argument supports the authorities Rav and R. Johanan. The Yerushalmi prohibits the levirate for the co-wife. The Babli disagrees, 109a.

(fol. 13b) **משנה ח**: שְׁנֵי אַחִים נְשׂוּאִין לִשְׁתֵּי יְתוֹמוֹת קְטַנּוֹת מֵת בַּעֲלָהּ שֶׁלְּאַחַת מֵהֶן תֵּצֵא מִשּׁוּם אֲחוֹת אִשָּׁה. וְכֵן שְׁתֵּי חֵרְשׁוֹת גְּדוֹלָה וּקְטַנָּה מֵת בַּעֲלָהּ שֶׁלַּקְּטַנָּה תֵּצֵא מִשּׁוּם אֲחוֹת אִשָּׁה. מֵת בַּעֲלָהּ שֶׁלַּגְּדוֹלָה רַבִּי לִיעֶזֶר אוֹמֵר מְלַמְּדִין אֶת הַקְּטַנָּה שֶׁתְּמָאֵן בּוֹ. רַבָּן גַּמְלִיאֵל אוֹמֵר אִם מֵיאֲנָה מֵיאֲנָה וְאִם לָאו תַּמְתִּין עַד שֶׁתַּגְדִּיל וְתֵצֵא הַלָּזוּ מִשּׁוּם אֲחוֹת אִשָּׁה. רַבִּי יְהוֹשֻׁעַ אוֹמֵר אִי לוֹ עַל אִשְׁתּוֹ וְאִי לוֹ לְאֵשֶׁת אָחִיו מוֹצִיא אֶת אִשְׁתּוֹ בְּגֵט וְאֵשֶׁת אָחִיו בַּחֲלִיצָה.

Mishnah 8: Two brothers are married to two underage orphan [sisters][83]. If the husband of one of them dies, the other one has to leave as wife's sister. And so for two deaf-mute [sisters][84]. If one is adult and the other underage, if the husband of the underage girl died, she has to leave as wife's sister. If the husband of the adult one died, Rebbi Eliezer said, one teaches the underage one to repudiate him[85]. Rabban Gamliel says, if she repudiated, she repudiated; otherwise she should wait until she becomes of age and the other one has to leave as wife's sister[86]. Rebbi Joshua says, woe to him for his wife, woe to him for his brother's wife! He has to send away his wife by a bill of divorce and his brother's wife by *ḥalîṣah*[87].

83 The word "sisters" is missing but is in the Mishnah in the Babli and in the independent Mishnah.

84 Their marriages are only rabbinically valid.

85 R. Eliezer holds that the biblical candidacy of the adult one forbids the rabbinically married one to her husband. If the underage girl repudiates her husband, her marriage never happened and the husband is free to marry his brother's widow in levirate.

86 Rabban Gamliel holds that candidacy has no effect on an existing marriage even if that marriage is only rabbinical. As long as the sister is underage, the older one cannot marry since she cannot get *ḥalîṣah*.

87 He holds with R. Eliezer that candidacy of the older forbids the younger one to her husband. But he also thinks that one never tells an underage girl to repudiate. He will

agree that if his wife repudiates him on her own, that he may marry her sister in levirate.

(fol. 13d) **מתניתא**: שְׁנֵי אַחִים נְשׂוּאִין כול׳. רִבִּי יוּדָן. כְּמָה דְאַתְּ אֲמַר תַּמָּן בָּעֵי. וְיַחֲלוֹץ צַד הַקָּנוּי שֶׁבָּהּ וְיִפְטוֹר צָרָתָהּ. אַף הָכָא. וְיַחֲלוֹץ צַד הַקָּנוּי שֶׁבַּקְּטַנָּה וְיַכְנִיס צָרָתָהּ. עַד דְּאַתְּ מַקְשֵׁי לֵיהּ עַל דְּרִבִּי לָעְזָר קַשִּׁייָתָה עַל דְּרִבִּי לִעֶזֶר. לֵיתְנֵי יָכוֹל לְמִיקְשֵׁי לָהּ עַל דְּרִבִּי אֱלִיעֶזֶר. דְּרִבִּי לִיעֶזֶר שַׁמּוּתִי. בֵּית שַׁמַּי אוֹמְרִים. אֵין מְמָאֲנִי׳ אֶלָּא אֲרוּסוֹת.

Mishnah: "Two brothers are married," etc. Rebbi Yudan: One may ask what one asked there. Should he not perform *ḥalîṣah* for the acquired aspect in her and free her co-wife? So here, should he not perform *ḥalîṣah* for the acquired aspect in the underage girl and free her (co-wife) [sister][88]? Before you find Rebbi Eleazar difficult, you might find Rebbi Eliezer difficult! You cannot find this difficult for Rebbi Eliezer, since Rebbi Eliezer is a Shammaite[89] and the House of Shammai say, one lets only the betrothed [women] repudiate[90]?

88 Would it not be possible (or required) to apply the argument of R. Eleazar and R. Abba bar Mamal in the previous Halakhah to the situation here? It is difficult to see why one should try to make the situation more complicated than it already is. The text is at least partially corrupt.

89 *Ševi'it* 9:9, *Terumot* 5:4, Babli *Niddah* 7b. R. Eliezer became a student of Rabban Yoḥanan ben Zakkai; in no sense can he be considered an orthodox representative of the House of Shammai.

90 Mishnah 1.

כְּקִינְיָינָהּ שֶׁלְּזוּ כֵּן קִינְיָינָהּ שֶׁלְּזוּ וּכְקִינְיָינָהּ שֶׁלְּזוּ כֵּן קִינְיָינָהּ שֶׁלְּזוּ. וְלֹא כֵן תַּמִּינָן קְטַנָּה וְחֵרֶשֶׁת. תַּנֵּי רִבִּי חִייָה. קְטַנָּה וְחֵרֶשֶׁת. מֵת בַּעַל הַקְּטַנָּה בַּעַל הַחֵרֶשֶׁת מוֹצִיאָהּ בְּגֵט וְהַקְּטַנָּה תַּמְתִּין עַד שֶׁתַּגְדִּיל וְתַחֲלוֹץ. וְתַחֲלוֹץ מִיַּד. לֵית יָכִיל בְּגִין דְּרִבִּי מֵאִיר. דְּרִבִּי מֵאִיר אָמַר. אֵין חוֹלְצִין וְאֵין מְייַבְּמִין אֶת

הַקְּטַנָּה שֶׁמָּא תִימָּצֵא אַיילוֹנִית. מֵת בַּעַל הַחֵרֶשֶׁת בַּעַל הַקְּטַנָּה מוֹצִיאָהּ בְּגֵט וְהַחֵרֶשֶׁת אֲסוּרָה אִיסּוּר עוֹלָם. עָבַר וּבָא עַל הַחֵרֶשֶׁת יוֹצִיא בְגֵט וְהוּתְּרָה. כְּהַהִיא דְאָמַר רִבִּי הִילָא. מִפְּנֵי תַקָּנָתָהּ.

Is the degree of acquisition of one equal to that of the other[91]? Did we not state "underage and deaf-mute"[92]? Rebbi Hiyya stated ""underage and deaf-mute"[93]: "If the husband of the underage girl died, the husband of the deaf-mute has to divorce her and the underage girl has to wait until she comes of age and perform *ḥalîṣah.*[94]" Why can she not perform *ḥalîṣah* immediately? She cannot because of Rebbi Meïr, since Rebbi Meïr said that one does not perform levirate or *ḥalîṣah* with an underage girl, since she might be found to be a she-ram[95]. "If the husband of the deaf-mute died, the husband of the underage girl has to divorce her and the deaf-mute is permanently forbidden[96]. If he transgressed and had intercourse with the deaf-mute, he divorces her and she becomes permitted[97]." This follows what Rebbi Hila said, in order to fix her status[98].

91 The Mishnah proclaims that underage and deaf-mute spouses have the same status. But this is not true, as exemplified by the case of two brothers marrying two fatherless sisters, one underage and one deaf-mute, when one of the brothers died childless. {It is assumed that the second sister was deaf-mute when she married, otherwise her marriage would be biblical but not her divorce.}

92 In the next Mishnah, also dealing with a case asymmetric in the rules.

93 Tosephta 13:6.

94 Possibly the degree of acquisition of the deaf-mute by the husband is less than that of an underage girl. Then the biblical candidacy of the underage would prohibit the deaf-mute for her husband. Therefore, he must divorce the deaf-mute.

95 But according to other authorities, she may perform *ḥalîṣah* immediately; cf. Chapter 12, Note 105.

96 She cannot be married in levirate since her sister's marriage may

have been valid. As a deaf-mute, she cannot perform *ḥalîṣah*. No man in the world is permitted to her.

97 Since the marriage of the underage girl is only rabbinic, the sister either was not married, then she can be married and divorced, or she was married, then she is freed by divorce after levirate.

98 One permits the levir to transgress rabbinic rules since otherwise the deaf-mute cannot be helped. In the inverse case, that the underage girl became the childless widow, it is not necessary to permit infraction of the rules since everything can be done abiding by the rules. All this case shows is that *on the rabbinic level*, there is a difference between underage and deaf-mute.

כֵּינִי מַתְנִיתָא. וְהַקְּטַנָּה תַּמְתִּין עַד שֶׁתַּגְדִּיל וְתַגִּיעַ לַפֶּרֶק וְתִינָּשֵׂא. אָמַר רִבִּי לָעְזָר. לֵית כָּאן תִּינָּשֵׂא אֶלָּא (fol. 14a) תִּתְאָרֵס. אָמַר רִבִּי יוֹחָנָן. זוֹ דִבְרֵי רַבָּן גַּמְלִיאֵל. הַמְקַדֵּשׁ אֲחוֹת יְבִמְתּוֹ נִפְטְרָה יְבִמְתּוֹ מִן הַחֲלִיצָה וּמִן הַיִּבּוּם. הֲוֵי הַהִיא דְתַנִּינָן תַּמָּן שׁוֹמֶרֶת יָבָם שֶׁקִּידֵּשׁ אָחִיו אֶת אֲחוֹתָהּ. דְּלֹא כְרַבָּן גַּמְלִיאֵל.

So is the Mishnah: The underage girl should wait until she grows up, reaches puberty, and is being married[99]. Rebbi Eleazar said, there is no "being married" here, only "being betrothed.[100]" Rebbi Johanban said, these are the words of Rabban Gamliel: If somebody gave *qiddušin* to his sister-in-law's sister, his sister-in-law was freed from *ḥalîṣah* and levirate. It follows that what we had stated there[101], "if somebody gave *qiddušin* to the sister of a woman waiting for her levir" does not follow Rabban Gamliel.

99 This refers to the statement of Rabban Gamliel that in the absence of repudiation, the underage girl should wait until she becomes of age. The statement is modified slightly to make clear that the marriage of the former underage girl must acquire biblical validity in order to free her sister.

100 In the Babli, 109b, that is very much in dispute.

101 Mishnah 4:10. The complications of that Mishnah are irrelevant for Rabban Gamliel.

רִבִּי חַגַּיי אָמַר קוֹמֵי רִבִּי זְעִירָה מְנַחֵם בְּשֵׁם רִבִּי יוֹחָנָן. הֲלָכָה כְּרִבִּי אֱלִיעֶזֶר אִם מֵיאֲנָה מֵיאֲנָה. רִבִּי לִיעֶזֶר אוֹמֵר. מְלַמְּדִין אֶת הַקְּטַנָּה שֶׁתְּמָאֵן בּוֹ וְאַתְּ אָמַר הָכֵין. רִבִּי זְעִירָה רִבִּי חִייָה בְּשֵׁם רִבִּי יוֹחָנָן. הֲלָכָה כְּרִבִּי יְהוֹשֻׁעַ אִם מֵיאֲנָה מֵיאֲנָה. רִבִּי יְהוֹשֻׁעַ אוֹמֵר אִי לוֹ עַל אִשְׁתּוֹ וְאִי לוֹ עַל אֵשֶׁת אָחִיו. וְאַתְּ אָמַר הָכֵין. רִבִּי הִילָא רִבִּי יוֹסֵי בְּשֵׁם רִבִּי יוֹחָנָן. הֲלָכָה כְּרַבָּן גַּמְלִיאֵל. מוֹדֶה רִבִּי יְהוֹשֻׁעַ לְרַבָּן גַּמְלִיאֵל. אִם מֵיאֲנָה מֵיאֲנָה וְאִם לָאו תַּמְתִּין עַד שֶׁתַּגְדִּיל. וְאִם לָאו מוֹצִיא אֶת אִשְׁתּוֹ בְּגֵט וְאֵשֶׁת אָחִיו בַּחֲלִיצָה.

Rebbi Ḥaggai said before Rebbi Ze'ira, Menaḥem in the name of Rebbi Joḥanan: Practice follows Rebbi Eliezer, if she repudiated, she repudiated. Rebbi Eliezer said, one teaches the underage one to repudiate him, and you say so[102]? Rebbi Ze'ira, Rebbi Ḥiyya, in the name of Rebbi Joḥanan: Practice follows Rebbi Joshua, if she repudiated, she repudiated. Rebbi Joshua says, woe to him for his wife, woe to him for his brother's wife! And you say so[103]? Rebbi Hila, Rebbi Yose[104] in the name of Rebbi Joḥanan: Practice follows Rabban Gamliel. Rebbi Joshua agrees with Rabban Gamliel, if she repudiated, she repudiated[105]; otherwise she should wait until she becomes of age. If not[105], he has to send away his wife by a bill of divorce and his brother's wife by *ḥalîṣah*.

102 The statement in the name of R. Joḥanan is inconsistent: R. Eliezer says one teaches the girl to repudiate!

103 The second formulation is also inconsistent.

104 Since R. Hila was one of the teachers of R. Yose, one has to read here: R. Yasa.

105 In the first case, the problem took care of itself. If the women do not want to wait, Rabban Gamliel will agree with Rebbi Joshua.

In the Babli, 110a, practice is stated to follow R. Eliezer without discussion.

משנה ט: מִי שֶׁהָיָה נָשׂוּי לִשְׁתֵּי יְתוֹמוֹת קְטַנּוֹת וָמֵת. בִּיאָתָהּ אוֹ(fol. 13b) חֲלִיצָתָהּ שֶׁלְּאַחַת מֵהֶן פּוֹטֶרֶת צָרָתָהּ. וְכֵן שְׁתֵּי חֵרְשׁוֹת. קְטַנָּה וְחֵרֶשֶׁת אֵין בִּיאַת אַחַת מֵהֶן פּוֹטֶרֶת צָרָתָהּ.

Mishnah 9: If somebody was married to two underage orphan girls and died, intercourse or *ḥaliṣah* of one of them frees her co-wife. The same holds for two deaf-mutes. An underaged girl and a deaf-mute: Intercourse of neither of them frees her co-wife.

(fol. 14a) **מתניתא**: מִי שֶׁהָיָה נָשׂוּי כול'. כְּקִינְיָינָהּ שֶׁלָּזוּ כֵּן קִינְיָינָהּ שֶׁלָּזוּ וּכְקִינְיָינָהּ שֶׁלָּזוּ כֵּן קִינְיָינָהּ שֶׁלָּזוּ. כֵּיצַד הוּא עוֹשֶׂה. רַב חִיָּיה בַּר אַשִׁי בְשֵׁם רַב. כּוֹנֵס אֶת הַחֵרֶשֶׁת וּמוֹצִיאָהּ בְּגֵט וְהַקְּטַנָּה תַּמְתִּין עַד שֶׁתַּחֲלוֹץ. וְתַחֲלוֹץ מִיַּד. לֵית יָכִיל בְּגִין דְּרִבִּי מֵאִיר. דְּרִבִּי מֵאִיר אָמַר. אֵין חוֹלְצִין וְלֹא מְיַיבְּמִין אֶת הַקְּטַנָּה שֶׁמָּא תִימָּצֵא אַיילוֹנִית. וְאִם בָּא עַל הַקְּטַנָּה מוֹצִיאָהּ בְּגֵט וְהַחֵרֶשֶׁת אֲסוּרָה אִיסּוּר עוֹלָם. עָבַר וּבָא עַל הַחֵרֶשֶׁת מוֹצִיאָהּ בְּגֵט וְהוּתְּרָה. אָמַר רִבִּי הִילָא. מִפְּנֵי תַקָּנָתָהּ. רִבִּי בּוּן בַּר חִיָּה בָּעֵי קוֹמֵי רִבִּי הִילָא. מַהוּ מִפְּנֵי תַקָּנָתָהּ. כְּמָה דְתֵימַר תַּמָּן. יַחֲלוֹץ צַד הַקָּנוּי שֶׁבּוֹ וְיִכְנוֹס צָרָתָהּ. אָמַר אוּף הָכָא. יַחֲלוֹץ צַד הַקָּנוּי שֶׁבָּהּ וְיַכְנִיס צָרָתָהּ. וְיַחֲלוֹץ צַד הַקָּנוּי שֶׁבִּקְטַנָּה וְיַכְנִיס אֶת הַחֵרֶשֶׁת. אָמַר לֵיהּ. כֵּן אָמַר רִבִּי שִׁמְעוֹן בֶּן לָקִישׁ. לֹא מָצִינוּ שְׁתֵּי יְבָמוֹת אַחַת חוֹלֶצֶת וְאַחַת מִתְייַבֶּמֶת. וּמָצִינוּ שְׁתֵּי יְבָמוֹת אַחַת חוֹלֶצֶת וְאַחַת יוֹצְאָה בְגֵט. אָמַר לֵיהּ. הֲוֵי הִיא דְתַנִּינָן תַּמָּן. מַאֲמָר לָזֶה וְחָלַץ לָזֶה הָרִאשׁוֹנָה צְרִיכָה גֵט.

[106]Is the degree of acquisition of one equal to that of the other? What does he do? Rav Ḥiyya bar Ashi in the name of Rav: He marries the deaf-mute and divorces her; the underage girl has to wait until she can perform *ḥalîṣah*." Why can she not perform *ḥalîṣah* immediately? She cannot because of Rebbi Meïr, since Rebbi Meïr said that one does not perform levirate or *ḥalîṣah* with an underage girl, since she might be found to be a she-ram. If he sleeps with the underage girl, he has to divorce her, and the deaf-mute is permanently forbidden. If he

transgressed and had intercourse with the deaf-mute, he divorces her and she became permitted." This follows what Rebbi Hila said, in order to fix her status. Rebbi Abun bar Ḥiyya asked before Rebbi Hila: What means, "in order to fix her status"? As you say there, he should perform *ḥalîṣah* for the aspect that was acquired in her and marry her co-wife; could he not perform *ḥalîṣah* for the aspect that was acquired in the underage girl and marry the deaf-mute[107]? He said to him, so says Rebbi Simeon ben Laqish: We never find two sisters-in-law of whom one performs *ḥalîṣah* and one is married in levirate. Do we find two sisters-in-law of whom one performs *ḥalîṣah* and one is divorced? He said to him, that happens. That is what we have stated there: "If he 'bespoke' one and performed *ḥalîṣah* with the other, the first one needs a bill of divorce"[108].

106 This refers to the last case in the Mishnah, an underage girl and a deaf-mute. It is again supposed that the underage girl was not married off by her father and the deaf-mute was already deaf-mute at the moment of marriage. In contrast to the Babli, the Yerushalmi does not try to determine the actual difference in the rabbinic status of the two marriages. The first part of the paragraph is exactly parallel to the preceding Halakhah, Notes 91-98.

107 This refers to the discussion in Halakhah 6 and supports the reading of Naḥmanides in Note 81. It is suggested there that in case of partial validity of a marriage there could be a partial *ḥalîṣah* which permits the co-wife for levirate; in our case there would be a solution which takes care of the deaf-mute without requiring the levir to commit a sin. {This also supports the position of Nahmanides that the Yerushalmi in Halakhah 6 choses R. Eleazar over R. Shammai.}

108 Mishnah 5:5, Note 73.

משנה י: פִּיקַחַת וְחֵרֶשֶׁת בִּיאַת הַפִּיקַחַת פּוֹטֶרֶת אֶת הַחֵרֶשֶׁת וְאֵין(fol. 13b) בִּיאַת הַחֵרֶשֶׁת פּוֹטֶרֶת אֶת הַפִּיקַחַת.

Mishnah 10: A hearing wife and a deaf-mute: The intercourse of the hearing woman frees the deaf-mute but the intercourse of the deaf-mute does not free the hearing woman[109].

109 If a man married to a hearing woman and a deaf-mute dies childless, the execution of biblical levirate by intercourse with the hearing widow frees the deaf-mute but the execution of rabbinic levirate by intercourse with the deaf-mute does not free the hearing widow.

(fol. 14a) **מתניתא:** פִּיקַחַת וְחֵרֶשֶׁת כול'. פִּיקַחַת וְחֵרֶשֶׁת. בִּיאַת הַפִּיקַחַת פּוֹטֶרֶת אֶת הַחֵרֶשֶׁת. אֵין בִּיאַת הַחֵרֶשֶׁת פּוֹטֶרֶת אֶת הַפִּיקַחַת אֶלָּא פּוֹסֶלֶת אֶת הַפִּיקַחַת.

Mishnah: "A hearing wife and a deaf-mute," etc. : A hearing wife and a deaf-mute. The intercourse of the hearing woman frees the deaf-mute. The intercourse of the deaf-mute does not free the hearing woman but disables the hearing woman[110].

110 She now is forbidden to the levir. But since the marriage of the deaf-mute was rabbinic only, the hearing woman cannot remarry without *ḥalîṣah*.

משנה יא: גְּדוֹלָה וּקְטַנָּה בִּיאַת הַגְּדוֹלָה פּוֹטֶרֶת אֶת הַקְּטַנָּה וְאֵין (fol. 13b) בִּיאַת הַקְּטַנָּה פּוֹטֶרֶת אֶת הַגְּדוֹלָה.

Mishnah 11: An adult wife and an underage wife. The intercourse of the adult woman frees the underage girl but the intercourse of the underage girl does not free the adult woman[111].

111 This and the corresponding Halakhah are the exact parallels to the preceding Mishnah and Halakhah. The Mishnah is required only because it is not known whether the rabbinic status of the underage wife is identical with that of the deaf-mute wife or not.

(fol. 14a) **מתניתא**: גְּדוֹלָה וּקְטַנָּה כול'. גְּדוֹלָה וּקְטַנָּה. בִּיאַת הַגְּדוֹלָה פּוֹטֶרֶת אֶת הַקְּטַנָּה וְאֵין בִּיאַת הַקְּטַנָּה פּוֹטֶרֶת אֶת הַגְּדוֹלָה אֶלָּא פּוֹסֶלֶת אֶת הַגְּדוֹלָה.

Mishnah: "An adult wife and an underage wife," etc. An adult wife and an underage wife. The intercourse of the adult woman frees the underage girl. The intercourse of the underage girl does not free the adult woman but disables the adult woman[111].

(fol. 13b) **משנה יב**: מִי שֶׁהָיָה נָשׂוּי לִשְׁתֵּי יְתוֹמוֹת קְטַנּוֹת וָמֵת. בָּא הַיָּבָם עַל הָרִאשׁוֹנָה וְחָזַר וּבָא עַל הַשְּׁנִייָה. אוֹ שֶׁבָּא אָחִיו עַל הַשְּׁנִייָה לֹא פָסַל אֶת הָרִאשׁוֹנָה וְכֵן שְׁתֵּי חֵרְשׁוֹת. קְטַנָּה וְחֵרֶשֶׁת בָּא הַיָּבָם עַל הַקְּטַנָּה וְחָזַר וּבָא עַל הַחֵרֶשֶׁת. אוֹ שֶׁבָּא אָחִיו עַל הַחֵרֶשֶׁת לֹא פָסַל אֶת הַקְּטַנָּה. בָּא הַיָּבָם עַל הַחֵרֶשֶׁת וְחָזַר וּבָא עַל הַקְּטַנָּה אוֹ שֶׁבָּא אָחִיו עַל הַקְּטַנָּה פָּסַל אֶת הַחֵרֶשֶׁת.

Mishnah 12: Somebody was married to two underage orphan girls and died. If the levir had intercourse with the first one[112] and then had intercourse with the second, or his brother had intercourse with the second[113], the first one was not disabled. The same holds for two deaf-mutes. An underage girl and a deaf-mute. If the levir had intercourse with the underage girl and then had intercourse with the deaf-mute, or his brother had intercourse with the deaf-mute, the underage girl was not disabled[114]. If the levir had intercourse with the deaf-mute and then had intercourse with the underage girl, or his brother had intercourse with the underage girl, the deaf-mute was disabled[115].

112 She then is married to him in levirate by biblical standards.

113 These acts are sinful, but since the first levirate was legitimate, the sins of others cannot influence the status of the blameless wife.

114 This is also the reading in the Babli of the Babylonian Gaonim and Maimonides. But the Western tradition, represented by Rashi, RaBaD, and the printed Babli text, reads: "the underage girl was disabled". This is explained as a rabbinic decree to assimilate this case to the next one. Since the Mishnaiot are formulated to express the non-symmetry of the situations, the Eastern reading is to be preferred.

115 This Mishnah very definitely holds that the status of the deaf-mute is inferior to that of the underage girl. If the underage girl had not been an orphan, she could have been a wife by biblical standards. The marriage of the deaf-mute is a purely rabbinic institution to ensure that she should have a home and not be an object of public sexual abuse. Therefore, the almost biblical levirate of the underage girl annuls the purely rabbinic levirate of the deaf-mute, forbids the latter to the levir, and leads to the problem of the permanently forbidden deaf-mute discussed in the preceding Halakhot. As a consequence, both widows are forbidden to the levirs.

A totally different tradition is preserved in Tosephta 13:7. There, it is held that if any levirate is not 100% biblical, any doubling forbids both widows for all levirs.

(fol. 14a) **מתניתא:** מִי שֶׁהָיָה נָשׂוּי כול׳. אֲפִילוּ לֹא בָא עַל הַקְּטַנָּה פּוֹסֵל אֶת הַחֵרֶשֶׁת. שֶׁאִילּוּ לֹא בָא עַל הַקְּטַנָּה וָמֵתָה הָיָה מוּתָּר בַּחֵרֶשֶׁת. וְעַכְשָׁיו שֶׁבָּא עָלֶיהָ אֲפִילוּ מֵתָה פָּסַל אֶת הַחֵרֶשֶׁת.

Mishnah: "Somebody was married." Even if he did not have intercourse with the underage girl, the deaf-mute is disabled[116]. If he did not have intercourse with the underage girl and she died, he would have been permitted the deaf-mute. But now that he did have intercourse with her, even if she died he had disabled the deaf-mute.

116 In the presence of an underage widow, the candidacy of the deaf-mute widow for levirate is not executable. As an earlier Mishnah stated,

intercourse with the deaf-mute does not free the underage girl. The candidacy of the deaf-mute could be resurrected only if the underage girl died before she was married by the levir.

It is obvious that if the case involves a biblically married woman and a deaf-mute or an underage girl, the same situation applies.

(fol. 13b) **משנה יג:** פִּיקַּחַת וְחֵרֶשֶׁת בָּא הַיָּבָם עַל פִּיקַּחַת וְחָזַר וּבָא עַל הַחֵרֶשֶׁת. אוֹ שֶׁבָּא אָחִיו עַל הַחֵרֶשֶׁת לֹא פָּסַל אֶת הַפִּיקַּחַת. בָּא הַיָּבָם עַל הַחֵרֶשֶׁת וְחָזַר וּבָא עַל הַפִּיקַּחַת אוֹ שֶׁבָּא אָחִיו עַל הַפִּיקַּחַת פָּסַל אֶת הַחֵרֶשֶׁת.

Mishnah 13: A hearing wife and a deaf-mute. If the levir had intercourse with the hearing woman and then had intercourse with the deaf-mute, or his brother had intercourse with the deaf-mute, the hearing woman was not disabled. If the levir had intercourse with the deaf-mute and then had intercourse with the hearing woman, or his brother had intercourse with the hearing woman, the deaf-mute was disabled.

(fol. 14a) **מתניתא:** פִּיקַּחַת וְחֵרֶשֶׁת. בָּא הַיָּבָם כול'. אֲפִילוּ לֹא בָא עַל הַפִּיקַּחַת פּוֹסֵל אֶת הַחֵרֶשֶׁת. שֶׁאִילּוּ לֹא בָא עַל הַפִּיקַּחַת וָמֵתָה הָיָה מוּתָּר בַּחֵרֶשֶׁת. וְעַכְשָׁיו שֶׁבָּא עָלֶיהָ אֲפִילוּ מֵתָה פָּסַל אֶת הַחֵרֶשֶׁת.

Mishnah: "A hearing wife and a deaf-mute. If the levir had intercourse," etc. Even if he did not have intercourse with the hearing woman, the deaf-mute is disabled[116]. If he did not have intercourse with the hearing woman and she died, he would have been permitted the deaf-mute. But now that he did have intercourse with her, even if she died he had disabled the deaf-mute.

(fol. 13b) **משנה יד**: גְּדוֹלָה וּקְטַנָּה בָּא הַיָּבָם עַל הַגְּדוֹלָה וְחָזַר וּבָא עַל הַקְּטַנָּה. אוֹ שֶׁבָּא אָחִיו עַל הַקְּטַנָּה לֹא פָּסַל אֶת הַגְּדוֹלָה. בָּא הַיָּבָם עַל הַקְּטַנָּה וְחָזַר וּבָא עַל הַגְּדוֹלָה אוֹ שֶׁבָּא אָחִיו עַל הַגְּדוֹלָה פָּסַל אֶת הַקְּטַנָּה. רִבִּי לָעְזָר אוֹמֵר מְלַמְּדִין אֶת הַקְּטַנָּה שֶׁתְּמָאֵן בּוֹ.

Mishnah 14: An adult wife and an underage one. If the levir had intercourse with the adult and then had intercourse with the underage one, or his brother had intercourse with her, the adult was not disabled. If the levir had intercourse with the underage widow and then had intercourse with the adult one, or his brother had intercourse with her, the underage one was disabled. Rebbi Eleazar says, one teaches the underage girl that she should repudiate him[117].

117 Since the levirate of the underage girl would be almost biblical, her intercourse is incestuous and also forbids the adult co-widow. The situation can be remedied if the marriage of the underage girl is eliminated.

(fol. 14a) **מתניתא**: גְּדוֹלָה וּקְטַנָּה. בָּא הַיָּבָם כול׳. אֲפִילוּ לֹא בָא עַל הַגְּדוֹלָה פּוֹסֵל אֶת הַקְּטַנָּה. שֶׁאִילוּ לֹא בָא עַל הַגְּדוֹלָה וָמֵתָה הָיָה מוּתָּר בַּקְּטַנָּה. וְעַכְשָׁיו שֶׁבָּא עָלֶיהָ אֲפִילוּ מֵתָה פָּסַל אֶת הַקְּטַנָּה.

Mishnah: "An adult wife and an underage one" Even if he did not have intercourse with the adult one, the underage one is disabled[116]. If he did not have intercourse with the adult woman and she died, he would have been permitted the underage one. But now that he did have intercourse with her, even if she died he had disabled the underage one.

רִבִּי לָעְזָר אוֹמֵר מְלַמְּדִין אֶת הַקְּטַנָּה שֶׁתְּמָאֵן בּוֹ. לְשֶׁעָבַר. הָא כַּתְּחִילָּה לֹא. רִבִּי מָנָא אָמַר לָהּ סְתָם. רִבִּי יִצְחָק בְּרֵיהּ דְּרִבִּי חִיָּיה כְּתוּבָה בְּשֵׁם דְּרִבִּי יוֹחָנָן. דְּרִבִּי מֵאִיר הִיא. דְּרִבִּי מֵאִיר אָמַר. אֵין חוֹלְצִין וְלֹא מְיַיבְּמִין אֶת הַקְּטַנָּה שֶׁמָּא תִימָּצֵא אַיְילוֹנִית.

"Rebbi Eleazar says, one teaches the underage girl that she should repudiate him." After the fact[118]. Therefore, not from the start! Rebbi Mana said it without attribution, Rebbi Isaac the son of Rebbi Ḥiyya the Scribe in the name of Rebbi Yoḥanan: This is Rebbi Meïr's, since Rebbi Meïr said that one does not perform levirate or *ḥalîṣah* with an underage girl, since she might be found to be a she-ram.

118 Why does R. Eleazar (ben Shamua, the Tanna) not recommend that the underage girl repudiate the levir immediately before any complications can arise? The conclusion is that in practice one does not have to wait before one instructs the underage widow to repudiate the former marriage. The Babli, 111b, concurs that one follows R. Eleazar.

(fol. 13b) **משנה טו**: יָבָם קָטָן שֶׁבָּא עַל יְבָמָה קְטַנָּה יִגְדְּלוּ זֶה עִם זֶה. בָּא עַל יְבָמָה גְדוֹלָה יְגַדְּלֶנּוּ. הַיְבָמָה שֶׁאָמְרָה בְּתוֹךְ שְׁלֹשִׁים יוֹם לֹא נִבְעַלְתִּי כּוֹפִין אוֹתוֹ שֶׁיַּחֲלוֹץ לָהּ. לְאַחַר שְׁלֹשִׁים יוֹם מְבַקְשִׁים מִמֶּנּוּ שֶׁיַּחֲלוֹץ לָהּ. וּבִזְמַן שֶׁהוּא מוֹדֶה אֲפִילוּ אַחַר שְׁנֵים עָשָׂר חוֹדֶשׁ כּוֹפִין אוֹתוֹ שֶׁיַּחֲלוֹץ לָהּ.

Mishnah 15: If an underage levir had intercourse with an underage sister-in-law, they should grow up together[119]. If he had intercourse with an adult sister-in-law, she should raise him[119]. If the sister-in-law claims within thirty days[120] that she was not copulated with, one forces him to perform *ḥalîṣah* with her[121]. After thirty days, one asks him to perform *ḥalîṣah* with her[122]. But if he confesses, one forces him to perform *ḥalîṣah* with her even after twelve months.

119 And stay married.

120 After he officially brought her into his house. The marriage ceremony of the levir is without meaning unless it is followed by the sex act.

121 It is obvious that she cannot

prove her claim by witnesses. But for the first thirty days, her claim carries a presumption of truth. Unless the levir can disprove her claim, she is not married in levirate and is freed by *ḥalîṣah*.

122 It is not credible that a woman would stay more than thirty days with a man who does not sleep with her. If the levir denies her claim, she would have to prove it. In the absence of proof, the court may counsel a separation but cannot force it.

(fol. 14a) **מתניתא:** יָבָם קָטָן כול׳. תַּנֵּי. טַעֲנַת בְּתוּלִים עַד שְׁלֹשִׁים יוֹם. דִּבְרֵי רִבִּי מֵאִיר. וַחֲכָמִים אוֹמְרִים. מִיָּד. מַה נָן קַיָּימִין. אִם בְּשֶׁבָּעַל. מִיָּד. אִם בְּשֶׁלֹּא בָעַל. אֲפִילוּ לְאַחַר כַּמָּה. אֶלָּא כֵן אֲנָן קַיָּימִין בִּסְתָם. רִבִּי מֵאִיר אָמַר. חֲזָקָה אָדָם מַעֲמִיד עַצְמוֹ שְׁלֹשִׁים יוֹם. וְרַבָּנִין אָמְרִין. אֵין אָדָם מַעֲמִיד אֲפִילוּ יוֹם אֶחָד. רִבִּי יִרְמְיָה בָּעֵי. מַהוּ שֶׁיְּהֵא נֶאֱמָן לוֹמַר עַל דְּרִבִּי מֵאִיר. הֶעֱמַדְתִּי עַצְמִי שְׁלֹשִׁים יוֹם בִּשְׁבִיל לַעֲשׂוֹת הַוְּלָד שְׁתוּקִי. נִישְׁמְעִינָהּ מִן הָדָא. הַיְבָמָה שֶׁאָמְרָה בְתוֹךְ שְׁלֹשִׁים יוֹם. לֹא נִבְעַלְתִּי. כּוֹפִין אוֹתוֹ שֶׁיַּחֲלוֹץ לָהּ. לְאַחַר שְׁלֹשִׁים יוֹם מְבַקְשִׁים מִמֶּנּוּ שֶׁיַּחֲלוֹץ לָהּ. (לְאַחַר שְׁלֹשִׁים.)[127] וְאָמַר רִבִּי לָעְזָר. דְּרִבִּי מֵאִיר הִיא. וְאָמַר רִבִּי לָעְזָר. לֹא שָׁנוּ אֶלָּא אֶצְלָהּ. הָא אֵצֶל צָרָתָהּ לֹא. כְּמָה דְתֵימַר תַּמָּן. לֹא הַכֹּל מִמֶּנָּה לַחוֹב לְצָרָתָהּ. אַף הָכָא לֹא הַכֹּל מִמֶּנּוּ לַחוֹב לִבְנוֹ.

Mishnah: "If an underage levir," etc. [123]It was stated: A claim of non-virginity may be brought within thirty days, the words of Rebbi Meïr. But the Sages say, immediately[124]. Where do we hold? If he copulated, immediately. If he did not copulate, even after a longer delay. But we must hold if it was not spelled out. Rebbi Meïr said, it is credible that a man may hold himself back for thirty days. But the Sages say, a man does not hold himself back even for one day[125]. Rebbi Jeremiah asked: According to Rebbi Meïr, would a man be believed to assert that he held himself back for thirty days in order to make the child fatherless[126]? Let us hear from the following: " If the sister-in-law claims within thirty days that she was not copulated with, one forces him to perform *ḥalîṣah* with her. After thirty days, one asks him to perform *ḥalîṣah* with her." (After thirty days.)[127] And Rebbi Eleazar said, this is Rebbi Meïr's[128]. And Rebbi Eleazar said, that refers only to her, but not to her co-wife[129]. As you say there[130], she is not believed to damage her co-wife, so here, he is not believed to damage his son.

123 The entire paragraph is from *Ketubot* Halakhah 1:4.

124 In the Babli, 111b, and the Tosephta, *Ketubot* 1:4: "A claim of non-virginity may be brought within thirty days, the words of Rebbi Meïr. Rebbi Yose says, if they were alone together, immediately; if they were not alone together, within thirty days (*Tosephta)*, indefinitely (*Babli*)."

The husband goes to court to annul the marriage, without divorce and without payment, claiming that he was lead to believe the bride to be a virgin when he found that she was not.

125 In the Babli, 112a, this is declared to be irrelevant for our Mishnah since a man will sleep with his bride immediately after the marriage ceremony but might be reluctant to touch his sister-in-law for some time.

126 If his wife becomes pregnant immediately after the marriage ceremony, can he declare in court that the child is not his since he did not sleep with his bride for some time?

127 Missing in *Ketubot*.

128 But the majority will accept the widow's claim only on the day after she entered the levir's house.

129 If the co-wife married an outside man based on the other's levirate marriage, she cannot cast aspersion on the validity of her co-widow's marriage without the testimony of two credible witnesse.

The Babli agrees, 112a, at least in the interpretation of Rashi and Rabbenu Ḥananel.

130 "There" is here, *Yebamot*; "here" is there, *Ketubot*; cf. Note 122.

(fol. 13b) **משנה טז**: הַנּוֹדֶרֶת הֲנָייָה מִיבָמָהּ בְּחַיֵּי בַעֲלָהּ כּוֹפִין אוֹתוֹ עַד שֶׁיַּחֲלוֹץ לָהּ. לְאַחַר מִיתַת בַּעֲלָהּ מְבַקְשִׁין מִמֶּנּוּ שֶׁיַּחֲלוֹץ לָהּ. אִם נִתְכַּוְונָה לְכָךְ אֲפִילוּ בְחַיֵּי בַעֲלָהּ מְבַקְשִׁין מִמֶּנּוּ שֶׁיַּחֲלוֹץ לָהּ.

Mishnah 16: If a woman made a vow during her husband's lifetime forbidding herself any usufruct from her levir[131], one coerces him until he performs *ḥalîṣah* with her. After her husband's death, one begs him that he should perform *ḥalîṣah* with her[132]. If she had [*ḥalîṣah*] in mind even during her husband's lifetime, one begs him that he should perform *ḥalîṣah* with her.

131 She made the vow when she did not think that her husband would die childless, but now she finds herself forbidden to marry the levir.

132 If she made the vow in order to prevent levirate, the court will not coerce the levir to abandon the biblical commandment of levirate. It is clear that the Mishnah became obsolete when preference changed from levirate to *ḥalîṣah*.

(fol. 14a) **מתניתא**: הַנּוֹדֶרֶת הֲנָייָה מִיבָמָהּ כול׳. כְּהָדָא. הוּא אוֹמֵר. בְּעַלְתִּי. וְהִיא אוֹמֶרֶת. לֹא נִבְעַלְתִּי. אַף עַל פִּי שֶׁחָזַר וְאָמַר. לֹא בָעַלְתִּי. לֹא הַכֹּל מִמֶּנּוּ. שֶׁכְּבָר מִשָּׁעָה הָרִאשׁוֹנָה אָמַר. בָּעַלְתִּי. אֲבָל אִם אָמַר מִשָּׁעָה הָרִאשׁוֹנָה. לֹא בָעַלְתִּי. שְׁנֵיהֶן יְכוֹלִין לַעֲקוֹר חֲזָקָה. חֲבֵרַיָּא בָעֵיי. מַה נָן קַייָמִין. אִם בְּמִשְׁנָה הָרִאשׁוֹנָה שֶׁמַּעֲנוּ שֶׁמּוּתָּר לְייַבֵּם. אִם בְּמִשְׁנָה אַחֲרוֹנָה שֶׁמַּעֲנוּ שֶׁמּוּתָּר לַחֲלוֹץ. שֶׁמַּעֲנוּ שֶׁכּוֹפִין. רַב הוּנָא בְשֵׁם רַב. וְהוּא שֶׁיְּהֵא הַגֵּט יוֹצֵא מִתַּחַת יָדוֹ לְתוֹךְ יָדָהּ. הוּא אָמַר. גֵּט אִשָּׁה. וְהִיא אוֹמֶרֶת. גֵּט יְבָמָה. בְּתוֹךְ שְׁלֹשִׁים יוֹם חֲזָקָה לֹא בָעַל כּוֹפִין אוֹתוֹ שֶׁיַּחֲלוֹץ לָהּ. לְאַחַר שְׁלֹשִׁים יוֹם מְבַקְשִׁין מִמֶּנּוּ שֶׁיַּחֲלוֹץ. רִבִּי יוֹסֵי בָעֵי. לְאַחַר שְׁלֹשִׁים יוֹם חֲזָקָה בָעַל. וְאַתְּ אָמַר כּוֹפִין. אֶלָּא כֵינִי. רַב הוּנָא בְשֵׁם רַב. וְהוּא שֶׁיְּהֵא הַגֵּט יוֹצֵא מִתַּחַת יָדוֹ לְתוֹךְ יָדָהּ. הוּא אָמַר. גֵּט אִשָּׁה. וְהִיא אוֹמֶרֶת. גֵּט יְבָמָה. בְּתוֹךְ שְׁלֹשִׁים חֲזָקָה לֹא בָעַל כּוֹפִין אוֹתוֹ שֶׁיַּחֲלוֹץ לָהּ. לְאַחַר שְׁלֹשִׁים יוֹם מְבַקְשִׁין מִמֶּנּוּ שֶׁיַּחֲלוֹץ לָהּ. כְּהָדָא. הוּא

אוֹמֵר. בָּעַלְתִּי. וְהִיא אוֹמֶרֶת. לֹא נִבְעַלְתִּי. פְּשִׁיטָה דְהוּא מַעֲלֶה לָהּ מְזוֹנוֹת. פְּשִׁיטָה שֶׁאֵינָהּ יוֹרְשָׁהּ. לֹא צְרִיכָה דְלֹא מַהוּ שֶׁיִּירַשׁ נִיכְסֵי אָחִיו. הִיא אוֹמֶרֶת. נִבְעַלְתִּי. וְהוּא אוֹמֵר. לֹא בָעַלְתִּי. פְּשִׁיטָה שֶׁאֵינוֹ מַעֲלֶה לָהּ מְזוֹנוֹת. פְּשִׁיטָה שֶׁהוּא יוֹרֵשׁ נִיכְסֵי אָחִיו. לֹא צְרִיכָה דְלֹא מַהוּ שֶׁיִּירָשֶׁנָּה.

Mishnah: "If a woman made a vow forbidding herself any usufruct," etc. [133]Consider the following: He said, I copulated, but she says, I was not copulated with. Even if he changed and then said, I did not copulate, he cannot be believed since from the start he had said, I copulated. But if from the start he said that he had not copulated, the two together can uproot the presumption[134].

The colleagues asked: What are we talking about? If following the early Mishnah[135], we have understood that one may marry in levirate. If following the later Mishnah, we have understood that one may perform *ḥalîṣah.* Where did we hear that one coerces[136]? Rav Huna in the name of Rav: That is, if a bill of divorce has passed from his hand to her hand[137]. He says, it is the bill of divorce of a wife. But she says, it is the bill of divorce of a sister-in-law[138]. Within thirty days, the presumption is that he did not copulate; one coerces him to perform *ḥalîṣah.* After thirty days, one asks him to perform *ḥalîṣah.*

Rebbi Yose asked, after thirty days, the presumption is that he copulated and you say one coerces[139]? But it must be the following: Rav Huna in the name of Rav: That is, if a bill of divorce has passed from his hand to her hand. He says, it is the bill of divorce of a wife. But she says, it is the bill of divorce of a sister-in-law. Within thirty days, the presumption is that he did not copulate; one coerces him to perform *ḥalîṣah.* After thirty days, one asks him to perform *ḥalîṣah.*

The following: If he says, I copulated, and she says, I was not copulated with, it is obvious that he has to sustain her[140]. It is obvious that he does not inherit from her[141]. The problem is whether he inherits his brother's property[142]. If she says, I was copulated with, and he says, I did not copulate, it is obvious that he does not have to sustain her[143]. It is obvious that he inherits his brother's property[144]. The problem is whether he inherits from her[145].

133 The entire Halakhah refers to Mishnah 15, not Mishnah 16.

134 The court must believe that they had no sexual relations and that she never became the levir's wife while living in his house.

135 *Bekhorot* 1:7 stating that in early times, levirate was preferred, but today *ḥalîṣah* is preferred.

136 *Deut.* 25:5-9 makes it clear that the levir can be compelled to appear in court but not that he can be compelled to do anything against his will.

137 In the Babli, 112a, this is the answer of Rav to the question why one does coerce him to perform *ḥalîṣah* if she already lives in his house, why does one not coerce him to sleep with her? Note that the colleagues prevented this question to be asked by referring to the later Mishnah.

138 As was determined earlier, in order to remarry she needs a bill of divorce for his "bespeaking" *and ḥalîṣah* for her candidacy of levirate.

139 The only difference between the colleagues and R. Yose is the formulation of the question. Since after 30 days the presumption is that she became his wife, why should he be asked to perform a useless *ḥalîṣah*? The answer is that he already gave the bill of divorce but that might not be enough to let the sister-in-law remarry.

140 He obligated himself since he asserts that she is his wife by biblical standards.

141 She asserts that she is not his wife.

142 If there are potential co-heirs, he inherits only if he is married to the widow.

143 If he asserts that he did not copulate, it is obvious that there are no eyewitnesses to back up her claim for support as a wife. Since in money matters the proof is on the claimant, she cannot enforce her claim.

144 This is not obvious. In fact, all classical commentators amend the text to read "he does not inherit" and the editor of the Leiden ms. here notes a corruption. Their reason is that the co-heirs can point to his denial of

acquisition. There is little reason to accept the argument and the correction since *Deut.* 25:5-6 makes it quite clear that the transfer of property is an automatic consequence of the transfer of the wife and her word is the only one that should carry weight in his family.

145 One the one hand, she asserts that he inherits from her. On the other hand, he renounces all his rights in any settlement with her family. No answers are given to the questions that never apply in practice.

חרש שנשא פרק ארבעה עשר

(fol. 14a) **משנה א:** חֵרֵשׁ שֶׁנָּשָׂא פִּיקַּחַת וּפִיקֵּחַ שֶׁנָּשָׂא חֵרֶשֶׁת אִם רָצָה יוֹצִיא וְאִם רָצָה יְקַייֵם כְּשֵׁם שֶׁהוּא כוֹנֵס בִּרְמִיזָה כָּךְ הוּא מוֹצִיא בִּרְמִיזָה. פִּיקֵּחַ שֶׁנָּשָׂא פִּיקַּחַת וְנִתְחָרְשָׁה (fol. 14b) אִם רָצָה יוֹצִיא וְאִם רָצָה יְקַייֵם. נִשְׁטַתְּתָה לֹא יוֹצִיא. נִתְחָרֵשׁ הוּא אוֹ נִשְׁתַּטָּה אֵינוֹ מוֹצִיא עוֹלָמִית.

Mishnah 1: A deaf-mute man who married a hearing woman or a hearing man who married a deaf-mute woman may divorce or stay married at will; just as he marries with sign language so he divorces with sign language[1]. A hearing man who married a hearing woman who then became deaf-mute may divorce or stay married at will[2]. If she became insane he shall not divorce[3]. If he became deaf-mute or insane, he can never divorce[4].

1 The marriage is only valid by rabbinic standards; a divorce is possible by rabbinic standards.

2 As explained in the next Mishnah, a divorce is effective by the action of the husband alone; the divorce is possible even if the wife is not able to act in law.

3 By rabbinic decree.

4 He is married under biblical standards. Even if he were able to communicate in sign language as a deaf-mute, he cannot execute acts under biblical standards.

הלכה א: חֵרֵשׁ שֶׁנָּשָׂא פִּיקַּחַת כול'. כֵּיצַד הוּא עוֹשֶׂה. רוֹמֵז וְהוּא נוֹתֵן לָהּ גִּיטָהּ. כְּשֵׁם שֶׁהוּא רוֹמֵז כָּךְ הוּא נִרְמָז.

Halakhah 1: "A deaf-mute who married a hearing woman", etc. How does he do it[5]? He communicates in sign language and gives her the bill of divorce. In the same way he communicates with others, others communicate with him.

5 How can he divorce? He has to tell the clerk to write the bill and the witnesses to sign and to witness the delivery of the documents. If the woman is deaf-mute, she has to be instructed to receive the documents in her hands. There is an opinion in Mishnah *Giṭṭin* 5:8 that he may communicate by lip reading.

מַתְנִיתָא בְּשֶׁקִּידְּשָׁהּ בַּכֶּסֶף. אֲבָל אִם קִידְּשָׁהּ בִּבְעִילָה קִידּוּשָׁיו מַעֲשֶׂה וְגֵירוּשָׁיו אֵינוֹ מַעֲשֶׂה.

The Mishnah applies if he[6] became betrothed to her by money. But if he became betrothed to her by copulation, his betrothal is an action but his divorce is not an action.

6 If the deaf-mute became betrothed to a woman by giving her an object of value, he is imitating an act reserved for competent adults. His marriage is deemed valid only by special rabbinic enactment. If an underage (otherwise normal) boy became betrothed by money's worth, his act does not have even a shadow of validity. But the betrothal of a woman by the sex act of a man, while impractical, is valid by biblical standards (*Deut*. 24:1). The marriage then can be undone only by an act valid by biblical standards, outside the reach of a deaf-mute.

רִבִּי לָעְזָר שָׁאַל לְרִבִּי יוֹחָנָן. אִשְׁתּוֹ שֶׁלַּחֵרֵשׁ וְשֶׁלַּשּׁוֹטֶה. אָמַר לֵיהּ. אֲפִילוּ אָשָׁם תָּלוּי אֵין בָּהּ. רִבִּי יַעֲקֹב בַּר אָחָא בְשֵׁם רִבִּי יוֹחָנָן רִבִּי הִילָא בְשֵׁם רִבִּי לָעְזָר. אֲפִילוּ אָשָׁם תָּלוּי אֵין בָּהּ. מִכֵּיוָן דְּאַתְּ אָמַר. אֲפִילוּ אָשָׁם תָּלוּי אֵין בָּהּ וּבָא אַחֵר וְקִידְּשָׁהּ נִתְפְּשׂוּ בָהּ קִידּוּשִׁין. גֵּירַשׁ מוּתֶּרֶת לְהִינָּשֵׂא לָרִאשׁוֹן. הָדָא הִיא דְתַנֵּי רִבִּי חִיָּה. אִשְׁתּוֹ שֶׁלַּחֵרֵשׁ שֶׁגֵּירְשָׁהּ חֵרֵשׁ וְהָלְכָה וְנִישֵּׂאת לְחֵרֵשׁ אוֹ לְפִיקֵּחַ. קוֹרֵא אֲנִי עָלֶיהָ לֹא יוּכַל בַּעֲלָהּ הָרִאשׁוֹן אֲשֶׁר שִׁלְּחָהּ לָשׁוּב לְקַחְתָּהּ. אִשְׁתּוֹ שֶׁלַּפִּיקֵּחַ שֶׁגֵּירְשָׁהּ וְהָלְכָה וְנִישֵּׂאת לְחֵרֵשׁ אוֹ לְפִיקֵּחַ. קוֹרֵא אֲנִי עָלֶיהָ לֹא

יוּכַל בַּעֲלָהּ הָרִאשׁוֹן אֲשֶׁר שִׁלְּחָהּ . אִשְׁתּוֹ שֶׁלַּחֵרֵשׁ שֶׁהָלַךְ לוֹ בַעֲלָהּ לִמְדִינַת הַיָּם. וּבָאוּ וְאָמְרוּ לָהּ. מֵת בַּעֲלֵיךְ. וְהָלְכָה וְנִישֵּׂאת לְחֵרֵשׁ אוֹ לְפִיקֵּחַ וְאַחַר כָּךְ בָּא בַעֲלָהּ. תֵּצֵא מִזֶּה וּמִזֶּה. אִשְׁתּוֹ שֶׁלַּפִּיקֵּחַ שֶׁהָלַךְ לוֹ בַעֲלָהּ לִמְדִינַת הַיָּם. בָּאוּ וְאָמְרוּ לָהּ. מֵת בַּעֲלֵיךְ. וְהָלְכָה וְנִישֵּׂאת לְחֵרֵשׁ וְאַחַר כָּךְ בָּא הַפִּיקֵּחַ. הֲוֵינָן סָבְרִין מֵימַר. יוֹצִיא הַחֵרֵשׁ וִיקַיֵּים הַפִּיקֵּחַ. עוֹד הִיא כְאִילֵּין קְנָסַיָּיה.

Rebbi Eleazar asked Rebbi Johanan: The wife of a deaf-mute or an insane? He said to him, that does not even need a reparation sacrifice for a possible sin[7]. Rebbi Jacob bar Aḥa in the name of Rebbi Johanan, Rebbi Hila in the name of Rebbi Eleazar: It does not even need a reparation sacrifice for a possible sin. Since you say, it does not even need a reparation sacrifice for a possible sin; if another man came and gave her *qiddušin*, they take hold of her[8]. If he divorced, is she permitted to remarry the first [husband]? That is what Rebbi Ḥiyya stated: About the wife of a deaf-mute who after being divorced by the deaf-mute went and married a deaf-mute or a hearing person, I am reading: "Her first husband who sent her away cannot come to take her back."[9,10] About the wife of a hearing person who after being divorced went and married a deaf-mute or a hearing person, I am reading: "Her first husband who sent her away cannot . . . ." If a deaf-mute's husband went overseas and they came and told his wife, your husband has died, and she went and married a deaf-mute or a hearing person, and then her husband returned, she has to leave both of them[11]. If the husband of a hearing wife went overseas and they came and told her, your husband has died, and she went and married a deaf-mute, and then her hearing [husband] returned, we would think that the deaf-mute should divorce her but the hearing person can keep her[12]. She is still under these disabilities[13].

7 Since the marriage has no biblical validity, adultery by the wife cannot be a biblical crime. There cannot be a sacrifice to atone for any transgression of rabbinic rules. The Babli agrees, 113a in the name of Samuel.

8 Cf. Chapter 5, Note 43. If the woman is not married by biblical standards, betrothal to another man needs a divorce.

9 *Deut*. 24:4.

10 This is a rabbinic decree.

11 Under the rules of Mishnah 10:1.

12 Since she was not really married and unmarried sex in the erroneous belief that she was a widow does not prevent the woman to return to her husband.

13 The long list of disabilities of Mishnah 10:1 is rabbinic and the rabbis enforce them for marriages concluded under rabbinic rules only.

נִשְׁתַּטָּה לֹא יוֹצִיא. דְּבֵית יַנַּאי אָמְרֵי. מִפְּנֵי גְדֵירָה. רִבִּי זְעִירָה וְרִבִּי אִילָא תְּרֵיהוֹן אָמְרִין. שֶׁאֵינָהּ יְכוֹלָה לְשַׁמֵּר אֶת גִּיטָּהּ. רִבִּי נְחֶמְיָה בַּר מַר עוּקְבָּן בְּרֵיהּ דְּרִבִּי יוֹסֵי אָמַר תְּלָתָא. עָבַר וְגֵירַשׁ. מָאן דְּאָמַר. מִפְּנֵי גְדֵירָה. גֵּירַשׁ. מָאן דְּאָמַר. שֶׁאֵינָהּ יְכוֹלָה לְשַׁמֵּר אֶת גִּיטָּהּ. אָסוּר. יֵשׁ לָהּ בֵּן וְאָב וְאָח. מָאן דְּאָמַר. מִפְּנֵי גְדֵירָה. אָסוּר. מָאן דְּאָמַר. שֶׁאֵינָהּ יְכוֹלָה לְשַׁמֵּר אֶת גִּיטָּהּ. יֵשׁ לָהּ אָב וִיכוֹלָה הִיא לִשְׁמוֹר אֶת גִּיטָּהּ. פְּעָמִים שׁוֹטָה פְּעָמִים חֲלוּמָה. מָאן דְּאָמַר. מִפְּנֵי גְדֵירָה. אָסוּר. מָאן דְּאָמַר. שֶׁאֵינָהּ יְכוֹלָה לְשַׁמֵּר אֶת גִּיטָּהּ. יֵשׁ לָהּ עִיתִּים וִיכוֹלָה הִיא לְשַׁמֵּר אֶת גִּיטָּהּ.

"If she became insane he shall not divorce." In the House of Rebbi Yannai they said, because of the fence[14]. Rebbi Ze'ira and Rebbi Hila both say, because she cannot preserve her bill of divorce[15]. Rebbi Nehemiah bar Mar Uqban (the son) [in the name][16] of Rebbi Yose explained three cases. If he transgressed and divorced her. According to him who said because of a fence, he divorced[17]. According to him who said because she cannot preserve her bill of divorce, it is forbidden[18]. If she has a son, or a father, or a brother. According to him who said because of a fence, it is forbidden. According to him who said because she cannot preserve her bill of divorce, she has a father and can preserve her bill of divorce. Sometimes she is insane and sometimes of lucid mind. According to him who said because of a fence, it is forbidden. According to him who said because she cannot preserve her bill of divorce, sometimes she can preserve her bill of divorce[19].

14 In the rabbinic literature (*Tosaphot* 113b *s. v.* יצתה, *Rašba* 113b, *Roš* 14:3, from where all later sources are derived) the reading is גְּרִירָה "towing, dragging". According to that reading, R. Yannai says that the divorce is rabbinically prohibited because on her own the insane could not defend herself and might be dragged away by any man for sexual abuse. According to the reading of the ms. and *editio princeps* גְּדֵירָה, R. Yannai asserts only that it is a rabbinic decree that the husband is forbidden to divorce her (cf. *Demai* Chapter 1, Note 89 for the equality גדירה = גזירה). The cases quoted by R. Nehemiah bar Mar Uqban support the ms. reading unequivocally.

In the Babli, 113b, R. Yannai is quoted as author of the statement attributed here to R. Ze'ira and R. Hila.

15 Since *Deut.* 24:1 requires that the divorce document be *in the hand* of the wife, a wife without a legal hand cannot be divorced. The Babli, 113b, agrees that a bill of divorce that cannot be delivered either to the woman or her representative is inactive.

16 Reading of *Roš*, *l. c.* The reading of the ms. is impossible.

17 His action was a transgression but is valid.

18 Unless the woman understands that she is divorced, she is not divorced.

19 According to both Talmudim [Yerushalmi *Terumot* 1:1 (Notes 52-55), *Giṭṭin* 7:1, fol. 48c; Babli *Roš Haššanah* 28a] a sporadically insane person is treated as a normal person in his intervals of lucidity.

משנה ב: אָמַר רִבִּי יוֹחָנָן בֶּן נוּרִי וְכִי מִפְּנֵי מָה הָאִשָּׁה שֶׁנִּתְחָרְשָׁה יוֹצְאָה וְהָאִישׁ שֶׁנִּתְחָרֵשׁ אֵינוֹ מוֹצִיא. אָמְרוּ לוֹ אֵינוֹ דוֹמֶה הָאִישׁ הַמְגָרֵשׁ לָאִשָּׁה הַמִּתְגָּרֶשֶׁת שֶׁהָאִשָּׁה יוֹצְאָה לִרְצוֹנָהּ וְשֶׁלֹּא לִרְצוֹנָהּ וְהָאִישׁ אֵינוֹ מוֹצִיא אֶלָּא לִרְצוֹנוֹ.

Mishnah 2: Rebbi Joḥanan ben Nuri said, why can a deaf-mute woman be divorced but a deaf-mute man cannot divorce? They told him, a divorcing man is not comparable to a divorced woman since a woman can be divorced with or against her will[20] but a man divorces only by his own will[21].

משנה ג: הֵעִיד רִבִּי יוֹחָנָן בֶּן גּוּדְגָּדָה עַל הַחֵרֶשֶׁת שֶׁהִשִּׂיאָהּ אָבִיהָ שֶׁהִיא יוֹצְאָה בְּגֵט אָמְרוּ לוֹ אַף זוֹ כַּיּוֹצֵא בָהּ.

Mishnah 3: Rebbi Joḥanan ben Gudgada[22] testified about a deaf-mute girl who was married off by her father[23] that she could be divorced by a bill of divorce. They said to him[24], that is an example.

20 By talmudic standards. By an institution of R. Gershon ben Jehudah (Mayence, about the year 1000), European Jews were forbidden to divorce without the wife's consent (except in cases where the law forces the husband to divorce).

21 If the court coerces a recalcitrant husband to give a divorce, they have to coerce him "until he says, I want to do it."

22 A Tanna, about one generation older than R. Joḥanan ben Nuri. His testimony is also in Mishnah *Idiut* 7:9, *Giṭṭin* 5:5.

23 When she was a minor and was passive in the marriage. She is married by biblical standards.

24 To R. Joḥanan ben Nuri, that in principle, the biblical marriage of an incompetent person can be dissolved by divorce.

מתניתא: הֵעִיד רִבִּי יוֹחָנָן בֶּן נוּרִי כול'. רִבִּי חֲנַנְיָה בְּעָא קוֹמֵי רִבִּי הִילָא. נִרְאִין דְּבָרִים בְּפִיקַּחַת שֶׁיֵּשׁ בָּהּ דַּעַת שֶׁהִיא יוֹצְאָה בֵּין לְדַעַת בֵּין שֶׁלֹּא לְדַעַת. וְחֵרֶשֶׁת שֶׁאֵין בָּהּ דַּעַת לֹא תֵצֵא אֶלָּא לְדַעַת. וְלֹא עֵידוּת הִיא. אַף זוֹ כְּיוֹצֵא

בָּהּ וּמוֹסִיפִין עַל הָעֵדוּת. וְרִבִּי חֲנַנְיָה סָבַר מֵימַר בְּפִיקַּחַת שֶׁהִשִּׂיאָהּ אָבִיהָ וְנִתְחָרְשָׁה. רִבִּי יוֹסֵה סָבַר מֵימַר בִּקְטַנָּה שֶׁהִשִּׂיאָהּ אָבִיהָ וְנִתְגָּרְשָׁה.

Mishnah: "Rebbi Johanan ben Nuri[25] testified," etc. Rebbi Hananiah asked before Rebbi Hila. The matters seem reasonable for a hearing woman of sound mind, that she is divorced with or without her acquiescence. But a deaf-mute woman who has no will should not be divorced except with her acquiescence. But is it not testimony "that is an example"; does one add to a testimony[26]? But Rebbi Hanania is of the opinion that this deals with a hearing girl who was married off by her father and became deaf-and-dumb[27]. Rebbi Yose is of the opinion that this deals with an underage girl[28] who was married off by her father and became divorced.

25 A scribal error.

26 If the Mishnah was included in *Idiut* it is proof that the testimony was checked and found truly to reflect old practice.

27 Since the marriage was valid by biblical standards, the divorce follows biblical rules.

28 Already deaf-mute. Since she is not an orphan, she can be married off legally, not only if deaf-mute but even if insane.

אָמַר רִבִּי יוֹחָנָן. לֵית כֵּן עַל רֹאשָׁהּ. אִית כֵּן עַל סוֹפָהּ. מַה אִית כֵּן עַל רֹאשָׁהּ. כְּשֶׁהָיָה חֵרֵשׁ בַּעַל הַחֵרֶשֶׁת פִּיקֵּחַ בַּעַל הַפִּיקַּחַת. אֲבָל אִם הָיָה חֵרֵשׁ בַּעַל הַפִּיקַּחַת פִּיקֵּחַ בַּעַל הַחֵרֶשֶׁת הָדָא הִיא דְתַנִּינָן דְּבָתַר דְּבָתַר דְּבַתְרָא.

Rebbi Johanan said[29], there is nothing to be learned from the beginning, but there is something to be learned from the end. What is there at the beginning? If the deaf-mute [brother] was the husband of the deaf-mute [woman] and the hearing the husband of the hearing. But if the deaf-mute [brother] was the husband of the hearing [woman] and the hearing the husband of the deaf-mute, that should have been stated at the very end.

29 That is a note only on the order of the following Mishnaiot. R. Joḥanan notes that it would have been more reasonable to start in both series (sisters or unrelated women) with the totally unproblematic case and to introduce the complications later.

משנה ד: שְׁנֵי אַחִים חֵרְשִׁים נְשׂוּאִים לִשְׁתֵּי אֲחָיוֹת חֵרְשׁוֹת אוֹ לִשְׁתֵּי אֲחָיוֹת פִּקְחוֹת אוֹ לִשְׁתֵּי אֲחָיוֹת אַחַת חֵרֶשֶׁת וְאַחַת פִּיקַחַת אוֹ שְׁתֵּי אֲחָיוֹת חֵרְשׁוֹת נְשׂוּאוֹת לִשְׁנֵי אַחִין פִּיקְחִין לִשְׁנֵי אַחִין חֵרְשִׁין לִשְׁנֵי אַחִין אֶחָד חֵרֵשׁ וְאֶחָד פִּיקֵּחַ. הֲרֵי אֵילוּ פְּטוּרִין מִן הַחֲלִיצָה וּמִן הַיִּיבּוּם. וְאִם הָיוּ נָכְרִיּוֹת יִכְנוֹסוּ וְאִם רָצוּ לְהוֹצִיא יוֹצִיאוּ.

Mishnah 4: Two deaf-mute brothers married to two deaf-mute sisters, or two hearing sisters, or two sisters of whom one is deaf-mute, the other hearing; or two deaf-mute sisters married to two deaf-mute brothers, or two hearing brothers, or two brothers of whom one is deaf-mute, these are free from *ḥalîṣah* and levirate[30]. If the women are unrelated, they must marry them, and, if they want to, they may send them away[31].

30 A sister cannot become the co-wife of a sister, Mishnah 1:1.

31 Since they cannot perform a valid *ḥalîṣah* if one of the parties at least is deaf-mute, and the two marriages are of equal status, they must marry in levirate. But after the marriage, there is no general obstacle to a divorce.

מתניתא: שְׁנֵי אַחִין חֵרְשִׁין כול'. צָרָתָהּ מָהוּ. נִישְׁמְעִינָהּ מִן הָדָא. בִּתּוֹ פִּיקַּחַת נְשׂוּאָה לְאָחִיו חֵרֵשׁ. צָרָתָהּ פְּטוּרָה מִן הַחֲלִיצָה וּמִן הַיִּיבּוּם.

Mishnah: "Two deaf-mute brothers," etc. What about her co-wife[32]? Let us hear from the following: If his hearing daughter was married to his deaf-mute brother, her co-wife is free from *ḥalîṣah* and levirate[33].

32 Since at least one party is deaf-mute, none of the marriages described in the Mishnah is of biblical validity (it is assumed throughout these Mishnaiot that the deaf-mute woman was not married to her hearing husband by her father during her minority.) It therefore is not self-evident that the exemptions of Mishnah 1:1 apply in these cases.

33 If the marriage was valid, then the co-wife of the daughter is free according to the House of Hillel (Mishnah 1-4). If the marriage was invalid, then there is no place for levirate. In the latter case, the co-wife is forbidden to the hearing brother by rabbinic decree.

(fol. 14b) **משנה ה:** שְׁנֵי אַחִין אֶחָד חֵרֵשׁ וְאֶחָד פִּיקֵחַ נְשׂוּאִין לִשְׁתֵּי אֲחָיוֹת פִּקְחוֹת מֵת חֵרֵשׁ בַּעַל הַפִּיקַחַת מַה יַּעֲשֶׂה פִּיקֵחַ בַּעַל הַפִּקַּחַת תֵּצֵא מִשּׁוּם אֲחוֹת אִשָּׁה. מֵת פִּקֵּחַ בַּעַל הַפִּקַּחַת מַה יַּעֲשֶׂה חֵרֵשׁ בַּעַל הַפִּקַּחַת מוֹצִיא אִשְׁתּוֹ בְּגֵט וְאֵשֶׁת אָחִיו אֲסוּרָה לְעוֹלָם.

Mishnah 5: Two brothers, one deaf-mute and one hearing, married to two hearing sisters. If the deaf-mute married to the hearing wife died, what shall the hearing [brother] married to the hearing wife do? [The widow] has to leave as the wife's sister. If the hearing [brother] married to the hearing wife died, what shall the deaf-mute married to the hearing wife do? He divorces his wife by a bill of divorce; his brother's widow is permanently forbidden[34].

(fol. 14b) **משנה ו:** שְׁנֵי אַחִין פִּקְחִין נְשׂוּאִין לִשְׁתֵּי אֲחָיוֹת אַחַת חֵרֶשֶׁת וְאַחַת פִּיקַחַת מֵת פִּיקֵחַ בַּעַל הַחֵרֶשֶׁת מַה יַּעֲשֶׂה פִּקֵּחַ בַּעַל הַפִּיקַחַת תֵּצֵא מִשּׁוּם אֲחוֹת אִשָּׁה. מֵת פִּקֵּחַ בַּעַל הַפִּיקַחַת מַה יַּעֲשֶׂה פִּיקֵּחַ בַּעַל הַחֵרֶשֶׁת. מוֹצִיא אִשְׁתּוֹ בְּגֵט וְאֵשֶׁת אָחִיו בַּחֲלִיצָה.

Mishnah 6: Two hearing brothers married to two sisters, one deaf-mute and one hearing. If the hearing [brother] married to the deaf-mute wife died, what shall the hearing [brother] married to a hearing wife do? [The widow] has to leave as the wife's sister. If the hearing [brother] married to the hearing wife died, what shall the hearing [brother] married to the deaf-mute wife do? He removes his wife by a bill of divorce and his brother's widow by *ḥalîṣah*[35].

34 The widow was married by biblical standards. She now is a candidate for levirate with the deaf-mute brother by biblical standards. Her biblical claim to the levir is stronger than the rabbinic claim of her deaf-mute sister. Therefore, from the moment of the hearing brother's death, the deaf-mute sister is forbidden to her husband as sister of a quasi-wife. The widow herself cannot be helped. She cannot be married in levirate since her levir is incapable of marrying by biblical standards. She cannot be freed to marry another man since her levir is incapable of performing *ḥalîṣah*.

35 Here again, the claim of the biblically married widow is stronger than that of the rabbinically married wife; but since he had rabbinically married the sister, the widow is rabbinically forbidden to him.

מתניתא: שְׁנֵי אַחִים פִּקְחִים כול׳. צָרָתָהּ מָהוּ. נִישְׁמְעִינָהּ מִן הָדָא. בִּתּוֹ חֵרֶשֶׁת נְשׂוּאָה לְאָחִיו פִּיקֵּחַ. צָרָתָהּ חוֹלֶצֶת וְלֹא מִתְייַבֶּמֶת.

Mishnah: "Two hearing brothers," etc. What about her co-wife[36]? Let us hear from the following: If his deaf-mute daughter was married to his hearing brother, her co-wife performs *ḥalîṣah* but not levirate[37].

36 This refers to a co-wife of the deaf-mute sister married to a hearing brother.

37 She cannot be freed automatically since her co-wife's marriage was not valid by biblical standards.

(fol. 14b) **משנה ז:** שְׁנֵי אַחִין אֶחָד חֵרֵשׁ וְאֶחָד פִּיקֵּחַ נְשׂוּאִין לִשְׁתֵּי אֲחָיוֹת אַחַת חֵרֶשֶׁת וְאַחַת פִּיקַּחַת מֵת חֵרֵשׁ בַּעַל הַחֵרֶשֶׁת מַה יַּעֲשֶׂה פִּקֵּחַ בַּעַל הַפִּיקַּחַת תֵּצֵא מִשּׁוּם אֲחוֹת אִשָּׁה. מֵת פִּקֵּחַ בַּעַל הַפִּיקַּחַת מַה יַּעֲשֶׂה חֵרֵשׁ בַּעַל הַחֵרֶשֶׁת מוֹצִיא אִשְׁתּוֹ בְגֵט וְאֵשֶׁת אָחִיו אֲסוּרָה לְעוֹלָם.

Mishnah 7: Two brothers, one deaf-mute and one hearing, married to two sisters, one deaf-mute and one hearing. If the deaf-mute [brother] married to the deaf-mute wife died, what shall the hearing [brother] married to a hearing wife do? [The widow] has to leave as the wife's sister. If the hearing [brother] married to the hearing wife died, what shall the deaf-mute [brother] married to the deaf-mute wife do? He removes his wife by a bill of divorce; his brother's wife is permanently forbidden[34].

מתניתא: שְׁנֵי אַחִין אֶחָד חֵרֵשׁ כול׳. צָרָתָהּ מָהוּ. נִישְׁמְעִינָהּ מִן הָדָא. בִּתּוֹ חֵרֶשֶׁת נְשׂוּאָה לְאָחִיו חֵרֵשׁ. צָרָתָהּ פְּטוּרָה מִן (fol. 14c) הַחֲלִיצָה וּמִן הַיִּיבּוּם.

Mishnah: "Two deaf-mute brothers," etc. What about her co-wife[38]? Let us hear from the following: If his deaf-mute daughter was married to his deaf-mute brother, her co-wife is free from *ḥalîṣah* and levirate.

38 The co-wife of the deaf-mute wife of the deaf-mute brother. She has no claim on the hearing brother married to a hearing wife.

(fol. 14b) **משנה ח:** שְׁנֵי אַחִין אֶחָד חֵרֵשׁ וְאֶחָד פִּיקֵּחַ נְשׂוּאִין לִשְׁתֵּי נוֹכְרִיּוֹת פִּקְּחוֹת מֵת חֵרֵשׁ בַּעַל הַפִּיקַּחַת מַה יַּעֲשֶׂה פִּקֵּחַ בַּעַל הַפִּיקַּחַת אוֹ חוֹלֵץ אוֹ מְיַיבֵּם. מֵת פִּיקֵּחַ בַּעַל הַפִּיקַּחַת מַה יַּעֲשֶׂה חֵרֵשׁ בַּעַל הַפִּיקַּחַת כּוֹנֵס וְאֵינוֹ מוֹצִיא לְעוֹלָם.

Mishnah 8: Two brothers, one deaf-mute and one hearing, married to two unrelated hearing women. If the deaf-mute [brother] married to a hearing wife died, what shall the hearing [brother] married to a hearing wife do? He performs either *ḥalîṣah* or levirate. If the hearing [brother] married to a hearing wife died, what shall the deaf-mute [brother] married to a hearing wife do? He marries [the widow] and never can divorce her[39].

מתניתא: שְׁנֵי אַחִין אֶחָד חֵרֵשׁ כול'. מַהוּ שֶׁתֹּאכַל בַּתְּרוּמָה. נִישְׁמְעִינָהּ מִן הָדָא. בַּת יִשְׂרָאֵל פִּיקַּחַת שֶׁנִּישֵּׂאת לְכֹהֵן חֵרֵשׁ אֵינָהּ אוֹכֶלֶת בִּתְרוּמָה. מֵת וְנָפְלָה לִפְנֵי הַיָּבָם. אִם הָיָה פִּיקֵּחַ אוֹכֶלֶת. חֵרֵשׁ אֵינָהּ אוֹכֶלֶת.

Mishnah: "Two brothers, one deaf-mute," etc. May she eat heave? Let us her from the following[40]: "A hearing daughter of an Israel who married a deaf-mute Cohen does not eat heave. If he died and she came before the levir, if he is hearing, she eats, deaf-mute does not eat."

39 His levirate is valid by biblical standards but his divorce would only be rabbinical.

40 Chapter 6, Halakhah 1, Notes 31-32.

(fol. 14b) **משנה ט**: שְׁנֵי אַחִין פִּקְחִין נְשׂוּאִין לִשְׁתֵּי נוֹכְרִיּוֹת אַחַת חֵרֶשֶׁת וְאַחַת פִּיקַּחַת מֵת פִּיקֵּחַ בַּעַל הַחֵרֶשֶׁת מַה יַּעֲשֶׂה פִּקֵּחַ בַּעַל הַפִּיקַּחַת כּוֹנֵס וְאִם רָצָה לְהוֹצִיא יוֹצִיא. מֵת פִּקֵּחַ בַּעַל הַפִּיקַּחַת מַה יַּעֲשֶׂה פִּיקֵּחַ בַּעַל הַחֵרֶשֶׁת אוֹ חוֹלֵץ אוֹ מְיַיבֵּם.

Mishnah 9: Two hearing brothers, married to two unrelated women, one deaf-mute and one hearing. If the hearing [brother] married to the deaf-mute wife died, what shall the hearing [brother] married to a hearing wife do? He marries [the widow][41], and if he wants to divorce, he divorces. If the hearing [brother] married to the hearing wife died, what shall the hearing [brother] married to the deaf-mute wife do? He performs either *ḥalîṣah* or levirate.

(fol. 14b) **משנה י:** שְׁנֵי אַחִין אֶחָד חֵרֵשׁ וְאֶחָד פִּיקֵּחַ נְשׂוּאִין לִשְׁתֵּי נוֹכְרִיּוֹת אַחַת חֵרֶשֶׁת וְאַחַת פִּיקַּחַת מֵת חֵרֵשׁ בַּעַל הַחֵרֶשֶׁת מַה יַּעֲשֶׂה פִּקֵּחַ בַּעַל הַפִּיקַּחַת כּוֹנֵס וְאִם רָצָה לְהוֹצִיא יוֹצִיא. מֵת פִּקֵּחַ בַּעַל הַפִּיקַּחַת מַה יַּעֲשֶׂה חֵרֵשׁ בַּעַל הַחֵרֶשֶׁת כּוֹנֵס וְאֵינוֹ מוֹצִיא לְעוֹלָם.

Mishnah 10: Two brothers, one deaf-mute and one hearing, married to two unrelated women, one deaf-mute and one hearing. If the deaf-mute [brother] married to the deaf-mute wife died, what shall the hearing [brother] married to the hearing wife do? He marries, and if he wants to divorce, he divorces[41]. If the hearing [brother] married to the hearing wife died, what shall the deaf-mute [brother] married to the deaf-mute wife do? He marries and can never divorce[39].

מתניתא: שְׁנֵי אַחִין פִּקְחִין כול'. שְׁנֵי אַחִין אֶחָד חֵרֵשׁ כול'. מַהוּ שֶׁתֹּאכַל בִּתְרוּמָה. נִישְׁמְעִינָהּ מִן הָדָא. בַּת יִשְׂרָאֵל פִּיקַּחַת שֶׁנִּתְאָרְסָה לְכֹהֵן פִּיקֵּחַ. לֹא הִסְפִּיק לְכוֹנְסָהּ לְחוּפָּה שֶׁלְּנִישּׂוּאִין עַד שֶׁנִּיתְחָרֵשׁ הוּא אוֹ עַד שֶׁנִּתְחָרְשָׁה הִיא. אֵינָהּ אוֹכֶלֶת בִּתְרוּמָה. מֵת וְנָפְלָה לִפְנֵי הַיָּבָם וַאֲפִילוּ חֵרֵשׁ. אוֹכֶלֶת. בְּזֶה יִיפֶּה כּוֹחַ הַיָּבָם מִכּוֹחַ הַבַּעַל. שֶׁהַיָּבָם חֵרֵשׁ מַאֲכִיל וְהַבַּעַל חֵרֵשׁ אֵינוֹ מַאֲכִיל.

Mishnah: "Two hearing brothers," etc. "Two brothers, one of them deaf-mute," etc. May she eat heave? [42]Let us hear from the following: "A hearing daughter of an Israel who became engaged to a hearing Cohen, who did not manage to bring her to the bridal chamber before he became deaf-mute or before she became deaf-mute, does not eat heave.

If he died and she came before a levir she eats even if he is deaf-mute. In this He increased the power of the levir over that of the husband since the deaf-mute levir enables her to eat, but the deaf-mute husband does not enable her to eat."

41 Since the widow is unable to perform *ḥalîṣah.* He may later divorce her since in that she is passive.

42 Chapter 6, Halakhah 1, Notes 34-35.

האשה שהלכה פרק חמשה עשר

(fol. 14c) **משנה א:** הָאִשָּׁה שֶׁהָלְכָה הִיא וּבַעֲלָהּ לִמְדִינַת הַיָּם שָׁלוֹם בֵּינוֹ לְבֵינָהּ וְשָׁלוֹם בָּעוֹלָם וּבָאת וְאָמְרָה מֵת בַּעֲלִי תִּינָּשֵׂא מֵת בַּעֲלִי תִּתְיַיבֵּם. אֵין שָׁלוֹם בֵּינוֹ לְבֵינָהּ וְשָׁלוֹם בָּעוֹלָם וּבָאת וְאָמְרָה מֵת בַּעֲלִי אֵינָהּ נֶאֱמֶנֶת. רִבִּי יְהוּדָה אוֹמֵר לְעוֹלָם אֵינָהּ נֶאֱמֶנֶת אֶלָּא אִם כֵּן בָּאת בּוֹכָה וּבְגָדֶיהָ קְרוּעִין. אָמְרוּ לוֹ אַחַת זוֹ וְאַחַת זוֹ תִּינָּשֵׂא.

Mishnah 1: A woman went overseas with her husband. If there was peace between him and her and there was peace in the world and came and said, "my husband died", she can remarry, "my husband died", she can marry in levirate[1]. If there was no peace between him and her but there was peace in the world, she cannot be believed[2]. Rebbi Jehudah says, she is never believed unless she comes crying with torn clothes. They said to him, in any case she can remarry.

1 Not only can she remarry but the local court will oversee the liquidation of the husband's inheritance on her word. Since the consequences of her remarrying while her husband is alive are so devastating (cf. Mishnah 10:1) we trust that she will not knowingly remarry if her husband is alive.

2 In the Babli and the independent Mishnah mss. there is another clause "if there was peace between him and her but no peace in the world." Since the first sentence requires two conditions, peace between him and her and peace in the world, it is clear that the other clause was omitted by an oversight of the scribe. This is confirmed by the Halakhah, which discusses why in case of war she is not believed without supporting evidence.

הלכה א: הָאִשָּׁה שֶׁהָלְכָה הִיא וּבַעֲלָהּ כול׳. כְּמָה דְאַתְּ אָמַר. אִם יֵשׁ עֵדִים שֶׁהִיא אֵשֶׁת אִישׁ. וְהִיא אוֹמֶרֶת. גְּרוּשָׁה אֲנִי. אֵינָהּ נֶאֱמֶנֶת. וְאָמַר אַף הָכָא כֵן. שַׁנְיָיה הִיא בְעֵידֵי מִיתָה. מֵאַחַר שֶׁאִם יָבוֹא הוּא מַכְחִישׁ. וּתְהֵא נֶאֱמֶנֶת לוֹמַר. מֵת יְבָמִי. לֵית יְכִיל. דְּתַנִּינָן (fol. 14d) שֶׁאֵין הָאִשָּׁה נֶאֱמֶנֶת לוֹמַר. מֵת יְבָמִי. שֶׁתִּינָּשֵׂא. וְלֹא. מֵתָה אֲחוֹתִי. שֶׁתִּיכָּנֵס לְבֵיתָהּ. אָמַר רִבִּי בָּא. בַּעֲלָהּ שֶׁנִּישֵּׂאת לוֹ לִרְצוֹנָהּ נֶאֱמֶנֶת. יְבָמָהּ שֶׁנָּפְלָה לוֹ עַל כָּרְחָהּ אֵינָהּ נֶאֱמֶנֶת. רִבִּי הוֹשַׁעְיָה בָּעֵי. הַגַּע עַצְמָךְ שֶׁנִּישֵּׂאת לוֹ עַל כָּרְחָהּ מֵעַתָּה לֹא תְהֵא נֶאֱמֶנֶת.

Halakhah 1: "A woman went with her husband," etc. Just as you say, [3]"if there are witnesses that she is a married woman and she says, I was divorced, she is not trustworthy;" would I say it is the same here? There is a difference for witnesses of death since if he comes he disproves [the testimony][4]. Then she should be trustworthy to say: "my levir died"! That is impossible since we have stated[5]: "A woman is not trustworthy if she says 'my levir died' to remarry, or 'my sister died' to enter her house[6]." Rebbi Abba said, she is trustworthy for her husband whom she married out of her free will; she is not trustworthy about her levir on whom she was thrown against her will. Rebbi Hoshaia asked, think of it, then she should not be trustworthy if she was forced to marry him[7]!

3 Mishnah *Ketubot* 2:4. This belongs to a series of statements illustrating the principle that "the mouth that prohibits is the mouth that permits". If nobody at that place knew that she had been married before, then if she asserts that she was married she forbids herself for every other male. If then she qualifies the statement that now she is no longer married because she is divorced, her testimony must be accepted since if one believes her that she was married one must believe her that she is divorced; if one does not believe her that she was married, one does not have to believe her that she is divorced but it makes no difference since as an unmarried woman she can contract marriage. But if there were witnesses who could testify that she was married, she has to prove her case by documents or witnesses if she wants

to remarry as a divorcee.

4 But if the husband comes and claims that he did not divorce her, it is his word against hers; she is not automatically proven to be a liar.

5 Mishnah 15:10. There is no relaxation of standards of proof before a court except in the case of testimony about a husband's death.

6 To marry her brother-in-law.

7 If she was married off by her father while she was underage. There is no mention in the Mishnah of a restriction on women marrying on their own. No answer is given to the question.

לֹא סוֹף דָּבָר כְּמִשְׁנָה הָאַחֲרוֹנָה שֶׁעֵד אֶחָד מַתִּירָהּ. וַאֲפִילוּ כְּמִשְׁנָה הָרִאשׁוֹנָה שֶׁאֵין עֵד אֶחָד מַתִּירָהּ הִיא מַתֶּרֶת עַצְמָהּ. מַה בֵּינָהּ לְעֵד אֶחָד. עֵד אֶחָד חָשׁוּד לְקַלְקְלָהּ. וְהִיא אֵינָהּ חֲשׁוּדָה לְקַלְקֵל אֶת עַצְמָהּ.

Not only according to the current Mishnah that a single witness can permit her[8], but even according to the earlier Mishnah that a single witness cannot permit her, she permits herself. What is the difference between herself and a single witness? A single witness is suspected to want to cause trouble to her; she is not suspected to want to cause trouble to herself[9].

8 Mishnaiot 16:7-8, a change in practice dated to the times of Trajan or Hadrian. In order to minimize the cases in which a woman is prevented from remarrying if the documentation of her husband's death cannot be completed, the standards of proof have been extremely relaxed.

9 Since Mishnah 10:1 requires her to satisfy herself that her husband is really dead. The Babli agrees, 93b.

עֵד אֶחָד מָהוּ שֶׁיְּהֵא נֶאֱמָן בִּשְׁעַת מִלְחָמָה. נִישְׁמְעִינָהּ מִן הָדָא. חַד בַּר נַשׁ בְּיוֹמוֹי דְּרִבִּי אֲמַר לֵיהּ. הֵן הַהוּא פְּלָן. אֲמַר לוֹן. מִית. הֵן הַהוּא פְּלָן. אֲמַר לוֹן. מִית. אֲמַר לֵיהּ. וְכוּלְּהוֹן מֵתִים. אֲמַר לוֹן. וְאִילּוּ הַוְיָן בְּחַיִין לָא הֲווֹן מֵייתֵי. רִבִּי יִרְמְיָה בְּשֵׁם רִבִּי חֲנִינָה. מַעֲשֶׂה בָא לִפְנֵי רִבִּי וְאָמַר. מָאן דְּנִישֵּׂאת

נִישְּׂאת. וּמָאן דְּלָא נִישְּׂאת לָא נִישְּׂאת. רִבִּי אַייְבוֹ בָּר נַגָּרִי. בִּשְׁעַת מִלְחָמָה הֲוָות. הָדָא אָמְרָה שֶׁעֵד אֶחָד נֶאֱמָן בִּשְׁעַת מִלְחָמָה.

Is a single witness trustworthy in wartime? Let us hear from the following: A person was living in the times of Rebbi. They asked him about X; he said, he died. They asked him about Y; he said, he died. They asked him, are they all dead? He answered, if they were alive would they not have come[10]? Rebbi Jeremiah in the name of Rebbi Ḥanina: The case came before Rebbi and he said, the ones married should stay married, the ones not married should not marry[11]. Rebbi Ayvo bar Naggari said, it happened in wartime. That implies that a single witness is trustworthy in wartime[12].

10 It seems that they were local residents.

11 Those who remarried based on the unsupported testimony of one witness may remain married; those who want a ruling of the court in that matter will not get one.

12 If the wife accepts his testimony. In the Babli, 115a, there is an inconclusive discussion which may be interpreted (cf. *RIF*, *Nimmuqe Yosef*, in Wilna ed. 32b-33a; *Meïri*, ed. Albeck, p. 436) to follow the Yerushalmi.

מַה בֵין שָׁלוֹם לְעוֹלָם לְבֵין מִלְחָמָה לְעוֹלָם. מִלְחָמָה בָעוֹלָם סְבוּרָה בוֹ שֶׁמֵּת וְלֹא מֵת. עַד כְּדוֹן בְּשֶׁהָיְתָה מִלְחָמָה בַצָּפוֹן וּבָאת מִן הַצָּפוֹן. בַּדָּרוֹם וּבָאת מִן הַדָּרוֹם. הָיְתָה מִלְחָמָה בַצָּפוֹן וּבָאת מִן הַדָּרוֹם. וְהִיא אוֹמֶרֶת. מִן הַצָּפוֹן בָּאתִי. וַאֲנִי אוֹמֵר. מִן הַדָּרוֹם בָּאת. וְהִיא אוֹמֶרֶת. מִן הַדָּרוֹם בָּאתִי. סְבוּרָה לְהַתִּיר אֶת עַצְמָהּ. הִיא אָמְרָה. עַל מִיטָּתוֹ מֵת. וַאֲנִי אוֹמֵר. לַמִּלְחָמָה הָלַךְ. הִיא אוֹמֶרֶת. עַל מִיטָּתוֹ מֵת. סְבוּרָה לְהַתִּיר אֶת עַצְמָהּ.

What is the difference whether peace is in the world or war is in the world? If war is in the world, she might think that he died although he is not dead[13]. So far if war was in the North and she came from the North, in the South and she came from the South. If there was war in the North and she came from the South; she says I am coming from the North, but I am arguing that you came from the South[14]. If she says, I am coming from the South, it is because she thinks to free herself[15]. If she says, he died on his bed, I am arguing that he went to war; it is because she thinks to free herself[16].

13 If most of individuals in his group are known to have been killed, she thinks that all have been killed. But her husband may have escaped or been taken prisoner. The same argument in the Babli, 114b.

14 The court will argue that she has no knowledge of what really happened.

15 She might lie to the court to make it appear that her husband never was near a dangerous place.

16 The Babli, 114b, accepts the testimony that the husband died in his bed even in a time of war.

אֵי זוֹ הִיא קְטָטָה. רִבִּי בָּא בְּשֵׁם רַב חִייָה בַּר אַשִּׁי. לֹא קִידַּשְׁתָּנִי וְלֹא גֵירַשְׁתָּנִי וְלֹא הָיִיתִי אִשְׁתְּךָ מִיּוֹמַיי. אֵין זֶה קְטָטָה. קִידַּשְׁתָּנִי וְגֵירַשְׁתָּנִי אֶלָּא שֶׁלֹּא נָתַתָּ לִי כְּתוּבָתִי. הֲרֵי זֶה קְטָטָה. אָמְרָה רִבִּי בָּא קוֹמֵי רִבִּי חִייָה בַּר אַבָּא. אָמַר לֵיהּ. בְּנִי. אֶלָּא אֲפִילוּ הִיא תוֹבַעַת בְּוַדַּאי לְהִתְגָּרֵשׁ.

What is a quarrel[17]? Rebbi Abba in the name of Rav Ḥiyya bar Ashi. "You never gave me *qiddušin*, you did not divorce me, I never was your wife," that is not a quarrel[18]. "You gave me *qiddušin*, you divorced me, but you never paid me what is owed me under my *ketubah*," that is a quarrel[19]. When Rebbi Abba said this before Rebbi Hiyya bar Abba, he said to him, my son, even if she clearly requests to be divorced.

17 This wording shows that the reading in the Mishnah before the authors of the Yerushalmi was not אֵין קְטָטָה בֵּינוֹ לְבֵינָהּ but שָׁלוֹם בֵּינוֹ לְבֵינָהּ וְשָׁלוֹם בָּעוֹלָם as in the Babli.

18 If everybody knows that she is married to him, that is talk which is not serious.

19 In the opinion of the Babli, 116a, she is disqualified from testifying about her husband's death only if the rabbinic court, which she pretends handled her divorce, denies the divorce ever took place. It is possible to read such an interpretation into the wording of the Yerushalmi.

רִבִּי יְהוּדָה אוֹמֵר לְעוֹלָם אֵינָהּ נֶאֱמֶנֶת אֶלָּא אִם כֵּן בָּאָה בוֹכָה וּבְגָדֶיהָ קְרוּעִין. מְתִיבִין לְרִבִּי יְהוּדָה. הַגַּע עַצְמָךְ שֶׁהָיְתָה אַחַת בּוֹכָה וְאַחַת שֶׁאֵינָהּ בּוֹכָה. לְזוֹ אַתְּ אוֹסֵר וּלְזוֹ אַתְּ מַתִּיר. הֲתִיב רִבִּי חֲנַנְיָה חֲבֵרוֹן דְּרַבָּנִין. הַגַּע עַצְמָךְ שֶׁיָּצָא בְנָהּ לִמְדִינַת הַיָּם וּמֵת שָׁם. אֲנִי אוֹמֵר. שֶׁמָּא הִיא מַזְכֶּרֶת וּבוֹכָה.

"Rebbi Jehudah says, she is never believed unless she comes crying with torn clothes." They objected to Rebbi Jehudah: Think of it, if one came crying, the other did not cry. To this one you forbid, to that one you permit[20]. Rebbi Ḥananiah, the colleague of the rabbis, objected: Think of it, maybe her son went overseas and died there, she remembers that and cries[21].

20 In the language of the Babli, 116b, the well-coached one will be permitted to remarry, the simple-minded one will be prevented.

21 There are many causes that might induce a woman to cry, not necessarily her husband's death.

(fol. 14c) **משנה ב:** בֵּית הִלֵּל אוֹמְרִים לֹא שָׁמַעְנוּ אֶלָּא בְּבוֹאָה מִן הַקָּצִיר בִּלְבַד. אָמְרוּ לָהֶן בֵּית שַׁמַּאי אֶחָד הַבָּאָה מִן הַקָּצִיר וְאֶחָד הַבָּאָה מִן הַזֵּיתִים וְאֶחָד הַבָּאָה מִמְּדִינַת הַיָּם לֹא דִבְּרוּ חֲכָמִים בְּקָצִיר אֶלָּא בַהוֹוֶה. חָזְרוּ בֵית הִלֵּל לְהוֹרוֹת כְּבֵית שַׁמַּאי.

Mishnah 2: The House of Hillel say, we heard only about one who came from the grain harvest[22]. The House of Shammai said to them, it makes no difference whether she comes from the grain harvest, or from the olive harvest, or from overseas. The Sages spoke about the grain harvest only because of what happened. The House of Hillel reversed themselves and taught following the House of Shammai.

22 The Mishnah is shortened in the Yerushalmi. In the Babli and the independent Mishnah mss. the text reads: "The House of Hillel say, we heard only about one who came from the harvest, *in the same district, and as it happened*. The House of Shammai said to them, it makes no difference whether she comes from the grain harvest, or from the olive harvest, *or from the grape harvest, or from another district*. The Sages spoke about the grain harvest only because what happened. The House of Hillel reversed themselves and taught following the House of Shammai.' It seems that the rule that the woman is permitted to testify on her own behalf was promulgated first in a case when the husband died of a heat stroke on the field and was immediately buried in place. {The cause of death was accepted as reasonable and the details of her testimony were subject to possible verification.} The House of Hillel restricts the precedent to exactly the circumstances of the first case.

(fol. 14d) **מתניתא:** בֵּית הִלֵּל אוֹמְרִים לֹא שָׁמַעְנוּ כול׳. אָמְרוּ לָהֶן בֵּית שַׁמַּי. וַהֲלֹא כָּל־הַשָּׁנָה כוּלָּהּ קָצִיר. הָא כְּאֵי זֶה צַד. יָצָא קְצִיר שְׂעוֹרִים וְנִכְנַס קְצִיר חִטִּים. יָצָא קָצִיר וְנִכְנַס בָּצִיר. יָצָא בָּצִיר וְנִכְנַס מָסִיק. נִמְצֵאת כָּל־הַשָּׁנָה כוּלָּהּ קָצִיר. וְקִיְּימוּ אֶת דִּבְרֵיהֶן. וְלָמָּה קָצִיר. אָמַר רִבִּי מָנָא. דְּאוֹנְסָא שְׁכִיחַ. שֶׁאֵין הַחַמָּה קוֹפַחַת עַל רֹאשׁוֹ שֶׁלְּאָדָם אֶלָּא בִשְׁעַת הַקָּצִיר. הָדָא הִיא דִכְתִיב וַיִּגְדַּל הַיֶּלֶד וַיְהִי הַיּוֹם וַיֵּצֵא אֶל אָבִיו אֶל הַקּוֹצְרִים. וַיֹּאמֶר אֶל אָבִיו רֹאשִׁי רֹאשִׁי וַיֹּאמַר אֶל הַנַּעַר שָׂאֵהוּ אֶל אִמּוֹ. וַיִּשָּׂאֵהוּ וַיְבִיאֵרוּ אֶל אִמּוֹ וַיֵּשֶׁב עַל בִּרְכֶּיהָ עַד הַצָּהֳרַיִם וַיָּמוֹת. וְרַבָּנָן אָמְרֵי. דְּרִיתְחָשָׁא שְׁכִיחַ. אָמַר רִבִּי יוֹסֵי בֵּירִבִּי בּוּן. סַכּוֹתָה לְרֹאשִׁי בְּיוֹם נָשֶׁק. בְּיוֹם שֶׁהַקַּיִץ נוֹשֵׁק אֶת הַחוֹרֶף. דָּבָר אַחֵר. בְּיוֹם נָשֶׁק זֶה נִשְׁקוֹ שֶׁלַּגּוֹג. דָּבָר אַחֵר. בְּיוֹם שֶׁשְּׁנֵי עוֹלָמוֹת נוֹשְׁקִין זֶה אֶת זֶה הָעוֹלָם הַזֶּה יוֹצֵא וְהָעוֹלָם הַבָּא נִכְנַס.

Mishnah: "The House of Hillel say, we heard only," etc. [23]The House of Shammai said to them: Is there not harvest the entire year? How is that? At the end of barley harvest starts wheat harvest. At the end of wheat harvest starts grape harvest. At the end of grape harvest starts olive harvest. That means, there is some harvest the year round. They accepted this argument. And why the grain harvest? Rebbi Mana said, because there accidents are frequent, for the sun only hits a person's head at grain harvest time. That is what is written[24]: "The child grew and some day it went to his father, to the harvesters. He said to his father, 'my head, my head'; who said to the servant, 'carry him to his mother'. He carried him and brought him to his mother where he sat on her knees until noontime, when he died." But the rabbis say, because snakes are abundant. Rebbi Yose ben Rebbi Abun said[25], "You shielded my head at the day of kissing," at the day summer and winter are kissing[26]. Another explanation: "At the day of weaponry," that is Gog's weaponry[27]. Another explanation, on a day when two worlds kiss one another, when this world leaves and the future world enters[28].

23 A similar *baraita* is quoted in the Babli, 116b.

24 *2K*.:18-20. He diagnoses the illness of the Sunamite's child as a sun stroke. This is accepted by most modern commentators.

25 *Ps*. 140:8. Usually, one would translate: "On the day of weaponry;" cf. Note 27.

26 There are no other sources in talmudic literature that would declare the autumn equinox a dangerous day.

27 *Ez*. 39, explained as prologue to the appearance of the Messiah, a descendant of David.

28 The day of death.

משנה ג: בֵּית שַׁמַּי אוֹמְרִים תִּינָּשֵׂא וְתִיטּוֹל כְּתוּבָּתָהּ. וּבֵית הִלֵּל(fol. 14c) אוֹמְרִים תִּינָּשֵׂא וְלֹא תִיטּוֹל כְּתוּבָּתָהּ. אָֽמְרוּ לָהֶן בֵּית שַׁמַּי הִיתַּרְתֶּם אֶת עֶרְוָה הַחֲמוּרָה וְלֹא תַתִּירוּ אֶת הַמָּמוֹן הַקַּל. אָֽמְרוּ לָהֶן בֵּית הִלֵּל מָצִינוּ שֶׁאֵין הָאַחִין נִכְנָסִין לַנַּחֲלָה עַל פִּיהָ. אָֽמְרוּ לָהֶן בֵּית שַׁמַּי וַהֲלֹא מִסֵּפֶר כְּתוּבָּתָהּ נִלְמוֹד שֶׁהוּא כוֹתֵב לָהּ שֶׁאִם תִּינָּשְׂאִי לְאַחֵר תִּיטְּלִי מַה שֶּׁכָּתוּב לִיךְ. חָֽזְרוּ בֵּית הִלֵּל לְהוֹרוֹת כְּבֵית שַׁמַּי.

Mishnah 3: The House of Shammai say, she should remarry and collect her *ketubah*[29]. The House of Hillel say, she should remarry but not collect her *ketubah*. The House of Shammai said to them, you permitted the stringent incest prohibition[30], should you not permit the lenient money matters? The House of Hillel said to them, we find that the brothers cannot access the inheritance on her testimony[31]. The House of Shammai said, we can infer that from the text of her *ketubah* document in which he writes[32]: "If you would be married to another man you shall take the amount I wrote for you." The House of Hillel reversed themselves and taught following the House of Shammai.

29 Since the husband is declared dead, she collects the widow's portion.

30 Adultery, which is considered incest. If the husband were alive, her second marriage would be adulterous.

31 Nowhere do we find that the requirement of proof either by two witnesses or by certified document is abrogated in money matters. The leniency of informal proof applies only to the case of a woman who otherwise would have to stay unmarried for the rest of her life.

32 I. e., he is required by rabbinical decree to write this sentence in her marriage document; if the sentence is missing it nevertheless is implied and enforced by the court; cf. *Ketubot* Chapter 4.

(fol. 14d) **מתניתא:** בֵּית שַׁמַּי אוֹמְרִים תִּינָּשֵׂא כול'. בָּנוֹת מַהוּ שֶׁיִּיכָּנְסוּ לִמְזוֹנוֹת עַל פִּיהָ.

Mishnah: "The House of Shammai say, she should remarry," etc. May the daughters claim upkeep based on her word[33]?

33 As will be explained later in the Halakhah, the standard text of the *ketubah* requires that "the sons will inherit and the daughters will be supported". Since her testimony activates the *ketubah*, the daughters should be able to claim support (and a dowry in case they marry). But since the claim of the daughters is made dependent on that of the sons, and the sons cannot claim the inheritance on basis of her testimony, the daughters should be unable to claim support. The question is not answered (which *in praxi* means that the daughters cannot collect.) The problem is not treated in the Babli.

בֵּית שַׁמַּי עָֽבְדִין כְּתוּבָּה מִדְרָשׁ. דְּבֵית שַׁמַּי דָֽרְשִׁין מִסֵּפֶר כְּתוּבָּתָהּ נִלְמוֹד. שֶׁהוּא כוֹתֵב לָהּ. שֶׁאִם תִּינָּֽשְׂאִי לְאַחֵר תִּיטְּלִי מַה שֶׁכָּתוּב לִיךְ. חָֽזְרוּ בֵית הִלֵּל לְהוֹרוֹת כְּבֵית שַׁמַּי. בֵּית הִלֵּל עָֽבְדִין כְּתוּבָּה מִדְרָשׁ. דָּרַשׁ הִלֵּל הַזָּקֵן לְשׁוֹן הֶדְיוֹט. הָיוּ כוֹתְבִין בְּאַלֶכְסַנְדְּרִיאָה שֶׁהָיָה אֶחָד מֵהֶן מְקַדֵּשׁ אִשָּׁה וַחֲבֵירוֹ חוֹטְפָהּ מִן הַשּׁוּק. וּכְשֶׁבָּא מַעֲשֶׂה לִפְנֵי חֲכָמִים בִּקְשׁוּ לַעֲשׂוֹתָן מַמְזֵירִים. אָמַר לָהֶן הִלֵּל הַזָּקֵן. הוֹצִיאוּ כְּתוּבַּת אִימּוֹתֵיהֶן. וְהוֹצִיאוּ כְתוּבַּת אִימּוֹתֵיהֶן וּמָֽצְאוּ כָתוּב בָּהֶן. לִכְשֶׁתִּיכָּֽנְסִי לְבֵיתִי תְּהַוְייָן לִי לְאִינְתּוּ כְּדַת מֹשֶׁה וִיהוּדָאֵי.

The House of Shammai insist on interpretation of the *ketubah*. As the House of Shammai explain, we can infer that from the text of her *ketubah* document in which he writes[32]: "If you would be married to another man you shall take the amount I wrote for you." The House of Hillel reversed themselves and taught following the House of Shammai. The House of Hillel insist on interpretation of the *ketubah*. [34]Hillel the Elder explained it, using the vernacular. In Alexandria they were writing that a man there became betrothed to a woman[35]. Another man abducted her from a public place[36]. When this came before the Sages, they intended to declare [the children] as bastards[37]. Hillel the Elder told them, bring your mothers' *ketubah*. They brough their mothers' *ketubah*. They found written there: "When you enter my house you shall be my wife according to the laws of Moses and the Jews[38]."

34 Tosephta *Ketubot* 4:9; a slightly different language in Babli *Baba Meṣi'a* 104a. In a slightly different arrangement the rest of the Halakhah is also in *Ketubot* 4:8.

35 In contrast to the usage in Judea, they did not execute the betrothal, *qiddušin*, by a gift but exclusively by contract.

36 And immediately marry her.

37 Since *qiddušin* make the girl a married woman in all aspects of criminal law. If somebody abducts a betrothed girl he commits adultery and the children are bastards.

38 This language makes the validity of the betrothal dependent on the fact of marriage, of the bride entering the groom's house. If the prospective bride was abducted before entering the groom's house, there were no *qiddušin* and the girl was free to marry any man.

רִבִּי לָעְזָר בֶּן עֲזַרְיָה עֲבַד כְּתוּבָּה מִדְרָשׁ. דָּרַשׁ רִבִּי לָעְזָר בֶּן עֲזַרְיָה הַבָּנִים יִירְשׁוּ וְהַבָּנוֹת יָזוֹנוּ. מַה הַבָּנִים אֵינָן יוֹרְשִׁין אֶלָּא לְאַחַר מִיתַת אֲבִיהֶן. אַף הַבָּנוֹת אֵינָן נִיזּוֹנוֹת אֶלָּא לְאַחַר מִיתַת אֲבִיהֶן.

Rebbi Eleazar ben Azariah insisted on interpreting the *ketubah*: [39]"Rebbi Eleazar ben Azariah explained: 'The sons shall inherit and the daughters shall be supported.[40] Since the sons can only inherit after their father's death, so the daughters can claim support only after their father's death."

39 Mishnah *Ketubot* 4:8. This Mishnah is rejected in *Ketubot* 4:8. The Babli, *Ketubot* 49a/b accepts the Mishnah but holds that a father who does not support his children has to be shamed in public.

40 A condition of the *ketubah*, incorporated in the text by reference even if not written.

רִבִּי מֵאִיר עֲבַד כְּתוּבָּה מִדְרָשׁ. דְּאָמַר רִבִּי מֵאִיר הַמְקַבֵּל שָׂדֶה מֵחֲבֵירוֹ שָׁמִין אוֹתָהּ כַּמָּה הִיא רְאוּיָה לַעֲשׂוֹת וְנוֹתְנִין לוֹ. שֶׁהוּא כוֹתֵב לוֹ. אִם אוֹבִיר וְלֹא אַעֲבִיד אֲשַׁלֵּם בְּמֵיטְבָא.

Rebbi Meïr insists on interpreting the contract text. As Rebbi Meïr said[41], if somebody accepts a field as a contractor[42], one estimates how much it is expected to yield and give to [the owner]. Because the standard contract reads: "If I let it lie fallow and do not work on it, I shall pay as if from the best."

41 Tosephta *Ketubot* 4:10. Essentially this text, but without attribution, is Mishnah *Baba Meṣi'a* 9:3.

42 He either works as a sharecropper or he leases the field for a fixed sum of money. In either case the contractor is required to keep the field in good condition so that at the expiration of the contract the owner can continue working the field as before without additional expense.

רִבִּי יוּדָה עֲבַד כְּתוּבָּה מִדְרָשׁ. תַּנֵּי בְשֵׁם רִבִּי יוּדָה. מֵבִיא הוּא אָדָם עַל יְדֵי אִשְׁתּוֹ כָּל־קָרְבָּן שֶׁהִיא חַייֶבֶת. אֲפִילוּ אָכְלָה חֵלֶב אֲפִילוּ חִילְּלָה אֶת הַשַּׁבָּת. וְכֵן הָיָה רִבִּי יוּדָה אוֹמֵר. פּוֹטְרָהּ אֵינוֹ חַייָב בָּהּ. שֶׁכֵּן הִיא כוֹתֶבֶת לוֹ. וְאוֹחְרָן דִּי אַתְיָין לָךְ מִן קַדְמַת דְּנָא.

Rebbi Jehudah insists on interpreting the contract text. [43]It was stated in the name of Rebbi Jehudah: A person brings for his wife any sacrifice she is obligated for[44], even if she ate suet or desecrated the Sabbath. Also, Rebbi Jehudah says, once he divorces her, he is no longer obligated for her, for she writes to him[45] "any other obligations that come to you from earlier times."

43 Tosephta *Ketubot* 4:11; a similar text *Sifra Meṣora' Parašah* 4(16). The Babli, *Baba Meṣi'a* 104a, presents a problem. The text of the *editio princeps* formulates the statement that he is responsible for "any other obligations that come to you from earlier times" as part of the *ketubah*

document; this is R. Jehudah's reason to require that the husband pay for all obligatory sacrifices due from his wife, even if the obligation predates the marriage. Rashi *ad loc.* changes the text to conform to the *Sifra* text; the changed text is that of the Munich ms. and all other Ashkenazic surviving mss.

44 Mishnah *Nega'im* 14:12. The majority hold that the husband has to pay only for his children and slaves. R. Jehudah holds that a wealthy husband has to pay for his wife's sacrifices in the way prescribed for wealthy people even if the wife has no money of her own. But he does not have to pay for her voluntary sacrifices.

45 In the receipt she gives for full payment of her *ketubah*.

רִבִּי יוֹסֵי עֲבַד כְּתוּבָּה מִדְרָשׁ. דָּרַשׁ רִבִּי יוֹסֵי. מָקוֹם שֶׁנָּהֲגוּ לַעֲשׂוֹת כְּתוּבָּה מִלְוֶה גוֹבָה אֶת הַכֹּל. לִכְפּוֹל אֵינָהּ גוֹבָה אֶלָּא מֶחֱצָה. רִבִּי לָעְזָר [הַקַּפָּר][46] אָמַר. אֵין אָדָם רַשַּׁאי לִיקַּח לוֹ בְּהֵמָה חַיָּה וְעוֹף אֶלָּא אִם כֵּן הִתְקִין לָהֶן מְזוֹנוֹת. רִבִּי יְהוֹשֻׁעַ בֶּן קָרְחָה עֲבַד כְּתוּבָּה מִדְרָשׁ. דְּאָמַר רִבִּי יְהוֹשֻׁעַ בֶּן קָרְחָה. הַמַּלְוֶה אֶת חֲבֵירוֹ לֹא יְמַשְׁכְּנֶנּוּ יוֹתֵר עַל חוֹבוֹ. שֶׁהוּא כוֹתֵב לוֹ. תִּשְׁלַמְתָּהּ מִן נִכְסַיי דִּיאַתְיָין לְיָדַי דְּאַקְנָה לְקַבֵּל דְּנָה.

Rebbi Yose insists on interpreting the contract text. Rebbi Yose explained: In a place where one treats the *ketubah* as a loan[47], she collects the entire amount. Where one doubles, she collects only half the amount. Rebbi Eleazar [the caper grower] said, nobody is permitted to buy domesticated or wild animals or birds unless he has food prepared for them[48]. Rebbi Joshua ben Qorḥa insists on interpreting the contract text, since Rebbi Joshua ben Qorḥa said, a person lending money to another person should not take pledges from him for more than the value of the loan since he writes for him: "It will be paid by the property that came to my hand that I shall acquire corresponding to this [sum]."[49]

46 From the parallel text in *Ketubot* 4:6.

47 If the *ketubah* is treated as a mortgage on the groom's real estate from the moment it is signed and due at the dissolution of the marriage, it

relegates all mortgages executed during the marriage to secondary status. Any real estate sold by the husband after he signed the *ketubah* is potentially subject to foreclosure by the wife if there is not enough real estate left in the husband's possession to satisfy her claim. Therefore, care must be taken in establishing the value of the *ketubah* in order to protect the innocent buyer. The value of the *ketubah* is the sum of three parts. (1) The basic sum of 200 *zuz* (defined in Mishnah *Peah* 8:8 as an amount which disqualifies its owner from public charity), (2) the voluntary amount added by the groom to that sum, and (3) the value of the dowry. It is stated here that the value of the dowry may be collected by foreclosure only if its value is correctly stated in the *ketubah* document. In places where the value of the dowry is routinely doubled, the document cannot be used against third parties for more than half the stated value.

A parallel text in Babli *Baba Meṣi'a* 104b and in Tosephta *Ketubot* 4:13; in the latter text (all sources) in the name of R. Yose the Galilean.

48 In *Ketubot*, this is also declared to be the interpretation of a document but the document is not indicated.

49 In *Ketubot*, the text is slightly different: "He who takes a pledge from his debtor shall take it only in court; he may not enter the debtor's house to take the pledge." The parallels in Babli *Baba Meṣi'a* 104a and Tosephta *Ketubot* 4:12 follow the text given here. The text in *Ketubot* seems to require that the value of the pledge should be determined by an official of the court. The second clause in that text is a biblical verse (*Deut*. 24:10).

רַב חוּנָא עֲבַד כְּתוּבָּה מִדְרָשׁ. דָּרַשׁ רַב חוּנָא. הַבָּנִים יִירְשׁוּ וְהַבָּנוֹת יִיזוֹנוּ. מַה הַבָּנִים יוֹרְשִׁין מִן הַמְּטַלְטְלִין אַף הַבָּנוֹת נִיזּוֹנוֹת מִן הַמְּטַלְטְלִין. שְׁמוּאֵל אָמַר אֵין הַבָּנוֹת נִיזּוֹנוֹת מִן הַמְּטַלְטְלִין. מַתְנִיתָא מְסַייְעָא לִשְׁמוּאֵל. בְּנָן נוּקְבָּן דִיהֲווֹן לֵיכִי מִינַּאי יְהַוְייָן יָתְבָן בְּבֵיתִי וּמִיתְזְנָן מִנִּיכְסַיי. וְתַנֵּי עֲלָהּ. מִמְּקַרְקְעֵי וְלֹא מִמְּטַלְטְלֵי. אָמַר רִבִּי בָּא בַּר זַבְדָּא. אַתְיָא דְּרַב הוּנָא כְּרִבִּי וְרִבִּי שְׁמוּאֵל כְּרִבִּי שִׁמְעוֹן בֶּן לָעְזָר. דְּתַנֵּי. אֶחָד נְכָסִים שֶׁיֵּשׁ לָהֶן אֲחֵרָיוּת וְאֶחָד נְכָסִים שֶׁאֵין לָהֶן אֲחֵרָיוּת נִפְרָעִין מֵהֶן לִמְזוֹן הָאִשָּׁה וְהַבָּנוֹת. דִּבְרֵי רִבִּי. רִבִּי שִׁמְעוֹן בֶּן לָעְזָר אוֹמֵר. נְכָסִים שֶׁיֵּשׁ לָהֶן אֲחֵרָיוּת הַבָּנִים מוֹצִיאִין מִן הַבָּנִים וְהַבָּנוֹת מִן

הַבָּנוֹת וְהַבָּנִים מִן הַבָּנוֹת וְהַבָּנוֹת מִן הַבָּנִים. וְשֶׁאֵין לָהֶן אֲחֵרָיוּת הַבָּנִים מוֹצִיאִין מִן הַבָּנוֹת וְאֵין הַבָּנוֹת מוֹצִיאִין מִן הַבָּנִים. אָמְרִין. חָזַר בָּהּ רַב חוּנָא. אָמְרִין. יָאוּת. כְּתוּבָּה דְּבַר תּוֹרָה וּמְזוֹן הַבָּנוֹת מִדִּבְרֵיהֶן. וְדִבְרֵיהֶן עוֹקְרִין דְּבַר תּוֹרָה. אֶלָּא בְּכֶסֶף כְּתוּבַּת אִימָּן פְּלִיגִין. וְכֶסֶף כְּתוּבַּת אִימָּן לֹא קַרְקַע הוּא.

Rav Huna insists on interpreting the contract text. Rav Huna explained: "The sons shall inherit but the daughters must be fed[50]." Since the sons inherit movables[51], the daughters also are fed from movables. Samuel said, the daughters are not fed from movables. A Mishnah supports Samuel: "The female children you shall have from me shall dwell in my house and be supported from my property.[52]" It was stated on this[53]: From real estate but not from movables. Rebbi Abba bar Zavda said: Rav Huna follows Rebbi and Samuel follows Rebbi Simeon ben Eleazar, as it was stated[54]: "One uses both guaranteed property[55] and non-guaranteed property[56] for the support of the wife and the daughters, the words of Rebbi. Rebbi Simeon ben Eleazar says, guaranteed property may be taken by sons from sons[57], by daughters from daughters[58], by sons from daughters[59], and by daughters from sons[60]. But non-guaranteed property may be taken by sons from daughters[61] but not by daughters from sons." They said, Rav Huna reversed himself[62]. They said, that was well done, *ketubah* is a biblical commandment[63] but support of the daughters is from their words[64]. May their words uproot a biblical commandment? It must be that they differ about the money contained in their mother's *ketubah*[65]. But is the money contained in their mother's *ketubah* not also real estate[66]?

50 Mishnah *Ketubot* 4:6.

51 Since the entire inheritance goes to the sons, it seems logical that the daughters should have a lien on the entire inheritance.

52 Mishnah *Ketubot* 4:11. This is one of the conditions stipulated in the marriage contract which does not have to be written down because the court will enforce it based on the existence of a *ketubah* alone. The obligation to support the daughters continues "until they are taken in marriage".

53 In the Babli, *Ketubot* 51a, this is stated in the name of the later Amora Rava and is undisputed. Rava himself rules in a practical case that if there was no real estate, the daughters must be fed in payment for the housekeeping duties they fulfill. {All these rules on the meaning of the *ketubah* contract are rabbinical and dependent on the circumstances. When the Jews lost their real estate after the Arab conquest of Iraq in the Eighth Century, the Geonim, the rabbinical authorities of that time, eliminated any mention of real estate in the rules of the *ketubah*.}

54 Babli *Ketubot* 51a, Tosephta *Ketubot* 4:18. The version of the Babli is the most elaborate; probably it is the latest version taking into account the objections that may be raised against the Yerushalmi version. The Tosephta version differs in language from both Talmudim; S. Lieberman (*Tosephta kiFshuṭah*, part 6, vol. 1 (New York 1967) p. 254 shows that the Tosephta is compatible with the Babli version.

55 "Property under threat of alienation". Real estate is always sold with a warranty that if the buyer loses the property (it is alienated) because of a pre-existing lien or mortgage, the seller will indemnify the buyer. Cf. *Peah* 3:8, Note 121.

56 Movables.

57 The court will adjudicate claims of unequal distribution of property between the heirs. (If there are no sons, the daughters legally have the status of sons.)

58 The daughters have a claim to a dowry which is fixed at 10% of the inheritance (*Ketubot*, Yerushalmi 6:6, fol. 30d; Babli 68a). If there are *n* daughters, for the first one has to reserve $^1/_{10}$ of the capital, for the second $^1/_{10}$ of the remaining $^9/_{10}$, etc. By the formula of the geometric progression, in all $1 - (^9/_{10})^n$ of the inheritance has to be set aside for the daughters. The younger daughters may claim an equal share with the oldest one in the distribution of dowry.

59 If the inheritance is large, the sons may try to convince the court that

the part reserved for the support of the unmarried daughters is too large.

60 If the inheritance is small, the daughters my apply to the court to reserve the entire inheritance for them. If the inheritance is large, the daughters may sue to invalidate any sale of real estate by the brothers which reduces the amount of capital available for their support. {This shows that the brothers have a monetary interest in marrying off their underage sisters.}

61 If they took from the inheritance.

62 The silence of the Babli in this matter supports this claim in the Yerushalmi.

63 This is the position of the Yerushalmi (for the marriage of a virgin), opposed by the Babli; cf. Chapter 7, Note 63.

64 It is part of the rabbinic *ketubah* text decreed by Simeon ben Sheṭaḥ in Hasmonean times which may show demotic Egyptian and Roman influences.

65 If there were sons of different mothers who predeceased the father, the original *ketubah* decree required that each set of full brothers first recover the full amount of their mother's *ketubah* before the rest was divided among all sons.

66 Since the entire *ketubah* must be satisfied by distribution of real estate (cf. Note 53).

הַיּוֹרֵד לְנִיכְסֵי אִשְׁתּוֹ וְנָתַן עֵינָו בָּהּ לְגָרְשָׁהּ וְקָפַץ (fol. 15a) וְתָלַשׁ מִן הַקַּרְקַע הֲרֵי זֶה זָרִיז וְנִשְׂכָּר. הַיּוֹרֵד לְנִיכְסֵי שְׁבוּיִין וְשָׁמַע עֲלֵיהֶן שֶׁהֵן מְמַשְׁמְשִׁין וּבָאִין וְקָפַץ וְתָלַשׁ מִן הַקַּרְקַע הֲרֵי זֶה זָרִיז וְנִשְׂכָּר. וְאֵילּוּ הֵן נִיכְסֵי שְׁבוּיִים. כָּל־שֶׁהָלַךְ אָבִיו אוֹ אָחִיו אוֹ אֶחָד מִכָּל־הַמּוֹרִישִׁן אוֹתוֹ לִמְדִינַת הַיָּם וְשָׁמַע עֲלֵיהֶן שֶׁמֵּתוּ וְיָרַד לוֹ לְנַחֲלָה. אֲבָל נִיכְסֵי נְטוּשִׁין מוֹצִיאִין אוֹתוֹ מִיָּדוֹ. וְאֵילּוּ הֵן נִיכְסֵי נְטוּשִׁין. כָּל־שֶׁהָלַךְ אָבִיו אוֹ אָחִיו אוֹ אֶחָד מִכָּל־הַמּוֹרִישִׁין אוֹתוֹ לִמְדִינַת הַיָּם וְלֹא שָׁמַע עֲלֵיהֶן שֶׁמֵּתוּ וְיָרַד לוֹ לְנַחֲלָה. אָמַר רַבָּן שִׁמְעוֹן בֶּן גַּמְלִיאֵל. שָׁמַעְתִּי הוּא שְׁבוּיִים הוּא נְטוּשִׁים. אֲבָל נִיכְסֵי רְטוּשִׁין מוֹצִיאִין מִיָּדוֹ. וְאֵילּוּ הֵן נִיכְסֵי רְטוּשִׁין. כָּל־שֶׁהָלַךְ אָבִיו אוֹ אָחִיו אוֹ אֶחָד מִכָּל־הַמּוֹרִישִׁין אוֹתוֹ לִמְדִינַת הַיָּם וְאֵין יָדוּעַ אֵיכָן הוּא. שְׁמוּאֵל אָמַר שָׁבוּי זֶה שֶׁיָּצָא שֶׁלֹּא לְדַעַת. שֶׁאִילּוּ יָצָא לְדַעַת הָיָה מְצַוֵּיהוּ. נָטוּשׁ זֶה שֶׁיָּצָא לְדַעַת.

תֵּידַע לָךְ שֶׁעִילָּה הָיָה רוֹצֶה לְהַבְרִיחוֹ מִנְּכָסָיו. הֲרֵי לְדַעַת יָצָא וְלֹא צִיוָּהוּ. רִבִּי אָחָא רִבִּי בָּא רַב יְהוּדָה בְשֵׁם שְׁמוּאֵל. הַמְטַלְטְלִין אֵין בָּהֶן מִשּׁוּם נִיכְסֵי רְטוּשִׁין. רִבִּי יַעֲקֹב בַּר אָחָא בְשֵׁם רַב יְהוּדָה. קָמָה עוֹמֶדֶת לְהִיקָּצֵר וּגְפָנִים עוֹמְדוֹת לְהִיבָּצֵר מִמְטַלְטְלִין הֵן. רַב שֵׁשֶׁת שָׁאַל. אִילֵּין דִּקְלַיָּא דְבָבֶל דְּלָא צְרִיכִין מֵרְכָּבָה לֹא מִסְתַּבְּרָא מֵיעַבְדִּינָן כְּקָמָה עוֹבֶרֶת לְהִיקָּצֵר וּגְפָנִים עוֹבְרוֹת לְהִיבָּצֵר.

[67]"If somebody who works his wife's property[68] has the intention of divorcing her and goes and takes from the ground, he is quick and is rewarded. If somebody who works the property of prisoners[69] heard that they prepare to return, goes and takes from the ground, he is quick and is rewarded. These are properties of prisoners: In any case where his father, brother, or any person from whom he might inherit, went overseas, he heard that they died, and he went to work the inheritance[70]. But property of abandoning persons one takes out of their hands. These are properties of abandoning persons: In any case where his father, brother, or any person from whom he might inherit, went overseas, he did not hear that they died, but he went to work the inheritance[71]. Rabban Simeon ben Gamliel said, I heard that there is no difference between prisoners and abandoning persons[72]. But property of broken persons one takes out of their hands. These are properties of smashed[73] persons: In any case where his father, brother, or any person from whom he might inherit, went overseas, and his whereabouts are not known." Samuel says, the prisoner is one who left involuntarily. If he had left voluntarily he would have given him instructions[74]. The abandoning person is one who left voluntarily. You should know that he had the intention of keeping [the relative] off his property since he left voluntarily and did not give him instructions[75]. Rebbi Aḥa, Rebbi Abba, Rav Jehudah in the name of Samuel: Movables do not fall under the rules of smashed people[76]. Rebbi

Jacob bar Aḥa in the name of Rav Jehudah: Standing grain ready to be harvested and grapes ready to be harvested are movables[77]. Rav Sheshet asked: Those date palms of Babylonia which do not need grafting[78], is it not reasonable that we should treat them like standing grain ready to be harvested and grapes ready to be harvested[79]?

67 Tosephta *Ketubot* 8:2-3. The Tosephta contains additional statements, found in the parallel in the Babli, *Baba Meṣi'a* 28b-29a.

68 His wife's paraphernalia property of which he receives the usufruct as payment for his investment in and work on the fields. If he divorces his wife before harvest, he loses all rights to the crop. He therefore has an incentive to harvest as early as possible.

69 Not only kidnap victims but a large class described in the next sentence. Both Talmudim, by endorsing Samuel's definition, take position against the very wide definition of this Tosephta.

70 He had a reason to work the fields to keep them producing; he is rewarded by the possibility of acquiring the yield even if he has to return the real estate.

71 He started to work the field without authorization; if the owner returns before the harvest, he loses his investment. (In the Tosephta he may claim to be rewarded for his investment in money and time by being made a sharecropper. The Babli explains that this applies only if the farmer is appointed by the court to take care of his relative's property. There is no hint of this in the Yerushalmi.)

72 He disagrees with the anonymous Tanna and assigns the yield to the person working the field.

73 The Babli refers to *Hos*. 10:14.

74 The relative who went to work the field may reasonably assume that he would have been appointed to care for the property if the kidnap victim had had time to communicate with him. Therefore, the courts will assign the yield to him.

75 Samuel disagrees with Rabban Simeon ben Gamliel and refuses the harvest to the relative working the field.

76 The absent person cannot reclaim usufruct the unauthorized relative had from his movables.

77 In the Babli, *Šebuot* 43a, the

parallel statement is attributed to the Tanna R. Meïr; the anonymous majority declares any ripe crop to be under the laws of real estate until harvested. That means that the editors of the Babli rejected the attribution of the statement to Samuel, their highest authority in civil law.

78 There, palm trees are so abundant that it is not necessary to take male flowers and hang them into the crowns of female trees. That means that the trees do not need hard work.

79 No answer is given. The problem is not treated in the Babli since it precludes the basis of the question.

(fol. 14c) **משנה ד:** הַכֹּל נֶאֱמָנִים לְהַעִידָהּ חוּץ מֵחֲמוֹתָהּ וּבַת חֲמוֹתָהּ וְצָרָתָהּ וִיבִמְתָּהּ וּבַת בַּעֲלָהּ. מַה בֵין גֵּט לְמִיתָה שֶׁהַכְּתָב מוֹכִיחַ. עֵד אֶחָד אוֹמֵר מֵת וְנִשֵּׂאת. וּבָא אַחֵר וְאָמַר לֹא מֵת הֲרֵי זוֹ לֹא תֵצֵא. עֵד אוֹמֵר מֵת וּשְׁנַיִם אוֹמְרִין לֹא מֵת אַף עַל פִּי שֶׁנִּשֵּׂאת תֵּצֵא. שְׁנַיִם אוֹמְרִים מֵת וְעֵד אֶחָד אוֹמֵר לֹא מֵת אַף עַל פִּי שֶׁלֹּא נִשֵּׂאת תִּינָּשֵׂא.

Mishnah 4: Everybody is accepted to be a witness for her[80] except[81] her mother-in-law, her mother-in-law's daughter, her co-wife, her levir's wife, and her husband's daughter[82]. What is the difference between a bill of divorce and death[83]? The document is the proof. If one witness says that he died and she remarried, then another comes and says that he is not dead, she shall not leave[84]. If one witness says that he died but two say that he did not die, even if she remarried she must leave. If two say that he died but one said that he did not die, even if she has not yet remarried she may remarry[85].

80 As explained in Mishnah 16:8, even slaves and in certain cases people who attest to hearsay are empowered to declare that the husband died and that the woman is a widow free to remarry.

81 It is assumed that these hate her and that they might give wrong information in order to forbid her to her husband.

82 From another wife.

83 It is stated in Mishnah *Giṭṭin* 2:8 that the women who are not empowered to testify to the husband's death are empowered to deliver her bill of divorce and to testify to its validity.

84 Once she has remarried, her marriage can be invalidated only by the (biblically valid) testimony of two independent credible witnesses. But if she has not yet remarried, it is the word of one against the other and she should not remarry until the situation is clear.

85 Since the testimony of two witnesses is valid by biblical standards (*Deut.* 19:15), the word of a single witness is disregarded.

(fol. 15a) **מתניתא:** הַכֹּל נֶאֱמָנִים לְהַעִידָהּ כול׳. תַּנֵּי. כְּשֵׁם שֶׁאֵינָן נֶאֱמָנוֹת עָלֶיהָ כָּךְ אֵינָהּ נֶאֱמֶנֶת עֲלֵיהֶן. בֶּן חֲמוֹתָהּ כְּבַת חֲמוֹתָהּ. בֶּן בַּעֲלָהּ כְּבַת בַּעֲלָהּ. צָרָתָהּ אֲפִילוּ נְשׂוּאָה. יבִמְתָּהּ אֲפִילוּ אֲחוֹתָהּ. אָמַר רִבִּי יוֹסֵי. מַתְנִיתָא אָמְרָה כֵן שֶׁלֹּא עָשׂוּ זְכָרִים כִּנְקֵיבוֹת. דְּתַנִינָן תַּמָּן. שֶׁאֵין הָאִשָּׁה נֶאֱמֶנֶת לוֹמַר. מֵת יְבָמִי שֶׁתִּינָּשֵׂא. וְלֹא מֵתָה אֲחוֹתוֹ. שֶׁתִּיכָּנֵס לְבֵיתָהּ. מִפְּנֵי שֶׁאֵין לָהּ בָּנִים. אֲבָל אִם יֵשׁ לָהּ בָּנִים נֶאֱמֶנֶת.

Mishnah: "Everybody is accepted to be a witness for her," etc. It was stated[86]: "Just as they cannot be trusted for her, so she cannot be trusted about them." Her mother-in-law's son is like her mother-in-law's daughter. Her husband's son is like her husband's daughter. Her co-wife, even if remarried[87]. Her levir's wife, even [if she is] her own sister[88]. Rebbi Yose said, a Mishnah says that they did not treat the males as they treat the females, as we have stated there: "because a woman is not trusted if she says, my levir died, that she should be free to remarry, nor that her sister died, to enter her house.[89]" Because she has no children. But if she has children, she is trustworthy.

86 Tosephta 14:1. The Babli, 117a, agrees implicitly since it states that it is not necessary to note that the daughter-in-law cannot be trusted since the mother-in-law is on the list.

87 She no longer has any interest in her former husband's marriage.

88 Who can never be married in levirate.

89 Mishnah 12. The Mishnah continues: "Nor can a man be trusted to say 'my brother died' in order to marry his wife, nor 'my wife died', in order to marry her sister." That means that the levir can be trusted if he says that his brother died if the latter had children. But the statement of the Mishnah, that the levir's wife is excluded from testimony, is absolute and not dependent on her being a candidate for levirate.

וְהַכְּתָב מוֹכִיחַ. וְלָא מִפִּיהָ מַאֲמִינִים אוֹתָהּ. שֶׁאִילּוּ לֹא אָמְרָה. בְּפָנַיי נִכְתַּב וּבְפָנַיי נֶחְתַּם. אַף אַתְּ שֶׁמָּא מַתִּירָהּ לְהִינָּשֵׂא. אָמַר רִבִּי יוֹסֵי בֵּירִבִּי בּוּן. כְּהַהִיא דְאָמַר רִבִּי בּוּן. אֵינוֹ חָשׁוּד לְקַלְקְלָהּ בִּידֵי שָׁמַיִם. בְּבֵית דִּין חָשׁוּד לְקַלְקְלָהּ. שֶׁמִּתּוֹךְ שֶׁהוּא יוֹדֵעַ שֶׁאִם בָּא (וְעֵידָיו עִמּוֹ) [וְעִרְעֵר עִרְעוּרוֹ][90] בָּטֵל אַף הוּא מַחְתִּמוֹ בְעֵדִים כְּשֵׁירִים. וְהָכָא מִתּוֹךְ שֶׁהִיא יוֹדַעַת שֶׁלֹּא עָשׂוּ בָהּ דְּבָרֶיהָ אֶצֶל חֲבֵירָתָהּ כְּלוּם אַף הִיא אוֹמֶרֶת אֱמֶת.

Does the document prove? Do we not have to believe what she says? If she did not say 'it was written in my presence, it was signed in my presence', would you permit her to remarry[91]? Rebbi Yose ben Rebbi Abun said, that parallels what Rebbi Abun said[92], one does not suspect him to vilify her in the eyes of Heaven; he is suspect to vilify her in the eyes of the court[93]. Since he knows that if he were to come [and object, his objection] would not be accepted[94], he has [the bill of divorce] signed by witnesses in good standing. And here, since she knows that her word does not count for the other woman, she will be truthful.

90 The text in parenthesis is the ms. text here; the text in brackets is R. Abun's original statement in *Giṭṭin* 1:1. The *Giṭṭin* text is the only one which makes sense.

91 Mishnah *Giṭṭin* 1:1 states that a

bill of divorce brought from far away is accepted by the local court only if the person delivering the bill testifies that it was executed in his presence and, therefore, he can be queried about the details of the execution. Without such testimony, the woman to whom the bill is addressed cannot be declared to be a divorcee free to remarry.

92 In Halakhah *Giṭṭin* 1:1.

93 If the husband would trick the messenger into delivering an invalid bill of divorce and the court would declare the woman free to remarry on that basis, the only consequence would be that the children of the divorcee from a second husband would be bastards in the eyes of Heaven. Since the divorce, once approved by a competent court, cannot be reversed, the second marriage will always be legitimate in the eyes of the public and the children will be legitimate and able to marry in the congregation. But the court has to be able to cross-examine him before it accepts the document to be sure that the husband had the bill signed by witnesses in good standing.

94 In the Babli, this is the argument of Rava (cf. Chapter 1, Note 19). Another opinion there holds that the excluded women may deliver a bill of divorce only locally since then their testimony is not needed, as the testimony is not directly mentioned in Mishnah *Giṭṭin* 2:8. Since the Babli accepts Rava's argument, it concurs that a bill of divorce duly accepted in a second court cannot be attacked by the husband.

עֵד אֶחָד אוֹמֵר כול׳. עֵד אֶחָד אוֹמֵר מֵת. וְנִשֵּׂאת. וּבָא אַחֵר וְאָמַר. לֹא מֵת. הֲרֵי זוֹ לֹא תֵצֵא. מִפְּנֵי שֶׁאָמַר מִשֶּׁנִּישֵּׂאת. הָא אִם עַד שֶׁלֹּא נִישֵּׂאת וְנִישֵּׂאת תֵּצֵא. אָמַר רִבִּי יוֹחָנָן. זוֹ דִבְרֵי רִבִּי מְנַחֵם בֵּירִבִּי יוֹסֵי. אֲבָל דִּבְרֵי חֲכָמִים בֵּין אָמַר מִשֶּׁנִּישֵּׂאת בֵּין שֶׁאָמַר עַד שֶׁלֹּא נִישֵּׂאת לֹא תִינָּשֵׂא. וְאִם נִישֵּׂאת לֹא תֵצֵא. רַב נַחְמָן בַּר יַעֲקֹב בְּשֵׁם רַב. נִישֵּׂאת עַל פִּי עֵדִים שְׁנַיִם אֲפִילוּ אָתוֹן. אָֽמְרִין לֵהּ. לֵית אַתְּ נוֹ.[95] רִבִּי שְׁמוּאֵל בַּר רַב יִצְחָק בָּעֵי. הַגַּע אַצְמָךְ שֶׁהוּא אָדָם מְסוּיָּים כְּגוֹן אִימִּי. אָמַר רִבִּי יוֹסֵי בֵּירִבִּי בּוּן. וְלֵית כְּמָן בַּר נַשׁ דָּמֵיי לְרִבִּי אִמִּי. אָתָא עוּבְדָא קוֹמֵי דְרַבָּנָן דְּתַמָּן. אָֽמְרִין לֵיהּ. לֵית (אתנו).[100] קָם אַבָּא בַּר בָּא וְלָחַשׁ גַּו אוּדְנֵהּ. אָמַר לֵהּ. בְּחַיֶּיךָ. הַב לָהּ גֵּט מִסָּפֵק. קָמוּ תַלְמִידוֹי דְרַב וּמְחוֹנֵיהּ. אָמַר. עַרְקְתָא יְקַד וְסַפְסְלָא יְקַד. שְׁמוּאֵל אָמַר. תַּמָּן הֲוֵינָא וְלָא עַרְקְתָא יָֽקְדָת וְלָא סַפְסְלָא יָֽקְדָת אֶלָּא אַבָּא הוּא דְלָקָה. וְקָם לֵהּ. אָתָא

עוֹבְדָא קוֹמֵי רִבִּי אִימִּי. אָמַר לֵיהּ. אִין בָּרִיא דְהִיא שַׁרְיָא לָךְ אֶלָּא תְהֵא יוֹדֵעַ דִּבְנֵיהּ דְּהַהוּא גַבְרָא מַמְזֵירָא קוֹמֵי שְׁמַיָּא וַהֲוָא רִבִּי זְעִירָא מְקַלֵּס לֵיהּ דוּ מֵקִים מִילְּתָא עַל בְּרָרָא.

"If one witness says," etc. "If one witness says that he died and she remarried, then another comes and says that he is not dead, she shall not leave." Because he said that after she had remarried. Therefore if [the second witness came] before she remarried, if she remarried she has to leave. Rebbi Joḥanan said, these are the words of Rebbi Menaḥem ben Rebbi Yose[96]. But the words of the Sages [are], whether he testified after she remarried or before she remarried, she should not remarry[97], but if she remarried she shall not leave. Rav Naḥman bar Jacob said in the name of Rav, if she was married by the testimony of two witnesses, even if he returns, one says to him, "you are not he.[98]" Rebbi Samuel ben Rav Isaac asked, think of it, if he is a famous person like Immi? Rebbi Yose ben Rebbi Abun said, is there nobody who would look like Rebbi Immi[99]? There came a case before the rabbis there. They said to him, "you are not he." Abba bar Abba[100] got up and whispered in his[101] ear saying, by your life, give her a bill of divorce because of the doubt. Rav's students got up and beat him. Somebody said, the whip is burning and the footstool is burning[102]. Samuel said, I was there, no whip was burning and no footstool was burning, but my father was hit[103] and got up[104]. There came a case before Rebbi Immi. He said to him[105], yes, it is sure that she is permitted to you but you should know that the child of this man is a bastard before Heaven. Rebbi Ze'ira was praising him because he made the situation clear.

95 The ms. indicates that the reading is either אתנו or את נו. The second reading is acceptable, לֵית אַתְּ הֲנוּ "you are not he". In Chapter 10, the

reading is תני

96 Tosephta 14:1.

97 Since a woman remarrying on the testimony of a single witness does so at her own peril as explained in Halakhah 10:1.

98 In this version, the court tells the returning husband that they do not know him. In the earlier version (Chapter 10, Note 129) the wife tells the returning husband that she does not know him.

99 The rule of Rav was also accepted in Galilee, with misgivings.

100 Samuel's father. The story implies that Abba bar Abba did outlive Rav since "the students of Rav" only appear in cases after Rav's death.

101 The second husband, who had married her on the testimony of two credible witnesses with the agreement of the court.

102 It is difficult to understand what this means; probably one should translate אמר as third person plural: They (Rav's students) said that Abba bar Abba should be whipped with a burning whip kneeling on a burning footstool because he denied the validity of their teacher's decision.

103 In the tumult.

104 He left without insisting that the matter of applying Rav's teaching should come to a vote. The Babli knows nothing of Rav's ruling nor of Abba bar Abba's opposition.

משנה ה: אַחַת אוֹמֶרֶת מֵת וְאַחַת אוֹמֶרֶת לֹא מֵת זוֹ שֶׁאוֹמֶרֶת מֵת תִּינָּשֵׂא וְתִיטּוֹל כְּתוּבָּתָהּ וְזוֹ שֶׁאוֹמֶרֶת לֹא מֵת לֹא תִינָּשֵׂא וְלֹא תִיטּוֹל כְּתוּבָּתָהּ. אַחַת אוֹמֶרֶת מֵת וְאַחַת אוֹמֶרֶת נֶהֱרַג רַבִּי מֵאִיר אוֹמֵר הוֹאִיל וּמַכְחִישׁוֹת זוֹ אֶת זוֹ הֲרֵי אֵילּוּ לֹא יִנָּשְׂאוּ. רַבִּי יְהוּדָה וְרַבִּי שִׁמְעוֹן אוֹמְרִין זוֹ וְזוֹ מוֹדוֹת שֶׁאֵינוֹ קַיָּים יִנָּשְׂאוּ.

Mishnah 5: One [wife] says[105], he died, the other one says, he did not die. The one who said that he died can remarry and collect her *ketubah*; the one who said that he did not die cannot remarry[106] nor collect her *ketubah*. If one said that he died, while the other one[107] said he was killed; Rebbi Meïr says, since they contradict one another, they[108] cannot remarry. Rebbi Jehudah and Rebbi Simeon say, since both agree that he is not alive they can remarry.

105 A man went overseas with his two wives; the wives return without the husband.

106 According to her own statement, a second marriage would be adulterous. The *ketubah* is due only at the dissolution of the marriage.

107 According to the understanding of the Halakhah, this refers to two unrelated women who testify about their common husband who has disappeared.

108 The wives who contradict one another.

(fol. 15a) **מתניתא:** הָאִשָּׁה שֶׁהָלְכָה הִיא כול׳. רִבִּי יַעֲקֹב בַּר אָחָא בְּשֵׁם רִבִּי יוֹחָנָן רִבִּי הִילָא בְּשֵׁם רִבִּי לָעְזָר. מוֹדֶה רִבִּי מֵאִיר בָּרִאשׁוֹנָה. אַשְׁכָּח תַּנֵּי. עוֹד הִיא בְּמַחֲלוֹקֶת. מַה בֵּין שְׁנִיָּיה מַה בֵּין רִאשׁוֹנָה. רִאשׁוֹנָה לֹא עָשׂוּ בָהּ דָּבָר זֶה אֵצֶל חֲבֵירָתָהּ כְּלוּם. אָמַר רִבִּי לָעְזָר. מוֹדֶה רִבִּי יוּדָה וְרִבִּי שִׁמְעוֹן בְּעֵדִים. מַה בֵּין עֵדִים מַה בֵּין צָרָה. לֹא עָשׂוּ דִבְרֵי צָרָה אֵצֶל חֲבֵירָתָהּ כְּלוּם. אָמַר רִבִּי יוֹחָנָן. אִילּוּ אֲמָרָהּ רִבִּי לָעְזָר מִנִּי שְׁמָעָהּ וַאֲמָרָהּ.

Mishnah: "A woman who went overseas with her husband,"[109] etc. Rebbi Jacob bar Aḥa in the name of Rebbi Joḥanan, Rebbi Hila in the name of Rebbi Eleazar: Rebbi Meïr agrees in the first case[110]. It was found stated: That is also in dispute. What is the difference between the second and the first cases? In the first case, did they not consider her word as nonexistent for her companion[111]? Rebbi Eleazar said, Rebbi Judah and Rebbi Simeon concede in the case of witnesses[112]. What is the difference between witnesses and the co-wife? Did they not consider the co-wife's words as nonexistent for her companion[111]? Rebbi Joḥanan said, if Rebbi Eleazar said this, he heard it from me and formulated it[113].

109 A misquote from Mishnah 7.

110 Of two co-wives giving conflicting testimony.

111 Nothing a wife says has any

legal consequences for her co-wife. (The Babli, 118a, quotes R. Johanan as holding that a quarrel whether the husband is dead or not is not a contradiction. That opinion is characterized as difficult to understand. The simple solution offered here is not mentioned; this implies that it is rejected.)

112 Witnesses who contradict one another in details that have no essential bearing on the case before the court are nevertheless legally contradicting one another, making their testimony worthless. In the Babli, 118a, R. Eleazar and R Johanan reject any distinction by R. Jehudah and R. Simeon between women and witnesses.

113 A frequent complaint of R. Johanan, that R. Eleazar should have formulated his statement for the permanent record as stating: R. Johanan says . . . .

תַּמָּן תַּנִּינָן. מִי שֶׁהָיוּ שְׁתֵּי כִיתֵּי עֵדִים מְעִידוֹת אוֹתוֹ. אֵלּוּ מְעִידִין אוֹתוֹ שֶׁנָּזַר שְׁתַּיִם וְאֵלּוּ מְעִידִין אוֹתוֹ שֶׁנָּזַר חָמֵשׁ. רַב אָמַר. בִּכְלָל נֶחְלְקוּ. אֲבָל בִּפְרָט כָּל־עַמָּא מוֹדֵיי שֶׁיֵּשׁ בִּכְלָל חָמֵשׁ שְׁתַּיִם שֶׁיְּהֵא נָזִיר שְׁתַּיִם. אָמַר רִבִּי יוֹחָנָן. בְּמוֹנֶה[114] נֶחְלְקוּ. אֲבָל בִּכְלָל כָּל־עַמָּא מוֹדֵיי. נֶחֱלֶקֶת הָעֵדוּת אֵין כָּאן נְזִירוּת. וְהֵידִינוּ כְלָל וְהֵידִינוּ מוֹנֶה. כְּלָל. הָהֵן אָמַר תַּרְתֵּיי וְהָהֵן אָמַר חָמֵשׁ. מוֹנֶה. הָהֵן אָמַר. חָדָא תַּרְתֵּיי וְהָהֵן אָמַר. תְּלַת אַרְבַּע וְחָמֵשׁ

[115]There, we have stated[116]: "If two groups of witnesses testified about him, one group testifying that he vowed two periods of *nezirut*[117], the other group testifying that he vowed five periods of *nezirut*.[118]" Rav said, they differ in the overall testimony. But in detail, everybody agrees that five contains two, that he has to be a *nazir* for two periods[119]. Rebbi Johanan said, they differ in counting. But in an overall testimony, everybody agrees that the testimonies contradict one another and there is no *nezirut*[120]. What is overall and what is counting? Overall, this one says two, the other one says five. Counting, this one says one, two, the other one says three, four, five.

114 Reading of the parallels in *Nazir* 3:7, *Sanhedrin* 5:2. The ms. reading here is בזמנה "in the timing".

115 From here to the end of the Halakhah, the text is also in *Nazir* 3:7, *Sanhedrin* 5:2.

116 Mishnah *Nazir* 3:7.

117 The vow to abstain from grape products, from impurity of the dead, and from hair cutting, *Num.* 6:1-21. If the person making the vow does not indicate the duration of the vow, it is for a period of 30 days (Mishnah *Nazir* 3:1).

118 "The House of Shammai say, this is conflicting testimony, there is no *nezirut*, the House of Hillel say, two is included in a totality of five, he must be a *nazir* for two periods."

119 What Rav calls detail, R. Joḥanan calls counting. Rav holds that the Houses of Shammai and Hillel disagree if one group of witnesses say that he vowed two periods and the other group say five periods. But if the first group testify that he vowed a first and a second time separate 30-day periods of *nezirut*, and the other group confirm this but add that he also vowed third, fourth, and fifth periods, then the testimony for the first two periods is concurrent and valid according to everybody. The Babli agrees, *Nazir* 20a/b, in the names of Rav and the Galileans.

120 R. Joḥanan holds that the testimony of 5 contradicts the testimony of 2 and the House of Hillel will agree that both testimonies are invalid. He holds that the House of Hillel consider a testimony on (1,2) to be contained in the testimony about (1,2,3,4,5), but the House of Shammai see the testimonies as contradicting one another.

רַב אָמַר.[121] הִכְחִישׁ עֵדוּת בְּתוֹךְ עֵדוּת לֹא בָֽטְלָה הָעֵדוּת. רִבִּי יוֹחָנָן אָמַר. הִכְחִישׁ עֵדוּת בְּתוֹךְ עֵדוּת בָֽטְלָה הָעֵדוּת. דִּבְרֵי הַכֹּל. הִכְחִישׁ עֵדוּת לְאַחַר עֵדוּת לֹא בָֽטְלָה הָעֵדוּת. רִבִּי יוֹחָנָן כְּדַעְתֵּיהּ. דָּמַר רִבִּי בָּא רִבִּי חִיָּיה בְּשֵׁם רִבִּי יוֹחָנָן. הוּחְזַק הַמּוֹנֶה. זֶה אָמַר. מִן הַכִּיס מוֹנֶה. וְזֶה אוֹמֵר. מִן הַצְּרוֹר מוֹנֶה. הִכְחִישׁ עֵדוּת בְּתוֹךְ עֵדוּת. וְאַף רַב מוֹדֶה שֶׁבָֽטְלָה הָעֵדוּת. מַה פְלִיגִין. בְּשֶׁהָיוּ שְׁתֵּי כִיתֵּי עֵדִים. אֵילּוּ אוֹמְרִים. מִן הַכִּיס מוֹנֶה. וְאֵילּוּ אוֹמְרִים. מִן הַצְּרוֹר מוֹנֶה. הִכְחִישׁ עֵדוּת בְּתוֹךְ עֵדוּת בָּטֵל הָעֵדוּת. וּכְרַב לֹא בָֽטְלָה הָעֵדוּת. אֵילּוּ אוֹמְרִים. לְתוֹךְ חֵיקוֹ מָנָה.[122] וְאֵילּוּ אוֹמְרִים. לְתוֹךְ פוּנְדָּתוֹ מָנָה[122]. דִּבְרֵי

הַכֹּל. הִכְחִישׁ הָעֵדוּת לְאַחַר עֵידוּת לֹא בָֽטְלָה עֵדוּת. זֶה אָמַר. בְּמַקֵּל הֲרָגוֹ. וְזֶה אָמַר. בְּסַיִיף הֲרָגוֹ. הִכְחִישׁ עֵדוּת בְּתוֹךְ עֵדוּת בָֽטְלָה הָעֵדוּת. וְאַף רַב מוֹדֶה שֶׁבָּֽטְלָה עֵדוּת. מַה פְלִיגִין. כְּשֶׁהָיוּ שְׁתֵּי כִיתֵּי עֵדִים. אֵלּוּ אָמַר. בְּמַקֵּל הֲרָגוֹ. וְאֵלּוּ אָמַר. בְּסַיְיף הֲרָגוֹ. הִכְחִישׁ עֵדוּת בְּתוֹךְ עֵדוּת בָֽטְלָה הָעֵדוּת. וּכְרַב לֹא בָֽטְלָה הָעֵדוּת. אֵילּוּ אוֹמְרִים. בְּדָרוֹם פָּנָה. וְאֵילוּ אוֹמְרִים. בְּצָפוֹן פָּנָה. דִּבְרֵי הַכֹּל. הִכְחִישׁ עֵדוּת לְאַחַר עֵדוּת לֹא בָֽטְלָה הָעֵדוּת. חֵיילֵיהּ דְּרַב מִן הָדָא. רִבִּי שִׁמְעוֹן וְרִבִּי יְהוּדָה אוֹמְרִין. הוֹאִיל וְזוֹ וְזוֹ מוֹדוֹת שֶׁאֵינוֹ קַייָם יִנָּשְׂאוּ. וְלֹא שְׁמִיעַ דָּמַר רִבִּי לָֽעְזָר. מוֹדֶה רִבִּי יוּדָה וְרִבִּי שִׁמְעוֹן בְּעֵדִים. מַה בֵין עֵדִים מַה בֵין צָרָה. לֹא עָשׂוּ דִבְרֵי צָרָה אֵצֶל חֲבֵירָתָהּ כְּלוּם. (דָּמַר רִבִּי יוֹחָנָן. אִם אֲמָרָהּ רִבִּי לָֽעְזָר מִנֵּי שְׁמָעָהּ וַאֲמָרָהּ.)[130] מַתְנִיתָא פְלִיגָא עַל רַב. אֶחָד חֲקִירוֹת וְאֶחָד בְּדִיקוֹת. בִּזְמַן שֶׁהֵן מַכְחִישִׁין (fol. 15b) זֶה אֶת זֶה עֵדוּתָן בְּטֵילָה. אָמַר רִבִּי מָנָא. פָּתַר לָהּ רַב עֵד בְּעֵד. אָמַר רִבִּי אָבִין. וַאֲפִילוּ תֵימַר כַּת בְּכַת. שַׁנְיָיא הִיא בְדִינֵי נְפָשׁוֹת. צֶדֶק צֶדֶק תִּרְדּוֹף.

Rav said, if testimony was contradicted in its essence, the testimony is not void[123]. Rebbi Johanan said, if testimony was contradicted in itself, the testimony is void in the opinion of everybody[124]. If testimony was contradicted in some aspects that belong after the fact, the testimony is not void[125]. Rebbi Johanan is consistent since Rebbi Abba, Rebbi Ḥiyya, said in the name of Rebbi Johanan, if it was agreed that he counted[126] but one [witness] said, he counted from a wallet and the other said, he counted from a bundle, that contradicts the essence of the testimony, and Rav will agree that the testimony is void. Where do they disagree? If there were two groups of witnesses, these say he counted from a wallet and the others say he counted from a bundle. That contradicts the essence of the testimony[127], the testimony is void but according to Rav, the testimony is not void[128]. These say, he counted into his bosom, the others say he counted into his money-belt; everybody agrees that is contradicting testimony after the main testimony, and the testimony is not void. If one [witness] said, he killed him with a mace, the other [witness] said, he killed him with a sword, that contradicts the essence of the testimony, the testimony is void and Rav will agree that the testimony is void[129]. Where do they disagree? If there were two groups of witnesses, these say he killed him with a mace and the others say, he killed him with a sword. That contradicts the essence of the testimony, the testimony is void but according to Rav, the testimony is not void. If these say, he ran away to the South and those say, he ran away to the North, everybody agrees that the testimony was contradictory in some aspects that belong after the fact, the testimony is not void[125]. The strength of Rav comes from the following: "Rebbi Jehudah and Rebbi Simeon say, since both agree that he is not alive they can remarry." He did nor hear that Rebbi Eleazar said, Rebbi Judah and Rebbi Simeon concede in the case of witnesses[112]. What is the difference between witnesses and the co-wife? Did they not consider the co-wife's words as nonexistent for her companion[111]? (Rebbi Joḥanan said, if Rebbi Eleazar said this, he heard it from me and formulated it[113].)[130] A Mishnah disagrees with Rav[131]: "Both in investigations[132] and in cross examinations[133], if they contradict one another their testimony is void." Rebbi Mana said, Rav will explain that as referring to single witness against single witness. Rebbi Abun said, even if you say groups and groups. There is a difference in criminal cases: "Justice, justice you shall pursue"[134].

121 Text from the parallels. Text here: רב אידי "Rav Idi".

122 Text from the parallel in *Sanhedrin* (this sentence missing in *Nazir*). Text here: המה.

123 The court may try to piece together an account of what really happened.

124 Both the testimony and the opposing testimony are eliminated from the record.

125 The example given below is

concurrent testimony how the murder was committed but conflicting testimony as to the direction of escape of the murderer, which is testimony to what happened after the criminal act was committed.

126 In some case before the court one needs to establish the fact that one party counted a certain amount of money.

127 For R. Joḥanan, concurrent testimony by several witnesses is biblical testimony binding on the court only if it holds up under cross examination; *Deut.* 19:18: "The judges have to investigate thoroughly".

128 In the first case, there was no testimony. If both witnesses had testified in a coherent way, the fact would have been established by two independent witnesses and would be testimony by biblical standards which is binding on the court. In the second case, Rav holds that both testimonies are binding by biblical standards and can be used to establish any fact that is uncontested between the two groups; in that example that one of the parties counted money.

129 In criminal cases, the testimony of a single witness has no standing; if the two testimonies do not combine in a meaningful way, there is no testimony (this example is quoted by Rav Ḥisda in the Babli, *Sanhedrin* 30b,41a). (In civil cases, a single witness also cannot testify but he can be used to ascertain circumstances.)

130 The text in parenthesis is from ms. A only; probably it is copied from above by an unthinking scribe.

131 Mishnah *Sanhedrin* 5:2.

132 The procedures before a Talmudic court are inquisitory. In a first stage the witnesses are queried about the alleged crime.

133 These are questions about matters of secondary importance put to each witness in the absence of the other to ferret out any prior understanding between the witnesses, which would invalidate the testimony, or inconsistencies in detail which would impair its standing.

134 *Deut.* 16:20. In criminal cases, proof beyond any reasonable doubt is required.

מתניתא: אֲמְרָה מֵת בַּעֲלִי כול׳. גִּידֵל בַּר מִנְיָימִין בְּשֵׁם רַב. בְּכָל־מָקוֹם שֶׁהִכְשִׁירוּ עֲדוּת הָאִשָּׁה בָּאִישׁ הָאִישׁ מַכְחִישׁ אֶת הָאִשָּׁה וְהָאִשָּׁה מַכְחֶשֶׁת אֶת הָאִישׁ. נִיתְנֵי. עֵד אוֹמֵר. מֵת. וְאִשָּׁה אוֹמֶרֶת. לֹא מֵת. אִשָּׁה אוֹמֶרֶת. מֵת.

וְעֵד אוֹמֵר. לֹא מֵת. [135]תַּנֵּיי דְבֵית רִבִּי כֵן. תַּנֵּי בְשֵׁם רִבִּי נְחֶמְיָה. הוֹלְכִין אַחַר רוֹב הָעֵדוּת. הֵיךְ עֲבִידָה. שְׁתֵּי נָשִׁים וְאִשָּׁה אַחַת עָשׂוּ אוֹתָן כִּשְׁנֵי עֵדִים וְעֵד אֶחָד. הָדָא אַתְּ אָמַר בְּאִשָּׁה וְנָשִׁים. אֲבָל אִם הָיוּ מֵאָה נָשִׁים וְעֵד אֶחָד כְּעֵד אִינּוּן.

Mishnah: "if she says 'my husband died'," etc[109]. Gidul bar Miniamin in the name of Rav: Anywhere they accepted the testimony of a woman parallel to that of a man, a man can contradict a woman and a woman can contradict a man. Then one should state: "A witness says that he died, and a woman says that he did not die; a woman said that he died and a witness said that he did not die." In the House of Rebbi they stated it this way. It was stated[136] in the name of Rebbi Neḥemiah: One follows the majority of the testimonies. How is that? Two women against one woman they considered as if there were two witnesses against one witness[137]. What you say refers to a woman and women. But if there were a hundred women against one [male] witness, they are like one witness[138].

135 From here to almost the end of the Tractate, there is no text from Ms. L available. The text given here is that of the *editio princeps*. For the rest of this chapter and part of the following, ms. A is available. The remainder of this paragraph is inconsistent there and reads:

וְתַנֵּיי דְבֵית רִבִּי כֵן. תַּנָּא בְשֵׁם רִבִּי נְחֶמְיָה. הוֹלְכִים אַחַר דֵיעוֹת. הֵיךְ עֲבִידָה. שְׁתֵּי נָשִׁים וְאִישׁ עָשׂוּ אוֹתָם כִּשְׁנֵי עֵדִים וְעֵד אֶחָד. הָדָה אָמְרָה בְּאִשׁ וְאִשָּׁה. אֲבָל אִם הָיוּ מֵאָה נָשִׁים וְעֵד אֶחָד עֵד בְּעֵד אִינּוּן.

"In the House of Rebbi they stated it this way. It was stated in the name of Rebbi Neḥemiah: One follows the opinions. How is that? Two women against one man they considered as if there were two witnesses against one witness. What you say refers to a man and a woman. But if there were a hundred women against one [male] witness, they are like one witness against one witness."

136 Tosephta 14:1; formulation as in ms. A and the Babli (88b, 117b; *Soṭah* 31b, 47b) against the reading of the Yerushalmi here and in *Soṭah* 6:4, 9:7.

137 Two concurring witnesses have biblical status. One witness contradicting two witnesses has no standing, assuming that all are of the same reliability.

138 The Babli presents two opinions. Everybody holds that in the weight of testimony there is no difference between 2 and 100 witnesses. The first opinion holds that if the women came first, the single male witness has no standing. The other holds that any number of women against a male whose credibility is unimpaired (i. e., he never was found in violation of *any* biblical commandment) are like testimony split 50-50. This is accepted by Maimonides (*Gerušin* 12:20). Anywhere the text uses "witness" instead of "man" it means a male of impeccable standing.

The reading of the *editio princeps*, בע־ אינון, is supported by R. Nissim Gerondi (Commentary to RIF *Ketubot*, §206): בעידי אינון.

משנה ו: עֵד אָמַר מֵת וְעֵד אֶחָד אָמַר לֹא מֵת אִשָּׁה אָמְרָה מֵת וְאִשָּׁה אוֹמֶרֶת לֹא מֵת הֲרֵי זוֹ לֹא תִינָּשֵׂא.

Mishnah 6: One witness said that he died, another witness said that he did not die; a woman said that he died, another woman said that he did not die; she may not remarry[139].

139 Two witnesses testify to opposite facts and the court sees no reason to believe the one more than the other. In that case there is no testimony and the wife of the disappeared husband cannot remarry.

(fol. 14c) **משנה ז:** הָאִשָּׁה שֶׁהָלְכָה הִיא וּבַעֲלָהּ לִמְדִינַת הַיָּם בָּאת וְאָמְרָה מֵת בַּעֲלִי תִינָּשֵׂא וְתִיטּוֹל כְּתוּבָּתָהּ וְצָרָתָהּ אֲסוּרָה. הָיְתָה בַת יִשְׂרָאֵל לַכֹּהֵן תֹּאכַל בִּתְרוּמָה דִּבְרֵי רִבִּי טַרְפוֹן. רִבִּי עֲקִיבָה אוֹמֵר אֵין זוֹ דֶרֶךְ מוֹצִיאַתָּהּ מִידֵי עֲבֵירָה עַד שֶׁתְּהֵא אֲסוּרָה לְהִינָּשֵׂא וַאֲסוּרָה מִלּוֹכַל בִּתְרוּמָה.

Mishnah 7: If a woman went overseas with her husband and she returns and says "my husband died", she can remarry and collect her *ketubah*, but her co-wife remains forbidden[140]. If she was the daughter of an Israel married to a Cohen[141], she should eat heave, the words of Rebbi Tarphon. Rebbi Aqiba says, in this way one does not remove her from sin unless she be forbidden to remarry[142] and forbidden to eat heave[143].

140 Since the testimony of a wife cannot be trusted in matters of her co-wife.

141 And she has no son on whose behalf she remains in the priestly clan and continues to eat heave.

142 Since perhaps her co-wife is ready to put herself in a perilous position in order to damage her co-wife.

143 Since perhaps the testimony of her co-wife was true.

(fol. 15b) **מתניתא:** חֲשׁוּדָה הִיא לְקַלְקֵל עַצְמָהּ כְּדֵי לְקַלְקֵל צָרָתָהּ. מֵעַתָּה אֲפִילוּ עַל עַצְמָהּ לֹא תְהֵא נֶאֱמֶנֶת. מִתּוֹךְ שֶׁהִיא יוֹדַעַת שֶׁלֹּא עָשׂוּ דְּבָרֶיהָ אֵצֶל חֲבֵירָתָהּ כְּלוּם אַף הִיא אוֹמֶרֶת אֱמֶת. מֵעַתָּה אֲפִילוּ עַל צָרָתָהּ תְּהֵא נֶאֱמֶנֶת. חֲשׁוּדָה הִיא לְקַלְקֵל עַצְמָהּ כְּדֵי לְקַלְקֵל צָרָתָהּ.

Mishnah. She is suspected to cause trouble to herself in order to cause trouble to her co-wife[144]. Then she should not be trustworthy even for herself! Since she knows that her word does not count for the other woman, she will be truthful[145]. Then she should be trustworthy even for her co-wife! [146]She is suspected to cause trouble to herself in order to cause trouble to her co-wife.

144 She is ready to forbid herself to her husband if it causes her co-wife to be equally forbidden.

145 Cf. Halakhah 4, Note 94.

146 Ms. A has an addition: אָמַר רִבִּי הִילָא חֲזוֹר לְקִילְקוּל הָרִאשׁוֹן חֲשׁוּדָה הִיא . "Rebbi Ila said, go back to the first trouble; she is suspected . . .".

משנה ח: אָמְרָה מֵת בַּעְלִי וְאַחַר כָּךְ מֵת חָמִי תִּינָּשֵׂא וְתִיטּוֹל כְּתוּבָּתָהּ (fol. 14c) וַחֲמוֹתָהּ אֲסוּרָה. הָיְתָה בַת יִשְׂרָאֵל לַכֹּהֵן תֹּאכַל בַּתְּרוּמָה דִּבְרֵי רִבִּי טַרְפוֹן. רִבִּי עֲקִיבָה אוֹמֵר אֵין זוֹ דֶרֶךְ מוֹצִיאָתָהּ מִידֵי עֲבֵירָה עַד שֶׁתְּהֵא אֲסוּרָה לְהִינָּשֵׂא וַאֲסוּרָה מִלּוֹכַל בַּתְּרוּמָה.

Mishnah 8: If a woman went overseas with her husband and she returns and says "my husband died and then my father-in-law died", she can remarry and collect her *ketubah*, but her mother-in-law remains forbidden[147]. If she was the daughter of an Israel married to a Cohen, she should eat heave, the words of Rebbi Tarphon. Rebbi Aqiba says, in this way one does not remove her from sin unless she be forbidden to remarry and forbidden to eat heave.

147 This is a complete parallel to the preceding Mishnah and shows that the same rules apply to all women who cannot be trusted with the testimony about a husband's death.

(fol. 15b) **מתניתא:** קִידֵּשׁ אַחַת. וּתְהֵא נֶאֱמֶנֶת לוֹמַר מֵת חָמִי. לֹא כֵן סָבְרִינָן מֵימַר. כְּשֵׁם שֶׁאֵינָן נֶאֱמָנוֹת עָלֶיהָ כָּךְ הִיא אֵינָהּ נֶאֱמֶנֶת עֲלֵיהֶן. אָמַר רִבִּי חֲנִינָא. תִּיפְתָּר שֶׁהָיָה חָמִיהָ כָן וְסִייְמָהּ.

Mishnah: "If he was betrothed to one.[148]" Should she not be trusted to say "my father-in-law died"? Did we not hold that just as they are not trusted about her so she is not trusted about them[86]? Rebbi Ḥanina said, explain it if her father-in-law was there and she described the circumstances[149].

148 Wrong quote, belonging to the next Mishnah.

149 Even if anything she says can be checked and nothing would have to be feared by accepting her testimony, she is not admitted to testify about the status of her mother-in-law

משנה ט: קִידֵּשׁ אַחַת מֵחָמֵשׁ נָשִׁים וְאֵין יָדוּעַ אֵיזוֹ קִידֵּשׁ כָּל־אַחַת(fol. 14c) אוֹמֶרֶת אוֹתִי קִידֵּשׁ נוֹתֵן גֵּט לְכָל־אַחַת וְאַחַת וּמַנִּיחַ כְּתוּבָּה בֵּינֵיהֶן וּמִסְתַּלֵּק דִּבְרֵי רִבִּי טַרְפוֹן. רִבִּי עֲקִיבָה אוֹמֵר אֵין זוֹ דֶּרֶךְ מוֹצִיאָתוֹ מִידֵי עֲבֵירָה עַד שֶׁיִּתֵּן גֵּט וּכְתוּבָּה לְכָל־אַחַת וְאַחַת.

Mishnah 9: If he became betrothed to one of five women but it cannot be ascertained to which of them he became betrothed, and each one says he became betrothed to me, he gives a bill of divorce to each of them, puts up the amount of one *ketubah* between them and removes himself, the words of Rebbi Tarphon[150]. Rebbi Aqiba says, in this way one does not remove him from sin unless he gives a bill of divorce and pays the *ketubah* to each of them[151].

150 Since in order to collect the money, the claimant would have to prove in court that she was betrothed (or, in the case discussed in Mishnah 10, that he was robbed). The circumstances of the case are that the proof is impossible. On the other hand, his admission that he became betrothed to one woman, or that he robbed a person, makes him liable to pay.

151 There is a moral obligation even if the court cannot enforce it. The Tosephta, 15:2, quoted in the Babli, 118b, has R. Simeon ben Eleazar state that R. Aqiba agrees with R. Tarphon in the case of betrothal or an acquisition but disagrees in the case of a consummated marriage and robbery.

(fol. 15b) **הלכה ט**: [(גָּזַל אֶחָד מֵחֲמִשָּׁה). אָמַר רִבִּי אָבוּן מַתְנִיתָה בְּשֶׁקִּדְּשָׁהּ בִּשְׁטָר אֲבָל אִם קִדְּשָׁהּ בְּכֶסֶף כָּל־עַמָּא מוֹדֵיי שֶׁיִּתֵּן גֵּט וּכְתוּבָּה לְכָל־אַחַת וְאַחַת.]

Halakhah 9: [(He robbed one of five people). Rebbi Abun said, the Mishnah deals with the case that she was betrothed by a document. But if he was betrothed by money, everybody agrees that he gives a bill of divorce and pays the *ketubah* to each of them.][152]

152 This text is only in ms. A; it is genuine since it is quoted by the twelfth Century author R. Isaac ben Abba Mari in Sefer Ha'ittur (ed. R. Meïr Jonah, vol. 1, 79b, Notes 121,122). In a parallel (anonymous) discussion, the Babli (118b) states that R. Aqiba insists on multiple ketubah payments only if the betrothal was by copulation (before witnesses, cf Chapter 5, Note 46), which is a biblically valid betrothal but rabbinically forbidden. According to that opinion, R. Aqiba declares the additional payments to be a fine; this seems to contradict the language of the Mishnah.

In the interpretation of the *Sefer Ha'ittur*, the document of betrothal would count as proof of a *ketubah*. Since each woman claims to have had such a document but lost it, they cannot enforce a claim and the two have to fight about one *ketubah*. If the betrothal was by money's worth, in the opinion of the Yerushalmi the divorcee can claim the basic amount of the *ketubah* even if the marriage was not consummated (*Ketubot* 5:1). Since in that case there was no negligence on the part of the woman, he has to pay. (The Babli would hold that one does not follow the Mishnah and in practice no *ketubah* is due until the marriage is consummated.)

(fol. 14c) **משנה י:** גָּזַל אֶחָד מֵחֲמִשָּׁה וְאֵין יָדוּעַ לְאֵי זֶה גָּזַל וְכָל־אֶחָד אוֹמֵר אוֹתִי גָּזַל מַנִּיחַ אֶת הַגְּזֵילָה בֵּינֵיהֶן וּמִסְתַּלֵּק דִּבְרֵי רִבִּי טַרְפוֹן. רִבִּי עֲקִיבָה אוֹמֵר אֵין זוֹ דֶרֶךְ מוֹצִיאַתּוּ מִידֵי עֲבֵירָה עַד שֶׁיְּשַׁלֵּם גְּזֵילָה לְכָל־אֶחָד וְאֶחָד.

Mishnah 10: He robbed one of five people, it is not known which of them he robbed and each one says "I was robbed", he puts up the amount of the robbery between them and removes himself, the words of Rebbi Tarphon[150]. Rebbi Aqiba says, in this way one does not remove him from sin unless he pays the amount of the robbery to each of them[151].

(fol. 15b) **מתניתא:** גָּזַל אֶחָד מֵחֲמִשָּׁה. אָמַר רִבִּי אַסִּי. מַהֲנִיתִין דְּרִבִּי עֲקִיבָה. דְּלֹא כְרִבִּי טַרְפוֹן. דְּתַנִּינָן תַּמָּן. [אָמַר][153] לִשְׁנַיִם. גָּזַלְתִּי אֶת אֶחָד מִכֶּם מָנֶה

וְאֵינִי יוֹדֵעַ אֵיזֶה מִכֶּם הוּא. אָבִיו שֶׁל אֶחָד מִכֶּם הִפְקִיד אֶצְלִי מָנֶה וְאֵינִי יוֹדֵעַ אֵיזֶה מִכֶּם הוּא. נוֹתֵן לָזֶה מָנֶה וְלָזֶה מָנֶה. שֶׁהוֹדָה מִפִּי עַצְמוֹ. רִבִּי יַעֲקֹב בַּר אָחָא בְשֵׁם רִבִּי יוֹחָנָן. דִּבְרֵי הַכֹּל הִיא. אוֹמֵר. צֵא יְדֵי שָׁמַיִם.[154] רִבִּי בָּא בְשֵׁם רַב יְהוּדָה. כָּאן שֶׁיֵּשׁ[155] עֵדִים יוֹדְעִים. כָּאן שֶׁאֵין[155] עֵדִים יוֹדְעִים. רִבִּי הִילָא[156] בְשֵׁם רִבִּי לָעְזָר. כָּאן בְּשׁוֹתְקִין. כָּאן בִּמְדַבְּרִים. רַב יִרְמְיָה בְשֵׁם רַב. כָּאן בְּשֶׁנִּשְׁבַּע. כָּאן בְּשֶׁלֹּא נִשְׁבַּע[157]. [158] [רִבִּי יוֹחָנָן אָמַר. אִם בְּשֶׁנִּשְׁבַּע][159] הָיָה לוֹ לַעֲשׂוֹת שְׁלִיחַ בֵּית דִּין וְלִמְסוֹר. רִבִּי יוֹחָנָן סָבַר מֵימַר. בֵּית דִּין שֶׁעֲשָׂאוֹ [גּוֹזֵל].[160] לֹא בֵית דִּין שֶׁעֲשָׂאוֹ נִגְזַל. רַב אָמַר בֵּית דִּין שֶׁעֲשָׂאוֹ נִגְזַל וְלֹא בֵית דִּין שֶׁעֲשָׂאוֹ גוֹזֵל. חֵילֵיהּ דְּרַב מִן הָדָא. דָּמַר רִבִּי שִׁמְעוֹן בֶּן לָעְזָר. בֵּית דִּין שֶׁעֲשָׂאוֹ נִגְזַל וְלֹא בֵית דִּין שֶׁעֲשָׂאוֹ גוֹזֵל. וְאִם לֹא הָיָה לִשְׁתּוֹק.[161] רִבִּי יִרְמְיָה סָבַר מֵימַר. הָיָה לוֹ לִשְׁתּוֹק וְלֹא [לְהוֹדוֹת].[162] רִבִּי יוֹסֵי סָבַר מֵימַר. הָיָה לוֹ לִשְׁתּוֹק וְלֹא לְהִשָּׁבַע. אָמַר רִבִּי יוּדָן. וַאֲפִילוּ תֵימַר דְּאִינּוּן אָמְרִין. הִיא שׁוֹתְקִין הִיא מְדַבְּרִים בִּגְ[זֵ]ילָה[163] מוֹדֵי בְּפִקָּדוֹן דְּשָׁתַק מִתְגַּר וּדְמִשְׁתָּעֵי [מַפְסִד].[164] דְּשָׁתַק מִתְגַּר מִן הָדָה. שְׁנַיִם שֶׁהִפְקִידוּ אֵצֶל אֶחָד זֶה מָנֶה וְזֶה מָאתַיִם. זֶה אוֹמֵר. מָאתַיִם שֶׁלִּי. וְזֶה אוֹמֵר. מָאתַיִם שֶׁלִּי. נוֹתֵן לָזֶה מָנֶה וְלָזֶה מָנֶה וְהַשְּׁאָר יְהֵא מוּנַּח עַד שֶׁיָּבֹא אֵלִיָּהוּ. דְּמִשְׁתָּעֵי [מַפְסִד][164] מִן הָכָא.[165] גָּזַלְתִּי אֶת אֶחָד מִכֶּם. וְאֵינִי יוֹדֵעַ אֵיזֶה מִכֶּם כו'.

Mishnah: "He robbed one of five people." Rebbi Assi said, there is a Mishnah which follows Rebbi Aqiba against Rebbi Tarphon. As we have stated there[166]: "If he said to two people, I robbed a mina from one of you but I do not know who of you it was; I received a deposit of a mina from the father of one of you but I do not know who of you it was; he gives to each of them a mina because he confessed himself." Rebbi Jacob bar Aḥa in the name of Rebbi Joḥanan: This is everybody's opinion. One says, to be clean before Heaven[167]. Rebbi Abba in the name of Rav Jehudah: Here, if witnesses know; there, if no witnesses know[168]. Rebbi Hila in the name of Rebbi Eleazar: Here if they are silent; there if they are talking[169]. Rebbi Jeremiah in the name of Rav: Here if he swore;

there if he did not swear[170]. Rebbi Johanan said, if he swore, he should have appointed an officer of the court and hand it over to him[171]. Rebbi Johanan seems to say, a court which determined that one was a robber, not a court which determined that one was robbed[172]. Rav said, a court which determined that one was robbed, not a court which determined that one was a robber[173]. The strength of Rav is from the following, that Rebbi Simeon ben Eleazar said, a court which determined that one was robbed, not a court which determined that one was a robber[174]. Otherwise he should have kept silent. Rebbi Jeremiah wanted to say, he should have kept silent and not confessed[175]. Rebbi Yose wanted to say, he should have kept silent and not have sworn[176]. Rebbi Yudan said, even following those who say that there is no difference between keeping silent and talking in matters of a robbery, for a deposit they agree that he who keeps silent is rewarded[177] and he who talks loses. He who keeps silent is rewarded from the following: "Two people deposited with the same person, one a mina and one 200 [tetradrachmas]. This one says, the 200 belong to me, and that one says, the 200 belong to me. He gives each one a mina and the rest shall lie with him until Elijah comes." He who talks loses, from this: "If he said to two people, I robbed[178] a mina from one of you but I do not know which one of you."

153 From ms. A, word missing in *editio princeps*.

154 In ms. A: אוֹמֵר לֵי צֵא. לָצֵאת יְדֵי שָׁמַיִם. "One says to him go, to be clean before Heaven." The addition of לצאת may be a gloss.

155 In ms. A: בשיש, בשאין.

156 In ms. A: אילא.

157 Ms. A adds: תַּמָּן אָמְרִין בְּשֵׁם רַב. כָּאן בְּשֶׁנִּשְׁבַּע. כָּאן בְּשֶׁלֹּא נִשְׁבַּע. "There (in Babylonia) they say in the name of Rav . . ." which must mean that this is the received explanation in Babylonia to the exclusion of any other since *Rav* Jeremiah was a Babylonian. The same language is in the parallel *Baba Meṣi'a* 3:3 (fol. 8d), a text from the hand of a different editor.

158 Here, ms. A and the parallel *Baba Meṣi'a* 3:3 have an addition: רִבִּי יִרְמְיָה בָּעֵי. אִם בְּשֶׁנִּשְׁבַּע. הָיָה לוֹ לִשְׁתּוֹק וְלֹא לִישָּׁבַע. It would seem that this is an extraneous addition from the redaction of *Baba Meṣi'a*, since R. Jeremiah is reported below to have another question and his text here is ascribed there to R. Yose.

159 Added from ms. A and the parallel *Baba Meṣi'a* 3:3; missing in *editio princeps*.

160 From ms. A and the parallel *Baba Meṣi'a* 3:3; *editio princeps* גזול.

161 The reading of ms. A is intelligible: וְאִם לָאו לֹא הָיָה לוֹ לִשְׁתּוֹק "otherwise, he should not have to be quiet."

162 Reading from ms. A. *Editio princeps:* לְהוֹרוֹת "to instruct".

163 Both in ms. A and in *editio princeps* the reading is גילה.

164 Reading from ms. A. *Editio princeps:* מִסְפָּר "number".

165 In ms. A corrected מן הדה "from the following", the more idiomatic expression.

166 Mishnah *Baba Meṣi'a* 3:3; Tosephta *Yebamot* 14:2.

167 Since one understands from the Mishnah that the person was not sued but made the statement on his own initiative, one tells him that while the court could not force him to pay more than one mina and let the parties involved fight about the distribution, to assuage his conscience he has to give to each of the parties the amount they might be entitled to. The Babli concurs, *Baba Meṣi'a* 37a.

168 The expression כאן . . . כאן makes it difficult to know to which statement one refers. In the interpretation of R. David Fränkel (קרבן העדה), the Mishnah *Yebamot* refers to a case where there are witnesses to the robbery but they cannot identify the victim, but in *Baba Meṣi'a* there are no witnesses at all. In the interpretation of R. Moses Margalit (פני משה), the Mishnah *Baba Meṣi'a* refers to a case where there are witnesses to the robbery but they cannot identify the victim, but in *Yebamot* there are no witnesses at all. In the latter interpretation, the fact that the robber confessed makes him liable to pay every claim as a matter of law, not of ethics. The first interpretation is more acceptable.

169 In *Yebamot*, there are no claimants (they are silent), in *Baba Meṣi'a* there are no claimants (they talk). R. Ṭarphon must agree in the second case that he pays since if he does not want to pay he would have to swear that he owes nothing; since he does not know whether he owes, he

cannot swear.

170 If he swore falsely that he did no rob anything. R. Tarphon will agree that he has to satisfy each individual claim against him.

171 He immediately could have deposited the money claimed with the court and let the claimants go to court to get the money (Mishnah *Baba Qama* 9:7).

172 The remedy of R. Johanan works only if the robber can choose the court to which he confesses before he is sued and where he deposits the amount he owes.

173 If the court has to be the one to which the victims apply, the robber cannot forestall suits against himself and cannot free himself of responsibility by delivering restitution to a court convenient to himself.

174 The opinion of R. Simeon ben Eleazar is not recorded elsewhere. The Babli, 118b, throws out the Mishnah *Yebamot* in favor of a *baraita* (found in shortened form in Tosephta *Yebamot* 14:2) in the name of R. Simeon ben Eleazar, which reduces the disagreement of R. Aqiba with R. Tarphon to the case (a) of a consummated marriage and (b) of a witnessed robbery.

175 Then he would not have to pay.

176 He would have to pay only once.

177 The root of מתגר is Aramaic אגר "reward".

178 Obviously, the proof is not from this but from the second half of the Mishnah quoted: "I received a deposit of a mina from the father of one of you but I do not know which one of you it was ...".

(fol. 14c) **משנה יא**: רָאשָׁה שֶׁהָלְכָה הִיא וּבַעֲלָהּ לִמְדִינַת הַיָּם וּבְנָהּ עִמָּהֶם בָּאָה וְאָמְרָה מֵת בְּנִי וְאַחַר כָּךְ מֵת בַּעֲלִי נֶאֱמֶנֶת. מֵת בַּעֲלִי וְאַחַר כָּךְ מֵת בְּנִי אֵינָהּ נֶאֱמֶנֶת וְחוֹשְׁשִׁין לִדְבָרֶיהָ וְחוֹלֶצֶת וְלֹא מִתְיַיבֶּמֶת. נִיתַּן לִי בֵן בִּמְדִינַת הַיָּם אָמְרָה מֵת בְּנִי וְאַחַר כָּךְ בַּעֲלִי נֶאֱמֶנֶת מֵת בַּעֲלִי וְאַחַר כָּךְ בְּנִי אֵינָהּ נֶאֱמֶנֶת וְחוֹשְׁשִׁין לִדְבָרֶיהָ וְחוֹלֶצֶת וְלֹא מִתְיַיבֶּמֶת.

Mishnah 11: A woman went overseas with her husband and her son[179]; if she returns and says, "my husband died and after that my son died," she is to be believed[180]. "My son died and after that my husband died," she is not believed but one takes her words into account and she performs *ḥalîṣah* but is excluded from levirate[181]. "I had a son overseas," she says[180], "my son died and after him my husband," she is believed[181]; "my husband died and after that my son," she is not believed but one takes her words into account and she performs *ḥalîṣah* but is excluded from levirate[182].

179 If at the moment of her departure the husband had died, she would have been free to marry outside the family. She then returns alone.

180 Her testimony does not change her prior status.

181 Assuming the son was an only child, the husband would have died without issue and she would be required to be married in levirate. She is not believed to have changed her known status (in the absence of documentary proof). But since she forbade herself any marriage other than to the levir, she has to be freed by *ḥalîṣah*.

180 She left with her husband when the husband was childless; at her departure she was a potential candidate for levirate.

181 She did not change her status with this testimony since she asserts that the husband died childless.

182 Since she declares herself forbidden for levirate, the levir cannot force her into marriage.

(fol. 15b) **מתניתא:** נִיתַּן לִי בֵן בִּמְדִינַת הַיָּם. רִבִּי חֲנַנְיָה בְּעָא קוֹמֵי רִבִּי אִילָא. מָן תַּנָּא חוֹשְׁשִׁין לִדְבָרֶיהָ חוֹלֶצֶת. רִבִּי טַרְפוֹן דְּלֹא כְרִבִּי עֲקִיבָא. אָמַר לֵיהּ. דִּבְרֵי הַכֹּל הוּא הָכָא אוֹף רִבִּי עֲקִיבָה מוֹדֶה בָהּ. מַה בֵינָהּ לְקַדְמִייָתָא. הָכָא תֵימַר אֵינָהּ נֶאֱמֶנֶת. וְכָה תֵימַר. נֶאֱמֶנֶת. [185](בְּשֶׁיָּצְתָה מִכְּלָל הֵיתֵר לְיִיבּוּם. וְ)הֵן דְּתֵימַר. אֵינָהּ נֶאֱמֶנֶת. בְּשֶׁלֹּא יָצְתָה מִכְּלָל הֵיתֵר לְיִיבּוּם.

Mishnah: "I had a son overseas." Rebbi Ḥanania asked before Rebbi Hila: Who is the one who stated that one takes her words into account and she performs *ḥalîṣah*? Rebbi Tarphon, but not Rebbi Aqibah[183]! He said to him, it is the opinion of everybody and even Rebbi Aqiba agrees to it. What is the difference betweeen this statement and the first one[184]? There, you say that she is not to be believed. But here, you say that she is believed! (When she left as included[186] in the permission of levirate. But)[185] where you say that she is not believed, when she left and was not included in the permission of levirate.

183 This refers to their disagreement in Halakhah 6, where R. Aqiba puts on her the disabilities she is under if her words are true and those she would be under if her words were not true. It would be expected that he holds the same in this case.

In both sources, the name is spelled עקיבא, this babylonism must have been in the common *Vorlage*.

184 Why are the cases switched, she is believed if she says that the husband died before the son in the first case but disbelieved for the same statement in the second.

185 This sentence is missing in ms. A; the ms. probably is correct since the introduction "she is believed if . . ." is missing.

186 כלל is what in modern mathematics is called a *set*. When she left with her son, she was not a member of the set of women potentially obligated for levirate.

(fol. 14c) **משנה יב**: נִתַּן לִי יָבָם בִּמְדִינַת הַיָּם אָמְרָה מֵת בַּעֲלִי וְאַחַר כָּךְ מֵת יְבָמִי. יְבָמִי וְאַחַר כָּךְ בַּעֲלִי נֶאֱמֶנֶת. הָלְכָה הִיא וּבַעֲלָהּ וִיבָמָהּ לִמְדִינַת הַיָּם אָמְרָה מֵת בַּעֲלִי וְאַחַר כָּךְ מֵת יְבָמִי יְבָמִי וְאַחַר כָּךְ בַּעֲלִי אֵינָהּ נֶאֱמֶנֶת שֶׁאֵין הָאִשָּׁה נֶאֱמֶנֶת לוֹמַר. מֵת יְבָמִי. שֶׁתִּנָּשֵׂא. וְלֹא. מֵתָה אֲחוֹתִי. שֶׁתִּיכָּנֵס לְבֵיתוֹ. וְאֵין הָאִישׁ נֶאֱמָן לוֹמַר מֵת אָחִי שֶׁיְּיַבֵּם אִשְׁתּוֹ וְלֹא מֵתָה אִשְׁתִּי שֶׁיִּשָּׂא אֶת אֲחוֹתָהּ.

Mishnah 12: "A levir was given to me overseas;[187]" if she said "my husband died and after that my levir" [or] "my levir died and after that my husband", she is to be believed. If she, her husband[188], and her levir went overseas, if she said "my husband died and after that my levir" [or] "my levir died and after that my husband", she is not to be believed, since no woman is believed if she says "my levir died" that she might marry [outside the family] nor "my sister died" that she might enter his house. Also the husband is not to be believed if he says "my brother died" that he might marry his wife in levirate, nor "my wife died" that he might marry her sister[189].

187 Her father-in-law had a son unknown at the place of her previous residence. She left when it was assumed that there was no possible levirate because there was no levir even though her husband was childless.

188 Who was childless.

189 Cf. Notes 6, 89.

(fol. 15b) אָמַר רִבִּי יוֹסֵי. מַתְנִיתָא אָמְרָה כֵן שֶׁלֹּא עָשׂוּ זְכָרִים כִּנְקֵיבוֹת. דְּתַנִינָן תַּמָּן. שֶׁאֵינָהּ נֶאֱמֶנֶת לוֹמַר. מֵת יְבָמִי. תִּינָּשֵׂא. וְלֹא מֵתָה אֲחוֹתִי. שֶׁתִּיכָּנֵס לְבֵיתָהּ. מִפְּנֵי שֶׁאֵין לָהּ בָּנִים. אֲבָל אִם יֵשׁ לָהּ בָּנִים נֶאֱמֶנֶת.

[190]Rebbi Yose said, a Mishnah says that they did not treat the males as they treat the females, as we have stated there: "because she is not trusted if she says, my levir died, that she should be free to remarry, nor that her sister died, to enter her house." Because she has no children. But if she has children, she is trustworthy.

190 This is from Halakhah 4, Note 89.

האשה שהלך פרק ששה עשר

(fol. 15b) **משנה א:** הָאִשָּׁה שֶׁהָלַךְ בַּעֲלָהּ וְצָרָתָהּ לִמְדִינַת הַיָּם וּבָאוּ וְאָמְרוּ לָהּ מֵת בַּעֲלֵיךְ לֹא תִינָּשֵׂא וְלֹא תִתְיַיבֵּם עַד שֶׁתֵּדַע שֶׁמָּא מְעוּבֶּרֶת הִיא צָרָתָהּ. הָיְתָה לָהּ חָמוֹת אֵינָהּ חוֹשֶׁשֶׁת. יָצָאת מְלֵיאָה חוֹשֶׁשֶׁת. רִבִּי יְהוֹשֻׁעַ אוֹמֵר אֵינָהּ חוֹשֶׁשֶׁת.

Mishnah 1: If a woman's husband and her co-wife went overseas and people came and told her 'your husband died", she cannot remarry or perform *ḥalîṣah* until she has ascertained whether this co-wife was pregnant[1]. If she had a mother-in-law, she does not have to suspect[2]. If the latter left pregnant[3], she has to suspect; Rebbi Joshua says, she does not have to suspect[4].

1 She cannot marry outside the family for the husband might have died childless. She cannot marry the levir for there might be a child born overseas. The Babli, 119a, notes that the expression היא צרתה "this co-wife" implies that she does not have to inquire whether her husband took yet another wife overseas.

2 When she last saw her mother-in-law, her husband was the only son. If the mother-in-law is far away, she does not have to inquire whether in the meantime the latter had another son.

3 And now the whereabouts of the mother-in-law are not known; no notice of a brother born to her husband was received.

4 The reason is detailed in the Halakhah.

(fol. 15c) הָאִשָּׁה שֶׁהָלַךְ בַּעֲלָהּ וְצָרָתָהּ לִמְדִינַת הַיָּם.[5] רַב שָׁאִיל לְרִבִּי חִייָה רוֹבָה. וְתַמְתִּין שְׁלֹשָׁה וְתַחֲלוֹץ מִיַּד. מַה נַפְשָׁךְ. אִם בֶּן קַייָמָה הוּא לֹא נָגְעָה בָהּ חֲלִיצָה. אִם אֵינוֹ בֶן קַייָמָה הֲרֵי חֲלִיצָתָהּ בְּיָדָהּ. אָמַר לֵיהּ לֹא שָׁנוּ[6] שְׁלֹשָׁה

חֳדָשִׁים אֶלָּא אֶצְלָהּ. הָא אֵצֶל צָרָתָהּ כַּמָּה תַּמְתִּין. ט חֳדָשִׁים. וְתַחֲלוֹץ מִיָּד. מַה נַפְשָׁךְ. אִם בֶּן קַיְימָא הוּא הָא לֹא נָגְעָה בָהּ חֲלִיצָה. אִים אֵין בֶּן קַיְימָא הוּא הֲרֵי חֲלִיצָה בְיָדָהּ. אָתָא רִבִּי יְהוּדָה בְּשֵׁם רִבִּי אֶלְעָזָר בְּשֵׁם רִבִּי חִייָה רוּבָא. שֶׁלֹּא תְהֵא צְרִיכָה כְרוּז לִכְהוּנָּה.

"If a woman's husband and her co-wife went overseas". Rav asked the elder Rebbi Ḥiyya: Why can she not wait three months and then immediately perform *ḥalîṣah*? As the case may be, if there was a live birth, *ḥalîṣah* did not affect her. If there was no live birth, she has *ḥalîṣah* in her hand![7] He said to him: They taught "three months" only for herself. If so, how long does she have to wait for her co-wife? 9 months.[8] After that, could she not immediately perform *ḥalîṣah*? As the case may be, if there was a live birth, *ḥalîṣah* did not touch her. If there was no live birth, she has *ḥalîṣah* in her hand?[9] There came Rebbi Jehudah in the name of Rebbi Eleazar in the name of the elder Rebbi Ḥiyya[10]: That she would not need a proclamation with regard to priesthood[11].

5 Text from ms. A. *Editio princeps*: האשה שהלכה, a misquote from the preceding chapter.

6 Reading of ms. A. In *editio princeps* a misprint: שני.

7 The plain language of the Mishnah implies that the woman is permanently forbidden marriage and levirate until there is proof of her co-wife's status. This seems to be unreasonable since *ḥalîṣah* would solve every problem as explained by Rav.

8 Any *ḥalîṣah* while her co-wife is pregnant would be invalid; cf. the parallel discussion in Halakhah 4:1, Note 4.

9 In the Babli, 119b, this is the tradition of Ze'iri, student of Rav and Rebbi Joḥanan.

10 The name tradition is garbled. There is no mention in any other source of a R. Jehudah younger than R. Eleazar; the double "in the name of" is irregular. In ms. A, the reading is: יהודה בן כיני (?) ר' לעזר בשם ר' חייה רובה. An acceptable reading would be (ר') יהודה בר בוני ר' לעזר בשם ר' חייה רובה "Rebbi Jehudah bar Buni, Rebbi

Eleazar, in the name of the elder Rebbi Ḥiyya." In the Babli, 119b, the rule is ascribed to R. Ḥanina, the explanation to Abbai and Ḥanina bar Abin.

11 In effect, she is never permitted to marry as long as her situation is not cleared up. The Babli explains that the prohibition is permanent since if it should turn out that the co-wife had a live child overseas, there might be persons who know about the *ḥalîṣah* ceremony and the marriage to a Cohen but were not informed about the proclamation that the *ḥalîṣah* was void. These persons would then think that the rabbis do no longer equate a woman after *ḥalîṣah* with a divorcee. The Babli does not permit the woman to waive her right to marry a Cohen. The position of the Yerushalmi in that last case is not known. Cf. also Chapter 4, Note 5.

חֲבֵרַיָּא בְּשֵׁם רִבִּי יוֹחָנָן. טַעֲמוֹן דְּרַבָּנִן. כִּי יֵשְׁבוּ. בְּוַדַּאי לֹא בְסָפֵק.

The colleagues in the name of Rebbi Joḥanan[12]: The reason of the rabbis: "When [brothers] dwell," certainly, not in a case of doubt[13].

12 Text from ms. A.; missing in *editio princeps.*

13 This refers to the statement of the Mishnah that, if the husband had no known brother when he left, the widow does not have to inquire whether his faraway father-in-law had another son.

יָצְאת מְלֵיאָה חוֹשֶׁשֶׁת. שֶׁהוּא סָפֵק אֶחָד.[14] סָפֵק זָכָר סָפֵק נְקֵיבָה. סָפֵק[15] מְדִּבַר תּוֹרָה לְהַחֲמִיר. רִבִּי יְהוֹשֻׁעַ אוֹמֵר אֵינָהּ חוֹשֶׁשֶׁת. שֶׁהֵן שְׁנֵי סְפֵיקוֹת. סָפֵק זָכָר סָפֵק נְקֵיבָה. סָפֵק בֶּן קַיָּימָה סָפֵק אֵינוֹ בֶן קַיָּימָה. שְׁתֵּי סְפֵיקוֹת מִדִּבְרֵי תוֹרָה לְהָקֵל.

"If the latter left pregnant, she has to suspect," since there is one doubt, whether it was a male or a female. A doubt in biblical matters has to be resolved in a restrictive way[16]. "Rebbi Joshua says, she does not have to suspect," since there is a double doubt. There are doubts whether it was a male or a female, and whether it was a live or a still birth[17].

14 Reading of ms. A. *Editio princeps*: אחר.

15 Reading of ms. A; missing in *editio princeps*.

16 The Babli agrees to this principle, *Beṣah* 3b.

17 While the Babli agrees to this principle, *Qiddušin* 75a, it disagrees in this particular case since the probability of a still birth is rather small. It is argued that if the Yerushalmi reason were true, it could be applied to the case of the co-wife and then the woman left at home would be free to remarry. The Babli explains the position of R. Joshua that the woman was known to be free from levirate when her husband left. Since the probability that the mother-in-law gave birth to a live son is less than 50%, the known prior state remains in force because the probability that it remained in force (that either the mother-in-law had a baby girl who cannot be a levir, or there was a still birth, or a termination of pregnancy) is greater than 50%.

(fol. 15b) **משנה ב:** שְׁתֵּי יְבָמוֹת זוֹ אוֹמֶרֶת מֵת בַּעְלִי וְזוֹ אוֹמֶרֶת מֵת בַּעְלִי זוֹ אֲסוּרָה מִפְּנֵי בַּעְלָהּ שֶׁל זוֹ וְזוֹ אֲסוּרָה מִפְּנֵי בַּעְלָהּ שֶׁל זוֹ. לָזוֹ עֵדִים וְלָזוֹ אֵין עֵדִים אֶת שֶׁיֵּשׁ לָהּ עֵדִים אֲסוּרָה וְאֶת שֶׁאֵין לָהּ עֵדִים מוּתֶּרֶת. לָזוֹ בָנִים וְלָזוֹ אֵין בָּנִים אֶת שֶׁיֵּשׁ לָהּ בָּנִים מוּתֶּרֶת וְאֶת שֶׁאֵין לָהּ בָּנִים אֲסוּרָה. נִתְיַיבְּמוּ וּמֵתוּ יְבָמִין אֲסוּרוֹת לְהִינָּשֵׂא. רִבִּי לָעְזָר אוֹמֵר הוֹאִיל וְהוּתְּרוּ לַיְּבָמִין הוּתְּרוּ לְכָל־אָדָם.

Mishnah 2: If each one of two sisters-in-law[18] says "my husband died", each one is forbidden because of the other's husband[19]. If one has witnesses but the other has no witnesses, the one who has witnesses is forbidden but the one who has no witnesses is permitted[20]. If one has children but the other has no children, the one who has children is permitted[21] but the one who has no children is forbidden. If they married in levirate[22] but the levirs died[23], they are forbidden to remarry. Rebbi

Eleazar said, since they were permitted to the levirs, they became permitted to any man.

18 The wives of two brothers.

19 Each of them can testify that her husband is dead but her testimony is not accepted for her sister-in-law (Mishnah 15:4). Neither of them can marry outside the family until the death of her levir is confirmed by another source.

20 If the husband of the sister-in-law was the only levir, his death confirmed by witnesses releases his brother's widow from levirate.

21 She is forbidden for levirate.

22 There were other brothers in addition to the two husbands. Since each woman is believed when she declares to be a widow, she must be believed that she has the right to be married in levirate.

23 They died childless and there are no other brothers. For the rabbis, the situation is now that of the first case, that the death of the first two brothers is only asserted by the women, each of whom is excluded as source of information regarding her sister-in-law.

(fol. 15c) **מתניתא**: שְׁתֵּי יְבָמוֹת. לָזוֹ בָנִים [עֵדִים][24] וְלָזוֹ אֵין כְּלוּם. זוֹ נִיתֶּרֶת בְּבָנִים וְזוֹ נִיתֶּרֶת בְּעֵדֶיהָ.

Mishnah: [25]Two sisters-in-law, of whom one has children and witnesses but the other has neither. The first one is permitted by children, the other one by her witnesses[26].

24 Reading of ms. A; missing in *editio princeps*. The reading of ms. A is required by the next sentence.

25 A similar text in Tosephta 14:3. There is no quote from the Mishnah here.

26 The widow with children can remarry outside the family. The widow without witnesses is believed if she states that she is a widow. Since her levir's death is certified by witnesses, she is free to marry outside the family.

מַה טַעְמָא דְרִבִּי לְעָזָר. מִשּׁוּם שֶׁאֵינָהּ חֲשׁוּדָה לְקַלְקֵל [עַצְמָהּ וּלְקַלְקֵל צָרָתָהּ לְאַחַר זְמָן אוֹ מִשּׁוּם שֶׁאֵינָהּ חֲשׁוּדָה לְקַלְקֵל][27] צָרָתָהּ כָּל־עִיקָּר. נִישְׁמְעִינָהּ מִן

הָדָא. הָאִשָּׁה שֶׁהָלְכָה הִיא וּבַעֲלָהּ לִמְדִינַת הַיָּם. וּבָאתָה וְאָמְרָה. מֵת בַּעֲלִי. תִּינָּשֵׂא וְתִיטּוֹל כְּתוּבָּתָהּ וְצָרָתָהּ אֲסוּרָה. וְסָבְרִינָן מֵימַר. חֲשׁוּדָה הִיא לְקַלְקֵל אֶת עַצְמָהּ כְּדֵי שֶׁתְּקַלְקֵל צָרָתָהּ. וְלֵית רִבִּי לָעְזָר פְּלִיג. הֲוֵי לֵית טַעֲמָא וְלֹא מִשּׁוּם שֶׁאֵינָהּ חֲשׁוּדָה לְקַלְקֵל צָרָתָהּ כָּל־עִיקָּר. וְחָשׁ לוֹמַר שֶׁמָּא שִׁילַּח לָהּ גִּיטָּהּ מִמְּדִינַת הַיָּם. הַגַּע עַצְמָךְ שֶׁהָיָה כֹהֵן. אָמַר רִבִּי אַבָּא בְּרִבִּי זְמִנָא.[28] חֲשׁוּדָה הִיא לַעֲשׂוֹת כַּמָּה חֲלָלִים כְּדֵי לַעֲשׂוֹת בְּנֵי צָרָתָהּ מַמְזֵרִין.

What is the reason of Rebbi Eleazar[29]? Is it because she is not suspected to cause trouble [to herself in order later to cause trouble to her co-wife or because she is not suspected to cause any trouble] to her co-wife? Let us hear from the following: [30]"If a woman went overseas with her husband and returns and says 'my husband died', she can remarry and collect her *ketubah*, but her co-wife remains forbidden." We explain it, saying that she is suspected to cause trouble to herself in order to cause trouble to her co-wife, and Rebbi Eleazar does not disagree[31]. It is impossible that the reason be that she is not suspected to cause any trouble to her co-wife. We could suspect that perhaps her husband sent her a bill of divorce from overseas[32]. Think of it, what if her [next] husband was a Cohen[33]? Rebbi Abba bar Rebbi Zemina said, she is suspected to produce several desecrated children in order to make bastards of her co-wife's children.

27 Reading of ms. A; missing in *editio princeps*. The text of the *editio princeps* also makes sense.

28 Reading of ms. A; in *editio princeps*: ר' בא בר זימנא. Everywhere else the name is בר זמינא.

29 In ms. A and the Tosephta which parallels the Mishnah (14:3), the name everywhere is R. Eliezer. The abbreviation ר"א used by several medieval authors in quotes of the Mishnah usually refers to R. Eliezer.

30 Mishnah 15:7.

31 Halakhah 15:7.

32 If she remarries as a divorcee, she has not sinned even though in reality she is a divorcee. But if her co-wife remarries on her testimony, the

co-wife's children will be bastards born in adultery.

33 As a divorcee, it is sinful for her to marry a Cohen and her children will be desecrated from priesthood, but the marriage is valid. The Babli, 120a, dismisses the thought that a woman would willingly desecrate her children.

(fol. 15b) **משנה ג:** אֵין מְעִידִין אֶלָּא עַל פַּרְצוּף פָּנִים עִם הַחוֹטֶם אַף עַל פִּי שֶׁיֵּשׁ סִימָנִין בְּגִיפוֹ וּבְכֵלָיו. אֵין מְעִידִין אֶלָּא עַד שְׁלֹשָׁה יָמִים. וַאֲפִילוּ רָאוּהוּ מְגוּיָּיד וְצָלוּב עַל הַצְּלִיב וְהַחַיָּה אוֹכֶלֶת בּוֹ אֵין מְעִידִין אֶלָּא עַד שֶׁתֵּצֵא נַפְשׁוֹ.

Mishnah 3: One testifies only on the appearance of the face[34] with the nose[35], even though there may be marks on his body and his clothing[36]. One testifies only up to three days[37]. Even if one saw him cut up or crucified on the cross, or an animal eating of him, one testifies[38] only after he has stopped breathing.

34 Greek πρόσωπος, ὁ, πρόσωπον, τό, "face, front, mask, bust" (meanings also found in Hebrew and Aramaic), also in Greek "dramatic or legal person, portrait". Since the Yerushalmi expresses only long vowels by written letters, the spelling in the Mishnah would permit a vocalization of פַּרְצוּף but Mandaic פארצופא confirms the spelling pronunciation *parṣuf*.

35 Positive identification of a corpse is only accepted if based on the recognition of the face.

36 This and the following Mishnaiot are the basis of a novel by S. J. Agnon, והיה העקוב למישור, translated into German as: *Und das Krumme wird gerade* based on the misidentification of a corpse as that of the absent husband; cf. Note 154.

37 After that time, the body starts to decompose and positive identification is no longer possible.

38 To the fact of death. Before a person has stopped breathing, there is always a chance that he might be saved.

מתניתא: אֵין מְעִידִין אֶלָּא עַל פַּרְצוּף פָּנִים וכו'. רַב יְהוּדָה אָמַר.(fol. 15c) הַחוֹטֶם עִם הַלְּסָתוֹת. וְאַתְיָא דָמַר רִבִּי יִרְמְיָה בְשֵׁם רַב. הַכָּרַת פְּנֵיהֶם עָנְתָה בָם. זֶה הַחוֹטֶם. אָמַר רִבִּי[39] חִייָא בַּר בָּא. מָאן דְּבָעֵי דְּלָא מִתְחַכְּמָא יְהִיב אִיסְפְּלָנִי עַל נְחִירֵיהּ וְלָא מִתְחַכֵּם. כְּהָדָה. בְּיוֹמֵי דְאֶרְסְקִינָס מַלְכָּא הֲוַיָן צִיפּוֹרָאֵי מִתְבָּעִין וַהֲווֹן יְהָבִין אִיסְפְּלָנִי עַל נְחִירֵיהוֹן וְאִינּוּן לָא מִתְחַכְּמִין. וּבְסֵיפָא אִיתְמַר עֲלֵיהוֹן לִישָׁן בִּישׁ וְאִיתְצַיְּדוֹן כּוּלְּהוֹן מִן בִּידוֹ.

Mishnah: "One testifies only on the appearance of the face," etc. Rav Jehudah said, the nose with the mandibles[40]. This follows what Rebbi[41] Jeremiah said in the name of Rav: "The recognition of their faces testified about them[42]," that is the nose. Rebbi Ḥiyya bar Abba said, if somebody does not want to be recognized, he should put a patch[43] on his nostrils, then he will not be recognized. As in the following[44]: In the times of king Ursicinus[45], some people from Sepphoris were under arrest warrants. They put patches on their nostrils and were not recognized. Finally they were denunciated and all caught because of lies.

39 In the Babli, the nose and the forehead.

40 Reading of ms. A. *Editio princeps*: רב.

41 This is the reading of both sources. One might expect that the reading should be "Rav", referring to Rav's colleague in Babylonia rather than to a Galilean Amora some 100 years later. However, in the Babli, the same argument and verse are quoted by Abbai and/or Rav Cahana II, one generation after Rebbi Jeremiah.

42 *Is*. 3:9.

43 Greek σπλήνιον, Latin *splenium*, cf. *'Orlah* 3:1, Note 20.

44 This is an editorial comment, on what happened some 50 years after R. Ḥiyya bar Abba's death. The same text appears in *Soṭah* 9:3.

45 The legate of Caesar Gallus in Palestine, about the year 350. His oppressive regime lead to a revolt centered in Sepphoris.

כְּתִיב. וַיַּכּוּ בָהֶם אֲבִיָּה וְעַמּוֹ מַכָּה גְדוֹלָה מְאֹד. אָמַר רִבִּי אַבָּא בַּר כַּהֲנָא. שֶׁהֶעֱבִיר הַכָּרַת פְּנֵיהֶם שֶׁל יִשְׂרָאֵל. הָדָא הִיא דִכְתִיב הַכָּרַת פְּנֵיהֶם עָנְתָה בָם

וגו׳. זֶה הַחוֹטֶם. רִבִּי אִמִּי אָמַר. שֶׁהוֹשִׁיב עֲלֵיהֶם מִשְׁמָרוֹת שְׁלֹשָׁה יָמִים עַד שֶׁנִּתְקַלְקֵל צוּרָתָן. הָדָה הִיא דִכְתִיב עָצְמוּ לִי אַלְמְנוֹתָיו מֵחוֹל יַמִּים. וְתַנֵּי כֵן אֵין מְעִידִין אֶלָּא עַל פַּרְצוּף פָּנִים עִם הַחוֹטֶם. כְּתִיב וְלֹא עָצַר כֹּחַ יָרָבְעָם עוֹד בִּימֵי אֲבִיָּה וַיִּגְּפֵהוּ יי וַיָּמוֹת. אָמַר רִבִּי שְׁמוּאֵל. אַתְּ סָבוּר שֶׁהוּא יָרָבְעָם. אֵינָהּ אֶלָּא אֲבִיָּה. וְלָמָּה נִיגַּף. רִבִּי יוֹחָנָן אָמַר. עַל שֶׁחִישֵּׁד אֶת יָרָבְעָם בְּרַבִּים. הָדָה הִיא דִכְתִיב וְאַתֶּם הָמוֹן רָב וְעִמָּכֶם עֶגְלֵי הַזָּהָב אֲשֶׁר עָשָׂה לָכֶם יָרָבְעָם לֵאלֹהִים. רִבִּי שִׁמְעוֹן בֶּן לָקִישׁ[46] אָמַר. עַל שֶׁבִּיזָּה אֶת אֲחִיָּה הַשִּׁילוֹנִי רַבֵּיהּ. וְדָה הִיא דִכְתִיב וַיִּקָּבְצוּ אֵלָיו אֲנָשִׁים בְּנֵי בְלִיַּעַל עַל דְּצַוָּח לַאֲחִיָּה הַשִּׁילוֹנִי [בְּלִיַּעַל].[47] וְרַבָּנִין אָמְרִין. עַל יְדֵי שֶׁבָּאת עֲבוֹדָה זָרָה לְיָדוֹ וְלֹא בִיעֲרָהּ. הָדָה הִיא דִכְתִיב וַיִּרְדּוֹף אֲבִיָּה אַחֲרֵי יָרָבְעָם וְיִלְכּוֹד מִמֶּנּוּ עָרִים אֶת בֵּיתְאֵל וְאֶת בְּנוֹתֶיהָ. וּכְתִיב וַיָּשֶׂם אֶת הָאֶחָד בְּבֵיתאֵל וְאֶת הָאֶחָד נָתַן בְּדָן.

It is written: "Abijah and his people inflicted a very great slaughter on them[48]." Rebbi Abba bar Cahana said, he destroyed the face recognition of the men of Israel. That is what is written, "the recognition of their faces testified about them," etc. That refers to the nose. Rebbi Immi said, he put up guards for three days until appearance was disfigured. That is what is written: "Your widows are more for me than the sand of the oceans[49]." It was stated in this respect: One testifies only on the appearance of the face with the nose. It is written: "Jeroboam was powerless for the rest of Aijah's days; the Eternal smote him and he died.[50]" Rebbi Samuel[51] said you think that this refers to Jeroboam, but it is Abijah[52]. Why was he smitten? Rebbi Joḥanan said, because he insulted Jeroboam in public[53]. That is what is written: "You are a great multitude and with you are the golden calves that Jeroboam made for you as gods." Rebbi Simeon ben Laqish said, because he denigrated his teacher Aḥijah from Shiloh. That is what is written: "And men, rascals, joined him,[54]" that he called Aḥijah from Shiloh a rascal. But the rabbis say, because an idol fell into his hand and he did not destroy it, that is what is written: "Abijah pursued Jeroboam and took from him cities, Beth El and its dependencies . . .[55]" and it is written: "He set up one in Beth El and one he dedicated in Dan.[56]"

46 Reading of ms. A. *Editio princeps* has the Babli form Resh Laqish.

47 From ms. A; missing in *editio princeps*.

48 *2Chr.* 13:13. The biblical text reads: וַיַּכּוּ בָהֶם אֲבִיָּה וְעַמּוֹ מַכָּה רַבָּה.

49 Since the slain warriors could no longer be identified, their widows could never remarry according to rabbinic rules.

50 *2Chr.* 13:20.

51 In *Gen. rabba* 65:16, 73:4, R. Samuel bar Naḥman. He and the authors quoted earlier attribute Abijah's early death to his mutilation of the bodies of the slain.

52 Abijah was king for only 3 years and must have died shortly after the battle; Jeroboam died two years after Abijah (*1K.* 15:25).

53 In the Babli, *Sanhedrin* 101b, R. Joḥanan is reported to have said that Jeroboam was punished for insulting Solomon in public.

54 *2Chr.* 13:7. The text there reads וַיִּקָּבְצוּ עָלָיו אֲנָשִׁים רֵקִים בְּנֵי בְלִיַּעַל "and loiterers, rascals, joined him."

55 *2Chr.* 13:19.

56 *1K.* 12:20.

אַף עַל פִּי שֶׁיֵּשׁ בְּגוּפוֹ וּבְכֵלָיו. וְלֹא כֵן תַּנֵּי. מְנַיִן לְאָחִיךָ שֶׁטָּעָה אַתָּה מַחֲזִירוֹ בֵּין בְּגוּפוֹ בֵּין בְּכֵילָיו. שַׁנְייָא הִיא שֶׁהַסִּימָנִין דַּרְכָּן לְהִשְׁתַּנּוֹת.

"Even though there are [marks] on his body and his clothing." Did one not state: From where that if your fellow man is lost, you return him both body and property[57]? There is a difference, because marks are apt to change.

57 The verse to which this refers is not indicated; it probably refers to *Deut.* 22:2 where the obligation to return a find is extended to include helping a person who is lost, since the end of the verse may be read "return him to himself." The essence of the verse is interpreted to mean that the obligation to return property exists only after the person who claims to be the owner was examined as to the validity of this claim (*Sifry Deut.* 223;

Mishnah *Baba Meṣi'a* 2:7); in *Midrash Tannaïm* (*Midrash Haggadol Deut*, ed. S. Fisch, p. 486) the implication is that one is required the look after the medical needs of indigents and travelers.. These sources imply that examination of marks on bodies and property is accepted in biblical law. Then the question is how the Mishnah here can declare this kind of investigation as invalid. The answer given here (and in the Babli, 120b and *Baba Meṣi'a* 27b) is that after death, bodily marks will rapidly change. The Babli in *Baba Meṣi'a* adds that clothing or documents found on a corpse are no proofs of identity since they may belong to someone else.

כֵּינִי מַתְנִיתָא. אֵין מְעִידִין אֶלָּא עַד לְאַחַר שְׁלֹשָׁה יָמִים. רִבִּי בָּא[58] בְּשֵׁם רַב פַּפַּי רִבִּי יְהוֹשֻׁעַ דְּסוּכְנִין בְּשֵׁם רִבִּי לֵוִי. כָּל־תְּלָתָא יוֹמִין נַפְשָׁא טַיְיסָא עַל גּוּפָא. סָבְרָה דְהִיא חוֹזֶרֶת לְגַוָּהּ. כֵּיוָן דְּהִיא חָמִית לֵיהּ דְּאִשְׁתַּנֵּי זִיוְהוֹן דְּאַפּוֹי הִיא שָׁבְקָא לֵיהּ וְאָזְלָה.[59] מִן תְּלָתָא יוֹמִין וּלְהַלָּן הַכֶּרֶס נִבְקַעַת עַל פָּנָיו וְאוֹמֶרֶת לוֹ. הֵילָךְ מַה שֶׁגָּזַלְתָּ וְחָמַסְתָּ. רִבִּי חַגַּי בְּשֵׁם רִבִּי יֹאשִׁיָּה מַיְיתֵי לָהּ מֵהָדָה קְרָא וְזֵרִיתִי פֶרֶשׁ עַל פְּנֵיכֶם וַאֲפִילוּ פֶּרֶשׁ חַגֵּיכֶם. בְּאוֹתָהּ שָׁעָה אַךְ בְּשָׂרוֹ עָלָיו יִכְאָב וְנַפְשׁוֹ עָלָיו תֶּאֱבָל.

So is the Mishnah: "One testifies only up to *after* three days[60]." Rebbi Abba in the name of Rav Pappai, Rebbi Joshua from Suknin in the name of Rebbi Levi: During the first three days, the soul hovers over the body because she thinks that she will return to it[61]. Once she sees that the splendor of his face changes after three days, she abandons him and goes away. After three days, the belly breaks open in his face and says to him, there is what you have robbed and extorted. Rebbi Haggai in the name of Rebbi Joshia brings it from that verse[62]: "I shall scatter your stomachs' contents in your faces," even "your holidays' stomach contents." At that moment, [63]"but his flesh will hurt him, his soul will mourn for him."

58 Reading of ms. A. *Editio princeps*: ר' בריה ורב פפי

59 Reading of ms. A. *Editio princeps*: ואלזא ליה

60 One testifies that the person was identified within a full 72 hours.

61 In the Babli, *Šabbat* 152b, the verse from Job quoted at the end of this sermon is taken as proof that the soul remembers this world until all flesh is decomposed.

62 *Ma.* 2:3.

63 *Job* 14:22.

מתניתין. וַאֲפִילוּ רָאוּהוּ מְגוּיָּיד. אֲנִי אוֹמֵר. בְּחֶרֶב מְלוּבֶּנֶת נִכְוָה וְחָיָה. וְצָלוּב עַל הַצְּלִיבָה.[64] אוֹמֵר אֲנִי. מַטְרוֹנָה עָבְרָה עָלָיו וּפְדָאָתוֹ. וְהַחַיָּה אוֹכֶלֶת בּוֹ. אֲנִי אוֹמֵר. נִתְרַחֲמוּ עָלָיו מִן הַשָּׁמַיִם. נָפַל לְבוֹר אֲרָיוֹת אֵין מְעִידִין עָלָיו. אוֹמֵר אֲנִי. נַעֲשָׂה לוֹ נִיסִּים כְּדָנִיֵּאל. נָפַל לְכִבְשָׁן הָאֵשׁ אֵין מְעִידִין עָלָיו. אוֹמֵר אֲנִי. נַעֲשָׂה לוֹ נִיסִּים כַּחֲנַנְיָה מִישָׁאֵל וַעֲזַרְיָה. נָפַל לְבוֹר מָלֵא נְחָשִׁים וְעַקְרַבִּים אֵין מְעִידִין עָלָיו. רִבִּי יְהוּדָה בֶּן בָּבָא אוֹמֵר. (fol. 15d) אוֹמֵר אֲנִי. חַבָּר הָיָה. נָפַל לְיוֹרָה בֵּין שֶׁל מַיִם וּבֵין שֶׁל שֶׁמֶן אֵין מְעִידִין עָלָיו. רִבִּי אַבָּא אָמַר. שֶׁל שֶׁמֶן מְעִידִין עָלָיו. שֶׁל מַיִם אֵין מְעִידִין עָלָיו.

Mishnah: "Even if one saw him cut up," I say he was burned by a red hot lance and survived[65]. "Or crucified on the cross," I say a noble lady passed by and redeemed him. "Or an animal was eating of him," I say that in Heaven they had mercy on him[66].

If he fell into a lion's den one does not testify about him[67], I say that miracles happened for him as they did for Daniel.

If he fell into a fiery oven one does not testify about him[68], I say that miracles happened for him as they did for Ḥanaiah, Mishael and Azariah.

If he fell into a cistern full of snakes and scorpions one does not testify about him; Rebbi Jehudah ben Baba said, I say he was a snake charmer[69].

If he fell into a boiling vat of water or oil, one does not testify about him. Rebbi Abba[70] said, of oil one testifies, of water one does not testify[71].

64 Reading of ms. A. *Editio princeps*: צלוב.

65 It is recognized that not the wound is the main danger but the infection by a dirty lance or sword. The Babli, 120b, quotes Tosephta 14:2 where R. Simeon ben Eleazar holds that even if wounded by a dirty instrument one may burn away the infected flesh so that the victim can survive. The position of the Yerushalmi is quoted there by Rava; cf. Chapter 1, Note 19.

66 It is known that animals obey the commandments of Heaven; cf. *1K*. 13:28.

67 Without seeing that the person is dead. The same statement is in Babli 121a/Tosephta 14:4.

68 In Babli 121a/Tosephta 14:4, "one testifies about him".

69 In Babli 121a/Tosephta 14:4: "If he fell into a cistern full of snakes and scorpions one testifies about him; Rebbi Jehudah ben Bathyra said, one takes into consideration that he might be a snake charmer." In the Yerushalmi version it is not clear why R. Jehudah ben Baba has to be mentioned if nobody disagrees with him; but both sources agree that one does not testify and the text cannot be amended.

70 In a few Medieval authors he is quoted as R. Aḥa, the Tanna who is quoted in Babli/Tosephta.

71 In Babli/Tosephta (*loc. cit.*) the discussion is about vats of oil and wine, where R. Aḥa holds that the overflow of wine caused by the human's drop into the vat might extinguish the flames. The majority disagrees since the alcohol in the wine acts as fuel. The Babli might agree with the Yerushalmi in the case of a vat of water.

(fol. 15b) **משנה ד:** רִבִּי יוּדָה בֶן בָּבָא אוֹמֵר. לֹא כָל־הָאָדָם וְלֹא כָל־הַמְּקוֹמוֹת וְלֹא כָל־הַשָּׁעוֹת שָׁווֹת. נָפַל בַּמַּיִם בֵּין שֶׁיֵּשׁ לָהֶן סוֹף בֵּין שֶׁאֵין לָהֶן סוֹף אִשְׁתּוֹ אֲסוּרָה. אָמַר רִבִּי מֵאִיר מַעֲשֶׂה בְאֶחָד שֶׁנָּפַל לְבוֹר הַגָּדוֹל וְעָלָה אַחַר שְׁלֹשָׁה יָמִים. אָמַר רִבִּי יוֹסֵי מַעֲשֶׂה בְסוּמָא שֶׁיָּרַד לִטְבּוֹל בִּמְעָרָה וְיָרַד מוֹשְׁכוֹ אַחֲרָיו וְשָׁהוּ כְדֵי שֶׁתֵּצֵא נַפְשָׁם וְהִשִּׂיאוּ אֶת נְשׁוֹתֵיהֶן. וְשׁוּב מַעֲשֶׂה בְעַסְיָא בְּאֶחָד שֶׁשִּׁילְשְׁלוּהוּ לַיָּם וְלֹא עָלָה בְיָדָם אֶלָּא רַגְלוֹ אָמְרוּ חֲכָמִים מִן הָאַרְכּוּבָּה וּלְמַעְלָה תִּינָּשֵׂא מִן הָאַרְכּוּבָּה וּלְמַטָּה לֹא תִינָּשֵׂא.

Mishnah 4: Rebbi Judah ben Baba says, not all people nor all places nor all times are the same[72]. If he fell into water, both enclosed and open, his wife is forbidden[73]. Rebbi Meïr said, if happened that someone fell into a large cistern and came up after three days[74]. Rebbi Yose said, it happened with a blind man who went to immerse himself in a cave, and his guide went after him, they stayed there the time to die [from drowning] and they permitted their wives to remarry[75]. It also happened in Assos[76] that one lowered a person into the sea and only his leg was recovered. The Sages said, if from the knee and higher, she can remarry[77], from lower than the knee she cannot remarry.

72 This refers to the end of the preceding Mishnah, that one testifies only within three days from the time of death. Both the Yerushalmi and the Babli tend to consider R. Jehudah ben Baba's statement as a restriction, that under some circumstances the time available for identification is less than three days.

73 This is the statement of R. Meïr. The other authorities permit the widow to remarry if the husband drowned in an enclosed body of water: a lake, or a cistern, or a cave.

74 A cistern is an enclosed container of water. If it is possible to survive in water for three days, then one can never assume that a person drowned unless his corpse was found.

75 This proves that practice does not follow R. Meïr in enclosed bodies of water.

76 Cf. *Kilaim* 9, Note 128.

77 An animal, which has lost a part of a leg that included the knee, is considered *ṭerefa*, unfit for human consumtion since it is as good as dead. The Mishnah extends the principle to humans that any wound or deficiency which makes an animal unfit for human consumption, if found in a human proves that that human must die unless immediate medical attention can be given.

(fol. 15d) רִבִּי יוּדָה בֶן בָּבָא. רִבִּי זְעִירָא רִבִּי חֲנַנְאֵל בְּשֵׁם רַב. הֲלָכָה כְרִבִּי יוּדָה בֶן בָּבָא. מִילֵּיהוֹן דְּרַבָּנִין פְּלִיגִין. דָּמַר רִבִּי יִרְמְיָה. מַעֲשֶׂה בְאֶחָד שֶׁנָּפַל לְיַרְדֵּן וְעָלָה לְאַחַר שִׁבְעָה עָשָׂר יוֹם. וְהִכִּירוּ שֶׁצִּפָּרְתוֹ הַצִּינָּה וְהִשִּׂיאוּ אֶת אִשְׁתּוֹ.

"Rebbi Judah ben Baba." Rebbi Ze'ira, Rebbi Ḥananel in the name of Rav: Practice follows Rebbi Judah ben Baba. The words of the rabbis disagree, since Rebbi Jeremiah said that it happened that someone fell into the Jordan and surfaced after seventeen days when he was recognized because the cold had shrunk him[78] so that they permitted his wife to remarry[79].

78 Following Rashba (commentary to Babli 120a) who reads צפדתו. *Maggid Mishneh* (on Maimonides, *Gerušin* 13:22) reads צרפתו "refined him".

79 The Babli, 121a, quotes a parallel ruling by Rava (cf. Chapter 1, Note 19) which does not mention the frigidity of the water as cause.

נָפַל לַמַּיִם בֵּין שֶׁיֵּשׁ לַהֶן סוֹף בֵּין שֶׁאֵין לָהֶן סוֹף אִשְׁתּוֹ אֲסוּרָה. דִּבְרֵי רִבִּי מֵאִיר. וַחֲכָמִים אוֹמְרִים. מַיִם שֶׁאֵין לָהֶם סוֹף אִשְׁתּוֹ אֲסוּרָה. שֶׁיֵּשׁ לָהֶם סוֹף אִשְׁתּוֹ מוּתֶּרֶת. אָמַר רִבִּי מֵאִיר. מַעֲשֶׂה שֶׁנָּפַל לְבוֹר הַגָּדוֹל וְעָלָה אַחַר שְׁלֹשָׁה יָמִים. אָמְרוּ לוֹ. אֵין מַזְכִּירִין מַעֲשֵׂה נִיסִּים. אָמַר רִבִּי. מַעֲשֶׂה בִשְׁנַיִם שֶׁיָּרְדוּ לִכְמוֹר מִכְמָרוֹת לַיַּרְדֵּן. לְעִיתּוֹתֵי עֶרֶב.[80] רָאָה אֶחָד מְחִילָה שֶׁל דָּגִים וְנִכְנַס לְתוֹכָהּ. וּבִקֵּשׁ לָצֵאת לֹא הָיָה מוֹצֵא[81] פִּיתְחָהּ שֶׁל מְעָרָה. וּבָא חֲבֵירוֹ וְעָמַד עַל פִּתְחָהּ שֶׁל מְעָרָה וְשָׁהָא כְדֵי שֶׁתֵּצֵא נַפְשׁוֹ וּבָא וְהִגִּיד בְּתוֹךְ בֵּיתוֹ. וּבְשַׁחֲרִית זָרְחָה הַחַמָּה וְהִכִּיר פִּתְחָהּ שֶׁל מְעָרָה וְיָצָא וּבָא וּמָצָא הֶסְפֵּד[82] קָשׁוּר בְּתוֹךְ בֵּיתוֹ. אָמַר רִבִּי עֲקִיבָה. מַעֲשֶׂה שֶׁעָשִׂיתִי מְפָרֵשׁ בְּיָם הַגָּדוֹל וְרָאִיתִי סְפִינָה אַחַת שֶׁשָּׁקְעָה בַּיָּם וְהָיִיתִי מִצְטָעֵר עַל תַּלְמִיד חָכָם אֶחָד שֶׁהָיָה בְתוֹכָהּ. וּכְשֶׁבָּאתִי לְמַגִּיזָה שֶׁל קַפּוֹדְקִיָּא וְהִתְחִיל מְקַדְּמֵינִי וְשׁוֹאֵל לִי שְׁאֵלוֹת נוּמְתִי לוֹ. הֵיאַךְ פְּלַטְתָּהּ. נוּמֶה לִי. רִבִּי. טְרָפַנִי גַּל לַחֲבֵירוֹ וַחֲבֵירוֹ לַחֲבֵירוֹ עַד שֶׁהֱקִיאָנִי לַיַּבָּשָׁה. בְּאוֹתָהּ שָׁעָה אָמַרְתִּי. גְּדוֹלִים דִּבְרֵי חֲכָמִים שֶׁאָמְרוּ. מַיִם שֶׁאֵין לָהֶן סוֹף אִשְׁתּוֹ אֲסוּרָה. מַיִם שֶׁיֵּשׁ לָהֶם סוֹף אִשְׁתּוֹ מוּתֶּרֶת.

"If he fell into water, both enclosed and open, his wife is forbidden, the words of Rebbi Meïr. But the Sages say, in open waters his wife is forbidden, in enclosed waters, his wife is permitted."[83] Rebbi Meïr said, it happened that someone fell into a large cistern and came up after three days. They said to him, one does not mention wonders[84].

Rebbi said, it happened that two went to put fish nets into the Jordan in the evening. One of them saw a fish cave and entered it. When he wanted to leave, he was unable to find the cave's entrance. His colleague waited at the entrance of the cave so long that he would be dead; he returned and reported to his house. Next morning when the sun shone, the man recognized the entrance of the cave, left, and found his house in mourning[85].

Rebbi Aqiba said, It happened that I was traveling on the ocean that I saw a ship sinking. I was sorry for a student Sage who was on that ship. When I came to Kappadocian Mazaga he greated me and asked me questions. I said to him, my son, how did you escape? He told me, Rabbi, one wave tore me to another, and another to another, until it vomited me[86] onto dry land. Then I said, how great are the words of the Sages who said, in open waters his wife is forbidden, in enclosed waters, his wife is permitted[87].

80 Reading of Ms. A. *Editio princeps*: לציתותי.

81 Reading of Ms. A. *Editio princeps*: מוציא.

82 Reading of Ms. A. *Editio princeps*: הספר.

83 The same text in Babli 121a, Tosephta 14:5.

84 The same text in Babli 121b. Wonders should not be considered in writing regulations (and anyhow, the widow is not permitted to remarry before 30 days have elapsed). In the opinion of the Babli, the wonder was that he survived three days without sleep. The Amoraic opinion is that there is no wonder since one may survive with occasional naps without drowning.

85 Babli 121a, Tosephta 14:6.

86 From *Jonah* 2:11.

87 Babli 121a, Tosephta 14:5.

אָמַר רִבִּי אַבָּהוּ. אִם הָיָה הַיָּם גַּלֵּינֵי וְהִבִּיט לְאַרְבַּע רוּחוֹתָיו וְרָאָה שֶׁאֵין שָׁם בְּרִייָה. מַשִּׂיאִין אֶת אִשְׁתּוֹ.

Rebbi Abbahu said, if the ocean was quiet[88], he looked around in all directions and saw that no creature was there, one lets his wife remarry[89].

88 Greek γαλήνη, ἡ "stillness of the sea". In Erubin 4:1 (fol. 21d) הים גלנו, Greek γαληνός, όν "calm (adj.)".

89 In the Babli, 121a, this is the definition of "enclosed waters", that from one point one can see the lake shore all around. In the discussion there, the anonymous editors agree that even a larger lake can be considered enclosed if at the time of the accident there was absolute calm.

וְשׁוּב מַעֲשֶׂה בְעַסְיָא בְּאֶחָד שֶׁשִּׁילְשְׁלוּהוּ הַיָּם וְלֹא עָלָה בְיָדָם אֶלָּא רַגְלוֹ. תַּנֵּי. רָצוּ לַחֲתוֹךְ סְפוֹגִים וּבָאוּ וּמָצְאוּ אוֹתוֹ שׁוּלְחָנִי בְעַכּוֹ. רִבִּי חַגַּי בָּעֵי קוֹמֵי רִבִּי יוֹסֵי. לֹא מִסְתַּבְּרָא נוֹתְנִין לוֹ שָׁהוּת כְּדֵי טְרֵיפָה. אָמַר לֵיהּ. אַף אֲנָא סָבוּר כֵּן.

"It also happened in Assos that one lowered a person into the sea and only his leg was recovered." It was stated: They wanted to cut sponges and found that banker in Acco[90]. Rebbi Ḥaggai asked before Rebbi Yose: Is it not reasonable that one allows time for him as for a torn animal[91]? He answered him, that is my opinion also.

90 Apparently, after a long time the remains of a banker who had disappeared at Assos on the Aegean sea were found by sponge divers near Acco on the Mediterranean.

91 Since the Mishnah states that a human can be presumed dead if he sustains a wound that would make an animal "torn" and unfit for consumption, it should be clear that this can be stated only after the wounded person has disappeared for at least a full 12 months since an animal is declared to be "torn" if it cannot possible survive a full 12 months. This is the interpretation of Don Vidal de Tolosa (מגיד משנה) and R. Isaiah II of Trani (ריא"ז). R. Joseph Caro (כסף משנה) holds that a human might survive more than 12 months (Maimonides, *Gerušin* 13:13) but in his Code (*Even Ha'ezer* 17:32) he follows Don Vidal.

(fol. 15b) **משנה ה:** אֲפִילוּ שָׁמַע מִן הַנָּשִׁים אוֹמְרוֹת מֵת אִישׁ פְּלוֹנִי דַּיּוֹ. רִבִּי יוּדָה אוֹמֵר אֲפִילוּ שָׁמַע מִן הַתִּינוֹקוֹת אוֹמְרִים הֲרֵי אָנוּ הוֹלְכִין לִסְפּוֹד וְלִקְבּוֹר אֶת אִישׁ פְּלוֹנִי בֵּין מִתְכַּוֵּן וּבֵין שֶׁאֵינוֹ מִתְכַּוֵּין. רִבִּי יוּדָה בֶּן בָּבָא אוֹמֵר בְּיִשְׂרָאֵל עַד שֶׁיְּהֵא מִתְכַּוֵּן וּבְגוֹי אִם הָיָה מִתְכַּוֵּן אֵין עֵדוּתוֹ עֵדוּת.

Mishnah 5: It is sufficient even if somebody heard women say, the man X died[92]. Rebbi Jehudah said, even if he heard children say, we go to lament and bury X, whether intentional or unintentional. Rebbi Jehudah ben Baba said, if he is a Jew, only if he intends [to testify][93]; but if a Gentile intends to testify, it is no testimony[94].

92 A woman can be permitted to remarry on the basis of hearsay testimony based on statements overheard from people who themselves would not be accepted as witnesses.

93 Only if he knows the consequences of his testimony and is presumed to be as accurate as possible.

94 He is suspected of ulterior motives; *Ps.* 144:8,11.

(fol. 15d) **הלכה ה**[95]: אֲפִילוּ שָׁמַע מִן הַנָּשִׁים. שָׁמַע קוֹל הַמְקוֹנְנוֹת מְיַבְּבָתוֹ בֵּין הַמֵּתִים אֵין עֵדוּת גָּדוֹל מִזּוֹ. מִקּמְּנְטָרִיסֵי הַמֶּלֶךְ. מֵת פְּלוֹנִי נֶהֱרַג פְּלוֹנִי. אֵין מַשִּׂיאִין אֶת אִשְׁתּוֹ. מִבֵּית דִּין שֶׁל יִשְׂרָאֵל.[96] מֵת פְּלוֹנִי נֶהֱרַג פְּלוֹנִי. מַשִּׂיאִין אֶת אִשְׁתּוֹ.

Halakhah 5: "Even if somebody heard women." If one heard lamenting women eulogizing him among the dead, there is no better testinony than that. From the king's *commentariensis*[97], "X died, X was killed", one does not let his wife remarry. From a Jewish court[98], "X died, X was killed", one lets his wife remarry.

95 From ms. A.

96 From ms. A. *Editio princeps*: שלישי "a third party". Cf. Note 98.

97 Latin *commentariensis* "one who makes out a list of prisoners" (*Cod. Just.* 9,4,4). His certification that a certain person convicted of a capital crime appears on his list is insufficient

since this might only indicate the civil death of the person, *viz.*, that from the emperor's prison the man was sold into slavery.

98 As indicated in Note 96, this reading is from ms. A; it is suspect since it appears in the Babli, *Giṭṭin* 28b. The reading was conjectured by the earlier commentators on basis of the Babli. (One ms. of *Giṭṭin* reads: "If one heard from a Jewish judge," cf. M. S. Feldblum, *Tractate Giṭṭin*, New York 1966). Both Babli readings make sense only if one assumes that the *baraita* dates at the latest to the first Century C. E. as detailed in the last Mishnah, before hearsay evidence became acceptable. But then the part dealing with the king's secretary of prisons also would not represent current practice. The difficulty the Babli has with explaining the rejection of indications from a government secretary and the text of the Yerushalmi here make it clear that both Talmudim accept the *baraita* as reflecting practice.

Therefore, the reading "third party court", while rejected by all commentators and questioned by the Academy of the Hebrew Language, seems to be the preferable one, appearing as, but not being, *lectio difficilior.* If we accept the reading, the evidence presented is still hearsay evidence.

אָבַד פְּלוֹנִי נַתְרֵי[99] פְּלוֹנִי אֵינוֹ בָעוֹלָם. אָבַד פְּלוֹנִי. אֵינָה אֲמַר. רְבַק מִן עָלְמָא. נַתְרֵי פְלוֹנִי. אֲנָא אֲמַר. אַתְרִין פְּלוֹנִי מַאֲכָל. פְּלוֹנִי אֵינוֹ בָעוֹלָם. טִיפַּח רוּחֵיהּ עֲלֵיהּ. שֶׁקָּעָא סְפִינָתוֹ בַיָּם. אַתְיָא כְּהָדָה דָמַר רַבָּא בַּר זַבְדָּא בְשֵׁם רַב. מַעֲשֶׂה בְּאַבָּא סִימַיי שֶׁשָּׁקְעָא סְפִינָתוֹ בַיָּם וְהוּא לֹא הָיָה בְתוֹכָהּ וְהָכָה כֵן.

X was lost, X was shaken off, X is not in the world[100]. "X was lost," I say he was embarrassed[101]. "X was shaken off," I say that X vomited his food[102]. "X is not in the world," he is lost in tought. "His ship sank in the sea;" that parallels what Rebbi Abba bar Zavida said in the name of Rav: It happened that Abba Simai's ship sank in the sea but he was not on it; here it is the same.

99 In the *editio princeps*, the statements appear twice, first as אָבַד פְּלוֹנִי נֶהֱרַג פְּלוֹנִי and then as given in the text. Ms. A has only the text as

given. In the entire paragraph, the spelling follows ms. A.

100 It is shown that these expressions do not necessarily imply that X is dead; his wife cannot remarry.

101 Arabic ربك.

102 He was sick and could not keep down his food.

אֵיזוֹ הִיא מִתְכַּוֵּין. רִבִּי יוֹחָנָן אוֹמֵר. כָּל־שֶׁמַּזְכִּירִין לוֹ אִשָּׁה. רִבִּי שִׁמְעוֹן בֶּן לָקִישׁ אָמַר. כָּל־שֶׁשּׁוֹאֲלִין אוֹתוֹ וְהוּא מֵשִׁיב. אָמַר רִבִּי חַגַּי לְרִבִּי יְהוֹשֻׁעַ בֶּן לֵוִי. זָכוּר רִבִּי בִּשְׁלֹשִׁין[103] וְכַמָּה זְקֵינִים שֶׁהָיוּ מַתְרִיסִין[104] כְּנֶגֶד רִבִּי הוֹשַׁעְיָה בְּיַד לְמֶעֱבַד כְּהָדָא דְרִבִּי שִׁמְעוֹן בֶּן לָקִישׁ וְהוּא לֹא מְקַבֵּל עָלָיו.

What means "intentional"? Rebbi Joḥanan said, anytime one mentions a woman[105]. Rebbi Simeon ben Laqish said, anybody one asks and he responds[106]. Rebbi Ḥaggai said to Rebbi Joshua ben Levi, does the Rabbi remember that [107]thirty and some Elders were up in arms against Rebbi Hoshaiah to follow the rule of Rebbi Simeon ben Laqish but he did not accept it[108]?

103 Reading of ms. A. *Editio princeps*: בשלישי "in the third.

104 Here ends ms. A.

105 If in a conversation one mentions any woman and somebody says, speaking of women I remember that here is a woman who became a widow and she does not know it yet. Such a statement is acceptable if made by a Jew but not by a Gentile.

106 In the Babli, 121b, R. Simeon ben Laqish states that the testimony of the Gentile is accepted if he wants to tell about the death of Mr. X if he did not know that X was married and that his testimony will let the widow remarry. R. Joḥanan points out that the case quoted here by R. Ḥaggai that R. Simeon ben Laqish's position was not accepted. The Babli accepts the Gentile only if he tells his story without ulterior motives.

107 In the Babli, 121b, the argument was with 85 Elders supporting what in the next generation would become R. Simeon ben Laqish's position.

108 The common position of R. Joḥanan and R. Hoshaia certainly defines practice, even against a majority of dissenting Elders.

רַב יְהוּדָה בְשֵׁם רַב. אֵין הֲלָכָה כְּרִבִּי יְהוּדָה בֶּן בָּבָא בְּיִשְׂרָאֵל. וּמִילֵּיהוֹן דְּרַבָּנִין אָמְרָן כֵּן. דַּמַר רִבִּי שְׁמוּאֵל רִבִּי אַבָּהוּ רִבִּי עֲקִיבָה בַּר אָחָא בְשֵׁם רִבִּי יָסָא. אֵין בּוֹדְקִין עֵידֵי מִיתָה בִדְרִישָׁה וַחֲקִירָה. מַעֲשֶׂה בְאֶחָד שֶׁבָּא לְהָעִיד לִפְנֵי רִבִּי טַרְפוֹן עַל הָאִשָּׁה שֶׁנִּישֵּׂאת. אָמַר לוֹ. בְּנִי. הֵיאַךְ אַתָּה מֵעִיד עַל הָאִשָּׁה שֶׁתִּינָּשֵׂא. אֲמַר לוֹ. רִבִּי. עִמָּנוּ הָיָה בִשְׁיָירָה וְיָרַד הַגַּיִיס עָלֵינוּ. וְנִתְלָה בְיִחוּר שֶׁל זַיִת וּפְשָׁחוֹ וְרָדַף הַגַּיִיס וְחָזַר. נוּמְתִּי לוֹ. בְּנִי. מְשַׁבְּחָךְ אֲנִי בַּאֲרִי. נוּמֶה לוֹ. יָפֶה כִיוַונְתָּ לִשְׁמִי. אֲנִי נִקְרָא בְעִירִי יוֹחָנָן בֶּן יוֹנָתָן אַרְיֵה מִכְּפַר שִׁיחְלָה. אֲמַרְתִּי לוֹ. בְּנִי. יָפֶה אָמַרְתָּ יוֹחָנָן בֶּן יוֹנָתָן אַרְיֵה מִכְּפַר שִׁיחְלָה. אָמַר לִי. לֹא כֵן אֲמַרְתִּי. אֶלָּא יוֹחָנָן בֶּן יוֹנָתָן אַרְיֵה מִכְּפַר שִׁיחְלָה. אֲמַרְתִּי לוֹ. וַהֲלֹא כָךְ אָמַרְתָּ. יוֹנָתָן בֶּן יוֹחָנָן אֲרִי מִכְּפַר שִׁיחְלָה. אָמַר לִי. לֹא כָךְ אֲמַרְתִּי. אֶלָּא יוֹחָנָן בֶּן יוֹנָתָן אֲרִי מִכְּפַר שִׁיחְלָה. לְאַחַר הַיָּמִים חָלָה וָמֵת. וּבָדַק רִבִּי טַרְפוֹן אֶת עֵדוּתוֹ וְהִשִּׂיאוּ אֶת אִשְׁתּוֹ. אוֹ נֵימַר. מִשּׁוּם מַה בְכָךְ. אַשְׁכַּךְ תַּנֵּי. אֵין בּוֹדְקִין עֵידֵי מִיתָה בִדְרִישָׁה וַחֲקִירָה. וּדְלָא כְרִבִּי טַרְפוֹן. דְּרִבִּי טַרְפוֹן אוֹמֵר. בּוֹדְקִין עֵידֵי מִיתָה בִדְרִישָׁה וַחֲקִירָה.

Rav Jehudah in the name of Rav: Practice does not follow Rebbi Jehudah ben Baba in the case of an Israel[109]. The words of the Rabbis say the same since Rebbi Samuel, Rebbi Abbahu, Rebbi (Aqiba) [Jacob][110] bar Aḥa said in the name of Rebbi Yasa, one does not subject witnesses to a death to cross-examination[111].

[112]It happened that somebody came before Rebbi Tarphon about a woman who wanted to remarry. He said to him, my son, how can you testify for the woman that she can remarry? He said to him, Rabbi, he was with us in a caravan when we were attacked by an armed gang. He hung himself at a branch of an olive tree, tore it off, ran after the armed gang and returned. I said to him, my son, I am praising you as a lion. He said to me, you got my name well; in my city I am called Joḥanan ben Jonathan the lion from Kefar Shiḥla[113]. I said to him, my son, you said very well Joḥanan ben Jonathan[114] the lion from Kefar Shiḥla. He said to

me, no, what I said was Joḥanan ben Jonathan the lion from Kefar Shiḥla. I said to him, did you not say Jonathan ben Joḥanan the lion from Kefar Shiḥla? He said to me, no, what I said was Joḥanan ben Jonathan the lion from Kefar Shiḥla. After some time he became sick and died; Rebbi Tarphon checked out his testimony and let his widow remarry[115]. It was found stated: "One does not subject witnesses to a death to cross-examination[116], against Rebbi Tarphon, since Rebbi Tarphon said, one subjects witnesses to a death to cross-examination.

109 It is not necessary that the death be reported in a formal testimony; the information is accepted even if gleaned in an accidental way.

110 ר' עקיבה is a scribal error.

111 "Questions and investigations" are required in criminal inquiries (*Deut*. 13:15). חקירות are obligatory questions to determine time and place of the crime without which no prosecution can be successful. דרישות are questions which depend on the circumstances of the case.

112 The same story in the Babli, 122b; a short version is in Tosephta 14:9.

113 In the Tosephta בפר שחרא, in the Babli בפר שיחיא.

114 It is obvious that one must read "Jonathan ben Joḥanan" as in the other two sources.

115 In the Babli, R. Tarphon cross-examined the witness only for the purpose of permitting the wife of the deceased to remarry.

116 In the Babli, 122b, that is the position of R. Aqiba.

(fol. 15b) **משנה ו:** מְעִידִין לְאוֹר הַנֵּר וּלְאוֹר הַלְּבָנָה וּמַשִּׂיאִין עַל פִּי בַת קוֹל. מַעֲשֶׂה בְאֶחָד שֶׁעָמַד עַל רֹאשׁ הָהָר וְאָמַר אִישׁ פְּלוֹנִי מִמָּקוֹם פְּלוֹנִי מֵת הָלְכוּ וְלֹא מָצְאוּ שָׁם אָדָם וְהִשִּׂיאוּ אֶת אִשְׁתּוֹ. וְשׁוּב מַעֲשֶׂה בְצַלְמוֹן בְּאֶחָד שֶׁאָמַר אֲנִי אִישׁ פְּלוֹנִי בֶּן אִישׁ פְּלוֹנִי נְשָׁכַנִי נָחָשׁ וַהֲרֵי אֲנִי מֵת וְהָלְכוּ וְלֹא הִכִּירוּהוּ וְהִשִּׂיאוּ אֶת אִשְׁתּוֹ.

Mishnah 6: One testifies by the light of a candle or by the light of the moon[117] and one permits to remarry on the basis of a disembodied voice[118]. It happened that one stood on a hilltop and called out that the man X from place Y died. They went and found nobody but let his wife remarry. It also happened at Ṣalmon[119] that somebody said, I am X, son of Y; a snake bit me and I am dying. They went there, did not recognize him, and let his wife remarry.

117 In judicial proceedings, testimony is accepted only during daytime.

118 This is a source of information without any standing in judicial proceedings.

119 An unidentified place, possibly Kafr Ṣalmeh in lower Galilee.

(fol. 15d) **מתניתא**: מְעִידִין לְאוֹר הַנֵּר. אָמַר רִבִּי חֲנִינָא. לִימְּדַנִי רִבִּי יוֹנָתָן. וְהֵן שֶׁרָאוּ בּוּבְיָה שֶׁל אָדָם. רִבִּי אָחָא בְּשֵׁם רִבִּי חֲנִינָא. תַּמָּן תַּנִּינָן. מִי שֶׁהָיָה מוּשְׁלָךְ בַּבּוֹר וְאָמַר כָּל־הַשּׁוֹמֵעַ אֶת קוֹלִי יִכְתּוֹב גֵּט לְאִשְׁתּוֹ. הֲרֵי אֵלּוּ יִכְתְּבוּ וְיִתְּנוּ. וָמַר רִבִּי יוֹנָתָן. וְהֵן שֶׁרָאוּ בּוּבְיָה שֶׁל אָדָם. רִבִּי אָחָא בַּר חֲנִינָה[120] חִנְנָה בְּשֵׁם רִבִּי חֲנִינָא. הָדָה דְתֵימַר בַּשָּׂדֶה. אֲבָל בָּעִיר אֲפִילוּ לֹא רָאוּ[121] בּוּבְיָה שֶׁל אָדָם. וְהֵן תַּנִּינָן. מִי שֶׁהָיָה מוּשְׁלָךְ בַּבּוֹר וְאָמַר כָּל־הַשּׁוֹמֵעַ אֶת קוֹלִי יִכְתּוֹב גֵּט לְאִשְׁתּוֹ. הֲרֵי אֵלּוּ יִכְתְּבוּ וְיִתְּנוּ. וְאָמַר רִבִּי יוֹנָתָן. וְהֵן שֶׁרָאוּ בּוּבְיָה שֶׁל אָדָם. אָמַר רִבִּי אָבוּן. הַמַּזִּיקִין מְצוּיִין בַּבּוֹרוֹת כְּדֶרֶךְ שֶׁמְּצוּיִין בַּשָּׂדוֹת.

Mishnah: "One testifies by the light of a candle." [122]Rebbi Ḥanina said, Rebbi Jonathan taught me, only if they saw a man's shadow. Rebbi Aḥa in the name of Rebbi Ḥanina: There[123], we have stated: "If somebody had been thrown into a cistern and said, anybody who hears my voice should write a bill of divorce to my wife, they should write and deliver," and Rebbi Jonathan said, only if the saw a man's shadow. Rebbi Aḥa bar Ḥanina, in the name of Rebbi Ḥanina: That means, in the fields, but in town even without a man's shadow. But did we not state: "If somebody had been thrown into a cistern and said, anybody who hears my voice should write a bill of divorce to my wife, they should write and deliver," and Rebbi Jonathan said, only if they saw a man's shadow? Rebbi Abun said, damaging spirits[124] are as frequent in cisterns as they are frequent on the fields.

120 Reading of the parallel. Here: R. Aḥa in the name of R. Ḥinena in the name of R. Ḥanina. The doubling of the expression "in the name of" is a sure sign of a corruption.

121 Reading of the parallel; the word is missing in the text here.

122 This paragraph is copied from *Giṭṭin* 6:6.

123 Mishnah *Giṭṭin* 6:6.

124 In the opinion of the Babli, *Giṭṭin* 66a, they can take on human shapes and even have a shadow. But since that shadow is the work of the spirit and not of physics, they have no half shadows (meaning that the shadows of spirits follow the rules of geometric, not of wave, optics.)

תַּמָּן תַּנִּינָן. הַמֵּסִית זֶה הֶדְיוֹט וְהַנִּיסֵּית זֶה הֶדְיוֹט. הָא חָכָם לֹא. מִכֵּיוָן שֶׁהוּא נִיסֵּית אֵין זֶה חָכָם. מִכֵּיוָן שֶׁהוּא מֵסִית אֵין זֶה חָכָם. מִכֵּיוָן שֶׁהוּא נִיסֵּית אֵין זֶה חָכָם. כֵּיצַד עוֹשִׂין לוֹ לְהַעֲרִים עָלָיו. מַכְמִינִים עָלָיו שְׁנֵי עֵדִים בְּנֵי אָדָם בַּבַּיִת הַפְּנִימִית וּמוֹשִׁיבִין אוֹתוֹ בַּבַּיִת הַחִיצוֹן וּמַדְלִיקִין נֵר עַל גַּבָּיו כְּדֵי שֶׁיְּהוּ רוֹאִין אוֹתוֹ וְשׁוֹמְעִין אֶת קוֹלוֹ. שֶׁכֵּן עָשׂוּ לְבֶן סַטְרָא בְּלוֹד שֶׁהִכְמִינוּ לוֹ שְׁנֵי תַלְמִידֵי חֲכָמִים וֶהֱבִיאוּהוּ לְבֵית דִּין וּסְקָלוּהוּ. וְכֹה תֹּמַר אָכֵן. שַׁנְיָיא הִיא דָמַר אֲנִי. אַף הָכָא אֲנִי. שֶׁלֹּא יִבְרַח וְיֵלֵךְ לוֹ וְיֵלֵךְ וְיַסִּית אֶת אֲחֵרִים עִמּוֹ.

[125]There, we have stated: "The seducer is a common person, the seduced is a common person." Therefore, not a Sage[126]? (Since he is seduced, he is not a Sage.)[127] Since he seduces, he is not a Sage. Since he is seduced, he is not a Sage. What does one do to be sly about him? One hides two witnesses, people[128], in an inner room and puts him into the outer room, lights a candle near him so they can see him and hear his voice. That is what they did to Ben Satra[129] in Lod, where they hid two

Sages, brought him to court, and stoned him. And here, you say so[130]? It is different because he said "I am". Here also, "I am"?[131] That he should not flee, go away, and continue to seduce others with him[132].

125 The parallel is in *Sanhedrin* 7:16. The Mishnah states that there are two kinds of missionaries for idolatry, the seducer (*Deut.* 13:7-12) and the expeller (*Deut.* 13:13-19). The seducer is the one who tries to bring individuals to idolatry whereas the expeller adresses himself to the public. They go under different rules and one cannot try a seducer as an expeller and vice-versa. The first part of the paragraph has no relevance for the topics of this Halakhah, only the second part does.

The expression תמן תנינן introduces a Mishnah. Here, it introduces a paraphrase of the Mishnah.

126 Is a thoroughly educated person immune from prosecution for idolatry?

127 Sentence out of place, missing in *Sanhedrin*.

128 A marginal gloss that entered the text, missing in *Sanhedrin*.

129 In *Sanhedrin*: Ben Sôtĕdā, in the Babli, *Sanhedrin* 67a, and Tosephta *Sanhedrin* 10:11: Ben Sātĕdā, explained there as "son of the adultress" (known as Miriam the women's hairdresser).

130 In the case in Sanhedrin, the single person whom the seducer wants to convert to idolatry is unable to testify since a single witness is insufficient in criminal proceedings. Therefore, he had to find supporting witnesses in secret. But if voice identification is sufficient to permit a woman to marry even though up to now she was a married woman forbidden under the penalties of adultery to everybody except her husband, then voice identification should be enough also in other criminal proceedings.

131 If the intended victim could get the seducer to identify himself as "I am . . ." then voice identification should be enough.

132 The previous argument is correct; also for the court it would have been enough to hide a single witness who would be the second witness after the intended victim. One chooses two hidden witnesses to have enough manpower to arrest the seducer and haul him into court.

תַּמָּן תַּנִּינָן. הַמֵּבִיא גֵט וְאָבַד מִמֶּנּוּ. אִם מְצָאוֹ עַל אָתַר כָּשֵׁר. וְאִם לָאו פָּסוּל. אֵיזֶהוּ עַל אָתַר. רִבִּי יוֹחָנָן אָמַר. כָּל־שֶׁלֹּא עָבְרוּ שָׁם שְׁלֹשָׁה בְנֵי אָדָם. עָבַר גּוֹי מָהוּ. נִישְׁמְעִינָהּ מִן הָדָא. אַבָּא בַר בַּר חָנָה אַייתֵי גִיטָא וָבַד[133] מִינֵּיהּ. אַשְׁכְּחֵיהּ חַד סִירְקִיי. אָתָא עוֹבְדָא קוֹמֵי רַבָּנָן וְאַכְשְׁרוּן. הָדָא אָמְרָה עָבַר גּוֹי כָּשֵׁר. נֹאמַר. סִימָן הָיָה לוֹ בָהּ. לֹא כֵן תַּנֵּי. אֵין סִימָנִין בְּגִיטִּין. בְּהַהוּא דְאָמַר. תַּרְתֵּי תְּלַת שׁוּרִין. בְּרַם הָכָא הֵ״י שֶׁבּוֹ הָיָה נָקוּד. רִבִּי עֶזְרָא[134] בָּעֵי קוֹמֵי רִבִּי מָנָא. הָכָא לָמָּה הוּא פָּסוּל. אֲנִי אוֹמֵר. אַחֵר הָיָה וְהָיָה שְׁמוֹ כִשְׁמוֹ. הַגַּע עַצְמָךְ שֶׁבְּדְקוּ אוֹתוֹ מָקוֹם וְלֹא מָצְאוּ שָׁם אַחֵר שֶׁשְּׁמוֹ כִשְׁמוֹ. אֶלָּא מִשּׁוּם חוֹמֶר הוּא בָּעֲרָיוֹת. וְהָא תַנִּינָן. הָלְכוּ וְלֹא מָצְאוּ שָׁם אָדָם וְהִשִּׂיאוּ אֶת אִשְׁתּוֹ. (fol. 16a) הָלְכוּ וְלֹא הִכִּירוּהוּ וְהִשִּׂיאוּ אֶת אִשְׁתּוֹ. אָמַר לֵיהּ רִבִּי מָנָא. כֵּן אָמַר רִבִּי שַׁמַּי רִבִּי אָחָא בְשֵׁם רִבִּי בּוּן בַּר חִיָּה. הָאִישׁ הַזֶּה שְׁנֵי גִיטִּין הָיוּ בְיָדוֹ. אֶחָד כָּשֵׁר וְאֶחָד פָּסוּל. אִיבֵּד אֶת הַכָּשֵׁר וְהִשְׁלִיךְ אֶת הַפָּסוּל. בְּשָׁעָה שֶׁמָּצָא אֲנִי אוֹמֵר הַפָּסוּל מָצָא.

[135]There, we have stated: "If somebody was bringing a bill of divorce and lost it, if he found it again immediately, it is valid; otherwise it is invalid." What is immediately? Rebbi Joḥanan said,[136] as long as less than three people passed by. [137]If a Gentile passed by, what is the rule[138]? Let us hear from the following: Abba bar bar Ḥana[139] was bringing a bill of divorce when he lost it. A Saracen found it. The case came before the rabbis and they declared [the bill] valid. That means, if a Gentile passed by, it is valid. May we say that he had an identifying mark on [the bill]? But was it not stated that there are no identifying marks on bills of divorce? That means, two or three lines. But here it had a *heh* which was pointed[140]. Rebbi Ezra asked before Rebbi Mana, why should it be invalid in that case? I would say, it was another bill executed for a person with the same name[141]. Think of it, if they investigated and did not find there another person with the same name! It must be that one is very strict in matters of possible incest[142]. But did we not state: "They went and found

nobody but let his wife remarry; they went there, did not recognize him, and let his wife remarry?[143]" Rebbi Mana said to him: So says Rebbi Shammai, Rebbi Aḥa in the name of Rebbi Abun bar Ḥiyya: This man[144] had two bills of divorce in his hand, one valid and one invalid. He lost the valid one after he had thrown away the invalid one. When he found it, I am saying that he found the invalid one.

133 Reading (shortened from ואבד) of the parallel in *Giṭṭin*. Reading here: ייבד.

134 Reading of the parallel in *Giṭṭin*. Reading here: R. Ze'ira. That reading is impossible since R. Mana II was a student of R. Ze'ira and R. Ze'ira was three generations removed from R. Mana I. But it is documented from other sources that R. Ezra was a student of R. Mana II.

135 This is a slightly defective copy of the text in *Giṭṭin* 3:3 (fol. 44d).

136 In *Giṭṭin*: R. Joḥanan said, as long as nobody passed by. R. Jacob bar Idi, R. Simeon bar Abba in the name of R. Joshua ben Levi: as long as three people did not pass by. In the Babli, *Giṭṭin* 27b/28a, the first opinion is quoted in the names of the Tanna R. Simeon ben Eleazar and the Amora R. Abba bar bar Ḥana. The most lenient opinion in the Babli allows for a caravan to come there and encamp.

137 From here to the end of the Tractate, the Leiden ms. is again available.

138 The question is not asked in the Babli; that Talmud must hold that a Gentile is included under the notion of "person".

139 He insists in the Babli that the presence of another person invalidates the bill of divorce.

140 In the Babli: If there was a hole in the parchment near a certain letter, that is a convincing mark. But one does not testify about shape, color, type of material, etc. The argument shows that the story of Rabba bar bar Ḥana does not imply that the Gentile is not a person.

141 If there were two couples in the same town where both husbands and wives had, respectively, the same names and patronymics, then it might be possible that both husbands divorced their wives at the same time and the bills of divorce were switched. Since a bill of divorce has to be written for a specific woman (*Deut.* 24:1) the switch invalidates both bills.

142 In this case, possible adultery if an invalid bill of divorce was delivered and the still married wife remarried as a divorcee.

143 How can one be super-strict in cases of bills of divorce when one is super-lenient in confirming the husband's death?

144 The one who lost the bill of divorce. In view of the Mishnah in *Yebamot*, the Mishnah in *Giṭṭin* is explained away by being reduced to a very special case unlikely to be realized.

(fol. 15c) **משנה ז:** אָמַר רִבִּי עֲקִיבָה כְּשֶׁיָּרַדְתִּי לִנְהַרְדֶּעָא לְעִיבּוּר הַשָּׁנָה מְצָאַנִי נְחֶמְיָה אִישׁ בֶּדָלָא אָמַר לִי שָׁמַעְתִּי שֶׁאֵין מַשִּׂיאִין הָאִשָּׁה בְּאֶרֶץ יִשְׂרָאֵל עַל פִּי עֵד אֶחָד אֶלָּא יְהוּדָה בֶּן בָּבָא נוּמֵיתִי לוֹ וְכֵן הַדְּבָרִים אָמַר לִי אֱמוֹר לָהֶם מִשְּׁמִי אַתֶּם יוֹדְעִים שֶׁהַמְּדִינָה הַזֹּאת מְשׁוּבֶּשֶׁת בִּגְיָיסוֹת מְקוּבָּל אֲנִי מֵרַבָּן גַּמְלִיאֵל הַזָּקֵן שֶׁמַּשִּׂיאִין אֶת הָאִשָּׁה עַל פִּי עֵד אֶחָד. וּכְשֶׁבָּאתִי וְהִרְצֵיתִי הַדְּבָרִים לִפְנֵי רַבָּן גַּמְלִיאֵל שָׂמַח לִדְבָרַי וְאָמַר מָצָאנוּ חָבֵר לִיהוּדָה בֶּן בָּבָא.

Mishnah 7: Rebbi Aqiba said, when I left the country for Nahardea[145] for the intercalation of the year[146], Nehemiah from Badala[147] found me and said to me, I heard that in the Land of Israel one does not let a woman remarry on the testimony of one witness, except Jehudah ben Baba[148]. I told him, that is so. He said to me: Tell them in my name, you know that this country is in bad shape because of armed bands[149]; I learned from Rabban Gamliel the Elder that one lets a woman remarry on the testimony of one witness. When I came and lectured about this before Rabban Gamliel[150], he was happy about my words and said, we found a colleague for Jehudah ben Baba[148,151].

145 The center of Jewish Babylonia at that time; reputed to have been the place of residence of King Jojachin after his release from prison.

146 It is difficult to determine the historical background of the Mishnah.

In general, intercalations (adding a month to the year) are the prerogative of the Synhedrion in the Land of Israel. Intercalations can be decreed outside the Land only if this is impossible in the Land. Rabban Gamliel the Elder must have died some time before 60 C. E.; his grandson Gamliel II cannot have become patriarch before the election of Galba as Roman Emperor and must have died some time before the outbreak of the war of Bar Kokhba. The only period in which R. Aqiba could act as representative of the Synhedrion in a situation in which this institution was paralyzed in Palestine would be in the latter part of Trajan's reign, in the time of the great revolution of the Jewish Diaspora against the Romans. The "armed bands" which hindered an old man to go to Jabne to testify might have been Roman units preparing to invade Mesopotamia in Trajan's last campaign.

147 In the Mishnah of the Babli בית דלי "the house of Aquarius". The place is unidentified.

148 In the independent Mishnah mss: Rebbi Jehudah ben Baba. The text of the Talmudim is preferable since the rabbis among themselves did not use titles, the use of a title would be inappropriate in the mouth of an old man who studied before the invention of the title of "Rebbi" in Rabban Johanan ben Zakkai's academy at Jabne.

149 And therefore, an old man like me cannot travel to the Land of Israel.

150 Rabban Gamliel II, known as Rabban Gamliel of Jabne.

151 His opinion is no longer that of a single Sage; it can be the opinion of the majority.

(fol. 16a) **מתניתא**: אָמַר רִבִּי עֲקִיבָה כְּשֶׁיָּרַדְתִּי לִנְהַרְדֵּעָא לְעַבֵּר אֶת הַשָּׁנָה מְצָאַנִי נְחֶמְיָה אִישׁ בֵּדָלָא כול'. מְצָאוּ כָתוּב בִּשְׁטָר. מֵת פְּלוֹנִי נֶהֱרַג פְּלוֹנִי. רִבִּי יִרְמְיָה אָמַר. מַשִּׂיאִין אֶת אִשְׁתּוֹ. רִבִּי בּוּן בַּר כָּהֲנָא אָמַר. אֵין מַשִּׂיאִין אֶת אִשְׁתּוֹ. מַתְנִיתָא מְסַייְעָא לְדֵין וּמַתְנִיתָא מְסַייְעָא לְדֵין. מַתְנִיתָא מְסַייְעָא לְרִבִּי יִרְמְיָה. עַל פִּי עֵדִים. לֹא עַל פִּי כְתָבָן וְלֹא עַל פִּי מְתוּרְגְּמָן וְלֹא עֵד מִפִּי עֵד. וְעַכְשָׁיו אֵין מַשִּׂיאִין עֵד מִפִּי עֵד. וְדִכְוָותָהּ עַל פִּי כְתָבָן וְעַל פִּי מְתוּרְגְּמָן מַסִּיאִין. וּמַתְנִיתָא מְסַייְעָא לְרִבִּי בּוּן בַּר כָּהֲנָא. יָפֶה כֹּחַ הָעֵדִים מִכֹּחַ הַשְּׁטָר וכֹחַ הַשְּׁטָר מִכֹּחַ הָעֵדִים שֶׁהָעֵדִים שֶׁאָמְרוּ. מֵת פְּלוֹנִי נֶהֱרַג פְּלוֹנִי. מַשִּׂיאִין אֶת אִשְׁתּוֹ. מְצָאוּ כָתוּב בִּשְׁטָר. מֵת פְּלוֹנִי נֶהֱרַג פְּלוֹנִי. אֵין מַשִּׂיאִין אֶת אִשְׁתּוֹ.

יָפֶה כֹּחַ הַשְּׁטָר מִכֹּחַ הָעֵדִים. שֶׁהַמַּלְוֶה אֶת חֲבֵירוֹ בְעֵדִים (fol. 16b) גּוֹבֶה מִנְּכָסִים בְּנֵי חוֹרִין. בִּשְׁטָר גּוֹבֶה מִנְּכָסִים מְשׁוּעֲבָדִים.

Mishnah: "Rebbi Aqiba said, when I left the country for Nahardea for the intercalation of the year, Nehemiah from Badala found me," etc. If it was found in a document: "X died, X was killed"; Rebbi Jeremiah said, one lets his wife remarry; Rebbi Abun bar Cahana said, one does not let his wife remarry. A *baraita* supports the one, a *baraita* supports the other. A *baraita* supports Rebbi Jeremiah: "By the mouth of witnesses," not on basis of their writings, not on the word of a translator, not on the testimony of a single witness[152]." Today, does one not let remarry on the testimony of a single witness[153]? Therefore also one lets remarry on basis of their writings and on the word of a translator. A *baraita* supports Rebbi Abun bar Cahana: The power of witnesses is greater than the power of a document and the power of a document is greater than the power of witnesses. Since if witnesses say, "X died, X was killed", one lets his wife remarry but if it was found in a document: "X died, X was killed", one does not let his wife remarry[154]. The power of a document is greater than the power of witnesses, since if somebody gives a loan before witnesses, he can foreclose only from unincumbered property; by a document, he can foreclose from mortgaged property[155].

152 The full *baraita* is found only here. In *Sifry Deut.* 188, on *Deut.* 19:15, "by the mouth of two witnesses or three witnesses the matter shall be determined", written testimony and translated testimony are excluded (the court which hears a criminal matter must be composed of judges able to hear the witnesses in their own languages). In that context, the lone witness does not have to be mentioned since he is excluded by the verse itself. In the Babli, *Yebamot* 31b, *Giṭṭin* 71a, only written testimony is excluded.

153 Next Mishnah. The biblical rules of testimony have been abrogated once and for all in the case of the presumed widow since in that case

there are no adversary proceedings and the biblical rules of testimony never applied.

154 However, it is not established whether this *baraita* follows or precedes the reform of Rabban Gamliel.

155 This is explained in Chapter 3, Notes 130-131. Cf. Mishnah *Baba Batra* 10:16.

(fol. 15c) **משנה ח:** מִתּוֹךְ דְּבָרִים נִזְכַּר רַבָּן גַּמְלִיאֵל שֶׁנֶּהֶרְגוּ הֲרוּגִים בְּתֵל אַרְזָה וְהִשִּׂיא רַבָּן גַּמְלִיאֵל אֶת נְשׁוֹתֵיהֶן עַל פִּי עֵד אֶחָד. וְהוּחְזְקוּ לִהְיוֹת מַשִּׂיאִין עֵד מִפִּי עֵד וּמִפִּי אִשָּׁה וּמִפִּי שִׁפְחָה.

Mishnah 8: During the discussion, Rabban Gamliel remembered that people had been killed at Tel Arza and Rabban Gamliel let their widows remarry on the testimony of a single witness. It was firmly established that one permits to remarry on the words of a witness reporting from another witness, and on the words of a woman or a slave girl[156].

משנה ט: רִבִּי לְעֶזֶר וְרִבִּי יְהוֹשֻׁעַ אוֹמֵר אֵין מַשִּׂיאִין אֶת הָאִשָּׁה עַל פִּי עֵד אֶחָד. רִבִּי עֲקִיבָה אוֹמֵר לֹא עַל פִּי אִשָּׁה וְלֹא עַל פִּי קְרוֹבִים.

Mishnah 9: Rebbi Eliezer and Rebbi Joshua say, one does not let a woman remarry on the testimony of a single witness. Rebbi Aqiba says, not on the testimony of a woman nor on that of relatives[157].

156 The text of these Mishnaiot is not well established. There are Mishnah texts which ascribe the decision about the men killed at Tel Arza to Rabban Gamliel the Elder, and the Babli adds the male slave as credible witness to a death. Hearsay evidence and that of women and slaves is not accepted in adversary proceedings. It seems that the quote of the Mishnah in the Halakhah is the correct one also for the Yerushalmi.

157 He must agree that a single male witness in good standing is acceptable to testify about a death since he was the messenger of that rule

in Mishnah 7. But he restricts the leniency to exactly the case he had heard in Nahardea and objects to the expansive interpretation given at Jabne.

In the Mishnah in the Yerushalmi, the fact that R. Aqiba also disqualifies slaves was forgotten by the scribe. The relatives accepted by the majority naturally exclude the 5 women barred in Mishnah 15:4.

(fol. 16b) **מתניתא**: רִבִּי אֱלִיעֶזֶר וְרִבִּי יְהוֹשֻׁעַ אוֹמְרִים. אֵין מַשִּׂיאִין אֶת הָאִשָּׁה כול׳. תַּנִּינָן הוּחְזְקוּ לִהְיוֹת מַשִּׂיאִין עֵד מִפִּי עֵד מִפִּי אִשָּׁה וְאִשָּׁה מִפִּי אִשָּׁה וּמִפִּי עֶבֶד וּמִפִּי שִׁפְחָה וּמִפִּי קְרוֹבִים. וְאַתְּ אֲמַר הָכֵין. מַתְנִיתִין בְּמִשְׁנָה הָרִאשׁוֹנָה.

Mishnah: "Rebbi Eliezer and Rebbi Joshua say, one does not let a woman remarry," etc. We have stated: "It was firmly established that one permits to remarry on the words of a witness reporting from another witness, and on the words of a woman, and a woman on the words of another woman, and from a slave or a slave girl." And you say so? Our Mishnah is of the prior Mishnah[158].

158 Mishnah 9 clearly contradicts Mishnah 8. Since Rebbis Eliezer and Joshua were the joint leaders at Jabne between the death of Rabban Joḥanan ben Zakkai and the accession of Rabban Gamliel, it is quite clear that their joint statement precedes the reform of Rabban Gamliel.

(fol. 15c) **משנה י**: אָמְרוּ לוֹ מַעֲשֶׂה בִּבְנֵי לֵוִי שֶׁהָלְכוּ לְצוֹעַר עִיר הַתְּמָרִים וְחָלָה אֶחָד מֵהֶם בַּדֶּרֶךְ וְהִנִּיחוּהוּ בַּפּוּנְדָּק וּבַחֲזָרָתָם אָמְרוּ לַפּוּנְדָּקִית אַיּוֹ חֲבֵירֵינוּ נוֹמַת לָהֶם מֵת וּקְבַרְתִּיו וְהִשִּׂיאוּ אֶת אִשְׁתּוֹ. אָמְרוּ לוֹ וְלֹא תְהֵא כֹהֶנֶת כַּפּוּנְדָּקִית. אָמַר לָהֶן לִכְשֶׁתְּהֵא הַפּוּנְדָּקִית נֶאֱמֶנֶת.

משנה יא: וְהַפּוּנְדָּקִית הוֹצִיאָה לָהֶן מַקְלוֹ וְתַרְמִילוֹ וְסֵפֶר תּוֹרָה שֶׁהָיָה בְיָדוֹ.

Mishnah 10: They said to him[159], it happened that Levites went to Zoar the town of date palms when one one them fell ill and they left him at an inn. On their return, they asked the woman innkeeper[160], where is our colleague? She told them, he died and I buried him[161]; and they let his widow remarry. They said to him[159], should not the wife of a Cohen[162] be like a woman innkeeper? He retorted, if she is in the position of the woman innkeeper

Mishnah 11: For the woman innkeeper delivered to them his stick, his back pack, and the Torah scroll that had been in his hand[163].

159 The other Sages to R. Aqiba.

160 A Gentile woman who most probably kept slave girls to act as prostitutes for her guests.

161 Since they asked, her answer is testimony which according to Mishnah 5 should not be accepted.

162 She is the paradigm of a decent Jewish woman. How can R. Aqiba accept the testimony of a Gentile woman of ill repute and refuse that of a Jewish woman in good standing?

163 Any woman who can deliver concrete proof of her words is accepted.

(fol. 16b) **מתניתא**: הַפּוּנְדָּקִית הוֹצִיאָה לָהֶן מַקְלוֹ וּמַנְעָלָיו וַאֲפוּנְדָּתוֹ וְסֵפֶר תּוֹרָה שֶׁהָיָה בְיָדוֹ. רִבִּי אָחָא בְשֵׁם רִבִּי חיננא עָשׂוּ אוֹתָהּ כִּי חַיָּה שֶׁהִיא נֶאֱמֶנֶת עַל אָתָר. אָמַר רִבִּי שְׁמוּאֵל בַּר סוֹסַרְטָא. עָשׂוּ אוֹתָהּ כְּגוֹי מְסִיחַ לְתוּמוֹ. חַד אֲרִיסְטוֹן בָּעֵי קוֹמֵי רִבִּי מָנָא. לֵית הָדָא פְלִיג עַל רִבִּי שִׁמְעוֹן בֶּן לָקִישׁ. דְּרִבִּי שִׁמְעוֹן בֶּן לָקִישׁ אָמַר. כָּל־שֶׁשּׁוֹאֲלִין אוֹתוֹ וְהוּא מֵשִׁיב. לֵית כָּן כְּהַהִיא דְאָמַר רִבִּי שְׁמוּאֵל בַּר סוֹסַרְטָא. אִית כָּאן כְּהַהִיא דָמַר רִבִּי חֲנִינָה. עָשׂוּ אוֹתָהּ כִּי חַיָּה שֶׁהִיא נֶאֱמֶנֶת עַל אָתָר.

Mishnah: "For the woman innkeeper delivered to them his stick, his shoes, his money belt, and the Torah scroll that had been in his hand.". Rebbi Aha in the name of Rebbi Hanina[164]: They treated her like a midwife who is trusted on the spot[165]. Rebbi Samuel bar Scsarta said, they treated her like a Gentile speaking simplemindedly. A gentleman asked before Rebbi Mana, does that not contradict Rebbi Simeon ben

Laqish, for Rebbi Simeon ben Laqish said, anybody one asks and he responds[166]! The statement of Rebbi Samuel bar Sosarta is impossible; one has the statement of Rebbi Ḥanina: They treated her like a midwife who is trusted on the spot.

164 This is the correct name, as given at the end of the paragraph. R. Aḥa is reported frequently to quote R. Ḥanina but not R. Ḥinena.

165 If a midwife testifies immediately at the birth which one of twin boys was born first, her testimony is accepted with all the consequences it has in matters of inheritance (*Qiddušin* Yerushalmi 4:2 fol. 65d; Babli 73b).

166 Cf. Note 106. This is R. Simeon ben Laqish's definition of intentional answer which disqualifies the statement of a Gentile. The Babli, 122b, explains the problem away by proposing that the innkeeper started to cry when she saw the Levites coming and informed them of the death when they inquired why she was crying.

Indices

Index of Biblical Quotations

Gen. 1:27,28 271, 276
2:7 176
2:24 98,468
4:19 269
16:3 272
17:13 329
17:14 333
20:12 468
31.:30 329
33:16,17 57
38:24 197
40:15 329
46:28 355
48:16 525

Ex. 4:26 329
6:20 468
12:9 317
12:44 326
12:45 315
12:48 281,319
21:9 436
21:20 284
21:26 283
23:17 333
30:19 502
30:32,33 459

Lev. 1:2 471
4:2 219
4:13 219
5:14 173
6:9 11
6:18 363
7:14 317
7:27 170
7:34 371
12:2 211
12:3 332
14:14,17 510
15:18 250
15:25 197
18:7 91
18:8 91
18:10 456,458
18:13 91
18:15 91
18:16 16
18:17 10,91,92,360, 451.455
18:18 454
18:22 375
18:27 88
18:29 18
19:20-22 249
19:29 460
20:9 464
20:14 92
20:17 173,454
20:18 216
21:1-4 264
21:7 86,160,163,254 259,268
21:8 87
21:9 460
21:13 157,266,352, 358
21:14 86,91,163,256, 268,352,358
21:15 249
22:4 314
22:10 314,315,318
22:11 230,390
22:12 302
22:13 157,307, 393,394,395
23:40 504
23:42 492
25:45 358
28:17,18 256

Num. 1:18 23
5:13 425
15:24 220
17:5 23
18:11 390
18:26,27 541
18:28 543
18:31 391
18:32 541
27:6 186
27:8 168
29:1 504
30:14 397

Deut. 7:3-4 99
14:21 324
16:20 615
17:13 36
18:6-7 480
18:12 470

Deut. 21:14 261
21:17 189
22:12 259
22:13 233,261
22:16 43
22:23 259,264
23:1 27,216,449, 453,461
23:2 260,339,349, 462
23:3 86
23:4 354
23:5 354
23:8 354
23:9 305,349,360
23:18 309
24:1 149
24:2 23,424
24:4 213,214,225, 381,574
24:14 324
25:5 18,20,33,36,56, 57,72,152,225,247
25:6 107,189
25:7 23,163,519
25:8 519
25:9 225,496,510, 513,516,519
25:10 490,519
26:14 314,318
28:57 502

1Sam. 25:41 539

2Sam. 9:10 99
12:8 94
17:25 356

1K. 12:20 638
13:28 641
15:18 98
15:25 638

2K. 4:9 88
4:27 88
16:2 442
18:2 442
18:20 592

Is. 3:9 636
26:18 197
28:9 62
33:11 197
39:1 98
45:22 356
46:6 33

Jer. 4:22 524

Hos. 4:4 365
4:10 269
10:14 603

Mic. 6:5 354

Zach. 8:18 67

Mal. 2:3 640
3:3 364

Ps. 9:18 57
34:11 62
37:25 62
89:3 454
137:8 394
140:8 592
144:8,11 646

Prov. 1:5 33
3:21 33
9:9 33
27:11 33
30:32 523

Job 14:22 640
24:11,18 269
39:1-2 200

Ruth 1:22 356
2:11 356

Eccl. 4:9 277

Esth. 9:24 98

Ezra 10:3 101

Dan. 10:21 523

1Chr. 2:17 356
8:8-11 355
13:14 211
23:15 271
26:4 211

2Chr. 6:10 211
13:7 638
13:13 638
13:19,20 638

Index of Talmudical Quotations

Babylonian Talmud

Berakhot 47b 479
63b 211

Sabbat 66a 505
112a 507,508
112b 507
118b 16
133b 337
134a 275
135a 485.486
136a 485,486
137a 334
137b 335,336
152b 640

Erubin 6b 69
46b 204

Roš Haššanah 14b
69
28a 504,575

Beṣah 3b 632

Megillah 5a 277

Mo'ed Qaṭan 23a 209

Ḥagigah 2a 333

Yebamot 3a 457
9a 27,28,32
10b 29
11a 408
11b 408,429
12a 40
12b 47
13b 58
14a 68
14b 58,67
16a 62,63
17a 55
17b 17,18,34,76
18a 76
18b 77
19b 79
20a 23,79,87
20b 85
21a 88,89,93,94
21b 91,93,95
22b 458
23a 99
23b 104
24a 104,107
25a 108
25b 113
26b 128
27a 58,123
27b 119,121
28a 124
28b 135,137
29a 141
29b 141,185
30a 146
31b 139,658
33b 158
34b 203
35a 203
35b 159
36a 165
37a 178
37b 177
38b 182
39a 182,184
39b 11,14,521
40a 13,187
40b 191
41a 119
41b 163
42a 208
42b 206
44b 212
45a 217,308
46b 321
48a 320,326
48b 321
50b 234
51a 228,245
51b 128
52a 74
52b 232
53a 128
54a 247
54b 256
55a 17
55b 248,249
56a 251,252,253
56b 430
57b 260
59a 262,265
59b 263
60a 264
61a 261,268
61b 265,270,271
62a 98
62b 271
64a 272
64b 274
65a 260,272,273
65b 276
66a 280

Yebamot 66b 287
67a 291,292,295
68a 304
68b 391
69a 305
69b 302
70a 314,318
70b 319
71a 314,315,334, 335
72a 328,329
74a 314,315
75a 341
75b 342,344
76a 344,345,373
76b 347
77a 356,358
77b 358,360
78a 347,358
78b 363
79b 367
80a 368,448,485
80b 369,447,484
81a 371
83b 375
84a 375,377
84b 378,379,380
85a 384,401
85b 387
87a 390
88b 399
89b 403
91a 405,412
92a 15,421
93b 423,587
95a 427,429,430
95b 434
96a 242
97a 450,461
98b 466,467
99b 475
100a 479
100b 483
101a 487,489,520
101b 491
102a 495,496,497, 499,501
102b 500
104a 501,504,511
104b 414
103a 490,502
105a 512,521,522
105b 516,517
106a 524
107a 529,533
107b 533,534
108a 535,539
109a 536,54
109b 555
110a 556
110b 5519
111a 246,551
111b 566
112a 566,569
113b 574
114b 589
115a 588
116b 590
117b 615
118a 611
118b 620,625
119a 629
119b 630,63'1
120b 639
121a 641,643,644
121b 644,648
122b 650,662

Soṭah 3b 479
9a 347
32b 363
42b 175

Ketubot 22b 416, 417
49a/b 595
51a 600
53b 540
60a 197
79b 285
81a 183
82b 184,293

Nedarim 74a 121
93a 514

Nazir 20a 612

Giṭṭin 18a 208
24b 497,500
27b/28a 655
28b 647
38b 479
41a 283
66a 652
71a 658

Qiddushin 4a 318
15a 511
17b 437
19a 438
63a 112
63b 142
69b 365
70a 365
70b 363
71b 64
73a 348
73b 662
78a 249
88b 424

Baba Qama 11b 283
89a 283,284
102a 206

Baba Meṣi'a 28b/29a 603
37a 624
39b 116
44b 283
104a 595,596,598

Baba Meṣi'a 104b 598
111b 324

Baba Batra 2b 513
16a 200
20a 485
55a 189
123b 285
141b 167
142a 168
176a 151,152

Shebuot 43a 603

Sanhedrin 2a 333
3a 493
30b 615
31b 520
54a 460
57b 469,470
58a 468
58b 470
67a 653
69b 442
75a 93
75b 455,457
76a 457,460

Makkot 5b 460
14a 460
14b 459
16a 487,448

Abodah Zarah 7a 206
20a 324
27a 329,331
36b 204
64b 321,323,324

Horaiot 8a 219

Zebaḥim 12a 335
50a 45
62a 318

Bekhorot 8a 200
19b 164

Keritut 3a 459
9a 325
14b 451
15a 452
17b 170,172

Arakhin 2a 333

Ḥulin 43a 69
82b 487
91a 487

Niddah 7b 553
8b 196
11b 206
27a 175
31a 298
38b 198,199
41b 250
46a 46,440
46b 300
52a 44,45,47
56b 63
65a 48
65b 274

Tosephta

Terumot 5:11 204

Shabbat 15:5 485
15:7 486
15:8 274, 275
15:9 331

Ḥagigah 1:1 333

Sukkah 2:3 69

Yebamot 1:1 74
1:2 50
1:7 18
1:9-10 58,59,67
1:13 69
2:1 84
2:4 385,387
2:6 369
3:1 73,79,88,93
4:5 108,113
5:1 124
5:7 148,155
5:8-9 158
6:2 178
6:3 126,165
6:6 204
6:7 208
7:3 228
7:5 245
8:1 304
8:4 278
8:5 272
8:6 272
9:1 287,291,295
9:3 298
9:4 299
10:1 253
10:2 375
10:3 342
11:2 369
11:7 411
12:7 487,488
12:9 493,494

Yebamot 12:11 495
12:12 516
12:13 524
12:15 521
13:1 535
13:5 550
13:6 554
13:7 561
13:9 539
14:1 606,609,616
14:2 624,625
14:3 408,633
14:4 641
14:5 643
14:6 643
14:9 650
15:2 620

Ketubot 1:4 566
2:2 418
4:9 595
4:11 596
4:13 598
4:18 600
8:2-3 603
9:1 184
14:1 416

Baba Batra 9:5 161

Sanhedrin 10:11 653
Abodah Zarah 3:13 331

Keritut 1:21 451
3:1 172
Bekhorot 5:1,14 288

Ḥulin 5:7 451

Kelim Baba Batra 4:2 507
4:5 505
Niddah 1:3 204
1:7 197
5:7 44
6:1 304
8:1-2 274

Yadaim 4:18 347

Other Talmudic Sources

Derekh Ereṣ rabba 88,89
Gen. rabba 11,100, 176,269,287,329,331,468,523,536,638
Num. rabba 100, 176,427
Eccl. rabba 100
Ruth rabba 175, 355
Lament. rabbati 262
Midrash Shemuel 175

Mekhilta
dR. Ismael 315,327,437,511
dR. Simeon bar Iohai 326,437,511
Midrah Tannaïm 491,520,639

Sifra 11,17,19,22,93, 256,259,260,265,280, 281,298,314,315,318, 331,332,371,373,380, 390,395,427,464,488,492,596
Sifry Num. 377,425,427
Sifry Deut. 18,24, 36,107,165,305,324, 354,361,429,491,511,520,638,658
Sifry Zuṭa 427

Tanḥuma 176
Tanḥuma Buber 271

Index of Greek, Latin, Hebrew and Arabic Words

βῆμα 523
γαλήνη, γαληνός 645
δίαιτα 57
ζῇ τὰ ἑπτά 176
ἰδιώτης 254
κῆρυξ 162
κόθορνος 501
κοινωνία 151

κοσμίδια 538
ὀρχιπέδη 327
σάνδαλον 490
σημεῖον 440
ὑποθήκη 283
φερνάριον 266

גלע 375
רכא 329
חקה 72
כלוג 180,288
פרצוף 635
צרר 21

commentariensis 646
conditum (vinum) 437
impilia 490
tiro 365

شراك 505
طلق 509
عرى 505

General Index

Abraham ben David, Rabad 371,561
Adultery, inadvertent 398
  questionable 471
  with minor's wife 439
Adults, undeveloped 448
Agnon, S.J. 635
Albeck, H. 377,588
Arukh 251,287,505
Asher ben Ieḥiel, Rosh 284,575

Bastard 15,52,215
Bespeaking 71
Bill of divorce, old 208
Bill of Indebtedness, questionable 151

Candidate 71
Caro, Joseph 645
Castrate 366
  congenital 368
Child, live 161
Claims, undecidable 417
Converts, Levirate of 465
Cross Examination 650

Damascus Document 2
David ibn Zimra 385
Divorce, forced 386
  invalidated 67,203
Dor, Z. M. 6,13,452
Dowry, claim to 600

Emergency Wills 168
Engagement, questionable 266
Epstein, J. N. 505

Fat, forbidden 413
Feldblum, M. S. 647
Firstborn, redemption of 405
Fraenckel, D. 7,16,85,512,624

Gentiles, impurity of 63,204
Gershom ben Jehudah 576
Gibeonites 86
Gift, to unborn 167

Ḥalîṣah 2
Ḥananel ben Ḥushiel 67
Harvest, status of 603
Hermaphrodite 373
Hermeneutical Rules 11,17,21,256,
315,317,360,361,456,462,492

Idols, damaged 321
Incest Prohibitions 9

Inheritance Rules 177,186,292
Intercouse, completed 246
Isaac ben Abba Mari 621
Isaac Fasi, Rif 284,401
Isaiah II of Trani 645

Jacob ben Asher, Ṭur 344
Josephus 262

Karaites 10
Ketubah 287
Kutscher, E. Y. 56

Lesbians 373
Levirate Marriage 16
Lieberman, S. 67,176,288,298,600
Löw, I. 501,508
Löwinger, A. 501
Luria, B. Z. 60

Maidenhood 48
Maimonides 281,385,561,617,643,645
Mamzer 1
Margalit, M. 16,85,104,292,624
Marriage, Alexandrian 595
  by intercourse 270
  classes 179,348,349
  formal 24
  of deaf-mute 554,558,571
  of underage male 444
  of underage female 38
  void 25
Meir Jonah 621
Meïri 7,377,588
Minor girl, emancipation 43,48,529
  marriage 526
  marriage age 537
  of incompetent 247
Minor male, fertile 442
  levirate 241
  marriage of 296,444
  sex act 154
Mishnah, Babylonian 164
Mortmain 278

Nahardea 656
Naḥmanides 97,280,551,558
Nazir 612
Neubauer, A. 65
Nissim ben Jacob 97
Nissim Gerondi 617

Paraphernalia 278
Patrilinear Descent 100
Peruṭah 67,512
Philo 469
Practice of Moses from Sinai 353
Precedence, rules of 204
Pregnancy, duration 199
Presumption, of ownership 498
Priestly districts 479
Prohibition, of commandment 83,85
  of sanctity 83,85
Property, of slave 280
Punishments 459,460
Purification Offering 219

Qiddushin 24
  questionable 147
  valid 233

Rabbinowicz, N. 203
Rashi 10,28,45,63,67,295,561,597
Reappearance, person declared dead 609
Remarriage 399,409,587
Repudiation 38

Sadducees 1,10
Samaritans 1,56,179,308,365
Schechter, A. 132
Seduced town 504
Set 627
Sexless 369
Shammai, House of 55
She-ram 25
Shelomo ibn Adrat, Rashba 7,128, 132,228,280,341,575,643
Šiṭṭah Mequbeṣṣet 325

Slaves, as witnesses 476
Sperber, D. 501
Status quo ante 626
Support, of children 595
Sussman, J. 6

Tithes, obligation of 293

Vidal de Tolosa 643

Wacholder, B. Z. 315
Wife's property 180
Witness, criminal 110
  imperfect 399
  unique 586
Woman's vow 114

YomTov Ishbili Ritba 400
Yosef ben Ḥabiba, Nimmuqe Yosef 401,588

Ziany,E. M. 6

www.ingramcontent.com/pod-product-compliance
Lightning Source LLC
Chambersburg PA
CBHW031841220426
43663CB00006B/463